Nineteenth-Century Literature Criticism

Guide to Gale Literary Criticism Series

For criticism on	Consult these Gale series
Authors now living or who died after December 31, 1959	*CONTEMPORARY LITERARY CRITICISM (CLC)*
Authors who died between 1900 and 1959	*TWENTIETH-CENTURY LITERARY CRITICISM (TCLC)*
Authors who died between 1800 and 1899	*NINETEENTH-CENTURY LITERATURE CRITICISM (NCLC)*
Authors who died between 1400 and 1799	*LITERATURE CRITICISM FROM 1400 TO 1800 (LC)* *SHAKESPEAREAN CRITICISM (SC)*
Authors who died before 1400	*CLASSICAL AND MEDIEVAL LITERATURE CRITICISM (CMLC)*
Black writers of the past two hundred years	*BLACK LITERATURE CRITICISM (BLC)*
Authors of books for children and young adults	*CHILDREN'S LITERATURE REVIEW (CLR)*
Dramatists	*DRAMA CRITICISM (DC)*
Hispanic writers of the late nineteenth and twentieth centuries	*HISPANIC LITERATURE CRITICISM (HLC)*
Native North American writers and orators of the eighteenth, nineteenth, and twentieth centuries	*NATIVE NORTH AMERICAN LITERATURE (NNAL)*
Poets	*POETRY CRITICISM (PC)*
Short story writers	*SHORT STORY CRITICISM (SSC)*
Major authors from the Renaissance to the present	*WORLD LITERATURE CRITICISM, 1500 TO THE PRESENT (WLC)*

ISSN 0732-1864

Volume 62

Nineteenth-Century Literature Criticism

Criticism of the
Works of Novelists, Poets, Playwrights,
Short Story Writers, Philosophers, and Other
Creative Writers Who Died between 1800
and 1899, from the First Published Critical
Appraisals to Current Evaluations

Gerald R. Barterian
Denise Evans
Editors

GALE

DETROIT • NEW YORK • TORONTO • LONDON

STAFF

Gerald R. Barterian and Denise Evans, *Editors*

James E. Person, Jr., *Contributing Editor*

Aarti D. Stephens, *Managing Editor*

Susan M. Trosky, *Permissions Manager*
Kimberly F. Smilay, *Permissions Specialist*
Sarah Chesney, *Permissions Associate*
Steve Cusack, Kelly A. Quin, *Permissions Assistants*

Victoria B. Cariappa, *Research Manager*
Michele P. LaMeau, *Research Specialist*
Julia C. Daniel, Tamara C. Nott,
Tracie A. Richardson, Cheryl L. Warnock, *Research Associates*

Mary Beth Trimper, *Production Director*
Deborah L. Milliken, *Production Assistant*

Gary Leach, *Desktop Publisher*
Randy Bassett, *Image Database Supervisor*
Robert Duncan, Michael Logusz, *Imaging Specialists*
Pamela A. Reed, *Photography Coordinator*

Contents

Preface vii

Acknowledgments xi

Preface

Since its inception in 1981, *Nineteenth-Century Literature Criticism* has been a valuable resource for students and librarians seeking critical commentary on writers of this transitional period in world history. Designated an "Outstanding Reference Source" by the American Library Association with the publication of its first volume, *NCLC* has since been purchased by over 6,000 school, public, and university libraries. The series has covered more than 300 authors representing 29 nationalities and over 17,000 titles. No other reference source has surveyed the critical reaction to nineteenth-century authors and literature as thoroughly as *NCLC*.

Scope of the Series

NCLC is designed to introduce students and advanced readers to the authors of the nineteenth century, and to the most significant interpretations of these authors' works. The great poets, novelists, short story writers, playwrights, and philosophers of this period are frequently studied in high school and college literature courses. By organizing and reprinting commentary written on these authors, *NCLC* helps students develop valuable insight into literary history, promotes a better understanding of the texts, and sparks ideas for papers and assignments. Each entry in *NCLC* presents a comprehensive survey of an author's career or an individual work of literature and provides the user with a multiplicity of interpretations and assessments. Such variety allows students to pursue their own interests; furthermore, it fosters an awareness that literature is dynamic and responsive to many different opinions.

Every fourth volume of *NCLC* is devoted to literary topics that cannot be covered under the author approach used in the rest of the series. Such topics include literary movements, prominent themes in nineteenth-century literature, literary reaction to political and historical events, significant eras in literary history, prominent literary anniversaries, and the literatures of cultures that are often overlooked by English-speaking readers.

NCLC continues the survey of criticism of world literature begun by Gale's *Contemporary Literary Criticism (CLC)* and *Twentieth-Century Literary Criticism (TCLC)*, both of which excerpt and reprint commentary on authors of the twentieth century. For additional information about *TCLC, CLC,* and Gale's other criticism series, users should consult the Guide to Gale Literary Criticism Series preceding the title page in this volume.

Coverage

Each volume of *NCLC* is carefully compiled to present:

- criticism of authors, or literary topics, representing a variety of genres and nationalities
- both major and lesser-known writers and literary works of the period
- 5-8 authors or 4-6 topics per volume
- individual entries that survey critical response to an author's work or a topic in literary history, including early criticism to reflect initial reactions, later criticism to represent any rise or decline in reputation, and current retrospective analyses.

Organization

An author entry consists of the following elements: author heading, biographical and critical introduction, list of principal works, excerpts of criticism (each preceded by a bibliographic citation and an annotation), and a bibliography of further reading.

- The **Author Heading** consists of the name under which the author most commonly wrote, followed by birth and death dates. If an author wrote consistently under a pseudonym, the pseudonym will be listed in the author heading and the real name given in parentheses on the first line of the biographical and critical introduction. Also located at the beginning of the introduction to the author entry are any name variations under which an author wrote, including transliterated forms for an author whose language uses a nonroman alphabet.

- The **Biographical and Critical Introduction** outlines the author's life and career, as well as the critical issues surrounding his or her work. References are provided to past volumes of *NCLC* in which further information about the author may be found.

- Most *NCLC* entries include a **Portrait** of the author. Many entries also contain reproductions of materials pertinent to an author's career, including manuscript pages, title pages, dust jackets, letters, and drawings, as well as photographs of important people, places, and events in an author's life.

- The list of **Principal Works** is chronological by date of first publication and identifies the genre of each work. In the case of foreign authors with both foreign-language publications and English translations, the English-language version is given in brackets. Unless otherwise indicated, dramas are dated by first performance, not first publication.

- **Criticism** in each author entry is arranged chronologically to provide a perspective on changes in critical evaluation over the years. All titles of works by the author featured in the entry are printed in boldface type to enable the user to easily locate discussion of particular works. Also for purposes of easier identification, the critic's name and the publication date of the essay are given at the beginning of each piece of criticism. Unsigned criticism is preceded by the title of the journal in which it appeared. Publication information (such as publisher names and book prices) and some parenthetical numerical references (such as page and line references to specific editions of works) have been deleted at the editors' discretion to provide smoother reading of the text. Footnotes that appear with previously published pieces of criticism are reprinted at the end of each essay or excerpt. In the case of excerpted criticism, only those footnotes that pertain to the excerpted text are included.

- A complete **Bibliographic Citation** provides original publication information for each piece of criticism.

- Critical excerpts are prefaced by **Annotations** providing the reader with a summary of the critical intent of the piece. Also included, when appropriate, is information about the critic's reputation, individual approach to literary criticism, and particular expertise in an author's works, as well as information about the relative importance of the critical excerpt. In some cases, the annotations cross-reference excerpts by critics who discuss each other's commentary.

- An annotated list of **Further Reading** appearing at the end of each entry suggests secondary sources on the author. In some cases it includes essays for which the editors could not obtain reprint rights.

Cumulative Indexes

- Each volume of *NCLC* contains a cumulative **Author Index** listing all authors who have appeared in Gale's Literary Criticism Series, along with cross-references to such biographical series as *Contemporary Authors* and *Dictionary of Literary Biography*. Useful for locating authors within the various series, this index is particularly valuable for those authors who are identified with a certain period but who, because of their death dates, are placed in another, or for those authors whose careers span two periods. For example, Fyodor Dostoevsky is found in *NCLC,* yet Leo Tolstoy, another major nineteenth-century Russian novelist, is found in *TCLC* because he died after 1899.

- Each *NCLC* volume includes a cumulative **Nationality Index** which lists all authors who have appeared in *NCLC*, arranged alphabetically under their respective nationalities.

- Each new volume in Gale's Literary Criticism Series includes a cumulative **Topic Index**, which lists all literary topics treated in *NCLC, TCLC, LC 1400-1800*, and the *CLC* Yearbook.

- Each new volume of *NCLC*, with the exception of the Topics volumes, contains a **Title Index** listing the titles of all literary works discussed in the volume. In response to numerous suggestions from librarians, Gale has also produced a **Special Paperbound Edition** of the *NCLC* title index. This annual cumulation lists all titles discussed in the series since its inception. Additional copies of the index are available on request. Librarians and patrons have welcomed this separate index: it saves shelf space, is easy to use, and is recyclable upon receipt of the following year's cumulation. Titles discussed in the Topics volume entries are not included in the *NCLC* cumulative index.

Citing *Nineteenth-Century Literature Criticism*

When writing papers, students who quote directly from any volume in Gale's Literary Criticism Series may use the following general forms to footnote reprinted criticism. The first example pertains to material drawn from periodicals, the second to material reprinted from books:

[1]T.S. Eliot, "John Donne," *The Nation and Athenaeum*, 33 (9 June 1923), 321-32; excerpted and reprinted in *Literature Criticism from 1400-1800,* Vol. 10, ed. James E. Person, Jr. (Detroit: Gale Research, 1989), pp. 28-9.

[2]Clara G. Stillman, *Samuel Butler: A Mid-Victorian Modern* (Viking Press, 1932); excerpted and reprinted in *Twentieth-Century Literary Criticism,* Vol. 33, ed. Paula Kepos (Detroit: Gale Research, 1989), pp. 43-5.

Suggestions Are Welcome

In response to suggestions, several features have been added to *NCLC* since the series began, including annotations to excerpted criticism, a cumulative index to authors in all Gale literary criticism series, entries devoted to criticism on a single work by a major author, more illustrations, and a title index listing all literary works discussed in the series.

Readers who wish to suggest authors, single works, or topics to appear in future volumes, or who have other suggestions, are cordially invited to write: The Editors, *Nineteenth-Century Literature Criticism,* 835 Penobscot Bldg., 645 Griswold St., Detroit, MI 48226-4094; call toll-free at 1-800-347-GALE; or fax to 1-313-961-6599.

Acknowledgments

The editors wish to thank the copyright holders of the excerpted criticism included in this volume and the permissions managers of many book and magazine publishing companies for assisting us in securing reproduction rights. We are also grateful to the staffs of the Detroit Public Library, the Library of Congress, the University of Detroit Mercy Library, Wayne State University Purdy/Kresge Library Complex, and the University of Michigan Libraries for making their resources available to us. Following is a list of the copyright holders who have granted us permission to reproduce material in this volume of *NCLC*. Every effort has been made to trace copyright, but if omissions have been made, please let us know.

COPYRIGHTED EXCERPTS IN *NCLC*, VOLUME 62, WERE REPRODUCED FROM THE FOLLOWING PERIODICALS:

Ariel: A Review of International English Literature, v. 10, April, 1979 for "Ghostly Rhetoric: Ambivalence in M. G. Lewis' 'The Monk'" by Robin Lydenberg. Copyright (c) 1979 The Board of Governors, The University of Calgary. Reproduced by permission of the publisher and the author.—*Dutch Quarterly Review,* v. 19, 1989. Reproduced by permission.—*Essays in Criticism,* v. XII, January, 1962 for "Literature and Politics I: Tom Paine and the Vulgar Style" by James T. Boulton. Reproduced by permission of the Editors of *Essays in Criticism* and the author.—*The Journal of Narrative Technique,* v. 5, May, 1975 for "The Monk: Matilda and the Rhetoric of Deceit," by Peter Grudin. Copyright (c) 1975 by *The Journal of Narrative Technique.* Reproduced by permission of the publisher and the author.—*Modern Language Notes,* v. 98, December, 1983. Copyright (c) 1983 by The Johns Hopkins University Press. Reproduced by permission of The Johns Hopkins University Press.—*Nineteenth-Century French Studies,* v. 12, Spring, 1984; v. 16, Spring, 1987-88. (c) 1984, 1988 by *Nineteenth-Century French Studies.* Both Reproduced by permission.—*Political Science Quarterly,* v. LVIII, September, 1938. Copyright 1938, (c) renewed, 1966 by *Political Science Quarterly* Editors. Reproduced by permission from *Political Science Quarterly.*—*Queen's Quarterly,* v. 79, Summer, 1972 for "The 'Reasonable' Style of Tom Paine" by Evelyn J. Hinz. Copyright (c) 1972 by the author. Reproduced by permission of the author.—*Studies in English Literature 1500-1900,* v. 34, Summer, 1994. Copyright (c) 1994 William Marsh Rice University. Reproduced by permission of the publisher.

COPYRIGHTED EXCERPTS IN *NCLC*, VOLUME 62, WERE REPRODUCED FROM THE FOLLOWING BOOKS:

Aldridge, A. Owen. From *Thomas Paine's American Ideology.* University of Delaware Press, 1984. Reproduced by permission.—Backscheider, Paula R. From an introduction to *The Plays of Elizabeth Inchbald, Volume 1.* Edited by Paula R. Backscheider. Garland Publishing, Inc., 1980. Introduction (c) 1980 by Paula R. Backscheider. All rights reserved. Reproduced by permission.—Castle, Terry. From *Masquerade and Civilization: The Carnivalesque in Eighteenth-Century English Culture and Fiction.* Stanford University Press, 1986. Copyright (c) 1986 by the Board of Trustees of the Leland Stanford Junior University. Reproduced with the permission of the publishers, Stanford University Press.—Clark, Harry Hayden in an introduction to *Thomas Paine.* American Book Company, 1944. Copyright, 1944, by American Book Company. Copyright (c) 1972 by Kathlene Clark. All rights reserved. Reproduced by permission of Houghton Mifflin Company.—Copleston, Frederick. *From A History of Philosophy, Volume VII, Fichte to Nietzsche.* Burns and Oates Limited, 1963. (c) Frederick Coopleston, 1963. Reproduced by permission.—Culler, Jonathan. *From Flaubert: The Uses of Uncertainty.* Cornell, 1974. Copyright (c) 1974 Elek Books Ltd. Copyright (c) 1985 by Cornell University. All rights reserved. Used by permission of the publisher, Cornell University Press. All additional uses of this material— including, but not limited to, photocopying and reprinting—are prohibited without the prior written approval of Cornell University Press.—Davidson, Edward H. and William J. Scheick. From *Paine, Scripture, and Authority: The Age of Reason as Religious and Political Idea.* Lehigh University Press, 1994. Copyright (c) 1994 by Associated University Press, Inc. All rights reserved. Reproduced by permission.—Fennessy, R. R. From "Paine Replies to Burke: Rights of Man," in *Burke, Paine and the Rights of Man: A Difference of Political*

PHOTOGRAPHS AND ILLUSTRATIONS APPEARING IN *NCLC*, VOLUME 62, WERE RECEIVED FROM THE FOLLOWING SOURCES:

Johann Gottlieb Fichte

1762-1814

German philosopher.

INTRODUCTION

Johann Gottlieb Fichte entered the field of German philosophy in the wake of Immanuel Kant (1724-1804) and just prior to G. W. F. Hegel (1770-1831). Consequently, his name often appears in critical works only to mark the distance between Kant and Hegel. Fichte was, however, an important thinker in his own right, as historians have acknowledged more and more in recent years. Fichte's explication of Kant, which long earned him credit for being his predecessor's best interpreter, also catalyzed Fichte's original philosophy, which depends on his concept of the *Wissenschaftslehre,* or "The Science of all Knowledge." Determined to make his system accessible to the German population at large, as well as to other specialists, Fichte lectured and wrote prolifically, producing many major works in his relatively short career. He excelled as a speaker, addressing himself to the public with a missionary zeal based on his belief that philosophy—practical philosophy—could change lives, as it had his. Fichte directed the force of his work against the implications of determinism, searching instead for the possibility of human freedom or agency. A disciple of political theorist Jean-Jacques Rousseau, Fichte applied his philosophical commitment to political causes as well, allying himself with the cause of the French Revolution in 1789. When Germany felt the threat of imperial French forces less than two decades later, Fichte devoted himself to fomenting German unity, thus earning a reputation as the "father of German nationalism."

Biographical Information

Fichte was born on May 19, 1762, in Saxony. The son of a poor ribbon weaver, Fichte was working as a goose herd by the age of eight. At this time, however, his precociousness won him an aristocratic mentor in Baron Ernest Haubold von Miltitz. The Baron provided Fichte first with a private tutor, then with entrance to a prestigious preparatory school, and finally with courses of study at the universities in Jena, Wittenburg, and Leipzig. Before Fichte finished his anticipated degree in theology, however, the generosity of the von Miltitz family ran out: the Baron's heirs withdrew financial support in 1784. Fichte had to abandon his studies in order to support himself as a tutor. Already an avid student of philosophy, he lived frugally in the hopes that he could stop teaching long

enough to pursue intellectual work. He has been described as advocating during this time a "metaphysical fatalism"—a determinism bereft of any belief in free will. His philosophical perspective shifted quite radically in the early 1790s, however, when he embarked on an in-depth study of Kant, whose thought dominated German philosophy. After a virtual conversion through Kant's work, Fichte decided to meet the master. Their first interview was lukewarm, so Fichte decided to demonstrate his devotion and skill with some written work. His *Attempt at a Critique of all Revelation* so impressed Kant that the latter recommended it to his publisher, who had it in print by 1792. When the first edition appeared, accidentally, without the author's name, it was taken to be a new work by Kant himself. Once Fichte took his rightful place in the spotlight, with Kant's blessing, his name won immediate, broad recognition.

Two years later, accompanied by his new wife, Fichte assumed a professorship at the University of Jena, where he quickly became a popular teacher. His private lectures drew a regular and sizable student attendance, while his public lectures—in itself a radical concept—sometimes drew audiences of 500. As he energetically pursued his teaching duties, Fichte continued to develop his philosophical system, consolidating his reputation as a Kantian even as he began to strike into new territory. His publications and lectures while at Jena ultimately focused on the idea of *Wissenschaftslehre,* the "first principle" that functioned as the linchpin to his entire philosophical system. The demands of his life at Jena, however, limited the time he had for writing, so that he was only able to outline the *Wissenschaftslehre* in print, often as an accompaniment to his lectures; he anticipated some point in the future when he would have the time to explain his philosophy in depth. That opportunity came, but through rather adverse events: Fichte's outspokenness and radical stances made him a controversial figure among his more conservative colleagues, the most hostile of whom painted him as anti-throne and anti-altar. Fichte did little to help matters: he tended to throw himself into public controversies, and his style of debate was aggressive and often described as petty. The tensions finally came to a head in 1799, when charges that he was an atheist prompted a forced resignation from his post. The situation cost Fichte many of his adherents and mentors, including Kant. Although the expulsion was a loss, Fichte was able to devote time to his writings, producing many of his most important treatises, including *The Vocation of Man,* which he began immediately in 1799. He produced new explanations of the *Wissenschaftslehre* in 1801, 1804, 1810, and 1813. He also found opportunities to continue his teaching career, working at the universities in Erlangen and Konigsberg before he was appointed dean of the philosophy faculty in Berlin in 1810, where he also served as rector from 1811 to 1812. He continued his political activities, throwing himself into the cause of German nationalism during the Napoleonic wars. In a sense, he even lost his life to the war: he died at the end of January, 1814, from the typhus his wife had contracted while nursing wounded soldiers.

Major Works

Although Fichte regarded his duties at Jena as limiting his opportunity to develop and articulate his philosophical system, it was a prolific period in his life. All of the significant works of the time, with the exception of *Some Lectures Concerning the Scholar's Vocation* in 1794, treated the *Wissenschaftslehre.* Fichte's earliest significant publication at Jena was his review of the philosopher G. E. Schulze's book *Aenesidemus;* the review was first published in *Allgemeine Literature-Zeitung* in 1794. The article presented, in its initial form, Fichte's own philosophical positions, especially the pivotal concept of the *Wissenschaftslehre.*

Fichte formally introduced himself to Jena with *Concerning the Concept of the Wissenschaftslehre, or, of So-called "Philosophy"* (1794). His *Foundations of the Entire Wissenschaftslehre* appeared in 1794. These, plus an *Outline* prepared for his students, only sketched the first principle on the expectation that he would later have time to publish a more thorough explication. In his two "Introductions" published in the *Philosophisches Journal* in 1797-98, titled *Attempt at a New Presentation of the Wissenschaftslehre,* Fichte attempted to expand his explications, but there still was much left to do. Although over twenty versions turned up in his papers after his death, Fichte never completed that all-encompassing statement of his basic principle; consequently, philosophers and historians have treated *Foundations* as the primary statement of the *Wissenschaftslehre.*

Instead of a complete statement of his principle, Fichte published many developments of the *Wissenschaftslehre,* demonstrating how it functioned in fields outside of abstract philosophy. *Foundations of Natural Right according to the Principles of the Wissenschaftslehre* (1796-97), which ultimately influenced Hegel, provided an application of the principle to natural law and the state. *The System of Ethical Theory according to Principles of the Wissenschaftslehre* (1798) did the same for moral law, stressing the importance of moral striving. Fichte planned similar volumes on aesthetics, religion, and the philosophy of nature, but they never materialized. Upon his dismissal from Jena, Fichte wrote *The Vocation of Man* (1800), which presented his idealist response to skepticism. Other significant works of this period include *The Closed Commercial State* (1800), a recommendation of a socialist state; *The Characteristics of the Present Age* (1806), a historical work; *The Way towards the Blessed Life* (1806), a theological work; and *Addresses to the German Nation* (1808), a collection of his speeches calling for German unity.

Critical Reception

Tom Rockmore identifies the years from 1790 to 1807 as Fichte's "brief moment of glory . . . when [his] was the brightest star in the philosophical firmament." That brightness was, however, very short-lived: recent scholars have noted the relative obscurity in which Fichte's work has suffered for almost two centuries. They attribute that insignificance to several causes, including the overshadowing figures of Kant and Hegel, and the complexity and difficulty of Fichte's prose style, which has sometimes made his work inaccessible to lay people as well to other philosophers. Responses to some of Fichte's earliest publications pointed out the opacity of his style. As his reputation grew, that problem became compounded by his tendency to write in a defensive fashion, often resorting to ad hominem attacks on his critics. The anger in his prose was, however, a reaction against criticisms that were also harsh and personal. Anti-Kantians of his own period took sharp aim at Fichte, abusing him and his writing; Kant-purists also criticized him, chastising his divergence from the master.

The neglect of Fichte's philosophical works may also be partly due to the popularity of his political writings in Germany. His philosophical reputation was at times obscured by his reputation as a "founding father of German nationalism." Outside of Germany, especially in the period encompassing the two world wars, that reputation damaged appreciation of his philosophical works. Where attention has focused on his philosophy, Fichte's detractors have cast him as a "subjective idealist," following the lead set by Kant in his rejection of Fichte in 1799. According to this critique, Fichte's works are subjective to the point of monstrous egotism. A reevaluation, however, gathered momentum in the second half of the twentieth century, spurred on mostly by critics in Germany, Italy, and France. Drawing on a definitive critical edition and the first publication of many of Fichte's posthumous papers, these critics have begun to consider Fichte as an original thinker in his own right and, consequently, to cast his ideas in increasingly complex terms. The fresh perspective spread to England and the United States, where it is evident in the wealth of publications made available in the 1980s and 1990s.

PRINCIPAL WORKS

Versuch einer Kritik aller Offenbarung [Attempt at a Critique of All Revelation] (philosophical treatise) 1792
Einige Vorlesungen über die Bestimmung des Gelehrten [Some Lectures Concerning the Scholar's Vocation] (philosophical treatise) 1794
Über den Begriff der Wissenschaftslehre [Concerning the Concept of the Wissenschaftslehre, or, of So-called "Philosophy"] (philosophical treatise) 1794
Grundlage der gesamten Wissenschaftslehre [Foundations of the Entire Wissenschaftslehre] (philosophical treatise) 1794-95
Grundlage des Naturrechts nach Prinzipien der Wissenschaftslehre [Foundations of Natural Right according to the Principles of the Wissenschaftslehre] (philosophical treatise) 1796-97
Attempt at a New Presentation of the Wissenschaftslehre (philosophical treatise) 1797-98
Das System der Sittenlehre nach den Prinzipien der Wissenschaftslehre [The System of Ethical Theory according to Principles of the Wissenschaftslehre] (philosophical treatise) 1798
Die Bestimmung des Menschen [The Vocation of Man] (philosophical treatise) 1800

Der geschlossne Handelstaat [The Closed Commercial State] (philosophical treatise) 1800
Darstellung der Wissenschaftslehre aus dem Jahre 1801 (philosophical treatise) 1801
Die Anweisung zum seligen Leben, oder auch Religionslehre [The Way towards the Blessed Life] (philosophical treatise) 1806
Die Grundzüge der Gegenwärtigun Zeitalters [The Characteristics of the Present Age] (philosophical treatise) 1806
Reden an die deutsche Nation [Addresses to the German Nation] (speeches) 1808

PRINCIPAL ENGLISH TRANSLATIONS

The Way towards the Blessed Life; or, The Doctrine of Religion (translated by William Smith) 1849
The Science of Rights (translated by A. E. Kroeger) 1869
The Science of Ethics as Based on the Science of Knowledge (translated by A. E. Kroeger) 1897
Addresses to the German Nation (translated by R. F. Jones and G. H. Turnbull) 1922
Foundations of the Entire Science of Knowledge (translated by Peter Heath and John Lachs) 1970
The Vocation of Man (translated by Peter Preuss) 1987
Fichte: Early Philosophical Writings (translated by Daniel Breazeale) 1988

CRITICISM

Robert Adamson (essay date 1881)

SOURCE: "'Wissenschafslehre' in Its Earlier Form," in *Fichte*, William Blackwood and Sons, 1881, pp. 125-88.

[*Adamson's work constituted the earliest substantial study of Fichte in English. The first half of his book covers Fichte's biography, and the second, his philosophies. The chapter excerpted below offers an explanation of the* Wissenschaftslehre *as it appears in Fichte's earlier writings. Beginning with Fichte's influences, Adamson describes Fichte as "Spinoza in terms of Kant."*]

The general aim or spirit of the *Wissenschaftslehre* having been determined, it becomes necessary to consider more particularly the nature of the problems presenting themselves for solution, and the method by which they are to be treated. As regards both points, the most valuable writings are the two **"Introductions to *Wissenschaftslehre,"*** and the **"Sonnenklarer Bericht."**[1]

1.—Dogmatism and Idealism.

The slightest reflection discloses to us the remarkable distinction in consciousness between two orders of representations[2] or phenomena, which we call, with some vagueness, inner and outer experience. With more precision we should say that, while some phenomena of conciousness present themselves as evidently the products of free mental activity, others appear in an order independent of us, and are characterised for us by the accompanying "feeling" of necessity which attaches to them. Now, the problem of philosophy— *i.e.,* of *Wissenschaftslehre*—is to explain experience, to render it intelligible; and all explanation consists in rendering a reason for the phenomena to be explained. The ground of experience, in the highest sense, is not to be sought beyond experience itself, but our reflection upon experience does undoubtedly proceed beyond it, since it regards the whole as matter to be accounted for. This procedure beyond experience is, in fact, the process familiarly known as abstraction. Philosophical theory, having presented to it the complex fact of the coexistence of inner and outer experience, abstracts from the condition of coexistence, and selects for isolated consideration, on the one hand, the Ego or conscious subject, on the other hand, the non-Ego or object simply. Whether such abstraction is a legitimate process may remain meanwhile undetermined,—the analysis of the problem itself will throw light upon the nature of the thoughts involved in it,— but by its means we reach the fundamental opposition of philosophical systems. Ego and non-Ego, subject and object, thought and being, are separate grounds, to which the whole of experience may be referred for explanation. Do we explain experience as the product of the non-Ego, we have the system which may be called Dogmatism; do we explain the whole as springing from the Ego, we have Idealism. Of the one, the typical example is the system of Spinoza, in which the order and connection of thoughts are explained by reference to that which does not contain in itself the element of self-consciousness,—where, therefore, the Ego appears as a mechanically determined unit in the sum total of things. Of the other, a representative may probably be found in Leibnitz, though much of the later Kantian speculation is only intelligible as a kind of half-understood idealism.[3]

Which of these counter-principles has right on its side? Does either satisfy the requirements of philosophical explanation? It is evident, on the one hand, that the dogmatic method, if true to itself, must, in the end, have resort to an absolutely unknown and unknowable thing as the non-Ego. The thing-in-itself is, in fact, the

solution offered by dogmatism; and such solution is defective in two ways. In the first place, while for a supposed external observer the existence of a non-Ego might furnish explanation of what presents itself in the consciousness of the subject—that is to say, of the limitation of the subject—no such explanation is possible for the subject himself. That he should *be* limited may possibly result from the existence of a non-Ego; that he should *know himself* as limited cannot be explained from the existence of the non-Ego simply. In the second place, the assumed non-Ego is for the thinking subject non-existent: no possible predicate can, by the subject, be attached to it which does not imply reference to the subject, and therefore relative, dependent existence. The non-Ego, as such, as thing-in-itself, is not in consciousness, and is, for the Ego, nothing.

Dogmatism thus furnishes no explanation. The opposed principle, that of idealism pure and simple, has at least one superiority: it selects, as ground of explanation, what is unquestionably in consciousness. The Ego, or subject, is known to be. But when the Ego, or subject, is taken *per se,* and the attempt is made to deduce from it the multiplicity of experience, we find a *hiatus* which is absolutely impassable, unless our method is at once guarded and comprehensive. An imperfect or half-understood idealism regards the Ego as merely subject, and is thus driven to the conception of self-consciousness as somehow one of the facts discoverable in intelligence. In this case, while it may be possible to explain that the Ego should know itself as limited, it is quite impossible to explain how it should know itself as limited by the non-Ego. As Fichte rightly puts it, "In vain shall we look for a link of connection between subject and object, if they are not first and simply apprehended as a unity. . . . The Ego is not to be regarded as subject merely, but as at once subject and object."[4]

If we translate Fichte's reasoning regarding idealism into other terms, it might be expressed thus. Idealist speculation has sought the ground of explanation in consciousness,—in that which is immediately and directly known to us. But in so doing, it has followed the same method which, when dealing with the thing-in-itself, gave rise to dogmatism. It has regarded consciousness as merely so much to be known,—as a series of states, *Vorstellungen,* from which nothing can possibly be extracted. It has not considered how consciousness comes to be, what conditions are necessarily implied in its existence, what are the laws under which it acts. Thus idealism drifts easily into a kind of psychological doctrine (as in Schmid, and later in Fries), or results in a sceptical phenomenalism (as in Maimon and in Hume).[5] Only one idealist system has really gone to the heart of the problem, and fairly considered how it is that, in consciousness, there appears the opposition between Ego and non-Ego; for only one philosophy has seized the principle that consciousness or intelligence as a whole is conditioned by self-consciousness, and that the laws under which self-consciousness are realised are at once the form and matter of intelligence. This is the critical or transcendental idealism of Kant,—a system imperfect in details, easily misunderstood, and requiring to be remodelled or restated before it can be made to yield adequate solution of the speculative problem.

Thus for Fichte there are historically but two reasoned systems of philosophy—that of Spinoza and that of Kant. The one is dogmatic,—that is, it neglects to give due weight to the principle of self-consciousness, and hence endeavours to explain existence by a notion which is limited, and applicable only within the experience of a self-conscious subject. The other is critical,—that is, it recognises the great truth that all consciousness is determined by self-consciousness, and so acknowledges the due limits of thought. If we were to express in a single word the characteristic feature of Fichte's system, we should describe it as "Spinoza in terms of Kant." That which was wanting in the critical philosophy, systematic development, is predominant in Spinoza; and, as will be seen, the theoretical part of the *Wissenschaftslehre* is nothing but an inverted or idealistic Spinozism. It has often been said that the influence of Spinoza over the course of Fichte's speculation became more significant in the second period of his literary activity; but even were this the case, one must not forget that in the earliest expositions of *Wissenschaftslehre,* comparison with Spinoza, and recognition of similarity with his thoughts, appear throughout. To understand the substance of Fichte's speculation, some note must be taken of these historical antecedents.

2.—Historical Antecedents: Spinoza and Kant.

To any one acquainted with Spinoza's system, Fichte's description of it as essentially "dogmatic" must at first appear erroneous; for by a dogmatic system Fichte understands one which deduces the order of conscious experience from a supposed order of things,—and it needs but slight knowledge of Spinoza to be aware that for him any implied contrast or relation between the order of ideas and the order of things has no place. It is necessary, however, to pass beyond the mere verbal definition of dogmatism on the one hand, and the mere statement of Spinoza's opinion on the other, if we are to discuss fairly the relation between them. That which characterises *dogmatism* as a philosophical method is not simply the distinction between ideas and things, but the nature of the notion or category by means of which either ideas or things are made comprehensible. In all cases of explanation, we find, as the residuum of analysis, some fundamental relation or thought by means of which the facts involved have become for us intelligible. Thus the notion

or relation of cause is involved in all explanations of physical change, and itself requires to be critically analysed in order that we may see what assumptions or underlying notions are implied in it. Now the notion which dogmatism applies to explanation of experience is briefly that of mutual determination,—what Kant called the category of Reciprocity. Each thing, or part of real experience, has its definite character by and through its relations to all other things. It is determined to be what it is, by virtue of the determinations of other things. A notion or category of this kind is evidently highly complex; and, indeed, as one might conjecture, it may be applied with much variety of signification. It may remain a purely mechanical category, implying only external relations of the things which compose a collective or aggregate whole; or it may be elevated so as to become the idea of a systematic whole, in which the relations of the parts are not mechanical.[6] The first significance, however, is that which characterises the use of the notion in the dogmatic method. For here things and ideas are regarded as alike in one respect, as being alike finite objects of possible cognition. Each external thing, each idea, is finite in its kind—*i.e.,* is capable of being limited, determined by another. Through this limitation by others, each has its definite being. It matters not, then, whether we regard things and ideas as composing two orders, of which one is cause, the other effect, or assert that things and ideas are both the same, looked at from different points of view; in either case we subject the facts to the same mode of explanation, regard each as a unit, marked off from others, and with only external relations to them, and explain the special characteristics of each as depending on the coexistence of all the others.

Now this notion of reciprocity or mutual determination is fundamental in Spinoza, and is that by which his system has gained its greatest influence over modern thought. It is true that it is not the only notion used by Spinoza,—in fact, the difficulties, even incomprehensibilities, of his metaphysics arise mainly from the conjunction of the notion of mutual determination with that of substance,—but it is a thought which is involved in scientific procedure as such, and through it Spinoza has been brought into the closest relations with modern scientific work. The phrases, more or less commonplace, by which the systematic unity of things is expressed,—such as, the order and uniformity of nature, the prevalence of law,—are merely expressions of what is contained in this notion of reciprocity. It is evident, further, that if we apply this notion to the explanation of experience, we must regard self-consciousness, the essence of the thinking subject, as merely one phenomenon, or state, or *thing,* determined by relations to other phenomena, and assume that these relations are of an external kind. Thus, for Spinoza, the peculiarity of self-consciousness vanishes; and even if we interpret liberally the obscure propositions ('Ethics,' ii. *Props*. 21 *et seq*.) in which the *Idea Mentis* is treated, it is evident that self-consciousness, as understood by him, is referred to that which lies outside of it and therefore mechanically determines it.

Fichte's criticism of this dogmatic method is in form and spirit identical with the later and more famous expression of Hegel. He has to point out that Spinoza omits altogether *criticism* of the notion of mutual determination—that is to say, omits to examine the nature and validity of the notion for our thinking. Had such criticism been undertaken, it would have become apparent that a category like reciprocity is entirely inadequate to express the relation of self-consciousness and the experience to which it is related; that substance and mode, Spinoza's supreme forms, are limited in their nature; and that there is no philosophic ground for procedure beyond self-consciousness. While signalising these faults, Fichte nevertheless recognises the high ideal of speculation which is disclosed in Spinoza's 'Ethics,' and draws largely on the Spinozistic method. Many of his fundamental principles, both in the earlier and the later periods of his thinking, are in form and matter identical with those of the 'Ethics.' There is no sufficient ground for asserting, as many writers have done, that the influence of Spinoza over Fichte increased, and that in the final period of the latter's philosophising his exposition is merely a mystical Spinozism. No closer connection is possible than that between the theoretical portion of the '***Wissenschaftslehre***' and the principles of Spinoza. The later works accentuate somewhat the religious aspect of the theory of knowledge, but imply no other theory; and however close in forms of expression the religious doctrines of the two thinkers may be, the radical opposition in their point of view is not to be forgotten.

This radical opposition in point of view was the natural and inevitable consequence of the critical philosophy. To understand the specific problems presented to Fichte, it is necessary to note with some care what the Kantian system had completed, and what it had left undone.

To Kant the problem of philosophy in general had presented itself under special aspects determined by historical circumstances,—in the main, however, under the aspect of a question as to the possibility of knowledge. This question he for the first time proposed to treat in its wider issues, as independent of psychology and of metaphysical assumptions. Beyond all doubt it was not given to Kant,—it is given to no thinker,—to free himself entirely from the notions and phraseology current at the time; and so it has come about that the 'Critique of Pure Reason,' the work in which the dogmatic method of English philosophy and of Leibnitz was first subjected to examination, shows in many of its main doctrines unmistakable traces of

the method against which it was directed. Thus, while Kant is making clear, on the one hand, that knowledge, for the self-conscious subject, cannot be explained by reference to a world of things thought as out of connection with self-consciousness, he still allows himself ambiguities of speech which might be interpreted to mean that the special content of knowledge, the matter, is explicable by reference to such things; and while he makes clear, on the other hand, that the conception of a mere stream of conscious states, as the phenomena of an individual subject, is in itself contradictory and absurd, he yet draws distinctions which might be taken to imply that the difference of subjective and objective in knowledge is one of kind, and not a subordinate form to be explained under the more comprehensive synthesis with which he started.

If, then, it be considered what was for Kant the fundamental principle of philosophical method, and how far the actual results of his system correspond with the requirements of the method, a summary view of the problems left for solution to the post-Kantian writers may readily be obtained. Now the fundamental principle, disguised under many strange fashions of speech in the 'Critique of Pure Reason,' is that already described as the principle of self-consciousness. All knowledge, all experience, *is* only for a self-conscious subject. Such a subject is not to be regarded as an individual, for the notion of individuality implies relations of a complex and quite distinct kind. It is the common element in all consciousness, that by which consciousness is what it is. If, therefore, the explanation of experience be proposed as the problem of philosophy, the method of procedure may be either an investigation of the idea of self-consciousness, the determination of the conditions under which it is possible, and the evolution in strict sequence of the elements which are embraced in it; or by an analysis of knowledge, of experience, as it presents itself in ordinary, empirical consciousness, and the determination of the features in it due to the presence of this central unity. The second method was that adopted by Kant, and the result has been somewhat unfortunate. For, in consequence of the method adopted, the several elements composing knowledge were discussed in isolation from one another and from their central unity, and were thus, almost of necessity, viewed not as elements in a synthesis, which have no existence save in and through their combination, but as independent parts of an integral or collective whole. Thus, in the 'Critique of Pure Reason,' the problem is stated in an ambiguous and confusing way; and in the 'Æsthetik,' more particularly, the central point of view is lost sight of in a quite subordinate issue. Knowledge, Kant sees clearly enough, is possible only as a synthetic combination in the unity of self-consciousness. The conditions or forms of such combination determine experience, or give general laws to it, but such determination is merely formal. Nothing can be presented in self-consciousness which contradicts or is out of harmony with these conditions, but the specific determination of this matter of knowledge is not to be deduced from the conditions themselves. Upon this view of the purely formal or logical function of the unity of thought rest the Kantian distinctions of the *a priori* and *a posteriori* elements in cognition, of form and matter, of sense and understanding, of empirical and transcendent reality, of phenomena and noumena. So far, then, as theory of knowledge goes, Kant, while bringing into the foreground the very first principle of cognition, fails to connect therewith the subordinate forms. Space and Time are shown, on special grounds, not to be explicable by reference to external things or to states of subjective experience, but they are placed in no intimate relation to the unity of self-consciousness. The conscious subject is *receptive,* and, if receptive, only under the pure forms of space and time. But how or why a self-conscious subject should appear to itself receptive; how or why, if receptive, it should be so in the forms of space and time,—are questions entirely unresolved. So when Kant undertakes the discussion of the key-stone to his position, the deduction of the categories or exposition of the forms of combination which make up the nature of the thinking subject, his procedure is equally external and haphazard. It is certainly shown that *categories* are implied in self-consciousness, but how or why they should be so implied—how or why there should be so many of them and no more—how they are connected with one another and form a system in human knowledge,—these questions, likewise, are left unsolved. Further, when the categories, having been deduced as the forms of the activity of the synthetic Ego, are brought into relation with the forms of receptivity, the results, though rich in consequences, leave much to be desired. The fusion into the unity of knowledge is a merely mechanical one. Categories as modes of understanding, schemata as modes of productive imagination, data of sense as modes of affection, are linked together, and appear to have a nature and existence independently of one another, and of the synthesis in which they are combined. The final result—the world of sense-experience determined throughout by intelligence, but in itself an empirically endless series of finite, limited objects—is not one which can satisfy the demand for unity of cognition. The constant striving to transcend the limits of this world of experience, to reach the final synthesis in which its relation to self-consciousness shall be deduced, is what Kant calls Reason. So far as cognition is concerned, the one result of reason is the empty notion of the thing in itself,—a notion which, unfortunately, was by Kant so expressed, and by the Kantians so understood, as to imply much of the old dogmatic theory which it had been the business of the 'Critique' to explode. Kant, however, is not to be credited with all that has been drawn from his speculations by writers who had never

grasped his fundamental principle. For him, the thing in itself, the expression of the infinite striving of self-consciousness, is discoverable only in self-consciousness, as its absolute law. The statement of this absolute law is certainly approached by Kant from the empirical point of view or by an analytic method, and the position assigned by him to the categorical imperative seems at first sight to sunder Reason entirely from the world of experience. Nothing, indeed, can make the Kantian moral theory perfectly coherent; but, with especial reference to Fichte and the later German philosophy, it must be stated with perhaps unnecessary definiteness, that only in the categorical imperative does the notion of the thing-in-itself hold any position as a reality in the Kantian metaphysics.[7] The final synthesis, so far as it was attempted by Kant, appears only in the 'Critique of Judgment,' in which, by means of the notion of End, a reconciliation is sought between the intelligible or moral world, the realm of things-in-themselves, and the world of experience, of phenomena. The ethical idealism with which the Kantian theory closes, comes nearer to the Fichtean position than can be made apparent without more lengthy analysis of Kant than is here possible; but even in it we find the same tendency to separation which is the harassing feature of all the Kantian work. Fichte, it must be held, was justified in his constant complaint that in Kant there were really three theories which are never amalgamated. "Kant," he remarks in an instructive passage in the **'Nachgelassene Werke,'** "had three absolutes. . . . In the 'Critique of Pure Reason,' sense-experience was for him the absolute ($=x$); and in regard to the ideas, the higher, intelligible world, he expressed himself in a most depreciatory fashion. From his earlier works, and from hints in the 'Critique' itself, it may certainly be inferred that he would not have halted at that position; but I will engage to show that these hints are mere inconsequences of reasoning, for if his principles were consistently followed out, the supersensible world must vanish entirely, and as the only noumenon there would remain that which is to be realised in experience. . . . The loftier moral nature of the man corrected his philosophical error, and so appeared the 'Critique of Practical Reason.' In it was manifested the categorical notion of the Ego as something in itself, which could never have appeared in the 'Critique of Pure Reason;' we have thus a second absolute, a moral world ($=z$). But all the phenomena of human nature were not thereby explained. The relations of the beautiful, of the sublime, and of end in nature, which palpably were neither theoretical nor moral notions, yet remained. Moreover, what is of much greater importance, the empirical world was now absorbed in the moral world, as a world in itself,—a just retribution, as it were, for the first victory of the empirical. There appeared, then, the 'Critique of Judgment,' in the introduction to which—the most remarkable portion of that remarkable work—it was acknowledged that the supersensible and the sensible worlds must have some common though undiscoverable root, which root is the third absolute ($=y$). I say a *third,* separate from the two preceding and independent, although giving unity to them; and in this I do Kant no wrong, For if this y is undiscoverable, it may *contain* the other two; but we cannot comprehend how it does so, or deduce them from it. If, on the other hand, it is to be comprehended, it must be comprehended as absolute; and there remain, as before, three absolutes."[8]

The Kantian philosophy, while definitely formulating the first principle of speculation, thus left unsolved a whole series of problems, all of them arising in connection with one line of thought, and furnishing the material for later efforts at systematic development of the principle from which it started. With more or less clearness the thinkers who immediately followed Kant undertook the solution of these problems, and their work to a large extent determined the character of the Fichtean system, and was incorporated into it. Thus Reinhold's constant demand for unity of principle is recognised by Fichte as an attempt in the right direction, though the principle selected by him, that of representation (*Vorstellung*) as the fundamental fact of consciousness, was incapable of yielding any result more satisfactory than had been presented in the Kantian philosophy. Reinhold evidently felt the difficulty of bringing subject and object into any connection whatsoever, if they were assumed as originally distinct. He therefore proposed to select as starting-point the existence of the conscious state or representation, in which subject and object are contained as factors, and endeavoured by analysis of this fact to deduce the several doctrines which in a less coherent form had been brought forward by Kant. But in the first place, as Fichte points out in the **'Review of Ænesidemus,'**[9] the primary datum of philosophical construction cannot be a fact or representation, but must be the simple and original activity by which the fact or representation comes to be; and in the second place, as had been made quite apparent by the sceptical criticism of 'Ænesidemus' (Schulze), the idea of *Vorstellung* involved that doctrine which above all others was a stumbling-block to the Kantians,—the doctrine that the matter or definite content of *Vorstellung* was determined *ab extra,* by things-in-themselves. So, too, Beck's acute restatement of the Kantian theory had brought into the clearest light the gross misconceptions which might readily arise from Kant's mode of stating his doctrines. To many of the Kantians, indeed, the theory of the *a priori* character of the forms of perception and thought had been nothing but a revival, in the crudest sense, of the old doctrine of innate ideas. To them Kant's idea of self-consciousness, as conditioning knowledge, had meant that the individual subject was somehow acted upon by things, and that in consequence of the *a priori* or innate mechanism of consciousness, the effects of such action took of necessity the forms of space and

time and the categories. Beck's admirable discussion of the Kantian distinctions between analytic and synthetic judgments, synthetic *a priori* and synthetic *a posteriori* truths, intuition and thought, phenomena and things-in-themselves, sufficiently showed that these were but excrescences on the Kantian doctrine, merely temporary expedients for bringing the real problems into light; while the definiteness with which he expressed the cardinal doctrine of Kant's theory, the original synthetic unity of self-consciousness, threw light on all the subordinate points. At the same time, Beck advanced no sufficient grounds for the original positing of the object, which according to him is the very essence of the activity of self-consciousness. His theory failed to explain how and why it is that for the subject there is necessarily the object, the non-Ego. It left still in isolation the separate elements which had been thrown together by Kant. Finally, the acute criticisms of Maimon, for whose talent Fichte expresses unbounded admiration, had shown to demonstration how utterly inconsistent with the genuine Kantian doctrine was the commonly received view of the thing-in-itself. He too, however, misconceived Kant's idea of self-consciousness, found himself perplexed by the problem of the relation between the categories or forms of thought and the given matter of sense, proceeded to accept experience as consisting of a given series of phenomenal states, with the attributes of space and time, rejected therefore all *a priori* truths except the mathematical or quantitative, and thus left untouched the deeper problems raised by the **Kritik**.

The way had thus been prepared for Fichte's endeavour to take up in a comprehensive fashion the speculative question as it had been formulated by Kant, and to work into an organic whole what had been left by Kant in a fragmentary form. The artificial and sometimes forced fashion in which the *Wissenschaftslehre* at first proceeded must not disguise from us the genuine nature of the task Fichte had set before him, or the principle which underlies it. Firm adherence to the idea of the transcendental method; determination to accept nothing, whether as fact, law, or notion, which is not deducible from self-consciousness and its necessary conditions,—such is the spirit of the Fichtean philosophy, and from it follows the demand for systematic unity of conception, for a single principle out of which the multiplicity of experience may be deduced, and therefore for a single, all-embracing philosophical science. It is this very consistency which renders the detailed study of the Fichtean system a matter of so much difficulty, for if the fundamental idea be not grasped,—and as Fichte truly says, his philosophy is either to be mastered at a stroke or not at all,—little or none of the help which even Kant affords is extended to the student. The familiar psychological distinctions which furnish natural divisions in the Kantian theory of knowledge, are entirely wanting in the *Wissenschaftslehre*. Sense, understanding, reason, are not assumed as rubrics under which special kinds of knowledge may be arranged, but are regarded as specific modes in the development or realisation of self-consciousness, and appear in their determined position in the series of necessary acts by which self-consciousness is realised. The notions by which popular or unphilosophical thinking manages to explain to itself the nature of things—*e.g.,* the notion of cause by which we think the relation of objects to the variable contents of our representations—are not accepted or permitted to pass until they have been deduced, or shown to arise in the development of the necessary conditions of self-consciousness. The Kantian categories, the anomalous position of which had given occasion to grave misunderstanding of the very meaning of the system, are not in any way assumed as pre-existing forms into which matter falls; but object as formed by the category, and category as form of the object, are deduced together.

If *Wissenschaftslehre* is to accomplish its object—the systematic evolution of all that enters into consciousness—its starting-point must be found in that which renders any consciousness or knowledge possible. Such starting-point, by its very nature, cannot be a demonstrable fact, nor can it be comprehended in strict logical fashion,—that is, brought under a notion. All certainty rests ultimately on immediate evidence or intuition. The first condition, therefore, of consciousness, must be realised by us in the form of intuition. But the said first condition of consciousness is manifestly the consciousness of self. "Along with whatever any intelligence knows," says Ferrier, whose statement may here be accepted in place of any more elaborate treatment, "it must, as the ground or condition of its knowledge, have some cognisance of itself." To the speculative inquirer, endeavouring to reconstruct that which is immediately given in experience, the first and common ground for all experience is the result of that act whereby the Ego or self becomes an Ego or self. Of the necessary implications of this fundamental activity and its product, nothing requires at first to be said; philosophy is simply the attempt to give a systematic and complete account of them. But no philosophy can transcend the fact; and any problem referring to that which is absolutely dissevered from the result of the fact, must be dismissed as in terms contradictory and absurd. To ask, for example, whether the activity by which the Ego becomes an Ego does not presuppose the prior existence, in reality,—in an objective fashion,—of the Ego, is merely to make the "wonderful assumption that the Ego is something different from its own consciousness of itself, and that something, heaven knows what, lying beyond this consciousness, is the foundation of it,"[11] and to introduce notions of a complex and hypothetical character, such as existence and time, into the explanation of that with reference to which only have such notions significance. Doubtless, to the popular consciousness, thought pre-

sents itself as merely one, and probably one of the least important, of the facts of experience,—as arising from and dependent on the nature of things. But philosophy and popular thinking move on different platforms, and most of the gravest errors in speculation arise from the transference of considerations which are in due place in one of them into the other, where they are absolute absurdities. The philosophical construction of the world of experience is not to be confused with the world of experience itself, nor is it to be taken as a natural—*i.e.,* psychological—history of the development of the individual mind.[12] If in the development of the necessary conditions of self-consciousness, it is shown how the notion of a non-Ego arises,—if feeling and representation are deduced,—it is not to be supposed that by such process of deduction these, as facts of experience, are *produced.* Production and genetic construction of the contents of consciousness are totally distinct. Life, as Fichte puts it, is non-philosophising, and philosophy is non-living.

The intuition of the activity, whose product is the reflex act of consciousness—an activity the exact nature of which will presently be considered—Fichte calls *intellectual intuition.* The name is unfortunate, both as regards his predecessor Kant, and as regards his successor Schelling, for, in their systems, the same term is employed to denote two quite diverse facts. In the critical philosophy, intellectual intuition was used to indicate the supposed mode of consciousness by which a knowledge of things-in-themselves might be obtained, and was therefore regarded as contradictory of the very principles of the system. Fichte has little difficulty in showing that, so far as this meaning of the term is concerned, there is no difference of opinion between Kant and himself; but he, at the same time, points out that the whole critical analysis rested upon the fact of the unity of consciousness (or, as Kant called it, the unity of apperception), and that for this unity no name was so appropriate as that of intellectual intuition. On the other hand, in Schelling's system, intellectual intuition was employed to denote the consciousness of the absolute, of the identity between subject and object; and, in so far, there is a certain resemblance between his use of the term and that of Fichte. There was, however, a fundamental difference between the two thinkers in regard to this identity of subject and object; and in his later writings, Fichte, to emphasise his opposition to Schelling, generally employed the expression, *free activity,* to denote the fundamental act and product of the Ego.

In calling the consciousness of the fundamental activity of the Ego intuition, Fichte had a twofold object. He desired to bring into prominence the fact that he is not starting with any abstract notion, but with the activity of the Ego—an activity not to be designated thought or will, or by any other complex, and therefore misleading, term; and further, to indicate from the outset what was the peculiar nature of the general method of *Wissenschaftslehre*. For an intuition is never a datum which is simply received in experience. It is invariably the product of a constructive act. The intuition of a triangle, for example, is the consciousness of a definite and necessarily determined procedure of construction within the limitations of space; and in this process of construction we see intuitively the connection of the elements,—we see how each subsequent portion of the construction is determined by what has preceded; and as the process is general, determined only by the conditions of space, we are at the same time aware of the generality of the result. Intuitive knowledge, therefore, is genetic, and *Wissenschaftslehre,* the systematic consciousness of what is contained in the fundamental intellectual intuition, must likewise be genetic in method. *Wissenschaftslehre* will show "that the fundamental proposition, posited and immediately known as existent in consciousness, is impossible unless under a further condition, and that this further condition is likewise impossible unless a third be added,—until the conditions of the first are completely developed, and the possibility of the same completely comprehended."[13] It will "construct the whole common consciousness of all rational beings in its fundamental characteristics, with pure *a priori* evidence, just as geometry constructs, with pure *a priori* evidence, the general modes of limitation of space by all rational beings. It starts from the simplest and most characteristic quality of self-consciousness, the intuition of the Ego,[14] and, under the assumption that the completely qualified self-consciousness is the final result of all the other qualifications of consciousness, proceeds until this is thoroughly deduced. To each link in the chain of these qualifications a new one is added, and it is clear, in the direct intuition of them, that the same addition must take place in the consciousness of every rational being. Call the Ego A. Then, in the intuition of the construction of A, it is seen that B is inseparably connected with it. In the intuition of the construction of B, it is equally clear that C is an inseparable link, and so on, till we reach the final member of A,—completed self-consciousness,—which manifests itself as complete and perfect."[15]

No commentary upon these passages seems necessary, save perhaps on the expression, "completed self-consciousness," of which, indeed, the system itself is the best explanation. On both sides, this notion of completed self-consciousness requires to be guarded or defined—with regard to its essence as *self*-consciousness, and with regard to its *completion*. To popular thinking, self-consciousness is identical with individuality,—with the knowledge of self as a personal, active being, related to others, and to a universe of things. But it is at once evident that knowledge of individuality in this sense is a complex fact, and a fact of which the ground or possibility must be sought in

the original act whereby the subject is conscious at all. "The Ego of real consciousness is always particular, and isolated: it is a person among other persons, each of whom describes himself as an Ego; and *Wissenschaftslehre* must develop up to the point at which such consciousness is explained. Totally distinct from this is the Ego from which *Wissenschaftslehre* starts; for this is nothing but the identity of the conscious subject with that of which it is conscious. Abstraction from all else that is contained in personality is necessary in order to attain this point of view."[16] Self-consciousness, in fact, is the common element in all knowledge and action, and therefore cannot in itself contain that which is special and particular to the individual. It is the ground of individuality; for without it there could not possibly be the developed, concrete consciousness of personality; but as ground, it is distinct from that which is conditioned by it. We may call it, if we choose, the pure Ego, or form of the Ego,—Fichte, as above noted, occasionally employs the untranslatable term *Ich-heit,*—but under whatever fashion of speech, we have to recognise in it the indispensable condition of all consciousness. Intellectual intuition lies at the basis of all more developed modes of mental action.

What, then, is to be understood by *completed* self-consciousness? Evidently, the realisation in consciousness of all that can be shown to be necessarily implied or involved in intellectual intuition as such. For it may very well happen that the peculiar activity of the Ego, in becoming conscious of itself, implies a number of intermediate stages,—such, for instance, as the definite separation of subject and object, self and not-self; the definite *representation* of each of these under special forms; the recognition of a plurality of individual active beings, with rights and duties; and all of these may speculatively be exhibited as following from, and dependent on, self-consciousness itself. In that case, completed self-consciousness would mean, not simply the abstract moment of self-identity, but the consciousness to which the individual may arrive, that he occupies a place in an ideal system of conscious beings, in an ideal order; that his finite existence is to be regarded as the continuous effort to realise what is implied in that position; and thus, that his individuality is lost or absorbed in the universal, rational order. All knowledge and the varied forms of law, of state mechanism, of moral duties, of religious beliefs, would thus appear to consciousness as necessary elements of the scheme or plan of the ideal world; and the consciousness of this ideal system, which it is the business of speculative philosophy to describe, would be completed self-consciousness. This is, in substance, the distinction which Fichte indicates between the Ego as intellectual intuition, and the Ego as idea. "The idea of the Ego has only this in common with the Ego as intuition, that in both the Ego is thought as not individual,—in the latter, because the form of the Ego is not yet defined to the point of individuality; in the former, conversely, because the individual is lost in thought and action according to universal laws. The two are opposed in this, that in the Ego as intuition only the form of the Ego is to be found, and no reference can be made to any special matter,—which indeed becomes conceivable only when the thought of a world arises in the Ego—while, on the other hand, in the Ego as idea, the whole matter of the Ego is thought. From the first, speculative cognition proceeds, and to the latter it tends: only in the practical sphere can the idea be posited as the ultimate goal of the efforts of reason. The first is original intuition, and becomes for us, when treated by thought, a notion (*Begriff*): the latter is idea only; it cannot be thought in a determinate fashion; it can never exist *realiter,* but we must continuously approximate to it."[17] It need not surprise us that Fichte, at this period of his philosophical reflection, should frequently use the term God as equivalent to the pure Ego, regarded as idea. Such a doctrine can appear startling only if we identify self-consciousness with individuality, and if we fail to see that were God not involved in self-consciousness, His existence must be for ever contingent or unnecessary for thought. We have here one of the points on which it is instructive to note the difference between Fichte's position and that of Spinoza. For Spinoza, as for philosophy in general, the supreme problem is to connect the particular with the system of which it is a part,—a problem which we may call the reduction of the many to one, or by what phrase we please. Now the one and the many are definitely described by Spinoza, but so separated as to render transition or union wellnigh impossible. As in the Eleatic system, so in that of Spinoza, the two elements fall asunder. It is true that Spinoza seems to have thought the problem solved by pointing to the impossibility of thinking the particular or finite, save as in relation to the infinite; but his treatment of this necessity of thinking is the weak point in his system. Modes of thought become for him so many finite objects, mutually determining and determined; and any relation to substance is thus, for them, impossible. To an intellect regarding finite modes from without, it might well be impossible to think of them, except as limitations of the infinite substance; but no such thought is possible for the finite modes themselves. The two notions with which Spinoza works— substance and mutual determination—are irreconcilable; and their subjective counterparts, understanding and imagination, are, in a similar fashion, left standing side by side.[18] It is on account of this failure to unite the two elements of his system that Fichte classes Spinoza as a dogmatist, and points out that his own doctrine, on the speculative side, is Spinozism, but, as containing the higher synthesis, an inverted or spiritualised Spinozism. The same criticism is contained in Hegel's pregnant remark, that Spinoza's error lay in regarding God as substance, and not as spirit.

Before passing to the more explicit statement of the development of self-consciousness—*i.e.,* to the systematic portion of the *Wissenschaftslehre*—it may be remarked that in this notion of the Ego as both abstract unity and concrete fulness, we have the transition from the Kantian to the later philosophy of Hegel. For Hegel as for Fichte, philosophy is the systematic development of thought from its most abstract moment to the fulness and wealth of real existence, and the culminating point is the complete consciousness of thought as that which, systematically developed, is the reality of existence. In treatment of many problems the two thinkers differ; in matter, and to a large extent in form, they are at one.

3.—First Principles of Wissenschaftslehre.

As science of science, or theory of that which is presupposed in all consciousness, *Wissenschaftslehre* must take its origin from that which is in itself unsusceptible of proof. Its first principle cannot be a proposition for which reasons can be advanced; it cannot even be the expression of a fact which is given in experience; but it must express that which lies at the basis of all experience, of all consciousness. The matter of the first principle must therefore be unconditioned, and equally so the form. We may indeed assume that alongside of this absolutely unconditioned first principle, two other propositions may be given, two expressions of necessary acts in the development of self-consciousness,—the one, unconditioned in form though determined as regards matter; the other, unconditioned in matter, though determined as regards form. More than these three there cannot be assumed; all other propositions in the theory of consciousness must be deducible from them.

What, then, is the first principle of the *Wissenschaftslehre?* Evidently, from the exposition already given of the nature of this science, the first principle can be nothing but an explicit statement of the very innermost nature of self-consciousness. For all consciousness, and therefore all experience, is determined by self-consciousness, and stands under it as its supreme condition. The first truth must therefore be the express statement of that fundamental activity by which consciousness comes to be. Beyond all doubt this fundamental activity is not to be thought as an object in consciousness, as one of the facts which we may discover by inner observation. As opposed to all the mechanical necessity under which facts appear for us, this activity is freedom as such,—pure action, which, indeed, is or has being, but is not to be regarded as being.

The explicit statement of this fundamental activity is reached in Fichte's first systematic work, the **Grundlage des Wissenschaftslehre,** by a somewhat artificial method; and unfortunately, the few pages containing the application of this method not only exhaust the ordinary student's knowledge of the system, but supply almost all that is given of Fichte's doctrine in the ordinary histories of philosophy. To this cause one must refer much of the misunderstanding which has undoubtedly existed regarding the true nature of Fichte's speculative work. The method is certainly artificial, but as the activity in question is absolutely unconditioned, there is not, as it were, any one defined road by which it is to be approached. Fichte, accordingly, proposes to take an undeniable fact of ordinary, empirical thought, and by criticism to show what is implied in it. The fact selected is the well-known logical or formal law of identity,—A is A. A is A; that is, independently of all material considerations as to what A may be, this at least is true, that it is itself,—it is A. But such a purely formal proposition makes no assertion regarding the positing or affirming of A. It asserts merely that *if* A is posited, then it is =A: in other words, it asserts the absolute and unconditioned validity of a certain *nexus* or bond =*x*. The *nexus* or bond, the law according to which we judge that A is A, is only in consciousness, is only for the Ego; consequently the proposition A = A may be expressed thus: A is for the Ego simply and solely by virtue of being affirmed or posited in the Ego; and the *nexus* (*x*), the ground of this identity, is the affirmation of the existence of the Ego, *I am*. Only in and for a consciousness that is aware of its own identity, can the law A = A have validity. The unity and identity of self-consciousness thus lies at the basis of all empirical consciousness, for all empirical consciousness falls under the rule, A = A. But if the proposition A = A, valid for all empirical consciousness, has validity only because it is grounded on the fact of the identity of self-consciousness, Ego=Ego, this identity must be the pure act of the Ego itself, the mere expression or product of the activity by which the Ego is the Ego at all. Self-affirmation, then, is given simply, unconditionally, as the being of the Ego. The Ego is, because it posits itself as being; it posits itself as being, because it is. The fundamental activity of all consciousness is thus the affirmation of itself by the Ego. "The Ego posits originally and simply its own being."[19]

The method of arriving at this first proposition,—one absolutely unconditioned in matter as in form, for the Ego is the common condition of all matter of consciousness in general, and the affirmation of its self-identity, the form of the proposition, is not prescribed to it from without,—is otherwise given by Fichte in his later expositions.[20] In them the reader is called upon to make the experiment of thinking any given object, and then of thinking the Ego. In the first act, the characteristic feature is the definite and recognised distinction in consciousness between the subject thinking and the object thought. In the second, it is equally plain that the Ego thought and the Ego thinking are one and the same. The activity of thought is reflected upon itself, and in this reflection upon self consists the very essence of the Ego, or of self-consciousness. "The procedure of *Wissenschaftslehre* is the following: it requires each one to note what he necessarily does when he calls himself, I. It assumes that every one who really performs the required act, will find that he *affirms himself,* or, which may be clearer to many, *that he is at the same time subject and object.* In this absolute identity of subject and object consists the very nature of the Ego. The Ego is that which cannot be subject, without being, in the same indivisible act, object—and cannot be object, without being, in the same indivisible act, subject; and conversely, whatever has this characteristic, is Ego; the two expressions are the same."[21]

Thus the first proposition is the explicit statement of that which underlies all consciousness,—of the act whereby consciousness is possible. It is the same proposition which implicitly had appeared in the critical philosophy under the term unity of apperception; but the full significance of it had not been developed by Kant. Beyond this truth no philosophy can go, and all true philosophy depends upon the recognition of it. Any metaphysical theorem which assumes an origin or cause for consciousness transcending this first, primitive affirmation of the Ego by itself, is self-convicted of incompleteness and absurdity.

It is perhaps needless to note that the Ego referred to is not to be identified with the individual or person. Each individual or person has in common the consciousness of self, without which he exists not at all; but to be individual or person, more is required than is contained in self-consciousness. Accordingly, as we shall later see, although Fichte will not deny to God self-consciousness in the sense here analysed, he will not admit that God is personal or individual. To identify any one thing or person with self-consciousness is absurd. Self-consciousness is not a thing or fact to be observed; just as little is God one among the objects of experience to be thought of as coexisting with finite spirits, conditioning or determining them, and in turn conditioned or determined by them. There is, and can be, from the position of pure thought, no God except the ideal system which is involved in self-consciousness, and in which finite spirits have a definite place and function.

The fundamental mode of activity, the position of the Ego by itself, if regarded *in abstracto,* is the logical law of identity—*i.e.,* no identity of object can be thought apart from the identity of the thinking self. If regarded as in application to objects, it is the category of reality. All reality is in and for the Ego. The categories are merely the necessary modes of action of self-consciousness viewed objectively, or in relation to the object.

Alongside of this first principle, which is unconditioned both in matter and in form, there may be placed for the purposes of the *Wissenschaftslehre* two further principles, one unconditioned in form but conditioned in matter, the other conditioned as to form but unconditioned as to matter. By an artificial procedure resembling that adopted in the case of the first principle, Fichte brings forward the second, on the nature and position of which the greatest misconception has prevailed.

As certainly as the proposition, A = A, appears in empirical consciousness, so certainly appears the allied but distinct proposition, Not-A does not = A. This proposition is not to be taken as a mere reduplication in negative form of the rule of identity; it is not equivalent to the judgment, Not-A = Not-A. For there is implied in it a new element, Not-A, and a totally new and distinct act, that of opposing to A its negative, Not-A. So far as matter is concerned, the proposition is determined; for if there is to be op-positing at all, that which is opposed to A can only be Not-A. But the form of the proposition, the act of negation, is not conditioned by the form of affirmation. Now, if we treat this proposition as we treated the first, resolving it into its ultimate terms, we have as result the opposition, in the Ego, of Ego and non-Ego. In the Ego, the non-Ego is opposed to the Ego. This second proposition is fundamental in the Fichtean philosophy, but at the same time its significance is not immediately evident. On the one hand, it is clear what is not to be understood by the non-Ego in question. The non-Ego is not the thing-in-itself. It is impossible and contradictory that the Ego should affirm for itself the being of that which, by definition, is not for the Ego. On the other hand, it is not yet plain, and, indeed, it only becomes plain from much later developments of the system, what is the precise nature of the act of oppositing or negating. The obscurity which rests over the proposition arises from two sources. In the first place, Fichte accepts, as given, a fact of empirical consciousness, the fact of difference or opposition, and shows that for a self-conscious subject, the ultimate ground of all difference is the distinction of self and not-self. No opposition or difference in empirical knowledge is conceivable, if the Ego has not in itself the moment of difference. As mere abstract statement of what is implied in real consciousness, the proposition has, therefore, unconditioned truth; but it has not thereby been made clear how real consciousness, which is determined or limited, is related to the pure unity of self-consciousness as such. All limitation is negation—this is fundamental for Fichte as for Spinoza, and in the second proposition the ground of the maxim is given—but it is not thereby explained why or how there should be limitation at all. In the second place, the all-important distinction between the abstract and concrete moments of self-consciousness is easily overlooked. Fichte is here giving expression to the most

abstract aspect of consciousness, which becomes real or concrete only after the introduction of many other elements. The non-Ego referred to is the abstract aspect of that which in the further movement of thought presents itself as the world of objects, but it is not in itself the concrete, represented world.

The first proposition, as was said, is not in Fichte's later expositions approached in the artificial manner adopted in the *Grundlage*; still less is this the case in regard to the second fundamental act. In the later works, specially in the *Darstellung aus dem Jahre, 1801*, and in the posthumous lectures, the statement is much more concrete and intelligible. Self-affirmation of the Ego is the primitive activity of consciousness. But such primitive activity is in itself but the ground of consciousness. The Ego, to be real, must be aware of its own activity as affirming itself. This becoming aware of its own activity Fichte calls *reflection;* and it is easily seen that the essential feature of reflection is self-limitation of the Ego. But limitation is negation; the Ego becomes aware of its own activity as self-positing only in and by opposition to self. Infinite activity—*i.e.,* activity related only to itself—is never, as such, conscious activity. "Consciousness works through reflection, and reflection is only through limitation."[22] So soon as we reflect upon the activity of the Ego, the Ego is necessarily finite; so soon as the Ego is conscious of its finitude, it is conscious of striving beyond these limits, and so of its infinitude. Were the question raised, Is the Ego, then, infinite? the Ego, by the very question, is finite. Is the Ego finite? then, to be aware of finitude, it is necessarily infinite; and so on, in endless alternation.

The abstract expression of this alternation between subject and object as in relation to one another, is contained in the third fundamental proposition,—that from which the *Wissenschaftslehre* definitely takes its start.

The second proposition has brought forward a non-Ego, which is in every respect the negative of the Ego. Whatever is affirmed regarding the one must be explicitly denied of the other. But, if we consider our two propositions, we shall find not only that they contradict one another, but that each proposition, taken in respect of the other, contradicts itself. For if the non-Ego is posited, the Ego is negated; but the Ego is absolute reality, and consequently the non-Ego is only posited through the Ego. The Ego, therefore, both posits and negates itself. It is in itself a contradiction, or unites contradictions in itself. It is evidently impossible that both can be negated; it is equally impossible that one should be negated by the other. The only solution is to be found in some act of the Ego by which it is limited as regards the non-Ego, and by which the non-Ego is limited as regards the Ego: the Ego shall, *in part,* negate the non-Ego; the non-Ego shall, *in part,* negate the Ego. So certainly, therefore, as the two fundamental propositions are true, as certainly can they be combined in the unity of self-consciousness, only if the Ego posit in itself a divisible Ego as limited by a divisible non-Ego. In this third proposition the form is conditioned, for by the needs of the prior maxims it is prescribed what the activity must be; the matter is unconditioned, for the notion by which the union is effected—that of limitation—is not prescribed beforehand. The third proposition, therefore, completes the principles of *Wissenschaftslehre:* henceforth each step in the evolution of self-consciousness can and must be proved to follow with demonstrative evidence from them.

Moreover, the connection of the three principles, and especially the mode by which the third of them was attained, shows clearly what must be the method of evolution. The very essence of self-consciousness, in its double moments of self-position and reflection, is the union of contradictory aspects. Thesis and antithesis are the formal expressions of the activity lying at the root of consciousness. But contradictions can only be for a self-conscious subject when united or contained in some more concrete synthesis. Limitation has manifested itself as the first synthesis; but, narrowly examined, the members there united will be seen to manifest new contradictions, which again require to be resolved into some richer, more concrete notion. The course of procedure is thus the continuous analysis of the antithetical moments of each notion, and the synthetical union of them: the goal is the complete synthetical union of the original opposition of the Ego and the non-Ego in consciousness. Term after term will be introduced, until at last the gap between these two is filled up, and the final synthesis either attained or the full ground for its unattainability made clear. The successive acts by which the new synthesis comes forward, yield, *in abstracto,* the forms of the categories, which will thus be deduced systematically, not accepted haphazard, as in the critical philosophy. The successive modes of consciousness, in and through which the categories receive application to objects, will be rigorously developed, and not taken from empirical psychology. *Wissenschaftslehre* is thus not only logic, in the highest sense of the term, but also a *phenomenology* or pragmatic history of consciousness.

Notes

[1] 'Werke,' vol. i. pp. 419-518; vol. ii. pp. 323-420.

[2] The term *Vorstellung* is used by Fichte, as indeed by all German writers, in various senses; and the ambiguity attaching to it is undoubtedly one of the main causes of the misunderstanding of his doctrine, as of the Kantian system. Here it is employed simply to denote some form of consciousness—something of which the subject is aware. Nothing is thereby decided as to the *mode of existence* of the representation. It is not meanwhile to be regarded as a subjective state— *i.e.,* as a modification of the individual, particular Ego.

[3] Berkeley, as Fichte rightly notes, is a *dogmatist;* but some phases of his speculation, and much of the philosophy which has rested itself on Berkeley, may be regarded as idealist. Fichte himself does not, in this reference, adduce Leibnitz as the type of idealism,— and there are certainly elements in Leibnitz which might lead one to class him otherwise.

[4] "Versuch einer neuen Darstellung," 'Werke,' vol. i. pp. 528, 529.

[5] It is not a little remarkable how slight appears to have been Fichte's acquaintance with Hume's writings. Scepticism, as a whole, indeed, plays but a small part in his system of thinking, and is generally dismissed with a species of contempt. Cf. 'Werke,' vol. i. p. 120 *n.*

[6] The double significance of this category is very apparent in the Kantian system.

[7] It is much to be regretted that, almost without exception, the best English expositions of Kant restrict themselves to an account of the 'Critique of Pure Reason.' Nothing but error and confusion can result from this arbitrary limitation. It is much as though one were to treat only the theoretical portion of *Wissenschaftslehre,* and leave untouched the fundamental problems of the practical side. That the Kantian theory appeared in three separate books, is no reason why we should treat it as three separate theories. The 'Critique of Practical Reason,' moreover, though simple enough in its details, stands more in need of elucidation and commentary, so far as its principle is concerned, than the 'Critique of Pure Reason.'

[8] 'Nachgelassene Werke,' vol. ii. pp. 102-104. See also 'Leben und Briefwechsel,' vol. ii. p. 177.

[9] 'Werke,' vol. i. p. 9. Cf. vol. i. p. 468.

[10] Beck's 'Einzig-möglicher Standpunckt' (Riga, 1796), though not written with much skill, is yet one of the best and most instructive commentaries on the 'Kritik,' and should be neglected by no student of Kant.

[11] 'Werke,' vol. i. p. 460.

[12] 'Werke,' vol. i. pp. 397-399. Cf. vol. v. pp. 333 *et seq.*

[13] 'Werke,' vol. i. p. 446.

[14] Fichte's expression, *Anschaung der Ich-heit,* is more exact, but, I think, untranslatable into English.

[15] 'Werke,' vol. ii. pp. 379, 380.

[16] 'Werke,' vol. ii. p. 382. Cf. 'Briefwechsel,' p. 166.

[17] 'Werke,' vol. i. p. 516. The distinction here taken between *Begriff* and *Idee* is, on the whole, Kantian. The passage implies much that can only be made intelligible through the system itself.

[18] Expositions of Spinoza are frequently imperfect from laying undue stress on one of these elements. Mr Pollock's recent very able statement entirely rejects or casts in the shade the first of them. Spinoza is treated throughout as working with the important scientific notion of mutual determination.

[19] 'Werke,' vol. i. p. 98.

[20] In the two "Introductions to Wissenschaftslehre," in the 'New Exposition,' and in the 'Sonnenklarer Bericht.' The posthumous "Exposition from the year 1801" ('Werke,' vol. ii. pp. 1-162) contains in its first part (¶1-29) a most elaborate but excessively complicated and obscure analysis of the same fundamental condition.

[21] 'Werke,' vol. ii. pp. 441, 442. Cf. 'Werke,' vol. i. pp. 522, 523, 529.

[22] 'Werke,' vol. i. p. 269. Cf. 'Darstellung, a. d. J., 1801, ¶17, 28, 29; 'Nachgelassene Werke,' vol. i. p. 79; vol. ii. pp. 339, 349.

One of Fichte's students at Jena describes him:

Fichte really was an impressive person. Jokingly, I often called him "the Bonaparte of philosophy," and there are many similarities between the two. This small, broad-shouldered man did not stand calmly at his lectern like a secular sage, but stood angrily and combatively. His unkept brown hair really stood out around the furrowed face, which resembled both the face of an old woman and that of an eagle. Whether standing or striding about upon his sturdy legs, he was always firmly planted in the earth upon which he stood, secure and immovable in the sense of his own strength. No gentle word passed his lips, nor did any laughter. He seemed to have declared war upon the world which stood over against his I and to be concealing his lack of grace and dignity with harshness. This, anyway, is the way it seemed to me.

Johann Georg Rist, in Lebenserinnerungen, *1880, reprinted in* Fichte: Early Philosophical Writings, *ed. by Daniel Breazeale, Cornell University Press, 1988.*

John Dewey (essay date 1915)

SOURCE: "Moral and Political Philosophy," in *German Philosophy and Politics,* G. P. Putnam's Sons, 1942, pp. 98-113.

[*Although Dewey's* German Philosophy and Politics *appeared in a revised edition in 1942, the chapters were revised as little as possible in order to retain their World War I perspective. In a view characteristic of the years spanning both world wars, Dewey presents Fichte as "the beginning" of modern German nationalism.*]

. . . Kant was enough of a child of the eighteenth century to be cosmopolitan, not nationalistic, in his feeling. Since humanity as a whole, in its universality, alone truly corresponds to the universality of reason, he upheld the ideal of an ultimate republican federation of states; he was one of the first to proclaim the possibility of enduring peace among nations on the basis of such a federated union of mankind.

The threatened domination of Europe by Napoleon following on the wars waged by republican France put an end, however, to cosmopolitanism. Since Germany was the greatest sufferer from these wars, and since it was obvious that the lack of national unity, the division of Germany into a multitude of petty states, was the great source of her weakness; since it was equally obvious that Prussia, the one strong and centralized power among the German states, was the only thing which saved them all from national extinction, subsequent political philosophy in Germany rescued the idea of the State from the somewhat ambiguous moral position in which Kant had left it. Since a state which is an absolute moral necessity and whose actions are nevertheless lacking in inherent moral quantity is an anomaly, the doctrine almost calls for a theory which shall make the State the supreme moral entity.

Fichte marks the beginning of the transformation; and, in his writings, it is easy to detect a marked difference of attitude toward the nationalistic state before and after 1806, when in the battle of Jena Germany went down to inglorious defeat. From the time of Fichte, the German philosophy of the State blends with its philosophy of history, so that my reservation of the latter topic for the next section is somewhat arbitrary, and I shall not try rigidly to maintain the division of themes.

I have already mentioned the fact that Kant relaxes the separation of the moral realm of freedom from the sensuous realm of nature sufficiently to assert that the former is *meant* to influence the latter and finally to subjugate it. By means of the little crack thus introduced into nature, Fichte rewrites the Kantian philosophy. The world of sense must be regarded from the very start as material which the free, rational, moral Ego has created in order to have material for its own adequate realization of will. Fichte had a longing for an absolute unity which did not afflict Kant, to whom, save for the concession just referred to, a complete separation of the two operations of legislative reason sufficed. Fichte was also an ardently *active* soul, whose very temperament assured him of the subordination of theoretical knowledge to moral action.

It would be as difficult to give, in short space, an adequate sketch of Fichte's philosophy as of Kant's. To him, however, reason was the expression of the will, not (as with Kant) the will an application of reason to action. *"Im Anfang war die That"* is good Fichteanism. While Kant continued the usual significance of the term Reason (with only such modifications as the rationalism of his century had made current), Fichte began the transformation which consummated in later German idealism. If the world of nature and of human relations is an expression of reason, then reason must be the sort of thing and have the sort of attributes by means of which the world must be construed, no matter how far away this conception of reason takes us from the usual meaning of the term. To Fichte the formula which best described such aspects of the world and of life as he was interested in was effort at self-realization through struggle with difficulties and overcoming opposition. Hence his formula for reason was a Will which, having "posited" itself, then "posited" its antithesis in order, through further action subjugating this opposite, to conquer its own freedom.

The doctrine of the primacy of the Deed, and of the Duty to achieve freedom through moral self-assertion against obstacles (which, after all, are there only to further this self-assertion) was one which could, with more or less plausibility, be derived from Kant. More to our present point, it was a doctrine which could be preached with noble moral fervor in connection with the difficulties and needs of a divided and conquered Germany. Fichte saw himself as the continuator of the work of Luther and Kant. His final "science of knowledge" brought the German people alone of the peoples of the world into the possession of the idea and ideal of absolute freedom. Hence the peculiar destiny of the German scholar and the German State. It was the duty and mission of German science and philosophy to contribute to the cause of the spiritual emancipation of humanity. Kant had already taught that the acts of men were to become gradually permeated by a spirit of rationality till there should be an equation of inner freedom of mind and outer freedom of action. Fichte's doctrine demanded an acceleration of the process. Men who have attained to a consciousness of the absolute freedom and self-activity must necessarily desire to see around them similar free beings. The scholar who

is truly a scholar not merely knows, but he knows the nature of knowledge—its place and function as a manifestation of the Absolute. Hence he is, in a peculiar sense, the direct manifestation of God in the world—the true priest. And his priestly function consists in bringing other men to recognize moral freedom in its creative operation. Such is the dignity of education as conducted by those who have attained true philosophic insight.

Fichte made a specific application of this idea to his own country and time. The humiliating condition of contemporary Germany was due to the prevalence of egoism, selfishness and particularism: to the fact that men had lowered themselves to the plane of sensuous life. The fall was the worse because the Germans, more than any other people, were by nature and history conscious of the ideal and spiritual principle, the principle of freedom, lying at the very basis of all things. The key to the political regeneration of Germany was to be found in a moral and spiritual regeneration effected by means of education. The key, amid political division, to political unity was to be sought in devotion to moral unity. In this spirit Fichte preached his ***Addresses to the German Nation***. In this spirit he collaborated in the foundation of the University of Berlin, and zealously promoted all the educational reforms introduced by Stein and Humboldt into Prussian life.

The conception of the State as an essential moral Being charged with an indispensable moral function lay close to these ideas. Education is *the* means of the advancement of humanity toward realization of its divine perfection. Education is the work of the State. The syllogism completes itself. But in order that the State may carry on its educational or moral mission it must not only possess organization and commensurate power, but it must also control the conditions which secure the possibility offered to the individuals composing it. To adopt Aristotle's phrase, men must live before they can live nobly. The primary condition of a secure life is that everyone be able to live by his own labor. Without this, moral self-determination is a mockery. The business of the State, outside of its educational mission, is concerned with property, and this business means insuring property to everyone as well as protecting him in what he already possesses. Moreover, property is not mere physical possession. It has a profound moral significance, for it means the subjugation of physical things to will. It is a necessary part of the realization of moral personality: the conquest of the non-ego by the ego. Since property does not mean mere appropriation, but is a right recognized and validated by society itself, property has a social basis and aim. It is an expression not of individual egotism but of the universal will. Hence it is essential to the very idea of property and of the State that all the members of society have an equal opportunity for property.

Hence it is the duty of the State to secure to its every member the right to work and the reward of his work.

The outcome, as expressed in his essay on **"The Closed Industrial State,"** is State Socialism, based on moral and idealistic grounds, not on economic considerations. In order that men may have a real opportunity to develop their moral personalities, their right to labor and to adequate living, in return for their labor, must be assured. This cannot happen in a competitive society. Industry must be completely regulated by the State if these indispensable rights to labor and resulting comfort and security of life as means to moral volition are to be achieved. But a state engaged in unrestricted foreign trade will leave its workingmen at the mercy of foreign conditions. It must therefore regulate or even eliminate foreign commerce so far as is necessary to secure its own citizens. The ultimate goal is a universal state as wide as humanity, and a state in which each individual will act freely, without state-secured rights and state-imposed obligations. But before this cosmopolitan and philosophically anarchic condition can be reached, we must pass through a period of the nationalistic closed state. Thus at the end a wide gulf separates Fichte from Kant. The moral individualism of the latter has become an ethical socialism. Only in and by means of a circle of egos or personalities does a human being attain the moral reason and freedom which Kant bestowed upon him as his birth-right. Only through the educational activities of the State and its complete regulation of the industrial activities of its members does the potential moral freedom of individuals become an established reality.

If I have devoted so much space to Fichte it is not because of his direct influence upon affairs or even upon thought. He did not found a school. His system was at once too personal and too formal. Nevertheless, he expressed ideas which, removed from their special context in his system, were taken up into the thought of cultivated Germany. Heine, speaking of the vogue of systems of thought, says with profound truth that "nations have an instinctive presentiment of what they require to fulfill their mission."

And Fichte's thought infiltrated through many crevices. Rodbertus and Lasalle, the socialists, were, for example, profoundly affected by him. When the latter was prosecuted in a criminal suit for his "Programme of Workingmen," his reply was that his programme was a distinctively philosophic utterance, and hence protected by the constitutional provision for freedom of science and its teaching. And this is his philosophy of the State:

> The State is the unity and coöperation of individuals in a moral whole. . . . The ultimate and intrinsic end of the State is, therefore, to further the positive unfolding, the progressive development of human

life. Its function is to work out the true end of man; that is to say, the full degree of culture of which human nature is capable.

And he quotes with approval the words:

> The concept of the State must be broadened so as to make the State the contrivance whereby all human virtue is to be realized to the full.

And if he differs from Fichte, it is but in the assertion that since the laboring class is the one to whom the need most directly appeals, it is workingmen who must take the lead in the development of the true functions of the State.

Pantheism is a philosophic nickname which should be sparingly employed; so also should the term Monism. To call Fichte's system an ethical pantheism and monism is not to say much that is enlightening. But with free interpretation, the designation may be highly significant in reference to the spiritual temper of the Germany of the first part of the nineteenth century. For it gives a key to the presentiment of what Germany needed to fulfill its mission.

It is a commonplace of German historians that its unity and expansion to a great state powerful externally, prosperous internally, was wrought, unlike that of any other people, from within outward. In Lange's words, "our national development started from the most ideal and approximated more and more to the real." Hegel and Heine agree that in Germany the French Revolution and the Napoleonic career were paralleled by a philosophic revolution and an intellectual empire. You recall the bitter word that, when Napoleon was finally conquered and Europe partitioned, to Germany was assigned the kingdom of the clouds. But this aërial and tenuous kingdom became a mighty power, working with and in the statesmen of Prussia and the scholars of Germany to found a kingdom on the solid earth. Spiritual and ideal Germany made common cause with realistic and practical Prussia. As says Von Sybel, the historian of the "Founding of the German Empire":

> Germany had been ruined through its own disintegration and had dragged Prussia with it into the abyss. It was well known that the wild fancies of the Conqueror hovered about the utter annihilation of Prussia; if this should take place, then east as well as west of the Elbe, not only political independence, but every trace of a German spirit, the German language and customs, German art and learning—everything would be wiped out by the foreigners. But this fatal danger was perceived just at the time when everybody had been looking up to Kant and Schiller, had been admiring Faust, the world-embracing masterpiece of Goethe's, and had recognized that Alexander von Humboldt's cosmological studies

and Niebuhr's "Roman History" had created a new era in European science and learning. In such intellectual attainments the Germans felt that they were far superior to the vanquisher of the world and his great nation; and so the political interests of Prussia and the salvation of the German nationality exactly coincided. Schleiermacher's patriotic sermons, Fichte's stirring addresses to the German people, Humboldt's glorious founding of the Berlin University, served to augment the resisting power of Prussia, while Scharnhorst's recruits and militia were devoted to the defense of German honor and German customs. Everyone felt that German nationality was lost if Prussia did not come to its rescue, and that, too, there was no safety possible for Prussia unless all Germany was free.

What a remarkable providence it was that brought together, as in the Middle Ages, on this ancient colonial ground, a throng of the most energetic men from all districts of Germany. For neither Stein nor his follower, Hardenberg, nor the generals, Scharnhorst, Bluecher and Gneisenau, nor the authors, Niebuhr, Fichte and K. F. Eichorn, nor many others who might be mentioned, were born in Prussia; yet because their thoughts centered in Germany, they had become loyal Prussians. The name Germany had been blotted from the political map of Europe, but never had so many hearts thrilled at the thought of being German.

Thus on the most eastern frontier of German life, in the midst of troubles which seemed hopeless, the idea of German unity, which had lain dormant for centuries, now sprang up in a new birth. At first this idea was held exclusively by the great men of the times and remained the invaluable possession of the cultivated classes; but once started it spread far and wide among the younger generation. . . . But it was easier to defeat Napoleon than to bend the German sentiments of dualism and individualism to the spirit of national unity.

What I have called the ethical pantheism and monistic idealism of Fichte (a type of philosophy reigning almost unchallenged in Germany till almost the middle of the century) was an effective weapon in fighting and winning this more difficult battle. In his volume on the "Romantic School in Germany," Brandes quotes from the diary of Hoffman a passage written in 1809.

> Seized by a strange fancy at the ball on the 6th, I imagine myself looking at my own Ego through a kaleidoscope. All the forms moving around me are Egos and annoy me by what they do and leave undone.

It is a temptation to find in this passage a symbol both of German philosophy and of the temper of Germany at the time. Its outer defeats, its weakness in the world of action, had developed an exasperated introspection. This outer weakness, coinciding, as Von Sybel points out, with the bloom of Germany in art, science, history, philology and philosophy, made the Ego of Germany the noblest contemporary object of contemplation, yet one surrounded with other national Egos who offended by what they did and what they did not do. Patriotism, national feeling, national consciousness are common enough facts. But nowhere save in Germany, in the earlier nineteenth century, have these sentiments and impulses been transformed by deliberate nurture into a mystic cult. This was the time when the idea of the *Volks-seele,* the *Volks-geist,* was born; and the idea lost no time in becoming a fact. Not merely poetry was affected by it, but philology, history and jurisprudence. The so-called historic school is its offspring. The science of social psychology derives from it at one remove. The soul, however, needed a body, and (quite in accord with German idealism) it formed a body for itself—the German state as a unified Empire.

While the idealistic period came first, it is important to bear in mind the kind of idealism it was. At this point the pantheistic allusion becomes significant. The idealism in question was not an idealism of another world but of *this* world, and especially of the State. The embodiment of the divine and absolute will and ideal is the existing world of nature and of men. Especially is the human ego the authorized and creative agent of absolute purpose. The significance of German philosophy was precisely to make men aware of their nature and destiny as the direct and active representatives of absolute and creative purpose.

If I again quote Heine, it is because, with his contempt for technical philosophy, he had an intimate sense of its human meaning. Of German pantheistic idealism, he wrote in 1833 while it was still in its prime:

> God is identical with the world. . . . But he manifests himself most gloriously in man, who feels and thinks at the same time, who is capable of distinguishing his own individuality from objective nature, whose intellect already bears within itself the ideas that present themselves to him in the phenomenal world. In man Deity reaches self-consciousness, and this self-consciousness God again reveals through man. But this revelation does not take place in and through individual man, but in and through collective humanity . . . which comprehends and represents in idea and in reality the whole God-universe. . . . It is an error to suppose that this religion leads men to indifference. On the contrary, the consciousness of his divinity will inspire man with enthusiasm for its manifestation, and from this moment the really noble achievements of true heroism glorify the earth.

In one respect, Heine was a false prophet. He thought that this philosophy would in the end accrue to the profit of the radical, the republican and revolutionary party in Germany. The history of German liberalism is a complicated matter. Suffice it in general to say that the honey the libertarians hived was appropriated in the end by the party of authority. In Heine's assurance that these ideas would in due time issue in action he was profoundly right. His essay closes with burning words, from which I extract the following:

> It seems to me that a methodical people, such as we, must begin with the reformation, must then occupy themselves with systems of philosophy, and only after their completion pass to the political revolution. . . . Then will appear Kantians, as little tolerant of piety in the world of deeds as in the world of ideas, who will mercilessly upturn with sword and axe the soil of our European life to extirpate the last remnants of the past. Then will come upon the scene armed Fichteans, whose fanaticism of will is to be restrained neither by fear nor self-interest, for they live in the spirit. . . . Most of all to be feared would be the philosophers of nature, were they actively to mingle. . . . For if the hand of the Kantian strikes with strong unerring blow; if the Fichtean courageously defies every danger, since for him danger has in reality no existence;—the Philosopher of Nature will be terrible in that he has allied himself with the primitive powers of nature, in that he can conjure up the domestic forces of old German pantheism; and having done so, aroused in him that ancient Germanic eagerness which combats for the joy of the combat itself. . . . Smile not at any counsel as at the counsel of a dreamer. . . . The thought precedes the deed as the lightning the thunder. . . . The hour will come, As on the steps of an amphitheater, the nations will group themselves around Germany to witness the terrible combat.

In my preoccupation with Heine, I seem to have wandered somewhat from our immediate topic: the connection of the idealistic philosophy with the development and organization of the national state of Germany. But the necessity of the organized State to care for the moral interests of mankind was an inherent part of Fichte's thought. At first, *what* state was a matter of indifference. In fact his sympathies were largely French and republican. Before Jena, he writes:

> What is the nation for a truly civilized Christian European? In a general way, Europe itself. More particularly at any time the State which is at the head of civilization. . . . With this cosmopolitan sense, we can be tranquil before the vicissitudes and catastrophes of history.

In 1807 he writes:

> The distinction between Prussia and the rest of Germany is external, arbitrary and fortuitous. The distinction between Germany and the rest of Europe is founded in nature.

The seeming gulf between the two ideas is easily bridged. The **"Addresses on the Fundamental Features of the Present Age"** had taught that the end of humanity on earth is the establishment of a kingdom in which all relations of humanity are determined with freedom or according to Reason—according to Reason as conceived by the Fichtean formula. In his *Addresses to the German Nation*, in 1807-08, the unique mission of Germany in the establishment of this kingdom is urged as a motive for securing national unity and the overthrow of the conqueror. The Germans are the sole people who recognize the principles of spiritual freedom, of freedom won by action in accord with reason. Faithfulness to this mission will "elevate the German name to that of the most glorious among all the peoples, making this Nation the regenerator and restorer of the world." He personifies their ancestors speaking to them, and saying: "We in our time saved Germany from the Roman World Empire." But "yours is the greater fortune. You may establish once for all the Kingdom of the Spirit and of Reason, bringing to naught corporeal might as the ruling thing in the world." And this antithesis of the Germanic and the Roman principles has become a commonplace in the German imagination. Moreover, for Germany to win is no selfish gain. It is an advantage to all nations. "The great promise of a kingdom of right reason and truth on earth must not become a vain and empty phantom; the present iron age is but a transition to a better estate." Hence the concluding words: "There is no middle road: If you sink, so sinks humanity entire with you, without hope of future restoration."

The premises of the historic syllogism are plain. First, the German Luther who saved for mankind the principle of spiritual freedom against Latin externalism; then Kant and Fichte, who wrought out the principle into a final philosophy of science, morals and the State; as conclusion, the German nation organized in order to win the world to recognition of the principle, and thereby to establish the rule of freedom and science in humanity as a whole. The Germans are patient; they have a long memory. Ideas produced when Germany was divided and broken were retained and cherished after it became a unified State of supreme military power, and one yielding to no other people in industrial and commercial prosperity. In the grosser sense of the words, Germany has not held that might makes right. But it has been instructed by a long line of philosophers that it is the business of ideal right to gather might to itself in order that it may cease to be merely ideal. The State represents exactly this incarnation of ideal law and right in effective might. The military arm is part of this moral embodiment. Let sentimentalists sing the praises of an ideal to which no actual force corresponds. Prussian faith in the reality and enforcement among men of the ideal is of a more solid character. As past history is the record of the gradual realization in the Germanic State of the divine idea, future history must uphold and expand what has been accomplished. Diplomacy is the veiled display of law clothed with force in behalf of this realization, and war is its overt manifestation. That war demands self-sacrifice is but the more convincing proof of its profound morality. It is the final seal of devotion to the extension of the kingdom of the Absolute on earth.

For the philosophy stands or falls with the conception of an Absolute. Whether a philosophy of absolutes is theoretically sound or unsound is none of my present concern. But that philosophical absolutism may be practically as dangerous as matter of fact political absolutism history testifies. The situation puts in relief what finally is at issue between a theory which is pinned to a belief in an Absolute beyond history and behind experience, and one which is frankly experimental. For any philosophy which is not consistently experimental will always traffic in absolutes no matter in how disguised a form. In German political philosophy, the traffic is without mask.

George Santayana (essay date 1916)

SOURCE: "Transcendentalism Perfected" and "Fichte on the Mission of Germany," in *Egotism in German Philosophy*, J. M. Dent and Sons Limited, and Charles Scribner's Sons, 1916, pp. 65-72 and 73-83.

[*In the two chapters below, Santayana addresses the irony that "Fichte, a prophet sprung from the people, a theoretical republican who quarrelled with his students for forming clubs and fighting duels, a fierce idealist full of contempt for worldlings, should have so perfectly supplied the Junkers and bankers with their philosophy." He illustrates how Fichte's transcendental idealism, translated by the philosopher into nationalism, could become the nationalism of German fascism.*]

Transcendentalism Perfected

Fichte purified the system of Kant of all its inconsistent and humane elements; he set forth the subjective system of knowledge and action in its frankest and most radical form. The ego, in order to live a full and free life, posited or feigned a world of circumstances, in the midst of which it might disport itself; but this imagined theatre was made to suit the play, and though it might seem to oppress the Will with all sorts of hindrances, and even to snuff it out altogether, it was really only a mirage which that Will, being wiser than

it knew, had raised in order to enjoy the experience of exerting itself manfully.

It would seem obvious from this that the Will could never be defeated, and that in spite of its name it was identical with destiny or the laws of nature: and those transcendentalists who lean to naturalism, or pass into it unawares, like Schelling or Emerson, actually understand the absolute Will in this way. But not so Fichte, nor what I take to be the keener and more heroic romantic school, whose last prophet was Nietzsche. The Germans, in the midst of their fantastic metaphysics, sometimes surprise us by their return to immediate experience: after all, it was in wrestling with the Lord that their philosophy was begotten. As a matter of fact, the will is often defeated—especially if we are stubborn in defining our will; and this tragic fact by no means refutes the Fichtean philosophy, which knows how to deal with it heroically. It conceives that what is inviolable is only what ought to be, the unconscious plan or idea of perfect living which is hidden in the depths of all life: a will not animated in some measure by this idea cannot exist, or at least cannot be noticed or respected by this philosophy. But when, where, how often and how far this divine idea shall be carried out is left unexplained. Actual will may be feeble or wicked in any degree; and in consequence the world that ought to be evoked in its maximum conceivable richness, may dwindle and fade to nothing.

The Will may accordingly be defeated; not, indeed, by imagined external things, but by its own apathy and tergiversation. In this case, according to the logic of this system (which is as beautifully thought out as that of Plotinus), the dissolving world will appear to be overwhelmingly formidable and real. In expiring because we have no longer the warmth to keep it alive, it will seem to be killing us; for the passivity of the ego, says Fichte, is posited as activity in the non-ego. That way of speaking is scholastic; but the thought, if we take the egotistical point of view, is deep and true.

So any actual will may perish by defect and die out; but actual will may also perish by sublimation. The true object of absolute Will is not things or pleasures or length of life, but willing itself; and the more intense and disinterested this willing is, the better it manifests absolute Will. The heroic act of dashing oneself against overwhelming obstacles may, therefore, be the highest fulfilment of the divine idea. The will dares to perish in order to have dared everything. In its material ruin it remains ideally victorious. If we consider the matter under the form of eternity, we shall see that this heroic and suicidal will has accomplished what it willed; it has not only lived perilously but perished nobly.

It is hardly necessary to point out how completely this theory justifies any desperate enterprise to which one happens to be wedded. It justifies, for instance, any wilful handling of history and science. The Will by right lays down the principles on which things must and shall be arranged. If things slip somehow from the traces, so much the grander your "scientific deed" in striving to rein them in. After all, you first summoned them into being only that you might drive them. If they seem to run wild and upset you, like the steeds of Hippolytus, you will, at least, not have missed the glory, while you lived and drove, of assuming the attitude of a master. Call spirits from the vasty deep: if they do not come, what of it? That will only prove the absolute self-sufficiency of your duty to call them.

What tightens this speculative bond between Fichte and the Nietzschean school is that he himself applied his theory of absolute Will to national life. This ego, which was identical with mind in general, he identified also with the German people. If the Germans suffered their national will to be domesticated in the Napoleonic empire, the creative spirit of the universe would be extinguished, and God himself, who existed only when incarnate in mankind, would disappear. It was evidently one's duty to prevent this if possible; and Fichte poured out all the vehemence of his nature into the struggle for freedom. The mere struggle, the mere protest in the soul, according to his system, would secure the end desired: self-assertion, not material success, was the goal. A happy equilibrium once established in human life would have been only a temptation, a sort of Napoleonic or Mephistophelian quietus falling on the will to strive.

I am not sure how far Fichte, in his romantic and puritan tension of soul, would have relished the present organisation of Germany. He was a man of the people, a radical and an agitator as much as a prophet of nationalism, and the shining armour in which German freedom is now encased might have seemed to him too ponderous. He might have discerned in victory the beginning of corruption.

Nevertheless we should remember that a perfected idealism has a tendency to change into its opposite and become a materialism for all practical purposes. Absolute Will is not a natural being, not anybody's will or thought; it is a disembodied and unrealised genius which first comes into operation when it begins to surround itself with objects and points of resistance, so as to become aware of its own stress and vocation. What these objects or felt resistances may be is not prejudged; or rather it is prejudged that they shall be most opposite to spirit, and that spirit shall experience its own passivity—one mode of its fated and requisite experience—in the form of an influence which it imputes to dead and material things.

The whole business of spirit may, therefore, well be with matter. Science might be mechanical, art might be cumbrous and material, all the instruments of life might be brutal, life itself might be hard, bitter, and obsessed, and yet the whole might remain a direct manifestation of pure spirit, absolute freedom, and creative duty. This speculative possibility is worth noting: it helps us to understand modern Germany. It is no paradox that idealists should be so much at home among material things. These material things, according to them, are the offspring of their spirit. Why should they not sink fondly into the manipulation of philological details or chemical elements, or over-ingenious commerce and intrigue? Why should they not dote on blood and iron? Why should these fruits of the spirit be uncongenial to it?

A theoretical materialist, who looks on the natural world as on a soil that he has risen from and feeds on, may perhaps feel a certain piety towards those obscure abysses of nature that have given him birth; but his delight will be rather in the clear things of the imagination, in the humanities, by which the rude forces of nature are at once expressed and eluded. Not so the transcendentalist. Regarding his mind as the source of everything, he is moved to solemn silence and piety only before himself: on the other hand, what bewitches him, what he loves to fondle, is his progeny, the material environment, the facts, the laws, the blood, and the iron in which he conceives (quite truly, perhaps) that his spirit perfectly and freely expresses itself. To despise the world and withdraw into the realm of mind, as into a subtler and more congenial sphere, is quite contrary to his idealism. Such a retreat might bring him peace, and he wants war. His idealism teaches him that strife and contradiction, as Heraclitus said, are the parents of all things; and if he stopped striving, if he grew sick of ambition and material goods, he thinks he would be forsaking life, for he hates as he would death what another kind of idealists have called salvation.

We are told that God, when he had made the world, found it very good, and the transcendentalist, when he assumes the Creator's place, follows his example. The hatred and fear of matter is perhaps not a sign of a pure spirit. Even contemplatively, a divine mind may perfectly well fall in love with matter, as the Moon-goddess did with Endymion. Such matter might be imagined only, as if Diana had merely dreamt of her swain; and the fond image might not be less dear on that account. The romantic poet finds his own spirit greeting him in rocks, clouds, and waves; the musician pours out his soul in movement and tumult; why should not the transcendental general, or engineer, or commercial traveller find his purest ideal in trade, crafts, and wars? Grim work, above all, is what absolute Will demands. It needs the stimulus of resistance to become more intensely conscious of Self, which is said to be its ultimate object in imagining a world at all. Acquisition interests it more than possession, because the sense of effort and power is then more acute. The more material the arts that engage it, and the more complicated and worldly its field of action, the more intense will be its exertion, and the greater its joy. This is no idealism for a recluse or a moping poet; it does not feel itself to be something incidental and fugitive in the world, like a bird's note, that it should fear to be drowned in the crash of material instruments or to be forced to a hideous tension and shrillness: shrillness and tension are its native element. It is convinced that it has composed all the movements there are or can be in existence, and it feels all the more masterful, the more numerous and thunderous is the orchestra it leads. It is entirely at home in a mechanical environment, which [?] can prove transcendentally to be perfectly ideal. Its most congenial work is to hack its way through to the execution of its World-Plan. Its most adequate and soul-satisfying expression is a universal battle.

Fichte on the Mission of Germany

When the ancient Jews enlarged their conception of Jehovah so as to recognise in him the only living God to whom all nature and history were subject, they did not cease to regard the universal power as at the same time their special national deity. Here was a latent contradiction. It was ingeniously removed by saying that Jehovah, while not essentially a tribal deity, had chosen Israel for his people by a free act of grace with no previous merit on their part; so that the pride of the Jews was not without humility.

No humility, however, is mingled with the claim which the Germans now make to a similar preeminence. "Modern critics," says Max Stirner, "inveigh against religion because it sets up God, the divine, or the moral law over against man, regarding them as external things, whereas the critics transform all these objects into ideas in the human mind. Nevertheless the essential mistake of religion, to assign a mission to man at all, is not avoided by these critics, who continue to insist that man shall be divine, or ideally human, or what not; morality, freedom, humanity, etc., are his essence." Now a divinity which is subjective or immanent evidently cannot choose any nation, save by dwelling and manifesting itself more particularly in them. They can be highly favoured only in that they are intrinsically superior, and on that account may be figuratively called vessels of election. Therefore, if the spirit which is in a nation is not one spirit among many in the world (as the primitive Hebrews supposed and as a naturalistic philosophy would maintain), but is the one holy and universal spirit, and if at the same time this spirit dwells in that nation preeminently, or even exclusively, humility on the part of this nation would evidently be out of place. Accordingly, the Germans cannot help bearing witness to the divine

virtues and prerogatives which they find in themselves, some of which are set forth by Fichte as follows:

The present age stands precisely in the middle of earthly time, between the era in which men were still self-seeking, earthly, and impulsive, and the coming era in which they will live for the sake of pure ideals. The Germans prefigure this better age, and are leading the rest of the world into it. They have created the modern world by uniting the political heritage of classical Europe with the true religion that lingered in Asia, and they have raised the two to a higher unity in their *Kultur*. From them is drawn the best blood of most other nations and the spiritual force that has fashioned them all.

The Germans have never forsaken their native land nor suffered seriously from immigration. Their language is primitive, and they have never exchanged it for a foreign one. Hence German alone is truly a mother-tongue. Its intellectual terms retain a vital and vivid connection with sensible experience. True poetry and philosophy, therefore, exist only in German. Captious persons who judge by mere crude feeling may fancy that German is not very melodious; but these matters cannot be rightly judged without reference to first principles, which in this case would prove that the sweetest language is that which exhausts all possible sounds and combines them in all available ways. Whether German or some other language comes nearest to this *a priori* ideal of euphony must be left for empirical observation to decide.

The German nature, being pure, deep, earnest, and bold, has instinctively seized upon the true essence of Christianity and discarded with abhorrence all the lies and corruption that obscured it. This essence is the imperative need of turning from the natural to the ideal life. The German knows that his own soul is safe; but this is not enough for him in his unselfishness. His zeal is kindled easily for warmth and light everywhere; and this zeal of his is patient and efficacious, taking hold on real life and transforming it. As he presses on he finds more than he sought, for he has plunged into the quick stream of life which forges ahead of itself and carries him forward with it. The dead heart of other nations may dream of gods in the clouds, or of some perfect type of human life already exemplified in the past and only to be approached or repeated in the future. The spirit of the German is no coinage of earth; it is the living source of all the suns, and rushes to create absolutely new things for ever. The German mind is the self-consciousness of God.

I do not see that the strain of war or the intoxication of victory could add much to these boasts, uttered by Fichte when, for the moment, he had abandoned all hope of military self-assertion on the part of his country, and relied on education and philosophy alone to preserve and propagate German righteousness. Even in detail, what he says often seems strangely like what official Germany is now saying. Even the hysterical hatred of England is not absent. In England Fichte did not see the champion of Protestantism, morality, and political liberty, nor the constant foe of Napoleon, but only a universal commercial vampire. His contempt for the Latin races, too, was boundless. In the matter of race, indeed, he entertained a curious idea that there must have been, from all eternity until the beginning of history, a primitive Normal People, a tribe of Adams and Eves; because according to a principle which he adopted from Calvinistic theology, if all men had been originally slaves to nature none could ever have become free. This Normal People were, of course, the ancestors of the Germans. Earth-born savage tribes must have existed also for the Normal People to subdue, since but for some such conquest the primitive equilibrium would never have been broken, Eden and the jungle would never have been merged together, and history, which is a record of novelties, would never have begun. The theory of evolution has rendered the reasons for such a view obsolete; but the idea that the bulk of mankind are mongrels formed by the union of blonde godlike creatures with some sort of anthropoid blacks, recurred later in Gobineau and has had a certain vogue in Germany.

Fichte, following Calvin and Kant, made a very sharp distinction between the life of nature and that of duty. The ideal must be pursued without the least thought of advantage. Trades, he says, must be practised spontaneously, without any other reward than longer vigils. The young must never hear it mentioned that any one could ever be incited or guided in life by the thought of his own preservation or well-being. Knowledge is no report of existing things or laws which have happened to be discovered. Knowledge is the very life of God, and self-generated. It is "an intellectual activity for its own sake, according to rules for their own sake." In plain English, it is pure imagination. But the method to be imposed on this madness is fixed innately, both for thought and for morals. Only frivolity can interfere with a unanimous idealism.

We must not suppose that this prescription of austere and abstract aims implies any aversion on Fichte's part to material progress, compulsory *Kultur,* or military conquest. German idealism, as we have seen, is not Platonic or ascetic, that it should leave the world behind. On the contrary, its mission is to consecrate the world and show that every part of it is an organ of the spirit. This is a form of piety akin to the Hebraic. Even the strictest Calvinists, who taught that the world was totally depraved, were able, in every sense of the phrase, to make a very good thing of it. They reclaimed, they appropriated, they almost enjoyed it. So Fichte gives us prophetic glimpses of an idealistic Germany conquering the world. The state

does not aim at self-preservation, still less is it concerned to come to the aid of those members of the human family that lag behind the movement of the day. The dominion of unorganised physical force must be abolished by a force obedient to reason and spirit. True life consists in refashioning human relations after a model innate in the mind. The glorious destiny of Germany is to bring forth and establish the world anew. Natural freedom is a disgraceful thing, a mere medley of sensual and intellectual impulses without any principle of order. It is for the Germans to decide whether a providential progress exists by becoming themselves the providence that shall bring progress about, or whether on the contrary every higher thought is folly. If they should fail, history would never blame them, for in that case there would be no more history.

The sole animating principle of history is the tendency towards a universal Christian European monarchy. This tendency is deeper than the plans of men and stronger than their intentions. "That a state, even when on the very point of making war, should solemnly assert its love of peace and its aversion to conquest, is nothing; for in the first place it must needs make this asseveration and so hide its real intention if it would succeed in its design; and the well-known principle *Threaten war that thou mayst have peace* may also be inverted in this way: *Promise peace that thou mayst begin war with advantage;* and in the second place the state may be wholly in earnest in its peaceful assurances, so far as its self-knowledge has gone; but let the favourable opportunity for aggrandisement present itself, and the previous good resolution is forgotten."

If the people are disinclined to obey the Idea, the government must constrain them to do so. All the powers of all the citizens must be absorbed in the state. Personal liberty could be turned to no good use when such individuality and variety of training as are good for the state have been provided for by its regulations. Nor must any idleness be tolerated. An ideal education must make men over so that they shall be incapable of willing anything but what that education wills them to will. The state may then rely upon its subjects, "for whoever has a well-grounded will, wills what he wills for all eternity."

As to foreign relations, the state, in obedience to its ideal mission, must conquer the surrounding barbarians and raise them to a state of culture. It is this process almost exclusively that has introduced progress into history. "What impels the Macedonian hero . . . to seek foreign lands? What chains victory to his footsteps and scatters before him in terror the countless hordes of his enemies? Is this mere fortune? No; it is an Idea. . . . The civilised must rule and the uncivilised must obey, if Right is to be the law of the world. . . . Tell me not of the thousands who fell round his path; speak not of his own early death. After the realisation of his Idea, what was there greater for him to do than to die?"

This enthusiasm for Alexander (which Hegel shared) is not merely retrospective. "At last in one nation of the world the highest, purest morality, such as was never seen before among men, will arise and will be made secure for all future time, and thence will be extended over all other peoples. There will ensue a transformation of the human race from earthly and sensual creatures into pure and noble spirits." "Do you know anything higher than death? . . . Who has a right to stand in the way of an enterprise begun in the face of this peril?"

It may seem curious that an uncompromising puritan like Fichte, a prophet sprung from the people, a theoretical republican who quarrelled with his students for forming clubs and fighting duels, a fierce idealist full of contempt for worldlings, should have so perfectly supplied the Junkers and bankers with their philosophy. But the phenomenon is not new. Plato, divine and urbane as he was, supplied the dull Spartans with theirs. Men of idealistic faith are confident that the foundations of things must be divine, and when, upon investigating these foundations, they come upon sinister principles—blind impulse, chance, murderous competition—they fanatically erect these very principles into sacred maxims. All strength, they are antecedently convinced, must come from God; therefore if deception, wilfulness, tyranny, and big battalions are the means to power, they must be the chosen instruments of God on earth. In some such way the Catholic Church, too, for fear of impiety, is seen blessing many a form of deceit and oppression. Thus the most ardent speculation may come to sanction the most brutal practice. The primitive passions so sanctioned, because they seem to be safe and potent, are probably too narrowly organised to sustain themselves long; and meantime they miss and trample down the best things that mankind possesses. Nevertheless they are a force like any other, a force not only vehement but contagious, and capable of many victories though of no stable success. Such passions, and the philosophies that glorify them, are sincere, absorbing, and if frankly expressed irrefutable.

The transcendental theory of a world merely imagined by the ego, and the will that deems itself absolute are certainly desperate delusions; but not more desperate or deluded than many another system that millions have been brought to accept. The thing bears all the marks of a new religion. The fact that the established religions of Germany are still forms of Christianity may obscure the explicit and heathen character of the new faith: it passes for a somewhat faded speculation, or for the creed of a few extremists, when in reality it dominates the judgment and conduct of the nation. No religious tyranny could be more complete. It has

its prophets in the great philosophers and historians of the last century; its high priests and pharisees in the government and the professors; its faithful flock in the disciplined mass of the nation; its heretics in the socialists; its dupes in the Catholics and the liberals, to both of whom the national creed, if they understood it, would be an abomination; it has its martyrs now by the million, and its victims among unbelievers are even more numerous, for its victims, in some degree, are all men.

An excerpt from Immanuel Kant's open letter on Fichte's *Wissenschaftslehre*, August 7, 1799:

. . . I hereby declare that I regard Fichte's ***Theory of Science*** [***Wissenschaftslehre***] as a totally indefensible system. For the pure theory of science is nothing more or less than mere logic, and the principles of logic cannot lead to any material knowledge. Since logic, that is to say, *pure logic,* abstracts from the content of knowledge, the attempt to cull a real object out of logic is a vain effort and therefore a thing that no one has ever done. If the transcendental philosophy is correct, such a task would involve metaphysics rather than logic. But I am so opposed to metaphysics, as defined according to Fichtean principles, that I have advised him, in a letter, to turn his fine literary gifts to the problem of applying the *Critique of Pure Reason* rather than squander them in cultivating fruitless sophistries. He, however, has replied politely by explaining that "he would not make light of scholasticism after all." Thus the question whether I take the Fichtean philosophy to be a genuinely critical philosophy is already answered by Fichte himself, and it is unnecessary for me to express my opinion of its value or lack of value. . . .

Immanuel Kant, in Kant: Philosophical Correspondence 1759-99, *University of Chicago Press, 1967.*

Richard Kroner (essay date 1948)

SOURCE: "The Year 1800 in the Development of German Idealism," in *The Review of Metaphysics,* Vol. I, No. 4, June, 1948, pp. 1-31.

[*In the excerpt that follows, Kroner recounts the history of German Idealism, focusing "on the year 1800 in which the period of Kant and Fichte waned and the period of Schelling and Hegel began."*]

I

The general import of the year 1800 as
the turning point in the development
of German Idealism

1. Introduction

The year 1800 was a fateful year in the philosophical movement which we are wont to call "German Idealism." "O'er what place does the moon hang to your eye, my dearest Sara? To me, it hangs over the left bank of the Elbe . . ."[1] Coleridge wrote to his wife on September 19 in 1798. His famous visit to Germany in this and the following year has not only a biographical but also a general historical significance. Coleridge and through him the English world became acquainted with the rising star of German Idealism. The years in which Coleridge stayed in Germany were years of a tremendous philosophical and spiritual struggle that reached its climax in 1800 when Schelling published his *System of Transcendental Idealism,* the title and charter of Philosophic Romanticism.

The Critique of Pure Reason had appeared in 1781; almost twenty years later it was completely forgotten and pushed aside by a movement that though originating from Kant's important work nevertheless came to results extremely alien to the intentions and the spirit of its initiator. How could this happen in such a short time? How could the epoch-making philosophic revolution brought about by Kant take such a strange turn? How could the critical principles be perverted to such a degree as to be completely denied eventually?

The term "German Idealism" usually suggests the great philosophic movement that was inaugurated by Kant and developed by his successors, particularly by Joh. Gottlieb Fichte, Fr. Wilh. Joseph Schelling and Georg Wilh. Fredr. Hegel. But we should not forget that the same period also generated composers and poets like Mozart and Beethoven, Schiller and Goethe; important critics like the two Schlegels, theologians like Schleiermacher, historians and philologists like W. v. Humboldt and Niebuhr. All these men and a large host of minor but still noted poets and scholars shared in the same German Idealism. "The secret of this golden age," Windelband says in his *History of Modern Philosophy,* "is to be found in the close cooperation of philosophic thought and poetic imagination."

When Coleridge travelled in Germany he had the impression that Kant and Fichte were the outstanding figures in the field of metaphysics, and that all universities were affected by the new philosophic fashion. "Throughout the universities of Germany," he wrote, "there is not a single professor who is not either a Kantian or a disciple of Fichte whose system is built on the Kantian and presupposes its truth; or lastly who, though an antagonist of Kant as to his theoretical work, has not embraced wholly or in part his moral system . . ."[2]

This statement is confirmed by all reports we know about this time. Everyone who had studied the *Critique of Practical Reason* was overpowered and transported by the moral gravity and sublimity of Kant's ideas; the whole nation admired and applauded the author. Every serious reader of Kant's works felt what Coleridge himself experienced and what he in his spiritual autobiography expressed in the following words: "The originality, the depth, and the adamantine chain of the lyric . . . , the clearness and evidence of those words . . . took possession of me as with the giant's hand."[3]

But in spite of this intense influence, or should I say, just by virtue of its enormous impetuosity, the Kantian philosophy evoked a movement which was not foreseen and even less wished for by its author. There is a certain analogy between the Kantian and the French Revolution. Both began by contesting the previous state of affairs and by introducing new points of view which thoroughly altered the face of all things. Both were driven forward by an inner dynamic impulse that modified gradually more and more the first program, and finally resulted in consequences strictly adverse to the original motives and ideals. There is indeed a striking analogy between the stages of the French Revolution and those of German Idealism. The philosophy of Kant can be compared with the opening action of the National Assembly, the philosophy of Fichte with the attitude of the Girondists and Extremists, the reaction instigated by Schelling with the constitution of the Directory and finally the all-embracing and absolute system of Hegel with the Empire of Napoleon.

It is the alarming and exciting story of this fateful course of spiritual events with which these lectures will deal. Of course, I cannot give an extensive report on all the single steps that finally led to the system of Hegel. I cannot discuss in detail all the controversies that took place between Kant and Fichte, Fichte and Schelling, Schelling and Hegel. I will concentrate on the year 1800 in which the period of Kant and Fichte waned and the period of Schelling and Hegel began. But before I refer to the works published in that year I will try to outline what was at issue between these two groups of thinkers and between these two periods of German Idealism. I will try to show that the implications of the great controversy were far reaching and of the uttermost significance.

Kant in a passage of his first *Critique* distinguishes the school concept of philosophy from its world concept. The school concept concerns the disputes of the students and scholars alone, the world concept the great issues of life and faith. The turning point of 1800 involved a change in philosophy, not only as a science, but as the expression of faith and as the answer to the eternal questions which ever anew stir and agitate the mind of man. The world concept of philosophy has to be taken into account, when we compare the period before 1800 with the period after that fateful year. The critical idealism of Kant underwent not only some technical or internal modifications, but the entire spirit of its principles, the style of its thought, the faith that was alive in it, altered. The world in which and for which Schelling and Hegel wrote is no more the same world in which Kant and Fichte built their systems. The year 1800 made this difference manifest.

Kant was and ever remained a child of the age of Reason or Enlightenment. Although the *Critique of Pure Reason* hastened the downfall of that age, it was at the same time its most mature product. Fichte's doctrine or theory of science, to be sure, foreshadows already the new century to a certain degree, but it still preserved the main principles of the Kantian philosophy. Fichte even overstressed and overemphasized the principles and thereby opened the eyes to their limit.

While Kant is still a representative of the Enlightenment, Fichte embodies the spirit of that movement which is called "Storm and Stress" in literature, and which characterizes the transition from the age of Enlightenment to the romantic period. Fichte, however, was still loyal to the banner of Kant's moral idealism. Like Kant, and even louder than Kant, he pronounced the freedom of the will as the highest of all principles, and faith in the moral order of the world as a postulate based on that principle.

Schelling resolutely left this ground. He shifted the centre of gravity from the ethical to an aesthetic idealism, from the respect of man as the moral agent to the cult of man as the creative genius in art; from a spiritually democratic to a spiritually aristocratic creed; from a position that in its religious consequences was akin to biblical theism, although of course in a rationalistic interpretation, to a position that had some affinity with naturalism and pantheism, and with the mythological religions of paganism.

What encouraged and inspired Schelling to dare this venturous leap from the place of ethical to that of aesthetic idealism was the imposing and commanding figure of his admired friend and model: Goethe. Goethe seemed to have achieved not only the perfection of classical beauty, he seemed also to represent the perfection of man, man in his consummate form.

A more radical and fundamental change can hardly be imagined, although it was the same tree of German Idealism that developed in three different appearances and forms. The metaphor of a tree may be permitted to compare Kant with its root, Fichte with its stem. Schelling with its leaves and blossoms and Hegel with its fruit. Kant indeed was the seed and root of the whole growth of German Idealism. All its thoughts, its theories, its achievements are potentially already existent in his system. Fichte sprang up from Kant as the trunk springs from the soil. This system rises in a straight and bold line striving upwards: his thought is stern, but somewhat barren, strong but somewhat tough, and hard, lofty but not pleasant. Schelling on the contrary is rich and brilliant, colorful and always delightful. For him the stem unfolds into the manifold of various shapes and colours and displays its vigour in beautiful pomp of ever new and surprising productions. In Hegel the ripe fruit of the plant appears, full of strength and savour, condensing as it were and recollecting the whole tree in itself, and representing the seed for future growth.

Of course, such an allegory should not be carried too far, or taken too literally, but it illustrates fairly well the unity and the difference between the main figures of German Idealism. It illustrates that Kant and Fichte belong to one another in a form more coherent than Fichte and Schelling, although Fichte dwells no longer in the subterranean depth of Kant. This philosophy seeks the light of a new speculative knowledge, but it does not reach it. It is only striving and longing for it. Schelling converts the strength and energy of the tree into a luminous splendour of many different systems. Hegel returns to the profundity of Kant, but now developed into a new self-sufficient and self-dependent organism.

2. Moral-aesthetic

A. Moral

When we leave the realm of comparisons and metaphors and turn to the thoughts of the German idealists, we can describe the contrast between the two main phases, that before and that after the year 1800, in different ways. I pointed out already that Kant and Fichte emphasize the ethical or moral aspect. They are idealists, because they believe in ideals as the summit and end not only of life but also of thought.

(a) *Ideals-reality.*

The opposition between reality and the sphere of ideals is basic in their systems. Reality as the realm of objects, as the world of sense, as that world that the natural sciences explore and explain is not ultimate, it is not the All, or the Universe.

Besides this visible or phenomenal world there is another hemisphere, the realm of aims and ends, of purposes and intentions, of duties and ideals. This practical world is by far more important, not only to us as willing and acting beings, but also to the thinking mind. For the thinking mind has to recognize and to acknowledge that duties and ideals cannot be derived from facts and events. They form a class of their own, a sphere that lies beyond the horizon and the reach of the natural sciences and of their merely theoretical knowledge. They are not objects of perception, they have to be conceived as objects of volition, as goals of the striving and longing will.

(b) *Reflection on practical principles.*

Kant and Fichte therefore are practical idealists. The philosopher has to adopt the place and the point of view taken by the common man who pursues his tasks, discharges his duties, and who feels responsibility for his actions and deeds. The common man is the moral man, however immoral his life may be, however he may fail to comply with his duties. For philosophy has to trust the principles which underlie the consciousness of the common man.

It is the business of philosophic thought to find out these principles, for the common man does not reflect upon them, he does not analyze his own consciousness, precisely because he is engaged in his practical affairs alone: the common man is the man of action, not the man of thought. But the philosopher, although he is obliged not to act practically but to think theoretically, nevertheless should analyze the practical consciousness and construe in theoretical terms the position of the men of practice. He cannot succeed, if he does not take into account the principles of action, and he can never exceed or transcend these principles.

(c) *Causality-Freedom.*

There is an ultimate gulf between natural causality and moral responsibility, between natural necessity and moral freedom, between phenomenal reality and ethical ideality. No speculative artifice, no metaphysical intuition, no dialectical method can ever bridge the gulf between these hemispheres. To our insight and thought, to our philosophic knowledge the gulf is final. Therefore we must base all our reflections and conclusions, all our principles and propositions on the fundamental and original truth of this duality. All we can say is, that it is our duty to instil the ideal into reality or to make the content of the ideal efficient and powerful in our will and in our actions. The distance between the brute facts and the ideal goal cannot be diminished or even annulled by any reflection or by any conclusion; it cannot be overcome by thought. It can be overcome only by the energy and the steadfastness of the will.

B. Aesthetic

Quite a different picture prevails in the second period of German Idealism. No longer the practical issues, the ideals of the moral man, the principles of volition and action dominate thought, but instead intuition and imagination, contemplation and speculation assume supremacy. Man is a genius, is more than other mortals are. He is akin to God. he is divine himself! The marvellous spell, the splendour and mystery of a masterpiece points to the divine origin of its maker. The great poet in a particular sense is created in the image of God, he is himself a creator, as God is the poet of the world immanent in his Word. Schelling in his system of 1800 conceived of poetry as the model, measure and standard of philosophic speculation; he transformed the practical or ethical idealism of Fichte, to which he ardently adhered in the beginning of his career, into an aesthetic idealism.

In Emerson's essays we find the American echo of this romantic creed. Emerson, like Schelling, insisted that the Beautiful is supreme. "In the eternal trinity of Truth, Goodness and Beauty," he says, "the Transcendentalist prefers to make Beauty the sign and head . . . The beauty of Nature reforms itself in the mind, and not for barren completion, but for new creation. In art Nature works through the will of a man filled with the beauty of her first works. The world thus exists to the soul to satisfy the desire of beauty. This element I call an ultimate end. Beauty in its largest and profoundest sense is one expression for the universe. God is the all-fair."

3. Intuition and Thought

The idealism of the first period of German Idealism centered in the ideal or in the ideals of striving and action; that of the second period in the idea or in the ideas of intuition and thought. This contrast did not appear for the first time in the story when it arose as a conflict between the German Idealists. It is an old struggle that was renewed on a new metaphysical level and in new conceptual forms. The contrast between Platonism and Aristotelianism is, though not exactly the same, very much akin, Plato's idealism culminated in the idea of the Good which is higher than anything that exists, and which is the idea of an ideal, the idea of a permanent goal, the model and pattern of all human planning and acting. The idealism of Aristotle, on the other hand, concerns not the ideals of action, but the structure of existence itself, the ideas which form and animate the real substances and which actualize themselves within the real processes of nature and of history.

In the Middle Ages a similar contrast and conflict divided those who held that the will of God is primary to his intellect, or in other words, that God himself is a practical idealist, from those who insisted that the intellect is superior to the will, that there is an eternal ideal order not only within the spirit of God, but also in his creation, and that this order is the highest subject of philosophical and theological speculation.

4. Devotional-Intellectual

When we consider this universal, historical antagonism, we can fully comprehend and evaluate the far-reaching consequences implied in the crisis of the year 1800. However, there is an even deeper and greater historical antagonism that reappears in the collision of the idealism of Kant and Fichte and that of Schelling and Hegel. an antagonism not only of philosophic schools, but of diametrically opposed tendencies within the Christian civilization. I might call them the devotional and the intellectual tendency. From the very beginning these two currents were present in Christianity, one represented by the life and faith of the community, the other by Christian dogma and doctrine of the theologians.

The ethical idealism of Kant and Fichte vindicates the supreme right of faith, of course in the form, not of Christianity, but of a faith based on moral reason and moral autonomy. The aesthetic and speculative idealism of the second period culminates in the theological logic of Hegel, which pretends to be the logic of that Logos who was in the beginning and was with God and was God, and by whom all things were made.[4] Coleridge, who was strongly influenced by the ethical idealism of Kant and Fichte, but also by the aesthetic romanticism of Schelling, after a period of serious inner conflicts, finally rejected the speculative systems of Schelling and Hegel altogether precisely because he regarded theology as a danger for the life of faith. In the Aids to Reflection he says: "This was the true and first apostasy—when in council and synod the Divine Humanities of the Gospel gave way to speculative systems, and religion became a science of shadows under the name of theology."[5]

5. *Reflective-Intuitive*

The contrast between the two periods can be conceived still in another way which concerns the method of the systems. When transcendental idealism was first introduced to America the so-called Transcendentalists of New England, guided by Emerson, depended completely without knowing it, on the version of Schelling. Emerson was impressed by the intuitive method which corresponded best with his poetic enthusiasm and his deification of nature. But he believed that Kant himself had used this method and that the term "transcendental idealism" was coined by Kant precisely to designate this method.

Mentioning Kant as the founder of Transcendental Idealism, he writes: "The extraordinary profoundness and precision of that man's thinking have given vogue to his nomenclature in Europe and America to that extent that whoever belongs to the class of intuitive thought is popularly called at the present day Transcendental."[6] Historically, nothing can be more remote from the truth than this statement. The character and spirit of Kant's critical philosophy is utterly opposed to any intuitive thought. In fact, Kant most definitely and explicitly excluded such a possibility. Human knowledge either rests upon sense experience or upon reflection and analysis of this experience, but it can attain to no kind of intuitive knowledge whatever. On the contrary human reason is restricted and barred from any comprehension of the things-in-themselves precisely because it is not intuitive. Kant even circumscribes the idea of a problematic divine intellect by assigning to it the capacity of intellectual intuition which the human mind does not possess.

Emerson probably never really studied Kant, but learnt about him from Coleridge, and Coleridge himself is not at all clear, when he refers to the transcendental method. Coleridge, as is well known, laid stress on the distinction between understanding and reason. Here again he confused reason and intuition as if both could be identified. But this is not the point in which the first period of German Idealism fundamentally varies from the second period.

Kant designates as reason not an intuitive power of man, but rather the capacity of conceiving the ideals or those ultimate goals of knowledge which can never actually be reached, although they determine the direction and close the horizon of all human cognition. The root of reason Kant therefore insists, is not theoretical, but practical, not intellectual, but moral, not intuitive, but active. Reason is at bottom willing and striving in the field of knowledge and science as well as in the field of volition and life.

Fichte began to speak of an intellectual intuition as the source of philosophic insight. But he did not mean a special kind of knowledge that would disclose the inner nature of things, the hidden ground of the Universe or something like this; he merely insisted that reflection and analysis is not based on outer sensation, but on inner intuition. He, even stronger than Kant, maintained the position that not intuition but action is the pith and core of the human Ego, and the only basis of the whole fabric of idealism. This idealism was therefore not intuitive, but moral, practical, and directed toward the ideal of absolute freedom.

Only Schelling in his system of Transcendental Idealism presumed that the philosopher should avail himself of an intuition which is able to grasp the original unity of all opposites in the absolute consciousness. And Hegel went even one step farther. He asserted that intuition penetrates into the core of ultimate reality, and that it can construe a system of absolute knowledge. In a way Hegel returned to Kant. For he recognized that intuition alone is helpless and that the claims of a merely intuitive knowledge cannot be vindicated by reason. He therefore synthesized the intuitive and discursive method in his dialectic. There is no insight based on intuition alone. Every immediate knowledge is also to be mediated by analysis and reflection. Hegel called this synthesis of intuitive and reflective, reason, and therefore his position that of reason, while he despised the method of Kant as that of the mere understanding. Coleridge was deeply impressed by the distinction between understanding and reason. But he did not discern that this distinction was not at all the same in Kant and his successors.

II
The Conflict between Fichte and Schelling in 1800

In the foregoing lecture I delineated the general character of the contrast between the position of Kant and Fichte and that of Schelling as presented in *The System of Transcendental Idealism*. Today I will describe the contrast, and particularly the controversy fought out between Fichte and Schelling, more in detail. Besides the system of Schelling an important and influential book was published in the same year by Fichte, **The Vocation of Man**. Schelling in his system made the first comprehensive attempt to defend his own position in its distinctive peculiarity by stern methodical means over against the great system of Fichte, first published in 1794 under the very inadequate title **Wissenschaftslehre**. While Schelling's system was written for professional philosophers alone, Fichte on the contrary addressed himself to all readers, as he said, "who are altogether able to understand a book."

Fichte in 1800 had already passed the zenith of his historic career as a speculative thinker. Although he continued to lecture privately on the first principles, thereby transforming his metaphysical system from year to year, the books he published showed him henceforth only as an orator and educator, as a philosophic politician and a speculative prophet. Schelling, on the other hand, was just about to ascend the throne of metaphysics proper. To use the phrase of John Hutchison Stirling: "Fichte . . . had two philosophical epochs, and if both belong to biography, only one belongs to history."[7] The year 1800 draws the line just between these two epochs. From 1794 until 1800 Fichte exercised absolute authority in the realm of metaphysics,[8] though by 1799 he had to resign his chair as professor in Jena because of alleged atheism.

To be sure, Schelling began to rival his older and learned colleague in the University of Jena already before 1800. He lectured on the philosophy of nature, and the students were irresistibly attracted by the powerful voice of this young teacher. Nature as conceived in the mind of Schelling ceased to be the mechanical order of material molecules ruled by the principle of causality and subject to mathematical equations. It was no longer the nature investigated and interpreted by Galileo and Newton, nature as the object of the natural sciences. It became instead the object of philosophy interpreted by speculative thought. This new idea of Nature had little in common with the concepts underlying the *Critique of Pure Reason*. It was more akin

to the picture given in Goethe's sketch bearing the title *Nature*. Schelling's view transfigured as with a magic wand the world of sense phenomena into a living being. No longer was mathematics the privileged instrument for deciphering the book of nature: it was rather intellectual intuition assisted by transcendental reflection. Nature was no longer opposed to the world of our human consciousness. The secret of nature and the secret of our consciousness, Schelling proclaimed, is one and the same secret, it is the central and all embracing secret of the universal soul. The human soul and the soul of the world are different not in kind, but only with respect to the stage of development in which the creative ground of all existence manifests itself.

The soul of nature forms and transforms itself according to the stages of its evolution. It strives after a certain goal as the human soul also does, and on its way it produces ever new phenomena, ever new effects as it gradually approaches its final end. There is an inner antagonism in nature as well as in the human Ego; the universal soul is alive only because it is divided against itself and endeavours to unite itself. This unity in difference or this difference in unity is the source and primeval condition of all activity and of all life. Opposite forces bear up the fundamental and original unity of nature; all processes in the universe, all movements, all changes occur only because of this inner discord, this internal strife. Nature works to reconcile herself, to overcome the antagonism of her poles, and thus to produce a perfect balance, a perfect harmony within herself. Matter and energy, magnetism and electricity, light and sound, the system of the stars as well as the chemical processes, gravitation as much as molecular forces have to be understood as manifestations of the same supreme principle that constitutes their inner soul. But the highest stage to which nature rises, is the world of organisms. Here the creative stream of productions results in a living unity in which all other natural substances and processes are bound together. The organism is the most advanced attempt of Nature to achieve her supreme end: the unity and harmony of herself.

Of course the plurality of organisms, the contrariness of the sexes, the complexity of different functions and processes within every individual organism, the struggle for self-conservation and self-propagation, the tension between the organic and the inorganic world, the exposure of all living beings to disease and death, all these features demonstrate obviously enough that even the amazing perfection of the organic structure and the wonder of life do not yet represent the final goal of the World Soul. Nature produces in the living organism her highest products. By reconciling the antagonistic poles of existence Nature achieves her most perfect form. But even so, this form is still utterly defective and imperfect. Nature is eventually compelled to transcend herself. It is on the stage of Mind

Title page of Das System der Sittenlehre nach den Prinzipien der Wissenschafslehre, *1798.*

that the universal soul aspires and attains to higher and ever higher good actions.

This famous philosophy of nature worked out and published by Schelling in the course of the years from 1798 to 1800 preceded *The System of Transcendental Idealism*. Fichte could believe and perhaps believed for a certain span of time that Schelling, who had begun to think and to write as Fichte's admirer and disciple, still adhered to the fundamental principles of the Lore of Science even at the moment when he built up his philosophy of nature. It is a matter of fact that Schelling himself, in the first rapture evoked by his new discoveries, did not yet fully recognize the abyss that opened between him and Fichte.

And yet, Schelling was already abandoning the position of Fichte when he set out to philosophize about nature. It is strange irony in the development of German Idealism that the fruit of Kant's careful and considerate restriction of human knowledge, his limi-

tation of reason by means of reason, i.e., the main result of his critical theory, became only an incitement to the boldest adventures human reason has ever undertaken. The key to this riddle is given us by reason itself. There is an indomitable and radical impetus in all knowledge not to stop before we arrive at the absolute fulfillment of its expressions, i.e., at the full truth.

All sceptical considerations, all attempts to draw a line between the realm of what we can and of what we cannot and shall never know confront an intrinsic difficulty. If there is such a line how can we find it out, and if we cannot find it out, how can we assert that it exists? Even if it should be true that the possibilities of our human understanding are limited, the possibility of knowing this limit also seems to be excluded. We can know only what is within our compass: but to know where this compass ends would imply standing simultaneously within and without it. Only he who has transcended the frontier can become aware of the frontier, but then it is no longer a frontier for him.

This intrinsic difficulty became the motive for an ever growing enlargement of knowledge until at the end Hegel's *Encyclopædia of the Philosophical Sciences* proclaimed that there is no possible limit at all to our knowledge. No one has more vehemently and more passionately wrestled with the intrinsic difficulty of drawing a line between the realm accessible to knowledge and that inaccessible to it than Fichte in his Lore of Science. Fichte recognized that this task was much harder than Kant had guessed. He recognized the full scope of the contradictions in which thought engages if it dares to draw that all-important line.

Fichte envisaged the dangers looming behind his own attempt. He felt that the limit of knowledge seemed to vanish inasmuch as the effort to grasp it was increased. He also saw the consequences that would inevitably result, should human reason succumb to the temptation of denying this limit. For if man imagines he has overcome in principle all barriers of knowledge, then the gulf between humanity and deity, between finitude and infinity, between imperfection and perfection can no longer be acknowledged and respected. Man then is tempted to deify himself and to repudiate the existence of any Being higher than himself. Man's religious awe and humility thus was at stake. Faith was imperiled.

Realizing the tremendous weight of his responsibility as a thinker, as a man of conscience and of faith. Fichte strove to warn Schelling and to keep him within the limits of finite knowledge—within the confines of human possibilities. But at the same time he himself experienced the driving impulse of Schelling's speculative intuition and the persuading force of the philosophy of nature. In this mood and in this situation he wrote his little book of 1800. The trend of thought there developed is not as straight forward and clearly directed towards a definite goal as the writings before 1800. Still it is the work of a master of philosophic meditation and argumentation, and it even contains some of Fichte's most fervent and most stirring utterances.

The *Vocation of Man* has three parts. Fichte depicts at first the position of pre-Kantian metaphysics. He calls this chapter *Doubt*. Before Kant metaphysical knowledge concerned the nature of things, not the nature of knowledge itself. It was based upon the presupposition that thought can succeed in construing the structure of being and in comprehending ultimate reality. But the more successful we are in this direction, the less can we understand ourselves. To the eyes of the understanding everything is conditioned by everything. The system of knowledge, if completed, is and must be a system in which necessity rules without any restriction whatsoever. In such a system freedom and action have no place; they lose their true meaning. Therefore an "intolerable state of uncertainty and ir-resolution" is the consequence.

The second part of Fichte's treatise has the title *Knowledge*. Here Fichte outlines Kant's theory of knowledge which turns the focus of metaphysics from the objects of knowledge towards the knowledge of the objects, or in other words, which inquires no longer into the nature of things but instead into the nature of the knowing subject or the thinking self. This new type of metaphysics is sceptical therefore as to our ability to know ultimate reality, but it has an excellence and an advantage lacking in the former, pre-Kantian position: it delivers man from the bondage of necessity; it shows the ascendency of the centrality of the consciousness, and thus it defeats doubt and restores the legitimate right of will and action.

But this is not yet the whole harvest of the new position. In saving the true meaning of freedom and the right of the personality thought opens a new horizon. While it destroys the illusions of metaphysical knowledge, it rehabilitates the claims of faith. The third and last part of Fichte's book is headed: *Faith*. It is in this chapter that Fichte advances a good deal to meet his younger fellow thinker whose philosophy of nature incited the ambition of knowledge anew and led a path to new possibilities of reconquering the lost terrain.

Fichte insists that not knowledge but faith alone can visualize the ultimate nature of things. None the less he borrows the colours of his picture from the Schellingian palette. In a letter dated December the 27th, i.e., at the end of the fateful year 1800. Fichte writes to Schelling[9] that he is well aware of the "needs of the time" urgently demanding an "enlargement of the Transcendental Philosophy even on its very prin-ciples," and that he has given some hints of that purpose in his *Vocation of Man*. He even goes so far as to concede that man as an individual originated from Nature, if we understand Nature not as the object of the natural sciences, but as the intellectual idea underlying the phenomena of sense perception.

Fichte describes the content of faith in words that strangely deviate from the frame of ethical idealism and approach the intuitive contemplation prevailing in Schelling's *System of Transcendental Idealism*[10]. But he does not completely forsake his ethical position. Faith suggests a new appeal not only of our duties and our moral activity as related to the infinite Will of God, but it grants us also a new vision of the world of sense. Whereas Fichte in all his writings before 1800 strongly emphasized that this world is ultimately nothing but the occasion of moral action for the free will of man, he now teaches (or preaches) that faith inspires us to look at the objects of sense perception with other eyes.

By faith we do not only perceive the world in the light of our duties, we penetrate through error and deformation into its inner truth and beauty. Nature is not only the raw-material of the moral edifice at which we as moral beings aim and for which we act, it is divine in itself, a living Universe that veils and reveals the life and the power of the Infinite. Fichte suddenly exchanges the style and tone of the thinker for those of the praying worshipper: "Sublime and Living Will! named by no name, compassed by no thought! I may well raise my soul to Thee, for Thou and I are not divided."

And he continues: "The life . . . clothed to the eye of the mortal with manifold sensuous forms, flows forth through me, and throughout the immeasurable universe of Nature. Here it streams as self-creating and self-forming matter through my veins and muscles, and pours its abundance into the tree, the flower, the grass. Creative life flows forth in one continuous stream, drop on drop, through all forms and into all places where my eye can follow it . . . All Death in Nature is Birth, and in Death itself appears visibly the exaltation of Life. There is no destructive principle in Nature, for Nature throughout is pure, unclouded Life . . . Death and Birth are but the struggle of Life with itself to assume a more glorious and congenial form" and so on. One would think it is no longer Fichte who speaks, that Fichte who disdained the world of sense. One would think it is Schelling or perhaps even Emerson who has written these lines, not Fichte.

While Fichte thus in the *Vocation of Man* tried to catch up with Schelling's Philosophy of Nature, Schelling himself finished and published the system in which he, with one daring leap, presented a solution of the problem of how the Transcendental Philosophy can be enlarged to meet the "needs of the time." He transfigured the philosophy of the knowing and willing consciousness into a philosophy of the creative genius in the realm of fine arts. Nature accomplishes her greatest and her finest product in producing the artist, for it is in the sphere of artistic beauty that the opposite poles of existence are perfectly integrated into one harmonious whole. Nature and Mind cooperate to this end. Their intrinsic identity is thereby revealed. The work of beauty therefore presents us with the moral and pattern of that perfection at which philosophy itself aims. It sets forth an image of ultimate reality.

The philosopher can accomplish his own work only by imitating the artist. He has to depart from the idea of an original consciousness in which the conflict between opposite forces necessarily arises; and he has to disclose the steps taken by that consciousness in overcoming its original disunity so as to reunify itself. In such a way philosophy can demonstrate why and how the divisions of sensation and understanding of theoretical and practical reason, of the world of sense and the world of ends, and all the contrasts within nature as well as within mind came from a primordial disintegration.

This whole method is justified ultimately by the testimony of Art, for Art shows us ostensibly that the opposites of the finite and the infinite, of the visible and the invisible, of the sensuous and the spiritual are at bottom united and can therefore be reunited by the artist in his work. This work is therefore the highest triumph of man and the greatest achievement of that universal mind which appears in all the forms of Nature. "To the philosopher," Schelling jubilantly announces, "Art is supreme, because it as it were opens to him the Holy of Holies, where in everlasting and original unity there burns, as it were in one flame, what is parted asunder in nature and history, and what in life and conduct, no less than in thinking, must forever flee apart. The view the philosopher artificially makes for himself of nature is for Art the original and natural. What we call nature is a poem which is locked up in strange and secret characters. Yet, could the riddle be disclosed, we should recognize in it the Odyssey of the mind which, strangely decisively, in seeking itself, flees from itself."[11]

Science has therefore as far as possible to return to poetry. The means most appropriate to this purpose would be a new mythology, for in mythology science and art were originally united. "As to how," Schelling concludes," a new mythology—which cannot be the invention of the single poet but of a new generation, as it were representing only a single poet—can itself arise, is a problem the solution of which is to be expected only from the future destinies of the world

and the further course of history." Schelling points here to a favourite idea of the early romantics, an idea which has today for us an ominous sound, as the destiny of the world and the course of history has been deeply and badly influenced by a new mythology opposed to biblical faith and its moral principles. It cannot be denied that there is a certain historical connection between the idea so ardently propagated by Schelling in his system of 1800 and the faith of contemporary Germany, although it would be foolish to call Schelling to account for what happens today.

The system of 1800 however has its historic significance not only in that it foreshadows the decline of the Christian faith in Germany and the insanity of Nazism, but also within the development of German Idealism. For it is the first attempt to establish that kind of idealism which would at the same time be a realism. Kant and Fichte pronounced the idealism of the Ideal, particularly the moral Ideal; Schelling and Hegel promoted the idealism of reality as such, of the ultimately Real. The absolute idea actualizes itself eternally. It is not only an ideal towards which man strives, that man labours to introduce into the real world and into his life; it is eternally realized, it is eternally present. The absolute Idea, Hegel insists, is not so weak as to represent a mere "ought", it really exists and works and is operative in all things real.

This view seems to agree better with Christian faith than the Idealism of the Ideal; it seems to be more religious than the merely moral creed. Indeed Hegel was convinced that his system had brought about the full reconciliation between philosophic speculation and religious revelation, between finite man and divine infinity. "Hegel," James Hutchison Stirling proclaims in his noteworthy book *The Secret of Hegel,* "is the greatest abstract thinker of Christianity and closes the modern world as Aristotle the ancient."[12] However, we have to remember the tension between the Christian faith and the Christian dogma, the life of the saints and the systems of the theologians. Even if it should prove true, that Hegel is the greatest abstract thinker of Christianity, still he cannot be called a Christian thinker for the simple reason that he regarded theology as the kernel of Christianity. Faith necessarily suffers from such an evaluation.

Moreover, one may rightly doubt whether Hegel was really a Christian theologian, for he seems to deny any distinction between God and the Logos, and pretends to construe the Logos in a merely logical way. Too much of romanticism and æstheticism is included in this attempt, to allow of it being accepted as a theological logic of Christianity.

In the year 1800 Hegel was nearer to the genuine Gospel as the original message of Christianity than he was as the author of the *Logic* and of the *Encyclopædia*. In that year he wrote down the latest of his early theological writings.

Notes

[1] *Letters of S. T. Coleridge,* ed. by E. H. Coleridge, Vol. I. p. 259.

[2] *Biogr. Lit.* Everyman's Libr. No. 11. p. 298.

[3] *ibid.,* p. 76.

[4] The logic, Hegel says, is "God as he is in his eternal essence before the creation of Nature and of a Finite Spirit" (Vol. I. p. 60).

[5] *op. cit.,* p. 126.

[6] Modern Libr. Ed. p. 93.

[7] *The Secret of Hegel,* I, p. 21.

[8] How great and dreaded his authority still was in 1800 can be seen from the fact that Schleiermacher in his review of *The Vocation Of Man* did not dare to criticise this book as severely and as ruthlessly as he condemned it privately (cp. my book *Von Kant bis Hegel,* vol. II, p. 68. fn. 2).

[9] Cp. *Von Kant bis Hegel.* II. p. 133.

[10] Cp. *l.c.* p. 73 f.

[11] Tr. by W. Wallace, in *The Logic of Hegel, Prolegomena,* p. 161.

[12] Vol. I. p. 116.

G. W. F. Hegel criticizes how Fichte related his concept of beauty to his philosophical system (1801):

It is remarkable how Fichte can express himself so well about beauty, when what he says is inconsistent with regard to his system; and he does not apply what he says to his system at all, but immediately proceeds to apply it wrongly to the idea of the ethical law.

G. W. F. Hegel, in The Difference Between Fichte's and Schelling's System of Philosophy, *State University of New York Press, 1977.*

Frederick Copleston (essay date 1963)

SOURCE: "Fichte," in *A History of Philosophy:* Volume VII, *Fichte to Nietzsche,* Burns and Oates Limited, 1963, pp. 32-58.

[*In his* A History of Philosophy, *Copleston devotes three chapters to explicating Fichte's philosophy. The excerpt that follows includes Copleston's review of Fichte's life and some of the fundamental tenets in his philosophy.*]

1. Johann Gottlieb Fichte was born in 1762 at Rammenau in Saxony. He came of a poor family, and in the ordinary course of events he could hardly have enjoyed facilities for pursuing advanced studies. But as a small boy he aroused the interest of a local nobleman, the Baron von Miltitz, who undertook to provide for his education. At the appropriate age Fichte was sent to the famous school at Pforta where Nietzsche was later to study. And in 1780 he enrolled as a student of theology in the University of Jena, moving later to Wittenberg and subsequently to Leipzig.

During his studies Fichte came to accept the theory of determinism. To remedy this sad state of affairs a good clergyman recommended to him an edition of Spinoza's *Ethics* which was furnished with a refutation by Wolff. But as the refutation seemed to Fichte to be extremely weak, the effect of the work was the very opposite of that intended by the pastor. Determinism, however, was not really in tune with Fichte's active and energetic character or with his strong ethical interests, and it was soon replaced by an insistence on moral freedom. He was later to show himself a vigorous opponent of Spinozism, but it always represented for him one of the great alternatives in philosophy.

For financial reasons Fichte found himself compelled to take a post as tutor in a family at Zürich where he read Rousseau and Montesquieu and welcomed the news of the French Revolution with its message of liberty. His interest in Kant was aroused when a student's request for the explanation of the critical philosophy led him to study it for the first time. And in 1791, when returning to Germany from Warsaw, where he had a brief and rather humiliating experience as tutor in a nobleman's family, he visited Kant at Königsberg. But he was not received with any enthusiasm. And he therefore attempted to win the great man's favour by writing an essay to develop Kant's justification of faith in the name of the practical reason. The resulting ***Essay towards a Critique of all Revelation (Versuch einer Kritik aller Offenbarung)*** pleased Kant, and after some difficulties with the theological censorship it was published in 1792. As the name of the author was not given, some reviewers concluded that the essay had been written by Kant.

And when Kant proceeded to correct this error and to praise the real author, Fichte's name became at once widely known.

In 1793 Fichte published his *Contributions designed to correct the Judgment of the Public on the French Revolution*. This work won for him the reputation of being a democrat and Jacobin, a politically dangerous figure. In spite of this, however, he was appointed professor of philosophy at Jena in 1794, partly owing to a warm recommendation by Goethe. In addition to his more professional courses of lectures Fichte gave a series of conferences on the dignity of man and the vocation of the scholar, which were published in the year of his appointment to the chair. He was always something of a missionary or preacher. But the chief publication of 1794 was the *Basis of the Entire Theory of Science* (*Grundlage der gesammten Wissenschaftslehre*) in which he presented his idealist development of the critical philosophy of Kant. His predecessor in the chair of philosophy at Jena, K. L. Reinhold (1758-1823), who had accepted an invitation to Kiel, had already demanded that the Kantian criticism should be turned into a system, that is to say, that it should be derived systematically from one fundamental principle. And in his theory of science Fichte undertook to fulfil this task more successfully than Reinhold had done.[1] The theory of science was conceived as exhibiting the systematic development from one ultimate principle of the fundamental propositions which lie at the basis of and make possible all particular sciences or ways of knowing. But to exhibit this development is at the same time to portray the development of creative thought. Hence the theory of science is not only epistemology but also metaphysics.

But Fichte was very far from concentrating exclusively on the theoretical deduction of consciousness. He laid great stress on the moral end of the development of consciousness or, in more concrete terms, on the moral purpose of human existence. And we find him publishing in 1796 the *Basis of Natural Right* (*Grundlage des Naturrechts*) and in 1798 *The System of Ethics* (*Das System der Sittenlehre*). Both subjects are said to be treated 'according to the principles of the theory of science'. And so no doubt they are. But the works are much more than mere appendages to the *Wissenschaftslehre*. For they display the true character of Fichte's philosophy, that is, as a system of ethical idealism.

Complaints have often been made, and not without reason, of the obscurity of the metaphysical idealists. But a prominent feature of Fichte's literary activity was his unremitting efforts to clarify the ideas and principles of the theory of science.[2] For instance, in 1797 he published two introductions to the *Wissenschaftslehre* and in 1801 his *Sonnenklarer Bericht, A Report, Clear as the Sun, for the General Public on the Real Essence of the Latest Philosophy: An Attempt to compel the Reader to Understand*. The title may have been over-optimistic, but at any rate it bore witness to the author's efforts to make his meaning clear. Moreover, in the period 1801-13 Fichte composed, for his lecture courses, several revised versions of the *Wissenschaftslehre*. In 1810 he published *The Theory of Science in its General Lines* (*Die Wissenschaftslehre in ihrem allgemeinen Umrisse*) and the *Facts of Consciousness* (*Tatsachen des Bewusstseins,* second edition, 1813).

In 1799 Fichte's career at Jena came to an abrupt end. He had already aroused some antagonism in the university by his plans to reform the students' societies and by his Sunday discourses which seemed to the clergy to constitute an act of trespass on their preserves. But his crowning offence was the publication in 1798 of an essay *On the Ground of our Belief in a Divine World-Order* (*Ueber den Grund unseres Glaubens an eine göttliche Weltregierung*). The appearance of this essay led to a charge of atheism, on the ground that Fichte identified God with a moral world-order to be created and sustained by the human will. The philosopher tried to defend himself, but without success. And in 1799 he had to leave Jena and went to Berlin.

In 1800 Fichte published *The Vocation of Man* (*Die Bestimmung des Menschen*). The work belongs to his so-called popular writings, addressed to the general educated public rather than to professional philosophers; and it is a manifesto in favour of the author's idealist system as contrasted with the romantics' attitude to Nature and to religion. Fichte's exalted language may indeed easily suggest a romantic pantheism, but the significance of the work was understood well enough by the romantics themselves. Schleiermacher, for example, saw that Fichte was concerned with repudiating any attempt to achieve a fusion of Spinozism and idealism, and in a sharply critical review he maintained that Fichte's hostile reaction to the idea of the universal necessity of Nature was really caused by his predominating interest in man as a finite, independent being who had at all costs to be exalted above Nature. In Schleiermacher's opinion Fichte should have sought for a higher synthesis which would include the truth in Spinozism while not denying moral freedom, instead of simply opposing man to Nature.

In the same year, 1800, Fichte published his work on *The Closed Commercial State* (*Der geschlossene Handelsstaat*) in which he proposed a kind of State socialism. It has already been remarked that Fichte was something of a missionary. He regarded his system not only as the philosophical truth in an abstract, academic sense, but also as the saving truth, in the sense that the proper application of its principles would lead to the reform of society. In this respect at least he resembles Plato. Fichte had once hoped that Free-masonry might prove an apt instrument for promoting moral and social reform by taking up and applying the principles of the *Wissenschaftslehre*. But he was disappointed in this hope and turned instead to the Prussian government. And his work was really a programme offered to the government for implementation.

In 1804 Fichte accepted the offer of a chair at Erlangen. But he was not actually nominated professor until April 1805, and he employed the interval by lecturing at Berlin on the *Characteristics of the Present Age* (*Grundzüge der gegenwärtigen Zeitalters*). In these lectures he attacked the view of romantics such as Novalis, Tieck and the two Schlegels. Tieck introduced Novalis to Boehme's writings, and some of the romantics were enthusiastic admirers of the mystical shoemaker of Görlitz. But their enthusiasm was not shared by Fichte. Nor had he any sympathy with Novalis's dream of the restoration of a theocratic Catholic culture. His lectures were also directed against the philosophy of Nature which had been developed by Schelling, his former disciple. But these polemics are in a sense incidental to the general philosophy of history which is sketched in the lectures. Fichte's 'present age' represents one of the epochs in the development of man towards the goal of history described as the ordering of all human relations with freedom according to reason. The lectures were published in 1806.

At Erlangen Fichte lectured in 1805 *On the Nature of the Scholar (Ueber das Wesen des Gelehrten)*. And in the winter of 1805-6 he gave a course of lectures at Berlin on *The Way to the Blessed Life or The Doctrine of Religion (Die Anweisung zum seligen Leben, oder auch die Religionslehre)*. At first sight at least this work on religion seems to show a radical change from the philosophy expounded in Fichte's early writings. We hear less about the ego and much more about the Absolute and life in God. Indeed, Schelling accused Fichte of plagiarism, that is, of borrowing ideas from Schelling's theory of the Absolute and trying to graft them on to the *Wissenschaftslehre,* oblivious of the incompatibility between the two elements. Fichte, however, refused to admit that his religious ideas, as set forth in *The Doctrine of Religion,* were in any way inconsistent with his original philosophy.

When Napoleon invaded Prussia in 1806, Fichte offered to accompany the Prussian troops as a lay preacher or orator. But he was informed that the King considered it a time for speaking by acts rather than by words, and that oratory would be better suited for celebrating victory. When events took a menacing turn Fichte left Berlin; but he returned in 1807, and in the winter of 1807-8 he delivered his *Addresses to the German Nation (Reden an die deutsche Nation)*.

These discourses, in which the philosopher speaks in exalted and glowing terms of the cultural mission of the German people,[3] have lent themselves to subsequent exploitation in an extreme nationalist sense. But in justice to him we should remember the circumstances in which they were delivered, namely the period of Napoleonic domination.

The year 1810 saw the foundation of the University of Berlin, and Fichte was appointed dean of the philosophical faculty. From 1811 to 1812 he was rector of the university. At the beginning of 1814 he caught typhus from his wife who had contracted the disease while nursing the sick, and on January 29th of that year he died.

2. Fichte's initial conception of philosophy has little in common with the romantic idea of the kinship between it and poetry. Philosophy is, or at least ought to be, a science. In the first place, that is to say, it should be a body of propositions which form a systematic whole of such a kind that each proposition occupies its proper place in a logical order. And in the second there must be a fundamental or logically prior proposition. 'Every science must have a fundamental proposition [*Grundsatz*]. . . . And it cannot have more than one fundamental proposition. For otherwise it would be not one but several sciences.'[4] We might indeed wish to question the statement that every science must have one, and only one basic proposition; but this is at any rate part of what Fichte means by a science.

This idea of science is obviously inspired by a mathematical model. Indeed, Fichte takes geometry as an example of a science. But it is, of course, a particular science, whereas philosophy is for Fichte the science of science, that is, the knowledge of knowledge or doctrine of knowledge (*Wissenschaftslehre*). In other words, philosophy is the basic science. Hence the fundamental proposition of philosophy must be indemonstrable and self-evidently true. 'All other propositions will possess only a mediate certainty, derived from it, whereas it must be immediately certain.'[5] For if its fundamental proposition were demonstrable in another science, philosophy would not be the basic science.

As will be seen in the course of the exposition of his thought, Fichte does not actually adhere to the programme suggested by this concept of philosophy. That is to say, his philosophy is not in practice a strict logical deduction such as could in principle be performed by a machine. But this point must be left aside for the moment. The immediate question is, what is the basic proposition of philosophy?

But before we can answer this question we must decide in what direction we are going to look for the proposition which we are seeking. And here, according to Fichte, one is faced with an initial option, one's choice depending on what kind of a man one is. A man of one type will be inclined to look in one direction and a man of another type in another direction. But this idea of an initial option stands in need of some explanation. And the explanation throws light on Fichte's conception of the task of philosophy and of the issue with which contemporary thought is faced.

In his *First Introduction to the Theory of Science* Fichte tells us that philosophy is called upon to make clear the ground of all experience (*Erfahrung*). But the word experience is here used in a somewhat restricted sense. If we consider the contents of consciousness, we see that they are of two kinds. 'We can say in brief: some of our presentations [*Vorstellungen*] are accompanied by the feeling of freedom, while others are accompanied by the feeling of necessity.'[6] If I construct in imagination a griffin or a golden mountain, or if I make up my mind to go to Paris rather than to Brussels, such presentations seem to depend on myself. And, as depending on the subject's choice, they are said to be accompanied by the feeling of freedom. If we ask why they are what they are, the answer is that the subject makes them what they are. But if I take a walk along a London street, it does not depend simply on myself what I see or hear. And such presentations are said to be accompanied by the feeling of necessity. That is to say, they appear to be imposed upon me. The whole system of these presentations is called by Fichte 'experience' even if he does not always use the term in this limited sense. And we can ask, what is the ground of experience? How are we to explain the obvious fact that a very large class of presentations seem to be imposed on the subject? 'To answer this question is the task of philosophy.'[7]

Now, two possibilities lie open to us. Actual experience is always experience of something by an experiencer: consciousness is always consciousness of an object by a subject or, as Fichte sometimes puts it, intelligence. But by a process which Fichte calls abstraction the philosopher can isolate conceptually the two factors which in actual consciousness are always conjoined. He can thus form the concepts of intelligence-in-itself and thing-in-itself. And two paths lie before him. Either he can try to explain experience (in the sense described in the last paragraph) as the product of intelligence-in-itself, that is, of creative thought. Or he can try to explain experience as the effect of the thing-in-itself. The first path is obviously that of idealism. The second is that of 'dogmatism'. And in the long run dogmatism spells materialism and determinism. If the thing, the object, is taken as the fundamental principle of explanation, intelligence will ultimately be reduced to a mere epiphenomenon.

This uncompromising Either-Or attitude is characteristic of Fichte. There is for him a clear-cut option between two opposed and mutually exclusive positions. True, some philosophers, notably Kant, have endeavoured to effect a compromise, to find, that is to say, a middle path between pure idealism and a dogmatism which ends in deterministic materialism. But Fichte has no use for such compromises. If a philosopher wishes to avoid dogmatism with all its consequences, and if he is prepared to be consistent, he must eliminate the thing-in-itself as a factor in the explanation of experience. The presentations which are accompanied by a feeling of necessity, by the feeling of being imposed upon or affected by an object existing independently of mind or thought, must be accounted for without any recourse to the Kantian idea of the thing-in-itself.

But on what principle is the philosopher to make his choice between the two possibilities which lie open to him? He cannot appeal to any basic theoretical principle. For we are assuming that he has not yet found such a principle but has to decide in what direction he is going to look for it. The issue must, therefore, be decided 'by inclination and interest'.[8] That is to say, the choice which the philosopher makes depends on what kind of a man he is. Needless to say, Fichte is convinced that the superiority of idealism to dogmatism as an explanation of experience becomes evident in the process of working out the two systems. But they have not yet been worked out. And in looking for the first principle of philosophy we cannot appeal to the theoretical superiority of a system which has not yet been constructed.

What Fichte means is that the philosopher who is maturely conscious of his freedom as revealed in moral experience will be inclined to idealism, while the philosopher who lacks this mature moral consciousness will be inclined to dogmatism. The 'interest' in question is thus interest in and for the self, which Fichte regards as the highest interest. The dogmatist, lacking this interest, emphasizes the thing, the not-self. But the thinker who has a genuine interest in and for the free moral subject will turn for his basic philosophical principle to intelligence, the self or ego, rather than to the not-self.

Fichte's preoccupation with the free and morally active self is thus made clear from the start. Underlying and inspiring his theoretical inquiry into the ground of experience there is a profound conviction of the primary significance of man's free moral activity. He continues Kant's insistence on the primacy of the practical reason, the moral will. But he is convinced that to maintain this primacy one has to take the path to pure idealism. For behind Kant's apparently innocent retention of the thing-in-itself Fichte sees the lurking spectre of Spinozism, the exaltation of Nature and the disappearance of freedom. If we are to exorcize this spectre, compromise must be rejected.

We can, of course, detach Fichte's idea of the influence exercised by 'inclination and interest' from his historically-conditioned picture of the initial option with which philosophers are faced. And the idea can then be seen as opening up fascinating vistas in the field of what Karl Jaspers calls 'the psychology of world-views'. But in a book of this kind one must resist the temptation to embark on a discussion of this attractive topic.

3. Assuming that we have chosen the path of idealism, we must turn for the first principle of philosophy to intelligence-in-itself. But it is better to drop this cumbersome term and to speak, as Fichte proceeds to do, of the *I* or ego. We are committed, therefore, to explaining the genesis of experience from the side, so to speak, of the self. In reality Fichte is concerned with deriving consciousness in general from the ego. But in speaking of experience, in the restricted sense explained above, he lays his finger on the crucial difficulty which pure idealism has to face, namely the evident fact that the self finds itself in a world of objects which affect it in various ways. If idealism is incapable of accounting adequately for this fact, it is evidently untenable.

But what is the ego which is the foundation of philosophy? To answer this question we obviously have to go behind the objectifiable self, the ego as object of introspection or of empirical psychology, to the pure ego. Fichte once said to his students: 'Gentlemen, think the wall.' He then proceeded: 'Gentlemen, think him who thought the wall.' Clearly, we could proceed indefinitely in this fashion. 'Gentlemen, think him who thought him who thought the wall', and so on. In other words, however hard we may try to objectify the self, that is, to turn it into an object of consciousness, there always remains an *I* or ego which transcends objectification and is itself the condition of all objectifiability and the condition of the unity of consciousness. And it is this pure or transcendental ego which is the first principle of philosophy.

It is clearly idle to object against Fichte that we cannot find a pure or transcendental ego by peering about. For it is precisely Fichte's contention that the pure ego cannot be found in this way, though it is the necessary condition of our being able to do any peering about. But for this very reason it may appear that Fichte has gone beyond the range of experience (in a wide sense) or consciousness and has failed to observe his own self-imposed limitations. That is to say, having reaffirmed the Kantian view that our theoretical knowledge cannot extend beyond experience, he now seems to have transgressed this limit.

But this, Fichte insists, is not the case. For we can enjoy an intellectual intuition of the pure ego. This is not, however, a mystical experience reserved for the privileged few. Nor is it an intuition of the pure ego as an entity existing behind or beyond consciousness. Rather is it an awareness of the pure ego or *I* principle as an activity within consciousness. And this awareness is a component element in all self-consciousness. 'I cannot take a pace, I cannot move hand or foot, without the intellectual intuition of my self-consciousness in these actions. It is only through intuition that I know that I perform the action. . . . Everyone who ascribes activity to himself appeals to this intuition. In it is the foundation of life, and without it is death.'[9] In other words, anyone who is conscious of an action as his own is aware of himself acting. In this sense he has an intuition of the self as activity. But it does not follow that he is reflectively aware of this intuition as a component element in consciousness. It is only the philosopher who is reflectively aware of it, for the simple reason that transcendental reflection, by which the attention is reflected onto the pure ego, is a philosophical act. But this reflection is directed, so to speak, to ordinary consciousness, not to a privileged mystical experience. Hence, if the philosopher wishes to convince anyone of the reality of this intuition, he can only draw the man's attention to the data of consciousness and invite him to reflect for himself. He cannot show the man the intuition existing in a pure state, unmixed with any component elements; for it does not exist in this state. Nor can he convince the other man by means of some abstract proof. He can only invite the man to reflect on his own self-consciousness and to see that it includes an intuition of the pure ego, not as a thing, but as an activity. 'That there is such a power of intellectual intuition cannot be demonstrated through concepts, nor can its nature be developed by means of concepts. Everyone must find it immediately in himself or he will never be able to know it.'[10]

Fichte's thesis can be clarified in this way. The pure ego cannot be turned into an object of consciousness in the same way that a desire, for example, can be objectified. It would be absurd to say that through introspection I see a desire, an image and a pure ego. For every act of objectification presupposes the pure ego. And for this reason it can be called the transcendental ego. But it does not follow that the pure ego is an inferred occult entity. For it manifests itself in the activity of objectification. When I say, 'I am walking', I objectify the action, in the sense that I make it object-for-a-subject. And the pure *I* reveals itself to reflection in this activity of objectification. An activity is intuited, but no entity behind consciousness is inferred. Hence Fichte concludes that the pure ego is not something which acts but simply an activity or doing. 'For idealism the intelligence is a doing [*Thun*] and absolutely nothing else; one should not even call it an active thing [*ein Tätiges*].'[11]

At first sight at least Fichte appears to contradict Kant's denial that the human mind possesses any faculty of intellectual intuition. In particular, he seems to be turning into an object of intuition the transcendental ego which for Kant was simply a logical condition of the unity of consciousness and could be neither intuited nor proved to exist as a spiritual substance. But Fichte insists that his contradiction of Kant is really only verbal. For when Kant denied that the human mind possesses any faculty of intellectual intuition, he meant that we do not enjoy any intellectual intuition of supersensible entities transcending experience. And the *Wissenschaftslehre* does not really affirm what Kant denied. For it is not claimed that we intuit the pure ego as a spiritual substance or entity transcending consciousness but simply as an activity within consciousness, which reveals itself to reflection. Further, apart from the fact that Kant's doctrine of pure apperception[12] gives us at any rate a hint of intellectual intuition, we can easily indicate the place, Fichte claims, at which Kant ought to have spoken of and admitted this intuition. For he asserted that we are conscious of a categorical imperative; and if he had considered the matter thoroughly, he should have seen that this consciousness involves the intellectual intuition of the pure ego as activity. Indeed, Fichte goes on to suggest a specifically moral approach to the topic. 'In the consciousness of this law . . . is grounded the intuition of self-activity and freedom. . . . It is only through the medium of the moral law that I apprehend *myself*. And if I apprehend myself in this way, I necessarily apprehend myself as self-active. . . .'[13] Once again, therefore, the strongly ethical bent of Fichte's mind finds clear expression. . . .

Notes

[1] From about 1797 Reinhold accepted and defended the philosophy of Fichte. But he was a restless spirit, and after a few years he turned to other lines of thought.

[2] It is perhaps needless to say that the word 'science' must be understood in the sense of 'knowledge' rather than according to the narrower modern use of the term.

[3] A. G. Schlegel had already spoken in a not dissimilar vein of Germany's cultural mission in a course of lectures given in 1803-4.

[4] *F,* 1, pp. 41-2; *M,* 1, p. 170. In this and similar references to Fichte's writings *F* and *M* signify respectively the editions of his *Works* by his son, I. H. Fichte, and F. Medicus.

[5] *F,* 1, p. 48; *M,* 1, p. 177.

[6] *F,* I, p. 423; *M,* III, p. 7.

[7] *Ibid.*

[8] *F,* I, p. 433; *M,* III, p. 17.

[9] *F,* I, p. 463; *M,* III, p. 47.

[10] *F,* I, p. 463; *M,* III, p. 47.

[11] *F,* I, p. 440; *M,* III, p. 24.

[12] See Vol. VI, pp. 253-6, 282-6, 391-2.

[13] *F,* I, p. 466; *M,* III, p. 50.

Bertrand Russell criticizes Fichte's use of subjectivism:

Kant's immediate successor, Fichte (1762-1814), abandoned "things in themselves," and carried subjectivism to a point which seems almost to involve a kind of insanity. He holds that the Ego is the only ultimate reality, and that it exists because it posits itself; the non-Ego, which has a subordinate reality, also exists only because the Ego posits it. Fichte is not important as a pure philosopher, but as the theoretical founder of German nationalism, by his *Addresses to the German Nation* (1807-8), which were intended to rouse the Germans to resistance to Napoleon after the battle of Jena. The Ego as a metaphysical concept easily became confused with the empirical Fichte; since the Ego was German, it followed that the Germans were superior to all other nations. "To have character and to be a German," says Fichte, "undoubtedly mean the same thing." On this basis he worked out a whole philosophy of nationalistic totalitarianism, which had great influence in Germany.

Bertrand Russell, in A History of Western Philosophy, *Simon and Schuster, 1945.*

Tom Rockmore (essay date 1980)

SOURCE: "Fichte's Theory of Man as Active Self," in *Fichte, Marx, and the German Philosophical Tradition,* Southern Illinois University Press, 1980, pp. 6-27.

[*In the excerpt that follows, Rockmore reviews Fichte's philosophy as it defined his notion of human activity. Rockmore concludes that "in Fichte's position the attempted solution to the problem of consciousness requires a view of man as an active being."*]

My intention in this chapter is to state Fichte's view of activity in the context of his wider position. In

Fichte's thought, the concepts of activity and man are inseparable, although neither is well understood. Accordingly, my task here will be to outline as clearly as possible Fichte's understanding of man as an active being. Although I shall refer to the relevant literature as the need arises, the primary emphasis here will be less on a definitive discussion of Fichte's concept of man as an active being than on the general exposition of this view in order to permit its analysis below.

There is good reason to believe that Fichte understood man as the central concern both in his own philosophy and in all human thought. In an early text, Fichte writes, "All philosophy, all human thought and teaching, its entire study . . . can be directed toward nothing other than the answer to the questions posed, especially to the last and highest: What is the vocation [*Bestimmung*] of man in general, and through what means can he best attain it?"[1] But somewhat paradoxically, aside from this single passage, Fichte only rarely mentions man. Rather, he formulates his position in terms of a concept of the self (*Ich*), which has no obvious connection with man. Perhaps for this reason, Fichte's contribution to the problem of man has received only scant attention.[2] It follows that, if we are to understand his view of human being, our immediate task is to grasp the concept of the self as Fichte's response to the problem of man.

Although this aspect of Fichte's thought has not attracted much notice, there is an interpretative tendency which should be indicated, since for the most part my own discussion will run counter to it. Fichte's thought begins from an analysis of the contents of consciousness in terms of a theory of the self. There are basically two schools of interpretation in the literature devoted to Fichte. One school, certainly the majoritarian tendency at the present time, holds that Fichte's thought is limited to the level of consciousness and self-consciousness, since it is unable to make the transition from subjectivity to objectivity. According to this view, which is largely but not wholly inspired by Hegel's reading of Fichte, the external world is no more than the result of the individual's mind. The German poet Friedrich Schiller's comment in a letter, that the individual is the complete source of all reality, is an early, but representative instance of this interpretative tendency.[3]

Needless to say, this way of reading Fichte is closely related to a widespread, but, in my opinion, unfair view of idealists in general, in which Fichte is frequently singled out as a chief offender, as purveyors of a patently ridiculous theory in which each individual plays the role of the divine creator. On the other hand, there is the less frequent tendency to interpret Fichte's view of the self as a theory of man. This can be represented by Dilthey's comment that what is new in Fichte is his grasp of the self, not as a being, but as

an active principle.[4] My own sympathies lie with this second approach. It will be my task here to indicate how, from an analysis of the contents of consciousness, Fichte develops a continuous argument which include such areas as ethics and social organization, as different aspects of the problem of man.

Prior to beginning the exposition, a textual matter should be mentioned. Fichte developed his theory of the self primarily in the *Wissenschaftslehre* (*WL*),[5] and in other texts related to this book. Fichte published several different and only partially compatible editions of this work during his lifetime, and there are several additional versions in his *Nachlass*. Since this book exists in different and in part incompatible editions, it will be necessary to choose one as a source of his views. In the following discussion, I shall rely heavily on the first edition of the *WL,* which appeared in 1794. Although to some extent arbitrary, this decision is not merely so, for this text is widely recognized as Fichte's major contribution and, despite subsequent revisions, it remained the fullest version of his view. It further continued to play a central role in the later development of his thought, since Fichte made abundant use of the position developed here as the theoretical basis from which to address other, more practical questions.

Although the theory of the self arguably receives its most ample discussion in the *WL*, this text is not sufficient by itself. It will need to be supplemented by others in order to reveal the full scope of Fichte's view of man as an active being. The justification is Fichte's apparent intention. Shortly after the appearance of the first edition of the *WL*, in a semipopular article Fichte wrote, "On the basis of the current [form of the] *WL* next Easter a detailed theoretical and practical science of knowledge will follow."[6] In fact the proposed publication took the form of a series of works addressed to related questions in terms of the analysis already developed in the *WL*. Just as in the *Phenomenology of Mind* Hegel moves from an analysis of consciousness and self-consciousness to society, morality, and history, so Fichte's thought ranges outward from a theory of consciousness to related problems. The difference is that while Hegel is able to state the related aspects of his theory in a single, encompassing work, Fichte develops his own view in a number of interrelated writings. But to isolate the *WL* from these related texts, as is sometimes done, is in effect to consider merely a fragment of the position.[7] For this reason, I shall emphasize the manner in which selected, later writings complete the view of the self first sketched in the *WL*.

Historical Background

To understand Fichte's thought, it is helpful to place it in historical perspective. In the period following

Kant's elaboration of the critical philosophy, a number of thinkers, among them Beck, Maimon, Schulze, and Reinhold, subjected it to criticism, often in view of its amelioration. Although there were others who shared his desire to reformulate the Kantian doctrine, Fichte was distinguished by his belief that he was the legitimate successor to Kant.

Fichte's identification with Kant easily surpassed a mere academic interest. His first publication, the *Kritik aller Offenbarung* [*Critique of all revelation*], through accident appeared anonymously. When published in 1792 it was almost immediately mistaken for the long-awaited Kantian work on religion. This instance of mistaken identity brought Fichte immediate fame when he was identified as the author. More to the point, Fichte thought of himself as a Kantian, indeed as the only one who really understood the critical philosophy, a claim he clearly carried to indefensible lengths. For instance Fichte even goes to the extreme of alleging that he understands Kant better than the latter understands himself, although the excessive immodesty of the remark is perhaps moderated if we recall that Kant made a similar comment about his relation to Plato. Kantian premises are further everywhere present in Fichte's thought. Indeed there seems to have been some confusion in Fichte's mind concerning the relation between Kant and himself, such as when in a letter Fichte suggests grandiosely that the critical philosophy in fact follows from his own premises. "It is the same with Kant, whose writings I firmly believe I have understood. It seems more and more likely that he reasons on the basis of my basic principles."[8]

But there is a touch of irony in his assertion that his own view is the completion of the critical quest. Kant, of course, prided himself on the painful architectonic form in which he couched his thought as necessary to its rigorous exposition, although it is precisely this side of the critical philosophy which numerous post-Kantian thinkers, including Fichte, found least appealing. For if he could agree with Kant's conclusions, Fichte found the manner in which they were stated to be lacking in systematic form. Fichte's task, as he saw it, was to give rigorous structure to the Kantian theory by restating it in systematic form.

The source of Fichte's revision of Kantianism can be understood through his relation to K. H. Reinhold and G. E. Schulze. Reinhold is important in the post-Kantian tradition as the first to suggest that a philosophical theory should be based on a single, self-evident principle. He developed this view under the title of Elementary Philosophy (*Elementarphilosophie*) in a number of works. Schulze was a skeptic who, writing under the pseudonym Aenesidemus, objected to the attempt to develop an epistemological theory in this manner on the grounds that no such principle could be found.

The immediate occasion for Fichte to state the first version of his theory was provided by his review of Schulze's study of Reinhold. In his *Elementarphilosophie* Reinhold had attempted to formulate the Kantian position through the introduction of a principle of presentation (*Vorstellung*). "In consciousness the presentation is distinguished by the subject from subject and object, and related to both."[9] Schulze properly objected to this proposition on the grounds that Reinhold had failed to observe the asymmetry in the relation of presentation to the subject and object of experience. Although the presentation occurs in and is in this sense identical with the subject, it differs from the object which it represents. In his review, although Fichte endorses Schulze's criticism, he rejects the skeptical conclusions the latter attempts to draw.

With Schulze's objection in mind, Fichte reformulates Reinhold's principle in his own language, as the claim that the "presentation is related to the object as an effect to its cause, and to the subject as an accident to its substance."[10] This statement is significant, because it gives, in the compass of a single sentence, the outlines of an ontology of consciousness in terms of two elements, subject and object, and their interrelation. It is this same ontology which Fichte further develops in the *WL* and which is the basis of his entire position.[11]

Philosophy, Experience, and Man as Self

Fichte's reworking of Kantian thought in terms of Reinhold's principle of presentation can be introduced through a comment on the aim of philosophy. If, as has been said, idealism is characterized by a simultaneous effort at total explanation and internal unity, then Fichte is an idealist.[12] In Fichte's view, philosophy must explain all experience, and an authentic or rigorous explanation can only be advanced on the basis of a single principle or hypothesis from which the remainder of the theory can be rigorously deduced. The concern to formulate a total explanation of experience in terms of a single concept is a constant theme in Fichte's thought. To grasp the attempt at total explanation in terms of a single underlying idea is to understand the intent motivating Fichte's position.

Like many philosophers, Fichte holds that the task of philosophy is coextensive with the explanation of experience. Fichte draws a basic distinction between two attitudes, that of philosophy and of life. According to Fichte, ordinary experience is insufficient to furnish its own explanation, which can only occur on a meta-experiential or philosophical level. The purpose of philosophy and indeed its only *raison d'être* is to run parallel to and to render everyday life intelligible. "The first standpoint is that of pure speculation; the second that of life and scientific knowledge [in a sense contrasted with that of the *Science of Knowledge*]. The second is intelligible only on the basis of the first" (*WL*, p. 31).

Fichte develops his theory in quasi-phenomenological fashion.[13] If we turn our attention away from the world and toward ourselves, we can see that our experience consists in the contents of consciousness, or presentations (*Vorstellungen*). Our presentations include two general classes. On the one hand, there are those presentations which are accompanied by a feeling of freedom. In contemporary terminology, perhaps the closest analogy would be imagining or free phantasy. Presentations accompanied by a feeling of freedom are contents of consciousness solely dependent on the individual, although in the post-Freudian world it seems doubtful that one would concede that anything occurs in consciousness for which the subject is wholly responsible. On the other hand, there are presentations accompanied by a feeling of necessity. These are contents of consciousness which, to an extent variable with the particular situation, may be said to have their origin in an external world. It is this latter form of presentation for which philosophy is to account. "The system of presentations accompanied by a feeling of necessity is also called *experience*. . . . Philosophy, in other words, must therefore furnish the grounds of all experience" (*WL*, p. 6). But since by virtue of his restriction of experience to these contents of consciousness accompanied by a feeling of necessity, Fichte has sharply limited the scope of his task, it is apparent that, at least initially, to explain experience is equivalent to accounting for one among the possible classes of the contents of consciousness.

If we take into account that Fichte conceives of the problem of experience in terms of a theory of consciousness, his approach has a certain plausibility. Just as, it has been argued, an infant can be aware of his surroundings as such only through the differentiation of the world from himself, so from the perspective of consciousness everything must be understood from the vantage point of the subject. The result is what might be called, in contemporary terms, a first-person ontology, or theory of being from the point of view of the experiential subject.

How is experience to be explained? According to Fichte, the ultimate constituent of reality, through which experience is to be understood, is the self (*das Ich*), a term chosen to designate the human individual as the conscious subject of experience. Using the interaction between subject and object as his basic experiential model, Fichte further distinguishes four kinds of self. From the perspective of the subject, Fichte recognizes both finite self and absolute self. Finite self is the human being as limited and hence defined through his interaction with the surrounding world. Fichte is unfortunately not entirely consistent in his use of this term, for which he frequently substitutes the word

"self," but some misunderstanding can be avoided if it is realized that he apparently has in mind the finite human individual considered as the subject of conscious experience.

Absolute self, on the contrary, is Fichte's term for the individual considered in theoretical abstraction from the man-world interaction that is the setting of all human experience. Since the absolute self is not accompanied by a feeling of necessity, it can never be an object of experience. It follows that to the extent that it can be thought and hence present in mind, absolute self is a free presentation. More to the point, the concept of absolute self, or absolute being, is invoked as a theoretical construct only in order to explain the possibility of experience.

Since the absolute self has often been misconstrued, it is useful to note that Fichte's understanding of this concept underwent revision in his later writings. Schelling reformulated the Fichtean concept of the absolute as the *Indifferenzpunkt* in his *System des transzendentalen Idealismus* (1800). Beginning in 1801, in large part, one may speculate, as a reaction to the celebrated *Atheismusstreit,* Fichte redefines the absolute in a manner closely similar to Schelling's concept of the absolute harmony between subjective and objective forms of activity.[14] But it must be emphasized that earlier, and certainly in the initial version of the *WL*, this term refers merely to a speculative concept devoid of all religious overtones, as Fichte makes clear. "The ***Science of Knowledge*** makes a careful distinction between absolute being and real existence, and employs the former merely as a basis, in order to explain the latter" (*WL*, p. 245).[15]

From the side of the object, Fichte distinguishes notself and absolute not-self. By the term "not-self," he refers to man's world as it is perceived in experience. Fichte also occasionally employs the term "absolute not-self" or even "thing-in-itself," although in a causal manner Kant could not sanction, to designate the surrounding world as that which does not appear in experience, but which may be thought of as the ground of experience. From this perspective, the absolute not-self can be said to provide the ontological underpinnings for experience in general.

It seems clear that Fichte's theory of the world, at least on the epistemological plane, is anything but detailed. In part for this reason, it was accorded a chilly reception by his contemporaries. Indeed, Fichte's failure to provide a more than highly abstract theory of the natural world is one of the reasons which led Schelling to develop his *Naturphilosophie,* and hence an important source of the controversy that separated Fichte from his contemporaries, Schelling and Hegel.[16]

Self and Activity

So far we have seen how Fichte developed an ontology in terms of concepts of self and not-self. He further attempted to comprehend man, understood as a self, as an active being. Since Fichte's aim is to understand the self in terms of its activity, it is to the latter view that one must turn in order to grasp his theory of man. The self's leading characteristic is that it is active or activity, and that this is so is the single presupposition to which Fichte will admit. "The self is absolutely active and merely active—that is our absolute presupposition" (*WL*, p. 221). For Fichte, selfhood and activity are synonymous terms. If we remember that in his view the term "self" stands for "human individual," it follows that, in a fundamental sense, one is not a human being except as one is active and to be active is to be a human being.

The claim that the self is active arises from the regressive nature of the discussion. The problem at hand is to explain the contents of consciousness accompanied by a feeling of necessity, or facts of experience, in terms of the self or experiential subject. Fichte's argument is based on the presupposition that experience can only be understood in terms of an active self. But it should be emphasized that Fichte's theory of activity is more than an assumption which he is constrained to make by the logic of his argument. For he claims that each of us can immediately verify our own activity in what he terms "intellectual intuition" on the level of self-consciousness.[17]

Fichte further develops a theory of the interactions between self and world, and self and other selves. In terms of his basic interactionist model of experience, he differentiates several forms of activity. According to Fichte, subject and object stand in a relation of interdetermination, which may be understood as a restatement of Kant's concept of relation. Each element of the relation determines and is determined by the other. But since self is defined as activity, only three basic forms of activity are possible. Either the subject acts to limit the object, or it is limited by the object, or it acts independently of the object. These three kinds of activity are called respectively positing, striving, and independent activity. To posit (*setzen*) literally means to set, to place, or to put (something). Positing is a positioning of something in regard to something else, and the verb suggests opposition. To strive (*streben*) means to struggle or aspire to, for, or after. Striving implies a perceived lack as well as an attempt to rectify it. Independent activity (*unabhängige Thätigkeit*) is in no sense determined by the subject-object relation, although it takes place within the bounds of this setting.

Positing is the form of activity through which Fichte accounts for consciousness. Fichte employs this con-cept in the sense of the necessary condition. "It is intended to express that *Act* [*Thathandlung*] which does not and cannot appear among the empirical states of our consciousness, but rather lies at the basis of all consciousness and alone makes it possible" (*WL*, p. 93). Fichte's point here is that although positing cannot be experienced, it must nevertheless be thought.

In a manner that recalls Kant's Copernican Revolution, Fichte further maintains that if the object of experience is to be known, the act through which it arises must be ordered according to the laws of the mind. Positing occurs according to three fundamental principles. The three fundamental principles, that is, identity, opposition, and grounding or quantitative limitation, should not be confused with the first principle, the hypothesis that the self is activity. The three fundamental principles may be characterized as quasi-logical laws in terms of which all experience must occur and hence can be explained. These principles invariably limit the manifestation of positing, and hence all experience, to a single paradigm of dialectically rational development. It follows that conscious experience must conform to laws of the mind, and there is no limit to our knowledge of the content of consciousness accompanied by necessity.

The regressive character of the inquiry resembles Kant's analytic approach in the *Prolegomena*. In this work Kant makes the key assumption that there is synthetic a priori knowledge and argues backward, or regressively, to its conditions. In the *WL* Fichte similarly argues from known facts to antecedent conditions or, in his terminology, from conditioned to condition. But since Fichte's theory presupposes that experience is limited to the contents of consciousness, he is obliged to proceed in terms of a specific fact, and not the existence of knowledge in general.

The problem which immediately arises is the selection of an appropriate fact from which to begin the analysis. Fichte begins in what can only be called pseudo-phenomenological fashion. To initiate the discussion, he proposes that we select any one fact of empirical consciousness "that everyone will grant us without dispute" (*WL*, p. 94) and, through abstraction, remove its empirical features. The difficulty is, of course, the specification of any such fact upon which general agreement could be obtained. But the problem is really no more than apparent, since it is patent that in his discussion Fichte is not so much interested in arriving at agreement regarding an initial fact, as in utilizing it as an example for the development of his analysis. In this sense, it makes no difference at all from what fact one begins, since the argument in no sense depends upon it.

The proposition advanced is none other than a form of the law of identity, which Fichte states as "A is A" and as "A = A" (*WL*, p. 94). Fichte uses this proposition to make a number of points in a very murky discussion, which can perhaps be summed up in two principal points. On the one hand, in a manner which partially echoes Kant's transcendental unity of apperception, Fichte maintains that a subject must be invoked as a necessary condition of any and all experience. From this perspective, the subject is no more than a quasi-logical concept which can and indeed must be thought of as accompanying all consciousness. With this quasi-Kantian point in mind, Fichte writes that the subject or absolute self is "a ground of explanation of all facts of empirical consciousness, that prior to all postulation in the self, the self itself is posited" (*WL*, p. 96). Thus, at least from the epistemological perspective, one must consider the subject qua logical principle as a prior and necessary condition of experience.

But Fichte has another, less Kantian card up his philosophical sleeve, a card which derives from his view of logic. It has been the usual practice, at least since Aristotle, to assume the validity of logical laws as a condition of all discussion. But Fichte parts company with the tradition by holding that the *Science of Knowledge*, which can in part be regarded as a logic of experience, is prior to logic *tout court*. This has certain consequences. For one thing, it means that, since the rules of logic must be assumed in all discourse, as Aristotle argues and Fichte concedes, philosophy is necessarily a circular enterprise, a conclusion Fichte readily acknowledges. But there is the further consequence that logical laws, which in Fichte's view can be derived only through abstraction from the content of experience, contain an implicit ontological reference. Applying this point to the concept of an epistemological subject, it follows that this concept is capable of an ontological interpretation.

Kant, as is widely known, laid great stress on the fact that the transcendental unity of apperception is a mere logical condition, in other words an epistemological subject only, to which no psychological interpretation can be attached. But Fichte argues that the logical concept at the base of experience is underlain by an actual subject, or finite human being. This can be seen in two ways. On the one hand, the proposition A is A is a judgment of personal identity, the validity of which can be confirmed by the subject in reflection. For in every case a condition of consciousness is that the subject can, through reflection, be self-aware. Further, the assertion of identity occurs through the coupling of subject and predicate in a judgment. Hence, the logical relation of identity must have as its basis the real subject which brings about the relation through mental activity.

The first or thetic principle, A = A, refers solely to the concept of the experiential subject. Fichte next introduces an antithetic principle, also called the principle of opposition. If there is to be consciousness, there must be something of which the subject is aware, something which stands out over against and opposes it and hence can be known. Now the principle of opposition cannot be deduced from the principle of unity. Accordingly, Fichte goes through a quasi-phenomenological analysis similar to that already described in order to deduce the concept of the object.

So far we have discussed concepts of thesis and antithesis, each of which was supposedly derived from the study of the conditions of consciousness. Now dropping any further pretensions to define his position from conscious experience, Fichte urges that if there is an antithesis, there must be a synthesis. As he puts it, analysis is the process of discovering the sense in which like things differ, and synthesis is the converse process of identifying the sense in which unlike objects resemble one another. Proposing that subject and object can be regarded as composed of scalar quantities, Fichte suggests that antithesis, or opposition between subject and object, can be overcome through a postulated mutual divisibility in which both poles of the subject-object relation limit and define their opposites through interaction. The advantage of this third principle is that it provides for the unity between subject and object requisite for the occurrence of consciousness.

After identification of Fichte's three fundamental principles, we can understand the use to which he puts them. In Fichte's hands, these principles are not a collection of logical rules, but the tools of a dialectical method, better known in its restatement in Hegel's thought. In Fichte's version of the dialectical method, the synthesis requires the antithesis and the antithesis the synthesis. The method is applied by developing two alternative ideas or propositions, both of which are shown to be true, but which are incompatible with one another. The synthesis of what, on closer inspection, is seen to be only apparently contradictory propositions, is achieved through the introduction of another proposition which "contains" the compatible elements of the other two propositions. This enables one to proceed to another synthesis, and so on. As a methodological device, the use of dialectic enables Fichte to generate his *Science of Knowledge* from the three principles discussed by constantly discovering new antitheses which require the introduction of new syntheses.

The topic to which Fichte immediately applies his dialectic method is the problem of consciousness. The argument here is too intricate to follow in detail, and I shall attempt to do no more than to summarize its main points. But if the discussion is to be understood, it must be borne in mind that Fichte's purported solution of this problem depends on the legitimacy of the analysis of the conditions of consciousness from both realistic and idealistic standpoints. Now this is perhaps a move which, on reflection, one may not want to grant Fichte, a decision which would rule his approach to the question out of order on strictly procedural grounds. But one must at least be aware that this is the method Fichte wants to follow if his argument is to be comprehended.

Fichte approaches the problem of consciousness through a quasi-visual image. Consider the following schema. The activity of the self streams outward until it is subjected to a check, at which point it is reflected back into the self. To the extent that its activity is hindered, the self is limited by the not-self, which may be considered as active in relation to a passive self. As passive, the self undergoes, or suffers, the activity of the not-self, of which it is the original cause. In more familiar terms, the relation between subject and object is that of cause to effect. What occurs in the subject is the result of the limitation of its activity due to the interaction with the world. The relation is an opposition between self and not-self, which corresponds to the second principle. The opposition is in a sense overcome by the result of the interaction, the effect of which is the awareness by the subject of its surroundings. In the substance-accident terminology sometimes employed by Fichte, the subject is a substance in which accidents, which correspond to modifications of consciousness, occur as the product of the subject-object interaction. This latter relation is one of synthesis, in which subject and object unite as a condition of consciousness. Synthesis corresponds to the third principle. But the possibility of synthesis is guaranteed by free or unhindered imagination. For although the subject is limited to the extent that it is determined by its interrelation with the object, to the extent that it is undetermined it is free to act. Imagination, or independent activity, is the absolute power by which subject and object are united within a single consciousness. But this unity is made possible by the original thetic subject (the active being or finite person), that is, the first principle which underlies both antithetic and synthetic subject-object relations.

The theory just outlined errs perhaps by attempting to account for too much. Even if one grants Fichte his assumption that the self is the sole source of activity, a presupposition which seems as highly improbable as it is necessary for his attempt to explain experience through a single proposition, at best Fichte can account for the facts of consciousness. What he cannot explain is the ontology underlying his theory, a fact of which he seems occasionally aware. He is unable, for instance, as he is well aware, to cast any light on the source of either self or not-self. In this spirit he notes that his theory is limited "in that it shows how neither does the mere activity of the self provide the ground of the reality of the not-self, nor the mere activity of the not-self provide the ground of passivity in the self" (*WL*, p. 164), as do other views, which he, however, characterizes as dogmatic forms of idealism and realism. Fichte's point here is that at best a theory can describe and interpret the interaction which in fact occurs, but must leave unexplained the source of the elements of the interaction. The latter is a problem whose solution falls outside the scope of philosophy, as he defines it. But this momentary modesty is not only uncharacteristic of Fichte's writings. It is also incompatible with his ascription of activity to the not-self and entire explanation of presentation, since his initial assumption concerns the activity of the absolute self. For as Fichte writes, in a somewhat clearer statement of his position, "The absolute self must therefore be cause of the not-self, insofar as the latter is the ultimate ground of all presentation; and the not-self must to that extent be its effect" (*WL*, p. 22).

At this point, we might pause to evaluate what seems to be a patently circular argument. Fichte's explanation of consciousness makes use of both idealistic and realistic perspectives. From an idealistic perspective, the self is completely autonomous, and there is hence no need to appeal to an external force or principle. Self and not-self are merely determinations within the unity of the self, and self as activity is cause both of itself and not-self. But this idealistic view of self as activity does not "solve" the problem of consciousness, since it fails to demonstrate how the self can be determined by the not-self, as required by the theory of consciousness. This can only be done from a realistic perspective, on the assumption of the reality of the not-self. For consciousness is explicable only if we assume that there exists an external force which reflects the activity of the self back into the self. Not-self determines self, since it provides the real opposition necessary for the reflection of the self's activity. This is the realistic side of the argument.

As a result of the dual perspective, Fichte's position is both realistic and idealistic. Fichte relates this dual perspective to a necessary circle proper to the finite individual. His approach to this circle consists in an attempt to understand it within the context of his theory, rather than in an attempt to explain it away. On the one hand, he acknowledges the impossibility of a complete account of consciousness and experience without the assumption of an independent given. However, whatever is only is for the individual as a presentation on the level of consciousness, not as it is in itself. Since the self as active is self-determining, it can be regarded as the source of the given. In this way only the demand of reason, that the self, in its reflection upon itself, consider that it is the source both of itself and all reality, is fulfilled.

Here, then, the principle: no ideality, no reality, and *vice versa* again receives confirmation or rather emerges into full clarity. As we can also put it, therefore: the ultimate ground of all consciousness is an interaction of the self with itself, by way of a not-self that has to be regarded from different points of view. This is the circle from which the finite spirit cannot escape, and cannot wish to escape, unless it is to disown reason and demand its own annihilation. (*WL*, p. 248)

The preceding account of consciousness contains a problem which should be addressed. The problem arises out of the onesided nature of a theory which centers on the limitation of the individual by his surroundings and the nature of this limitation. The dual perspective from which this limitation is considered harbors a double view of the subject. From the realistic side, the subject is understood as a finite being, whose activity is limited through the opposition furnished by the external world. This is the finite individual, who is the subject of experience, the human being who in fact exists. From the idealistic side, the subject is understood as a theoretical construct, whose activity is, in accordance with Fichte's view of positing, entirely unlimited, or infinite. This form of subjectivity is of course not experienced nor is it experienceable. Rather, it has the status of a theoretical construct required to make the argument work. The problem is to relate the two sides of subjectivity in order to arrive at a single, coherent view.

As Kant before him, Fichte seeks the resolution for conflicts which arise within the context of a theoretical analysis on the practical level. According to Fichte, it is a fact of experience, verifiable through introspection, that the individual is confronted by a real and independent world, which stands over against and limits his activity. Fichte further suggests that it is a "fact" about human nature that the individual is unable to tolerate any restrictions to his activity. Human existence can be understood as an uninterrupted effort to overcome and to abolish all such restrictions. "The self strives to fill out the infinite" (*WL*, p. 254).

From the point of view of the human individual, the importance of striving is that it grounds a theory of self-development. As is his practice, Fichte considers self-development and self-realization from both real and ideal perspectives. The result is a quasi-Spinozistic deductive psychology. Realistically speaking, an individual can escape neither his context nor his limited status as a finite being. At best the surrounding world can be modified in ways consistent with the needs of individual development. The opposition of the individual and his world result in feelings, which Fichte defines as the subjective manifestation of the inability of striving to reach its goal. The feeling of the self's inability to act is accompanied by a longing for the

required determination. Yet since a finite being can never actually expand out to infinity, satisfaction—or the real attainment of the desired determination—can be no more than partial. But on the ideal level, limitations are only apparent. Here it may be said that striving leads to complete realization or fulfillment, which Fichte calls harmony, through the generation of opposition to feelings. But a change in feeling signifies a change in that which opposes it. Harmony results from the fact that the drive and the activity are one and the same, although only ideally so. And it should be stressed, lest Fichte's view seem merely silly, that the fulfillment mentioned here is ideal precisely because the form of striving in question does not relate to a real object.

As an attempt by the individual to surpass what is in the direction of what should be, striving has moral implications. Thus, in Fichte's position as in Kant's epistemology theory leads to and is completed by morality. There is further an obvious comparison to be made between Kant's and Fichte's ethical theories. The similarity is that in both views freedom is a presupposition of morality. For Fichte, the human individual is limited to his relation to the world. It follows that man is free only to the extent that he is not limited by his surroundings. But insofar as man is unlimited, he is completely autonomous in the Kantian sense of the term. Morality is possible because, as a free but limited being, the individual can freely act within the limits of his surroundings according to the moral law. But Fichte's view differs from Kant's in that it preserves autonomy as a condition of morality without the requirement, unrealizable in practice, that the moral subject be thought of as a totally free and completely unconstrained being. Further it should be noted that Fichtean striving is wider than Kantian morality since all practical activity falls under this heading, whereas in Kant's view only activity based on the categorical imperative is moral.

But whatever advantage Fichte's ethical view might possess with respect to Kant's, it seems difficult to defend the concept of striving in the precise sense in which it is formulated by Fichte. Since striving is by definition deprived of causal efficacy, human agency can at best be limited to no more than rational self-orientation. This overrestrictive definition can perhaps be explained in the following way. One may speculate that the residual rationalist tinge in Fichte's position, especially as related to Spinozism, would seem to prohibit a quantification of the causal principle. Yet Fichte's failure to see that causality is possible in a restricted form is nevertheless astonishing, given his own concept of mutual limitation and its relation to the grounding principle, as the latter depends upon the very concept of quantification here in question. The other reason may be that, following Kant, Fichte could not see his way clear, on pain of upsetting the possibility of natural science, to limit causality in the world of experience to make room for freedom, as Kant had limited knowledge to make room for faith.

Despite the evident difficulties with which Fichte's concept is beset, it would seem that a simple reformulation of its definition would resolve many of them. Fichte ought to have left open the possibility for striving to be causal or at least to attain causality, since it is manifestly true that in certain situations at least some actions are causally efficacious, even if all are not. He would still have been able to maintain that striving occurs in response to a desire constitutive of man's being and would not have lost the possibility of excluding certain forms of activity, such as positing, from the realm of conscious, voluntary action. He could then argue consistently, as he at times in the *WL* and frequently in other writings somewhat inconsistently attempts to do, that while complete domination of man over nature of himself is never in fact attained, this is a goal which is constantly and ever-increasingly realized in practice, as man expands the sway of his control of his environment.

But whatever the reason invoked to explain this definition, it would seem that it cannot be defended as it stands. In the short run it seems clear that the ability to act accordingly to principles is a human capacity, even if it is somewhat infrequently exercised. Further, it has been persuasively argued by many thinkers that in the long run human history records a gradually increasing mastery of man over nature as the cumulative result of the activity of many individuals, acting in concert or alone. In this connection, it is comforting to note that Fichte is rather consistent in his manifest disregard of the consequences of his definition of striving for his view of the self, which he regards, both in the *WL* and elsewhere, as a being able to undertake practical activity. Indeed, that man possesses this capacity is a necessary element of the attempt to relate the absolute and theoretical sides of the self through practical activity.

After this discussion of striving, we can understand Fichte's belief that practical activity provides the necessary junction between the absolute and theoretical perspectives previously described. Fichte makes this argument in two steps. On the one hand, as a practical being the individual attempts, in response to an inner drive, to overcome all possible obstacles to his activity and to become an actually infinite being. Hence the concept of self-development presupposes for its intelligibility an idea of the self as ideally unlimited, namely, an absolute self. In this way the practical side of human being may be said to relate to its wholly speculative or absolute aspect. On the other hand, through its striving the individual is constantly confronted by a real world, which stands over against and opposes it. But by virtue of the argument summarized in the

deduction of presentation, that which opposes the self furnishes both the material and the opportunity for knowledge. So the practical aspect of individuality also relates to man's theoretical nature. In other words, both the absolute and theoretical sides of man are conjoined through practical activity. Hence Fichte can write that "we have at last discovered the point of union we were seeking between the absolute, the practical and the intellectual characters of the self" (*WL*, p. 244).

This phase of the discussion recalls Kant's similar preoccupation, but there is a difference which should be noted. Kant's intent is to determine the relative precedence to be accorded to different kinds of experience in order to avoid what he sometimes terms a conflict (*Streit*) between the various faculties. Fichte is interested in a somewhat different question. He is not so much concerned to avoid a conflict among faculties, although he certainly does not overlook this problem, as he is to demonstrate their possible coexistence in a finite human being. In this regard his primary motivation would seem to be to provide for a unitary conception of the human individual in terms of the various forms of activity which can be attributed to it in correlation with types of human experience.

Man as an Active Being

A résumé of the view of man which emerges from this complicated train of reasoning can now be rapidly sketched. In a discussion which begins with the problem of the conditions of knowledge and experience, Fichte considers man from two perspectives. As a finite human being, the individual person is both a theoretical, namely, a subject of consciousness, and a practical, or moral, being. As a real finite being, man is limited through his relation to the external world. The concept of absolute being is further invoked on the philosophical or meta-experiential level, as a philosophical concept useful in the explanation of experience. To the types of man or self Fichte associates kinds of activity. As theoretical man posits, as practical he strives, and as absolute he acts in theoretical independence of his surroundings. The concept of an ideally existent absolute being is justified as a means to understand the experience of the really existent finite being. Forms of activity need to be subtended by activity in general, and from the side of realism man is above all a practical being. But from the idealistic perspective, the concept of pure activity is identified with the absolute self, an acknowledged philosophical construct in Fichte's discussion. Yet since from this perspective a view of man follows from the concept of absolute self, Fichte may be said to "deduce" the concept of the individual from that of the absolute. As he notes in a letter: "My absolute self is clearly not the individual. . . . But the individual must be deduced from the absolute self."[18] But one should of course not lose sight of the fact that the pretended deduction only works since Fichte "smuggles in" the concept of the individual in abstract form as the presupposition of the theory.

So far we have been concerned with that portion of Fichte's position which appears in the first version of the *WL*, its introductions, and prior writings. It is obvious that the concept of man is here stated merely in the context of his relation to a featureless surrounding world, which has no apparent relation to a social context or other men. To be sure, in the *WL* there is a single passage in which the concept of interpersonal relations is obscurely invoked. "We thus envisage an activity extraneous to the self (= — Y), equal and akin to this activity of the self" (*WL*, p. 230). But this is hardly a full treatment of the problem. For this reason, it might be thought that Fichte somehow overlooks or fails to account for the social side of human being.

That Fichte does not at this point devote more attention to interpersonal relations is not surprising, but rather consistent with his understanding of his task. Although the narrow focus of the discussion has the effect of imparting a solipsistic tinge to his argument, the attempt to state a theory of experience solely from within the perspective of the individual's conscious awareness virtually precludes satisfactory discussion of man's social being. Yet one should be aware that Fichte's later emphasis on the interpersonal nature of human being does not mark a shift in the basic position.[19] There is rather a shift in emphasis.

The shift in emphasis has two major aspects. One aspect concerns the evolution of Fichte's original position, whose first full statement occurs in the *WL*. The further evolution of Fichte's original position can be attributed to several factors, including his own desire to improve the imperfect manner in which his theory was originally stated, his concern to respond to criticism raised by his contemporaries, and the development in his own mind of the goal and nature of philosophy. As a result, Fichte is perhaps the only major philosopher whose central work exists in more than half a dozen, only partially compatible versions, the consequence of his continued efforts to improve upon earlier statements of his own position.

The evolution of Fichte's position is not merely in degree, but in kind. In writings after the celebrated *Atheismusstreit*, for instance, he tended to emphasize the religious dimension of his thought in a manner which was not wholly consistent with his earlier position and further made stronger claims for knowledge in the traditional philosophical sense than can be defended in his earlier view. Accordingly, a consequence of the later change of his position was to bring it into closer alignment with the development from Kant to Hegel, in which his own thought is often, but errone-

ously, regarded as a mere transitional link, not worthy of consideration for its own sake.[20]

The complex issue of the later evolution of Fichte's position and its relation to his earlier thought represents an as-yet-unsettled problem which is the topic of much interest in the literature. But although an account of the later development of Fichte's philosophy would be interesting, it must be omitted since the ulterior modifications of Fichte's views tended to diminish the parallel between his and Marx's respective positions under consideration here.[21] But I do want to mention aspects of the later Fichtean view of man which are continuous with Fichte's earlier thought, since they are relevant to the present discussion.

In later works Fichte applies his view of man as an active being to various problems and gives increasing emphasis to social considerations. In the latter respect Fichte's basic point seems to be that "man . . . only becomes a man among men."[22] It follows that the concept of social interaction is built into the concept of individuality. For man is always in or must be considered in relation to a social setting, and hence cannot reasonably be conceived of in isolation from other human beings. Fichte develops his understanding of man's social aspect in several directions. One point he makes is that, as Hegel later observes, man is only fully aware of himself through the awareness of others. In other words, the condition of self-consciousness is that others recognize me as a human being. And Fichte goes on to stress that man develops only within a social context, although he notes that existing nations need fundamental reorganization if man is ever to reach the goal of becoming fully freely active among other freely active individuals.

Fichte further applies his view of man as an active being to ethics and morality. As Hegel will do later, Fichte draws a distinction between these two spheres. In Fichte's position, the distinction rests on the difference between independent and practical forms of activity. The former is completely unrestrained as to its occurrence and has no necessary effect on the individual's surroundings, since it is by definition independent of the subject-object relation of experience. It hence takes place on the level of mind only. The latter occurs within the space allotted to the individual by his context and is, again by definition, an attempt to enlarge the available space for man's free activity. "The concept of rights applies only to that which externalizes itself in the sensuous world; that which has no causality in the sensuous world, but rather remains within the interior of the mind belongs to another standard of judgment, that of morality."[23]

Fichte develops his theory of morality in *Das System der Sittenlehre* (1798). Although this work bears a strong Kantian imprint, it is essentially a critique of the

Kantian position. Here, as elsewhere, Fichte is strongly concerned to give systematic form to what he regards as an unsystematic Kantian view. The discussion deals at length with the concept of duty (*Pflicht*) in relation to the concept of morality. Duty is portrayed as an abstract idea which has currency only within this realm, but within this realm it is the prime motivating force. Not surprisingly, Fichte even claims to provide the foundation for, as well as the correct deduction of, the categorical imperative.

But one ought not to overlook the critical thrust of this reworking of the Kantian position. It is significant that the locus of moral activity is restricted to the sphere of individual consciousness, since this is to imply that formal morality in fact has and can have no real application. Hence Fichte notes that moral freedom is merely a theoretical idea and he observes that the efficacy of morality is no more than that of the causality of its concept. For the restriction of its sphere of influence solely to the level of the individual's self-determination means that morality is deprived of a role on the social level. Morality is therefore an ideal concept which has meaning under the condition of perfect rationality only, and hence admits of no real application.

Fichte's criticism of the Kantian moral theory is elaborated from the perspective of social reality. A realistic analysis must proceed from the standpoint of free human relations. Its principal task is to understand the possibility of free human activity within a social context. Fichte elaborates his theory of social interaction in the *Grundlage des Naturrechts (Rechtslehre)* (1796). The title is, as Fichte later points out, somewhat misleading, since it implies erroneously that he holds a theory of natural right. But Fichte later corrected this impression in the second edition of the book when he writes that "natural right is a right of reason, and should be so called."[24]

Following Rousseau, Fichte maintains that the essential justification of community is the free association of individuals who come together on the basis of a contract. Now if there is a community, there must be rights. Rights include both the restriction of individuals' actions with respect to one another and the reciprocal recognition of certain privileges, or positive rights to something. Among the most fundamental rights is that of property, by which Fichte means the right to the means necessary for life. This basic right, which is grounded in the original contract, depends for its validity upon the ability of the individual to live from his work. In the event that this is not possible, then the contract is regarded as broken, which is another way of stating that under certain conditions the right to revolt and, if necessary, to revolution, exists. In practice this means the justification of individual rights is that in a social context, where each is limited, each

profits from the existence of mutual limitations. But if and when the individual can no longer profit from the limitation of his range of action, then all such limits are to be regarded as removed.

As mentioned, the purpose of the **Rechtslehre** is to discuss the conditions of the possibility of the free association of social beings. A further question is the condition of the development of social freedom. Fichte addresses himself to this problem in a little-known book, **Der geschlossene Handelsstaat** (1800), which was intended as a continuation of the **Rechtslehre**. This work has unfortunately for the most part either been ignored or noticed only to point out its utopian character. Fichte was himself aware of this possible line of criticism, since he notes that it is highly unlikely that any state would freely agree to adopt the suggestions he makes here. And Struensee, to whom the book is dedicated, states in a letter to its author that "even you doubt whether this ideal can be reached."[25]

But it would be wrong to regard this book as wholly impractical. For the central idea, that the state must make use of economic closure in order to attain independence and hence provide for the real possibility of rational interpersonal relations, is not utopian. The difficulty arises mainly in the transition to this kind of national organization. And although the details of Fichte's analysis have been improved on in subsequent political theory, this work retains permanent importance as the first serious discussion in the German tradition of the economic conditions of social freedom.

As the discussion has now reached the stage of the reorganization of social relations, this is perhaps an appropriate place to break off the exposition. In this chapter I have sought to outline Fichte's understanding of man as an active being in the wider context of his position. In rapid outline I have reconstructed the train of thought by which Fichte moves from a regressive and transcendental analysis of the conditions of consciousness to questions of individuality and human interaction. I have further stressed throughout the continuity of the argument in the earlier and later writings, through demonstration of the fact that in Fichte's position the attempted solution to the problem of consciousness requires a view of man as an active being. Marx's position is very different from Fichte's. But it is fascinating to observe that his conception of man as an active being is similar to Fichte's theory of the self. . . .

Notes

[1] Johann Gottlieb Fichte, *Fichtes Werke,* ed. I. H. Fichte, 11 vols. (Berlin: Walter De Gruyter, 1971), 6, p. 294.

[2] The signal exception is Wilhelm Weischedel, *Der Aufbruch der Freiheit zur Gemeinschaft* (Leipzig: Meiner, 1939). See also Heinz Heimsoeth, *Fichte* (Munich: E. Reinhardt, 1923).

[3] "According to Fichte's verbal statements, which were not mentioned in his book, the self creates through its representations; and all reality is only in the self. The world is to the self like a ball, which the self has thrown out and then caught again through reflection [*Reflexion*]." Letter from Schiller to Goethe of October 28, 1794 in Johann Christian Friedrich Schiller *Briefwechsel zwischen Schiller und Goethe,* ed. H. Hauff, 2 vols. (Stuttgart: Cotta'sche Buchhandlung, 1856), 1:26. A more sophisticated, but similar interpretation is stated by Josiah Royce, *Lectures on Modern Idealism* (1919; reprint ed., New Haven: Yale University Press, 1964), p. 97: "That this self of philosophy is not the individual man of ordinary life appears from the very outset of Fichte's discussion. The individual man of ordinary life is one of the beings to be defined by philosophy, and is certainly not the principle of philosophy."

[4] "In what sense does Fichte signify the beginning of something new? In that he begins from the intellectual intuition of the self, not however as a substance, a being, a givenness, but rather through this intuition, that is, he understands this striving for deepening (*diese angestrebte Vertiefung*) of the self in itself as life, activity, energy and, accordingly, the corresponding concepts of energy as opposition, etc., the realisation in itself." Wilhelm Dilthey, *Gesammelte Schriften* (Stuttgart: Tübner, 1961), 7: 148.

[5] Johann Gottlieb Fichte, *Fichte: Science of Knowledge (Wissenschaftslehre) with First and Second Introductions,* ed. and trans. Peter Heath and John Lachs (New York: Appleton-Century-Crofts, 1970). (Hereafter cited in text as *WL*.)

[6] *Intelligenzblatt der Allgemeinen-Literatur-Zeitung,* no. 113 (October 1794).

[7] For an example of the tendency to approach the *Wissenschaftslehre* apart from the wider context of Fichte's thought, see Dieter Henrich, *Fichtes ursprüngliche Einsicht* (Frankfurt: Vittorio Klostermann, 1966).

[8] Letter from Fichte to Reinhold of March 1, 1794, in Johann Gottlieb Fichte, *J. G. Fichte. Briefwechsel,* ed. Hans Schulz, 2 vols. (Hildesheim: Georg Olms, 1967), 1:341.

[9] Karl Leonhard Reinhold, *Beyträge zur Berichtigung bisheriger Missverständnisse der Philosophie,* 2 vols. (Jena: Manke, 1790), 1:267: "In consciousness the representation (*Vorstellung*) is distinguished from both subject and object, and related to both."

[10] *Fichtes Werke,* 1:18.

[11] Adolph Schurr makes a similar point when he writes, "During the process of working out [*Ausarbeitung*] the review of Aenesidemus Fichte conceived the foundation [*Fundament*] upon which his *Foundation [Grundlage]* was [later] built." *Philosophie als System bei Fichte, Schelling, und Hegel* (Stuttgart: Frommann-Holzboog, 1974), p. 12.

[12] Martial Gueroult notes, "The effort towards totality is equalled only by the effort toward real and internal unity, which is opposed—even in a Schelling—to eclecticism or arbitrary syncretism." *L'Evolution et la structure de la doctrine de la science chez Fichte,* 2 vols. (Paris: Société d'éditions Les Belles Lettres, 1930), 1:3.

[13] I have no intention of suggesting that Fichte was a phenomenologist *avant la lettre* in the sense this term has been given by such writers as Husserl and Heidegger. Here as elsewhere, unless otherwise specified, by "phenomenological" is meant the somewhat different, but not unrelated sense in which this term applies also, but not only, to Hegel. For a discussion, which however conflates the phenomenological sides of Husserl's and Hegel's positions, see Alexandre Kojève, *Introduction à la lecture de Hegel* (Paris: Gallimard, 1947).

[14] "The absolute is neither knowledge, nor is it being, nor is it identity, nor is it the indifference of both; rather, it is throughout only and simply the absolute." *Fichtes Werke,* 2:13.

[15] This point has frequently been misconstrued. On the whole, Wundt seems correct, when he writes, "The concept of God has no intrinsic place in the *Wissenschaftslehre* of 1794, but is only appealed to occasionally for purposes of comparison" (*sondern wird nur gelegentlich zum Vergleich herangezogen*). Wilhelm Wundt, *Fichteforschungen* (Stuttgart: F. Frommann, 1929), p. 275.

[16] Schelling stated the need for a philosophy of nature as follows: "Fichte considered idealism from a fully subjective perspective, and I considered it from a fully objective perspective. Fichte's idealistic principle remained on the reflective standpoint; on the contrary, I put forward the idealistic principle from the standpoint of production." *Darstellung meines Systems der Philosophie* in *Schellings Werke,* ed. Manfred Schröder (Munich: Beck and Olden-bourg, 1927), 3:5. For a recent study of the relation between Fichte and Schelling, see Reinhard Lauth, *Die Entstehung von Schellings Identitätsphilosophie in der Auseinandersetzung mit Fichtes Wissenschaftslehre, 1795-1801* (Munich: Alber, 1975).

[17] For an account of Fichte's view of intellectual intuition, see Alexis Philonenko, "L'Intuition intellectuelle chez Fichte," in *Akten der Fichte-Tagung* (Proceedings of international conference at Zwettl, Austria, in press).

[18] Letter from Fichte to Jacobi of August 30, 1795, from Osmannstadt in *J. G. Fichte, Briefwechsel,* 1:501.

[19] The argument has been made that Fichte is a pioneer in the attempt to understand social interaction. See C. Hunter, *Der Interpersonalitätsbeweis in Fichtes früher angewandter praktischer Philosophie* (Meisenheim: a.M. Glan: Hain, 1973).

[20] For the classic expression of this interpretation, see Richard Kroner, *Von Kant bis Hegel* (Tübingen: Siebeck, 1921—24) two volumes. For criticism of the Hegelian-inspired reading of Fichte's position, see Peter Baumanns, *Fichtes ursprüngliche System: Sein Standort zwischen Kant und Hegel* (Stuttgart: Frommann-Holzboog, 1972).

[21] For a recent, general introduction to Fichte's thought as a whole, see Pierre-Philippe Druet, *Fichte* (Namur: Seghers, 1977). For a more specialized, recent discussion, see Wolfgang Janke, *Fichte: Sein und Reflexion. Grundlagen der kritischen Vernunft* (Berlin: Walter De Gruyter, 1970). For the most detailed analysis of the structure of the *Wissenschaftslehre* of 1794, see Alexis Philonenko, *La Liberté humaine dans la philosophie de Fichte* (Paris: Vrin, 1966).

[22] *Fichtes Werke,* 3:39.

[23] Ibid., p. 55.

[24] Ibid., 10:498. Marianne Weber's failure to note this correction leads her unfortunately to perceive an analogy on this point between the positions of Fichte and Marx, when in fact there is none. See *Fichtes Sozialismus und sein Verhältnis zum Marx'schen Doktrin.*

[25] Letter from Fichte to Struensee of November 9, 1800, in *J. G. Fichte, Briefwechsel,* 2:288.

Patrick Gardiner (essay date 1982)

SOURCE: "Fichte and German Idealism," in *Idealism: Past and Present,* edited by Godfrey Vesey, Cambridge University Press, 1982, pp. 111-26.

[*In the following essay, Gardiner considers Fichte's claim that his works are arguments for human freedom. This purpose might be difficult to believe, Gardiner contends, until one puts Fichte's writings into historical and cultural context.*]

Fichte's reputation at the present time is in some respects a curious one. On the one hand, he is by common consent acknowledged to have exercised a dominant influence upon the development of German thought during the opening decades of the nineteenth century. Thus from a specifically philosophical point of view he is regarded as an innovator who (for good or ill) played a decisive role in transforming Kant's transcendental idealism into the absolute idealism of his immediate successors, while at a more general level he is customarily seen as having put into currency certain persuasive conceptions which contributed—less directly but no less surely—to the emergence and spread of romanticism in some of its varied and ramifying forms. On the other hand, however, it is noticeable that detailed consideration of his work has not figured prominently in the recent revival of concern with post-Kantian thought as a whole which has been manifested by philosophers of the English-speaking world. Although his name is frequently mentioned in that connection, one suspects that his books may not be so often read. In part this may be due to his particular mode of expounding his views, which at times attains a level of opacity that can make even Hegel's obscurest passages seem comparatively tractable. It is also true that Fichte's principal theoretical works—if not his semipopular writings—are largely devoid of the allusions to scientific, historical, psychological or cultural matters with which his German contemporaries were prone to illustrate their philosophical doctrines and enliven their more abstract discussions: there is a daunting aridity about much of what he wrote which can raise nagging doubts in the modern reader's mind about the actual issues that are in question. Yet the fact remains that by the close of the eighteenth century his ideas had already made a profound impact, capturing the imagination of a host of German thinkers and intellectuals. The problem therefore arises as to what preoccupations, current at the time, they owed their indubitable appeal and to what puzzles they were welcomed as proffering a solution. If these can be identified, it may become at least partially intelligible that Fichte should have been widely regarded as having provided a framework within which certain hitherto intractable difficulties could be satisfactorily reformulated and resolved. Let me accordingly begin by saying something about them.

Fichte once described his own philosophy as amounting from beginning to end to no more than an 'analysis of the idea of freedom'. However that may be, it is undoubtedly true that from an early stage in his philosophical career the question of whether, and if so in what sense, human freedom could be vindicated assumed an overwhelming importance in his eyes and that it continued in one form or another to haunt him for the rest of his life. Nor was he alone in this. Thus he came to intellectual maturity in the seventeen-eighties, during a period when the belief that the operations of the human mind were as susceptible to mechanistic explanation in terms of invariant regularities or laws as those of physical nature had in many quarters achieved an almost axiomatic status. Upholders of such a view, which was associated in the first instance with representatives of the Enlightenment in France but which also found eloquent adherents elsewhere, may have differed amongst themselves as to the precise nature and foundations of the laws in question. None the less, that were united in the conviction that in the final analysis all that men thought and did could be explained as the necessary consequences of antecedent factors—whether physiological, psychological or environmental—which determined them as rigorously as those that governed occurrences in the inanimate sphere investigated by the natural sciences; only irrationality or a misplaced vanity could lead people to imagine that they were somehow exempt from the causal uniformities that manifested themselves throughout the universe and whose ubiquity had been triumphantly demonstrated by the successes of Newtonian physics. If followed that there was no acceptable alternative to treating the human world, in all its aspects, as a mechanically ordered system wherein traditional doctrines of 'free will' had no place: the latter must either be ruthlessly re-interpreted in the interests of intellectual hygiene or else simply discarded, along with other outdated theological and metaphysical dogmas, as the contemptible remants of pre-scientific superstition. If these consequences were repugnant to orthodox religious opinion this was hardly a matter for surprise, still less for regret.

Yet while there were some, in Fichte's time as in our own, who were prepared happily, even eagerly, to embrace such a conclusion, there were others (especially in Germany) for whom it was a source of intense disquiet; moreover, their discontent, though partly influenced by religious concerns, by no means wholly derived from these. Two further considerations, both of which later found expression in Fichte's own writings and struck a responsive chord in his readers, may be picked out as being of particular significance in the present context.

The first involved a deep distaste, not easy to define with any precision but nevertheless profoundly felt, with an overall picture of the universe in which human existence was seemingly conceived as a mere appendage of nature and where nature itself was presented in a way that reduced it ultimately to no more than an abstract system of interacting material particles—'the same old atoms shuffling about in accordance with the same old laws', as one modern commentator has succinctly put it.[1] Apart from anything else, a picture of this kind was considered to rob human life of the spontaneity and variety which were its distinctive features and to obscure something to which all history, including that of the sciences themselves, bore wit-

ness at every point—the palpable creativity of the intellect and its capacity for transforming both itself and the world in novel and unpredictable ways. The second consideration, though not unconnected with the first, was more specific and pertained to the asseverations of immediate practical experience. Thus it was all very well to speak as if doctrines affirming the freedom of the will belonged to the prehistory of human knowledge and could be treated as so much metaphysical lumber which we should be far better off without. It was not clear, however, that those who adopted this confident tone had understood the full implications of what they were proposing. For the ideas they dismissed in so cavalier a fashion could not properly be portrayed as if they were no more than the ghosts of antiquated theory, with about as much relevance to everyday thought and behaviour as the abstractions and rarefied essences of the schoolmen. On the contrary, they remained alive and active, being intrinsic to our awareness of what it was to participate as purposive agents in the world and representing an essential component of the structure within which our practical consciousness as a whole, and in particular our moral consciousness, was set. When such points were recognised and taken into account, the suggestion that to accept a thorough-going determinism need entail no radical dislocation of our ordinary beliefs acquired—to put it mildly—a paradoxical air. How far was it really possible to do so without undermining the entire conception of ourselves as autonomous sources of deliberation and choice, capable of determining our behaviour in accordance with reasons which we had freely decided upon or endorsed? Was not such a supposition, even if it were granted that it could be coherently entertained, destructive of the very notion of human action as this was customarily used and understood?

It was, of course, precisely contentions of the latter kind that were accorded primacy of place in the moral philosophy of Kant. Unlike some of his compatriots, however, Kant did not think that it was justifiable, or indeed possible, blankly to reject the determinist thesis out of hand; rather he believed that an account of man's status as a rational and practical being could be provided which fully accommodated the considerations just mentioned without in any way impugning the legitimacy of treating human behaviour as being at the same time subject to invariant causal laws. The materials for resolving the alleged dilemma were in fact to be found in the doctrines of transcendental idealism, according to which a fundamental distinction must be drawn between the phenomenal world, or reality as it appears to a conscious subject, and the noumenal or 'intelligible' world of things as they are in themselves. Regarded as empirical entities we necessarily belong to the former realm and as such must be conceived of as conforming to the same ordering principles as those that govern the rest of nature; to that extent the scientifically minded theorists associated with the Enlightenment had been correct. But, notoriously, this was for Kant by no means the whole story. For he also maintained that another standpoint could be adopted that transcended the limits of a purely naturalistic approach and from which human beings might be viewed, not as phenomenal 'appearances' falling under the causality of nature, but rather as non-empirical centres of consciousness and will; in this sense they could be regarded as members of the noumenal sphere, capable of issuing and obeying laws which were 'independent of nature' and which had their source in reason alone. Moreover Kant claimed, somewhat obscurely, that these two distinguishable ways of looking at ourselves were entirely compatible with one another and that no clash need therefore occur between, on the one hand, the scientific conception of what went on in the human world and, on the other, those assumptions about the reality of freedom which were, he fully agreed, integral to our outlook as practical and moral beings; as he himself put it, 'that our reason has causality, or at least that we represent it to ourselves as having causality, is evident from the *imperatives* which in all matters of conduct we impose as rules upon our active powers'.[2]

In a general way, and whatever Kant might have thought it appropriate to affirm at the empirical level about human beings and their activities, his own version of idealism appeared to his contemporaries to involve a drastic transformation of the terms in which it had become customary to present the relation between the human mind and the natural order. Prevalent views typically subordinated the former to the latter and portrayed consciousness, under both its cognitive and its practical aspects, in a manner that conformed to the interpretative scheme which had been successfully applied to the investigation of the natural world; hence the various mechanistic models and hypotheses that had been introduced to explain thought and action alike. In place of these Kant had elaborated notions which stressed the creative and constructive functions of the intellect, such functions being envisaged as in some fashion set apart from the realm of nature and as contributing to its overall character. Theoretically speaking, they were seen as responsible for the pervasive structure and form, though not for the sensory content, which the world of experience as a whole displayed; while at the level of practice they were to be understood as generating rational principles which could prescribe courses of action opposed to those prompted by the sensuously conceived inclinations and passions emphasized by much Enlightenment psychology. Mind and nature had thus been pictured in a profoundly changed perspective. Kant himself might have believed that, in so presenting them, he had not really put in question the essential insights embodied in the Enlightenment position; his aim had rather been one of providing a corrective to certain limitations

inherent in it, both by removing defects in its theory of knowledge and by making room for dimensions of human thought which it tended to ignore or override. To Fichte, however, it seemed that the innovations introduced carried far-reaching implications which even their author had not adequately appreciated. Only when these had been fully explored and developed, and their misleading association with the relics of superseded doctrine finally severed, could their truly revolutionary import at last become manifest. Fichte claimed to have performed such a service in his own philosophy. To this claim we must now turn.

Fichte first encountered Kant's ideas through the *Critique of Practical Reason,* which he read in his late twenties, and it was this work above all others that made a lasting impact upon his mind. His own philosophical reputation originally derived from a contribution to critical theology so deeply influenced by Kantian conceptions that it was taken to be by the master himself; when its true authorship became known he was appointed to a professorship at Jena at the early age of thirty-two. During the same year (1794) the first version of his most famous book, the ***Science of Knowledge*** (***Wissenschaftslehre***), appeared, and in this case he went out of his way to stress its Kantian affiliations through two Introductions to the work which he appended three years later. In the first of these he expressed his indebtedness to Kant's revisionary achievement in philosophy, while in the second he argued for the view that what he had written was 'perfectly in accordance with the teaching of Kant' and that this had been 'increasingly confirmed by the continuing elaboration of his system'.[3] Yet he was at the same time quite aware that such an opinion was by no means shared by reviewers and critics of the ***Wissenschaftslehre***, many of whom dissented from it and one of whom had cited Kant himself as firmly dissociating his position from Fichte's own. In reply, Fichte was mainly content to argue that, since Kant's basic these had been generally misunderstood, it was not surprising that their true relation to his own philosophy had been correspondingly misapprehended; while if Kant, too, had demurred, it might be because that 'reverend sage' had not read Fichte's actual writings and had relied instead on inaccurate expositions of them. In any case he wished to insist that his system was in all essentials continuous with the Kantian.

Despite the vehemence of his language one wonders how far Fichte really believed this. Admittedly his attitude towards those who disagreed with him was seldom conspicuously temperate; but the peculiar irritation he showed in the present instance may have been due to an uneasy sense that his claims must appear to the most sympathetic reader as somewhat lacking in plausibility. It was one thing to hold that he had taken as his starting point certain leading Kantian themes; it was another to assert that the conclusions he had reached were consistent with Kant's own doctrines. The latter contention was extremely hard to square with any natural interpretation of Kant's views, if only because Fichte's thinking seemed to have issued in the construction of a speculative ontology which was sharply at variance with Kant's conception of philosophy as a preeminently critical enterprise directed towards establishing the scope and determinate limits of human reason. Such an outcome, however unexpected, had—as we shall see—two principal sources. Partly it arose through emphasizing and exploiting the libertarian and idealist strands in the Kantian theory, especially its insistence upon the autonomy of the self and upon the contribution made by the subject to the character of experience. And partly it derived from an attempt to eliminate what Fichte was not alone in conceiving to be a glaring inconsistency in Kantian epistemology, although he was exceptional in attributing it to Kant's interpreters rather than to Kant himself: this was the claim, already referred to, that there exist noumena or things in themselves upon which the realm of phenomenal appearance is in some way dependent. The consequence was a system that stood to its predecessor in a relation not without parallels in the genealogy of philosophical theories. Certain features characteristic of its ancestor were preserved in an accentuated form; others, by contrast, had either not survived at all or else re-emerged in so altered a shape as to be barely recognizable. In any event, the face it presented to the world seemed beyond question to be a new one. And if there were some whom it disturbed or dismayed, there were also those over whom it exerted a powerful fascination.

Fichte made his central preoccupation with the problem of freedom apparent at the outset, when he declared that the outstanding philosophical issue of his time concerned the status of what he called 'dogmatism'. For him dogmatism covered an amalgam of notions which he sometimes explicitly connected with a Spinozist conception of reality but which he also employed in a more general way to embrace all scientifically inspired attempts to provide materialistic or mechanistic accounts of human consciousness and behaviour. Such accounts, whatever form they might take, were viewed by him as constituting a *prima facie* threat to the validity of ideas like choice and responsibility which were fundamental to our experience as moral beings; thus far, at least, his concerns may be said to have paralleled those shown by Kant when confronted by similar considerations. But Fichte's reaction was altogether more extreme. In the first place, he implied—unlike Kant—that some element of spiritual weakness, of temperamental passivity or inertia, attached to the upholders of such interpretations of the human condition; the idea of being a mere appendage or product of nature, acted upon rather than acting and forever governed by factors beyond their control, possessed a certain lure for many persons

who were by no means averse to regarding themselves as helpless objects rather than as self-determining subjects—'the majority of men', he wrote at one point, 'could sooner be brought to believe themselves a piece of lava in the moon than to take themselves for a *self*'.[4] Thus he often spoke as if there were something perverse and self-deceiving, and not just mistaken, in adhering to beliefs of this sort. Fichte's reaction was, however, more extreme in a further respect and one that was of greater relevance to the development of his own system. Kant had attempted to mediate between a deterministic and a libertarian outlook, holding that we could consistently treat ourselves from a theoretical standpoint as subject to the natural order and from a practical one as essentially free; for him, moreover, it was characteristically within contexts demanding the exercise of moral reasoning and choice that we found ourselves committed to a libertarian position. Fichte's philosophy, on the other hand, involved a wide-ranging and comprehensive extension of Kant's conception of the practical dimension of human consciousness, an extension which took as its point of departure the direct intimations of subjective self-awareness and which finally issued in a perspective on life and experience that was far removed from anything to be found in what Kant himself had written. It is true that Fichte did not wish to deny that it was possible, and for certain purposes quite legitimate, for us to regard ourselves under an aspect in which we appeared as what he called 'organized creations of nature'; he did not, however, believe—for reasons which he never perhaps made sufficiently clear—that this entailed a radical dualism of the kind enshrined in the Kantian attempt to show how the respective requirements of the theoretical and the practical consciousness could be rendered mutually coherent. Rather, he implied that it was necessary at the outset to acknowledge the primacy of the practical standpoint, according priority to the crucial part played by the notion of agency in any adequate account of our role in the world and of the terms in which we conceived it. And it is here, if anywhere, that one touches upon the nerve of his thought, the focal point from which his claims to originality as a philosopher who exercised a potent influence upon subsequent speculation ultimately derived. Yet the contention as it stands is a vague one, open to more than one interpretation. How should it be understood?

As an initial step towards unravelling what Fichte had in mind it is necessary to look at his account of the concept which he himself treated as fundamental. This was the notion of the 'I' (*das Ich*)—the self or ego—which represented an ineliminable component of every aspect of our conscious life and which could be immediately recognized through what Fichte was prone to term 'intellectual intuition'. The latter expression, with its rationalist associations and the suggestion it carries of referring to a faculty of non-empirical cognition, might lead one to suppose that he had in view something recondite or mysterious. He hastened to inform his readers, however, that this was not so. What he was talking about was, on the contrary, wholly familiar and such that a moment's reflection would show it to occur in the most mundane everyday experience. To grasp what was meant we need only consider what was involved in doing something, however trivial; for it amounted (in Fichte's words) to 'the immediate consciousness that I act, and what I enact: it is that whereby I know something because I do it'.[5] In this sense, it could be affirmed that whenever we engaged in activity of any sort we were aware of ourselves as performing, or as intending to perform, whatever it was that was in question; such consciousness of ourselves as active, which was primitive and underived, both accompanied and at the same time was distinguishable from our knowledge of the actual content—the observable or describable features—of what we did or proposed to do. If, for example, I decide to put into effect some course of action, subsequently carrying it out, then I am certainly aware of what is aimed at and of its eventual realization. But (Fichte thinks) we shall seriously distort the situation if we portray it as being one in which all that happens, all that I am conscious of, is a sequence of discrete presentations—in this case, the idea of a certain thing's being performed followed by a perception of the actual performance. Such a picture, reminiscent of the accounts offered by empiricists like Hume, treats consciousness as an 'inert stage on which presentations succeed one another', and it is quite unacceptable. For it omits something indispensable, namely, my concurrent awareness of myself as the 'active principle' that is responsible for the formation of the intention and for its fulfilment in reality alike. It is precisely because of the continuing awareness I possess of my 'real efficacy' that I treat the intention as being more than simply an ideational content which happens to be followed by a sensory presentation involving my behaviour. Yet that would be all that it could conceivably be for me if my consciousness were reducible to a flow of impressions, passively apprehended, on the Humean pattern. Fichte believed that the latter model was in fact profoundly untrue to the pervasive conception we have of ourselves in the course of our ordinary experience: 'I cannot take a step, move hand or foot, without an intellectual intuition of my self-consciousness in these acts; only so do I know that *I* do it, only so do I distinguish my action, and myself therein, from the object of the action before me'.[6]

In putting forward such phenomenological points—which in some ways invite comparison with those propounded by his French contemporary, Maine de Biran—Fichte was none the less insistent that he should not be taken as trying to revive the idea that self-consciousness implied awareness of the ego as some kind of immaterial or mental 'substance'; whatever his dissent from him on other counts, on this one he was in agreement with Hume. The 'intuition' referred to was of 'sheer activity', not of a 'static' thing or entity, and he thought that all attempts to reify the self, to freeze it within the categories of objective existence and to endow it with substantial properties was already to take a fatal step on the road to 'dogmatism' and the denial of the subject's essential freedom. Instead we were obliged to think of ourselves as 'self-active', 'not as determined by things but as determining them'[7]—a notion which, as he acknowledged, had strongly Kantian overtones. For all that, however, his own account embodied a significant shift in outlook and emphasis. Not only was Kant's theory of the self formulated within the framework of an obscure dualism, according to which deterministic assumptions still held good at the purely cognitive level. It was also stated in a fashion that implied further divisions: the theoretical use of reason was contrasted with its practical employment, while within the sphere of the practical itself a fundamental distinction was drawn between behaviour governed by respect for the moral law and behaviour motivated by purely sensuous inclination. Fichte, in effect, drastically simplified this picture and in doing so radically changed its outlines.

In the first place, he treated awareness of self-activity as a residual but none the less irreducible and pervasive feature of consciousness under all its varying forms; such awareness was sufficient, without transcending the bounds of experience, to preclude us from assimilating ourselves to the category of merely objective or 'natural' phenomena. Secondly, he asserted that there was no justification for insulating our moral propensities from our non-moral ones; both could in the end be traced back to the same volitional source, the behaviour that issued from them representing simply the distinguishable ways in which we were capable of expressing ourselves as unitary beings. Thirdly, and perhaps most significantly, he implied that a true recognition of our essentially active nature as revealed by self-consciousness set in a quite fresh light the general question of how we apprehend reality and attempt to understand it. Traditional distinctions between knowing and doing, which neatly separated the two into independent compartments, appeared less convincing when we were seen to be primarily centres of activity, the initiators of projects which we sought to realize in concrete form. For, once this was granted, it was no longer plausible to assume that our habitual modes of approaching and interpreting experience could be considered in isolation from the needs and interests that informed our attitudes as purposive agents. As Fichte put it in his essay, *The Vocation of Man*, 'we do not act because we know, but we know because we are called upon to act—the practical reason is the root of all reason'.[8] Cognition being ultimately dependent upon practical demands and requirements, it followed that the forms taken by the first could not adequately be comprehended without reference to the second; the practical orientation of our thinking had a vital bearing upon the ways in which we grasped, ordered and conceptualized what was presented to us and upon the classifications we found it natural to impose. In this manner the world as we experienced it was not the 'neutral', self-sufficient domain it was typically portrayed as being. On the contrary, when viewed as the field of our diverse needs, aims, and—Fichte was at pains to stress—moral aspirations, it was in a crucial sense 'our world', falling within a perspective that could not fail to reflect these at every turn. At the level of day-to-day living, phenomena were characteristically apprehended 'through want, desire and enjoyment': 'not by the mental conception', Fichte wrote, 'but by hunger, thirst and their satisfaction, does anything become for me food and drink'.[9] And it was partly in the light of similar considerations that he claimed that, from an ethical standpoint, 'my world is the object and sphere of my duties, and absolutely nothing else; there is no other world for me, and no other qualities of my world than what are implied in this'.[10] Governed throughout by my moral preoccupations, it inevitably bore their imprint.

Thus far, and with these aspects of his thought before us, it is not unreasonable to see Fichte as the forerunner of a host of philosophers, ranging from the pragmatists of the last century to existentialist and analytic writers of the present one, who have—albeit in widely varying ways—emphasized the role played by agency in shaping and structuring human knowledge and who have protested that exclusively contemplative models of cognition have been responsible for pervasive errors in epistemology. Both Heidegger and Sartre, for instance, have underlined the extent to which the world of everyday life is necessarily experienced in 'instrumentalist' terms, our apprehension of what we find being filtered through the complex network of tasks and practical concerns which determines our approach to it and from which whatever we perceive derives its particular significance or 'meaning'; in Sartre's words, 'since the world reveals itself across our conduct, it is the intentional choice of the end which reveals the world, and the world is revealed as this or that (in this or that order) according to the end chosen'.[11] And if such points are often reminiscent of what Fichte had to say on the same theme, so too—although from a quite different angle—are the recurrent suggestions in Wittgenstein's later work that the quest after indubitable foundations in the sense typified by much traditional epistemology is misconceived, and that the process of cognitive justification comes to an end, not in certain propositions 'striking us immediately as true', but rather in our readiness to act in certain ways.[12] At one point Wittgenstein quotes from Goethe's *Faust* the dictum 'In the beginning was the deed', and this could almost serve as a motto for Fichte's own approach to problems of the kind that philosophers have

frequently raised regarding the status of our fundamental beliefs. In our capacity as agents, Fichte maintained, we found ourselves unavoidably committed to an interpretation of experience which was not in the final analysis susceptible to justification in theoretical terms and which instead had its roots in the demands we made as beings with concrete purposes to fulfil and projects to realize: it was here, not elsewhere, that we should look for an answer to the sceptical doubts apt to assail us when we indulged in free-floating reflection of the sort that involved an abstraction from the practical dimensions of our life and thought. For within the context of practical endeavour and moral striving questions concerning the reality of what we encountered in consciousness, of a world or 'non-ego' set over against the active subject or self, lost all force and substance and could not even properly be said to arise; we were bound to posit such a world in the course of fulfilling our aims or duties and could not coherently envisage ourselves as agents without it. As Fichte himself expressed the point, in so far as 'we are compelled to believe that we act, and that we ought to act in a certain manner, we are compelled to assume a certain sphere for this action'; ultimately it was from 'this necessity of action' that our 'consciousness of the actual world' proceeded, and not the other way about.[13]

Yet, whatever the intrinsic interest or merits of such claims, it would none the less be wrong to suppose that they represented all, or even the major part, of what Fichte finally wished to maintain. It might be true that, when discussing the structure and conditions of ordinary experience, he offered an account in which the primacy of agency was stressed. It was, however, no part of his purpose to question the role played in such experience by the idea of an objectively conceived natural order; rather, as has just been seen, the latter was treated by him as a necessary correlative or counterpart of the notion we have of ourselves as active subjects. But this was only part of the story. For he also believed that it was possible to provide an interpretation of existence as a whole which transcended the everyday standpoint and according to which the primordial activity of the ego as revealed in self-consciousness could be shown to have much more extensive and dramatic implications than any mentioned so far. To understand his reasons for making this claim we must go back once more to Kant, in this case to the doctrine of things in themselves.

That doctrine (it will be recalled) involved the contention that, while the overall *form* of the phenomenal realm derived from the operations of the intellect, the sensuous representations that constituted, so to speak, its 'filling' had a non-empirical source or 'ground' which was necessarily inaccessible to consciousness: to this extent, the world of nature was only in part of our own making, its sensory content having an independent origin. But was such a theory plausible, or even intelligible? In Fichte's view it was utterly unacceptable, amounting to a 'reckless' attempt to combine elements that had been drawn from two inherently opposed philosophical positions: from materialism the notion of 'things in themselves making impressions upon us', from idealism the notion of 'all existence arising solely out of the thinking of the intellect'.[14] Furthermore, it stood in palpable conflict with a cardinal thesis which Kant had repeatedly proclaimed throughout the *Critique of Pure Reason,* the thesis, namely, that categories of the understanding, like *substance* and *cause,* could not validly be employed outside the field of possible experience. Hence there could be no warrant for using them to arrive at 'the assumption of a something distinct from the self, as a ground of the empirical content of knowledge'.[15] Yet this was just what the theory in question required us to do.

In general, indeed, Fichte considered the doctrine of the *Ding an sich* to be so radically confused, so sharply at variance with the central tenets of the critical teaching, that he was reluctant to ascribe it to Kant himself, preferring instead to lay the blame on commentators who in his opinon had misconstrued those passages in the *Critique* where the notion of noumena was discussed. Such an interpretation of Kant's intentions, whereby he was to be seen as simply articulating a presumption of ordinary thought rather than as propounding an ontological claim of his own, has not found many adherents, either in his time or since; but however that may be, the objections Fichte brought against the doctrine itself retain their pertinence. And, if their force is granted, it is not too hard to understand why his own thinking took a direction which, in its eventual outcome, involved a total reversal of the priorities he attributed to the scientifically inspired theorists of his day. For he did not challenge what he conceived to be the essence of the Kantian view, in which it was affirmed that the entire spatio-temporal realm of phenomena existed purely for the subject and had no independent reality. On the contrary, he spoke as if it were clearly true. But if so, and if at the same time one eliminated the obverse conception of things in themselves, there appeared to be no alternative to opting for a thorough-going and unadulterated idealism according to which the world of experience under all its aspects derived from the operations of the ego alone. Primacy in the fullest sense would thereby be ascribed to the active subject; instead of the latter's being treated as if it were in some way subordinate to nature, it would be necessary to regard the natural world itself as being ultimately no more than the expression or manifestation at the level of the empirical consciousness of an ungrounded and spontaneous spiritual activity. It was with such considerations in mind that Fichte felt justified in concluding that 'to the idealist, the only positive thing is freedom'.[16]

Fichte was, of course, aware that an uncompromising commitment to idealism along the lines proposed might appear to pose a problem in the light of his earlier, equally uncompromising, insistence upon the part played in our ordinary experience by the notion of an objective world. Yet his various attempts to deal with it, both in the *Wissenschaftslehre* and elsewhere, are not easy to follow. Part of the difficulty arises from the indeterminacy of his fundamental concept of the self or ego, an indeterminacy which frequently leaves it unclear whether it is intended to carry implications of the sort customarily associated with its use in everyday contexts or whether, on the other hand, it is to be interpreted in a fashion that involves a more or less complete severance from these. In so far as he initially implied that his system was founded upon the direct deliverances of self-consciousness and nothing more, it is scarcely surprising that he was taken by some of his original readers to be propounding an extreme and paradoxical solipsism, with everything in the Fichtean universe traced back to Fichte himself. This was a criticism which—again perhaps unsurprisingly—he bitterly resented, and he went out of his way to repudiate it as constituting a gross misrepresentation of his whole position. For it overlooked (he maintained) the vital distinction he wished to draw between the 'finite' or personal subject of everyday life and what he was prone to term, by contrast, the 'infinite' or 'absolute' subject. It was the second, not the first, that was the ultimate creative agency, expressing itself under one aspect in the form of finite centres of self-conscious activity and under the other in the form of phenomenal objects and events. As finite subjects, we are necessarily aware of ourselves as being affected or impinged upon in certain ways; in Fichte's words, we are apprised of 'something *given* to reflection, as the material of presentation', without being conscious of 'the manner in which it arrived there'.[17] The suggestion here seems to be that, through an opaque process involving what is sometimes referred to as 'the productive imagination', the absolute ego gives rise to sensory representations which are susceptible to a projective interpretation in the shape of an objectively conceived spatio-temporal world. Thus our everyday 'firm conviction of the reality of things outside us' can be accommodated within the framework of a philosophical theory which entails no departure from a fundamentally idealist standpoint.

While such an account of his position may have protected Fichte from the particular objection he was concerned to rebut, it is nevertheless hard to square with his original contention that all knowledge is necessarily confined to what lies within the sphere of consciousness. Nor, in the end, was it easily reconcilable with other claims he wished to make regarding our relations both to nature and to each other. And such difficulties were, indeed, symptomatic of a more general lack of tidy fit between the epistemological and ontological departments of his system which was to become increasingly manifest. As we have already noticed, there was from the beginning a discernible tension between his professed adherence to the cognitive principles laid down by Kant and the speculative impulse by which so much of his own thinking was actually guided and propelled. In the subsequent development of his philosophy the gap separating the two widened, with the more critical and epistemologically oriented elements in his thought tending progressively to recede into the background. What replaced them was a metaphysical interpretation of reality as a whole, an interpretation which was imbued with teleological and ethical ideas and which represented a kind of massive projection, on a cosmic scale, of of what he conceived to be the true nature and destiny of human beings in the world.

Thus the notion of an absolute subject or self, which lay at the centre of Fichte's comprehensive vision, can be said to reflect his conviction that the categories of agency and will formed the basis of any scheme in which the significance of human life and consciousness could be adequately presented. Certainly nature, regarded as a system of interconnected phenomena, would also play an indispensable role in such a scheme, but it would only do so in a manner that exhibited it as being a prerequisite for the constructive activity and self-development of free autonomous persons. As dramatized by Fichte, this was transformed into the claim that the world in general must be envisaged as a dynamic self-differentiating totality, the natural sphere now being portrayed as a direct or immediate manifestation of the absolute ego rather than as something merely posited by it through the mental processes of the finite human subject. In a sense it could still be affirmed that—as he once put it—'the world is the product of my whole spirit', but only if this was understood to mean that I, as a particular individual, was constituted by the same self-active principle that expressed itself, on the one hand, through the medium of other conscious agents like myself and, on the other, in the shape of an opposed realm of nature against which I must exert my will. So conceived, the spiritual character of reality in no way implied that it should be regarded as a seamless or harmonious whole: its inner 'striving' essence entailed conflict and division, such division being, so to speak, self-generated and involving it in a continual struggle to overcome constraints and obstacles that had their source in its own primordial activity. Human beings were the vehicles of this process and, as such, could fulfil themselves only by pitting themselves against a resistant natural world whose ultimate function was to afford them the opportunity for realizing their potentialities as free self-determining beings. A close colleague of Fichte—F. K. Forberg—once described him as teaching on every possible occasion that 'action, action, action' was the proper destiny of man, and this indeed is the message that his philosophical system seems continually to proclaim. Despite, however, his emphasis upon the unitary character of the human psyche, he was also anxious to stress that man only attained his full stature when his conduct and motivation were of a certain kind. For action, as he understood it, implied the vindication at the level of self-conscious experience of the spontaneous creative principle which underlay reality in general; and for that to be adequately achieved human behaviour must exhibit a complete independence of the influence of external factors—it must (in his words) be a manifestation of 'absolute self-activity'. In practice, this meant that the agent's motivation should be governed by laws which he, as a self-conscious subject, imposed upon himself and made the ground of his conduct. But conduct so actuated was, for Fichte, nothing less than moral conduct; it was only when what was done was performed simply on the basis of 'an immediate consciousness of our determinate duty' that we fulfilled our true vocations as agents in the world. Thus the practical conclusion of Fichte's metaphysic was a form of ethical idealism, designed to confirm the reliance of the ordinary person upon the direct deliverances of his conscience. Whatever his divergences from Kant in other respects, here at least he remained true to the spirit of his master.

From a present-day standpoint, Fichte's speculative excursions inevitably appear bizarre and invite the question of why, in order to protect human freedom against the threat allegedly posed by what he stigmatized as 'dogmatism', he should have felt compelled to propound so sweeping and all-embracing a theory. Nor is it always clear what kind of freedom he principally had in mind: the notion that we are free inasmuch as our actions are not subject to natural necessitation tended, as he proceeded, to give way to more 'positive' interpretations of the concept, such as those in which it implied self-legislation and the determination of behaviour by principles of our own making. As I have tried to show, however, his far-reaching claims take on a more intelligible aspect when they are viewed against the background of Kant's own contentions and the problems they might be felt to raise. If some of Fichte's attempts to deal with these seem less convincing, they were none the less prompted by genuine difficulties and dilemmas. Nor, in the end, is it hard to understand the attraction of what he wrote for a large number of his contemporaries. In place of conceptions of the human mind and consciousness which many found implausible or artificial, he substituted a dynamic one which gave precedence to the ideas of action and volition; moreover, in doing so he helped to focus attention upon aspects of our psychic life whose significance for the human studies came to be increasingly appreciated, particularly in Germany, as the century wore on. At the same time, he provided an account of man's place in the world which possessed a strong appeal for those who felt oppressed by materialist or determinist doctrines and who welcomed what they regarded as a less dispiriting portrayal of the relation in which men stood to the natural order. The claim that both the human sphere and the realm of nature are in some sense the expression of an identical subject or 'absolute spirit'; the accompanying suggestion that as individuals we participate in a process whereby that spirit is involved in an unremitting struggle, constantly seeking to master or transcend what it has itself produced: these were seminal ideas which struck deep roots and which were to re-emerge—though in vastly different forms—in the philosophies of Schelling, Hegel and Schopenhauer. But that is another story.

Notes

1 A. O. Lovejoy, *The Reason, the Understanding, and Time* (Baltimore: Johns Hopkins Press, 1961), 150.

2 *Critique of Pure Reason,* A547, B575.

3 *Science of Knowledge, with the First and Second Introductions,* ed. and trans. P. Heath and J. Lachs (New York: Appleton-Century-Crofts, 1970), 43.

4 Ibid., 162. In his tendency to treat philosophical views as owing their appeal to emotional or temperamental factors, and not merely to intellectual considerations, Fichte anticipated a variety of other nineteenth-century writers, including Kierkegaard and Nietzsche.

5 Ibid., 38.

6 Ibid., 38.

7 Ibid. 41.

8 *Fichte's Popular Works,* I, trans. W. Smith (London: Trübner & Co., 1889), 421.

9 Ibid., 418.

10 Ibid., 419.

11 J.P. Sartre, *Being and Nothingness,* trans. H. E. Barnes (London: Methuen, 1957), 477.

12 L. Wittgenstein, *On Certainty,* trans. D. Paul and G. E. M. Anscombe (Oxford Basil Blackwell, 1969), PP. 110, 148, 204, 342.

13 *Fichte's Popular Works,* I, 421.

14 *Science of Knowledge,* p. 56.

15 Ibid., 54.

16 Ibid., 69.

17 Ibid., 208.

Daniel Morrison (essay date 1993)

SOURCE: "Women, Family, and State in Fichte's Philosophy of Freedom," in *New Perspectives on Fichte,* edited by Tom Rockmore and Daniel Breazeale, Humanities Press, 1996, pp. 179-91.

[*In the following essay, which was presented in 1993 and first published in 1996, Morrison sets forth the apparent contradiction in Fichte's treatment of women—they both have rights and do not have rights—and then demonstrates how Fichte's assumptions allowed for this apparent paradox.*]

I. Introduction

As Fichte called his philosophy the first system of freedom, it would be interesting to know his position on the rights of women as it can be argued that the position of women in society is a sensitive barometer of the freedom and rights within the society as a whole. It also happens to be the case that the position of women in Fichte's philosophy has largely been ignored.[1]

Fichte discusses women at length in ***The Science of Rights***[2] and in ***The Science of Ethics***.[3] What he says in these works regarding women, their rights, and their place in society may appear contradictory and difficult to fit into twentieth century political categories. The main task of this paper will be to overcome the apparent contradictions presented by Fichte and to offer the most generous reading possible for this position which has been largely ignored, perhaps for the simple reason that it is so odd. One of the few English-language authors who mentions Fichte's position on women devotes less than one sentence to the subject. With great condescension he notes of ***The Science of Rights*** that "its flaws are many; some, such as the discussion of women's rights, may amuse us."[4]

II. The Problem: Conflicting Positions

A. Thesis—Women Have Full Rights

I begin by reviewing the two apparently contradictory positions Fichte holds with regard to women. You will pardon me for quoting Fichte at length, as it is best to let him speak for himself on this matter. He writes:

If the only ground of all legal rights is reason and freedom, how can a distinction exist between two sexes which possess both the same reason and the same freedom?[5]

Thus

> . . . both sexes, as moral beings, ought to be equal.[6]

Neither can it

> . . . be maintained that women are inferior to men in regard to talents of mind.[7]

Indeed,

> . . . all great revolutions . . . either emanated from, or at least were led and considerably modified by, women.[8]

From the general principle that rights derive from reason and freedom, Fichte concludes that women have all the natural rights men have, including the rights to vote, to appear in court, to own property, to choose and leave one's spouse, and to engage in the arts, professions, and commerce.

Living nearly two centuries after the publication of **The Science of Rights** such an array of rights seems reasonable, modest, and perhaps minimal. But when this book was published in 1796, such rights were known to no women anywhere in the world and were enjoyed by few men. Fichte recognized a woman's right to vote even before he himself was able to exercise that right.

B. Anti-thesis—Women Have No Rights

In what appears to be contrary to this liberal position regarding the rights of women, Fichte makes the following claims:

> The female sex stands one step lower in the arrangement of nature than the male sex; the female sex is the object of power of the male sex.[9]

Further he writes:

> . . . the one sex [is] purely active and the other purely passive.[10]

You can guess which one is which.

From these "facts" about the nature of the two sexes, Fichte draws conclusions about marriage and the relationship between men and women within that institution. He claims that the wife:

> . . . should renounce to [her husband] all her property and all her rights. Henceforth she has life and activity only under his eyes and in his business. She has ceased to lead the life of an individual; her life has become a part of the life of her [husband]. (This is aptly characterized by her assuming his name.)[11]

Fichte has assured us that women have the full collection of natural rights but now he tells us that a wife must give up these rights to her husband. This submission to and submergence in the husband is unconditional. The very "conception of marriage involves the most unlimited subjection of the woman to the will of the husband."[12] Indeed, it is a "woman's destiny . . . to submit."[13] Unconditional submission of the wife to the husband requires not only that the husband exercise her rights for her and own and control her property, but the wife's own person, her very self, is owned by the husband. As Fichte writes: "The woman does not belong to herself, but to the man."[14]

In Fichte's view of marriage, the wife disappears from public view and remains sequestered in the home. The husband "lives in all her public life, and she retains for herself only a house life."[15] Not only does the wife disappear from public view, but she also disappears in her own estimation. Fichte claims that "a rational and virtuous woman can be proud only of her husband and children; not of herself, for she forgets herself in them.[16] Of course, Fichte does not take this submission of the wife to the husband to be in any way demeaning or indicative of the diminished worth of a woman. On the contrary, Fichte takes the submission of a woman to her husband to be the very source of her worth. He claims that the wife's "whole dignity depends upon her being completely subject and seeming to be so subject, to her husband."[17] To will otherwise would be a sign of mental disease or moral perversion as a wife "cannot rationally will to be free."[18]

Fichte has other equally provocative things to say about women outside of marriage. Thus, though he insists that men and women are equal with regard to reason and talents of mind, he says that "really learned women . . . are usually pedantic."[19] We can conclude this review with what must be Fichte's most withering comment: "No women are known to have been philosophers."[20]

, III. Synthesis—Species Nature

A. Sex and Nature

To begin a discussion of why male and female are regarded differently by Fichte, we must look first at the origin of the distinction between the sexes. To state the obvious, sexual dimorphism serves to propagate the species. Fichte took sexual reproduction to be universal, apparently unaware of asexual reproduction. The division of the generative forces of nature into two separate parts somehow stabilizes the species. Fichte seems to have thought that asexual reproduction would be chaotic.

The division of the generative forces is not equal. The female has a superior role in reproduction; she contains all the conditions necessary for reproduction, with the exception of the first moving principle. That first moving principle is located in the male and Fichte's description of it brings to mind a fuse which has been removed from the bomb for the sake of safety. To be sure, both male and female are needed for reproduction, but the male supplies only one of many conditions necessary for reproduction and the remainder of those conditions are contained in the female.

While the female has the superior position in reproduction, her position is inferior in sexual intercourse. As Fichte puts it: "In the union of the sexes for the propagation of the race only the one sex should be active and the other altogether passive."[21] This observation might strike us as problematic, but what Fichte is indicating here is, at one level, simply a physiological fact. Fichte, however, draws conclusions beyond the mere shape of organs and these conclusions we may find unpalatable.

In an anatomical sense, the female sexual organs are receptors and are intruded upon by the male sexual organ. It is also true that a man may force himself upon a woman in a way that a woman cannot force herself upon a man. All of this is obvious, but Fichte extends the passive or receptive nature of female sexuality beyond the physical aspects into psychological and social domains of sexuality. Psychologically, the female sex drive itself is a drive to submission and passivity. Socially, the passivity of women in courtship is natural and not conventional. Thus Fichte says that women have the right to court men, just as men have the right to fly. The point of this sarcasm is that women cannot court and men cannot fly—not for legal or moral reasons, but simply because it defies nature.

As feminine sexuality is purely passive and reason is always purely active, there arises a conflict between the sexual and rational natures in women. Such a conflict is not present for men as their sexual nature is purely active and conforms with their rational nature. Note that Fichte departs from the nearly universally held position that sexuality and rationality are at odds with one another. Masculine sexuality and rationality are fraternal twins born of the same root: activity.

While the active sexuality of males agrees with reason, we are still confronted by the problem of the passive sexuality of females which is at odds with reason's activity. "As reason rules in woman, . . . the sexual impulse cannot appear as an impulse to be purely passive, but must change itself into an impulse to be likewise active."[22] The conflict between passive sexuality and active rationality is overcome by a transformation of feminine sexuality from a passive into an active form. In its original form, feminine sexuality is a drive to passive submission, it is a drive to surrender control of one's body to another, "to surrender herself, not for her own sake, but for the sake of the other."[23] So that sex and reason may coexist in women, the sex drive is sublimated, to borrow a term from Freud, whose theory Fichte anticipates by a century, into love. Love is a faculty allied with the will and not physical inclinations and thus it is by nature active and free. This faculty does choose submission to the beloved, but this is a choice which the woman actively and freely makes; it is not a choice which she suffers as a result of her physical nature.

Fichte identifies the faculty of love as the highest point of nature and the one point of contact between reason and nature. Nature is below reason, but love, which is of nature, is that which gives rise to reason, as I will explain below. Love arises as a natural consequence of the conflict between reason and sexuality in women. It is acquired by men only subsequent to their marriage to a loving woman. It is only within marriage that man learns love and love becomes reciprocal. Once a husband learns love, he seeks to please his wife in all matters, just as the wife seeks to please the husband. Thus love, as an active and willful submission to the interests of the beloved, is natural to women, is acquired by men in marriage and becomes the first reciprocal norm of human intersubjectivity.[24]

This first reciprocal norm arises out of sexual dimorphism in rational creatures and is the ground of all human community. Mating alone does not produce lasting relationships among human beings. Rather it is love which is necessary for the emergence of the first human community, i.e., the family. Upon that first community, all higher order communities are built, culminating in the state. Rights arise only within the state and thus if we are to discuss the rights of women, we must make our way first through the family to the state and then examine the position of women within that highest order human community. But first we turn to the family.

B. Family

The family is a natural unit which exists to propagate the species. It begins with the marriage of one man to one woman. The man and the woman enter into marriage with very different purposes. A man enters marriage to alleviate his lust. To be sure, that lust may be somewhat ennobled by the high regard he has for his betrothed, but the groom is quite incapable of love and will only learn love inside marriage itself. The woman, on the other hand, can properly marry for no reason other than love. For a woman to enter marriage, she must be firmly of the opinion that her beloved is the most loveable of all men and that her love for him will never wane. If she is not of such an opinion, then her marriage is mere concubinage.

As the family is a natural unit, so also in marriage a natural union, one which precedes the existence of the state. Marriage is the state of cohabitation under the conditions of the love of the woman—the love of the man will follow with time. Civil marriage ceremonies serve only to make public what has already taken place. A woman is married only when she loves her husband and thus should she cease to love him, she is no longer married. Like civil marriage, civil divorce serves only to make public what has taken place in the heart of the woman.

In marriage and divorce, as with reproduction, the woman takes precedence over the man, indeed the man appears to be something of an appendage to the process. It is the woman's love which makes or breaks the marriage; the wooing, pleading, and protestations of men are all for naught. Thus a woman need never sue for divorce for never can the love of a woman be contested in court, whereas a man can divorce his wife only with great difficulty.

Men driven by lust and women driven by love seek to fulfill their private ends, but through the selfish acts of individuals, nature fulfills her own purpose, a purpose which transcends the individual. Nature's end is the propagation of the species and this end is accomplished by individuals intending to fulfill private purposes, not the purposes of their species. Thus we see the first transcendence of the individual in marriage. Though often misunderstood on this count, Fichte consistently called for the overcoming of the individual in ever-higher transcendent orders. This begins with marriage and ends in a mystical union with God.

Sexual reproduction is responsible for bringing man into being as a physical creature. As marriage and the family are a context for sexual reproduction, it is clear that the first and most obvious function of the family is the propagation of the species. But as this purpose could be accomplished without such permanent arrangements as marriage and family, we must look beyond mere propagation for the greater purpose of the natural structures of marriage and the family.

The family is not only the context of the physical birth of humans, it is also the context of their spiritual birth—their coming to reason and freedom. This spiritual birth is the product of education, for which the primary obligation falls to the family.[25] Education for Fichte is not the acquisition of information or the memorization of the conclusions arrived at by other minds, rather it is the development of moral character and reason—it is training for freedom. One of the duties of the family to the state is the education of the children. The family is obliged to deliver well-formed citizens to the state. Though education may at some point be taken over by the state, the young child is entirely formed within the confines of the family.

It is in the family that we are born both as physical creatures and as rational creatures. And as the physical birth of man is dominated by women, so is the spiritual birth of man. Indeed, while physical birth requires the cooperation of the male, the conditions of spiritual birth, and therefore of civil society and the state, seem to lie entirely in the female. Though Fichte does not explicitly claim that the female is the mother of mankind as a spiritual or rational species, it is an unavoidable consequence of what he says regarding women and reason. To make out the case for women as the mother of spirit, and therefore of the state, I anticipate my discussion of rights, which follows shortly. A parenthetical argument to demonstrate that reason, freedom, and the state owe their origins to the faculty of love, found naturally in women, begins with four Fichtean principles:

> 1. Reason emerges only in society. All beings outside of society are not rational.

> 2. Prior to entry into society, men possess unbounded freedom.

> 3. To enter into society, one's freedom must be restricted. But as society is a community of free beings, such a restriction may not negate one's freedom. Thus there must be a free self-restriction of members of society.

> 4. Free self-restriction is accomplished only through reason—indeed it is the first indication of the presence of reason.

From these four points we can see that reason is a condition of society and at the same time society is a condition of reason. The way out of this circle is supplied by women in their faculty of love.

Love, as you will recall, is the highest point of nature and it is the single point at which nature and reason coincide. Love originates in sublimated female sexuality and results in the active and free choice of submission to the desires of the beloved. Thus love is the free self-restraint of brutish unlimited freedom which is required for the emergence of society, which, in turn, is where men become rational. Love is the condition of the possibility of any human community, the first such community being the family. And as freedom, spirit, and reason arise only in community, love is responsible for the existence of these as well. Finally we can note that as love is the point at which nature and reason coincide, love is itself the first appearance of reason, and thus reason first appears in women, for the faculty of love is nature to women, while it is acquired by men.

Thus far we have seen that women play the dominant role in reproduction, which is the birth of man's body, in education, which is the birth of man's spirit, and in civilization, which is the birth of communities of men. Women alone possess the faculty necessary for the emergence of communities, the first of which is the family. From this small community will ultimately arise the state, which in its triumphant form will constitute the rational community of all mankind. Such an all-embracing rational community would be the realization of the moral world order, which Fichte tells us in "**On the Foundation of Our Belief in a Divine Government of the Universe**" is equivalent to God. Thus we may finally conclude that woman is not only the mother of man's body, spirit, family, community, and state, but that she is also the mother of God.[26]

C. State

The state is the rational nexus of free beings. It is a structure which serves to preserve the freedom of men in a finite form by regulating men in the exercise of their unbounded natural freedom. When men exercise their full measure of natural freedom, their actions bring them into conflict with other men in the exercise of their freedom.

The state has as its highest purpose the fulfillment of the purposes of reason. This entails drawing men into the highest realization of freedom. Such freedom is not the brutish *Wilkür* of man in the state of nature, but rather of men regulating all their actions according to reason.

The ordering of man's actions within the state requires the division of the total domain of human action into separate domains in which individuals exercise their freedom. These domains are those of rights, property, offices, licenses, and concessions. Thus when we ask about the rights of women, we are asking about what portion of the total domain of human action is accorded by the state to women.

As we said above, the sole condition for the possession of rights is the possession of reason. Women and men possess the same reason and thus possess the same rights. Fichte's account of women in the state is odd in that he argues that while women have the same rights as men, they ought not exercise those rights. It must be made clear that this "ought" is a moral ought. The state as envisioned by Fichte does not legally deny women the exercise of their rights. Were the state to deny women the exercise of their rights, they would have no rights, which would then place the state in conflict with reason itself.

Rights, and the laws which safeguard them, concern only public life. These laws serve to keep the operation of individual wills from coming into conflict with each other. In a domain where there is but one will, such a conflict is impossible and thus there can be no application of rights or need for law. A domain where there is but one will we call private, and in a private domain there are no rights and no laws. Thus there are no laws regulating the internal actions of individuals—no civil laws regulating one's thinking.

Each individual constitutes within himself a private domain where civil law does not apply. But in addition to the individual, there is another private domain, that is, the family. The reason for this is that there is, according to Fichte, but one will in the family. Fichte takes quite seriously the idea that in marriage, two become one. The one will of the family is neither the will of the husband nor that of the wife, but is rather a free collaboration of the two in love. As there is but one will in the family, there are no rights within the family. This is made manifest by the fact that there can be no lawsuit brought between husband and wife. Should such a suit be brought, it would indicate the presence of two wills, and not one, and thus the marriage is *de facto* dissolved, though it remains intact *de jure*.

The individual is a private domain, who when he enters the public domain, begins to exercise his rights. The family is also a unit in the private domain and when it enters the public domain, it speaks with one voice and one will. For Fichte, the husband is the public representative of the family. Thus it is the husband who exercises the rights of the family. In doing so, he does not speak or act for himself as an individual. In the case of voting rights, the husband votes not for himself, but for the family as a whole. It is the duty of the husband to be affected by the opinions of his wife. The wife does not cast the ballot, but she votes in her husband with whose will her own is united.

What Fichte offers here is representative suffrage. The husband votes for a group of individuals, all of whom share a common will. In this system women are no more disenfranchised than someone who does not sit in Congress and vote on laws directly. Indeed, it is the case that Fichte expands the franchise to include children. He suggests a proportional representation whereby the vote cast by the head of a family of four would have twice the weight of the vote cast by the head of a family of two. This is quite sensible as voting is a mechanism for shaping the future and large families have a greater stake in the future than do small families.

As the husband is the representative of the family in the exercise of voting rights, so he is also the family's representative in the exercise of all rights of the family. The husband is the only member of the family who has a public life—and his public life is not individual; it is not his own, but it is corporate and representational; it is his family's.

Though Fichte understands the public domain to be the province of men, there are cases in which women may enter the public domain in order to exercise their rights. Firstly, if a husband refuses to exercise the rights of the family, the wife may do so in his stead. As is the case with husbands in the public domain, wives who step forward to exercise rights in the public domain do so not in their own name, but under the auspices of the family. And secondly, widows and unmarried adult women exercise all their own rights, as they are the heads of their own households.

For each household there is but one voice in public life. Where there is husband and wife, the husband ought to be the voice of the family. Where the household is headed by a woman, she speaks for the household. Though it may seem odd to us, Fichte's vision of the household having but one public voice has much to recommend it. When the family or the household speaks with one voice, it reflects a unity of will born of love which is the ground of all civil society and the state. When it is not an individual, but a group of individuals sharing a common will, that is the private unit, the encounter with the public domain takes place through love and not self-interest. Before the husband enters the public domain to exercise the rights of the family, he has already had the edifying exercise of sublimating his own will to the interests of the family as a whole.

Today the individual is the sole private unit which enters the public domain. Such an individual has not had the experience of the self-restriction born of love which characterizes the unitary family, and thus he enters the public domain as a wild beast whose actions are kept in check, not by self-restraint and love, but by fear of the state's punitive apparatus. This is why the dissolution of the family, as an aggregate of individuals joined in love and sharing a common will, results in the collapse of civil society and the state.

D. Women Vis-a-Vis the State

The family is a crucial element in any discussion of individuals and the state, of the private and the public, for the family participates in both realms. It is a private realm which is collective; it is an aggregate of individuals self-governed by love. But while Fichte's formula of the relationship between the public and the private domains as mediated by the family sheds some light on the question of individual rights and freedoms, we have thus far managed to avoid the crucial question: What reasons can Fichte offer for his claim that the man and not the woman ought to be the family's representative in the public domain? The short answer to this question is: None. On this point, Fichte's position seems to be little more than a reflection of the prejudice of his age. This is surprising as Fichte offers so many original and forwardlooking insights into the position of women. Indeed it would seem from what Fichte has said that if only one of the two sexes can enter the public domain, it should be the female, for in her lies the very conditions of society. From what Fichte has said we would have to conclude that if there were only men in the world, there would be no society. Since there is no apparent reason for the man representing the family in public, I can only speculate that Fichte gives him this job because all other important tasks, i.e., birth of man, education of man, birth of spirit, creation of the family, state and God, all fall to women. If the male is to have more dignity than just a fuse in a population bomb, we must allow him a public life.

IV. Conclusion

For us, the denial of access to the public domain is such an important issue because of our fixation on the individual. For Fichte, individuals are to be overcome and subsumed into larger wholes. For Fichte, individuals are not complete creatures; neither male nor female is fully human. Each sex is a partial creature and each becomes most fully human only in marriage. In marriage two become one, two wills become a single will. Nature split the species into two halves for more orderly procreation. And nature overcomes this split in marriage. Only in marriage do humans, male and female, approach their "species being," to use a term of Marx's, whose theories Fichte anticipates in many ways.

As individualists, we cherish the rights and freedoms of individual humans. For Fichte the individual is not an end in itself, but is a means to reason's higher end. Fichte says very strongly that "it is the absolute destination of each individual of both sexes to marry. Physical man is neither man nor woman, but both; and it is the same with the moral man."[27] In marriage, we extinguish our individuality and learn to overcome ourselves. This is a moral duty, as it is a means for the realization of the ends of reason, which can never be accomplished in a fractured, individuated state.

Fichte's position on marriage also sheds light on the question of the nature of the I from which his system springs and around which it revolves. For Fichte "an unmarried person is only half a man" and is thus inadequate as the starting point of his absolute philosophy.[28] The I cannot be an individual human, but we first move in the direction of this I, which is a regulative ideal, in marriage, where all of the physical and rational elements of mankind are joined under a single unifying will.

Notes

[1] One of the few authors working in English who have addressed Fichte's position on women is Susan Shell, who discusses women's rights in her essay, "'A Determined Stand': Freedom & Security in Fichte's *Science of Right*," *Polity*, XXV, 1, Fall 1991, pp. 95-122.

[2] *Grundlage des Naturrechts nach Prinzipien der Wissenschaftslehre* (1796); translated as *The Science of Rights* by A. E. Kroeger (London: Truebner & Co., 1889), reprinted with a preface by Willis T. Harris (London: Routledge and Kegan Paul, 1970). Citations are from the Kroeger translation.

[3] *Das System der Sittenlehre nach den Principien der Wissenschaftslehre* (1798); translated as *The Science of Ethics* by A. E. Kroeger (London: Kegan Paul, Trench, Truebner & Co., 1897). All citations are from the Kroeger translation.

[4] Charles M. Sherover's introduction to *The Science of Rights*, p. xxi.

[5] *Science of Rights*, p. 439.

[6] *Science of Rights*, p. 396.

[7] *Science of Rights*, p. 448.

[8] *Science of Rights*, p. 442.

[9] *Science of Rights*, p. 396.

[10] *Science of Rights*, p. 393.

[11] *Science of Rights*, p. 402.

[12] *Science of Rights*, p. 417.

[13] *Science of Rights*, p. 403.

[14] *Science of Rights*, p. 418.

[15] *Science of Rights*, p. 418.

[16] *Science of Rights*, p. 444.

[17] *Science of Rights*, p. 441.

[18] *Science of Rights*, p. 441.

[19] *Science of Rights*, p. 448.

[20] *Science of Rights*, p. 450.

[21] *Science of Ethics*, p. 343.

[22] *Science of Ethics*, p. 343-344.

[23] *Science of Ethics*, p. 344.

[24] Some think the function I ascribe to love, as the first norm of intersubjectivity, is played by the summons. The summons is the free act which calls to the unfree person to exercise his freedom. A free person calls the unfree and the chain of summonings reaches back to the first free man and then to God walking in the Garden of Eden. Fichte says that "when one arrives—as one must—at [the thought of] a first individual, one must also assume the existence of an even higher incomprehensible being." [NM 352; B 178].

The summons and love, as I describe it in this paper, share the function of bringing freedom and reason into being. It is my position, however, that priority belongs to love and that the reasons for this are implicit in Fichte, though he himself seems to have given more attention to the summons. I can only briefly indicate why love has priority over the summons. (1) The structures of summoning depends upon the external. The free person has to be called to freedom—he does not rise to it by himself. (2) The summons leads to a regress back to God as the source of freedom and reason. Love is natural and it is better to choose a natural over a supernatural explanation. (3) As freedom and reason in the system of summonses are transmitted from one man to another, anyone not in the line of summonings (a kind of apostolic succession) can never be free. This model leads to very few free men and would leave entire geographical regions devoid of freedom and reason. (4) Because love, a self-restraining attribute known to women and learned by men, is natural, it is available in all places at all times. Love is an originary summons, a summons which is not itself the result of another prior summoning, but one which arises out of nature itself. Thus, there is no need for a chain of regress, which may be broken, and which must lead back to a God who is physically known to man (for the physical domain is the *Spielraum* of freedom).

[25] A good account of the roles of the family and the state in education is presented in *The Educational Theory of J. G. Fichte: A Critical Account, Together with Translations*, by G. H. Turnbull, (London: University Press of Liverpool, 1926).

[26] J. G. Fichte, "On the Foundation of our Belief in a Divine Government of the Universe," trans. Paul

Edwards in *19th Century Philosophy*, ed. Patrick L. Gardiner, pp. 19-26 (New York: Free Press, 1969).

[27] *Science of Ethics*, p. 346.

[28] *Science of Ethics*, p. 247.

FURTHER READING

Breazeale, Daniel. "Fichte's *Aenesidemus* Review and the Transformation of German Idealism." *The Review of Metaphysics* XXXIV, No. 3 (March 1981): 545-68.

Examines the moment and content of Fichte's review in order to establish its significance in Fichte's thought, as well as Breazeale's assertion that it "marks a genuine watershed in the history of German Idealism."

Breazeale, Daniel and Tom Rockmore, eds. *Fichte: Historical Contexts/Contemporary Controversies.* Atlantic Highlands, N.J.: Humanities Press, 1994, 271 p.

Presents a selection of essays on Fichte that reflect the resurgent, late twentieth-century interest. Includes essays by the editors and by Robert Williams, Jere Paul Surber, and Frederick Neuhouser.

Breazeale, Daniel and Tom Rockmore, eds. *New Perspectives on Fichte.* Atlantic Highlands, N.J.: Humanities Press, 1996, 233 p.

Updates the editors' previous volume, particularly stressing new approaches to Fichte. Includes essays by the editors and by Wayne M. Martin, Jere Paul Surber, and George J. Seidel.

Engelbrecht, H. C. *Johann Gottlieb Fichte: A Study of His Political Writings with Special Reference to His Nationalism.* New York: Columbia University Press, 1933, 221 p.

Attempts to provide an objective analysis of Fichte as a political philosopher, in light of his prominence as the author of *Reden an die deutsche Nation* and the fact that numerous German factions have used this work to promote their own causes.

Everett, Charles Carroll. *Fichte's Science of Knowledge: A Critical Exposition.* Chicago: S. C. Griggs and Company, 1892, 287 p.

Detailed critique of Fichte's *Principles of the Complete Science of Knowledge.*

Heath, Peter, and John Lachs. Preface to *J. G. Fichte: Science of Knowledge,* edited and translated by Peter Heath and John Lachs, pp. vii-xviii. Cambridge: Cambridge University Press, 1982.

This preface to Fichte's "Introductions" was first published in 1970. Beginning by recapping the problems with Fichte's style, the authors nevertheless present his works as rewarding reading. They also characterize Fichte's system as "tenable idealism" and summarize his concept of the "self."

Hegel, G. W. F. *The Difference Between Fichte's and Schelling's System of Philosophy.* Trans. H.S. Harris and Walter Cerf. Albany: State University of New York Press, 1977, 213 p.

A famous and influential work, originally published in 1801, by the young Hegel. Includes his "Exposition of Fichte's System," which the author contends is not a system.

Hohler, T. P. *Imagination and Reflection: Intersubjectivity, Fichte's* Grundlage *of 1794.* The Hague, Boston, and London: Martinus Nijhoff Publishers, 1982, 159 p.

Argues that Fichte was the first thinker responsible for bringing reflection and imagination—elements already central to philosophy—to bear on the problem of intersubjectivity.

Lachs, John. "Fichte's Idealism." *American Philosophical Quarterly* 9, No. 4 (October 1972): 311-18.

Defines the specific character of Fichte's critical idealism, which Lachs identifies as dependent on Fichte's concept of a "single, unconditioned self."

Martin, Wayne M. "Fichte's Anti-Dogmatism." *Ratio* V, No. 2 (December 1992): 129-46.

Reviews critical treatment of the opposition between idealism and dogmatism in Fichte's work. Martin reaches his own conclusion in this discussion by arguing that Fichte conceived of *realism* as entirely compatible with idealism.

Rose, Paul Lawrence. "The German Nationalists and the Jewish Question: Fichte and the Birth of Revolutionary Antisemitism." In *Revolutionary Antisemitism in Germany from Kant to Wagner,* pp. 117-32. Princeton, N.J.: Princeton University Press, 1990.

Analyzes the form that anti-Semitism takes in Fichte's work and explains how Fichte's anti-Semitism figured into the rise of German nationalism.

Surber, Jere Paul. *Language and German Idealism: Fichte's Linguistic Philosophy.* Atlantic Highlands, N.J.: Humanities Press, 1996, 190 p.

Treats Fichte's generally neglected work "On the Linguistic Capacity and the Origin of Language" (1795). Surber characterizes the work as an anomaly in German Idealism and an anticipation of post-structuralist ideas about language.

Talbot, Ellen Bliss. *The Fundamental Principle of Fichte's Philosophy.* New York: Macmillan, 1906, 140 p.

Examines Fichte's philosophies in-depth and challenges some standard interpretations of the earlier criticism.

Thompson, Anna Boynton. *The Unity of Fichte's Doctrine of Knowledge.* Boston: Ginn and Company, 1895, 215 p.

> Attempts to achieve an understanding of Fichte's science of knowledge by following his thought process. Thompson claims that in order to fully grasp Fichte's system, the reader must "not only follow Fichte, but . . . follow him with sympathy."

Weissberg, Liliane. "A Philosopher's Style: Reading Fichte's 'Geist und Buchstab.'" In *Fictions of Culture: Essays in Honor of Walter H. Sokel,* by Steven Taubeneck, pp. 117-32. New York: Peter Lang, 1991.

> Considers Fichte's ideas and style at once in order to demonstrate that the opacity of his style stems from his philosophy itself.

Williams, Robert R. *Recognition: Fichte and Hegel on the Other.* Albany: State University of New York Press, 1992, 332 p.

> Contends not only that the "problem of the other" was central to Fichte's system of idealism, but moreover that Fichte "explicitly formulated the problem of the other."

Additional coverage of Fichte's life and career is contained in the following source published by Gale Research: *Dictionary of Literary Biography,* **Vol. 90.**

Gustave Flaubert

1821-1880

French novelist, short story writer, and playwright.

For additional information on Flaubert's complete career, see *NCLC*, Volume 2; for a discussion of the novel *Madame Bovary*, see *NCLC*, Volume 10; for a discussion of the novel *Sentimental Education*, see *NCLC*, Volume 19. A single-work entry updating the criticism on *Madame Bovary* will appear in an upcoming *NCLC* volume.

INTRODUCTION

Considered among the most influential novelists of the nineteenth century, Flaubert is frequently associated with the realist and naturalist schools of fiction and is best known for his masterpiece *Madame Bovary* (1857). A meticulous literary craftsman, Flaubert diligently researched his subjects and infused his works with psychological realism with the goal of achieving an objective prose style "as rhythmical as verse and as precise as the language of science."

Biographical Information

Flaubert was born in Rouen, where his father was chief surgeon at the city hospital and his mother was a respected woman from a provincial bourgeois family. As a youth, Flaubert attended school at the Collège Royal de Rouen. It was during a summer vacation with his family in Trouville that Flaubert met Elisa Schlésinger, a married woman for whom he harbored a lifelong infatuation. In 1838, Flaubert began *Mémoires d'un fou*, a reflective essay in which he recounted the agonies and frustrations of his love for Schlésinger. Shortly after, between 1841 and 1842, he composed the short novel *Novembre* (*November*), which relates the slow death of the main character. Upon receiving his baccalaureate degree, Flaubert honored his parents' wishes and reluctantly registered for law school in Paris, despite his stronger interest in literature. In 1844, however, he experienced an attack of what is now believed to have been epilepsy; he subsequently abandoned his law studies and devoted himself entirely to writing. In 1845, Flaubert completed the first draft of *L'éducation sentimentale* (1869; *Sentimental Education*), which contrasts the respective rewards of love and art. Following the death of both Flaubert's father and sister in 1846, Flaubert moved to the family home at Croisset, near Rouen, with his mother and his infant niece. In 1849, he completed the first version of *La tentation de Saint Antoine* (1874; *The Temptation of Saint Antony*), a novel inspired by a painting by the elder Brueghel. When Flaubert's friends

Maxime Du Camp and Louis Bouilhet rejected the work's excessive lyricism and lack of precision, Flaubert was persuaded to abandon historical subjects and turn to a project that would be contemporary in content and realistic in theme. The result was the composition of *Madame Bovary,* which occupied Flaubert from 1851 to 1856. While writing *Madame Bovary,* Flaubert corresponded regularly with Louise Colet, his "muse" and mistress; his letters to Colet closely document the slow, laborious development of his novel. *Madame Bovary* was first published in serial form in the *Revue de Paris* from October 1 through December 15, 1856. An obscenity trial ensued, and Flaubert was charged with offenses against public and religious morals. Flaubert's defense argued successfully that the novel was indeed a moral work, however, and Flaubert was acquitted. Published in book form two months after the trial, *Madame Bovary* enjoyed widespread sales and significant critical commentary. Flaubert's artistic focus expanded during the later years of his career; his works include the historical novel *Salammbô* (1862), the political drama *Le*

candidat (1874; *The Candidate*), and the short fiction collected in *Trois contes* (1877; *Three Tales*). Additionally, he realized the completion of two major works that had consumed many years of his career—*Sentimental Education* and *The Temptation of Saint Antony*. With the exception of occasional trips abroad and to Paris, Flaubert lived at his family's home in Croisset until his death in 1880.

Major Works

Through painstaking attention to detail and the process of extensive revision, Flaubert developed a dispassionate but psychologically accurate prose style that has subsequently served as a respected model for innumerable writers. During the process of writing *Madame Bovary*, for example, Flaubert composed at most a few paragraphs each day, which he would repeatedly revise in an effort to achieve stylistic perfection. He rejected the use of synonyms; instead, he searched for *le seul mot juste*, or the most precise word, to convey each thought. Partly because of its breakthrough status in the evolution of the objective narrative voice, *Madame Bovary* is considered Flaubert's masterpiece—the most influential French novel of the nineteenth century. History is an important element of such works as *Sentimental Education*, which historians as well as literary critics have regarded as a record of daily life in France during and immediately following the July Monarchy. According to Flaubert, the goal of this work was the writing of "the moral history of the men of my generation." Historical fiction is also the focus of *Salammbô*, which Edmund Wilson characterized in 1948 as "gruesome and extravagant," depicting the "savage and benighted barbarians" of Carthage "[who] slaughtered, lusted and agonized superbly." Contrasting with the exoticism of Flaubert's historical fiction, such noted works as *Madame Bovary* and *Sentimental Education* delineate the concerns of the French bourgeoisie, displaying an autobiographical impulse. Emile Faguet argued in 1899 that each of Flaubert's works was inspired by a particular tendency or "mania" in the author's temperament. Faguet attributed the novel *Bouvard et Pécuchet* (1881), for instance, to one of Flaubert's primary manias: his "horror of stupidity and at the same time [his] sort of fascination [with] stupidity." Another important theme that runs throughout Flaubert's oeuvre is a concern with the experience of human failure. Particularly in *Madame Bovary, Salammbô,* and *Sentimental Education,* Flaubert explores the failure of bourgeois characters to achieve love, happiness, and distinction, and their subsequent renunciation of idealistic dreams. Paul Valéry viewed Flaubert's long-term project *The Temptation of Saint Antony* as "a personal antidote against the boredom (which he admits) of writing his novels of contemporary manners, erecting stylistic monuments to the banality of provincial bourgeois life." Valéry linked *The Temptation of Saint Antony* with Goethe's

Faust, emphasizing the theme of man versus the devil in both works. Flaubert also addressed religious themes in *Three Tales,* which presents three stories ranging in setting from contemporary France to classical antiquity, each of which explores the concept of sainthood and the Christian idea of the trinity. While some critics have interpreted the work as moralistic, others have posited that the volume demonstrates Flaubert's belief that history can be divided into three distinct phases: paganism, Christianity, and *muflisme*, which refers to Flaubert's conception of the nineteenth century as an era marked by the petty values and lifestyles of the bourgeoisie.

Critical Reception

Flaubert's breakthroughs in approaches to narration instigated negative criticism during the nineteenth century, usually on moral grounds. *Madame Bovary*, for example, was widely faulted for its pessimistic view of provincial life and for what was seen as the complete absence of goodness· in his characters. Another revolutionary work, *Sentimental Education,* was also attacked for what many critics perceived as questionable morality, the lack of a strong hero figure, and an awkward and disjointed structure. It was only at the end of the nineteenth century with the emergence of ethics and aesthetics as separate fields that critics began to evaluate Flaubert's works on the basis of artistry rather than morality. Twentieth-century critics have consistently praised the technical virtuosity of Flaubert's writing—his use of style, structure, imagery and symbolism. Flaubert's writing process itself has also been the subject of continuing study, with letters and various drafts of his works being examined in order to gain an understanding of his approach to craft. In recent years, some critics have been concerned with the question of Flaubert's modernity and his perceived role as the father of the modern novel. Victor Brombert, for example, has argued against viewing Flaubert as "the direct ancestor of the *nouveau roman*," arguing that his works reject the application of critical systems of poetic theory. Another area of reexamination among contemporary Flaubert critics has been the significance of the theme of stupidity in his satirical works. Diana Knight, for example, has argued that Flaubert "suggests an important connection between moral and aesthetic values in [his] so-called 'simple' characters."

PRINCIPAL WORKS

Mémoires d'un fou [essay] 1838
Novembre [*November*] [short novel] 1841-42
Premiere Education sentimentale [*The First Sentimental Education*] (novel) 1845
Madame Bovary: Moeurs de province [*Madame*

Bovary: A Tale of Provincial Life] (novel) 1857

Salammbô (novel) 1862

L'éducation sentimentale: Histoire d'un jeune homme [*Sentimental Education: A Young Man's History*] (novel) 1869

Le candidat, comédie en 4 actes [*The Candidate: A Humorous Political Drama in Four Acts*] (drama) 1874

La tentation de Saint Antoine [*The Temptation of Saint Anthony*] (novel) 1874

Trois contes: Un coeur simple; La légende de Saint-Julien l'hospitalier; Hérodias [*Three Tales*] (short fiction) 1877

Bouvard et Pécuchet (novel) 1881

Correspondance. 4 vols. (letters) 1887-93

Oeuvres complètes. 28 vols. (novels, short stories, essays, letters) 1910-54

***Dictionnaire des idées reçues* [*Flaubert's Dictionary of Accepted Ideas*] (prose) 1913

*First version of the work later published in 1869 as *L'éducation sentimentale.*

**First separate publication. Originally published with *Bouvard et Pécuchet.*

CRITICISM

Jonathan Culler (essay date 1974)

SOURCE: "Values," in *Flaubert: The Uses of Uncertainty,* Cornell University Press, 1974, pp. 157-232.

[*In the following excerpt, Culler discusses the function of "stupidity" in Flaubert's themes, symbols, narrative strategies, and characters. Culler connects the idea of stupefaction with Flaubert's notion of the experience of "reverie" and the incomprehensible as the goal of art.*]

Mit der Dummheit kämpfen Götter selbst vergebens.

SCHILLER

BÊTISE ET POÉSIE. Il y a des relations subtiles entre ces deux ordres. L'ordre de la bêtise et celui de la poésie.

VALERY[1]

A. Stupidity

At the age of nine, in a letter that one is pleased to regard as prophetic, Gustave discovered his first literary project: 'comme il y a une dame qui vient chez papa et qui nous contes toujours de bêtises je les écrirai' (i, 1).[2] And write them he did, for the rest of his life. His final compilation, the ***Dictionnaire des idées reçues,*** was not published until after his death, but he began collecting specimens for it early on and in 1850 he already speaks of it as well under way. But even when not working specifically on this project he spent much of his time wading through stupidity in his research for other novels: ***Madame Bovary***—'Je suis dans les *rêves de jeune fille* jusqu'au cou' (ii, 372); ***Saint Antoine***—'Actuellement, je fais parler tous les dieux à l'étatd'agonie. Le sous-titre de mon bouquin pourra être: "le Comble de l'insanité"' (vi, 276); ***L'Education sentimentale***—'Rien n'est épuisant comme de creuser la bêtise humaine!' (v, 317); and ***Bouvard et Pécuchet***—'La bêtise de mes deux bonshommes m'envahit' (vii, 189).[3] Writing was always an immersion in stupidity, partly, as he explained, because he wished to attempt 'le comique d'idées' (viii, 26).

But such an explanation barely touches the surface. Stupidity, both as a category of his own thought and as a component of his literary practice, is very much at the centre of Flaubert's world. . . .   Narrative strategies display varieties of stupidity: descriptions which serve no apparent purpose, devices for isolation and decomposition, characters who are themselves stupid in their perceptions and responses, episodes which refuse to range themselves under ostensible themes. The reader of Flaubert's novels might well agree with his statement that 'We suffer from only one thing, la Bêtise, but it is formidable and universal' (vi, 307). Yet stupidity, though the 'unique objet de son ressentiment', was also very nearly the unique object of his joy. To find a perfect example was, as Henry James said, 'his nearest approach to natural bliss'.[4] What was this ubiquitous stupidity? Why should it be so important? To provide some kind of answer seems incumbent upon anyone pretending to an understanding of his work.

The ***Dictionnaire des idées reçues,*** the most obvious guide to stupidity, is prefaced by an epigraph from Chamfort which suggests one approach to the problem: 'Il y a à parier que toute idée publique, toute convention reçue est une sottise, car elle a convenu au plus grand nombre' (II, 303).[5] Received ideas are stupid because, in their ignorance, the majority will accept ideas that are untrue and, in their intellectual laxness, will distort and oversimplify any true ideas that happen to come their way. The elite know better and because of their superior knowledge can recognize 'sottises' of this kind. Some of the entries in the ***Dictionnaire*** are stupid in that we can formulate the 'correct' alternative. *Omega:* second letter of the Greek alphabet, because one says 'the Alpha and the Omega'.[6] *Gulf-stream:* famous town in Norway, newly discovered. *Rousseau:* Jean-Jacques and Jean-Baptiste are brothers, like the two Corneilles.

Merging into this category are the facile generalizations which illustrate a willingness to content oneself with the most rudimentary knowledge without pursuing the topic further. *Architectes:* all fools; always forget the stairways in houses. *Estomac:* all illnesses come from the stomach. *Koran:* Book by Mohammed which talks only of women. *Serpents:* all poisonous. *Peru:* country where everything is made of gold. That such ideas are stupid there can be little doubt, but they seem weak stuff indeed for a book that was to be Flaubert's revenge on his age and the repository, as he said, of all his hatred.

It is possible, however, that these entries had a specific role to play in the book. The original plan was to include a preface which would explain that the work was designed to promote respect for order, tradition, and convention, in a word 'right thinking'; this was to be done in such a way 'que le lecteur ne sache pas si l'on se fout de lui, oui on non' (ii, 238). When the bourgeois reader found palpable stupidities alongside his own thoughts and beliefs he would be disconcerted and uncertain how to respond. The more egregious cases would help to point to the *bêtise* of those entries reflecting a bourgeois view of the world. True stupidity, we might suppose, was the bourgeois ideology.

Some entries clearly fit this hypothesis. *Hugo:* was wrong to get himself mixed up in politics. Who speaks here? The semi-cultured partisans of order and the Second Empire who will pay lip-service to culture but are pleased that Napoleon III had reestablished business as usual. *Magistrature:* splendid career for a young man. That, as Flaubert's own case shows, was very much the idea of the professional middle-classes. *Police:* bastions of society. After the great divide of 1848 it is clear who says that. *Drapeau (national):* the very sight of it is moving. Not to the left-wing, but perhaps to both the moderate republicans and the reactionaries who say the French must be governed by the sword (*Sabre*). But neither of these is the royalist who still hopes for the *Fusion des branches royales. Idéal:* completely useless. *Ingénieur:* best career for a young man. These come from the new technocratic and positivistic stratum of the middle-class, who neither find *Ruins* romantic nor say that *Music* makes you dream. How do they relate to those for whom *Spiritualism* is the best philosophical system? The man who rails against the age (*Epoque*) and complains that it is not poetic is not the same as he for whom wealth is all-important (*Richesse*) and business takes precedence (*Affaires*). As one collects more evidence the problems increase. One must say, at the very least, that if all these ideas be bourgeois, the bourgeoisie is a class with a highly confused ideology. But Sartre's conclusion seems more apt: 'more than a thousand entries and who feels that he is the target? No one.'[7]

Sartre goes on to argue that Flaubert himself, as much as anyone else, is the target. Many of the ideas are undoubtedly his, but this only strengthens one's growing conviction that the identification of stupidity does not depend on one's ability to formulate the "correct" alternative view. Stupid opinions are not those of the bourgeoisie as opposed to other, preferable opinions. And hence the entries of the ***Dictionnaire*** neither represent a coherent view of the world, nor are they rendered stupid by being set against another coherent ideology.

Flaubert's enterprise, in fact, seems very much that of the mythologist, as Roland Barthes has since defined it. To analyse the contemporary myths of bourgeois culture is not to claim that they are necessarily false but only that their historical and conventional character has been obscured by a society which attempts to transform its particular culture into a universal nature.[8] A Rolls-Royce has a great many properties which, given the qualities that are sought in motor-cars, make it a prize specimen, but the Rolls-Royce is still a mythical object: the symbol of excellence and status. It bears an objective relation to wealth in that only the wealthy can afford one, but when we pass from that relation to one of connotation and make it 'signify' wealth, we have entered the realm of myth. The mythologist attacks a kind of fetishism which takes various associations, however sound their factual basis, and makes them the 'natural' meanings of or responses to an object or concept.

In this perspective Flaubert's choice of a dictionary format becomes thoroughly appropriate. One looks something up in order to discover its social meaning. *Chapeaux:* 'protester contre la forme des.' The *action* of complaining about the form of a hat is not necessarily stupid. What is stupid is to make this an automatic and socially-coded response; to make it what one should think whenever hats are mentioned. *Basques:* are the best runners. This may be true, but to make it, as it were, the meaning of *basques,* the socially-required response, is to limit freedom and curiosity in ways which cannot but seem stupid.

The majority of Flaubert's entries are of this sort: stupid, not because the facts on which they rely are false but because the particular meanings offered do not exhaust an object or concept and because they place it in a self-enclosed system of social discourse which comes to serve as reality for those who allow themselves to be caught up in it. This social text allows contradictory meanings so that discussion may take place. *Imprimerie:* one may say either that it is a marvellous discovery or, if someone else has got his word in first, maintain that it has done more harm than good. *Prêtres:* sleep with their maids and have children whom they call their nephews—'C'est égal, il y en a de bons, tout de même' is the proper response. The novels, of course, are full of this sort of thing. Discussions consist of a ritualistic exchange of clichés in which the world is no longer of any moment, replaced as it is by a limited set of phrases.

There are, therefore, many items which merit their entry in the dictionary only when they are considered not as responses in a particular situation but as possible responses which society has, in its semiotic wisdom, elevated to the status of natural meanings. *Palmier:* gives local color. The object has disappeared, taken up in a social language which suppresses all but one of its possible qualities. *Catholicisme:* has had a very favourable influence on the arts; which is true, but stupid if that is all one can find to say about it. The tangential association or consequence, made a natural response, loses its redeeming features as response. For example, *Diamant:* 'and to think that it is really just coal!' As a spontaneous response to a scientific fact, as wonder that the black and the opaque can become, through a natural agency bordering on the magical, the sparkling and the translucent, this is wholly admirable. It translates a certain attachment to the evidence of the senses and the logic of every day objects and a willingness to explore the unusual. But as a socially-determined association it is of no interest. It is, in fact, no more than a sentence.

If stupidity were ignorance, one might take one's stand on the side of knowledge; if stupidity were bourgeois, one might range oneself with the aristocracy or with the people; but if stupity is cultural language made nature, where can one stand to combat it? How does one gain purchase against clichés which are grounded in truth but have been made the constituents of a world? Flaubert's first attempts to define a posture in which he could rail against stupidity was his invention, with various schoolfellows, of that enigmatic giant, le Garçon.

Our evidence about him is pitifully slight. Some twenty letters make brief reference to him as common property and the Goncourts provide an uncomprehending account of what Flaubert told them; but such as it is the evidence at least indicates that the Garçon was both subject and object. To play the Garçon was to perceive the world in a particular way and laugh at the stupidity of others, but it was also, simultaneously, to make oneself a stupid and grotesque object.

The Garçon's parentage is Flaubert out of Rabelais— or at least out of Rabelais as interpreted in one of Gustave's youthful essays: the vicious satirist who has undertaken destructive mockery. Everything that had been respected he demolished. All human conditions 'pass before the colossal sarcasm of Rabelais, which whips and brands them, and they all emerge bloody and mutilated from beneath his pen' (I, 183). But he was object as well as subject. His laughter, which was so terrible, 'c'est la statue du grotesque' (I, 180). While mocking others he made himself so disgusting that the eighteenth century might judge his works 'a mass of the most obscene garbage that a drunken monk could vomit up'. It had to be thus, writes Flaubert. Setting himself up against the world, Rabelais reveals the stupidity of others by their reactions to his books.

Similarly, Rabelais' giants are both instruments and objects of ridicule; they both exemplify the human qualities which we see magnified in them and set themselves against the ordinary run of men, whom they present to us as pitiful creatures indeed. The Garçon was designed as a modern Pantagruel, who would himself be obscene, stupid, ridiculous, but who would also and simultaneously destroy, by his colossal laughter, the world on which he looked.

The Garçon is not therefore, as some have suggested, the archetypal bourgeois, Homais grown giant. He utters *idées reçues* on the appropriate occasions but with such conceit and bellowing that interlocutors who are not in on the joke become annoyed. And he can take up any other position sufficiently gross and ridiculous for him to make a spectacle of himself. The Goncourts tell a story of Flaubert, at one of Princesse Mathilde's soirées, challenging the sculptor Jacquemart who had told a story concerning Egypt and fleas. Determined to prove that he himself had had more fleas, Flaubert succeeded in engaging Jacquemart in violent argument, to the annoyance and discomfiture of everyone.[9] And such annoyance, it is important to note, would be directed not simply at Flaubert but also at themselves for failing to preserve a detached and amused calm. Making himself ridiculous, the Garçon brings others to see themselves as ridiculous: 'By his shouts and paradoxes he makes emerge the bourgeois who lurk beneath the skin of these aristocrats and artists. Only those bourgeois do not like to be shown their true nature.'[10]

When one plays the Garçon, one makes oneself object voluntarily so as to make others become objects involuntarily. A letter of 1850, written from Cairo, reveals the basic mechanism. Bouilhet, who had out of friendship been visiting Flaubert's mother regularly, is thanked profusely and most tenderly. But don't think yourself obliged to give up all your Sundays, Flaubert continues, or to go to so much trouble. My mother, I know, appreciates your visits so much she'd gladly pay a hundred francs a time. That phrase sets him off on another course:

> Il serait gars de lui en faire la proposition. Vois-tu le mémoire que fourbirait le Garçon en cette occasion: 'Tant pour la société d'un homme comme moi. Frais extraordinaires: avoir dit un mot spirituel . . . avoir été charmant et plein de bon ton. Etc.' (ii, 217).[11]

If one were playing the Garçon one could display self-satisfaction and unmask one's relations with others.

Bouilhet's visits are presumably undertaken out of duty rather than pleasure, so that to present a bill would be to reveal the true state of affairs which is ordinarily masked by polite formulae. But the Garçon, we are told, would not simply present a bill; that would put him into the situation of professional men whose time we buy but with whom we expect to entertain human relations during that period that is ours. The Garçon details his fees, like a doctor charging extra for each reassuring word, adding a supplement for delicacy. Every moment of his behaviour is an object to be weighted and paid for. He is making, quite literally, a spectacle of himself, not merely revealing the sordid truth of a human relationship but exacerbating it. Like Rameau's nephew, he attains a version of freedom in and through alienation: making himself object in his every moment, he laughs in his Gargantuan way at both himself and his interlocutor. The latter, outraged, finds the tormentor invulnerable in his laughter and cannot avoid being discomfited, for the useless anger has been provoked and controlled by the Garçon. Playing a reprehensible role, he pulls the strings which make others puppets.

Laughter is the Garçon's mode of existence, and the man who laughs is strong among the strong, especially if his laughter be outrageous. 'Je me récrie, je ris, je bois, je chante ah ah ah, et je fais entendu le rire du Gârcon, je tape sur la table, je m'arrache les cheveux, je me roule par terre' (i, 24-5).[12] One must either join in the laughter, which makes one feel self-conscious and foolish, so excessive is it, or one must allow bourgeois indignation to mount and become a spectacle oneself. Either way, the Garçon disconcerts; he pulls the strings. And if one would experience this paradoxical duality one might try, as experiment, what Flaubert often did to avoid boredom: look at oneself in the mirror and laugh one's most outrageous laugh. One is both subject and object of ridicule and can experience in one of its purest forms the stupidity of the human species.

'Comment épingler la bêtise sans se déclarer intelligent?' asks Barthes.[13] How can one prick stupidity without claiming supreme intelligence? One solution, which the Garçon outlines, is to 'se déclarer bête' and display one's stupidity with a blatant and provocative self-confidence. The Garçon has no positive position; in him, as Sartre observes, materialism makes fun of romanticism and vice versa. Everything is grist to his mill, or at least any position that takes itself seriously. The stupidity of the Garçon is both a mode of comprehension and a property of all that he comprehends.

But the Garçon was an attempt at a lived rather than written solution; it is noteworthy that he appears in none of Flaubert's books—though Yuk, the God of the grotesque in *Smarh* is obviously a relative—for he is a Homeric figure whose epic stature would sort ill

with the modes of stupidity that Flaubert's novels express. The structure of the Garçon, however, can be traced in the conception of *Bouvard et Pécuchet*. It was to be, Du Camp reports, an encyclopaedia of human stupidity, and when he asked for an explanation Flaubert replied, 'Je veux produire une telle impression de lassitude et d'ennui, qu'en lisant ce livre on puisse croire qu'il a été fait par un crétin' (I, 35).[14] The book is not to present intelligence mocking stupidity but stupidity both as object and as mode of comprehension. To write the book is itself stupid, as Flaubert felt only too clearly. Representation of the world in sentences is a particularly pointless and gratuitous activity.

Indeed, one might say that as an incarnation of stupidity the Garçon leaves out of account one crucial factor: the stupidity of language. The *Dictionnaire des idées reçues* implies, as I have already suggested, that stupidity is a mode of language, or rather that social language is itself stupid: it is not the instrument or vehicle of a spontaneous response to the world, it is not something lived but something given, a set of codified responses. We do not understand the world or even come to grips with it. We talk about it in phrases which interact with one another in a self-enclosed system. Language, in short, is part of the practico-inert: a set of objects with which man plays but which do not speak to him.

The alphabetical listing of the *Dictionnaire* makes this point quite nicely. The order is purely arbitrary or linguistic only, unlike those medieval and renaissance compendiums which attempted to reproduce in their arrangement the order of the world. Sentences are simply juxtaposed, as isolated bits of linguistic matter. We can glimpse here Flaubert's basic attitude towards language: one does not speak, one does not construct sentences to express one's relation to the world and to others; one is spoken. Social discourse is always there already and when addressed one need only pick out the response which the system of discourse provides. Whether or not Sartre is right in attributing this attitude to childhood traumas and difficulties in learning to read, it is well documented from the novels themselves, which offer a sense of 'the grotesque stupidity of things said, whatever they may be.'[15] Anything one says is a linguistic object placed on display, and if one looks at it long enough, just as when one repeats a word until it becomes meaningless, its stupidity will become apparent. Cutting speech off from its origins in practical life, Flaubert treats it as a set of phrases rather than the accomplishment of human intentions. 'It's going to rain', says Emma to Léon, who is taking his leave. 'I have a raincoat,' he replies. 'Ah!' (I, 614). Nothing is said. Sentences stand, empty and detached.

To say anything is to take up a banal social discourse. Hence the self-conscious, citational mode of Flaubert's own letters. The sentences he writes are not his, and by distancing himself from them, supplying possible sources—'comme dirait M. Prudhomme', 'comme dit l'épicier'—he protects himself from the stupidity which contaminates any speech. The hope that after reading the **Dictionnaire des idées reçues** 'no one would dare speak, for fear of saying one of the phrases which were to be found in it' (iii, 67) was simply a desire for revenge and the hope that the despair of language which he had so long experienced might be visited on others.

A melancholy reflection in **Par les champs et par les grèves** provides a nice summary of man's relationship to language. Something rather ordinary surprised me and made me laugh, Flaubert says. It was a telegraph box on a tower in Nantes with a ladder leading up to it.

> Quelle drôle de vie que celle d'un homme qui reste là, dans cette petite cabane à faire mouvoir ces deux perches et à tirer sur ces ficelles; rouage inintelligent d'une machine muette pour lui, il peut mourir sans connaître un seul des événements qu'il a appris, un seul mot de tous ceux qu'il aura dits. Le but? le but? le sens? qui le sait? . . . Un peu plus, un peu moins, ne sommes-nous pas tous comme ce brave homme, parlant des mots qu'on nous a appris et que nous apprenons sans les comprendre (II, 484).[16]

Language lifted away from the world becomes a self-contained system of empty phrases which we exchange and transmit but which we neither invent nor investigate.

This should not imply, however, that for Flaubert man has a rich inner and outer life prior to language, a treasure so particular that no social discourse can capture it. There is, indeed, much evidence to the contrary. Emma's desires are created by a language of romance and she finds nothing in her life to fulfil the promise of those words, 'félicité', 'passion', and 'ivresse', which had seemed so splendid in books (I, 586). Frédéric *admires* passion (estimait par-dessus tout la passion) (II, 13) and hopes to reproduce in his own life the love whose image a culture offers him. Bouvard and Pécuchet spend a fortnight attempting introspection after lunch: 'they searched in their consciousness, at random, hoping to make great discoveries there, and made none, which surprised them greatly' (II, 271). The emptiness of language is paralleled by an inner emptiness.

Indeed, it is as though, having lifted language away from human praxis and intentionality in order to make it stupid, Flaubert, in a crucial but rather devious move, had re-established connections between language and thought on the one hand and language and the world on the other, in order to render thought and world as

stupid as language. Whereas stupidity seemed at first the result of a gap between language and the world, the property of a language that was substituted for the world, now, by contamination, it becomes a property of active attempts to manipulate language in what is called 'thought' and also a property of a world of objects which refuses to be composed by language.

Before exploring the links between these varieties of stupidity and considering the possibilities of synthesis we must try to define, in turn, the stupidity of thought and the stupidity of objects.

'Oui, la bêtise consiste à vouloir conclure', wrote Flaubert in a famous letter. 'Stupidity is wanting to conclude. We are a thread and want to know the pattern' (ii, 239). The attempts of intelligence to master the world, to seek out causes and offer explanations, are a form of stupidity. Homais, after all, is stupid *because* he is intelligent, because he attempts to keep up with contemporary science and make his own contribution to it, to display his awareness of knowledge and help others towards the benefits of it. But the stupidity of thought is even more apparent in **Bouvard et Pécuchet,** where Flaubert lists and explores the theories of the best authorities in a wide range of fields, all of which pretend to some kind of explanatory validity and all of which prove contradictory and inept. 'Stupidity is not on one side and intelligence on the other' (iv, 83); such an opposition seems impossible. Those who still believe in sorcerers and divining rods may be stupid, but where does one stand to combat such an opinion; is there a correct opposing view?

> As for combating it, why not combat the contrary, which is quite as stupid as it is? There are a whole crowd of such topics which annoy me just as much whatever way they are approached . . . Thus Voltaire, mesmerism, Napoleon, the French Revolution, Catholicism, etc. Whether one speak good or ill of them I am equally irritated. Most of the time conclusions seem to me acts of stupidity (iii, 153-4).

That irritation is the law that governs **Bouvard et Pécuchet**. One opinion is set against another with no attempt to adjudicate between them. What should be done in the garden? 'Puvis recommends marl, Roret manual opposes it . . . Tull exalts tillage at the expense of fertilizer, but Major Beetson suppresses fertilizer in favour of tillage' (II, 211). All theories are rendered equivalent by their failure. That these failures may be due sometimes to want of understanding, at other times to the general perverseness of a recalcitrant Nature, and at still others to the incompetence of the authorities themselves, does not materially affect the case. Oppositions between the theories are effectively neutralized as they take their place with one another in paradigms of stupidity.

Some critics, struck no doubt by the ineptness of the two protagonists and by the subtitle, 'Du défaut de méthode dans les sciences', have assumed that human knowledge is not itself under attack; but that subtitle is highly ironic, since method is perhaps the only thing Bouvard and Pécuchet do not lack. When tackling a new discipline they send off for the best authorities, read and compare them, and attempt to test their conclusions. What probably influences critics on this point is the fact that so much of what is reported seems pseudo-science and so much of what we respect as science is absent, but this is scarcely Flaubert's fault. He would joyfully have included an account of nuclear physics and sub-atomic particles in his list of theories of matter, and one can imagine Bouvard and Pécuchet riding around the district in trains trying to test the theory of relativity. Stupidity is not a property of incorrect theories but rather the inevitable coefficient of the whole attempt to master nature through knowledge.

Indeed, Flaubert's remarks on science in other contexts make it clear that what he admires is an attempt to establish facts. He is attracted to Positivism precisely insofar as it appears to have abandoned a search for causes and contented itself with exhaustive taxonomic descriptions. Explanation, in his view, lies outside the province of science and any attempt to attain it is a step into the abyss of stupidity. 'Note that the sciences began to make progress only when they set aside the notion of cause' (iv, 357). 'Try to hold firm to science, to pure science: love facts for themselves' (iv, 399). The only kind of knowledge worthy of respect is that which presents and classifies facts and, offering no conclusions or explanations, cannot be translated into action. Attempts to relate knowledge and activity are instances of presumptuous stupidity. Hence medicine for Flaubert, as Sartre notes, is not an attempt to master disease and cure the sick (which makes one wonder what sort of example Flaubert's father presented) but only dissection and naming of parts, analysis without synthesis. The notion that the search for causes is anti-scientific (v, 148) and deplorable is related, of course, to Flaubert's rejection of practical life, but it cannot avoid affecting the artistic life he has adopted. As a general denigration of synthesis, it is particularly inimical to the pursuit, in novels, of thematic conclusions. Nor does it promote a desire for organization.

This seems apparent in Flaubert's ambiguous attachment to binarism. His predilection for pairs has been noted by most critics, though as I have suggested above, many of his oppositions are factitious and unproductive. Binary opposition—'cette logique élémentaire qui est comme le plus petit commun dénominateur de toute pensée'[17]—is a metaphor for all thought in its ability to bring order into any disorder. It is not surprising that for Flaubert it should be linked with *bêtise*

since any application of it presumes to isolate crucial features in simple antitheses and hence to move towards conclusions with a minimum of intellectual effort. One remembers the passage in the first ***Education sentimentale*** where Henry, the provincial newly-arrived in Paris, watches the faces of passengers in the omnibus, 'establishing between them similarities and antitheses' (I, 279). That is stupid both as an attempt to grasp and comprehend the world and as an intellectual construction which takes place in a language lifted away from the world which does not allow itself to be organized so easily.

Yet Flaubert himself is very much wedded to the binary principle, especially when drawing up plans. The project for a novel on 'Un ménage parisien sous Napoléon III' is rigidly symmetrical: 'Madame catches Monsieur deceiving her; then Monsieur catches Madame deceiving him—jealousy. She wishes she had married a true lover who had become a great man; he wishes he had married a tart who had become very rich.' And opposed to them, 'in the background his sister and her husband, a respectable and perfectly egotistical household.'[18] The task of writing such a novel would thus become one of struggling with the stupidity of his symmetrical plan.

The problem of binarism may serve as a useful pivot on which to turn from the stupidity of intellect to the stupidity of the world, for precisely because of his dislike of facile antitheses and his tendency to make oppositions unproductive, Flaubert can in descriptions use binarism as a device of anti-synthesis: doubling objects without allowing this to produce meaning. He is at irritatingly great pains, Claude Duchet writes,

> to note objects in pairs, so that they thereby take on connotations of penetrating stupidity and repetitive monotony: 'she remained leaning on the edge, between two pots of geraniums', 'she rested her elbow alongside her plate, between the two smoking candles'; or even connotations of satisfied plenitude, as if the bourgeois thought in pairs.[19]

Citing numerous examples, he concludes that we are dealing with both a stylistic tic and a vision of the world.

> One could even say that one of the reasons for Flaubert's hatred of boots is that they call for double notation . . . Passing from clothes to person, the figure two decomposes bodies, as it were, into fascinating objects of flesh. Here is Charles by the fireside, 'his two hands on his stomach, his two feet on the andirons'. Here are the country-folk at the fair in their Sunday-best, like bourgeois in stiff collars and white cravats: 'et l'on appuyait ses deux mains sur ses deux cuisses.'[20]

The unnecessary numerical specifications add an element of gratuitous facticity and produce, as Duchet suggests, somewhat grotesque but fascinating objects. They are stupid because of their particularity.

It might seem that Flaubert displays here a sense of stupidity closely related to Valéry's:

> La 'bêtise' de tout se fait sentir. Bêtise, c'est-á-dire particularité opposée à la généralité. 'Plus petit que' devient le signe terrible de l'esprit. Le Démon des possibles ordonnés.[21]

Bêtise is what escapes the ordering intellect, whatever makes itself felt as a particularity which falls outside the concept and is simply there. Yet with 'smaller than', one of those many demons of logical possibility which are at the mind's beck and call, one can order any pair and thereby denature the objects in question. Stupidity would seem to be opposed to organization, but Valéry at least recognizes that such an opposition is at best ambiguous: 'Démon' and 'terrible' indicate reservations about the value of easy organization. But he would not go so far as to bring these operations under the aegis of stupidity, and it is here that Flaubert shows a much deeper understanding of the constraints on and requirements of a sophisticated literary theory of *bêtise*.

He understands, that is to say, that in literature there is never a question of objects which escape the organizing powers of language and mind. Stupidity cannot be an absence of organization. If it is to be a literary category one must reflect on the ways in which absence of organization may be signified and therefore one cannot think of stupidity as a residue which, by definition, does not makes its way onto the page. Stupidity is already a type of organization. The use of pairs, 'his two arms on his two thighs' or whatever, offers a rudimentary disposition which holds out no possibilities for development and comes thereby to signify the purely factual and fatuous. The stupidity of objects is itself a mode of organization, and one might say that for Flaubert, as opposed to Valéry, 'le Démon des possibles ordonnés" is *bêtise* itself.

Viewed in this way, Flaubert's binary predilections become wholly comprehensible—or at least insofar as the attractions of stupidity are ever fully comprehensible. The stupidity of objects is dependent on a sense of possible order, of which doubling is the most elementary index, and a failure to fulfill the expectations such possibilities arouse. The stupidity of the world, in Flaubert, is always the coefficient of a rudimentary order, whether that of the syntax which pretends to compose items into a coherent proposition, or that of the more elaborate objects described at some length.

Emma's wedding cake and the elaborate toy which was destined for the Homais children but did not find its way into the final text due to the insistence of Bouilhet, are excellent instances of stupidity as a co-efficient of organization.[22] The former, of course, is ridiculous in its mixture of styles and in the contrast between its elements and what they represent: 'a castle-keep in Savoy cake, surrounded by tiny fortifications in angelica, almonds, raisins, and orange quarters; . . . jam lakes and nutshell boats' (I, 584). It was 'une pièce montée qui fit pousser des cris', a deliberate spectacle which is doubly alienated and fetishistic: first, because its form is so divorced from its practical purposes (it will, after all, be eaten), and secondly, because its ingredients are made to serve functions which are not their own. The toy, however, is an even purer example of stupidity and its attractions: a scale model of a town and all the activities taking place within it, it is also nonfunctional and purely representational. 'Both the height of gratuitousness and highly essential', as Thibaudet says,[23] such an object holds attractions which anyone who has been fascinated by an architectural scale model or an elaborate electric train set can understand. One takes pleasure in discovering the accuracy of representation and the means by which it has been achieved. Perfectly useless, such objects with their high degree of organization, are directly and unabashedly mimetic, presenting us with a whole and allowing us to explore its parts. Lévi-Strauss even argues that the 'modèle réduit' is the very type of the work of art, whose intrinsic virtue is to compensate for the reduction of spatial dimensions by the addition of new dimensions of intelligibility.[24]

That is, of course, the traditional defence of mimetic art, but Flaubert's objects illustrate the stupidity of this kind of intelligibility. Blocking the discourse of the text—that is why Bouilhet insisted on the excision of the long description of the toy—they offer a high degree of organization which leads nowhere. Closed, autonomous, absolute, 'these objects are *there*: the observer, flustered and fascinated, cannot question these monuments to the genius of stupidity, these complacent and flowering arabesques.'[25] They figure the absurdity of representational art itself; language divorced from its human origins and goals but retaining a high degree of organization as it accedes to the condition of the practico-inert.

It should be clear that for Flaubert the attractions of such objects lie in their stupidity; one stands fascinated before them, *béant* or *ébahi,* because they have no function, prove nothing. The mind is released from any commitment to practical life and can simply explore.

Stupidity of this kind is a property of aesthetic objects also: 'Masterpieces are stupid; they present a tranquil face, like the very productions of nature, like large animals or mountains' (ii, 451). The masterpiece does not display intelligence or reach towards conclusions but offers itself with no ostensible purpose. The *bêtise* of novels is, however, more than a version of negative capability; they command attention, as a mountain does when it rises before one, and are not subsumed by any human project. Their tranquil appearance, a kind of bovine placidity, does not actively invite interpretation, as would a surface complexity that bespoke figured secrets. They are *de trop;* one may play around them but does not exhaust them.

Inexhaustibility is, for Flaubert, a compelling property of both art and stupidity.

> What seems to me the highest thing in art (and the most difficult), is not to evoke laughter, or tears, or lust, or anger, but to work as nature does: that is to say, to *induce reverie.* And the most beautiful works have in fact this quality. They are of serene aspect and incomprehensible. As for their technique, they are immobile like cliffs, stormy like the ocean, full of foliage, greenery, and murmurs like woods, sad like the desert, blue like the sky. Homer, Rabelais, Michelangelo, Shakespeare, Goethe seem to me *inexorable.* Such works are unfathomable, infinite, multifarious. Through little gaps one glimpses precipices; there is darkness below, dizziness (iii, 322-3).

This passage brings about, under the aegis of stupidity, a combination of terms which requires some elucidation. Why choose natural metaphors to discuss the workings of masterpieces? What is the relationship between reverie, incomprehension, and profundity? An answer would enable us to attack that enigmatic account of the temptations of stupidity which obsessed Flaubert for most of his life: *La Tentation de Saint Antoine.*

First of all, incomprehension was for Flaubert the road to reverie. Henry in the first *Education sentimentale* 'sat for a whole hour reading the same line of a newspaper' (I, 279), and that this should be called 'reading' rather than, say, 'staring', is quite significant. 'I reread this week the first act of *King Lear*', Flaubert reports. Shakespeare 'stupifies and exalts me'; 'je n'y vois qu'une immensité où mon regard se perd avec des éblouissements' (iv, 46). This 'vastness where the gaze loses itself in dizziness' is the experience of reading that Flaubert desires. Reading is an act of passing through the text ('through little gaps one glimpses precipices'), not synthesizing it, but either looking for stupid phrases which command admiration (that is research) or seeking between the lines for something which, as Sartre says, lends itself to his 'directed reverie'.[26] He claims to have been completely flattened for three days after reading Act III, scene i of *Lear,* but his comments make clear that he is discussing another scene and that he has not only misinterpreted it but failed to grasp elementary facts about the plot (iv, 18).

The image of Flaubert sitting before these texts in an inspired and devouring reverie recalls the one picture of serious intellectual effort that he offers us in his works: the German mathematician in the first *Education sentimentale.* 'Shahutsnischbach . . . was always working at mathematics, mathematics were consuming his life, he understood nothing about them. Never had M. Renaud had a more studious or stupid young man' (I, 293). Again the choice of words is revealing. The student is not involved in one of those intellectual tasks which would be possible without understanding, nor is it simply that he has great difficulty and must therefore work harder to keep up. 'Il n'y comprenait rien' and yet 'il travaillait toujours au mathématiques.' One thinks of the hours the young Flaubert spent staring at his law books, taking nothing in, understanding nothing, because he was merely reading sentences, contemplating them, and finding them stupid.[27] Or of the considerable periods he spent 'studying' Greek but never attacking the verbs, because, as Sartre says, he did not want to understand and cherished the opacity of texts which provoked reverie the more readily because they were incomprehensible.[28]

If the highest goal of art is to *faire rêver* then it is quite appropriate that masterpieces should be incomprehensible and that Flaubert should have sought in his own writing to set obstacles in the way of synthesis. Whether incomprehension results from the stupidity of the subject or of the object is perhaps a minor matter, since the goal is a mental activity that is self-directing. The subject is to find no instructions in the object. Understanding is a participatory movement which grasps the object either as the result of human intentions or as a form with a teleological intentionality of its own. Either way, one organizes it with respect to a purpose or function. Reverie, then, is the result of contemplating the object under another aspect, denying or failing to reach the purpose which would integrate it. Treating potentially purposive objects as mere material stimuli, reverie rejects understanding and seeks stupidity.

Whence Flaubert's predilection for natural metaphors. One cannot understand a stone or a mountain. One can understand facts about them or problems that are posed when a human project or discourse operates on them, providing a focus, asking a question. 'Why is the stone this colour?' But natural objects have no such focus in themselves, and hence the task of science, as Flaubert sees it, is merely to note and describe, not to understand. 'That's the beauty of the natural sciences: they do not wish to prove anything. Consequently, what breadth of facts and immense space for thought? One ought to treat men like mastodons or crocodiles' (iii, 154). To treat men in this way is to deny the relevance of that immense fund of knowledge one has by virtue of being a man oneself. Refusing to understand them, one transforms them into curiosities available for contemplation and reverie. This is Flaubert's habitual procedure. He is annoyed when people whose lives impinge on his own talk or behave stupidly, but as soon as he can achieve sufficient distance and take the sentences or behaviour as natural specimens which need not be understood, they can be cause for joy and reverie. The stupidity which transforms the human into the non-human neutralizes annoying qualities and produces an opacity which is a source of value.

Inexorable and 'impitoyables', masterpieces offer the mind none of the consolations of easy recuperation. They do not address it, and so any message to be drawn from them must be constructed by the mind in self-conscious fashion. Like the reading of rocks or clouds, interpretation is an activity always threatened by its possible gratuitousness, and the placidity of great works only heightens the threat. The ending of *Candide,* Flaubert remarks, 'that tranquil conclusion, stupid like life itself' is for me the striking proof of Voltaire's genius. Neither melodrama nor synthesis, neither tragedy nor success, the ending is calm and even mediocre. Tailing off, explicitly rejecting reflections on the final state of affairs, it asserts its own reality and stops there, 'stupid like life itself' (ii, 398).

But for Flaubert it is also profound, no doubt because of Candide's own refusal to think. Thought itself, the adventures of a mind attaching itself to a particular problem and working towards some end, is not profound. Depth, for Flaubert, is not a determinate space; it is not, for example, the attribute of a thought which, difficult to grasp, holds itself back from the mind, inviting it to traverse a space in order to accede to it. Depth is rather the result of superficiality; one breaks through a thin and brittle surface and finds that there is no bottom below: 'such works are unfathomable . . . there is darkness below, dizziness.' Indeed, it is when one regards something as stupid, when one severs it from a human context which might serve as a bottom beyond which one need not explore, when one thus makes it a pure surface phenomenon, that it becomes properly profound. What could be more stupid, after all, than the 'bêtise sublime' of carving one's name in huge letters on Pompey's column? The name itself, 'Thompson', is quite meaningless, yet it stares one imperiously in the face, looms before one as a surface which one does not know how to deal with. 'It can be read a quarter of a league away. There is no way to see the column without seeing the name 'Thompson' and consequently without thinking of Thompson.' There is in Flaubert's reaction a hint of jealousy: 'This idiot has become part of the monument and perpetuates himself with it', but it is due above all to his admiration for the profundity of this stupidity. 'Not only that, he overwhelms it by the magnificence of his gigantic letters.' These letters testify for him to the 'serenity' of stupidity, and he concludes that 'Stupid-

ity is something unshakeable. Nothing attacks it without breaking itself against it. It is of the nature of granite, hard and resistant' (ii, 243).

Sartre has written some brilliant pages on Flaubert's response to Thompson: Flaubert finds confirmation of his sense of writing as 'l'acte pur de bêtise' and of its triumph as a correlate of its stupidity. But Sartre is wont to stress the gesture of Thompson the man, who instead of admiring a work of art used it to his own ends, stole the glory that rightfully belonged to another, and succeeded both because matter itself, the stone of the column, lent him permanence and because 'la matière du dedans, celle que s'est coulée dans les coeurs, lui confère l'immortalité'.[29] But to treat it in this way is already to make it less stupid, or rather to make oneself more stupid; for Thompson did not, after all, achieve anything. All that is immortalized is a name borne by many others, and it is precisely that absence of efficacy which gives his inscription its profound stupidity. It stands before the viewer as a surface, a *signifiant* with an absent *signifié*. To treat the inscription as a calculated act designed to achieve a particular goal is to supply a meaning, to understand it, and thereby to negate the gratuitous stupidity which makes it fascinating.

This aspect of stupidity's attraction is borne out by a letter to George Sand in which, while discussing beauty as the goal of art, he gives a most curious illustration.

> I remember once how moved I was and what violent pleasure I felt when looking at a wall of the Acropolis, a completely bare wall. Well, I wonder whether a book, quite apart from what it says, could not produce the same effect. In the precision with which parts are fitted together, the rarity of its elements, the high polish of the surface, the harmony of the whole, is there not an intrinsic virtue, a kind of divine force, something eternal like a principle? (I speak as a Platonist.) (vii, 294).

It would, of course, be his *livre sur rien,* placid and tranquil, which did not address man; just a blank wall, which is one of our models of stupidity. It would be profound because it would be only a surface that provoked reverie in the spectator, 'écrasé sans savoir pourquoi' (iii, 62). One can catch glimpses of a divine order, but if one tried to express that order one would fall back into the mode of *bêtise.*

If one attempts to bring together the various manifestations of this ubiquitous concept one discovers that it cannot be defined in terms of a few common properties which all its instances share. It is not, for Flaubert, a positively defined concept which he can simply apply. Were that the case it would not occupy the role in his mental and artistic life that it does. It is a concept which, as the French allows us to say, 'le travaille et qu'il travaille'. It works or exercises him and he must, in turn, work it, as one works metal or stone. Indeed, the concept seems to contain within itself the whole structure of Flaubert's intellectual adventure. The best way to grasp this complex structure is perhaps to show how it differs from irony as Kierkegaard defines it.

It might seem, Kierkegaard writes, that as 'infinite absolute negativity' irony were identical with doubt. But 'doubt is a conceptual determination while irony is the being-for-itself of subjectivity.'[30] As a youth Flaubert was given to doubt: 'how many long and monotonous hours have I spent in thinking, in doubting' (I, 230). Doubt applies to a proposition or attitude that men have adopted and questions it in the name of something else; it implies at least the possibility of an alternative positive statement. With doubt the subject feels oppressed because he must attempt to penetrate the phenomena in question and offer a mode of discourse of his own, committing himself in some way, if only to justify his refusal to go beyond doubt. Irony, however, at least in Kierkegaard's sense, implies no positive alternative. The subject feels free. He 'is always seeking to get outside the object, and this he attains by becoming conscious at every moment that the object has no reality.' Whereas doubt leads one to do battle, 'with irony the subject constantly retires from the field and proceeds to talk every phenomenon out of its reality in order to save himself, that is, in order to preserve himself in his negative independence of everything.'[31]

Irony is purely an attitude of mind which, though it may talk phenomena out of their reality, does not predicate other qualities of its objects because that would already imply a positive determination of some sort. Flaubert's stupidity, on the other hand, is both a mode of perception and a quality of objects, an attempt to free oneself from the world coupled with an oppressive consciousness of the reality of that world. More complex and in a sense more realistic than irony, it incorporates some residue of doubt and involves, one might say, three stages.

The first stage corresponds roughly to the initial perception of both the doubter and the ironist: the recognition that the being of society lies in its discourse. Clichés, propositions, theories, assumptions, are all attempts to organize the world through language, to master it, to humanize it, and to give it a meaning. One might react by doubting the truth of propositions and values, but that would require explanation. One might quote them ironically, but that gives one little purchase against them. After all, according to Kierkegaard, Socrates had to die because he became so totally identified with irony that there was no way left for him to live. If one wishes to give some substantial realization to one's sense of the incompleteness and partiality of

society as constituted by its modes of discourse, if one wishes to show the foolishness of its attempts to create natural signs, one must develop another strategy.

That strategy is the second stage of stupidity. Stupidity is a mode of perception which makes things stupid. Take anything, a sentence, an activity, and isolate it, cut it off from the human intentions and goals that might give it a meaning, treat it, in short, as an object, and it will become stupid by virtue of the very stupidity and failure of understanding with which one regards it. Shaving, perfectly comprehensible in terms of human physiology and social conventions, becomes ridiculous when considered in and of itself. Phrases set down in the dictionary, taken out of social contexts where they might translate a response which was not wholly reprehensible, become mythical objects. The Garçon, by his own stupidity, provokes responses in others which make them pure automata and also displays the stupidity of those whom he imitates. Stupidity as a mode of perception is not simply the free attitude of irony, which makes little contact with its objects; it produces, rather, a correspondence between mind and its objects so that both come to partake of the same quality. The world is ordered but, seen *sub specie inanitatis,* that order is without point.

The movement of this second stage, which by stupidly dehumanizing and fragmenting the world permits one to see it as stupid without delineating positive alternatives, enables one to accede to the third stage, at which stupidity becomes a positive quality. It is as though by characterizing the world as stupid Flaubert has saved it for himself. The operation which reduces it to a surface and makes it a series of signs without meaning leaves the subject free before it. It remains the world and therefore carries the presumption of importance and order, but once that is shown to be, precisely, an empty presumption, the subject is free to fill it in the activity of reverie. He can glimpse a 'divine' order beneath a surface whose 'bottom' has been destroyed by stupidity in its second phase. The attempts to create natural signs have been undermined, and the subject can now prize innocent placidity, blankness, tranquillity, a simple being-there: versions of stupidity which serve as *signifiants* to empty *signifiés* which he can explore without naming: 'cela est sans fond, infini, multiple.'

Viewed in this way, Flaubert's sense of stupidity helps to bring together a good many diverse pronouncements and attitudes: the desire to write 'un livre sur rien', the comparison between masterpieces and natural objects, the practice of realism and the hatred of ordinary life, the ambiguous attitude towards clichés and absurd statements, his view of himself as analyst despite his failure to undertake analysis. This complex structure permits one to understand that stupidity oppresses because it locates the observer in the human and imposes on him the task of disengaging himself, distancing himself, making stupidity a mode of perception, in order to break free. But it also exhilarates because that task can be accomplished and leaves one, at least momentarily, with a feeling of freedom.

I should like to think that Flaubert's obsession with *Saint Antoine,* an obsession which he himself clearly did not understand, was due to the fact that it was to be a synthesis of his attitudes towards stupidity. But whether or not such an hypothesis has any bearing on the psychology of the author, it is crucial, I would maintain, to the psychology of the reader. For *La Tentation de Saint Antoine* is so blatantly stupid a work, especially when the three texts are placed side by side, that unless one attempts to read it as symptom, and as symptom of the ways in which the problems of stupidity may work themselves out in literature, it is difficult to summon up the stamina to proceed.

If the example of *Bouvard et Pécuchet* is anything to go by, one might postulate that the *Tentation* too was designed to be exasperating and incomprehensible, 'un livre sur rien' in that all these phantoms and temptations amount, finally, to nothing. As a monstrous excrescence the work poses in rather too imperious a fashion the question of what is stupid, how stupidity relates to temptation, and whether it is a desire for knowledge or stupidity that makes one tempted by the monstrous. For the reader who follows the title and attempts to use it to structure the book the problems of reading are acute. We know something of temptations because we presume to a knowledge of human psychology, but the traditional lures of sex, wealth, and power are represented by pasteboard figures who are easily summoned and quickly dismissed, and the remaining temptations seem notable primarily for their grotesqueness and stupidity. The question which the reader is forced to ask himself is whether he is wrong in thinking these figures stupid and in discounting for that reason their power as temptations, or whether he is right in thinking them stupid but wrong in assuming that this makes them less effective as temptations.

We might expect to find an answer in the psychology of the Saint himself, for it is he, after all, who is being tempted, and we ought to be able to discover in his response an attitude towards the figures that pass before him, which, if it does not satisfy as an attitude which we might ourselves adopt, would at least provide some point of departure that would permit us to make our way through the pages with greater conceptual ease. But in fact the Saint has no psychology. We cannot tell whether he is stupid or intelligent, whether he is particularly credulous, for the simple reason that he is not adequately situated. A contemplative, outside the world of action, supposed already to hold the world for nought, outside of time in his freedom of vision, he escapes any standard of *vraisemblance* one might wish to apply to him. At the one point, for example, when he seems to enter the human condition by finding Apollonius boring, it then appears, just as we begin to think that his modes of thought are ours, that he was seriously tempted after all. Fortunately our theory of stupidity can come to the rescue and provide the much-needed guidance.

Like *Bouvard et Pécuchet,* the *Tentation* is a citational work. Jean Seznec has identified many of its sources and Michel Foucault has stressed the importance in the work of a multilayered dialectic of text and vision.[32] The word made flesh passes before Saint Antoine just as sentences pass before Bouvard and Pécuchet. The characters attempt to assimilate the word in different ways: Bouvard and Pécuchet, in the mode of *faire,* move through the word to practical activity, whereas Saint Antoine, in the mode of *être,* seeks a condition, a belief that will inform his existence. But in both cases the text juxtaposes its citations in paradigms of non-functional contradictions which make all views seem stupid. And whereas for Bouvard and Pécuchet this is cause for despair and annoyance, since they do not know what to do and whatever they do seems to fail, for Saint Antoine, who is approaching the citations in a different mode, the problem seems more acute and at the same time more foolish. Since he has no practical goal like grafting fruit trees or making radishes grow he could simply turn away from these juxtaposed visions. Why does he not do so?

The answer, at least in part, might be a purely empirical one: he is alone and bored and has nothing better to do. But as the temptations progress and the narration continues at the second level of stupidity, isolating and juxtaposing them, making them objects, Saint Antoine begins to accede to the third level of stupidity and find them attractive *because* rather than in spite of their foolishness. If one attempts to trace this movement one finds that one proceeds through most of the versions of stupidity encountered elsewhere in Flaubert.

First of all, for example, we encounter intelligence and theory as manifestations of *bêtise.* Hilarion, who replaces in the final version the eighth mortal sin of 'logic' that appeared in earlier versions, overwhelms Antoine in argument by citing scripture, bringing out contradictions in it and in the Christian tradition. He then brings before Antoine a babble of heretics all shouting contradictory precepts and doctrines:

> *Marcion*: le Créateur n'est pas le vrai Dieu!
> *Saint Clément d'Alexandrie*: La matière est éternelle!
> *Bardesanes*: Elle a été formée par Sept Esprits planétaires.

Les Herniens: Les anges ont fait les âmes!
Les Priscillianiens: C'est le Diable qui a fait
 le monde!

         (I, 536)[33]

When Antoine asks, 'Who was Jesus?' he receives thirteen different replies. And when he calls them liars they reply in chorus:

> Nous avons des martyrs plus martyrs que
> les tiens, des prières plus difficiles, des
> élans d'amour supérieurs, des extases
> aussi longues.
> *Antoine*: Mais pas de révélation! pas de
> preuves!
> Alors tous brandissent dans l'air des
> rouleaux de papyrus, des tablettes de
> bois, des morceaux de cuir, des bandes
> d'étoffe (I, 540).[34]

We are clearly confronted here with a distancing and reductive mode of perception which reduces theories to ridiculous objects.

Then we encounter the comical pride and boring self-satisfaction of Apollonius, who speaks at such great length of his life, works and virtues (echoed by his foolish acolyte, Damis), that even Antoine becomes bored: 'What are they getting at?' 'They babble on as if they were drunk'; 'Excuse me, strangers, it is late'; 'Stop it'; 'Enough' (I, 548-9). But when he is gone Antoine admits,

> Celui-là vaut tout l'enfer! Nabuchodonosor ne
> m'avait pas tant ébloui. La Reine de Saba ne m'a
> pas si profondément charmé. Sa manière de parler
> des dieux inspire l'envie de les connaître (I, 551).[35]

It is perhaps here that he begins to feel the attractions of stupidity, for immediately afterwards, as all the images that men have worshipped pass before him and Hilarion, they enjoy themselves tremendously, holding their sides with laughter. But his development is by no means complete, for as the images come nearer to human forms 'they irritate Antoine more' and he finally recoils in horror from a huge iron statue, like that in *Salammbô,* whose innards contain a furnace for the sacrifice of children.

Next we have *bêtise* as solidified language in the person of the Buddha. 'I too have done astounding things', he begins, an old man recounting his youth. 'I used to eat only one grain of rice per day—*and* the grains of rice in those days weren't as big as they are today.' Or, 'I remained immobile for six years'. All this is recounted in rather a comic mode: 'Having defeated the Devil, I spent twelve years living exclusively on perfumes'; then, since I had acquired the five virtues, the eighteen substances, etc., I became the Buddha.

"All the gods bow; those with several heads bow them all simultaneously.'

The Buddha is followed by other Gods, who first interest and then tire Antoine; but at the end, after Jehovah, comes the Devil who, bearing him off to the heavens, offers knowledge. His lesson is that the world has no goal and God is 'la seule substance', matter itself. And this, once Antoine is back on earth, seems the last necessary step in his education in stupidity. All matter is finally divine, but it does not have immediate meaning, for the forms it takes are epiphenomena. Hence there is no reason to try to understand them; one may regard them simply as matter, as objects in which or through which reverie may glimpse the transcendental *signifié* of the divine. And so, as the monsters pass before him—les Nisnas, les Blemmyes, les Cynocéphales, le Sadhuzag, le Martichoras—he feels a natural horror but also a definite attraction. And when the Catoblépas, a black buffalo with the head of a pig that drags on the ground at the end of a long thin neck, speaks to him, he is sorely tempted: 'Sa stupidité m'attire.' Surrounded by monsters of all kind, animal, vegetable, and mineral, he finds suddenly, like Jules in his terrifying encounter with the dog, that 'il n'a plus peur' and he shouts out his desire to become one with the universe, to take on all the forms he has observed, 'être en tout, . . . être la matière!' (I, 571).

The fact that the sun then rises, bearing on its face the image of Christ, and that Antoine returns to his prayers, renders highly ambiguous the problem of temptation: has God at the last moment saved him from his desire to become matter, or is the sunrise merely an ironic comment on the structure of temptation which will require Antoine to begin his cycle again? The tale of temptation does not conclude, but the moments of Flaubertian stupidity give the work a certain unity. The attitude of mind which makes the vast collection of heresies, theories, images, and objects into instances of stupidity does not dispense with them but makes them more powerful as temptations, since in them the mind can attain the kind of exaltation and freedom which Antoine expresses in his final paragraph. The supreme accomplishment of stupidity as both a property of objects and a mode of vision would be to overcome all alienation by making the actual forms of the world disappear and allowing the mind itself to create the world out of a universal and undifferentiated matter. But to state that proposal would be itself stupid, which is perhaps why the drama cannot conclude.

I write at length of stupidity not because of a strong interest in Flaubert's mental pathology but because the structure of the concept seems to give an organization to attitudes which determine Flaubert's literary practice. In recognizing the importance of the concept I am not claiming, with Sartre, that Flaubert was always defined for himself as a stupid man, *l'Idiot de la famille,* though in comparison with analytically-minded contemporaries like Kierkegaard and Marx he was, as Valéry said, 'a very tolerable artist but without much grace or profundity of mind'.[36]

What I should want to maintain, though, is that a desire not to understand, not to grasp the purposes that language, behaviour, and objects serve in ordinary practical life, is one of the determining features of Flaubert's writing. Granted, he puts it somewhat differently: 'A force de vouloir tout comprendre, tout me fait rêver' (i, 192). But he recognizes that understanding has been displaced by reverie, though he might prefer to think of reverie as beyond understanding. And he grasps also the connection with stupidity, for he moves immediately to deny it: 'Il me semble, pourtant, que cet ébahissement-là n'est pas la bêtise.' He is right in that it is not mere foolishness but complex stupidity as a mode of perception and source of value, which transforms 'le bourgeois', as he says, into 'quelque chose d'infini'. Stupidity, as a refusal to understand, negates ordinary meaning to replace it with an open and exploratory reverie. To see how this was done in the novels one must consider the style which was to make the world stupid while remaining itself an object of admiration. To comprehend the world without understanding it, to treat men, for example, as mastodons or butterflies and to fix them sprawling on a pin, was the task of Flaubertian irony.

Notes

[1] 'With stupidity the Gods themselves struggle in vain.' 'Stupidity and Poetry. There are subtle relationships between these two orders; the order of stupidity and the order of poetry.'

[2] The mis-spellings are Flaubert's. 'Since there's a woman who comes to Papa's house and who always tells us stupid things I will write them.'

[3] 'I am up to the neck in young girls' dreams.' 'At the moment I'm making all the gods speak on their death-beds. The subtitle of my book could be: "The height of insanity." ' 'Nothing is so exhausting as delving into human stupidity.' 'I am overrun by the stupidity of my two chaps.'

[4] *Selected Literary Criticism,* [ed. M. Shapira (Penguin, Harmondsworth, 1968)], p. 187.

[5] 'One can bet that any public notion, anything conventionally accepted, is a stupidity, since it has suited the greatest number.'

[6] Henceforth in citing the *Dictionnaire des idées reçues* I shall simply italicize the word under which the entry is to be found.

[7] [Jean-Paul Sartre, *L'Idiot de la famille* (Gallimard, Paris, 1971-), 4 vols], I, 635.

[8] See the 'Postface' to Barthes' *Mythologies* (Seuil, Paris, 1957).

[9] E. and J. de Goncourt, *Journal,* 17 December 1873.

[10] Sartre, *L'Idiot de la famille,* II, 1245.

[11] 'It would be bloody good fun to propose it to her. Can you imagine the bill the Garçon would make out in this situation? "For the company of a man like myself, so much. Extra charges: for having made a clever remark, for having been charming and polite, etc."'

[12] 'I shout aloud, I laugh, I drink, I sing out, ha! ha! ha! ha! ha! ha!, and I give the Garçon's laugh, I beat on the table, I pull out my hair, I roll on the floor.'

[13] [Roland Barthes, *S/Z* (Seuil, Paris, 1970)], p. 212.

[14] 'I want to produce such an impression of weariness and boredom that one might believe in reading the book that it had been written by an imbecile.'

[15] Sartre, *L'Idiot de la famille,* II, 1505.

[16] 'What a strange life a man must lead who stays there, in that little cabin, moving the two keys and pulling the wires; the unintelligent cog in a machine which is mute for him, he can die without having known any of the events he has been informed of, any of the many words he has transmitted. The point? the point? the significance? Who knows? . . . Are we not all, a bit more or less, like this worthy fellow, speaking words we have been taught and which we learn without understanding them?'

[17] Claude Lévi-Strauss, *Le Totémisme aujourd'hui* (PUF, Paris, 1962), p. 130.

[18] Marie-Jeanne Durry, *Flaubert et ses projets inédits,* [(Nizet, Paris, 1950)], p. 349.

[19] 'Roman et objects: l'exemple de *Madame Bovary,*' *Europe* 485-7, 'Flaubert', (Sept-Nov, 1969), p. 186.

[20] 'People were resting their two hands on their two thighs.' *Ibid.,* p. 187.

[21] 'The "stupidity" of everything makes itself felt. Stupidity, that is to say particularity as opposed to generality. "Smaller than" becomes the awful sign of mind. The demon of possible orderings.' *Oeuvres* (Pléiade, Paris, 1960), II, 64.

[22] Cf. *Madame Bovary—Nouvelle version,* ed. J. Pommier and G. Leleu (Corti, Paris, 1949), p. 458;

and Maxime du Camp, extract from *Souvenirs littéraires,* in Flaubert, *Oeuvres complètes* [ed. Bernard Masson (Seuil, Paris, 1964), 2 vols.], I, 29.

[23] [Albert Thibaudet, *Gustave Flaubert* (Gallimard, Paris, 1935)], p. 96.

[24] *La Pensée sauvage* (Plon, Paris, 1962), pp. 34-6.

[25] Michel Crouzet, 'Le Style épique dans *Madame Bovary'*, *Europe* 485-7 'Flaubert' (Sept-Nov, 1969), p. 159.

[26] Though I am much indebted to Sartre's brilliant discussion of reading (*L'Idiot de la famille,* II, 2028-42), I should like at least to dissociate myself from the reasoning by which he decides that Flaubert does not read books from beginning to end.

[27] Cf. Sartre, *L'Idiot de la famille,* II, 1703-6.

[28] *Ibid.,* II, 2042.

[29] *L'Idiot de la famille,* I, 628, Cf. I, 626-9.

[30] *The Concept of Irony,* p. 274.

[31] *Ibid.*

[32] Seznec, *Les Sources de l'episode des dieux dans la Tentation de Saint Antoine* (Vrin, Paris, 1940) and *Nouvelles Etudes sur la Tentation de Saint Antoine* (Warburg Institute, London, 1949). Foucault, 'La Bibliothèque fantastique' in *Flaubert,* ed. Raymonde Debray-Genette (Didier, Paris, 1970).

[33] '*Marcion:* The Creator is not the true God!

Saint Clement of Alexandria: Matter is eternal!

Bardesanes: It was created by the seven Planetary Spirits.

The Hernians: The angels made souls!

The Priscillianians: The Devil made the world!'

[34] 'We have martyrs more martyred than yours, more difficult prayers, better outbursts of love, and trances at least as long.

Antoine: But no revelation, no proofs!

Then all wave in the air papyrus rolls, wooden tablets, scraps of leather, cloth strips.'

[35] 'That one is worth all the rest of hell. Nebuchadnezzar did not dazzle me as much, nor the Queen of Sheba charm me so deeply. His way of speaking of the gods makes one want to know them.'

[36] *Oeuvres,* I, 613. . . .

Michal Peled Ginsburg (essay date 1983)

SOURCE: "Representational Strategies and the Early Works of Flaubert," in *Modern Language Notes,* Vol. 98, No. 5, December, 1983, pp. 1248-68.

[*Focusing in particular on Flaubert's early works, Ginsburg attempts in the following essay to demonstrate "how the problematic nature of representation and of the self dictates a certain number of narrative strategies which then determine the plot, themes, and narrative voice of [Flaubert's] works."*]

The radical change which Flaubert criticism has undergone in recent years has as one of its effects the possibility of seeing for the first time the work of Flaubert as a whole. Not only because certain works are finally admitted into the canon, but mainly because it becomes more and more evident that beyond the superficial differences which seem to oppose the **Tentation de Saint Antoine** to **Madame Bovary** or **Madame Bovary** to **Bouvard et Pécuchet** the Flaubertian text has some constant features which give it its particularity.

I will argue that these features result from narrative strategies Flaubert adopts in order to overcome basic problems of representation created by his text. It should be stated from the outset that my analysis itself is inscribed within (and even shaped by) a growing awareness in recent criticism of the problematic nature of representation.[1] This theoretical awareness has as one of its "sources" the practice of certain writers, among them Flaubert, while on the other hand it generates new readings of those writers, "creates" a new Flaubert. This interchange between text and theory, where each can be seen as generating and determining the other, is one of the issues at stake in the problematization of the concept of representation. The questioning, or "deconstruction," of the concept of the representation involves a demonstration that the opposition between experience and representation (or, in terms of literary analysis, between text and interpretation) is generated by a mis-recognition of the derived nature of experience and of the originative character of representation, that is to say, the mis-recognition of the impossibility to separate and oppose these terms. A similar critique would apply to the concept of the subject where not only the primacy of the self over language is put into question but where also it can be argued that while the subject projects (or creates) an image of himself, it is this image which creates him, constitutes him as a self.[2] These "theoretical" problems are in some way or another already thematized in the text of Flaubert, especially through his preoccupation with the relation between experience and language. What I intend, however, to show in this paper is how the problematic nature of representation and of the self dictates a certain number of narrative strategies which then determine the plot, themes, and narrative voice of his works.

These strategies can be discerned quite easily in the early works where the search for an adequate mode of narration is all too clear: the ***Mémoires d'un fou, Novembre,*** and the first ***Education sentimentale.*** Each of these works is composed of heterogeneous elements: in the ***Mémoires*** the fifteenth chapter, relating the story of the two English girls, is written in an ironic style that contrasts with the tone and narrative tradition of the rest of the work.[3] In ***Novembre*** the confessional mode is broken by the interpolated story of Marie, and with the second narrator the narration changes from first to third person. The ***Education*** is narrated partially in the first person (letters), partially in the third. This absence of narrative unity is not simply the result of lack of craftsmanship in the young Flaubert. The narrative impasses which dictate the change in narrative mode result from a basic problem in generating the text and this problem lingers in Flaubert's work to the end. An analysis of the early narratives will help us understand the subsequent works of Flaubert.

I

The problem of representation which Flaubert faces is clearly formulated in the Dedication of the ***Mémoires:*** "Ces pages . . . renferment une âme toute entière. Est-ce la mienne? est-ce celle d'un autre?"[4] Having completed his autobiographical text, the narrator doubts whether he is really its subject matter, and as a reader of his own text he finds himself alienated from himself. The "I" plays here the roles of narrator, character, and reader, but this fusion does not generate unity. Though he writes about himself, the narrating-I necessarily creates a character which, once created, seems to have a life of its own and hence escapes his control: "Ces pages . . . renferment une *âme* toute entière . . . peu à peu, en écrivant . . . l'*âme* remua la plume et l'écrasa" (p. 230, my emphasis). The "soul," by being represented, becomes independent and different from the narrator who, hence, at the end no longer recognizes himself in it. This feeling of alienation, the loss of the self through self-representation, which the retrospective Dedication formulates so clearly, is present throughout the ***Mémoires*** and governs its movement.

From the beginning of the ***Mémoires*** one finds that writing involves externalizing part of oneself and giving that projected part a certain independence. The process of projection is made manifest by the visual nature of the act of narration. In the ***Mémoires,*** from the moment the narrator starts to narrate, he *sees.* And as he tells about himself, or more precisely about the writer he is trying to become, it is not surprising that he does not simply see himself, but rather sees himself seeing, that is to say, sees himself as one who sees a spectacle which his imagination has created:

Je fus au collège dès l'âge de dix ans . . .

J'y vécus . . . seul et ennuyé . . .

Je me vois encore, assis sur les bancs de la classe, absorbé dans mes rêves d'avenir, pensant à ce que l'imagination d'un enfant peut rêver de plus sublime . . .

Je me voyais jeune, à vingt ans, entouré de gloire . . . je voyais l'Orient et ses sables immenses, ses palais que foulent les chameaux avec leurs clochettes d'airain; je voyais les cavales bondir vers l'horizon rougi par le soleil; je voyais des vagues bleues, un ciel pur, un sable d'argent; je sentais le parfum de ces océans tièdes du Midi; et puis, près de moi, sous une tente, à l'ombre d'un aloès aux larges feuilles, quelque femme à la peau brune, au regard ardent, qui m'entourait de ses deux bras et me parlait la langue des houris.

(p. 232)

The structure *en abîme* of this passage (in which the narrator sees a school boy who sees a young man who sees an oriental scene) suggests that in Flaubert both reminiscing and imagining—autobiography and fiction—have the structure of a spectacle, are both an externalization of part of the self which the self then can watch. The difference between the two is only in the degree of differentiation and independence which the spectacle is given. The oriental scene would no longer be an "autobiographical" account of the imagining of an (imaginary) young man, and become a "story" of oriental passion if the woman—the spectacle which the self has projected—could gain some life of her own, that is to say, become independent and different from her creator. However, as the Dedication has shown, such differentiation also takes place in autobiography, so that every autobiography is to some extent fictive. This awareness jeopardizes the whole enterprise of the ***Mémoires,*** which is based on the assumption that the self can translate its own unique story into language.

Moreover, the logic of the structure is such that the more the spectacle is differentiated, the more it is independent of its creator—the more fictive it is—the more it can generate a narrative. This means that in Flaubert the intention to narrate is always in conflict with the narcissistic interest of the subject to unite with his own mirror image.

For Flaubert creating means projecting a part of the self, giving birth to an image which can be called "I," "a madman," "woman," "the world," and so on. This image, in order to live, must become differentiated from the self; it becomes actually so different that, as the Dedication has shown, it cannot be recognized as an image of the self anymore. The mirror image is hence threatening and inherently hostile since it usurps the place of the self and thus annihilates it. The creation of the spectacle entails an aggressive conflict between creator and spectacle, between the "I" and a hostile world: the fellow students who ridicule him, the father who mutilates him, the castrating woman. What is important to note is that in Flaubert the representation of the world as antagonistic is not simply the restatement of the romantic cliché of the individual singularity in danger of being destroyed by a world that does not understand it; it is, rather, a necessity of the representation.

The narrator of the *Mémoires* can see only one solution to the threat presented by the spectacle he has created: he destroys his creation, eliminates the spectacle. The sequence of the two dreams the narrator relates (chapters IV and V) articulates the threat which the differentiated spectacle represents for the self and the destruction of the created image which follows. In the first dream the spectacle the narrator has projected (the "vision" he sees) threatens to mutilate him. Hence, in the second dream the mother, the mirror image, is destroyed. The mother is clearly the narrator's narcissistic double: trying to see her when she calls for help he looks at his own reflection in the water: "j'étais avec ma mère qui marchait du côté de la rive; elle tomba. . . . Je me penchai à plat ventre sur l'herbe pour regarder, je ne vis rien; les cris continuaient" (p. 233). It is true that in this passage the elimination of the other is not represented as a deliberate murder but as an inevitable catastrophe; but its voluntary aspect will become apparent as it is repeated.

The rhythm of the *Mémoires* is that of creation, differentiation, fear of this differentiation, and elimination. As the annihilation of the created spectacle rules out continuation of the story, the whole cycle must start again.

The narrator of the *Mémoires* tries out different strategies that would allow the narration to continue without endangering him. When he evokes his past, for example, he is careful not to give the spectacle he creates so much life that he cannot control it: the past is hence presented as dead: "une série de souvenirs . . . passent tous confus, effacés comme des ombres. . . . souvenirs calmes et riants . . . vous passez près de moi comme des roses flétries . . ." (p. 235). In the main episode, that of Maria, the narrator attempts to keep a strenuous balance between existence and annihilation of the mirror image. The narrator first encounters Maria when he saves her coat from the water, the water from which he did not want to (or could not) save his mother. But Maria is "saved" only to be repeatedly in danger of drowning and her footsteps are constantly being wiped out by the waves ("La vague a effacé les pas de Maria," p. 237). In addition, though described as a rather large, dark woman, with

"expression mâle et énergique" (*ibid.*), Maria remains a shadow because the narrator refuses to give her flesh and blood. The very thought of her as a living body, full of desire, fills him with rage (p. 239). Instead of giving her a voice of her own, he simply reports that she talked and that "Maria et moi nous étions parfaitement du même sentiment en fait d'art" (p. 238). Giving her a voice of her own would be to establish, side by side with her similarity to himself, her complete otherness, her existence as a separate entity independent of him and hence a threat to his unity and integrity as a self. Maria remains a fleshless, voiceless figure, object of a platonic love, because the narrator cannot face making her a living creature; but, on the other hand, he cannot sustain a narrative around this spectral figure. Hence, the narrative stops and starts again with the story of the two English girls.

This episode too begins with the creation of a spectacle:

> Parmi tous les rêves du passé, les souvenirs d'autrefois et mes réminiscences de jeunesse, j'en ai conservé un bien petit nombre, avec quoi je m'amuse aux heures d'ennui. A l'évocation d'un nom tous les personnages reviennent, avec leurs costumes et leur langage, jouer leur rôle comme ils le jouèrent dans ma vie, et je les vois agir devant moi comme un Dieu qui s'amuserait à regarder ses mondes créés.
>
> (pp. 239-40)

The spectacle is described as both alive (the characters can act in front of him) and dead ("comme un cadavre," p. 240). We have seen that this is an aggressive measure by which the narrator protects himself against his creation. But the distinctiveness of this episode is that the annihilation of the spectacle is brought about neither by placing it on the border between existence and death, nor by characterizing it as ephemeral and insubstantial. Rather, the narrator protects himself against his narration by showing its imaginary and inauthentic character.

The main text of the *Mémoires* is based on the assumption that the self can tell its own story in language. The narrator presents himself as a madman, "image hyperbolique d'une singularité, d'une subjectivité exacerbée"[5] and in dwelling on the story of his youth, virginity, and first love, he presents himself and his desires as original and hence authentic. He trusts in the capacity of language to express his subjectivity and therefore posits an adequacy between the subject and his language: "Seulement tu croiras peut-être, en bien des endroits, que l'expression est forcée et le tableau assombri à plaisir; rappelle-toi que c'est un fou qui a écrit ces pages . . ." (p. 230). The particular character of language is accounted for by the individuality of the person who uses it. In the episode of the two English girls, however, this notion of originality, in matters both of love and of literary expression, is consciously and deliberately undermined.

The audience of friends to whom the narrator tells this episode serves as an ironic deflation of the narrator's beliefs: "par hasard, j'avais du papier et un crayon, je fis des vers . . . (Tout le monde se mit à rire)" (p. 241); "—Voilà que tu vas devenir bête, dit un des auditeurs en m'interrompant" (p. 240). The notion of spontaneity and hence originality and authenticity of expression is undermined by being exposed as in itself a literary cliché. Instead of a genuine, original desire, which can be spontaneously expressed in language, we find that self, desire, and language are inauthentic, a result of imitation and self-suggestion:

> . . . mais ces vers, pour la plupart étaient faux . . .

> Je me battais les flancs pour peindre une chaleur que je n'avais vue que dans les livres; puis, à propos de rien, je passais à une mélancolie sombre et digne d'Antony . . . et je disais à propos de rien:

> Ma douleur est amère, ma tristesse
>   profonde,
> Et j'y suis enseveli comme un homme en la
>   tombe.

> (p. 241)

The narrator realizes that language, whether that of the poets or that of his own poems, rather than expressing his desire, creates it, bringing into being his image as a desiring self. In other words, he sees that he does not have a self that precedes its (re)presentation in language. But this (re)presentation which creates him also brings about, as he has already discovered, his death, since he cannot recognize himself in the self he has created. The precarious situation between life and death which his creation occupies is thus a necessary feature of representation. The self discovers that it is always already double, alienated from itself, aggressive and subject to aggression, in a precarious balance between life and death.

In the *Mémoires,* however, this insight remains without consequences; after a moment of lucidity the narrator falls back into mystification, claiming that doubling and fictionality are the result of representation and not features of experience itself. Hence, when he realizes that his work is a failure, he says: "quelle vanité que l'art! vouloir peindre l'homme dans un bloc de pierre ou l'âme dans des mots, les sentiments par des sons et la nature sur une toile vernie . . ." (pp. 242-43). But the insights of the episode of the two English girls are not lost; they are further developed in *Novembre.*

II

Novembre repeats in many ways the movement of the *Mémoires.* It also starts with the doubling of the self and the creation of a spectacle. On the first page of *Novembre,* for example, one reads: "ma vie entière s'est placée devant moi comme un fantôme . . . mes pauvres années ont repassé devant moi . . . une ironie étrange les frôlait et les retournait pour mon spectacle . . ." (p. 248); "la vie m'apparaissait de loin avec des splendeurs et des bruits triomphaux . . ." (p. 249). But what *Novembre* makes explicit is the erotic character of the experience of doubling. The narrator externalizes a part of himself that, under its feminine form, he wants to join sexually:

> Oh! que ne pouvais-je presser quelque chose dans mes bras, l'y étouffer sous ma chaleur, ou bien me dédoubler moi-même, aimer cet autre être et nous fondre ensemble. . . .

> Mes lèvres tremblaient, s'avançaient, comme si j'eusse senti l'haleine d'une autre bouche, mes mains cherchaient quelque chose à palper . . . et je remuais les cheveux autour de ma tête, je m'en caressais le visage . . . j'aurais voulu . . . être la fleur que le vent secoue, la rive que la fleuve humecte, la terre que le soleil féconde.

> (p. 258)

It is this erotic-narcissistic doubling, with its rhythm of differentiation and assimilation, which generates the main part of *Novembre,* the episode with the prostitute Marie.

Marie is clearly the narrator's specular opposite: "ta vie et la mienne, n'est-ce pas la même?" (p. 269); "sans nous connaître, elle dans sa prostitution et moi dans ma chasteté, nous avions suivi le même chemin, aboutissant au même gouffre; pendant que je me cherchais une maîtresse, elle s'était cherché un amant, elle dans le monde, moi dans mon coeur; l'un et l'autre nous avaient fuis" (p. 268). Marie is his mirror image not only on the erotic but also on the narrative level. She is a "narrator" who uses the cliché language of the novels and poems that created the desire of the narrator: " 'Ange d'amour, de délices, de volupté, d'où viens-tu? où est ta mère? à quoi songeait-elle quand elle t'a conçu? rêvait-elle la force des lions d'Afrique ou le parfum de ces arbres lointains, si embaumants qu'on meurt à les sentir?' " (p. 262). She fictionalizes him, makes him the idealized subject of her own narration in the same way that in the *Mémoires* he created a fiction of Maria: she creates him as an idealized man and lover ("ange d'amour"), attributes to him a perfect mistress ("il me semblait qu'avec ces mots elle me faisait une maîtresse idéale," *ibid.*), and describes all the cliché situations of a "roman d'amour": " 'Ta maîtresse t'aime, n'est-ce pas? . . . Comment vous voyez-vous? est-ce chez toi, ou chez elle? est-ce à la promenade, quand tu passes à cheval? . . . au théâtre, quand on sort et qu'on lui donne son manteau? ou bien la nuit, dans son jardin?'" (*ibid.*).

Marie then is a double in which the narrator can see himself. But she is also a double which is well developed and alive: being a prostitute, Marie, unlike Maria of the *Mémoires*, is necessarily given a bodily existence, and again, unlike Maria, she has a voice and a life of her own which she herself narrates. Thus what was desperately avoided in the *Mémoires* can take place here: the double takes on flesh and bone to such an extent that it threatens to annihilate the narrator. Not only on the erotic level, where Marie's desire seems to gain frightening dimensions: " 'Oui, oui, embrasse moi bien, embrasse-moi bien! tes baisers me rajeunissent . . .' Et elle s'appuya la bouche sur mon cou, y fouillant avec d'âpres baisers, comme une bête fauve au ventre de sa victime" (p. 263), but also on the level of narration. After all, from a certain point on, it is Marie who becomes the narrator, usurping the first person.

Thus the double which the "I" has created, by gaining life and independence, threatens to annihilate him both erotically and verbally (both as a hero and as a narrator). In other words, the "I" is faced with the necessity of giving up "romantic" autobiography, which proved to be impossible, for the sake of "realistic" fiction. During the Marie episode he is not yet ready for this. He hastens to eliminate Marie as a vital force and keeps her as a memory, well under his control. Though Marie is much more alive and independent than Maria, a step forward towards "creation," the same destiny awaits both. But the difference between them is important and influences the course which each work takes.

In both works, after the disappearance of the desired object (in the *Mémoires* this disappearance is still attributed to chance while in *Novembre* its deliberate nature is clear[6]), desire increases: "je ne l'aimais pas alors, et en tout ce que je vous ai dit, j'ai menti; c'était maintenant que je l'aimais, que je la désirais; que, seul sur le rivage, dans les bois ou dans les champs, je me la créais là, marchant à côté de moi, me parlant, me regardant" (p. 246), writes the narrator of the *Mémoires*. Similarly, in *Novembre:* "A mesure que le temps s'éloignait, je l'en aimais de plus en plus; avec la rage que l'on a pour les choses impossibles, j'inventais des aventures pour la retrouver, j'imaginais notre rencontre . . ." (p. 270).

These two passages establish a dichotomy between the "real" woman and a "fictive" image which the self creates in the absence of the real object. We know, however, that the "real" object is just as much an imaginary, narcissistic projection. The difference between the "real" and the "imaginary" lies only in the degree of independence the image is granted. The "real" object has been eliminated because its potential difference threatened the integrity of the self; but its annihilation made any further narration impossible. The way the narrator tries now out of this impasse is that of preserving his creation by pretending that it is alive, and hence able to generate a story, while never losing sight of the fact that as a created image it depends on him and cannot threaten him. The same solution of an imaginary substitute is attempted in both *Novembre* and the *Mémoires*, but the imaginary substitute which has satisfied the "I" of the *Mémoires* no longer satisfies the "I" of *Novembre*. In the *Mémoires* we read:

> Un jour je revenais, vers le crépuscule, je marchais à travers les pâturages couverts de boeufs, je marchais vite, je n'entendais que le bruit de ma marche qui froissait l'herbe; j'avais la tête baissée et je regardais la terre. Ce mouvement régulier m'endormit pour ainsi dire, je crus entendre Maria marcher près de moi; elle me tenait le bras et tournait la tête pour me voir, c'était elle qui marchait dans les herbes. Je savais bien que c'était une hallucination que j'animais moi-même, mais je ne pouvais me défendre d'en sourire et je me sentais heureux.
>
> (p. 246)[7]

The narcissistic-onanistic experience, result of the elimination of the other, is satisfactory. Not so in *Novembre:* "Une fois, je marchais vite dans un pré, les herbes sifflaient autour de mes pieds en m'avançant, elle était derrière moi; je me suis retourné, il n'y avait personne. . . . et je suis retombé seul, abîmé, plus abandonné qu'au fond d'un précipice" (pp. 270-71). The "I" who panicked at the strength of his creation, seeing that giving life and independence to it necessarily entails his elimination as a desiring and speaking self, killed his own creation so that he could safely employ himself in imaginary pleasures. The impact, the "reality" of Marie was, however, too strong and the narrator realizes that his attempt, erotic and verbal, is a failure: "C'est pour me la rappeler que j'ai écrit ce qui précède, espérant que les mots me la feraient revivre; j'y ai échoué, j'en sais bien plus que je n'en ai dit" (p. 271).

Hence the end of *Novembre*. The narrator realizes that in order to exist as the other, as his narcissistic projection, the third person, he has to die as an "I." He therefore dies and out of his ashes the second narrator is born.

The second narrator begins by keeping his distance from the first narrator, the subject of his discourse. He does not use the text as an occasion to narrate his own experience or express his own feelings but limits himself to narrating, with some criticism, the life of a character, the first narrator. But gradually he discovers more and more affinity with his character and the critical attitude yields to a feeling of solidarity: "Il avait aussi trop de goût pour se lancer dans la critique; il était trop poète, peut-être, pour réussir dans les lettres" (pp. 273-274). Along with this change in attitude comes a change in the mode of narration: the second narrator starts expressing his own opinions and not only reporting those of the first narrator. His own narrative voice mixes with what he reports and the "je" at times becomes ambiguous:

> Il pensait sérieusement qu'il y a moins de mal à tuer un homme qu'à faire un enfant: au premier vous ôtez la vie . . . mais envers le second, disait-il, n'êtes-vous pas responsable de toutes les larmes qu'il versera depuis son berceau jusqu'à sa tombe? sans vous, il ne serait pas né, et il naît, pourquoi cela? pour votre amusement, non pour le sien à coup sûr; pour porter votre nom, le nom d'un sot, *je* parie? autant vaudrait l'écrire sur un mur . . .

> (p. 273, my emphasis)

It is symptomatic that the fusion between narrator and character occurs in a discussion of birth and murder, creation and destruction, the two poles between which the narration of *Novembre* and the *Mémoires* oscillates.

The menacing power of Marie and the death of the first narrator indicate the dangers that representation entails for the integrity of the self. They operate within the opposition self/representation, experience/language. But *Novembre* actually undermines the opposition between language and experience, which it itself plays out, by showing that doubling and lack of originality, both of which seemed to be the result of the translation of experience into language, already exist on the level of experience. Experience itself has the structure of representation.

Like the *Mémoires, Novembre* starts with the illusion of the originality of experience: "Comme le premier homme créé, je me réveillais enfin d'un long sommeil, et je voyais près de moi un être semblable à moi . . . et en même temps je sentais pour cette forme nouvelle un sentiment nouveau dont ma tête était fière . . ." (p. 251). This belief, however, is soon in conflict with the awareness of the non-originality of desire: "Ces passions que j'aurais voulu avoir, je les étudiais dans les livres" (p. 251).[8] *Novembre* thus restates the conclusions of the episode of the two English girls which the last part of the *Mémoires* tries to obfuscate: as language (both one's readings and one's writings) creates desire, one can say that experience doubles language just as much as language doubles experience. On the levels both of language and of experience *Novembre* shows a disillusionment about the possibility of authenticity and originality. Its sub-title is "Frag-

ments de style quelconque" because, in opposition to the *Mémoires*, style can no longer be seen as a mirror of the self. To the impossibility of original language is linked the impossibility of virgin-desire, thematized in the love episode with the prostitute Marie.[9]

In this respect, again, the difference between the *Mémoires* and *Novembre* becomes clear when we compare two similar episodes. Towards the end of both stories the hero returns to the scene of a crucial experience. This visit dramatizes the structure of memory, the movement of autobiography, and therefore can be taken, in each case, as an emblem of the text as a whole. In the *Mémoires* the visit is an experience of sameness and difference: the place is the same and yet different because the beloved is not there: "Je revoyais le même océan avec ses mêmes vagues . . . ce même village . . . Mais tout ce que j'avais aimé, tout ce qui entourait Maria . . . tout cela était parti sans retour" (p. 246). The pathos of the scene emerges from this opposition between present lack and past plenitude, echoing the view of the *Mémoires* that not experience itself but its doubling in language is faulty and inauthentic. In *Novembre*, on the other hand, the narrator is struck by a more radical form of dispossession: " 'O mon Dieu, se dit-il, est-ce qu'il n'y a pas sur la terre des lieux que nous avons assez aimés, où nous avons assez vécu pour qu'ils nous appartiennent jusqu'à la mort, et que d'autres que nous-mêmes n'y mettent jamais les yeux!' " (p. 276).[10] There never was a place one could call one's own. Lack is not a matter of having lost something, but of never really owning anything. Experience itself, and not simply its representation in language is the scene of loss and division.

Moreover, while the visit at the end of the *Mémoires* is to a place where the narrator-hero was, in however ambiguous and transitory way, in the presence of the "object" of desire, the visit at the end of *Novembre* is to a scene which already in its "first" occurrence was a repetition, to a place where the hero has already felt himself as double and different from himself. The alienation which seemed to characterize representation (and differentiate it from experience), exists already on the level of experience and the lack of coincidence of the self with itself is not simply the result of literary creation but the result of consciousness, which is itself a writing. From the moment there is memory, or desire, or language, that is to say, from the very moment there is a self, the self is divided from itself, double and alienated from itself, and this division is experienced as a loss, but as a loss which has always already occurred and cannot be avoided or made good.

Loss and alienation can be avoided only at the price of narcissistic sterility and destruction; they can however be accepted and manipulated as a source of production. This realization dictates the relation between narrator and character in the first *Education sentimentale*.

III

On one level the first *Education* tells the familiar story of the gradual differentiation between the self and its mirror image which the previous works acted out in spite of their creator. Starting out as specular opposites ("toi, tu voulais une pâle Italienne en robe de velours noir, avec un cordon d'or sur sa chevelure d'ébène, la lèvre superbe, l'allure royale, une taille vigoureuse et svelte, une femme jalouse et pleine de voluptés; moi j'aimais les profils chrétiens des statuettes gothiques, des yeux candidement baissés, des cheveux d'or fin comme les fils de la Vierge," p. 288), Jules and Henry end up utterly different (of a difference which is no more reducible to an economy of the same): "Ils ne pensaient de même sur quoi que ce soit et n'envisageaient rien d'une manière semblable" (p. 366). But the peculiarity of the *Education sentimentale* is that it has as its *starting point* the complete separation between Jules and Henry. And because Jules and Henry are from the very beginning separated, each of them is independent of the other, "free" to live as he finds fitting, and not subjected to the other. While in the previous works the assumption was that a unique self, by the necessities of consciousness, memory, and writing, gave birth to an image of itself of which, as its own creation, it could dispose as it found fitting, the *Education* posits as a point of departure a duality, a division, that is present from the beginning, prior to any act of desire, memory, or writing. This change is a radicalization of the insights gained in the *Mémoires* and *Novembre* where it was shown that the mirror image creates the self just as much as the self creates its mirror image, that a character can become a narrator and a narrator a character, and that language and experience are each the origin of the other. The point of difference between the first *Education* and the *Mémoires* is not so much that one is a novel and the other an autobiography, one in the third person, the other in the first; rather, the difference between the two lies in the fact that in the first *Education* the narrator has stepped out of the narcissistic circle and instead of contemplating his mirror image (as did the second narrator in *Novembre*) sees himself as divided into two.

As the opposition creator/created, narrator/character, self/mirror image proved to be imaginary, the relation between Jules and Henry has to be defined in different terms. As we have seen, the conflict which dictated the movement of the previous narratives is that between, on the one hand, a narcissistic attempt of self to defend its (imaginary) integrity and unity by repressing any indication of its division from itself, and, on the other hand, an awareness that this narcissistic attempt leads to sterility and death and that only by

accepting and exploiting its own alienation can the self continue to live and narrate. In the *Education* these two conflicting attitudes are each developed to its logical end, the first in the figure of Henry, and the second in that of Jules. What was previously represented as different movements in the same story is now seen as two separate and independent possibilities. Through an acceptance of his division (his death as a unique and unified self), the narrator can get out of the vicious circle where projection is always followed by annihilation, creation by destruction.

Henry is the representation of the narcissistic self which refuses, in order to protect its unity, any loss of itself. He does not externalize any part of himself and hence does not see himself as other or in the other. While Jules, experiencing his alienation and difference from himself, "sees" the world as a book where he can read his past ("Etrange sensation du sol que l'on foule! On dirait que chacun de nos pas d'autrefois y a laissé une ineffaçable trace, et qu'en revenant sur eux nous marchons sur des médailles où serait écrite l'histoire de ces temps accomplis, qui surgissent devant nous" p. 350), Henry "looks" at a world totally strange and incomprehensible to him. Arriving at Paris, at the beginning of the novel, Henry walks in the streets and looks:

> Ne sachant que faire les premiers jours, il rôdait dans les rues, sur les places, dans les jardins . . . il s'asseyait sur un banc et regardait les enfants jouer ou bien les cygnes glisser sur l'eau. . . . il regardait les devantures des boutiques de nouveautés . . . il admirait le gaz et les affiches. . . .

> . . . il s'arrêtait, aux Champs-Elysées, devant les faiseurs de tours et les arracheurs de dents; sur la place du Louvre, il passa un jour beaucoup de temps à contempler les oiseaux étrangers. . . .

> Il montait sur les tours des églises et restait longtemps appuyé sur les balustrades de pierre qui les couronnent, contemplant les toits des maisons . . .

> Il entrait dans un café et restait une heure entière à lire la même ligne d'un journal.

> (p. 279)

This passage makes clear the difference between the act of "seeing" (of the *Mémoires,* of *Novembre,* of Jules) and the act of "looking" of Henry. While "seeing" is a projection, a creation of a spectacle, "looking" is a passive fascination with external objects which seem totally incomprehensible because they do not correspond to anything inside. But Henry is not entirely the "idiot" who gazes at incomprehensible objects, passively, open-mouthed; sometimes he looks actively, making sense of what he sees around him, or, in other words, creating a world, projecting a spectacle:

> Il se faisait transporter en omnibus d'un quartier de Paris à l'autre, et il regardait toutes les figures que l'on prenait et qu'on laissait en route, établissant entre elles des rapprochements et des antithèses. . . .

> Il allait au bois de Boulogne, il regardait les jolis chevaux et les beaux messieurs, les carrosses vernis et les chasseurs panachés, et les grandes dames à figure pâle . . . il rêvait, en les contemplant, à quelque existence grasse, pleine de loisirs heureux . . . il se figurait les salons où elles allaient, le soir, décolletées, en diamants. . . .

> *(Ibid.)*

But these moments of imagination and creation are immediately checked and repressed: "Mais, à chaque joie qu'il rêvait, une douleur nouvelle s'ouvrait dans son âme, comme pour expier de suite les plaisirs fugitifs de son imagination" (*ibid.*). The pleasures of the imagination are forbidden for Henry, and by censoring them he gradually eliminates them completely. This is the aspect of annihilation of the spectacle which we have seen in the earlier works and which is now followed to its logical conclusion.

The same repression of creation in the interest of narcissistic unity can be seen in Henry's relation to his past. The retrospective moments in Henry's story are never moments in which he sees his own past self, himself as another. He sees his past in the same way that he sees the world: as a collection of external objects that amaze or amuse him but never show him his own face. After having spent a vacation at home Henry goes back to Paris and passes again the route he has taken six months before, when he first left for the capital:

> Henry s'ennuya pendant toute la route. . . . il se blottit à sa place, se roula sur lui-même comme un limaçon dans sa coquille, et se mit à penser. Il se laissait aller au mouvement de la voiture, qui se balançait doucement comme un navire, au galop de ses six chevaux; il regardait les arbres qui passaient le long de la portière et les mètres de cailloux couchés au bord du fossé. Pour passer le temps, il regarda aussi la mine avinée du gros homme qui dormait et les favoris rouges de l'Anglais.

> En revoyant les lieux qu'il avait vus pour la première fois il y avait six mois, il songea à ce temps passé et à tous les événements qui s'étaient écoulés depuis; cela l'amusa une grande heure.

> (p. 311)

Unlike Jules, or the narrator of the *Mémoires* or *Novembre,* who would have read in this scene their difference from themselves, Henry remains absorbed in external objects and even the regular movement of the carriage, with its lulling effect, does not create the usual movement of self-reflective doubling. The return journey of Henry and Emilie provides an even more striking example. The voyage is a repetition of the voyage to America: they come back on the same boat, take the same cabin, pass the same towns and villages. But unlike the hero of *Novembre* in his visit to X . . . , they do not read in this repetition their difference from themselves: "Du Havre à Paris ils passèrent par les mêmes villages, ils revirent les mêmes arbres, verts comme autrefois et toujours jeunes; ils avaient fleuri deux fois depuis qu'ils ne les avaient vus" (p. 347). Characteristically, the moments that Henry cherishes the most are "ces moments qui s'écoulent vaguement, doucement, sans laisser dans l'esprit aucun souvenir de joie ni de douleur" (p. 284).

Jules, as we have said, represents the other possibility, that of exploiting alienation as a creative power. He starts with the particular Flaubertian predicament of projection. In the third chapter, when he reminiscences in a letter to Henry about their past life and dreams, he evokes the image of the theater where one is in the position of "contemplant sa pensée vivre sur la scène" (p. 280). For Jules, as for the narrator of the *Mémoires,* love is related to the theater, and the desired woman, Lucinde, is the actress, the woman-spectacle. He is subject to auto-suggestion and his words create his desires: "il s'exaltait en écrivant, devenait éloquent à force de parler, s'attendrissait lui-même . . ." (p. 308). But after the disappearance of Lucinde (which is parallel to the disappearance of the woman-spectacle, Marie or Maria, in the earlier works), things change.

In the twenty-first chapter Jules, alone, dreams: he projects his desires, makes them alive, and contemplates them. But this projection, rather than being an attempt to capture himself in the object of his contemplation, becomes an act of renouncement. The act of imagination is seen not as a way of recovering a lost unity, but as a dispersion of the self in the world it created, a loss of the self which emptied itself out in a way which prevents dialectical recuperation. This is because Jules does not arrest his attention on one particular image; his imagination proliferates and shows him different possibilities. The spectacle that Jules creates is full of life, but nevertheless he does not enter into an erotic-narcissistic relation with it as was the case with Marie. Instead, Jules shifts his attention from one image to another and creates a multiplicity of objects: as they are all his image, his projection, none can give him back a unified image of himself. The movement of creation and annihilation, life and death gives way to dispersion, a renouncement of one image for the sake of the possibility of creating another. To limit oneself to one image is to enter into the narcissistic field of love and aggression; in this chapter (which prefigures already the *Tentation de Saint Antoine*) this movement is changed into one of temptation and renouncement and that guarantees the inexhaustible proliferation of creation.

Another change with respect to the earlier works can be seen in the twenty-sixth chapter of the *Education* which describes Jules' encounter with the dog. The full meaning of this passage emerges from a comparison with similar passages in the *Mémoires* and *Novembre:* in all three works we find key passages where a walk in the country, near water, in the grass, describes the act of projection, the creation of the other, mirror image and imaginary object of desire. One may cite two passages from the *Mémoires,* four from *Novembre,* and finally the episode with the dog from the first *Education:*

> Ailleurs, c'était dans une campagne verte et émaillée de fleurs, le long d'un fleuve;—j'étais avec ma mère qui marchait du côté de la rive; elle tomba.
>
> (*Mémoires,* p. 233)

> Un jour je revenais, vers le crépuscule, je marchais à travers les pâturages couverts de boeufs, je marchais vite, je n'entendais que le bruit de ma marche qui froissait l'herbe; j'avais la tête baissée et je regardais la terre. Ce mouvement régulier m'endormit pour ainsi dire, je crus entendre Maria marcher près de moi; elle me tenait le bras et tournait la tête pour me voir, c'était elle qui marchait dans les herbes.
>
> (*Mémoires,* p. 246)

> Je rêvais la douleur des poètes . . . des pages, où d'autres restaient froids, me transportaient . . . je me les récitais au bord de la mer, ou bien j'allais, la tête baissée, marchant dans l'herbe, me les disant de la voix la plus amoureuse et la plus tendre.
>
> (*Novembre,* p. 251)

> Je suis sorti et je m'en suis allé à X . . . ; . . . j'ai d'abord marché dans les sentiers qui serpentent entre les blés; j'ai passé sous des pommiers, au bord des haies; je ne songeais à rien, j'écoutais le bruit de mes pas, la cadence de mes mouvements me berçait la pensée. . . .

> . . . l'esprit de Dieu me remplissait, je me sentais le coeur grand, j'adorais quelque chose d'un étrange mouvement, j'aurais voulu m'absorber dans la lumière du soleil et me perdre dans cette immensité d'azur. . . .
>
> (*Novembre,* p. 256)

> J'allai au bord de la rivière; j'ai toujours aimé l'eau . . .

> . . . écoutant le bruit de l'eau et le frémissement de la cime des arbres, qui remuait quoi qu'il n'y eût pas de vent, seul, agité et calme à la fois, je me sentis défaillir de volupté sous le poids de cette nature aimante, et j'appelai l'amour! Mes lèvres tremblaient, s'avançaient, comme si j'eusse senti l'haleine d'une autre bouche . . .

> L'herbe était douce à marcher, je marchai; chaque pas me procurait un plaisir nouveau, et je jouissais par la plante des pieds de la douceur du gazon. . . .

> Tout à coup je me mis à fuir . . .
>
> (*Novembre,* p. 258)

> Une fois, je marchais vite dans un pré, les herbes sifflaient autour de mes pieds en m'avançant, elle [Marie] était derrière moi; je me suis retourné, il n'y avait personne.
>
> (*Novembre,* p. 270)

> A peu près dans ce temps-là, il arriva à Jules une chose lamentable; il était sorti dans les champs, il se promenait, les feuilles roulaient devant ses pas, s'envolaient au vent, bruissaient sous ses pieds; c'était le soir, tout était calme . . .

> il marchait et pas un autre bruit n'arrivait à ses oreilles.

> Sa pensée seule lui parlait . . .

> Il releva la tête . . .

> Il entendit quelque chose courir dans l'herbe, il se retourna, et tout à coup en chien s'élança sur lui . . .

> Jules reprit sa route . . . il marchait vite, le chien le suivait . . . Le vent soufflait, les arbres, à demi dépouillés, inclinaient leurs têtes et faisaient fouetter leurs rameaux, les feuilles des haies tressaillaient. . . .

> Le chien s'enfuit . . .

> "Il est encore là", se disait-il, et il entendait en effet, derrière lui, toujours quelque chose qui sautillait et courait sur ses talons; il se retournait, il n'y avait personne.
>
> (*Education,* pp. 349-353)

In all these passages the hero is alone and enclosed within himself. His head lowered, he is not concerned with the "real" world outside him; rather, lulled by the sound of his own steps in the grass or by his voice, he projects an image—his mother, Maria, loving nature, Marie—which attracts him erotically. Thus the dog appears in the same landscape as the imaginary other, object of desire; this is why in most of the passage it is referred to as feminine "la bête," "elle." The appearance of the dog is the result of an act of projection as is the appearance of the object of desire and the reaction to it is the same as to the feminine other—fear and attraction.

But the difference between the dog episode and the scenes from the *Mémoires* and *Novembre* is as striking as the similarity. If in the earlier works the self tries to avoid or to destroy the difference between itself and the image it necessarily has to create, in the *Education* the narrator realizes that the most important thing is to keep this difference. This means that the other keeps its basic quality of otherness and is thus inassimilable and unknown. Jules tries in various ways in this episode to understand the dog, make him known, and in this way to abolish the difference between the dog and himself.[11] But these attempts all fail and opening the door to the dog at the end of the chapter, Jules has to accept the dog's otherness and real difference from himself. The dog is an independent creature; it is, one might say, the first real *character* that Flaubert has created. One should note that strictly speaking the dog is a character created by *Jules* and not by the narrator. The scene in this respect announces and repeats the structure *en abîme* which characterizes all the works of Flaubert, and which is most evident in the *Tentation de Saint Antoine*. The possibility of the created world to proliferate and in its turn to create new worlds is a sign of its life and independence of the self which created it. We have seen it already in *Novembre,* when Marie became a narrator and told her story. But while in *Novembre* this life and creativity of the mirror image was dreaded as threatening to the self (when Marie said that she might have a child the narrator fled away, p. 270), in the first *Education* and in later works it is embraced as the only way in which the self, aware of its doubleness, of the fact that it does not exist prior to its (re)presentation of itself as another, can assure its existence by allowing the process of creation and representation to continue.

IV

We have seen how, in his early works, Flaubert adopts certain narrative strategies in order to overcome problems of representation created by his own text. These strategies give shape to the narrative, dictating its plot, characters, themes, and narrative voice. Though we stopped short of the major works we have already seen why and how the most important features of the text come into being: the so-called "objectivity" of Flaubert—his "absence" as a subject from the narrative; the structure *en abîme;* the opacity, incomprehensibility, or lack of significance of his characters;

the serial structure (of temptations in *Saint Antoine,* of lovers, in *Madame Bovary,* of objects of desire, in *Un coeur simple,* of subjects of knowledge, in *Bouvard et Pécuchet*). There is thus a strong and meaningful continuity rather than a break, between the early and the late Flaubert, between the autobiographical writings and the novels, the "romantic" works and the "realistic" ones. The late "realistic" novels are the logical development, the radicalization, of the insights of the early "romantic" autobiographies. Realistic fiction in Flaubert is the (re)presentation of the self as different from itself and not entirely known or controllable.

Notes

[1] This study is a part of a manuscript dealing with the relation between self and discourse in the entire work of Flaubert. The basic argument of this analysis is that the literary text is not a reformulation of a pre-existing meaning which determines it but is rather an "original substitute." This theoretical stance which is taken as a point of departure for the reading of Flaubert is inspired by the work of Jacques Derrida and by psychoanalytical theory, especially in its reformulation by Jacques Lacan. For a discussion of the status of the subject and of discourse in "post-structuralist" thought in general, see Josué V. Harari, "Critical Factions/Critical Fictions," in *Textual Strategies: Perspectives in Post Structuralist Criticism* (Ithaca: Cornell University Press, 1979), pp. 17-72.

[2] This relation between self and mirror image was elaborated by Jacques Lacan. See "Le Stade du miroir comme formateur de la fonction du Je," in *Ecrits* (Paris: Seuil, 1966), pp. 93-100.

[3] Jean Bruneau, *Les Débuts littéraires de Gustave Flaubert 1831-1845* (Paris: Armand Collin, 1962), pp. 254-257.

[4] Gustave Flaubert, *Œuvres complètes* (Paris: Seuil, Coll, L'Intégrale, 1964), I, 230. All references to the works of Flaubert are to this edition and will be given in the text.

[5] Shoshana Felman, "Modernité du lieu commun: en marge de Flaubert: *Novembre,"* *Littérature,* No. 20 (1975), pp. 34-35.

[6] Marie J. Diamond, *Flaubert: The Problem of Aesthetic Discontinuity* (Port Washington, Wisconsin and New York: National University Publication, 1975), pp. 63-64.

[7] For a detailed analysis of this scene, see Jean-Paul Sartre, *L'Idiot de la famille* (Paris: Gallimard, 1971), II, pp. 1526-1528.

[8] See also p. 250: "J'avais tant lu chez les poètes le mot amour, et si souvent je me le redisais pour me

charmer de sa douceur, qu'à chaque étoile qui brillait dans un ciel bleu, par une nuit douce, qu'à chaque murmure du flot sur la rive, qu'à chaque rayon de soleil dans les gouttes de la rosée, je me disais: 'J'aime! Oh! J'aime!' et j'en étais heureux . . ." and p. 269: " . . . j'ai écrit des lettres adressées à n'importe qui, pour m'attendrir avec la plume et j'ai plueré . . ."

[9] Felman, pp. 39-40.

[10] Felman discusses the relation between this visit and the concept of cliché as "lieu commun."

[11] Jonathan Culler, *Flaubert: The Uses of Uncertainty* (Ithaca: Cornell University Press, 1974), pp. 64-66.

A caricature of Flaubert by Eugene Giraud.

Victor Brombert (essay date 1984)

SOURCE: "Flaubert and the Temptation of the Subject," in *Nineteenth-Century French Studies,* Vol. 12, No. 3, Spring, 1984, pp. 280-96.

[*In the following essay, Brombert discusses the concept of the literary subject in Flaubert's works and* *refutes critical "distortions" and "overstatements" which view Flaubert "not only as the direct ancestor of the* nouveau roman, *but as one of the fathers of literary 'modernity'." Brombert argues against applying specific theoretical systems of poetics to Flaubert's works.*]

—Les plus grands . . . reproduisent l'Univers.

—Oh! les *sujets,* comme il y en a.

From Constantinople, during his travels in search of near-Eastern exotica, Flaubert announced to his friend Louis Bouilhet that he has found three literary subjects: a night of Don Juan that would blend worldly and mystical love; the story of Anubis, the woman who wanted to be embraced by a god; the life of a young Flemish virgin who vegetates, dreams, and masturbates in her prosaic provincial setting.[1] Alert readers of Flaubert will recognize germs of *Salammbô, Un Cœur simple,* even *Madame Bovary.* The range seems impressive. Yet interestingly, what worries Flaubert, as he explains to Bouilhet, is that the three subjects are fundamentally one and the same. This sameness annoys him ("ça m'emmerde considérablement"), but also appears to him as an unavoidable law. "On ne choisit pas ses sujets, ils s'imposent," he explains to George Sand a number of years later.[2]

Two important ideas emerge from these letters separated by almost twenty years: the *unity* as well as the *necessity* of a literary project—which is another way of referring to the inner, intimate configuration of a work. Not the least of Baudelaire's achievements as critic is to have perceived, immediately upon the publication of *Madame Bovary,* that there existed a powerful thematic link between this novel and a work as apparently dissimilar as *La Tentation de Saint Antoine,* which he described, with uncanny acumen, even though he knew only the published fragments, as the "chambre secrète" of Flaubert's mind.[3] Baudelaire's very positive stress on resemblance and sameness must have reassured and delighted Flaubert. The diversity and multiplicity of subjects were seen to serve a thematic center. Baudelaire was in a sense answering Flaubert's anxiety expressed in the letter to Bouilhet—an anxiety that corresponds to the deeper search for his literary self during the Oriental journey. "Il me faut connaître la qualité de mon terrain et ses limites avant de me mettre au labourage."[4] The concern for the three subjects is part of a more lasting concern for the very nature and function of a literary subject.

In this one hundredth year of Flaubert's death, it is perhaps time to dispel some misunderstandings that have affected recent discussions of the author's attitude toward the concept of the *subject.* Overstatements, if not downright distortions, have indeed invaded a certain criticism bent on viewing the author of

Madame Bovary not only as the direct ancestor of the *nouveau roman,* but as one of the fathers of literary "modernity".[5] The status of the subject is of particular import, as it affects the notion of referentiality, the production of meaning, and the possibilities of symbolic interpretations.

Contemporary criticism is fond of quoting Flaubert's proclaimed desire to write a book with hardly a subject, a book about nothing at all ("un livre sur rien") that would be held together through sheer power of structure and style. A number of other sallies or paradoxes have been found useful in this effort to enlist Flaubert in the cause of modernity. "On peut écrire n'importe quoi aussi bien que quoi que ce soit," Flaubert affirmed to Louise Colet whom he liked to impress with his literary extremism. Or: " . . . je voudrais faire des livres où il n'y eût qu'à *écrire* des phrases . . .". It is almost as though Flaubert coined the by now commonplace chiasmatic opposition between the story of an adventure and the adventure of a story. Did he not, in speaking about his own uneventful life, describe the act of writing as the real drama, " . . . où les phrases sont des aventures".[6] All this feeds the prevailing notions that Flaubert is interested above all in form; that he engages, as an *experimenter,* in a game of literary structures; that his fiction, projecting the bad conscience of the traditional novel, is committed to the ultimate disappearance of the personage; that he is the first of the nonfigurative novelists, that his books reflect essentially the problematics of textuality.

On the occasion of this hundredth anniversary, *Le Monde* (April 25, 1980) ran a short article entitled "Le premier écrivain moderne." The article, signed Gérard Genette, sums up the modernistic doxa: Flaubert, though choosing the medium of the novel, attempts to escape from the tyranny of storytelling; he not only subverts narrative movement, but eludes meaning, and aims at undecidability; he reaches toward the essence of literature which perversely is its own disappearance. His is the tragedy of a vocation which ultimately tends toward a spoken silence. Genette thus usefully synthesizes what various recent critics have chosen to find and to stress in Flaubert: Maurice Blanchot, the intransitive nature of the literary work; Pierre Bergounioux, the elusiveness of the center of meaning; Claude Burgelin, the self-referential nature of the text; Jonathan Culler, the fundamental questioning of the communicative act. And even Sartre, though he continued until the last to believe in intentionality and meaning, has seen Flaubert as one of the original Knights of Nothingness.[7]

All this is not sheer critical fantasy and willful (or wishful) reading. Flaubert's literary habits and pronouncements, even if one discounts the consciously playful or aggressive nature of some of the paradoxes,

do provide more than a hint of the essentially ironic, perverse, and aporetic nature of his literary idiom. The dogmas of impersonality (" . . . il ne faut pas *s'écrire*"), of the autonomous value of art, of the priority of language (words precede experience), all seem to undermine the conventional notion that literature is *about something,* and that the subject is centrally important. Here again Baudelaire's article anticipates the most recent assessments. Flaubert, according to him, set out to prove that all subjects are indifferently good or bad, that everything depends on literary prowess. This observation, made in 1857, is the more remarkable since Baudelaire could not possibly have known Flaubert's correspondence, and since the latter never expressed his theoretical views in print (though he may, of course, have communicated some of his ideas in unrecorded conversations). But for us, who read his finest letters as rich theoretical texts on the art of the novel, Baudelaire's insight seems to be almost too obvious. For throughout his correspondence, Flaubert repeatedly questions the prestige of the subject and appears to deny the mimetic function of literature.[8]

The insignificance of the subject is by him affirmed not merely as a challenge to the vulgarian and utilitarian thinking of the *caboches épicières,* but as axiomatic: " . . . il n'y a pas en littérature de beaux sujets d'art." Style, form, and point of view (they are often interchangeable) are all that count; and their efficacy and prestige grow in inverse proportion to the deflation of subject matter: " . . . le style étant à lui tout seul une manière absolue de voir les choses." Increasingly so, it would seem, Flaubert moves toward the esthetics of formalism. In a letter to George Sand, in 1876, he wonders why a book, independently of what it purports to say, could not produce the same architectural effect as a Greek temple, through the precision work of its articulations, the texture of its surfaces, the harmony of its structure—thus reaching out toward a form of abstract perfection. But even much earlier, at the time he was still at work on *Madame Bovary,* he could assert that from the point of view of "pure Art" one might say that the subject did not exist.[9]

Such statements amount to a declaration of independence of art. If Flaubert irascibly maintains that the word *subject* is without meaning ("ne veut rien dire"), it is because long before Edouard in Gide's *Les Faux-Monnayeurs,* he is convinced that the truly great works are those that are least dependent on an external reality: " . . . les oeuvres les plus belles sont celles où il y a le moins de matière." The creative pride behind such affirmations casts light on the provocative final sentence of *La Légende de Saint Julien L'Hospitalier:*

> Et voilà l'histoire de saint Julien L'Hospitalier,
> telle à peu près qu'on la trouve sur un vitrail
> d'église dans mon pays.

Not only is the referred to reality here an art work in its own right (the stained glass window of the Rouen Cathedral), but between text and what it refers to no true mimetic relation exists. Flaubert in fact comments revealingly on this fake relation and on the importance of the discrepancy. In a letter to Gustave Charpentier, he imagines with delight the puzzlement of the reader had an illustration of the cathedral window been added to the text: "En comparant l'image au texte on se serait dit: 'Je n'y comprends rien. Comment a-t-il tiré ceci de cela?' "[10]

Of course, Flaubert abhorred the very idea of having his books illustrated. And the gap betwen text and referential reality, as he sees it, not only serves the prerogatives of art, but intensifies the power to perplex and bewilder. The combination of ironic and poetic mystification is a potent temptation for Flaubert. He repeatedly stated that the loftiest art works, the ones that unleash the power to dream, are also *incomprehensible*. Hence the lasting ambition to conceive works that would puzzle and even madden the reader. Two years before his death, he put it explicitly: "C'est mon but (secret): ahurir tellement le lecteur qu'il en devienne fou." The aim was already formulated years before he published his first novel. In a letter to Bouilhet, he dreams of a text so written that the reader would be totally disconcerted (" . . . que le lecteur ne sache pas si on se fout de lui, oui ou non.")[11]

Since this particular declaration of intent relates to the projected *Dictionnaire des Idées Reçues,* one might wish to read it as indicative of a satirical thrust. But much as he admired Voltaire, and despite many satirical elements in his work (Homais, the Club de l'Intelligence, Bouvard and Pécuchet—who, it is worth recalling, are at their most inept when searching for a method to discover literary subjects!), despite telling satirical gifts, one should pay heed to Flaubert's affirmation that he never set out to write satire intentionally. The resistance to his own satirical vein is no doubt, in part, a form of resistance to socio-political encroachments. If Flaubert had an almost visceral aversion (*dégoût physique*) to newspapers, if he found "militant" writing nauseating, this is a sign of a general retreat from the notion of engaged literature. Satire is always, in some form or other, concerned with, and committed to, the problems of the "real" world.[12]

But there is another reason why Flaubert, as artist, almost instinctively mistrusted and eluded satire. And this has to do precisely with an underlying fusion of poetic and ironic objectives—the desire to enigmatize the poetry of his vision. Irony inverts, subverts, camouflages, dissimulates, and recreates, ultimately producing an elegant self-conscious code. Even when communicating, it remains strangely private. Satire on the other hand, pretending to repudiate the Muse for the public weal, is openly indignant, denounces visible vices and follies, and explicitly or implicitly affirms the permanence and priority of a social reality.[13] Viewed in a certain perspective, satire and irony (though one may occasionally serve the other) are hardly compatible in their essence.

The anti-representational, anti-mimetic bias of Flaubert is further sustained by an early conviction that art and life are distinct, even antagonistic realities, that the former is clearly superior to the latter. From his earliest texts on, he repeatedly suggested that life cannot measure up to books. He openly declared his preference for a factitious existence ("vie factice"). Hence the advice given to Louise Colet to indulge not in real debauches, but in those of the imagination. 'Il faut se faire des harems dans la tête, des palais avec du style." Writing is perceived, all at once, as derivative, legitimate self-defense, and hostile substitute for life. Nonliving becomes, as it were, the pre-condition of the artist's vocation. Conversely, non-writing appears as a form of death: " . . . ma non-écriture [. . .] me pèse", he confides to Jules Duplan in a depressed mood. More dramatically still, in a letter to Mᴵˡᵉ Leroyer de Chantepie: " . . . *Pour ne pas vivre,* je me plonge dans l'Art, en désespéré."[14]

Statements such as these help understand why Flaubert's esthetic bias so often takes the form of the very opposite of what his contemporaries, perhaps because it suited them, chose to praise as his "realism."[15] For Flaubert's peculiar love-hate relation to reality nurtures his anti-mimetic stance, making him at times stress the unbreachable hiatus between art and life ("L'art n'est pas la réalité [. . .] il faut bien choisir"), at others point to the need for transcendence: "La Réalité, selon moi, ne doit être qu'un tremplin." Not only is "exact narration" considered impossible and undesirable, but literature's superiority over the plastic arts is largely attributed to its nonreferential status. One might ponder the following declaration in a letter to Duplan: " . . . une femme dessinée ressemble à une femme, voilà tout" [. . .] tandis qu'une femme écrite fait rêver à mille femmes."[16]

One could go on and on marshalling evidence. From where we stand, a century after his death, Flaubert can only too easily be made to loom as a prophet of modernism. There is, however, something partial and self-serving in this critical perspective. To be sure, Flaubert the "homme-plume", as he called himself, lived out the writer's craft as a total vocation; he approached each work as a new problem, as a new challenge; he sought, in the literary experience, the essence of literarity. And between this literarity and the subject matter there existed for him a fundamental gap. Art he always saw as a matter of *excess*: that which could not be made to correspond. He was, at the same time, haunted by the specter of repetition, the paralyzing and silencing effect of any linguistic act, the fear and consolation of being no more than a redundant scribe. Much like the budding poet in **Novembre,** who discovers that he is only a *copyist,* much like Frédéric who is discouraged by the numerous literary echoes he detects in his own writings, Flaubert himself is plagued by the pervasiveness of the *déjà-dit.* Only with him, this self-consciousness turns into an ironic and parodistic strategy that blurs genres and becomes, one might say, creatively deconstructive. And the case for Flaubert's modernity is further strengthened by his deliberate view of himself as a transitional figure, preparing and anticipating the literature of the future. With arrogant humility, he liked to see himself as achieving "ce qu'il y a de plus difficile et de moins glorieux: la transition."[17]

Yet there is something simplistic and downright falsifying in a critical position that sets up Flaubert as the progenitor and exemplar of modernity. His fascination with the past, his allegiance to classical culture, his reverence for those he calls the "pères de l'Art" are demonstrably keener than any of his attitudes towards the to-be-created future. Homer and Shakespeare are literally referred-to as co-workers with God: they are the conscience of the world. Throughout his life, and increasingly so as his own art matured, he felt that only the classics deserved to be read and studied. "Acharnez-vous donc sur les classiques [. . .] ne lisez rien de médiocre," he advises Amélie Bosquet. "Lisez les classiques [. . .] vous avez lu trop de livres modernes," he admonishes another correspondent. As a first rule of literary hygiene, he urges the daily reading of great texts of the past: " . . . *tous* les jours [. . .] lire un *classique* pendant au moins une bonne heure." More significantly, as Sartre so well put it, Flaubert saw himself, while alive, as already posthumous, as integrated into the free-masonry of all the great dead writers of the past, as writing uneasily not for the future (and even less so for the present) but for all those readers who have already, or will have, their place in the vast cemetery of culture.[18] One might add that, temporally speaking, the *futur antérieur* is the symbolic tense of Flaubert's literary calling.

It could be argued, perhaps too cleverly, that a particular type of uneasy relation to past culture is precisely a characteristic of modernity. But such an argument would hardly dispose of deeper contradictions. Flaubert, it should be noted, was quite aware of some of them. "Il y a en moi [. . .] deux bonshommes," he declared: one is in love with lyric outbursts or *gueulades,* the other is determined to observe reality, to seek out and analyze the truth ("qui fouille et creuse le vrai"). He himself diagnosed the compartmentalization of his mind, allowing the most scabrous contradictions to co-exist: "je vis par casiers; j'ai des tiroirs, je suis plein de compartiments." Flaubert's correspondence, so justly praised for its theoretical interest, is in fact a fascinating web of contradictions, of confusing overlaps and blurrings. The key notions of *representation* and *reproduction*—at times opposed to each other, and others almost interchangable—are shifting in meaning and context. The notion of illusion is ill defined, and the concept of *truth,* whether in the guise of "vrai" or "vérité," remains thoroughly inconsistent. "Du moment qu'une chose est vraie, elle est bonne," he writes late in life to George Sand, echoing an early conviction that all great works do reveal a truth ("la vérité qu'elles manifestent et qu'elles exposent"). But his reaction to Zola's *L'Assommoir,* which he qualifies as "ignoble" to the Princess Mathilde, rings another bell. "Faire vrai ne me paraît pas être la première condition de l'art." And pondering over the poor reception of **L'Education sentimentale,** he comes up with an altogether ambiguous statement: "c'est trop vrai et [. . .] il y manque: la fausseté de la perspective."[19]

Granted that some of these inconsistencies have to do with changing contexts and changing interlocutors, it remains that Flaubert's theoretical pronouncements, unless one systematically represses the ones that do not "fit" into a system, seriously complicate the task of defining his critical position. This is especially so if one examines Flaubert's unsteady and constantly shifting attitudes towards the priorities of art and experience. On the one hand, the inferiority of experience is posited as a pre-condition of art: it is the poet's voice, not lived life, that is to provide the raw material for reverie. But on the other hand, experience is considered ineffable, too overwhelming to be spoken. In Beyrouth, looking at the sea and snow-capped mountains, he scorns the nerve ("toupet") of those who dare write descriptions. The one literary lesson of his Oriental trip, he claims, will have been to discourage him for ever writing a single line on the Orient. The impossible mimesis: again looking at the sea, he muses on how radically false any attempted artistic "reproduction" would be. The vanity of art in the face of reality impressed him during his earliest literary efforts. "Quelle vanité que l'art," he writes in **Mémoires d'un fou,** "vouloir peindre l'homme dans un bloc de pierres ou l'âme dans des mots, les sentiments par des sons et la nature sur une toile vernie." The Unsayable haunts the young writer, struck by the inadequacy of language. "Pauvre faiblesse humaine! avec tes mots, tes langues, tes sons, tu parles et tu balbuties"—while the essence of the experience cannot be expressed.[20]

This inexpressible experience, often defined as the *Idea,* is thus surprisingly perceived as beyond words, indeed as independent from words. Flaubert goes so far as to suggest—and this may seem strange in our era of linguistically oriented criticism—the existence of a style without words. The narrator of **Mémoires d'un fou** has learned Byron by heart—in French. The fact that it was a translation does not seem to matter. "La traduction française disparaissait devant les pensées seules, comme si elles eussent eu un style à elles sans les mots eux-mêmes." The corollary of this wordless style is obvious: an experience that lies beyond words, beyond art. "Vaguement je convoitais quelque chose de splendide que je n'aurais su formuler par aucun mot, ni préciser dans ma pensée sous aucune forme . . ."[21]

The problematic relation, in this sentence, between the words "chose", "mot", and "forme" does point to a wavering between two fundamental frustrations: the unattainability of unmediated experience and the futility of the mediation of writing. Flaubert's drama as writer will somehow remain situated between two opposing negations: the denial of the subject and the discredit of linguistic expression. The ambiguity outlasts his adolescence. While writing **Madame Bovary,** he observes, in a manner that seems to displace *bovarysme* from the character to the act of writing: "Nous avons trop de choses et pas assez de formes." Just as Emma's dreams are too big for her house, so Flaubert suffers from a sense of oppressive limitation. The over-abundance of available subject matter ("oh! les *sujets,* comme il y en a . . .") becomes as crushing and as paralyzing to the anguished writer as the endless cortège of heresies in **La Tentation** is to the anguished saint. Already in the first **Education sentimentale,** the one he completed when he was 24 years old, Flaubert had commented on the relation between wealth of subjects and artistic paralysis. The Nineteenth-Century with its Revolutionary background, its Napoleonic saga, its collapsing and reborn regimes, its ideological fermentation, provided a dizzying marketplace of topics. But this wealth itself strikes the young Flaubert as a threatening plethora: " . . . de cette surabondance de matériaux résulte l'embarras de l'art."[22]

We are compelled to return to the central issue of the subject and its status. For if it is indeed tempting to draw up a catalogue of Flaubert's pronouncements deflating the import of the subject, thus lending support to the declared ambition to write a book "about nothing," it is possible also to come up with a no less telling list of conflicting statements, all of which proclaim the subject's centrality. "Il faut que tout sorte du sujet . . . ," he peremptorily informs Louise Colet. It is hard to imagine a more categorical statement. What Flaubert means is that the literary devices, in a viable work, derive from the conceptual thrust of the subject. The subject as matrix: we are far removed from the notion of the generative power of language and rhetoric. Flaubert says as much in a colorful letter to Louis Bouilhet. Literary know-how (the *ruses,* the *ficelles*), and sophisticated self-consciousness are not enough. Masterpieces are conceived only when there is an organizing central principle which Flaubert defines as "l'âme de la chose," and more specifically as the "idée même du sujet." And he pursues this with a series of bold erotic metaphors to stress his misgivings about a literary virtuosity that remains impotent: "Nous gamahuchons bien, nous langottons beaucoup, nous pelotons lentement, mais baiser! mais décharger pour faire l'enfant!"[23]

The conviction that there exists an original bond between subject matter and creativity lies behind countless comments on the importance of the subject. When Flaubert writes that the secret of masterpieces is the concordance between the subject and the temperament of the author, when he repeatedly hopes to find a subject suitable for his own particular temperament ("un sujet dans *ma voix*"), when he flatly states that for a book to be oozing with truth the author must be pregnant with his topic ("bourré de son sujet"), what is involved is the belief in the generative power of the subject. He could not be more explicit about this than in a letter of 1861 to Mme Roger des Genettes; "Un bon sujet de roman est celui qui vient tout d'une pièce, d'un seul jet. C'est une idée mère d'où toutes les autres découlent." The belief in the subject's matricial virtue would explain why, in flagrant contradiction to the claim that there are no "beautiful" subjects, that all subjects can be indifferently good or bad, Flaubert nonetheless remains stubbornly faithful to the notion that the African desert is more inspiring a subject than a vegetable garden or the even more pedestrian *trottoir.* And this would explain why he can get angry with his friend Feydau for supporting precisely the paradoxical notions he himself so often advocated: "Pourquoi tiens-tu à m'agacer les nerfs en me soutenant qu'un carré de choux est *plus* beau que le désert." This disputation with himself has its fictional projections. Thus Pellerin, in **L'Education sentimentale,** whose ideas echo Flaubert's own pronouncements, yet seem to mock them, at the same time rejects the doctrine of realism ("Laissez-moi tranquille avec votre hideuse réalité!"), and reaffirms the priority of the subject's intrinsic value: "Mieux vaut [. . .] le désert qu'un trottoir."[24]

The reaffirmation of the subject's pre-eminence would also explain why, despite disclaimers, Flaubert never gave up an interest in satire, why topicality remained a steady temptation and why, far from signing the death warrant of the personage, he continued to believe in the independent, non-textual reality of his own characters.

The satiric impulse goes back to pre-literary days, when Gustave and his Rouen schoolfriends invented the pre-Ubuesque figure of the Garçon, at once mocker and mocked, an early embodiment of Flaubertian laughter. The Garçon, vulgar and parodistic, seems to undermine and negate. This negation itself is, however, a program; it corresponds to the explicit identification of the roles of thinker and demoralizer: " . . . si jamais je prends une part active au monde ce sera comme penseur et démoralisateur." Jules, the artist as a young man in the first **Education sentimentale,** feverishly collects satirical topics, *matière à satire*: Academicians, police officials, Fourierists and Saint-Simonians, nouveaux riches, Victor Cousin and Pierre Leroux, the platitudes and the hypocrisies of the day. Jules even considers the caricature of caricature, while the author himself parodies the tone of Montesquieu's *Les Lettres persanes*. Quite deliberately, Flaubert accepts, via Jules, the challenge and topicality of the satirical tradition, as he observes that the Turcarets of the Stock Exchange, the Diafoirus at the School of Medicine, and the Brid'oison at the Palais de Justice, are still powerfully alive. The desire to focus satirically on the sociopolitical reality of his own period also comes through in many a letter. Not only does the 19th-century Bourgeois appear to the young writer as a most tempting *enormity* ("Qu'est-ce que celui de Molière à côté?"), but the political utopias of his day strike him as a particularly fertile comic terrain. "Il y a là-dedans des mines de comique immenses, des Californies de grotesque." And it is worth recalling that at the end of his life, as a sequel to the historically rooted *Education sentimentale,* Flaubert had in mind projects (*Napoléon III, Le Préfet*) dealing with life under the Second Empire.[25]

Equally noteworthy is Flaubert's continued belief in the extra-textual reality of his characters. In a letter to Taine, he makes a revealing comment about the unwritten presence of his personages: "Il y a bien des détails que je n'écris pas. Ainsi Homais est légèrement marqué de petite vérole." The unwritten physical detail matters, however, less than the pre-textual or extra-textual, psychological individuation. Flaubert, in his early thirties, speaks of himself proudly as "un vieux psychologue comme moi." He will continue to view the creative effort of the novelist as an inductive process leading to the reconstruction or reproduction of a psychological reality which has a pre-existent, independent status. He in fact congratulates himself precisely on this psychological intuition and reconstruction. "*Bovary* sera [. . .] la somme de ma science psychologique"—and, as he explains to Louise Colet, "n'aura une valeur originale que par ce côté." Even more telling, for it clearly denies the priority of formalistic concerns, is the following appraisal of his achievement in *Madame Bovary:* "Le lecteur ne s'apercevra pas, je l'espère, de tout le travail psychologique caché sous la forme, mais il en ressentira l'effet." This notion of form as hiding a deeper truth certainly does not give much support to linking Flaubert's name to the generation of the *nouveau roman,* a generation that so scornfully denounced what Robbe-Grillet called "les vieux mythes de la profondeur."[25]

Thus, Flaubert himself places curious difficulties in the way of any attempt to canonize him as an apostle of a formalistic, self-referential, intransitive literature devoted to the problematics of its own textuality, a literature whose subject, as Jean Ricardou wants us to believe, is "le fonctionnement du livre" and nothing else.[26] And the greatest difficulties Flaubert places in the way of a post-mortem conversion to this brand of fashionable "modernity" has to do with his insisting that the prime function of literature is to *reproduce* and *represent.*

Reproduction and representation are, of course, far from the same thing, though they tend to overlap in Flaubert's usage. The greatest poets, Flaubert asserts, reproduce the world ("reproduisent l'Univers"). But with equal axiomatic assurance, he declares that the greatest geniuses have never done anything but *represent.* Though the two notions blur, their distinct meanings for Flaubert can be traced. When he refers to reproduction, it seems quite obvious that he means something both more precise and more limited than a totalizing of experience, *a speculum mundi*. The reproduction is, first, that of material reality. His literary self, as he puts it, wants to "faire sentir presque *matériellement* les choses qu'il reproduit." The outer physical reality must come into focus, it is the objective: " . . . il faut que la réalité extérieure entre en nous [. . .] pour la bien reproduire." And Flaubert not only advocates, but practices the close observation of the physical model. While at work on *Un Coeur simple,* he kept a stuffed parrot on his desk, "afin de 'peindre' d'après la nature."[27]

Three images—the eye, the mirror, and the mime—preside over the Flaubertian doctrine of reproduction. Seeing sharply comes first. For anything at all to become interesting, it is enough, he is convinced, to look at it for a long time. Beyond the "voluptuous sensation" that comes with the contemplation of the object, the steady gaze has to do with the conception and delineation of the object as subject. If Flaubert is so pleased to have what he calls a "myopic" vision ("Je sais voir, et voir comme voient les myopes, jusque dans les pores des choses"), it is because he is convinced that all great works depend on the abundance of functional details ("détails intrinsèques au sujet"). This reaffirmation of the subject's centrality and of the detail's specific role in the larger economy of the work, suffices to cast strong doubt on Roland Barthes' somewhat hasty contention that the concrete detail in Flaubert, serving only the illusion of reality ("l'effet de réel"), remains resistant to any structure or meaning.

Flaubert's symbolic myopia is in fact the prerequisite for a larger vision. Flaubert speaks of the need to become the eye of the world (" . . . être oeil, tout bonnement"), to lose oneself in the subject, much as saint Anthony dreams of becoming matter. "A force quelquefois de regarder un caillou, un animal, un tableau, je me suis senti y entrer." The great literary artist, in turn, provides his reader with a supreme ocular and specular experience. Upon reading Shakespeare "on n'est plus homme, on est oeil." The mirror image serves indeed as a mediation between the visionary eye and the spectacle of external reality. "Soyons des miroirs grossissants de la vérité externe." Appropriately, the transition between the reflecting eye and the spectacle is provided by the metaphor of the imitative actor, and more specifically the *mime.* "L'artiste doit contenir un saltimbanque," states the aging Flaubert. But the imitative process depends first of all on the ability to observe. "Pour être un bon mime, il faut [. . .] *voir* enfin les personnes, en être pénétré."[29]

But this mimetic function of art, precisely because of the mediating specular and theatrical metaphors, does not really imply *a reproduction* of a fixed reality. It is here that the other key term, *representation,* serves not as a contradiction but a corrective. Art, says Flaubert, is representation: "nous ne devons penser qu'à représenter." Yet even to "represent" such immaterial realities as "les Passions" or as "l'humanité de tous les temps," Flaubert feels driven to the most painstaking documentation: on agricultural fairs for *Madame Bovary,* death by thirst for *Salammbô,* the symptoms of croup for *L'Education sentimentale,* provincial sites for the setting of *Bouvard et Pécuchet.* Flaubert's principle remains invariable: " . . . connaître les choses avant de les décrire." That of course includes books. The powerful attraction to erudition is, however, not a mere yearning for a sheltered life spent counting "des pattes de mouches;" it corresponds to the conviction that only encyclopedic knowledge can give literary mastery. "Il faudrait tout connaître pour écrire . . ." And Flaubert stresses the encyclopedic nature of this literary documentation: " . . . les livres d'où ont découlé les littératures entières, comme Homère, Rabelais, sont des encylopédies de leur époque . . ." What lurks behind this respect for knowledge and its fecundating power is not only the potential of caricature (and self-caricature) which Flaubert was to exploit fully in *Bouvard et Pécuchet,* but the conviction that no matter how omnipresent the specter of eternal redundance, there is a worthwhile something-to-be-written, that the subject exists, and that it can be communicated—though perhaps only in an enigmatic, or as Flaubert puts it, "incomprehensible" manner. This indeed, for Flaubert, is the paradox of the subject: "J'ai besoin de dire des choses incompréhensibles."[30]

Flaubert himself provides the qualifier to his perplexing relation with the "subject." In the same sentence that prominently features the word *sujet,* the word *illusion* appears as the ironic companion. Literary form, he explains, is achieved only when "l'illusion du sujet nous obsède." Illusion may even be seen to achieve priority in Flaubert's theory of mimesis. "La première qualité de l'Art et son but est l'*illusion.*" Though he boasted that *Madame Bovary* would make his fellow Normans roar with indignation because of the absolutely life-like *couleur normande,* Flaubert was obviously not a dupe of the mimetic fallacy. Writing to Léon Hennique, shortly before his death: "Me croyez-vous assez godiche pour être convaincu que j'aie fait dans *Salammbô* une vraie reproduction de Carthage, et dans *Saint Antoine* une peinture exacte de l'Alexandrisme?" Raymonde Debray-Genette has very shrewdly made the point that when Flaubert speaks of reproduction, the verb "to reproduce" comes heavily loaded with connotations of craft and artifice. What is to be imitated is not nature itself but its devices. It is because of this *artistic* imitation of nature that art appears as a second nature, an analogue. Or rather, it is nature itself that here functions as the metaphor for artistic creation: " . . . habituons-nous à considérer le monde comme une oeuvre d'art, dont il faut reproduire les procédés dans nos oeuvres." The verb "reproduire" is thus emphatically linked to literary technique (*procédés*) rather than a fixed reality.[31]

Mutability is indeed of the essence. Transmutation, recasting, transformation, metamorphosis, are the key images associated with the creative act. "Je désire [. . .] transformer par l'Art [. . .] tout ce que j'ai senti." Or again: " . . . je suis dévoré maintenant par un besoin de métamorphoses. Je voudrais écrire tout ce que je vois, non tel qu'il est, mais transfiguré . . ." . One might justifiably claim that the profound and unifying *subject* of Flaubert is not this or that character in a given setting, but the struggle against the very conditions of existence by means of what he himself defines as the "refonte plastique et complète par l'Art."[32]

Raymonde Debray-Genette scores another important point: the *structures imaginaires* are indeed far more significant in a given textual space than the imperatives of the so-called subject.[33] But it should be added that such structures are the pre-condition for thematic unity, that elaboration of the themes represents the real subject of the work. To be sure, this thematic subject, ultimately the organizing principle of the writer's total vision, is harder to define; it always partially eludes both reader and writer, camouflaging its powerful singularity behind a surface variety. Hence Flaubert's bafflement at the fundamental resemblance of the three widely different topics he describes in his letter from Constantinople. Hence also his uncomfortable, yet exhilerating feeling that what he has to say must necessarily remain *indisable.*

And this precisely is the merit of thematic reading and thematic criticism when, at their best, they focus on textual strategies: they decipher, through a careful reconnaissance of linguistic and figural patterns, the *hidden subject* of the work. This "other" subject which, in the case of Flaubert, centers on the superiority of artifice and imagination over life, cannot be reduced to what has come to be known as textual self-referentiality. Just as the book "about nothing" is not the same as the book about pure textuality, so the writing of fiction is a self-projecting as well as self-transposing activity: " . . . un livre est pour moi une manière spéciale de vivre;" and more clearly still: " . . . je me suis toujours mis dans tout ce que j'ai fait. A la place de **Saint Antoine** c'est moi qui y suis."[34]

It is most revealing that Flaubert, in his fiction, avoided the portrayal of the artist as hero. This figure makes the briefest appearance—and at that in a work Flaubert refused to publish. Jules, in the first **Education sentimentale,** achieves a kind of salvation through suffering, solitude, and the struggle with the demon of Art. But even in this novel, the artist hero appears only in order to disappear. The priority of art implies, it would seem, the death of the artist. "A mesure que je me détache des artistes, je m'enthousiasme devantage pour l'art." If Flaubert confesses to having disseminated himself in his works ("mon moi s'éparpille (. . .) dans les livres"—" . . . j'ai toujours péché par là . . ."), this only strengthens the latent hostility to the artist-hero.[35]

Yet it could be argued that, in the deepest sense, all of Flaubert's writings extol the artist. Even the caricatures of Pellerin or of Bouvard and Pécuchet, deal—perversely to be sure—with ideals and ideas dear to the author. And "bovarysme," this yearning for the unattainable, this confrontation of dream and reality, is certainly not Emma's monopoly. Baudelaire once again was uncannily perceptive when he identified Emma, in pursuit of the ideal, as the "poète hystérique." Of course, Emma's flaw is that she uses art to feed her dreams, instead of placing her dreams in the service of art. In a subtle way, Frédéric and Madame Arnoux move closer, if only by preterition, towards an esthetic posession of their own existence. During their last encounter, they become the narrators of their own past ("Ils se racontèrent leurs anciens jours.") Abstracted from their passion, they place themselves at the supreme vantage point of a transcending future anterior: "N'importe, nous nous serons bien aimès." Albert Thibaudet, as perceptive a reader as Flaubert could have hoped for, went so far as to hint at Frédéric and Mme Arnoux's status as proto-novel-ists: at the end they possess their dream instead of being possessed by it. The *livre sur rien* may well turn out to deal latently but powerfully with a subject and with meanings that go beyond intransitivity and the sophisticated playfulness of a non-signifying sig-nifier![36]

Flaubert himself, for those who care to listen, provides ample warning against the abuses of reductive and dogmatic criticism. The first warning relates to his belief in genius, and calls for humility. It is a great sin indeed to be "sans vénération pour le génie." The second warning has to do with the tyranny of all systems that would bend masterpieces to their arro-gant theoretical dictates. It is because he is convinced that every genuine work projects its own poetics, that he develops a "dédain complet de toutes les poétiques du monde." As for the third warning, it is perhaps the most important. There is no substitute for fair, sensi-tive, and intelligent reading, " . . . cela demande tant d'esprit que de bien lire."[37]

Notes

[1] Gustave Flaubert, *Correspondance,* ed. Jean Bruneau (Paris: Gallimard, *Pléiade,* 1973), I, 708. From here on referred to as *Pléiade.*

[2] *Correspondance de Gustave Flaubert,* 9 vols. (Paris: Conard, 1926-33), VI, 2. From here on referred to as *Corr.*

[3] Gustave Flaubert, *Oeuvres complètes* (Paris: Gallimard, *Pléiade,* 1963), 657.

[4] *Pléiade,* 708.

[5] For a reaction to some of these overstatements, P. M. Wetherill "Flaubert et les distortions de la critique moderne," *Symposium,* Fall 1971, 271-279; and Louis Fournier, "Flaubert et le 'Nouvau Roman': un cas de paternité douteuse", *Amis de Flaubert,* 52, May 1978.

[6] *Corr.* II, 345; III, 249, 248; IIIa, 96.

[7] Maurice Blanchot, *L'Entretien infini,* Gallimard, 1969, 492; Pierre Bergounioux "Flaubert et l'autre," *Communications,* 19, 1972; Claude Burgelin "La Flaubert-olâtrie," *Littérature,* 15, October 1974, 5-16; Jonathan Culler, *Flaubert. The Uses of Uncertainty,* Cornell University Press, 1974, 13; Jean-Paul Sartre, *L'Idiot de la famille,* Gallimard, vols. I, II, 1971 passim. For perspectives on Flaubert's modernity, see also Jean Rousset, "*Madame Bovary* ou le 'livre sur rien' ", in *Forme et Signification,* Corti, 1962; Nathalie Sarraute, "Flaubert le précurseur," *Preuves,* Feb. 1965; Jeanne Bem, "Sur le sens d'un discours circulaire," *Littérature,* 15, October 1974.

[8] *Corr.,* IV, 164; *Oeuvres complètes,* Pléiade, 1963, 652.

[9] *Corr.,* VII, 322; III, 249; II, 345; VII, 294; II, 345.

[10] *Corr.,* IV, 225; II, 345; VIII, 207.

[11] *Corr.,* III, 322; VIII, 175. *Pléiade,* I, 679.

[12] *Corr.,* VII, 281; III, 330, 355.

[13] For a short and useful theoretical discussion of satire, see Alvin Kernan's fine chapter, "A Theory of Satire" in *The Cankered Muse,* Yale University Press, 1959.

[14] *Corr.*, III, 45, 351; V, 91; IV, 356.

[15] Jean-Paul Sartre, in *L'Idiot de la famille,* has given complex analyses of the fundamental (and wilful) misunderstanding.

[16] *Corr.*, S.IV, 52;V, 26. The hierarchy of the arts was obviously a conviction of Flaubert. See his letter to Turgenev: " . . . je vous soupçonne de vouloir [. . .] entendre de la musique ou voir de la peinture, *arts inférieurs.*" [S.IV.59].

[17] *Corr.*, II, 364; *Novembre '79, L'Education sentimentale,* Garnier-Flammarion, 1969, 59; *Corr.*, II, 279.

[18] *La Première Education sentimentale,* Editions du Seuil, 1963, 244. *Corr.*, I, 302; VIII, 300; II, 353. For a concise discussion by Sartre of the "posthumous" stance of both Flaubert and Baudelaire, see his "Introduction" to Baudelaire's *Ecrits intimes,* Editions du Point du Jour, 1946.

[19] *Corr.*, II, 343; IV, 5; VII, 285; *La Première Education sentimentale,* op. cit. 237; *Corr.*, VII, 351; VIII, 309.

[20] *Pléiade,* I, 652, 637; *Mémoires d'un fou,* 46, 58.

[21] *Mémoires d'un fou,* 15, 65.

[22] *Corr.*, III, 157, 66. *La Première Education sentimentale,* op. cit. 246.

[23] *Corr.*, II, 439; *Pléiade,* I, 627-628.

[24] *Corr.*, IV, 464; III, 268; IV, 215, 463, 212; *L'Education sentimentale,* Garnier-Flammarion, 1969, 81.

[25] *Pléiade,* I, 37; *La Première Education sentimentale,* op. cit., 246-251; *Pléiade,* I, 680, 679. *Corr.*, S. II, 92; III, 100; II, 457; IV, 3; Alain Robbe-Grillet, "Une Voie pour le roman futur," *Nouvelle Nouvelle Revue Francaise,* July, 1956, 77-84.

[26] "L'Aqueduc et le Piédestal," *Tel Quel,* Summer 1964, 18, 87-88.

[27] *Corr.*, I, 385; V, 111; II, 343; III, 269; VII, 331.

[28] *Corr.*, I, 192, 178; II, 343. Roland Barthes, "L'Effet de réel," *Communications II,* 84-89.

[29] *Corr.*, II, 169; III, 210; I, 339; III, 384; IX, 3; S. 11.

[30] *Corr.*, III, 21; V, 338; S. II, 118; VII, 230; IV, 249; IV, 52. *Pléiade,* I, 495.

[31] *Corr.*, III, 388, 344, 161; VIII, 374. Raymonde Debray-Genette, "Flaubert: Science et Ecriture," *Littérature,* 15 October 1974, 41-51. *Corr.*, III, 138.

[32] *Corr.*, III, 317, 320; IV, 18.

[33] Raymonde Debray-Genette, "Du Mode narratif dans les 'Trois Contes'," *Littérature,* 1971.

[34] *Corr.*, IV, 357; II, 461.

[35] *Corr.*, II, 38; VI, 441; II, 461.

[36] *Oeuvres Complètes,* Pléiade, 654; Albert Thibaudet, *Gustave Flaubert,* Gallimard, 1935, 150.

[37] *La Première Education sentimentale,* op. cit., 262, 237; *Corr.*, III, 45. I wish to express my debt to Charles Carlut's most useful concordance and repertory *La Correspondance de Flaubert. Etude et répertoire critique,* Ohio State University Press, Columbus, 1968.

Diana Knight (essay date 1985)

SOURCE: "The Merits of Inarticulacy," in *Flaubert's Characters: The Language of Illusion,* Cambridge University Press, 1985, pp. 25-40.

[*In the following essay, Knight examines Flaubert's "simple" characters who lack the ability to articulate their experiences effectively, and argues that Flaubert "suggests an important connection between moral and aesthetic values" in these types of characters.*]

Although his 'weak vessels' have often attracted critical disapproval, Flaubert himself suggests an important connection between moral and aesthetic values in so-called 'simple' characters:

> Les mots sublimes (que l'on rapporte dans les histoires) ont été dits souvent par des simples. Ce qui n'est nullement un argument contre l'Art, au contraire, car ils avaient ce qui fait l'Art même, à savoir la pensée concrétée, un sentiment quelconque, *violent,* et arrivé à son dernier état d'idéal. 'Si vous aviez la foi, vous remuerez des montagnes' est aussi le principe du Beau.
>
> (*Correspondance* [hereafter, *Corr.*]
> (B) II, p. 785 (1957))

Flaubert writes into his works an almost explicit argument on behalf of such characters, whose simplicity invariably takes the form of an extreme linguistic disadvantage. If language itself is sometimes blamed for difficulties of self-expression,[1] inarticulate characters are more usually seen to have a personal problem. It is not that the right words do not exist, but that they do not have access to them. They are not good at translating their experience of the world into speech, and are especially unable to use language to communicate with other people. Nor is this because their thoughts are too profound for expression—the same characters clearly lack intellectual capacity as well. Yet Flaubert uses them to incarnate positive values such as single-mindedness, silence, immobility and imaginative sympathy. These values seem, in Flaubert, to possess a traditional moral sense, but all also have aesthetic connotations. At the same time, Flaubert undermines, at the level of theme and plot, the normally accepted function of spoken language as an instrument of self-expression and communication. He does this through a debunking of various forms of verbal facility, accompanied by a sustained caricature of any intellectual outlook on the world as boring pedantry.

Sartre's influential analysis of the ubiquitous but slippery concept of 'la Bêtise' (*L'Idiot* I, pp.612-48) suggests that it originates as a quality of language, but is best characterized as a refusal to synthesize—stupidity is basically an attitude which makes things stupid. It is powerful because no position can be adopted to combat it, that is, its identification has nothing to do with formulating a more sensible alternative view (for example, opposing sound opinions to the silly ones of the bourgeoisie). Intelligence is neither a foil for stupidity nor an analytical weapon against it, but is invariably put forward by Flaubert as a sub-species of stupidity itself. Herein lies all the subtle difference between Balzac's treatment of a bourgeois fool like Célestin Crevel in *La Cousine Bette* and Flaubert's of M. Homais. For as Sartre suggests in an outstanding analysis of Homais, Flaubert's masterstroke is to make Homais the incarnation of intelligence (p.642).

A fierce criticism of easy eloquence, verbosity, and pedantry is pursued right through Flaubert's works. He claims to have no liking for 'les doctrinaires d'aucune espèce' (*Correspondance. Supplément* [hereafter, *Corr. Suppl.*] IV, p. 84 (1878)), and describes eloquence as 'une chose qui me laisse absolument froid' (*Corr. Suppl.* IV, p. 63 (1878)). This is a personal position maintained throughout his life and declared as early as 1837:

> Il y a des jours où je donnerais toute la science des bavards passés, présents, futurs, toute la sotte érudition des éplucheurs, équarisseurs, philosophes, romanciers, chimistes, épiciers, académiciens, pour deux vers de Lamartine ou de Victor Hugo. Me voilà devenu bien anti-prose, anti-raison, anti-vérité car qu'est-ce que le beau sinon l'impossible, la poésie si ce n'est la barbarie—le cœur de l'homme.

> (*Corr.* (B) I, pp. 24-5)

He builds into his fiction a long line of complacent smooth talkers: Ernest, Paul and the later Henry prefigure the better-known examples of Lheureux and Rodolphe. Flaubert's method is often to set up a contrast between a pair of characters, whereby some version of pompous verbosity acts as a foil for apparent ignorance, ineloquence or simplicity. Straightforward examples abound in a rather obvious way in the early works.

Giacomo, the illiterate, manic book collector of **Bibliomanie** is above all a silent man, apparently by choice: 'Cet homme n'avait jamais parlé à personne, si ce n'est aux bouquinistes et aux brocanteurs; il était taciturne et rêveur' (I, p. 78). This causes him to be despised and misunderstood, but, standing in court accused of arson, theft and murder: 'il était calme et paisible, et ne répondit pas même par un regard à la multitude qui l'insultait'. This dignified silence is set in relief by the nature of the prosecutor's speech which precedes it: 'le Procureur se leva et lut son rapport; il était long et diffus, à peine si on pouvait en distinguer l'action principale des parenthèses et des réflexions', and that of his own 'clever' lawyer—'il parla longtemps et bien; enfin, quand il crut avoir ébranlé son auditoire . . .'—who makes the tactical error of producing the second Bible (I, p. 82).

In **Quidquid volueris** a clear contrast is set up between Djalioh and Paul. Djalioh cannot read or write, and while it is not made clear whether he is actually dumb, he appears to be so for all practical purposes. He cannot make himself understood, and although the narrator suggests that his strange and incoherent violin music at the wedding is some form of self-expression, this music in no way explains him to his audience: 'Tout le monde se mit à rire, tant la musique était fausse, bizarre, incohérente' (I, p. 108). Yet the richness which lies behind his inarticulacy is made explicit for the reader:

> Si c'était un mot ou un soupir, peu importe, mais il y avait là-dedans toute une âme! [. . .] Oh! son cœur était vaste et immense, mais vaste comme la mer, immense et vide comme sa solitude [. . .] Il avait en lui un chaos des sentiments les plus étranges; la poésie avait remplacé la logique, et les passions avaient pris la place de la science.

> (pp. 104-5)

He is all poetry, passion and capacity for love, while Paul is a cold, rational person, who has even created Djalioh by way of a scientific experiment: 'l'homme sensé, celui qu'on respecte et qu'on honore; car il monte sa garde nationale, s'habille comme tout le monde, parle morale et philanthropie' (p. 103). Paul translates his shallow feelings into easy words, while Djalioh's experience remains non-verbal and unformulated, and Flaubert heavily underlines the moral lesson which he means his reader to draw from the contrasts:

> Voilà le monstre de la nature qui était en contact avec M. Paul, cet autre monstre, ou plutôt cette merveille de la civilisation, et qui en portait tous les symboles, grandeurs de l'esprit, sécheresse du cœur. Autant l'un avait d'amour pour les épanchements de l'âme, les douces causeries du cœur, autant Djalioh aimait les rêveries de la nuit et les songes de la pensée [. . .] où l'intelligence finissait, le cœur prenait son empire; il était vaste et infini, car il comprenait le monde dans son amour.
>
> (p. 105)

Mazza and Ernest, of **Passion et vertu,** an obvious first sketch of Emma and Rodolphe, represent the same dichotomy, for Mazza lives in a world of emotion, while Ernest is all judgement and reason: 'C'était un de ces gens chez qui le jugement et la raison occupent une si grande place qu'ils ont mangé le cœur comme un voisin incommode' (I, p. 120). Like Rodolphe, Ernest is a skilful talker who knows how to exploit language for purposes of seduction, how to flatter Mazza and to out-argue her scruples:

> —Il faut que je l'aime. [her husband]
>
> —Cela est plus facile à dire qu'à faire, c'est-à-dire que si la loi vous dit: 'Vous l'aimerez', votre cœur s'y pliera comme un régiment qu'on fait manœuvrer ou une barre d'acier qu'on ploie des deux mains, et si moi je vous aime . . .
>
> [. . .] il faudra que je ne vous aime plus parce qu'il le faudra, et rien de plus; mais cela est-il sensé et juste?
>
> —Ah! vous raisonnez à merveille, mon cher ami.
>
> (pp. 114-15)

Once he feels the need he can even persuade himself out of any feelings of love he may have (again resembling Rodolphe regretfully renouncing Emma): 'La lettre était longue, bien écrite, toute remplie de riches métaphores et de grands mots . . . Pauvre Mazza! tant d'amour, de cœur et de tendresse pour une indifférence si froide, un calme si raisonné!' (p. 119). The young Flaubert cannot resist spelling out the moral lesson behind the contrast of eloquence and ineloquence: 'Quel trésor que l'amour d'une telle femme!' (p. 123).

In the 1845 **L'Éducation sentimentale** Alvarés's silent love for Mlle Aglaé rings what is beginning to sound like a typical note: 'il aurait épuisé l'éternité à tourner, comme un cheval au manège, autour de cette idée fixe et immobile, il n'en parlait plus, mais dans le silence de son cœur il se consumait solitairement' (I, p. 319). And Flaubert comes near to doing something important with Shahutsnischbach, who is not just awkward but arguably Flaubert's first really stupid character. He makes his *début* arriving late at Mme Renaud's dinner party, in his everyday clothes and covered in chalk: 'étonné, confus, ébahi, ne sachant s'il devait s'en aller ou rester, s'enfuir ou s'asseoir, les bras ballants, le nez au vent, ahuri, stupide' (p. 286). Later we learn why Shahutsnischbach is the only young man of the household not to be in love: 'il travaillait toujours aux mathématiques, les mathématiques dévorait sa vie, il n'y comprenait rien. Jamais M. Renaud n'avait eu de jeune homme plus studieux . . . ni plus stupide; Mendès lui-même le regardait comme un butor' (p. 293). When M. Renaud makes a silly joke: 'Alvarès et Mendès rirent, Shahutsnischbach ne comprit pas' (p. 295), and at Mme Renaud's ball the stupid but good-natured German: 'resté dans l'anti-chambre, aidait les domestiques à passer les plateaux de la salle à manager dans le salon' (p. 301). For in the strange interlude where Henry sadistically 'beats up' M. Renaud in the street, Shahutsnischbach, who happens to be passing ('pour une commission que Mme Renaud lui envoyait faire'), shows a contrasting kindness:

> Et le bon Allemand, en effet, le réconfortait de son mieux, il alla lui-même dans la cour, y mouilla son mouchoir sous la pompe, revint auprès de M. Renaud et lui essuya le sang qui était resté le long de sa figure; il s'offrit pour courir lui chercher un médecin, pour acheter quelque drogue s'il en avait besoin, pour aller avertir chez lui, pour tout ce qu'il voudrait, n'importe quoi. En songeant que, jusqu'à cette heure, à peine s'il l'avait regardé et qu'il le méprisait même pour son manque d'esprit, le père Renaud se sentait le cœur navré et était pris de l'envie de le serrer dans ses bras, de l'embrasser comme son fils.
>
> (p. 349)

Built into the final development of Henry and Jules is a very marked contrast between verbal facility and its lack. Henry ends up by becoming a man of the world, only really believing in feelings which can be expressed. His superficial intelligence is characterized by its easy processing of language:

> Il croit bien connaître le théâtre, parce qu'il saisit á première vue toutes les ficelles d'un mélodrame et les intentions d'une exposition [. . .] il passe pour avoir le tact fin, car il découvrira l'épithète heureuse, le trait saillant ou le mot hasardeux qui fait tache [. . .]
>
> Il a un avantage sur ceux qui voient plus loin et qui sentent d'une façon plus intense, c'est qu'il peut justifier ses sensations et donner la preuve de ses assertions; il expose nettement ce qu'il

éprouve, il écrit clairement ce qu'il pense, et dans le développement d'une théorie comme dans la pratique d'un sentiment, il écrase les natures plus engagées dans l'infini, chez lesquelles l'idée chante et la passion rêve.

(p. 365)

Such articulacy is typically combined with a complete inability to understand people different from himself, and of this, we know, Flaubert disapproves:

Il n'estimait pas ceux qui se grisent avec de l'eau-de-vie, parce qu'il préférait le vin: il trouvait le goût de la pipe trop fort, parce qu'il fumait des cigarettes [. . .] il ne comprenait pas les gens qui meurent d'amour, lui qui avait tant aimé et qui n'en était pas mort.

(p. 364)

But his opposite, Jules, is shown to have moved right away from the verbal domain, especially as an artist: 'la discussion lui était devenue impossible, il n'y avait à son usage de mode de transmission psychologique que l'expansion, la communication directe, l'inspiration simultanée' (p. 360).

Playing the various characters of **Madame Bovary** off against each other is an altogether more complicated business, largely because of the ambivalent treatment of Emma and Charles. A clear undermining of pompous verbosity is nevertheless apparent, which sets in relief some famous worldless characters. At the very centre of the novel (middle chapter of middle part), Flaubert inserts, in the set-piece 'symphony' of the agricultural show, the description of the old peasant woman receiving her medal. Catherine Leroux is often commented upon, normally to emphasize the contrast between the complacent bourgeoisie and 'ce demi-siècle de servitude' (I, p. 625). But I should prefer to underline her silence and immobility. By frequenting farm animals all her life she has assumed their dumb placidity. Whereas the gaping crowd is shown drinking in the ridiculous speeches against a background of mooing cows, Catherine Leroux is so frightened by the noise, bustle and confusion, that her reaction is simply to stand quite still, not knowing what else to do. In a scene carefully constructed so as to oppose the absurd parallel exploitation of the official speeches (to seduce the crowd), and of Rodolphe (to seduce Emma)—both are shown to be equally effective—the implicit moral worth of the old woman who does not even understand language is foregrounded, the more so given the reaction of the audience: '—Ah! qu'elle est bête!'. Abuse of language for various reasons is so widespread throughout the novel (Lheureux's selling technique, Homais's journalistic powers, the campaign to persuade Charles to operate on the club-foot), that characters who hardly speak should be prized by the reader quite simply for not misusing language.

M. Homais's view of the relative values of silence and speech is made clear on his first appearance in the novel, through his disdain for Binet's uncommunicativeness:

pendant tout le temps que l'on fut à mettre son couvert, Binet resta silencieux à sa place, auprès du poêle; puis il ferma la porte et retira sa casquette, comme d'usage.

Ce ne sont pas les civilités qui lui useront la langue! dit le pharmacien, dès qu'il fut seul avec l'hôtesse.

—Jamais il ne cause davantage, répondit-elle; il est venu ici, la semaine dernière, deux voyageurs en draps, des garçons pleins d'esprit qui contaient, le soir, un tas de farces que j'en pleurais de rire: eh bien! il restait là, comme une alose, sans dire un mot.

—Oui, fit le pharmacien, pas d'imagination, pas de saillies, rien de ce qui constitue l'homme de la société!

(p. 600)

The particular combination of talkativeness and useless knowledge that distinguishes Homais throughout the novel is characterized by his preferred version of social intercourse with the Bovarys:

Ensuite, on causait de ce qu'il y avait *dans le journal*. Homais, à cette heure-là, le savait presque par cœur; et il le rapportait intégralement, avec les réflexions du journaliste et toutes les histoires des catastrophes individuelles arrivées en France ou à l'étranger. Mais le sujet se tarissant, il ne tardait pas à lancer quelques observations sur les mets qu'il voyait. Parfois même, se levant à demi, il indiquait délicatement à Madame le morceau le plus tendre, ou, se tournant vers la bonne, lui adressait des conseils, pour la manipulation des ragoûts et l'hygiène des assaisonnements; il parlait arome, osmazôme, suc et gélatine d'une façon à éblouir.

(p. 607)

Flaubert takes particular pleasure in deflating Homais when he is given the task of breaking the news that Emma's father-in-law has died: 'Il avait médité sa phrase, il l'avait arrondie, polie, rhythmée, c'était un chef-d'œuvre de prudence et de transition, de tournures fines et de délicatesse; mais la colère avait emporté la rhétorique' (p. 659). Perhaps the abrupt outburst which is substituted in the event is a salutary one, for when Homais writes to Emma's father to tell him she is dead: 'par égard pour sa sensibilité, M. Homais l'avait rédigée de telle façon qu'il était impossible de savoir à quoi s'en tenir' (p. 687). The preferability of Père Rouault's own uneducated style of letter-writing is surely apparent: 'Les fautes d'orthographe s'y enlaçaient les unes aux autres, et Emma poursuivait la pensée douce qui caquetait tout au travers comme une poule à demi cachée dans une haie d'épine' (p. 632).

Charles's generally distracted and wordless grief makes the ending of the novel moving in a way that Flaubert quite explicitly intended,[2] and it is only when 'il la regardait avec des yeux d'une tendresse comme elle n'en avait jamais vu' that Emma at last consecrates his value with her 'tu es bon, toi!' (p. 681). Indeed one interpretation of the finding of the autopsy on Charles would surely be that he is allowed the fictional privilege of dying of a broken heart. Less dramatic than Salammbô's death, it is equally strongly motivated, and the cruelly ambiguous 'Il l'ouvrit et ne trouva rien' (p. 692), which both sets the seal on his moral worth and on his 'stupidity', captures the possible connection between the two.

Critics have more readily noticed that Charles speaks in clichés than that such a central character can barely speak at all. In the first part of the novel, despite his large part in the plot, he is especially wordless—direct conversations that exist in the early drafts have been removed by Flaubert to give greater emphasis to Charles's occasional stutterings.[3] It is not that he is a secretive, deliberately silent person; by nature he is relatively expansive and tells Emma everything. He simply has no command of language. The famous 'Charbovari' scene presents a lasting image of Charles: introduced to the reader as 'un nom inintelligible' (p. 575), he cannot even pronounce his own name. He is aware of his own problem to the extent that he dare not ask for Emma's hand in marriage: 'la peur de ne point trouver les mots convenables lui collait les lèvres' (p. 582). Indeed he is right and when the moment comes can manage only to stammer out 'Père Rouault . . . Père Rouault'. If he is a social failure at his wedding it is because he is unable to keep up with the jokes, puns and obligatory allusions, for their medium is linguistic. In fact in so far as Charles is transformed by the wedding night, it is his powers of speech that are temporarily improved: 'Mais Charles ne dissimulait rien. Il l'appelaient ma femme, la tutoyait, s'informait d'elle à chacun' (p. 584).

Though Emma's language is clichéd and while her tragedy is partly tied up with the misunderstanding or abuse of words, she is not properly speaking inarticulate, and is quite at home in a verbal atmosphere. In many ways she serves as a contrast for Charles here. While Charles is totally nonplussed by his medical studies and can only pass his examinations by learning the answers by heart, Emma can understand all the difficult parts of the catechism at school, and can send out well-phrased letters to Charles's clients. She notices and easily fits into the social conventions at La Vaubyessard, whereas Charles spends five hours at the card tables 'à regarder jouer au whist, sans y rien comprendre' (p. 592). The first reported conversation between them shows how easily Emma can out-argue Charles:

> —Les sous-pieds vont me gêner pour danser, dit-il.
>
> —Danser? reprit Emma.
>
> —Oui!
>
> —Mais tu as perdu la tête! on se moquerait de toi, reste á ta place. D'ailleurs, c'est plus convenable pour un médecin, ajouta-t-elle.
>
> Charles se tut.
>
> (p. 591)

It is because Emma needs to converse with someone that she becomes dissatisfied with Charles, and although at first she wishes that he would understand her need, she more or less writes him off for good when 'il ne put, un jour, lui expliquer un terme d'équitation qu'elle avait rencontré dans un roman' (p. 588).

Flaubert points out that Emma is at least partly seduced by Rodolphe's verbal 'galanterie': 'C'était la première fois qu'Emma s'entendait dire ces choses; et son orgueil, comme quelqu'un qui se délasse dans une étuve, s'étirait mollement et tout entier á la chaleur de ce langage' (p. 627). It is because Charles is so incapable of using the clichéd language of love with which she is familiar that she can never understand that he loves her (Flaubert's rough notes state plainly that Charles adores Emma far more than Léon and Rodolphe ever do, and that though clumsy and without imagination, he is 'sensible' (Pommier and Leleu, 1949, pp. 3 and 21)). Emma's most serious personal failing is her inability to understand any experience other than her own: 'guère tendre, cependant, ni facilement accessible à l'émotion d'autrui' (p. 597), and:

> incapable, du reste, de comprendre ce qu'elle n'éprouvait pas, comme de croire à tout ce qui ne se manifestait point par des formes convenues, elle se persuada sans peine que la passion de Charles n'avait plus rien d'exhorbitant. Ses expansions étaient devenues régulières; il l'embrassait à de certaines heures.
>
> ·(p. 589)

At the climax of her disgust with him she denigrates him as 'cet homme qui ne comprenait rien, qui ne sentait rien!' (p. 637), and her mistake is obviously supposed to lie in thinking that the two activities of intellectual understanding and feeling have any necessary connection. Critical discussions of Charles as the clumsy and stupid husband who cannot cater for Emma's needs therefore miss at least half of the point. This was spelled out by Flaubert in a grandiloquent description of Charles to be found in earlier versions of the novel. In this passage—deleted perhaps for the very reason that it overemphasizes one *half* of the final, ambivalent Charles—Rodolphe, at their final meeting, scorns Charles for not hating him:

> Car il ne comprenait rien à cet amour vorace se précipitant au hasard sur les choses pour s'assouvir, à la passion vide d'orgueil, sans respect humain, ni conscience, qui plonge tout entière dans l'être aimé, accapare ses sentiments, en palpite, et touche presque aux proportions d'une idée pure, à force de largeur ct d'impersonnalité.

(Pommier and Leleu, 1949, p. 641)

This is precisely the treasured moral ideal of universal sympathy which Emma lacks:[4] 'Il fallait qu'elle pût retirer des choses une sorte de profit personnel; et elle rejetait comme inutile tout ce qui ne contribuait pas à la consommation immédiate de son cœur,—étant de tempérament plus sentimentale qu'artiste' (I, p. 586). In fact my own reading of the much glossed 'c'est la faute de la fatalité' (p. 692) would be that if it is the ultimate cliché it is also the ultimate act of generosity. For as seen in his wishes for her burial and in his much changed behaviour after her death, Charles more or less succeeds in understanding Emma, 'raising' his ideals to the level of literary romances, passionate affairs etc. These words could be seen to represent the final insight into her world and are a generous self-sacrifice, for Charles himself is not so trite.

But one character is ahead of Charles in understanding Emma's value system, for her desire for a tilbury and groom is attributed to *Justin:* 'C'était Justin qui lui en avait inspiré le caprice, en la suppliant dc lc prendre chez elle comme valet de chambre' (p. 665). Indeed if Charles, in contrast with Léon and Rodolphe, lies awake all night after Emma's funeral, it is Justin's grief which is given the privileged position as he lies sobbing at the graveside. Justin is Charles's silent shadow in that he echoes his values, and, as Flaubert makes quite specific in the text, he too offers adoring but unvoiced devotion of which Emma remains unaware: 'Elle ne se doutait point que l'amour, disparu de sa vie, palpitait là, près d'elle, sous cette chemise de grosse toile, dans ce cœur d'adolescent ouvert aux émanations de sa beauté' (p. 647). He is almost a caricature of Charles in that he is even more incompetent linguistically.[5] When Homais calls him a 'petit sot' for fainting 'Justin ne répondait pas' (p. 618), when in disgrace over the key to the arsenic his only response to Homais's noisy scene and 'Parle, réponds, articule quelque chose?' (p. 658) is a few stutterings,

and his copy of *L'Amour conjugal* (like the geography book that provides Félicité's literary education in *Un Cœur simple*), needs pictures by way of explanation. He comes and goes so quietly that it is indeed easy to overlook him: 'Il montait avec eux dans la chambre, et il restait debout près de la porte, immobile, sans parler' (p. 647). Just as on the Sunday expedition to the flax mill his role is to carry the umbrellas and to wipe the children's shoes clean, his devotion is never articulated, but (again like Félicité's), shows itself in acts of service: 'et Justin, qui se trouvait là, circulait à pas muets, plus ingénieux à la servir qu'une excellente camériste. Il plaçait les allumettes, le bougeoir, un livre, disposait sa camisole, ouvrait les draps' (p. 665). As this reference to the sheets suggests, it is the erotic and sensuous qualities of Emma which fascinate him, for example her hair, and it could be suggested that he shares with Charles the role of creating and preserving Emma's 'mystery', even when her rather silly interior has been made available to the reader. Justin's greatest satisfaction is always to watch Emma, and his imaginative sympathy has the power to transform reality: 'Et aussitôt il atteignit sur le chambranle les chaussures d'Emma tout empâtées de crotte—la crotte des rendez-vous—qui se détachait en poudre sous se doigts, et qu'il regardait monter doucement dans un rayon de soleil' (p. 638). That Flaubert regards this power as an artist's privilege is suggested when he writes to Maupassant: 'La poésie, comme le soleil, met l'or sur le fumier' (*Corr.* (C) VIII, p. 397 (1880)).

The values associated with inarticulate characters—silence, stillness and single-mindedness—are clearly built into the presentation of character in the 1869 **L'Éducation sentimentale**. The simple but loyal Dussardier, though a minor character, appears at enough crucial points in the novel to act as a symbol for its guiding moral thread. He is introduced stammering 'Où est mon carton? Je veux mon carton [. . .] Mon carton!' (II, p. 19), he is incapable of understanding the stories by means of which Frédéric and Hussonnet try to help him out of trouble at the police station, and his erudition is limited to two books. But his dream is to love one woman for life, his hatred for authority is unswerving, and, more faithful than his friends to his earlier cry of 'Vive la République!' (p. 114), he is struck down on 2nd December as he towers above the police in a quite immobile pose: 'un homme,—Dussardier, remarquable de loin à sa haute taille, restait sans plus bouger qu'une cariatide' (p. 160). He is rewarded in the next line with a martyr's death: 'Il tomba sur le dos, les bras en croix.'[6]

Frédéric's persistent attachment to Mme Arnoux may well act on the reader as it does on Deslauriers: 'La persistance de cet amour l'irritait comme un problème. Son austérité un peu théâtrale l'ennuyait maintenant' (p. 97). Yet Frédéric's story embodies a deliberate tension between concentrated and diffuse experience, as he dabbles in painting, literature, business and politics, frittering his energies among four women between whom he seems unable to choose. Arnoux, Rosanette and many of Frédéric's Parisian acquaintances clearly provide the temptation of diffusion, and the semi-fidelity despite everything to Mme Arnoux is surely, in this context, a positive force. Part of Flaubert's problem is to build moral value into Mme Arnoux, despite her husband and, up to a point, despite Frédéric himself. This he does through the particular nature of Frédéric's perception of her, and through her place in the structure of the novel. By constructing the novel around her (through a complicated network of reminders), he obliges the reader to join in Frédéric's original desire to 'vivre dans son atmosphère' (p. 26), an atmosphere which is not only poetic and emotional, but essentially moral: 'la contemplation de cette femme l'énervait, comme l'usage d'un parfum trop fort. Cela descendit dans les profondeurs de son tempérament, et devenait presque une manière générale de sentir, un mode nouveau d'exister' (p. 33).

If Frédéric's 'Je n'ai jamais aimé qu'elle!' is less than totally convincing (p. 157), Mme Arnoux is nevertheless presented to the reader as a coherent force in the novel. The varieties of dispersion which act as a foil for her simplicity are invariably related to noise and unnecessary speech. Without being inarticulate Mme Arnoux is basically quiet, gentle and unaffected. Criticized by Frédéric for using bourgeois maxims, she protests that she has no pretensions to anything else. She has no special love of literature, she uses straightforward language, she is superstitious—'croyait aux songes' (p. 38)—and enjoys commonplace pleasures like walking bareheaded in the rain. The very first vision of her is presented against a background of the noise, bustle and confusion of the departure of the boat. The talkative Arnoux fits naturally into this scene, involving everyone around him in his fragmentary conversation, giving advice, expounding theories, relating anecdotes. Mme Arnoux's 'apparition' is immediately preceded by a squalid description of the mess on the deck, of the noise and constant movement of the passengers and the captain:

> Le pont était sali par des écales de noix, des bouts de cigares, des pelures de poires, des détritus de charcuterie apportée dans du papier [. . .] on entendait par intervalles le bruit du charbon de terre dans le fourneau, un éclat de voix, un rire; et le capitaine, sur la passerelle, marchait d'un tambour à l'autre, sans s'arrêter.
>
> (p.9)

While everyone else mixes, laughing, joking and drinking together, dressed in old, worn and dirty travelling clothes, Mme Arnoux sits alone and silent, her light-coloured dress standing out against the blue sky. She is sewing, that is doing something useful, but above all she is still. Frédéric observes her for some minutes in the same pose, and on his last view of her as the boat arrives: 'Elle était près du gouvernail, debout. Il lui envoya un regard où il avait tâché de mettre toute son âme; comme s'il n'eût rien fait, elle demeura immobile' (p.11). The immobile pose of this first scene is established almost as a leitmotif which appears throughout the novel, and on one occasion the continuity is even pointed out: 'Elle se tenait dans la même attitude que le premier jour, et cousait une chemise d'enfant' (p.56). That these values are not necessarily obvious ones is shown up in the scene where Deslauriers dismisses his mistress: 'Elle se planta devant la fenêtre, et y resta immobile, le front contre le carreau. Son attitude et son mutisme agaça Deslauriers' (p.73).

One especially memorable tableau of Mme Arnoux is during her fête at Saint-Cloud, where she is placed on a rock with a flaming sunset behind her, while the other guests wander around somewhat aimlessly, and Hussonnet on the river bank skims stones on the water. In his correspondence Flaubert twice uses this as an image to imply moral dispersion: 'Ah! mes richesses morales! J'ai jeté aux passants les grosses pièces par la fenêtre, et avec les louis j'ai fait des ricochets sur l'eau' (*Corr.* (B) I, p. 290 (1846)). Louise Colet's idea of a communally directed review is dismissed in the same terms: 'On bavarde beaucoup, on dépense tout son talent à faire des ricochets sur la rivière avec de la menue monnaie, tandis qu'avec plus d'économie on aurait pu par la suite acheter de belles fermes et de bons châteaux' (*Corr.* (B) II, p.291 (1853)). Appropriately it is Hussonnet who is chosen to skim stones, for as the newspaper owner he emerges as a rival to Mme Arnoux for Frédéric's time, attention and money. At Rosanette's ball he is made by Flaubert to stand in Frédéric's line of vision and thus to interrupt his thoughts—as the sight of the chandelier from the *Art industriel* stirs old memories of Mme Arnoux, Frédéric is suddenly distracted by 'un fantassin de la ligne en petite tenue' who has planted himself in his path, congratulating him and calling him 'colonel'. This turns out to be Hussonet in fancy dress (pp.49-50). It is also specified that the dispersal of Hussonet's talents in all directions is linguistic: 'Hussonnet ne fut pas drôle. A force d'écrire quotidiennement sur toute sorte de sujets, de lire beaucoup de journeaux, d'entendre beaucoup de discussions et d'émettre des paradoxes pour éblouir, il avait fini par perdre la notion exacte des choses, s'aveuglant lui-même avec ses faibles pétards' (p.84).

Frédéric is described as coming to resemble Arnoux more and more, and undoubtedly Arnoux is the character who most consistently leads Frédéric in the direction of dissipation and moral decline. Frédéric's first visit to the *Art industriel* is an introduction to Arnoux's typical environment: the rooms are packed, nobody can move or breathe amidst the cigar smoke and dazzling light, and all is bustle and activity against a background of different conversations. This moral chaos is carried over into the description of the evening at the Alhambra, where even the talkative Arnoux is outdone:

> Mais ses paroles étaient couvertes par le tapage de la musique; et, sitôt le quadrille ou la polka terminés, tous s'abattaient sur les tables, appelaient le garçon, riaient; les bouteilles de bière et de limonade gazeuse détonaient dans les feuillages, des femmes criaient comme des poules; quelquefois, deux messieurs voulaient se battre; un voleur fut arrêté.

(p. 35)

It is Arnoux who takes Frédéric to Rosanette's ball, a fancy-dress party-cum-orgy clearly intended to symbolize the superficial pleasures of a diffuse and essentially worthless experience which is again, at one point, quite specifically related to language:

> Une horloge allemande, munie d'un coq, carillonnant deux heures, provoqua sur le coucou force plaisanteries. Toutes sortes de propos s'ensuivirent: calembours, anecdotes, vantardises, gageures, mensonges tenus pour vrais, assertions improbables, un tumulte de paroles qui bientôt s'éparpilla en conversations particulières.

(p. 53)

When the whole party collapses in exhaustion, it is appropriately a moment of sudden silence which shows up the real value of the ball, as someone opens a window and daylight transforms the scene: 'Il y eut une exclamation d'étonnement, puis un silence' (p.54). The costumes and flowers are all wilting, there are drink stains everywhere, hair-styles have collapsed and make-up runs down perspiring faces. The frenzied excitement is no more than a sordid chaos, and Frédéric not surprisingly fails, in his half-drunken stupor, to recognize the 'deux grands yeux noirs' which were not, of course, anything to do with the ball.

The clearest reinstatement of an inarticulate character in any of Flaubert's works takes place in *Un Cœur simple*. If the problem of irony in this story can be put aside for the time being, it is clear at least that the straightforward linear plot raises a completely illiterate and ineloquent servant to the position of central character and main focus of interest. She is quite uneducated apart from Paul's explanations of a picture book geography, where she speaks directly, as in the bull incident, it is in very short sentences, and she is so silent and orderly that she seems to function automatically. Her life is made up of regular work and devoted service, her fondness for those around her is constantly shown in small acts of kindness, and her reaction to the grief of Victor's death leads her to contain her sorrow and keep on working. Though she starts out with a certain amount of common sense (her suspicion of Théodore's promises, her dealings with Mme Aubain's tenant farmers and visitors), as the story progresses she appears more and more stupid.

The chief foil for Félicité is M. Bourais, the pedantic culmination of Flaubert's long line of self-satisfied 'knowledgeable' characters, whom Mme Aubain regards as an authority to consult on all important matters (on the bathing at Trouville, on the choice of a school for Paul). Flaubert completes the undermining of such characters by making Bourais a cheap villain who is finally exposed, a disgracing of 'intelligence' all the greater in that it is the parrot Loulou (a caricature of Félicité in his relations with language), who is given the privilege of seeing through him from the start, laughing at him every time he sees him and humiliating him to such an extent that Bourais has to arrive at Mme Aubain's by stealth (with his hat covering his face). The contrast between Félicité and Bourais is underlined when she asks him to show her where Victor is on the map. Bourais, wrapped up in lengthy explanations of longitudes and so on, is enormously amused when asked to point out Victor's house: 'et il avait un beau sourire de cuistre devant l'ahurissement de Félicité [. . .] Bourais leva les bras, il éternua, rit énormément; une candeur pareille excitait sa joie; et Félicité n'en comprenait pas le motif, elle qui s'attendait peut-être à voir jusqu'au portrait de son neveu, tant son intelligence était bornée!' (p.171).[7] But Flaubert makes plain the relative values of their different versions of 'understanding'. Félicité does not need Bourais's intellectual approach to the world; indeed it is *because* of her ignorance that she is able to follow Victor in her imagination. She is thirsty on his behalf when it is hot, frightened for him when there is a storm, and her simplicity is enhanced by a genuine interest: her attempts to visualize Havana involve clouds of tobacco 'à cause des cigares' (p.171.)

Félicité's heart and imagination dominate her whole conception of reality; for example because Virginie and Victor are linked in her heart she imagines that their destiny must be the same. Similarly her understanding of religion takes place on the level of imagination and emotion, as she reduces Christian imagery to her own surroundings:

> Les semailles, les moissons, les pressoirs, toutes ces choses familières dont parle l'Évangile, se trouvaient dans sa vie; le passage de Dieu les avait sanctifiées; et elle aima plus tendrement les agneaux par amour de l'Agneau, les colombes à cause du Saint-Esprit [. . .] C'est peut-être sa lumière qui voltige la nuit aux bords des marécages,

son haleine qui pousse les nuées, sa voix qui rend les cloches harmonieuses; et elle demeurait dans une adoration, jouissant de la fraîcheur des murs et de la tranquillité de l'église. (p.170)

When the priest tells stories from the Bible she can vividly imagine Paradise and the Great Flood, and 'pleura en écoutant la Passion'. But when it comes to dogma: 'elle n'y comprenait rien, ne tâcha même pas de comprendre' (p.170). Her sympathetic understanding is such that she can forgive Mme Aubain for sending Virginie away to the convent, and for thinking her daughter so much more important than Victor. The height of this power comes at the moment of Virginie's First Communion when Félicité identifies with Virginie so closely that she feels she has become her: 'avec l'imagination que donnent les vraies tendresses, il lui sembla qu'elle était elle-même cette enfant' (p.170).[8] Her qualities are those which Flaubert elsewhere attributes to the artist. Like Justin's her love can transform the ugliest of realities: she forms a fetishistic attachment to Virginie's hat although it has been eaten away by vermin, loves the stuffed Loulou all the more and kisses him farewell regardless of his worm-eaten state, and devotedly tends the cancer-ridden Père Colmiche. Certainly Emma Bovary could not have accepted and pitied the blind beggar, and the importance of this particular theme is shown by the fact that, in *La Légende de Saint Julien l'Hospitalier,* Julien's accession to sainthood seems ultimately to be dependent on his willing and selfless embrace of the leper. The enormous effort over self required by Julien sets in full relief Félicité's entirely spontaneous selflessness, which is quite without personal motive. While her 'sainthood' emerges largely through association with the saints of the other stories of the *Trois Contes,* Flaubert would evidently consider it deserved: though (or because) an inarticulate servant cut off from the world, she is rewarded with an experience that is the richer and the more complete for being imaginary.

Notes

[1] Especially in the early works, and normally in the context of artistic creation: 'Comment rendre par des mots ces choses pour lesquelles il n'y a pas de langage?' (I, p.238); 'Pouvez-vous dire par des mots le battement du cœur?' (p.247). Such remarks can be classified of course under the familiar Romantic cliché of the incommensurability of language and experience; however, Flaubert's insistence upon this theme far outlives his imitations of Romantic literature.

[2] 'il faut que mon bonhomme [. . .] vous émeuve pour tous les veufs' (*Corr.* (B) II, p.346 (1853)).

[3] For example on the return journey from La Vaubyessard ([Pommier, Jean, and Gabrielle Leleu (eds.), 1949. *'Madame Bovany'. Nouvelle Version*

précédée des scénarios inédits (Paris, Corti)], pp. 218-19).

[4] 'cette faculté de s'assimiler à toutes les misères et de se supposer les ayant est peut-être la vraie charité humaine. Se faire ainsi le centre de l'humanité, tâcher enfin d'être son cœur général où toutes les veines éparses se réunissent, . . . ce serait à la fois l'effort du plus grand et du meilleur homme?' (*Corr.* (B) II, p. 346 (1853)).

[5] As for Charles, much of Justin's direct speech is removed from the drafts, for example the discussion about the tilbury and groom (Pommier and Leleu, 1949, p.536).

[6] In a draft Dussardier is described as follows: 'Ce gros garçon avait l'âme plus délicate qu'une marquise. Avec ses fortes épaules & ses bons yeux, il rappelait les forgerons que l'on voit au bord des routes, tenant sur leurs bras un petit enfant [. . .] Quoiqu'il n'eut pas d'esprit Fred. goûtait dans sa compagnie un certain charme' (B.N. n.a.fr. 17605, fol. 167[r]).

[7] Discussing this Culler claims: 'We are amused, no doubt, but we do not want to class ourselves with Bourais by joining in his amusement. We prefer to be won over by her innocence and unpretentiousness, valuing the sense of our own broadmindedness that comes from protecting or defending one so charmingly vulnerable' ([Culler, Jonathan, 1974. *Flaubert: The Uses of Uncertainty* (London, Elek)], p.209). Doubtless my view of inarticulacy leaves me open to the dreadful charge of 'protecting the charmingly vulnerable', and I can only rely on the reader's good will to protect my own vulnerability on this issue.

[8] Whereas when she takes communion herself the next day the experience is less real: 'Elle la reçut dévotement, mais n'y goûta pas les mêmes délices' (p.170).

Annie Rouxeville (essay date 1987-88)

SOURCE: "Victorian Attitudes to Flaubert: An Investigation," in *Nineteenth-Century French Studies,* Vol. 16, Nos. 1-2, Fall-Winter, 1987-88, pp. 132-40.

[*In the following essay, Rouxeville examines elements of critical controversy that surrounded Flaubert's oeuvre during the Victorian era, noting in particular the Victorian rejection of pessimism and an absence of moral purpose in Flaubert's works.*]

A study of the critical reviews published on Flaubert between 1850 and 1950 reveals that the acceptance of his work in England was slow and difficult.[1] Apart from a few articles published as a result of the Bovary trial, there was little criticism on Flaubert until the seventies. The violent controversies which took place around Flaubert reached a climax in England in the late eighties. This fact is reflected in the periodical literature in which one notes a greater concentration of articles on Flaubert in the late eighties and early nineties, when the critics seemed to attain a certain degree of unanimity in their praise of his novels. At the beginning of the twentieth century Flaubert's novels were unquestionably accepted as classics and, as a consequence, the critical reviews of his artistic theories became practically non-existent, while the interest in his work was sustained by a number of new translations.

From 1857 onwards Flaubert had had passionate supporters among the most distinguished writers of the time like Meredith, George Moore, Swinburne, R. L. Stevenson, Walter Pater who discovered Flaubert's correspondence, and, of course, Henry James. However, although the critical reviews they published on Flaubert were far from negligible, the fact remains that they were few and far between, if the fact that they were spread over a period of fifty years is taken into consideration. Some periodicals had totally ignored Flaubert in the latter part of the century. Four of the most influential ones, namely the *Edinburgh Review, Blackwood's Edinburgh Magazine,* the *Cornhill* and the *Spectator,* did not so much as mention Flaubert's name for half a century. Since these four reviews were all popular, it meant that a large section of the reading public had no knowledge of Flaubert's works, as none of his books had been translated before 1886. The best reviews were often published in less popular periodicals like the *Westminster Review,* the *Pall Mall Gazette, Nineteenth Century* or *Notes and Queries.* Why, in a period of such extraordinary brilliancy in critical literature, were there so few estimations of such a stimulating author?

The answer to this question is partly provided by Victorian attitudes, in particular to the French and their literature. It was commonly accepted at the time that French novels were fascinating but that their spirit was foreign to the genius of the English. The *Pall Mall Gazette* had noticed the very French tone of Flaubert's novels which often made them completely antipathetic to the English reader.[2] Henry James, too, thought that "it is not in the English character of vision to see things as Mr. Flaubert sees them,"[3] while George Saintsbury accounted for the difference of tone by the fact that "there is too much healthy beefiness and beeriness in the English temperament to permit it to indulge in sterile pessimism."[4] It is well known that, except for an elite, the Victorians made little effort to understand current artistic trends. The public at large was not ready to accept Flaubert's works, nor was it ready to accept that a novel could be a work of art in its own right and have its own inner significance. The idea that novels were entertaining but conventional stories with some sort of a moral purpose still lingered on. What was good and right was made obvious and was usually represented by one likeable character in the novel. The noticeable absence of such a character in Flaubert's works was much criticised by English reviewers. The substance of Flaubert's novels was indeed the source of many criticisms levelled against their author but certain clues to the lack of success Flaubert experienced in England are also to be found in the English controversy over Realism which centralised various streams of opposition to existing standards in literary, moral, aesthetic and philosophical matters for approximately half a century. Although it was not as tumultuous as it had been on the continent, the importance of this controversy in the history of English literature and thought is beyond question.

The Victorians witnessed the scandal and subsequent success of **Madame Bovary** with a somewhat detached interest, as there seemed to be little chance of contamination in England. In fact a clash was inevitable when the French Realist movement met Victorianism in the heyday of its glory. George Saintsbury was the first critic to show a truly appreciative attitude towards the new trend. He tried to give a definition of the word 'Realism,' then to give an appraisal of Flaubert's works in the context of the Realist movement which was gradually finding its way into Victorian England. According to him, Realism was "the faithful patience and the sense of artistic capacity which lead a man to grapple boldly with his subject, whatever that subject may be, and to refuse *tanquam scopulum* easy generalities and accepted phrase."[5] To accept this definition is, of course, to classify Flaubert as a Realist. Yet in the minds of the majority of people the word 'Realism' still meant the deliberate choice of unpleasant topics.

The controversy gradually took shape as more views were expressed in periodical literature. It is this increasing interest in Realism that explains why the first translations of Flaubert appeared in 1886. The origins of the controversy in England go back to 1885 when the London publisher Henry Vizetelly issued several Realist novels and in particular translations of Zola which provoked more angry comments than any other Realist works because of their alleged immorality and bestiality.[6] In 1886 more translations of Realist works appeared including this time **Madame Bovary** and **Salammbô**. All these swelled the chorus of indignation against Realism on the one hand, and admiration for the new art on the other. Immediately after the publication in translation of Zola's novels, the outcry was such that the National Vigilance Association felt it was its duty to intervene and arranged for a motion to be tabled in the House of Commons asking "that the laws against obscene publications . . . should be vigorously enforced and, if necessary, strengthened." The fact that the motion was carried unanimously no doubt reflected the popular attitude of the time. The chief offender, Henry Vizetelly, was subsequently prosecuted. The same pattern of accusations as for Baudelaire and Flaubert in 1857 was repeated in England with Vizetelly in 1888. The publisher was fined and bound over not to break the law for 12 months. The National Vigilants, taking very seriously their rôle of guardians of English morality, did not feel their action had been pervasive enough and attacked the Realists again, this time on a much broader front. Henry Vizetelly was prosecuted a second time for selling 11 books, among which were novels by Zola, Maupassant and Flaubert. After further consideration the original list was amended and *Madame Bovary* did not appear on the final list. This time the publisher was sent to prison.

As had been the case with *Madame Bovary* in France in 1857, the scandal brought success to Realist works which became best-sellers in the eighties and nineties.

Flaubert had become the object of English detestation because he had been the first writer who could conveniently be identified with Realism. The reproaches he incurred from the English public after the publication of his first novel had, in fact, been commonly addressed to French novels in general before *Madame Bovary*.[7] During his lifetime Flaubert was overshadowed in England by the dominant figures of Balzac and Victor Hugo. Moreover he was the victim of certain unfortunate coincidences such, for instance, as the publication of *Salammbô* at the same time as *Les Misérables*. Hugo's novel created a great stir and, as a result, *Salammbô* never really emerged from obscurity. Flaubert had to be cleared of accusations that English critics really meant for Hugo or Balzac and, by the time he was beginning to be appreciated as a novelist distinct from his precursors, critics had already started associating him with Zola and he found himself engulfed in the wave of hysteria caused by the publication of translations of Zola's novels. Although Zola was considered to be far more reprehensible than Flaubert by the English critics, they could trace the source of pollution back to the master of Realism. Apart from a very few critics who made a distinction between Flaubert's efforts and the literary trends of the period,[8] the majority included him in a tumultuous controversy which, strictly speaking, did not concern him.

In the same way as Victor Hugo had been made a scapegoat for the whole French nation in the earlier part of the century, so Gustave Flaubert carried the brunt of English wrath and became the embodiment of all French evils, personal, moral and political in the latter. Amongst other extra-literary circumstances the acceptance of his work in England was hindered by the political boycott of *Madame Bovary*. In France the accusation of offending public morals brought

against Flaubert's first published novel had been the pretext for suspending the *Revue de Paris* which, in the eyes of the government of the day, was far too liberal. It is interesting to find a corresponding attack on *Madame Bovary* in England where some of the accusations brought against the novel definitely had a more political than literary flavour. The *Saturday Review* denounced in *Madame Bovary* "the garbage of which we are invited to partake by the reviewer of the official journal of the French Empire."[9] Nor was this attack launched on the Imperial regime an isolated criticism. In its review of *Salammbô,* the *Saturday Review* indicted the book as the "foulest fungus which has yet appeared on the unhealthy tree of Imperialism."[10] Such expressions of resentment did not stem from the *Saturday Review* alone. The *Nineteenth Century,* in an article on Gustave Flaubert and George Sand, recalled the circumstances of the publication of *Madame Bovary:* "on its publication in 1857, the Second Empire, like all governments who attain to power with not very clean hands, wished to show the extreme orthodoxy of its moral and religious views, and endeavoured to suppress the book."[11] As late as 1890, the *Quarterly Review* confirmed that in the minds of many English readers political accusations were linked with attacks on Realism.[12]

A mixture of resentment, hatred and contempt for the French political scene thus coloured the judgements of English critics and the reading public, and obviously influenced their acceptance of Flaubert's works. The success of the latter can be said to have been very dependent on Franco-English relations of a social, political and literary order but, above all, it was a slow and difficult process because Flaubert had shocked English opinion on aesthetic, moral and philosophical grounds.

From 1857 the words 'ugly,' 'disgusting,' 'revolting,' 'repellent,' etc., had been applied very frequently to Flaubert's own individual output. One of George Saintsbury's very few criticisms of Flaubert was that he indulged in repulsive detail to an unnecessary extent. Even Henry James did not altogether approve of Flaubert's choice of subjects:

> Into all that makes life ignoble and vulgar and sterile, M. Flaubert has entered with an extraordinary penetration. The fullness and flatness of its all suffocate us; the pettiness and ugliness sicken us. . . . Everything in the book is ugly.[13]

The effect Flaubert's works produced on the reader was usually thought to be one of weariness as there was nothing in the novel to relieve its ugliness and flatness, and not one character for whom the reader could feel admiration and sympathy. Matthew Arnold in an article on Tolstoy and his work drew a comparison between *Anna Karenina* and ***Madame Bovary***. Referring to the latter, he noticed that there was "not a personage in the book to rejoice or console us; the springs of freshness and feeling are not there to create such personages," and Matthew Arnold concluded that ***Madame Bovary*** was a work of 'petrified feeling': "The treasures of compassion, tenderness, insight, which alone amid such guilt and misery can enable charm to subsist and to emerge are wanting to Flaubert."[14]

The charm Matthew Arnold alluded to seems to have been one of the preoccupations of the reading public in the Victorian era. Henry James in an American review of *la Tentation de Saint Antoine* had already alluded to the strange lack of charm in this book.[15] A few years later he wrote in *French Poets and Novelists:* "that a novel should have a certain charm seems to us the most rudimentary principle," and, to him, *Madame Bovary* as well as *Salammbô, L'éducation Sentimentale* and *La Tentation de Saint Antoine* were lacking in it.

Another point of critical controversy on Flaubert was the morality of his works. Except towards the end of the century the fields of ethics and aesthetics were ill-defined by the Victorians and public opinion was divided on the issue of morality in art. The majority of critics adopted a conventionally Victorian attitude and the outcry caused by the alleged immorality of Flaubert's work took a long time to abate. These criticisms were certainly very representative of the attitude of the reading public as well as that of the critics. The precise nature of this attitude is, of course, difficult to define, since the average reader does not usually record his observations on literary matters for the benefit of future generations, but there exists an interesting letter written on 23 June 1857 and addressed to Flaubert by Mrs Gertrude Tennant, née Collier, a former friend of the Flauberts. Although there had not been any contact between the Colliers and Flaubert for several years, Flaubert had sent Gertrude a copy of his first published novel. Mrs Tennant was so genuinely shocked that she sent him a very moralising letter in which she shows herself mainly concerned with the moral duties of a writer:

> . . . je ne ferai pas de phrases, mais je vous dirai tout bonnement que je suis émerveillée que vous, avec votre imagination, avec votre admiration pour tout ce qui est beau, que vous ayez écrit, que vous ayez pu prendre plaisir à écrire quelque chose de si hideux que ce livre! Je trouve tout cela si mauvais! . . . Je ne comprends pas comment vous ayez [sic] pu écrire tout cela!—où il n'y a absolument rien de beau, ni de bon![16]

This curt reception and final rejection of the book, coming from an intelligent and educated woman, was probably a typical reaction among the Victorian ladies who could read French. The outburst of horror was certainly a spontaneous reaction as the book had not yet been reviewed in England except for a brief hostile article in the *Saturday Review* on 6 June 1857.

After the publication of ***Madame Bovary,*** some critics had been appalled by its immorality; conversely others had seen in it a deliberately moral work. Henry James thought it was a

> . . . great work capable of being applied to educational purposes. It is an elaborate picture of vice, but it represents it as so indefeasibly commingled with misery that in a really enlightened system of education it would form exactly the volume to put into the hands of young persons in whom vicious tendencies had been distinctly perceived, and who were wavering as to which way they should let the balance fall.[17]

In fact, the moralising intention detected in ***Madame Bovary*** was considered by Fitzjames Stephen as the main fault of the book:

> . . . perhaps the worst feature of ***Madame Bovary*** is the obvious intention on the part of the author to write rather a moral book . . . the real immorality which is involved in such a tale as ***Madame Bovary*** lies in the want which it presumes in its readers of any moral distinctions at all. . . .

The reviewer considered the book to be immoral because it showed the consequences of adultery if discovered, but it did not show that adultery in itself was "vile, hateful and treacherous."[18]

Amongst general disapproval there remained a few English critics who firmly believed that morals had nothing to do with art. In 1857 Meredith had stated his belief that ***Madame Bovary*** was not immoral.[19] The lines of his judgement had been followed by George Saintsbury and Henry James in the seventies and by the followers of the 'Art for Art's Sake' school in the nineties.

However, a number of those critics who defended Flaubert from a variety of accusations made on moral grounds, themselves attacked him on philosophical grounds. The accusation of pessimism was indeed a frequent one. Some critics like E. Newman deplored it but excused Flaubert by attributing this disposition to his nervous disease. Surprisingly none of them understood at the time that his predisposition to pessimism derived from his deep-rooted hatred of life. Most of them thought of it only as the inevitable consequence of French Decadence. The French no longer believed in God, no longer believed in moral values and, as a result, French literature in general and Flaubert's work in particular were marked by pessimism and nihilism. This, together with the determinist explanation of human behaviour, was the root cause of the outcry against *Madame Bovary*.

The first aspect of Flaubert's work to be generally appreciated in England was his style. As early as 1863, the *Saturday Review,* whose ferocity was well known, disparaged *Salammbô* but made concessions regarding the style which was referred to as "forcible and clear." As the years passed more and more critics praised Flaubert's prose and his painstaking craftsmanship. Most of them, however, did not understand that it was an absurdity to divorce ideas and their expression. The English public gradually became more tolerant and even admiring as regards the subject matter of Flaubert's novels. Gradually, the objections disappeared: first those of a moral order, then those of a more philosophical order. The causes for this progressive change of attitude towards Flaubert were manifold.

Victorianism had changed over the second half of the century, and was indeed very different in the nineties from what it had been in the sixties. It was slowly moving towards greater freedom and independence. The controversy over Realism which had ended in a partial victory for the Realist had been reflected in the periodical literature of the time. Controversial articles on the problems of literature and its relationship to science, morals and philosophy were found in most reviews during the eighties. As Realism became less of a burning issue the articles devoted to the problems it involved naturally decreased in number. At the same time the theories of Art for Art's Sake recruited more and more followers in England. The general artistic trends of the time were such as to encourage the appreciation of Flaubert's works. New principles of art were exposed in periodicals and it became accepted that morality was no more the concern of art than it was that of science. Moreover, the subject matter of fiction became less restricted by conventions and writers had more scope to treat it. In 1894, A. Waugh wrote in the *Yellow Book* that

> . . . it is . . . the privilege, it is more, it is the duty of the man of letters to speak out, to be fearless, to be frank, to give no ear to the Puritans of his hour, to have no care for the objections of prudery.[20]

The reviewer was very conscious of the duty of the man of letters on whom posterity relies for an accurate picture of the history of his time. In the case of Flaubert, the relationship between his writing and the scientific age is obvious, and it had been pointed out by Sainte-Beuve in his first article on Flaubert. With the progress of materialism which entailed a certain amount of pessimism, Flaubert's work became more

readily accepted and indeed novels as a whole became more and more appreciated in the late nineteenth century. Flaubert himself had helped to make the novel a recognised literary genre. J.C. Tarver summed up the position of the novel in 1895 by saying that

> . . . the novel from being the resource of idle moments, the dissipation of indolent minds, a thing to be preached against, and put away on Sundays, has become the chosen instrument of the greatest thinkers of our age, of our most earnest preachers. Those who object to the works of George Eliot because they are so disagreeable, to *Madame Bovary* because it is so cruel, and declare that such things ought not to be written, are simply stoning the prophets in order to be rid of them in their home-truths.[21]

When the first novels by Flaubert appeared in England, they were too bold for the majority of English readers. Their gradual acceptance was subject to the changing values in England, to the evolution of thought, and to a genuine interest in the philosophy of the Realists which reflected a deep pessimism in native English writers themselves. Although it may be said that Flaubert's influence far exceeded his popularity in Victorian England, it is also unquestionably true that he was considered by the intellectual elite not only one of the masters of fiction but also one of the main forces of liberation in nineteenth-century art.

Notes

[1] A. Rouxeville, "The Reception of Flaubert in Victorian England," *Comparative Literature Studies* 14 (1977): 274-284.

[2] Anonymous, no title, *Pall Mall Gazette* 31 (1880): 10-11.

[3] H. James, *French Poets and Novelists* (London: Macmillan & Co., 1893) 199.

[4] G. Saintsbury, "The Present State of the Novel," *Fortnightly Review* 42 (1887): 410-417.

[5] G. Saintsbury, "Gustave Flaubert," *Fortnightly Review* 23 (1878): 575-595.

[6] W.C. Frierson, "The English Controversy over Realism in Fiction, 1885-95," *PMLA* 43 (1928): 533-550.

[7] Anonymous, "English Novels," *Fraser's Magazine* 44 (1851): 375-391.

[8] W.S. Lilly, "The New Naturalism," *Fortnightly Review* 38 (1885): 240-256.

[9] Anonymous, "French Literature," *Saturday Review* 3 (1857): 523-525.

[10] Anonymous, *"Salammbô,"* Saturday Review 15 (1863): 309-311.

[11] N.H. Kennard, "Gustave Flaubert and George Sand," *Nineteenth Century* 20 (1886): 693-708.

[12] Anonymous, "Realism and Decadence in French Fiction," *Quarterly Review* 171 [1890]: 57-90.

[13] See note 3.

[14] M. Arnold, "Count Leo Tolstoi," *Fortnightly Review* 42 (1887): 783-799.

[15] Anonymous, "Flaubert's *Temptation of Saint Anthony,*" *The Nation* 34 (1874): 241-246.

[16] J. Bruneau, *"Madame Bovary* jugée par un fantôme de Trouville," *Revue de Littérature Comparée* 31 (1957): 277-279.

[17] See note 3.

[18] Anonymous, *"Madame Bovary,"* Saturday Review 4 (1857): 40-41. The reviewer refers here to the well-known sentence: "Emma retrouvait dans cet adultère toutes les platitudes du mariage," later changed to the safer "l'adultère." See B.F. Bart, "Louis Bouilhet, Flaubert's 'accoucheur'," *Symposium* 17 (1963): 183-202.

[19] G. Meredith, "Belles Lettres," *Westminster Review* 12 (1857): 585-604.

[20] A. Waugh, "Reticence in Literature," *Yellow Book* 1 (1894): 201-219.

[21] J. C. Tarver, *Gustave Flaubert as Seen in His Works and Correspondence* (Westminster: Constable, 1895).

Lisa Lowe (essay date 1991)

SOURCE: "Nationalism and Exoticism: Nineteenth-Century Others in Flaubert's *Salammbô* and *L'Education sentimentale,*" in *Macropolitics of Nineteenth-Century Literature: Nationalism, Exoticism, Imperialism,* edited by Jonathan Arac and Harriet Ritvo, University of Pennsylvania Press, 1991, pp. 213-42.

[*In the following essay, Lowe discusses "the French tradition of orientalism" and the treatment of "otherness" in Flaubert's works. Lowe argues that "Flaubert's corpus, considered as a series of orien-talist moments, reflects the divided and conflicted nature of nineteenth-century French culture itself."*]

Orientalist Text as Cultural Artifact

The necessarily diverse ways in which we construct and approximate the "macropolitical" field in nineteenth-century studies vary not only according to the national culture through which one approaches the field, but certainly also according to the nature of the materials through which one reads, reconstitutes, and perhaps, invents the "macropolitical"—whether they be historical, literary, or para-literary materials. The "macropolitical" can be extrapolated then as a heterogeneous composite of the diversity of "micropolitical" descriptions; we arrive at one sense of "macropolitics" through a variety of analyses of specific textual moments in the nineteenth century. In my study, I consider the means and strategies through which different types of otherness—national, cultural, historical, and sexual—are rhetorically postulated and parodied in the texts of Flaubert. Flaubert's texts are cultural artifacts that dramatize some of the dynamics peculiar to the nineteenth-century culture by which they are produced, and which they, in turn, produce; the urgent concerns with a national identity distinguishable from culturally, economically, and sexually different Others, emerges at this moment from French involvements in North Africa and the rivalries between France and other continental nations, as well as from the conflicts between classes and ideologies within the unstable French state itself. Figurations of the oriental, the woman, and the barbarian masses, as Others of a national bourgeois identity, textualize the desires of French national identification in an age of instability, as much as this textualizing contributes to, and further determines, the convention of establishing a national identity in the projection of different Others. The orientalism in Flaubert's texts does not merely indicate how an Orient is constructed as an Other of the Occident as a means of establishing a coherent European national identity; it also provides some illustrative statements about the kinds of macropolitical circumstances which generate the narratives of Occident and Orient, male and female, and bourgeois and worker, in nineteenth-century France.

The importance of the Orient as a *topos* in Flaubert's work has been noted in a number of recent studies both of Flaubert and of orientalism.[1] Particularly the *Voyage en Orient* (1849-52), an account of Flaubert's travels through Egypt and the Middle East, and *Salammbô* (1862), his novel set in Carthage after the First Punic War, occupy influential positions in the French tradition of orientalism. It is a tradition that includes literatures as different as eighteenth-century travel fictions by Montesquieu or Voltaire, nineteenth-century narratives of pilgrimages to the Orient by Volney or Chateaubriand, the diversely orientalist twentieth-century novels of Pierre Loti, André Malraux, or Marguerite Duras, and the more theoretically self-conscious representations of Japan and China by Roland Barthes or Julia Kristeva. The Orient evoked in the last three centuries of French literature is alternately figured as a powerfully consuming unknown, a forbidden erotic figure, a grotesquely uncivilized world of violence, and a site of incomprehensible difference. In all senses, the place of the Orient is a richly literary space, where French culture inscribes its various myths and preoccupations by invoking an imaginary and culturally different Other.

The diversity of narratives about the Orient reflects different states of urgency in the history of French nationalism; the importance of defining a fixed and prominent identity among other western European nations changes in different ages, and the French representations of the Orient vary as territories, boundaries, and empires change. In eighteenth-century travel literature, for example, the Orient is often figured as a metaphorical reflection of a notion of occidental Self, geographically displaced onto a fictional land; the colonial concern with land and empire is expressed in this geographical trope. In contrast, during the nineteenth-century, the Orient is frequently represented as a female figure, and the narrative of Occident and Orient is figured in the rhetorical framework of the romantic quest; the female Orient is a metonymical reduction of what is different from and desired by the masculine European subject. For example, in *Salammbô,* the occidental regard for a constructed oriental opposite is not only eroticized, but figured as the quest for the forbidden female priestess Salammbô; the spatial logic of eighteenth-century travel literature—which asserts the geographical centrality of Europe and distances non-European Others—becomes, in the nineteenth century, a hetero-erotic and gendered relationship. Orientalist techniques of figuration resonate and collude with the nineteenth-century literature which constitutes women as romantic and sexual objects. The projection of Others as not simply culturally but sexually different constitutes a figuration of social and political crises in a rhetorical register of sexuality: for example, the instability of the regimes oscillating between revolution and reaction after 1789, the crisis of class definition in a bourgeois age, the changes in family, gender, and social structure in a time of rapid industrialization, urbanization, and emigration—these may all be figured in the concerns with the centrality and coherence of masculine individuality over and against a powerfully different feminine Other. The problematic tensions within the French identity are rhetorically condensed into the *topoi* and rhetorics of cultural difference between France and other nations, and the sexual difference between male and female.

In 1853, Flaubert wrote to Louise Colet of the Egyptian courtesan, Kuchuk-Hânem, one of the subjects of the *Voyage en Orient*. His description of "la femme orientale" is paradigmatic of the vivid intersection and collusion of the discourses of orientalism and colonial domination, and that of romantic desire and the sexual domination of women: "La femme orientale est une machine, et rien de plus; elle ne fait aucune différence entre un homme et un autre homme . . . C'est nous qui pensons à elle, mais elle ne pense guère à nous. Nous faisons de l'esthétique sur son compte."[2] In Flaubert's letter, "la femme orientale" is invented as an exaggerated sensuality and sexuality against which "civilized man" may be distinguished, but in this invention, she only generates sexuality, she is unable to comprehend its pleasures. There is no correspondence between "la femme orientale" and women of North Africa and Asia; rather, the representation "la femme orientale" is a metonymy of an invented opposite to an imagined European masculinity, an otherness whose referent is not femininity but rather the construction of masculinity based upon the notion of masculine desire. Further, the equation of the oriental woman and the highly prized object of the industrialized nineteenth century, the machine, reduces and dehumanizes Kuchuk-Hânem, and renders her the technology, and sexual pleasure the surplus value, for which the "femme/machine" is exploited. But the portrait of the Egyptian woman is a representation of a European masculine desire to master, and in the unsuccessful mastery of "her"—"she" does not recognize Flaubert, he does not succeed in inscribing himself on the oriental world, it overwhelms him, is complete without him—it is an equal and concomitant statement about the Frenchman's anxiety about a failure of this desire, against which the desire to master is articulated.

The last decade of criticism on orientalism,[3] particularly since Edward Said's influential study (*Orientalism,* 1979), suggests that these literary Orients are invented, and that "the cultures and nations whose location is in the East" are dominated by means of these fictions, or constructed misrepresentations. Orientalism is a discourse, Said argues, which is, on the one hand, homogenizing—the Orient is leveled into one indistinguishable entity; and is, on the other hand, anatomizing and enumerative—the Orient is an encyclopedia of details, divided and particularized into manageable parts; the discourse manages and produces information about an invented Other, which locates and justifies the power of the knowledgeable European Self. My essay, following Said's notion of orientalist discourse, considers a moment of the French orientalist tradition to describe how texts, as cultural artifacts, construct cultural narratives about the relationship between Occident and Orient. However, I depart from Said's critique in several respects. First, European productions and managements of difference are not limited to inscriptions of cultural difference, but take the forms of ascriptions of gender, class, caste, race, and nation, as well. For example, in different texts by Flaubert, the oriental figures enunciate the structuring themes of quite different discourses: the representation of Kuchuk-Hânem in the *Voyage en Orient* (1850) and *Corres-*

pondance (1853) figures her oriental otherness in both racial and sexual terms; whereas in *Salammbô* (1862) the drama of the barbarian oriental tribes builds upon a concurrent discourse about the French working class revolts of 1848; and in *L'Education sentimentale* (1869), the oriental motif is invoked as a figure of sentimental and romantic desire, offering a literary critique of this *topos*. In this sense, I would like to foreground gender and class as two equally important valences of difference within nineteenth-century French orientalism, to propose that the constructions of "woman" as the Other of man, and the barbarian mass as the Other of the bourgeois commercial class, are ideological tropes as powerful as the orientalist constructions, and to suggest that, in this regard, marxist and feminist theories provide crucial methods of deconstructive reading.[4]

Secondly, if we understand from this observation of the importance of class and gender that inscription and domination are not uniform, but multivalent, operating through a plurality of discourses at different moments, this heterogeneity contradicts the notion of orientalist discourse as discrete, monolithic, and mastering. The cultural text of Flaubert's orientalism exemplifies that any "discourse of orientalism" is bound up with, indeed reanimates some of the structuring themes of, other discourses that emerge in the nineteenth century: e.g., the colonial and scientific discourses concerning "race," the medical discourses about "sexuality," the commercial discourses of industry and class. Further, discourses are not univocal, they include not only dominant formations, but challenges to those dominant formations. The orientalizing formations articulated in Flaubert's *Salammbô* and *Voyage* are reiterated and parodied at another moment in the corpus, in *L'Education sentimentale*. Flaubert's divided corpus exemplifies one instance of the greater discursive field that is heterogeneous, dynamic, and dialectical. The notion of orientalist discourse as mastering generates readings that render orientalist texts unequivocally appropriative or dominant with regard to the one cultural Other treated by the texts; whereas a consideration of orientalist discourse as a heterogeneous, rather than homogeneous, series of rhetorics, tropes, and literary traditions through which the management and production of many Others take place, permit us readings in which we trace not only the desires for mastery, but the critiques of these desires as well. In other words, the critique of orientalism is not simply a late twentieth-century post-colonial critical position retrospectively applied to a tradition: the societies and historical moments which produced these texts are already divided and already self-critical, and the tensions between the desires of orientalism and the failures of these desires are already thematized within the texts of these societies. In this sense, my readings of Flaubert's corpus do not consider it as a unified, purely "colonizing" corpus which exemplifies a mis-

representation and appropriation of women, non-Europeans, and the working class; rather, my reading concentrates on the ways in which the various texts reflect different states of conflict in the history of French nationalism. While the *Voyage, Correspondance,* and *Salammbô* exemplify nineteenth-century orientalisms which figure the Orient as female or barbarian Others, the later work, *L'Education sentimentale,* thematizes and critically observes orientalism; the narrative of *L'Education* thematizes Frédéric's use of the oriental motif, and calls attention to it as an emblem of Frédéric's sentimentalism. As my reading of the novel's final reminiscence of the bordello of "La Turque" suggests, orientalism is ultimately targeted in *L'Education* as a regressive *topos* of sentimentality, a posture of subjective and cultural instability in the figuration of an Other. Flaubert's corpus, considered as a series of orientalist moments, reflect the divided and conflicted nature of nineteenth-century French culture itself; the orientalism of the various texts is multivalent and heterogeneous, expressing a plurality of ideologies. The texts of orientalism themselves contain critiques of orientalist logics and rhetorics.

Thirdly, it seems necessary to revise and render more complex the thesis that an ontology of Occident and Orient appears in a consistent manner throughout all cultural and historical moments,[5] because the operation which grants this kind of uniform coherence and closure to any discourse risks misrepresenting the far more heterogeneous conditions and operations of discourses. When Michel Foucault posits the concept of "discursive formations"—the regularities in groups of statements, institutions, operations, and practices—he is careful to distinguish it as an *irregular* series of regularities which produce objects of knowledge. In other words, a phenomenon, such as the notion of the Orient, is said to be constituted by a "regularity"—the conjunction of statements and institutions (maps, literary narratives, treatises, missionary reports, diplomatic politics, etc.) pertaining to the Orient; however, the manner in which these materials conjoin to produce the category "Orient" is unequal to the conjunction constituting it at another historical moment, or in another national culture.[6] In a like manner, I would argue against the "historical desire" to view the occidental conception of the oriental Other as an unchanging *topos,* the origin of which is European man's curiosity about the non-European world. The misapprehension of an identical construction of an object through time does not adequately appreciate that the process through which an object of difference—the Orient—is constituted, is enabled precisely by the non-identity through time of such notions, Occident and Orient. That is, the identification of a static dualism of identity and difference as the means through which a discourse expresses domination and subordination, upholds the logic of the dualism and fails to account for the "differences" (internal discontinuities, heterogeneity) inherent in each term. In the case of orientalism, the misunderstanding of uniformity prohibits a consideration of the plural and inconstant referents of both terms—Occident and Orient; the binary opposition of Occident and Orient is a misleading perception which serves to suppress the specific heterogeneities, inconstancies, and slippages of each individual notion.[7]

In addition, the assumption of a unifying principle—even one that we must assume to be partly true, that the representation of the Orient expresses the colonial relationships between Europe and the non-European world—leaves uninvestigated the necessary possibility that social events and circumstances other than the relationships between Europe and the non-European world are represented in the literature about the Orient, and that the relative importances of these other conditions differ over time and by culture. Allegorizing the meaning of the representation of the Orient as if it were exclusively and always an expression of European colonialism analyzes the relationship between text and context in terms of a homology, an overdetermining of meaning such that every signified must have one signifier, and every narrative one interpretation. Such a totalizing logic represses the heterologic possibilities that texts are not simple reproductions of context—indeed that "context" is plural, unfixed, unrepresentable—and that orientalism may well be an apparatus through which a variety of concerns with differences are figured. I consider the "Orient as Other" as a literary trope that may register a variety of national crises—at one time, the race for colonies; at others, class conflicts and workers' revolts, or changes in the sexual roles in a time of rapid urbanization and industrialization. Orientalism facilitates the inscription of many different kinds of differences as oriental otherness, and the use of oriental figures at one moment may be distinct from their use in another historical period, in another set of texts, or even at another moment in the same corpus.

A very important and necessary political statement is contained in the thesis that orientalism is an expression of European imperialism. Yet, when we polemically propose that the discourse of orientalism is both discrete and monolithic, this falsely isolates the discourse and ignores the condition that discourses are never singular; discourses operate in conflict, they overlap and collude, they do not produce fixed or unified objects. For this reason, my essay treats orientalism as one discourse in a complex intersection. My reading of the heterogeneity of orientalism, based on this nineteenth-century moment represented by the corpus of Flaubert, does not dispute the orientalist criticism that argues that there is a discernible history of European representation and appropriation of the Orient; I do, however, problematize the assumption that orientalism *monolithically* constructs the Orient as Other of the Occident. The purpose of making this distinction is to challenge the critical perception of a single univocal discourse that dominates and controls forms of cultural difference. My essay ultimately rejects the totalizing paradigm that grants such authority to a managing discourse, because this kind of paradigm tends to understand all forms of resistance to be contained within the discourse.

The Orient as Woman: **Salammbô** *and Kuchuk-Hânem*

The novel **Salammbô** concerns the Carthaginian priestess Salammbô and Mâtho, the leader of the mercenary army who falls in love with her. Salammbô is the daughter of the Carthaginian ruler Hamilcar and is betrothed by her father to a rival leader. In the story of Mâtho's impossible desire for Salammbô, the oriental woman is exoticized as distant, forbidden, and inaccessible, and is objectified as the prize or bounty of Mâtho's war against Carthage. The Barbarians' efforts, under Mâtho's leadership, to penetrate barricaded Carthage, to puncture the city's aqueduct, and to steal the sacred veil of Tanit are contemporary with Mâtho's growing desire for the virgin priestess Salammbô; the simultaneity of the two conquest themes contributes to the figuration of the oriental city of Carthage as the woman, Salammbô. The cultural and historical alterity of Carthage as the Orient, are figured in the sexual alterity of Salammbô, as woman. Salammbô is, as woman, a complicated representation of multivalent and intersecting inscriptions: she is a forbidden object of desire as well as a material object of exchange, the barricaded city and the virgin priestess, the infinite beauty of "la nature" and the sacred, violent, oriental world. She is a fiction of European man's Other, represented as the seducer and recipient of Mâtho's desire, as the prey and object of men's social exchange in war, and as a metonym of the wealthy city of Carthage who starves its mercenary children.

Two separate descriptions of Salammbô's entrances emblematize her different functions in the novel as eroticized woman and as object of exchange in war. The first occurs when she enters the courtyard where the mercenary soldiers are feasting at her father's house in his absence. During the feast, the soldiers have proclaimed the injustice of the Carthaginian republic in having neglected to pay them for their labor during the war with Rome. They curse Hamilcar's wealth and power; they kill the sacred fish of the Barca family.

> Enfin elle descendit l'escalier des galères. Les prêtres la suivirent. Elle avança dans l'avenue des cyprès, et elle marchait lentement entre les tables des capitaines, qui se reculaient un peu en la regardant passer.
>
> Sa chevelure, poudrée d'un sable violet et réunie en forme de tour selon la mode des vierges

chananéenes, la faisait paraître plus grande. Des tresses de perles attachées à ses tempes descendaient jusqu'au coins de sa bouche, rose comme un grenade entr'ouverte. Il y avait sur sa poitrine un assemblage de pierres lumineuses, imitant par leur bigarrure les écailles d'une murène. Ses bras, garnis de diamants, sortaient nus de sa tunique sans manches, étoilée de fleurs rouges sur un fond tout noir. (12)

In this passage, Salammbô is described in a vertical descension, from her hair, to her mouth, her breasts, her arms, and finally her ankles. The descriptive gaze of the narrator anatomizes, particularizes, and sequesters isolated parts of Salammbô. The gems of her "costume" are an ironically conspicuous display of her market value as an object, her significance as Hamilcar's daughter. The attention to the "perles," "pierres lumineuses," and "diamants" of Salammbô's dress marks her as the embodiment of Hamilcar's hoarded wealth, the "war-chest" desired by the mercenary soldiers as she enters the scene. And yet the narration remains at a distance from her; the gaze does not penetrate into the interior of Salammbô, but remains fastened upon the jewels, textures, and fabrics of her dress. Salammbô, although described in particulars, is not a character in the immediate world of the novel as others might be, but rather a represented figure which calls attention to itself as representation, unknowable, eccentric, and extravagant to the narrator and the mercenary soldiers. Salammbô is compared to "un tour," "une grenade," and "une murène"; while the metaphors attempt to capture Salammbô, she is nonetheless rendered quite strange by these comparisons. The metaphor of the tower evokes height, but at the same time, the comparison renders the woman excessively tall and unfamiliar, almost dwarfing the men below. Salammbô is paradoxically distanced and isolated, objectified and desired by the narrative description. "Salammbô" is a figure for contradiction; she is concrete and worldly, like her gems, but she has a remote unworldly aspect which resists possession and referentiality.

The *topos* of the descending oriental woman, both eroticized and materially objectified, appears also in the *Voyage en Orient* in Flaubert's first encounter with the Egyptian courtesan, Kuchuk-Hânem.[8]

Sur l'escalier, en face de nous, la lumière l'entourant et se détachant sur le fond bleu du ciel, une femme debout en pantalons roses, n'ayant autour du torse qu'une gaze d'un violet foncé.

Elle venait de sortir du bain, sa gorge dure sentait frais, quelque chose comme une odeur de térébenthine sucrée. . . .

Ruchiouk-Hânem est une grande et splendide créature, plus blanche qu'une Arabe, elle est de

Damas; sa peau, surtout du corps, est un peu cafetée. Quand elle s'asseoit de côté, elle a des bourrelets de bronze sur ses flancs. Ses yeux noirs et démesurés, ses sourcils noirs, ses narines fendues, larges épaules solides, seins abondants, pomme. (487-88)

Between 1849 and 1851, Flaubert traveled in Egypt and the Middle East. Among his most notable portraits is the one of Kuchuk-Hânem, who appears in both the letters from Egypt and the *Voyage en Orient*. Kuchuk-Hânem is said to be the model for Salammbô, and Flaubert wrote *Salammbô* upon his return from his travels. And yet the Orient that Flaubert writes about in his travels and articulates in the letters about Kuchuk-Hânem is an Orient received from cultural myths and a literary tradition. As with the descent of Salammbô, the Egyptian woman enters the narrative gaze from an elevated position on the staircase. There is an allusion to her height, as well, in "[elle] est une grande et splendide créature." However, it is not simply in her height that she is rendered strange. She is called a "créature," as if she is a different species, not human, animal. Further, her eyes are "noirs et démesurés," and their scale and color seem to make them icons of her difference. The perspective from which the Egyptian woman is regarded is a disturbingly immediate one, and the writer of the *Voyage* emphasizes her otherness not through the use of distancing metaphors (as in the passage introducing Salammbô) but through the intimacy of the bodily and sensual detail in the descriptions of her race and her sex. In "Quand elle s'asseoit de côté, elle a des bourrelets de bronze sur ses flancs," the narrator constitutes not only her otherness as an Egyptian in the attention to the color of her skin "un peu cafetée," but her otherness as a woman, as an erotic object scrutinized very near, as well. A perspective of close proximity is utilized to aestheticize her image, to reduce her as object; the very details—"n'ayant autour du torse qu'une gaze d'un violet foncé," "seins abondants, pomme"—establish and privilege the artist's eye and constitute Kuchuk Hânem as object. It is upon the objectivity of Kuchuk-Hânem that the subjectivity, the "métier" and identity of Flaubert, is established.

In the passage describing Salammbô's second descent, she greets her father Hamilcar when he returns to Carthage after the First Punic War.

Salammbô descendait alors l'escalier des galères. Toutes ses femmes venaient derrière elle; et, à chacun de ses pas, elles descendaient aussi.

Hamilcar s'arrêta, en apercevant Salammbô. Elle lui était survenue après la mort de plusieurs enfants mâles. D'ailleurs, la naissance des filles passait pour une calamité dans les religions du Soleil. (139-40)

The two descents—the one before the mercenary soldiers, Mâtho, and Narr'Havras, the other before Hamilcar—indicate two dimensions of Salammbô's objectification as woman. In the first passage, she is a remote, inaccessible sexual object; in the second, as she greets her father, she is a material object of exchange, useful only to Hamilcar as wealth to barter. In the first, the woman is beloved, sought, and desired; in the second, she is daughter, disdained and exchanged for a better price. The objectification of the woman as material possession is particularly evident in Hamilcar's attitude toward Salammbô when he receives the rumor that his daughter may have lost her virginity to the leader of the Barbarian tribes. Hamilcar's rage at imagining his daughter's violation mixes with his anger about the theft of the sacred veil, as well as his indignation that his properties and riches have been mismanaged in his absence: "malgré ses efforts pour les bannir de sa pensée, il retrouvait continuellement les Barbares. Leurs débordements se confondaient avec la honte de sa fille" (153). For Hamilcar, hearing of his daughter's alleged rape is equal to his discovery that property from his home has been stolen. It is the combined effect of acknowledging all of his losses—his material loss of property, as well as the loss of ownership of Salammbô, which the hypothetical loss of her virginity represents to him—which moves Hamilcar to accept the command of the Carthaginian armies against the Barbarian tribes. When Hamilcar enlists the aid of the Numidian tribes, he offers his daughter as bride to Narr'Havras, the Numidian king, saying "En recompense des services que tu m'as rendus, Narr'Havras, je te donne ma fille." Narr'Havras' gratitude is described: "[Il] eut un grand geste de surprise, puis se jeta sur ses mains qu'il couvrit de baisers." (235) Salammbô is the prize, the bounty, exchanged between men at war. The economy of war between men is based upon the woman as territory which is bartered and exchanged. The man is granted the possession of the woman when he kills for another man. Although "ses mains" is somewhat ambiguous in its reference, it is presumably Hamilcar's hands which Narr'Havras kisses; through the exchange of Salammbô, the two men are erotically united.[9] Salammbô is described as being "calme comme une statue, semblait ne pas comprendre" (235)—she is the token whose receipt seals the contract that the Numidians will kill for the Carthaginians.

French Barbarians in *Salammbô*

Salammbô takes place in 240 BC, after Carthage loses to Rome in the First Punic War, when the various North African tribes who had been employed as mercenaries by Carthage revolt against the Carthaginian Republic. The novel describes the wars between Carthage and these Barbarian tribes. At the time of the First Punic War, Rome and Carthage are competitors for trade in the western Mediterranean. Although a

world which is historically and geographically other to nineteenth-century France is evoked, it is not difficult to recognize in *Salammbô* echoes of themes from Flaubert's France. Just as Carthage is a commercial republic competing with Rome for markets and empire, so too is early nineteenth-century France an emerging commercial force, threatening and being threatened by Great Britain. Napoleon's defeats by the British are echoed in Carthage's repeated defeats, under Hamilcar, and then his son Hannibal, in the First (264 BC), Second (218-201 BC) and Third (149-146 BC) Punic Wars. The decline of Carthage is due as much to its losses to Rome as to the revolt of the Barbarian tribes of North Africa, just as the instability of France after its international losses in the periods of bourgeois revolt (1830) was shaken further by the workers' revolts during the Revolutions of 1848. Yet while the Roman Republic is a forceful determinant in the war between Rome and Carthage and its mercenaries, Rome is conspicuously absent from the novel, which focuses strictly on the war between Carthage and the Barbarians.[10] Rather than figuring France's Roman Other, the Barbarian tribes in *Salammbô* may be understood as a simultaneous figuration of the two "internal" and "external" Others constituted as threats by French bourgeois society in the mid-nineteenth-century; on the one hand, the volatile and emergent French working class whose concerns erupt in 1848, and on the other hand, the North African colonies violently occupied by French armies in the 1830s and 1840s. The extreme brutality of the battle scenes in *Salammbô* alienates the slaughter of rioting masses in 1848 onto a very distant historical setting, at the same time that the location of the violence in North Africa curiously "confesses" the equally violent French activities in North Africa and Egypt during the first half of the nineteenth century. The French occupation and military subjugation of Algeria in the 1830s and 1840s, which included systematic massacres of the native populations, is defamiliarized in the portrait of Carthage's commercial and military exploitation of the nomad peoples outside the walls of the city. Internal class violence and external nationalistic violence are thematized in the novel, but the responsibility for those violences is quite apart from France when it is detoured into the oriental world of Carthage and the surrounding Barbarian tribes. A world of war—determined by commercial greed and the desire for empire, and founded upon the subjugation of other lands and other people—is removed by the exotic context of *Salammbô*.

The fascination with the themes of war in the novel—the subjugation of many races of people by the Carthaginian Republic, the penetration of the walled-in city, war as the alliances and enmities among men, the status of women as the bounty of the war between men—reveals a particular displacement of both French fascination with, and denial of its own nineteenth-century war efforts, in North America, Africa, and continental Europe, as well as in France itself. Because the historically distant Orient is not contemporary with modern Europe, the slaughter of the warring factions can be distanced and aestheticized. In the novel's juxtaposition of two powerful populations, Carthage and the Barbarians, the structure of the novel portrays each as equal to the other: each is involved in a frenzy of violence, each disapproves of the other's violence, and does not recognize that the other community's barbarism is thoroughly present within their own group. In the wars between Carthage and the Barbarians, the novel itself thematizes the process by which one group's violence is expelled in the image of the threatening and different Other.

The dynamic by which one group is constituted as "outside" or Other to the hegemonic culture is represented by the description of the nomad peoples who live just outside of Carthage. These nomads are described as Mâtho and the Barbarians approach the walls of the city.[11]

> Il y avait en dehors des fortifications des gens d'une autre race et d'une origine inconnue,— tous chasseurs de porc-épic, mangeurs de mollusques et de serpents. Ils allaient dans les cavernes prendre des hyènes vivantes, qu'ils s'amusaient à faire courir le soir sur les sables de Mégara, entres les stèles des tombeaux. Leur cabanes, de fange et de varech, s'accrochait contre la falaise comme des nids d'hirondelles. Ils vivaient là, sans gouvernement et sans dieux, pêle-mêle, complètement nus, à la fois débiles et farouches, et depuis des siècles exécrés par le peuple, à cause de leurs nourritures immondes. (*Salammbô*, 60-61)

This passage contains an inventory of the means by which a group of nomads who live outside the walls of the city are classified and constituted as Other—as barbarian—by the Barbarians themselves, who are approaching the fortifications. They are described as "d'une autre race," a difference and exteriority marked by their position outside the walls of the city of Carthage, and "d'une origine inconnue," beyond Mâtho's people's territory of information and experience. They are outside of history, and eccentric to culture and civilization. They retreat into caves to hunt "leurs nourritures immondes"; they eat prohibited, unclean, wild foods, like porcupines, shellfish, and snakes. Their dwellings, "de fange et de varech," are made of materials which are coded as primitive and natural. Hayden White discusses the cultural function of the Other as "savage" as a "technique of ostensive self-definition by negation. . . . If we do not know what we think 'civilization' *is,* we can always find an example of what it is not."[12] In a complementary observation, Mary Louise Pratt notes that there are very particular ethnographic "tropes"—literary figures or commonplaces—which characterize the reports of

European anthropologists encountering native, "primitive" cultures.[13] This description of the nomads as "sans gouvernement et sans dieux . . . complètement nus" exemplifies a number of tropes, used throughout the eighteenth and nineteenth centuries, for constituting cultural and historical otherness as a chaotic "nature," before language, society, and law. The notion of the "primitive" which evolves throughout European philosophical, political, and literary discourses (like the notions of the "oriental") comprises a genealogy of myths, a series of signifiers, which refer to the desire of European culture to define itself through negation, in terms of what it fears it is, and desires not to be. Rousseau's descriptions of primitive man in the state of nature in the second *Discourse,* or Montesquieu's Troglodytes in the *Lettres persanes,* express less about the origins of western civilization than they do about the dilemma of national self-representation and French cultural desires during the Enlightenment. To the extent that these tropes are recognizable as established rhetorics for constituting difference, *Salammbô* thematizes its own orientalism and the displacement of French barbarism—against both North African and working class Others—into a novel about oriental violence. That the novel levels the two sides of the conflict between Carthage and the Barbarians, revealing each to be equally barbaric, suggests that nationalism and war depend upon the representation of one's own barbarism in the Other. The "othering" of the nomads by the Barbarians is repeated in the attitudes of Carthage and the Barbarians towards one another: the disdain for the Other, the inability to recognize the Other's crimes as one's own.

Carthage's violence towards the Barbarians is described in sensualized, particularized detail, as are the Barbarian tortures of Carthaginians. Descriptions of the brutality waged by one group against the other are also present in the accounts of the slaughter of soldiers and workers during the June battles of 1848 in *L'Education sentimentale,* and suggest that the battle scenes in *Salammbô* are curious statements about the failures and loss of human life in 1848, as well as symptoms of the preoccupation with and unsuccessful denial of the French massacres in North Africa. But of interest is the remarkable rhetorical equality of Carthaginian and Barbarian tortures of their foes. Both sides are grotesque and barbaric, and neither more so than the other. The equality of the two warring groups suggests a reflection of the one group's sadism in the brutality of the Other. Carthage's torture of the Barbarians is described:

> Les deux milles Barbares furent attachés dans les Mappales, contre les stèles des tombeaux; et des marchands, des goujats de cuisine, des brodeurs et même des femmes, les veuves des morts avec leurs enfants, tous ceux qui voulaient, vinrent les tuer à coups de flèche. On les visait lentement,

pour mieux prolonger leur supplice: on baissait
son arme, puis on la relevait tour à tour; et la
multitude se poussait en hurlant. . . .

Puis on laissa debout tous ces cadavres crucifiés,
qui semblaient sur les tombeaux autant de statues
rouges. (184)

The sadism of the Barbarian troops is likewise described in painful detail:

Les hommes y vinrent ensuite, et ils les
suppliciaient depuis les pieds, qu'ils coupaient
aux chevilles, jusqu'au front, dont ils levaient des
couronnes de peau pour se mettre sur la tête. . . .
Il envenimaient les blessures en y versant de la
poussière, du vinaigre, des éclats de poterie:
d'autres attendaient derrière eux; le sang coulait
et ils réjouissaient comme font les vendangeurs
autour des cuves fumantes. (241)

In both passages, one community of soldiers perceives
the other community, and there is a condemnation of
the lack of conscience, of the extent to which the
torturers are unmoved by their own violence and the
suffering of the Other. In the first passage, describing
the Carthaginian tortures, the prisoners are a spectacle
for the by-standers to enjoy, and several merchants
make profits by selling to the crowds the arrows with
which they will render the "cadavres crucifiés." In the
second, describing the Barbarians putting vinegar and
irritants in the soldiers' wounds, the torturers are
described as being as joyful as winemakers. Neither
faction is privileged in the representation of the fascination with the other's violence, and in this sense, in
Flaubert's text *Salammbô* the workers' revolts are as
cynically condemned as they are in *L'Education
sentimentale*. The mutual fascination and equality of
violence represent a description of the means by which
Others are regarded and objectified in the constitution
of the national class and cultural identity. The manner
in which Carthage constitutes the Barbarians as sacrilegious and sexually violent, and the Barbarians consider Carthage to be cruel and hoarding, are themselves emblems of the process by which the oriental
world of *Salammbô* is produced, and enjoyed as a
spectacle of displaced violence, by the novel.

The Oriental Motif as Sentimentalism: *L'Education sentimentale*

Flaubert's texts reflect the divided and conflicted nature of the nineteenth-century culture in which they
are produced and which they, in turn, produce. As
cultural products, a variety of ideologies coexist within
Flaubert's texts just as a multiplicity of positions compete within the culture; in this sense, the orientalism in
Flaubert's texts is multivalent and heterogeneous, ex-

pressing a plurality of often contradictory concerns.
For example, Flaubert may have traveled to and written about the Orient as an attempt to escape from
bourgeois society and to find a position from which to
criticize French society; in this sense, the appearance
of the Orient in his work is one representation of
cultural self-criticism, of an anti-bourgeois position.[14]
But the figuration of the oriental as Other in Flaubert's
texts equally textualizes the cultural preoccupation with
defining a coherent national identity—and bourgeois
identity—at a moment when its stability is challenged
by external rivalries with other nations, and internal
upheaval and social dislocations during and following
the revolutions of 1848. As I suggest earlier, the construction of the Orient as "les Barbares" in *Salammbû*
is, on a cultural level, a bourgeois projection of the
internal threat in 1848 by workers and revolutionaries
(and continuing beyond 1848 to the Paris Commune),
as much as the figuration of the Orient as an exteriority
may equally register French anxiety about the wars
between the French and other nations. In addition to
the plurality of ideological positions represented, the
narrative styles of the texts are themselves complexly
ironic and divided. In *L'Education sentimentale*
(1869), for example, the "style indirect libre"[15] for
which Flaubert is so famous, merges narratorial and
subjective modes to achieve the greatest elimination of
distance between narrator and character. The result is
a subtly ironic narrative that in one description preserves the subjective perspective of Frédéric's thoughts
as it simultaneously represents a narratorial commentary and critique of that perspective, through mimicry
of Frédéric's idiom and through the ironic juxtaposition of different contexts in which these idioms occur.
Thus, while Frédéric has a penchant for oriental symbols, and orientalism is present in *L'Education* as an
aspect of Frédéric's world, at the same time, I suggest that the orientalist posture which associates the
Orient with eroticism is established in the narrative as
Frédéric's posture; and as a mark of Frédéric's sentimentalism, the use of the oriental motif is mocked,
parodied, and ultimately criticized.

Oriental motifs—a painting of a Turkish odalisque by
Ingres, a Chinese parasol, an Egyptian tarbouche—
occur in the novels as fragments of an exotic world
elsewhere, signifiers of "l'au-delà," references to oriental contexts eccentric to the scenes in which they
are invoked. These motifs accompany and come to
characterize the young man's erotic interest: Léon
imagining the finds in Emma's shoulders "la couleur
ambrée de l'*Odalisque au bain*"; the harpist playing
"une romance orientale, où il était question de poignards,
de fleurs et d'étoiles" during Frédéric's first sight of
Madame Arnoux; or the "chaînette d'or" between the
ankles of Salammbô seen by Mâtho when she first
enters the group of soldiers. As fragments, they quote
from the detailed iconographies of other orientalist texts
which associate certain motifs with the Orient: nude

slaves, daggers, gold ankle chains. They are incomplete, partial quotations, and their fragmentary natures underscore their standing as marks of incompletion, and hence, as marks of desire. For example, in *Madame Bovary* (1856), Léon's imagination of Emma's shoulders as those of the Turkish odalisque in Ingres's painting does not refer to a woman in a Turkish harem. In imagining Emma as Ingres's subject, Léon expresses his desire by invoking an already established association of the oriental and the erotic; the erotic relationship of present lover and absent beloved, and eroticism as the transgression of prohibition and taboo, are expressed in an oriental motif. The association of orientalism and this particular type of eroticism is not coincidental, for the two situations of desire—the occidental fascination with the Orient, and the young adulterer's passion for Emma Bovary—are structurally similar. Both paradigms depend upon a binary structure which locates the Other—as woman, as oriental scene—as inaccessible, different, beyond. In addition, Léon's desire for Emma reveals desire as fundamentally a matter of cultural quotation, or the repetition of cultural signs; the metaphor of Emma's shoulders as those in Ingres's painting is twice-distanced: itself a quotation of an orientalist painting, it signifies orientalism in order to signify erotic desire. Just as Emma learns her desiring posture from popular novels,[16] Léon casts this moment of his desire in an orientalist and equally literary mode. Ironically enough, Ingres never traveled to North Africa or the Near East, but derived the colors and textures for his bathers, odalisques, and Islamic interiors "from the eighteenth-century illustrations and the descriptions found in the letters of Lady Mary Wortley Montagu and in Montesquieu's *Lettres persanes* (1721)."[17] In the sense that Ingres received his Orient from literary sources, it is a "literary" Orient that he painted, and Léon's notion of desire is as "literary" as that of Emma. The oriental motif is the distinguishing mark of sentimentalism in Flaubert—a sentimentalism which longs for a memory of earlier innocence, an impossible union, a lost wholeness in which European culture is faithfully reflected in its oriental Other. This paradigm of sentimentalism, represented by the oriental motif, is exemplified, critically observed, and ultimately mocked by the occurrences of the motifs in *L'Education sentimentale*.

The oriental motif, though perhaps not central to *L'Education*, emerges nonetheless as the mark which characteristically expresses and initiates Frédéric's erotic desire. The first time Frédéric meets Madame Arnoux aboard the steamboat, a harpist plays an oriental ballad. The narration of this scene begins, "Il la supposait d'origine andalouse, créole peut-être," which establishes the figuration of Madame Arnoux as exotically Other as Frédéric's perceptive mode, and this passage describing the oriental melody, though undesignated by a pronoun as belonging to Frédéric, continues his romantic idiom and postures. The throb-

bing of the boat's engine makes loud and uneven noises so that the harpist must play louder to compensate:

> les battements de la machine coupaient la mélodie à fausse mesure; il pinçait plus fort: les cordes vibraient, et leur sons métalliques semblaient exhaler des sanglots et comme la plainte d'un amour orgueilleux et vaincu. (41)

Frédéric's adulterous desire for Madame Arnoux is signified, as is Léon's in *Bovary*, by the quotation of fragments from orientalism; not only is the ballad a fragment, an emblem of incompletion and desire, but in this image, the Orient of its origin is also associated with a lost, threatened past. Frédéric's impossible passion for Madame Arnoux is personified in the sobbing sounds of the plucked notes as the musician attempts to be heard over the engine noises. In this image, the narrative observes Frédéric's conflation of several kinds of censorship and prohibition: the noises from the engine impinge upon the delicate sounds of the ballad, as the bourgeois Arnoux obstructs Frédéric's passion for Arnoux's wife, and even more grandly, as western industrial society supersedes an earlier oriental age of plenitude and sensuality. Frédéric's plight is dramatized as the plight of a lost, earlier oriental civilization. Desire is figured in a romantic opposition: an earlier temporality is juxtaposed with a corrupted present, an unknown plenitude opposed to a known world. The oriental ballad is always already tortured and sad; from the first moment, Frédéric's desire for Madame Arnoux is already characterized as loss and impossibility. Frédéric's idealization of Madame Arnoux is continually characterized by an exaggerated drama about loss, and is underscored by the hyperbolic language used to express his infatuation: "Plus il la contemplait, plus il sentait entre elle et lui se creuser des abîmes. Il songeait qu'il faudrait la quitter tout à l'heure, irrévocablement, sans avoir arraché une parole, sans lui laisser même un souvenir!" (43) The intensity of Frédéric's desire is represented by the growing enormity of the abysses he imagines opening between them; the moment of contact with her is overdetermined by the inevitable subsequent separation. The narrative critically observes Frédéric creating his sublime sentiment for Madame Arnoux by dramatizing her inaccessibility in the inversion of two moments—the future in which Madame Arnoux is gone is substituted for the present moment of contact. She is constituted as already lost, the moment of contact thoroughly desired because it is irrevocably past. The oriental motif is the mark under which Frédéric's sentimentalizing posture takes place.

The oriental motif occurs at other moments in the novel, as well. Frédéric's passion for Madame Arnoux is continually associated with travel to distant oriental lands: he imagines that he and Madame Arnoux will travel to "des pays lointains . . . au dos des dromadaires, sous le tendelet des éléphants" (101), and he dreams of her "en pantalon de soie jaune, sur les coussins d'un harem" (102). Later, a bawdy party attended by Frédéric and his young friends takes place in "moresque" rooms, under "une toiture chinoise" where Hussonet speaks the now typical conflation of the erotic and the oriental by suggesting "un raout oriental" (105). When he is not able to attend Madame Arnoux's birthday, Frédéric selects for her "une ombrelle . . . en soie gorge-pigeon, à petit manche d'ivoire ciselé, et qui arrivait de Chine." (112) The motifs are completely heterogeneous fragments—camels and elephants, bits of Moorish interiors, a Chinese silk parasol with carved handle—they are incomplete quotations of disparate orientalisms, and their fragmentary qualities as *motifs* call attention to their importance as signifiers and as marks of desire. Further, the orientalist texts themselves, to which these motifs refer, also represent postures of incompletion, ultimately sentimental paradigms which constitute the invented Orient as a sublime ideal, a lost otherness, a time and space removed from the occidental world. The oriental motif calls attention to itself as a signifier which does not correspond or refer to "cultures and nations whose location is in the East,"[18] and, in effect, does not signify except to signify orientalism (a larger tradition of postures of incompletion). It is an emblem of the desire to signify desire, as if the structure and character of desire is—as Lacan suggests[19]—a perpetual series of linguistic and social postures of incompletion, which does not find its completion in objects but renews itself in the signification of other desiring postures. That the novel represents desire as inhering in the metonymic substitution of one signifying posture for another is echoed in Frédéric's voyage from one love interest to another: from the infatuation with Madame Arnoux, to the desire for Rosanette, to the interest in Madame Dambreuse. Frédéric's love-choices parallel his efforts to rise into the society of the "haute bourgeoisie"; he wishes to signify himself and his social standing by the possession of women from particular classes (or women possessed by other men of particular classes); his efforts are unsuccessful, and the progress of his desire is the repeated substitution of one woman for another, or one signifying posture for another. Indeed, in a single day, he visits all three women, going from one residence to the next (IIc:ii), and on the day of the fateful rendezvous with Madame Arnoux on la rue Tronchet, Frédéric makes love with Rosanette "dans le logement préparé pour l'autre" (307).

After Frédéric has deserted Rosanette, spurned Madame Dambreuse, and refused finally to consummate his love with a much older Madame Arnoux, the novel ends with Frédéric's "atrophie sentimentale" (394). The Revolutions of 1848 have given way to the installation of Louis Napoléon in 1851. It is not only the young men in the novel who do not achieve their ambitions, but their society does not achieve the ideals of equality and liberty—lost first in 1789 and now again in 1848. Frédéric's disillusionment in love corresponds to the political disillusionment after the virtual restoration of the old structures of wealth and privilege during the Second Empire. The failure of the revolutions and the betrayal of revolutionary ideals by the bourgeoisie is most poignantly figured when Frédéric witnesses the death of his working-class friend Dussardier at the hands of Sénécal, a former revolutionary turned "agent de police." Frédéric's long desire for and pursuit of Madame Arnoux is one model of sentimental idealism observed throughout the novel, but the novel also draws an analogy between Frédéric's education in love and the political education of the French society which has suffered two thwarted efforts at revolutionary social change. Frédéric's love quest, a process of desire already marked by the loss of the object, is compared to the story of the failure of the revolutions of 1848 to achieve the egalitarian society already desired and lost in 1789.[20] In this metaphor of the young man's sentimentalism and his society's aspirations, the revolution and its political idealism are judged severely.

The oriental motif which marks Frédéric's and Deslauriers' reminiscence of the bordello at the end of the novel, provides the final commentary on the oriental figuration of erotic desire. The two friends' remembrance of their first visit to a house of prostitution in 1837 is introduced by an explanation of how the woman who ran the house had come to be called "la Turque": many people believed her to be a Muslim from Turkey, and as this "ajoutait à la poesie de son établissement" (444), she was from that point known as "la Turque." Hearsay embellished the house with an exotic flair, endowing it with an intriguing erotic quality.

> Ce lieu de perdition projetait dans tout l'arrondissement un éclat fantastique. On le désignait par des périphrases: "L'endroit que vous savez,—une certaine rue,—au bas des Ponts." (445)

Frédéric and Deslauriers recall that the townspeople would use euphemisms when speaking of the house of prostitution. Ambiguous, non-referential phrases like "l'endroit que vous savez" were used to signify the prohibited site of sexuality. "La Turque" also serves the purpose of a periphrasis, a turning or deferring of meaning, used to signify the unknown sexuality within the house of prostitution. The oriental motif of "la Turque" does not refer to the woman who manages the house (indeed, she does not appear in their reminiscence), nor does it refer to Turkey; "la Turque" is the periphrasis used by the young boys to signify the plenitude of unknown women and sexual practices. It is also the *motif* under which Frédéric and Deslauriers reconstitute the adolescent position of curiosity, still uninterrupted by failure and disillusionment. The remembered scene has value as a reconstructed moment of pure idealism and innocence: Frédéric presents a bouquet "comme un amoureux à sa fiancée" (445), and, flustered by the presence of so many women, he ultimately flees.[21] Frédéric leaves the establishment of "la Turque" a virgin, still inexperienced, with all desire and all disappointment ahead of him. The irony of this final scene in which Frédéric and Deslauriers invoke a lost moment of plenitude, is punctuated by their final declarations: "C'est là ce que nous avons eu de meilleur!" In a characteristically romantic strategy, the two friends perform a dialectic of presence and absence, rhetorically substituting a constructed past— "c'est là"—for their fallen, corrupted present states. The invocation of the house of "la Turque" as the place where they had their happiest times replaces their condition of loss with a reconstituted plenitude of adolescent virginity. The novel portrays Frédéric in an endless repetition of these desiring postures, marked by the oriental motif, as an unsignifying signifier of incompleteness. This final use of the motif suggests Frédéric's ultimate lack of change; though older, more weary—having lived under Louis Philippe, through the revolutions, and now under Napoléon III—Frédéric invokes once more the adolescent oriental motif to recall an earlier state of desire.

Flaubert's texts—especially the representations of the Egyptian courtesan in the *Voyage en Orient* (1850) and *Correspondance* (1853), and *Salammbô* (1862)— exemplify a nineteenth-century orientalism which figures the Orient as an erotic female Other. The later work, *L'Education* (1869), departs from this orientalism, thematizing rather than strictly exemplifying the orientalist posture; the narrative observes Frédéric's use of the oriental motif, and calls attention to it as an emblem of Frédéric's sentimentalism. The scene in which Frédéric remembers "la Turque" is entirely in contrast to Flaubert's description of the courtesan Kuchuk-Hânem in the *Voyage* and the *Correspondance*. The scene from *L'Education* exposes Frédéric's invention of oriental exoticism as sentimentality. In a sense, it offers us a retrospective critique of orientalism within the Flaubertian corpus itself, while the earlier description of "la femme orientale" in the *Correspondance* most vividly exemplifies the orientalizing posture which both desires and debases its culturally and sexually different object. To the degree that orientalism and sentimentalism are equated in *L'Education,* the narrative criticizes the ultimate delusion and regression of the orientalist posture. It is as if the various texts in the "oeuvre" of the author Flaubert were themselves different orientalist moments on a continuum in which, to greater and greater degrees, the narrative calls attention to orientalism as a posture, and ironically contextualizes that posture. With *L'Education,* the orientalist imagery is no longer performed by the narrative, but is instead mocked as a function of the protagonist. The final reminiscence of a reconstituted ideal moment under the signifier of "la Turque" (the name itself is a received hearsay, a periphrastic reference to another orientalist text), illustrates the utility of the oriental motif as sentimentalism, as much as the reminiscence emphasizes how the oriental motif indeed fails to signify throughout the novel. The narrative's use of the oriental motif to signify Frédéric's sentimentalism is appropriate, because the individual paradigm of sentimentalism is structurally similar to the cultural paradigm of orientalism: each substitutes an invented otherness for a present condition of failed self-possession or unstable cultural identity.

Orientalist Criticism

It is not sufficient to merely characterize the shapes, rhetorics, and postures of French orientalism, however, for, in a sense, these criticisms may contribute further to a static notion of the "discourse of orientalism." I would prefer instead to apply my readings of Flaubert—as plural, conflicted multivalent texts in which representations of class, culture, and gender overlap and intersect in a variety of ways—towards the project of challenging the very idea of a "discourse of orientalism."

At particular moments in critical theory in the United States, the notion of "the Other" has been powerful, illuminating, transformative. For example, in feminist debates, these moments are marked by the publication of works such as Juliet Mitchell's *Psychoanalysis and Feminism* (1974), or Nancy Chodorow's *Reproduction of Mothering* (1978), or Gayatri Chakravorty Spivak's important introduction to her translation of Jacques Derrida's *Of Grammatology* (1976). Similarly, Edward Said's *Orientalism* (1979) and his analysis of the construction of "the Orient as Other" initiated a questioning of scholarly assumptions in several academic disciplines—in modern and classical literary studies, in history—not the least of which is a serious ongoing interrogation of ethnographic practices within the field of anthropology.[22] Analyses of how races, cultures, economic groups, or sexualities are marked and figured as "other," or as the subordinated counterpart of dominant privileged categories, are absolutely essential to our current project of cultural criticism. Yet I believe we risk certain dangers in continuing to use monolithic notions of both "discourse" and "the Other": on the one hand, the production of more of this kind of theory may enunciate and be deeply implicated in the powerful hegemonies it seeks to criticize; and, on the other hand, these theories may greatly underestimate other points and positions of struggle and resistance operating in the discourse at all moments. The view that a dominant discourse produces and manages the Other, univocally appropriating and containing all dissenting positions within it, underestimates the tensions and contradictions within a discourse, the continual play of resistance, dissent, and accommodation by different positions. This type of dominant discourse theory minimizes the importance of minority group counter-representations and counter-ideology, and continues to subsume the minority to the majority. The idea that a dominant discourse monochromatically misrepresents and produces a minority ties us too strictly to the very literal notion that cultural politics and ideological changes are always a matter of numbers (a greater number has a greater voice), and perpetuates the over-determined mythology that minority interests are always represented by the majority. This cannot be the case if we recognize that local regions of economic, sexual, and racial minorities are continually resisting and contesting particular uses of the classification of "otherness" and thematizing the very misuse of the classification as a powerful means of altering its function. To begin to account for this resistance while continuing to recognize the functioning category of the "Other" in discourse, I believe we must consider instead the heterogeneity of acts of representation. On the one hand, marks of difference and otherness are multivalent; the mark of difference which is at one time a mode of exclusion may at another historical moment or in another set of social relations be an enabling mark of inclusion.[23] On the other hand, discourses are what I would call "heterotopical"; discourses are heterogeneously and irregularly composed of statements and restatements, contestations and accommodation, generated by a plurality of writing positions at any given moment. The theoretical problem facing us in cultural criticism is not how to fit anomalous positions into a fixed dualistic conception of dominant ideology and counter ideology, or discourse and counter-discourse. Rather, it is the other way around; heterogeneities and pluralities are givens in culture. These non-equivalences and non-correspondences are not the objects to be explained; they must constitute the beginning premise of any analysis.

It is my contention that the accepted usage of the idea of a closed discourse which manages and produces a single object has left the dynamics of dissent, intervention, resistance, and change inadequately theorized. In other words, the use of the notion of a dominant discourse is incomplete if not accompanied by a critique which explains why some positions are easily co-opted and integrated into apparently-dominant discourses, and why others are less likely to be appropriated. I believe that the critical work identifying a "discourse of otherness" should include a discussion of reification and hegemony, as well as an analysis of how the reification of categories such as "otherness" and "difference" incorporates within them the very logics of domination and subordination, hegemony and counter-hegemony. The premise that representations

of difference and otherness are multivalent—that they can be at one time marks of exclusion, at other times used in arguments for enfranchisement, and still at others appropriated again as different means of exclusion—has direct ramifications for how we, in literary and cultural criticism, construct our future arguments. For when the *topos* of "the Orient as Other" is used as a mode of argument to analyze the power of orientalism, this mode of argument itself may contribute to the very logic it seeks to criticize. In this sense, the ultimate aim of my essay is to challenge and resist the "logic of otherness" and to historicize the critical strategy of identifying the representations of otherness as a discursive mode of production itself. For if we understand the "logic of otherness" as an apparatus in which is inscribed a logic of domination and subordination, then we must also question the continuing efficacy of using this logic as a critical method. By interrogating the utility and responsibility of the concept of "the discourse of the Other," we can begin to rethink the notion of discourse and work toward the theorizing of change and resistance within discourse.

Notes

[1] Jean Bruneau, *Le "Conte oriental" de Gustave Flaubert* (1973); Edward Said, *Orientalism* (1979); Richard Terdiman, *Discourse/Counter-Discourse* (1985); Naomi Schor, *Breaking the Chain: Women, Realism and the French Novel* (1985).

[2] Flaubert, *Correspondance* in *Oeuvres complètes de Gustave Flaubert,* 313-14.

[3] The 1984 Essex conference on the Sociology of Literature, entitled "Europe and Its Others" and focused on representations of colonial and imperial power, is a fine example of the aftermath of orientalist criticism and the attention given to Said's work. Topics covered in the published volume of papers include orientalist painting, Flaubert in Egypt, Islam and the idea of Europe, the Chinese and Japanese in the USA, aspects of India under the British, and multiculturalism in Australia. Said, also, presents a reconsideration of *Orientalism* in the light of its reception. (Colchester: University of Essex, 1985.)

The Group for the Study of Colonialist Discourse, out of the University of California, Santa Cruz and Berkeley, is a network responsible for concentrating and generating some recent anti-colonialist criticism and other responses to orientalism.

"Race," Writing and Difference, ed. Henry Louis Gates, Jr. (1986) constitutes another forum responding to the implications and consequences of Said's theory of otherness.

The debates in anthropology and cultural criticism represented in two collections of essays, *Writing Culture: The Poetics and Politics of Ethnography,* ed. James Clifford and George Marcus (1986), and *Anthropology as Cultural Critique: An Experimental Moment in the Human Sciences,* ed. George Marcus and Michael M. J. Fischer (1986), are also clearly marked by Said's work. Indeed, of all the modern disciplines, perhaps it is the anthropological project of one culture authoritatively rendering another culture, which has been most shaken by Said's notion of orientalist discourse.

4 Notable and important work that explores this nexus of colonialist discourse with discourses about class and gender includes Malek Alloula, *The Colonial Harem* (1986); Gayatri Chakravorty Spivak, *In Other Worlds* (1988); Lata Mani's work on the discourse on "sati" in nineteenth-century Bengal; Trinh T. Minh-ha, *Woman, Native, Other: Writing Postcoloniality and Feminism* (1989). See also *Inscriptions* Nos. 3/4 (1988) entitled "Feminism and the Critique of Colonial Discourse."

5 This is one implication of Said's *Orientalism,* in which he writes: "Orientalism is a style of thought based upon an ontological and epistemological distinction made between 'the Orient' and (most of the time) 'the Occident.' . . . in short, Orientalism as a Western style for dominating, restructuring, and having authority over the Orient." (2-1) The inference that Orientalism is a constant and monolithic discourse is illustrated by others' interpretations of Said: e.g., James Clifford, 1988; B. J. Moore-Gilbert, 1986. Moore-Gilbert, for example, argues for the need to reappraise Said's presentation of orientalism as monolithic by calling attention to the incongruity between the West's relationship to Arabs and Islam and Britain's relationship to India.

However, in the work subsequent to *Orientalism,* Said has turned his attention to situations of post-colonial emergence, making it clear that he is not a proponent of the kind of monolithic rendering that does not account for resistance. See "Identity, Negation and Violence," *New Left Review* (December, 1988); and the forthcoming *Culture and Imperialism.* At the same time, Said's work does continue to stress the homogeneity and dominance of an imperialism of a single character, and to de-emphasize what I would consider equally important, the heterogeneity of different imperialisms and specific resistances.

6 With the idea of an "irregular series," Foucault emphasizes that both the conditions of discursive formation and the objects of knowledge are neither identical, static, nor continuous over time. In this way, Foucault devises a project that avoids some of the primary idealities of traditional historical study—the desire for origins, unified developments, or causes and effects. Conceiving of history as an irregular series of discursive formations is an alternative method that takes into account non-linear events, discontinuity, breaks, and the transformations of both the apparatuses for producing knowledge and what is conceived of as "knowledge" itself. After having rejected four hypotheses concerning the unifying principles of a discursive formation—reference to the same object, a common style in the production of statements, constancy of concepts, and reference to a common theme—Foucault characterizes the active principle of discourse as "dispersion."

> Whenever one can describe, between a number of statements, such a system of dispersion, whenever, between objects, types of statement, concepts, or thematic choices, one can define a regularity (an order, correlations, positions and functionings, transformations), we will say, for the sake of convenience, that we are dealing with a *discursive formation.* . . . The conditions to which the elements of this division (objects, mode of statements, concepts, thematic choices) are subjected we shall call the *rules of formation.* The rules of formation are conditions of existence (but also of coexistence, maintenance, modification, and disappearance) in a given discursive division. (*Archaeology of Knowledge* 38)

7 This is borne out most simply in the different meanings of the "Orient" over time: in many eighteenth-century texts, the Orient signifies Turkey, the Levant, and the Arabian peninsula occupied by the Ottoman Empire, now known as the Middle East; in the nineteenth-century literature, the notion of the Orient additionally refers to North Africa; and in the twentieth century, more often to Central and Southeast Asia. Notions such as "French culture," "the British Empire," or "European nations," are replete with ambiguity, conflicts, and non-equivalences, as well. And we will see that the nineteenth-century British literature about India is marked by an entirely different set of conventions, narratives, figures, and genres, from the French literature about Egypt and North Africa of the same period. For the British and French cultural contexts for producing such literatures at that particular moment are distinct: not only are there many non correspondences between the individual national cultures and literatures, but in the nineteenth century, Britain's century-old colonial involvement in Indian culture, economy, and administration, and France's more recent occupation of North Africa, exemplify non-equivalent degrees of rule and relationship.

8 Flaubert, *Voyage en Orient* in *Oeuvres complètes de Gustave Flaubert,* 487-88. The name of "Kuchuk-Hânem" appears variously and inconsistently in the *Voyage* and the *Correspondance.*

[9] In a most interesting manner, in *La femme dans les romans de Flaubert: mythes et idéologie* (1983), Lucette Czyba associates the reduction of Salammbô as an object of exchange with the homoeroticism of war. She argues that "La femme est la proie, la victime désignée dans l'univers de violence masculine et sadique qui caractérise la guerre et qui mêle indissolublement la volupté à la mort." (130) Czyba suggests that the sadism of war in *Salammbô,* may be the obverse aspect of erotic bonding between men. Both male "eros" and "thanatos" have the common characteristic of excluding women from a closed society of men; the two parts of the war economy are compatible and mutually productive.

[10] In *Improvisation sur Flaubert* (1984), 117, Michel Butor suggests that Carthage is "la face cachée de la Rome antique," at once denied and suppressed by Rome, the precursor of France, and yet signifying Rome, and by implication, France. One may think of Carthage as the oriental Other of Rome, the Other of Christianity and classical antiquity. The absenting of Rome decenters Rome as the western origin, and presents the French tale in the oriental disguise of Carthage.

[11] All quotations from *Salammbô, Madame Bovary,* and *L'Education sentimentale* are from editions of Garnier-Flammarion, Paris.

[12] Hayden White, "The Forms of Wildness: Archaeology of an Idea," and "The Noble Savage Theme as Fetish," in *Tropics of Discourse* (1978), 150-96.

[13] Mary Louise Pratt, "Fieldwork in Common Places," in *Writing Culture,* ed. Clifford and Marcus (1986), 27-50.

[14] This interpretation of Flaubert's orientalism is offered by Richard Terdiman in *Discourse/Counter-Discourse,* Part II, Chapter 5.

[15] The discussions of Flaubert's style are many. For particularly lucid explications, see: Roy Pascal, *The Dual Voice: Free Indirect Speech and Its Functioning in the Nineteenth-Century European Novel* (1977); Dominick LaCapra, *"Madame Bovary" on Trial* (1982).

[16] That Emma takes her particular notion of romantic desire from the clichés of popular novels, and from the songs she sang in the convent as an adolescent, has been noted by many critics, including: Victor Brombert, *Flaubert* (1971); Jonathan Culler, *Flaubert: The Uses of Uncertainty* (1974); Tony Tanner, *Adultery in the Novel* (1979).

[17] From *The Orientalists: Delacroix to Matisse,* ed. MaryAnne Stevens (1984), 17, catalogue to the exhibit of nineteenth-century orientalist paintings at the National Gallery in Washington, D.C. in 1984. The exhibit included in its collection several paintings of odalisques by Jean-Auguste-Dominique Ingres even though he, like many orientalist painters, "never travelled to North Africa or to the Near East."

[18] Said, *Orientalism* (1979).

[19] The notion of the "signifying chain" is clearly articulated in "Agency of the Letter in the Unconscious or Reason Since Freud," *Ecrits* (1977), 146-78.

Lacan's subject is situated in and by language, language being the most determining structure in the Symbolic, or social realm. Lacan discusses signification in the Symbolic as a process in which every signifier corresponds not to a signified, but to another signifier: "no signification can be sustained other than by reference to another signification" (150) Desire inheres in the chain of signifiers, and more particularly in the incommensurability of word and thing, the failure of metaphoric similitude and the determined succession of metonymic associations. "It is in the word-to-word connection that metonymy is based." (156) The metonymic structure, or the connection between signifier and signifier "permits the elision in which the signifier installs the lack-of-being in the object relation, using the value of 'reference back' possessed by signification in order to invest it with the desire aimed at the very lack it supports." (164).

[20] For a discussion of historical representation in Flaubert's novel and Marx's *Eighteenth Brumaire of Louis Bonaparte* see Hayden White, "The Problem of Style in Realistic Representation: Marx and Flaubert," in *The Concept of Style* (1979), 213-22.

[21] Faced with so many women available to him, the young Frédéric is speechless, and when the women laugh, he flees thinking they are mocking him: "d'un seul coup d'oeil, tant de lemme à sa disposition, l'émurent tellement, qu'il devint très pâle et restait sans avancer . . . il s'enhuit." (445) Victor Brombert, *Flaubert* (1971), 98-100, has noted that the final reminiscence of the bordello is "un résumé en miniature" of many of the previous themes in the novel: Frédéric's flight when confronted with choices is a tendency echoed throughout the novel, in his repeated inability to choose a woman to whom he can be committed or a vocation to which he can be tied, in his fear of humiliation and his obsession with reputation.

[22] The significant debates in anthropology are represented in two volumes: Clifford and Marcus (1986); Marcus and Fischer (1986). For Said's response to these debates, see "Representing the Colonized: Anthropology and its Interlocutors."

[23] By "multivalent," I mean that marks denoting social class, race, culture, or gender differences acquire distinct significances in different contexts; these marks may in one period or culture be used to exclude and marginalize a social group, while in another they may be appropriated as marks of privilege or empowerment. I

discuss the problem of multivalence with regard to the position of Asian Americans in the university, in "Differences: Theory and the University."

Stuart Hall has remarked that the names "black" and "coloured" signify quite differently in the distinct contexts of England and the Caribbean. He observes that in the English system, organized around a binary dichotomy which reflected the colonizing order of "white/not-white," the terms "black" and "coloured" are more or less synonymous, while in the Caribbean system, where race is organized in an ascending spectrum of classifications, "black" and "coloured" denote different points on the scale rising towards the ultimate "white" term. See "Signification, Representation, Ideology: Althusser and the Post-Structuralist Debates," *Critical Studies in Mass Communication* (June, 1985).

Another example is the construction of "race" in contemporary U.S. society, which has changed since the 1950s, as the result of many factors, including the civil rights movements of the 1950s and 1960s. In *Racial Formation in the United States: From the 1960's to the 1980's* (1986), Michael Omi and Howard Winant argue persuasively that previous paradigms for analyzing racial formation—an ethnicity-based theory, a class-based theory, and a nation-based theory—are not sufficient. Omi and Winant theorize a process of "racial formation," in which social, economic, and political forces determine the content and importance of racial categories and racial meanings, through the examination of the different meanings of race from the 1950s to the 1980s.

There is also multivalence and non-correspondence in the signification of gender. For example, in middle-class literary discourse in early eighteenth-century England, the classification of female connoted domesticity, sexual fidelity, passive virtue. By the early nineteenth century, when female authority had asserted itself in the domestic sphere, in courtship, in family relations, marks of femininity had different meanings and different categories of female identity emerged. For study of the role of gender in culture and its relation to political change in eighteenth- and nineteenth-century England, see Nancy Armstrong, *Desire and Domestic Fiction* (1987).

Works Cited

Alloula, Malek. *The Colonial Harem*. Trans. Myrna Godzich and Wlad Godzich. Minneapolis: University of Minnesota Press, 1986.

Armstrong, Nancy. *Desire and Domestic Fiction*. New York and Oxford: Oxford University Press, 1987.

Brombert, Victor. *Flaubert*. Paris: Seuil, 1971.

Bruneau, Jean. *Le "Conte oriental" de Gustave Flaubert*. Paris: Denöel, 1973.

Butor, Michel. *Improvisation sur Flaubert*. Paris: Editions de la Différence, 1984.

Clifford, James. *The Predicament of Culture: Twentieth-Century Ethnography, Literature, and Art*. Cambridge, Mass.: Harvard University Press, 1988.

Clifford, James and George Marcus, eds. *Writing Culture: The Poetics and Politics of Ethnography*. Berkeley: University of California Press, 1986.

Culler, Jonathan. *Flaubert: The Uses of Uncertainty*. Ithaca, N.Y.: Cornell University Press, 1974.

Czyba, Lucette. *La Femme dans les romans de Flaubert: mythes et idéologie*. Lyon: Presses Universitaires de Lyon, 1983.

Flaubert, Gustave. *Oeuvres complètes de Gustave Flaubert*. Volumes 10 and 13. Paris: Club de l'Honnête homme, 1973.

———. *Madame Bovary*. Paris: Garnier Flammarion, 1979 (1856).

———. *L'Education sentimentale*. Paris: Garnier Flammarion, 1969 (1869).

———. *Salammbô*. Paris: Garnier Flammarion, 1961 (1862).

Foucault, Michel. *The Archaeology of Knowledge*. Trans. A. M. Sheridan Smith. New York: Pantheon, 1972.

Gates, Henry Louis, Jr., ed. *"Race," Writing and Difference*. Chicago: University of Chicago Press, 1986.

Hall, Stuart. "Signification, Representation, Ideology: Althusser and the Post-Structuralist Debates." *Critical Studies in Mass Communication* (June, 1985).

Lacan, Jacques. *Ecrits*. Trans. Alan Sheridan. New York: Norton, 1977.

LaCapra, Dominick. *"Madame Bovary" on Trial*. Ithaca, N.Y.: Cornell University Press, 1982.

Mani, Lata. "The Construction of Women as Tradition in Early Nineteenth-Century Bengal." In *Minority Discourse*. Ed. Abdul Jan Mohamed and David Lloyd. Oxford: Oxford University Press, 1990.

Marcus, George and Michael M. J. Fischer, eds. *Anthropology as Cultural Critique: An Experimental Moment in the Human Sciences*. Chicago: University of Chicago Press, 1986.

Minh-ha, Trinh T. *Woman, Native, Other: Writing Postcoloniality and Feminism*. Bloomington: Indiana University Press, 1989.

Moore-Gilbert, B. J. *Kipling and "Orientalism."* London: Croom Helm, 1986.

Omi, Michael and Howard Winant. *Racial Formation in the United States.* London: Routledge, 1986.

Pascal, Roy. *The Dual Voice: Free Indirect Speech and Its Functioning in the Nineteenth-Century European Novel.* Manchester: Manchester University Press, 1977.

Said, Edward. *Orientalism.* New York: Random House, 1979.

————. "Identity, Negation and Violence." *New Left Review* (December, 1988).

————. "Representing the Colonized: Anthropology and its Interlocutors." *Critical Inquiry* (Winter, 1989).

Schor, Naomi, *Breaking the Chain: Women, Realism and the French Novel.* New York: Columbia University Press, 1985.

Spivak, Gayatri Chakravorty. *In Other Worlds.* London: Routledge, 1988.

Stevens, MaryAnne, ed. *The Orientalists: Delacroix to Matisse.* London: Weidenfeld and Nicolson, 1984.

Tanner, Tony. *Adultery In the Novel.* Baltimore: Johns Hopkins University Press, 1979.

Terdiman, Richard. *Discourse/Counter-Discourse: The Theory and Practice of Symbolic Resistance in Nineteenth-Century France.* Ithaca, N.Y.: Cornell University Press, 1985.

White, Hayden. *Tropics of Discourse.* Baltimore: Johns Hopkins University Press, 1978.

————. "The Problem of Style in Realistic Representation: Marx and Flaubert." In *The Concept of Style.* Ed. Berel Lang. Philadelphia: University of Pennsylvania Press, 1979.

FURTHER READING

Biography

Bart, Benjamin F. *Flaubert.* Syracuse: Syracuse University Press, 1967, 791 p.
    Updates previous biographies of Flaubert in light of the availability of new Flaubert manuscript materials and revisions of critical assessments of Flaubert's place in literature.

Criticism

Brombert, Victor. *The Novels of Flaubert: A Study of Themes and Techniques.* Princeton, N. J.: Princeton University Press, 1966, 301 p.
    Includes general critical discussion of Flaubert's literary temperament and his use of themes and narrative techniques. Each chapter focuses on one of Flaubert's major works.

Foucault, Michel. "Fantasia of the Library." In *Language, Counter-Memory, Practice: Selected Essays and Interviews,* edited by Donald F. Bouchard, translated by Donald F. Bouchard and Sherry Simon, pp. 87-109. Ithaca: Cornell University Press, 1977.
    Describes *La Tentation de Saint Antoine* as a long-term project which contributed to the genesis of Flaubert's linguistic style in *Madame Bovary, Salammbô,* and *Bouvard et Pécuchet.* This essay originally appeared in 1967 in *Cahiers Renaud-Barrault.*

Ginsburg, Michal Peled. *Flaubert Writing: A Study in Narrative Strategies.* Stanford: Stanford University Press, 1986, 207 p.
    Argues that unlike "such authors as Balzac or Stendhal, Flaubert seems to have a problem generating his text and keeping it going." Ginsburg explores the following questions: "What is this difficulty [of Flaubert's] in generating the text? How is it circumvented? How do this problem and the strategies used to overcome it shape the narrative?"

Haig, Stirling. "History and Illusion in Flaubert's *Un Coeur simple.*" In *The Madame Bovary Blues: The Pursuit of Illusion in Nineteenth-Century French Fiction,* pp. 116-43. Baton Rouge: Louisiana State University Press, 1987.
    Examines how "personal event" and "illusion" are imposed in *Un Coeur simple* as "the gauge of truth," then traces the pattern of discourse in the story and examines its "semantic relationship with the thematics of *Trois Contes* and of Flaubert's work as a whole."

LaCapra, Dominick. "Collapsing Spheres in Flaubert's *Sentimental Education.*" In *History, Politics, and the Novel,* pp. 83-110. Ithaca: Cornell University Press, 1987.
    Reads Flaubert's *Sentimental Education* as a social document and a "historical event." Notes that "around the time he was composing *The Sentimental Education,* Flaubert seemed to overlay an escapist dedication to art with a bitter critique of universal suffrage and a defense of a cultural and political elite."

McKenna, Andrew J. "Allodidacticism: Flaubert 100 Years After." *Yale French Studies,* No. 63 (1982): 227-44.
    Argues that Flaubert's characters Bouvard and Pécuchet

are "perhaps the most comical and . . . the most disquieting" pedagogical figures in French literature.

Porter, Dennis. "Flaubert and the Difficulty of Reading." *Nineteenth-Century French Studies* 12, No. 3 (Spring 1984): 366-78.

Examines the perception of some critics that Flaubert contributed to the increased "self-awareness" of the nineteenth-century novel and therefore played a crucial role in the increased "complications" of the reading process.

Prendergast, Christopher. "Flaubert: The Stupidity of Mimesis." In *The Order of Mimesis: Balzac, Stendhal, Nerval, Flaubert,* pp. 180-211. Cambridge: Cambridge University Press, 1986.

Argues that the critical "assimilation of Flaubert to the 'modern'" is a function of viewing his art as "resolutely 'non-figurative', or indeed as actively anti-figurative."

Ramazani, Vaheed K. *The Free Indirect Mode: Flaubert and the Poetics of Irony.* Charlottesville: University Press of Virginia, 1988, 159 p.

Attempts to address the lack of an "intensive study of free indirect discourse as an instrument of irony in Flaubert's fiction." Evaluates "pertinent critical arguments in the fields of ironology and narratology, and brings the fruits of that analysis to bear on a model text, *Madame Bovary.*"

Schor, Naomi, and Henry F. Majewski, eds. *Flaubert and Postmodernism.* Lincoln: University of Nebraska Press, 1984, 219 p.

Presents a collection of essays concerned with the following question: "what does [Flaubert] represent for the postmodernist generation now at the forefront of contemporary thought?"

White, Hayden. "The Problem of Style in Realistic Representation: Marx and Flaubert." In *The Concept of Style,* edited by Berel Lang, pp. 213-29. University of Pennsylvania Press, 1979.

Examines the function of style as a feature of literary realism by comparing Flaubert's novel *Sentimental Education* with Marx's history *The Eighteenth Brumaire of Louis Bonaparte.*

Additional coverage of Flaubert's life and career is contained in the following sources published by Gale Research: *Nineteenth-Century Literature Criticism*, Vols. 2, 10, and 19; *DISCovering Authors; Short Story Criticism*, Vol. 11; *World Literature Criticism, 1500 to the Present;* and *Dictionary of Literary Biography*, Vol. 119.

Elizabeth Inchbald

1753-1821

(Born Elizabeth Simpson) British playwright, novelist, critic, and editor.

INTRODUCTION

After beginning her career as an actress in London during the late 1700s, Elizabeth Inchbald turned to writing, becoming a prominent dramatist, novelist, and critic in London literary and theatre circles. Her success grew out of her insightful characterizations and depictions of intense emotions. Considered by some critics to be a simple reflection of her time, her work had been neglected until a recent rejuvenation of interest in her criticism as well as in her novels—*A Simple Story* (1791) and *Nature and Art* (1796)—the latter of which are valued for their concern with social and moral reform.

Biographical Information

Elizabeth Simpson was born near Bury St. Edmunds, in Suffolk, into a large, Roman Catholic, farming family. Although she received no formal education, she was intelligent and avidly interested in literature. When she was eighteen and in spite of a pronounced stammer, she secretly left home to pursue an acting career in London. After two months, in June of 1772, she married Joseph Inchbald, an older actor, and frequently played opposite him in touring companies until his death in 1779. The following year she signed a four-year acting contract with Covent Garden; she also made acting appearances at the Haymarket and in Dublin. In order to maintain a steady income, she began writing. Her first play to be produced was the farcical comedy *A Mogul Tale* (1784); her comedy *I'll Tell You What* was produced the following year to popular acclaim. Between 1784 and 1805, nineteen of her dramatic works (either original plays or adaptations) appeared on the London stage. Her celebrity and financial security were assured by continuing popular success, although her work was considered overly sentimental or didactic by some critics, and scandalous by others. By the turn of the century, she had retired from her acting career, in which she had achieved only moderate renown, in order to focus upon writing, but she retained strong connections to the theater, including friendships with Sarah Siddons, Tate Wilkinson, and John Philip Kemble. As a well-established and independent literary figure, Inchbald also pursued politi-

cal interests, particularly the education of women, and the defense of theater against religious attacks. She was also associated with the prominent Jacobin intellectuals Thomas Holcroft and William Godwin. Reflecting her increased interest in religion, her final years were spent in a Roman Catholic residence; she died in 1821.

Major Works

Inchbald's dramatic works and novels reflect the sensibilities of her time, and in her critical prefaces to the plays collected in *The British Theatre* she addressed conventional values and also displayed a keen insight into the crafting of dialogue, setting, and character. Her plays are primarily comedies and farces, many of which illuminate the humor, as well as the pathos, of domestic life and romantic love; the most popular of these include *I'll Tell You What* (1785), *Such Things Are* (1787), *Animal Magnetism* (1788), and *Every One Has His Fault* (1793). She also adapted and translated many plays from France and Germany. Her best-known drama, *Lovers' Vows* (1798) is an adaptation of August von Kotzebue's *Das Kind der Liebe,* and is the play rehearsed in Jane Austen's *Mansfield Park.* Inchbald often drew from her own experience as an actress in constructing her plays, and her timing, attention to detail, plot design, and use of props enhanced the development of mood and the expression of emotion. Inchbald wrote a total of twenty plays, and during her lifetime all but two of these were produced, and all but five were published. Her two major novels, *A Simple Story* and *Nature and Art*, met with moderate success. Slightly polemical in tone, they focus on the consequences of a lack of education for women. Both works follow, over the span of two generations, the development and repercussions of romantic love. The plots and characters of these novels reflect a profound attachment to the conventions of sentimental fiction, even as Inchbald portrayed the problems inherent in the contemporary ideal of domesticity. This has led some critics to assert that Inchbald appropriated events and characters from her own experience for use in her plays and novels. In 1805 Inchbald was asked to write critical and biographical prefaces for the 125 plays collected in twenty-five volumes of *The British Theatre.* Though she did not participate in the selection of these plays, her contribution of critical introductions was significant—at the time it was commonly believed that women did not possess the critical faculties to evaluate another's work, and many of her contemporaries took offense at her assessments. Four years later she edited two collections of dramatic works: *A Collection of Farces* and *The Modern Theatre.* She also contributed numerous critical articles and reviews for a number of British publications, including the *Artist* and the *Edinburgh Review.*

Critical Reception

Although Inchbald's contemporaries considered her work to be examples of popular sentimentalism rather than serious literature, recent critics have argued that she profoundly subverted the conventional values of her day, particularly in her two novels. As a playwright and novelist, Inchbald focused on the situation of women, portraying the tragic consequences—the perversion of feminine sensibility into obsessive love and inner conflict—of a lack of education for women. She also attributed redemptive powers to femininity, particularly when it is cultivated and utilized for social and moral reform. In addition, scholars note that her use as well as mockery of the devices of sentimental fiction prefigure the demise of the ideal of domesticity, and indicate a self-conscious manipulation of conventional literary devices. However, many commentators criticize her convoluted plots and her frequently didactic tone. There is a general consensus that her achievement rests not only in her early success as a dramatist, novelist, and critic, but in her ability to

characterize intense emotion and the dynamics of private life.

PRINCIPAL WORKS

A Mogul Tale (drama) 1784
I'll Tell You What (drama) 1785
Such Things Are (drama) 1787
Animal Magnetism (drama) 1788
A Simple Story. 4 vols. (novel) 1791
Every One Has His Fault (drama) 1793
Nature and Art. 2 vols. (novel) 1796
Lovers' Vows [adaptor and translator; from the drama *Das Kind der Liebe* by August von Kotzebue] (drama) 1798
The British Theatre; or, A Collection of Plays. 25 vols. [writer of critical and biographical prefaces] (dramas) 1806-09
A Collection of Farces and Other Afterpieces. 7 vols. [editor] (dramas) 1809
The Modern Theatre: A Collection of Successful Modern Plays, as Acted at the Theatres Royal, London. 10 vols. [editor] (dramas) 1809-11
The Plays of Elizabeth Inchbald. 2 vols. [edited by Paula R. Backscheider] 1980

CRITICISM

William McKee (essay date 1935)

SOURCE: "The Technique of Her Novels" and "The Art of Her Novels," in *Elizabeth Inchbald: Novelist,* The Catholic University of America, 1935, pp. 55-74 and 75-102.

[*In the excerpt that follows, McKee examines the plot design and character development of* A Simple Story *and* Nature and Art. *(Only those footnotes pertaining to the excerpt below have been reprinted.)*]

The Broken Plot of *A Simple Story*

We turn now to an examination of those theories set forth by critics in explanation of what they consider Mrs. Inchbald's sacrifice of unity in *A Simple Story.* The reader will remember that, in reviewing events of this novel, attention was called to a break in the narrative and to the lapse of seventeen years between the first and second half of the work. The first to undertake an explanation of this *cesura* was James Boaden. In various parts of the *Memoirs* he has suggested several solutions. He tells us that Mrs. Inchbald intended to write a novel and its sequel and then decided to combine them into one story.[5] Again he offers another explanation: in excusing the long lapse of time between the two parts of a novel he is praising, he recalls a like lapse of time in Shakespeare's *A Winter's Tale* and, assuming that this play was well known to Mrs. Inchbald since she frequently played Shakespearean parts, he immediately jumps to the conclusion that *A Winter's Tale* served as a model for *A Simple Story*.[6] There are, it is true, certain points of similarity between these works, but had there been no seventeen-year lapse perhaps Boaden would not have noticed them, for the parallel between the play and the novel is far from complete. With as much reason, he might have suggested the original of *A Winter's Tale,* Robert Greene's *Pandosto,* as the source of *A Simple Story*. *Pandosto* was almost as well known in Mrs. Inchbald's day as was *A Winter's Tale,* and seems to have been extremely popular in England throughout the century. The fact that there are at the present time in the British Museum alone ten editions dated before 1800[7] is proof of the favor in which *Dorastus and Fawnia,* the title under which *Pandosto* was issued, was held by the eighteenth century reader. Mrs. Inchbald could have been familiar with this love tragedy. I do not mean here to put forth any claim for *Pandosto* as the source of *A Simple Story,* but I do wish to point out that Boaden's claim for *A Winter's Tale* as its source is not convincing. Evidently he does not take his own explanation too seriously, for in another place and in another connection he seems to imply that the years were passed over by Mrs. Inchbald in order to avoid the necessity of describing a seduction scene.

S. R. Littlewood approaches the problem in a different way and suggests that the death of Joseph Inchbald, during the period of the novel's composition, may explain the hiatus.[8] He does not emphasize this claim, nor does he stress the point, and therefore, he may not have been entirely convinced that his theory was valid.

Now, we know that the novel was completed in 1779, three months after the death of Mrs. Inchbald's husband. Just how much of the tale, as we have it today, was included in that first draft there is no way of telling. If Mrs. Inchbald originally wrote the work in four volumes, and if the break came between the second and third volumes, then the theory which Littlewood advances is hardly sound. It puts too great a burden upon the author, for it necessitates her writing two volumes in the time between the death of her husband and the date three months later, when she was looking for a publisher. But if, on the other hand, there was in the original only that part of the story dealing with Miss Milner, such a theory might be plausible. We have already seen how *A Simple Story* originated in Mrs. Inchbald's fancy when she met John Kemble; how she saw herself and Kemble as the heroine and hero of the tale, and built her plot around that idea. All

this romancing took place before the death of Joseph Inchbald. It well could be that when her husband died Mrs. Inchbald's wounded conscience would not permit her to carry the story further with herself as heroine, and so she broke off and began with a new generation. At any rate Littlewood's solution is a more reasonable one than that advanced by Boaden.

One might, taking a hint from Littlewood, advance still another theory. It could be assumed that the latter half of the novel was written during one of those periodic estrangements between the author and John Kemble, and that she, in a spirit of vindictiveness toward her friend, transformed Dorriforth into a tyrant. Perhaps one would not like to go so far as to say that Mrs. Inchbald was capable of this, but her treatment of William Godwin at the time of Mary Wollstonecraft's death does show that she could harbor the bitterest resentment.[9]

I am not convinced by any of these theories. If one is to make a fair judgment upon *A Simple Story* and its plot one should endeavor to discover the author's point of view and approach the question from that angle. Some of the critics, I fear, have not done this, because they have accepted the common opinion that *A Simple Story* is a purpose novel, which primarily it is not, as I shall show in a subsequent chapter. If one remembers that the plot of the novel is built around Mrs. Inchbald and her friend, John Kemble, and forgets for the moment the didactic material which was added at a later date, the problem of the broken plot does not offer such great difficulty. One may now view it in an entirely different light. As I see it, Mrs. Inchbald began her novel with the idea in mind that if she and John Kemble had been free to marry and had done so, they could never have lived together in peace and happiness, regardless of how much love there may have existed between them. From this starting point she worked out her theory that the marriage of two irreconcilable characters, such as herself and Kemble, must inevitably bring disaster and end in tragedy. As the idea of the novel grew in her mind she may have seen that the whole theory would be strengthened and the tragedy made the greater if she demonstrated that disaster would fall not only upon the first but upon the second generation as well. To do this she introduced a second heroine and a second hero.[10] The fact that she used a like device in *Nature and Art,* to show the development of an idea in two generations, gives strength to this point. Perhaps the scheme does not lend itself to an artistic treatment but that need not concern us here. The thing to be noted is that if such were Mrs. Inchbald's purpose, and if she handled her plot logically, then many of the objections raised against her workmanship are not entirely justified. Let us examine the objections.

Littlewood has this to say:

There does not seem to be any exact reason for this double generation of heroines. The moral remains the same, and the character of the daughter, though it does not repeat that of the mother, hardly intensifies the point of view. In short, the whole of the second part is something of an anti-climax.[11]

This same writer then adds:

> None the less, it is indubitably to the second part that we owe the Charlotte Brontë inspiration [in *Jane Eyre*]. So—if for that alone—it was worth having.[12]

Edith Birkhead expresses a similar opinion. She says:

> Because of her imperfections, Miss Milner is much more interesting and life-like than that pallid waxwork, her daughter, who observes the emotional etiquette prescribed for the sentimental heroine with painful exactitude.[13]

These of course are points of view arising from the notion that *A Simple Story* is a treatise upon the education of women. If it were a novel of this type, such objections would be reasonable; for the kind of education received by a mother does not necessarily determine the kind the daughter is to receive; and therefore, "the double generation" would be superfluous and the broken plot would be inexcusable.

There is, however, another critic who commented upon the novel at the time of its publication, and who, in my opinion, saw the work as the author intended it should be understood. This anonymous reviewer says of the broken plot:

> To give a picture of Lord Elmwood, in all these trying circumstances, as well in his conduct to his wife, who has dishonored him, as to his daughter, who was his issue by that wife, is the main design of Mrs. Inchbald's *Simple Story*. It is this that gives unity of design to the whole fable and makes it one unbroken narrative; not two stories woven together, which has been erroneously observed.[14]

Unity in the Novels

This brings us now to a discussion of unity in the novels. In *A Simple Story* is the break in the middle destructive of unity, or is the early reviewer correct in his contention? Before answering the question it is desirable that we have a statement of the method by which unity must be obtained. I choose Professor Hamilton's declaration upon the subject, because the rule which he lays down is comprehensive enough to include any work of fiction, while at the same time it is sufficiently limited as not to admit of license in plot construction. He says:

> Unity in any work of art can be attained only by a definite decision of the artist as to what he is trying to accomplish, and by a rigorous focus of attention on his purpose to accomplish it,—a focus of attention so rigorous as to exclude consideration of any matter which does not contribute, directly or indirectly, to the furtherance of his aim.[15]

On a preceding page I stated what I considered was Mrs. Inchbald's aim in writing her first novel. If my contention is correct, and I believe that it is, that she meant to show how marriage between two irreconcilable characters brings tragedy, not only upon the first but upon the second generation as well, then the break in plot hardly seems to be destructive of unity. The plot is simple and straightforward. Nothing, with the exception of the didactic material, and that is small in extent and foreign to the novel, is introduced to distract from the author's purpose. The plot moves forward with no digressions, and without hesitation. Mrs. Inchbald carries the reader from the first to the second part of the novel in such a way that he is scarcely conscious of the lapse of time, for the interest is immediately centered upon Lord Elmwood and his daughter as it had been earlier upon Lord Elmwood and the mother of that daughter. The author might have filled up the intervening time with narrative, but the events she would have recorded would have contributed little intensity to her point of view. Certainly, the seduction of the heroine would have added nothing to the furtherance of the plot. Besides, Richardson had already given the world an abundance of such scenes, and it is refreshing to find Mrs. Inchbald independent enough to pass over this favorite expedient of her time. The only other event of interest in the seventeen years was Lord Elmwood's dismissal of his daughter. Presenting this before the reader would have given opportunity for showing the inflexible tyranny of the hero, but Mrs. Inchbald treats this fully in another connection and therefore, there is no necessity of the revelation at this point.

What the author does it simply to ignore time and to center attention upon causality. By this she succeeds in doing what she set out to do. She focuses attention upon her purpose so "as to exclude consideration of any matter which does not contribute" to the furtherance of her aim. She introduces only such incidents as are intended to emphasize the cause of the tragedy. Since the exchange of heroines and the break in the plot in no way violate the author's original intention, the plot of *A Simple Story* has unity, and those who have attacked it have missed the whole point of the tale.

In the case of *Nature and Art,* strangely enough, there has been no serious attack upon the plot. It is precisely here that the attack should have been made, rather than upon the plot of *A Simple Story,* for it is here that Mrs.

Inchbald violates her original intention. She begins with Rousseau's idea of the man of *nature* and the man of *art*. She undertakes to show through the working out of the plot that the man of *nature* is superior to the man of *art*. When she is half way through the novel the fate of the heroine so absorbs her interest that she largely forgets her sociological intent, and, instead of making the novel a treatise upon the disasters resulting from a false system of education, she makes it a tragedy of an outcast in the London streets. In other words, Mrs. Inchbald saw from the beginning what situations she would introduce into the plot, but as the story unfolded itself she became engrossed in a single situation and allowed her plot to fall into the background and to be forgotten. At the very end of the novel she tried to remedy this by gathering up the threads and finishing as she had intended, but the effect is anything but pleasing. Whatever interest one may have had at the beginning in the complication of events is lost as the author follows the misfortunes of Hannah Primrose. When the plot is again taken up, it is too late to re-arouse that interest. One does not care what becomes of the Henrys, the Williams, and Rebecca Rymer. Unity of design has been destroyed. In spite of the fact that Mrs. Inchbald accounts for time in this novel, and in spite of the fact that she carries her heroine through from her introduction until she is disposed of, nevertheless, from the standpoint of plot construction she shows herself a better workman in her first novel than in her second. In *A Simple Story* the reader feels that the novelist is leading him to a definite culmination, while in *Nature and Art* he is never quite certain where he is being conducted. This is because the author, in wandering away from her original design, failed to build up to a totality of effect in her plot, and therefore, she violated a fundamental principle of unity.

Relation of Character to Plot

In introducing characters into plot Mrs. Inchbald is hardly more skillful than she is in securing unity. What originality she shows is in the type of character chosen, rather than in the position given to the character. She follows the conventions of her time in *A Simple Story* and presents a hero and his friend, a heroine and her confidante, and a villain. When in this novel she departs from the conventional form in the use made of characters she frequently exhibits a weakness in technique and confuses the reader. One expects that the hero and heroine will be the important and unifying characters, but this is not the scheme followed. The task of unifying the plot is given almost exclusively to the hero. He is carried through from beginning to end, and in him Mrs. Inchbald works out her theory that the passion of love in the human heart may be a tyrant. Instead of exalting the heroine, as might be expected, she gives the next place of importance to the heroine's confidante. This is especially true in the latter half of the novel, although in the first half the confidante plays

an important rôle as well.[16] She is assigned a place of importance from beginning to end, and shares honors with the hero in bringing order out of chaos. Of course, the position of the heroine is not minimized to any great extent, but her significance grows less and less as the theme is worked out until she is finally dismissed when the novel is about half complete. With the introduction of a new heroine the position of this character is somewhat altered. Instead of being the complement to the hero, she is now a character of no great importance, being simply one in whom is exhibited the ultimate disaster of misdirected love. However, the greatest inconsistency is shown in the function given to the hero's friend. In the earlier part of the story this character, and not the villain as might be expected, represents a retarding force to the smooth succession of events. In fact one is never quite sure whether he is not more villainous than the villain himself. At least one is sure that he is usurping the prerogative of the villain. All this is changed in the later development when the friend is transformed into an accelerating force and becomes a kind of second hero. With the change in rôle played by the hero's friend, Mrs. Inchbald divides the responsibility of retarding the action between the unyielding will of the hero and a second villain, whom she introduces in this part of the novel. In the clash of these two forces she brings *A Simple Story* to its culmination.

In *Nature and Art,* Mrs. Inchbald shows no advance in mastery of technique. As a matter of fact her technique is more faulty than in her earlier novel. Perhaps it was necessarily so, since she was writing a novel in which she had nothing more than an academic interest, and therefore, she had no vital theme to present. To work out a plan whereby she might emphasize Rousseau's theory of a decadent culture and its deleterious effects upon the individual, puzzled her and led her into difficulties. In advancing the theory, she formulated no clearly defined plan. She neither reasoned from cause to effect, nor from effect to cause. She saw the effect which she wished to emphasize, but instead of working back in a logical manner to the cause, she jumped to the cause immediately; and then ignoring logic she attempted to bridge the gap between cause and effect and failed, with the net result that the two ends of the novel do not meet.

Specifically, Mrs. Inchbald works in this way: to give force to Rousseau's doctrine she introduces two characters of equal gifts, and develops them under different influences, with the intention of revealing the man of *nature* as a superior being to the man of *art*. She sees that the characters when introduced are mature and that their habits of life are pretty well fixed. It would be more forceful, therefore, if two characters were to be subjected from youth to the influences of *nature* and *art,* and their careers traced. This scheme our author adopts and introduces a second generation of sons. The *art* generations, father and son, she intends to develop into villains, and the *nature* generations, likewise father and son, into heroes. The presence of the sons gives occasion for the female characters. Two are brought forward, both of whom Mrs. Inchbald calls heroines.[17] She then discovers, according to her plan, that she has two villains, two heroes, and two heroines. This immediately constitutes the difficulty of giving proper space in the novel to six major characters. The author surmounts this by reducing one villain, two heroes, and one heroine to the rôle of minor characters, at the same time raising the remaining villain to the rôle of hero, and throwing him into conflict with the remaining heroine. By this scheme she loses sight of her original intention, and ends by representing respectability as tyrannizing over love. It is here that Mrs. Inchbald fails to make the two ends of the novel meet, and as a result she is compelled to carry her other characters through to the end and to dispose of them in a huddled manner, much as Goldsmith disposed of his characters at the end of *The Vicar of Wakefield.*

In the disposal of characters Mrs. Inchbald leaves much to be desired in both novels. She introduces many with the intention of giving them a prominent place, and then leaves them at loose ends when they cannot be used effectively. For example, in *A Simple Story* Rushbrook is introduced as a child, obviously with the idea of making him, as he grows up, a second Dorriforth, without Dorriforth's faults. The novel offers no opportunity for doing this, and as a consequence Mrs. Inchbald has to carry him through the entire work in order to have a proper man at hand for the heroine to marry at the denouement. In *Nature and Art* the two Henrys and Rebecca Rymer are brought into the story and then "go dead while the author is at work."[18] This lack of facility in manipulating the people of her novels led Mrs. Inchbald to compel some of her characters to do double duty. We have seen in *A Simple Story* that Dorriforth is both hero in and antagonist to the plot. The Dean in *Nature and Art* is villain first and hero afterwards. In other words, when these characters are disposed of, it is in a manner contrary to what the novelist had led the reader to expect, and therefore, the reader is to be pardoned if he feels that the writer of the tales has permitted some of the characters to wander into ways not marked out for them.

The reason for Mrs. Inchbald's failure in this respect is not difficult to find. Her experience as an actress and playwright made her always the dramatist but never the novelist. She thought of her novels in terms of the drama. She manipulated her characters as on a stage rather than in the broad expanse of life. The drama demands that the *dramatis personae* be introduced early in the play and that their relationships be pointed out. They may then be dismissed and called in when needed. We find that in both *A Simple Story* and *Nature and*

Art, this scheme was followed. What to do with them after they were introduced our author did not always know. She could not dismiss them to the wings. If the characters were to be used again she had one expedient which she most frequently fell back upon,—that was, an indefinite place called a farmhouse in the country. For example, in *A Simple Story,* Harry Rushbrook, during the displeasure of his uncle Dorriforth, is sent to a farmhouse in the country; Lady Elmwood and her daughter Matilda flee to a farmhouse in northern England; at the time of Matilda's second exile she is sent to a farmhouse at some distance from Elmwood castle; the elder Henry, in *Nature and Art,* goes first to an island but when he returns to England he, with his son Henry and his son's wife Rebecca, retires to a farm. There they are left to meditate. Occasionally the scheme was varied, some characters being disposed of by death and others being forgotten, but all in all the farmhouse was the most important wing in Mrs. Inchbald's theatre. Of course, her major characters she carried through to the end and disposed of them naturally, but only her major characters.

Locale and Style

There are two other respects in which Mrs. Inchbald's dramatic experience shows itself in her technique. The first is in the relation of locale to plot, and the second, in her style of writing. As for locale it has almost no influence upon plot. The scene of both works is laid in England, but the scene might have been laid almost anywhere in Europe without affecting seriously the train of events. She takes her reader from city to country and back again, but the reader is hardly conscious of the change. There is nothing in locale to color or affect the action. It is confined to the limits of a stage, which in the novel, is usually a drawing or dining room. This is especially true in *A Simple Story,* and true to a limited degree in *Nature and Art.* In the latter novel there is less confinement to the inside of houses, but there is no more expanse of the field of action than in the former. One may say, therefore, that locale is completely ignored in the construction of plot and for it is substituted names, such as London, Elmwood castle, the country, an island. None of these places is presented to the reader's consciousness, but, on the contrary, they appear rather as a notice of location which one might read on a playbill.

In Mrs. Inchbald's style of writing we see again the influence of her stage experience. E. M. Forster has said that "the specialty of the novel is that the writer can talk about his characters as well as through them or can arrange for us to listen when they talk to themselves".[19] This, naturally, the dramatist cannot do to the same extent as the novelist, and this our author does not do. Her novels are made up almost exclusively of dialogue. The plot is worked out in the give and take of the characters in conversation. When, upon occasions, she attempts to talk about her characters she is ill at ease. It is as if the novelist, as an actress, has turned to her audience, and in some embarrassment is explaining what to expect when next the actor appears. The explanations are stilted and self-conscious. What is true of such explanations is equally true of the running narrative between scenes of the novel. The narration is out of place and awkward. As a workman Mrs. Inchbald has but one tool, dialogue, and this only she knows how to use with any degree of skill.

As a technician, Mrs. Inchbald never advanced beyond the apprentice stage in novel writing. The intensity of her theme in *A Simple Story* enabled her to write a unified novel, but not a good one. In *Nature and Art* the absence of a theme in which she was vitally interested caused her to violate the first principle of unity. She tried to subject her characters to plot, with the result that they never quite fitted into the life she had prepared for them. She saw the novel as an extended drama, but knew not how to handle it because it was extended. She began as an amateur, and finished as she had begun, without ever having mastered the mechanics of novel writing.

. . . . .

The Art of Her Novels

Mrs. Inchbald as an artist is little better than she is as a technician. Her achievement in this particular bears the marks of the amateur writer. In her use of materials she scarcely produces the illusion of reality. She does not seem to be able to manipulate her characters or control her situations. Professor Horne has said of *A Simple Story* that

> The book offers a most interesting study of an unconscious power, of a half-formed art.[20]

In order to illustrate the truth of this statement we shall examine our author's finished product.

Character Portrayal

The male characters in *A Simple Story* and *Nature and Art* are semi-strangers to their creator. These she does not understand. Dorriforth and Sandford, the Henrys and the Williams present a problem with which she is not able to cope. As a result she treats them almost entirely from an objective point of view. She judges man by his actions; motives she leaves untouched, or when, on occasions, she tries to analyze them, her analysis is inaccurate.

The reason for this difficulty becomes clear when one looks into the life of the author. Mrs. Inchbald was never particularly successful in judging the characters of the various men who came into her life. There was scarcely a woman of her day who had more admirers, many of whom wished to marry her,[21] and yet one may say that all these admirers remained strangers to her. Perhaps she understood John Kemble best of all, but even that understanding did not enable her to continue in unbroken friendship with him. It may be that her childish conduct toward William Godwin arose from a belief that she knew him so well that she could direct his actions. Even though she would not herself marry him, she evidently believed he would not marry without consulting her. When he did, she acted with a petulance that was unworthy of her. In one of her suitors, Sir Charles Bunbury, she placed all confidence, but he proved a trifler in the end. A Colonel Glover was the most worthy of all her friends. Although he was a man of family and wealth, she, nevertheless, treated him with indifference, while at the same time she continued to be friendly with men who were, in no sense, deserving of her. When her friends warned her against any bad associates she disregarded their warnings, ending an unhappy friendship usually in tears and heartaches. She never seemed able to distinguish between the sincere man and the trifler. Mrs. Inchbald was a woman of contradictions. In her life she was sceptical toward the Colonel Glovers, but toward the Bunburys she was charitable. This inability to understand character is reflected in her novels.

The characters of *A Simple Story* admirably illustrate this peculiarity. For example, Dorriforth's outstanding traits are pride and selfishness, yet in the novel these are called integrity. Mrs. Inchbald does not succeed in convincing the reader that he is good, although she insists that he is. Sanford, on the other hand, is intended to be a man of rough exterior and generous heart, but he appears for the most part as an unmannered boor. The author calls him a holy man, but only his faults are apparent. Even the villain, Lord Frederick, is not villainous. Although the fact is emphasized that he is a gallant and therefore bad, the evil in his character appears to be the result of unfair treatment, and consequently, in spite of all Mrs. Inchabald's efforts, he wins the sympathy of the reader. None of these characters fits effectively into the place prepared for it by the author.

In *Nature and Art* there is some improvement. The characters talk like men even though they do not always act like men. While the love which the elder Henry bears for his brother William is introduced naturally and with genuine pathos, Henry is never quite the man of nature he is intended to be. Young Henry shines for a time and then degenerates into a nonentity. The younger William, in the few glimpses afforded the reader, never rises to a position of reality. By far the best of all the male characters in this second novel is the Dean and Bishop. He is not an individual, but as a type he is well drawn, and he serves to keep alive a story that might otherwise have expired from sheer debility.

A more careful examination of the character of Dorriforth in *A Simple Story* will suffice to illustrate Mrs. Inchbald's deficiency in the portrayal of male character.

The hero is introduced to the reader with an appropriate description of his appearance. In fact, he is the only character so described, but the novel loses nothing by the omission. In spite of Mrs. Inchbald's efforts Dorriforth remains indistinct in appearance, and moves about as if behind a thin veil, without once giving the reader a full view of his countenance. The author says of him:

> But that the reader may be interested in what Dorriforth says and does, it is necessary to give some description of his person and manners. His figure was tall and elegant, but his face, except a pair of dark bright eyes, a set of white teeth, and a graceful fall in his clerical curls of brown hair, had not one feature to excite admiration—yet such a gleam of sensibility was diffused over each, that many people mistook his face for handsome, and all were more or less attracted by it—in a word, the charm, that is here meant to be described, is a *countenance*—on *his* [sic] you read the feelings of his heart—saw all its inmost workings—the quick pulses that beat with hope and fear, or the gentle ones that moved in a more equal course of patience and resignation. On this countenance his thoughts were pourtrayed; and as his mind was enriched with every virtue that could make it valuable, so was his face adorned with every expression of those virtues—and they not only gave a lustre to his aspect, but added a harmonious sound to all he uttered; it was persuasive, it was perfect eloquence; whilst in his looks you beheld his thoughts moving with his lips, and ever coinciding with what he said.[22]

Such a description in itself might be considered meritorious and sufficient for the author's purpose, but an intimate knowledge of the character as it is developed compels me to assert that it is no description at all, since it is at complete variance with the Dorriforth represented in the novel. In other words, the character Mrs. Inchbald has in mind never finds its way into the story. The eighteenth century writers were fond of the man of sensibility, and this somewhat mythical figure has ever since resisted all attempts at analysis.[23] Certainly this novel adds nothing to an understanding of him. Black eyes, white teeth, and clerical curls of brown hair do not make of any person a man of sensibility. Such an idea is absurd, but it is not more absurd than the qualities attributed to the hero. Nor does a face which gives away every thought of the mind make a man all that the author seems to imply. She hardly thought so herself, for throughout the novel she labors her character to make him "Dorriforth the pious, the good", and in spite of all that she says he remains from introduction to conclusion a contradiction of Mrs. Inchbald's declaration. In this character, and likewise in the others, she lacks the power of so directing the action that the good and evil will emerge into the light and be seen in proper relief. It is this weakness that accounts for her forever telling the reader what qualities are to be admired and what detested.

Two passages of *A Simple Story* will illustrate the point just made. Both are intended to throw light upon the character of the hero. The first represents him as Mrs. Inchbald conceived him, but not as she succeeded in presenting him to the reader. She says:

> Every virtue which it was his vocation to preach, it was his care to practice; nor was he in the class of those of the religious, who, by secluding themselves from the world, fly the merit they might have in reforming mankind. He refused to shelter himself from the temptations of the layman by the walls of a cloister, but sought for, and found that shelter in the center of London, where he dwelt, in his own prudence, justice, fortitude, and temperance.[24]

Such is the man presented by the author for the admiration of the reader. But the reader is not to be blamed if he does not admire, for that "virtue which it was his care to practice" makes Dorriforth refuse to see his sister when she is dying, and to neglect her orphan child; it causes him to place prohibitions upon his ward's actions for no other reason than his own selfish satisfaction; it makes him publicly insult Lord Frederick Lawnley whose only crime is an ardent love for Miss Milner; it makes him feared by every servant in his house; it makes him bend to his own will the will of every person near him; in short, it makes of him such a person as no one would wish to live with, and no woman should wish to marry. All that may be said in his behalf is that he is extremely polite to those who never cross him, and kind to those who accept his opinions. This gentleman is intended to represent the admirable hero of the first half of the story and not the tyrant of the second.

Now the passage which accurately describes the man is this:

> Although Dorriforth was the good man that he has been described, there were in his nature shades of evil—there was an obstinacy which he himself, and his friends termed firmness of mind; but had not religion and some opposite virtues weighed heavily in the balance, it would frequently have degenerated into implacable stubbornness.[25]

No doubt the latter passage was introduced to foreshadow the character in its later development; as such it is good art with which we can have no quarrel. But why does Mrs. Inchbald insist on the first description, presenting Dorriforth, so she believes, as a model gentleman? In spite of her constant protests that he is good he acts always as the man described in the second passage. Dorriforth, the guardian and priest, is in reality as stubborn as Lord Elmwood, the husband and tyrant. He does not change, but only develops the intensity of his essential character. All through the early chapters he strains at the leash and tries to express himself as he is, and all through these chapters the author holds him in check. Never once does she depict him as giving free rein to his passions until the last half of the novel. In this part of the work Dorriforth seems to break loose and run away from the writer. It might be argued that since Mrs. Inchbald had introduced this man as a priest she felt that she should represent him as noble and good, so long as he remained in that office. But the point is that she only called him *good* while she portrayed him on the page as *bad*. What is true in this instance is true of all Mrs. Inchbald's male characters. She could not make them behave as she wished. She failed to understand the inner workings of the minds of these gentlemen she had created, and failed because she had little knowledge of male psychology.

When we turn to an analysis of female characters we find that Mrs. Inchbald is more at home in their company, although even here not quite at ease. She approaches these characters subjectively and analyzes their motives, thus giving to her females a greater plausibility than is to be found in the male characters. Miss Milner, Miss Woodley, Mrs. Horton, Lady Matilda, and Hannah Primrose, while not admirably drawn, are at least not poorly drawn. They stand out as human beings, but with the exception of Mrs. Horton, they are hardly individualized, hardly living. As for poor Rebecca Rymer, she is too anemic to be noticed. Miss Milner and Hannah Primrose touched the author's own life and for this reason she understood their personal peculiarities. Even Miss Woodley, the over-conscientious Catholic, she must have observed in some English boarding-house. Mrs. Inchbald's greatest weakness in the delineation of female characters seems to be that she understood more of the source of woman's foibles than she did of her deeper feelings. It may be that for this reason she was a successful writer of comedy of manners[26] and a failure as a novelist.

Just as the treatment of the hero in *A Simple Story* served to illustrate Mrs. Inchbald's handling of male character in general, so an analysis of the heroine in the same novel will illustrate her method with female character. Here we find a trace of Richardson's influence in that the author attempts to lay bare the heart of Miss Milner and to assign motives for her actions. Immediately she gets into a difficulty similar to the one experienced with Dorriforth. This time it is Miss Milner's appearance and personality that get in the way,

just as Dorriforth's goodness got in her way. She insists that the heroine is beautiful and charitable, but fails to make the reader aware of that beauty and charity. But in spite of this fault she does develop the character of Miss Milner logically, and makes her actions the result of what she is essentially. The reason she is able to do this is that now she is writing of the kind of person whom she knows. One may go so far as to say that Miss Milner is about the only kind of person whom the author does know. Generally speaking, the heroine is Mrs. Inchbald with a new name. She was herself a coquette, and she likewise makes Miss Milner a coquette, as passages culled here and there will, I hope, make clear. The first one I have chosen refers to a time before Dorriforth has seen his ward. Inquiring of an acquaintance what he should expect of this young lady he is told that

> . . . she's young, idle, indiscreet, and giddy, with half a dozen lovers in her suite; some coxcombs, others men of gallantry, some single, and others married.[27]

In commenting upon the shortcomings of the heroine Mrs. Inchbald says:

> . . . if she had more faults than generally belong to others, she had likewise more temptations.[28]

And again:

> She was beautiful; she had been too frequently told the high value of that beauty, and thought every moment passed in wasteful idleness during which she was not gaining some new conquest. She had a quick sensibility, which too frequently discovered itself in the immediate resentment of injuries or neglect.[29]

An illustration of how these qualities show themselves in the heroine's actions is to be found in her conduct toward Dorriforth soon after she learns that he is in love with her. She gambles with his affections in the hope of arousing his jealousy, mistaking it for love:

> Are not my charms even more invincible than I ever believed them to be? Dorriforth, the grave, the pious, the anchorite Dorriforth, by their force, is animated to all the ardour of the most impassioned lover—while the proud priest, the austere guardian is humbled, if I but frown, into the veriest slave of love. She then asked, "Why did I not keep him longer in suspense? He could not have loved me more, I believe; but my power over him might have been greater still. I am the happiest of women in the affection he has proved to me, but I wonder whether it would exist under ill-treatment? If it would not, he still does not love me as I wish to be loved—if it would, my triumph, my felicity, would be enhanced."[30]

The author's comment upon this passage is:

> These thoughts were phantoms of the brain, and never, by system, put into action; but, repeatedly indulged, they were practiced by casual occurrences; the dear-bought experiment of being loved in spite of her faults, (a glory proud women ever aspire to) was, at present, the ambition of Miss Milner. Unthinking woman! she did not reflect, that to the searching eye of Lord Elmwood, she had faults, with her utmost care to conceal or overcome them, sufficient to try all his love, and all his patience. But what female is not fond of experiments? To which, how few do not fall a sacrifice![31]

Miss Milner, acting upon her theory of proving a true lover, puts Lord Elmwood to the test. She attends a masquerade in defiance of his prohibition. Upon her return her lover threatens to release her from the engagement between them. A quarrel ensues and Miss Milner observes to her confidante:

> "That after what had passed between her and Lord Elmwood, *he* must be the first to make a concession, before she herself would condescend to be reconciled." "I believe I know Lord Elmwood's temper," replied Miss Woodley, "and I do not think he will be easily induced to beg pardon for a fault which he thinks *you* have committed." "Then he does not love me . . . tenderness, affection, the politeness due from a lover to his mistress demands his submission."[32]

The passages quoted reveal one side of the heroine's nature; but there is another side which is equally important. After Mrs. Inchbald has described her beauty, she says of her:

> She had, besides, acquired the dangerous character of a wit; but to which she had no real pretentions, although the most discerning critic, hearing her converse, might fall into this mistake. Her replies had all the effect of repartee . . . Her words were but the words of others, and, like those of others, put into common sentences; but the delivery made them pass for wit, as grace in an ill-proportioned figure will often make it pass for symmetry.
>
> . . . . .
>
> Miss Milner had the quality peculiar to wits, of hazarding the thought that first occurs, which thought, is generally truth.[33]

The thing that Mrs. Inchbald here says passed for wit in the heroine is the thing that passed for wit in Mrs. Inchbald's own life. In reality this so-called wit is nothing more than a quickness in repartee, a cleverness in conversation. Its use in the development of character is infrequent in the novels. In fact, the quality is given to but two of the characters, and is con-

fined to the period of youth. Probably Mrs. Inchbald did not consider it as a quality belonging to youth alone, but as she carried her characters along in the complication she neglected to emphasize this particular side of the personality. At any rate, she did make use of it in the early development of Miss Milner's character in *A Simple Story,* and in the early development of young Henry's character in *Nature and Art.* One passage from *A Simple Story* will suffice to illustrate Mrs. Inchbald's use of this quality in her novels.

The occasion of the following conversation is the guardian's attempt to force an admission or a denial from his ward that she loves Lord Frederick. Sandford is by to assist at the inquisition, and Miss Woodley has been called in as a witness. Dorriforth begins:

> "Under this consideration, I wish once more to hear your thoughts in regard to matrimony, and to hear them before one of your sex, that I may form an opinion by her constructions." To all this serious oration, Miss Milner made no other reply than by turning to Mr. Sandford, and asking, "if he was the person of her own sex, to whose judgment her guardian was to submit his own?" "Madam," cried Sandford angrily, "you are come hither upon serious business." "Any business must be serious to me, Mr. Sandford, in which you are concerned; and if you had called it *sorrowful,* the epithet would have suited as well." "Miss Milner," said her guardian, "I did not bring you here to contend with Mr. Sandford." "Then why, Sir, bring him hither? for where he and I are, there must be contention." "I brought him hither, Madam, or I should rather say, brought you to this house, merely that he might be present on this occasion, and with his discernment relieve me from a suspicion, that my own judgment is neither able to suppress nor to confirm." "Are there any more witnesses you may wish to call in, Sir, to remove your doubts of my veracity? if there are, pray send for them before you begin your interrogations."[34]

Little more of Miss Milner's character is revealed in the novel than may be gleaned from these passages. Occasionally there are glimpses of noble sentiment and genuine charity, but these are far too few to convince the reader of the nobility of the heroine. The general impression that remains after a reading of the novel is that she was foolish, vain, and extremely susceptible to flattery. It was a combination of these qualities that brought on her ultimate tragedy, and the modern reader after being treated to an excess of silly caprices in this woman, sheds not a tear when she is finally eliminated from the second half of the tale. This overemphasis upon the caprices of Miss Milner leads me to say that Mrs. Inchbald was better acquainted with woman's foibles than with her soul. In other words, she was a poor psychologist in her character drawing.

Such criticism of the characters in Mrs. Inchbald's novels, particularly those in *A Simple Story,* does not mean that as they were conceived, they had nothing of greatness about them. Some of them were great, but not sufficiently developed to leave a lasting impression on the reader. Dorriforth, Miss Milner, the Dean, and Hannah Primrose could have taken their places with the great figures of fiction had they received a more thorough treatment. Even Miss Woodley, with her kind heart and charity, reminds one of Goldsmith's Dr. Primrose. Mrs. Horton, had her character been more fully treated, would have been the equal of Fielding's minor characters. It seems that Mrs. Inchbald had the power of inventing great figures of fiction, but that she lacked the ability to draw them as she conceived them. They always remain indistinct and static. They are individuals, but are not humanized. They remind one of the figures in a Hogarth painting, for, like Hogarth's characters, they have the stamp of the eighteenth century upon them; they are caught and held fast in a pose or an attitude, and seem never to have been live, dynamic individuals.

Furthermore, the characters in *A Simple Story* have no purpose in life. The men seem to exist for no other reason than to spend their time in the company of fine ladies, and the ladies' chief function appears to be to listen to the wisdom of the men, and to stand in awe of them. One would like to feel there was some business in life outside the four walls of a house, but Mrs. Inchbald affords the reader no such opportunity. Her people are always in the drawing or dining room in earnest conversation. When this conversation breaks up the heroine with her confidante retires to her apartment to sigh, sew, weep, or talk of love; the hero with his friend goes to his study to read or talk upon some point of philosophy. The characters do not, in any sense, live in the fullness of life.

In *Nature and Art* the characters are slightly more concerned with living than are those in the earlier novel, but the extra-literary purpose in this work serves to destroy their naturalness. This is seen in the characters of the two brothers. Mrs. Inchbald ignores inherent traits in order to show that her people are the product of environment. The two brothers at their introduction are said to have the qualities of "honesty, sobriety, and humility", but William is returned from the university a proud, haughty, and selfish man, the transformation, of course, being attributed to an artificial training. In treating the characters of the cousins the author at times makes character depend upon heredity, at other times upon environment and training. As a sensible woman of wide experience she knew that character is not entirely dependent upon environment and training, that heredity plays its rôle,—and so, forgetting her didactic intent for the moment, she occasionally permitted her good judgment to dictate what she wrote. However, such evidence of good judgment appears too infrequently to allow her to present living individuals.

On the whole the characters in Mrs. Inchbald's novels are stiff and artificial. Their affectation is a constant annoyance to the reader. Frequently their very names have an unpleasant sound and do not invite one to an intimate acquaintance. One may read through the whole of *A Simple Story* without once meeting the Christian name of Miss Milner. The sound of *Dorriforth* is harsh and unpleasant. In *Nature and Art* the multiplying of the Williams and Henrys leads to confusion, and leaves the impression that the characters themselves are a heterogeneous lot, and in reality that is what they are. . . .

Notes

. . .[5] James Boaden, *Memoirs of Mrs. Inchbald,* Vol. I, p. 264.

[6] *Ibid.,* Vol. I, p. 277.

[7] P. G. Thomas (Editor), *Greene's Pandosto—The Original of Shakespeare's Winter's Tale.* Introduction, p. ix.

[8] Samuel Richardson Littlewood, *Elizabeth Inchbald and Her Circle,* p. 75.

[9] J. Boaden, *op. cit.,* Vol. II, p. 30.

[10] Apparently Mrs. Inchbald introduced Rushbrook with the idea of making of him a second hero but failed to carry out her purpose.

[11] S. R. Littlewood, *op. cit.,* p. 76.

[12] *Loc. cit.*

[13] Edith Birkhead, "Sentiment and Sensibility in the Eighteenth-Century Novel." *English Association—Essays and Studies,* Vol. XI, p. 108.

[14] *Monthly Review, Enlarged Edition,* April 1791, Vol. IV, p. 436. G. L. Joughin expresses a similar opinion when he says: "If *A Simple Story* is a fusion of two novels it must be a fundamental one. The identity of the characterizations precludes the possibility of the two parts representing two early separate works." *The Life and Work of Elizabeth Inchbald,* p. 302.

[15] Clayton Hamilton, *A Manual of the Art of Fiction,* p. 61.

[16] It will be recalled that Defoe again and again in the pages of *Moll Flanders* attributes the downfall of his heroine to the fact that she had never had a confidante. The importance which Mrs. Inchbald gives to this character suggests that she was taking Defoe's dictum seriously.

[17] *Nature and Art* (Philadelphia, 1796), Vol. I, p. 78.

[18] Edward Morgan Forster, *Aspects of the Novel,* p. 143.

[19] *Ibid.,* p. 127.

[20] Charles F. Horne, *The Technique of the Novel*, p. 176.

[21] In spite of Mrs. Shelley's assertion that Mrs. Inchbald's admirers were unwilling to take a poor actress and playwright as a wife, Boaden insists again and again that Mrs. Inchbald had frequent proposals of marriage.

[22] *A Simple Story* (1908), pp. 9-10.

[23] Edith Birkhead, "Sentiment and Sensibility in the Eighteenth-Century Novel." *English Association—Essays and Studies,* Vol. XI, pp. 96-97.

[24] *A Simple Story* (1908), p. 5.

[25] *Ibid.,* p. 31.

[26] Allardyce Nicholl, *A History of Late Eighteenth Century Drama,* Preface, p. vi.

[27] *A Simple Story* (1908), p. 11.

[28] *Ibid.,* p. 15.

[29] *Loc. cit.*

[30] *Ibid.,* p. 123.

[31] *Loc. cit.*

[32] *Ibid.,* p. 147.

[33] *Ibid.,* pp. 15 and 16.

[34] *Ibid.,* pp. 49-50.

Works Cited

Birkhead, Edith, "Sentiment and Sensibility in the Eighteenth-Century Novel." *English Association—Essays and Studies,* Vol. 11, pp. 92-116, Oxford, 1925.

Boaden, James, *Memoirs of Mrs. Inchbald,* Vols. 1 and 2, London, 1833.

[Defoe, Daniel], *Moll Flanders,* New York, 1929.

Ernle, Lord (Prothero, Rowland Edmund), *The Light Reading of Our Ancestors,* London, 1927.

Forster, Edward Morgan, *Aspects of the Novel,* New York, 1927.

Gregory, Allene, *The French Revolution and The English Novel,* New York, 1915.

Hamilton, Clayton, *A Manual of the Art of Fiction,* New York, 1922.

Horne, Charles F., *The Technique of the Novel,* New York, 1908.

[Inchbald, Mrs. Elizabeth], *A Simple Story,* London, 1908.

_____, *Nature and Art,* Philadelphia, 1796.

Joughin, G. Louis, *The Life and Work of Elizabeth Inchbald.* (Unpublished manuscript in the Harvard University Library.)

Littlewood, Samuel Richardson, *Elizabeth Inchbald and Her Circle,* London, 1921.

Monthly Review. Enlarged Edition, April, 1791, Vol. 4, pp. 434-38.

[Nicoll, Allardyce], *A History of Late Eighteenth Century Drama,* Cambridge, 1927.

Thomas, P. G. (Editor), *Greene's Pandosto—The Original of Shakespeare's Winter's Tale,* New York, 1907.

Paula R. Backscheider (essay date 1980)

SOURCE: Introduction to *The Plays of Elizabeth Inchbald,* Volume I, edited by Paula R. Backscheider, Garland Publishing, Inc., 1980, pp. ix-xlv.

[*In the following essay, Backscheider provides a historical account of Inchbald's career as a playwright and novelist.*]

Elizabeth Inchbald was a strange combination of consuming ambition and personal charm. In spite of a severe speech defect, she worked her way from the theatres of Edinburgh, Aberdeen, Bristol, and York to Covent Garden, where in her first season she played such roles as Mariana in *Measure for Measure,* Lavinia in *The Fair Penitent,* and Anne Bullen in *Henry VIII.*[1] Her husband, the actor Joseph Inchbald, coached her as they traveled, and her vanity, impatience, and relentless demands led her biographer, James Boaden, to surmise that she must have felt remorse after his death.[2] By 1786, she was an established theatrical presence, soon to be the intimate of Colman, Kemble, Harris, Holcroft, Godwin, Mrs. Jordan, and Mrs. Siddons.

She entertained a string of suitors into her forties and inspired her acquaintance Mrs. Wells to describe her early behavior as striking:

> When she was at the theatre, at such a low salary, she conducted herself with so much propriety that even the very scene-shifters and dependents about it treated her with the most marked respect: and every person there declared there was a something in her which they found it impossible to ascertain. . . . [3]

Yet she was capable of saying unforgivable things to her closest friends and could write Godwin on the death of his wife,

> I did not know [Mary Wollstonecraft]. I did not wish to know her: as I avoid every female acquaintance, who has no husband, I avoided her. Against my desire you made us acquainted. With what justice I shunned her, your present note evinces, for she judged me harshly.[4]

She closed the shutters to prevent distractions and worked so tirelessly that her friends marveled, yet she sat up night after night with a sick maid.[5] She bargained with managers and helped Kemble negotiate his sixth of a share of Covent Garden, yet she cried when she saw the signs of age in her mirror.[6] No one who knew her was surprised at the number of revisions of *A Simple Story* or at its skillful combination of the characterization of an arch-flirt with themes of moral seriousness. Likewise, she could provoke another woman to say "that when Mrs. Inchbald came into a room, and sat in a chair in the middle of it as was her wont, every man gathered round it, and it was vain for any other woman to attempt to gain attention."[7] Yet her profitable investments and pious retirement seemed equally true to her personality. Her beauty, her suitors, her acts of benevolence, her moodiness, and her achievements as playwright and novelist made her one of the best-known citizens of London in the 1790's, and her retirement and work with the aged in the Priory confirm the rigid morality present in her character from her youth.

The plays in this volume [*The Plays of Elizabeth Inchbald*] testify to her diligence and her personality. Stage-worthy, varied, and distinguished by insight into human relationships, they rest firmly upon her careful observations of what works on the stage, her experience with English and continental drama, and her own opinions about people. In this introduction, I shall set her playwriting in the context of her life and professional situation and then define and discuss her particular strengths as a dramatist.

Her Career

Mrs. Inchbald was a reliable and prolific playwright during a time in which the English stage was dominated by revivals of earlier plays and the work of a few men, many of whom owned shares in their home theatres.[8] Fourteen of her twenty-one surviving plays ran ten or more nights in their first season, and six ran twenty or more. *Such Things Are* (1787) played twenty-two nights, *Every One Has His Fault* (1793) thirty-two nights, and *Lovers' Vows* (1798) forty-two. *The Midnight Hour* (1787) played ten nights the first season and thirty-six the next. The 1788-89 season alone saw six of her plays performed, and during the week of 16 March 1790, *The Child of Nature, Such Things Are,* and *The Midnight Hour* were all performed at Covent Garden.[9] She explained her success in part as the theatre's voracious appetite for material and London's renewed interest in original plays: "A new play, which, from a reputed wit of former times, would not, with success, bring him a hundred pounds, a manager will now purchase, from a reputed blockhead, at the price of near a thousand. . . ."[10] In fact, however, Mrs. Inchbald was a shrewd observer of contemporary theatre, a canny craftsman, and a sensitive student of human nature. Some of the most experienced and successful dramatists of the age helped her revise her work, made suggestions, and offered her material.

Just as she had worked tirelessly to become an actress (carrying a small cloth bag of words to pronounce and reciting her parts in the fields), so did she work to establish herself as a playwright.[11] Her success as an actress was modest, and evidence indicates that her beauty compensated for her lack of talent.[12] The death of Joseph in 1779 made her financial situation precarious, and she finished a version of the novel *A Simple Story* and began writing an unidentified farce in that year.[13] It was 1791 before the novel was published and 1784 before she received 100 guineas for *The Mogul Tale,* her first play to be performed. This long apprenticeship and her nervousness testify to her ambition and pride. Wearing a mask, she heard the play read from the Green Room. In order to disguise her authorship, she played the role of Selima on opening night, but her agitated stammer nearly gave her away.[14] Later she was to observe that an actor risks sullying a "reputation hardly earned, and dearly prized" when his first play is performed.[15] She describes the anxiety felt by Addison and O'Keeffe as their plays were performed and concludes

> The sound of clamorous plaudits raises his spirits to a kind of ecstacy; whilst hisses and groans, from a dissatisfied audience strike on the ear like a personal insult, avowing loud and public contempt for that, in which he has been labouring to show his skill.[16]

She did not suffer embarrassment, however. The farce *The Mogul Tale* played ten nights at the Haymarket in its first season and continued to be performed a few times each season throughout the century. Although Genest could remark that "it met with considerably more success than it deserved," the play turns upon a situation sure to raise laughter and suspense: three Englishmen accidentally land in the Great Mogul's harem.[17] The audience was sure to applaud when the cobbler must impersonate the pope and speak such lines as "Please your Mogulship, I will talk to her in private—perhaps I may persuade her to comply with your princely desires, for we Popes have never any conversation with women except in private."

Inchbald's second play, a full-length comedy that Colman titled *I'll Tell You What,* ran twenty nights in the 1784-85 season.[18] On 13 May, a benefit paid her £101 and played to 1,095 spectators; on 17 May, the play was performed "By Command of their majesties." *Appearance is against Them,* a two-act farce, and *The Widow's Vow,* another farce, rapidly followed. These plays were less original. *Appearance is against Them* and *I'll Tell You What* use the same device, a person hidden in a closet, to make the same point, that appearances can be deceiving; *The Widow's Vow* is based on *L'Heureuse Erreur,* a successful piece by Joseph Patrat.[19]

The late eighteenth-century theatre and Mrs. Inchbald were often pressed for material. She admired Susannah Centlivre's invention and observed several times how difficult it is to write more than one excellent play: "good plays are difficult to produce; and those, who write often, must divide the materials, which would constitute one extraordinary, into two ordinary dramas."[20] Inchbald had already learned to use the stock techniques of comedy such as hidden auditors and compromising situations and to base a play upon a single joke. *The Widow's Vow* turns on the heroine's promise to remain single. Those around her contrive a means for her to change her mind without ridicule or melancholy. Act I ends with her suitor dressed as a woman and promises some of the delight of *Twelfth Night,* but Act II fails to exploit the situation and ends with bombastic threats between the suitor and the heroine's uncle Carlos.

About her next full-length play, she wrote,

> The writer of this play was, at the time of its production, but just admitted to the honours of an authoress, and wanted experience to behold her own danger, when she attempted the subject on which the work is founded. . . . A bold enterprise requires bold execution; and as skill does not always unite with courage, it is often advantageous, where cases are desperate, not to see with the eye of criticism: chance will sometimes do more for rash self-importance, than that judgment, which is the parent of timidity.[21]

This play, *Such Things Are,* characterized the famous philanthropist and reformer John Howard as Haswell, who was played by Pope. The reception was extraordinarily favorable, and Mrs. Inchbald declared herself "happy beyond expression."[22] The royal family attended the play, and she claimed that it earned her over £900. Act II is a fine study of audience manipulation. The embittered Zedan steals. Haswell's pocketbook, becomes acquainted with him, and returns the wallet on bended knee; according to contemporary reports this never failed to draw groans, then tears, and then wild applause. The shrewd observation that Englishmen are not like Haswell but "the worst of them are good enough to admire him" both explains part of the play's

appeal and shows a typical Inchbald assessment of human nature.

The Midnight Hour, a short intrigue comedy, had ten performances in its first season (it opened 22 May 1787) and thirty-six in its next.[23] Taking advantage of the sub-genre, Spanish setting, the play is three acts of constant motion.[24] *The Critical Review* observed "Mrs. Inchbald understands the use of walls, hedges and pavillions,"[25] and the play's rapid pace depends upon such devices as bribes, disguises, trunks, and songs in code.

The same year that this play was introduced, her first failure, *All on a Summer's Day,* was performed. Damned the first night, this five-act comedy, like most of Inchbald's plays, is well set up. Wildlove has seduced Louisa, the woman he cannot forget, and Lady Carrol has carried on a correspondence with young Mooneye as though she were single. Louisa arrives for a visit, and Mooneye's father brings Lady Carrol's letters to her husband, who she pretends is her father. *The London Review and Literary Journal* remarked that *All on a Summer's Day* "seems to have been not finished with that care which the reputation she has acquired demanded from her" and prints a letter in which Inchbald explains that she yielded to Harris's urging and allowed him to produce the play "*contrary to my inclination,* and *even contrary to my most earnest entreaties.*" She notes that Harris meant well and that he had persuaded her to stage successful pieces such as *The Midnight Hour* which she otherwise would not have.[26]

Returning to farce after this piece, she found success with three adaptations, *Animal Magnetism, The Child of Nature,* and *The Married Man.*[27] Each depends upon a single joke that supplies complication and intrigue. Both *Animal Magnetism* and *The Married Man* make vanity the source of humour; the aging suitor, the doctor, believes the wand that carries "animal magnetism" makes him irresistible to women, and in *The Married Man,* Sir John has been hiding the fact that he is married for two years. Both are exposed in the end and laughed out of their follies. *The Child of Nature* is a more serious play; Amanthis has been kept from all company by her guardian and, in her simplicity and goodness, defines love for all of the other characters.

The adaptation of Dumaniant's *La Nuit aux Aventures, The Hue and Cry* (1791) appears to be yet more serious since it begins with an account of a duel between the heroine's cousin and her fiancé, but the second act, played in a jail cell, is pure farce. Reviving the comedy of trunks in a Spanish setting, both the cousin and the fiancé (and their servants) find themselves in the jail cell meant only for the cousin. Unfortunately the two acts raise mixed expectations, and the duel lacks the dramatic interest necessary to give the play the centripetal force that the wand gives *Animal Magnetism.* It was damned on the first night. In the same year, the Haymarket produced *Next Door Neighbours,* like her recent plays, an adaptation.[28] This play reflects Inchbald's fascination with doubles, an idea prominent in her second novel, *Nature and Art* (1796). By juxtaposing the wealthy, idle George and the hard-pressed Eleanor, Inchbald tests their virtue and manages a very neat play with a happy ending.

Young Men and Old Women (1792) hung on for six performances at the Haymarket, and although it is styled a farce on the manuscript page,[29] it illustrates her deepening psychological concerns. Mr. Knaveston has nearly broken the engagement between Miss Prejudice and Sylvan, and Inchbald again explores the dangers of deceit and impressions based on appearances. Miss Ambilogy, a well-conceived comic character, has been caught in one lie, and her brother now insists that he believes nothing she says. In fact, he insists on crying, "Bravo!" each time he thinks she is lying. Miss Ambilogy, however, is entirely honest, and Inchbald does not exploit her comic potential.

The strangely violent *The Massacre,* which Boaden explains was never intended for the stage, was printed in 1792 but was suppressed. The play is a reaction to the Reign of Terror in France and a rare instance of Inchbald's writing explicitly about her deep political interests. Eusébe Tricastin has escaped the Paris mob only to be caught and tried near his home. He and his father are saved by the courageous Glandeve who affirms the meaning of justice and the right of free thought, but his wife and children are killed and brought in on a bier. As Gary Kelly said, Inchbald was "always a feeling rather than a thinking liberal,"[30] and *The Massacre* translates her outrage and shock into the means of expression she found most congenial.

The next five years brought Inchbald yet more success and testify to the range of her dramatic powers. *Every One Has His Fault* ran thirty-two nights in its first season, *The Wedding Day* nineteen, *Wives as They Were* twenty-four, *Lovers' Vows* forty-two, and *To Marry, or Not to Marry* seventeen. All explore social problems that Ibsen and Shaw might have been reluctant to stage. Combining sentiment, strong moral principles, expert characterization, and well-executed plots, these plays consider such topics as adultery, revenge, domestic unhappiness, and loneliness. Inchbald's own life had been filled with contact with suffering; her sister Debby had died after a rather dissolute life in 1794, and George Inchbald had been killed in a duel in 1795. Furthermore, dramatic tastes favored such plays. Arthur Murphy characterized the age as "this grave, this moral, pious age" in the epilogue to his 1776 play, *Three Weeks after Marriage.*[31] Inchbald could combine the popular sentimental plot tinged with touches of broad humor with consideration of serious social problems. *Wives as They Were* presents an old-fashioned couple with an apparently tyrannical hus-

band; the rake Bronzely, however, is unable to seduce the wife and is reformed by her example. The rake's tricks, his extravagantly romantic speeches to the wife, and his embarrassment and confusion make good scenes. The other plot balances the same types of humor and precept; Dorrillon, in disguise, is horrified at his daughter's behavior. She is rude and eventually threatened with arrest for gambling debts, but her sincere concern for her father wins him over. Their angry, witty sparring yields to affection and respect.

The Wise Man of the East returns to Inchbald's earlier technique of drawing upon a gimmick, and often a pseudo-scientific one. The Wise Man, Ava, pretends he can get in touch with the dead and wants Claransforth to ask to see his father. The subplot concerns the poverty of the Metlands; the resolution of the play restores the Metland's money, reveals that Ava is Claransforth's father, and culminates in Claransforth's engagement to Ellen Metland. It, like *Lovers' Vows,* was adapted from a play by Kotzebue, and the sentiment and suffering are typical of the German's plays.[32] The first night the play shocked the audience and was not well-received, and Inchbald's revisions modify the play to give the audience the happy ending they had come to expect in their theatre. One critic noted,

> The body of Ellen was on the first night exhibited, newly taken out of the river, on a shutter; but the disgustfulness of the scene, added to the absurdity of preaching over the poor girl for nearly an hour, instead of putting in practice the mode of treatment recommended in such cases by the Humane Society, being too glaring to pass, even in a play manufactured from Kotzebue. . . .[33]

The revision has Ava rescue the deranged Ellen, and the suspense involves restoring her reason. This play, like *Lovers' Vows* and *Every One Has His Fault,* dramatizes the destructive effects of poverty and desperation. Characters who can bear their own poverty act in irrational and extreme ways when they see those they love in misery. Even the firmest principles and great fortitude can be shaken by the needs of wives, elderly parents, and siblings. In this way, Inchbald could present good people and yet stage the behavior of the more interesting bad.

Strangely enough, Inchbald's unacted play, *A Case of Conscience,* may be her best. Written around 1800 for the Kembles but never performed because of John Philip Kemble's extended trip to the continent and disruptions in the theatres' managements, the play portrays the hideous, brooding, delayed revenge of a jilted lover, the confused anger and remorse of the heroine, and the jealous anxieties of a husband transformed into a monster. Although it veers away from the apparently inevitable harsh conclusion of earlier tragedy and takes refuge in the late eighteenth-century's acceptance of remorse and reform, it develops concentrated emotional force. Salvador is a villain, Gothic in his imagination, evil, and energy. The other characters are equally well-drawn, and the plot moves relentlessly toward a horrible conclusion.

It was 1805 before Inchbald saw another play of hers acted.[34] *To Marry, or Not to Marry* opened at Covent Garden with Kemble in the lead. Genest described the play as follows:

> this Comedy ('tho somewhat of too serious a cast) does Mrs. Inchbald great credit—it is chaste and simple—there are no farcical incidents—no songs, nor processions—no broken English—no striking situation—no particular stage effect—in a word, none of those meretricious Arts, by which the favour of the public has been so successfully courted. (VII, 669)

As such, it summarizes the direction her drama took after 1791. Her career began with farces and afterpieces characterized by gimmicks, improbabilities (acceptable in farce but not in comedy), bustle, mistakes, and contrivances. Except for *Such Things Are* and *All on a Summer's Day,* her themes are light. Concerned with mistaken assumptions, awkward situations, and courtship, these early plays give way to the more sophisticated plots, mature characters, and serious social themes of the later plays. Appropriately, she created parts for Quick in the 80's and Lewis and Kemble in the 90's. In her "Remarks," Inchbald explains,

> Plays of former times were written to be read, not seen. Dramatic authors succeeded in their aim; their works were placed in libraries, and the theatres were deserted.— Now, plays are written to be seen, not read—and present authors gain their views; for they, and the managers, are enriched, and the theatres crowded.

> To be both seen and read, at the present day, is a degree of honour, which, perhaps, not one comic dramatist can wholly boast, except Shakespeare.[35]

Her own plays were shaped by the demands of the audience, the realities of the late-century theatre, her rather modest ambitions, and practical experience on the stage. The size of the theatres, the poor illumination, and the psychological effect of the proscenium-arch stage demanded that she hold the audience with variety and emotion rather than with subtlety and intimacy. The Restoration playwright could position his characters so that three sets of characters could talk, providing counterpoint or reflection for each other, or he could have a Sir Fopling Flutter stroll about as much a part of the audience as the play. The proscenium arch, however, framed the action and made the audience spectators. After all, Covent Garden held 2,500 and was oblong; in 1792, Thomas Harris had it renovated to hold 3,013 in its "lyral form." Drury Lane, altered by Adams in 1777, was rebuilt and opened in

1794 with a capacity of 3,611. Although trained actors probably had no difficulty projecting their voices adequately, small touches, gesture and voice nuance, must have been difficult, and certainly only part of the stage was suitable for sustained, serious dialogue.[36] Inchbald once complained that the English have "no attention, no curiosity, till roused by some powerful fable, intricate occurrences, and all the interest variety creates," while the French will listen to long speeches.[37] Well aware of her medium, she adjusted action, plot, and character to changing tastes and available players.

Her Achievement

Inchbald's strengths as a dramatist were her sure grasp of the stage's potential, her ability to write good dialogue, and her creation of characters. Her sense of timing and pace seldom failed her, and she was a master of stage effects. When she wanted to, she could produce frantic action and wild comedy or elicit tears.[38] Her dialogue could be colloquial and comic or witty and incisive or clear and natural. Her characters ring with authenticity; they behave and speak in familiar ways yet they are usually individuals. Some of the minor characters are highly original humours characters although even they usually display strikingly human qualities.

Her twelve years of acting served her well. She knew the small touches that draw bursts of laughter or gasps of alarm as well as the larger strokes that sustain interest and bear theme. When Nicolas is taken away in a trunk and tilted and tumbled in *The Midnight Hour,* when Lighthead decides to give Lady Mary's shawl to Lady Loveall in *Appearance is Against Them,* and when Lady Priory enters with the corner of cloth snipped from Bronzely's coat in *Wives as They Were,* the playwright could count on the delight of the audience. Props and costumes contribute to the fun in her able hands. The wand in *Animal Magnetism,* the trunks in *The Midnight Hour* and *The Hue and Cry,* and the telescope in *The Widow's Vow* concentrate the joke, and audiences must have relished the extravagant costumes of George in *Next Door Neighbours* and Twineall in *Such Things Are,* the harem costumes in *Mogul Tale,* and the disguises of Sylvan and Knaveston in *Young Men and Old Women* and of the marquis in *The Midnight Hour.* The shawl in *Appearance is against Them* focuses interest to the point that Genest remarked that the play should have been titled *The Shawl,*[39] and the marquis's disguise in *The Widow's Vow* brings about the resolution.

The situations that Inchbald creates consistently motivate entertaining action. Numerous characters are forced into disguises they would never choose for themselves as the balloonists become an ambassador and the pope in *The Mogul Tale* and the suitors become fortune tellers in *The Hue and Cry.* Although Inchbald once wrote of breeches parts that "reason assures us, that they could seldom, if ever, have concealed their sex by such stratagem,"[40] her own plays include several male characters disguised as women. The novelty of this and the awkwardness of the actor perhaps led her to use this strategy. Characters are often discovered in compromising situations and punished for their assumptions about others, illustrating the moral of *Appearance is against Them:* "These adventures shall then be a warning to us, never to judge with severity, while the parties have only appearances against them." Closets, screens, adjoining rooms repeatedly hold embarrassed auditors. Elementary dramatic irony adds to the comedy; because the marquis's disguise as a mantua-maker is so transparent in *The Midnight Hour,* humour comes both from the general's lack of suspicion and our sense that discovery is imminent. The confrontation between the disguised marquis and the uncle in *The Widow's Vow* flirts with the real threat of violence because we know the marquis is a proud man and the uncle a coward.

At other times, serious themes depend upon similar situations. The impotent, comic rages of Dorrillon in *Wives as They Were* and of Sir John in *The Married Man* expose these characters' pompous sense of self-importance. The easy movement of Act II of her early *I'll Tell You What* reveals unhappy marriages, disappointments, and longing for conventional happiness through quarrels, intrigues, and speeches marked by obvious bravado. In *Such Things Are,* the force of Haswell's personality becomes more convincing because of the incident when Zedan steals his pocketbook; the recognition of the extent of the sultan's remorse depends upon his comprehension of Arabella's suffering and faithfulness. Similarly in *The Wise Man of the East,* Claransforth's basic goodness convinces because he can say,

> Living, though my father stript me of my wealth, and sent me back to plod on a wretched spot, where all society is banished, still I should rejoice to see him. But dead—I wou'd not that my folly should disturb, or my curiosity even treat with irreverence, his honoured dust (II).

Later he will refuse to have any share of the plan to defraud the Metlands. The poignancy of George's speeches about his father and the sincerity of Miss Dorrillon in *Wives* and of Frederick in *Lovers' Vows* reveal character and strip away the disguises and defenses of the fathers.

Inchbald's control and versatility developed with experience. The bustle and abundance of action of her early plays gave way to sensitivity to pause and even stillness as well. In *Every One Has His Fault* (1793), Inchbald creates a tableau effect in order to build emotional impact. The scene in which Edward chooses to go with his mother moves in a series of deliberately affecting freezes. First Edward quietly follows his mother, Eleanor, across the stage, then pulls her gown; she turns, and they look at each other. When Edward realizes Eleanor is his mother, he kneels; then Eleanor kneels at her father's feet. Lord Norland, the father, demands that Edward choose between him and his mother; Edward studies them both for some time, then slowly advances to shake his grandfather's hand and tell him good-by. These four pauses tend to emphasize the recognition scenes and the bonds between the characters. The final freeze as Edward chooses illustrates the difficulty of the decision and momentarily leads the audience to believe that Edward has chosen Lord Norland. The domestic scenes of the Metlands in *The Wise Man* and of Eleanor and Henry in *Next Door Neighbours* juxtapose harmony and poverty. Both plays take advantage of the framing effect of the proscenium-arch stage and use slow scene openings so that the image of happiness and awareness of threat are imprinted on the audience's minds. When Lawley begins to strip the Metland home for debt, the earlier scenes come to mind as pitiable contrasts. *To Marry, or Not to Marry* alternates the pace of comedy with the measured movement of melodrama. Hester's naive enthusiasm and unconventional opinions and Oswin's passion for quiet and distaste for marriage provide humor, but the return of the wronged and vengeful Lavensforth changes the play's complexion. Although theatrical tastes embraced such mixed-mode plays, *To Marry* integrates characters, plots, and theatrical forms far more smoothly than Inchbald's early plays and more effectively than all but the best of her contemporaries.

Well aware of the contributions and limitations of players, Inchbald wrote acting pieces above all. She knew that gesture and expression could be more important than dialogue. *The West Indian,* she explained, is better on the stage because "Many of the characters require the actor's art, to fill up the bold design, where the author's pen has not failed, but wisely left the perilous touches of a finishing hand, to the judicious comedian."[41] Of Holcroft's *Road to Ruin,* she says, "There is merit in the writing, but much more in that dramatic science, which disposes character, scenes, and dialogue, with minute attention to theatric exhibition. . . ."[42] Some of the parts of which she was aware of the difficulties were Rosalind in *As You Like It,* Falstaff in *Merry Wives of Windsor,* and Glenalvon in *Douglas.* She insisted that good acting could determine the interpretation of character as it does for Alicia in *Jane Shore,* which, when correctly acted, becomes a portrait of terrible remorse.[43] She understood the limitations of acting as well. Certain moods and emotions were too subtle for the stage; for example, she explains that *The Winter's Tale* is better read because the conversations between Florizel and Perdita "have more tenderness, than the fervour, of love; and consequently their passion has not the force of expression to animate a multitude, though it is properly adapted to steal upon the heart of an individual."[44] The method of having the play read by the actors, submitting an acting copy to the examiner, and printing an edition several days after the production opened allowed a kind of collaboration between playwright, manager, and players unknown on the modern stage. Comparison of Larpent manuscripts and the printed plays reveals a few changes, some toward less colloquial language and most in regularizing punctuation and typography.[45] The plays themselves show sensitive attention to the skills of various actors and room for interpretation and enhancement in most of the parts. Twineall and Elvirus in *Such Things Are* are but two examples, one of extravagant conceit and the other of dignified manhood. Convinced that modern audiences would not tolerate long speeches and that modern actors could not depict pathetic, subtle emotions without becoming insipid and plaintive, Inchbald avoided these pitfalls. Substituting remorse for revenge and spirit for passivity, she presents reform rather than poetic justice. Insisting that the modern woman is resourceful and fairly well educated, her heroines are strong characters. Even Amanthis in *The Child of Nature* can distinguish virtue and act firmly.

That Inchbald could write for Quick, Lewis, and Kemble testifies to her versatility and understanding of the players' strengths. Quick was unsurpassed in the parts of rustics and simpletons and, by Mrs. Inchbald's time, of old men. His small, active body, his squeaky voice, and his ability to portray whimsey distinguished his roles for thirty-six years. Trained by Oliver Carr, the man who claimed to have taught Garrick at Goodman's Fields, and by Foote, Macklin, and Colman, Quick created the roles of Tony Lumpkin (*She Stoops to Conquer*), Bob Acres (*The Rivals*), Isaac Mendoza (*The Duenna*), Crockletop (*Modern Antiques*), Sir George Thunder (*Wild Oats*), and Silky (*Road to Ruin*). In Inchbald's plays, he was the original doctor in *Animal Magnetism,*[46] Walmsley in *Appearance is against Them,* Sir Ralph Mooneye in *All on a Summer's Day,* Tremor in *Such Things Are,* the general in *The Midnight Hour,* Solus in *Every One Has His Fault,* the rhyming butler in *Lovers' Vows,*[47] and Lord Priory in *Wives as They Were.* In each case, the part requires a sympathetic depiction of eccentricity. Each is a bit subject to ridicule, each has a problem, each displays weakness yet has basic goodness and strength of principles. For example, Tremor is the bickering husband whom his wife compares unfavorably to Lord Flint; he fears the sultan and flatters him hypocritically yet he admires Haswell and shows pity for Elvirus and Aurelia. Inchbald admired Quick's work and praised his animation, particularly his ability to appear agitated, and created parts that exploited this talent.[48]

William Lewis, in contrast, was a versatile, serious actor. He could be whimsical or gentlemanly, playful or sentimental. His most successful role was that of Mercutio, a part ideally suited for his mercurial, lively, light, and graceful demeanor. Of Lewis, Inchbald wrote that he "had the talent to display all the bold features of the vulgar citizen, whilst his own constitutional refinement prevented the audience from feeling themselves in bad company."[49] Making use of this ability to appear debauched while retaining the foundation of good character, he played Sir Robert Ramble in *Every One Has His Fault,* Claransforth in *The Wise Man,* and Bronzely in *Wives as They Were.*

The play she wrote for the Kembles, *A Case of Conscience,* displays yet another mode for her. She had played opposite John Philip Kemble, been his close friend, and seen him in scores of roles by the time she wrote the part of Romono for him. The greatest tragedian until Kean, Kemble's expressive countenance, regal bearing, good looks, and intelligence more than compensated for his occasionally asthmatic voice. Although he played the hero in almost every Shakespearian play, he seems to have excelled as Hamlet, Lear, King John, and especially Coriolanus, and in Roman and Gothic parts. Those who saw him praised his dignity and sympathy for such "Roman" sentiments as fortitude, Stoicism, masculine tenderness, and loyalty.[50] One admirer noted that "He wore classical drapery with unrivalled ease and elegance, and his features were both noble and expressive."[51] His Coriolanus, Cato, and Orestes (*The Distrest Mother*) won universal acclaim. His first triumph was in Dublin, where he played Raymond in Jephson's *Count of Narbonne.* This work, an adaptation of Walpole's *Castle of Otranto,* allowed full play to his brooding, intense interpretation of tragedy. He went on to play the part in London and to add those of Mentevole and Sextus in Jephson's *Julia* and *Conspiracy,* Montgomerie in Cumberland's *Carmelite,* the lead in Thompson's *The Stranger,* Percy in "Monk" Lewis's *Castle Spectre,* and Aurelio in Boaden's adaptation of *The Monk, Aurelio and Miranda.* Sir Walter Scott observed that Kemble was at his best when representing characters with "a predominating tinge of some over-mastering passion."[52] Kemble was noted for intensity and particularly for pertinent by-play, the ability to enhance a part with gestures and facial expressions.[53] Roles such as that of Orestes allowed him to display the grandeur of a disordered mind, and Inchbald's role for him draws upon the Gothic and upon the kind of brooding fixation one of the characters describes as "a gloomy sullenness overspreads his features, varied by flashes of indignant rage."[54] As Romono becomes so bitter that he mistreats his beloved wife and turns his son over to the Inquisition, the mannered and somber style of Kemble would have been most effective.

Inchbald's dialogue is consistently serviceable and often distinguished. Attuned to the stage and acting and perceptive about human nature, she possessed great versatility. Because of her speech impediment, she must have been unusually sensitive to the demands for precise, clear speech. Those words she painstakingly carried about and lines she repeated tirelessly to Joseph alerted her to difficult sound combinations and impractical sentence structures. Much of her dialogue is ordinary, workmanlike prose. The bickering of the Placids in *Every One Has His Fault,* the tenderness of the Priories in *Wives as They Were,* and the concern of the Metlands when Ellen is missing in *Wise Man* are examples of her middle style. The eloquence of Almanza and Oswin in *The Child of Nature* and *To Marry* respectively and the elevation of the sorrow of Irwin in *Every One Has His Fault* and of Frederick in *Lovers' Vows* give the characters dignity and affective force. Inchbald's own stinging pragmatism gives aphoristic ring to such lines as Tremor's that most men are good enough to admire Haswell, and Lady Ramble's that she should behave so that she makes no "offering to the tinselled shrine of love."[55] Elizabeth Inchbald's moral sentiments often carry tart truth; *Every One* ends with Harmony wishing people would always speak well of others behind their backs, and *The Married Man* concludes that no title is more honorable than "married man" if a man "fills the station" as he ought.

Some of Inchbald's dialogue echoes William Congreve and anticipates Oscar Wilde. We see her ability to write repartee as early as *The Mogul Tale, I'll Tell You What,* and *The Widow's Vow.* In *I'll Tell You What,* Lady Euston parodies women of fashion and dramatizes the ways she has humiliated rakes. Lisette, the clever servant in *Animal Magnetism,* dashes off a reply to the marquis for Constance to send before she receives his letter, then chides Constance for wanting to read it, "No, don't examine your thoughts. . . ." Inchbald could slant into nonsense laced with social commentary worthy of the Cecily Cardews and Bessie Saunderses of the late nineteenth century. Lady Mary describes her shawl,

> —it came over but last night from India—has been on the seas seven months—was in that terrible storm of October last.—Little did I think, when I heard of those dreadful wrecks, and the many souls perished, that I had a shawl at sea. . . .

Lord Norland complains that the British should be able to stop robbery, and Harmony exclaims, "Provisions are so scarce!" Lady Contest remarks, "I am very fond of particular business," and Oswin complains that he is being forced to marry "to accommodate two nonentities; one of whom will be gone out of the world [his uncle Danberry] and the other not come into it [the baby son]."[56] Timing raises many lines above the ordinary. In *I'll Tell You What,* Cyprus has asked for French horns to divert him; shortly after his wife is discovered with George, Bloom enters and says, "The horns are ready." One of her most entertaining scenes is in *Such Things Are;* Twineall teaches the Tremors the art of fashionable conversation, defined as speaking without any words.[57]

Above all else, Inchbald's plays explore relationships between people. She presents parents and children, husbands and wives, neighbors, and friends, and in-

sists upon the influences people have upon each other. Good people warm the hearts of those around them, making those who meet them better, but the mean-spirited and particularly the tyrannical cause those around them to wither and contract. As characters' lives touch they find human misunderstandings, old mistakes, and constricting social attitudes, and for a few moments, the dross of the late eighteenth-century sentiments and the restrictions of the short, lugubrious drama fade, and Inchbald's insights into human psychology shine. She shows no fear of presenting unpleasant situations—illegitimacy, divorce, poverty—and insists upon the responsibilities people have for one another. Remorse, reform, and reconciliation close her plays, and characters assume a sober, affectionate relationship, a realistic picture of the best that human beings can be.[58]

The situations and characters in *I'll Tell You What* prefigure those of Inchbald's later plays. Sir George, Major Cyprus, and Anthony become stock characters for her. Sir George Euston has discovered his wife, Harriet, in her closet with Cyprus, divorced her, and remarried. Anthony, his uncle, has disowned his son, and Cyprus is scheming to seduce George's second wife. Harriet tricks George into visiting her, and he is caught hiding in her closet. From this, he learns that judgments based on appearances can be wrong. Cyprus is humiliated when the new Lady Euston exposes his scheme, and he and Harriet separate. Lady Euston has demonstrated the way to resist such men as Cyprus, and Harriet suffers the punishment of the indiscreet, acrimonious wife. Anthony rescues a poor woman who happens to be his daughter-in-law and forgives his son. He, like George, is virtuous but severe and yet finds forgiveness a happier attitude than what he has labeled justice. Unlike her less skilled contemporaries, Inchbald usually supplies a unifying theme. In this play, the plot lines share the concept of a "critical minute," specifically the discoveries in the closets and Anthony's rescue. Both discoveries end marriages and represent deeper domestic disharmonies and immoralities. The rescue motivates a moving description of the desperation of a fallen woman and an appeal for charity toward such victims. The play concludes with a comic dilemma (what is the relationship of the child of a first husband to the mother's second husband while the father is living) and the serious contention that all are related by the *"kindred ties* of each others passions, weaknesses, and imperfections."

In *Every One Has His Fault,* Eleanor is destitute, and her husband becomes deranged and robs Lord Norland, the father who disowned her. Norland's sister has recently been divorced from Sir Ramble; their friends, Placid, who wants a separation from his wife, and Solus, who wants to marry, complete the household. Here we see the worst effects people have on each other: The Placids and Miss Spinster carp and fret, Irwin and Eleanor face disgrace and ruin, and Solus, Norland,

and the Rambles are dissatisfied and lonely. By dwelling on each person's virtues and insinuating that each person says good things about the others, Harmony reconciles them all. His benign lies lead to Solus's marrying a better-tempered Miss Spinster, the Rambles' re-marriage, Placid's announcement that he will now rule his wife, and Norland's embracing his daughter and her family. Harmony has made them aware of the good in everyone, and when he tries to confess his lies, they agree that everyone has faults and should be forgiven. Harmony becomes the means by which each character does what he most wants to do; aware that fear of ridicule restrains even the best impulses, Inchbald provides characters willing to be eccentric who can set the example for others who might wish to break with conventional behavior.

Inchbald's late plays feature more villainous characters. Baron Wildenhaim has seduced Agatha and left her pregnant and alone. Years later, their son returns from the army to find Agatha a homeless indigent and, in desperation, demands a dollar from the baron. The baron sentences him to death. Inchbald uses two characters to bring the baron to reform. The count, the man intended for his daughter Amelia, is a fool and explains his earlier debaucheries as the kind of thing young men do. The baron concludes, "I am, indeed, worse than he is, as much as the crimes of a man exceed those of an idiot." Such sensitivity testifies to his basic goodness and makes him amenable to the virtuous and modest Anhalt's guidance. Romono in *A Case of Conscience* has found a miniature of his beloved wife in Cordunna's papers along with evidence that Cordunna is the father of Romono's son Oviedo. Romono becomes convinced that this is so and drives his wife, Adriana, to leave and allows the Inquisition to take Oviedo. He masters his grief and love for his wife and son with a harsh allegiance to what he calls justice but is overcome with joy when he learns Adriana is innocent. Finally, Oswin, the protagonist of *To Marry,* is a darker character than is immediately apparent. In his youth, he testified against Lavensforth, perhaps more for political motives than for justice's sake. He is rigid, judgmental, and imposing, but the irrepressible Hester and the generosity of Lavensforth change him from a solitary man into an affectionate one.

Inchbald seems to have been fascinated by the stern, nearly tyrannical, father figure. Like Dorriforth in *A Simple Story,*[59] the heroes sacrifice love and mercy for "justice." Acting out of a sense of personal betrayal rather than an understanding of human frailty, they punish and cut off those closest to them. They find surrogates for their affection as Norland does with his grandson, or they take disguises and continue to hope that their love will be justified as Dorrillon and Ava do. The effort their severity requires is always apparent, and the audience, therefore, can sympathize with their pain while condemning the suffering they cause.

Deprived of expressing their love, they are somber men whose disciplined lives hint at the restlessness beneath. For all his protests, Oswin seems eager to leave his library and concern himself with his sister, with Willowear, and with Hester. Amanthis admonishes her guardian Almanza, "Learn, my lord, to be less suspicious; affect less generosity and moderation, and be less ungrateful and unjust." These lines contain the lesson Inchbald continually dramatizes. Her patriarchs are not truly generous because they are suspicious, jealous of others, and judgmental. They *affect* moderation, but both moderation and generosity appear when their affections are unengaged, when they are relatively indifferent. Rather than accepting and pardoning those about whom they care most, they evaluate and blame. Their dignity and the appearance of rectitude mean more than anything else.

Lord Priory in *Wives as They Were* brings the risks of the marriage relationship to the stage. He is a firm husband; he describes the hours he makes his wife keep, the diversions he denies her, even the way he locks her in her room. When she leaves with Bronzely, he questions whether he has been too authoritarian or whether he is now being too lenient. His agitation and doubts grow, but she rewards his love and trust, insisting that Bronzely makes her appreciate her husband all the more. Lord Priory, in contrast to other Inchbald characters, believes her and welcomes her back wholeheartedly; he represents the firm but trusting patriarch. Dorrillon represents the more typical Inchbald problem father.[60] In disguise, he watches his daughter with varying degrees of disappointment, rage, and hope. His sense of justice determines his turning her over to the constable representing her creditors, but he follows her to offer her money to reform.

Inchbald presents the motives and effects of these characters' severity remarkably well considering the form and brevity of the late eighteenth-century comedy. Rather than being harsh and cold by nature, the men have usually been deeply in love and have held unrealistically high expectations for those objects of their affection. A bit like Matt Bramble, they are hypersensitive, but like *A Simple Story*'s Dorriforth, they protect themselves with an imposing exterior. The sultan in *Such Things Are* has lost his adored Arabella and become an unfeeling ruler whose prison is filled with innocent people. When Haswell restores Arabella, the sultan learns that others love as he and reforms. His basic goodness and deep remorse justify the happy ending and make the unifying theme of powerful love affecting.

The tyrannical characters touch all those around them. They keep most people at a distance, and the bravest and most perceptive remark as Harmony does to Norland, "I pity you." On those they love, however, they have a more powerful effect. The most admirable stand firm, but the weakest sink into crime, madness, and despair. Eleanor in *Every One Has His Fault,* Miss Dorrillon, and Eleanor Splendorville in *Next Door Neighbors* ask for help, but there are limits to what they will sacrifice. None will commit a dishonest act or one that might injure someone else. Eleanor will not take evidence of her husband's crime from their son, Eleanor Splendorville sees her father return to prison rather than compromise herself with George, and Miss Dorrillon refuses to take the money because she might return to her irresponsible habits. Irwin, Henry, and Ellen Metland become temporarily deranged. Older wives like Agatha and Adriana grieve and find themselves in desperate circumstances. Once the patriarchs have found a middle way between severity and carelessness, the women yield and the relationships become harmonious. Even Arabella can forgive the sultan, and Adriana, Romono; Miss Dorrillon becomes an obedient and charming daughter, and Hester a forthright and respectful fiancée. The frivolity and indiscretion that characterized their early behavior becomes loyal, compassionate maturity.[61] Because of the high-principled outsider and the worthiness of the wife or child, the male character comes to allow his innate benevolence to dominate, and he and all around him grow into fuller, happier human beings.

Inchbald goes beyond her contemporaries to explore the psychology of relationships; not only does she show her characters' reactions to events, but she reveals the conflicts and motives within them. She believed that some interpersonal situations play better than others. In her "Remarks," she observed,

> It is supposed by the rigidly pious, who never frequent a theatre, that the power of love is painted on the stage in the most glowing and bewitching colours—when, alas! the insipidity of lovers, in almost every play, might cure the most romantic youth and damsel of the ardour of their mutual attachment.[62]

Inchbald chose to write about conjugal love, a love she found more conducive to the arousal of sympathy and suspense. The years of companionship threatened, the shared pleasures and hardships, the strains on the bond, the hopes, and the difficulties of age, children, and poverty interested her far more than the perils of getting acquainted and the obstacles to courtship. The efforts to save a marriage appeared more praiseworthy to her than any girl's schemes to get married. She could make mutual respect and abiding affection convincing, but passion eluded her. Wildlove and Louisa, Elvirus and Aurelia are among her least successful characters; the remembered love of Romolo and Adriana, of the baron and Agatha, of the sultan and Arabella move the audience far more. As they talk of the past and then wound each other in the present, they illustrate a more familiar and more lamentable human condition.

Inchbald has discovered a number of ways to reveal otherwise hidden feelings. Harriet's sad or angry comparisons between her first and second marriages express her discontent, her regret, and her guilt. She leaves her second husband and finds hope in the fact that she can yet be good. In *The Wedding Day,* Contest has married a woman for her youth, and she has married him for his money. Both realize the mistake, their incompatibilities, and yet acknowledge the fulfillment of their ambitions. Again Inchbald can bring the complexities of such a relationship to the stage and work within the audience's expectations. Their bickering brings out their disappointment and their motives, and the resolution pleases the audiences. Inchbald also uses children to reveal the depth of love for a dead spouse, long-forgotten resentments, and fears that the child will repeat nearly buried past follies. Frederick in *Lovers' Vows* works this way for both parents.

The appeal of Elizabeth Inchbald and her theatre eludes many modern scholars. The peculiar combination of maudlin sensation, farcical elements, exposition reduced to stark statement, and coincidences hardly seems like good drama to us. The theatre, however, served well the purposes of popular art forms. Inchbald can amuse and entertain; *Animal Magnetism* and *The Midnight Hour* would play well today. She presents real problems, familiar problems: indiscreet wives, philandering husbands, acrimonious couples, estranged children, extravagant sons and disobedient daughters. She explores the forbidden: the temptation to commit adultery, the desperate amateur robbery, the attempt to break up a friend's engagement, and cruelty springing from ambition or indifference. Believing in the basic goodness of mankind, Inchbald used events to lead otherwise admirable people into difficulty. The remorse such people feel gave her a powerful private emotion that could be dramatized. Finally, Inchbald champions conventional morality and provides happy endings. The audience could see the good rewarded and returned to happiness and the bad reformed or, if not punished, isolated so that they could do no harm. To the end of her life, Inchbald chose the techniques of theatre rather than the art of the "closet"; of *Lovers' Vows,* she wrote, " . . . the rigid criticism of the closet will be but a slender abatement of the pleasure resulting from the sanction of an applauding theatre."[63] The result of such a belief is a collection of acting pieces, admirable for their variety of incidents, movement, pace, ingenuity but neither profound nor dazzling literature.

Notes

[1] Unless otherwise noted, information about productions comes from *The London Stage* (Carbondale: Southern Illinois University Press, 1968), III, 1-3.

[2] James Boaden, *Memoirs of the Life of Mrs. Inchbald* (London, 1833), I, 96. *Cf.* G. Louis Joughin, *The Life and Work of Elizabeth Inchbald* (Harvard dissertation, 1932), pp. 22-23, 28.

[3] *Memoirs of the Life of Mrs. Sumbel,* quoted in Joughin, p. 41.

[4] C. Kegan Paul, *William Godwin: His Friends and Contemporaries* (Boston: Roberts, 1876), I, 277.

[5] Boaden, I, 269, and II, 44-45.

[6] Boaden, II, 64-65; 126 and 292-293.

[7] Paul, I, 73. This story is in some doubt; not only is the source Mary Shelley, but a suspiciously similar story is told about Mrs. Inchbald and Mrs. Siddons; in this case, Mrs. Inchbald feared being eclipsed; see Frances Ann Kemble, *Record of a Girlhood* (London: Bentley, 1879), II, 49.

[8] In the seasons 1783-1784 through 1786-1787, when Inchbald was beginning her career, Drury Lane, Covent Garden, and the Haymarket averaged three new plays each a season. Of these, four were by Holcroft, three by Colman the Younger, four by Cumberland, and two each by Reynolds, O'Keeffe, and Inchbald. In the seasons 1792-1793 through 1796-1797, when Inchbald was at the height of her success, Drury Lane averaged five new productions, Covent Garden six, and the Haymarket two; of these nine were by Cumberland, six by Reynolds, six by O'Keeffe, five by Holcroft, and three by Colman the Younger.

Allardyce Nicoll concludes, "In surveying Mrs. Inchbald's work as a whole, we cannot deny the fact that her plays are as good as any of her time, and that one, at least, *I'll Tell You What,* really challenges comparison with the comedies of Goldsmith and Sheridan." *A History of Late Eighteenth-Century Drama 1750-1800* (Cambridge: University Press, 1927), p. 150. John Genest sums up her career thus: "as a dramatic writer, she was little inferiour to any of her contemporaries, and even superiour to most of them. . . ." *Some account of the English Stage, from the Restoration in 1660 to 1830* (Bath: Carrington, 1832), VII, 669.

[9] George Joughin lists number of performances for each play in its first calendar year in "An Inchbald Bibliography," University of Texas *Studies in English,* 14 (1934), 73.

[10] Elizabeth Inchbald, ed., *The British Theatre,* "Remarks" to *Every One Has His Fault* (London, 1808), XXIII, 2.

[11] A number of her contemporaries remarked on her industriousness. Boaden says, "she laughed at the toil of common mortals," I, 264; see also the biography serialized in the *Monthly Mirror,* especially May 1797, II, 259; Joughin, 54-56; George Daniel, "Remarks" on *The Midnight Hour* in Cumberland's *British Theatre* (London, [1885]), 7-8.

[12] "Her defects as an actress were generally forgiven in respect to her personal attraction. . . ." *Monthly Mirror*

(June 1797), III, 331. See also *The World,* 20 January 1787, and *The Edinburgh Rosciad* (Edinburgh, 1775), p. 13.

[13] She wrote several farces before *The Mogul Tale,* including *The Ancient Law* and *Polygamy* (Boaden, I, 137 and 154, and Joughin, 142). For a titillating account of Joseph's death and a description of Elizabeth's youthful beauty, see Tate Wilkinson, *The Wandering Patentee* (York, 1795), II, 56-64. Joughin says Joseph died of acute indigestion, p. 30.

[14] Boaden, I, 186 and 189.

[15] *British Theatre,* "Remarks" to Kemble's *The Point of Honour,* XXIV, 2. See the account of her nervousness in *Memoirs of the Life of Mrs. Sumbel* (London, 1811), II, 199-202.

[16] *British Theatre,* "Remarks" to Addition's *Cato,* VIII, 5. Her ambition is obvious in her enraged reaction to Wilkinson's request to use *Such Things Are* for his benefit at York, *Wandering Patentee,* III, 32-35, and in the preface to *A Simple Story,* J. M. S. Tompkins, ed. (London: Oxford U. Press, 1967), p. I:

> . . . it has been her fate to devote a tedious seven years to the unremitting labour of literary productions—whilst a taste for authors of the first rank has been an additional punishment, forbidding her one moment of those self-approving reflections which are assuredly due to the industrious.

[17] Genest, VI, 316; *The Mogul Tale* and Frederick Pilon's *Aerostation* (1784) exploit the interest in ballooning aroused by the Montgolfier brothers' invention of a practical balloon in 1783.

[18] The manuscript copy of the play in the Larpent collection has the title inserted with a caret in Inchbald's handwriting.

[19] Willard A. Kinne briefly describes the types of changes Inchbald makes in her adaptations in *Revivals and Importations of French Comedies in England 1749-1800* (New York: Columbia U. Press, 1939), pp. 190-193, 197-199, 205, 209-210, and 223-226. See also Joughin, 150, 156-161 *et passim.*

[20] *British Theatre,* "Remarks" on Holcroft's *Road to Ruin,* XXIV, 5.

[21] *British Theatre,* "Remarks" to *Such Things Are,* XXIII, 2.

[22] Boaden, I, 240, and Wilkinson, III, 32-35; Wilkinson describes how the merit of the play ended a theatre riot.

[23] The play was adapted from *Guerre Ouverte; ou, Ruse Contre Ruse* by Antoine Jean Bourlin *dit* Dumaniant.

[24] Inchbald explains that plays set in a foreign country "particularly when that country is Spain, have a license to present certain improbabilities to the audience" and that the English "in bringing the Spaniards upon the stage, have always given them a great deal to do, and scarcely any thing to say." "Remarks" to Cowley's *Bold Stroke for a Husband,* XIX, 2, and Cibber's *Love Makes a Man,* IX, 3.

[25] *Critical Review* (December 1787), p. 479.

[26] *London Review* (December 1787), pp. 502-503.

[27] *The Child of Nature* is an adaptation of *Zélie; ou, L'Ingénue* by the Comtesse de Genlis; *The Married Man* is an adaptation of *Le Philosophe Marié* by Philippe Néricault *dit* Destouches. The evidence that *Animal Magnetism* is an adaptation comes from Boaden who says Le Texier (who imported plays for Harris) got the play soon after *The Hue and Cry,* that he got it from Paris, and that Inchbald finished the adaptation in sixteen days, I, 256. Also *Monthly Mirror* (July 1797), IV, 12.

[28] This time she adapts two French plays, *L'Indigent* by Louis Sébastien Mercier and *Le Dissipateur* by Destouches.

[29] The manuscript, reproduced in this edition, is titled *Lovers, No Conjurors;* Inchbald's source is Jean Baptiste Louis Gresset's *Le Méchant.*

[30] Gary Kelly, *The English Jacobin Novel, 1780-1805* (Oxford: Clarendon Press, 1976), p. 113.

[31] Epilogue to *Three Weeks after Marriage* (1776) in *The Plays of Arthur Murphy,* Richard Schwartz, ed. (New York: Garland, 1979), II, 433.

[32] *Lovers' Vows* is from *Das Kind der Liebe,* and *Wise Man of the East* from *Das Schreibepult.* Inchbald describes the changes she makes in the preface to *Lovers' Vows;* see also E. S. deBeer, "*Lovers' Vows:* The Dangerous Insignificance of the Butler," *N&Q* 207 (1962), 421-422, and Marcella Gosch, "'Translators' of Kotzebue in England," *Monatshefte für deutschen Unterricht,* 31 (1939), 175-183; Joughin, pp. 274-277.

[33] Thomas Dutton, *The Wise Man of the East; or, The Apparition of Zoroaster the son of Oromases to the Theatrical Midwife of Leicester-Fields* (London, 1800), p. 53. This satiric attack purports to aim at theatrical taste and Kotzebue rather than at "that intelligent lady (whose talents no person can hold in higher estimation than himself)," p. vii.

[34] Inchbald had given up the adaptation of *Deaf and Dumb* only to see Hill make a hit of it and had seen Boaden's translation of Caigniez's *Judgement de Salomon* acted in preference to hers, Boaden, II, 48-50 and 59-61.

[35] *British Theatre,* "Remarks" to Reynolds's *The Dramatist,* XX, 2.

[36] Gestures probably helped audiences interpret action much as referee's signals do distant football fans; for descriptions of the still highly stylized gestures, see Henry Siddons, *Practical Illustrations of Rhetorical Gesture and Action* (London, 1807), and Aaron Hill, *An Essay on the Art of Acting* in *The Works of the Late Aaron Hill,* 2nd edition (London, 1753), IV, 339—398; Hill describes ten emotions and seven variations on the passion of love. See also Samuel Foote, *A Treatise on the Passions* (London, [1747]).

[37] *British Theatre,* "Remarks" on *The Distressed Mother,* VII, 2.

[38] Not a sentimental dramatist, Inchbald does not sacrifice humor nor does she manipulate plot to emphasize sensibility. Pertinent discussions of sentimental drama can be found in Larry Carver, "Introduction" to *The Plays of Hugh Kelly* (New York: Garland, 1980); Nicoll, pp. 144-152; Arthur Sherbo, *English Sentimental Drama* (East Lansing: Michigan State U. Press, 1957), pp. 1-14, 21, 71, 83-87, and 100-101; Robert D. Hume, "Goldsmith and Sheridan and the Supposed Revolution of 'Laughing' against 'Sentimental' Comedy" in *Studies in Change and Revolution,* Paul Korshin, ed. (Menston: Scholar, 1972), pp. 237-276.

[39] The manuscript copy in the Huntington's Larpent collection bears this title.

[40] *British Theatre,* "Remarks" on *Recruiting Officer,* VIII, 4.

[41] "Remarks," XVIII, 5.

[42] "Remarks," XXIV, 2.

[43] "Remarks," X, 4-5.

[44] "Remarks," III, 4.

[45] See "A Note on the Texts," and note 56. Only *The Mogul Tale* and *The Wise Man of the East* differ considerably and in important ways; for other plays, there may be numerous differences, but they are unimportant (punctuation, capitalization, synonyms; see *The Widow's Vow,* titled *The Neuter* in the manuscript version, and *Animal Magnetism*). Most of the plays show only slight variations. Such differences are characteristic of eighteenth-century plays; as Dougald MacMillan says, the relationship of the Larpent manuscript "on the one hand to the acted version and on the other hand to the published work raises complicated problems that can be solved only individually. The Larpent text, thus, may represent a state of composition either later or earlier than the first acted version.

An examination of the manuscript will show the Examiner's copy seldom conforms entirely to the published text." "Prefatory Note" to *Catalogue of the Larpent Plays in the Huntington Library* (Pasadena: San Pasqual Press for the Huntington Library, 1939), p. viii. See also Tom Davis and Susan Hamlyn, "What do we do when two texts differ?" in *Evidence in Literary Scholarship,* René Wellek and Alvaro Ribeiro, eds. (Oxford: Clarendon, 1979), pp. 263-279, especially 267; and Hume, pp. 257-258.

[46] George Daniel writes, "Little Quick was the original *Doctor:* his rubicand face, with its rich comic expression, his Sancho Panza-like figure, and his voice, bearing some affinity to the squeak of a Barthemy-fair trumpet, invested the character with a degree of drollery that it has not exhibited since." [He held] "absolute sway over our risible faculties." Cumberland's *British Theatre* (London, n.d.), XIV, 7.

[47] Inchbald admitted she had no talent for rhyme. The butler's lines are by Palmer, son of one of the proprietors of the Bath Theatre, although Inchbald gives Taylor credit for the lines. The song in *The Wedding Day* is a translation of Anacreon's Third Ode.

[48] "Remarks," *cf. Deserted Daughter,* XXIV, 4, and *The Duenna,* XIX, 4.

[49] "Remarks," Holcroft's *Road to Ruin,* XXIV, 4-5.

[50] See Walter Donaldson, *Theatrical Portraits* (London, 1870), pp. 90-96, especially the poem by Harry Stoe Van Dyke; Frederick Pollock, ed., *Macready's Reminiscences* (London, 1875), I, 135-136, and William C. Russell, *Representative Actors* (London, 1872), pp. 241-242.

[51] Quoted in the *DNB,* X, 1261.

[52] Quoted in *Representative Actors,* p. 248.

[53] This is a common observation. See William Hazlitt, *The Collected Works of William Hazlitt,* A. R. Waller and Arnold Glover, eds. (London: Dent, 1903), VIII, 379; Thomas Gilliland, *The Dramatic Mirror* (London, 1808), II, 813; Bertram Joseph, *The Tragic Actor* (London: Routledge & Kegan Paul, 1959), pp. 191-193.

[54] Kemble's restrained declamatory style was broken by flashes of activity and vehemence that electrified audiences; see Alan Downer, "Players and the Painted Stage," *PMLA* 61 (1946), 523-533, and *Macready's Reminiscences,* pp. 194-195. Inchbald was well aware of his limitations; she said, "Garrick was an artist and an actor—Kemble is merely an artist. The former could imitate the manners of the whole human-race—the latter can describe only their passions" ("Remarks" to *The Wheel of Fortune,* XVIII, 5). She praises Kemble in her "Remarks" on *King John* (I; she compares Garrick and Kemble here as well), *Coriolanus* (V), and *The Mountaineers* (XXI).

[55] Examples from *Such Things Are* and *Every One Has His Fault* respectively.

[56] Examples from *Appearance is against Them, Every One Has His Fault, The Wedding Day,* and *To Marry, or Not to Marry* respectively.

The line from *The Wedding Day* appears in the edition *A Collection of Farces and other Afterpieces,* selected by Inchbald (London, 1809), but not in the 1794 London edition. In fact, these lines indicate the textual problems the editor faces. The Larpent manuscript reads,

> Hannah: Yes, madam, an elderly Gentlewoman—but refused to leave her name—She begg'd very hard she might have the pleasure to see you the next time she came as she said she had particular business.
>
> Lady Contest: Then pray let me see her—for I am fond of particular business.
>
> (Act II, p. I)

The 1794 edition is different:

> Hannah: Yes, madam, an elderly gentlewoman; but she refused to leave her name—she said she had particular business, and wanted to speak to you in private.
>
> Lady Contest: Then pray let me see her when she comes again. (p. 24)

Only in this edition does Lady Contest ask if anyone else has called. The 1806 edition in Inchbald's *Farces* has elements of both of these versions:

> Hannah: Yes, Madam, an elderly gentlewoman; but she refused to leave her name. She begg'd very hard she might have the pleasure of seeing you the next time she came, as she said she had particular business, and wanted to speak to you in private.
>
> Lady Contest: Then pray let me see her when she comes again; for I am very fond of particular business. (p. 56)

This edition omits Hannah's reply, and John enters immediately. Only in this edition do the male servants have names.

[57] Inchbald explains that she modeled Twineall on Lord Chesterfield's finished gentleman. Compare Sir Pertinax in Macklin's *The Man of the World.* "Remarks" to *Such Things Are,* XXIII, 4.

[58] Nicoll points out that her contemporaries enjoyed seeing the "follies and vices of fashionable life put upon the stage, but they were not content to witness

the inevitable consequences of that folly and vice," p. 109. Because Inchbald's characters are irresponsible rather than evil, their reform is not unrealistic.

[59] Pertinent analyses of Dorriforth may be found in Katharine M. Rogers, "Inhibitions on Eighteenth-Century Women Novelists," *ECS* 11 (1977), pp. 69-71, and my "Woman's Influence," *SNNTS,* 11 (1979), 9-10 and 15-16.

[60] For a contemporary reaction to Dorrillon, see the *Monthly Mirror* (June 1979), III, 303-304.

[61] In another place, I have discussed the treatment of vivacious women by women writers, see "Woman's Influence," p. 17.

[62] "Remarks" to *The Good Natur'd Man,* XVII, 4; "Love is a fervid passion to feel, but an insipid one to see," "Remarks" to Congreve's *The Mourning Bride,* XIII, 2. She finds the lovers in *Conscious Lovers* equally "insipid" and defends the superiority of conjugal love; see also "Remarks" on *Venice Preserv'd,* XII, 4.

[63] This is true to a large extent of her novels, both of which are full of dialogue and theatrical touches such as the moment when Clementine glances in her mirror to see how rage becomes her in *Nature and Art.* J. M. S. Tompkins discusses dramatic elements in the introduction to *A Simple Story,* pp. vii-ix, as does Kelly who says, "Mrs. Inchbald could be said to have translated the new naturalistic style of acting . . . into the techniques of fiction," p. 79.

Terry Castle (essay date 1986)

SOURCE: "Masquerade and Utopia II: Inchbald's *A Simple Story,*" in *Masquerade and Civilization: The Carnivalesque in Eighteenth-Century English Culture and Fiction,* Stanford University Press, 1986, pp. 290-330.

[*In the essay that follows, Castle characterizes* A Simple Story *as subversive because it both uses and mocks sentimental literary conventions.*]

Moving from [Fanny] Burney's novel to Elizabeth Inchbald's *A Simple Story*, one travels a great distance. Inchbald offers the reader a new terrain, a fictional world that has been utterly transformed. The difference is in part aesthetic. [Burney's] *Cecilia,* for all its interest, can scarcely be called an artistic success. The work is at once constricted and over-elaborate, hesitant and diffuse. Five volumes extenuate the underlying imaginative dilemma: Burney's language manages to seem both dilated and emotionally imprecise. The style of *Cecilia* is the linguistic equivalent of anomie: clichéd, bleached out, the rhetoric of enervation. Despair speaks here in the borrowed phrases of

sentimental fiction; repetition has become a verbal as well as psychological syndrome. Burney's familiar plot takes shape, fittingly, in a language of ennui, replete with tics and backtracking.

Inchbald's novel, by contrast, is a tour de force—a small masterpiece neglected far too long. Without exaggeration the case might be made for *A Simple Story* as the most elegant English fiction of the century. (And one need not exclude any of Sterne here.) The emotional exactitude, the subtlety of imaginative statement, make it one of the finest novels of any period. Inchbald shares the profound interiority of Jane Austen and Henry James; hers is also a world of the utmost intelligence and wit. Yet here too, paradoxically, is the same freedom—the exquisite extremism—one associates with Emily Brontë. *Wuthering Heights* may be the work *A Simple Story* most anticipates, not only because of the similar double narrative structure (each fiction takes place over two generations), but because of the way Inchbald succeeds in communicating, with startling economy, reserves of the most intense feeling. Inchbald's modern editor, J. M. S. Tompkins, matches the spare, beautiful idiom of her subject when she notes that *A Simple Story* "had . . . for its generation, and still has for readers who can learn its language, an overpowering sense of reality."[1]

The differences between Burney and Inchbald are biographical as well as aesthetic. In contrast with Burney's polite fiction-making, sudden fame, and entry into literary and court circles, Inchbald's somewhat raffish theatrical career, as well as her Catholicism and her Jacobin sympathies, set her apart from many contemporaries. James Boaden's *Memoirs of Mrs. Inchbald* (1833) attractively summarizes her exploits, which included associations with Godwin's circle, theatrical love affairs, and at a masquerade in 1781, a notorious appearance dressed as a man. Boaden asserts that many of the "frolics" of Inchbald's heroine, Miss Milner, including the masquerade that figures so subtly in *A Simple Story,* had their origin in Inchbald's own sometimes dare-devil career.[2]

The contrast extends to the two novelists' reputations. In comparison with Burney, Inchbald is usually treated as a strictly minor literary figure; she has received none of that moderate yet continuous critical scrutiny accorded the author of *Evelina.* Readers are more likely to recall that one of Inchbald's plays, *Lovers' Vows* (1798), is featured discreditably in *Mansfield Park* than they are to have read either her drama or her fiction. *A Simple Story* itself has had an obscure literary half-life; though it has always had admirers (from Mrs. Edgeworth to Lytton Strachey), it has never been a part of the canon of indispensable eighteenth-century texts. Like its witty, intractable protagonist, the novel has preserved a certain renegade status, but has hardly been well known.[3]

It is tempting to speculate that some of this neglect may be due to Inchbald's sardonic rendering, verging on parody, of a conventional world of eighteenth-century literary representation. Hers is not a vision that flatters the symbolic order. This impatience with "things as they are" lends her fiction, even now, a certain ideological illegibility. We do not yet know, perhaps, how to read her fully, for *A Simple Story* is a restlessly anti-authoritarian, even avant-garde work. It insistently satirizes conventionality, self-restriction, physical and psychic inhibition—the morbid state, in Freudian terms, of civilization itself. Much of the power of the novel lies in its dramatization of liberation from the restraints imposed by culture. Inchbald's is a world in which impulses toward contact—starting with those of the body itself—triumph over taboo. Ordinary gestures have a marvelous affective power here; they dismantle internalized structures of alienation. Human longings find an answer; human needs confound and circumvent sclerotic patterns of decorum and politesse. It is debatable whether the twentieth century, the most frightening epoch of alienation to date, is any better equipped than the eighteenth to confront Inchbald's radical vision of consummation.

But the libertarian impulse has too its specifically feminist dimension, for this is a world, above all, of female gratification. What Burney can only intimate, in a disjunctive episode of pleasure later abjured, is at the heart of Inchbald's fiction. *Cecilia* remains legible in an ideological sense; for all its impacted moral anguish, it validates the familiar cultural and literary themes of female *Bildung*. But *A Simple Story* offers an unfamiliar image of female plot. Here the heroine's desires repeatedly triumph over masculine prerogative; familial, religious, and psychic patterns of male domination collapse in the face of her persistent will to liberty. In both a social and a literary sense, Miss Milner (the first and most potent of *A Simple Story*'s two heroines) could be said to embody an unprecedented feminine destiny. She is never, to borrow a word from *Clarissa*, successfully "enwomaned." She escapes that symbolic emasculation Simone de Beauvoir has identified with the process of being made female in patriarchal society.[4]

The mysterious last words of Inchbald's fiction sum it up. There, as though by way of explanation for her remarkable tale, Inchbald acknowledges that Miss Milner never received

A PROPER EDUCATION

The words are set off in the text like a strange, incomprehensible charm. They call attention to precisely what has been absent from the start—any prescriptive rendering of female socialization. One is not surprised to learn of Inchbald's associations with Mary Wollstonecraft, for *A Simple Story* sometimes reads like a fantastic, exuberant transformation of the *Vindication*. Even the traces of Wollstonecraft's occasional self-pity have been removed. This story of failed "education" is also a lyrical assault, a rhapsody of transgression, in which masculine authority is insistently demystified, female aspiration rewarded, and the conventional world of eighteenth-century representation transformed in consequence.

If I seem to describe a carnivalized fictional landscape, that is precisely my intention. Inchbald's novel has, indeed, its requisite masquerade scene: like her contemporaries Inchbald turns at a compelling moment in her fiction to the conventional topos of liberty. Given her political sympathies, one might anticipate this gravitation toward the imagery of reversal. What is perhaps unexpected, however, is the transformation she works upon it, for in one important sense—the instrumental—the episode seems no longer strictly necessary. Literally speaking, Inchbald's masquerade scene is barely a scene at all. She presents nothing in the way of conventional masquerade spectacle—indeed, her "set piece" is over in a sentence or two. Likewise, in contrast with Fielding's or even Burney's use of the topos, the masquerade in *A Simple Story* generates little intrigue to speak of—no theatrical structure of enigma and revelation—though it will prompt the final ethical and psychological confrontation between Miss Milner and her fiancé, Dorriforth.

Inchbald has a less pressing need for the externalized scenery of transgression because the pattern of her narrative is already powerfully transgressive.[3] The fictional world itself globalizes carnivalesque impulses. One of the paradoxes of *A Simple Story* is that it shows us the traditional imagery of scandal on its way toward obsolescence: a minimalist carnivalesque. Inchbald does not turn to the set piece for instrumental purposes, for she no longer needs its hidden mediation. The subversive technical functions served by such scenes in Richardson, Fielding, and Burney are in Inchbald's novel implicit in the narrative as a whole. She renders transgression directly; it is the very essence of her plot. Likewise, ordinary life, rather than the colored crystal of the masquerade, has become the supercharged site of pathos, liberty, and delight.

What, then, is the meaning of the scene? Inchbald invokes the masquerade quite explicitly as an emblem of liberation. This, for the first time in eighteenth-century English fiction, is a politicized carnivalesque, a consciously utopian image—the signature, if not the instrument, of an incorrigibly feminist plot. Like the rape of Clarissa (though bearing an entirely different emotional weight), Inchbald's masquerade could be called an abstract vignette: it pervades the text in which it is not, strictly speaking, represented. Like an object in a dream one cannot quite see yet knows is there, it condenses the radical concerns of Inchbald's fiction.

I have already intimated the nature of these concerns: *A Simple Story* is a story of law and its violation. It is about the breaking of vows, the crossing of boundaries, the reversal of prohibitions. The rhythm of the fiction is repetitive without seeming repetitive. Each half of the novel is structured as a chain of violations. The pattern of rebellion is linked to the struggle for power between men and women: the law is masculine, the will that opposes feminine. In the first half of the novel, Dorriforth, the somber guardian and priest, gradually gives way to the ardor and yearning for intimacy of his ward, Miss Milner; in the second half, in his new incarnation as Lord Elmwood, the embittered widower and father, he yields again, this time to the poignant emotional pleas of his daughter Matilda, whom he has earlier banished from his sight. [The February 1791 edition of *A Simple Story* appeared in four volumes. Throughout this chapter I speak loosely of the first and second halves of the novel: the story of Miss Milner occupied the first two volumes in the original edition; the story of Matilda the second two. The page citations in this chapter, however, refer to the Oxford edition (1967), which was based on the 1791 edition but published in a single volume.] Patriarchal injunctions—against passion, connection, presence—are repeatedly overturned.

Female energy, in Inchbald's vision, has the power to transform space. Her fictional landscape is always initially organized according to a repressive masculine logic of permitted and proscribed zones. The reader of *A Simple Story* cannot help recalling, for example, the Bluebeard-like manner in which Dorriforth, in both sections of the novel, subdivides the physical world and forbids his female ward entry into certain tabooed spaces. To penetrate the proscribed realm, for the woman, is to risk separation from the beloved other—a physical and existential alienation of the most extreme kind. In the first half of the novel, the masquerade is the primary forbidden zone. Dorriforth will threaten to leave Miss Milner "forever" if she attends this event against his will. In the second half the forbidden zone shifts indoors and becomes part of the domestic scene. Matilda cannot enter the rooms in her father's country house, which he inhabits himself, or come into his sight; if she does, she will forfeit his invisible protection and be "debarred" from him forever (p. 213).

The irony, however, is that threatened punishments are never executed—or at least never completely executed—in Inchbald's imaginative world. Transgressions take place, for whether by accident or design, the heroine always goes where she is not supposed to. But the violation of masculine law results, not in the expected separation, but in the collapse, the voiding, of proscription itself. Banishment is transformed, at the last minute, into ecstatic, extra-logical union. The system of safe and forbidden zones, they symbolic articulation of space (which one might take as Inchbald's paradigmatic externalization of patriarchal oppression) falls away in the face of female passion and will. The result is utopian—a physical order without negativity, a realm of ideal freedom.[4]

Granted, this structure of taboo and violation, masculine proscription and feminine transgression, could conceivably coexist with a more conventional treatment of the carnivalesque if Inchbald's heroine were a different sort of character. The reification of the masquerade as a forbidden zone is after all nothing new in eighteenth-century fiction, and Dorriforth's injunction against the event is entirely in keeping with conventional moral pronouncements on the subject. Ordinary eighteenth-century heroines guarantee their integrity by what might be called their nonvolitional relationship to their masquerade adventures. Pamela and Amelia are forced to go to masquerades by indiscreet husbands, though Amelia escapes with a ruse; Cecilia is swept up in the occasion, but again not exactly of her own free will. Cecilia does not go to the masquerade; it comes to her, when her guardians transform their house into an assembly room. Technically speaking, the virtuous heroine avoids the taboo zone of the carnivalesque, though she does, as though by accident, end up in it.

The result of such passive trespass, as we have seen, is almost always comic and almost always linked to the plot of heterosexual romance. One may find a lover (*Cecilia, Sir Charles Grandison*); or an earlier erotic union may be repeated in displaced form (*Pamela, Amelia*). Whatever difficulties emerge from the unwilled violation of masculine norms also create a core of narrative interest and carry the novel toward its conclusion. The naturalization of the heroine's carnivalesque union with her lover—her *amor impossibilia*—is typically the essential problem masquerade fiction seeks to resolve. [Parodic forms of the masquerade *amor impossibilia* appear in *Roxana* (Roxana's briefly scandalous liaison with the "Duke of M———"), *Tom Jones* (the relationship of Lady Bellaston and Jones), and *Memoirs of a Woman of Pleasure* (the sexual encounter between the prostitute Emily and a homosexual). Each of these sets of relations mimics the improper coupling motif found elsewhere in eighteenth-century masquerade fiction yet avoids the conventional sentimental pathos and lengthy extenuation associated with it in a work like *Cecilia*. The social, economic, and libidinal incongruities represented in these three episodes are only cynically and temporarily resolved, and narrative closure comes by other means.]

The first point to be made about Inchbald's masquerade, however, is that not only is the heroine's relation to it not passive, but the episode seems to play no catalytic part in the romance plot of the novel at all. This plot—an extremely indecorous one—has already arrived at a point of apparent closure before the masquerade takes place, near the end of the first half. We recollect the situation. Miss Milner, the beautiful, vivacious heiress, has fallen in love with her guardian, the dignified and austere young Jesuit priest Dorriforth, in whose household she has been residing since the death of her father. After a period of secret infatuation Miss Milner reveals her love to Miss Woodley, her spinster companion, who at first opposes the scandalous attachment. But the fortuitous death of Dorriforth's cousin, Lord Elmwood, suddenly makes Dorriforth the new heir, and necessitates that he give up his priestly vows and marry. After a series of complications (including a period of separation during which Miss Milner attempts to let go of her desire), Miss Woodley informs Dorriforth of Miss Milner's love for him. In a scene of remarkable, restrained emotional intensity, he discovers his own suppressed passion for Miss Milner and is subsequently swiftly and rapturously engaged to her.

What such a summary (which accounts, roughly, for only the first third of the novel) leaves out is the sustained erotic tension, the frisson at the heart of Inchbald's psychological drama. (A similar tension is present in the second half of the novel, though in perhaps even more elemental form, deriving as it does from the charged Oedipal attachment between Dorriforth/Elmwood and his daughter.) Much of this tension grows out of the reader's persistent sense of obstacle—of the overwhelming ethical and psychic obstructions impeding the union of Miss Milner and her guardian. The heroine's passion thrives on, indeed at times seems indistinguishable from, the barriers she faces: hers is a transgressive liaison par excellence.

Yet it is precisely this tension that Inchbald establishes without the mediation of the conventional turn into the carnivalesque. She needs no episode, no moment of fugue or phantasmagoria, to prompt the plot of subversive desire. Instead, she takes this plot as a given, identifying Miss Milner from the start—the moment of her arrival in Dorriforth's house—with the impulses of inappropriate longing. In Inchbald's most radical break with fictional convention, character itself provides the impetus for the *amor impossibilia*. Thus we learn that Miss Milner is beautiful and self-indulgent, possessed of a "quick sensibility," yet prone to "vanity" and "an inordinate desire of admiration." She has "acquired the dangerous character of a wit" and revels in insouciance (15). Yet she possesses too a capacity for deeper response, an imaginative connection with the world that coexists, in the words of one character, in a kind of "intricate incoherence" with her love of the merely delightful. Despite an "immoderate enjoyment of the art of pleasing, for her own individual happiness, and not for the happiness of others," Miss Milner has too a kind of problematic, heartbreaking sweetness: "Still had she a heart inclined, and oftentimes affected by tendencies less unworthy; but those approaches to what was estimable, were generally arrested in their first impulse by some darling folly" (19). This devastating combination of attributes makes her a disruptive force from the beginning—the "stranger in the house" (in Tony Tanner's evocative phrase) who will bring both ecstasy and chaos into the lives of her hosts. After meeting Miss Milner for the first time, Sandford, the irascible older priest who is Dorriforth's spiritual ad-

viser and tutor, instantly condemns her as "incorrigible" and advises that a "proper match" be found for her immediately and "the care of so dangerous a person given into other hands" (42).

By psychologizing the transgressive impulse, turning it inward and rendering it part of her heroine's passionate nature, Inchbald makes it part of the scenery of everyday life. It ceases to be the function of any discontinuous or dreamlike "Evening's Intrigue." Everything follows, instead, from Miss Milner herself. She embodies sexual energy in a house of celibates, disturbing—sometimes farcically—that polite *ménage à quatre* composed of the two sober priests, Dorriforth and Sandford, and two pious "unseductive innocent females," the landlady (Mrs. Horton) and Miss Woodley (7). But Miss Milner also embodies an inchoate political energy—a spirit of anti-authoritarianism. She is no respecter of petty tyrants; her supper-table skirmishes with the blimpish Sandford (who baits her sadistically while at the same time pretending to ignore her presence) are models of particular daring:

> "There are very different kinds of women," (answered Sandford, directing his discourse to Mrs. Horton,) "there is as much difference between some women, as between good and evil spirits."
>
> Lord Elmwood asked Miss Milner again—if she took an airing?
>
> She replied, "No."
>
> "And beauty," continued Sandford, "when endowed upon spirits that are evil, is a mark of their greater, their more extreme wickedness.—Lucifer was the most beautiful of all the angels in paradise—"
>
> "How do you know?" said Miss Milner. (117)

But by far and away the most important aspect of Miss Milner's character is her yearning, intractable and unerring, for that which is taboo. She longs, as though by reflex, for that which is denied her, banned by convention, edict, or scruple. She is undoubtedly capricious and often desires what is forbidden precisely because it is forbidden. She exemplifies what Georges Bataille calls the "absurd proposition" at the heart of desire—that "the forbidden is there to be violated."[5] "Monastic vows, like those of marriage," Miss Milner overhears someone remark early in the novel, "were made to be broken" (21).

Miss Milner's passion for Dorriforth is illicit on several counts. He is a Catholic priest, bound to vows of chastity, and thus in social terms an obviously unsuitable love object. But her attachment also could be said to violate literary convention. The attraction she feels for the man who is also her legal guardian represents one of Inchbald's characteristic breaks with ordinary novelistic decorum. The guardian/ward relationship is typically a sacrosanct one in English fiction of the period—sentimental in form and nonsexual in nature.[6] The exclusively noneroticized nature of this particular male/female bond is usually marked symbolically by an age difference or the marital status of the guardian. No one expects, for example, the aged Mr. Villars in Burney's *Evelina* to fall in love with the heroine, or she with him; theirs is a purely familial attachment. Likewise, in *Cecilia,* none of Cecilia's three guardians, Harrel, Delvile senior, and Briggs, represents a sexual possibility; each is married or elderly, or both. To imagine an eroticization of the guardian/ward bond, in English literature at least, is to diverge abruptly into the realms of pornography and burlesque; one thinks of certain perverse situations in Cleland, or that obscene relationship depicted, in the next century, in the anonymous pornographic novel *Rosa Fielding: A Victim of Lust* (1876). The guardian/ward relationship of the Lord Chancellor and Phyllis in Gilbert and Sullivan's *Iolanthe* is merely ludicrous. On the rare occasion when such a relationship does become a serious possibility, as in *Bleak House,* between Esther and Jarndyce, it is invariably neutralized as soon as possible.[6]

The situation is different in French writing. There the guardian/ward bond has always been treated more ambiguously, and its subversive narrative possibilities explored. The eroticized relation between M. de Climal and the heroine in Marivaux's *La Vie de Marianne* (1731) set a precedent for eighteenth-century French literature; Laclos and Rousseau offered variations on the theme later in the period. The point is worth making because it suggests something about Inchbald's characteristically "un-English" imaginative concerns. What Lytton Strachey referred to as her "French" manner might indeed be traced to her interest in the transgressive erotic pattern per se. She is far more at home in a tradition that includes Prévost, Rousseau, Stendhal, Flaubert, and Proust, finally, than that of English sentimental fiction, with its heavily didactic emphasis and more indirect representations of sexual desire.

The influence of Rousseau is particularly striking. The charged guardian/ward relationship in *A Simple Story* at times resembles the teacher/pupil dyad of Saint-Preux and Julie in *La Nouvelle Héloïse;* Abelard and Heloise provide the larger intertextual link. One is not surprised to find Inchbald invoking these exemplary French lovers early on in her novel. During a conversation with the heroine and her guardian, after Miss Milner laughs at a pleasantry made by Dorriforth, the jealous rake Lord Frederick Lawnley interjects a sneering Popean reference:

> From Abelard it came,
> And Heloisa still must love the name. (22)

Miss Milner instantly recognizes the hidden aptness of the quotation and has to hold her head out a window

"to conceal the embarrassment these lines had occasioned." In his oblivion Dorriforth, however, is untouched. "Whether from inattention to the quotation, or from a consciousness it was wholly inapplicable, [he] heard it without one emotion of shame or of anger" (22).

If Miss Milner is aware, in some sense, of the Frenchness of her passion, no one else in the fictional world is—not at first. She is indeed like a character from a French novel who has strayed by accident into an English one. Without her, Dorriforth's placid household might seem to foreshadow a host of comic vicarages in later English fiction, from Trollope to Barbara Pym. (The Catholic element is unusual, but Inchbald gives even this a distinctly unsensational cast.) Miss Milner disturbs the familiar microcosm. She embodies literary as well as social discontinuity, from which Inchbald draws a range of comic and pathetic effects.

No one knows how to read Miss Milner. Dorriforth certainly cannot, nor can he imagine any way of apprehending their relationship other than as a version of the familiar guardian/ward bond. He comports himself toward her at first as though he too were a character in a novel—the personification of the good paternal guardian. He sees his own role in purely conventional terms: to arrange a marriage for her with some suitable person. Yet she remains an oddly disturbing charge. Dorriforth is distressed by those aspects of her character that violate the literary paradigm he knows—her propensity for the frivolous, her inability to commit herself to any serious ties (she unaccountably breaks off an engagement to Lord Frederick Lawnley), her disquieting erotic power. She is hardly a self-effacing Burney heroine. In the first part of the novel, he is repeatedly oppressed by feelings of responsibility for her that he does not yet recognize—and has no way of interpreting—as desire.

Miss Woodley likewise misreads her wildly, but as the heroine in a sentimental romance. Thus when Miss Milner becomes melancholy, Miss Woodley immediately assumes that she must be in love with Lord Frederick, the feckless peer who has fought a duel on her behalf. Miss Woodley's misdirected diagnosis of Miss Milner's case is an epitome of vulgarity: "'Her senses have been captivated by the person and accomplishments of Lord Frederick,' said Miss Woodley to herself, 'while her understanding beholds his faults, and reproaches her passion—and, oh!" cried she, 'could her guardian and Mr. Sandford know of this conflict, how much more would they have to admire than condemn!'" (46).

Of course, Miss Woodley's banal fantasy of troubled passion in no way matches the scandal of Miss Milner's real attachment. Miss Milner's ringing confession, proffered "with a degree of madness in her looks," that she loves her guardian—"with all the passion of a mistress, and with all the tenderness of a wife"—leaves Miss Woodley aghast, as though witness to an act of sacrilege. For Miss Woodley, "the violation of oaths, persons, or things consecrated to Heaven, was, in her opinion, if not the most enormous, the most horrid of crimes" (73). She attributes her friend's monstrous passion to the failings of her Protestant education: "Had she been early taught what were the sacred functions of a Roman ecclesiastic, though all her esteem, all her admiration, had been attracted by the qualities and accomplishments of her guardian; yet education would have given such a prohibition to her love, that she had been precluded from it, as by that barrier which divides brother and sister" (74). Miss Milner lacks a sense of taboo; her love for Dorriforth is equivalent, in Miss Woodley's eyes, to incest.

Miss Woodley prescribes drastic measures, installing herself as a belated voice of moral decorum. Miss Milner will go to Bath and purge herself of her passion. The necessary "barrier" between Miss Milner and Dorriforth will be restored geographically if not emotionally. "You *shall part,*" Miss Woodley admonishes, frightening her friend with dreadful images of Dorriforth's reaction, should he discover her love: "What astonishment! what confusion! what remorse, do I foresee painted on his face!—I hear him call you by the harshest names, and behold him fly from your sight forever, as an object of his detestation" (88-89). One way or another, banishment and loss, she argues, represent the life of the future.

Just at this point, however, the point of maximum difficulty and estrangement (for Miss Milner does go to Bath, and falls abruptly into an agony of despair), Inchbald's narrative turns inside out and moves toward an unexpected, temporarily euphoric closure. The news of Dorriforth's inheritance and release from priestly vows comes to Miss Milner at Bath, and instantly provides her with a sense of enthralling, even sublime anticipation: "she felt, while every word was speaking, a chill through all her veins—it was a pleasure too exquisite, not to bear along with it the sensation of exquisite pain" (102).

One last obstacle obtrudes, however. The new Lord Elmwood, still unapprised of his ward's love, seems likely to marry Miss Fenton, a neighborhood heiress. Miss Woodley—now, like an ambiguous character in a folktale, on the side of Miss Milner and vicariously caught up in her friend's passion—wonders briefly if Miss Milner should not just marry Lord Frederick, to save herself needless suffering. This final crisis, soon resolved, is nonetheless significant because it prompts the heroine to articulate her most compelling manifesto of passion to date—a theory, in fact, of transgressive desire. Miss Milner's unself-conscious celebration of the forbidden object is unprecedented in polite English fiction: "What, love a rake," she exclaims, "a man of professed gallantry? impossible.—To me, a common rake is as odious, as a common prostitute is

to a man of the nicest feelings.—Where can be the pride of inspiring a passion, fifty others can equally inspire? Or the transport of bestowing favours, where the appetite is already cloyed by fruition of the self-same enjoyments?" (120). When Miss Woodley is shocked, Miss Milner, in a grandiloquent flurry, offers a thrilling credo: "My dear Miss Woodley . . . put in competition the languid love of a debauchee, with the vivid affection of a sober man, and judge which has the dominion? Oh! in my calendar of love, a solemn lord chief justice, or a devout archbishop ranks before a licentious king" (120).

We detect again the Rousseauian note: like Rousseau, Inchbald offers an aestheticization of instinct, a civilization of eros, that seems inescapably modern.[7] We might agree with Miss Woodley's tactful observation later, when she finally discloses her friend's love to Lord Elmwood, that "Miss Milner's taste is not a depraved one; it is but too much refined" (129). But Miss Milner's remarkable declaration may also bring to mind the characteristic formulations of an even more notorious contemporary. It might seem odd at first glance to juxtapose Inchbald with the Marquis de Sade, but her conceptualization of the erotic has a strange kinship with the subversive projections of the consummate *encyclopédiste* of the perverse. (*A Simple Story* appeared in the same year as *Justine.*) In Inchbald too, the forbidden is sought—and found—over and over again. Desire constructs itself in relation to an endlessly self-extending set of prohibitions; there is always another "sober man," another proscribed object or activity to spur passion. With its intimations of a repetitive, continuously renewable desire, Miss Milner's "calendar of love" bears more than a passing likeness to pornographic almanacs like *The 120 Days of Sodom* (1785). We are in a realm of potentially infinite gratification, a Fibonacci series of pleasurable violations.

Inchbald's heroine dreams of carnivalesque ends—metamorphosis, scandal, euphoria—without the carnival. And paradoxically enough, she achieves them. After Miss Woodley's timely hints (125-31), the new Lord Elmwood recognizes that he himself is the unknown lover for whom the heroine yearns: "Again he searched his own thoughts, nor ineffectually as before.—At the first glance the object was presented, and he beheld *himself*" (130). The *amor impossibilia* is miraculously redeemed: in a transport of passion, the former priest becomes Miss Milner's "profest lover." The house of celibacy is likewise transformed: after the lovers' betrothal (a scene that Inchbald with typically Jamesian delicacy omits), "every thing and every person wore a new face" (136).

As Inchbald's last image suggests, this could indeed be called a masquerade story without the masquerade. The narrative situation bears a displaced resemblance to the popular eighteenth-century masquerade fantasy of the *parodia sacra,* in which priests and cardinals turned out to be libertines in disguise, and "Sweet Devotees" the harlots of Drury Lane. The comic idea implicit in ecclesiastical travesty was that repression could transform itself, in an instant, into concupiscence, and sacred personages behave as licentiously as anyone else. Dorriforth's transformation from priest to lover is at least metaphorically analogous. Granted, Dorriforth hardly fits the stereotype of the secretly lustful cleric; he has only the most attenuated kinship with a wholly parodic character, say, like Ambrosio in Lewis's *The Monk.* For a long time Dorriforth's sexual desire is entirely unconscious; he has no hidden designs upon his ward. But he does undergo a gradual transformation of sensibility—a kind of sentimental education—that one might take as the psychological equivalent of carnivalesque transformation. Perhaps it is not surprising, in this novel of failed female education, that Inchbald's male characters should be insistently re-educated in just this way: that they learn to forgo austerity and emotional detachment for a new life of passion and adhesiveness. Dorriforth must yield, as it were, to the impure power of eros. Thus he enacts the familiar story of metamorphosis—from chastity to sexuality, from celibate to lover. He becomes a kind of carnivalesque icon in the novel, a mediator between socioerotic categories.[8]

Yet it is right here, after the carnivalesque union of Miss Milner and Dorriforth has apparently already been accomplished, that Inchbald invokes the masquerade topos: the very point at which such a turn must seem most irrelevant and threatening. Still "lost in the maze of happiness that surrounded her," Miss Milner receives a masquerade invitation from "Mrs. G———" (151). Everything seems back to front; the pattern of normal eighteenth-century narrative development seems inverted. We seem to move into dangerously uncharted psychological waters. Given Miss Milner's intractable mixture of love and wildness, one cannot help fearing the worst. Indeed, the episode promises at first to be the most damaging revelation to date of the heroine's idiosyncratic character—an epitome of the "intricate incoherence" that defines her nature.

Inchbald prepares us for just such a limited, almost clinical psychological demonstration. We learn, for example, that Miss Milner's pride, incorrigibility, and love of the taboo have not vanished as a result of her engagement; rather, the very complacency of her happy new condition seems to have intensified her restiveness. Even before the chance to go to a masquerade presents itself, she is building up to new heights of perversity. Disregarding Dorriforth's commands, she renews her "fashionable levities," begins keeping late hours, and runs up bills for "toys that were out of fashion before they were paid for" (139). Like a child she insistently tests the limits of her lover's patience. Dorriforth, it must be said, at first finds something fascinating in the situation. "Blinded by his passion," he is intrigued by the novelty of finding his ward, who

had "ever been gentle," transformed into "a mistress, sometimes haughty; and to opposition, always insolent." Miss Milner is "charmed to see his love struggling with his censure—his politeness with his anxiety" (139). Yet the reader has a sense of escalating emotional danger. In an aside to Sandford (who remains resolute in his dislike of the heroine), Dorriforth articulates the basic threat of the narrative—that should Miss Milner continue to challenge his authority over her, he will decide whether to marry her after all "or—*banish me from her forever*" (142).

On some level it is just such a threat, and the renewal of obstacles to passion, that Miss Milner courts. Bored with satisfaction, she interrogates her "flattering" heart in ever more provocative ways: "Are not my charms" she muses, "even more invincible than I ever believed them to be? Dorriforth, the grave, the sanctified, the anchorite Dorriforth, by their force is animated to all the ardour of the most impassioned lover—while the proud priest, the austere guardian, is humbled, if I but frown, into the veriest slave of love" (138). Miss Milner wonders if her lover's devotion would survive "ill treatment." "If it would not," she concludes, "he still does not love me as I wish to be loved" (138).

Inchbald does not sentimentalize this desire at all; indeed, she takes the risk that some of her readers will, like Sandford, lose all patience with the heroine and condemn her yearnings as simply obnoxious. Certainly Miss Milner might be viewed in conventional moral terms as an example of unprincipled hedonism: she wishes for an "enhanced" erotic pleasure, founded upon the domination of her lover (138). While affirming that her heroine's fantasies of power remain "mere phantoms of the brain," never "by system put into action," the narrator also allows that "repeatedly indulged, they were practised by casual occurrences; and the dear-bought experiment of being beloved in spite of her faults, (a glory proud women ever aspire to) was, at present, the ambition of Miss Milner" (138).

At the same time, however, one cannot escape a sense of the deeper sexual and ideological struggle here shaping itself between Inchbald's characters. For all her faults, Miss Milner never loses the reader's sympathy. Her sensitivity invariably redeems her, while her spirit animates an otherwise intensely repressive domestic scene. Inchbald herself seems to understand her heroine's narcissism and how it compensates for a lack of any real power within the fictional world. For Miss Milner is invariably treated as a child by those around her. Seen objectively, her frivolity can be described as understandable frustration in the face of unjust social restraint, while her need for independence is simply that of any psychologically viable adult. It is not clear that the wish to be "beloved in spite of her faults" is a sin—or, the ironic aside on "proud women" notwithstanding, that her creator means us to see it so.

Dorriforth is in every respect a far more prideful character: rigid in opinion, priggish, and self-absorbed; his portrait verges everywhere on the satiric. He, just as much as his fiancée, seeks power and dominance; the only difference is that his narcissism is veiled by a mantle of patriarchal prestige. He assumes obedience as his unquestioned right, and like a threatened despot, grimly contemplates his future with an unpacified Miss Milner: "the horror of domestic wrangles—a family without subordination—a house without economy—in a word, a wife without discretion, had been perpetually present to his mind" (142). In this paradigm of patriarchal analysis, order depends, quite baldly, on the subordination of female subjects.

Such passages remind us that the conflict between the heroine and her lover is, after all, a political as well as psychological one. Inchbald seems to intuit the historic implications of the sexual antagonism she delineates here. Indeed, from the twentieth-century perspective her characters resemble nothing less than exemplary figures—representative opponents in a new and unprecedented cultural struggle. Their dispute anticipates that moral, legal, and psychic conflict, repeatedly enacted in Western civilization from the late eighteenth century on, between entrenched masculine authority and aggressive female aspiration. [That Inchbald's imagination tends toward the kind of dichotomizing or emblematic oppositions I mention here—a sort of binary patterning—is borne out by the title and narrative structure of her subsequent novel *Nature and Art* (1796), the story of the contrasting sensibilities of two brothers and their equally dissimilar sons.]

Of course, Inchbald does not make it clear at the start how this ideological conflict will work itself out, or indeed on which side—Dorriforth's or Miss Milner's—her own imaginative investment will ultimately be made. The turn toward the carnivalesque, as usual in eighteenth-century fiction, seems merely ominous at first, particularly when the narrator offers the following peculiar and seemingly proleptic warning: "In the various, though delicate, struggles for power between Miss Milner and her guardian, there was not one person witness to these incidents, who did not suppose, all would at last end in wedlock—for the most common observer perceived, ardent love was the foundation of every discontent, as well as of every joy they experienced.—One great incident, however, totally reversed the prospect of all future accommodation" (151).

The fiction seems to promise nothing but reversal—the catastrophic undoing of the plot of heterosexual romance. Miss Milner has received her tickets for the masked ball at the house of "the fashionable Mrs. G———" with "ecstasy" and set her mind to go (151). Dorriforth predictably forbids her to attend. The emotional stakes are instantly raised. Miss Milner says flatly, "she should certainly go," while Dorriforth retreats into a state of incommunicative sorrow and anger, outraged that she should "persist, coolly and deliberately in so direct a contradiction to his will" (155). His previous threat to end their engagement hangs implicitly in the air. Yet he also holds on to the belief that she will not really go, and as though to test her, absents himself from the house on the evening of the masquerade. Immediately Miss Milner leaves for Mrs. G———'s, in the company of the excited Miss Woodley (156).

The moment is without parallel in serious eighteenth-century fiction. This is hardly passive trespass. No other contemporary heroine, not even Defoe's Roxana, chooses her masquerade adventure in quite this way, with such premeditation and daring. Here is the great "proof" Miss Milner has hoped for—the critical event that will clarify the extent of her power. As she tells Miss Woodley, "As my guardian, I certainly did obey him; and I could obey him as a husband; but as a lover, I will not" (154). The "old sentiments"—her odd, strangely heroic love of liberty and risk—inexorably impel her toward the world of the masquerade, despite the tragic alienation it threatens to produce. The occasion has become a casus belli. "If he will not submit to be my lover," she exclaims proudly, "I will not submit to be his wife—nor has he the affection I require in a husband" (154).

The scene stands out as the most self-consciously politicized invocation of the carnivalesque in eighteenth-century literature. As a narrative event Inchbald's masquerade has only one real purpose: to disclose relations of power, of dominance and submission. More than in any previous work it emerges as an explicitly symbolic domain, a ground of power over which masculine will and feminine desire contend. Dorriforth is the first to encode the event in this manner; by defining the masquerade as a forbidden zone, he makes it over into a rhetorical occasion. Significantly, he gives no reason why the masquerade should be off-limits to the heroine; unlike, say, Dr. Harrison in *Amelia,* he has no moral rationale, no didactic gloss upon the occasion to justify his injunction. Its sole importance for him, it seems, is as an abstract topic upon which he can express his authority. He is in love with the basic gesture of power—what Elias Canetti has called the gratifying, irrational "sting of command."[9]

In turn Miss Milner apprehends that the masquerade somehow embodies her freedom. In one sense it does not matter what the occasion is, in and of itself. Simply to go there has meaning enough. The masquerade has in a sense become pure gesture. It signifies the reassertion of autonomy, the countermanding of patriarchal whim. For the rebellious heroine, it is the way she takes charge of her destiny, however dire the consequences.

Paradoxically, this thematic transparency seems to render any conventional depiction of the masquerade unnecessary. For the first time Inchbald puts its ideological content uncompromisingly on view. But the spectacle itself becomes peculiarly irrelevant after such a demonstration; indeed it seems hardly to need narrating at all. Freed of its traditional moral ambiguities and contradictions, the enacted masquerade loses something of its mystique. It has become a recognizably feminist enterprise.

With the exception of one important detail, Inchbald's masquerade is thus the least visual, the least present to the reader, of any contemporary fictional episode. We learn only, somewhat ironically, that Miss Milner does not really enjoy Mrs. G———'s ball: "the crowd and bustle" fatigue her, and she is afflicted by an unexpected and touching tristesse. The delicate ambivalence suggested here is typical of Inchbald's rendering of her character. Thus "though she perceived she was the first object of admiration in the place," the narrator observes, "yet there was one person still wanting to admire; and the remorse at having transgressed his injunctions for so trivial an entertainment, weighed upon her spirits, and added to its weariness" (161). Returning home at daybreak, Miss Milner is wistful and pensive—a lost Watteau figure—embodying the spirit of post-saturnalia, its ashes and ennui.

The heroine's fleeting urge here to be seen and "admired" by Dorriforth is an important one; I shall return to it in a moment. It is connected with Inchbald's one concession to conventional iconography: the description of Miss Milner's masquerade costume, representing the goddess Diana. This "elegant habit," which the heroine complements with a pair of "buskins" and by curling her hair "in falling ringlets," is suggestive in several ways. It is literally suggestive, "for although it was the representative of the goddess of Chastity, yet from the buskins, and the petticoat made to festoon above the ankle, it had, on the first glance, the appearance of a female much less virtuous" (155). But at the same time the gender of the costume seems curiously indeterminate. Several characters are not sure whether Miss Milner's disguise is meant to represent a man or a woman. When Sandford, waiting with the angry Dorriforth for her to return from the masquerade, interrogates the servants about what sort of costume she left the house in, the footman describes her wearing "men's cloaths" (including boots), but the maid swears she saw her in "a woman's dress" (160). Like that "Hermaphroditical mixture" of garments worn by the heroine Harriet in Griffin's farce *The Masquerade; or, An Evening's Intrigue* (1717), Miss Milner's costume is at once ambiguously sexual and sexually ambiguous.

The ambiguity here is related to the fact that the heroine impersonates Diana, the most androgynous and sexually elusive of classical goddesses. It makes sense in an obvious way that Miss Milner, enamored of the dramas of control, should choose to represent her. For Artemis/Diana, huntress and amazon, protector of virgins and wild animals, has always had associations

with ancient matriarchy and cults of the mother-goddess; in the eighteenth century she was often seen as a profoundly disturbing embodiment of female power. [Artemis/Diana was originally a fertility goddess similar to the Minoan "Lady of the Wild Things" and the Phrygian Cybele. On her putative connection with matriarchal religion, see J. J. Bachofen, *Myth, Religion, and Mother Right;* and Robert Graves, *The White Goddess.* Given her embodiment of militant female chastity, Diana's eighteenth-century associations are complex. Taking a cue perhaps from Ovid's unsympathetic account of Diana's transformation of Actaeon (*Metamorphoses,* Book III, ll. 138-252), eighteenth-century male artists and composers often treat her as the representative of unnatural denial, erotic self-preoccupation, or female homoeroticism. See Jean Hagstrum's comments on Joseph Bodin de Boismortier's cantata *Diane et Actéon* (1732) and Watteau's *Diana at Her Bath* in *Sex and Sensibility,* p. 288. Diana may have held a less prejudicial place in the contemporary female imagination, however, as Inchbald's treatment suggests. Aileen Ribeiro comments on the popularity of the Diana costume in eighteenth-century English fancy dress portraits in *Dress Worn at Masquerades in England,* pp. 261-64. In Volume III of her *Memoirs,* the notorious Irish courtesan Margaret Leeson describes her appearance at a masquerade as the "Goddes of Chastity, Diana, huntress of the woods."] But more important, Diana also symbolizes autonomous female sexuality—a sexuality without reference to men or male authority. More than Aphrodite, whose charm across the epochs depends upon a world of masculine desire, the "Goddess of Chastity" personifies utopian femininity. Diana is free of ordinary structures of sexual subordination, her erotic inaccessibility a form of mastery. Thus her most famous encounter with a man, the unwitting voyeur Actaeon, is a parable of supernatural female integrity: to see (and desire) the goddess is to metamorphose and die.

The associations with celibacy and power linger, perversely at first, in subsequent scenes. To be sure, when Dorriforth sees Miss Milner, still in costume, on the morning after the masquerade, the power of the goddess seems in abeyance. Unlike Actaeon and his response to Diana, Dorriforth seems oblivious to Miss Milner's beauty, and remains implacable in his will to punish. The long-threatened order of banishment is given. He vows that "in a few days we shall part"—forever (163).

Dorriforth charges his lover with making herself unrecognizable, as it were, to patriarchy. Ruling that he will not see her, he also implies that he cannot; he cannot see her now in the existential sense, and cannot acknowledge either their history or their love. With her act of rebellion she has made herself unknown to him. When in her grief at his injunction, she calls out that her dead father would regret Dorriforth's severity, the former priest declares that she should "'appeal to your father in some other form, in that' (pointing to her dress) 'he will not know you'" (164-65). Her masquerade adventure has made all men blind to her. In the most profound sense the Father no longer knows who she is. [The interplay, in this passage and elsewhere, between fathers, father surrogates, and daughters is Shakespearean in resonance. Boaden notes that Inchbald may have modeled *A Simple Story* in part on *The Winter's Tale*. The complex relations between Miss Milner, Matilda, and Dorriforth certainly resemble those of Hermione, Perdita, and Leontes in several respects (*Memoirs of Mrs. Inchbald*, I, 277). But *King Lear* also comes to mind, particularly in the painful image here of the father's blindness to his daughter. In the second half Elmwood will literally refuse to see or be seen by his daughter. This projection of terrifying emotional themes through the imagery of blindness is very similar to the process Stanley Cavell describes in his classic essay "The Avoidance of Love: A Reading of *King Lear*."]

In this crucial moment, "divided between grief and anger," Miss Milner rallies and accepts the fate she has brought upon herself. "Lord Elmwood," she cries, "you think to frighten me by your menaces, but I can part with you; heaven knows I can—your late behavior has reconciled me to a separation" (164). The symbolism of her costume (which she is of course still wearing) is most potent here: in one sense she has indeed chosen Diana-like chastity in preference to enslavement to another's will. She is reconciled to alienation—to moral and psychic invisibility—if only to preserve her liberty.

Inchbald here temporarily reconstructs a familiar and cruel dichotomy: female independence seems incompatible with sexual rewards; the heroine cannot have both power and the love of her fiancé. The masquerade hints at freedom, but its consequences, in the real world of men, are dystopian. Freedom in one realm entails loss in another; carnivalesque pleasures cannot be imported into the patriarchal household. To wear the signs of utopia in everyday life—to bring the masquerade home—is to provoke estrangement and hatred, and a devastating end to "engagements."

We recognize the emotional logic; it was painfully at work in Burney. But even here, at the nadir of her heroine's fortunes, Inchbald begins to work a subversive change on this logic and thus alters its dehumanizing force. Her heroine refuses to capitulate and in so doing challenges literary as well as domestic decorum. This refusal alone gives an intoxicating twist to the clichéd plot of female destiny, for whatever happens, Miss Milner has demonstrated an essential imperturbable strength. The masquerade has indeed been her test—an agon—but unlike Cecilia she chooses liberty over ease, and the rigors of self-determination over the comforts of the disenfranchised.

Granted, despite Inchbald's subtle revisionism the narrative threatens to give itself over to the conventional

dysphoria. The masquerade, "scene of pleasure" (161), now seems, after all, to have brought about a very real punishment—the imminent loss of Dorriforth's love. But one senses the instability in Inchbald's version of this crudely retributive structure. Dorriforth presents his decision to leave Miss Milner with ceremonial violence, as though it were incontrovertible; yet given the psychic economy at work elsewhere in the fiction, we may wonder if it really is. In a sense he simply re-creates the earlier, eminently unstable time in their history when they were officially unavailable to each other as lovers. The vow to separate reproduces the conditions of the monastic vow: it imitates taboo, sets up a boundary, and makes him once more inaccessible. Yet it also sets up, as before, the possibility of violation. As we have seen, vows have little ultimate force in *A Simple Story;* they are "made to be broken" (21). And this vow seems especially to invite violation. For not only Miss Milner but Dorriforth himself must now contend with the transgressive desire that prohibitions, by their very nature, seem to entail. Given what has gone before—and Dorriforth's own metamorphosis from "proud priest" to "profest lover"—he is now as conscious as she of the potential for transformation and transgression. Swearing to part, yet caught up still in a passionate, complicated interest in one another, Dorriforth and Miss Milner are the perfect candidates for carnivalesque reunion.

And this, of course, is what Inchbald provides. She approaches her remarkable climax with some of her most beautifully understated narrative effects. In a painfully formal letter to the heroine, Dorriforth reveals his intention to leave for Italy "for a few years." This Goethe-like journey, he hopes, will reconcile him "to the change of state I am enjoined; a change, I now most fervently wish could be entirely dispensed with" (175). But during the week of his travel preparations, which he exhorts Miss Milner not to disturb with "further trial" of his feelings, the tension grows steadily between them. They avoid speaking but remain agonizingly aware of one another's presence—conversing, as it were, through the silences of metonymy. Mute objects take on intensely communicative power. When dinner guests, for example, ask Dorriforth if he indeed plans to leave the following Tuesday, Miss Milner's "knife and fork," the narrator observes, give "a sudden spring in her hand," though "no other emotion witnessed what she felt" (178). Later, when she stumbles upon Dorriforth's trunks, "nailed and corded, ready to be sent off to meet him at Venice," she runs to a far corner of the house to sob in despair (180). Dorriforth discovers her and they communicate silently:

> She instantly stifled her tears, and looked at him earnestly, as if to imply, "What now, my Lord?"

> He only answered with a bow, which expressed these words alone: "I beg your pardon." And immediately withdrew.

Thus each understood the other's language, without either uttering a word. (180-81)

The tension reaches a breaking point on the evening before Dorriforth's departure. Dorriforth himself gives no sign of any change of heart, but nonetheless one senses odd, inexplicable intimations of reversal. Most strikingly, Sandford, formerly the heroine's nemesis, becomes suddenly and unaccountably affectionate toward her, as though sympathizing with her for the first time. His gestures of concern seem authentic: Inchbald does not present them, as she easily might have, as mere senile flourishes or marks of hypocritical triumph. At dinner the old cleric offers the distraught Miss Milner a biscuit, "the first civility he had ever in his life offered her" (182), and when he invites her to breakfast with them the next day (a request in which Dorriforth silently concurs), he addresses her softly as "my dear." However bafflingly inconsistent his kindness, his expression seems to her "most precious" (186).

In the "wondrous" scene of resolution the next morning, Sandford plays the part of deus ex machina. Barely suppressed hysteria is the order of the day here. Miss Milner spills her coffee at the jingling sound of carriage wheels in the drive; Dorriforth jerks himself up from the breakfast table "as if it was necessary to go in haste" (190). He grips Miss Milner's hand in farewell; she responds with a sudden storm of grief. Then Sandford miraculously intervenes. As though by sorcery, the lovers stand "petrified" by his stark, tolling admonition: "'Separate this moment,'—cried Sandford—'or resolve never to be separated but by death'" (190). Without pause the old priest seizes a Bible, and after hearing their mutual declarations of love, tendered in "wonder" by Dorriforth and in "a trembling kind of ecstasy" by Miss Milner, marries them on the spot (191).

Such is not the point of ultimate closure: Miss Milner and Dorriforth have a second legal ceremony a few days later, at which point the narrator educes, without explanation, the strange detail on which the first half of *A Simple Story* suspends—the discovery that the ring that Dorriforth, in haste, places on the heroine's finger is a "mourning ring" (193). I will return briefly to this ambiguous coda (with which Inchbald apparently intended to link the two originally disparate halves of her fiction) in my concluding remarks on the second part of the novel and the relationship between Dorriforth/Elmwood and his daughter Matilda.

But in another sense one may treat the heroine's marriage as definitive, in that it completes the narrative sequence initiated by the masquerade episode and places the earlier incident in its most comprehensive light to date. Granted, reflecting back on the masquerade from the vantage point of the marriage scene, one may be conscious at first only of the now-familiar pattern of teleological reversal—the fact that, as in Richardson

and Fielding, the "fatal masquerade" is here not so fatal after all. The ball at Mrs. G———'s seems in retrospect a Fortunate Fall, promoting repetition of the most pleasurable kind. For without the post-masquerade alienation between Miss Milner and Dorriforth, obviously, there can be no euphoric reconciliation: the heroine's temporary loss of her lover makes it possible, as it were, for her to have him all over again. The situation is on the surface much like that in *Pamela*. With Miss Milner's impromptu marriage, as in the scene of Pamela's "éclaircissement" with B., "every joy was doubled by the expected sorrow" (193). Like that "fairer Paradise" mentioned by Milton in *Paradise Regained*— the renovated paradise of comedy—Miss Milner's is an improved state of ecstasy, carrying all the surplus delights of secondariness, its pathos and relief.

Here too, in this new version of the Richardsonian "happy turn," one senses profound affinities with the psychological world of romance. Like Richardson, Inchbald allegorizes comic mutability in a way that has struck some readers as unnovelistic—too abrupt, fantastic, and implausible according to strictly realistic canons. "The sustained portraiture of coherent but changing character over a long period," Inchbald's editor J. M. S. Tompkins argues, is not the novelist's strong point.[10] While granting the point, one might describe the seeming incoherence another way—not as the author's failing but as a manifestation of that generic ambiguity we have already noted in a number of eighteenth-century masquerade novels. The movement toward romance, toward an antinaturalistic wish-fulfillment structure, may be, as I hypothesized earlier, a formal side effect of the carnivalesque—the generic equivalent of those processes of transformation it initiates elsewhere in eighteenth-century narrative. Certainly, after the masquerade in *A Simple Story,* as in *Pamela,* phantasmic imperatives seem at least as strong as impulses toward conventional verisimilitude. Characters do metamorphose wildly here. Sandford is only the most obvious example of what could be called Inchbald's proto-romantic nonconservation of character. Dorriforth himself has unmistakable affinities with the shape-shifting, psychologically ambivalent beings of romance.[11] But Miss Milner's marriage too, like that of Pamela and B., has a quality of general uncanniness, reminiscent of both magical quest-narrative and wish-fulfillment dream. One detects, in the narrator's summing-up, the complacent, anonymous euphoria of fairy tale: "Never was there a more rapid change from despair to happiness—to happiness most supreme— than was that, which Miss Milner and Lord Elmwood experienced within one single hour" (193).

At the same time, however, Inchbald makes an important and arguably self-conscious modification of the Richardsonian romance precedent. If the marriage scene represents a kind of fairy-tale repetition—Inchbald's return to the carnivalesque plot of union—it is also, to borrow Kermode's phrase, repetition with a difference. For the marriage in no way compromises Miss Milner's central gesture of defiance, the provocative trip to the masquerade. This symbolic assertion of autonomy goes unpunished. Significantly, in the amazing love scene itself, no mention is made of the masquerade excursion. The heroine neither begs forgiveness for her transgression nor promises her fiancé any kind of future subservience. Inchbald instead treats Miss Milner's role in the rapprochement highly ambiguously. When Dorriforth plaintively asks Miss Milner if she will "in marriage, show me that tender love you have not shown me yet?" she responds only in the equivocal, nonbinding, feminine language of gesture: "She raised him from her feet, and by the expression of her face, the tears with which she bathed his hands, gave him confidence" (192). She gives little away, and makes no vows, even in this ostensibly conventional moment of erotic surrender.

Far more than *Pamela,* Inchbald's fiction politicizes the repetition-compulsion at the heart of the romance. Twice in the narrative Dorriforth is changed—from severity to softness, from icon of inaccessibility to enraptured lover. But his second transformation differs subtly from the first, confirming, like an experimental datum, Miss Milner's now-complete moral and psychic ascendancy. Via the great intervening "proof" of the masquerade, she has challenged his authority—and won. And precisely because of this crucial episode, the process of repetition modulates into one of supplementation. In *Pamela* the shock of socioerotic reversal symbolized in Pamela's marriage is mitigated by her ultimately slavish deference to her new husband's will. Hers in the end is the traditionally reactionary euphoria of the romance, a euphoria of the erotic alone, signified by the palpable inequalities of her married condition. But Inchbald alters the ideological force of the marriage plot itself. Her iconoclasm shows up most plainly in this work of embedded revisionism: Miss Milner's second union with Dorriforth is better than the first, not just because it redeems her status as a heroine of the erotic, but because, most remarkably, it has also become the sign of her control over her own destiny. [The situation may recall those masquerade comedies known to Inchbald from her work on the London stage. Hannah Cowley's *The Belle's Stratagem* (1781) seems in particular to have a bearing on *A Simple Story.* The hero's name, Doricourt, resembles Dorriforth's; the masquerade at Lady Brilliant's suggests the type of affair held by Mrs. G—— in Inchbald's novel. Inchbald edited the play for the *British Theatre* series (London, 1808), and in prefatory remarks admired its "charm" and "humour." Of the central masquerade episode she wrote, "who does not scorn that romantic passion, which is inflamed to the highest ardour, by a few hours conversation with a woman whose face is concealed? And yet, who does not here sympathize with the lover, and feel a strong agitation, when Letitia, going to take off her mask,

exclaims, in a tremulous voice,—'This is the most awful moment of my life'?" Nostalgia is a keynote in her summation: "the mention of powder worn by the ladies, their silk gowns, and other long exploded fashions, together with the hero's having in Paris 'danced with the Queen of France at a masquerade,' gives a certain sensation to the reader, which seems to place the work on the honourable list of ancient dramas." ("Remarks," *The British Theatre,* XIX, 4-5.)]

With this fortunate termination, the utopian promise of the masquerade episode is realized. Miss Milner has, as it were, brought the masquerade home after all. Like the goddess, she has in fact metamorphosed Dorriforth—for the second time—and carnivalized his household. No longer the precinct of authoritarianism, the patriarchal realm metamorphoses into a space of compassion, sensuality, and delight. Inchbald's imagery of relief still carries the power it held for contemporaries: "Cold indeed must be the bosom," wrote her biographer, Boaden, "that does not sympathise with the bride, when she sees the carriage that was to bear her lover for ever from her arms drive away empty from the door."[12]

And this remains the preeminent meaning of the carnivalesque in Inchbald's fiction: it spills over into the real world of the characters. Inchbald does not really need to dwell on masquerade scenery, or even on the controversial pattern of human relations the masquerade temporarily engenders, for she is interested in these relations only so far as they re-create themselves—after rewarding delay—permanently, in the fictional world itself. She uses the topos to write the first feminist romance. The masquerade, finally, is both the token of utopian aspirations and the lyrical mechanism through which Inchbald grants her heroine everything— the double euphoria of carnival, love and power, in the shape of the everyday.

It may seem that I have exaggerated the revolutionary aspects of Inchbald's conclusion, particularly since it is not, after all, the final conclusion. *A Simple Story* continues into the next generation, with the history of Lord Elmwood (formerly Dorriforth) and his daughter Matilda. What to make of Inchbald's curious joining section, in which we learn in a cursory paragraph or two that the former Miss Milner, after her marriage, has a brief adulterous affair and is exiled for life, along with her baby daughter, to a "dreary" seat in Scotland by her now-embittered husband? Fifteen years have passed when the second half of Inchbald's fiction commences, and the grief-stricken Lady Elmwood, still in exile, is on her deathbed. She dies a few pages later, and the story of her adolescent daughter comes abruptly to the fore. Do these dismaying developments qualify our sense of euphoric patterning in Inchbald's narrative?

Certainly if we insist that *A Simple Story* is somehow all of a piece—a plausible, logically consistent work of art—the vagaries of the second half may force us to modify our notions regarding Inchbald's formal sense of her fiction. With her odd ligature she dispenses with a number of conventional novelistic desiderata at one blow: temporal continuity, the single recognizable point of closure, overriding organic unity. What follows does not lack power; indeed, readers may disagree with Tompkins, who finds Matilda's story inferior to Miss Milner's. For Matilda's story combines folk motif and family romance in ways prefiguring the starkly super-charged structures of Romantic poetry and fiction. Here, certainly, is Inchbald at her most self-consciously sub-lime. In the figure of the now-terrible Lord Elmwood, a man paralyzed by compressed love and rage, in Matilda's Oedipal absorption with this invisible tyrant-father, we see the outlines of classic Romantic psychodrama, from *Prometheus Unbound* to *Wuthering Heights*.

Still the fate of Miss Milner remains perplexing. But it does not, I think, undermine the argument I have been making regarding Inchbald's use of the carnivalesque and her ultimate commitment to the utopian structures of the romance. In fact, the problem may illuminate a final important feature of the masquerade theme in *A Simple Story*—one with literary and cultural repercussions in the history of the carnivalesque generally.

To be sure, one might dispense with the problem of continuity by a simple appeal to textual history: the two halves of the 1791 edition may originally have been unrelated. The "mourning ring" omen at the end of the first part seems an afterthought, stuck in to make a rather awkward link to an altogether separate tale. Boaden asserted that the first version of the novel ended with Miss Milner's marriage, and her modern editor Tompkins concurs, suggesting that the novelist "fused" two disparate works that she had on hand in order to "extend a tale that was slender and brief beside the growing bulk and complexity of the novel at the end of the century." As for the alarmingly swift demise of Miss Milner / Lady Elmwood in the second half, Tompkins argues that Inchbald was "reluctant to enter into the collapse of the marriage she had imagined," and was therefore quickly "thrown on the next generation" and Matilda's story.[13]

Such comments make sense, though one objects to the genetic fallacy that because Inchbald's novel was origi-nally an amalgam, we need not treat Lady Elmwood's death as any more than a belated connective device— as part of a secondary fiction, as opposed to a primary fiction. Tompkins's remark that Inchbald was unable to imagine a tragic end for Miss Milner and turned instead to her daughter suggests a more provocative way of relating the two halves. Matilda is indeed in many respects a surrogate for the novel's original hero-ine and takes her mother's place, in the reader's mind as well as in the narrator's, with remarkable celerity.

Onomastics play a subtle affective part here. Sublimi-nally, perhaps, it is difficult to recognize the heroine of the first part—"the once gay, volatile Miss Milner" (199)—in the shadowy and evanescent figure of Lady Elmwood. The substitution in the realm of reference sug-gests an actual substitution of persons. So strong at times is the effect of discontinuity that we seem to be reading about a different woman altogether—someone, as the narrator puts it, "no longer beautiful—no longer beloved— no longer—tremble while you read it!—virtuous" (194). Similar pseudo-erasures occur elsewhere. In the same linking passage, we find that "Dorriforth, the pious, the good, the tender Dorriforth," is lost in Lord Elmwood, "an example of implacable rigour and injustice" (195).

By contrast, Matilda (whose name, on a primitive phonic level, seems consonant with her mother's) seems strangely familiar—continuous with "the first female object of this story" (194). (The reader never learns Miss Milner's first name, yet one would not be sur-prised to find it the same as her daughter's, given the hints of characterological blending elsewhere. Later, at the first sight of his grown daughter, Lord Elmwood will refer to her by mistake as "Miss Milner.") When Matilda is introduced, the reader has the sense of a re-turn to origins, to the beginning of Miss Milner's story. Matilda is seventeen, the narrator observes, "of the same age, within a year and a few months, of her mother when she became the ward of Dorriforth" (220). Miss Woodley (who is now Matilda's confidante, just as she was her mother's) sees the young woman as Lady Elmwood "risen from the grave in her former youth, health, and exquisite beauty" (221). Perhaps it is less disturbing to read of the demise of a charismatic char-acter when she is so quickly replaced—by herself. We are prepared for an *apophrades,* a return of the dead.

This hint of phantasmic substitution clues the reader in to what is surely the most important fact, critically speaking, about the second half: that its underlying narrative structure, or what one might call its symbolic plot, is almost identical to that of the first half. Matilda's story not only resembles her mother's, it is a displaced recapitulation. For Matilda too transgresses against patriarchal dictate, and she too is threatened with emotional banishment. Yet she too forms, at the last gasp, an eminently gratifying union, and with the same man, no less, who figures so prominently in Miss Milner's history—Dorriforth/Elmwood, her own father.

The repetition clarifies Inchbald's emotional idée fixe, the obsessive pattern of proscription/violation/reward. The second half condenses the wish-fulfillment struc-tures of the first. Like her mother's story, Matilda's story is predicated on the official inaccessibility of Dorriforth/Elmwood. Elmwood has agreed to let his daughter live at Elmwood Castle after her mother's death on condition that she never enter the rooms he himself occupies, or come into his sight while he is in residence. Any transgression will result once again in instant banishment. "If," he tells Sandford, "whether by design or accident, I ever see or hear from her; that moment my compliance to her mother's supplication ceases, and I abandon her once more" (213). The pronouncement is structurally analogous to his priestly vow in the first half, for it crystallizes his physical and emotional distance. With this highly neurotic psychic blackmail, the stricken Elmwood legislates against love itself, armoring himself against human contact even as he claims to protect his unfortunate daughter.

Also embedded in the same prohibition is the "forbidden zone" motif of the first half. Her father's quarters in Elmwood Castle function for Matilda in the same way the masquerade room did earlier for her mother—as a locale into which she must not pass. One recognizes too Inchbald's proto-Romantic negotiation with folk material; Bluebeard is only the most notorious popular example of the pathological controller of space.[14] And like his former injunction, Elmwood's second prohibition seems to invite violation. Matilda tests her father's command in subtle, obsessive ways, haunting his library in his absence, gazing at portraits of him, listening for the sounds of his carriage. And in the end, we recall, she does indeed transgress, by walking into him on a stairway. Of course, she does not premeditate this meeting; it seems accidental, though the narrator gives powerful indications that it has resulted from her unconscious search. Seeing him, Matilda swoons into his arms with an involuntary cry of "Save me!" while Elmwood, likewise by reflex, calls out the name of his dead wife and in a terrible state of unlocking grief presses his daughter convulsively "to his bosom" (274).

Here the underlying narrative pattern of the first half repeats itself almost exactly. The violation of patriarchal taboo brings on its requisite punishment—banishment—yet this punishment is immediately undone by a further unexpected reversal. Inchbald's narrative spins giddily through the turns. Elmwood, despite his emotional response, swiftly exiles Matilda to yet another remote cottage, thus reinstitutionalizing the distance between them. As before, the order of separation is but the necessary prelude to reunion. Matilda is abducted by a minor character, Lord Margrave; Elmwood is stricken with remorse and rescues her. Reconciled to his love for her, he joyfully carries her back to Elmwood Castle. Matilda, seeing her father changed from a repressive tyrant into an affectionate companion from whom she receives "a thousand proofs of . . . love," experiences a vision of natural rebirth: the snowy November fields appear green to her, "the trees in their bloom," and every bird seems to sing "the sweetest music" (331).

With this characteristic gesture, as though reversing an electromagnetic field, Inchbald brings about the romance solution, transforming polarization into attraction, drawing her characters together just as their separation seems imminent. The burgeoning November of the last pages is indeed the green world of romance,

the beautiful image of Inchbald's permanent World Upside-Down. For the second time in *A Simple Story*, patriarchal violence is quelled, and feminine delight made paramount. We sense again, compellingly, that for this author the romance conclusion is the only conclusion: she seems unable to tolerate any restriction on her heroine's happiness. In this charmed recapitulation Inchbald undoes the problematic "death" of Miss Milner, relives her own charismatic story, and achieves, like Richardson, a sequel that is also the spectral reenactment of its utopian original.

Yet as this rapid summary shows, the second half of the novel does without one important element present in the first—any reference to the carnivalesque. In Inchbald's second version of the romance, the forbidden zone is no longer externalized. Unlike her mother, Matilda does not go anywhere in order to transgress—anywhere, that is, outside Elmwood Castle. She seeks out no "promiscuous" occasion, no suspect public diversion. Rather, the realm of transgression is inside: it is within the house of the father, part of domesticity itself. A simple meeting on a staircase serves all the functions of the masquerade episode in the first half. Saturnalia has moved inward.

How to account for the interesting absence of the carnivalesque? Some naïve explanations come to mind: one could argue that Inchbald did not wish to repeat the plot of the first half so exactly; one may see traces here of a vestigial didacticism. Several commentators have suggested that Inchbald wished to present Matilda as an improved Miss Milner, guilty of no melodramatic acts of self-assertion, and as one whose "proper education" in virtue surpasses her mother's. The compromising scenery of the carnivalesque might be deemed inappropriate to this new Eve.[15]

But such responses (besides foreshortening numerous ambiguities in Matilda's character) underrate the historical shift taking place here. Matilda's story represents not a disavowal but an internalization of the carnivalesque. The transformational energy of the masquerade in the second half moves into the private world of the bourgeois houschold, and on a subjective level, into the realm of individual psychology. From the beginning the transgressive space is within—part of home itself—rather than a scene one visits, the *theatrum mundi* "out there."

Theoretically speaking, the change is remarkable. Inchbald turns from the mediating figure of the masquerade to the direct expression of primary content. The movement is characteristic of her imagination. The second half of *A Simple Story* shows a general tendency toward increasingly unmediated representation, in the psychological as well as the formal sense. The psychoanalytic reading illustrates this well. Though both halves of the novel are structured by the Oedipal romance, there is a striking difference in degree of symbolic mediation. In the first half the heroine's Oedipal attachment is mediated by Dorriforth, the "most beloved friend" of her dead father. She promises, on their first meeting, "ever to obey him as her father" (13), and he fulfills all the legal and emotional functions of the paternal surrogate. By contrast, the object of Matilda's desire is in fact her father: there is no displacement of Oedipal interest onto a secondary figure. One senses Inchbald moving closer and closer, in the second half, to an unmediated presentation of a basic wish fulfillment.[16]

Inchbald's internalization of utopian desire also has larger literary and cultural dimensions. The tendency of her fiction to do away with external agents—to psychologize transformational or transgressive impulses and locate their expression within the familial setting—anticipates formal and thematic developments in nineteenth-century fiction. There too, the carnival topos will gradually become obsolete; that is, novelists will rely on it less and less as the outside mediator of controversial psychosexual or political content. The masquerade episode loses importance as the objective correlative of scandal at the moment the novel gains in interiority and self-consciousness. Transgressive longings are centralized, so to speak, in the novels of Eliot, Flaubert, Tolstoy, and James; they haunt the ordinary, complacent realms of bourgeois domesticity, becoming part of the psychopathology of everyday life. In particular, as in Inchbald, the hidden dreams of women come poignantly, and sometimes sensationally, to the fore.[17]

I will return to nineteenth-century adaptations of the carnivalesque in the Epilogue; it is enough here to note Inchbald's typical radicalism. Granted, what I have been calling her internalization of the carnivalesque may reflect too the more obvious historical fact that the masquerade was a dying institution in the 1790's, and had already lost much of its éclat for the writers and readers of realistic fiction. Even in the first half of *A Simple Story,* the representational interest the masquerade holds for Inchbald is slight, as though she were already on her way to dispensing with the iconography of the event even as the transvalues its moral and sexual meanings. Though Inchbald makes the masquerade in some sense the crucial episode in Miss Milner's history, she does so more by allusion, paradoxically, than by representation. In the second half even the allusion is gone. . . .

Notes

[1] See the introduction to the Tompkins edition of Inchbald, p. vii.

[2] Boaden, I, 140-41. On Inchbald's political affiliations with Godwin, Thomas Holcroft, and the other English Jacobins, see Kelly. See Zall for a brief summary of Inchbald's career.

[3] On Jan. 14, 1810, Mrs. Edgeworth wrote to Inchbald, "I never read a novel that . . . so completely possessed me with the belief in the real existence of all the people it represents. . . . I am of the opinion that it is by leaving more than most other writers do to the imagination, that you succeed so eminently in affecting it. By the force that is necessary to repress feeling, we judge of the intensity of the feeling, and you always contrive to give us by intelligible but simple signs the measure of this force" (cited by Tompkins, introduction to Inchbald, pp. vii-viii). Lytton Strachey edited *A Simple Story* in 1908 for the *Oxford Miscellany.*

[4] de Beauvoir, p. 249.

[5] Bataille, p. 71.

[6] On *Rosa Fielding* (1876), see Marcus, chap. 5. Conscious of the irregularity of eroticized guardian/ward bonds, Dickens does not allow the projected marriage of Esther and her aged guardian, Jarndyce, to take place; at the end of the novel Jarndyce unselfishly gives his ward over to her real love, Woodcourt. The moment marks a return to normative, desexualized guardian/ward relations. "I clasped him round the neck," writes Esther, "and hung my head upon his breast, and wept. 'Lie lightly, confidently, here, my child,' said he, pressing me gently to him. 'I am your guardian and your father now. Rest confidently here.'" (*Bleak House,* p. 649.)

[7] According to Boaden, I, 287, Inchbald began a translation of the *Confessions* in 1790; but there are many affinities, Boaden himself compares Miss Milner's story to that of Sophia in *Émile.*

[8] Dorriforth's sentimental education at the hands of Miss Milner may be seen as a fruitful reversal of the conventional pattern in earlier eighteenth-century fiction in which women characters are educated into sexual passion by male tutors. The early part of *Moll Flanders* (the story of Moll and the Elder Brother), *Pamela,* and *Memoirs of a Woman of Pleasure* offer variations on the theme; *Clarissa* treats it ironically, through Lovelace's frustrated attempts to animate his "charming frostpiece." Inchbald's novel initiates a new tradition in which these implicit tutor/student roles between men and women are reversed. Later Charlotte Brontë would play upon similar reversals in *Villette.* The hero's education into sexual desire at the hands of an older woman is a mainstay, obviously, in nineteenth-century French fiction; one thinks of Benjamin Constant, Stendhal, and Flaubert.

[9] See Canetti, sec. 8 ("The Command. Flight and Sting").

[10] Tompkins, introduction to Inchbald, p. xvi.

[11] Heathcliff comes to mind as the obvious nineteenth-century example. See Frye's comments on Brontë and the romance tradition, pp. 304-7. Boaden repeatedly

refers to Inchbald's production as a romance (see, for example, *Memoirs,* I, 288, 290).

[12] Boaden, I, 276.

[13] *Ibid.,* p. 264; Inchbald, p. 344 (Tompkins note).

[14] The tale of Bluebeard, which here lends a sinister shading to Elmwood's character, was well known in the eighteenth century thanks to many contemporary editions and translations of Perrault's *Contes du temps* (1696). Inchbald's theatrical associate George Colman the Younger wrote a play called *Blue Beard* in 1798, a few years after *A Simple Story.* The folk motif of the forbidden chamber, classified under the general heading "Tabu" and the secondary heading "Unique prohibitions and compulsions: The one forbidden thing," is no. C611 in Stith Thompson's *Motif-Index.*

[15] Readers have disagreed profoundly about Miss Milner's moral status. Boaden scoffed at any didactic reading of *A Simple Story* and cherished its heroine's vivacity and charm. More recently, however, Kelly has attacked Miss Milner's "lack of moral discipline" and described Matilda's story as an attempt "to atone for her mother's error" (pp. 73-74). Such splits may reflect deeper ideological differences: in Kelly's case, pervasive antifeminism (he speaks of the "excessive and rebellious" heroines of Wollstonecraft and the "hysterical incoherence" afflicting the work of women Jacobin novelists) seems in part to inform his highly judgmental interpretation of Miss Milner's character.

[16] One's sense of Oedipal drama in *A Simple Story* is intensified by the knowledge that Inchbald's father died when she was seven. During the composition of her novel Inchbald was simultaneously involved in writing an autobiography, which she later burned (in 1819) on the advice of her Catholic confessor. See Boaden, II, 231; and Tompkins, introduction to Inchbald, p. xxx.

[17] Tanner discusses this centralization and domestication of transgressive impulses. See, in particular, his remarks on the symbolic functions of "la maison paternelle" in Rousseau's *La Nouvelle Héloïse,* pp. 120-33, and his analysis of Flaubert's *Madame Bovary,* pp. 233-367.

Works Cited

Bachofen, J. J. *Myth, Religion, and Mother Right.* Trans. Ralph Manheim. Princeton, N.J., 1967.

Bataille, Georges. *L'Erotisme.* Paris, 1965.

Beauvoir, Simone de. *The Second Sex.* Trans. H. M. Parshley. New York, 1961.

Boaden, James. *Memoirs of Mrs. Inchbald.* 2 vols. London, 1833.

Burney, Frances. *Cecilia; or, Memoirs of an Heiress.* 4th ed. 5 vols. London, 1784. [Cited by volume and page numbers.]

Canetti, Elias. *Crowds and Power.* Trans. Carol Stewart. New York, 1962.

Cavell, Stanley. "The Avoidance of Love: A Reading of *King Lear.*" In *Must We Mean What We Say?* Cambridge, Eng., 1976, pp. 267-353.

Cleland, John. *Memoirs of a Woman of Pleasure.* Ed. Peter Sabor. Oxford, Eng., 1985.

Cowley, Hannah. *The Belle's Stratagem.* London, 1781.

[Defoe, Daniel]. *Roxana: The Fortunate Mistress.* Ed. Jane Jack. Oxford, Eng., 1981.

Dickens, Charles. *Bleak House.* Ed. Morton Dauwen Zabel. Boston, 1956.

Fielding, Henry. *Amelia.* Ed. Martin C. Battestin. Middletown, Conn., 1983. [Cited by book and chapter numbers.]

_____. *Tom Jones.* Ed. Sheridan Baker. New York, 1973. [Cited by book and chapter numbers.]

Frye, Northrop. *Anatomy of Criticism.* Princeton, N.J., 1957.

Graves, Robert. *The White Goddess.* New York, 1948.

Griffin, Benjamin. *The Masquerade; or, An Evening's Intrigue.* London, 1717.

Hagstrum, Jean H. *Sex and Sensibility: Ideal and Erotic Love from Milton to Mozart.* Chicago, 1980.

Inchbald, Elizabeth. *A Simple Story.* Ed. J. M. S. Tompkins. London, 1967. [Cited by page number.]

Kelly, Gary. *The English Jacobin Novel, 1780-1805.* Oxford, Eng., 1976.

Leeson, Margaret. *The Memoirs of Margaret Lesson, Written by Herself.* 3 vols. Dublin, 1797.

Marcus, Steven. *The Other Victorians: A study of Sexuality and Pornography in Mid-Nineteenth-Century England.* New York, 1964.

[Ribeiro, Aileen]. *The Dress Worn at Masquerades in England, 1730-1790, and Its Relation to Fancy Dress in Portraiture.* New York, 1984.

[Richardson, Samuel]. *Pamela; or, Virtue Rewarded.* Ed. Peter Sabor. New York, 1979. Penguin ed.

_____. *Pamela*. Part 2. Ed. George Saintsbury. London, 1914. [Cited by page number.]

_____. *Sir Charles Grandison*. 3 vols. Ed. Jocelyn Harris. London, 1972. [Cited by volume and page numbers.]

Tanner, Tony. *Adultery in the Novel: Contract and Transgression*. Baltimore, 1979.

Thompson, Stith. *Motif-Index of Folk Literature*. 6 vols. Bloomington, Ind., 1955.

Zall, Paul M. "The Cool World of Samuel Taylor Coleridge: Elizabeth Inchbald; or, Sex and Sensibility." *The Wordsworth Circle,* 12 (1981), 270-73.

Roger Manvell (essay date 1987)

SOURCE: "Critic and Historian of the British Drama," in *Elizabeth Inchbald: England's Principal Woman Dramatist and Independent Woman of Letters in 18th-Century London,* University Press of America, 1987, pp. 127-45.

[*In the essay that follows, Manvell examines Inchbald's critical prefaces to* The British Theatre—*a collection of British drama from Shakespeare to the end of the eighteenth century—claiming that her interpretations generally reflect conventional social values of her time.*]

By the turn of the century Elizabeth Inchbald had become one of the most respected of writers in the mainstream of literary output in England. It was a transitional period in English writing, with the powerful influence of the French revolution of the 1790s only too evident, like a sting in the tail. In an age that seemed to enjoy both writing and reading literary and dramatic criticism on a higher level than the immediate and ephemeral reports in the press, Elizabeth could also hold her own as a critical essayist. Her position was so well established by the early 19th century for her to be invited to become a regular contributor to the newly-established *Quarterly Review,* though she chose not to do so, since by this time, when she was in her mid-fifties, her energies had become limited.

It was therefore no surprise when in 1806 she was invited to write critical and biographical introductions to a generous selection of representative plays from Shakespeare's time to the close of the 18th century which were regarded by the publisher as being of sufficient note to be anthologized in a series which appeared at first periodically and was later finally assembled in 1808 in 25 volumes, each including five plays—125 in all. It would seem that these plays were not selected by Elizabeth in the first place, but by the publisher, and that the choice, looked at with hindsight

almost two centuries later, might appear somewhat arbitrary. No doubt at the time the choice was based on the popularity the pieces had enjoyed in the late 18th-century theatre (often through association with some star performance rather than as a result of pure dramatic merit), or on the achievement of a satisfactory sale at the time of their initial publication. In the case of Shakespeare, however, 24 of his plays were included, filling the first five volumes in the series, with Ben Jonson's *Every Man in his Humour* (the only one of his plays represented) completing the fifth volume. Marked omissions are Marlowe, Webster and Ford, while the Restoration dramatists are comparatively thinly represented in heavily bowdlerized versions. On the other hand, Cibber and Rowe have four plays each, Cumberland five, and Colman the Younger no less than eight. Elizabeth herself has five plays included—one a translation from Kotzebue—filling Volume XX.

Elizabeth explains the terms of her commission in an open letter dated March 1808 and addressed to George Colman the Younger, who had complained about certain points in her critical introduction to his father's plays and his own:

> I accepted an overture, to write from two to four pages, in the manner of preface, to be introduced before a certain number of plays, for the perusal, or information, of such persons as have not access to any diffuse compositions, either in biography or criticism, but who are yet very liberal contributors to the treasury of a theatre . . . One of the points of my agreement was, that I should have no control over the time or the order in which these prefaces were to be printed or published, but that I should merely produce them as they were called for, and resign all other interference to the proprietor or editor of the work. . . . Nor did the time or space allotted me, for both observations and biography (for biography of the deceased was part of my duty, and not introduced at my discretion), admit of any farther than an abridgement, or slight sketch, of each.[1]

What in fact Elizabeth offers her readers amounts in all to some 20,000 or more words, giving basic biographical accounts of the dramatists and some background to their plays, together with often acute and pointed criticism from the point of view of a woman of the theatre. She is very well aware of the difference between scripts written for professional production— plays which flesh-and-blood players must perform successfully to flesh-and-blood audiences who have given of their time and money to patronize the living theatre—and plays that are literary exercises, written, as she puts it, for the 'closet,' not the stage. She is full of praise for memorable performances by star players in theatrically effective parts. While Shakespeare remains the dominating figure among British dramatists (with his 24 works reproduced as against everyone else being represented by anything between one to eight plays), Dr. Johnson figures as the most respected critic, whom she frequently cites. But she is never afraid to criticize on her own account, even the plays of contemporary dramatists she knows personally. George Colman the Younger was indeed, as we have seen, stung to reply to her strictures, and his open letter of reproach and her equally open reply appear in the 21st volume. It should be remembered that women commentators or critics (as distinct from creative writers) were virtually unknown in the early 19th century; writing as late as 1833, Boaden in the *Memoirs* says, 'There is something unfeminine . . . in a lady's placing herself in the seat of judgment.' Her comments, he says, made her unpopular with her contemporaries, and 'added but little to her fortune and nothing whatever to her fame.' Her initial retaining fee amounted to only 60 guineas, and she even appears to have tried to get released from her contract. Boaden claims that the pieces were written 'with slender preparation.'[2]

Elizabeth's values are unmistakably those of the late 18th century. As Prof. Allardyce Nicoll, for example, points out in the volume of his *History of the English Drama* devoted to the later 18th century, audiences had changed somewhat from the rough and rowdy houses of an earlier age; they were 'quieter and less uproarious' than the patrons of the Restoration period, who had clamoured in response to plays like unruly adolescents, even invading the stage itself. Audiences in Elizabeth's time preferred 'highly decorous comic operas,' 'moral melodramas' and 'decorous sentimental comedies' which emphasized 'poetic justice.' They liked productions which involved spectacular settings that displayed the artistry of the stage designer and scene painter. They were inspired by 'sensibility,' the catchword of the time; audiences were expected to demonstrate openly that they were men and women of feeling combined with the niceties of prudery, so that commentators such as Elizabeth could use in describing such emotional responses the word 'genteel.'[3]

Not that members of these same audiences could not become rowdy with disapproval at times and dispute from the auditorium with actors on the stage. Holcroft, writing in the 1780s, describes the drunks who could get into the theatre and cause disturbances ('the nightly intrusion of unhappy and improper persons'), while a Prologue to a play by Mrs. Cowley in the 1790s refers to the pressure of bodies in the pit:

Ah! ah! you're here, and comfortably tight?

Well squeez'd and press'd, I see—from left to right.

Audiences could only too easily grow inattentive and chatter during the performance. Elizabeth, with the memories of an actress as well as of a dramatist, was well aware that she and her fellow players depended on the dramatists not only to give them playable plays

which could hold the attention of at any rate the bulk of the audience, but work which would not offend the growing body of genteel, middle-class people who came to the theatre as families and did not want to have their ears (or those of their adolescent daughters) offended by the obscene and scurrilous dialogue that had once delighted the city rakes and their doxies in earlier times.

Elizabeth herself stood in the van of these reforms, which unhappily went hand in hand with the decline of creative vitality in dramatic writing. Only in comedy, particularly the comedy of manners, did the dramatists of the late 18th century hold their own, among them Elizabeth. Again and again she emphasizes the importance of playwrights supplying plays suitable for polite audiences: of *Romeo and Juliet* she says, 'it seldom attracts an elegant audience.' 'The company,' she adds, 'will not come to a tragedy, unless to weep in torrents—and *Romeo and Juliet* will not draw even a copious shower of tears.' Southerne's *Isabella* (in which Sarah Siddons failed in her first, youthful debut for Garrick in London), was more to their taste; it was a tragedy that 'effectually wrung the hearts of those who possess nice sensibility.' She is happy that in Mrs. Cowley's *The Belle's Stratagem,* 'the persons of importance . . . are all elegant, or, at least, well bred.' She praises Steele's *The Conscious Lovers* because it is 'elegantly written, highly refined,' and notes that Garrick adapted Wycherley's *The Country Wife* as *The Country Girl* by 'expunging those parts . . . which an improved taste delicately rejects.' In matters of taste, anything 'coarse,' including even dialogue in dialect— which was sometimes introduced by some dramatists, such as Holcroft or Colman the Younger for the benefit of 'low' comedians—was to be rejected. She pleads with Colman in her preface to his *John Bull* to 'leave the distortion of language to men who cannot embellish it like yourself,' merely to provide dialogue suitable for low comedy. Dialect, she writes, belongs to 'common life,' and is but 'language . . . deformed,' which on the stage produces 'uncouth sounds' that 'pervade . . . the ear.' She castigates Cibber for *She Wou'd and She Wou'd Not*—'This comedy has neither wit nor sentiment—it has, instead, swearing, lying, and imposture,' though she praises it afterwards for its 'dexterous' plot and 'bold characters.' And in the preface to her friend, Thomas Holcroft's play, *The Road to Ruin,* she says:

> Coarse manners, like old age, should always be counterfeit on the stage: when either of these is inherent in the actor himself, as well as in the character he represents, the sensitive part of the audience are more afflicted than entertained.

Similarly, she stresses the need for the theatre to establish and sustain its moral standards. This puts her in something of a dilemma when faced with the coarser elements in Shakespeare's plays, and with the wits of the Restoration whose plays still survived on the later 18th century stage, though severely pruned and altered. She is unsparing in her condemnation of the immorality of these plays:

> Of Farquhar's *The Beaux' Stratagem:* The well drawn characters, happy incidents, and excellent dialogue, in *The Beaux' Strategem,* are but poor atonement for that unrestrained contempt of principle which pervades every scene. Plays of this kind are far more mischievous than those, which preserve less appearance of delicacy. Every auditor and reader shrinks from those crimes, which are recommended in unseemly language, and from libertinism united with coarse manners; but in adorning vice with wit, and audacious rakes with the vivacity and elegance of men of fashion, youth, at least, will be decoyed into the snare of admiration.

> Of Mrs. Centlivre's *A Bold Stroke for a Wife:* The authoress of this comedy should have laid down her pen, and taken, in exchange, the meanest implement of labour, rather than have imitated the licentious example given her by the renowned poets of those days. . . . Nor can her offence be treated with excessive rigour in reference to the present time by those who consider that this very play of *A Bold Stroke for a Wife* is now frequently performed to an elegant, yet applauding audience.

Of Gay's *The Beggar's Opera* she writes that, 'it has the fatal tendency to make vice alluring.'

On a more positive note, what Elizabeth looked for in all plays, but especially in those of her contemporaries, was 'credibility' and a closeness to 'Nature.' She applied this to Shakespeare, objecting on this account to both *Romeo and Juliet* and *Cymbeline;* of the latter she says:

> the impossibility, that half the events in this play could ever occur, cannot be the sole cause of its weak effect. Shakespeare's scenes are frequently such, as could not take place in real life; and yet the sensations which they excite are so forcible, that improbability is overpowered by the author's art, and his auditors are made to feel, though they cannot believe. No such magic presides over the play of *Cymbeline* as to transform reason into imagination.

Credibility remains a constant theme in Elizabeth's assessment of more contemporary drama; she praises the authenticity of George Lillo's realistic drama, *Fatal Curiosity,* in spite of the violence in it against which she warns both readers and spectators:

> From the first scene of this tragedy to the last, all is interesting, all is natural—occurrences, as in real life, give rise to passions; passion inspires new thoughts, elevates each sentiment, embellishes the language, and renders every page of the production

either sweetly pathetic, or horribly sublime. . . . Mr. Colman was a warm admirer of Lillo's works, and of this play in particular. He caused it to be rehearsed with infinite care; and, from the reception of the first two acts, and part of the third, he had the hope that it would become extremely popular—but, on the performance of a scene which followed soon after, a certain horror seized the audience, and was manifested by a kind of stifled scream. After having shuddered at this tragedy, even as a fiction, it is dreadful to be told,—that the most horrid event which here takes place, is merely the representation of a fact which occurred at a village on the western coast of England.[4]

She praises the naturalistic characterization of Goldsmith's *She Stoops to Conquer,* though the improbability of certain events makes it in her opinion more like farce than comedy:

> *She Stoops to Conquer* had indeed more the quality of farce than of a regular, five-act drama: but, although some of the incidents are improbable, there is not one character in the piece, which is not perfectly in nature—The reader will find his country friends in the whole family of the Hardcastles; and, most likely, one of his town acquaintances in the modest Mr. Marlow.—From the most severe judge, to the name of farce can be this comedy's sole reproach; and he must even then allow, that it is an extremely pleasant one; and a far better evening's entertainment, than the sentimental comedies of Kelly and other dramatists of that day—at which the auditors were never incited either to laugh or to cry.

Elizabeth often expresses, too, the specific point of view of a woman. Of *Henry IV, Part I* she writes:

> This is a play which all men admire; and which most women dislike. Many revolting expressions in the comic parts, much boisterous courage in some of the graver scenes, together with Falstaff's unwieldy person, offend every female auditor; and whilst a facetious Prince of Wales is employed in taking purses on the highway, a lady would rather see him stealing hearts at a ball, though the event might produce more fatal consequences.

In her comments on Nathaniel Lee's *The Rival Queens* she writes, very interestingly:

> Dryden's Octavia is, however, much less refined than Lee's Statira. The first pardons her husband's love to Cleopatra, and is willing to accept his reluctant return, with an alienated heart;—whilst the last makes a solemn vow, never more to behold the man who loves her to distraction, because he has given her one proof of incontinence. There is deep knowledge of the female heart evinced in both these incidents. A woman is glad to be reconciled to the husband, who does not love her, upon any conditions—whilst the wife, who is beloved, is outrageous if she be not adored. Yet Lee should have considered, that such

delicate expectations of perpetual constancy, as he has given to his pagan queen, Statira, were not, so late as his own time, prevalent, even among Christian queens. The consorts of Charles II and Louis XIV, saw as many partakers of their royal spouses' love, as the Sultana of Constantinople, and with equal patience.

As a successful writer of comedy, she is particularly concerned with its nature and with the distinction between comedy, farce, comic opera, and burlesque, the various forms of lighter entertainment prevalent at the time.[5] Of Arthur Murphy's comedy, *All in the Wrong,* she writes:

> Molière's genius has been of use to many of our comic dramatists, who, at the time Mr. Murphy wrote, enriched their works with his wit and humour, without calling themselves translators, but merely occasional debtors to his primary invention. . . . The dialogue of *All in the Wrong* is of a species so natural, that it never in one sentence soars above the proper standard of elegant life; and the incidents that occur are bold without extravagance or apparent artifice, which is the criterion on which judgment should be formed between comedy and farce.

Broad farce she considered inelegant, as her comments introducing George Colman the Younger's comedy, *John Bull,* make clear:

> The irresistible broad humour, which is the predominant quality of this drama, is so exquisitely interspersed with touches of nature more refined, with occasional flashes of wit, and with events so interesting that, if the production is not of that perfect art which the most rigid critic demands, he must still acknowledge it is as a bond, given under the author's own hand, that he can, if he pleases, produce, in all its various branches, a complete comedy.

> The introduction of farces into the entertainments of the theatre has been one cause of destroying that intimate comedy, which such critics require. The art which has been accustomed to delight in painting of caricature, regards a picture from real life as an insipid work. The extravagance of farce has given to the Town a taste for the pleasant convulsion of big laughter, and smiles are contemned as the token of insipid amusement.

Comedy requires an exact judgment, acute observation of manners, and above all the elegancies of wit. Of Richard Cumberland's comedy, *The Brothers,* she says:

> To give blunt repartee, or other humourous dialogue, to characters in low life; to produce variety of comic accidents, by which a petty tradesman, a sailor, or a country clown, shall raise a peal of laughter, is the easy attainment of every whimsical writer; but to exhibit the weak side of wisdom, the occasional foibles which impede the full exertion of good sense,

the chance awkwardness of the elegant, and mistakes of the correct; to bestow wit on beauty, and to depict the passions, visible in the young, as well as in the aged;—these are efforts of intellect, required in the production of a good comedy, and can alone confer the title of a good comic author.

She also comments shrewdly on the basic technical problem of adapting novels to the theatre in the case of Colman the Younger, whose version of Godwin's novel, *Caleb Williams,* retitled *The Iron Chest,* she discusses:

> Narrative, on the stage, must never be diffuse; the play must be comprised in a certain number of pages; and, when the foundation of a fable is of the magnitude of murder, any abridgment of circumstances, requisite to make description both clear and probable, must be of fatal import to all the scenes so founded. British spectators of a tragedy, moreover, even wish to behold the assassin's dagger reeking, before they listen to his groans of remorse; and the offence received, is sometimes demanded in exhibition, ere they will sympathize in the thirst of vengeance.

With all these values in mind, it is interesting to see which dramatists emerge best from Elizabeth's evaluation, always keeping in mind that the choice of the plays was predetermined for her. On Shakespeare she avoids offering much generalized comment, preferring in the main to quote Johnson, and relying specially on describing the effectiveness, or otherwise, of the key parts on the stage as played by Garrick, Kemble, Henderson, and others. As we have seen, she does not favor *Romeo and Juliet* because (she claims) it is not pleasing to an 'elegant audience,' and because what happens in the play strains credibility, as does the action in *Cymbeline.* Although the characterization in *Henry IV, Part I* is drawn from nature, the dialogue she finds offensive to genteel taste, whereas *Henry V* and *Henry VIII* are excellent precisely because they emphasize moral issues, as indeed, she says, does *Macbeth.* However, she singles out the acting parts which have proven most successful with audiences; though Garrick failed as Romeo, and as King John, he succeeded as Faulconbridge and Richard III; Henderson made a fine Falstaff, while Kemble was outstanding as Jaques, as the Duke in *Measure for Measure,* as Macbeth and Coriolanus, among many other Shakespearean parts.

She makes an interesting point about censorship affecting the final act of *Richard III*:

> In the reign of William and Mary, the whole first act of this play was omitted in representation, by order of the licenser; who assigned as his reason— that the distresses of Henry VI, who is killed in the first act, by Richard, would put weak people too much in mind of King James II, who was then living an exile in France.

She speaks, too, about the censoring of certain lines from *Coriolanus* during the 1790s—the key period of the revolution in France—since, 'certain sentences in this play are . . . of dangerous tendency at certain times,' because of possible repercussion from 'the lower order of people.' However, the lines recently withheld have now been restored, she adds.

She comments, too, on the revisions imposed on Shakespeare's plays, especially in the case of *King Lear:*

> Tate alters the Play of *King Lear,* and instead of suffering the good Cordelia to die of grief, as Shakespeare had done, he rewards her with life, love, and a throne. Addison, in his Spectator, condemns him for this; Dr. Johnson commends him for it; Both showing excellent reasons. Then comes Steevens, who gives a better reason than all, why they are all wrong.[6]

Her character descriptions are often apt and clear. She speaks of King John's 'grovelling mind,' and of other Shakespearean characters, such as:

> *Coriolanus*: Here . . . the likeness of a stubborn schoolboy, as well as of the obstinate general of an army, is so exquisitely delineated, that every mental trait of the one can be discerned in the propensities of the other, so as forcibly to call to the recollection, that children are the originals of man.

> *Antony and Cleopatra*: The reader will be also introduced to the queen of Egypt, in her undress, as well as in her royal robes; he will be, as it were, admitted to her toilet, where, in converse with her waiting-woman, she will suffer him to arrive at her most secret thoughts and designs: and he will quickly perceive, that the arts of a queen with her lover, are just the same as those practised by any other beauty—'If you find Antony sad,' cries Cleopatra, to her female attendant, 'say I am dancing; if he is in mirth, report that I am suddenly sick.'

> These natural contrivances of artful woman, labouring to make her conquest and her power secure, are even outdone in truth of description, by that fretful impatience, with which she is tortured, in the absence of Antony from Egypt: By the gloom which the poet has spread throughout her whole palace, whilst he is away: and by the silly sentences, which, during this restless period, she is impelled to utter.

> 'Where think'st thou he is now? stands he, or sits he? Or does he walk? or is he on his horse?'

> Silly sentences to all who never were in love, but sensible, and most intelligent to all who ever were.

> Equal to the foregoing conversation, is that in which this impassioned queen makes anxious enquiry concerning the charms of her rival Octavia. But these

minute touches of nature by which Shakespeare proves a queen to be a woman are, perhaps, the very cause why Dryden's picture of the Egyptian court is preferred on the stage before this. There are things so diminutive, they cannot be perceived in a theatre; whilst in a closet, their very smallness constitutes their value.

The Restoration dramatists represented here—Farquhar, Vanbrugh, and Congreve especially—trouble her. She responds to their talents as dramatists and dialogue writers, while she deplores the licentious indulgences their plays represent. Even severe adaptation cannot, she thinks, veil the immorality of the situations and motivations involved. She even castigates Gay's *The Beggar's Opera,* as we have seen. She does not appear to rate Beaumont and Fletcher, or for that matter Dryden, very highly as dramatists, while among the playwrights she considers to be too literary is Addison, whom she admires more as a Christian gentleman than as a dramatist. Moving nearer her own time, she is much more ready to admire the best work of Cibber, Rowe, Southerne, Lillo (the latter for originality), Goldsmith, Holcroft and the Colmans, though none escapes criticism when she feels this is due. Among women dramatists she praises Mrs. Centlivre (though decidedly not for the moral implications of her plays), Joanna Baillie, and to a lesser degree, Mrs. Cowley.

Her praise of Sheridan, the leading dramatist of wit and elegance in her time, is generous. She prefers *The School for Scandal* to *The Rivals*—the only play, apart from Sheridan's comic opera, *The Duenna,* the editors included in *The British Theatre* selection.

> *The Rivals* is an elegant, an interesting, a humorous, and most entertaining comedy; but in neither fable, character, nor incident, is it, like *The School for Scandal*—inimitable. If Mrs. Malaprop, Acres, Sir Lucius, and some other personages in this drama were not upon the stage before *The Rivals* was acted, they have all appeared there, in various dramas, many a time since. But where can Sir Peter and Lady Teazle, where can the Surface family be found, either in original or copy, except in *The School for Scandal?* Where can be traced the plot or events of that extraordinary play, or where even the shadows of them. . . .

> Sir Anthony Absolute is generally counted the most prominent, though Faulkland is, no doubt, the most original character in the comedy. One particular circumstance adds extreme interest to this part. It is supposed by the author's most intimate friends that, in delineating Faulkland, he took a discerning view of his own disposition, in all the anxious tenderness of a youthful lover; and has here accurately described every sentiment, every feeling, which at that trying period of his life, agitated his troubled heart. The very town of Bath, just before the writing of this play, had been the identical scene of all his restless hopes and fears.

The impressive language, the refined notions, the enthusiastic, yet natural passion of Faulkland for Julia, with all the captivating charms of mind and expression which has been here given to this object of adoration, are positive vouchers that some very exalted idea of the force of love, if not its immediate power over himself, had at that time possession of the poet's fancy.

Elizabeth does not approve of the character of Mrs. Malaprop, and addresses us directly in the 20th century when dealing with her:

> Against the illiterate Mrs. Malaprop, common occurrence and common sense protest. That any Englishwoman, for these five hundred years past, in the habit of keeping good company, or any company, could have made use of the words—*extirpate* for *exculpate, exhort* for *escort,* and *malevolence* for *benevolence*—seems too far removed from probability to make a reasonable auditor smile.

> When future generations shall naturally suppose that an author of Mr. Sheridan's reputation drew men and women exactly as he found them; this sketch of a woman of family and fortune, at the end of the eighteenth century, will assure the said generations that the advance of female knowledge in Great Britain was far more tardy than in any other European nation.

Occasionally, plays out of the ordinary offer her opportunities for comment on unconventional subjects. *George Barnwell, or The London Merchant* (1731), George Lillo's tragedy based on a popular ballad, represented for her a 'new species of pathetic drama.' The author of this tragedy was a tradesman,' she writes, 'which might influence his taste for the description of scene of humble life.' She traces the ups and downs in favor that this tragedy in prose about humble people experienced with audiences used only to witnessing the destructive passions of the great. She holds Lillo in high regard, and quotes Fielding's commendation of him as a man, written when he died in 1739. Then again, the opera, *Inkle and Yarico,* by George Colman the Younger opened up, like Southerne's *Oroonoko,* the subject of slavery. Of this she says:

> This opera was written, when the author was very young, and, should he live to be very old, he will have reason to be proud of it to his latest day, for it is one of those plays which is independent of time, of place, or of circumstance, for its value. It was popular before the subject of the abolition of the slave trade was popular. It has the peculiar honour of preceding that great question. It was the bright forerunner of alleviation to the hardships of slavery.

Similarly, Richard Cumberland's *The Jew* (1794) introduced a subject hitherto absent in the English theatre, where Jews were normally seen by tradition as either villains or comic characters, as in *The Jew of Malta* and *The Merchant of Venice.* Elizabeth comments:

> When a zealous Christian writes in favour of a Jew, it is proof of the truest christianity. The author of this play has done more than befriend one unfortunate descendant of Abraham; he has taken the twelve tribes of Israel under his protection. The bravery of this enterprise was equal to its charity— the execution has been masterly—and complete success the reward of that compassion which incited him to his labour. . . . The play, in its formation, is adverse to the public taste, and in its sentiments contrary to public prejudice; still the public were charmed with it.

Finally, it is natural she should take constant pleasure in describing actors at work. Impressions of acting are peculiarly difficult to reconstruct for readers who have never seen the original performer, but Elizabeth is never afraid to try. Her recollection of the Kemble-Siddons production of *Macbeth* at the Theatre Royal, Drury Lane, inspires her:

> To those who are unacquainted with the effect wrought by theatrical action and decoration, it may not be superfluous to say—the huge rocks, the enormous caverns, and blasted heaths of Scotland, in the scenery; the highland warrior's dress, of centuries past, worn by the soldiers and their generals; the splendid robes and banquet at the royal court held at Fores; the awful, yet inspiring music which accompanies words assimilated to each sound; and above all, the fear, the terror, the remorse; the agonizing throbs and throes, which speak in looks, whispers, sudden starts, and writhings, by Kemble and Mrs. Siddons, all tending to one great precept—*Thou shalt not murder.*

Above all, she enjoys celebrating John Philip Kemble, whose performances shine again through the energy of her prose, and span the whole series of volumes. He excels, she claims, in Shakespeare, being second only to Garrick, to whose genius as an actor she frequently refers, for example, his Gloucester in *Richard III:*

> Garrick, Henderson, Kemble, and Cooke, have all in their turn been favoured with the love, as well as the admiration of the town for acting Richard. . . . Garrick appears to have been the actor, of all others, best suited for this character. His diminutive figure gave the best personal likeness of the crooked-back king. He had, besides, if tradition may be relied on, the first abilities as a mimic; and Richard himself was a mass of mimicry, except in his ambition and his cruelty.

Among the many parts to which she makes special reference in describing Kemble is his performance as the King in *King John:*

> The part of King John is held most difficult to perform. John is no hero, and yet he is a murderer; his best actions are debased by meanness, deceit, or cowardice, and yet he is a king. Here is then to be portrayed, thirst of blood, without thirst of fame; and dignity of person, with a groveling mind. . . .

The genius of Kemble gleams terrific through the gloomy John. No auditor can hear him call for his

'Kingdom's rivers to take their course through his burn'd bosom,'

and not feel for that moment parched with a scorching fever.

As we have seen, she praises his performance in *Macbeth* and among other Shakespearean roles:

Of Jaques in *As You Like It:* Kemble's Jaques is in the highest estimation with the public: it is one of those characters in which he gives certain bold testimonies of genius, which no spectator can controvert. Yet the mimic art has very little share in this grand exhibition.

Of Coriolanus: Kemble 'renders the utmost summit of the actor's art.'

As for other plays than Shakespeare's, she admires especially his work

As Osmyn in Congreve's *The Mourning Bride:* Kemble looks nobly, majestically, in Osmyn, and reminds the audience of the lines,

—Tall pillar rear its marble head,
Looking tranquility. . . .
And shoots a chillness to the trembling heart.

As Zanga in Young's parallel to Shakespeare's *Othello, The Revenge:* This character is of such magnitude, and so unprotected by those who surround him, that few performers will undertake to represent it; a less number still have succeeded in braving the danger. Mr. Kemble stands foremost among those, and draws some splendid audiences every year, merely to see *him,* though the intervals between his exits and entrances are sure to be passed in lassitude.

The many introductions for *The British Theatre* series were to be the only substantial undertaking in dramatic or literary criticism Elizabeth was to publish. In doing so, in the earliest years of the 19th century, she established professional standards for the woman critic that had no previous parallel. In particular, her comments were valuable because they revealed in virtually every instance the knowledge and experience of an actress who over a number of years had enjoyed the privilege of working with and observing at the closest range the performances of the best players of the time, not now and then but on hundreds of occasions, behind the scenes and on the stage, as participant and as member of an audience in the theatres of London and the provinces.

Notes

The introductory comments written by Elizabeth Inchbald for the 25-volume anthology of plays, *The British*

Theatre (1808) form the primary source for this chapter. Since the five plays making up each volume with their introductions are page-numbered individually, the many comments quoted in this chapter can only be referred to by indicating the number of the volume in which each play appears. They are listed below in alphabetic order of title; dates are given for plays from the Restoration period to the early 19th century:

All in the Wrong (Murphy, 1761), Vol. XV

Antony and Cleopatra (Shakespeare), Vol. IV

As You Like It (Shakespeare), Vol. III

The Beaux' Stratagem (Farquhar, 1707), Vol. VIII

The Beggar's Opera (Gay, 1728), Vol. XII

The Belles' Stratagem (Mrs. Cowley, 1780), Vol. XIX

A Bold Stroke for a Wife (Mrs. Centlivre, 1718), Vol. XI

The Brothers (Cumberland, 1769), Vol. XVIII

Cato (Addison, 1713), Vol. VIII

The Conscious Lovers (Steele, 1722), Vol. XII

The Country Girl (Garrick, 1766), Vol. XVI

Cymbeline (Shakespeare), Vol. IV

De Monfort (Joanna Baillie, 1798), Vol. XXIV

The Dramatist (Reynolds, 1789), Vol. XX

The Duenna (Sheridan, 1775), Vol. XIX

George Barnwell (The London Merchant, Lillo, 1731), Vol. XI

Henry IV, Part I (Shakespeare), Vol. II

Henry V (Shakespeare), Vol. II

Henry VIII (Shakespeare), Vol. III

Inkle and Yarico (Colman the Younger, 1796), Vol. XX

The Iron Chest (Colman the Younger, 1796), Vol. XXI

Isabella, or the Fatal Marriage (Southerne, 1694), Vol. VII

The Jew (Cumberland, 1794), Vol. XVIII

John Bull (Colman the Younger, 1803), Vol. XXI

King John (Shakespeare), Vol. I

King Lear (Shakespeare), Vol. IV

The London Merchant (Barnwell, Lillo, 1731), Vol. XI

Macbeth (Shakespeare), Vol. IV

Measure for Measure (Shakespeare), Vol. III

The Mountaineers (Colman the Younger, 1793), Vol. XXI

The Mourning Bride (Congreve, 1697), Vol. VIII

Oroonoko (Southerne, 1695), Vol. VII

The Revenge (Young, 1721), Vol. XII

Richard III (Shakespeare), Vol. I

The Rival Queens (Lee, 1677), Vol. VI

The Rivals (Sheridan, 1775), Vol. XIX

The Road to Ruin (Holcroft, 1792), Vol. XXIV

Romeo and Juliet (Shakespeare), Vol. I

She Stoops to Conquer (Goldsmith, 1773), Vol. XVII

She Wou'd and She Wou'd Not (Cibber, 1702), Vol. IX

Wheel of Fortune (Cumberland, 1795), Vol. XVIII

Notes for this chapter indicated by superior figures follow:

[1] See *The British Theatre,* Vol. XXI.

[2] The prefaces were, of course, intended for the general reader, not the scholar, or the literary or dramatic critic.

[3] For this and the quotations following, see Allardyce Nicoll, *A History of English Drama 1660 to 1900,* Vol. III, pp. 5, 10, 15-16.

[4] George Lillo's play, *Fatal Curiosity* (or, *Guilt its own Punishment,* 1736, but presented by Elizabeth Inchbald as altered by Colman, 1783), is described by Allardyce Nicoll as an example of 'sentimentalized bourgeois drama.' It is a domestic tragedy of three acts written in verse. Set in Penryn, near Falmouth in Cornwall, and based on what is alleged to have been a real-life incident, it involves an elderly couple, Wilmot and his wife Agnes, who live on in penury, believing that their son, who has in the past gone away to India, is now dead. But Young Wilmot returns. He chooses to visit his parents in disguise, taking with him a casket of jewels. The sight of this wealth destroys their consciences, and, like Macbeth and Lady Macbeth, they are driven by want to murder their guest, Agnes urging

her husband to commit the crime. When they realize the truth, that it is indeed their own son that they have murdered, Old Wilmot turns on his wife and kills her, and then commits suicide. Colman modified the violence in the play, toning down the dialogue.

[5] It should not be overlooked that Elizabeth Inchbald was herself the writer of farces as well as comedies. She included *Child of Nature, The Wedding Day,* and *The Midnight Hour* in her self-selected *Collection of Farces and other Afterpieces* collected into seven volumes in 1809.

[6] See for example, M. W. Black and M. A. Shaaber, Shakespeare's *Seventeenth Century Editors 1632-1685,* New York, MLA, 1937; Montagu Summers (ed.), *Shakespeare Adaptations: The Tempest, The Mock Tempest, King Lear,* New York, Haskell House, 1966; *Davenant's Macbeth* from the Yale Manuscript, edited by Christopher Spencer, New Haven, Yale University Press, 1961; and Nahum Tate, *The History of King Lear,* edited by James Black, Lincoln, University of Nebraska Press, 1975.

Works Cited

Boaden, James. *Memoirs of the Life of John Philip Kemble.* London, 1825.

————. *Memoirs of Mrs. Siddons.* London, 1827.

————. *The Life of Mrs. Jordan.* London, 1831.

————. *Memoirs of Mrs. Inchbald.* London, 1833.

[Inchbald, Elizabeth. Prefaces in *The British Theatre.* London: Longman, Hurst, Rees, & Orme, 1806-1808.

————. (Ed.) *A Collection of Farces and other Afterpieces.* London: Longman, Hurst, Rees, & Orme, 1809.]

Kelly, Gary. *The English Jacobin Novel, 1780-1805.* London: Oxford University Press, 1976.

Littlewood, Sam. R. *Elizabeth Inchbald and her Circle.* London: Daniel O'Connor, 1921.

McKee, William. *Elizabeth Inchbald.* Ph.D. Thesis, Washington, 1935.

Nicoll, Allardyce. *A History of the English Drama 1660-1900: Vol. III, Late 18th Century Drama.* Cambridge University Press, 1955.

————. *Introduction to Lesser English Comedies of the 18th Century.* Oxford University Press, 1927. The volume contains Elizabeth Inchbald's play, *Everyone has his Fault.*

Park, B. R. *Thomas Holcroft and Elizabeth Inchbald: Studies in the 18th Century Drama of Ideas.* Ph.D. Thesis for the Faculty of Philosophy, Columbia University, 1952.

Mary Anne Schofield (essay date 1990)

SOURCE: "Elizabeth Inchbald and Jane West," in *Masking and Unmasking the Female Mind: Disguising Romances in Feminine Fiction, 1713-1799,* University of Delaware Press, 1990, pp. 175-87.

[*In the following excerpt, Schofield contends that Inchbald manipulated sentimental images of women in her novels and in doing so, subverted traditional romantic conventions. (Only those footnotes pertaining to the excerpt below have been reprinted.)*]

By the end of the century, the masquerading romances had a decidedly different look from those of the earlier years. The adventures of the heroine still made up the mainstay of the romance plot, and the writers continued their feminist bias by depicting the abduction, disguises, rapes, attempted rapes, and escapes of their female protagonists, with little to relieve the intensity of the attacks. . . . What makes the later novels even more grim is not just the continued harassment of the heroines but the author's rational, outspoken critique of this tortured, romance form. (The nonfiction tracts of the period support this increased outspokenness, though there had been little amelioration of the feminine situation.)[1]

The rhetorical structure also indicates an increased awareness of the feminine plight. Rather than Haywood's technique of euphoric plot subversion and distortion, the later writers such as Fielding, Lennox, and Smith maintain the happily-ever-after ending, but precede it with so many "adventures" that the reader can hardly believe the heroine will survive. These "adventures" are patterned on the real-life exploits of the authors themselves who clearly define and state their positions in their numerous prefaces. It is impossible to mistake the feminist attitude—in real life, as in fiction, women are harassed, exploited, and subjugated. Fielding, Lennox, and Smith speak directly to these conditions. Elizabeth Inchbald and Jane West, however, exploit the romance rhetoric completely by thoroughly inverting the form itself.

Elizabeth Inchbald's (1753-1821) *A Simple Story* (1791)[2] appears as the most stylized of these late eighteenth-century romances. It becomes literally "a romance's romance," though such esoteric labels did not hinder its popularity, which required a second printing just three months after its initial publication. Maria Edgeworth writes to Inchbald that the realistic elements in the novel were unsurpassed: "I never read a novel that . . . so completely possessed me with the belief in the real existence of all the people it represents."[3] Such believable detail can be used because realism had already been introduced by Fielding, Lennox, and Smith, but Inchbald's Miss Milner is a far cry from Pamela. She is full of faults; she is vain, willful, a tease. She despises men and yet manages to catch one of the most important bachelors of the town. Unlike the qualified euphoric tone of the midcentury novelist, Inchbald presents characters who lead tragic lives. She cannot draw delightful young women with minor faults who are educated by the men. Forthright and outspoken, her women, Miss Milner and Agnes Primrose especially, can only be punished by the controlling male ideology for the position they adopt. The following year Mary Wollstonecraft would publish *A Vindication of the Rights of Woman,* making explicit the demands and judgments that Inchbald was able to present only fictionally.

Occupying much the same place of importance as Fielding's *The Cry* (1754), with its outspoken analysis and critique of the romance genre, so *A Simple Story* also exploits and explodes the romance convention. Inchbald achieves these results this time not by analytically dissecting the genre but instead by actually creating, first, the romance itself with a seventeen-year lapse in the story (between the two volumes) and, second, the tragic fate of the heroine.

Inchbald begins *A Simple Story* demurely enough by borrowing Charlotte Smith's unmasking technique and writing about herself in the preface:

> It has been the destiny of the writer of this Story, to be occupied throughout her life, in what has the least suited either her inclination or capacity—with an invincible impediment in her speech, it was her lot for thirteen years to gain a subsistence by public speaking—and, with the utmost detestation to the fatigue of inventing, a constitution suffering under a sedentary life, and an education confined to the narrow boundaries prescribed to her sex, it has been her fate to devote a tedious seven years to the unremitting labour of literary productions. (1)

After an extensive career in the theater,[4] Inchbald turns her attention to the novel, most specifically to investigate educational issues. She is quite candid as she remarks about the type of education she herself had, and it is just this concern that provides the main plot of *A Simple Story,* for here Inchbald provides another treatment of the ubiquitous "young woman's entrance into the world" narrative. Like her volatile predecessors, Inchbald wants to uncover the shocking naïveté of her female readers and educate them out of their complacency. Like Miss Milner, they must enter the world fully cognizant of their needing to deal with unscrupulous men. If nothing else, *A Simple Story* presents stark realism.

Miss Milner is introduced by a well-seasoned slightly jaundiced narrative voice, who observes: "Yet let not our over-scrupulous readers be misled, and extend their idea of her virtue so as to magnify it beyond that which frail mortals commonly possess; nor must they cavil, if, on a nearer view, they find it less" (14). Miss Milner is human, and, initially, controlled only by vanity. Early on, she learns to put on a good face to the outside world. Because she is so young, decisions are left to her guardian.

> How much do different circumstances not only alter the manners, but even the persons of some people! Miss Milner in the drawing room at Lord Elmwood's surrounded by listeners, by admirers (for even her enemies beheld her with admiration), and warm with their approbation and applause—and Miss Milner, with no giddy observer to give a false eclat to her actions, left destitute of all but her own understanding, (which severely condemns her), and upon the point of receiving the censure of her guardian and friend, are two different beings.—Though still beautiful beyond description, she does not look even in person the same.—In the last mentioned situation, she was shorter in stature than in the former—she was paler—she was thinner—and a very different contour presided over her whole air, and all her features. (50)

Miss Milner is not really disguising; it is only the priest, Sandford, friend of Dorriforth, who thinks Miss Milner is other than she appears, and he spends most of his time trying to trap her in a plot that will reveal what he thinks is her true nature. No other level exists in Miss Milner, however, that cannot be discovered and excused because of her age. Dorriforth favors an alliance with Sir Edward Ashton; Miss Milner appears to favor Lord Frederick Lawnley. The object of her affection is immaterial; power and control are at issue here. Initially, Dorriforth "was charmed to find her disposition so little untractable" (33) and thinks this bodes well for "the future prosperity of his guardianship" (33). Yet he is only seeing a masked Miss Milner. It is Miss Woodley (another woman) who is able to unmask her and who discovers an extraordinary mature and sophisticated woman underneath the ingenue who boldly, unabashedly asserts (concerning her relationship with Dorriforth): "I love him with all the passion of a mistress, and with all the tenderness of a wife" (72). She has uncovered the heart of the woman.

When Miss Milner, at last, confronts Dorriforth alone, she casts all disguises off:

> In his presence, unsupported by . . . a third person, every grace she had practised, every look she had borrowed, to set off her charms were annihilated, and she became a native beauty, with the artless arguments of reason, only for her aid.—Awed thus, by his power, from everything but what she really was, she never was perhaps half so bewitching as in those timid, respectful, and embarrassed moments she passed alone with him. (82)

Miss Milner is able to "read" this scene correctly; Dorrisforth is not. She is aware that the issue is one of power and control. And she wants to have it.

She continues to not express her affection for Dorriforth, but resorts to more and more subterfuge to mask her true feelings and test her power over him. She baits him; she determines to go to the masquerade though strictly forbidden. She constantly forces Dorriforth/Elmwood to take a position vis-à-vis her femininity.

Both Woodley and Dorriforth force Miss Milner to mask; like the controlling feminine ideologies, they must keep the woman in her place and that means she must be disguised. Dorriforth can only comprehend her if she is the pupil and he the instructor. When he learns of Miss Milner's love for him, *he* discards *her* mask of powerlessness and replaces it with one of romantic though still male-controlled love:

> Within a few days, in the house of Lord Elmwood, every thing and every person wore a new face.— His Lordship was the profest lover of Miss Milner— she, the happiest of human beings—Miss Woodley partaking in her joy—while Mr. Sandford was lamenting with the deepest concern, that Miss Fenton had been supplanted. (136)

With this declaration, power and control shift. Now Miss Milner masks herself:

> Perfectly secure of the affections of the man she loved, her declining health no longer threatened her; her declining spirits returned as before; and the suspicions of her guardian being now changed to the liberal confidence of a doating lover, she now again professed all her former follies, all her fashionable levities, and indulged them with less restraint than she had ever done. . . . she, who as his ward, had been ever gentle, and (when he strenuously opposed) always obedient; he now found as a mistress, sometimes haughty; and to opposition, always insolent. (139)

Inchbald presents a story of iconographic masquerade in this late-century tale, which culminates in the first volume with the masked ball given by the fashionable Mrs. G————. Miss Milner had never attended a masquerade and was anxious to go; Lord Elmwood forbids her attendance. "'I am sure your lordship,' continued she, 'with all your saintliness, can have no objection to my being present at the masquerade, provided I go as a Nun. . . . that is a habit . . . which covers a multitude of faults'" (152). When he refuses to attend, saying he will not "play the buffoon at a masquerade" (153), Miss Milner resolves that nothing will stop her from attending short of being physically locked into Lord Elmwood's house. Instead of the nun disguise, she decides to go as Diana, but Miss Woodley "was astonished at her venturing on such a character— for although it was the representative of the goddess of

Chastity, yet from the buskins, and the petticoat made to festoon far above the ankle, it had, on the first glance, the appearance of a female much less virtuous" (155).

Such behavior tests Dorriforth to the limit, and Miss Milner finally forces his hand; it is a power struggle to the end. When he writes and severs their engagement and almost the entire relationship, "her tones sunk into the flattest dejection.—Not only her colour, but her features became changed; her eyes lost their brilliancy, her lips seemed to hang without the power of motion, her head drooped, and her dress was wholly neglected" (179). Strangely enough, the denouement of this volume finds Dorriforth/Elmwood marrying Miss Milner, with a slight hint of doom to follow, since in the haste of the ceremony, the only ring that he had to give her was a mourning ring. In other words, the wedding did nothing to explain or consolidate the issue of power.

The second volume begins after a seventeen-year hiatus, with Lady Elmwood on her deathbed; her virtuous life has been thrown away on a life of dissipation that has lead to her early death. The plot focuses on the fate of Dorriforth and Miss Milner's daughter, Lady Matilda. Supervised by an older Miss Woodley, Miss Matilda practices deception from the first because she is secretly loved by Dorriforth's ward, Lord Rushbrook. Unlike her mother, Matilda is forced physically to hide her person when either Dorriforth/Elmwood is living in the country house or when Rushbrook comes for a visit. She willingly accepts the situation that puts her in male control; in fact, she seems to welcome it. Because she indulges in disguise, Miss Matilda is also subject to the romance heroine's mask, and, predictably, she is abducted by Lord Margrave's henchmen in an effort to make her submit to his offers. But the seduction is too informal, too predictable; Miss Matilda remains too calm. It is as if she is a character playing a part.

In the second portion of the story, Inchbald has given the reader an allegorization of the first part. It is the working out of Miss Milner's history in the disguise of her daughter that brings the reader to the necessary sense of denouement that fiction demands, to a sense of closure. The honesty of the daughter more than makes up for the disguise and guile of the mother. Inchbald's moralizing is obvious: in terms of the male ideology, Miss Milner is an example of what not to be; she cannot be controlled. Her daughter provides the man with a heroine, the one who willingly accepts domination. Part One exhibits the negative effects of masquerade, while Part Two strips away the disguise and shows the true worth of the heroine according to male law. Part One tries to present the feminine text, while Part Two is the man's story. Because of the highly contrived and artificial seventeen-year hiatus that occurs between the sections, Inchbald consciously presents a "made artifact" to the reader. The archetypal suspension of disbelief is called into question as the reader watches her conscious creation of a story that unmasks the masquerade and the romance to reveal the bare bones of the romance genre. *A Simple Story* is a deceptively simple fable.

Inchbald's *Nature and Art* (1795)[5] continues this deceptive presentation, again turning large issues of revolution and the treatment of women into almost allegorically stylized, simplistic fare. *Nature and Art,* perhaps patterned on Thomas Day's *Sandford and Merton,* is the story of two brothers, William and Henry, and the account of their adolescence and mature lives together, with a more detailed story of the lives of their sons, cousins William and Henry. The elder, Henry, is an accomplished violinist; William attends the university and becomes a clergyman. Henry marries a singer; William becomes even more snobbish and finally marries a woman of consequence, the Lady Clementina. The brothers drift apart. Henry's wife dies within a year, and William's Lady Clementina becomes more and more vain and haughty. After his wife's death, Henry goes to Africa with his infant son; eleven years later, Little Henry is sent to London to be taken care of by his uncle and aunt because of serious uprisings in Africa. The major portion of the book, then, focuses on the different educations of the two cousins. The two characters speak a different language: William, like his father, thinks of only himself; Henry, however, considers others. As Inchbald notes, Henry "would call *compliments, lies—reserve* he would call *pride—stateliness, affection—* and for the words *war* and *battle,* he constantly substituted the word *massacre*" (27:246; emphasis added). This difference in the characters' rhetoric extends, naturally, to their life philosophies as well. When they reach their twentieth year, the men fall in love: Henry with Rebecca, the fourth daughter of the curate of the parish; William with Agnes, the daughter of a poor cottager in the village. William aims only at seduction and triumph; Henry, virtuous devotion. Henry finds a chaste, sublime mate in Rebecca, whereas William disguises, seduces, and abandons poor Agnes Primrose.

Inchbald gives us a moral allegory here about the use and abuse of disguise and power. Her presentation is stylized; her preference is clear, as she writes when William and Henry return to their summer estate:

> While Henry flew to Mr. Rymer's house with a *conscience* clear, and a *face enlightened* with gladness; while he met Rebecca with open-hearted friendship and frankness, which charmed her soul to peaceful happiness; William *skulked around* the cottage of Agnes, *dreading detection;* and when towards midnight he found the means to obtain the company of the sad inhabitant, he grew impatient at her tears and sobs, at the delicacy with which she withheld her caresses, that he burst into bitter upbraidings at her coyness; and at length . . . abruptly left her. (27: 286-87; emphasis added)

Agnes "felt herself debased by a ruffian—yet still, having loved him when she thought him a far different character, the blackest proof of the deception could not erase a sentiment formed whilst she was deceived" (27:287). Inchbald, however, writes so the reader will not be "deceived." She exposes the romantic expectations of her reader claiming that "Rebecca Rymer and Agnes Primrose are its heroines" (27:270) and tells the reader to read on for more moral instruction than romantic escapism.

Further, she writes to expose the intense cruelty of men and their legal system. In the recounting of Agnes's tale of seduction (the story of the rake and the wanton), all the blame is attached to the man. Agnes is seduced by William, abandons her baby, is made to appear first before the dean (the grandfather of the child), reclaims the child but is forced to leave the village and leads a life ultimately ending in a brothel, only at the last to appear before Judge William, who sentences her to death. Faced with this barrage of male authority and power, Agnes "was still more disconcerted; said, and unsaid; confessed herself the mother . . . declared she did not know, then owned she *did* know, the name of the man who had undone her, but would never utter it" (27:318-19). As William delivers his verdict, "she shrunk, and seemed to stagger with the deadly blow; writhed under the weight of *his* minute justice (27:350). Her deathbed confession (27:352ff.) is a further indictment of the male system, for she still shoulders the blame and accepts the responsibility. Inchbald, however, is not done with her castigation of the male for she has even the virtuous Rebecca judged by the male (the Dean and William), browbeaten, and punished.

This surely is not a romance world that Inchbald presents. Like *A Simple Story,* she has pared down the romance rhetoric so one is faced with the skeleton structure, the stark confrontation between a man and woman. Inchbald does not disguise the romance tale; with no fanfare, she unmasks it and offers no panacea to her female readers. Unlike the midcentury Pamela, no happy-ever-after ending occurs for the heroine of the 1790s. All the Inchbald heroine can do is survive. Inchbald satirizes the sentimental, romantic midcentury romance. . . .

Notes

[1] See Katherine Rogers, *Feminism in Eighteenth-Century England* (Urbana: University of Illinois Press, 1982).

[2] Elizabeth Inchbald, *A Simple Story,* 4 vols., (1791; reprint in one volume, London: Oxford University Press, 1967). Subsequent citations are noted parenthetically in the text.

[3] Ibid., p. vii.

[4] See Dale Spender, *Mothers of the Novel: 100 Good Women Writers before Jane Austen* (London: Pandora,

1986) for an excellent discussion of Inchbald's stage career.

[5] Elizabeth Inchbald, *Nature and Art,* in *The British Novelists.* ed. Mrs. Barbauld (1794; reprinted, London: Rivington, et al. 1820), vol. 27.

Katharine M. Rogers (essay date 1991)

SOURCE: "Britain's First Woman Drama Critic: Elizabeth Inchbald," in *Curtain Calls: British and American Women and the Theater, 1660-1820,* edited by Mary Anne Schofield and Cecilia Macheski, Ohio University Press, 1991, pp. 277-90.

[*In the essay that follows, Rogers examines Inchbald's role as a professional drama critic, focusing on the difficulties she faced as one of the first female critics and what her criticism reveals about her own literary work.*]

When the publisher Longman decided, in October 1805, to bring out a collection of 125 current acting plays, he asked the popular dramatist Elizabeth Inchbald to provide biographical-critical prefaces. It was an unconventional request for the time, for while women were commonly allowed the fancy and sentiment which produce imaginative literature, they were supposed to lack the judgment required for criticism. Even though Inchbald exerted herself to find merit and soften strictures, especially in the plays of living authors (many of whom were her personal friends), the mere fact that she criticized the work of men angered them and caused her anxiety.[1] In 1808, as *The British Theatre* was nearing completion (it was published over several years), George Colman the Younger took offense at her mild criticism of several of his plays (which actually she judged much more favorably than they deserved) and published an insufferably patronizing letter of reproof.[2] She reprinted it, together with her reply, before his play *The Heir at Law* in the ensuing volume of *The British Theatre* (vol. 21). Mortified that his works have been "somewhat singed, in passing the fiery ordeal of feminine fingers," Colman charges that she missed their actual deficiencies only to find fault in the wrong places; why didn't she apply to him to enlighten her: "I should have been as zealous to save you trouble, as a beau to pick up your fan." Even worse, she had ventured to mention that the elder George Colman's dramatic writing had declined after his initial success: "is this *grateful*" the son ejaculates, "is it *graceful,* from an ingenious lady, who was originally encouraged, and brought forward, as an authoress, by that *very man,* on whose tomb she idly plants this poisonous weed of remark, to choke the laurels which justly grace his memory?"[3] The absurd disproportion between Colman's indignation and the mildness of her criticism shows that he was outraged simply by her presuming to judge her male colleagues; his reproach of ingratitude, that he expected a woman to be grateful for being granted any professional opportunity.

Inchbald's answer opens on a distressingly defensive note, as she deplores having let a publisher persuade her to write criticism, which she describes as "the cursory remarks of a female observer." However, she goes on to answer Colman's arguments far more competently than he had answered hers, and to point out that her obligations to his father consisted only of the attention any theater manager would give to the work of a beginning dramatist. Moving to the attack, she hints delicately that insecurity must underlie Colman's touchiness, "a degree of self-contempt, which I may be pardoned for never having supposed, that any one of my 'manly contemporaries in the drama' could have indulged," and adroitly uses his own play to deflate masculine pretensions based on superior formal education, as she yields to men, and to him in particular, "all those scholastic honors" which he "so excellently described" in his own dramatic character, the comic pedant Dr. Pangloss.

Inchbald's prefaces are most interesting for what they reveal about herself—as an individual and as a woman who had achieved great success in a man's world and yet was intent on maintaining femininity as her contemporaries defined it. Sometimes she enlivens her biographical sketches with insights derived from her own experience. In her essay on *Hamlet,* for example, she imagines Shakespeare as a brilliant youth escaping to the city from a stultifying provincial atmosphere, just as she herself had. She uses her biography of Susannah Centlivre to justify a woman's undertaking the masculine profession of playwriting (*The Busy Body*). Her own experience of earning her living by writing makes her sympathize with the hack dramatist John O'Keefe, who wrote more than was good for his reputation. Critics, she observes, censure writers as if they always published for glory works which they were proud of, but actually they may be pressed by financial need to bring out what their own judgment condemns, all the while "sinking under the shame of their puerile works, and discerning in them more faults, from closer attention and laudable timidity, than the most severe of their censurers can point out" (*The Castle of Andalusia*).[4]

As an experienced actress and playwright, Inchbald understood what worked in the theater—why, for example, Centlivre's comedies were more successful than *The Way of the World.* She appreciated good acting roles and recognized the actor's contribution to the creation of character on stage. Thus Thomas Morton's *A Cure for the Heart Ache,* though undistinguished as literature, illustrates fine theatrical craftsmanship because the characters were designed to be embodied by actors: hence they "exactly please upon the stage, the sphere alone for which they were formed." As a playwright, she considered technical problems such as how

to devise incidents to develop the basic conceptions of fable and character or how to sustain dramatic probability even when the plot takes an unlikely turn: distracting the audience by fixing their attention "solely upon every beauty which the dramatist displays," as in the masquerade scene in Hannah Cowley's *The Belle's Stratagem,* where the hero improbably falls in love with the heroine after a few hours of conversation.

Starting life as a farmer's daughter, Inchbald could never have accumulated her considerable fortune without rigorous hard work, self-discipline, and economy; her task was doubly hard in light of the limited opportunities open to women. Even after she had achieved success, she lived in modest lodgings and often did her own heavy housework, so as to be sure of maintaining her independence and her ability to help numerous distressed relatives. Accordingly, she had great contempt for financial irresponsibility. Arthur Murphy, she remarks acidly, was accustomed to the comforts of a gentleman and "had not strength of mind to yield up the ease and elegance, which affluence alone should bestow, for the content and pride of freedom and independence. But to reproach" him for this "would be treating him harshly, according to the rules of custom, though with perfect justice, according to the principles of honor and fortitude" (*All in the Wrong*). Her list of Murphy's successive means of support brings out by contrast the resources that were not available to women: after "the powers of invention forsook" him, he translated Tacitus, then got a government sinecure and finally, when he was even more infirm, a generous pension.

Her praise of Richard Cumberland for sympathetically presenting a Jewish hero would be expected from a liberal eighteenth-century humanitarian, but her praise of *The Jew* as a defense of misers as well is distinctively her own: "Mr. Cumberland has in one single part, rescued two unpopular characters from the stigma under which they both innocently suffered." Actually, it is likely that Cumberland emphasized Sheva's penny-pinching in order to give a little comic relief to his noble character and tearful story. But Inchbald makes it an exemplary characteristic; she describes the miser in her own image, as one who stints himself to "preserve a sane and purified mind" and to bestow more upon his neighbor. She goes on to note, accurately, that "indiscriminate profusion has been the dramatic hero's virtue in every comedy." Amiable wastrels like Sheridan's Charles Surface, redeemed by their benevolent impulses and spared the consequences of their thoughtless extravagance, abound in the drama of the period, but are conspicuously absent from her plays.

Though Inchbald was influenced by the sentimentalism of her period, she was consistently hard-headed about money. Thus she was not taken in by the specious morality of Edward Moore's *The Gamester,* which represents as amiable and essentially virtuous a man who ruins his family by gambling. She demolishes the sense and morality of this popular and admired tearjerker, which glorifies the uncritical devotion of the hero's wife. "An audience mostly supposes, that she performs an heroic action as a wife" when she hands over her last piece of property to her husband; "but readers call to mind, she is a mother," who is "yielding up the sole support of her infant child, to gratify the ideal honor of its duped and frantic father." An audience should "be taught, that charity without discrimination is a sensual enjoyment, and, like all sensuality, ought to be restrained" (Colman the Younger's *John Bull*). Though her own plays generally include a little delicate distress, she never confuses well-judged charity with heedless profusion.

Nor does she glorify romantic infatuation. When romantic love appears in her comedies—and it is not a prominent theme—it is a settled or a rationally grounded affection. Love may, as it is supposed, "engage every heart"; but it is conjugal love that raises a really deep interest (*Venice Preserved*). Inchbald sees the passion of Romeo and Juliet as adolescent infatuation rather than ideal love and therefore concludes that the play, however excellent and charming, is not deeply moving. On the other hand, the love of Othello and Desdemona is profoundly so, since Shakespeare convinces us that it was well founded. Congreve's *The Mourning Bride* does not touch the heart because the love on which it centers, "though . . . substantiated by wedlock . . . still . . . is merely bridal; neither cemented by long friendship, [nor] offspring." In her own comedies, she is more concerned with realistic marital problems than with the difficulties of young lovers, which furnished most dramatic plots in her time.

Inchbald's emphasis on marriage over courtship reflects the priorities of a mature, experienced woman, even as her insistence on economy reflects woman's traditional role of conserver. She also expresses an intelligent woman's irritation at men's tendency to idealize folly or insipidity in women: she is disgusted with the hero of Thomas Holcroft's *The Road to Ruin* for falling in love with an arrant fool, and she remarks that "Elegance in Charlotte Rusport, and beauty in Louisa Dudley, are the only qualities which the two actresses, who represent those parts, require" (Cumberland's *The West Indian*). She uses the experience of Sarah Siddons, who succeeded on the London stage only after her judgment was formed, to demonstrate that mature intelligence can make women more attractive (*Isabella, or The Fatal Marriage*). Inchbald finds Sheridan's illiterate Mrs. Malaprop too far-fetched to be funny and attacks the cliché that the life of an unmarried woman must be barren and joyless (Thomas Morton's *The Way to Get Married*). Her woman's viewpoint also appears in her distaste for the aggressively masculine values that male dramatists have traditionally glorified. In Corneille's *Horace* she finds the lover

Curiatius, whose courage is "joined with sensibility and tenderness," to be "superior, both as a man and a hero, to Publius Horatius, the brother," whose "rugged bravery, . . . never feels beyond its own selfish glory" (William Whitehead's *The Roman Father*, adapted from *Horace*). She notes that women do not generally like *Henry IV, Part I* and *Cato* because of these plays' predominantly masculine values.

Unfortunately, she was not always so independent. She was self-conscious about daring to be a critic, and perhaps, as a beautiful woman used to charming men, she was particularly reluctant to displease them. In any case, her prefaces do include placatory tributes to conventional ideals and stereotypes of womanhood. Though she justifies Centlivre's professional authorship and even the irregularities of her life, Inchbald condemns the immorality of *A Bold Stroke for A Wife* (which actually is quite clean), even though she concedes it was no worse than other plays of its time. "Though her temptations, to please the degraded taste of the public, were certainly more vehement" than those of contemporary males who did not write to eat, "yet, the virtue of fortitude is expected from a female, when delicacy is" in question; and she "should have laid down her pen, and taken, in exchange, the meanest implement of labor, rather than have imitated the licentious example" of others. Luckily for herself, Inchbald was not put to this test, since audiences in her time preferred the strict sexual morality and refined speech of her own comedies. On other occasions, she repeated ancient slurs on women: they are naturally deceitful and mischief-making (*Coriolanus*); they are greedy for praise and unable to keep a secret (Beaumont and Fletcher's *Rule a Wife and Have a Wife*). Contrary to the evidence of her own writing, she says women are liable to fall into "bad grammar, false metaphors and similes, with all the usual errors of imperfect diction" (***Lovers' Vows***).

The critical principles of Inchbald's prefaces reflect the assumptions of her time, though she applies them with perceptiveness and flexibility. Late eighteenth-century critics prized interrelated values of naturalness or probability, gentility, and morality. Probability requires incidents which occur in normal life, full of "little touches of refined nature," and passions "such as commonly govern mankind" rather than violent stagy ones (Colley Cibber's *The Careless Husband*). Inchbald praises Murphy's *All in the Wrong* because its dialogue "never in one sentence soars above the proper standard of elegant life; and the incidents . . . are bold without extravagance or apparent artifice." In one particularly skillful scene, "unlooked-for accidents" produce the highest comic effect, and yet all has "arisen from causes consonant with the general events of life."

Probability in character required avoidance of extremes. Though Inchbald greatly admired Congreve's *Love for Love*, she faulted many of its characters for exaggeration (as well as immorality): too heavy insistence on idiosyncrasies produced by temperament or occupation makes characters unbelievable. Holcroft's *The Road to Ruin* is supremely effective theatrically because it represents paternal and filial affection "with infinite power, and yet without one inflated or poetic sentence.—The scenes between Dornton and his son are not like scenes in a play, but like occurrences in the house of a respectable banker, who has a dissipated, though a loving and beloved, son." Characters should also illustrate a realistic mixture of virtues and vices. When Cibber endowed a licentious coxcomb with frankness and valor (Clodio in *Love Makes a Man*), he showed "justice, or rather judgment" unusual among authors. Carlos in the same play might seem unnaturally wise and good, but Cibber makes him so young and studious that "he appears like one whom temptations have yet never reached, rather than" one preternaturally immune to them. Inchbald admires the human reality of Shakespeare's Antony and Cleopatra and points out that this elicits from us "more lenity to their faults—more reverence for their virtues" than we feel for the stilted public figures in Dryden's *All for Love*. Mixed characters are also more useful in providing moral lessons (Murphy's *The Way to Keep Him*).

Inchbald often comments on the difficulty of portraying good characters without making them insipid, and, in her preface to Massinger's *A New Way to Pay Old Debts,* illuminates this problem with the insight of a practicing dramatist. Virtuous people have fewer turbulent passions and more control over those they have, and are not subject "to those grand exhibitions for a theater—remorse, or despair." And yet an author must create situations for them that will excite "sensations which awaken interest." It requires fertile invention to devise "Bold and unlooked for occurrences, [which] will raise conflicts in the most peaceful bosom" and surprise a good person into succumbing to temptation.

In her own plays, Inchbald generally avoided perfect characters. This was wise, since she was not able to make them interesting. Mr. Haswell in *Such Things Are* is colorless, though he derives some force from being based on a real-life hero, the prison reformer John Howard. Lady Eleanor Irwin in *Every One Has His Fault* is defined as a model wife, mother, and daughter, her appeal coming solely from her stock pathetic situation. On the other hand, Mr. Harmony, in the same play, is a successful comic character because he is not perfect: his universal benevolence is just a bit ridiculous because it is powered less by principled philanthropy than by a compulsive need to dispel ill-will and unpleasantness. In general, Inchbald's characters meet her standard of naturalness. They are typically well bred, often intelligent, but not extraordinary—neither preternaturally witty, nor distorted by a prevailing humor.

Yet improbability may be excused if it produces sufficiently beautiful imaginative or emotional effects.

Leontes' unfounded jealousy is unbelievable, but it occasions such noble behavior and such affecting suffering in his wife that "the extravagance of the first is soon forgotten, through the deep impression made by the last" (*The Winter's Tale*). Inchbald may have been aiming at an analogous effect by setting her *Such Things Are* in Sumatra. Only in such a place can she show a Sultan, made cruel and self-absorbed by the loss of his beloved wife, keeping that very woman in prison for years because he is too callous to care who may be languishing in his dungeons. Through this melodramatic fable, Inchbald can make vivid her plea for prison reform in England.

Refinement, the second great principle, meant avoidance not only of bawdry, but of anything "low"—vulgar characters or slapstick humor. Inchbald consistenty faulted dialect characters, because they were lower class and because their incorrect English was too easy a source of comedy, and never used them in her own work. She praises Cumberland's *The West Indian* for "wholly refined" language and "perfectly delicate" ideas, for bestowing wit and humor "on persons of pleasing forms and polite manners." This skill "divides, like a gulf, the superior, from the inferior, dramatist." It is easy to raise a laugh by the blunt repartee or comic accidents of characters in low life, "But to exhibit the weak side of wisdom, the occasional foibles which impede the full exertion of good sense; the chance awkwardness of the elegant, and mistakes of the correct . . . —these are efforts of intellect . . . [which] can alone confer the title of a good comic author" (Cumberland's *The Brothers*). Inchbald's dislike of the "low" led her to overvalue the younger Colman's *Inkle and Yarico* and to undervalue his genuinely amusing *The Heir at Law*. The first play is finer in her eyes because it is free of crude, dialect-speaking characters and full of high-flown moral declarations, and its characters are exaggerated in the direction of sentimental virtue rather than comical humors.[5] She can't help enjoying Dr. Pangloss, a caricatured pedant in *The Heir at Law,* but she must justify him on moral grounds: "when solemn sentences and sprightly wit are found ineffectual, the ludicrous will often prove of import."

Fortunately, however, Inchbald's dramatic practice was not so rigorous as her theory. She worried in the preface to *Such Things Are* that Sir Luke and Lady Tremor, two of the most amusing characters, were "low"; and so they are, if marital squabbles and the humble origins of Lady Tremor, whose father was a grocer, make them so. But they are not coarse or crude; their humor comes from their characters rather than from class mannerisms such as vulgar accents; their fighting involves poking at foibles rather than abuse; and they do not jar with the more refined characters, Twineall, Lord Flint, and Haswell. They are very funny, and it is happy for the play that she did not purify them into elevated but insipid gentility.

Inchbald shared in the overpreoccupation with moral teaching typical of her time. Even when she praises a play as light entertainment—for example, Morton's *A Cure for the Heart Ache*—she takes care to point out that it teaches a useful lesson and makes admirable moral reflections along the way.[6] She climaxes her appreciative description of the awe-inspiring Kemble-Siddons production of *Macbeth* by calling it "one of the most impressive moral lessons which the stage exhibits." She is horrified by "that unrestrained contempt of principle which pervades every scene" of *The Beaux' Strategem,* meaning chiefly Mrs. Sullen's adulterous intentions. In her own plays, she approves the good, reproves the bad and sets up edifying scenes; but in general she upholds a sound moral system based on honesty and humanity, and eschews the blatant moral declamations which studded the plays of many contemporaries. She follows sentimental morality by presenting human nature as essentially good and preferring to reform rather than reject misbehaving characters, but she refrains from presenting worthless characters redeemed by benevolent impulses.

Inchbald deviated from the norm only in her relatively enlightened presentation of unhappy fallen women (in serious drama only, where they can suffer adequately for their sins). In the preface to her highly successful adaptation of August von Kotzebue's *Lovers' Vows,* she points out that Agatha, the unwed mother in the play, suffered greatly, and that those who condemn her ultimate reunion with her lover "forget there is a punishment called *conscience,* which, though it seldom troubles the defamer's peace, may weigh heavy on the fallen female and her libertine seducer." The morality of Benjamin Thompson's *The Stranger,* another adaptation from Kotzebue, may not be perfect; but it shines in comparison with that of so-called pious Protestants or patriots who defame their opponents so "that the nation may hate them without offence to brotherly love."

Inchbald's critical principles suggest the limitations of drama in her period, both her own and that of others. There was far too much emphasis on negative virtues: plays must not violate the probability of ordinary life; they must avoid any hint of vulgarity; they must not present any character or action that could possibly provide a bad example.[7] Strongly marked characters may be considered improbable; low-life characters and farcical incidents are vulgar; a cynical view of human nature is unrefined and immoral; wit is apt to challenge accepted standards of morality or propriety. The result of such apprehensions is liable to be insipid correctness. Inchbald was capable of seeing this very fault in her own *To Marry, or Not to Marry,* despite its popular success. Here, she acknowledges, in avoiding farcical incidents, broad jests, dialect, songs and processions, she also avoided wit and humor.[8] She points out that her major characters "are all justly drawn, but not with sufficient force for high dramatic effect." They have neither the psychological depth required to make realistic drama of character interest-

ing, nor the intensity and exaggeration necessary for comic or satiric effects; nor does the play contain any other sources of entertainment.

Drama so concerned with gentility could hardly deal incisively with serious issues. In general, Inchbald seems to have accepted sentimental benevolence as a substitute for social criticism, at least in plays: she takes the younger Colman's *Inkle and Yarico* to be an indictment of slavery, even though all it really teaches is that it is not nice to sell one's Indian common-law wife. Her own radical opinions (she was a friend of Godwin and Holcroft) rarely appear in either plays or prefaces. The only examples are her relatively lenient attitude toward fallen women (if repentant and if found in German drama), her attack on prison abuses in *Such Things Are* (tactfully set in Sumatra, not England), and her acid comment on the complacent patriotic sentiments that were a staple of contemporary plays: "The author tells us truly, that, 'we have in England, palaces for poverty, and princely endowments for calamity'—the English are charitable, but they are too apt to boast of their benevolent endowments: a higher boast would be, to have fewer paupers who require them" (Morton's *The School of Reform*).

A desire to deal seriously with the problems of male-female relationships, together with reluctance actually to do so, may underlie Inchbald's dissatisfaction with her *Wives as They Were, and Maids as They Are* (even though it was, like most of her plays, very successful). Her preface to this comedy is her most detailed analysis of her own work. It has a good fable and characters, she says; but she did not execute her design effectively because she failed to develop it with appropriate incidents: some are insipid and some improbable, and there are jarring shifts in tone. She resorted to farce (though she well knew that its extravagance would be out of keeping with her basically realistic portrayal) and then, successively, to "the serious, the pathetic, and the refined comic." In particular, she failed to devise appropriate incidents to illustrate the extraordinary marriage of Lord and Lady Priory. She did not succeed in "gratifying certain expectations indiscreetly raised."

These accurately noted technical deficiencies result from Inchbald's inability to maintain consistently the realistic manner that suited both her subject and her personal style. *Wives as They Were,* which centers on the relationship between a lively daughter and her dictatorial father and that between a selfish, domineering husband and his resigned wife, raises challenging issues about male authority and female duty. But no dramatist writing for the conventional theater of 1797 could deal realistically with such actual social problems. Accordingly, Inchbald resorts to fantastic situations and easy dramatic effects. She contrives a plot whereby the daughter lives in the same house as her father but does not recognize him as such, so that her refusals to obey him are not a challenge to paternal authority. She indicates that Lady Priory, a cool, sensible woman, has reasons for submitting to her husband, even though she is neither weak nor devoted to him; but she does not analyze the woman's motivation or her situation so as to make her attitude plausible. She leads the couple to a confrontation, but lets it tail off into conventional sentiments. She illustrates the Priory marriage with fantastic detail because presenting it realistically would raise uncomfortable questions about the actual patriarchal marriages of the time. In lieu of developing the serious issues, Inchbald diverts her readers with pointless farcical episodes, such as a confusion between the dignified father and a young rake produced by an unmotivated exchange of coats at the end of act 2, or with factitious pathos, such as Miss Dorrillon's effusive reaction to the false tale that her father is in debtor's prison (5.2). The problem with the play is not so much shifts in tone or fluctuations in quality as it is discrepancy between stimulating ideas and conventional development.[9]

Inchbald did recognize the pressure of convention on the theater, although not explicitly in connection with her own work. In her preface to Colman's *John Bull,* she remarked that the dramatist "must please at first sight, or never be seen more" and therefore must address the audience's "habits, passions, and prejudices, as the only means to gain this sudden conquest of their minds and hearts." Hannah Cowley, her successful contemporary, made the same point in the prefatory "Address" to her own comedy *A School for Greybeards:* unlike a novelist, who can follow nature freely, the dramatist feels "encompassed in chains" when she writes, which check her in her "happiest flights, and force" her "continually to reflect, not, whether *this is just?* but, whether *this is safe?*" (1786, vi-vii). The contrast between possibilities in drama and the novel is strikingly illustrated by Inchbald's own Miss Dorrillon, who, as the author notes in her preface, is of the same type as Miss Milner of her **Simple Story.** Miss Milner is far more affecting and convincing, not only because of the wider scope for development afforded by the novel, but also because of the novelist's greater freedom to present a heroine with obvious faults as an intensely sympathetic character.[10]

Notes

[1] The gentleness of Inchbald's criticism appears when we contrast her *British Theatre* prefaces with Richard Cumberland's in a similar collection, *The British Drama* (1817). Cumberland delighted in tearing plays apart on grounds of improbability or immorality. (It is true that he was not dealing with living authors apart from himself.) Nevertheless, even James Boaden, Inchbald's admiring biographer, deplored her writing of criticism, on the grounds that it was to her interest "to conciliate everybody" and that "There is a something unfeminine . . . in a lady's placing herself in the seat of judgment" (1833, 2:84).

[2] Inchbald's overestimation of George Colman the Younger was general in the time. E.g., Thomas Gilliland wrote of Colman that "no one stands more prominent, or deserves to rank higher. . . . His works contain great beauties of thought, neatness of diction, and a potent share of morality . . ." (1808, 1:297-98).

[3] All quotations but the last one from Hannah Cowley on p. 288 are from Inchbald's prefaces in *The British Theatre* and the two letters printed before *The Heir at Law.* Since all of these are short (no more than five pages) and the volumes are not continuously paged, I have simply indicated in context or parentheses the play to which the relevant preface belongs.

[4] Personal experience may also account for her interpretation in the moral she draws from Olivia's infatuation with Viola in *Twelfth Night,* on "the imprudence of women, in placing their affections, their happiness, on men younger than themselves"; this probably reflects her unhappy passion for the actor John Philip Kemble, who was four years younger than she. Her Catholic religious affiliation may be seen in her disgust at the crimes committed by Henry VIII and Cardinal Wolsey "under the pretense of religious duty" and in her unusual sympathy with the deposed Catholic King James II, deserted by his Protestant daughters (*Henry VIII, King Lear*). Her definition of "the grand moral" of *Lovers' Vows* as "to set forth the miserable consequences which arise from the neglect, and to enforce the watchful care, of illegitimate offspring" may reflect her difficult relationship with Mr. Inchbald's illegitimate son.

[5] She did occasionally notice excesses in gentility: Richard Steele's Bevil and Indiana "sink into insipidity, through the lifeless weight of mere refinement" (*The Conscious Lovers*).

[6] Cf. Gilliland: Morton's "plays carry under the alluring vehicle of pleasure, a potent share of ethics, and when fascinating an audience, the antidote to immorality insensibly steals on the mind, and leaves an indelible impression of some useful lesson" (1808, 1:471). On the emphasis on morality in the drama in general, see Thomas Holcroft in *The English Review* of May 1783: the contemporary theater contributes "to humanize the heart, and correct the manners," by ridiculing follies, giving "the most beautiful precepts for . . . conduct," alluring "to the practice of virtue by declamations conveyed" in poetical thoughts and attractive language, and "exhibiting dreadful examples of the dreadful consequences of vice" (Gray 1931, 298).

[7] Charles Lamb astutely recognized that the essential failings of late eighteenth-century comedy as practiced by Inchbald and Holcroft were excessive moralizing and restriction to "common life" ("On the Artificial Comedy," Renwick, 1963, 234).

[8] The pressures on Inchbald as a dramatist and her superior penetration as a critic are illustrated by John

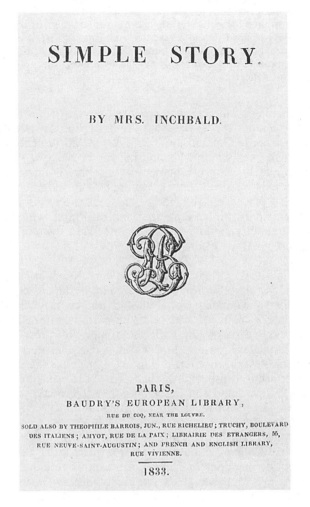

SIMPLE STORY.

BY MRS. INCHBALD.

PARIS,
BAUDRY'S EUROPEAN LIBRARY,
RUE DU COQ, NEAR THE LOUVRE.
SOLD ALSO BY THEOPHILE BARROIS, JUN., RUE RICHELIEU; TRUCHY, BOULEVARD
DES ITALIENS; AMYOT, RUE DE LA PAIX; LIBRAIRIE DES ETRANGERS, 55,
RUE NEUVE-SAINT-AUGUSTIN; AND FRENCH AND ENGLISH LIBRARY,
RUE VIVIENNE.

1833.

Title page to A Simple Story.

Genest's unqualified admiration for this play: "This comedy . . . does Mrs. Inchbald great credit—it is chaste and simple—there are no farcical incidents—no songs, nor processions—no broken English—no striking situation—no particular stage effect—in a word, none of those meretricious arts, by which the favor of the public has been so successfully courted" (1832, 7:669).

[9] Similarly, in *I'll Tell You What* and *Every One Has His Fault,* she raised the issue of divorce, but abstained from developing it to any conclusion.

[10] Genest provides an indication of contemporary audience reaction to Miss Dorrillon: he found her "not a pleasing character" (1832, 7:309).

Works Cited

Boaden, James. 1833. *Memoirs of Mrs. Inchbald.* 2 vols. London: Richard Bentley.

Cowley, Hannah. 1786. *A School for Greybeards: or, the Mourning Bride*. London: G. G. J. and J. Robinson.

Cumberland, Richard, ed. 1817. *The British Drama: A Collection of the Most Esteemed Dramatic Productions*. 14 vols. London: C. Cooke.

Genest, John. 1832. *Some Account of the English Stage, from the Restoration in 1660 to 1830*. 10 vols. Bath: Thomas Rudd.

Gilliland, Thomas. 1808. *The Dramatic Mirror: Containing the History of the Stage . . . A Biographical and Critical Account of All the Dramatic Writers, from 1660; and Also of the Most Distinguished Performers, from the Days of Shakespeare to 1807*. 2 vols. London: C. Chapple.

Gray, Charles Harold. 1931. *Theatrical Critics in London to 1795*. New York: Columbia Univ. Press.

Inchbald, Elizabeth, ed. 1808. *The British Theatre; or, A Collection of Plays, Which Are Acted at the Theaters Royal, Drury Lane, Covent Garden, and Haymarket*. With Biographical and Critical Remarks by Mrs. Inchbald. 25 vols. London: Longman, Hurst, Rees, and Orme.

———. 1980. *The Plays*. Ed. Paula R. Backscheider. 2 vols. New York: Garland. Renwick, W. L. 1963. *English Literature 1789-1815*. New York: Oxford Univ. Press.

Anna Lott (essay date 1994)

SOURCE: "Sexual Politics in Elizabeth Inchbald," in *Studies in English Literature, 1500-1900,* Vol. 34, No. 3, Summer, 1994, pp. 635-48.

[*In the following essay, Lott claims that Inchbald questioned the patriarchal social mores of late eighteenth-century and early nineteenth-century Britain.*]

Of Elizabeth Inchbald's collection of biographical and critical prefaces to popular plays, her near-contemporary biographer James Boaden wrote: "There is something unfeminine . . . in a lady's placing herself in the seat of judgment."[1] Merely by acting as critic, Inchbald challenged basic assumptions about gender roles, and Boaden's reaction to the essays, he claims, is typical of the response Inchbald received. The essays, he asserts, "added but little to her fortune and nothing whatever to her fame."[2] Inchbald's contribution within a burgeoning circle of drama critics did indeed, as Boaden's dismissive remarks suggest, meet with a disappointing response from some of her male colleagues, particularly from George Colman the Younger and D-G (George Daniel, the reviewer of John Cumberland's collection titled *Cumberland's British Theatre*).[3] But Boaden ignores the overwhelming popular success of the collection of plays and reviews:[4] Inchbald did, in spite of Boaden's insistence to the contrary, increase her fame with this collection (it is still widely available in libraries throughout England and the United States).

The essays in Inchbald's collection conveyed a distinctly feminist message that was, I believe, largely responsible for the resistance of Boaden and others. Inchbald's entire corpus of work was boldly radical, and her defiant stance toward social norms distressed readers like Boaden, although in many cases Boaden seemed as bothered by Inchbald's acting career as he was by her writings. Boaden condemns, for example, one of Inchbald's earliest portrayals, the role of Calista in Nicholas Rowe's *The Fair Penitent*. He apologizes both for Rowe's recalcitrant character and for Inchbald's personal behavior, and in his assessment, he allows little distinction between the actress and her role:

> [In December of 1772, Inchbald acted] Anne Bullen, Cordelia, and even Calista in *The Fair Penitent,* where, by the way, she is no penitent, but an audacious, ungenerous wanton, enlightened only as to her true interests when the lamp of life feebly glimmers to its close.[5]

That Boaden would respond with such discomfort to Inchbald's mere portrayal of Calista, a fictional half-hearted penitent, suggests that his later dismissal of her essays might have sprung from a similar aversion to Inchbald's revolutionary intentions. In what is still the most complete account of Inchbald's life and work, Boaden refused to acknowledge that Inchbald, throughout a widely varied career (culminating with the collection of essays that Boaden dismisses), was a major voice against the very constraints Boaden wished to uphold.[6]

In the twentieth century, Inchbald's biographers have imitated Boaden in their lukewarm response to her essays. William McKee does not mention Inchbald's collection, and S. R. Littlewood treats the essays with disdain, remarking that "Mrs. Inchbald simply did not understand Shakespeare."[7] Recently, critics such as Katharine M. Rogers and Roger Manvell have presented more sympathetic accounts of Inchbald's collection, although these accounts either ignore or downplay Inchbald's feminist message.[8] Rogers suggests that the essays reveal much about Inchbald's life and attitudes, "a woman who had achieved great success in a man's world and yet was intent on maintaining femininity as her contemporaries defined it." But Rogers's essay ultimately condemns Inchbald's agenda as disappointingly placatory toward "conventional ideals and stereotypes of womanhood." Inchbald, Rogers argues, "was self-conscious about daring to be a critic, and perhaps, as a beautiful woman used to charming men, she was particularly reluctant to displease them."[9]

It is difficult to imagine that the author of *A Simple Story,* who had spent her life challenging accepted gender roles, was suddenly cowed by the theatrical powers. Inchbald actually tended to view her femininity, and the beauty and charm inherent in it, as a prerogative that allowed her to speak more directly and incisively than men. She responded to the critical essays in the *Edinburgh Review* thus:

> I must own I enjoy this kind of satire very much— nor have I the slightest objection to the subject of it; but perhaps I should if I were a man. But for a woman to expose the want of literary talent I conceive no reproach, provided she is not led to publish through self-conceit.[10]

Inchbald continued to insist on her own particular right, as a woman, to "expose the want of literary talent," when George Colman the Younger reacted violently to her own essays about his and his father's plays. In response to his angry remarks she simply reminds him that she is, after all, only a woman: "The judgment on which I placed my reliance on this occasion was—that many readers might be amused and informed, whilst no one dramatist could possibly be offended, by the cursory remarks of a female observer."[11]

Inchbald's rhetorical stance is powerfully duplicitous. By taking a self-consciously deferential stance, claiming that a woman's words should not be offensive— should not, in fact, even be taken seriously—Inchbald effectively diffuses and deflects Colman's criticism and any further criticism before it can occur. Her very real critical power, however, is evident by the popularity of her collection, especially when we realize that the essays were printed and Inchbald's message conveyed in spite of her colleagues' angry protests.

Inchbald's remarks were threatening, not only to dramatists like Colman, but also to other critics like D-G, who scornfully mentions Inchbald's criticism of certain tragic scenes in Arthur Murphy's *The Grecian Daughter*. D-G does not acknowledge Inchbald's admiration for the play's structure (Inchbald remarks that "incidents arise progressively from each other, till the last great incident of all"); nor does he concede her approval of the play's valorous heroine (Inchbald admires the woman who "performs that which a whole army has in vain attempted"). Although D-G's disapproval of Inchbald's essay does not specifically address her clearly feminist agenda, his obvious disdain for her work, along with his own review of *The Grecian Daughter,* suggests that his critical intentions were radically different from Inchbald's.[12] Inchbald's review of Murphy's play stresses what she views as a reversal of gender roles (she attests that "the men's characters have been all sacrificed by the author to the *valour* of the woman" [my emphasis], vol. 15). D-G writes of the heroine in terms that are also congratulatory, but more conventionally feminine (Euphrasia has a *virtue* that "transcends even [the traits of] patriotism and philosophy" that D-G has earlier attached specifically to men, and Fanny Kemble played the part with "the tenderest *pathos* and tragic reality of *feeling* that are inseparable in true genius" [my emphasis]).

By invoking and criticizing Inchbald's essay, D-G invites comparison with his own essay, a gesture that suggests the content of Inchbald's reviews was more revolutionary than has previously been acknowledged, particularly when we remember that her reviews were intended to appeal to and influence a popular audience. Inchbald's essays, like her novel, *A Simple Story,* celebrate women who exist outside of familial constraints, refusing, despite strong pressure, to confess to misdeeds. The essays present overtly sharp judgments about Inchbald's society and woman's essentially limited role in it.

Inchbald's essays appeared during a time, shortly before the burnings of the Covent Garden and Drury Lane Theaters,[13] when the moral purpose of the theater was most in question, and her collection answered a general cry for the reformation of what was widely viewed as a corrupt art. Prince Hoare, Inchbald's friend and fellow critic, published an essay in 1810 in his journal *The Artist* in which he argues that theater's moral purpose could be revived by educating the London audience to respond properly to the plays.[14] Hoare hopes that

> this may be possible (and the experiment is at least worth the trial) to preserve, in a limited portion of those representations the existence of such elevated and honourable effort, as may tend to form a continually improving standard of popular taste. This may be effected either by the aid of the state, or of powerful individuals; and in our own country, where the state is for the most part nearly quiescent in regard to the arts, and powerful individuals are the strong arm of their support, the latter are chiefly to be looked to with confidence.[15]

Although Prince Hoare does not specifically address the critical essay as a means to the reform he supports,[16] I believe that Inchbald's efforts as a critic went a long way toward establishing Hoare's standard of public taste, and that she was one of the powerful individuals he looked to with such confidence.

Inchbald's own support of the theater (even after she had given up her acting career), and her insistence that it could have a didactic aim, are evident in an essay recently attributed to her by Patricia Sigl.[17] The essay was written shortly after the Covent Garden and Drury Lane disasters and was published in Prince Hoare's journal *The Artist.*[18] Inchbald signs her piece, "A Christian, but no Fanatick," and in it she defends the theater against attacks from Catholics and Methodists. The essay claims an explicitly didactic purpose for the theater, as does the other essay Inchbald published (and signed) in *The Artist,* although Inchbald's signed essay claims that the novel is more effective as a didactic tool.[19]

Boaden notes with relief that Inchbald chose not to write any more critical essays after *The British Theatre* was completed in 1808: "the unpleasant effect, resulting to herself alone from these prefaces, deterred her from the exercise of that power which she had so much enjoyed in *The Edinburgh Review.*"[20] The power that Boaden granted Inchbald was not only the privilege of judging a play, but also the ability to influence the responses of others. The didactic nature of the eighteenth-century critical essay allowed the reviewer a certain authority not only over playwrights but over audiences as well. Critical essays were meant to outline a proper moral response, and this was the power that attracted Inchbald. Richard Cumberland, editor and reviewer of *The British Drama* (a collection of plays similar to *The British Theatre*). claimed an explicitly didactic purpose for his essays. Condemning *The Beaux Stratagem,* he protests that

> I cannot make so light of a duty which I owe to the reader, or of a responsibility which bears upon myself, as to let it pass from under my review without a mark'd protest against its positive defect in point of moral. If what I am now writing is destined to meet the eye of any reader, young and inexperienced in dramatic compositions, let such either stop with me if curiosity can be controlled, or be prepared to admire the brilliancy of the dialogue without approving of the principles of the speakers in the following scenes.[21]

Inchbald's own didactic intentions were no less strong, although her purpose differed widely from Cumberland's. With her reviews, Inchbald could reclaim the theater as a didactic medium by defining the moral of a play, thereby shaping her audience's principles and focusing their expectations.

Inchbald, as she makes clear in her letter to George Colman the Younger, did not choose the plays that are included in the collection, but merely acted in the capacity of biographer and critic for plays chosen by her publisher, Longman. Because Inchbald reviewed plays that she did not necessarily approve of or like, her critical and moral judgments of the plays sometimes extended to the audiences who were making them popular. To watch a play that assumes certain confining parameters for women was, for Inchbald, implicitly to perpetuate those structures. Inchbald's essay on Thomas Morton's *The Way to Get Married,* for example, cautions a female playgoer against submitting to existing social constraints by regarding marriage as "the summit of her wishes" (vol. 25). The qualities that Morton contends will help a woman find a husband would be equally useful for a woman who remains unmarried. Whether or not a female auditor finds a husband, the virtues recommended in *The Way to Get Married* will "bestow on her that respect from the world, and that joy in her own breast, of which, commonplace remarks and false conclusions, have, for centuries past, been studious to deprive all aged spinsters." And Inchbald encourages her audience more generally to value unmarried women. Her essay on Sheridan's *The Rivals* condemns an audience who would credit Sheridan's unflattering portrait of the unmarried Mrs. Malaprop (vol. 19).[22]

Inchbald's stance becomes more obvious when her views are compared to those of other women critics such as Anna Seward. Seward's ideal was the "oppressed . . . injured, and angelic spirit" of Richardson's Clarissa.[23] Although Inchbald probably admired Clarissa for different reasons, she most assuredly would not have admired Seward's version of Clarissa as an oppressed spirit who does nothing to influence her unfortunate predicament. In Inchbald's essay on the popular play *Lady Jane Grey* (a play whose lesson is similar to that of Seward's essay), Inchbald questions the value of merely maintaining one's position within a limiting situation—waiting, essentially, to be freed by death. Lady Jane is, Inchbald contends, too virtuous to inspire imitation, lamenting in her review that "it is scarcely possible to be heroical like Lady Jane." For Inchbald, Lady Jane's "calm contempt for either living or dying," her passive acquiescence to her horrible fate, serves to promote rather than to thwart the aims of her oppressors.[24]

Inchbald was more interested in and more charitable toward depictions of women who violated or appeared to violate existing standards of behavior—women who were forced, as a result, to live on the literal and figurative fringes of society. These women held a special fascination for Inchbald merely by their survival apart from the constrictions of the family. Of Hermione in *The Winter's Tale,* who is forced at least into the appearance of abandoning all human contact, Inchbald adoringly remarks that she confers "honour and interest upon Leontes merely by his keeping such excellent company."[25] Leontes' jealous frenzy is "rendered interesting by the sufferings it brings upon [Hermione]" (vol. 3). And in her annotated copy of *The British Theatre,* Inchbald argues that Queen Katharine of Shakespeare's *Henry VIII,* another heroine forced from her home, is "one of the finest female characters in the English Drama."[26]

But Inchbald was perhaps most fascinated with the character of Jane Shore, a role she herself acted many times.[27] According to Nicholas Rowe's play, Jane Shore, the legendary adulteress, had been forced to walk the streets barefoot as a punishment and was subsequently left to starve. Inchbald finds fault with the play, insisting that Jane Shore "lived to an advanced age" after she had been expelled from polite society. The story of Jane Shore's premature death is, Inchbald argues, "the fiction of an old ballad." To support her claim, Inchbald cites Thomas More, who "assures his readers, that, in the reign of Henry VIII. forty years after her humiliating punishment was inflicted, he has frequently seen her gathering herbs, in a field near the city, for her nightly repast" (vol. 10).

For Inchbald, Jane Shore is truly worthy of emulation, because she, unlike Clarissa and Jane Grey, is able to survive, even to thrive, outside of the rigid social structures that condemn her. Inchbald notes, significantly, that Jane Shore was "extremely old and shrivelled; without one trace of her former beauty." Jane Shore's beauty is, for Inchbald, an emblem of eighteenth-cen-

tury attempts to essentialize female identity. Jane Shore's ability to live, unrecognized, without her former beauty is a triumph because she is able to create a self in spite of and in opposition to common definitions and perceptions of "woman." Her "death" at the end of Rowe's play is metaphorical—she is permanently ostracized from a domestic sphere. But rather than simply waiting for providence to rescue her from this social separation, Jane Shore finds the means to exist apart from the social constrictions that bind and finally kill other lesser heroines.

Inchbald did acknowledge existing social expectations for women.[28] Her essays often celebrate violators like Jane Shore, but when forced to generalize (especially about comedies), Inchbald agreed with the common understanding that adultery, particularly female adultery, was morally wrong.[29] But her refusal to condone adultery does not finally contradict her admiration for women excluded (through their own fault or not) from the domestic sphere. Her defense of August von Kotzebue's *The Stranger* (adapted and translated by Benjamin Thompson) exemplifies the pointed nature of her social criticism even when couched in an apparent confirmation of current mores (prohibitions against adultery, for one).[30] In Kotzebue's play, the heroine Mrs. Haller, mistakenly believing that her husband has been unfaithful, commits adultery and is later confronted and forgiven by her husband. Inchbald defends the play from detractors who had argued that its moral was flawed since a confessed adulteress is forgiven and reunited with her husband.[31] But Inchbald does not attempt to defend the play's fallen woman. Mrs. Haller. Instead Inchbald argues that Mrs. Haller's guilty return to her husband will serve as a more severe punishment than if she had been forced to stay away from her family. "What woman of common understanding and common cowardice," demands Inchbald, "would dare to dishonor and foresake her husband, if she foresaw she was ever likely to live with him again?" (vol. 24).

Inchbald's warning to the adulterous wife is equivocal. Is her dreadful punishment the guilty horror of facing an angry husband or is the punishment simply the horror of facing a husband at all? The role of contrite penitent was, I believe, actually a common one held by eighteenth-century women, even those who had been faithful to their husbands.[32] Inchbald attributes any sympathy the play's audience might feel for Mrs. Haller to her convincingly penitent confession. A spectator might be persuaded to forgive Mrs. Haller by "these distressful and repentant testimonies, preparatory to the reunion of husband and wife."

But Inchbald speculates that a more perceptive spectator might realize that Mrs. Haller's reunion with her husband is no kind of happy ending for a fallen woman. This spectator would "never [conceive], that from an agonizing, though affectionate embrace, any farther endearments will ensue than those of participated sadness, mutual care of their joint offspring, and to smooth each other's passage to the grave." Inchbald's ideal spectator would recognize the far-reaching consequences of Mrs. Haller's testimony, beyond the momentary relief of forgiveness; would realize that Mrs. Haller's guilt, and her husband's awareness of it, will make familial existence miserable for Mrs. Haller; would understand that Mrs. Haller's confession and the Stranger's (the disguised husband's) forgiveness reinforces an authoritarian relationship between the Stranger and Mrs. Haller, based on the revelation of her guilty secret.

What Inchbald knew was that by receiving Mrs. Haller's confession, the Stranger benefits from a political economy that grants him a discursive authority within the listener/confessor relationship. Though Mrs. Haller is momentarily unburdened by her confession and the Stranger's forgiveness, it is the Stranger who ultimately profits from Mrs. Haller's admission; the Stranger's new knowledge allows him an irreversible position of authority. Mrs. Haller's own testimony reifies her sexual act, forcing her to accept "fallen woman" as the essential and defining part of her self.

Michel Foucault has explored the implications of the confession, "the obligatory and exhaustive expression of an individual secret."[33] Foucault argues that

> The confession is a ritual of discourse in which the speaking subject is also the subject of the statement; it is also a ritual that unfolds within a power relationship, for one does not confess without a presence (or virtual presence) of a partner who is not simply the interlocutor but the authority who requires the confession, prescribes and appreciates it, and intervenes in order to judge, punish, forgive, console, and reconcile. . . . And this discourse of truth finally takes effect, not in the one who receives it, but in the one from whom it is wrested.[34]

Inchbald seems instinctively aware of the power wielded by a listener over the one from whom the confession is wrested or even volunteered. She notes that Jane Shore's enemies, instead of simply punishing her, accuse her first of witchcraft and adultery (and presumably try to force a confession). And it is in Jane Shore's refusal to confess—not in her superior virtue or innocence—that Inchbald seems to locate her particular strength. Inchbald carefully avoids the issue of Jane Shore's actual guilt or innocence, remarking simply that Jane Shore was "charged with the crime of adultery; an accusation it was in vain to deny." Inchbald's refusal to acknowledge Jane Shore's guilt seems especially radical when we remember that the ritual of Jane Shore's sincerely penitent confession and subsequent forgiveness was generally cited as the reason for the play's popularity. Samuel Johnson admired the play, and argued that "the wife is forgiven because she repents, and the husband is honoured because he forgives. This therefore is one of the pieces which we still welcome on the stage."[35]

The power that Inchbald believed a woman could gain simply by refusing to confess is nowhere more evident than in her novel *A Simple Story*. Inchbald's rebellious heroine, Miss Milner, seems almost calculated to resemble Jane Shore, the heroine Inchbald so loved to portray on the stage. Like Jane Shore, Miss Milner (now Lady Elmwood) leaves her home after she has committed adultery, and like Jane Shore, Miss Milner leaves before she is forced to confess her crime to her husband. Bored by her husband's extended absence from home, Miss Milner "[flies] from the present tedious solitude, to the dangerous society of [her paramour, Lord Frederick]."[36] When Miss Milner's husband returns suddenly, she realizes that her exciting affair might, after all, have been a mistake, but she refuses to accept as a punishment the constrictions implicit in a penitent confession. Rather than attempt any sort of reconciliation that would involve a testimony revealing her guilty secret, she "[flees] the place at his approach; [flees] his house, never again to return to a habitation *where he was the master*" (my emphasis).[37] Miss Milner's refusal to accept expected familial boundaries is revolutionary, and it places her in solid company with Inchbald's favorite dramatic heroines— Jane Shore, Hermione, and Katharine of Aragon.

Miss Milner's refusal to confess her affair is encoded in her behavior throughout the first part of the novel. Before her disastrous marriage, Miss Milner struggles to maintain control over her guardian/lover Dorriforth simply by not confessing her most private desires to him. Acting as Miss Milner's guardian, Dorriforth tries to coerce his ward to tell him whom she has given her heart to, and her refusal to confess denies him the secure authority he believes he deserves. Dorriforth is able to discover that he is himself the object of Miss Milner's love only when her woman confidante betrays her secret. Dorriforth—not coincidentally a Catholic Priest, one who is accustomed to hearing confessions—must accept Miss Milner's powerful silence in place of the confession he desires.

Inchbald's essays were written after *A Simple Story,* and they follow quite logically from the novel's more detailed exploration of gendered power struggles in the eighteenth century. Inchbald's work, of course, is not always pessimistic. The first half of *A Simple Story,* for example, which Inchbald had wanted to publish as a complete novel, ends before Miss Milner's affair. Miss Milner's power before her marriage seems real and exciting, even though the second half of *A Simple Story* (which I believe must be read as a revisionary complement to part 1) presents a more pessimistic scenario, with Miss Milner's affair and subsequent banishment from her home.[38] Such an ending suggests that even if a marriage or reunion appears initially to promise future well-being, a woman who remains in her home will be forced inevitably to accept the constraints that heroines like Miss Milner and Jane Shore reject. Many of Inchbald's critical essays carry overt variations on this pessimistic view of the eighteenth-century family. Inchbald locates masculine strength in the power to exact a confession and feminine strength in the power to resist giving self-revealing or self-damning testimonies. In Inchbald's view, a woman could maintain her self-regard only by refusing to speak, and any speech act other than silence would result in terrific constraints.

Inchbald's message was bold and direct, and it would have been threateningly specific to an audience accustomed to the reinforcement of existing gender constraints. It is little wonder that her biographer, James Boaden, and her fellow dramatists George Colman the Younger and George Daniel, reacted so violently to the essays. The scenario Inchbald presents is drastically bleak: "Though love may sometimes make a man, too often, it undoes a woman."[39]

Notes

[1] The series of plays along with Inchbald's prefaces appeared periodically beginning in 1806 and was assembled in 1808 in twenty-five volumes under the title *The British Theatre.* James Boaden, *Memoirs of Mrs. Inchbald: Including her Familiar Correspondence with the most distinguished persons of her time,* 2 vols. (London: Richard Bentley, 1833), 2:84.

[2] Boaden, 2:87.

[3] George Colman the Younger was particularly offended by Inchbald's judgment of his own plays and those of his father, and he published an angry letter of reproof which Inchbald answered. In Inchbald's 1808 diary (Folger Library MS M.a. 155), she reports revisions of her response to Colman in February and March of 1808. It was returned to her from the printer on 8 June. Inchbald's letter was published in vol. 21 of *The British Theatre.* D-G, review of Arthur Murphy's *The Grecian Daughter,* in *Cumberland's British Theatre,* ed. John Cumberland, 30 vols. (London: Ludgate Hall, 1828), vol. 25. All further reference to *Cumberland's British Theatre* will be to this edition. Like Inchbald's collection, these reviews are short and not continuously paginated, so I will identify the preface and play by volume number.

[4] Inchbald's collection was financially successful. According to the publisher Longman, it sold many copies. Inchbald was later paid for the use of her name in conjunction with a series entitled *The Modern Theatre,* and Inchbald was invited to become a regular contributor to the *Quarterly Review.* Even so, Boaden attributes her reluctance to write any more essays after the completion of *The British Theatre* to her unhappiness with the response her essays had received (2:114).

[5] Boaden, 1:42. Boaden, who could not have been more than eleven years old when Inchbald played Calista for the first time, probably could not have seen or evalu-ated Inchbald's performance, and his insistent association of Inchbald with the character she portrayed is striking.

[6] Boaden was quick to insist that Inchbald, in spite of her rather inappropriate (by his standards) flirtatious behavior, was never sexually promiscuous. His deep concern with Inchbald's reputation implies a moral standard that Inchbald would not necessarily have espoused. He worries (rather belatedly), for example, that "the situation of an actress is exposed beyond parallel to temptations of every kind" (Boaden, 1:109).

[7] William McKee, *Elizabeth Inchbald, Novelist* (Washington DC: Catholic University of America, 1935). S. R. Littlewood, *Elizabeth Inchbald and Her Circle: The Life Story of a Charming Woman* (London: Daniel O'Connor, 1921), p. 111.

[8] Katharine M. Rogers, "Britain's First Woman Drama Critic: Elizabeth Inchbald," *Curtain Calls: British and American Women and the Theater; 1660-1820,* ed. Mary Anne Schofield and Cecilia Macheski (Athens: Ohio Univ. Press, 1991), pp. 277-90. Rogers's essay is the most thorough and sympathetic account of Inchbald's prefaces to date. She argues that Inchbald follows other late-eighteenth-century critics in emphasizing the "interrelated values of naturalness or probability, gentility, and morality" (p. 282). And the essay carefully and sympathetically considers the implications of these values for Inchbald's work. See also Roger Manvell, *Elizabeth Inchbald: England's Principal Woman Dramatist and Independent Woman of Letters in Eighteenth-Century London* (Lanham, NY and London: Univ. Press of America, 1987). Manvell summarizes and quotes at length from the prefaces.

[9] Rogers, pp. 278 and 281.

[10] Quoted in Boaden, 2:101.

[11] Letter to Colman in vol. 21 of *The British Theatre* (London, 1808). All further references to *The British Theatre* will be to this edition. Because the essays are short and the pagination not continuous, I will identify the preface and play by volume number.

[12] D-G extends his scorn to Inchbald's own comedies, many of which, he argues, "as Mr. Puff says, 'there is no laughing at.'"

[13] Covent Garden was burned on 20 September 1808 and Drury Lane on 24 February 1809. Patricia Sigl ("Prince Hoare's Artist and Anti-Theatrical Polemics in the early 1800s: Mrs. Inchbald's Contribution," *Theatre Notebook* 44, 2 [1990]: 62-73) cites these disasters as the impetus for an essay appearing in Prince Hoare's *The Artist* that she attributes to Inchbald.

[14] Prince Hoare, "Reform of our Stage," *The Artist: A Collection of Essays Relative to Painting, Poetry, Sculpture, Architecture, the Drama, Discoveries of Science, and Various Other Subjects,* ed. Prince Hoare, 2 vols. (London, 1810), vol. 2, no. 20, pp. 392-416.

[15] Hoare, pp. 410-11.

[16] Hoare hoped that subscribers would fund the theater. On this point see Sigl, p. 63.

[17] Sigl, passim.

[18] Inchbald, letter "To *The Artist,*" *The Artist,* 2. no. 9, 15 May 1809, pp. 138-53.

[19] Inchbald, letter "To *The Artist,*" *The Artist,* 1, no. 14, 13 June 1807, pp. 9-19. Reprinted as an Appendix by William McKee in *Elizabeth Inchbald,* p. 153. Inchbald also contributed a short essay to *The Artist* as part of an issue devoted "To the Memory of John Opie," *The Artist,* 1, no. 7, 25 April 1807, pp. 22-23.

[20] Boaden, 2:114.

[21] Richard Cumberland, *The British Drama,* 14 vols. (London: C. Cooke, 1817), 6:xxii.

[22] Rogers notes that Inchbald deviates from social norms in her reviews of these two plays, but Rogers considers Inchbald's unorthodox stand an anomaly, remarking that "unfortunately she was not always so independent" (p. 281).

[23] Anna Seward, Essay 25 in *Variety* (1787; essays 25 and 26 rpnt. in Ioan Williams, ed., *Novel and Romance, 1700-1800: A Documentary Record* [New York: Barnes and Noble, 1970], pp. 357-66, 361).

[24] Lady Jane Grey's dispassionate morality was often a difficult issue for Rowe's audience. John Bell (*The British Theatre,* 35 vols. [London, 1791], vol. 31) says of the play that "in pathetic power it is infinitely below his Shore; yet the resignation of Jane may affect those whose moral rectitude might refuse in the former play their sympathy to the sufferer; stained by illicit conduct, and only expiating ingratitude by penury and pain."

[25] In her essay on *The Winter's Tale,* Inchbald also admires the widowed Paulina who, like Inchbald's other favorite heroines—Queen Katharine, Hermione, Jane Shore—maintains her dignified self-regard even when separated from her husband. Rogers attributes Inchbald's interest in Paulina and Hermione, and Inchbald's disapproval of Perdita, to her genuine interest in mature love. According to Rogers, Perdita (and Romeo and Juliet) are too young to inspire real interest (p. 281).

[26] Annotated copy of Inchbald's edition of *The British Theatre,* ca. 1806, Folger Library MS W.a. 70, n.p., opposite title page to *Henry VIII.*
[27] Inchbald reports in her diaries for 1776, 1780, 1781, 1783, and 1788 (Folger Library MS M.a. 149-51, n.p., passim) that she acted the part of Jane Shore periodically throughout the last quarter of the eighteenth century, often with her husband playing the deceived Shore

until his sudden death on 6 June 1779.

[28] Inchbald's condemnation of, for example, *The Beaux Stratagem* (vol. 8) and *The Provoked Wife* (vol. 5), was in keeping with the moral standards of her day. More striking is her disapproval of Calista in *The Fair Penitent* (the role Boaden so vehemently declaimed against), who, she argues, is not sufficiently or credibly penitent. But rather than dwell on Calista's penitence (or lack thereof), Inchbald condemns her taste in choosing the "skipping, dancing, worthless" Lothario over his honorable rival, and she hopes that the women of her own audience will be "better qualified than heretofore to chuse their lovers and husbands" (vol. 16).

[29] Perhaps, as Rogers has suggested (p. 285), Inchbald's morality was simply a concession to the standards of the day. But Inchbald remained a devout Catholic all of her life, and her stance may well have been genuine.

[30] Rogers mentions Inchbald's defense of *The Stranger,* remarking that Inchbald "deviated from the norm only in her relatively enlightened portrayal of unhappy fallen women (in serious drama only where they can suffer adequately for their sins)" (p. 285). I argue that Inchbald's attitude toward adulterous women is less significant than her consideration of the consequences of adultery or supposed adultery.

[31] D-G argues in his own review of *The Stranger (Cumberland's British Theatre)* that Mrs. Haller's fall from virtue "is but lamely imagined" (vol. 14). The essay seems to respond directly to Inchbald's more radical interpretation.

[32] Richard Cumberland (*The British Drama,* 6:xxi) locates true feminine virtue in the confession. Of Lady Townly's confession in *The Provok'd Husband,* her "awaking to a consciousness of her misconduct," Cumberland writes: "what [Lady Townly] rightly terms 'the story of her heart,' . . . [is] a story which every young woman of beauty, birth, and fashion, ought to lay to her heart, every parent and guardian recommend as a lesson." Inchbald's treatment of the confession in her essay on *The Stranger* seems to speak directly to Cumberland's moral lesson. Inchbald also approves of the final scene in *The Provok'd Husband,* but she avoids discussing the confession ritual. She remarks only that Cibber's attitude toward "female frailty" is more compassionate than that of Vanbrugh, who died before he finished the play. Vanbrugh had intended to punish his heroine by having her "repudiated by her husband, and all her honorable friends, as a proper warning to the unthinking wives of the period" (vol. 9).

[33] Michel Foucault, *The History of Sexuality, Volume I: An Introduction,* trans. Robert Hurley (New York: Pantheon Books, 1978), p. 61.

[34] Foucault, pp. 61-62.

[35] Samuel Johnson, *Life of Rowe* in *Lives of the Poets,*

ed. George Birkbeck Hill, 3 vols. (Oxford: Clarendon Press, 1905), 2:69-70.

[36] Elizabeth Inchbald, *A Simple Story,* intro. Jane Spencer, ed. J. M. S. Tompkins (London: Oxford Univ. Press, 1988), p. 196.

[37] Inchbald, *A Simple Story,* p. 197.

[38] Mary Anne Schofield (*Masking and Unmasking the Female Mind: Disguising Romances in Feminine Fiction, 1713-1799* [Newark: Univ. of Delaware Press, 1990]) has recently argued that part 2 of *A Simple Story* is an "unmasking" of the romance genre, an allegorical representation of the unhappy nature of the heroine's plight (pp. 175-82). For another reading of Matilda's situation see Terry Castle's *Masquerade and Civilization: The Carnivalesque in Eighteenth-Century Culture and Fiction* (Stanford: Stanford Univ. Press, 1986), in which she argues that Matilda's marriage is a feminine victory over masculine law (pp. 320-30). See also Jane Spencer's introduction to *A Simple Story.* Spencer characterizes the second half of the novel as a restoration of "feminine propriety and narrative closure" (p. xx).

[39] Inchbald, *The British Theatre,* vol. 1, remarks on Colley Cibber's *Love Makes a Man.*

FURTHER READING

Bibliography

Joughin, G. Louis. "An Inchbald Bibliography." *Studies in English: The University of Texas Bulletin,* No. 14 (July 8, 1934): 59-74.

    Contains production and publication information for Inchbald's plays and novels. Only those works that were available publicly (whether printed or staged) are listed.

Biography

Littlewood, S. R. *Elizabeth Inchbald and Her Circle: The Life Story of a Charming Woman (1753-1821).* London: Daniel O'Connor, 1921, 135 p.

    Detailed biographical account of Inchbald's life from her early years in Suffolk, through her literary accomplishments, to her increasing interest in religion toward the end of her life.

Zall, Paul M. "The Cool World of Samuel Taylor Coleridge: Elizabeth Inchbald; or Sex and Sensibility." *The Wordsworth Circle* XII, No. 4 (Autumn 1981): 270-73.

    Biographical account tracing Inchbald's professional career as an actress, playwright, and novelist.

Criticism

Ford, Susan Allen. "'A name more dear': Daughters, Fathers, and Desire in *A Simple Story, The False Friend,* and *Mathilda.*" In *Re-visioning Romanticism: British Women Writers, 1776-1837,* edited by Carol Shiner Wilson and Joel Haefner, pp. 51-71. Philadelphia: University of Pennsylvania Press, 1994.

    Analysis of the theme of illicit attraction to the patriarchal figure in novels by Inchbald, Mary Darby Robinson, and Mary Wollstonecraft Shelley, all of which subtly disrupt the conventional ideal of domesticity.

Kelly, Gary. "Elizabeth Inchbald." In *The English Jacobin Novel: 1780-1805,* pp. 64-113. Oxford: Clarendon Press, 1976.

    Argues that Inchbald's use of personal experiences in her novels served as a model for later nineteenth-century writers.

Macheski, Cecilia. "Herself as Heroine: Portraits as Autobiography for Elizabeth Inchbald." In *Curtain Calls: British and American Women and the Theater; 1660-1820,* edited by Mary Anne Schofield and Cecilia Macheski, pp. 34-47. Athens: Ohio University Press, 1991.

    Examines Inchbald's use of portraits—rather than written words—to form her autobiography.

Patterson, Emily H. "Elizabeth Inchbald's Treatment of the Family and the Pilgrimage in *A Simple Story.*" *Etudes Anglaises* XXIX, No. 2 (April-June 1976): 196-98.

    Examines the novel's non-traditional treatment of the family and the pilgrimage, which the critic believes borders on subversive.

Sigl, Patricia. "Prince Hoare's *Artist* and Anti-Theatrical Polemics in the Early 1800s: Mrs. Inchbald's Contribution." *Theatre Notebook* XLIV, No. 2 (1990): 62-73.

    Examination of Inchbald's defense of the English theatre world against religious censorship and criticism.

Spencer, Jane. Introduction to *A Simple Story,* by Elizabeth Inchbald. Ed. J. M. S. Tompkins, pp. vii-xx. Oxford: Oxford University Press, 1988.

    Examines the theme of womanhood, focusing in particular on the character of the coquette and the idea of female self-assertion.

Additional coverage of Inchbald's life and career is contained in the following source published by Gale Research: *Dictionary of Literary Biography,* **Vol. 39.**

The Monk

M. G. Lewis

The following entry presents criticism of Lewis's novel *The Monk* (1796). For a discussion of Lewis's complete career, see *NCLC*, Volume 11.

INTRODUCTION

Perhaps the most notorious English horror novel of the eighteenth century, M. G. Lewis's *The Monk* is considered one of the finest examples of Gothic fiction in the language. Sensationalistic and graphic in its depiction of violence and human sexuality, the novel created a scandal in England soon after its publication, and caused its author, then a member of the House of Commons, to be branded licentious and perverse. Extravagant and melodramatic in style, the work details the exploits of Ambrosio, a wayward monk whose excessive pride and vanity lead to murder, a pact with Satan, and his eternal damnation. *The Monk* is said to be composed from a variety of sources, many of them German, while its main plot comes from the story of Santon Barisa, which appeared in *The Guardian* in 1713. Lewis acknowledged his debts on many of these accounts, partially to divert possible charges of plagiarism, and included in his novel several pieces of original and translated verse, including the ballad "Alonzo the Brave and Fair Imogen." Although this and other poems are largely overlooked by modern scholars, *The Monk* is generally considered Lewis's masterpiece and one of the most fully realized visions of Gothic horror.

Plot and Major Characters

Ambrosio, the monk of the novel's title and a foundling of mysterious past and parentage, has risen to the position of abbot of the Capuchins, becoming a well-respected figure in medieval Madrid, revered by the populace. At the monastery a young novitiate named Rosario approaches Ambrosio and reveals that he is actually a woman named Matilda de Villanges, whose love for Ambrosio has led her to disguise herself in order to be nearer to him. The two consummate a sexual relationship, though Ambrosio later feels remorse and disgust for his actions. After his interlude with Matilda, while visiting the nearby convent of St. Clare, Ambrosio discovers that Agnes, a nun, desires to elope with her lover, Don Raymond de las Cisternas. The monk discloses this information to Mother St. Agatha, prioress of the convent, who punishes Agnes by imprisoning her in a dungeon beneath the convent. Later, Ambrosio travels to the house of the ailing Donna

Elvira Dalfa and there falls in love with her young daughter, Antonia. With the aid of Matilda and her knowledge of black magic, the monk summons a demon so that he might violate the girl. Ambrosio returns to Donna Elvira's house, kills her, and abducts Antonia, now unconscious through the action of a magical potion. In the meantime, Agnes's brother, Lorenzo, accuses Mother St. Agatha of murdering his sister and wins a warrant for her arrest. An angry mob forms in response to the accusation, and the crowd razes the convent, murdering the prioress and many innocent nuns. Amid the chaos, Lorenzo enters the convent grounds in search of his sister. When he finds her she is close to death and clutches the decaying body of her dead child. Hearing the screams of a young girl nearby, Lorenzo discovers Antonia's ravished and stabbed body and observes her attacker, Ambrosio, as he flees; later he notifies the Inquisition of Ambrosio's crimes. Ordered to be burned at the stake, Ambrosio, at the urgings of Matilda, makes a pact with Satan, exchanging his soul for freedom. The devil appears and saves him from the flames of the Inquisition, only to reveal that in killing Donna Elvira and raping Antonia, he has murdered his own mother and committed incest with his sister. The story ends as the monk's forfeit soul is cast into hell.

Major Themes

Scholars observe that the thematic character of *The Monk* departs somewhat from that of the traditional Gothic novel. And while it favors the evocation of grotesque horror rather than the rendering of a sentimental theme of justice based upon divine Providence, Lewis's novel nevertheless presents a critique of human vice and explores the conflict between religion and human sexuality. This conflict is dramatized in the character of Ambrosio through the juxtaposition of the monk's pride and destructive sexual appetite with the innocent virtue of Antonia and the forthrightness of Lorenzo. Many commentators note, however, that the dullness of the novel's virtuous characters fails to match the depth and complexity of Ambrosio and Matilda, and instead locate evidence of the novel's primary theme in the psychological exploration of its fallen protagonist and his accomplice. Likewise, many have observed that Matilda's strong will and intelligence make her far more compelling than her counterpart Antonia, despite her manipulative behavior and demonic nature. Others have commented on Lewis's attempts to establish an unsettling parallel between the violence of the riotous mob in his novel and that of the French Revolution, or on his deft integration of legends and folk tales, such as those of the Bleeding Nun and the Wandering Jew, in order to illicit terror and add universal appeal to his story.

Critical Reception

First published in 1796, *The Monk* created a considerable stir and earned Lewis instant fame, even infamy, as its author—though none of his later works received the same notoriety as this, his first novel. Labeled obscene by a cast of critics, including Samuel Taylor Coleridge—who acknowledged that despite its immorality the novel was the "offspring of no common genius"—it was nevertheless extremely popular, and went through five editions before the end of the century. The controversy that the first edition sparked prompted Lewis to expurgate certain passages from these later printings, though scholars now agree that his changes were largely superficial. Coleridge's criticism of the work on one point was taken up by James Mathias, who emphasized the lewdness and irreligion of the work, especially of a scene in which Antonia reads an edited version of the Bible given to her by her mother. In 1800 the Marquis de Sade wrote that *The Monk* was a product of the revolutionary atmosphere of the late eighteenth century, while in the twentieth century critics have reevaluated the influence of the work on the writers of the Romantic movement.

Modern scholars have since observed that *The Monk* represents a successful synthesis of the techniques and materials used by Gothic horror writers, leading many to take a renewed interest in the work. Recent critics have applied the tools of psychological criticism to it, examining its sexual imagery and applying biographical information about Lewis's childhood development and psyche to understanding the novel.

CRITICISM

"A Friend to Genius" (essay date 1797)

SOURCE: "An Apology for *The Monk*," in *Monthly Mirror*, Vol. 3, April, 1797, pp. 210-15.

[*In the following essay, the anonymous critic maintains that* The Monk *expounds lessons of virtue, rather than of vice, as many reviewers have contended.*]

It is with no inconsiderable pain that I have remarked the numerous attacks which have been made by the host of critics on the ingenious author of *The Monk,* for the supposed vicious tendency of that excellent romance. The author is universally allowed to be endowed with nature's best gift, genius, and in the work before us is generally acknowledged to discover throughout an imagination, rich, powerful, and fervid. This able writer is, however, attacked on a point which, I am sure, must make him feel little satisfaction in the applause which his genius commands. It is asserted by almost all the critics who have sat in judgment on this admirable performance, that its *tendency* is to deprave the heart, to vitiate the understanding, and to enlist the passions in the cause of vice. Differing as I do with these censors, as to this and other objections, I wish, through the medium of your impartial publication, to rescue his production from this undeserved obloquy. I have not the pleasure of Mr. Lewis's acquaintance, and I know not how this apology may be received on his part, but the defence of genius is the common cause of all men of the least pretensions to literature; and every person who can enjoy works of taste, has the right of rescuing them from unmerited attacks. I should, as little as the critics, wish to be the apologist of vice, or the defender of lasciviousness; but justice requires that error, and error of such magnitude, as it regards Mr. Lewis's character, should be detected and exposed.

The error of the principal objection to this romance, viz. that of its vicious *tendency,* appears to me entirely to arise from inaccuracy of observation of the author's work, of the human heart, and of the meaning of the word tendency. It is not a temporary effect, produced upon the imagination or the passions, by particular passages, which can fairly be cited as the tendency of the work; we must examine what are the probable general results from the whole, and not judge from these partial and fleeting effects.

In this view, I maintain, this beautiful romance is well calculated to support the cause of virtue, and to teach her lessons to man. I am not old enough to have my heart steeled against the effects of the strongest of the human passions, nor young enough to riot in lascivious description, or wanton in the regions of obscene imagery. I can feel as disgusted as the critics with such defects; but I entreat these *grey bearded* gentleman to consider again whether there are any such images in the work before us. The lessons of virtue which I see in the Monk, are striking and impressive. In the character of Ambrosio we see a man delineated of strong passions, which have been for a long period subdued by as strong resolution; of a natural disposition to virtue, but, like all other men, with some portion of vice, which has been fostered by the situation into which his fate had thrown him; he is haughty, vindictive, and austere. The greatest error of which he is guilty, is too great a confidence in his own virtue, too great a reliance on his own hatred of vice. We are taught by his conduct that this unbounded confidence, by blinding the mind as to the real consequences which result, lays the foundation for vice, and opens an easy road to great excesses. We have again a very forcible illustration in Ambrosio, a man of the strongest understanding and the highest powers of reason, of the danger of receding even in the least from the path of virtue, or giving way in the slightest degree to the insidious approaches of vice. *C'est le premier pas qui coute,* is a truth long established, and is well illustrated in the present instance. We see and feel strongly this danger, and the lesson is the more forcible, in proportion to the strength of understanding which is shown in the Monk. We learn that when once a man ventures into the pool of vice, that he plunges deeper and deeper till he is completely overwhelmed. These are striking and impressive lessons.

There are many other moral lessons which are inculcated by the work in the strongest manner; the tendency, therefore, i. e. the general effect likely to result, is favourable to the cause of virtue and morality. We are however told, that "the temptations of Ambrosio are described with a libidinous minuteness, which leaves the painful impression of great acquirements and splendid genius, employed to furnish poison for youth, and a provocative for the debauchee." [Critical Review, for February, 1797.] If this were the case, I must give up my author in part, though still the tendency of the whole would be good. But I deny the fact. I request that the character and circumstances of Ambrosio may be seriously considered. To a man of strong understanding, austerity of manners, and great self command, strong temptations must be offered. If the author had made the Monk sink under a slight temptation, he would have offended against the laws of probability, and shocked the reason of his readers. I ask if it be possible to describe such temptations as were calculated to seduce such a man, with greater delicacy and decorum than our author has done: and I will take for example the strongest instances—the conclusion of chapter 2. vol. I. p. 253 of vol. 2. and his attack on Antonia in p. 36 and 37 of vol. 3. The answer, I am persuaded, must be—No! Highly coloured as these passages are, I maintain that no heart but one already depraved, could rise from them, if the preceding part of the work had been perused, with the least impurity. The mind that could draw food for vicious appetites from this work, must have made no little progress in the paths of profligacy and debauchery; so strong are the entrenchments erected before the heart, by the *general tendency* of the work.

The previous part is calculated to prevent all the evil which may arise from warmth of description, by the interest we take in observing the gradual progress of vice in Ambrosio's bosom, and the hatred we of course must feel for this insiduous adversary. The work can be read only by three descriptions of persons; either those whose minds, by habitual vice, are prepared to turn every the least hint to the purposes of food for their depraved appetites, or as incitements to their dormant desires, which require stimulants; or those who are wavering between vice and virtue, whose minds may be led to either, by interesting their passions strongly for one or the other; or else, young, innocent, and undepraved persons. The first deserve not notice: purity itself would be poison to their hearts, and the modestest allusion would excite depraved ideas. The passions of the second will be, I contend, excited more strongly to virtue than to vice by **The Monk,** because the horrors consequent on his vicious conduct are so strongly pourtrayed, as to destroy the momentary effect, if any were produced, of the passages which are rather warm in description. The last, from the very supposition of their being yet innocent and unpolluted, and in consequence ignorant, can not have improper ideas excited, or their passions roused to vice; as, in the first place, they will not be able to understand as much as our *knowing* critics, nor can the confused notions of felicity which may be excited destroy the purity of their minds, or the effect of the moral lessons inculcated. The writer of this paper felt not a single loose idea excited by the warmest passages, so perfectly had he imbibed the moral lessons which the author has so forcibly brought forward.

The critics themselves seem aware of this tendency of the work, and therefore endeavour to deprive the author of the defence, by roundly asserting that "a romance is incapable of exemplifying moral truth; and that he who could rise superior to all earthly temptation, and whom the strength of the spiritual world alone would be adequate to overwhelm, might reasonably be proud, and would fall with glory." As applied to *The Monk*, there are two errors in this assertion. The reader of this romance has no reason to imagine, till the greater part of the mischief has been done, that any but earthly temptations are used against the hero. The fall of Ambrosio is precisely that which would happen to any man of a similar character, assailed as he was by the fascinating arts of a woman, skilled in exciting the strongest passions, and endowed with the most attractive charms. We see the gradual progress she makes in undermining his virtue by merely human means. His feelings, his gratitude, and finally the strong desires of human nature are all combined to ensure his fall. But still the temptations appear to be no more than human. We see where a man of truly virtuous principles would have commenced resistance; we observe and lament his first deviation from the path of virtue; and cannot withhold our wishes that he may remain firm when the first disposition to yield manifests itself. Matilda appears to be merely a woman, though a woman of the greatest charms, and of an extraordinary character; but still there is nothing improbable or unnatural in the means of temptation, nothing that a man of a strong mind and pure virtue would not have resisted. The lesson therefore is taught and deeply imbibed before the discovery of supernatural agency is made, and that discovery does not and cannot eradicate the morality before inculcated.

Nor is it true in general that moral truth cannot be conveyed in romance. The general sense of mankind is against the critics in this assertion. From the earliest ages fiction, and incredible fiction, has been thought a proper vehicle for moral instruction, from the fables of Æsop, to the tales, allegories, and visions of modern days. The religion itself which these gentlemen profess inculcates the notion that Lucifer is the author of all our vicious propensities, and that he is the continual seducer of man. An allegorical representation of this being visibly interfering is no more therefore than adopting popular belief, and turning it to the purposes of instruction. It is no more improbable, on the notion of this great tempter, that a man should yield to his agency, when he himself assumes the human figure, than when he is supposed, as he is, to inhabit the bodies of all the vicious, and supply the crafty and artful with the means of operating on inferior minds. We do not the less blame Eve, because we are told that she yielded to the temptation of the serpent.

As to the minor objections made to the conduct of parts of the story, and defects of style and description, I feel not myself called on to defend, my object not being to establish the literary but moral excellence of the work. The only remaining objection which I shall attempt to answer is that "our author has contrived to make his romance pernicious, by blending, with an irreverent negligence, all that is most awfully true in religion, with all that is most ridiculously absurd in superstition. He takes frequent occasion, indeed, to manifest his sovereign contempt for the latter, both in his own person and in that of his principal characters; and that his respect for the former is not excessive we are forced to conclude from the treatment which its inspired writers receive from him."

In support of this observation we have a garbled passage quoted by the critics, in which the author has noticed with too much warmth, we must confess, some of the passages of the bible, which are undoubtedly improper for the eye of a young female. It is not fair to quote this passage without adding the eulogiums which the author has passed on the morality of the sacred writings, both in that passage and others in the work. Whether the author be or be not a Christian, is not the inquiry, but whether there be any foundation for the observation made on the indecency of some parts of our religious code; this the critics are obliged to allow is the case in one instance, viz. Ezekiel chap. 23. There are also other examples which must be in the eye of every man who has read these writings with attention. The indiscriminate perusal of such passages as occur, in which every thing is called by its vulgar name, in which the most luxuriant images are described, as in Solomon's Song, must certainly be improper for young females. So fully aware were the Jews of this truth, that they prohibited the reading of Solomon's Song, till a certain age, when the passions are in subjection. The warmth of expression is too great, but we may pardon this, since we see a desire of preventing the mischievous effects of even the most generally excellent productions.—The author, so far from deserving to be stigmatized as an enemy to Christianity, appears to me to be acting as one of its best friends, when he endeavours to prevent the mischief which may ensue from mixing what may be improper for young minds, with the rest of a work so generally excellent in its morality, so pure in its doctrines. The mischief which might be produced would be the greater, because of the reverence with which young persons are generally taught to regard the sacred writings. The impressions of such images as are blamed, would be the more deeply engraven on the mind, as they believe that nothing can be learned there but purity and innocence. I should have thought that these critics might have overlooked an error into which they themselves have fallen to a still greater excess: for they cannot allow the moral tendency of the romance to plead the pardon of two or three passages, which appear to them to be too luxuriant, and too replete with wanton imagery.

I have thus, Sir, endeavoured to shew that the attacks made on Mr. Lewis are unfounded, and that when the critic stares and trembles to find the author of *The Monk* a legislator, his horror is not reasonable; and that with propriety we may apply to those men who can drink vice at the fountain of the Monk, the expression of this very critic: "The most innocent expressions may become the first link in the chain of association, when a man's soul has been poisoned and depraved by the habit of reading lewd and voluptuous tales; and we believe it not absolutely impossible that he might extract pollution from the word of purity, and turn the grace of God into wantonness."

I hope I have succeeded in showing, that "the author has not endeavoured to inflame the fleshy appetites, and then to pour contempt on the only book which would be adequate to the task of reclaiming them." If I have not failed in this object, I shall feel a satisfaction in having employed a leisure hour in a task so delightful as rescuing from disgrace, in my opinion unmerited, a man of such talents, taste, and brilliancy of imagination, as the author of **The Monk**. I hope this attempt will not be displeasing to him who is the most concerned, nor fail of its effect on the public mind. My motives are, however, pure; I know I am as great an enemy to licentiousness as the critics themselves, and I trust I have shewn myself

A FRIEND TO GENIUS

Monthly Review (review date 1797)

SOURCE: Review of *The Monk*, in *Monthly Review*, Vol. 23, August, 1797, p. 451.

[*In the following review, the critic describes the literary sources of* The Monk, *adding that obscenity "pervades and deforms the whole organization of this novel."*]

This novel has a double plot. The outline of the monk Ambrosio's story was suggested by that of the *Santon Barsisa*, in the Guardian: the form of temptation is borrowed from the *Devil in Love* of Cazotte; and the catastrophe is taken from *the Sorcerer*. The adventures of Raymond and Agnes are less obviously imitations; yet the forest-scene near Strasburgh brings to mind an incident in Smollet's Ferdinand Count Fathom: the bleeding Nun is described by the author as a popular tale of the Germans; and the convent-prison resembles the inflictions of Mrs. Radcliffe. This may be called plagiarism; yet it deserves some praise. The great art of writing consists in selecting what is most stimulant from the works of our predecessors, and in uniting the gathered beauties in a new whole, more interesting than the tributary models. This is the essential process of the imagination, and excellence is no otherwise attained. All invention is but new combination. To invent well is to combine the impressive.

Of the poetry, we have been best pleased with *the Water-Ring*, and with *Alonzo the brave and the fair Imogene*, the latter of which is written in a manner much resembling and little inferior to the Lenardo and Blandine of Bürger. A vein of obscenity, however, pervades and deforms the whole organization of this novel, which must ever blast, in a moral view, the *fair* fame that, in point of ability, it would have gained for the author; and which renders the work totally unfit for general circulation.

Coleridge on Lewis's *The Monk*:

The sufferings which [Lewis] describes are so frightful and intolerable, that we break with abruptness from the delusion, and indignantly suspect the man of a species of brutality, who could find a pleasure in wantonly imagining them; and the abominations which he pourtrays with no hurrying pencil, are such as the observation of character by no means demanded, such as 'no observation of character can justify, because no good man would willingly suffer them to pass, however transiently, through his own mind.' The merit of a novellist is in proportion (not simply to the effect, but) to the *pleasurable* effect which he produces. Situations of torment, and images of naked horror, are easily conceived; and a writer in whose works they abound, deserves our gratitude almost equally with him who should drag us by way of sport through a military hospital, or force us to sit at the dissecting-table of a natural philosopher. To trace the nice boundaries, beyond which terror and sympathy are deserted by the pleasurable emotions,— to reach those limits, yet never to pass them,—*hic labor, hic opus est.* Figures that shock the imagination, and narratives that mangle the feelings, rarely discover *genius*, and always betray a low and vulgar *taste*.

Samuel Taylor Coleridge, in The Critical Review, *February, 1797, reprinted in* Coleridge's Miscellaneous Criticism, *ed. by Thomas Middleton Raysor, Harvard University Press, 1936.*

Montague Summers (essay date 1938)

SOURCE: "Matthew Gregory Lewis," in *The Gothic Quest: A History of the Gothic Novel*, 1938. Reprint, Russell and Russell, Inc., 1964, pp. 202-308.

[*In the following excerpt, Summers details the composition, contemporary critical reception, plot, style, sources, translations, adaptations, and literary influence of* The Monk. *Only those footnotes pertaining to the excerpt below have been reprinted.*]

Towards the end of February, 1793, Lewis returned to England, and resumed his residence at Christ

Church. His keeping of terms must have been irregular, at least, on account of this absence in Germany, but none the less he proceeded B.A., 1794, and M.A., 1797. During the Easter vacation he was in Scotland, where he paid a long visit to Lord Douglas at Bothwell Castle and was also the guest of the Duke of Buccleuch. He was still occupying himself with making ballads, and was further engaged upon a translation of Schiller's *Kabale und Liebe* (1784) which, however, was not published until 1797. During the Hilary term of 1794 Lewis was at Oxford, but he did not come up for the summer since his father obtained him the position of an attaché to the British embassy at the Hague, whither Lord St. Helens[16] was returning from his ambassadorship at Madrid to succeed Lord Auckland,[17] who during the French revolution had been ambassador extraordinary to Holland.

Lewis arrived at the Hague on Thursday night, May 15th, 1794, where after a few days at an inn he removed to pleasant lodgings over a grocer's shop near the ambassador's hotel. Although eventually he got into a very agreeable Parisian coterie which used to assemble three times a week at the house of Madame de Matignon, Lewis found the Hague insupportably dull,—"I am certain that the devil *ennui* has made the Hague his favourite abode" he tells his mother—and it was only the fact that he was "horribly bit by the rage of writing," which saved him from falling into such low spirits as almost threatened to become a serious malady. His letters now are full of literary chit-chat, books he has read or is planning to write; a refusal to allow G. G. and J. Robinson, the well-known house of Paternoster Row, to publish his poem by bits and bits in magazines; the description of a little farce he has just penned on the subject of two twin brothers, one a rake-hell, and the other a broad-brim quaker, who are constantly mistaken for each other. The scenes were so arranged that the brothers never meet on the stage, and the dual rôle was, in fact, especially designed for a numerical actor, Jack Bannister,[18] who produced the piece, *The Twins; or, Is it He or his Brother,* on the occasion of his benefit at Drury Lane, Monday, April 8th, 1799. "It was a whimsical and pleasant entertainment," says the *Biographia Dramatica,* but it was not adopted by the house, nor has it been printed.

At the end of April, 1794, had appeared Mrs. Radcliffe's *The Mysteries of Udolpho,* which Lewis commenced reading before he set out on his journey and finished immediately after his arrival at the Hague. It is, he cries, "in my opinion, one of the most interesting books ever published." It is significant, however, that he regarded the first nine chapters, as comparatively insipid, and yet these very passages with their exquisite descriptions of mountain scenery are among the finest of Mrs. Radcliffe's work. His imagination, however, was set afire by the lone Castle amid the far Appenines,

those awful halls of dread where the dark Montoni was lord of life and death. Once more inspired to continue his own romance "in the style of *The Castle of Otranto,*" he set to work to extricate the dying man from his difficulties, but finding himself unable to carry the story further, he was soon obliged yet again to lay it on one side.[19]

Not to be baffled, he wisely determined to begin altogether anew, on an entirely fresh track and this time things went smoothly, for on September 23rd. he triumphantly asks his mother: "What do you think of my having written, in the space of ten weeks, a romance of between three and four hundred pages octavo? I have even written out half of it fair. It is called **The Monk,** and I am myself so much pleased with it that, if the booksellers will not buy it, I shall publish it myself." Two months after, his last letter from the Hague, November 22nd, tells Mrs. Lewis that he will not send her the manuscript of **The Monk** since he prefers to hand it to her himself when they meet in London. "For my own part, I have not written a line excepting the Farce, and **The Monk,** which is a work of some length, and will make an octavo volume of 420 pages. There is a great deal of poetry inserted," and so as a *bonne bouche* he encloses a copy of the "Inscription in an Hermitage" which occurs in Chapter II. (In the printed text of **The Monk** there are some few trifling variants.) As Lewis signed his octosyllabic Preface, Imitation of Horace,[20] Epistles, Book I, Ep. 20, "Hague, Oct. 28th, 1794," we may assume that he then completed his fair copy, and his pages were ready for the press.

Lewis' father now recalled him to England, and in December Matthew Gregory was back in London. He spent the Christmas of 1794 at Devonshire-place.

Very soon he set about finding a publisher for his romance, nor did he experience much difficulty in the quest. In March, 1796,[21] **The Monk** was first published, in three volumes, duodecimo, by John Bell, 148 Oxford Street, at nine shillings. It was re-issued in April[22] at half a guinea, whilst in October of the same year appeared a second edition, so designated on the title-page. The third, fourth, and fifth editions, all severally distinguished on their titles, followed in 1797, 1798, and 1800. In the fourth and fifth editions the title was changed to **Ambrosio, or The Monk.** Bell's advertisement, however, on the last leaf of *The Castle Spectre,* published, octavo, early in 1798, runs: "*In a few Days will be published,* By Joseph Bell, No. 148, Oxford Street, The Fourth Edition, *With considerable Additions and Alterations,* Of The Monk, A Romance, In Three Volumes. By M. G. Lewis, Esq. M.P. Author Of The Castle Spectre, Etc. *Price 10s. 6d.*"

In March, 1797, Bell found it necessary to inform the public that a few copies of the Second Edition still remained. "The Book has been reported out of print, and as a Grand Ballet has been brought forward, taken from the above work, many people may wish to see the book before the performance; and as it will be some months before a new edition can be ready to supply the demand, he has given this notice."

The Grand Ballet to which he makes reference was *Raymond and Agnes; or, The Castle of Lindenburgh,* "a New Grand Ballet Pantomime of Action," produced at Covent Garden on Thursday, March 16th, 1797, which proved a great success and drew the whole town, so that Mathias exclaimed in horror: "And one of our publick theatres has allured the publick attention still more to this novel, by a scenick representation of an Episode in it. *O Proceres Censore opus est, an Haruspice nobis!*"[23] The Episode of the Bleeding Nun indeed immediately captured the imagination of all perfervid romantics, and as early as 1799 it was extracted and separately printed in chap-book form as *The Castle of Lindenburg; or the History of Raymond and Agnes.*[24]

The differences between the first issue of *The Monk,* March, 1796, and the second issue, April, are very evident. Several errors of the first issue will be found to be duly corrected in the second, and there are distinctive bibliographical variations into which it is hardly necessary to enter here.[25] One extremely important point remains. Volume III of the first issue concludes the text with the death of Ambrosio immediately after he is dashed upon the sharp rocks by the demon and rolls from precipice to precipice. A short horizontal line is drawn, and there follows a passage of somewhat obvious morality which begins: "Haughty Lady, why shrunk you back when yon poor frail-one drew near?" In the second issue, after Ambrosio has fallen from a terrific height into the abyss, there follows a description of his agonies during six days, until his mangled corpse is swept away by the rising flood of waters. The paragraph of the Haughty Lady does not appear.

In the Second Edition of *The Monk* we find the shorter ending of the first issue together with the Haughty Lady paragraph. This is repeated in the third edition (1797), in the fourth edition, "with considerable additions and alterations" (1798), and in the fifth edition, "with considerable additions and alterations" (1800.)

The longer conclusion with Ambrosio's sufferings appears in the Dublin edition, 2 volumes, 1796; and also in the T. and H. Purkess illustrated edition of 1859.

It is difficult to surmise why Lewis should have preferred the rather abrupt ending and the little tag of trite morality to the more violent yet far more effective description. It has been suggested that possibly he thought the latter, however awesome, might be recognized as too obviously resembling the catastrophe of *Die Teufelsbeschwörung* in the *Sagen der Vorzeit* of Veit Weber (G. P. Leonhard Wächter).[26]

Mr. Louis F. Peck was, I believe, the first to point out that the well-known Waterford edition, 3 vols., 12mo, dated 1796, has 1818 watermarks, and since Lewis died in 1818 it seems tolerably certain that in consequence of his decease some enterprising printer, presaging that the obituary notices would awaken fresh interest in *The Monk,* resourcefully landed a number of "first editions" on the market.[27]

In a note, written in 1798, as an addendum to an existing note in his *Pursuits of Literature* (The Fourteenth Edition, 1808, p. 247), Matthias, quoting from *The Monk,* pp. 247-8, the passages regarded as profane, which describe how Ambrosio examines Antonia's Bible and his reflections thereon, says: "I refer to the *third* edition of *The Monk*[28]; for it must never be forgotten, that *three* editions of this novel have been circulated through the kingdom, without *any* alteration whatsoever, which fear or, as I hope, a better principle has induced Mr. Lewis to make, since this denunciation was first published (1798)."

Ambrosio; or the Monk, "By M. G. Lewis, Esq. M.P. Fifth Edition, in 3 Vol. Price 12*s.* in boards," is advertised by Bell in the Second Edition, 1801, of *Tales of Wonder.* Bell also advertised this Fifth Edition of *The Monk* at the end of *Adelmorn the Outlaw,* 8vo, 1801, but adds: "N.B. The *First Edition of the above Romance* may be had at the Publisher's, price One Guinea."

To exaggerate the success and scandal of *The Monk* were impossible. Lewis at once became famous, and a celebrity he remained. "The first names in rank and talent sought his society; he was the lion of every fashionable party." This he found extremely agreeable, for Sir Walter Scott tells us: "Lewis was fonder of great people than he ought to have been, either as a man of talent or a man of fortune. He had always dukes and duchesses in his mouth, and was particularly fond of any one who had a title. You could have sworn he had been a *parvenu* of yesterday, yet he had been all his life in good society."[29] After all, when fame comes at twenty, a little touch of snobbishness is a pardonable fault;[30] nor was Matthew Gregory the real snob, for, even if he loved gilded salons and coronets, he did a thousand kind turns to those who were insignificant and poor; nor did he ever treat his inferiors in purse, talent or station with the slightest discourtesy or ill-breeding. A more generous, a more civil gentleman never existed.

In these days of *Ulysses* and *Lady Chatterley's Lover,* and—for aught I know—even duller bawdry, that *The*

Monk should have given offence may well seem incomprehensible. Yet such indeed proved the case. Never was such a clamour, such an outcry, heard since Troy Town fell, or the geese hissed upon the Capitol, for at the noise one might have believed that the very pillars of religion and decency were shaken to the dust and crumbled away, that the reign of Cotytto had returned, that the altars of Priapus were set up in St. Paul's. Even a hundred years after it had first appeared, at the end of the nineteenth century, I can well remember that *The Monk* was spoken of as a lewd book and still regarded with sternest disapproval. Thus in *The Imperial Dictionary of National Biography* (1890) Francis Espinasse, with a gesture of repugnance, condemned this famous fiction as "shamelessly voluptuous." *The Monk* definitely took its place with pornography, among the volumes labelled "Curious," Facetiæ," "Erotica." It was classed with *Hic et Hæc, The Romance of Lust, Miss Coote* and *The Recollections of a Mary-Ann*. Amazing as it may appear even to-day, the crusted old tradition is sturdily maintained.[31]

There is, indeed, something a little extraordinary—one is tempted to write something morbid—in the persistence with which so uncritical and so unsound a prejudice survives; but, instructive as the diagnosis might prove, it hardly concerns us now, for our business is with the contemporary reception of *The Monk*. The attack was not immediate, but when the storm burst it bellowed none the less tempestuous and loud. The earliest reviews were favourable. "The author of this romance has amplified the character of the Santon[32] Barsissa in the Guardian, in a most masterly and impressive manner. We really do not remember to have read a more interesting production. The stronger passions are finely delineated and exemplified in the progress of artful temptation working on self-sufficient pride, superstition, and lasciviousness. The author has availed himself of a German tradition which furnishes an episodical incident, awful, but improbable. The whole is very skilfully managed, and reflects the highest credit on the judgement and imagination of the writer. Some beautiful little ballads are interspersed, which indicate no common poetical talents." With more flippancy than politeness the *Analytical Review*[33] remarked of Matilda: "The whole temptation is so artfully contrived, that a man, it would seem, were he made as other men are, would deserve to be d——d who could resist such devilish spells, conducted with such address, and assuming such a heavenly form."

Lewis, however, was only too soon to discover how "the odious task of writing" entails upon its professors "envy, slander, and malignity," and that an author is merely "an object of newspaper animadversion and impertinence," a bitter fatality which seems as inevitable to-day as ever it was a century and a half ago. *The Critical Review*[34] suspected the writer of the new romance "of a species of brutality," whilst the abominations contained in these pages were clearly "such as no observation of character can justify, because no good man would willingly suffer them to pass, how transiently, through his own mind." It warned all fathers that *The Monk* "is a romance, which if a parent saw in the hands of a son or daughter, he might reasonably turn pale." In fine the whole work could be summed up as "a poison for youth, and a provocative for the debauchee." *The Monthly Review*[35] severely reprehended "the vein of obscenity which corrupted the entire narrative." *The Scots Magazine*[36] was indignant at the evil influence of such romances, scattered far and wide by indefatigable circulating libraries. This cant, which could be repeated to weariness, might not perhaps cause any great surprise coming from paltry reviewers, but it is painful to find that Moore affected to think *The Monk* "libidinous and impious," whilst Byron set down in his *Journal*, Monday, December 6th, 1813, such remarks as the following: "I looked yesterday at the worst parts of the *Monk*. These descriptions ought to have been written by Tiberius at Caprea—they are forced—the *philtered* ideas of a jaded voluptuary. It is to me inconceivable how they could have been composed by a man of only twenty—his age when he wrote them. They have no nature—all the sour cream of cantharides. I should have suspected Buffon of writing them on the death-bed of his detestable dotage. I had never redde this edition, and merely looked at them from curiosity and recollection of the noise they made, and the name they had left to Lewis. But they could do no harm."[37]

It is at least amusing to think of Tiberius, crowned with laurel lest the lightning should strike him, in a garden at Capri, while dwarfs and peacocks strutted round him, and the flute-player mocked the bearer of the censer, reading not the shameful books of Elephantis,[38] but writing upon his *tabulæ* with ivory style the first draft of the Gothic chapters of *The Monk*.

Keenly as Lewis felt the acrimonious and unwarranted attacks upon his romance, he was the more deeply hurt on account of the vexation thereby caused to his father, who expressed himself as in no small degree displeased and distressed. The very manly, affectionate and straightforward letter which the young author addressed to Mr. Lewis on February 23rd, 1798, has several times been printed,[39] and it must have proved more than sufficient to set his father's mind at rest. That it did so seems certain from the fact that the excellent relations existing between them were not disturbed; and if Mr. Lewis regretted what he might consider his son's imprudence, he must at any rate have taken a just pride in his literary reputation and renown. Matthew Gregory in the course of his letter assures his father of the rectitude of his intentions; his experience now shows him to have been in the wrong when he published the first edition of *The Monk,* but it was the lack of knowledge of a youth of twenty which gave offence; he has made the only reparation in his power by carefully revising the work and expurging every syllable on which could be grounded the slightest construction of immorality, a charge not brought against the sentiments, characters, or general tendency of the work, but merely against some careless expressions and descriptions considered a little too warm, "a few ill-judged and unguarded passages."

The charge of irreligion was, perhaps, more serious. Yet to support this only one passage, which he is heartily sorry was ever published, had been or could be produced. In this respect he has been most unfairly treated. It is true that the expressions he used were much too strong, and he now sees that their style is irreverent. None the less the passage was only intended to convey that certain parts of the Bible should not be read before such an age as the student is capable of benefiting by its precepts and admiring its beauties. It also suggested the propriety of not putting certain passages before the eyes of very young persons. He never for a moment intended, and he believed he had sufficiently guarded against, any idea of attacking the Sacred Volume. None the less he has given offence, and he can only assure his hostile critics on this score that they have totally mistaken both himself and his principles. He is sorry for having given offence, and requests the pardon of his father for the uneasiness which this business has caused a parent whom he so regards with such true affection.

Before we examine more particularly the passage in question, which was condemned as impious and profane, it will not be impertinent to glance briefly at the censure of Lewis by Thomas James Mathias, since it was this very alleged irreverence which so grossly scandalized the satirist and stirred his hottest wrath.

Mathias, who was major-fellow of Trinity College, Cambridge, in 1776, proceeded M.A. the following year. He received the appointments of sub-treasurer and then treasurer to Queen Charlotte, the wife of George III; was created F.S.A. and F.R.S. in 1795; and in 1812 became librarian of Buckingham Palace. In 1817 he visited Italy, and translated freely from the Italian into English, obtaining a wide reputation as an Italian scholar. He died in 1835.

The Pursuits of Literature, a satirical poem, was published in Four Dialogues; the First in May, 1794; the Second and Third in June, 1796; and the Fourth in July, 1797. It was equipped with an immense lumbering apparatus of Introduction and Notes, whilst as it went on its way through sixteen editions[40] numerous alterations, corrections and additions were made, not only in the text but in the commentary. In the Fourth Dialogue, after returning to a most unreasonable and abusive onslaught on the celebrated Richard Payne Knight, and his "foul Priapus," as Mathias courteously terms this great scholar's *An Account of the Remains of the Worship of Priapus lately existing in Isernia,*[41] the poem continues:

> But though that *Garden-God* forsaken dies;
> Another Cleland see in Lewis rise.
> Why sleep the ministers of truth and law?
> Has the State no control, no decent awe,
> While each with each in madd'ning orgies vie,
> Panders to lust, and licens'd blasphemy?
> Can Senates hear without a kindred rage?
> Oh, may a Poet's light'ning blast the page,
> Nor with the bolt of Nemesis in vain
> Supply the laws, that wake not to restrain.

John Cleland, the son of Colonel Cleland, the Will Honeycomb of *The Spectator,* was born late in 1709,[42] and admitted to Westminster School in 1722. Whilst quite young he obtained the appointment of British Consul at Smyrna, and in 1736, having entered the service of the East India Company, he resided for a time at Bombay. Upon his return to London he wrote several novels and plays, the most famous of his works being that to which Mathias here refers, *Memoirs of a Woman of Pleasure.* Owing to the voluptuousness of the descriptions Cleland was called before the Privy Council and officially reprimanded, but when he pleaded his poverty, on condition that he would not write another romance of this nature he was granted an annual pension of £100. He died in Petty France, on January 23rd, 1789, aged eighty.[43]

The Memoirs of a Woman of Pleasure, which is perhaps better known under the title *Fanny Hill,* is certainly a masterpiece of English erotic literature, but to suggest that there is any comparison or point of contact between Cleland's work and **The Monk** is egregious nonsense. It would hardly be possible to name any two works of fiction which less resemble one another in every particular.

In a bombast note Mathias thus belabours **The Monk**: "The publication of this novel *by a Member of Parliament* is in itself *so serious an offence to the public* that I know not how the author can repair this breach of public decency, but by suppressing it himself: or he might omit the indecent and blasphemous passages in another edition." (This note was written in July, 1797, and in the previous year Lewis had taken his seat in Parliament for Hindon, Wilts.) "Novels of this seductive and libidinous tendency," continues Mathias, "excite disgust, fear, and horror."[44]

The Preface to this Fourth Dialogue is even more vituperative and denunciatory. "There is one publication of the time too peculiar and too important to be passed over in a general reprehension. There is nothing with which it may be compared. A legislator in our own parliament, a member of the House of Commons of Great Britain, an elected guardian and defender of the laws, the religion, and the good manners of the country, has neither scrupled nor blushed to depict, and to publish to the world, the arts of lewd and systematic seduction, and to thrust upon the nation the most open and unqualified blasphemy against the very code and volume of our religion. And all this, with his name, style, and title, prefixed to the novel or romance called 'THE MONK.'" There is appended a huffing ruffling note: "At first I thought that the name and title [M.P.] of the author were fictitious, and some of the public papers hinted it. But I have been solemnly and repeatedly assured by the Bookseller himself, that it is the writing and publication of M. LEWIS, Esq. Member of Parliament. It is sufficient for me to point out Chap. 7 of Vol. 2. As a composition, the work would have been better, if the offensive and scandalous passages had been omitted, and it is disgraced by a diablerie and nonsense fitted only to frighten children in the nursery. I believe this SEVENTH CHAPTER of Vol. 2 is indictable at Common Law." Mathias cites the prosecutions of Edmund Curll and Cleland, continuing with all the meretricious adjuvants of capitals and italics to express his horror and detestation: "To the passages of obscenity (which certainly I shall not copy in this place) Mr Lewis has added BLASPHEMY AGAINST THE SCRIPTURES."[45] He then quotes in full from *The Monk* the famous episode where Ambrosio finds Antonia reading the Bible. "'How,' said the Prior to himself, 'Antonia reads the Bible, and is still so ignorant?'" The Prior discovers, however, that Antonia's mother has provided a copy of the Scriptures "copied out with her own hand," from which are omitted those passages she considered unsuitable for young persons to study.

Surely this principle, denounced by Mathias as "unqualified blasphemy," is none other than that which suggested such publications as *Line upon Line, Bible Stories for the Young,* and a hundred similar redactions. Some seven years ago, for example, the Regius Professor of Divinity in the University of Cambridge, in conjunction with two other Fellows of the University, edited not only a "Children's Bible," but even "A Little Children's Bible," both of which are most grievously mutilated, whilst the text, "That of the Authorized Version," even ventures on "occasional corrections." Moreover, the University Press did not blush to announce: "It is hoped to publish later, in the same style, a School Bible, suitable for older boys and girls. This will be, in effect, the Authorized Version with considerable omissions."

Lewis never intended anything more than this.[46] We may perhaps allow (as he himself acknowledges) that he expresses himself a little roughly and awkwardly in this passage, but that he should therefore be assailed as a blasphemer, a scoffer and unhallowed sacrilegist, threatened and coarsely denounced, can only be ascribed to an excess of that fanatical exhibitionism which shatter-brained cranks so love to stimulate and indulge. This indeed is the root of the whole matter, for we can hardly read a score of lines (with their cumbrous baggage of notes) from *The Pursuits of Literature* without recognizing that we have to deal with a mind almost dangerously unbalanced. The rancour and enmity this "Satirical Poem" displays are certainly morbid, and had Max Nordau only known of these ebullitions with what glee would this *fané* journalist have instanced, in support of his pesudo-literary mock-psychiatrical theories, Thomas James Mathias as a first-class *fin-de-siècle* degenerate, with what gusto would he have dwelt upon the hysteria, the paroxysms of piety, the graphomania, egomania, *paraphrasia vesana,* and the whole fardel of nonsense tricks.

Lewis was very naturally chagrined at such an outrageous assault; albeit he treated "the fury of the 'Pursuits of Literature,' &c.," with deserved contempt.

Nor did Lewis lack defenders, for in 1798 was published anonymously "Impartial Structures on the Poem called 'The Pursuits of Literature,' and particularly a Vindication of the romance of *The Monk*." Lewis' youngest sister, Sophia, wrote a brief defence of *The Monk,* but without her name and unacknowledged. Lewis, however, was not obliged by these champions, for, to use his own phrase, he strongly disliked "flaming eulogium," and he also entertained some degree of prejudice against female authorship.

It was acutely observed at the time that, if the composition of *The Monk* was in any way a reproach to the author, then the unbounded popularity of this romance was a far stronger reflection upon public taste.

An amusing anecdote is told: "When 'Monk' Lewis's sensational romance was in universal request, a Mrs. Lord, who kept a circulating library in Dublin, enriched it with sufficient copies for her customers old and young. . . . A highly correct *paterfamilias* having reproved her for imperilling the morality of the metropolis by admitting such a book in her catalogue, she naively replied: 'A shocking bad book to be sure, sir; but I have carefully looked through every copy, and *underscored* all the naughty passages, and cautioned my young ladies what they are to skip without reading it.'"

Actually about eighteen months after the appearance of *The Monk* the Attorney-General was instructed by the Society for the Suppression of Vice to move for an injunction to prevent the sale of the book. A rule *nisi* was even obtained, but it was never made absolute, and certain passages being modified, the prosecution dropped.

Famous and frequently reprinted as **The Monk** is, it may not be entirely superfluous to remind ourselves very briefly of the principal incidents in the story. Ambrosio, the Monk, is Abbot of the Capuchins at Madrid, and revered throughout the city for his sanctity. A son of mystery, his parentage is unknown, since whilst an infant he was found by the brethren laid at their abbey door, a gift, they like to think, from heaven. The youngest novice of the house, Rosario, becomes a particular favourite with the abbot, who one evening when they are together in the gardens to his horror and amaze discovers that his companion is a woman. The lady declares herself to be Matilda de Villanegas, the daughter of a noble house, passionately avowing that she has for his dear love alone penetrated the cloistral walls. As her cowl falls back he recognizes in her radiant beauty a sacred picture which some two years before had been bought by the monks, and which has been the object of his increasing adoration.[47] Matilda confesses that she thus conveyed her portrait to his notice. After a brief, but fierce struggle, the celibate yields to the overwhelming temptation and seeks satisfaction in her wanton embraces. Howbeit anon comes satiety, and then disgust. Ambrosio is requested to attend a widow, a stranger to Madrid, who is sick, Donna Elvira Dalfa. At the house of his new penitent he sees and becomes violently enamoured of her daughter, Antonia, a lovely maiden of fifteen. Matilda consents to aid his designs and help debauch the innocent object of his hot desires. In order to complete these ends she summons a fallen angel, and at midnight in the dark vaults of the monastery the monk takes part in impious rites. By means of a magic spell he gains admittance to Antonia's chamber and is about to violate her, when Elvira interrupts the ravisher. In order to escape he murders the hapless woman, and, unsuspected, regains his cloister. By Matilda's contrivance he then administers a soporific draught to the orphan Antonia, and being taken for dead she is conveyed to the vaults for sepulchre. Here Ambrosio waits her hour of wakening, and in spite of her cries effects his lustful purpose. To conceal his crime in a wild frenzy he stabs her, but the fact is almost immediately discovered. With Matilda he is thrown into the dungeons of the Inquisition, and accused of horrid crimes, murder, rape, and sorcery. Torture is applied, a full confession being extorted from the fears of his accomplice, when both are condemned to the stake. Matilda obtains freedom by devoting herself to the demon, and at the last moment Ambrosio also vows himself to the fiend on the condition of instant release. He is borne to the wilds of the Sierra Morena where the mocking spirit informs him that Elvira, whom he slew, was his mother, Antonia whom he raped and killed was his sister. The condition of release has been fulfilled, no more will be granted. The wretched monk is then hurled into the abyss.

With these main incidents is threaded the love story of Don Raymond de las Cisternas and Agnes de Medina Celi. Raymond on his travels meets Agnes in Germany at the Castle of Lindenberg, which is haunted by the Bleeding Nun. Owing to a variety of circumstances they are separated, and Agnes, at Madrid, is forced to join the sisterhood of S. Clare. Ambrosio, who discovers the secret of her love, denounces her to the domina, Mother S. Agatha, a very severe old superior, who, enraged at the scandal, gives out she is dead and condemns her to perpetual imprisonment in the vaults. A kindly nun, Mother S. Ursula, manages to convey the truth to Raymond, and Agnes is released, Ambrosio and Matilda being found in the subterranean corridors by the rescuing party.

There is one very weak point in the story which Lewis could easily have cleared up, but he apparently forgot or was not at the pains to disentangle. This results in a contradiction. Matilda is represented throughout as a woman who has fallen in love with the Monk, who has skilfully contrived that her portrait under the guise of a sacred subject shall be brought to his notice, who has recourse to magic in order to effect her ends, and who only escapes from the prisons of the Holy Office by an impious contract. At the end the fiend tells Ambrosio that his blind idolatry of the picture was made largely instrumental in his seduction and fall. "I bade a subordinate, but crafty spirit assume a similar form, and you eagerly yielded to the blandishments of Matilda." This runs counter to the whole tenour of the narrative. We cannot accept the temptress as a female Mephistopheles. If Matilda was a succubus, many of the preceding incidents are impossible and out of gear. The whole discrepancy, which is serious, could have been obviated by the omission of the one sentence quoted above, and the story would have gained. I like to think that this vaunt of the demon is a mere oversight, and, in reading, I delete it—at least mentally—from the text.[48]

There are indeed many other manifest errors. To the profound—and in the case of Lewis distorted and almost farcical—ignorance of the religious orders, of convents and the enclosed life, which marks nearly all the Gothic romances detailed attention has already been drawn, so this point need hardly be dwelt upon here. It is not impertinent perhaps to repeat that the Monk himself is not a monk, but a Franciscan friar; and not an Abbot, but the Guardian of a Capuchin house. Incidentally the Capuchins during the course of the narrative are often described as "monks," whilst Ambrosio is called "the friar." The community of Poor Clares, than whom no nuns observe a stricter enclosure, leave their convent to visit the church, and even join in a grand procession through the midnight streets of the capital. The abbess is invariably termed the prioress, a trifling blunder in view of such grosser absurdities.

It has been shrewdly observed that in the work of Lewis "Convent life is represented from the point of view not of an ultra-Protestant but of a Voltairean freethinker," and the reviewer who announced that Matthew Gregory Lewis "is the spiritual parent of Maria Monk and all that grisly brood" was certainly very wide of the mark.

Nor is *The Monk* without some lighter strokes. Leonella is an amusing character with her exposition on the differences between the two sexes—happily interrupted by the arrival of the preacher—her amorous casting of nets for Don Christoval, the billet-doux she writes in red ink to express the blushes of her cheek, the pastoral dress she dons to receive her supposed admirer, when she is discovered simpering over the *Diana* of Jorge de Montemayor, nor is she a whit too farcical. The loquacious Jacintha is well drawn, an admirable sketch of a landlady, and indubitably from the life. There is humour too in the gossip of the religious at the grate when Theodore sings a ballad of Denmark: "Denmark, say you?" mumbled an old nun. "Are not the people all blacks in Denmark?"

"By no means, reverend lady; they are of a delicate pea-green, with flame-coloured hair and whiskers."

"Mother of God! Pea-green?" exclaimed sister Helena: "Oh! 'tis impossible!"

"Impossible," said the porteress, with a look of contempt and exultation: "Not at all: when I was a young woman, I remember seeing several of them myself."

Nor does Lewis for his Spanish scene rely merely upon references to "the Prado," Murcia, Cordova, to *Amadis de Gaul, Tirante the White, Don Galaor,*[49] to Lope de Vega and Calderon, to pilgrimages to S. James of Compostella, nor does he seek to obtain 'local atmosphere' with ejaculations such as "By St. Jago!" His art reaches much higher than such empty histrionics, and it has been well said: "Lewis is content with a few dusky strokes, but they evoke the torridities of Southern life. Nothing could be better in this vein than the opening of *The Monk* describing the excited crowd gathered in the Capuchin Church at Madrid to hear the great preacher Abbot Ambrosio. You can almost hear the fans whir and smell the stale incense."

It is indeed a remarkable tribute to the power of *The Monk* that in spite of all the imperfections, and indeed improprieties, in regard to the cloister, faults and ignorances which might well have proved fatal to the romance, the genius of Lewis shows itself so extraordinary that it makes nothing of them, and when we are reading his pages, so great is their fascination, the blemishes simply cease to be. The interest of the narrative enthralls and hurries one from incident to incident. His convents, his monks and nuns I regard as harmless, a mere fairyland of melodramatic adventure, delightfully mysterious and transpontine, having no relation at all to reality. I will not spare to quote a severe enough critic, although I cannot endorse his disapproval, but I echo the final praise: "Besides copious use of magic, incantations, and spirits to carry on his story, and his wanton gloating over scenes of luxury and license (hideously complicated by matricide and unconscious incest), Lewis resorted to an even more revolting category of horrors—loathsome images of mortal corruption and decay, the festering relics of death and the grave. But even when its startling defects and blemishes are fully admitted, *The Monk* remains in every way a marvellous production for a boy of twenty."

Mrs. Radcliffe is the romanticist of the Gothic novel; Lewis the realist. His pictures of voluptuous passion are necessary to the narrative; the violence of the orgasm but serves to balance and throw in high relief the charnel horrors. The comeliest forms of man and maid entwined in quivering embrace that Aretine might have imaged in his shameless sonnets, the long rapture of warm honeyed kisses such as Secundus sung, the full swift pulse of life, beauty, love, desire, all these are suddenly shadowed by the dark pall of mortality; those eyes that sparkled with lust's flame must fade and close in night, those hands whose touch was as a draught of heady wine must palsy, grow cold, and decay, the worm must pasture on those corrupting limbs where lovers' teeth once bit the white flesh in frenzy of sadistic appetite.

In his "Advertisement" Lewis thus acknowledges his sources: "The first idea of this Romance was suggested by the story of the *Santon Barsisa,* related in *The Guardian*. The *Bleeding Nun* is a tradition still credited in many parts of Germany; and I have been told that the ruins of the earth of Lauenstein, which she is supposed to haunt, may yet be seen upon the borders of Thuringia. The *Water King,* from the third to the twelfth stanza, is the fragment of an original Danish ballad; and *Belerma and Duranderte* is translated from some stanzas to be found in a collection of old Spanish poetry, which contains also the popular song of *Gayferos and Melesindra,* mentioned in *Don Quixote*. I have now made a full avowal of all the plagiarisms of which I am aware myself; but I doubt not many more may be found of which I am at present totally unconscious."

The story of the hermit Barsisa is to be found in No. 148 of *The Guardian,* August 31st, 1713. Satan, enraged by the surpassing holiness of Barsisa, contrives that the daughter of a king shall be sent to him to heal of her sickness. The beauty of the princess tempts the santon to violate her. Afterwards, at the fiend's suggestion, he kills his victim, burying her in his grotto, where the body is found. Barsisa is seized, and upon

The Temptation of Ambrosio, from Lewis's The Monk.

gust Sauer, the editor of Grillparzer (Vol. I, 1909) is inclined to suppose that many of these ghost stories were suggested by *Der Höllische Proteus oder tausendkünstige Versteller, vermittelst Erzahlung der vielsaltigen Bilderwechselungen erscheinender Gespenster,* of Erasmus Franciscus, first published at Nüremburg, 8vo, 1695.[52]

The Water King, the ballad sung by the disguised page, Theodore, to the nuns, is a free adaptation of *Der Wassermann* from J. T. von Herder's *Stimmen der Völker in Liedern,* for which collection it was taken from *Et Hundsede udvalde Danske viser, förögede med det andet Hundrede* of Peder Syv, Copenhagen, 1695, which derives from Andel Sörensen Vedel's *100 udvalgte Danske viser.* It was reprinted in *Tales of Wonder.*

Belerma and Durandarte is chanted by Matilda to the convalescent Ambrosio. It will be readily remembered how Don Quixote witnesses (and interrupts) the motion of Don Gayferos and the fair Melisandra. The story, says Lockhart, is told at great length in the Spanish Cancioneros.

The Monthly Review[53] in June, 1797, angrily endeavoured to strip **The Monk** of any originality. "The form of temptation," the critic declared, "is borrowed from that of *The Devil in Love* by Cazotte; and the catastrophe is taken from *The Sorcerer* . . . the forest scene near Strasburg brings to mind an incident in Smollett's *Ferdinand Count Fathom* . . . and the convent prison resembles the inflictions of Mrs. Radcliffe."[54]

Jacques Cazotte was born at Dijon in 1720. Most of his life was spent as a Civil Servant, and during the Reign of Terror he was arrested and executed in September, 1792. *Le Diable Amoureux,* his most famous work, appeared in 1772. An English translation was anonymously published in 1793, whilst in 1810 an inferior version, *Biondetta or the Enamoured Spirit* was "dedicated without permission to M. G. Lewis, Esq." In the ruins of Portici Don Alvaro Maravillas invokes a spirit, who appears first in the form of a camel, and then as a spaniel. The dog is changed into a page, Biondetto, who is in reality a female, that is to say a succubus, Biondetta. She exhibits the most passionate love for Alvaro, but after many adventures by a violent effort he renounces her and she vanishes as a black cloud. We learn that all that has happened was a phantasmagoria, and that the evil spirit had led Alvaro to the edge of the precipice when he was saved. Myself I can see no sort of connexion between Cazotte's story and **The Monk.** The horrid wiles of the succubus may be read of in almost any demonologist.

the gallows he adores the Evil One who promises in return to save him from death, but who immediately mocks and abandons his wretched prey. "Le Santon," says the French original, "dementit en un moment une vertu de cent années."

Lewis undoubtedly found the Legend of the Bleeding Nun[50] in a tale by Johann Karl August Musaeus,[51] *Die Entführing,* published in the *Volksmärchen der Deutschen,* Gotha, 1787, Part V, pp. 247-276. Musaeus, who was a professor in the gymnasium at Weimar, was personally known to and had often discussed German literature with Lewis when "the Monk" was residing in that town. Rudolf Fürst, *Vorläufer der modernen Novelle,* Halle, 1897, pp. 88-99, draws attention to a story by Naubert in her *Die neuen Volksmärchen der Deutschen,* 1789-92, entitled *Die wiesse Frau,* which tells of Neuhaus Castle in Bohemia, haunted by the ghost of Count Rosenberg's mistress. Fürst, p. 188, also mentions a legend not unlike *The Bleeding Nun* in Gajetan Tschink's *Wundergeschichten sammt dem Schlüssel zu ihrer Erklarung,* 1792. Au-

The catastrophe of **The Monk** and the doom of Ambrosio (particularly, as noted before, in the amplified form) are, it is true, closely modelled upon *Der Teufelsbeschwörung,* a romance by George Philipp Ludgwig Leonhard Wächter,[55] who wrote under the name of Veit Weber. This work was translated into English by Robert Huish as *The Sorcerer,* "A tale from the German of Veit Weber," and published at 4s. in one volume by Johnson, 1795.

The adventures with the robbers in Baptiste's cottage may derive a hint, but nothing more than the barest hint from Chapters XX and XXI of *Ferdinand Count Fathom,*[56] when Ferdinand being "overtaken by a terrible tempest, falls upon Scylla, seeking to avoid Charybdis." The episode is conceived and related in full Gothic vein by Smollett, but Lewis not so much improves a mere outline, but gives the whole situation an entirely different and original turn. Lewis himself was copied both in fiction and upon the stage times without number.[57]

When Lewis was writing the extravagantly transpontine melodrama of his Convent scenes, he clearly had not forgotten Monvel's lurid *Les Victimes cloîtrées* and Marsollier's *Camille, ou le Souterrain,* both of which pieces he mentions in a letter to his mother[58] as having seen in Paris during his stay there in the summer of 1791, when they awakened his liveliest interest. Although he does not speak of other similar plays, it is obvious that he had also seen or read several more "anticlerical" dramas, such, for example, as Baculard d'Arnaud's *Euphémie,* the *Convent* of Olympe de Gouges, and the notorious *Julie, ou la Religieuse de Nisme* by Pougens, in which latter the description of Julie in the dungeon very nearly resembles the picture of the imprisoned Agnes in **The Monk**.

The first literary record of a doomed wanderer, the "Wandering Jew," occurs in the *Flores Historiarum* of Roger of Wendover, a monk of S. Albans, who died in 1237. Hence with some slight amplification it was incorporated in the *Historia Major* of Matthew Paris who died in 1259. The account is given on the authority of a certain Armenian Bishop who visited England in 1228 and who related how he had himself met the Wanderer. A similar version, also on the authority of the Armenian Bishop, is recorded by the Flemish chronicler, Philippe Mousket, Bishop of Tournai, about 1243.

The story was well known in Italy at the beginning of the thirteenth century, and originally came from Jerusalem, where a legend of a witness of the Crucifixion, doomed to an accursed immortality, was current in very early times. The Wanderer is given many names, and there are many variants of the tale identifying him with several characters. The popularity of the story during the last three centuries is in the first place mainly due to a German chap-book, *Kurtze Beschreibung und Erzehlung von einem Judem mit*

Namen Ahasverus, 1602. The narrative is told by a Lutheran pastor, Paulus von Eitzen, who died in 1598, and who stated that at Hamburg in the year 1542 he had met the Jew Ahasuerus from whose lips he had the story. Whence or why the name Ahasuerus is not clear. In old English tradition the Wanderer is called Cartaphilus, a door-keeper of Pilate's house, who seeing the Saviour go forth carrying His Cross, struck Him crying: "Go faster, why dost Thou linger?" Whereupon the Lord made reply: "I go indeed, but thou shalt tarry until I come again." Not a few persons have met this figure of mystery, the Wandering Jew, and have left their witness. I see no reason to doubt the facts, although naturally legend has grown up about them and literature has used them in many guises.[59]

A French version, *Historie admirable d'un Juif Errant,* dating from the seventeenth century, adds striking particulars. The theme of the Wandering Jew attracted Goethe, and Christian Schubart's poem *Der Ewige Jude,* 1787, was read with admiration by Lewis. About 1810 it was Shelley, or Thomas Medwin, who "picked up, dirty and torn, in Lincoln's Inn Fields," a fragment of an English version of Schubart's poem in *The German Museum,* Vol. III, 1803. Shelley at once conceived and Medwin joined with him in a long metrical romance, something in the style of Scott, on the subject of the Wandering Jew. When seven or eight cantos were written, Shelley essayed various publishers, but four cantos of the poem first appeared in *The Edinburgh Literary Journal* for 1829 with Shelley's preface, dated January, 1811. The four cantos (in a different version and with the sanction of Mrs. Shelley) were also printed as "an unpublished poem" in *Fraser's Magazine* three years after they had been given in *The Edinburgh Literary Journal.* Medwin, whose account of the collaboration is unsatisfactory and inconsistent, claimed to have written almost entirely by himself the first three, if not indeed the first four, cantos, and the vision in the third canto he acknowledged was taken from **The Monk**. Shelley, we know, was a fervent admirer of **The Monk,** and many authorities believe that Shelley wrote practically the whole of this poem, *The Wandering Jew,* although as being Medwin's work it has been excluded (but improperly) from the more important editions of Shelley.

Medwin's poem, *Ahasuerus the Wanderer,* 1823, has no traces of the earlier piece.

Lewis, in addition to Schubart's poem, had read Reichardt's romance, *Der Ewige Jude,* 1785, and also Heller's *Briefe des Ewigen Juden,* two volumes, 1791. Above all, he was profoundly impressed by Schiller's *Der Geisterseher,* which was first printed in *Die Rheinische Thalia,* 1789, and which in England[60] had so powerful an influence, for as one critic asked[61]: "Who can look without awe at the inscrutable Armenian, or contemplate, unless with a heart-thrill, the terrific agony which his cunning and his science are able to evoke?"

A well-known journalist of the day, Andrew Franklin, produced at Drury Lane on May 15th, 1797, *The Wandering Jew; or, Love's Masquerade.* This is a mere farce, "containing much low humour, and little probability,"[62] in which Atall—the name is taken from Colley Cibber's *The Double Gallant, or, The Sick Lady's Cure*[63]—disguises himself as the Wandering Jew. That this character was chosen serves to show the popularity of Lewis' work. Franklin's scenes were received with loud laughter and applause, and when printed, octavo, 1797, the little piece ran through four editions within the year.

George Daniel, the famous book collector and critic, sweepingly enough said: "The chief merit that belongs to 'The Monk' is in bringing together an accumulation of supernatural horrors, and skilfully arranging them in an interesting tale—for it can boast of scarcely one atom of *originality*—it is *German* from beginning to end."[64]

In Ludwig Herrig's *Archiv für das Studium der Neueren Sprachen und Literaturen* (Alois Brandl und Heinrich Morf), Vol. CXI; new Series XI; 1903, Georg Herzfeld has an article *Die eigentliche Quelle von Lewis' 'Monk'* (pp. 316-323), in which he attempted to show that **The Monk** was for the greater part taken verbatim from an anonymous German romance *Die blutende Gestalt mit Dolch und Lampe, oder die Beschwöhrung im Schlosse Stern bei Prag,* Vienna and Prague,[65] no date. He quoted parallel passages as proving a word for word translation, and when his views were questioned by Otto Ritter[66] he did not hesitate to reassert and emphasize his supposed discovery.[67] Actually the whole question of priority is settled by an announcement of *Die blutende Gestalt* in the *Weiner Zeitung,* March 22nd, 1799, as "shortly to be published." Now Herzfeld's knowledge of *Die blutende Gestalt* was derived from an article, *Ein Schauerroman als Quelle der Ahnfrau,*[68] by L. Wyplel, who showed that Grillparzer's play *Die Ahnfrau* was taken from this source. Accordingly the editor of Grillparzer, August Sauer, compared the first German translation of **The Monk** by F. von Oertel, Leipzig, 1797-98 with the Prague romance, a collation which promptly established beyond all question that actually *Die blutende Gestalt* was derived from von Oertel's translation.[69] There are, of course, variants. Ambrosio in the German becomes a wizard astrologer; the Abbess (domina) of S. Clare is a Baroness of high lineage; the mystic myrtle is a rose-branch: names are changed; Agnes is Berta; Mother Ursula, Brigritta; and other details are altered. It is interesting to note that the anonymous author of *Die blutende Gestalt* published a sequel, no date (238 pages), *Der Geist*

Lurian im Silbergewand oder das Gericht über Ambrosio.

As we have just seen, the first German translation of **The Monk** appeared in 1797-8; a second version was published at Berlin in 1799 as *Mathilde von Villanegas, oder der weibliche Faust*; a third at Magdeburg in 1806 as *Der Mönch, oder die siegende Tugend*; a fourth at Hamburg in 1810 as *Der Mönch, Eine schauerlich abentheuerliche Geschichte.* In France *Le Moine,* Paris, 4 volumes, 1797, was said to be translated from the fourth English edition by a mournival of names, Deschamps, Després, Benoît and Lamare; Paris, an VI (1797), 4 vols., **The Monk** was translated as *Le Jacobin espagnol, ou Histoire du moine Ambrosio et de la belle Antonia, sa sœur*; in 1838 was issued a new translation, *Le Moine,* said to have been made by the Abbé Morellet, who died in January, 1819; two years later *Le Moine* newly translated by Léon de Wailly from the first English edition was published by Delloye; in 1878 **The Monk** was translated as *Le Moine, ou les Nuits du Cloître*; in 1880 as *Le Moine, ou les Nuits du Couvent*; whilst in 1883 *Le Moine incestueux,* "roman imité de l'anglais," being in effect an abridgement of **The Monk** by Edouard Ploert, was published by the Libraire anticléricale. Most of these translations and adaptations ran into many editions,[70] and the popularity of **The Monk** in France is proved to have been quite extraordinary. In French literature the romance of Lewis had an immense influence.[71] In Spain a version of **The Monk,** published in 1822 as *El Fraile, o historia del padre Ambrosio y de la bella Antonia,* is taken at second-hand from *Le Jacobin espagnol.* **The Monk** was also translated and adapted into Italian, and also (from the French) into Swedish, and other languages.

"Raymond and Agnes; or the Castle of Lindenberg," a grand and interesting ballet, taken from **The Monk**, and arranged for the stage, by Mr. Farley, was performed at Covent Garden with great success on March 16th, 1797. "The music of this ballet, which was interspersed with airs and choruses" was composed by William Reeve, actor, organist, and composer.[72]

Raymond and Agnes, the Travellers benighted, or the Bleeding Nun of Lindenberg,[73] by Henry William Grosette, in two acts, was performed at the London minor theatres in 1809.[74] It is ascribed to Lewis himself, but this I think is doubtful, although in its kind it is an extremely skilful dramatization of the story. The principals in the printed cast are: Don Felix, Cooper; Don Raymond, F. Vining; Theodore, F. Sutton; Conrad, Sutton; Baptista, O. Smith; Robert, Grimaldi; Jaques, T. Blanchard; Claude, Turnour; Marco, T. Matthews; Agnes, Miss Cawse; Cunegonde, Mrs. Davenport; Ursula, Miss Smith; Marguerette, Mrs. W. Vining; and the Bleeding Nun, Miss Nicolls. This would seem to be a Covent Garden cast of 1826.

Raymond and Agnes, a "grand romantic English Opera in three acts," the words by Edward Fitzball, and the music by E. J. Loder, was produced in Manchester, 1855, and at the S. James' Theatre, London, on June 11th, 1859.

Aurelio and Miranda, by James Boaden, "A Drama in Five Acts with Music,"[75] produced at Drury Lane on Saturday, December 29th, 1798, was *"avowedly founded on the Romance of the MONK."* Boaden's attempt set out *"to dramatize the leading incidents of the Romance, without recourse to supernatural agency,"* a vital omission which has given the whole play a completely different turn from the book, and which in my opinion by depriving the incidents of their ultimate design and dominant motif, nothing less than eviscerates Lewis' chapters, leaving a very spiritless and tame performance. On the other hand, one has to recognize that this is very much in the vein of producers who prefer to eliminate the witch-scenes from *Macbeth,* and would no doubt discard the Ghost from *Hamlet.*

Aurelio and Miranda is a mixture of prose and blank verse. The licenser of plays had obliged Boaden to change the intended name of his play *Ambrosio,* thus hoping no doubt to exorcise some of the freedom of the romance. Aurelio (Ambrosio) was played by Kemble, and Miranda-Eugenio (Matilda-Rosario) by Mrs. Siddons. However, in the play Miranda is no succubus, not even a witch, but the sister of Don Christoval; and when in the last scene Aurelio cries:

> The secret of my noble birth reveal'd, . . .
> Dispenses me from the monastic state;

Miranda promptly rejoins:

> Away reserve, and maidenly resentment.

Wedding bells are distinctly heard, and the curtain falls upon what to me appears a very disgusting spectacle. The audience obviously shared my views for Kelly tells us: "It was no sooner found out that Miranda was a virtuous woman, instead of a demon, than many in the pit and galleries evinced dissatisfaction."[76]

The first scene is *The Cathedral Church of Madrid,* "and many thought it indecorous to represent a church on the stage," finely painted though it was by Capon. Curiously enough "the powerful objection was the unearthly appearance of Kemble as the monk." It was considered sacrilegious "for Mr. Kemble, as Aurelio, to make himself look so like a *divinity,*" to which it was wittily retorted that the play would have been all the better if Mrs. Siddons as Miranda, had only proved to be the *devil.* Boaden's drama was acted but six nights.

In France *The Monk* was frequently dramatized,[77] and the playwrights showed themselves far more mettled in their sensationalism than the English theatre. Rather than whittle away the theme like Boaden to a paltry nothing, they strove to accumulate horrors on horror's head, and they did not fall far short of their aim. In 1798, the very year that *The Monk* was translated into French, on the 7th nivoise an VI, in Christian language December 27th, 1797, at the Théâtre de l'Émulation was produced *Le Moine* a "comédie" founded upon the romance, adapted by Cammaille Saint-Aubin, "plan et pantomime de Ribié, musique de Froment." The piece, however, proved to be too extravagant and grotesque, driving melodrama headlong into the realms of farce. Not only was a ballet interpolated in the dark monastic dungeons, but at the end Ambrosio was whirled away by a monstrous hippogriff to a Phlegthontian inferno, where fiends brandishing huge links danced the hey amid showers of golden fire.

Le Moine, for all these caperings and sulphureous effects, was poorly received, and shortly after was considerably abbreviated, but even thus failed entirely to attract.

On the 30th Thermidor, an X; 17th August, 1802, at the opening of the Théâtre de la Gaieté under the direction of Ribié *Le Moine* was revived with alterations as a melodrama in three acts. A good deal of the ridiculous extravaganza had been wisely shorn, and, indeed, only the second act, complete in itself, of the original was presented.[78]

The fact is that *The Monk* proves so rich in incident and adventure that the practised dramatist will choose and select from Lewis' chapters, and not attempt to bring the whole story to the boards. Thus *C'est le Diable, ou la Bohemienne* by Cuvelier de Tyre produced at the Ambigu on November 18th, 1798, was very successful. A little earlier, too, *La Nonne de Lindenberg, ou, la Nuit merveilleuse,* a tragi-comedy in five acts, by Cailleran and Coupilly, given at the Théâtre des Jeunes-Artistes on June 24th, in spite of the opposition of a fierce cabal,[79] enjoyed an amazing run.[80] From this Saint-Aubin and Ribié learned a lesson, and their next venture, an episode taken from *The Monk, Marguerite, ou, les Voleurs,* was in only one act.

Lewis' romance had naturally attracted the attention of the master melodramatist, Guilbert de Pixérécourt, who penned a *Moine, ou la victime de l'Orgueil,* which was offered to the Théâtre de la Gaieté in 1798, but not acted owing to the number of plays adapted from the English romance which were then actually running. None the less, his "drame lyrique" in two acts, *La Forêt de Sicile,* taken from *The Monke,* was produced at the Théâtre des Jeunes-Associés in the same year and achieved a veritable triumph, whilst in the following January it was transferred to the Théâtre de Montausier. The piece had caused some trouble with the authorities and was for a time prohibited, but it now appeared with various alterations and a changed catastrophe. On March 28th, 1800, *Ambrosio,* an anonymous drama in five acts, was given at the Odéon, and in the same year Prévost's *Le Jacobin espagnol* had a temporary success on the Paris stage.

As may well be believed the French theatre was sufficiently stocked from the source of **The Monk** for a good thirty years, but after the Revolution of July, 1830, **The Monk** enjoyed a veritable S. Luke's summer of popularity, for on May 28th at the Odéon, L.-M. Fontan produced *Le Moine* "drame fantastique en quatre actes et huit tableaux," a melodrama transferred on July 13th to the Porte-Saint-Martin. Frédéric Lemaître and Mlle. Juliette supported the leading characters. The catastrophe is better managed, but almost as outrageous as that of Saint-Aubin's play.

Le Dominicain, ou le Couvent de l'Annonciation, which was produced at the Ambigu-Comique on March 9th, 1832, was written by Fontan in collaboration with A. Chevalier. The principal rôle, Père Jéronimo, seems drawn from a mixture of Ambrosio and Schedoni. Jéronimo contrives to enclose in a convent a young girl whom he desires. When he attempts to rape her she poinards him, a little after to discover she has killed her own father.

La Nonne Sanglante, a drama in four acts by Anicet Bourgeois and J. Maillan, produced at the Porte-Saint-Martin, February 17th, 1835, only takes the figure of the nun from Lewis. Stella, who is believed dead, haunts Conrad her presumed assassin. This "grand et terrible mélodrame" concludes with a terrific conflagration. The spectacle had an immense success, and in May, 1864, was revived at the same theatre, achieving an equal popularity. The piece was judged very powerful and effective.

On October 18th, 1854, was produced at the Opéra, *La Nonne Sanglante,* which Gounod, who composed the music, describes in his *Mémoires d'un artiste,* Paris, 1896.

"Ma troisième tentative musicale au théâtre fut la *Nonne sanglante,* opéra en cinq actes de Scribe et Germain Delavigne . . . *La Nonne Sanglante* fut écrite en 1852-53; mise en répétition le 18 octobre, 1853, laissée de coté et successivement reprise à l'étude plusieurs fois, elle vit enfin la rampe le 18 octobre, 1854, un an juste après sa première répétition. Elle n'eut que onze représentations, après lesquelles Roqueplan fut remplacé à la direction de l'Opéra par M. Crosnier. Le nouveau directeur ayant déclaré qu'il ne laisserait pas jouer plus longtemps une "pareille ordure," la pièce disparut de l'affiche et n'y a plus reparu depuis. . . . Je ne sais si la *Nonne Sanglante* était susceptible d'un succès durable; je ne le pense pas: non que ce fut une œuvre sans effet (il en avait quelques-uns de saisissants); mais le sujet était trop uniformément sombre; il avait, en outre, l'inconvénient d'être plus qu'imaginaire, plus qu'invraisemblable: il était en dehors du possible, il reposait sur une situation purement fantastique, sans réalité, et par consequence sans intérêt dramatique."

The favourite *morceaux* of *La Nonne Sanglante* are the Marche Nuptiale; "De mes Fureurs déplorable Victime"; "Dieu nous commande l'ésperance"; "C'est Dieu qui nous appelle"; "Du Seigneur, pâle fiancée"; "Un page de ma sorte"; and "O l'erreur qui m'accable!"

A far more famous Opera than *La Nonne Sanglante* has borrowed important matter from **The Monk,** for the libretto of Meyerbeer's *Robert le Diable,* produced at the Académie Royale, Paris,[81] on November 21st, 1831, was also written by Scribe and Delavigne. The fearfully impressive scene of the haunted convent, when, at the invocation of the demoniac Bertram, the abbess Elena and her troop of spectral nuns rise from their accursed tombs to dance in horrid revelry and tempt Robert to pluck the fateful talisman, the mystic branch of cypress from Berta's marble hand, the exultation of the fiends, the midnight horror and woe, all are from Lewis. This cypress bough which gains Robert admission to the apartment of the Princess Isabella, and enchains in slumber her attendance of knights and ladies, is, of course, the myrtle Matilda procures for Ambrosio. Unlike the monk, Robert resists his final temptation and refuses to sign the infernal scroll wherewith Bertram seeks to win him to himself.

It might seem difficult to decide whether it was Ann Radcliffe or Matthew Gregory Lewis who exerted the more powerful effect upon the temper and shaping of the Gothic Novel as it went its varied course, and since actually the influence of the former was far greater than that of the author of **The Monk,** it may appear a paradox to say that none the less it was the latter upon whom contemporary writers of fiction the more closely modelled certain prominent aspects of their work. The reason for this lies in the very practical consideration that the romances of Lewis were found to be far easier to copy, although we may add that the prentice pens showed themselves apter to reproduce and even to exaggerate his faults rather than to exhibit a tithe of his vigour and power, fastening upon his weakness and unable to reach after his strength.

The followers of both Mrs. Radcliffe and Lewis are legion, and very often the imitation is not only confined to theme, characters, incidents, all of which are repeated again and again in a hundred chapters with exemplary fidelity, but there are also very distinct verbal echoes to be heard, dialogue at second-hand which merely differs from the original by a bombast word inserted here and there, or a phrase dropped out for the worse.

In all essentials, it must be emphasized, Mrs. Radcliffe and Lewis differ very widely from one another. They have certain romantic subject-matter in common, but so entirely opposite are their several methods of approach and treatment that although casually they may appear at some points to contact this similarity is extremely superficial and proves but a deceptive glamour of resembling. Both employ picturesque properties, convents, castles, the Holy Office. Such a figure as the austere and stately Abbess of San Stephano in *The Italian,* although altogether improbable and exceptional, is barely possible; such a figure as Lewis' domina of S. Clare, Mother St. Agatha, is altogether chimerical, fantastic, and absurd. Lewis recked nothing of Mrs. Radcliffe's suspense, her sensibility, her landscape pictures which are not the least lovely passages of her genius. Indeed, he pronounced these uncommonly dull, and fervently wished that they had been left out, and something substituted in their room.[82] Certes' *The Mysteries of Udolpho* influenced him, but not so much as he thought and liked to make himself believe. Mrs. Radcliffe shrank from the dark diablerie of Lewis; his matricides, incests, rapes, extremely shocked her; never did she admit his mouldering cerements and atomies; his Paphian encounters would have cruddled her very ink. Her terrors were spiritual, and for that reason her influence has most clearly shown itself in the writings of those authors whose natural reserve and a certain delicacy of talent would not have tolerated the high colouring and eroticism of *The Monk*. By his very violence, his impassioned realism, Lewis is widely separated from Mrs. Radcliffe and her school. It is the more pity that these two great writers have been so frequently and so erroneously confounded, and their work all lumped together as if they had exhibited precisely the same characteristics, developed the same style, and elaborated the same sensationalism. It is true that in their own day many minor novelists with a curious lack of perception repeatedly endeavoured to combine *Udolpho* and *The Monk* in their pages, to make one peerless heroine of Emily and Antonia, to bring an Ambrosio Montoni upon the scene, but these attempts were foredoomed to failure; the pieces do not fit; there are awkward creaking joints, and untenoned mortises, discrepancy, contradictions even and incongruity both in the narrative and the springs of action. . . .

Notes

[16] Alleyne Fitzherbert, Baron St. Helens (1753-1839), the famous diplomatist. He was envoy extraordinary at The Hague, 1789; ambassador at Madrid, 1791-94.

[17] William Eden, first Baron Auckland, 1744-1814.

[18] 1760-1836. He was accounted an excellent actor. Says Boaden: "I have seen no actor at all near him where he was fully himself." Oxberry considered him "the best actor on the stage." Among his many original parts were Don Ferolo Whiskerandos in *The Critic,* and Walter in *The Children in the Wood,* both of which were esteemed masterpieces.

[19] In his fuliginous book with the fierce title *La Carne, La Morte e il Diavolo nella letteratura romantica!* (discreetly and appropriately translated, be it noted, into English as *The Romantic Agony*) Signor Mario Praz, amongst other errors in reference to Lewis, confuses *The Monk* with the first unfinished romance (see p. 60 of *The Romantic Agony,* English translation by Angus Davidson, 1933). I might hesitate, however, to suggest that Signor Praz is at fault, since Mr. Wyndham Lewis, in *Men Without Art,* p. 175, in reference to *The Romantic Agony,* spoke of "This gigantic pile of satanic bric-a-brac, so industriously assembled, under my directions by Professor Praz." This was repeated by Mr. Stephen Spender, *The Destructive Element,* p. 206. But Signor Praz wrote hotly to *The Times Literary Supplement,* August 8th, 1935, "to point out" that Mr. Wyndham Lewis' words were "grossly misleading." He added: "I am afraid I must disclaim the honour of being ranked as his disciple, sorry as I am to deprive him of this satisfaction." *Actum est de* Mr. Wyndham Lewis! After all it does not in the least matter who is responsible for such disjointed gimcrack as *The Romantic Agony.*

[20] The Sosii were celebrated booksellers in Rome. Lewis aptly has "Stockdale, Hookham, or Debrett."

[21] *Monthly Magazine or British Register,* March, 1796. The List of new publications. In *The Life and Correspondence of M. G. Lewis,* 1839, Vol. I, p. 151, there is a bad blunder in regard to *The Monk*: "The first and greatest era in the literary life of Lewis was the publication of 'Ambrosio, or The Monk,' which event took place in the summer of 1795." Several writers have repeated the error that 1795 is the date of the first edition of *The Monk.* Thus Elton, *A Survey of English Literature, 1780-1830,* 1912, Vol. I, p. 215. Railo, *The Haunted Castle,* 1927, p. 89. Rudolf Schneider, *Der Mönch in der englischen Dichtung bis auf Lewis's "Monk,"* 1795, 1927, p. 168. Herr Brauchli, *Der englische Schauerroman um 1800,* 1928, pp. 200, 235, 254. Miss J. M. S. Tompkins, *The Popular Novel in England, 1770-1800,* 1932, p. 278. E. A. Baker, *The History of the English Novel,* Vol. V (1934), p. 205. Both Baker, who is responsible for an edition of *The Monk* (1907), and Railo fall into a further mistake when they assert that the original title of Lewis' romance was *Ambrosio, or The Monk.*

[22] *Monthly Magazine or British Register,* April, 1796. I have generally used the copy of *The Monk* which belonged to Francis Douce (1757-1834), and which is preserved in the Bodleian Library, Shelfmark, Douce: L. 307. This contains some interesting contemporary notes and cuttings.

[23] *The Pursuits of Literature.* The Sixth Edition. 1798, pp. 196-7. The quotation is from Juvenal, Satire II, 121.

[24] Printed and Sold by S. Fisher, No. 10, St. John's Lane, Clerkenwell, also Sold by T. Hurst, No. 32, Paternoster Row. The frontispiece has "*London. Pub. Decr. 4th, 1799, by S. Fisher.*" 98 pages. A printer's ornament on p. 4 is the same as that upon the title-page of Will's *Horrid Mysteries,* 4 vols., Lane, 1796.

[25] An interesting article upon the Bibliography of *The Monk,* by Mr. Louis F. Peck, *The Times Literary Supplement,* Thursday, March 7th, 1935, was followed by an important letter from Mr. Frederick Coykendall, who furnishes ample bibliographical details of the two issues. See also the letters in *The Times Literary Supplement,* 1935, of Mr. W. Roberts, March 14th; and Mr. E. G. Bayford, March 28th.

[26] It is not altogether easy to find a reprint of the text of the second issue of *The Monk* with the longer conclusion. Thus an "Unabridged Reprint of the First Edition," 2 vols., London, no date, but about 1890, has the shorter version and the Haughty Lady.

[27] In the nineteenth century numberless reprints of *The Monk*—all cheap and some clandestine—appeared as *Rosario, or The Monk,* and *Rosario, or The Female Monk.* They were often crudely illustrated with "penny dreadful" woodcuts, and were widely read by juveniles. A copy before me, London, The Temple Company (*c.* 1899) has: *Rosario: or, The Female Monk.* A Romance. (Reprinted from the Waterford Edition.) By Monk Lewis.

[28] 1797, Vol. II, pp. 247-8.

[29] *Byron's Works. Letters and Journals,* ed. Rowland E. Prothero, Second Impression, 1903. Vol II, p. 317, note.

[30] "His vanity is *ouverte,*" said Byron of Lewis, "and yet not offending." *Ibid.,* pp. 356-7.

[31] Miss J. M. S. Tompkins, *The Popular Novel in England, 1770-1800* (1932), p. 278, exclaims against this "scandalous book," and informs us that "the union of lasciviousness and terror . . . was first thoroughly worked by M. G. Lewis in *The Monk* (1795)." I fear that this "union" assuredly did not wait until the final decade of the eighteenth century. Miss Tompkins'

distaste for Lewis' work has, unfortunately, led her into several errors. She remarks, p. 245, note I, that "*The Monk* was begun during Lewis's stay in Germany, and finished under the influence of *The Mysteries of Udolpho,*" which is not the case. She is not aware that so far from two-thirds of *The Monk* being "taken, almost word for word, from a German romance, *Die Blutende Gestalt mit Dolch und Lampe,*" this very romance, published in 1799, is merely an adaptation of the German version of *The Monk,* by F. von Oertel, 1797-8. One regrets to find that, although in 1907 he furnished an Introduction to a reprint of *The Monk,* Dr. E. A. Baker with no uncertain sound lends his voice to the chorus of condemnation. Thus we are informed that Lewis "betrays the perverted lusts of a sadist." He had "not merely a voracious but a morbid appetite." The crimes of Ambrosio are described "with a gluttonous fullness." The episode of Agnes and Don Raymond "is treated with the same revolting frankness" as the main theme. And so on and so forth. *History of the English Novel,* Vol. V (1934), pp. 205-11.

[32] Santon, from the Spanish *santo,* a Mohammedan recluse or hermit.

[33] Vol. XXIV, p. 403; 1796.

[34] XIX, 1796, pp. 194-200.

[35] February, 1799, pp. 111-15.

[36] LIV, 1802, p. 548.

[37] *Byron's Works, ed. cit. Letters and Journals,* Vol. II, p. 368.

[38] Elephantis was a Greek poetess, quae libris suis expressit "Poikila tes Aphrodites kai akolasias schemata." See Suetonius, *Tiberius,* xliii; Martial, XII, 43; Priapeia, iii.

[39] *Life and Correspondence of M. G. Lewis,* Vol. I, pp. 154-8.

[40] I use the Sixth Edition, 1798, and the Fourteenth Edition, 1808, as representative texts.

[41] 4to, 1786, for the Dillettanti Society.

[42] Nichols, *Literary Anecdotes,* Vol. II, 1812, pp. 457-8. 1707 is sometimes given as the date. See also *The New Monthly Magazine,* 1819, July 1st, p. 512. The bibliography of the *Memoirs of a Woman of Pleasure* is very obscure. The first edition, 2 vols., "for G. Fenton in the Strand," has no date, but is 1747 or 1748. The third edition is 1749. In 1750 Griffiths the bookseller (who is doubtless G. Fenton) published an expurgated edition, 12mo, as *Memoirs of Fanny Hill.*

There have been numberless reprints, mostly clandestine and private. The Isidore Liseux edition was published in 1888. There are at least nine French translations, and several Italian adaptations, of which one, *La Meretrice,* Cosmopoli (Venice), about 1764, is by Count Carlo Gozzi. A German translation, *Das Frauenzimmer von Vergnugen,* is given in Volume I of *Priapische Romane,* Berlin, 1791; Leipzig, 1860 and 1872.

[43] For Cleland see further *New Monthly Magazine,* July 1st, 1819, p. 512.

[44] *The Pursuits of Literature,* 14th edition, 1808, p. 366. The italics are those of Mathias.

[45] *Ibid.,* p. 245, and note (*b*), pp. 245-6.

[46] Since I am unwilling to trench upon any theological discussion here I will merely remark in a note that I do not wish to seem to express approval of or defend the passage in *The Monk* which gave (perhaps not unjustifiably) offence on these grounds.

[47] Praz, *The Romantic Agony,* English translation, 1933, pp. 180-1, suggests that this incident may have inspired a passage (omitted from the final text) in Flaubert's *La Tentation de Saint Antoine*: "Il ouvre son missel et regarde l'image de la Vierge," whereupon the devil whispers obscene thoughts in the Saint's ear.

[48] Only Miss Birkhead, *The Tale of Terror,* 1921, p. 67, seems to have noticed that with regard to Matilda "Lewis changes his mind about her character during the course of the book, and fails to make her early history consistent with the ending of the story."

[49] In a famous passage which gave great scandal. Rather than have allowed Antonia to read certain episodes of the Old Testament, Elvira "would have preferred putting into her daughter's hands *Amadis de Gaul,* or *The Valiant Champion, Tirante the White;* and would sooner have authorized her studying the lewd exploits of *Don Galaor,* or the lascivious jokes of *Damsel Plazerdimivida.*" Lewis had the names from Don Quixote's library, *Don Quixote,* Part I, chapters i and vi. Don Galaor is the brother of Amadis de Gaul. Plazirdemavida is a maid of honour to the Princess Carmesina in *Tirante the White.*

[50] It was even suggested that he had taken the incident of the Bleeding Nun from a romance of Madame de Genlis, *Les Chevaliers du Cygne,* Hamburg, 3 vols., 1795. Two friends, Isambard and Oliver, pass the night at an inn, and the former hears gentle footsteps in his companion's room, whilst a voice murmurs: "Olivier! C'est en vain que tu veux me fuir; je te suivrai partout." Later attempting to catch a glimpse of this nocturnal visitant, Isambard is horrified to see

a carious skeleton, all dabbled with blood, whilst tortured groans disturb the air. Tome I, ch. vi, p. 41; and ch. vii, pp. 60-2. Lewis however, explicitly stated that he had not read *Les Chevaliers du Cygne* until *The Monk* was printed and just about to appear, as indeed the several dates of the French and English romances amply demonstrate. Madame de Genlis was in fact drawing upon the same story by Musaeus as Lewis used.

Praz, *The Romantic Agony,* p. 209, imagines that the Bleeding Nun may have been the original of Gautier's *La Morte Amoureuse!*

[51] 1735-87.

[52] Also 8vo, 1708. Graesse, *Bibliotheca Magica,* Leipzig, 1843, pp. 86, 130, 134. For a reproduction of the frontispiece of this rare book see Soldan-Heppe, *Geschichte der Hexenprozesse,* München, 1912, Band II, 376.

[53] Vol. XXIII, p. 451.

[54] Otto Ritter, in an article "Studien zu M. G. Lewis' Roman 'Ambrosio or the Monk,'" *Archiv für das Studium der Neueren Sprachen and Literaturen,* Band CXI (New Series XI), 1903, pp. 106-21, is rather belated in drawing attention to these similarities. The influence of Bürger on Lewis' ballads the author of *The Monk* was proud openly to acknowledge. To talk of the compact with the Demon as a "Faust-theme" seems a little absurd, in view of the many historical records of such horrid bargains. See my *History of Witchcraft* and *Geography of Witchcraft, passim.*

[55] Born November 25th, 1762; died January 8th, 1835.

[56] Published in 1753.

[57] Such plays as *The Woodman's Hut* and *The Miller and bis Men* obviously owe their inspiration to Lewis.

[58] *Life and Correspondence of M. G. Lewis,* Vol. I, pp. 60-1.

[59] I have not, of course, attempted to do more than barely touch the fringe of the subject. There should further be consulted Neubaur's *Die Sage von ewigen Juden,* 2nd ed., Leipzig, 1893; Albert Soergel's *Ahasver-Dichtungen seit Goethe,* 1905; and (for literary allusions) Theodor Kapstein, *Ahasverus in der Weltpossie,* Berlin, 1906. Miss Alice M. Killen has a study *L'évolution de la légende du Juif errant* in the *Revue de littérature comparée,* January-March, 1925, pp. 5-36. Of romances upon the subject of, or which introduce the Wandering Jew, among the most famous is *Le Juif Errant* (1845), of Marie-Joseph-Eugène Sue, who read and was influenced by *The Monk.*

[60] The earliest English translation was 1795, "*The Ghost-Seer, or Apparitionist,* an interesting fragment." Lewis, of course, knew the original.

[61] Standard Novels, Colburn and Bentley, No. IX, 1831, *The Ghost-Seer,* Vol. I, p. 8.

[62] *Biographia Dramatica,* 1812, Vol. III, p. 389; No. 9.

[63] Produced at the Haymarket on November 1st, 1707. 4to, 1707. This comedy was a stock play throughout the eighteenth century, and was revived at the Haymarket as late as March, 1848. Although he has served the dish cleverly enough, Cibber (as his wont) offers far from original fare. Atall, the "Double Gallant," masquerades as Mr. Freeman and Colonel Standfast.

[64] *Cumberland's British Theatre,* Vol. XV, 1827, *The Castle Spectre,* Remarks, p. 10. Of great significance and importance as were German influences upon the Gothic novel in general, and upon Lewis in particular, it is, of course, possible disproportionately to overstress this point at the expense of the originality of British authors. Thus in his *The Revolutionary Ideas of the Marquis de Sade,* 1934, p. 101, *Note,* Mr. Geoffrey Gorer criticizes M. Maurice Heine, who "claims priority for de Sade in the use of Gothic trappings to the adventure novel, on the historical ground of the dates of his books, compared with those of Mrs. Radcliffe and 'Monk' Lewis." Mr. Gorer proceeds: "This seems to me difficult to justify, when the work of Clara Reeve and the wide diffusion of such German books as Boden's *Children of the Abbey* are taken into account." Clara Reeve (1729-1807) wrote: *Original Poems* (1769); *The Phœnix* (1772); *The Champion of Virtue* (1777), reprinted as *The Old English Baron* (1778); *The Two Mentors* (1783); *The Progress of Romance* (1785); *The Exiles* (1789); *The School for Widows* (1791); *Plans of Education* (1792); *Memoirs of Sir Roger de Clarendon* (1793); and *Destination: or Memoirs of A Private Family* (1799). *Fatherless Fanny* is not by Clara Reeve. Horace Walpole writing to the Rev. William Mason upon April 8th, 1778, jeered *The Old English Baron* as *Otranto* "reduced to reason and probability! It is so probable, that any trial for murder at the Old Bailey would make a more interesting story." In the same letter he damns it as a "*caput mortuum,*" Walpole's *Letters,* ed. Toynbee, Vol. X, Oxford, 1904, pp. 216-17. Again (*ibid.,* p. 302) Walpole speaks of *The Old English Baron* as "stripped of the marvellous" and "the most insipid dull nothing you ever saw." Miss J. M. S. Tompkins hits the mark when she emphasizes the "homely and practical streak that differentiates *The Old English Baron* from any other Gothic story whatever," *The Popular Novel in England,* 1932, p. 229. She further (p. 231) points out that Clara Reeve's *Memoirs of Sir Roger de*

Clarendon "is wholly unlike the Gothic Romances in the middle of which it appeared" (1793). Professor Raleigh, in *The English Novel* (fifth edition, 1904, p. 227), justly observes that Miss Reeve deliberately diluted romance with prosiness. "In her relation to the romantic movement she thus appears as a reactionary." In fact Mr. Gorer has made such an extremely bad shot when he hazarded "the work of Clara Reeve" that one must be excused if one doubts whether he has any acquaintance at all with this lady's writing.

"Such German books as Boden's *Children of the Abbey.*" This sentence I frankly do not understand. Is Boden the German author from whom a book *anglice,* "Children of the Abbey," was translated? Is Boden the English translator? What is the German title of the book which he translated? Who is this Boden? Is he Joseph Boden, the Indian judge-advocate, who founded the Boden professorship of Sanscrit at Oxford?

The Children of the Abbey, 4 vols., 1798, is by Mrs. Regina Maria Roche, *née* Dalton. It is certainly not a "terror" but a "sensibility" novel, and was an especial favourite, being frequently reprinted until at least the end of the nineteenth century. It is British to the core, in every page, in every turn. I have never heard of, nor can I find a German original, if that is what Mr. Gorer intends. One is entitled, I think, to express some scepticism, but should a German novel exist—whether or not by Boden—from which Mrs. Roche translated her *The Children of the Abbey,* I shall be most interested to learn all details, and I await the reading of the book with considerable curiosity.

[65] Wien und Prag bey Franz Haas; 262 pages. A copy is to be found in the Wiener Stadtbibliothek.

[66] In an article, *Die angebliche Quelle von M. G. Lewis' "Monk"; Archiv für das Studium,* Vol. CXIII, pp. 56-65.

[67] *Noch einmal die Quelle des "Monk"; Archiv,* Vol. CXV, pp. 70-3.

[68] *Euphorion,* VII, p. 725.

[69] Sauer, *Grillparzers Werke,* I, 1909, definitely proves that the German romance is merely an adaptation of certain chapters from *The Monk.* Rudolf Schneider, in his very superficial compilation, *Der Mönch in der englischen Dichtung bis auf Lewis's "Monk,"* 1795, Leipzig, 1928 (Palaestra 155), pp. 168-75, repeats Herzfeld's errors at some length. His list of Titles influenced by *The Monk* is faulty to a degree. Evidently he had no knowledge of the books he catalogues in the most haphazard way. Misled by the word "Recluse," he regards Zara Wentworth's *The*

Recluse of Albyn Hall (which he calls *Albin Hall*) as a clerical novel, and he obviously takes Mrs. Meeke's *Veiled Protectress* for a nun!

[70] Alice M. Killen, *Le Roman Terrifiant*, Paris, 1923, Bibliographie, pp. 227-8.

[71] Fernand Baldensperger, *Le Moine de Lewis dans la Littérature française*; *Journal of Comparative Literature*, 1903.

[72] M. J. Young, *Memoirs of Mrs. Crouch*, 1806, Vol. II, p. 257. S. M. Ellis, *The Life of Michael Kelly*, 1930, p. 259. note 1.

[73] Cumberland's *British Theatre*, No. 38. Also Dicks' *Standard Plays*, No. 268.

[74] At Norwich, November 22nd, 1809.

[75] 8vo., 1798 (bis); Third Edition, 8vo, 1799. Pub. Bell.

[76] S. M. Ellis, *The Life of Michael Kelly*, 1930, pp. 258-9.

[77] Alexis Pitou has an interesting article, *Les Origines du mélodrame français à la fin du XVIII siècle*, in the *Revue d'Histoire littéraire de la France*, 1911.

Prosper Mérimée's *Une Femme est un Diable*, which certainly borrows the central idea from *The Monk*, was published in his *Théâtre de Clara Gazul*, 1825, and designed for the closet.

[78] Alexis Pitou in the *Revue d'Histoire littéraire*, 1911, pp. 279-80.

[79] *Chronique des petits théâtres de Paris*, tom. I, p. 214.

[80] Ch.-M. Des Granges, *Geoffrey et la critique dramatique*, p. 402.

[81] It was almost immediately given in England under various piratical forms. Edward Fitzball and J. B. Buckstone were first in the field with a Musical Drama, *Robert le Diable; or, The Devil's Son*, Adelphi Theatre, January 23rd, 1832. A few weeks later, on February 13th, Sadlers Wells followed with a burletta, *Robert le Diable; or, The Devil's Son*. On Monday, February 20th, 1832, *The Demon Duke; or, The Mystic Branch*, was produced at Drury Lane, and the following night, Tuesday, Covent Garden gave *The Fiend Father; or Robert of Normandy*. The Royal Pavilion presented a burletta, *The Demon Father; or The Devil and his Son*, on March 12th, 1832.

Robert le Diable was produced in French at Her Majesty's on June 11th, 1832; and in Italian at the same theatre on May 4th, 1847, when Jenny Lind in the rôle of Alice made her first London appearance. On March 1st, 1845, this "great Catholic work," as it has been aptly termed, arranged by Bunn, had been given at Drury Lane. The more recent English adaptation of the libretto is by John Oxenford.

Mlle. Taglioni won a supreme triumph by her mystic dance as the Abbess Elena in *Robert le Diable*.

[82] Lewis in a letter from The Hague to his mother, May 18th, 1794. *Life and Correspondence of M. G. Lewis*, Vol. I, p. 123. . . .

Elliot B. Gose, Jr. (essay date 1972)

SOURCE: "*The Monk*," in *Imagination Indulged: The Irrational in the Nineteenth-Century Novel*, McGill-Queen's University Press, 1972, pp. 27-40.

[*In the following essay, Gose undertakes a psychoanalytic survey of* The Monk, *noting its "unresolved tensions" of "sexual conflict, violated taboos, and self-destructive impulses."*]

According to Freud we must look behind conscious daydreaming, as well as behind unconscious sleep dreaming, for keys to the unsatisfied primitive desires of the self.[1] According to Jung, when investigating such fantasy, we sometimes find ourselves in the presence of a vision that transcends the bounds of the immediate self and its limitations.[2] If we admit the premise of either theory, we are likely to find ourselves approaching fiction as something other than literature. We may if we wish search a novel for keys to the author's psychological problems, or for certain archetypes, universal "superhuman" types, or character relations. But if we do we will have subordinated art to psychological theory. If, on the other hand, we expect a certain kind of novel to reflect distinguishing psychic traits of its author and are not surprised to discover in it mythic patterns, we shall find psychoanalysis a help in approaching fiction, as I shall try to demonstrate in this chapter.

In the last analysis, neither Freud's approach nor Jung's can, in my opinion, provide the grounds for an aesthetic judgement. As Jung admits, a work of great archetypal interest may not have great artistic merit. **The Monk** is by no means devoid of artistic merit, but it is certainly not in a class with *Wuthering Heights* or *Bleak House*. Although it did play a part in establishing the tradition that made them possible, it contains in imperfect form the elements that they brought to artistic greatness.

We shall find in Lewis' novel all the qualities Chase outlined for a romance: because it is set in the past, its action will not gain much "resistance from reality." Because its characters are "rather two-dimensional types" they will be shown "in ideal relation" and will often act as "a function of plot." The "astonishing events" in which they are caught will contribute not to a realistic effect but to "mythic, allegorical, and symbolic forms."

Fortunately or unfortunately, we lack the evidence to probe very deeply into Lewis' childhood. We can, however, see indications of a psychic split having taken place early in his life. His parents separated in 1781, when he was six, his mother going to live with a music master. Although he stayed with his father and followed his footsteps by attending Westminster School and Oxford, and then entering the Civil Service, his sensibility followed his mother. She enjoyed music and the theatre and wanted to be an author. When young, her son would parade before her mirror "arrayed in a long train, and loaded with all the gauze and feathers that lay within his reach." Once he returned from the theatre and "imitated the actress's shriek with . . . thrilling accuracy." As Lewis' first and very sympathetic biographer commented, "Being the constant companion of his mother—a timid and sensitive woman, whose youthful appearance, when he grew up into boyhood, caused her not unfrequently to be looked upon as his sister—he gradually partook of her own romantic temperament, and somewhat undecided character."[3]

From early childhood, a confusion of sexual roles appears evident in Lewis.[4] In his novel we shall find a study of the disintegration of an "undecided character." Evidence connecting Lewis' nature with that of his hero-villain, Ambrosio, is not hard to find. We know for instance that Lewis suggested a resemblance between himself and Mrs Radcliffe's villain, Montoni.[5] Montoni is also an important source for Ambrosio. In addition we shall see as we analyse *The Monk* how Lewis' naiveté in presenting dreams, daydreams, nightmares, and supernatural scenes affords a relatively clear view of his conflicts. The pattern these elements make is no prettier than the details through which they are rendered, but it is an important pattern, opening up as it does irrational motifs evident in the stuff of Romantic poetry and in a significant number of post-Romantic novels.

The first hint of confused sexual identity comes out in the monk Ambrosio's attraction to Rosario, a young novice whom he loves "with all the affection of a father."[6] Rosario finally reveals himself as a woman, Matilda, who entered the monastery out of love for Ambrosio. After saving his life by sucking the poison out of a deadly bite on his hand, she manages to seduce him. Afterward she confesses that the poison, now in her, cannot be countered by any natural means. But there is some hope. She has been brought up by an enlightened uncle: "Under his instructions my understanding acquired more strength and justness than generally falls to the lot of my sex" (p. 82). In short, she knows something of black magic, and it turns out she will need the aid of the devil if she is to escape death by poisoning. As she leads Ambrosio to the underground burial vaults where she will call up Satan, she assumes "a sort of courage and manliness in her manners and discourse, but ill calculated to please him" (p. 233). Lewis seems at once conscious of the paradoxical relation and confused about it: Ambrosio "regretted Rosario, the fond, the gentle, and submissive; he grieved that Matilda preferred the virtues of his sex to those of her own" (p. 234). The appeal of the effeminate is brought out again later when Ambrosio first sees the devil: "He beheld a figure more beautiful than fancy's pencil ever drew. It was a youth seemingly scarce eighteen, the perfection of whose form and face was unrivalled. He was perfectly naked; a bright star sparkled upon his forehead, two crimson wings extended themselves from his shoulders, and his silken locks were confined by a band of many-coloured fires" (p. 273).

Even when we shift our focus in the novel to male-female relations that are seemingly less ambiguous, we find strange patterns emerging. We may begin with the previous scene in which Ambrosio meets Satan, a scene admired by Coleridge for its demonic "blue trembling flame" that "emitted no heat."[7] In fact, a "cold shivering" that seizes Ambrosio anticipates the unexpected conclusion of the plot about to be hatched in the vault. To ensure the success of Ambrosio's plan to ravish the heroine, Antonia, Satan gives the monk a myrtle (a flower sacred to Venus) which will send Antonia into "a death-like slumber" (p. 275). But, when the time comes, Ambrosio is successful only to the point of kissing Antonia's lips. At that point her mother, Elvira, rushes in so distraught that Ambrosio finds it necessary to strangle her.

> The blood was chilled in her veins: her heart had forgotten to beat; and her hands were stiff and frozen. Ambrosio beheld before him that once noble and majestic form, now become a corse, cold, senseless, and disgusting.

> This horrible act was no sooner perpetrated, than the friar beheld the enormity of his crime. A cold dew flowed over his limbs. . . . Antonia now appeared to him an object of disgust. A deadly cold had usurped the place of that warmth which glowed in his bosom (pp. 297-98).

But the cold has only temporarily triumphed over the warmth of Ambrosio's passion. He again casts Antonia into a deathlike sleep, this time with a drug. Then he has her placed in the catacombs where Matilda had invoked the devil. When she awakens there, he finally ravishes her in a scene which strengthens the connection between lust and lifelessness. At first he tries to woo her:

> "This sepulchre seems to me Love's bower. . . . Your veins shall glow with the fire which circles in mine."
>
> . . . Her shroud being her only garment, she wrapped it closely round her.
>
> "Unhand me, father!" she cried. . . . "Why have you brought me to this place? Its appearance freezes me with horror!" (p. 366).

Afterward he tells her,

> "Wretched girl, you must stay here with me! Here amidst these lonely tombs, these images of death, these rotting, loathsome, corrupted bodies! Here shall you stay, and witness my sufferings; witness what it is to be in the horrors of despondency, and breathe the last groan in blasphemy and curses!—And whom am I to thank for this? What seduced me into crimes, whose bare remembrance makes me shudder? Fatal witch! was it not thy beauty? Have you not plunged my soul into infamy?" (p. 369).

Crude as the theatricality of this speech may be, its bald phrase "fatal witch" is a clue to the imaginative patterns which give *The Monk* its unhealthy power.

The real witch in Ambrosio's life is Matilda, who turns out to be in league with Satan. If Matilda and Antonia are enchanting witches, Elvira is that other kind, the old crone, who, like the incubus of conscience, turns cold with fear a man's warmest attempt at wish fulfilment. As I see it, the inevitable replacement of the enchantress by the crone is a central dilemma of Lewis' imagination.

These implications are evident in what Coleridge thought the most compelling part of the novel, the incidents in the section connected with the Bleeding Nun. Visiting in Bavaria, Don Raymond falls in love with a young Spanish woman, Agnes, whose jealous aunt finally denies him entry to her castle. Agnes decides to fly with him to avoid being forced into a nunnery, and she conceives the plan of dressing up as the Bleeding Nun, a ghost who appears once every five years at the castle. On the appropriate night, Don Raymond meets a figure dressed as the nun and swears that he is hers as long as "blood shall roll" in his veins. She turns out to be the actual ghost. He recalls, "I gazed upon the spectre with horror too great to be described. My blood was frozen in my veins. I would have called for aid, but the sound expired ere it could pass my lips. My nerves were bound up in impotence, and I remained in the same attitude inanimate as a statue"

(p. 170). Like the Ancient Mariner's Nightmare Life-in-Death, "who thicks men's blood with cold," this witch has Don Raymond in her power and will not let him go until he is reconciled with God. She visits him every night at the same hour for several months, until "the Great Mogul" appears on the scene.

With his help Don Raymond is freed from enchantment in a scene parallel to the one in which Ambrosio is introduced to Satan. But, whereas Don Raymond is guided by a mysterious old man back to a normal life, Ambrosio was guided by a mysterious young woman into a liaison with the devil. And, whereas Ambrosio faced Satan's cold to gain a deceptively easy means of satisfying his hot lust, Don Raymond is liberated from cold by the hot cross on the forehead of the mysterious stranger, who is later identified as the Wandering Jew.

Ambrosio's pursuit of Antonia and Don Raymond's more rewarding attempt to unite with Agnes have similar patterns: each desires an appealing woman but is frustrated by the deadly and chilling intervention of another woman. A similar sequence, wish fulfilment displaced by terror, is present in a scene near the beginning of the novel. Lorenzo, the brother of Agnes and one of two youthful heroes in the subplot, has just met Antonia and fallen in love with her. He goes into "the gothic obscurity of the church" and abandons "himself to the delusions of fancy." These melt into a sleeping dream in which Antonia appears dressed for a wedding. Lorenzo realizes that he is to be the groom.

> But before he had time to receive her, an unknown rushed between them: his form was gigantic; his complexion was swarthy, his eyes fierce and terrible; his mouth breathed out volumes of fire, and on his forehead was written in legible characters—"Pride! Lust! Inhumanity!"
>
> Antonia shrieked. The monster clasped her in his arms, and springing with her upon the altar, tortured her with his odious caresses. She endeavoured in vain to escape from his embrace. Lorenzo flew to her succour; but, ere he had time to reach her, a loud burst of thunder was heard. Instantly the cathedral seemed crumbling into pieces; the monks betook themselves to flight, shrieking fearfully; the lamps were extinguished, the altar sunk down, and in its place appeared an abyss vomiting forth clouds of flame. Uttering a loud and terrible cry the monster plunged into the gulph, and in his fall attempted to drag Antonia with him. He strove in vain. Animated by supernatural powers, she disengaged herself from his embrace; but her white robe was left in his possession. Instantly a wing of brilliant splendour spread itself from either of Antonia's arms. She darted upwards, and while ascending cried to Lorenzo, "Friend! we shall meet above!" (pp. 53-54).[8]

We have here one of those allegorical scenes which Chase saw as characteristic of romance. The monster stands for Ambrosio's faults as a man and a priest; his treatment of Antonia foreshadows Ambrosio's ultimate rape of her. The allegory also embodies Lewis' conscious anti-Catholicism (the labels on the monster's forehead referring beyond Ambrosio to the system which produced him), but more important it embodies an unconscious tension in Lewis' psyche and in the novel, a tension between idyllic daydream and destroying nightmare.

The marriage in the church represents the hopeful daydream, while death in the catacombs becomes the dominant (indeed, triumphant) extension of the nightmare ending of the dream. We have already investigated Ambrosio's rape of Antonia in the catacombs. Taking rape as soulless love, we saw it as the yoking of lustful daydream and deathly nightmare. More characteristic, however, is the separation of the two, the hopeful ascent toward light in opposition to the disintegrating descent into darkness. In Lorenzo's dream, the descent caused by the lustful monster is balanced by the ascent of the angelic Antonia. In the death of Ambrosio, we will find an equivalent to the monster's descent. But, although Ambrosio's fall is balanced by the happy marriages of both Lorenzo and Don Raymond, the subplot does not ascend easily toward light.

Forced into a nunnery back in Spain, Agnes is found by Don Raymond, with whom her passion reaches a climax which has an unfortunate, if natural, consequence. The prioress discovers that Agnes is pregnant and locks her deep in the underground burial vaults. There she gives birth to a child that dies immediately. "It soon became a mass of putridity, and to every eye was a loathsome and disgusting object, to every eye but a mother's," says Agnes loyally (p. 393). She also tells us that, when first chained in her prison, her "blood ran cold" as she was struck by "the cold vapours hovering in the air, the walls green with damp" (p. 390). She is found and rescued by her brother Lorenzo, who had believed her dead. As he descends toward her, the cold is again emphasized: "Coldly played the light upon the damp walls, whose dew-stained surface gave back a feeble reflection. A thick and pestilential fog clouded the height of the vaulted dungeon. As Lorenzo advanced, he felt a piercing chillness spread itself through his veins" (p. 355).

In one sense Lorenzo is descending into the abyss about which he had earlier dreamed, and the imagery of light and dark is as pronounced as it was in that dream. The entrance to Agnes' prison is hidden by a statue in the main part of the catacomb. Significantly, that statue is of St Clare, the patron saint of the order to which Agnes belongs. With the statue removed, "A deep abyss now presented itself before them, whose

thick obscurity the eye strove in vain to pierce. The rays of the lamp were too feeble to be of much assistance. Nothing was discernible, save a flight of rough unshapen steps, which sank into the yawning gulph, and were soon lost in darkness" (pp. 353-54). The symbolism of St Clare, "Saint Light," hiding a harsh reality of darkness behind her appearance of benevolence and light, is appropriate both to Lewis' conscious anti-Catholicism and to the unconscious ambiguity of his feelings about women.

In Lorenzo's early dream, after the appearance of the monster, "the cathedral seemed crumbling to pieces; . . . the lamps were extinguished, the altar sunk down, and in its place appeared an abyss" (p. 53). Similarly, in the later action, Lorenzo and his followers have descended into the vaults after the convent connected with them has been pulled down and burned by an angry mob. "Lorenzo was shocked at having been the cause, however innocent, of this frightful disturbance," of this "scene of devastation and horror" (p. 345). Like the monster in his dream, he plunges into the gulf below him, but he does so on a kind of redemptive quest.

The overt success of the quest can be measured by the reaction of Agnes when Lorenzo tells her she can at last ascend: "Joy! Joy! I shall once more breathe the fresh air, and view the light of the glorious sunbeams!" (p. 358). Then as they climb, "the rays of the lamp above, as well as the murmur of female voices, guided his steps" (p. 359). For the first time, light appears to triumph over darkness. If, in fact, we consider Lorenzo's experience as an archetypal one, we can see the possibility of a less pathological interpretation of the novel than we have so far been able to find.

Whereas the monster, like Ambrosio, goes down in the pit to be damned, Lorenzo descends into the depths like a hero to offer help. His actions even follow the pattern set by numerous heroes of folktale and myth, as these patterns have been abstracted by mythographers such as Frobenius, Rank, Jung, Lord Raglan, and Joseph Campbell.[9] The journey down into darkness is an important part of this pattern. Jung points out that, although the descent is what Freud would call a regression, it is undertaken with a positive aim. He emphasizes that the hero goes back to the womb in order that he may be reborn, renewed, made strong again.[10]

Since Lorenzo descends through the statue of a woman, Jung's symbolism could be said to hold good for the beginning of his quest. The psychoanalysts would see any movement back to the mother as running into the incest taboo. The overcoming of this taboo is usually represented by the hero's defeating a monster before he can return. The fact that Lorenzo is not forced to face any such monster bodes ill not so much for him as for the story (or its author). As though unconsciously aware of the pattern and its demands, Lewis gives Lorenzo a second chance to face a monster, by having him called back into the catacombs after he rescues Agnes. This time he almost confronts Ambrosio, the monster he should slay to round out the heroic pattern (or, from another point of view, to bring into more effective contact the twin strands of Lewis' plot). But instead Ambrosio escapes and Lorenzo is left with his own love, Antonia, who has just been raped by Ambrosio. She dies in his arms. Clearly something has gone wrong with the archetypal pattern.

In myth the darkness into which the hero descends is always dangerous, but it is also, as Jung shows, a source of life. In *The Monk,* however, it is a place of death only, really a tomb rather than a womb. This fact aligns the novel with an important subpattern that develops when the mythic success pattern is frustrated. As outlined by Joseph Campbell, this subpattern clearly fits *The Monk*. Where an

> Oedipus-Hamlet revulsion remains to beset the soul, there the world, the body, and woman above all, become the symbols no longer of victory but of defeat. A monastic-puritanical, world-negating ethical system then radically and immediately transfigures all the images of myth. No longer can the hero rest in innocence with the goddess of the flesh; for she is become the queen of sin. "So long as a man has any regard for this corpse-like body," writes the Hindu monk Shankaracharya, "he is impure, and suffers from his enemies as well as from birth, disease and death. . . . Throw far away this limitation of a body which is inert and filthy by nature."[11]

The moral that is conscious in the writings of the Hindu monk is largely unconscious in Lewis' work, as the happy ending to Lorenzo's story indicates.

Lorenzo has put his sister in the care of "the beautiful Virginia de Villa-Franca" (p. 348), whom he considers "as a ministering angel descended to the aid of afflicted innocence" (p. 361). Although he goes into a decline after the death of Antonia, soon Virginia wins him over by her "beautiful person, elegant manners, innumerable talents and sweet disposition" (p. 399). In other words, the happy ending may be seen as an attempt by Lewis to break out of the "world-negating" pattern in which he had immured Lorenzo. But Virginia is a *deus ex machina,* a character functioning more on the level of wish fulfilment than of engaged imagination.

The main impression made upon the reader is of the involvement of love with death in *The Monk*. Matilda risks death to gain Ambrosio (when they make love

the first time, a deadly poison is in her veins). Both times that Ambrosio attempts to seduce Antonia, she is first put in a deathlike sleep. The second time, the stage is set appropriately: "By the side of three putrid half-corrupted bodies lay the sleeping beauty" (p. 363). Don Raymond gets the ghost of a corpse the first time he thinks he has Agnes. And Lorenzo, after bringing his sister back from near death in which natural love has placed her, is rewarded by the death of his beloved Antonia. Considering the consistency and force of this pattern, we must attribute success to *The Monk* as an artistic embodiment of certain tensions in Lewis' mind. These tensions reach an effective if morbid resolution in the last chapter of the novel.

While Ambrosio awaits the burning ordained for him by the Inquisition, the devil appears again, not as the beautiful youth of daydream, who had earlier helped seduce the monk to the delights of *contra naturam,* but as a nightmarish reality.

> in all that ugliness which since his fall from heaven had been his portion. His blasted limbs still bore marks of the Almighty's thunder. A swarthy darkness spread itself over his gigantic form: his hands and feet were armed with long talons. . . . Over his huge shoulders waved two enormous sable wings: and his hair was supplied by living snakes, which twined themselves round his brows with frightful hissings. . . . Still the lightning flashed around him, and the thunder with repeated bursts seemed to announce the dissolution of Nature (p. 412).

The last phrase, "the dissolution of Nature," sums up the main direction of the novel, toward descent and disintegration. Life has been drawn irresistibly down into the catacombs to become one with the "rotting, loathsome, corrupted bodies" there. And a similar fate is in store for Ambrosio. Rescued by Satan, he is taken out of the prison to be set upon a precipice in the mountains, where "the disorder of his imagination was increased by the wildness of the surrounding scenery" (p. 417). He has found an environment appropriate to his temperament.

Although Ambrosio is unsatisfyingly passive at the end, he has dared enough to earn Lewis' implied comparisons with Orestes and Tantalus, if not with Prometheus.

> Darting his talons into the monk's shaven crown, [Satan] sprang with him from the rock. The caves and mountains rang with Ambrosio's shrieks. The daemon continued to soar aloft, till reaching a dreadful height, he released the sufferer. Headlong fell the monk through the airy waste; the sharp point of a rock received him; . . . . . bruised and mangled, he rested on the river's banks. Life still existed in his miserable frame: he attempted to raise himself; his broken and dislocated limbs refused to perform their office, nor was he able to

quit the spot where he had first fallen. The sun now rose above the horizon; its scorching beams darted full upon the head of the expiring sinner. Myriads of insects were called forth by the warmth; they drank the blood which trickled from Ambrosio's wounds; he had no power to drive them from him, and they fastened upon his sores, darted their stings into his body, covered him with their multitudes, and inflicted on him tortures the most exquisite and insupportable. The eagles of the rock tore his flesh piecemeal, and dug out his eye-balls with their crooked beaks. A burning thirst tormented him; he heard the river's murmur as it rolled beside him, but strove in vain to drag himself towards the sound. Blind, maimed, helpless, and despairing, venting his rage in blasphemy and curses, execrating his existence, yet dreading the arrival of death destined to yield him up to greater torments, six miserable days did the villain languish. On the seventh a violent storm arose: the winds in fury rent up rocks and forests: the sky was now black with clouds, now sheeted with fire: the rain fell in torrents; it swelled the stream; the waves overflowed their banks; they reached the spot where Ambrosio lay, and, when they abated, carried with them into the river the corpse of the despairing monk (pp. 419-20).

After plunging from the heights to the abyss, Ambrosio experiences sunlight not as the "glorious sunbeams" which Agnes looked forward to earlier, but as the wrath of God. The warmth caused by the sun is no longer his own hot lust for carnal experience; rather it calls forth insects which ravish his helpless body. Even the water of life which he desires, finally brings only death to him. It took six days for God to make the world; on the seventh he rested in peace. It takes six days for Ambrosio to disintegrate completely, physically and spiritually; on the seventh he dies in a storm.

The perversion of nature which Lewis made the moral basis of his conscious didacticism in the novel is also imaged in the development of its thematic patterns. Despite the presence of light and the ascent of some characters toward it, the controlling force in *The Monk*, and the one experienced by its readers, is demonic. All the supernatural visitants have rejected God, and even the one who frees Don Raymond from the Bleeding Nun was damned at Christ's death. Of the ten dreams described or referred to in the novel, six are nightmares, the other four being voluptuous fantasies of the type referred to earlier as leading to a nightmarish retribution. This triumph of the nightmare indicates the plight of Lewis' trapped psyche. In his novel, love leads to lasting union only within the accepted social framework, and then only at the cost of Agnes' natural child or Lorenzo's first love. All the lovers become enmeshed in the machinations of the nunnery and monastery, two institutions which in the novel breed inhumanity while attempting to mask it. Lewis exposes the "truth," rationally by observing that these institu-

tions separate male and female, symbolically by connecting them through the doors that lead from each to the underground burial vaults. But behind the rational distaste lurks a deeper reason for separating the sexes. Lewis could not bring them together convincingly in fulfilled natural love. Behind the loved one as female there stands a jealous aunt, a righteous mother, a damned incubus. Even the loved one as a male turns from a charming lad into a domineering woman or a punishing demon.

Coleridge began his review of *The Monk* with the following sentence: "The horrible and the preternatural have usually seized on the popular taste, at the rise and decline of literature" (*Miscellaneous Criticism*, p. 372). If we think of Coleridge's three great poems, the supernatural comes to mind immediately. The horrible has been less noticeable since he cut from the 1798 version of "The Ancient Mariner" a number of stanzas with a gothic charnel effect. From this point of view, Romantic poetry is the rising form, the gothic novel the declining one. Poetry picks up and transmutes most of the standard gothic accoutrement: horror, terror, the supernatural, the Middle Ages, the sublime, the demonic, incest.[12] Scott, unable to compete in poetry with Byron's dark, soulful hero, turns to the novel, which he reorients towards a more mundane use of the past with more conventional characters and situations. In effect the literary impetus shifts from the novel to poetry. But, with the artistic shift back to the novel after Byron's death in 1824, the techniques and attitudes of romanticism will help bring about a change in the nature of fiction.

The important aesthetic question raised by *The Monk* is one Coleridge tried to solve in the best part of his review. Coleridge's comments, reminiscent of Walpole's much earlier insight, are also a foreshadowing of his famous statement about the suspension of disbelief. In the review he asserted that "The romance-writer possesses an unlimited power over situations; but he must scrupulously make his characters act in congruity with them. . . . We feel no great difficulty in yielding a temporary belief to any, the strangest, situation of *things*. But that situation once conceived, how beings like ourselves would feel and act in it, our own feelings sufficiently instruct us; and we instantly reject the clumsy fiction that does not harmonise with them" (p. 373). In a certain kind of novel we do not ask for a probable environment. We gladly throw away the mirror of exterior nature, partly through joy in the liberation of imagination, but also, Coleridge intimates, because we except to find out something about our interior nature. It is to this world that Lewis must be true. But, contrary to Coleridge's dictum, and perhaps to common sense, he need not give us deep or consistent characters. That is, any one character may act from shallow or incongruous emotions, but because Lewis embodied in his action powerful emotional and thematic patterns we respond to them intuitively. The sensational sequence of events evokes at least a general sense of unease in the average reader, a response we have seen as based on Lewis' embodying the tensions of his psyche in patterns of sexual conflict, violated taboos, and self-destructive impulses.

Although *The Monk*, with its unresolved tensions, stands as a paradigm of excess, the gothic novel unquestionably did establish the practice of patterned fantasy and psychologically significant settings and action, a practice which influenced many important English novelists in the nineteenth century. A similar case may be made for the fairy tale, another influential form of romance and one we shall consider in the next chapter. One of the triumphs of the novel as a literary form in Victorian times was to transplant the patterns of romance into a nineteenth-century setting.

Notes

[1] Sigmund Freud, "The Relation of the Poet to Daydreaming" (1908), in *Delusion and Dream,* ed. Philip Rieff (Boston: Beacon Press, 1956).

[2] Carl Jung, *Symbols of Transformation* (New York: Pantheon Books, Inc., 1956). Jung points out that Freud had earlier opened up this line of thought.

[3] *The Life and Correspondence of M. G. Lewis* (London: H. Colburn, 1839), 2 Vols., I, 12, 44, 28. Peck (p. v) identifies the author as Mrs Cornwall Baron-Wilson.

[4] John Berryman takes Lewis' homosexuality for granted in his introduction. Peck (pp. 65-66) is doubtful, arguing that William Kelly, the youth whom Lewis undertook to sponsor in 1802, was only ten at the time. There is more evidence than Peck admits. See André Parreaux, *The Publication of The Monk: A Literary Event 1796-1798* (Paris: M. Didier, 1960), p. 119. Peck is, however, justified in his caveat that homosexuality covers too broad a range to be applied without defining. My case is simply that homoerotic emotions are apparent in Lewis' biography and writing. Whether he ever acted on them need not concern us.

[5] See the letter to Lewis' mother in the back of Peck's biography, p. 208.

[6] Matthew G. Lewis, *The Monk* (New York: Grove Press, 1959), p. 67. Edited by Peck, introduced by John Berryman.

[7] In the *Critical Review* (February 1797). Reprinted by Thomas M. Raysor in *Coleridge's Miscellaneous Criticism* (London: Constable, 1936), p. 373.

[8] The parallel with the end of *Clarissa* struck even Lewis, who in the fourth and fifth editions mentioned it in a footnote. See Peck's list of Variant Readings, p. 425, *The Monk*. See also Watt's analysis of *Clarissa*.

[9] Leo Frobenius, *Das Zeitalter des Sonnengottes* (1904); Otto Rank, *The Myth of the Birth of the Hero* (1914); Carl Jung, *Psychology of the Unconscious* (1916); Lord Raglan, *The Hero* (1936); Joseph Campbell, *The Hero with a Thousand Faces* (1949).

[10] *Symbols of Transformation,* pp. 293-94, 308, 330, 335, 408, 419-20.

[11] *The Hero with a Thousand Faces,* (New York: Meridian Books, 1956), p. 123.

[12] Railo treats the evolution of these themes in *The Haunted Castle* (London: G. Routledge & Sons, 1927). See also Peter L. Thorslev, Jr., *The Byronic Hero* (Minneapolis: University of Minnesota Press, 1962). See also Robert Hume, "Gothic versus Romantic: a Revaluation of the Gothic Novel," *PMLA,* 84 (March 1969).

Peter Grudin (essay date 1975)

SOURCE: "*The Monk:* Matilda and the Rhetoric of Deceit," in *The Journal of Narrative Technique,* Vol. 5, No. 2, May, 1975, pp. 136-46.

[*In the following essay, Grudin assesses the "formal coherence" of* The Monk, *claiming that evidence for its structural unity exists in an interpretation of Matilda as a demonic being.*]

> I charge thee to return and change thy
>   shape;
> Thou art too ugly to attend upon me.
> Go, and return an old Franciscan friar,
> That holy shape becomes a devil best.
>   (*Doctor Faustus,* iii, 25-28)

Until recently Matthew Gregory Lewis' *The Monk* has hardly sustained the critical and popular interest it inspired when it first appeared in 1796 when Coleridge, one of the novel's earliest reviewers, found it so attractive and appalling.[1] Subsequent changes in taste and literary decorum soon relegated the novel to relative obscurity. During most of the twentieth century those who have discussed it have barely outnumbered those who have actually read it, and the work has been confined to surveys of the Gothic novel and reading lists of Ph.D. candidates.

In the last few years, however, *The Monk* has enjoyed a revival among serious critics. John Berryman helped to stimulate this interest in his introduction to the novel, where he found it puzzlingly evocative of *Wuthering Heights*.[2] Robert Kiely has demonstrated that its themes, tensions and subsequent formal imperfections make it an important token of the romantic tradition in the English novel.[3] An influential student of the *"fantastique"* as a genre, Tzvetan Todorov, finds the novel a model for his notions of the equivocally surreal (*"fantastique"*) and the unequivocally surreal (*"merveilleux"*).[4] Peter Brooks finds it indicative of a change in intellectual climate. For him it conveys the idea that " . . . ethics has implicitly come to be founded on terror rather than virtue," and that "God' is simply one figure in a manicaeistic daemonology."[5]

This new stature, and the ambitiousness and variety of this recent criticism place a considerable strain upon the text itself. To use the work as a token of changes in intellectual climate, or to discuss it as representative of a genre is to assume that the text itself is basically comprehensible and coherent. Yet basic coherence is exactly what more conservative critics have found lacking in *The Monk*. Kiely even finds this lack of consistency to be characteristic of romantic fiction. Thus for him, as for the other recent critics, the question of formal coherence should be prior to all other problems. It is necessary, therefore, to reopen the question, to ask whether this novel makes sense. The resolution of this problem can then be applied to less fundamental treatments, and to the place of this novel within Gothic fiction.

One major charge leveled against *The Monk* is that the long episode of Raymond and Agnes (the story of the bleeding nun) is extraneous, and this charge is largely valid. The interpolation has no causal connection to the rest of the work. If it contributes anything, it does so by analogy. Don Raymond's persecution by this carnal, persistent, and lascivious revenant is a parody before the fact of Ambrosio's liaison with Matilda.

But this parallel suggests a contrast. Don Raymond, who had mistaken this monster for the lovely Agnes, is soon disabused. Such is not the case for Ambrosio. The real nature of his paramour, the central agent in the action of the novel, is long a mystery to him, and has remained one for readers. Montague Summers, one of the most enthusiastic of these, was dismayed to find so important a character presented so inconsistently.

Summers based his critique of Matilda on contradictory statements about her identity. At the end of the novel Satan reveals the nature of Ambrosio's temptress. Noting the Monk's idolatry of a painting of the Madonna, Satan " . . . bade a subordinate but crafty spirit assume a similar form."[6] Thus Ambrosio is de-

ceived, and lured to damnation by a tempter who combines Marlowe's Mephistopheles with Helen.

But Satan's explanation is diametrically opposed by Matilda's earlier claims. She contends that the Madonna looks like her because she had modelled for the painting, and that she had done this, and entered the monastery disguised as the novice Rosario, because of her idolatry of the Monk. Her claims thus deny any supernatural agency. She presents herself as mortal, as tempted rather than tempter, and her subsequent practice of witchcraft does not contradict these claims. She can still define herself as a mortal woman who has turned to the black arts in order to satisfy earthly passions.

For Summers the contradition posed by the claims of Satan and Matilda was hopelessly irreconcilable. He was appalled to find that Satan's ultimate revelation " . . . runs counter to the whole tenor of the narrative . . . and, in reading," he found it necessary to " . . . delete it—at least mentally—from the text."[7] Although they may not admire this tactic of deleting the problematic, both Berryman and Edith Birkhead accept this view.[8] Kiely, to whom paradox is not anomaly in romantic fiction, is undismayed: "When it is revealed that the model for the painting has been the wanton Matilda who dressed in monk's clothing in order to be near Ambrosio, we see that the portrait is merely another disguise. Whatever Matilda really is—a witch of Satan, a figment of Ambrosio's imagination, a woman possessed by lust—art can only hint at and we can only guess" (Kiely, p. 109).

Perhaps a more pertinent question would be: Is Matilda peculiar to the imagination that created *The Monk,* or is she a token derived from a once notorious type? Moreover, can the identification of this type help to solve the seeming anomalies in Matilda's nature and actions? In fact, art can more than hint at her true nature. Whether she is a mortal, as she claims to be, or a fiend in human shape, as Satan would have it, is a question that the text of *The Monk* can place beyond conjecture.

Matilda's initial actions excite little suspicion. In fact, the transvestite disguise which she exploits in order to enter Ambrosio's monastery is by no means peculiar; as a literary device it is overly familiar. Her protests that she had long adored the Monk from a distance, moreover, are certainly consistent with what we already know about Ambrosio's notoriety and adulation among the female populace of Madrid.

As Matilda encounters difficulties, however, her means become more and more extraordinary. Ambrosio struggles against the temptations she offers him. At a crucial moment he is so stricken with a last convulsion of "virtue" (more a fear of discovery and disgrace) that he commands Matilda to leave the monastery. Apparently willing to comply with his demand, she begs only for a last memento—a flower blooming in the lush gardens where they meet. Here the parallel to Faust is momentarily replaced by a sly allusion to *Genesis,* as Ambrosio, plucking the flower, is stung by a serpent whose venom is fatal. His doctor despairs of a cure; he is saved only by Matilda's seemingly selfless intervention: she sucks forth the venom and thus introduces the poison into her own system. Once Ambrosio learns of this sacrifice, and that he must both become her lover and endorse her appeal to Satan in order to save her, gratitude becomes the irresistible rationalization for lust. The virtuous prior breaks his vows and begins a dangerous flirtation with the dark powers.

Episodes such as this one force us to choose between alternatives: either this sequence of events is serial and coincidental, or it is systematic and designed. The first alternative suggests cheap melodrama. Matilda's despair provokes a request that just happens to lead to her success. But such blatant fortuitousness is exactly what makes such a reading suspect. The sequence beginning with Matilda's last wish and leading to the fulfillment of her desires suggests that she and the serpent are both figuratively and literally in collusion. This should be obvious to the reader and may seem too obvious to Matilda herself. Almost immediately after her "sacrifice" she tries to reenforce the idea that she is pure of prescience and deceit, and innocent of anything darker than her love for Ambrosio.

As the Monk recovers, Matilda soliloquizes on the purity and hopelessness of her passion. She precedes her confession with a performance upon the lute, and Ambrosio decides to test her sincerity by feigning sleep. Supposedly unaware of his pretense Matilda feels free to bare her soul; with characteristic resourcefulness, moreover, she manages to bare portions of her person as well. Thus, as she plays her lute, her cowl slips back far enough to expose, for the first time, " . . . two coral lips . . . ripe, fresh, and melting, and a chin, in whose dimples seemed to lurk a thousand Cupids." The sleeves of her habit interfere with her performance; thus she must draw them up, and expose " . . . an arm, formed in the most perfect symmetry, the delicacy of whose skin might have contended with the snow in whiteness" (p. 98). Glimpsing all this through half-closed lids, the Monk decides, naively, that pretense is no longer possible. He calls out to her, and she is so surprised by the sound of his voice that she moves her head suddenly. This, of course, causes her cowl to fall back completely and to reveal to Ambrosio " . . . the exact resemblance of his admired Madonna!" (p. 101).

Ambrosio's famous intellect is no match for this dramatic conspiracy of the verbal, the musical, and the visual. Readers, however, may recognize an ironic distancing in the playful, trite, and overblown rhetoric of the narrator's description, and may disagree with Birkhead's view that this scene completely exonerates Matilda (Birkhead, p. 67). Moreover, our purview includes an earlier episode in which Matilda had reenforced similar rhetoric with a similar demonstration. She had tried to move the resistant Monk by attempting suicide, and had compounded pity with lust by presenting the point of her dagger to a peerless, and needlessly exposed, breast. Thus when, before her confession, she salts its rhetorical potential with this artful strip-tease, repetition creates emphasis, and this emphasis combines with coincidence to excite our suspicions. It is difficult to believe that the revelation of her innocence and purity and the revelation of her body are merely coincidental. This leads us to wonder whether she really believes that Ambrosio is sleeping. Such tantalizing art seems intended for an audience that is attentive, and vulnerable. The love-lorn maiden who can apply such providence to the plucking of a flower, seems to shape other actions as though she could foresee their consequences as well.

Thus the means by which Matilda achieves her end suggest abnormal consciousness on her part. Far more suggestive of a non-human sensibility is the end itself. It is not simple sexual gratification; no sooner has the virtuous prior succumbed than she encourages him to abandon her.

As soon as Ambrosio has yielded, Matilda foresakes the role of mistress for that of procuress. She directs the Monk's newly aroused passions towards the conspicuously chaste Antonia. The anomalousness of Matilda's action is paralleled by the seemingly arbitrary choice of Antonia. But this choice turns out to be darkly logical: eventually Ambrosio is forced to murder this girl's mother, Elvira, and he rapes and murders Antonia herself. Thus he unknowingly commits matricide and incest. Matilda's intrinsic role in this process, and her strange abandonment of a lover won with such labor and art, suggest that her interest is not in the man, but in his perdition.

This gratuitous malevolence makes Matilda's nature puzzling indeed. But as the novel perfects the puzzle it has already begun to hint at a solution. As we begin to doubt that Matilda, because of her capacities and ends, is a mortal, the novel begins to suggest what she really is.

These hints inhere in her particular mode of alienating the Monk, for here she finally removes the last layer of a disguise that had begun with her impersonation of Rosario. In order to redirect Ambrosio's passions, she must first divert them from herself, and here her tactics are, once again, truly remarkable. "But a few days had passed, since she appeared the mildest and softest of her sex, devoted to his will and looking up to him as a superior being. Now she assumed a sort of courage and manliness in her manners and discourse, but ill calculated to please him . . . he grieved that Matilda preferred the virtues of his sex to those of her own . . ." (pp. 233-234). The progression from effeminate novice to voluptuous woman ends with the virago. Tactically this change is perfectly designed for her strange and gratuitously malign ends. But if it is part of a larger design of deceit, it has its own candor. If Matilda is not a mortal, this sexual proteanness combines with other characteristics and motives to suggest, specifically, what she really is. She is a token of the incubus-succubus proper to venerable and notorious theories of damnation and the pact between mortals and the infernal powers.

The motif of the Satanic contract is obvious within the novel. Ambrosio's commerce with Matilda leads him to progressively irredeemable sins, and finally, following her alleged example, he signs his soul over to Satan. Moreover, Lewis took care to situate his narrative in Spain and to place it within the historical context of the Spanish Inquisition. Matilda's role is consistent with the mythology suggested by the plot and its context.

Lewis' fictional inquisitors, in deciding questions of witchcraft and Satanism, would have referred constantly to the "Bible" of such matters: the *Malleus Malificarum (Hexenhammer)* (1487) of Heinrich Kramer and Jacob Sprenger. Within this work they could find the four primary proofs of witchcraft, the last of which is that witches must indulge "in every kind of carnal lust with Incubi and Succubi and all other manner of filthy delights."[9] This proof was relatively invulnerable to dispute. As the almost equally influential Francesco Maria Guazzo says in his *Compendium Maleficarum* (1596), "Almost all the theologians and learned Philosophers are agreed, . . . that witches practice coition with demons, the men with Succubus devils and the women with Incubus devils."[10] This act was a *sine qua non* to the pact between mortal and Satan. For the demon, intercourse was no end in itself, but a means to the enslavement and subsequent damnation of the mortal (*Malleus*, p. 25).

This explains the supposed anomalousness of Matilda's motives. But theories about the incubus-succubus can also explain her puzzling androgyny. When Milton tells us that " . . . Spirits when they please/ Can either Sex assume, or both; . . ." (*P.L.* I, 424-425), he is positing a trait most proper to the incubus-succubus. In fact, the term is hyphenated because it denotes alternate forms of the same essence. When a mortal woman was the object, the fiend assumed a male form ("*incubus*," lying upon); the succubus ("*suc*[sub] *-cubus*," lying beneath) serviced the male human (*Malleus*, p. 25; *Compendium*, p. 30). If, and this is highly doubtful, Lewis was innocent of these works, almost any handbook on demonology, *The Encyclopedia Brittannica*, or a contemporary dictionary could have provided him with this information.[11]

Thus whatever "new" ideas we may abstract from this Gothic novel, we must recognize that its treatment of sexual license and damnation is derived from venerable doctrine. The very problems inherent in the work force us outside of it for their solution. This solution replaces the idea of a pregnant ambiguity with the realization of a clever irony. Ambrosio is not the victim of accident; he is thoroughly "deceived by sin". If his career is Satanic, it is only because his progress is controlled by a greater power. It is appropriate, therefore, that the truth about his actions be revealed to him by "The Father of Lies". A final analysis of the motives underlying Satan's candor and Matilda's deceit can complete the explanation latent in the novel's allusiveness.

Satan's revelations are cautiously timed. Ambrosio does not learn the truth until he has formally and irrevocably sold his soul, and he does this in order to escape from prison. Satan immediately informs him that the fatal contract was sealed only minutes before the Monk's reprieve was to arrive. He announces the truth about Ambrosio's ties to Antonia and Elvira, and tells him what Matilda really is. Thus the ironies of the Monk's career are used as an instrument of torture, a prelude to his physical torments before death and to the eternity of woe that awaits him. Truth becomes a potent weapon in the hands of Satan, who can use it at last because he has nothing further to gain by concealing it.

However, Satan's success and subsequent candor are predicated upon Matilda's persistent deceit. All of her potent rhetoric has been based on the idea that she is a mortal. Her final mode of persuasion, example, still demands this imposture: she claims that she has gained freedom from the Inquisition by selling her soul. The example is effective because Ambrosio remains ignorant of her true identity. Here, as throughout the novel, Matilda must maintain her disguise, for to reveal her true nature would be nothing less than to reveal her true purpose.

Here Matilda's career is at odds, for once, with that of an earlier figure upon whom she may have been modelled: the seductive Biondetta of Jacques Cazotte's *Le Diable Amoureux* (1772),[12] and the difference is significant. Biondetta waits only for the perfection of her seduction before identifying herself to her victim: "Je suis le Diable. . . ." In **The Monk** so immediate a revelation would have been premature. Incest and matricide obviously do not insure Ambrosio's damnation; a formal pact is necessary. Thus the success of Matilda's design is precarious until her victim has sold his soul. As Berryman notes, damnation is difficult to achieve in this novel. The opacity of Matilda's disguise and the extent to which she must sustain it imply that this demon, derived from an old convention. operates in a universe where another convention, salvation, is still viable.

In its undercutting of Matilda's rhetoric *The Monk* forges a rhetoric of its own. We can see, for instance, that Pride is no more responsible for Ambrosio's fall than is Idolatry. The entire process of perdition is precipitated by his adulation of a graven image, the portrait of the Madonna; this is the moral breach through which Matilda can reach him. Lewis thus takes a rather conventional Protestant stand against the dangers of Catholic "superstition".

A more interesting meaning lurks in the relationships connecting beauty, eros, and sin. To identify eros and sin was certainly nothing new, but Lewis' treatment of the problem suggests human impotence in the face of greater forces. One reason that Ambrosio cannot resist temptation is that it is not only attractive, but unrecognizable. His problem is much like Eve's. He cannot see the nature and consequences of his disobedience because he is ignorant of the true nature of his tempter. His initial transgressions do not lead him, however, into a world of chaos; they propel him into an artful and systematic labyrinth in which he must sin at every turning and in which the ball of thread handed to him by his paramour can lead only to the center. His conscious surrender to sexual passion entails an unconscious surrender to uncontrollable gratiutously pernicious forces, but his progress is anything but arbitrary. His error is defined and controlled by the structure of an old and familiar moral cosmos.

If the defrocking of Matilda creates a new base for criticism of *The Monk*, it must also be applied to readings already in print. The solution to Lewis' clever puzzle has implications for students of the romantic novel, of the fantastic as a genre and, especially, for those interested in this work as a reflection of contemporary changes in outlook. That Matilda is demonstrably consistent creates a new respect for the formal coherence of *The Monk*. Thus the idea that the work operates through " . . . accumulations of strikingly realized scenes rather than from a logical knitting together of events" (Kiely, p. 102) becomes vulnerable. If formal incoherence is a hallmark of the romantic novel, Matilda is a very inappropriate example of that characteristic.

Of course, the interpolation of "The Bleeding Nun" remains unintegrated and helps to validate Kiely's theories. This very lack of integration can also be of use to the student of genre because it can help to demonstrate the two kinds of "Gothic" content the novel exploits. This episode relies largely on motifs borrowed from pagan folklore. Its structure is reminiscent of old ballads like "Sweet William's Ghost" and "The Suffolk Miracle", as well as contemporary literary treatments like Burger's *Lenore*. When the nun brushes against the Christian world (she is eventually exorcised by the Wandering Jew) she must flee in dismay. The world of ghosts and ghouls is subordinated to a world tangential to Christianity. Moreover, the narrative structures and beliefs of folklore are relatively unsystematic and must be structured by the writer. Lewis' attempt to structure this material is a failure—the episode is more evocative of laughter than of fear. Thus the genius of a Coleridge or Emily Brontë is conspicuously lacking here. Lewis succeeds when systematic doctrines inform his story. He is really a conservative writer who looks backward to *Paradise Lost* rather than forward toward *Frankenstein* and *Moby Dick,* works which create their own Gothic worlds.

This distinction between two kinds of Gothic in *The Monk* is related to problems of practical criticism. All Gothic works pose questions of identity and causality, but they answer these in various ways. Ann Radcliffe, to Scott's disgust and Jane Austen's profit, insisted upon explaining away her supernatural occurrences. Thus a traditional distinction exists between her works and works like *Lenore* and *Melmoth the Wanderer,* tokens of the *"merveilleux",* where the reality of the supernatural remains inviolate, because other elements conspire to reenforce it. There is no need to ask who Melmoth really is; the novel tells us.

The story of Ambrosio and Matilda is distinct from these. It is only comprehensible when the reader, taking its hints, becomes privy to the doctrines underlying the narrative. But this leads us to a third distinction. The critical techniques which work with Matilda seem to have been of dubious success when applied to her great successor, the Lady Geraldine. All of the apparent strangeness of Matilda's nature and motivation can be explained when she is seen as a simple token of an identifiable type. Such approaches to Geraldine, however, have produced very unsatisfactory results.[13] This is because she is so highly synthetic. Her nature and motives remain unsolved because she incorporates so many and such diverse figures of dark supernaturalism. Matilda is a puzzle; Geraldine is a mystery.

These distinctions are relevant not only to the Gothic, but to the more inclusive category of the "fantastic". Todorov stresses the usefulness and importance of *The Monk* by his frequent references to it. His treatment of the work, however, is misleading and uncovers a flaw in his theory. Although he is obviously interested in questions of ambiguity in the *"fantastique,"* he begs the question of Matilda's real nature. Thus, he does not see that metamorphosis is intrinsic to her activities. This misperception is one of several leading him to assert, with a confidence that almost belies its inappropriateness, that eros and metamorphosis are two themes that never coincide in a fantastic work.[14]

Thus Ambrosio is not alone in his misperception of Matilda's nature. Her dark influence is still alive in contemporary criticism. Her deceit has had its greatest success, moreover, when she is seen as a spokesman for changes in historical sensibility. Peter Brooks seems to take her at her word. He asserts that her " . . . masterstroke is to have her own portrait painted in the disguise of the Madonna . . ." (Brooks, p. 257), and thus suggests that he accepts her other fictions as well. As with the Monk, such credulity can have serious consequences.

In constructing his thesis that terror has replaced virtue in the world of this novel, and that God has become just another supernatural cause of fear, Brooks relies heavily on Matilda's arguments against the idea of salvation. She tells the Monk that God has abandoned him because of his initial sin and that fear alone prevents him from appealing to Satan. She finds the basis for his resistance "Absurd" and Brooks concurs: "If he [Ambrosio] can advance so illogical an argument, it is because he retains a vestigial belief in the Christian paradox of salvation" (Brooks, p. 251). But the whole plot of the novel implies the persistence of this vestige. We must be cautious in equating Matilda's arguments with the rhetoric of the work. Ambrosio's eventual acceptance of them leads to rather unenviable consequences. When Matilda turns theologian, we must remember who, or rather "what", is speaking—and why.

Thus if Brooks is finally correct in his discussion of a post-sacred universe proper to the end of the eighteenth century, he is right for the wrong reasons. The author of **The Monk** may not have believed in God, but then again, he may not have believed in Satan and his subordinates either. Lewis' interest was not in creating a new universe, but in exploiting the givens of an old one. Unwilling to rely solely on the shopworn machinery of castles, armor and crypts, he created a Gothic atmosphere with a fidelity that Walpole and Radcliffe never achieved. His novel recreates a world that is theologically as well as physically archaic. If **The Monk** is a post-Enlightenment novel, it demands the reader's familiarity with pre-Enlightenment ideas.

Notes

[1] Samuel Taylor Coleridge, "*The Monk,* A Romance, by M.G. Lewis," *The Critical Review,* XIX (Feb., 1797), 194-200, reprinted in *Coleridge's Miscellaneous Criticism,* ed., Thomas Middleton Raysor (London: Constable, 1936), pp. 370-378. For a picture of the state of Gothic studies as of 1969, see Robert D. Hume, "Gothic Versus Romantic: A Revaluation of the Gothic Novel," *PMLA,* LXXXIV, 282.

[2] John Berryman, "Introduction," *The Monk,* by Matthew Gregory Lewis (New York: Grove Press-Evergreen, 1952), p. 27. Subsequent references to this introduction will appear within parentheses both in the text and in notes.

[3] Robert Kiely, *The Romantic Novel in England* (Cambridge, Mass.: Harvard, 1972), pp. 98-117. Subsequent references will appear within parentheses. In his introduction Kiely poses question of incongruity, pp. 14-15, and its formal analogues in romantic fiction, p. 17.

[4] Tzvetan Todorov, *Introduction a la littérature fantastique* (Paris: Editions du Seuil, 1970), pp. 133-134, 138-139, 143. Subsequent references will appear within parentheses. Todorov defines the fantastic as " . . . l'hésitation eprouvée par un etre qui ne connaît que des lois naturelles face a un événement en apparence surnaturel . . ." (p. 29). This equivocation is to be shared by the reader (p. 46). He classifies the explained supernaturalism of Ann Radcliff as *"étrange"* and the accepted supernaturalism of *Melmoth the Wanderer* as *"merveilleux"* (pp. 46-47).

[5] Peter Brooks, "Virtue and Terror: The Monk," *ELH,* XL, 249-263. Subsequent references will appear within parentheses.

[6] Matthew Gregory Lewis, *The Monk,* Louis Peck, ed. (New York: Grove Press-Evergreen, 1952), p. 418. Subsequent references will appear within parentheses in the text.

[7] Montague Summers, *The Gothic Quest, A History of the Gothic Novel* (London: The Fortune Press, n.d.), p. 221. Subsequent references will appear within parentheses.

[8] Edith Birkhead, *The Tale of Terror* (London: Constable, 1921), p. 67. Also see Alice M. Killen, *Le Roman Terrifiant ou roman noir de Walpole à Anne Radcliffe et son influence sur la littérature francaise jusqu'en 1840* (Paris: Champion, 1923), p. 41. Berryman, p. 16.

[9] Heinrich Kramer, James Sprenger, *Malleus Malificarum,* trans., Montague Summers (London: Rodker, 1928) p. 20. Subsequent references will appear within parentheses.

[10] Francesco Maria Guazzo, *Compendium Malificarum,* trans. E.A. Ashwin (1929: rpt. New York: Barnes & Noble, 1970), p. 30. Subsequent references will appear within parentheses. Also see Ernest Jones, *On the Nightmare* (New York: Liveright, 1971), especially Chapter III, "Incubus and Incubation".

[11] Lewis was notorious for his interest in the occult and demonism. See Devendra P. Varma, *The Gothic Flame* (New York: Russell & Russell, 1957), p. 149, where Joseph Glanvill's *Saducismus Triumphatus* (1689), is mentioned as Lewis' favorite reading. The third edition of *The Encyclopedia Brittannica* makes a prominent mention of the *Malleus* in its article on witchcraft. Even the most superficial sources available to Lewis would have cited this, the first and most important of the tracts on witchcraft.

[12] Jacques Cazotte, *LeDiable Amoureux* (Paris: Grasset, 1921). This work was long viewed as the source of most of *The Monk*. Certainly the quantity and quality of the parallels is suspicious. Louis Peck, however, exonerates Lewis partially. (See Louis Peck, "*The Monk* and Le Diable Amoureux," *MLN,* LXVIII, 406-408.) If Cazotte and Lewis were basing their stories on identical doctrines, the parallels can be justified without question of influence, and this minor but persistent critical problem can be solved.

[13] A good example of this kind of reductiveness is Arthur H. Nethercot, *The Road to Tryermaine* (Chicago: University of Chicago Press, 1939). Nethercot's conclusion that Geraldine is a vampire is persistently influential. However, the existence of so many valid readings which contradict this leads to the conclusion that Geraldine is composed of a variety of supernatural types. One of the most prominent of these is the succubus.

[14] See John Reichert, "More than Kind and Less than Kind: On the Limits of Genre Theory," *The Yearbook of Comparative Studies,* ed., Joseph Strelka (University Park: Pennsylvania State University Press, 1975) n. 15. Reichert demonstrates how Todorov's own evidence gives the lie to his conclusions.

Robin Lydenberg (essay date 1979)

SOURCE: "Ghostly Rhetoric: Ambivalence in M. G. Lewis' *The Monk*," in *Ariel: A Review of International English Literature,* Vol. 10, No. 2, April, 1979, pp. 65-79.

[*In the following essay, Lydenberg investigates "Lewis's ambivalence toward his authorial responsibility" as moral judge in* The Monk.]

The Gothic novel is rarely, if ever, celebrated for its stylistic or thematic subtlety, and Matthew Gregory Lewis' ***The Monk*** is usually considered one of the more exaggerated and crude examples of the genre. Such assessments, however, overlook a basic ambivalence shared by most Gothic novelists towards the supernatural and sexual extravagance associated with this mode of popular fiction.[1] The consistency with which a Gothic novelist of such major influence as Ann Radcliffe collapses her supernatural and superstitious fictions with rational explanations suggests that ambivalence towards the excesses of Gothic terror may be characteristic of the genre itself.[2]

This ambivalence is particularly interesting in Lewis' work because his discomfort with the sexual and fantastical elaborations of his own novel reflects a deeper uncertainty about his role as a writer. Lewis' repeated ironic undercutting of the trappings of Gothic fiction, which he nevertheless persists in employing to maximum effect, reveals the same tentativeness which leads him to affect a flippancy and indifference towards all literary activity. A close examination of the style and content of ***The Monk*** will show that Lewis is threatened not so much by the powers of sexual passion and the unbridled imagination as by the dangerously affective powers of literature and rhetoric.

Lewis' correspondence with his mother indicates that he undertook most of his early literary projects as business ventures that might supplement his allowance. The popular demand for Gothic romance in dramatic and fictional form encouraged him to persevere in what promised to be a lucrative genre. Lewis demonstrates a shrewd sense of how to make money by pirating untranslated works for the stage and adding or expanding unnecessary roles in order to interest influential actresses. Indeed, he seems to have had hardly any literary pretensions, to the extent that he could remark casually to his mother, "If these projects do not make money, I am sure they will find amusement for *you,* who will be partial to every thing I either write or do."[3]

Lewis continues to disclaim any artistic commitment to his literary work, but his creative energy and ambition begin to grow in spite of himself. He finally admits that he is "horribly bit by the rage of writing."[4] The intense burst of literary activity he experiences during the summer of 1794 may be attributed to his discovery of Ann Radcliffe's *The Mysteries of Udolpho,* which he describes as one of the most interesting books ever published. This novel inspires him to return to his own unfinished romance with a renewed, although still ambivalent, respect for the genre he had merely exploited in the past.

Because Lewis' ambivalence is focused ultimately on his authorial role, he can never reconcile it, as Radcliffe does, by a simple shift from a supernatural to a realistic fictional world. The pattern of ambivalence established by his parodying of the hyperbolic qualities of Gothic fiction is repeated in his reluctance to accept the role of moral authority demanded by the very conventional social satire that pervades ***The Monk.*** Lewis may be distinguished from other Gothic novel-

Lewis, from the portrait by H. W. Pickersgill.

ists by the extent of the ironic distance he establishes between himself and all aspects of his narrative.

Lewis makes his ambivalence evident even before his narrative opens, in the playful poem with which he prefaces *The Monk*. In this poem the author chastises his book for its "vain, ill-judging" decision to venture out onto the public market. He prophesies a terrible fate for his novel, in imagery which suggests the most gloomy Gothic tortures:

> Soon as your novelty is o'er
> And you are young and new no more,
> In some dark dirty corner thrown,
> Mouldy with damps, with cobwebs strown
> Your leaves shall be the book-worm's prey
> Or sent to chandler-shop away,
> And doomed to suffer public scandal,
> Shall line the trunk or wrap the candle.[5]

The graveyard atmosphere of decrepitude and suffering, already quite familiar by the end of the eighteenth century, is reduced here to a literary joke. Lewis evokes not a fate of despair and death, but a fate worse than being remaindered—being unread. Dissociating himself from his book, disclaiming any responsibility for its reception, he attempts to establish by satiric exag-

geration his superiority to the very devices of Gothic terror he will use in his novel.

As I hope to demonstrate in this paper, despite this initial mockery of the machinery of dungeons, cobwebs and devouring worms, Lewis uses the same equipment quite seriously in the body of his novel, arousing the reader's indignation with scenes of human misery at the hands of merciless cruelty. The contradiction between Lewis' stance in the prefatory poem and in the novel which follows it reveals more than an ambivalence towards the sensational devices of the Gothic genre. We must recognize in this contradiction the author's fear of being identified and characterized by his novel: a fear of his reader's responses to the text and the assumptions about its creator.

Just as he denied responsibility for the rash appearance of his "vain, ill-judging" book, Lewis disclaims himself as a creature of frailties, extremes and contradictions:

> By few approved, and few approving,
> Extreme in hating and in loving;
> Abhorring all whom I dislike,
> Adoring who my fancy strike;
> In forming judgements never long,
> And for the most part judging wrong;
> In friendship firm but still believing
> Others are treacherous and deceiving . . .
> More passionate no creature living,
> Proud, obstinate, and unforgiving.
>
> (p. 34)

While this self-caricature stresses his moral failings, his unreliability and unpredictability, the actual voice which Lewis adopts in the narrative is one of moral authority judiciously tempered by reason, tolerance and understanding. He is uncomfortably aware that not only his novel but his very character will be exposed to scrutiny, and by painting such a negative portrait of himself he may hope to anticipate and discourage public criticism. The eagerness with which Lewis assures the reader that when he wrote *The Monk* he "scarce had reached his twentieth year" betrays the discomforts of a young man with the responsibilities inherent in the authorial role of moral example or arbiter. In response to the scandal that followed the publication of his novel, he defends himself to his father on similar grounds: "Let me, however, observe that TWENTY is not the age at which prudence is most to be expected."[6]

The ambivalence established by the preface is reinforced by continual shifts of tone within the narrative. Lewis alternately traces the tragic consequences of superstition and romantic delusion and then undercuts his serious moral warnings with scenes of farcical exaggeration. In one scene, for example, he brings together the stock comic landlady Jacintha Zunega, whose superstition is merely ridiculous, with the young heroine who will be superstition's tragic victim. This innocent girl is herself "susceptible of terror" and "superstitious prejudice," but unlike Jacintha ("miserable slave to fear and superstition") Antonia attempts to master what she considers her weakness.

Lewis establishes his heroine, on the night following her mother's sudden death, in a setting guaranteed to excite her imagination:

> It was the dead of night; she was alone, and in the chamber once occupied by her deceased mother. The weather was comfortless and stormy; the wind howled around the house, the doors rattled in their frames, and the heavy rain pattered against the windows. No other sound was heard. The taper, now burnt down to the socket, sometimes flaring upwards, shot a gleam of light through the room, then sinking again seemed upon the point of expiring. (p. 309)

Antonia unwisely seeks respite from her bereavement and this gloomy setting in a Gothic ballad which summons the worm-eaten spectre of Alonzo the Brave into the already macabre atmosphere of the darkened bedroom. Her mind unsettled and her senses aroused, she first hears only "imaginary noises," but finally she sees a vision of her dead mother, who announces that she and her daughter will be reunited within three days. Because Lewis has established Antonia so explicitly in this scene as a reader of Gothic tales, the reader of *The Monk* may detect in this episode a gentle warning and mockery of his own imaginative susceptibility. However, not only is Elvira's ghost never clearly dismissed as Antonia's hallucination, but the prophecy she pronounces is proved tragically accurate.

The ambivalence which leads Lewis alternately to ridicule and nourish the superstitious imaginations of his characters and his readers seems carefully manipulated. Antonia's account of the apparition of her mother's ghost sends the terrified Jacintha to the Capuchin Church seeking protection. Her response quickly shifts the tone of the narrative from pathos and melodrama to farce. Jacintha's terror proves a source of unexpected imaginative invention; for although she has seen nothing, she is able to describe the spectre in detail as "a great tall figure at by elbow whose head touched the ceiling! The face was Donna Elvira's . . . but out of its mouth came clouds of fire; its arms were loaded with heavy chains which it rattled piteously, and every hair on its head was a serpent as big as my arm" (p. 316). In contrast to Antonia's painful and helpless convulsions after seeing the ghost, the presence of mind that enables Jacintha simultaneously to conjure this spirit and calculate mentally the possible economic repercussions of running a haunted guest-house renders the scene quite comic.

In a serious scene at the end of his novel, Lewis himself conjures a vision remarkably similar to Jacintha's description of Elvira's ghost. When Ambrosio has been tortured to the brink of death by the Inquisition and is only hours away from the final *Auto da Fe,* the monk calls upon the Devil in despair. Lewis indicates that Satan, no longer needing to seduce the monk with his benign beauty, appears stripped of his "romantic disguise." The description Lewis offers here seems to be based on the same patchwork of dark conventions used by the ignorant Jacintha: "His blasted limbs still bore marks of the Almighty's thunder. A swarthy darkness spread itself over his gigantic form: his hands and feet were armed with long talons. Fury glared in his eyes, which might have struck the bravest heart with terror. Over his huge shoulders waved two enormous wings: and his hair was supplied by living snakes, which twined themselves around his brows with frightful hissings" (p. 412).

What separates Lewis and Jacintha—both indulgers in the elaboration of fanciful fictions—is Lewis' superior style and greater familiarity with literary tradition. He has read Milton's *Paradise Lost* and gleaned from that poet's epic Satan a certain metaphorical power, but the essential gimmickry is the same: snakes, immensity, darkness, clouds and thunder. The affinity established between Jacintha and Lewis brings the author within the scope of the mockery of superstition which is directed against his characters and readers. As in the prefatory poem, Lewis seems anxious to disqualify himself as a possible model of the rational mind which resists the lure of the supernatural.

It is only through the character of the levelheaded and sympathetic Agnes that Lewis is able to express an unambiguous denunciation of popular superstition. Agnes' description to her lover of the family tradition of the ghost of the bleeding nun who haunts the Castle of Lindenberg is unhampered by any secret predilection on her part for such tales of terror. The legend, she explains, extends its influence from the ignorant to the educated, for even her noble aunt "would sooner doubt the veracity of the Bible than that of the bleeding nun." Agnes ridicules such misplaced faith by relating in a "tone of burlesqued gravity" the circumstances of the ghost's periodic appearance: "It was accompanied with shrieking, howling, groaning, swearing, and many other agreeable noises of the same kind . . . now she howled out the most horrible blasphemies, and then chaunted *De Profondis* as orderly as if still in the choir. In short, she seemed a mighty capricious thing" (p. 152-3).

Just as Lewis exposes the reader and even himself to the warnings within the narrative—both satiric and melodramatic—he does not allow even his "normative" model[7] to stand aloof from the fiction. While Agnes treats with broad burlesque the ghost and its terrified spectators, this same laughable weakness of superstition has dangerous consequences in her own life. Because of a secret and "fatal vow" of her mother's, Agnes lives as a virtual prisoner first in her aunt's house and later in the convent of St. Clare. The extremes of suffering to which she eventually is subjected in the convent, and which can be traced directly to the "grossest superstition" of her parents, would seem to demand that Lewis adopt an unequivocal denunciation of superstition. Surprisingly, he continues to indulge his readers and himself in mystery and the supernatural, to the extreme of staging repeated appearances of the ghost of the bleeding nun.

Lewis' ability to reflect his ambivalence in his narrative style allows him to venture into these dangerous areas. The ghostly conjurings in *The Monk* hover between terror and hilarity, their titillation is theatrical and mannered, self-consciously literary and aesthetically playful. Even one of Lewis' most vicious critics recognized that his novel contained "diablerie and nonsense fitted only to frighten children."[8] A closer examination of the bleeding nun episode, which so captured the imagination of the popular audience that it was circulated separately as a chap-book, will reveal how Lewis safely indulges his readers in innocent terror.

When the unwelcome ghost materializes punctually at the bedside of Agnes' lover, Raymond is petrified with horror—but the reader is not. As in several similar scenes in the novel, this supposed object of terror is presented to us as a composite of clichés: "Her countenance was long and haggard; her cheeks and lips were bloodless; the paleness of death was spread over her features; and her eye-balls fixed steadfastly upon me were lustreless and hollow. I gazed upon the spectre with horror too great to be described. My blood was frozen in my veins. I would have called for aid but the sound expired ere it could pass my lips . . . I remained in the same attitude inanimate as a statue" (p. 170). Lewis is temporarily indulging his reader's taste for the supernatural only to dispel and discredit these "imaginary dangers" and "ideal terrors" with a more terrible reality. A narration of the *real* life of the bleeding nun, Beatrice de las Cisternas, immediately follows Lewis' rather ineffective conjuration of her ghost, and the account of her cruelty and depravity is all the more terrifying because it does not resort to the clichés and machinery of Gothic terror.

Perhaps the most effective juxtaposition of the terror generated by artifice and superstition with the horror evoked by actual danger and evil occurs in the riot scene at the Convent of St. Clare. The violent response of the populace to Mother St. Ursula's revelation of the crimes of the Domina forces several nuns to seek shelter in the vaults. When the chivalrous Lorenzo discovers them they are more terrified of ghosts than of the murderous mob, and indeed he too soon hears a sepulchral moaning in the corridors. Determined to discover the real source of these sounds, Lorenzo examines the nearby statue of St. Clare, which rumbles threateningly at his touch. The superstitiousness of the nuns has been nurtured by the Domina with terrifying and "marvelous stories" about the power and sanctity of this statue, and they recoil from Lorenzo's transgression. The mysterious movements of the statue, however, are revealed to be no more than a mechanical device which uncovers the hidden entrance to a deeper vault. Here is entombed the evidence of a more horrifying reality of Agnes' long imprisonment and suffering. The Domina has used the gullibility of the novices to guarantee the secrecy of her ruthless discipline; and the imaginary ghosts who "complain and groan and wail in accents that make [one's] blood run cold" seem benign spectres beside the cruel nuns who have caused the sufferings of the starving and delirious Agnes.

While Lorenzo's skepticism about the supernatural enables him to uncover the truth and rescue Agnes, his refined youth leaves him exposed to a different kind of self-deception. As his lower classes are fed on the popular culture of folk magic, Lewis' aristocratic young men perceive their world, anachronistically, through the distorted lenses of early Romanticism. The most explicit example Lewis offers of the dangers of nurturing romantic illusions is the story of Elvira's marriage to a man above her social station and the couple's subsequent exile from Spain. Elvira tells her story as a warning to the aristrocrat Lorenzo against setting his heart on an "unequal alliance" with Antonia. The "fond romantic vision" of an *égoisme à deux* which led Elvira's husband to imagine they could forsake country and parents, defy class conventions and still find happiness, seems to offend Lewis' sense of the necessarily social nature of man.

The fact that Lorenzo is not deterred by Elvira's warnings might seem to indicate that Lewis does believe in the steadfastness of romantic love. When Antonia is murdered and her lover despairs, however, the narrator assures us sarcastically that no one dies of a broken heart. Indeed we do witness in the course of the novel the miraculous recovery and subsequent marriage of several despairing lovers. Even Lewis' account of the multiple marriages which provide the happing ending of his novel is muted by a cynicism startling in a young man of twenty: "The remaining years of Raymond and Agnes, of Lorenzo and Virginia, were happy as can be those allotted to mortals, born to be the prey of grief, and sport of disappointment" (p. 400).

The recovery and marriage of disappointed lovers and the sober advice of characters like Elvira and Agnes serve as a check against the excesses of a romantic idealism in which, despite his skepticism, Lewis cannot refrain from indulging. Though he gently mocks the pleasures the young men find in romantic melancholy, Lewis himself clearly cannot resist the allure of these sentiments and the poetic freedom of style they permit. Temperamentally an Enlightenment conservative like Diderot, Lewis is impatient with the romantic misanthrope, the rousseauesque soulful solitary, but his descriptions of moments of sublime isolation are extended and polished. By allowing these romantic interludes only when the action of the novel has been temporarily suspended, Lewis maintains the same separation of life and art which renders his ghosts harmless. The success of Lewis' use and abuse of Gothic and romance conventions depends on a very delicate balance of his readers' involvement in and detachment from the fiction.

The same delicate balance of reader response is necessary to the success of Lewis' social as well as his aesthetic pedagogy. Consistent with his alternation of comic and tragic treatments of terror and sentimentality, Lewis' social commentary falls within the tradition of the gentler satirists like Fielding and Sterne, who would temper ridicule with sympathy, chastisement with laughter. While the Gothic and romance genres pose certain dangers for the impressionable reader, the novel of social satire often poses more threatening difficulties for the author himself. Lewis shares with earlier satirists an uncertainty as to his ability to separate humane satire from heartless moralizing and vicious mockery.

In the opening scene of *The Monk* Lewis' characterization of the secular and fashionable piety of the people of Madrid is playful and generalized: "The audience now assembled in the Capuchin Church was collected by various causes, but all of them were foreign to the ostensible motive. The women came to show themselves, the men to see the women: some were attracted by curiosity to hear an orator so celebrated; some came, because they had no better means of employing their time till the play began . . . and one half of Madrid was brought thither by expecting to meet the other half" (p. 35). After this opening scene, however, the focus of the narrative moves inward, becoming personal rather than public, and Lewis' satiric style begins to deviate from that of his predecessors.

When the object of ridicule shifts from vanity and affectation to human cruelty and evil, the satirist's balance is more difficult to maintain. Lewis' acute awareness that severe moral authority often produces an immovable and inhuman ethic is evident in his characterization of Ambrosio. The curse Agnes levels against her merciless judge may well serve as a reminder to the censorious reader and to the author himself against such intolerance of human weakness. The severity of the crimes which accumulate with a vertiginous rapidity in the final chapters of the novel would seem to demand that Lewis accept and assert his role as moral judge. Even here, however, the author manages to introduce contradiction and equivocation, focusing more on the dangers inherent in the assertion of moral authority than on the repercussions of moral transgression itself.

With a novelist's instinctive aversion to direct moralizing, Lewis dramatizes his own dilemma as a social critic in the situation of one of his characters. Having learned from Mother St. Ursula of the death of his sister at the hands of the Domina and her confederates, Lorenzo resolves to use the public forum of the convent procession to "unmask the hypocrites" of the church, to convince his countrymen that "a sanctified exterior does not always hide a virtuous heart." Like Lewis, Lorenzo plans to achieve his moral goal indirectly through a narrative. Prepared with armed support to subdue the crowd's initial outrage at his charges against the Domina, Lorenzo sets the stage for the good nun's revelation of the truth. The "sanctified exterior" and "artificial glory" of the ostentatious procession give way to the ugly and detailed story of Agnes' imprisonment and murder. The narrative is extended but effective; and almost as if the length of its concentrated attention necessitates an equivalent and violent reaction, the indignant crowd explodes in a "moment of popular frenzy" even before Mother St. Ursula has finished her *récit*. The moral intentions which motivated the confrontation are swept away by the mob's mindless violence, and the unmasking of hypocrisy and revelation of truth produce only "barbarous vengeance" and "vindictive fury" (pp. 334-44).

Lorenzo's horror at having been the cause of this paroxysm of violence may reveal in exaggerated form Lewis' own fear of the responsibility of seizing moral authority in his narrative. With grotesque irony, the merciless murder of the Domina by the rioters, enraged by the account of *her* cruelty, is based on a mistaken accusation: Agnes is still alive. Those who, in moral righteousness, seek to expose the contradiction between appearance and reality are unknowingly armed with a truth which is itself not what it seems. For in the world of *The Monk* even the truth is uncertain, and as Robert Kiely has pointed out, it is a world so filled with "uncontrollable energy" that one may "find [oneself] unexpectedly on the side of the flood."[9] In the convent riot scene, the "uncontrollable energy" at work is the very rhetoric of moral authority which wields a frightening power over its audience, producing a force which can easily escape the control and intention of the orator.

Lewis' distrust of the power of rhetoric is further reflected in the essential part which eloquence plays in seduction and damnation in the novel. The unguarded innocence of Antonia and the degenerate and determined lust of Ambrosio, which make possible the grotesque rape and murder in the climactic scene, begin to develop within the innocent confines of the Capuchin Church during the monk's initial pious and moving oratory. In the precise language which he later reserves for Ambrosio's awakening sexuality, Lewis describes the effects of the monk's eloquence on his listeners as an invasion of sensations "till then unknown." While he is first endangered only by the arrogant pride which his oratorical success engenders, Ambrosio's exposure to his own sexuality, for which he is so ill prepared, proves far more threatening.

But the process of damnation in **The Monk** is neither swift nor simple; and it is not the demands of the body which ultimately enslave Ambrosio, but rather the ingenious casuistry of the seductive Mathilde—woman or daemon. One recent critic reasons that Ambrosio's damnation is the work of no earthly woman, for Mathilde's power is achieved through the traditional sexual possession practiced by witches: "For the demon intercourse was no end in itself but a means to the enslavement and subsequent damnation of the mortal."[10] I would argue, however, that Mathilde's satanic ancestry is perhaps more clearly reflected in her insidious mastery of another traditional weapon of the devil—the rhetoric of persuasion. The most urgent concern of Lewis' fiction, then, may not be violent sexuality or supernaturalism, but the power of eloquence.

The violence of much of the critical response that greeted the publication of **The Monk** testifies to the powers of realization and persuasion that Lewis himself achieved. For many of his contemporaries, the crimes described in the novel became so threatening and immediate that not only was the book denounced for its "libidinous minuteness" but the author himself was maligned as betraying a "species of brutality."[11] Even modern readers, less likely to confuse the author's fictions with his moral conduct, attest to the strength of Lewis' style by their continual appreciation of **The Monk** despite its unfashionable length.

The devilish art of rhetoric is M.G. Lewis' medium, and if we are to believe his assertion that the novel was written in ten weeks, he had an uncanny control of that medium for a youth of twenty. His success, however, proved rather frightening, for he only narrowly escaped the type of prosecution which crowned

the publication of Baudelaire's *Les Fleurs du Mal* and Flaubert's *Madame Bovary* half a century later. Surprised and alarmed by the scandal incited by his book, Lewis wrote a letter of apology to his father in which he disclaims any intention to affect the moral conduct of his readers in the direction of good *or* evil:

> [It] never struck me that the exhibition of vice, in her temporary triumph, might possibly do as much harm as her final exposure and punishment would do good. To do much good, indeed, was more than I expected of my book; having always believed that our conduct depends on our own hearts and characters, not upon the books we read or the sentiments we hear. But though I did not expect much benefit to arise from the perusal of a trifling romance, written by a youth of twenty, I was in my own mind quite certain that no harm could be produced by a work whose subject was furnished by one of our best moralists.[12]

It is difficult to believe that Lewis could have so grossly underestimated the power of his "trifling romance." If this letter is more than a mere gesture of filial diplomacy, it is further evidence of Lewis' ambivalence towards his authorial responsibility.

Lewis was well aware that he was living in a time in which art and life often collided; fiction, whether deliberately or innocently, was producing repercussions in personal, social and political reality. During a trip to Germany in 1792 he wrote to his mother: "Among other people to whom I have been introduced, are the sister of Schweter, the composer, and M. de Goethe, the celebrated author of *Werter;* so that you must not be surprised if I should shoot myself one of these fine mornings."[13] Characteristically, Lewis dissolves the danger of eloquence with a witticism, but it is a joke grounded in the grim reality of the numerous suicides which were actually carried out in imitation of Goethe's romantic hero. This tragic repercussion of the widespread confusion of literature and life was perhaps one of the spectres haunting Lewis' own imagination as he composed with such convoluted ambivalence his Gothic fantasies.

Notes

[1] Two critical texts which do examine the ambivalence of Gothic fiction are Frederick Garber's "Meaning and Mode in Gothic Fiction," in *Racism in the Eighteenth Century* (Cleveland: Press of Case Western Reserve University, 1973), and Robert Kiely's *The Romantic Novel in England* (Cambridge: Harvard University Press, 1972).

[2] See Tzvetan Todorov's definition of the genre as *based* on the uncertainty of its characterization in *Introduction à la littérature fantastique* (Paris: Editions du Seuil, 1970).

[3] Margaret Baron-Wilson, *The Life and Correspondence of Matthew Gregory Lewis* (London: H. Colburn, 1839), p. 60.

[4] *Ibid.,* p. 128.

[5] Matthew G. Lewis, *The Monk* (New York: Grove Press, 1959), p. 33. All subsequent references to *The Monk* cite this edition and will appear as page numbers in my text.

[6] *Life and Correspondence,* p. 157.

[7] This concept is elaborated on by Robert Hume in "Gothic vs. Romantic" *PMLA,* March 1969. Hume sees Lorenzo and Raymond as stabilizing personalities within the novel, characters whose perspective parallels the "everyday outlook" of the reader. It seems to me that Lewis' ridicule of their bouts of romantic melancholy and superstition would deny them such stature within the narrative. The more consistent nature of Agnes seems a more likely "normative" model, if there is one within the uncertain world of *The Monk.*

[8] T. J. Mathias, *The Pursuits of Literature,* 8th edition, (London, 1798). See pages 241-3 and 347-8.

[9] Robert Kiely, *op. cit.*

[10] Peter Grudin, "*The Monk:* Matilda and the Rhetoric of Deceit" in *Journal of Narrative Technique,* 5, no. 2 (May 1975), 140.

[11] See *Coleridge's Miscellaneous Criticism* (Folcroft Press, 1936), pp. 370-72.

[12] *Life and Correspondence,* p. 156.

[13] *Ibid.,* p. 72.

Gudrun Kauhl (essay date 1989)

SOURCE: "On the Release from Monkish Fetters: Matthew Lewis Reconsidered," in *Dutch Quarterly Review,* Vol. 19, No. 4, 1989, pp. 264-80.

[*In the following essay, Kauhl examines the motif of transgression, as both a psychological and a political fact in* The Monk.]

In the Madrid of the Inquisition, "a city where superstition reigns with such despotic sway",[1] a young man (Raymond) loves a girl (Agnes) who has been destined for a monastic life from her birth; they experience separation and loss, but in the end they obtain the consent of their families and get married. A second young man, the monk Ambrosio, is led to a radical break with the religious tradition in which he believed; guided by "philosophy" towards his self-realization (which involves the murder of his mother and the rape and murder of his sister Antonia) he finally faces death as his punishment. A third young man (Lorenzo) falls in love with a girl (Antonia), who is socially not his equal. He loses her (she is murdered by the monk), but in the end he finds some quiet happiness in a marriage which was favoured by his family all along. A story of transgressions thus ends with two deaths and two marriages.

Transgression and punishment—transgression followed by an eventual liberation: the tension between these two endings characterizes the historical moment in which the novel was written and published. *The Monk* (1796) imaginatively explores the indecisions and anxieties to which the development of the French Revolution gave rise (Paulson, p. 536). The limited extent to which any option against the authority of the past still appeared viable can be seen in the story of Agnes. Although there is a final transition from "despotism" to "liberty", it does not imply a radical questioning of traditional institutions. By enforcing the mother's decision that her daughter be dedicated to a saint, representatives of these institutions (the Family and the Church) almost cause Agnes's destruction. Representatives of these institutions, however, also cooperate in order to help her and finally grant her a life of her own. In passing from the tutelage of the first group to the protection of the second, Agnes never leaves the realm of established authority. Similarly, she herself never challenges the law in an abstract sense. She regards her own desires as "culpable" (pp. 417), she pleads for "mercy" (pp. 47 ff.) and not for individual rights, and she is pardoned in an act of mercy.

While emphasizing this basic continuity between past and present, the story of Agnes also contains a glimpse of more radical historical possibilities. The reversal of her fate is accomplished in an act of open insurrection: the destruction of the convent in which she was kept. The relevant chapter is headed by a quote from Cowper's "Charity" which celebrates the "altar" of "sacred Liberty" (p. 343): the chapter itself shows a frenzied mob that pursues "innocent" and "guilty" alike (pp. 356-57), and the disillusionment of one protagonist who had originally wished to free the people from "monkish fetters" (p. 345). By illustrating that an unbounded self-assertion, a "cult of self,"[2] is as much the implied adversary in this novel as the unbounded "despotism" of "superstition" this scene creates a context for the ambivalent rendering of Ambrosio's story.

The life of "the monk" is completely defined by the monastery to which he belongs. He has no known history apart from it. He has lived there ever since he was found as a little child at the monastery door. He has even made a vow never to go outside, never to leave the boundaries of "his own precincts" (p. 30). His devotion, "the singular austerity of his life", is such that his name has come to designate a myth: Ambrosio is the "Man of Holiness", "a present . . . from the Virgin" (pp. 16-17).

The text establishes this reputation without affirming it. Instead we are told by a detached voice that Ambrosio's knowledge "*is said to be* the most profound, his eloquence the most persuasive"; that he "*has never been known* to transgress a single rule of his order"; that the "smallest stain *is not to be discovered* upon his character"; and that "He *is reported* to be so strict an observer of Chastity, that He knows not in what consists the difference of Man and Woman": "The common People therefore esteem him to be a Saint." (p. 17; italics added).

This commentary does not only refer to possible tensions between appearance and reality, since everything that is said about Ambrosio is quite pointedly based upon appearance only. Neither does it simply emphasize possible tensions between knowledge and ignorance, since Ambrosio's knowledge, though it is said to be most profound, would not contain important areas of self-experience. Presented by a sceptical voice, it comments above all on the characteristics of myth: that history, the historical complexity of a situation has drained out of it.[3]

The novel unfolds those aspects which were not contained in the original myth of the monk, just as Ambrosio begins to achieve that knowledge which did not seem to belong to "his own precincts" of the monastic tradition. In the murder of his mother and the rape of his sister he will discover his unknown origin and his unknown sexual nature at the same time. Significantly, this development is presented as the story of a temptation, in which every step is finally seen to have been manipulated by the devil. The traditional pattern confirms Ambrosio's own basic attitude, since Ambrosio himself experiences his own desires as transgressions. Imprisoned in the myth of the monk, he is led into secrecy, violence, and crime.

That Ambrosio's plight *and* the relevance of the story-pattern are to be seen in a historical perspective is made explicit in a lengthy commentary which describes the monk's early education:

> [Ambrosio's] Instructors carefully repressed those virtues, whose grandeur and disinterestedness were ill-suited to the Cloister. Instead of universal benevolence He adopted a selfish partiality for his own particular establishment: He was taught to consider compassion for the errors of Others as a crime of the blackest dye: The noble frankness of his temper was exchanged for servile humility; and in order to break his natural spirit, the Monks terrified his young mind, by placing before him all

the horrors with which Superstition could furnish them: They painted to him the torments of the Damned in colours the most dark, terrible, and fantastic, and threatened him at the slightest fault with eternal perdition (p. 237).

The commentary makes use of contemporary ideas concerning the corrupting influence of human institutions on human nature, and it expands them by presenting story-telling itself as a potentially corrupting institution. Ambrosio's life repeats the pattern of transgression and punishment because he belongs to a world which repeats and therefore perpetuates stories of temptation and perdition.

Developed one step further, this statement can help to define the central problem posed by *The Monk*. It is a novel about the destructive influence of past patterns of thought and at the same time it repeats the identical patterns. One element of the equations which are contained in the commentary remains empty. If Ambrosio's story shows human nature in a perverted form, what future stories will there be which realize his natural benevolence, compassion, noble frankness etc.? Instead the terms of the equation are silently changed. We do get a future story, but it is based on the principle of liberty *as opposed to* all the things Ambrosio might have "naturally" been.

The principle of liberty is introduced by Matilda, the woman who has been sent by the devil in order to tempt Ambrosio. She calls on the monk to discard all the "ridiculous prejudices" and "vulgar errors" of the past and to dare his happiness (p. 268). Her enlightened "natural philosophy" (p. 267) does not acknowledge any principle of action which would impose limits on her desire for self-preservation and self-gratification:

> I will enjoy unrestrained the gratification of my senses: Every passion shall be indulged, even to satiety; Then will I bid my Servants invent new pleasures, to revive and stimulate my glutted appetites! I go impatient to exercise my newly-gained dominion. I pant to be at liberty (pp. 428-29).

As illustrated by the career of the monk, this credo implies the destruction of all traditional boundaries between right and wrong. Murder itself, the murder of those witnesses who could impede the monk's onward movement, is transformed by it into "so insignificant a crime" (p. 390), if not into a "fortunate event" (p. 306). In emphasizing again this limited understanding of the word as an unbounded assertion of self, Matilda's celebration of "liberty" creates a point of reference for the ambivalent ending of the novel.

At the end Ambrosio dies. He signs the contract with the devil, and he is destroyed by the devil. Imprisoned by the Inquisition for his crimes, he had given his soul to be released; he had not demanded "life, and power, and pleasure" (p. 441) as well. Both tendencies of the novel are assembled in this ending. From one point of view, Ambrosio is still "too much the Monk" (p. 234) to envisage any alternative values; from another point of view these values themselves, which are translatable as the better-known "life", "liberty", and "happiness", can only be obtained in a bargain with "the devil". In the ambivalent political game of the novel, the original significance of the story of the tempter is first cancelled (since it would appear only conditionally true of the times that were shaped by it), and then reaffirmed.

There is a hidden alternative ending to Ambrosio's story. We are told that the guards were coming with his final pardon at the very moment that he signed the contract with the devil (p. 440). Ambrosio is destroyed not for his excessive crimes but because unlike Agnes he did not believe in the possibilities of mercy and therefore left the realm of the law. This ending where judgment is passed on the characters and where a merciful judgment is promised to all already points to the underlying psychological pattern. It shapes even the story of Lorenzo, who is the least conspicuous and apparently least "guilty" of the protagonists.

Lorenzo occupies a central position in two chapters only (Book I, Chapter 1; Book III, Chapter 3). The first chapter of the first book tells of his meeting with Antonia in the Church of the Capuchins. He falls in love with her at first sight; he means to marry her. Although he has heard that Antonia's social position is questionable, he so much believes in the liberal attitude of his family that he does not even think of not consulting them. Staying in the church after the service, Lorenzo dreams of his wedding-day. His dream is suddenly transformed into a nightmare: an "Unknown", a "Monster" (p. 28) rushes between bride and bridegroom and attacks and destroys Antonia. Lorenzo wakes up to discover that a secret exchange is being carried on in front of him within the church: a stranger hides a letter under the statue of the patron saint, and the letter is taken up by one of the nuns. The nun is Lorenzo's sister, the stranger his close friend Raymond.

A dream, a nightmare, a discovery—the three main narratives of *The Monk* are already foreshadowed in the first chapter. Lorenzo will follow his dream and will try to obtain the families' consent to his marriage; the nightmare will be acted out by Ambrosio. The glimpse of the hidden letter on the other hand leads to the unfolding of the past story of Raymond and Agnes. Lorenzo listens to Raymond's story and learns to accept it, so much so that he begins to assist the friend in his attempts to free the sister. In Book III, Chapter 3, he

is on the scene when the Domina is murdered and her convent destroyed. It is he who explores the building and who discovers Agnes, only to realize at the same time how his own hopes have been undone. In a still further recess of the building he finds his dying love, raped and stabbed by the monk.

Lorenzo's life appears primarily shaped by others, by his friendship for Raymond and by the unknown actions of the monk; his story is subordinated to these two more central stories. Even in the two scenes which focus on him he appears less as an actor than as the observer and witness of the actions of others. Nonetheless it can be argued that his experiences at the beginning of the novel are the centre from which all later developments radiate: the experience of love is followed by a momentary vision of sexuality as violence and by a sudden recognition that secret exchanges have already been going on all the time.

Raymond's narrative retrieves the past. There had indeed already been secret contacts with a girl who was debarred from all sexual experience by her guardians (the mother, the aunt, the governess, the prioress) and who was made inaccessible by the thick walls of the building (the castle, the convent) in which she was kept. In spite of these imposing barriers first contacts had been established: secret exchanges in the presence of "the saint". They had however culminated in a disturbing episode. There came a moment when Raymond believed himself finally released from all restricting influences, only to discover in the veiled woman with whom he had escaped from the castle a spectre from the primordial past:

> She lifted up her veil slowly. What a sight presented itself to my startled eyes! I beheld before me an animated Corpse. Her countenance was long and haggard; Her cheeks and lips were bloodless; The paleness of death was spread over her features, and her eye-balls fixed stedfastly upon me were lustreless and hollow (p. 160).

The sight transfixed him:

> My blood was frozen in my veins. I would have called for aid, but the sound expired, ere it could pass my lips. My nerves were bound up in impotence, and I remained in the same attitude inanimate as a Statue (p. 160).

Raymond confesses that for long nights afterwards the spectre and Agnes would present themselves alternately to his dreams, thereby pointing out the significance of this past experience: it poses the question of the loved one's true identity.

When Lorenzo finally enters the convent, he indeed rediscovers his sister in a strangely altered shape:

As Lorenzo advanced, He felt a piercing chillness spread itself through his veins. The frequent groans still engaged him to move forwards. He turned towards them, and by the Lamp's glimmering beams beheld in a corner of this loathsome abode, a Creature stretched upon a bed of straw, so wretched, so emaciated, so pale, that He doubted to think her Woman. She was half-naked: Her long dishevelled hair fell in disorder over her face, and almost entirely concealed it. One wasted Arm hung listlessly upon a tattered rug, which covered her convulsed and shivering limbs: The Other was wrapped round a small bundle, and held it closely to her bosom (p. 369).

Again the attributes of the object invade the observer:

Lorenzo stopped: He was petrified with horror. He gazed upon the miserable Object with disgust and pity. He trembled at the spectacle; He grew sick at heart: His strength failed him, and his limbs were unable to support his weight (p. 369).

Raymond's past experience and Lorenzo's experience are related to each other as question and answer, suspicion and confirmation. Raymond was faced by the spectre of a "bleeding nun", a woman who first appeared completely veiled in her nun's attire, her only distinguishing mark a bleeding wound on her breast; the vision of this mutilated figure was then replaced by a focus on her unveiled face, which is the face of a corpse. Lorenzo discovers his sister "wretched", "emaciated", "pale", close to death. The vision of her wasted body (which appears to him as the body of an undifferentiated "Creature" that has lost its identity as "Woman") is gradually replaced by a focus on the "small bundle" which she holds closely to her breast. "Unveiled" at last, it discloses the dead body of her child, a "mass of putridity", in its "livid corruption" an "emblem of mortality" (pp. 412-13).

The two women are linked by the identity of their stories: they both broke the primary law imposed upon them, the law of chastity. They are also linked by the identity of their attributes (the wounded, mutilated creature/the corpse/the wasted, emaciated creature/the corrupting flesh) which can again be rearranged into an identical story: mutilation leading to death and corruption. Both women finally spread the threat of their contagion. In different traditional symbolizations (the "face"/the "child") and by means of different transpositions to an upper part of the body (the face/the breast)[4] the descriptions capture an experience of sexual difference as negation. The other (Woman) is apprehended as a mutilated self; in a metonymic shift the fear of self-annihilation (re)characterizes "it" as dissolving/corrupting, death-like.

The same process of discovery is repeated in Lorenzo's own love story. In the vaults of the convent he encounters not only his lost sister, but also his lost love, one more woman who re-emerges on the point of death with deep wounds on her breast. In his initial vision Lorenzo dreamed how a monster rushes into the church to attack Antonia:

Antonia shrieked. The Monster clasped her in his arms, and springing with her upon the Altar, tortured her with his odious caresses. She endeavoured in vain to escape from his embrace. Lorenzo flew to her succour, but ere He had time to reach her, a loud burst of thunder was heard. Instantly the Cathedral seemed crumbling into pieces . . . the Altar sank down, and in its place appeared an abyss vomiting forth clouds of flame. Uttering a loud and terrible cry the Monster plunged into the Gulph, and in his fall attempted to drag Antonia with him. He strove in vain. Animated by supernatural powers She disengaged herself from his embrace; But her white Robe was left in his possession. Instantly a wing of brilliant splendour spread itself from either of Antonia's arms. She darted upwards, and while ascending cried to Lorenzo, "Friend! we shall meet above" (p. 28).

The religious meaning of the vision (that sinfulness will lead to damnation) appears foregrounded. The sequence of events, however, implies a different kind of story: that desire will lead to an experience of absence; that the "white robe" (associated with the "dazzling whiteness" [p.9] of Antonia's flesh) can be grasped while an unattainable essence will escape; that the "crumbling away" of the walls of the "sacred building" will reveal a deep "abyss", a void.

This suspicion, already adumbrated in the initial vision, is confirmed in Lorenzo's central experience in a lengthy process of exploration. The scene is the festival of St Clare, patron saint of the convent in which Agnes has disappeared. A huge church procession is held and the people watch in reverence. Their reverence is however suddenly transformed into a frenzied violence as the accusation is spread that inhuman things have been going on inside. Lorenzo witnesses the destruction of the Domina, attacked by a furious mob until her body is "no more than a mass of flesh, unsightly, shapeless, and disgusting" (p. 356); he experiences the frenzy of the people directing itself against the convent, battering the walls, throwing lighted torches into the windows, forcing the gates of the "holy Mansion" (p. 208) into which the eyes of men never before intruded.

Lorenzo himself joins in the exploration which leads him down the stairs into the long passages and distant vaults which form the labyrinthine cemetery of St Clare's. He is led on to a statue of the saint in the middle of the labyrinth. Myth protects the sacred figure: whoever dares to touch it will nevermore be able to disengage himself. Lorenzo examines it and discovers that it hides a "deep abyss", a "yawning Gulph" (p. 367). Inspection however proves that the abyss is not quite so deep; it leads on into further vaults and there Lorenzo will at last find Agnes and Antonia.

The exterior of the "holy Mansion" hides the dark stairs that lead into the subterranean labyrinth; the figure of the saint hides the abyss that leads into the secret vaults: the exploration repeats the experience already contained in the initial "nightmare" of Antonia. The object, however, is no longer the same. The imagined attack on Antonia has been replaced by the witnessed attack on the Domina.

Raymond in love with Agnes has to encounter the presence of the "bleeding nun"; Lorenzo in love with Antonia is to "witness" the destruction of the Domina. Both experiences converge in the same knowledge: the negation inscribed in the figure of the "nun" in the opposition between the flesh and its putrefaction is repeated in the opposition between the building and the void which characterizes the "sacred" mansion of the Domina. In the game of experience, all women (Agnes, Antonia) are assimilated to the likeness of that untouchable primal presence that "upon inspection" (p. 368) was found already to bear the mark of violation.

The transformation points to the mystery of its cause. The hidden cause almost surfaces in the story of the third protagonist, the monk Ambrosio. On his way to Antonia he is confronted by the presence of her mother, who is also his own unknown mother, and he kills her:

> Turning round suddenly, with one hand He grasped Elvira's throat so as to prevent her continuing her clamour, and with the other, dashing her violently upon the ground, He dragged her towards the Bed. Confused by this unexpected attack, She scarcely had power to strive at forcing herself from his grasp: While the Monk, snatching the pillow from beneath her Daughter's head, covering with it Elvira's face, and pressing his knee upon her stomach with all his strength, endeavoured to put an end to her existence. He succeeded but too well. Her natural strength increased by the excess of anguish, long did the Sufferer struggle to disengage herself, but in vain. The Monk continued to kneel upon her breast, witnessed without mercy the convulsive trembling of her limbs beneath him, and sustained with inhuman firmness the spectacle of her agonies . . . The Monk took off the pillow, and gazed upon her. Her face was covered with a frightful blackness: Her limbs moved no more; the blood was chilled in her veins; Her heart had forgotten to beat, and her hands were stiff and frozen (pp. 303-304).

Community of attributes links Elvira to the other women in the novel. The unveiling of her face echoes the unveiling of the "bleeding nun", the sight of her face—a "frightful blackness", later remembered as "livid" (p. 337)—links her to the "livid corruption" of Agnes' child (p. 413), the "convulsive trembling of her limbs" is repeated in the "convulsed and shivering limbs" of Agnes (p. 369). The identical reaction, the same sense of impending annihilation, connects Ambrosio and the other young men in the novel. Nonetheless his experience does not only repeat the stories of the others; Ambrosio acts, and his acting adds a decisive element. The murder of his mother, which is a distorted reenactment of a sexual scene, precedes the shocked recognition of mutilation and the fear of self-annihilation as its cause.[5]

Lorenzo and Raymond shrink back from the recognition of this slowly emerging memory which binds all desire to incestuous desires. Their innocent versions read that Raymond was suddenly faced by a spectre from a past in which he himself was no participant; Lorenzo only witnessed the actions of "unknown monsters" and unknown "mobs". The aims of Ambrosio, who is left to repeat the same primordial experience in his meeting with Antonia, will remain "unknown" to both of them.[6] Instead they both return to their families and the security of inexperience. Raymond will marry Agnes, who has left her "child" behind, and Lorenzo will marry Virginia, a girl who during church processions convincingly played the role of the saint.

In *The Monk*, the two movements described above, the political and the psychological, are closely interconnected: they appear as different expressions of the same urge to question the validity of "the law". The overstepping of the monastery's boundaries involves Ambrosio in the murder of his mother (which has sexual implications) and in the rape of his sister. The transgression of the (metaphoric) boundaries established by tradition is consummated in incestuous relationships, bringing together what had traditionally been kept apart. Philosophy appears implicated in this process, because "Philosophy's deceitful vapours" (p. 426) have blurred all distinctions between right and wrong. Criticism and inquiry are also behind the central political event, the frenzied attack on the convent: Lorenzo comes to realize that his wish to free the people from their "monkish fetters" of belief and to "unmask" the reality of the past (pp. 345-46) was the "innocent" cause of this "frightful disturbance" (p. 358).

In the organization of the text the culminating scenes of the different lines of action form a sequence: the murder of the mother (III,1) and Ambrosio's second approach towards the sister (III,2) are followed by the murder of the Domina and the attack upon her convent (III,3), and this again is followed by (although actually simultaneous with) the rape of Antonia (III,4). The linking of the scenes establishes an overt connection between political and sexual violence, but it also points to a more basic association of ideas. The political eruption is contextually assimilated to the sexual scenes, just as (from a different point of view) the assault on the convent itself is an architectural symbolization of these other scenes. Inversely, the monk's incestuous desire links him (who is his sister's brother and her lover at the same time) to that "world of Monsters", of as yet "nameless" things in which Edmund Burke found the essence of the Revolution.[7]

The bond between "incest", "the revolution", and "philosophy", which is implied in *The Monk*, is more overtly rendered in two further texts which were published in the same decade: Burke's *Reflections on the Revolution in France* (1790) and Sade's *La Philosophie dans le boudoir* (1795). They both testify to the not merely personal, contemporary relevance of the incest-motif. *La Philosophie* is written as a dialogue, in which the superstitions and prejudices of a young girl are subjected to a process of "philosophical" criticism by her partners in the boudoir. She discards the convictions with which her mother brought her up and at the same time gains access to hitherto forbidden sexual experiences. "Philosophical" discourse, leading to a destruction of established beliefs, alternates with a demonstration of its "ethical" consequences, paradigmatically rendered in the transgression of sexual taboos.

The "philosophical" sequence aims at questioning the validity of all moral judgments. In the context of historical research and of the voyages of exploration the categories of good and evil reappear as words only— "ces mots"—whose application perpetually changes: "Ah! n'en doutez pas . . . , ces mots de vice et de vertu ne nous donnent que des idées purement locales."[8] In the context of natural history they disappear altogether. "Murder" for example disappears, since it is reinterpreted as one of the modes of destruction which is a primary law of nature; "destruction" itself is only apparent since it is in truth only a variation of the forms of nature (pp. 107-108). The principle of the conservation of matter is at the basis of this argument.

Nature—"qui n'est autre chose que la matière en action" (p.70)—is, in a manner reminiscent of Holbach, presented as continually transforming, continually rearranging the given materials (pp.68ff.). This game of transformation, for which Buffon's research into extinct species is quoted as a further proof (p.160), contradicts all belief in the immutability of species, in their "special creation" and preordained place in the universe; it above all characterizes man's alleged central significance in the creation as an invention of his presumption. The implied opponent is the traditional account of genesis; in opposition to it mankind is redefined as an ephemeral product of natural processes:

> Nous estimant les premières créatures de l'univers, nous avons sottement imaginé que toute lésion qu'endurerait cette sublime créature devrait nécessairement être un crime énorme; nous avons cru que la nature périrait si notre merveilleuse espèce venait à s'anéantir sur ce globe, tandis que l'entière destruction de cette espèce, en rendant à la nature la faculté créatrice qu'elle nous cède, lui redonnerait une énergie que nous lui enlevons en nous propageant . . . (p. 108).

The scientific theory blurs all difference between man and the creation in general. Whereas mankind is just one of the forms which matter in motion could assume, an individual is just a piece of flesh, "ce morceau de chair, quelque animé qu'il fût" (pp. 123ff.). The impact of the natural sciences is echoed in that destruction of lexical difference which is one of the basic strategies of *La Philosophie*.

"A queen is but a woman; a woman is but an animal; and an animal not of the highest order", Burke wrote in a passage of his *Reflections* which comments on the forcible transfer of the royal family from Versailles to Paris and on the possibility of their future execution. The passage illustrates the political consequences of that equation of traditionally distinct categories brought about by the "new conquering empire of light and reason" (p. 171). The complete passage reads:

> On this [new] scheme of things, a king is but a man; a queen is but a woman; a woman is but an animal; and an animal not of the highest order. All homage paid to the sex in general as such, and without distinct views, is to be regarded as romance and folly. Regicide, and parricide, and sacrilege, are but fictions of superstition, corrupting jurisprudence by destroying its simplicity. The murder of a king, or a queen, or a bishop, or a father, are only common homicide; and if the people are by any chance, or in any way gainers by it, a sort of homicide much the most pardonable, and into which we ought not to make too severe a scrutiny (p. 171).

Regicide, parricide, and sacrilege, the murder of a king, a father, a bishop, are "only common homicide", to be judged according to the utility of the moment, just as the queen is a woman is an animal, potentially to be treated as such. The destruction of the social hierarchy ("the queen" = "a woman") corresponds to the destruction of the traditional world view epitomized in the idea of the *scala naturae* ("the queen" = "an animal").

The novel unfolds those aspects which were not contained in the original myth of the monk, just as

Ambrosio begins to achieve that knowledge which did not seem to belong to "his own precincts" of the monastic tradition. In the murder of his mother and the rape of his sister he will discover his unknown origin and his unknown sexual nature at the same time. Significantly, this development is presented as the story of a temptation, in which every step is finally seen to have been manipulated by the devil. The traditional pattern confirms Ambrosio's own basic attitude, since Ambrosio himself experiences his own desires as transgressions. Imprisoned in the myth of the monk, he is led into secrecy, violence, and crime. . . .

The "full scandal" of these revaluations[9] is realized as soon as the paradigmatic axis, along which the particular is continually being submerged in the more general category, is left and as the field of new syntagmatic possibilities is opened up. This is the function of the sexual scenes which are embedded in the philosophical discourse of *La Philosophie*. They culminate in a final scene in which the daughter in a last step of her education sexually assaults her mother: "Venez, belle maman, venez, que je vous serve de mari" (p. 278). In a transgression of gender distinctions and in a violation of the combination rules within the family, the girl is at the same time her mother's daughter and her mother's husband. In a comparable, though (comparatively) less strident way Burke presents the violent attack on the queen with its overt sexual connotations as the essence of the revolution: the bed of the queen is pierced "with an hundred strokes of bayonets and poniards", while she barely manages to escape "almost naked" (p. 164).

Can we account for this alignment of "incest", "philosophy", and "the revolution"? In a manner suited to clarify this aspect, Lévi-Strauss[10] discussed the "systems of kinship" not as a mirroring of biological links but as a system of social rules which encompasses the naming of the elements ("le système des appellations") and all possible combinations between them ("le système des attitudes").[11] Whatever the concrete modifications of the system, it contains the prohibition on incest, which is here understood in its positive aspect as "une règle de réciprocité",[12] as its decisive first step: "la prohibition de l'inceste exprime le passage du fait naturel de la consanguinité au fait culturel de l'alliance."[13] As soon as the barrier against incest is imaginatively grasped as a rule, as concomitant with a system of oppositions (between, for example, "les épouses, femmes acquíses" and "les soeurs et les filles, femmes cédées"[14]), its violation can with a limited number of elements signify the destruction of all social systems. As a universal rule, its transgression can serve as a universal model for the inauguration of a counterorder.

In the texts discussed above, this alternative world is evoked in order to be rejected. In Burke, the sexual assault on the queen/mother is momentarily visualized in a symbolic scene (the poniards pierce the bed), and is at the same time denied through a reference to the "real-life" story: actually the queen manages to escape and to reach the security of her husband's protection. In **The Monk**, the young men recoil from the realization of that memory which threatens them with Ambrosio's punishment. Even in Sade, where the mother is indeed for a short time included in the story of the boudoir, this final barrier remains: her inclusion is explicitly no voluntary participation, and in its sequel (she is infected with syphilis and then sewn up) it is tantamount to her final exclusion from all processes of sexual exchange such as was willed by the absent father. Comparable to the conception of Lévi-Strauss, where "incest" marks that irrecoverable noplace before culture,[15] it is not an attainable alternative that is foregrounded in these texts but an idea of transgression that appears fascinating and fearful at the same time.

Notes

[1] Matthew Lewis, *The Monk,* ed. Howard Anderson, The World's Classics edn, 1986, p. 7: all references in the text are to this edition. In preparing this paper, I have found the following studies especially stimulating: Peter Brooks, "Virtue and Terror: *The Monk*", *ELH,* 40 (1973), 249-63; Elliott B. Gose, jun., *Imagination Indulged,* Montreal & London 1972, ch. 2; Robert Kiely, *The Romantic Novel in England* Cambridge, Mass., 2nd edn, 1973, ch. 5; Eve Kosofsky Sedgwick, "The Character in the Veil: Imagery of the Surface in the Gothic Novel", *PMLA,* 96, 2 (1981), 255-70; Ronald Paulson, "Gothic Fiction and the French Revolution", *ELH,* 48 (1981), 532-54; Ignacy Trostaniecki, "La Poétique du Caché dans *Le Moine de M.G. Lewis*", *Recherches Anglaises et Américaines,* 6 (1973), 43-59.

[2] See Marilyn Butler, *Jane Austen and the War of Ideas,* Oxford, 1975, ch. 4, "The Anti-Jacobins".

[3] See Roland Barthes, "Myth Today", in *A Barthes Reader,* ed. Susan Sontag, London, 1982, pp. 102-105.

[4] See Sigmund Freud, *The Interpretation of Dreams,* in: *The Standard Edition of the Complete Psychological Works of Sigmund Freud,* gen. ed. James Strachey, vols 4 and 5, London, 1953, rpt with corrections 1958, 6th ed, 1973: vol. 5, p. 357 ("the child"), p. 387 ("the face"), and p. 346 (the architectural symbolism). See also the dream of "the barrel-maker's boys" (in vol. 4, p. 201), the dream of the "little one" (in vol. 5, pp. 362 ff.), and the dreams about buildings and landscapes (in vol. 5, pp. 364 ff.).

[5] See Sigmund Freud, "The Dissolution of the Oedipus Complex", *The Standard Edition of the Complete Psychological Works of Sigmund Freud,* gen. ed. James Strachey, vol. 19, London, 1961, 7th ed. 1975, pp. 173-79; "Some Psychical Consequences of the Anatomical Distinction between the Sexes", *SE,* vol. 19, pp. 248-58.

[6] For a different reading of Lorenzo's story as a "redemptive quest" which fails, see Gose, pp. 34 ff.

[7] See Edmund Burke, *Reflections on the Revolution in France* (1790), ed. Conor Cruise O'Brien, Penguin, 1968, 3rd edn, 1976, pp. 9, 14, 31n, 187: all references in the text are to this edition.

[8] [Donatien-Alphonse-François] Marquis de Sade, *La Philosophie dans le boudoir* (1795), ed. Yvon Belaval, Paris, 1976, p. 79: all references in the text are to this edition.

[9] See Roland Barthes, *Sade Fourier Loyola,* Paris, 1971, p. 141.

[10] Claude Lévi-Strauss, *Les structures élémentaires de la parenté,* Paris, 1949; and *Anthropologie Structurale,* Paris, 1958, chap. II "L'analyse structurale en linguistique et en anthropologie".

[11] See Lévi-Strauss, *Anthropologie Structurale,* pp. 40-41, 45-47, 61-62.

[12] See Lévi-Strauss, *Les structures élémentaires,* p. 79.

[13] *Ibid.,* p. 36.

[14] *Ibid.,* pp. 174-75.

[15] *Ibid.,* p. 31.

FURTHER READING

B[aker], E. A. Introduction to *The Monk: A Romance,* by M. G. Lewis, edited by E. A. Baker, pp. vii-xvii. London: George Routledge & Sons, 1929.
> Underscores the novel's historical significance as "the most notorious exemplar of the 'Gothic' school of romance."

Brooks, Philip. "Notes on Rare Books." *The New York Times Book Review* (27 January 1935): 21.
> Recounts the publication history of *The Monk* for the benefit of rare book collectors.

Conger, Syndy M. "An Analysis of *The Monk* and Its German Sources." In *Romantic Reassessment: Matthew G. Lewis, Charles Robert Maturin and the Germans, an Interpretive Study of the Influence of German Literature on Two Gothic Novels,* edited by James Hogg, pp. 12-125. Salzburg Studies in English Literature, edited by Erwin A. Stürzl, no. 67. Salzburg: Universität Salzburg, 1977.
> Explores the nature and extent of Lewis's reliance on German sources in writing *The Monk.*

Coykendall, Frederick. "Lewis's *Monk.*" *The Times Literary Supplement,* No. 1734 (25 April 1935): 276.
> Addendum to Peck's article on variations in later editions of *The Monk.*

Hume, Robert D. "Gothic Versus Romantic: A Revaluation of the Gothic Novel." *PMLA* 84, No. 2 (March 1969): 282-90.
> Mentions *The Monk* as part of a survey of Gothic narrative technique.

Irwin, Joseph James. "*The Monk.*" In *M. G. "Monk" Lewis,* pp. 35-59. Boston, Mass.: Twayne Publishers, 1976.
> Presents an overview of *The Monk,* surveying criticism of the novel as well as its characters and Gothic devices.

Parreaux, André. "The Poetry of *The Monk.*" In *The Publication of The Monk: A Literary Event; 1796-1798,* pp. 49-56. Paris: Librairie Marcel Didier, 1960.
> Traces the contemporary popularity and immediate influence of Lewis's ballads in *The Monk.*

Paulson, Ronald. "Gothic Fiction and the French Revolution." *ELH* 48, No. 3 (Fall 1981): 532-54.
> Includes an estimation of *The Monk* in relation to its historical contexts, seeing the work as symbolic of the act of political liberation.

Peck, Louis F. "Lewis's *Monk.*" *The Times Literary Supplement,* No. 1727 (7 March 1935): 148.
> Briefly details textual variations in the first through fifth editions of *The Monk.*

——. "*The Monk* and *Le diable amoureux.*" *Modern Language Notes* LXVIII, No. 6 (June 1953): 406-08.
> Analyzes the similarities between *The Monk* and Jacques Cazotte's novel *Le diable amoureux.*

Review of *The Monk; a Romance. Monthly Mirror* 2 (June 1796): 98.
> Short review of *The Monk* which calls the work "very skilfully managed."

Review of *The Monk. Scot's Magazine* LXIV (July 1802): 545-48.
> Finds *The Monk* a "loathsome story" which fails as a supposed cautionary tale because the author seems to revel in the perverse acts of his novel's characters. This review is signed "W.W."

Sedgwick, Eve Kosofsky. "The Character in the Veil: Imagery of the Surface in the Gothic Novel." *PMLA* 96, No. 2 (March 1981): 255-70.

> Evaluates imagery of sex and of the flesh, and assesses the thematic consequences of this symbolism in *The Monk* and Ann Radcliffe's *Mysteries of Udolpho* and *The Italian.*

Additional coverage of Lewis's life and career is contained in the following sources published by Gale Research: *Nineteenth-Century Literature Criticism,* **Vol. 11; and** *Dictionary of Literary Biography,* **Vols. 39 and 158.**

Thomas Paine

1737-1809

(Born Thomas Pain) English pamphleteer and essayist.

INTRODUCTION

Thomas Paine, a largely self-educated Englishman who was a corset-maker by trade, has been recognized as a primary force in the American Revolution since its instigation in 1775; he was similarly influential in the French Revolution, sparked in 1789. Several commentators have credited Paine with turning the tide of American opinion from tepid colonial discontent to the revolutionary conviction necessary for independence. Unlike other leading men of the revolution, such as John Adams, Benjamin Franklin, Alexander Hamilton, and Thomas Jefferson, Paine enjoyed none of the advantages of wealth, such as social status and extensive formal education. Paine, however, turned his disadvantages into advantages, positioning himself as the spokesman of the American populace—a population he moved profoundly with the publication of the pamphlet *Common Sense: Addressed to the Inhabitants of America* early in 1776, a work that was in itself revolutionary in its vernacular style and directness. Because of his many writings and efforts on behalf of newly-emerging democratic governments, Paine has become emblematic of the modern struggle for human rights and social justice. He was also considered to be ahead of his time in his critiques of slavery, unfair labor practices, gender inequality, and even cruelty to animals.

Biographical Information

Paine was born in the small village of Thetford in England on January 29, 1737. His father was a Quaker and a middle-class tradesman—he made stays for women's corsets. At a time when only upper-class men received an extensive formal education, Paine had only six years of the typical English curriculum—English, Latin, Greek, mathematics—before he had to go to work with his father in the family business. At nineteen (some biographers say sixteen), he joined in England's war effort against France, signing on with the privateer ship *The King of Prussia*. In 1757, he began supporting himself as a staymaker, living for two years first in London, then Dover, then Sandwich, where he married Mary Lambert in 1759; within a year, she passed away. Paine began his career as a civil servant in 1761, when he became an excise officer—a customs official—in Lincolnshire, a post he

held with only one brief interruption until 1774. He married again in 1771, to Elizabeth Ollive of Lewes. It was also during this year that he began to display evidence of his future calling, when he took up the cause of excise officers who felt they received an unfair wage. Paine wrote a pamphlet, *The Case of the Officers of Excise* (1772), to argue on their behalf and, in 1772-1773, went to London to lobby Parliament, unsuccessfully, for consideration. All he won for his effort, however, was a permanent dismissal from his post in 1774. That same year, he and his wife opted for a separation.

On the verge of bankruptcy, Paine went to London, where he became acquainted with Benjamin Franklin, who convinced him to try his luck in the British colonies in North America. Paine began his American career in Philadelphia, where he became a writer for a monthly periodical called the *Pennsylvania Magazine*. (Paine added the "e" to his surname after his arrival in America.) Paine had never stopped pursuing his education. He read everything he could find and attended lectures in every city in which he lived. He socialized with men more learned than himself, many of them scholars, and consulted with them informally as tutors. Paine's early success at the *Pennsylvania Magazine*—he became editor in 1775—was largely due to his style, which was uncommonly accessible to a general readership. Nonetheless, Paine left the journal, it is believed, in the fall of 1775. He was, all the same, already at work on his first significant work, a slim pamphlet called *Common Sense.* Published in January of 1776, it captured in succinct and persuasive prose otherwise unexpressed revolutionary sentiment. Although military conflict between Great Britain and the colonies had begun in the spring of the previous year, most Americans still sought some form of reconciliation with England. *Common Sense,* as most commentators since have argued, laid to rest the colonial mindset, replacing it with the fervent desire for national independence. The work sold over 100,000 copies in its first two months, and, published anonymously, was assumed to be the work of men much more well-known and well-educated than Paine, including John Adams and Franklin.

Without employment in 1776, Paine dedicated his body as well as his pen to the revolutionary cause, joining up with the Pennsylvania militia. He continued writing to his very broad, enthusiastic audience, penning sixteen pamphlets under the title *The Crisis,* or *The American Crisis,* the first of which appeared at the end of 1776. The publication of these pamphlets continued through to April 1783, when the war ended. Paine left the army at the beginning of 1777, convinced that he was not serving the revolution best in that capacity. Instead he became a commission secretary to several government bodies, including the Continental Congress. He served the Congress until 1779, when political complications forced him out of that position; he was then elected clerk of the Pennsylvania Assembly. Despite his successes as a pamphleteer and his many positions, Paine found himself once again penniless at the war's end in 1783: he had given all his profits from his publications to support the war. The states of Pennsylvania and New York and the new nation, via Congress, made him several gifts of cash and land. By the end of the decade Paine had become involved in many new projects, including a passion for bridge design; the latter took him to France in 1787, just as the revolutionary fervor there was mounting. He remained in Paris until July of 1791, serving the French Revolution in many capacities, even though he did not speak the language at all.

Edmund Burke, a prominent English statesman, published his influential criticism of France, *Reflections on the Revolution in France,* in 1790. Many defenders of France published responses, but the most significant of these replies was Paine's, the first part of which appeared in 1791. Completed in 1792, *Rights of Man: Being an Answer to Mr. Burke's Attack on the French Revolution* sold millions of copies in France and England. As with *Common Sense,* this publication made Paine both revered and despised in his homeland. Consequently, Paine's attempt to resettle in London was cut short; he fled in 1792, just ahead of the officers seeking his arrest on charges of high treason. He was convicted *in absentia.* Taking sanctuary in France, Paine was elected to several positions in the National Assembly and appointed to the committee responsible for framing the new constitution. The tenor of the French Revolution, however, diverged from Paine's values as it moved into a bloodthirsty phase commonly known as the "Terror," during which "enemies of the people"—both members of the former ruling class and less radical revolutionaries—were imprisoned and guillotined. Speaking against the planned execution of Louis XVI, the deposed king, Paine found himself incarcerated by the end of 1793, where he remained until James Monroe, the American ambassador to France, secured his release late in 1794. Restored to his position in the French government soon after, Paine remained in France until 1802. He produced his last significant pamphlet, *Agrarian Justice,* in 1797.

Paine immigrated to America again in 1802, although his reputation with Americans had been greatly damaged by several of his publications from the previous decade: *The Age of Reason: Being an Investigation of True and Famous Theology* (1794-1795), which critiqued organized religion and struck many readers as blasphemous, and the *Letter to George Washington, President of the United States of America, on Affairs Public and Private* (1796), which viciously attacked a man revered by Americans. Nonetheless, he remained in the United States until he passed away, largely unnoticed, on June 8, 1809.

Major Works

Although Paine produced articles and pamphlets almost nonstop after his arrival in colonial America, certain works stand out for their influence both at the time of their publication and over the ensuing centuries. Some, including *Common Sense* and *Rights of Man,* have become almost legendary, inspiring activists engaged in causes years after Paine's death; President Abraham Lincoln, for example, read Paine's works as he fought to end slavery in the United States.

Paine's writings share a generally consistent viewpoint and goal; although scholars can chart some changes in Paine's thinking, the framework of his perspective remained stable over the years. His style also remained largely the same, always remarkable for its difference from the dominant prose of the era, which consisted of complex sentences proposing complex arguments, written by highly-educated men for an audience of other highly-educated men. Paine, on the other hand, wrote to the broad mass of people in England and America, most of whom would have only as much as, if not less than, his six years of formal schooling. Consequently, his sentences were much more simple and direct, and his arguments turned on one or two accessible principles and pursued persuasion through clarity and repetition. He avoided the allusions and metaphors typical of prose for the highly literate, and chose instead references that would be available to common laborers and tradespeople. Sharing these standards, his major works differed from one another primarily in their focuses, which were often determined by the moment in which they were written.

Common Sense not only marks the real starting point of Paine's career as a pamphleteer in 1776, it also typifies his work. Rather than proposing any new political philosophies, *Common Sense* was remarkable for gathering up, in a sharp and powerful statement, the scattered strands of revolutionary thought. Once presented to the American public in this form, these arguments for America's need to cut itself free, both politically and economically, from the monarchy of the British Empire, instigated the drive to independence. A no-holds-barred critique of monarchy, *Common Sense* argued that Americans owed no loyalty to King George III or any hereditary ruler. Historians also credit Paine with maintaining the revolutionary spirit throughout the war years, from 1776 to 1783, with the many issues of *The American Crisis,* each of which offered further critiques of England and justifications for the American fight. The first issue began with the now legendary declaration that "These are the times that try men's souls."

With *Rights of Man*, published in 1791 and 1792 as a reply to Edmund Burke's *Reflections on the Revolution in France*, Paine's criticisms of hereditary government became their most explicit and demanding. His attacks on the monarchy and the aristocracy, meant to inspire the English populace to their own acts of revolution, also roused the ire of the ruling classes: unlike his previous works, this one was declared treasonous and caused his exile from England. Part I offers an explanation of the purpose of government, which Paine saw as essentially democratic—that is, it could exist legitimately only by the consent of the governed. Part II constituted an undisguised call for English subjects to topple the monarchy and create a constitutional democracy. In *The Age of Reason,* Paine turned his anti-establishment gaze on religious institutions, arguing that organized religions perpetuate oppression and ignorance. He espoused, instead, a deistic faith based on reason and consistent with a scientific view of nature. Many of the views he expressed shared the basic assumptions of other thinkers of the era; nonetheless, Paine incurred much more anger than did other rationalists, particularly with his direct efforts to refute many of the central tenets of Christianity. Although some critics would consider this his final significant work, other major works include *Agrarian Justice,* written in 1797, which most clearly articulates Paine's economic views. Written in the context of land reform debates in post-revolutionary France, the pamphlet suggests methods to eliminate the exploitation of laborers and to achieve a more equal distribution of wealth.

Critical Reception

By the time Paine passed away, he had fallen far from the pinnacle of his celebrity in revolutionary America. Even in the land where he had contributed the most directly to the success of the nation, he had become forgotten at best and despised at worst. He had contributed to this fall himself in a variety of ways, particularly with the publication of *The Age of Reason* and the *Letter to George Washington,* but his loss of public favor was also due to certain detractors. James Cheetham, most prominently, cemented an unpopular image of Paine with a biography published in 1809; that work set Paine's image for at least another century. Despite some isolated efforts to reassess Paine's image in the nineteenth century, and the admiration of some respected readers, including Abraham Lincoln, Paine's reputation held its taint through even the beginning of the twentieth century, when Theodore Roosevelt repeated the old charge that Paine was a "filthy little atheist."

It remained for scholars in the twentieth century to rediscover Paine and his work. Such scholars gradually developed a new view of the significance and complexity of Paine's writings. For these critics, discussions generally turned on several key issues. Early in this century, for example, there was still considerable debate about Paine's originality as a political thinker, many critics seeking to undermine his value by pointing out that the content of his works was largely derivative. More recently, however, it has become commonplace to find Paine's significance in his ability to articulate those ideas in original and fundamentally "democratic" language. Scholars such as Olivia Smith, for example, identify Paine as the progenitor of a written vernacular that addressed and even helped bring into being a mass audience. A changing perception of Paine may also be due simply to the passage of time: political and religious views that once shocked even other revolutionaries now strike many readers as comfortably progressive and self-evident.

PRINCIPAL WORKS

The Case of the Officers of Excise (political pamphlet) 1772

Common Sense: Addressed to the Inhabitants of America (political pamphlet) 1776

The American Crisis (political pamphlets) 1776-1783

Rights of Man: Being an Answer to Mr. Burke's Attack on the French Revolution (political treatise) 1791-1792

The Age of Reason: Being an Investigation of True and Famous Theology (political treatise) 1794-1795

Letter to George Washington, President of the United States of America, on Affairs Public and Private (political pamphlet) 1796

Agrarian Justice (political pamphlet) 1797

The Writings of Thomas Paine, 4 vols. (anthology, edited by Moncure Daniel Conway) 1894-1896

Six New Letters of Thomas Paine (letters to newspaper editor) 1939

The Complete Writings of Thomas Paine, 2 vols. (anthology, edited by Philip S. Foner) 1945

CRITICISM

Frederick Sheldon (essay date 1859)

SOURCE: "Tom Paine's First Appearance in America," in *Highlights in the History of the American Press: A Book of Readings,* edited by Edwin H. Ford and Edwin Emery, University of Minnesota Press, 1954, pp. 100-11.

[*In the second part of his* Atlantic Monthly *biography of Paine (from November, 1859), excerpted below, Sheldon recounts the revolutionary's role in the French Revolution and his efforts to inspire democratic fervor in England. As in his previous article, Sheldon summarizes the content of Paine's major works and illustrates the dramatic political situations in which he wrote.*]

When Tom Paine came to America in 1774, he found the dispute with England the all-absorbing topic. The atmosphere was heavy with the approaching storm. The First Congress was in session in the autumn of that year. On the 17th of September, John Adams felt certain that the other Colonies would support Massachusetts. The Second Congress met in May, 1775. During the winter and spring the quarrel had grown rapidly. Lexington and Concord had become national watchwords; the army was assembled about Boston; Washington was chosen commander-in-chief. Then came Bunker's Hill, the siege of Boston, the attack upon Quebec. There was open war between Great Britain and her Colonies. The Americans had drawn the sword, but were unwilling to raise the flag.

From the beginning of the troubles the Colonists had been consistent in their acts. Public meetings, protests, burnings in effigy, tea-riots, militia levies, congresses, skirmishes, war, followed each other in regular and logical succession—but theoretically they did not make out so clear a case. They had fine-drawn distinctions, not easy to appreciate at this day, between taxes levied for the purpose of raising revenue and duties imposed for the regulation of trade. Parliament could lay a duty on tobacco in a seaport, but might not make the weed excisable on a plantation, could break down a loom in any part of British America, could shut out all intercourse with foreign nations by the Navigation Act, but had not the legal right to make the Colonial merchant write his contracts or draw his bills on stamped paper. As to independence, very few desired it. "Independence," it was the fashion to say, "would be ruin and loss of liberty forever." The Colonists insisted that they were the most loyal of subjects; but they had men and muskets ready, and were determined to resist the obnoxious acts of Parliament with both, if necessary. These arguments of our ancestors led them to an excellent conclusion, and so far are entitled to our respect; but logically we are afraid that King George had the best of it.

Before many months had passed, lagging theory was left so far in the rear by the rapid course of events that the Colonists felt it necessary to move up a new set of principles to the van, if they wished to present a fair front to the enemy. They had raised an army, and taken the field. Unless they declared themselves a nation, they were confessedly rebels. And yet almost all hesitated. There was a deep-seated prejudice in favor of the English government, and a strong personal liking for the people. Even when it was known that the second petition to the King—Dickinson's "measure of imbecility"—was disregarded, as it deserved to be, and that the Hessians were coming, and all reasonable men admitted that there was no hope for reconciliation, they still refused to abandon the pleasing delusion, and talked over the old plans for redress of grievances, and a constitutional union with the mother country. With little or no belief in the possibility of either, they stood shivering on the banks of the Rubicon, that mythical river of irretrievable self-committal, hesitating to enter its turbid waters. A few of the bolder "shepherds of the people" tried to urge them onward; but no one was bold enough to dash in first and lead them through. Paine seized the opportunity. He had a mind whose eye always saw a subject, when it could perceive it at all, in its naked truth, stripped of the non-material accessories which disturb the vision of common men. He saw that reconciliation was impossible, mere rebellion folly; and that, to succeed in the struggle, it was necessary to fight Great Britain as an equal, nation against nation. This course he recommended in *Common Sense,* published in January, 1776.

Paine told the Colonists in this pamphlet that the connection with the mother country was of no use to them, and was rapidly becoming an impossibility. "It is not in the power of England to do this continent justice. The business of it is too weighty and too intricate to be managed with any tolerable degree of convenience by a power so distant. *To be always running three or four thousand miles with a tale or a petition, waiting four or five months for an answer, which, when obtained, requires five or six more to explain it in, will in a few years be looked upon as folly and childishness.*" As to the protection of England, what is that but the privilege of contributing to her wars? "Our trade will always be a protection." "Neutrality is a safer convoy than a man-of-war." "It is the true interest of America to steer clear of European contentions, which she can never do while by her dependence on Britain she is made the make-weight in the scale of European politics."

According to *Common Sense,* not only was a separation necessary and unavoidable, but the present moment was the right time to establish it. "The time hath found us." The materials of war were abundant; the union of the Colonies complete. It might be difficult, if not impossible, to form the continent into a government half a century hence. Now the task is easy. The interest of all is the same. "There is no religious difficulty in the way." "I fully believe that it is the will of the Almighty that there should be a diversity of religious opinions among us. *I look upon the various denominations among us as children of the same family, differing only in what is called their Christian names.*" All things considered, "nothing can settle our affairs so expeditiously as an open and determined declaration of independence." "This proceeding may at first appear strange and difficult. A long habit of not thinking a wrong gives it a superficial appearance of being right"; but in a little time it will become familiar. "And until independence is declared, the continent will feel itself like a man who continues putting off some unpleasant business from day to day, yet knows it must be done; hates to set about it, wishes it over, and is continually haunted with the thoughts of its necessity." To this he thought it necessary to add a labored argument against kings from the Old Testament, which may possibly have had much weight with a people some of whose descendants still triumphantly quote the same holy book in favor of slavery.

The King's speech, "a piece of finished villany," in the eyes of true patriots, appeared in Philadelphia on the same day as *Common Sense*. Thus Paine was as lucky in his time of publication as in his choice of a subject. All contemporaries admit that the pamphlet produced a prodigious effect. Paine himself says, "The success it met with was beyond anything since the invention of printing. I gave the copyright up to every State in the Union, and the demand ran to not less than one hundred thousand copies." The authorship was attributed to Dr. Franklin, to Samuel Adams, and to John Adams.

It is hardly necessary to mention that the movement party, with General Washington at its head, considered Paine's "doctrines sound, and his reasoning unanswerable." Even in England, Liberals read and applauded. The pamphlet was translated into French. When John Adams went to France, he heard himself called *le fameux Adams,* author of *Common Sense*.

It soon became apparent that the people were charged with Independence doctrines, and, like an electrified Leyden jar, only waited for the touch of a skillful hand to produce the explosion. *Common Sense* drew the spark. The winged words flew over the country and produced so rapid a change of opinion, that, in most cases, conservatives judged it useless to publish the answers they had prepared. One or two appeared. None attracted attention. About five months later, Congress declared independence; "as soon," Paine wrote, "as *Common Sense* could spread through such an extensive country." In a few years Paine asserted and believed that, had it not been for him, the Colonial government would have continued, and the United States would never have become a nation.

If we countermarch and get into the rear of Time, to borrow an expression from *The Crisis,* and, placing ourselves in January, 1776, look at *Common Sense* from that date, we may understand without much difficulty why it produced so great an impression. Paine, as later, when he brought out the *Rights of Man,* caused a chord to vibrate in the popular mind which was already strung to the exact point of tension. The publication was not only timely—it was novel. Paine founded a new school of pamphleteering. He was the first who wrote politics for the million. The learned political dissertations of Junius Brutus, Publicus, or Philanglus were guarded in expression, semimetaphysical in theory, and Johnsonian in style. They were relished by comparatively few readers; but the shrewd illustrations of *Common Sense,* the homely force of its statements, and its concise and muscular English stirred the mind of every class. Even Paine's coarse epithets, "Common Ruffian," "Royal Brute of Britain," and the like, which offended the taste of the leaders of the American party—for party-leaders were gentlemen in 1776—had as much weight with the rank-and-file as his arguments.

Paine became suddenly famous. General Charles Lee said "that he burst upon the world like Jove, in thunder." His acquaintance was sought by all who were of the true faith in Independence; and when, soon afterward, he visited New York, he carried with him letters from Dr. Franklin and John Adams, introducing him to the principal residents "as a citizen of the world, the celebrated author of **Common Sense**." Had he been a man of fortune or American-born, he might have reached a place in the foremost rank of the Fathers of the Country. But nativism was powerful, and position important at that time, as Lee and Gates and even Hamilton himself experienced. The signature **Common Sense,** Paine preserved through life. It became what our authorlings, who ought to know better, will persist in calling a *nom de plume*—a Yankee affectation, unknown to French idioms.

In the autumn of 1776, Paine joined the army as volunteer aide-de-camp to General Greene, and served through the gloomy campaign which opened with the loss of New York in September. He remained in the field until the army went into winter-quarters after the battles of Trenton and Princeton. It was not as a combatant that Paine did the States good service. He played the part of Tyrtaeus in prose—an adaptation of the old Greek lyrist to the eighteenth century and to British America—and cheered the soldiers, not with songs, but with essays, continuations of **Common Sense**. The first was written on the retreat from Fort Lee, and published under the name of **The Crisis,** on the 23d of December, when misfortune and severe weather had cast down the stoutest hearts. It began with the well-known phrase, "These are the times that try men's souls." "The summer soldier and the sunshine patriot will in this crisis shrink from the service of his country; but he that stands it now deserves the love and thanks of man and woman. . . . But after all," he continues, "matters might be worse. Howe has done very little. Fort Washington and Fort Lee were no loss to us. The retreat was admirably planned and conducted. General Washington is the right man for the place, 'with a mind that can even flourish upon care'." He closes with a cheerful sketch of the spirit and condition of the army, attacks the Tories, and appeals to the Colonies for union and contributions.

This **Crisis** produced the best effect at home; in England it had the honor of being burned by the hangman. The succeeding issues were brought out at irregular intervals, whenever the occasion seemed to demand Paine's attention; some of them not longer than a leader in a daily paper; others swollen to pamphlet dimensions. They were read by every corporal's guard in the army, and printed in every town of every State on brown or yellow paper; for white was rarely to be obtained. In their hours of despondency, the Colonists took consolation and courage from the **Crisis**. "Never," says a contemporary, "was a writer better calculated for the meridian under which he wrote, or who knew how to adapt himself more happily to every circumstance. . . . Even Cheetham admits, that to the army Paine's pen was an appendage almost as necessary and as formidable as its cannon."

The next campaign opened gloomily for the Colonies. The Tories felt certain of victory. In the political almanac of that party, 1777 was "*the year with* three gallows in it." The English held New York and ravaged the Jerseys on their way to Philadelphia. Howe issued a proclamation "commanding all congresses and committees to desist and cease from their treasonable doings," promising pardon to all who should come in and take the oath of allegiance. Paine met him with a **Crisis**. "By what means," he asked, "do you expect to conquer America? If you could not effect it in the summer, when our army was less than yours, nor in the winter, when we had none, how *are* you to do it? If you obtain possession of this city, [Philadelphia] you could do nothing with it but plunder it; it would be only an additional dead-weight on your hands. You have both an army and a country to contend with. You may march over the country, but you cannot hold it; if you attempt to garrison it, your army would be like a stream of water running to nothing. Even were our men to disperse, every man to his home, engaging to reassemble at some future day, you would be as much at a loss in that case as now. You would be afraid to send out your troops in detachments; when we returned, the work would be all to do." Paine then turns to those who, frightened by the proclamation, betrayed their country, and paints their folly and its punishment. In speaking of them, he calls upon the Pennsylvania Council of Safety to take into serious consideration the case of the Quakers, whose published protest against breaking off the "happy connection" seemed to Paine of a treasonable nature. "They have voluntarily read themselves out of the Continental meeting," he adds, with a humor, doubtless, little relished by the Friends, "and cannot hope to be restored to it again, but by payment and penitence."

In April, Paine was elected, on motion of John Adams, Secretary to the Congressional Committee on Foreign Affairs, with a salary of seventy dollars a month. When Philadelphia surrendered, he accompanied Congress in the flight to Lancaster. The day after the affair at Brandywine, a short **Crisis** appeared, explaining the accidents which had caused the defeat of the Continentals, and insisting that the good cause was safe, and that Howe's victories were no better than defeats. Paine was right. The Americans were gaining more ground in Northern New York than they had lost in Pennsylvania. Burgoyne, who,

> Unconscious of impending fates,
> Could push through woods, but not through Gates

had capitulated. The news reached Philadelphia on the 18th of October.

This winter ought to have closed the war. The alliance with France, Burgoyne's capture, two campaigns without useful results, Washington's admirable patience and management at Valley Forge, with starvation and mutiny in the ranks and disaffection to his person in the officers of the Gates faction, ought to have convinced every Englishman in America that the attempt to reduce the Colonies was now hopeless. Paine was so indignant with the reckless obstinacy of the British government that he conceived the idea of carrying the war into England with pen and paper—weapons he began to think invincible in his hands.

"If I could get over to England," he wrote to his old chief, General Greene, "without being known, and only remain in safety until I could get out a proclamation, I could open the eyes of the country with respect to the madness and stupidity of its government." Greene had no confidence in the success of this appeal to the English people, and advised Paine not to attempt it.

In the meantime the French fleet had arrived, bringing M. Gérard, the first foreign minister to the United States, and with him trouble to Thomas Paine. It is well known that the French government employed Beaumarchais, the author of the *Barber of Seville,* as their agent to furnish secret supplies to the American insurgents, and that Beaumarchais imagined a firm, Rodrigue Hortalez & Co., who shipped to the United Colonies munitions of war furnished by the King, and were to receive return cargoes of tobacco, to keep up mercantile appearances. Silas Deane, a member of Congress from Connecticut, represented the Americans in the business. In 1777, Congress, out of patience with Deane for his foolish contracts with foreign officers, recalled him. He returned, bringing with him a claim of Beaumarchais for the cargoes already shipped to the United States. As Deane could produce no vouchers, and Arthur Lee had cautioned Congress against his demands, the claim was laid on the table until the vouchers should be presented.

Deane, confiding in the support of his numerous friends, appealed to the public in a newspaper. Congress bore this indignity so amiably—refusing, indeed, by a small majority to take notice of it—that Henry Laurens, the president, who had laid Deane's appeal before them for their action, resigned in disgust, and was succeeded by John Jay. But Paine, whose position as Foreign Secretary enabled him to know that the supplies had come from the French government, and not from Beaumarchais, answered Deane in several newspaper articles, entitled **"Common Sense to the Public on Mr. Deane's Affairs."** In these he exposed the whole claim with his usual unmitigated directness. M. Gérard immediately announced officially that Paine's papers were false, and called upon Congress to declare them so and to pay the claim. Party feeling ran high on this question—a foreshadowing of the French and English factions fifteen years later. Congress passed a resolution in censure of Paine. Mr. Laurens moved

that he be heard in his defense; the motion was lost, and Paine resigned his office. A motion from the Deane party to refuse his resignation and to discharge him was also lost, the Northern States voting generally in Paine's favor. His resignation was then accepted.

As the French government persisted in denying that the King had furnished any supplies, Congress admitted the debt, and in October, 1779, drew bills on Dr. Franklin in favor of Beaumarchais, for two millions and a half of francs, at three years' sight. Beaumarchais negotiated the bills, built a fine hotel, and lived *en prince.* But neither he nor Deane was satisfied. They still demanded another million.

We have no doubt that Paine was correct in his facts, however injudicious it may have been to use them in his position. Deane's best friends gave him up, before many years had passed. M. de Loménie, in his interesting sketch of Beaumarchais, has tried hard to show the justice of his demands on the United States, but without much success. He does not attempt to explain how Beaumarchais, notoriously penniless in 1775, should have had in 1777 a good claim for three millions' worth of goods furnished. The American public looked upon Paine as a victim to state policy, and his position with his friends did not suffer at all in consequence of his disclosures. Personally, he exulted in his conduct to the end of his life, and took pleasure in watching and recording Deane's disreputable career and miserable end. "As he rose, like a rocket, so he fell like a stick," a metaphor which has passed into a proverb, was imagined by Paine to meet Deane's case. The immediate consequence of Paine's resignation was to oblige him to hire himself out as clerk to an attorney in Philadelphia. In his office, Paine earned his daily bread by copying law-papers until he was appointed clerk to the Assembly of Pennsylvania.

Early in May, 1780, while the Assembly of Pennsylvania was receiving petitions from all parts of the State, praying for exemption from taxes, a letter was brought to the speaker from General Washington, and read to the House by Paine as clerk. It stated simply that the army was in the utmost distress from the want of every necessary which men could need and yet retain life; and that the symptoms of discontent and mutiny were so marked that the General dreaded the event of every hour. "When the letter was read," says Paine, "I observed a despairing silence in the House. Nobody spoke for a considerable time. At length a member, of whose fortitude I had a high opinion, rose. 'If,' said he, 'the account in that letter is true, and we are in the situation there represented, it appears to me in vain to contend the matter any longer. We may as well give up first as last.' A more cheerful member endeavored to dissipate the gloom of the House, and moved an adjournment, which was carried."

Paine, who knew that the Assembly had neither money nor credit, felt that the voluntary aid of individuals could alone be relied upon in this conjuncture. He accordingly wrote a letter to a friend in Philadelphia, a man of influence, explaining the urgency of affairs, and inclosed five hundred dollars, the amount of the salary due him as clerk, as his contribution towards a relief fund. The Philadelphian called a meeting at the coffee-house, read Paine's communication, and proposed a subscription, heading the list with two hundred pounds in good money. Mr. Robert Morris put his name down for the same sum. Three hundred thousand pounds, Pennsylvania currency, were raised; and it was resolved to establish a bank with the fund for the relief of the army. This plan was carried out with the best results. After Morris was appointed Superintendent of Finances, he developed it into the Bank of North America, which was incorporated both by act of Congress and by the State of Pennsylvania. Paine followed up his letter by a *Crisis Extraordinary*. Admitting that the war costs the Colonists a very large sum, he shows that it is trifling, compared with the burdens the English have to bear. For this reason it would be less expensive for the Americans to raise almost any amount to drive the English out than to submit to them and come under their system of taxation.

Our ancestors read the *Crisis Extraordinary,* and understood every word of it, we may be sure. Paine's lucidity of statement is never more remarkable than when he handles financial questions. But conviction did not work its way down to the pocket. Few men gave who could avoid it, and each State appeared more fearful of paying, by accident, a larger sum than its neighbor, than of the success of the British arms. Congress, finding it at last almost impossible to get money or even provisions at home, resolved to resort again to the financial expedient which has proved so often profitable to this country, namely, to borrow in Europe. Colonel Laurens, son of the late President of Congress, was appointed commissioner to negotiate an annual loan from France of a million sterling during the continuation of the war. Paine accompanied him at his request.

They sailed in February, 1781, and were graciously received by King Louis, who promised them six millions of livres as a present and ten millions as a loan. In little more than ten years, the American secretary, who stands respectfully and unnoticed in the presence of his Majesty of France, will sit as one of his judges in a trial for life! Is there anything more wonderful in the transmutations of fiction than this? Meanwhile, the future member of the Convention, as little dreaming of what was in store for him as the King, sailed for Boston with his principal. They carried with them two millions and a half in silver—a great help to Washington in the movement southward, which ended with the capitulation of Yorktown. While in Paris, Paine was again seized with the desire of invading England, incognito, with a pamphlet in his pocket, to open the eyes of the people. But Colonel Laurens thought no better of this scheme than General Greene, and brought his secretary safely home again.

Cornwallis had surrendered, and it was evident that the war could not last much longer. The danger past, the Colonial aversion to pay Union expenses and to obey the orders of Congress became daily stronger. The want of a *Crisis,* as a corrective medicine for the body politic, was so much felt, that Robert Morris, with the knowledge and approbation of Washington, requested Paine to take pen in hand again, offering him, if his private affairs made it necessary, a salary for his services. Paine consented. A *Crisis* appeared which produced a most salutary effect. This was followed a few days later by another, in which a passage occurs which may be quoted as a specimen of Paine's rhetorical powers. A rumor was abroad that England was treating with France for a separate peace. Paine finds it impossible to express his contempt for the baseness of the ministry who could attempt to sow dissension between such faithful allies. "We sometimes experience sensations to which language is not equal. The conception is too bulky to be born alive, and in the torture of thinking we stand dumb. Our feelings, imprisoned by their magnitude, find no way out; and in the struggle of expression every finger tries to be a tongue." It will be difficult to describe better the struggle of an indignant soul with an insufficient vocabulary.

When peace was proclaimed, Paine, the untiring advocate of independence, had a right to print his "Io Paean." The last *Crisis* announces "that the times that tried men's souls were over, and the greatest and completest revolution the world ever knew gloriously and happily accomplished." "America need never be ashamed to tell her birth, nor relate the stages by which she rose to empire." But it is to the future he bids her look, rather than to the past. "The remembrance of what is past, if it operates rightly, must inspire her with the most laudable of all ambition, that of adding to the fair fame she began with." "She is now descending to the scenes of quiet and domestic life,—not beneath the cypress shade of disappointment, but to enjoy in her own land and under her own vine the sweet of her labors and the reward of her toil. In this situation may she never forget that a fair national reputation is of as much importance as independence,—that it possesses a charm that wins upon the world, and makes even enemies civil,—that it gives a dignity which is often superior to power, and commands reverence where pomp and splendor fail." As indispensable to a future of prosperity and dignity, he warmly recommends the Union. "I ever feel myself hurt," he says, "when I hear the Union, that great

Palladium of our liberty and safety, the least irreverently spoken of. It is the most sacred thing in the Constitution of America, and that which every man should be most proud and tender of." Thus he anticipated by seventy-five years our "Union-savers" of 1856, few of whom dreamed that their pet phrases, or something very like them, originated with Thomas Paine.

Frederick Sheldon (essay date 1859)

SOURCE: "Thomas Paine in England and in France," in *The Atlantic Monthly,* Vol. IV, No. XXVI, December, 1859, pp. 690-709.

[*In the following essay (from December of 1859) Sheldon charts the first part of Paine's career as a pamphleteer. Hailing Paine as a primary force in the American move toward independence, Sheldon wrote against popular opinion of his day, which still tended to dismiss Paine's importance and integrity.*]

[While he was in England in the late 1780s, Paine's] soul was engrossed by the contemplation of the wonderful event which was daily developing itself in France. Bankruptcy had brought on the crisis. In August, 1788, the interest was not paid on the national debt, and Brienne [Archbishop of Toulouse] resigned. The States-General met in May of the next year; in June they declared themselves a national assembly, and commenced work upon a constitution under the direction of Sièyes, who well merited the epithet, "indefatigable constitution-grinder," applied to Paine by Cobbett. Not long after, the attempted *coup d'état* of Louis XVI. failed, the Bastille was demolished, and the political Saturnalia of the French people began.

It is evident, that, in the beginning, Paine did not aspire to be the political Prometheus of England. He rather looked to the Whig party and to Mr. Burke as the leaders in such a movement. As for himself, a veteran reformer from another hemisphere, he was willing to serve as a volunteer in the campaign against the oppressors of mankind. He had adopted for his motto, "Where liberty is not, there is my country,"— a negative variation of Franklin's saying, which suited his tempestuous character. As he flitted to and fro across the Channel, observing with sharp, eager eyes the progress of "principles" in France, gradually there arose in his mind the thought that poor, old, worn-out England might be regenerated by these new methods. "The French are doubling their strength," he wrote, "by allying, if it may be so expressed, (for it is difficult to express a new idea by old terms,) the majesty of the sovereign with the majesty of the nation."

Paris swarmed with enthusiastic "friends of humanity," English, Scotch, and Irish. Among them Paine naturally took a foremost position, being an authority in revolutionary matters, and a man who had principles on the subject of government. In spite of his contempt of titles, he wrote himself, "Secretary for Foreign Affairs to the Congress of the United States," slightly improving upon the office he had actually held, to suit the sound to European capacity,—showing that in this, likewise, he possessed a genuine American element of character. Lafayette thought much of him, used his pen freely, and listened to his advice. The Marquis, warm-hearted, honest, but endowed with little judgment and a womanish vanity, was trying to make himself the Washington of a French federative republic, and felt happy in having secured the experienced services of Mr. Paine. He wrote to his great master,— "*Common Sense* is writing a book for you, and there you will see a part of my adventures. Liberty is springing up around us in the other parts of Europe, and I am encouraging it by all the means in my power." Paine was in Paris when the Bastille was taken. Lafayette placed the key in his hands, to be transmitted to Washington. Paine wrote to the President, "That the principles of America opened the Bastille is not to be doubted, and therefore the key comes to the right place." Washington, returning his thanks to Paine for the key, added,—"It will give you pleasure to learn that the new government answers its purposes as well as could have been reasonably expected." Yes! and still answers reasonable purposes to this day. In the mean while dozens of French constitutions, "perfections of human wisdom," have been invented, set up, and crushed to atoms. . . .

Before 1789, there was no particular discontent in England. Some talk there had been of reform in the representation, and the usual complaints of the burden of taxation. The Dissenters had been trying to get the Corporation and Test Acts repealed, without much success. But nothing beyond occasional meetings and petitions to Parliament would have occurred, had it not been for the explosion in France, then, as since, the political powder-magazine of Europe. The Whig party had seen with pleasure the beginning of the French reforms. Paine, who had partaken of Mr. Burke's hospitality at Beaconsfield, wrote to him freely from Paris, assuring him that everything was going on right; that little inconveniences, the necessary consequences of pulling down and building up, might arise; but that these were much less than ought to be expected; and that a national convention in England would be the best plan of regenerating the nation. Christie, a foolish Scotchman, and Baron Clootz (soon to become Anacharsis) also wrote to Burke in the same vein. Their communications affected his mind in a way they little expected. Mr. Burke had lost all faith in any good result from the blind, headlong rush of the Revolution, and was appalled at the toleration, or rather, sympathy, shown in England, for the riots, outrages, and murders of the Parisian rabble. He began writing the *Reflections,* as a warning to his countrymen. He was led to enlarge the work by some remarks made by Fox and Sheridan in the House of Commons; and more particularly by some passages in a sermon preached at the Old Jewry by Dr. Price. Eleven years before, this scientific divine, by a resolution of the American Congress, had been invited to consider himself an American citizen, and to furnish the rebellious Colonists with his assistance in regulating their finances. He had disregarded this flattering summons. Full of zeal for "humanity," he eagerly accepted the request of the Revolution Society to deliver their anniversary sermon. In this discourse, the Doctor, the fervor of whose sentiments had increased with age, maintained the right of the nation "to cashier the king," choose a new ruler, and frame a government for itself. The sermon and the congratulatory addresses it provoked were published by the society and industriously circulated.

Mr. Burke's well-known *Reflections* appeared in October, 1790. The book was hailed with delight by the conservatives of England. Thirteen thousand copies were sold and disseminated. It was a sowing of the dragon's teeth. Every copy brought out some radical, armed with speech or pamphlet. Among a vulgar and forgotten crowd of declaimers, the harebrained Lord Stanhope, Mary Wolstonecraft, who afterward wrote a "Vindication of the Rights of Women," and the violent Catharine Macaulay came forward to enter the ring against the great Mr. Burke. Dr. Priestley, Unitarian divine, discoverer of oxygen gas, correspondent of Dr. Franklin, afterward mobbed in Birmingham, and self-exiled to Pennsylvania, fiercely backed Dr. Price, and maintained that the French Revolution would result "in the enlargement of liberty, the melioration of society, and the increase of virtue and happiness." The "Vindiciæ Gallicæ" brought into notice Mr. Mackintosh, an opponent whom Burke did not consider beneath him. But the champion was Thomas Paine. At the White Bear, Piccadilly, Paine's favorite lounge, where Romney, who painted a good portrait of him, Lord Edward Fitzgerald, Colonel Oswald, Horne Tooke, and others of that set of clever, impracticable reformers used to meet, there had been talk of the blow Mr. Burke was preparing to strike, and Paine had promised his friends to ward it off and to return it. He set himself to work in the Red-Lion Tavern, at Islington, and in three months, Part the First of the *Rights of Man* was ready for the press. Here a delay occurred. The printer who had undertaken the job came to a stop before certain treasonable passages, and declined proceeding farther. This caused the loss of a month. At last, Jordan, of Fleet Street, brought it out on the 13th of March, 1791. No publication in Great Britain, not Junius nor Wilkes's No. 45, had produced such an effect. All England was divided into those who, like Cruger of Bristol, said "Ditto to Mr. Burke," and those who swore by Thomas Paine. "It is a false, wicked, and seditious libel," shouted loyal gentlemen. "It abounds in unanswerable truths, and principles of the purest

morality and benevolence; it has no object in view but the happiness of mankind," answered the reformers. "He is the scavenger of rebellion and infidelity."—"Say, rather, 'the Apostle of Freedom, whose heart is a perpetual bleeding fountain of philanthropy.'" The friends of the government carried Paine in effigy, with a pair of stays under his arms, and burned the figure in the streets. The friends of humanity added a new verse to the national hymn, and sung,—

> God save great Thomas Paine,
> His Rights of Man proclaim
> From pole to pole!

This pamphlet, which excited Englishmen of seventy years ago to such a pitch of angry and scornful contention, may be read safely now. Time has taken the sting from it. It is written in that popular style which was Paine's extraordinary gift. He practised the maxim of Aristotle,—although probably he had never heard of it,—"Think like the wise, and speak like the common people." Fox said of the *Rights of Man*, "It seems as clear and as simple as the first rule in arithmetic." Therein lay its strength. Paine knew exactly what he wanted to say, and exactly how to say it. His positions may be wrong,—no doubt frequently are wrong,—but so clearly, keenly, and above all so boldly stated, and backed by such shrewd arguments and such apposite illustrations, that it is difficult not to yield to his common-sense view of the question he is discussing. His plain and perspicuous style is often elegant. He may sometimes be coarse and rude, but it is in the thought rather than in the expression. It is true, that, in the heat of conflict, he is apt to lose his temper and break out into the bitter violence of his French associates; but even the scientific and reverend Priestley "called names,"—apostate, renegade, scoundrel. This rough energy added to his popularity with the middle and the lower classes, and made him doubly distasteful to his opponents. Paine, who thought all revolutions alike, and all good, could not understand why Burke, who had upheld the Americans, should exert his whole strength against the French, unless he were "a traitor to human nature." Burke did Paine equal injustice. He thought him unworthy of any refutation but the pillory. In public, he never mentioned his name. But his opinion, and, perhaps, a little soreness of feeling, may be seen in this extract from a letter to Sir William Smith:—

> He [Paine] is utterly incapable of comprehending his subject. He has not even a moderate portion of learning of any kind. He has learned the instrumental part of literature, without having ever made a previous preparation of study for the use of it. Paine has nothing more than what a man, whose audacity makes him careless of logical consequences and his total want of honor makes indifferent to political consequences, can very easily write.

The radicals thought otherwise. They drank Mr. Burke's health with "thanks to him for the discussion he had provoked." And the student of history, who may read Paine's opening sketch of the French Revolution, written to refute Burke's narrative of the same events, will not deny Paine's complete success. He will even meet with sentences that Burke might have composed. For instance: Paine ridicules, as Quixotic, the fine passage in the "Reflections on the Decay of Chivalry"; and adds, "Mr. Burke's mind is above the homely sorrows of the vulgar. He can only feel for a king or for a queen. The countless victims of tyranny have no place in his sympathies. He is not affected by the reality of distress touching upon his heart, but by the showy resemblance of it. He pities the plumage, but forgets the dying bird."

The French constitution,—"a fabric of government which time could not destroy and the latest posterity would admire." This was the boast of the National Assembly, echoed by the English clubs. Even Mr. Fox, as late as April, 1791, misled by his own magniloquence, spoke of it as "the most stupendous and glorious edifice of liberty which had been erected on the foundation of human integrity in any time or country." Paine heartily concurred with him. Such a constitution as this, he said, is needed in England. There is no hope of it from Parliament. Indeed, Parliament, if it desired reforms, could not make them; it has not the legal right. A national convention, fresh from the people, is indispensable. Then, *reculant pour mieux sauter,* Paine goes back to the origin of man,—a journey often undertaken by the political philosophers of that day. He describes his natural rights,—defines society as a compact,—declares that no generation has a right to bind its successors, (a doctrine which Mr. Jefferson, and some foolish people after him, thought a self-evident truth,)—hence, no family has a right to take possession of a throne. An hereditary rule is as great an absurdity as an hereditary professorship of mathematics,—a place supposed by Dr. Franklin to exist in some German university. Paine grew bolder as he advanced: "If monarchy is a useless thing, why is it kept up anywhere? and if a necessary thing, how can it be dispensed with?" This is a pretty good specimen of one of Paine's dialectical methods. Here is another: The French constitution says, that the right of war and of peace is in the nation. "Where else should it reside, but in those who are to pay the expense? In England, the right is said to reside in a metaphor shown at the Tower for sixpence or a shilling." Dropping the crown, he turned upon the aristocracy and the Church, and tore them. He begged Lafayette's pardon for addressing him as Marquis. Titles are but nicknames. Nobility and no ability are synonymous. "In all the vocabulary of Adam, you will find no such thing as a duke or a count." The French had established universal liberty of conscience, which gave rise to the following Painean statement: "With respect to what are called denominations of religion,—if every one is left to judge of his own religion, there is no such thing as a religion which is wrong; but if they are to judge of each other's religion, there is no such thing as a religion that is right;—and therefore all the world is right or all the world is wrong." The next is better: "Religion is man bringing to his Maker the fruits of his heart; and though these fruits may differ from each other, like the fruits of the earth, the grateful tribute of every one is accepted."

To encounter an antagonist like Burke, and to come off with credit, might stimulate moderate vanity into public self-exposure; but in Paine vanity was the besetting weakness. It was now swollen by success and flattery into magnificent proportions. Franklin says, that, "when we forbear to praise ourselves, we make a sacrifice to the pride or to the envy of others." Paine did not hesitate to mortify both these failings in his fellow-men. He praises himself with the simplicity of an Homeric hero before a fight. He introduces himself, without a misgiving, almost in the words of Pius Æneas,—

> Sum Thomas Paine,
> Famâ super æthera notus.

"With all the inconveniences of early life against me, I am proud to say, that, with a perseverance undismayed by difficulties, a disinterestedness that compels respect, I have not only contributed to raise a new empire in the world, founded on a new system of government, but I have arrived at an eminence in political literature, the most difficult of all lines to succeed and excel in, which aristocracy, with all its aids, has not been able to reach or to rival." "I possess," he wrote in the Second Part of the ***Rights of Man***, "more of what is called consequence in the world than any one of Mr. Burke's catalogue of aristocrats." Paine sincerely believed himself to be an adept who had found in the rights of man the *materia prima* of politics, by which error and suffering might be transmuted into happiness and truth. A second Columbus, but greater than the Genoese! Christopher had discovered a new world, it is true, but Thomas had discovered the means of making a new world out of the old. About this time, Dumont, the Benthamite, travelled with him from Paris to London. Dumont was irritated with "his incredible *amour-propre* and his presumptuous self-conceit." "He was mad with vanity." "The man was a caricature of the vainest of Frenchmen. He believed that his book on the ***Rights of Man*** might supply the place of all the books that had ever been written. If it was in his power, he would destroy all the libraries in the world without hesitation, in order to root out the errors of which they were the deposit, and so recommence by the ***Rights of Man*** a new chain of ideas and principles." Thus Paine and his wild friends had reached the point of folly in the reformer's scale, and, like so many of their class since, made the fatal mistake of supposing that the old world knew nothing.

When Dumont fell in with Paine, he was returning from a flying visit to Paris, invigorated by the bracing air of French freedom. He had seen Pope Pius burned in effigy in the Palais Royal, and the poor King brought back a prisoner from Varennes,—a cheerful spectacle to the friend of humanity. He was on his way to be present at a dinner given in London on the 14th of July, to commemorate the taking of the Bastille; but the managers of the festivity thought it prudent that he should not attend. He wrote, soon after, the address ready by Horne Tooke to the meeting of the 20th of August, at the Thatched House tavern. So enlightened were the doctrines set forth in this paper, that the innkeeper declined receiving Mr. Tooke and his friends on any subsequent occasion. On the 4th of November, he assisted at the customary celebration of the Fifth by the Revolution Society, and gave, for his toast, *The Revolution of the World.*

Meanwhile, Paine had reloaded his piece, and was now ready for another shot at kings, lords, and commons. A thousand guineas were offered for the copyright and refused. He declined to treat as a merchantable commodity principles of such importance to mankind. His plan was, to publish Part the Second on the day of the opening of Parliament; but Chapman, the printer, became frightened, like his predecessor, at a treasonable paragraph, and refused to go on. A fortnight passed before work was resumed, and the essay did not appear until the 16th of February, 1792. It combined, according to the author, "principles and practice." Part the First was now fully expounded, and enlarged by a scheme for diminishing the taxes and improving the condition of the poor, by making weekly allowances to young children, aged people, travelling workmen, and disbanded soldiers. This project of Paine, stated with the mathematical accuracy which was a characteristic of his mind, sprang from the same source as the thousand Utopianisms which form the ludicrous side of the terrible French Revolution.

Part the First was dedicated to Washington; Part the Second bore the name of Lafayette. It is evident, from the second dedication, that Paine had kept pace with the railway speed of the Revolution, and had far outstripped the Marquis, who was not born to lead, or even to understand the period he attempted to direct. The foremost men of 1792 had no time to wait;— "Mankind are always ripe enough to understand their true interest," said Paine; adding words which seemed to quiet Englishmen of fearful significance:—

"I do not believe that monarchy and aristocracy will continue seven years longer in any of the enlightened countries of Europe."—"When France shall be sur- rounded with revolutions, she will be in peace and safety."—"From what we can learn, all Europe may form but one great republic, and man be free of the whole."—"It is only a certain service that any man can perform in the state, and the service of any individual in the routine of office can never exceed the value of ten thousand pounds a year."—"I presume that no man in his sober senses will compare the character of any of the kings of Europe with that of George Washington. Yet in France and in England the expenses of the Civil List only for the support of one man are eight times greater than the whole expense of the Federal government of America."—"The time is not very distant when England will laugh at itself for sending to Holland, Hanover, Zell, or Brunswick, for men, at the expense of a million a year, who understand neither her laws, her language, or her interest, and whose capacities would scarcely have fitted them for the office of a parish constable. If government could be trusted to such hands, it must be some easy and simple thing indeed, and materials fit for all the purposes may be found in every town and village in England."

Here is treasonable matter enough, surely; and no wonder that Mr. Chapman judged it prudent to stop his press.

Paine sent fifty copies to Washington; and wrote to him that sixteen thousand had been printed in England, and four editions in Ireland,—the second of ten thousand copies. Thirty thousand copies were distributed by the clubs, at their own expense, among the poor. Six months after the appearance of the **Second Part,** Paine sent the Society for Constitutional Information a thousand pounds, which he had received from the sale of the book. He then gave up the copyright to the public. The circulation of this tract was prodigious. The original edition had been printed in the same form as Burke's "Reflections," in order that the antidote might be bound up with the bane. The high price preventing many from purchasing, Paine got out a cheap edition which was retailed at sixpence all over England and Scotland. It is said that at least one hundred thousand copies were sold, besides the large number distributed gratuitously. An edition was published in the United States. It was translated into French by Dr. Lanthenas, a member of the National Convention, and into German by C. F. Krämer. Upon English readers of a certain class it retained a hold for many years. In 1820, Carlile, the bookseller, said, that in the preceding three years he had sold five thousand copies of the *Rights of Man.* Perhaps Cobbett's resurrection of the bones of the prophet brought the book into fashion again at that time. It may yet be read in England; but in this country, where a citizen feels that his rights are anything he may choose to claim, it is certainly a superfluous publication, and seldom met with.

In England, in 1792, Burke and Paine revived the royalist and republican parties, which had lain dormant since 1688. A new body of men, the manufacturing, entered the political field on the republican side. The contest was embittered not only by the anger of antagonism, but by the feeling of class. A radical of Paine's school was considered by good society as a pestilent blackguard, unworthy of a gentleman's notice,—much as an Abolitionist is looked down upon nowadays by the American "Chivalry." But the strife was confined to meetings, resolutions, and pamphlets. Few riots took place; none of much importance. The gentlemen of England have never wanted the courage or the strength to take care of themselves.

The political clubs were the principal centres of agitation. There were two particularly active on the liberal side: the Revolution Society, originally founded to commemorate the Revolution of 1688, and the Society for Constitutional Information, established for the purpose of bringing about a reform in the representation. But the revolutionary changes in France had quickened their ideas, and had given them a taste for stronger and more rapid measures. They now openly "resolved" that England was "a prey to an arbitrary King, a senile Peerage, a corrupt House of Commons, and a rapacious and intolerant Clergy." A third club, the Corresponding Society, was younger and more violent, with branches and affiliations all over England on the Jacobins' plan, and in active correspondence with that famous institution. The middle and lower classes in manufacturing towns, precursors of the Chartists of 1846, belonged to this society. Their avowed objects were annual parliaments and universal suffrage; but many members were in favor of a national convention and a republic. The tone of all three societies became French; they used a jargon borrowed from the other side of the Channel. They sent deputations to the National Convention, expressing their wish to adopt the republican form in England, and their hope of success. The Corresponding Society even sent addresses of congratulation after the massacres of September. Joel Barlow, the American, a man of the Paine genus, without his talent or honesty of purpose, went as Commissioner of the Society for Constitutional Information to the Convention,—carrying with him an address which reads like a translation from the French, and a thousand pair of shoes, with the promise of a thousand pair a week for six weeks to come.

On the other side there were, of course, numerous Tory associations, counter clubs, as violent as their republican antagonists, whose loyal addresses to the throne were duly published in the Gazette.

The probability of a revolution now became a subject of general discussion. Government, at last convinced that England, in the words of Mr. Burke, "abounded in factious men, who would readily plunge the country into blood and confusion for the sake of establishing the fanciful systems they were enamored of," determined to act with vigor. A royal proclamation was issued against seditious writings. Paine received notice that he would be prosecuted in the King's Bench. He came immediately to London, and found that Jordan, his publisher, had already been served with a summons, but, having no stomach for a contest with the authorities, had compromised the affair with the Solicitor of the Treasury by agreeing to appear and plead guilty. Such pusillanimity was beneath the mark of Paine's enthusiasm. He wrote to M⁽ᶜ⁾Donald, the Attorney-General, that he, Paine, had no desire to avoid any prosecution which the authorship of one of the most useful books ever offered to mankind might bring upon him; and that he should do the defence full justice, as well for the sake of the nation as for that of his own reputation. He wound up a long letter by the very ungenerous insinuation, that Mr. Burke, not being able to answer the *Rights of Man*, had advised legal proceedings.

The societies, checked for a moment by the blow struck at them, soon renewed their exertions. The sale of the *Rights of Man* became more extended than ever. Paine said that the proclamation served him for an advertisement. The Manchester and Sheffield branches of the Constitutional Society voted unanimously addresses of thanks to him for his essay, "a work of the highest importance to every nation under heaven." The newspapers were full of speeches, votes, resolutions, on the same subject. Every mail was laden with congratulations to the Jacobins on the coming time,—

> When France shall reign, and laws be all repealed.

To the Radicals, the Genius of Liberty seemed to be hovering over England; and Thomas Paine was the harbinger to prepare his way.

Differences of opinion, when frequently expressed in hard words, commonly lead to hard blows; and the conservative classes of England were not men to hold their hands when they thought the proper time had come to strike. But the party which looked up to Paine as its apostle was not as numerous as it appeared to be from the noise it made. There is never a sufficiently large number of reckless zealots in England to do much mischief,—one of the greatest proofs of the inherent good sense of that people. Dr. Gall's saying, *"Tout ce qui est ultrà est bête,"* is worth his whole phrenological system. Measures and doctrines had now been pushed so far that a numerous and influential body of liberals called a halt,—the prelude of a union with the government forces.

Luckily for Paine, his French admirers stepped in at this critical moment to save him. Mons. Audibert, a municipal officer from Calais, came to announce to him that he was elected to the National Convention for that department. He immediately proceeded to Dover with his French friend. In Dover, the collector of the customs searched their pockets as well as their portmanteaus, in spite of many angry protestations. Finally their papers were returned to them, and they were allowed to embark. Paine was just in time; an order to detain him arrived about twenty minutes after his embarkation.

The trial came on before Lord Kenyon. Erskine appeared for the absent defendant. The Attorney-General used, as his brief, a foolish letter he had received from Paine at Calais, read it to the jury, made a few remarks, and rested his case. The jury found Paine guilty without leaving their seats. Sentence of outlawry was passed upon him. Safe in France, he treated the matter as a capital joke. Some years later he found that it had a disagreeable meaning in it.

The prophet had been translated to another sphere of revolutionary unrest. His influence gradually died away. He dwindled into a mere name. "But the fact remains," to use his own words, "and will hereafter be placed in the history of extraordinary things, that a pamphlet should be produced by an individual, unconnected with any sect or party, and almost a stranger in the land, that should completely frighten a whole government, and that in the midst of its triumphant security."

Paine might have published his "principles" his life long without troubling many subjects of King George, had it not been for their combination with "practice" in France,—whither let us now follow him.

When he landed at Calais, the guard turned out and presented arms; a grand salute was fired; the officer in command embraced him and presented him with the national cockade; a good-looking *citoyenne* asked leave to pin it on his hat, expressing the hope of her compatriots that he would continue his exertions in favor of liberty. Enthusiastic acclamations followed,— a grand chorus of *Vive Thomas Paine!* The crowd escorted him to Dessein's hotel, in the Rue de l'Égalité, formerly Rue du Roi, and shouted under his windows. At the proper time he was conducted to the Town Hall. The municipality were assembled to bestow the *accolade fraternelle* upon their representative. M. le Maire made a speech, which Audibert, who still had Paine in charge, translated. Paine laid his hand on his heart, bowed, and assured the municipality that his life should be devoted to their service. In the evening, the club held a meeting in the Salle des Minimes. The hall was jammed. Paine was seated beside the President, under a bust of Mirabeau, surmounted by the flags of France, England, and the United States. More addresses, compliments, protestations, and frantic cries of *Vive Thomas Paine!* The *séance* was adjourned to

the church, to give those who could not obtain admission into the Club Hall an opportunity to look at their famous representative. The next evening Paine went to the theatre. The state-box had been prepared for him. The house rose and *vivaed* as he entered.

When Calais had shouted itself hoarse, Paine travelled towards Paris. The towns he traversed on the road thither received him with similar honors. From the capital he addressed a letter of thanks to his fellow-citizens. Although he sat for Calais in the Convention, he had been chosen by three other departments. Priestley was a candidate for Paris, but was beaten by Marat, a doctor of another description. He was, however, duly elected in the department L'Orne, but never took his seat. Paine and Baron Clootz were the only foreigners in the Convention. Another stranger, of political celebrity out of doors, styled himself American as well as Paine,—*Fournier l'Américain,* a mulatto from the West Indies, whose complexion was not considered "incompatible with freedom" in France,—a violent and blood-thirsty fellow, who shot at Lafayette on the *dixsept Juillet,* narrowly missing him,—led an attacking party against the Tuileries on the *dix Août,* and escaped the guillotine to be transported by Bonaparte.

In Paris, Paine was already a personage well known to all the leading men,—a great republican luminary, "foreign benefactor of the species," who had commenced the revolution in America, was making one in England, and was willing to help make one in France. His English works, translated by Lanthenas, a friend of Robespierre and co-editor with Brissot of the "Patriote Français," had earned for him the dignity of *citoyen Français,*—an honor which he shared with Mackintosh, Dr. Price, the Priestleys, father and son, and David Williams. He had furnished Lafayette with a good deal of his revolutionary rhetoric, had contributed to the Monthly Review of the Girondists and the "Chronique de Paris," and had written a series of articles in defence of representative government, which Condorcet had translated for him. Paine was a man of one idea in politics; a federal republic, on the American plan, was the only system of government he believed in, and the only one he wished to see established in France. Lafayette belonged to this school. So did Condorcet, Pétion, Buzot, and others of less note. Under Paine's direction they formed a republican club, which met at Condorcet's house. This federal theory cost them dear. In 1793, it was treason against the *une et indivisible,* and was punished accordingly.

After the flight to Varennes, Paine openly declared that the King was "a political superfluity." This was true enough. The people had lost all respect for the man and for the office. None so base as to call him King. He was only the *pouvoir exécutif,* or more commonly still, *Monsieur Veto.* Achille Duchâtelet, a young officer who had served in America, called upon Dumont to get him to translate a proclamation drawn up by Paine, urging the people to seize the opportunity and establish a republic. It was intended to be a **Common Sense** for France. Dumont refusing to have anything to do with it, some other translator was found. It appeared on the walls of the capital with Duchâtelet's name affixed. The placard was torn down by order of the Assembly and attracted little attention. The French were not quite ready for the republic, although gradually approaching it. They seemed to take a pleasure in playing awhile with royalty before exterminating it.

The Abbé Sièyes was a warm monarchist. He wrote in the "Moniteur," that he could prove, "on every hypothesis," that men were more free in a monarchy than in a republic. Paine gave notice in Brissot's paper, that he would demolish the Abbé utterly in fifty pages, and show the world that a constitutional monarchy was a nullity,—concluding with the usual flourish about "weeping for the miseries of humanity," "hell of despotism," etc., etc., the fashionable doxology of patriotic authors in that day. Sièyes announced his readiness to meet the great Paine in conflict. This passage of pens was interrupted by the publication of Part Second of the **Rights of Man**. Before Paine returned to Paris, the mob had settled the question for the time, so far as the French nation were concerned.

Paine had also taken a leading part in some of the politico-theatrical entertainments then so frequent in the streets of Paris. At the festival of the Federation, in July, 1790, when Clootz led a "deputation" of the *genre humain*, consisting of an English editor and some oolored persons in fancy dresses, Paine and Paul Jones headed the American branch of humanity and carried the stars and stripes. Not long after, Paine appears again marshalling a deputation of English and Americans, who waited upon the Jacobin Club to fraternize. Suitable preparations had been made by the club for this solemn occasion. The three national flags, united, were placed in the hall over the busts of Dr. Franklin and Dr. Price. Robespierre himself received the generous strangers; but most of the talking seems to have been done by a fervid *citoyenne*, who took *la parole* and kept it. "Let a cry of joy rush through all Europe and fly to America," said she. "But hark! Philadelphia and all its countries repeat, like us, *Vive la Liberté!*" To see a man of Paine's clear sense and simple tastes pleased by such flummery as this shows us how difficult it is not to be affected by the spirit of the generation we live with. How could he have supposed that the new heaven upon earth of his dreams would ever be constructed out of such pinchbeck materials?

It was now the year 1. of the Republic. The *dix Août* was over, the King a prisoner in the Temple. Lafayette, in his attempt to imitate his "master," Washington, had succeeded no better than the magician's apprentice, who knew how to raise the demon, but not how to manage him when he appeared. He had gone down before the revolution, and was now *le traître Lafayette*, a refugee in Austria. Dumouriez commanded on the north-eastern frontier in his place. France was still shuddering at the recollection of the prison-massacres of the *Septembriseurs*, and society, to use the phrase of a modern French revolutionist, was *en procès de liquidation*.

Paine got on very well, at first. The Convention was impressed with the necessity of looking up first principles, and Paine was emphatically the man of principles. A universal republic was the hope of majority, with a convention sitting at the centre of the civilized world, watching untiringly over the rights of man and the peace of the human race. Meantime, they elected a committee to make a new constitution for France. Paine was, of course, selected. His colleagues were Sièyes, Condorcet, Gensonné, Vergniaud, Pétion, Brissot, Barrère, and Danton. Of these nine, Paine and Sièyes alone survived the Reign of Terror. When, in due time, this constitution was ready to be submitted to the Convention, no one could be found to listen to the reading of the report. The revolution had outstripped the committee. Their labors proved as useless as the Treatise on Education composed by Mr. Shandy for the use of his son Tristram;—when it was finished, the child had outgrown every chapter.

Thenceforward, we catch only occasional glimpses of Paine. In the days of his glory, he lived in the fashionable Rue de Richelieu, holding levees twice a week, to receive a public eager to gaze upon so great a man. His name appears at the *fête civique* held by English and Irish republicans at White's Hotel. There he sat beside Santerre, the famous brewer, and proposed, as a sentiment, "The approaching National Convention of Great Britain and Ireland." At this dinner, Lord Edward Fitzgerald, then an officer in the British service, gave, "May the 'Ça ira,' the 'Carmagnole,' and the 'Marseillaise' be the music of every army, and soldier and citizen join in the chorus,"—a toast which cost him his commission, perhaps his life. We read, too, that Paine was struck in a *café* by some loyal, hotheaded English captain, who took that means of showing his dislike for the author of the **Rights of Man**. The police sternly seized the foolish son of Albion. A blow inflicted upon the sacred person of a member of the Convention was clearly sacrilege, punishable, perhaps, with death. But Paine interfered, procured passports, and sent the penitent soldier safely out of the country.

Speaking no French, for he never succeeded in learning the language, Paine's part in the public sittings of the Convention must have been generally limited to eloquent silence or expressive dumbshow. But when the trial of the King came on, he took a bold and dangerous share in the proceedings, which destroyed what little popularity the ruin of his federal schemes had left him, and came near costing him his head. He was already so great a laggard behind the revolutionary march, that he did not suspect the determination of the Mountain to put the King to death. Louis was guilty, no doubt, Paine thought,—but not of any great crime. Banishment for life, or until the new government be consolidated,—say to the United States, where he will have the inestimable privilege of seeing the working of free institutions;—once thoroughly convinced of his royal errors, morally, as well as physically uncrowned, he might safely be allowed to return to France as plain Citizen Capet: that should be his sentence. But the extreme left of the Convention and the constituent rabble of the galleries wanted to break with the past, and to throw a king's head into the arena as wager of battle to the despots of Europe. The discovery of the iron safe in the palace offered, it was thought, sufficient show of evidence for the prosecution; if not, they were ready to dispense with any. The case was prejudged; the trial, a cruel and an empty form. There were two righteous men in that political Gomorrah,—Tronchet and the venerable Malesherbes. They offered their services to defend the unfortunate victim. Who can read Malesherbes's noble letter to the President of the Convention, without thinking the better of French nature forever after?

A fierce preliminary discussion arose in the Convention on the constitutional question of the King's inviolability. Paine had no patience with the privileges of kingship and voted against inviolability. He requested that a speech he had prepared on the subject might be read to the House at once, as he wished to send off a copy to London for the English papers. This wretched composition was manifestly written for England. Paine had George III. in his mind, rather than Louis XVI. Here is a specimen of the style of it,—interesting, as showing the temper of the time, as well as of Member Thomas Paine:—

> Louis, as an individual, is an object beneath the notice of the Republic. But he ought to be tried, because a conspiracy has been formed against the liberty of all nations by the crowned ruffians of Europe. Louis XVI. is believed to be the partner of that horde, and is the only man of them you have in your power. It is indispensable to discover who the gang is composed of, and this may be done by his trial. It may also bring to light the detestable conduct of Mr. Guelph, Elector of Hanover, and be doing justice to England to make them aware of it. It is the interest of France to be surrounded by republics, and that revolutions be universal. If Louis XVI. can serve to prove, by the flagitiousness of government in general, the necessity of revolutions, France ought not to let slip so precious an opportunity. Seeing no longer in Louis XVI. but a weak-minded and narrow-spirited individual, ill-bred, like all his colleagues, given, as it is said, to frequent excesses of drunkenness, and whom the National Assembly raised again imprudently to a throne which was not made for him,—if we show him hereafter some pity, it shall not be the result of the burlesque idea of a pretended inviolability.

A secretary read this speech from the tribune,—Paine standing near him, silent, furnishing perhaps an occasional gesture to mark the emphasis. The Convention applauded warmly, and ordered it to be printed and circulated in the departments.

When the King was found guilty, and it came to the final vote, whether he should be imprisoned, banished, or beheaded, the Girondins, who had spoken warmly against the death-penalty, voted for it, overawed by the stormy abuse of the galleries. Paine, coarse and insolent, but not cowardly or cruel, did not hesitate to vote for banishment. He requested the member from the Pas de Calais to read from the tribune his appeal in favor of the King. Drunau attempted to do it, but was hooted down. Paine persisted,—presented his speech again the next day. Marat objected to its reception, because Paine was a Quaker, and opposed to capital punishment on principle; but the Convention at last consented to the reading. After alluding to the all-important assistance furnished by Louis XVI. to the insurgent American Colonies, Paine, as a citizen of both countries, proposed sending him to the United States. "To kill Louis," wrote Paine, "is not only inhuman, but a folly. It will increase the number of your enemies. France has but one ally,—the United States of America,—and the execution of the King would spread an universal affliction in that country. If I could speak your language like a Frenchman, I would descend a suppliant to your bar, and in the name of all my brothers in America present to you a petition and prayer to suspend the execution of Louis." The Mountain and the galleries roared with rage. Thuriot exclaimed,—"That is not the true language of Thomas Paine."

"I denounce the translator," shrieked venomous Marat; "these are not the opinions of Thomas Paine; it is a wicked and unfaithful translation."

Coulon affirmed, solemnly, that he had seen the original in Paine's hands, and that it was exact. The reader was finally allowed to resume. "You mean to send an ambassador to the United States. Let him announce to the Americans that the National Convention of France, from pure friendship to America, has consented to respite the sentence of Louis. Ah, Citizens, do not give the despot of England the pleasure of seeing sent to the scaffold the man who helped my beloved brethren of America to free themselves from his chains!"

Soon after the execution of the King, Paris fell into the hands of the lowest classes. Their leaders ruled with terrible energy. Chàbot's *dictum,—"Il n'y a pas de crimes en révolution,"* and Stable-keeper Drouet's exclamation,—*"Soyons brigands pour le bonheur du peuple,"* contain the political principles which guided them. Marat thundered away in his paper against Brissotins, Girondins, federalism, and moderantism. The minority members, thus unpleasantly noticed, went armed; many of them dared not sleep at home. Soon came the arrest of the *suspects.* The 31st of May, *cette insurrection toute morale,* as Robespierre called it, followed next. The Convention was stormed by the mob and purged of Brissotins and Girondins. The *Comité de Salut Public* decreed forced loans and the *levée en masse.* Foreigners were expelled from the Convention and imprisoned throughout France. Mayor Bailly, Mme. Roland, Manuel, and their friends, passed under the axe. The same fate befell the Girondins, a party of phrase-makers who have enjoyed a posthumous sentimental reputation, but who, when living, had not the energy and active courage to back their fine speeches. The *reductio ad horribile* of all the fine arguments in favor of popular infallibility and virtue had come; neither was the *reductio ad absurdum* wanting. The old names of the days and months and years were changed. The statues of the Virgin were torn from the little niches in street-walls, and the busts of Marat and Lepelletier set up in their stead. The would-be God, *soi-disant Dieu,* was banished from France. Clootz and Chaumette, who called themselves Anacharsis and Anaxagoras, celebrated the worship of the Goddess of Reason. Bonfires of feudality; Goddesses of Liberty in plaster; trees of liberty planted in every square; altars *de la patrie;* huge ragdolls representing Anarchy and Discord; Cleobis and Biton dragging their revered parents through the streets; *bonnets rouges, banderolles, ça iras, carmagnoles, fraternisations, accolades;* the properties, as well as the text of the plays, borrowed from Ancient Greece or Rome. What a bewildering retrospect! A period well summed up by Emerson:—"To-day, pasteboard and filigree; to-morrow, madness and murder." *Tigre-singe,* Voltaire's epigrammatic definition, describes his countrymen of the Reign of Terror in two words.

Neglected by all parties, and disgusted with all, Paine moved to a remote quarter of Paris, and took rooms in a house which had once belonged to Mme. de Pompadour. Brissot, Thomas Christie, Mary Wolstonecraft, and Joel Barlow were his principal associates. Two Englishmen, "friends of humanity," and an ex-officer of the *garde-du-corps* lodged in the same building. The neighborhood was not without its considerable persons. Sanson, most celebrated of headsmen, had his domicile is the same section. He called upon Paine, complimented him in good English upon his **Rights of Man**, which he had read, and offered his services in a polite manner.

When the Reign of Terror was fully established, the little party seldom left their walls, and amused themselves as best they could with conversation and games. The news of the confusion and alarm of Paris reached them in their retreat, as if they were miles away in some quiet country residence. Every evening the landlord went into the city and brought back with him the horrible story of the day. "As to myself," Paine wrote to Lady Smith, "I used to find some relief by walking in the garden and cursing with hearty good-will the authors of that terrible system that had turned the character of the revolution I had been proud to defend."

After some weeks, the two Englishmen contrived to escape to Switzerland, leaving their enthusiasm for humanity behind them. Two days later, a file of armed men came to arrest them. Before the month was out, the landlord was carried off in the night. Last of all came the turn of Paine. He was arrested in December, by order of Robespierre, "for the interest of America, as well as of France, as a dangerous enemy of liberty and equality." On his way to the Luxembourg, he stopped at Barlow's lodgings and left with him the First Part of the **Age of Reason**, finished the day before. The Americans in Paris applied to the Convention for Paine's release, offering themselves as security for his good conduct during his stay in France. They rounded off their petition with a phrase of the prisoner's,—"Ah, Citizens! do not give the leagued despots of Europe the pleasure of seeing Thomas Paine in irons." This document was presented by a Major Jackson, a "volunteer character," who had come to Europe with a letter of introduction to Gouverneur Morris, then minister, from Mr. Jefferson. Instead of delivering his letter to Morris, Jackson lodged it with the *Comité de Salut Public* as a credential, and represented his country on the strength of it. The Convention, careless of the opinion of the "leagued despots," as well as of Major Jackson, replied, that Paine was an Englishman, and the demand for his release unauthorized by the United States. Paine wrote to Morris to request him to demand his discharge of the citizen who administered foreign affairs. Morris did so; but this official denied that Paine was an American. Morris inclosed this answer to Paine, who returned a shrewd argument in his own behalf, and begged Morris to lay the proofs of his citizenship before the minister. But Morris disliked Paine, and his own position in France was far from satisfactory. It is probable that he was not very zealous in the matter, and shortly after Paine's letter all communication with prisoners was forbidden.

The news of the outer world reached these unfortunates, penned up like sheep waiting for the butcher, only when the doors of the dungeon opened to admit a new *fournée,* or batch of victims, as the French pleasantly called them. They knew then that the revolution had made another stride forward, and had trodden these down as it moved on. Paine saw them all—Ronsin, Hébert, Momoro, Chaumette, Clootz, Gobel,

COMMON SENSE:

ADDRESSED TO THE

INHABITANTS

OF

AMERICA.

On the following interesting

SUBJECTS.

I. Of the Origin and Design of Government in general,
with concise Remarks on the English Constitution.

II. Of Monarchy and Hereditary Succession.

III. Thoughts on the present State of American Affairs.

IV. Of the present Ability of America, with some miscellaneous
Reflections.

Written by an ENGLISHMAN.
By Thomas Paine

Man knows no Master save creating HEAVEN,
Or those whom choice and common good ordain.
THOMSON.

PHILADELPHIA, Printed
And Sold by R. BELL, in Third-Street, 1776.

Title page for Paine's Common Sense, *1776.*

the crazy and the vile, mingled together, the very men he had cursed in his garden at St. Denis—pass before him like the shadows of a magic-lantern, entering at one side and gliding out at the other,—to death. A few days later came Danton, Camille, Desmoulins, and the few who remained of the moderate party. Paine was standing near the wicket when they were brought in. Danton embraced him. "What you have done for the happiness and liberty of your country I have in vain tried to do for mine. I have been less fortunate, but not more culpable. I am sent to the scaffold." Turning to his friends,—*"Eh, bien! mes amis, allons y gaiement."* Happy Frenchmen! What a consolation it was to them to be thus always able to take an attitude and enact a character! Their fondness for dramatic display must have served them as a moral anæsthetic in those scenes of murder, and have deadened their sensibility to the horrors of their actual condition.

In July, the carnage had reached its height. No man could count upon life for twenty-four hours. The tall, the wise, the reverend heads had been taken off, and now the humbler ones were insecure upon their shoulders. Fouquier-Tinville had erected a guillotine in his court-room, to save time and transportation. Newsboys sold about the streets printed lists of those who were to suffer that day. *"Voici ceux qui ont gagné à la loterie de la Sainte Guillotine!"* they cried, with that reckless, mocking, blood-thirsty spirit which is found only in Frenchmen, or, perhaps, in their fellow-Celts. It seemed to Paine that Robespierre and the Committee were afraid to leave a man alive. He expected daily his own summons; but he was overlooked. There was nothing to be gained by killing him, except the mere pleasure of the thing.

He ascribed his escape to a severe attack of fever, which kept him out of sight for a time, and to a clerical error on the part of the distributing jailer. He wrote this account of it, after his return to America:—

> The room in which I was lodged was on the ground-floor, and one of a long range of rooms under a gallery, and the door of it opened outward and flat against the wall, so that, when it was opened, the inside of the door appeared outward, and the contrary when it was shut. I had three fellow-prisoners with me,—Joseph Van Huile of Bruges, Michel and Robin Bastini of Louvain. When persons by scores were to be taken out of prison for the guillotine, it was always done in the night, and those who performed that office had a private mark by which they knew what rooms to go to and what number to take. We, as I have said, were four, and the door of our room was marked, unobserved by us, with that number in chalk; but it happened, if happening is a proper word, that the mark was put on when the door was open and flat against the wall, and thereby came on the inside when we shut it at night, and the destroying angel passed by it.

Paine thought his escape providential; the Orthodox took a different view of it.

After the fall of Robespierre, in Thermidor, seventy-three members of the Convention, who had survived the Reign of Terror, resumed their seats. But Paine was not released. Monroe had superseded Morris in August, but had no instructions from his government. Indeed, as Paine had accepted citizenship in France, and had publicly acted as a French citizen, it was considered, even by his friends, that he had no claim to the protection of the United States. Paine, as was natural, thought differently. He wrote to Monroe, explaining that French citizenship was a mere compliment paid to his reputation; and in any view of the case, it had been taken away from him by a decree of the Convention. His seat in that body did not affect his American *status,* because a convention to make a constitution is not a government, but extrinsic and antecedent to a government. The government once established, he would never have accepted a situation under it. Monroe assured him that he considered him an American citizen, and that "to the welfare of Thomas Paine Americans are not nor can they be indifferent,"—with which fine phrase Paine was obliged to be satisfied until November. On the fourth of that month he was released. The authorities of Thermidor disliked the Federalist government, and Paine was probably kept in prison some additional months on account of Monroe's application for his discharge.

He left the Luxembourg, after eleven months of incarceration, with unshaken confidence in his own greatness and in the truth of his principles,—but in appearance and in character another man, with only the tatters of his former self hanging about him. A certain elegance of manner and of dress, which had distinguished him, was gone. He drank deep, and was noisy. His fondness for talking of himself had grown to such excess as to destroy the conversational talents which all his contemporaries who speak of him describe as remarkable. "I will venture to say that the best thing will be said by Mr. Paine": that was Horne Tooke's prophecy, talking of some proposed dinner-party.

Demoralized by poverty, with ruined health, his mind had become distorted by physical suffering and by brooding over the ingratitude and cruel neglect of the American people, who owed, as he really believed, their very existence as a nation to him. "Is this what I ought to have expected from America," he wrote to General Washington, "after the part I have acted towards her?" "I do not hesitate to say that you have not served America with more fidelity or greater zeal or more disinterestedness than myself, and perhaps not with better effect." Henceforth he was a man of two ideas: he engrafted his resentment upon his **Rights of Man**, and thought himself carrying out his theory while indulging in his wrath. He poured the full measure of his indignation upon the party who directed affairs in the United States, and upon the President. In two long letters, composed after his release, under Monroe's roof, he accused Washington of conniving at his imprisonment, to keep him, Paine, "the marplot of all designs against the people," out of the way. "Mr. Washington and his new-fangled party were rushing as fast as they dared venture into all the vices and corruptions of the British government; and it was no more consistent with the policy of Mr. Washington and those who immediately surrounded him than it was with that of Robespierre or of Pitt that I should survive." As he grew more angry, he became more abusive. He ridiculed Washington's "cold, unmilitary conduct" during the War of Independence, and accused his administration, since the new constitution, of "vanity," "ingratitude," "corruption," "bare-faced treachery," and "the tricks of a sharper." He closed this wretched outbreak of peevishness and wounded self-conceit with the following passage:—

And as to you, Sir, treacherous in private friendship (for so you have been to me, and that in the day of danger) and a hypocrite in public life, the world will be puzzled to decide whether you are an apostate or an impostor,—whether you have abandoned good principles, or whether you ever had any.

The remains of the old Convention invited Paine to resume his place in their assemblage. A committee of eleven, unaided by his experience, had been working at a new constitution, the political spring-fashion in Paris for that year. It was the plan since known as the *Directoire,* reported complete about the time Paine reappeared in the Convention. Disapproving of some of the details of this instrument, Paine furbished up his old weapons, and published **A Dissertation on the First Principles of Government**. This tract he distributed among members,—the *libretto* of the speech he intended to make. Accordingly, on the 5th of July, on motion of his old ally, Lanthenas, who had managed to crawl safely through the troubles, permission was granted to Thomas Paine to deliver his sentiments on the "Declaration of Rights and the Constitution." He ascended the tribune for the last time, and the secretary read the translation. He began, of course, with rights; but qualified them by adding, that, when we consider rights, we ought always to couple with them the idea of duties,—a happy union, which did not strike him before the Reign of Terror, and which is almost always overlooked. He then brought forward his universal political specific and panacea,—representative government and a written constitution. "Had a constitution been established two years ago," he said, "(as ought to have been done,) the violences that have since desolated France and injured the character of the Revolution would, in my opinion, have been prevented." There is nothing else in his speech of interest to us, except, that, in attacking a property qualification, which was wisely inserted in the new system, he made use of the *reductio-ad-absurdum* illustration so often attributed to Dr. Franklin:—"When a broodmare shall fortunately produce a foal or a mule that by being worth the sum in question shall convey to its owner the right of voting, or by its death take it from him, in whom does the origin of such a right exist? Is it in the man or in the mule?"

The new government went into operation in September, 1795. Bonaparte's lesson to the insurgents of Vendémiaire, in front of the Church of St. Roche, followed immediately after. On the 26th of October, the Convention was dissolved, and Paine ceased to be a legislator for France.

He was no longer an object of consideration to Frenchmen, whose faith in principles and in constitutions was nearly worn out. Poor and infirm, indebted to Monroe's hospitality for a lodging, he remained eighteen months under the roof of the Embassy, looking for an opportunity to get back to America. Monroe wished to send him as bearer of dispatches before the dissolution of the Convention. But a member of that body could not leave France without a passport from it. To apply for it would have announced his departure, and have given the English government a chance to settle the old account they had against him. After Monroe had returned to the United States, Paine engaged his passage, and went to Havre to embark; but the appearance of a British frigate off the port changed his plans. The sentence of outlawry, a good joke four years before, had now become an unpleasant reality. So he travelled back to Paris, full of hate against England, and relieved his mind by writing a pamphlet on the *Decline and Fall of the English System of Finance*, a performance characteristic of the man,—sound, clear sense mixed with ignorance and arrogance. He attempted to show arithmetically that the English funding system could not continue to the end of Mr. Pitt's life, supposing him to live to the usual age of man. The calculation is ingenious, but has not proved to be as accurate as some of Newton's. On the other hand, his remarks on paper money are excellent, and his sneer at the Sinking Fund, then considered a great invention in finance, well placed:—"As to Mr. Pitt's project for paying off the national debt by applying a million a year for that purpose while he continues adding more than twenty millions a year to it, it is like setting a man with a wooden leg to run after a hare;—the longer he runs, the farther he is off." The conclusion is one of his peculiar flourishes of his own trumpet:—"I have now exposed the English system of finance to the eyes of all nations,—for this work will be published in all languages. As an individual citizen of America, and as far as an individual can go, I have revenged (if I may use the expression without any immoral meaning) the piratical depredations committed on the American commerce by the English government."

From Monroe's departure until the year 1802, little is known of Paine. He is said to have lived in humble lodgings with one Bonneville, a printer, editor of the "Bouche de Fer" in the good early days of the Revolution. He must have kept up some acquaintance with respectable society; for we find his name on the lists of the *Cercle Constitutionnel,* a club to which belonged Talleyrand, Benjamin Constant, and conservatives of that class who were opposed to both the *bonnet-rouge* and the *fleur-de-lis.* Occasionally he appears above the surface with a pamphlet. Politics were his passion, and to write a necessity of his nature. If public matters interested him, an essay of some kind made its way into print. When Babœuf's agrarian conspiracy was crushed, Paine gave the world his views on *Agrarian Justice.* Every man has a natural right to a share in the land; but it is impossible that every man should exercise this right. To compensate

him for this loss, he should receive at the age of twenty-one fifteen pounds sterling; and if he survive his fiftieth year, ten pounds *per annum* during the rest of his life. The funds for these payments to be furnished by a tax on inheritances.

Camille Jourdain made a report to the Five Hundred on priests and public worship, in which he recommended, *inter alia,* that the use of church-bells and the erection of crosses be again permitted by law. This reactionary measure excited Paine's liberal bigotry. He published a letter to Jourdain, telling him that priests were useless and bells public nuisances. Another letter may be seen, offering his subscription of one hundred francs to a fund for the invasion of England,—a favorite project of the Directory, and the dearest wish of Paine's heart. He added to his mite an offer of any personal service he could render to the invading army. When Carnot, Barthélémy, and Pichegru were expelled from power by the *coup d'état* of the 18th Fructidor,—a military demonstration against the Republic,—Paine wrote an address to the people of France and to the French armies, heartily approving of the summary method that had been adopted with these reactionists, who must have their bells and their priests. He did not then perceive the real significance of the movement.

On one remarkable occasion, Paine made a full-length appearance before the French public,—not in his character of a political philosopher, but as a moralist. Robespierre, a few days before his fall, declared atheism to be aristocratic, reinstated *l'Être suprème,* and gave a festival in his honor. There religious matters had rested. Deism, pure and simple, was the faith of true republicans, and the practice of morality their works. But deism is a dreary religion to the mass of mankind, and the practice of morality can never take the place of adoration. The heart must be satisfied, as well as the conscience. Larévillière, a Director, of irreproachable character, felt this deficiency of their system, and saw how strong a hold the Catholic priesthood had upon the common people. The idea occurred to him of rivalling the churches by establishing regular meetings of moral men and women, to sing hymns of praise to the Almighty, "one and indivisible," and to listen to discourses and exhortations on moral subjects. Haüy, a brother of the eminent crystallogist, assembled the first society of Theophilanthropists, (lovers of God and man,) as they called themselves. They held their meetings on the day corresponding to Sunday. They had their manual of worship and their book of canticles. Their dogmas were the existence of one God and the immortality of the soul. And they wisely said nothing about matters which they did not believe. Paine, who in his *Age of Reason* had attempted to prepare a theology *ad usum reipublicæ,* felt moved by the spirit of morality, and delivered a sermon to one of these Theophilanthropist congregations. His theme was the existence of God and the propriety of combining the study of natural science with theology. He chose, of course, the *a-posteriori* argument, and was brief, perhaps eloquent. Some passages of his discourse might pass unchallenged in the sermon of an Orthodox divine. He kept this one ready in his memory of brass, to confound all who accused him of irreligion:—

> Do we want to contemplate His power? We see it in the immensity of the creation. Do we want to contemplate His wisdom? We see it in the unchangeable order by which the incomprehensible whole is governed. Do we want to contemplate His mercy? We see it in His not withholding His abundance even from the unthankful. In fine, do we want to know what God is? Search not written books, but the Scriptures called the Creation.

If it were possible to establish a new *cultus,* based upon mere abstract principles, Frenchmen, we should say, would be about the last people who could do it. This new worship, like any other play, drew well as long as it was new, and no longer. The moral men and women soon grew tired of it, and relapsed into the old faith and the old forms.

The end of all this child's play at government and at religion came at last. Bonaparte, checked at Acre by Sir Sydney Smith, left the East, landed in France in October, 1799, sent a file of grenadiers to turn Ancients and Five Hundred out of their halls, and seated himself in the chair of state.

After this conclusive *coup d'état,* Paine sunk out of sight. The First Consul might have examined with interest the iron bridge, but could never have borne with the soiled person and the threadbare principles of the philosopher of two hemispheres. Bonaparte loved neatness and elegance, and disliked *idéologues* and *bavards,* as he styled all gentlemen of Paine's turn of mind.

In 1802, after the peace with England, Paine set sail from Havre to end his days in the United States. Here we leave him. We have neither space nor inclination to sum up his virtues and his vices in these columns, and to give him a character according to the balance struck. We have sketched a few outlines of his history as we have found it scattered about in newspapers and pamphlets. Our readers may make up their own minds whether this supposed ally of the Arch Enemy was as black as he has been painted.

Leslie Stephen (essay date 1893)

SOURCE: "Thomas Paine," in *Fortnightly Review,* Vol. LIV, No. CCCXX, August 1, 1893, pp. 267-81.

[*In the following essay, Stephen's review of Paine's major works substantiates his contention that Paine*

> **Thomas Jefferson, third president of the United States, in a letter to Francis Wayles Eppes (1821):**
>
> You ask my opinion of Ld. Bolingbroke and Thomas Paine. They were alike in making bitter enemies of the priests and Pharisees of their day. Both were honest men; both advocates for human liberty. Paine wrote for a country which permitted him to push his reasoning to whatever length it would go: Ld. Bolingbroke in one restrained by a constitution, and by public opinion. . . . These two persons differed remarkably in the style of their writing, each leaving a model of what is most perfect in both extremes of the simple and the sublime. No writer has exceeded Paine in ease and familiarity of style; in perspicuity of expression, happiness of elucidation, and in simple and unassuming language. In this he may be compared with Dr. Franklin: and indeed his **Common Sense** was, for awhile, believed to have been written by Dr. Franklin, and published under the borrowed name of Paine, who had come over with him from England. . . .
>
> *Thomas Jefferson, in* The Family Letters of Thomas Jefferson, *edited by Edwin Morris Betts and James Adam Bear, Jr., University of Missouri Press, 1966.*

argued in a direct and formulaic fashion that emphasized one or two clear-cut hypotheses.]

For some three generations the name of Paine has been regarded by the respectable classes as synonymous with vulgar brutality. Mr. Moncure Conway has recently published a biography [*The Life of Thomas Paine* (1899)—listed in the "Further Reading" section] intended to destroy this orthodox legend. He has carefully collected all available information, and probably knows all that can now be known upon the subject. He states in his preface that a book of mine published some years ago accepted certain scandals about Paine, and as I misled at least one of my readers, I think it a duty to confess my error frankly. My description of Paine's last years was taken from a statement by a witness whom Mr. Conway has proved to be utterly unworthy of credit. Mr. Conway, indeed, admits that at one period Paine drank brandy to excess; but the malignity of a personal enemy, taking advantage of the general prejudice against Paine as a freethinker, produced a caricature which should be no more taken for a likeness than Gillray's drawings for faithful portraits of Pitt or Fox. I am the more sorry to have been unintentionally an accomplice, because in any case the charges were but slightly relevant. Paine's brandy is less to the purpose than Pitt's port, and much less to the purpose than Coleridge's opium. Patriots may reverence Pitt, and philosophers and poets may love Coleridge in spite of weaknesses which really affected their careers. But Paine's lapse into drink, such as it was, did not take place till his work was substantially done; and his writings were the product of brains certainly not sodden by brandy, but clear, vigorous, and, in some ways, curiously free from passion.

Mr. Conway's book raises another question: What was the real value and significance of Paine's work? Paine, of course, more than any one else, represents for Englishmen the principles of 1789; and in particular the connection of those principles with the War of Independence in America. What, then, were his antecedents and his achievements? To answer fully would involve a prolonged discussion of many controverted points; but I will try to put briefly the impression made by Mr. Conway's full account of his career.

Paine, in the first place, was the son of a poor Quaker in Thetford. The Quaker spirit undoubtedly had much to do with his development. He was, like Franklin, a Quaker *minus* the orthodox creed, as in later years Carlyle was a Calvinist who had dropped the dogma. With the mysticism, indeed, which distinguished the earlier members of the sect, Paine had no sympathy. It was replaced in him as in Franklin by the metaphysical Deism of the eighteenth century. But he certainly imbibed the practical sentiment which made Quakers take so honourable and conspicuous a part in all the philanthropic movements of his time, and shared their aversion to all forms and ecclesiastical institutions. The Quaker religion, he declared in *The Age of Reason,* was that which approached most nearly to true Deism. A contempt for the pomps and vanities of the world, an enthusiasm for the brotherhood of mankind, and a reverence for the rights of individual consciences, may be expressed in terms of George Fox as of Thomas Paine. For the "inner light" we have only to substitute a metaphysical dogmatism, less emotional but equally imperative.

Paine, however, from his youth must have hung very lightly to any religious sect. There are vague indications that he preached, but his sermons, if any, are with the snows of last year. Nor is there the least proof that he was specially affected by the sight of those evils of the day upon which Mr. Conway insists. A lad of nine years old was probably more pleased by the drums of the regiments returning from the Highlands—if, indeed, any of them passed through Thetford—than shocked by the blood-stained uniforms of the instruments of Cumberland's vengeance. Certainly at the age of eighteen or nineteen he became for a short time a privateersman, which would hardly be the choice of a premature philanthropist. His career as a staymaker and afterwards as an exciseman is naturally obscure. We can see dimly that he had ambitions and that he neglected his business. He was a member of a jovial political club at Lewes, wrote songs and comic poems, and argued with great vivacity on behalf (it seems) of Wilkes and liberty. English radicalism was slowly stirring to life after the profound calm of the middle of the century. Paine, we may guess, read the English

translations of Rousseau's *Social Contract* and discourse on the *Inequality of Mankind,* which were the prophetic utterances of the newborn spirit. If he did not read them he learnt their formulæ. He became conspicuous enough among his fellows to be put forward as their spokesman in an agitation for an increase of salaries. The position was dangerous; for, of all classes of men, excisemen were the last who could count upon popular sympathy, and a request for more money rarely conciliates superiors. It is not surprising that Paine soon found himself an exciseman out of place. He had one resource. Paine's intellectual temper was that of a mathematician, and he had at some period acquired a knowledge of science. He got some teaching from two self-educated men, Benjamin Martin and the well-known astronomer, James Ferguson, who both gave lectures in London. It was possibly through them that he became known to Franklin, already famous for having snatched the lightning from heaven, and soon to snatch the sceptre from kings. Armed with a letter of introduction from Franklin, Paine sailed to Philadelphia, towards the end of 1774, intending to set up a school. He became editor of a magazine at the humble salary of £50 a year; but within a few months found much livelier occupation.

When Paine reached America a Congress was already sitting in Philadelphia. The skirmish at Lexington (19th April, 1775) and the battle at Bunker's Hill (17th June) were followed by the choice of Washington to be Commander-in-Chief of the provincial armies. Paine during the autumn wrote his *Common Sense,* which appeared in January, 1776, and made him famous at a blow. In three months 120,000 copies were sold, and it became the recognised manifesto of the revolutionary party. An exciseman, with such training only as was to be had at Thetford, had become the spokesman of a nation in which hardly a year before he had been almost a foreigner. What was the secret of his success? In the first place, it was that Paine was endowed with the most valuable instinct that a journalist can possess. Americans had up to the last moment been declaring that they had no wish for separation. Franklin asserted that he had heard no such desire expressed by "any person drunk or sober." Paine says much the same elsewhere, but in the pamphlet he also says that he never met a man in England or America who did not expect that separation would come sooner or later. A newspaper, it is said, has thriven by saying a little better what everybody is already saying. It is a still greater triumph to say what everybody is going to say to-morrow, but does not quite dare to say to-day. A quaint illustration of the obvious principle occurs in Coleridge's *Literary Remains.* When reading Leighton, he says, he seems to be "only thinking his own thoughts over again." On the next page he expresses the same opinion by saying that he almost believes Leighton to have been actually an inspired writer. Nothing is so impressive as a revelation of our own thoughts. When armed resistance had actually begun, when the colonists had formed a league and chosen a commander-in-chief, it must, one would suppose, have been hard for any man to keep up the pretence of disavowing a wish for independence. It could be merely a way of throwing the responsibility upon the mother country; and the time for such special pleading passed with the first outbreak of war. What was needed then was a clear, distinctive unveiling of the hitherto masked conviction. Paine, in a literary sense, was the man who "belled the cat." He had an audience ready to hail him as a prophet because he was an echo, not of their words, but of their thoughts. But he also put the case with a clearness and vigour which is the more remarkable from his entire want of literary experience. His method is characteristic. There is less than one might expect of such rhetoric as is called inflammatory. A native American would probably have dwelt more upon specific grievances, but Paine had no special personal knowledge of such things. He takes them for granted rather than expatiates upon them. He speaks like a man insisting upon an absolutely demonstrable scientific truth. The thesis which he has to establish is simply, "It is time to part"; and the proof is drawn from the obvious designs of Providence as manifested in geography. It is absurd to suppose that a continent can be perpetually governed by an island. Nature does not make a satellite bigger than its primary planet. When the quarrel has once broken out compromise becomes obviously absurd. Such differences cannot be patched up by any settlement. To come to terms for the moment could only be to leave the quarrel to the next generation. England is small, America a vast continent; therefore English rule of America is in a position of unstable equilibrium. Once upset it, and you can never again balance the pyramid on its apex. That is the substance of an argument which undoubtedly deserves, too, the title of "Common sense." It rests upon broad undeniable facts and is, of course, backed up by sufficient reference to the abominations of British government. But Paine also provides his argument with certain prolegomena which supersede any reference to expediency. Sir Henry Maine has traced the social contract theory from its sources in Roman jurisprudence to its transfiguration by Rousseau. Rousseau, he says, transmitted it to Jefferson. It appears, therefore, in the Declaration of Independence, upon which Paine had, perhaps, some influence. He had expounded it fully in *Common Sense*. Starting from the natural equality of man and the regular hypothesis of a small body of men meeting "in some sequestered part of the earth," and making a bargain as to their rights, we get at once a clean-cut theory of government and a demonstration of the gross absurdity of kings and aristocrats. It is plainly impossible to prove the value of the British constitution by *a priori* reasoning. To Paine, therefore, the American revolution was already the promulgation of the "rights of man" in the most absolute form. The colonies revolted, according to him, not because charters had

been infringed or specific injuries inflicted upon merchants, but in virtue of principles as true as the propositions of Euclid, and applicable not only to Englishmen or Americans, but to man as man. So long as all patriots were agreed to turn out George III., it mattered little what metaphysical principles they chose to postulate as the ground of their claims, whether they fought in the name of the great charter or of the rights of man. The more sweeping the principle announced the more effective the war-cry. Paine's doctrine covered claims enough, and if it covered rather too many, that was for the moment unimportant. He could speak as if his enemies were not only wanting in prudence but denying the plainest dictates of pure reason.

Paine, it must be added, acted in the spirit of his doctrines through the war. At intervals he published the series of pamphlets called collectively *The Crisis,* which, though of such various degrees of merit, show the same characteristic quality. If overweening confidence in one's opinions is a doubtful merit in a philosopher, it is undoubtedly valuable in the supporter of a precarious enterprise. "These are the times that try men's souls" was the opening—it became proverbial—of the most famous of these productions. It was written at a time when the cause was apparently in great danger, and it was followed by an unexpected success. Washington, it is said, had the paper distributed to be read throughout his army, and in that sign they conquered. The secret of Paine's power is given in a phrase from the same paper: "My own line of reasoning is to myself as straight and clear as a ray of light." Paine himself took part in active service until he was appointed secretary to a committee of Congress; and his words have not unfrequently the genuine ring as of one speaking actually under fire. The unanimous opinion of his companions, and especially Washington's declarations, leave no doubt that they did more than any other pamphlets to rouse the American spirit. Paine, with the calm self-complacency pardonable, perhaps, in a man who had thus suddenly sprung into fame, held in later years that his own pen had done as much service as Washington's sword. He might fairly claim whatever credit belongs to the man who throws himself unflinchingly into the defence of a great cause. He had got into certain difficulties in his official character which showed at worst that a desire to expose a dishonest transaction had led him to disregard diplomatic proprieties. He had blurted out a statement about French help to the colonies previous to the declaration of war, which had to be disavowed, and which forced him to resign his post. But he had staked his fortunes unreservedly on the issue of the war and deserved reward the more that he had gained nothing by his pamphlets. He had given up the copyright of his publications to increase their circulation; and the reward which he ultimately received was certainly not extravagant. New York generously presented him with an estate which it took from a Tory, and Pennsylvania gave him £500.

When the plain issue of the war was finally settled, Paine's occupation was gone. Work had to be done in which mathematical demonstrations of the rights of man were irrelevant. To form the separate colonies into a nation, to reconcile their jealousies and make such compromises as would practically work, was a task for men of very different qualities. The *Federalist,* now the most famous literary record of the guiding principles of that achievement, belongs to another order of thought. The writers follow the lead of Montesquieu instead of Rousseau; and any comparison with Paine's work would be absurd. His merit was to have raised a war-cry, and the merit of Hamilton and his colleagues to bring sound judgment to bear upon an intricate practical question. Paine fell back upon his scientific tastes: he designed an iron bridge, and the design seems to have had some real value as an engineering improvement. It was apparently the absence of the necessary manufacturing appliances in America which brought him back to England in 1787. Englishmen who had read his pamphlets must have felt it rather difficult to suppress certain spasms of patriotic resentment. A colonist might be excused for denouncing "Mr. Guelph" and Lord North and the British aristocracy generally, but a born Englishman might have refrained from declaring that his countrymen were cowards and brutal butchers. He marked his return by a pamphlet, ***Prospects on the Rubicon,*** written in support of the French policy of the time and demonstrating to his own satisfaction the complete incapacity of England, burthened with an accumulation of debt, to carry on a war against France. In France, he was already observing signs of internal harmony and development. As an enemy of Pitt, Paine naturally became intimate with various classes of the English Opposition. He saw not only Horne Tooke, a survivor of the old Wilkes agitations, and Godwin, the most conspicuous representative of revolutionary principles in England, but the aristocratic Whigs, Fox and Burke, who had a bond of sympathy with an American patriot. The outbreak of the French revolution, however, soon brought about the famous duel with Burke. Burke's *Reflections* and Paine's ***Rights of Man*** are the typical expressions of the antagonistic spirits. A friend of Hazlitt (if I remember rightly) had the two books bound together as giving between them an admirable system of politics. I fear that a little more than a binder's skill is required to fuse two such opponents. And yet, the proposal was not without its meaning. Burke is indeed called a renegade in the radical tradition and some people still insinuate that he apostatized to gain a pension. I do not understand how any one who has ever read Burke can accept such a view. Coleridge (in the *Biographia Literaria*) declares, and, as I should say, with undeniable truth, that Burke's views upon the American and the French revolutions are scientifically deduced from identical principles. Mr. Morley has insisted upon the same obvious fact. Approval of one "revolution" is held by some people to

involve approval of every "revolution." Mr. Morley, to take the nearest parallel to Burke in our own times, approves of Home Rule. Is he, therefore, bound to approve of State socialism and nationalization of the land? Mr. Morley would hardly admit the inference. It would only follow if he also accepted the dogma that whatever a majority wishes is therefore right. Now, Burke not only repudiated any such doctrine, but from his first writings based his whole argument on the most explicit reprobation of the whole doctrine of *a priori,* as he called these "metaphysical" rights. The *Vindication of Natural Society* (1756) gives the very pith of all that he urged during the American war and the French revolution. He objected to the English system in America because it had become intolerable. The attempt to keep adults under a tutelage suitable for children was absurd not because it conflicted with the rights of man, but because experience proved it to be futile. But a "revolution" which meant the rupture of a worn-out tie had only a name in common with a "revolution" which meant a vast social upheaval, confiscation of property and the total destruction of every tie that had held men together. Burke and the followers of Rousseau were agreed upon one particular issue: but a false premiss, as logicians tell us, may lead to a right conclusion. I may admit that you have a right of way across my fields; but if you assert that the same right permits you to walk into my house and share my spoons, I may deny your argument without inconsistency.

The whole pith of Burke's teaching, indeed, is his anticipation of what we should now call the historical method; and in that consists, as I should say, his superlative merit. He saw with unequalled clearness the necessity of basing all political economy upon the truths now recognised by every philosophical writer, that the state is an organism developed by slow processes, and depending for its vitality upon the evolution of corresponding instincts. He therefore urged, with more accuracy than his contemporaries, the vast importance of the crash which was taking place before his eyes. It was to him the avatar of the evil spirit which he had denounced more than thirty years before, and which was now becoming a real power to be reckoned with. If his judgment was wrong, it at least did not err by underrating the significance of the phenomena. He saw that what was happening was no mere superficial change of forms, but a world-shaking catastrophe. So far, those who sympathise with the revolution should be the first to do justice to his misfit. To the respectable British Whig, the meeting of the States-General meant that France was about to follow in the steps of its fathers of 1688: to pass a bill of rights, and adopt a judicious system of checks and balances. And what did it mean to Paine? He certainly did not stop at the Whig view. The revolution was the revelation of the new gospel of humanity. All the evils from which men had suffered were due to kings, nobles, and priests. The "old governments," he says, rested first on superstition, then on force, and the new governments will rest upon reason. Governments such as now exist could only have been founded "by a total violation of every principle, sacred and moral." The obscurity in which their origin is buried (the part, that is, that we know nothing about) "implies the iniquities and disgrace with which they began." The scales have dropped from men's eyes. We see how they led, and could but have led, to war and extortion. "If we would delineate human nature with a baseness of heart, and hypocrisy of countenance that reflection would shudder at and humanity disown, it is kings and cabinets that must sit for the portrait." War, terrorism, and tyranny will now disappear. Government has been regarded as a mystery; but it is in truth the easiest of subjects. The "meanest capacity," once put in the right path, cannot be at a loss. "There is not a problem in Euclid more mathematically true than that hereditary government has not a right to exist." These last phrases are from a ***Dissertation*** published in 1795, after Paine had himself had practical experience of imprisonment under the revolutionary government. Nothing, it is clear, could shake his faith. He still held that the violence which "injured the character of the revolution" was due simply to the want of a proper constitution on the American precedent. He is writing to insist that no limits should be imposed upon the acceptance of universal suffrage. The Reign of Terror would never have happened if a few more paper bonds had been framed. Paine, in fact, illustrated the remarks which Burke had made with his usual force, in his *Reflections,* upon the total want of experience of the set of lawyers, curates, and scribblers who had undertaken the government of France. Paine, when elected to the Convention, knew, so far as appears, nothing of French history; nothing of the real organization of the country; he could not even speak the language; and he had never been there except on two or three brief visits on business. He had no more qualifications for representing France than for ruling at Calcutta. But from his point of view, any knowledge of that kind was superfluous. Two or three abstract principles and an easy deduction were enough to set a man up to reconstruct a ruined government. If such consequences follow as Burke anticipated, it is a mere accident, to be remedied for the future by applying your formula more systematically. Lay down the equality of man and prove the absurdity of hereditary rule—and what more do you want? In 1798 Paine subscribed to the expenses of a descent upon England, and had, thinks Mr. Conway, a "happy vision of standing once more in Thetford, and proclaiming liberty in the land." His dream of this blessed consummation survived some years later, when Napoleon was at Boulogne. Paine was possibly "simple-hearted," as Mr. Conway puts it, but on the whole it is not difficult to understand why this kind of philanthropy caused the antipathy of Englishmen, to whom a Paine, acting as Napoleon's prophet, was scarcely

an encouraging vision. Cobbett, about the same year, was collecting a list of atrocities said to have been performed by French liberators in other countries. Paine indeed honourably did his best to prevent such practical applications of revolutionary principles. He was not one of the philanthropists who become blood-thirsty on provocation. He tried to save Louis from the scaffold, and came near to losing his head with his friends the Girondists in consequence. The strange thing is, creditable or otherwise, that his experience of massacres neither made him ferocious nor produced the slightest influence upon his theories. He was what we politely call an idealist—a man who lives in a region beyond all reach of facts or experience.

This, however, is but one side of the question. To speak of Paine as a political philosopher is to mistake dogged assertion of crude theories for grasp of argument. To compare him as a reasoner with Burke, whose thoughts have influenced all subsequent speculation, is absurd. Paine's service was simply to express with singular clearness—a suicidal clearness at times—certain theories which did and do exercise an enormous influence. Nor is it the question whether that influence is to be set down as simply good or simply bad. Such a judgment seems to me to be out of place. Men in times of revolution have to take one side or the other, and to answer the debating society question whether it is or is not "justifiable." But from a historical view it seems as idle to pack our judgments into a simple "bad" or "good," as to approve or condemn an earthquake. It represents one of the facts, an essential fact of the whole social process, which has to be explained, if possible, and to be estimated like any other inevitable transformation. We have to ask how the movement can be best directed, not whether it would be better if it did not exist at all. It was Burke's merit to see more clearly than his contemporaries how vast were the issues involved. But Burke, though a philosopher, was a philosopher in a rage, or rather in a storm of passion which led him to the bounds of sanity. The inconsistency which might have been laid to his charge was really that he did not carry out his own principles. He would not see that so vast a catastrophe required explanation as well as denunciation. It was not to be accounted for by the wickedness or folly of leaders, or by the erroneous teaching of Rousseau or the philosophers. They could only be formidable as the mouthpieces of a sentiment accumulating through all classes and indicating a disease of the whole organism. In the tornado of Burke's passionate eloquence all such considerations disappear, and he forgets a principle which he had most clearly recognised in earlier days, that a revolution in some sense justifies itself. It may not prove that the remedies are appropriate, but it demonstrates the existence of the evil. Burke talks of the revolution, therefore, as unreasonably as Paine spoke of kings and princes. It appears to him as a diabolical and supernatural intrusion: something inexplicable historically, and to be reasoned with only by cannonballs. He ought to propose remedies, and can only advise extirpation. He falls into the mere sentimentalism which Paine fairly exposed in his best-known sentence: Burke, he would say with some truth, "pitied the plumage and forgot the dying bird." Burke idealises the British Constitution till, in defiance of his own doctrine of expediency, it becomes almost an end in itself. Paine has the advantage not only of keeping his temper and arguing calmly, but of holding, at least in appearance, the higher position morally. Burke gives some excuse even for some complete misapprehensions. He of course did not really maintain the puerile argument imputed to him by Paine, which converted the revolution settlement into a kind of social compact, binding all future generations. The very essence of his position was the absurdity of all such theories. But in opposing to Paine the historical basis, the necessity of "prescription" and the inestimable value of social traditions, he bowed before the great Whig idol with a reverence which might well be taken for superstition. In attacking the metaphysical theory of abstract rights, he really seemed to Paine to be arguing that men had no rights at all, or that a country was to be ruled for the personal advantage of kings and priests. Briefly, Burke's sweeping denunciations imply an ignoring of the cardinal fact that, after all, the revolution implied a demand for justice and a challenge to existing systems to show that they discharged a useful function. Burke was upon unassailable ground when he showed the great danger of an abrupt breach with historical traditions, or when he exposed the meagreness and preposterous dogmatism of a treatment of political problems which would apply the same rule to London or Paris or Timbuctoo. He sufficiently exposes some of Paine's schoolboy arguments by quoting them. But he leaves Paine after all in the position of a man demanding upon what right government is based and getting no satisfactory answer. In that respect Paine was successful in the same way as he had been in the **Common Sense** pamphlet. He formulated briefly and pithily the demand which subjects were putting to their rulers, and to which the rulers had to give some better answer than an appeal to tradition. Paine's challenge was no doubt the more successful by reason of its defects in the eyes of a philosopher. He had to meet the popular instinct, and his statement was, as a successful popular argument must be, a condensation of the confused thoughts of his readers. Paine, as in his other writings, dwells little upon special concrete grievances. He gives no catalogue of grievances; kings are themselves a grievance. He does not dwell, for example, upon the wrongs of the peasantry or the injuries inflicted by the privileges of the noblesse. He is simply pointing out that the whole system of monarchy, aristocracy, and priestcraft is *ab initio* absurd. It must collapse as soon as you ask it for a reason. When Godwin, a few years later, published his *Political Justice,* the book which made the greatest mark at the time among the more educated classes, it is said that ministers declined to prosecute because a book which cost a guinea could not be dangerous. They might have added that a book which, though thin enough in its speculation, required some real reflection for its comprehension, was equally sure to be innocuous. Tocqueville, discussing the question why general ideas are so popular in democratic countries, gives as one reason that they save the trouble of thinking. An argument which requires refinement and distinctness flies above the ordinary reader, and an argument which requires a knowledge of facts can always be met by opposite facts. Paine was safe from such blunders. He had a skill, unsurpassed in his own country, and which might almost convince us that he was a Frenchman, for presenting clearly, tersely, and often with great epigrammatic force, what purports to be a self-evident truth, and what is really one way of putting an undeniably forcible demand. His merits will of course be judged according to the prejudices of the readers. But he put, as no one else put it in England, the challenge which had to be met by the existing order; and I must leave it to others to decide whether the terrible disappointments which punish the idealist for his supreme indifference to facts are to be considered as more or less than a compensation for the singularly vigorous appeal for some moral groundwork of political order.

Paine's last work of any significance, *The Age of Reason,* the book which finally alienated the respectable world and caused the isolation of his later years, is but another illustration of the same power. Amid the political catastrophes which he was powerless to control, while the heads of his friends were falling by the guillotine, Paine quietly sat down to expose the mystery of priestcraft as he had exposed the mystery of monarchy. His argument may be said once more to consist in bringing into clear daylight the genuine opinion of the classes which he addressed. English theologians were accustomed to boast that they had confuted the deism of the earlier half of the century. What they had really done was to assimilate it. They had made room for it tacitly till their orthodox dogmas were little more than a conventional superstructure upon which they laid as little stress as was convenient. The deism of Toland and Tindal was substantially the same philosophy which Samuel Clarke, the most philosophical divine of his day, contrived to make the substance of his teaching with only some slight injury to his orthodoxy. By the end of the century, the ablest writers, such as Paley and Paine's antagonist, Bishop Watson, were substantially theists of one stamp or another, whose orthodoxy was a mere formality, and who tried explicitly to minimize the differences which divided them from avowed Unitarians. Watson, according to De Quincey, talked Socinianism at his own table, and ridiculed the New Testament miracles as cases of legerdemain. De Quincey is not famous for accuracy; and there is more to be said on behalf of this position, in which theology was at least infiltrated with a good deal of common sense, than needs now to be insisted upon. Paine, however, deserves the credit of knowing his own mind more clearly, and speaking it with the most uncompromising courage. His theology, of course, is of the same substance as his politics. In both cases he is content with simply the embodiment of a single *a priori* dogma. The existence of God is proved by the necessity of supposing a first cause, and that once done we have a theological as we had before a political Euclid. Paine, however, takes another step, in which theologians declined to accompany him. He protests that the God of genuine theists cannot be identified with the Jehovah of the Hebrews, with the barbarous deity who sanctioned massacres and punished children for the sins of their parents. He protests, therefore, against the anthropomorphic and traditional creed, in the name of moral sentiment; and in the long list of writers who, before and since his time, have done the same, it would be, I think, impossible to mention any one who speaks with more conviction or gives terser expression to his arguments. I need not argue at length the question about Paine's brutality. That he was at times brutal is undeniable. "I have shown," he says, in concluding his second part, "that the Bible and Testament are impositions and forgeries"; and, of course, such a position supposes the support of some tolerably rough weapons. It is, perhaps, more tenable than the opposite theory that every word of the Bible was directly inspired by the Holy Ghost; but we have passed beyond that alternative and know all that has to be said about it. It is rather Freethinkers than the orthodox who should complain of any coarseness which has brought needless opprobrium upon their cause; though they may apologize for it on the ground that a poor man must be allowed to make such retorts as are open to him against threats of hellfire, or even informations from the Attorney-General. The only question is, What was the essential implication as to Paine's character and influence? Is he to be set down as a mere cynic, the man who attacks theology because he is dead to the nobler emotions which, as we all now admit, it endeavoured to satisfy, or a man of high moral feeling, who objected to it because it involved unworthy "accretions"?

Paine, according to his own account, wrote his book against the atheists as much as against the superstitious. In point of fact, however, the greater part of the book is at least as available for the atheist as for the deist. It is an attack upon the authenticity of the Bible, and an attack, it must be added, of remarkable shrewdness. Paine had read little; according to one of his admirers, indeed, the only book which he had read carefully was the Bible. He refers to a few authorities, among others to Conyers Middleton, one of his ablest predecessors, though a predecessor in a mask, and he only became acquainted with Middleton after writing the part published in his life-time. It is impossible to say how far he derived hints from the English deists, or from Voltaire or his followers, or from any of the writers who had taken the same line. Even when anticipated, he seems to be generally writing only from his own observation. It is the more remarkable that he anticipates a good many criticisms, obvious enough when once started, but requiring no little independence and directness of thought in the unguided investigator. So, for example, he remarks upon the inconsistency between the two narratives of the Creation [Letter to Erskine], and points out that in one narrative (he had only the English Bible before him) the phrase "Lord God" is substituted for "God" in the other. He has noted, therefore, the distinction made by later criticism between the Jehovist and Elohist. This and other remarks tending to justify a later than the accepted date for the composition of the Old Testament imply great acuteness in a self-taught critic, and would be accepted now even by professors of divinity. They show how much can be done by a man who has once resolved to look at facts freshly and for himself. *The Age of Reason* naturally became a textbook for all who, upon whatever grounds, objected to the Bible and the orthodox creeds, and the attempts to suppress it gave it fame and notoriety. The old deists had ceased to be read, but their spirit revived in a book certainly not inferior in vigour to the ablest of them, and making points which have only been strengthened by more learned criticism. It was a symptom and a stimulant of the revolt against a superstitious belief, which had become a mere survival. But it leaves open the question as to what should be called the constructive part of Paine's teaching. Did it, as he held, make for deism or for atheism? Was he a forerunner, for example, of the excellent Robert Elsmere, or really more in harmony with Bradlaugh, or with Comte?

To answer that question satisfactorily would take me a great deal too far. I must be content with a few words. Paine undoubtedly was a deist; and the really dignified part of his book is the refusal to admit that his deism could be worthily represented by the old superstitious symbols. As a deist, Paine became the founder of a society of theophilanthropists, which apparently had a brief and not very vigorous existence. Could it be expected to thrive, or to thrive upon Paine's lines? To me it seems that such metaphysical deism, made out of a single dogma dependent upon very questionable reasoning, has, necessarily, a very crazy constitution. If Paine had assimilated the old deist teaching, he seems hardly to have heard of the scepticism of Hume. The weakness of his political theories is shown in his refusal to allow for the stupidity and wickedness of mankind. The whole blame of tyranny and superstition must be thrown upon kings and priests, as if they were really supernatural elements intruded into the world and not an effect as much as a cause. When he is actually suffering from atrocities he refuses to believe that they are anything but accidents, due to the want of a proper constitution. He still holds by the abstract "man," the perfectly reasonable and sensible creature who only requires to be relieved of an incubus to enter upon the millennium. Such politics may be reasonable but they are not businesslike. Proceeding on the same method he tries to reform theology by simply abolishing the devil. But the devil is really an essential part of the machinery. When Bishop Watson answered him with Butler's argument, that Nature is cruel as well as Jehovah, he was really touching upon Paine's weak point, though the argument was a dangerous one. A religion, theological or positive, must take into account the facts which suggested the doctrine of human corruption. If we are to believe in God as the first cause, which is Paine's view, we must admit that he causes priests and kings, and superstition, and cruelty, and disease, and struggles for existence as much as the pleasant elements of the world in which we live. If the first cause is to be relieved of that responsibility, we require some subtler reasoning than Paine's to make a working theory. Mere optimism can only end in some sort of "theophilanthropical" moonshine; it may generate a good deal of very pretty eloquence, but it cannot generate a creed which will express the deepest human instincts. The mystic who can mistake emotion for logic may find a refuge of his own; but Paine's deism, a quasi-mathematical dogma, a theory which is nothing if not pure logic, and which has yet such a portentous gap in its logical apparatus, has not, I suspect, the seed of much vitality.

The main secret of Paine's strength is, I think, the same throughout. Like other men who have made a remarkable success, he combined qualities not often found together. He was an idealist, endowed with a strong vein of vigorous common sense. He was by nature a man of science, who imagines the method of Euclid to be applicable to all topics of speculation, and so falls in love with a good mathematical axiom that he despises the trifling difficulty of applying it to concrete facts. The facts have to bend or to be ignored. The type is common enough in the French theorists of the revolutionary movement, but there is something generally uncongenial about it to our rougher English minds. We rather hate symmetry, and our suspicions are roused by any appearance of logic. But a good many Englishmen were glad to see the sentiments round which we were blundering, packed so neatly into a definite formula and backed by good downright hard hitting. The dumb instinct of the people of England had come to suspect that the British Constitution was not the perfection of human wisdom; that even Burke's rhetoric could not make rotten boroughs beautiful; and that even the Thirty-nine Articles did not fully represent what men thought and felt. But this vague opinion had expressed itself in compromises and with reserves, and in a characteristically

clumsy fashion; while Paine's audacious dogmas enabled it to become conscious of its own meaning. It thus discovered what it had meant all the time. It had without knowing been philosophical and profound, capable of taking all the airs of abstract demonstration; and yet, for Paine's common sense always kept within reach of facts, capable of hitting such downright blows at its enemies as gladden the heart of the oppressed. I cannot take Paine seriously as a philosopher, but I think that those who share his views may fairly take a pride in some qualities of their champion.

C. E. Merriam, Jr. (essay date 1899)

SOURCE: "Thomas Paine's Political Theories," in *Political Science Quarterly,* Vol. XIV, No. 3, September, 1899, pp. 389-403.

[*In the essay that follows, Merriam outlines the basic tenets of Paine's political thought, defining at length his concepts of human nature and government. Merriam contends that Paine viewed government as a necessary evil, tolerable only in a democratic form.*]

The political theories of Thomas Paine were struck off in the course of a career that extended over the revolutionary quarter of the eighteenth century and persistently followed the storm centre of the revolutionary movement.[1] In January, 1776, he issued his famous pamphlet *Common Sense*—the strongest plea that was made for American independence; in the same year appeared *The Forester's Letters*—Paine's side of a controversy with Dr. William Smith, of Philadelphia; from 1776 to 1783 appeared thirteen letters under the heading of *The American Crisis,* and in 1786 the *Dissertations on Government, the Affairs of the Bank and Paper Money*.

In the same period Paine had served as aid to General Greene, as secretary of the Congressional Committee for Foreign Affairs and as clerk of the Pennsylvania Assembly. In 1787 he returned to England, where he published in 1791-92 *The Rights of Man,* as a reply to Burke's reactionary *Reflections on the Revolution in France.* Like his *Common Sense,* this production of Paine was extensively circulated and became widely influential. So obnoxious was its radicalism to the government that the author was prosecuted for "scandalous, malicious and seditious libel," and upon trial was outlawed.

Before his case was heard, however, Paine passed over to France, where he entered the National Convention in the capacity of representative. In this new scene of activity the irrepressible agitator played, as elsewhere, a conspicuous part. He was a member of the committee which framed the Constitution of 1793,[2] and was active in the proceedings against Louis XVI, though he opposed the execution of the king. Among his writings during his stay in France were an *Anti-Monarchical Essay* (1792), the *Age of Reason* (1794-95), a *Dissertation on First Principles of Government* (1795) and *Agrarian Justice* (1797).

Paine returned to America in 1802 and plunged at once into the conflict against the Federalists, with a series of letters *To the Citizens of the United States* (1802-3). He also wrote on the proposed constitutional convention in Pennsylvania (1805). These last years of Paine's life were not happy. His bitter letter to Washington[3] and the radical doctrines of the *Age of Reason* had estranged many of his friends and had made him many enemies, so that the career of the author of *Common Sense* closed in comparative obscurity and neglect.[4]

It is the purpose of this paper to examine the political ideas for which this ubiquitous revolutionist carried on so long, so vigorous and so frequently successful a propaganda. Did he "breathe the political atmosphere" of Rousseau and Locke? and was his genius "from the first that of an inventor"?[5] Or did he merely "prate about the rights of man"?[6] These are questions that may be answered by a study of Paine's writings in their relation to general political theory.

A fundamental distinction in the political theory of Paine is that drawn between society and government.[7] The social condition he regards as the natural state of man, the governmental as purely artificial. Men are attracted into society, on the one hand, by certain wants which can be satisfied only by means of social coöperation and, on the other, by that love for society and social relations which is implanted in men from birth. Life in society, then, Paine regards as perfectly natural and normal. It is in this social state, moreover, that Paine finds the basis for the natural rights upon which his whole system rests. Burke, who was as much afraid of political change as Plato, had in his *Reflections* contended for government in accordance with historical precedent. To this argument Paine agreed; but, said he, if the justification for government is to be found in precedent, we must not stop short of the first and foremost precedent. In this search he finds that

> it is authority against authority all the way till we come to the divine origin of the rights of man at the creation. Here our inquiries find a resting place and our reason finds a home.[8]

If, then, we are to follow precedent, the state of man at the creation stands first in the series. But man, fresh from the hands of nature, possesses a body of original or natural rights, such as liberty, equality, *etc.*[9] That there may be no lack of connection between the primitive and the present state, Paine goes on to show

that every child born into the world has the same kind of rights, as if "posterity had been continued by creation instead of generation." The state of nature, then, affords the first great precedent.

In this state of society men might have lived in peace and happiness without government, had the "impulses of conscience" been "clear, uniform and irresistibly obeyed."[10] Men are, however, morally weak and imperfect, and hence required some restraining power. This is found in government, which is defined as "a mode rendered necessary by the inability of moral virtue to govern the world."[11] Unconsciously following the theory of St. Augustine, Paine declares that "government, like dress, is the badge of lost innocence. The palaces of kings are built upon the ruins of the bowers of paradise." Government was in his eyes a "necessary evil": "the more perfect civilization is, the less occasion has it for government." Little importance is attached to what he terms "formal government." The security of the people, their comfort and their progress, depend much more upon society than upon government. Social usage and custom, the mutual relations of men and their mutual interests, are of far greater influence than any political institutions, however perfectly constructed or skillfully operated. Government is needed only in those few cases where society cannot conveniently act. There are even instances where all the ordinary functions of government have been performed by society alone, as in the American colonies during the first years of the Revolutionary War.[12] On the whole, society is "a creature of our wants," government of our "wickedness"; society is a blessing, government is an evil; society is a "patron," government a "punisher."

The transition from society to government is effected by a contract between members of the society.[13] By the terms of this agreement, each individual retains all the rights which he is able to enforce, such as "rights of the mind," and the right to act for one's own happiness where this is not in conflict with the happiness of others. Rights which one possesses but is unable to enforce are deposited in the "common stock"; and, as Paine says, the individual "takes the arm of society in preference to his own." After the formation of government every man has two classes of rights: natural rights, by virtue of his membership in the human race; civil rights, by virtue of his membership in civil society.

Paine denied, as Rousseau had denied, the existence of a contract between people and government;[14] for such a contract would suppose the existence of a government before it had a right to act. The government could not logically be a party to the contract which created it. The only contract between government and people which Paine would admit is that the people should pay their governors as long as they retain them in the popular service.

In the classification of the forms of government, Paine does not always adhere to the same canons of distinction. In one place he declares that there is but one species of man and one element of power; and that, therefore, "monarchy, aristocracy and democracy are but creatures of the imagination, and a thousand such may be contrived as well as three."[15] Again, from an historical point of view, there have been three classes of governments: first, government by superstition, in which the rulers and the priesthood are in close alliance; second, government by brute force, in which authority is obtained by conquest; and, third, government based on the rights of man.[16] The classification most commonly used divides government into two groups: government by "hereditary succession" and government by "election and representation."[17] Monarchy and aristocracy fall under the first of these classes; democracy, under the second.

For government by "hereditary succession" Paine, like Rousseau, had a deep-seated dislike. All hereditary government he looked upon as tyranny. There is no justification for such government on the basis either of right or of utility. In support of the legitimacy of the hereditary form, it might be urged that such a right was derived from the contract to which Paine stood committed; but to this he would reply that no one generation of men has power to bind another. A nation is in a constant state of change: infants are daily born into it and the aged are daily leaving; and in this ever-running flood of generation there is no part superior in authority to another. "Man," he argues, "has no property in man; neither has one generation a property in the generations that are to follow." Or, as otherwise expressed:

> Our ancestors, like ourselves, were but tenants for life in the great freehold of rights. The fee absolute was not in them, it is not in us: it belongs to the whole family of man through all ages.[18]

Paine suggests that "all laws and acts should cease of themselves in thirty years; it would prevent their becoming too numerous or voluminous."[19]

Again, it might be maintained that the right to hereditary succession had been acquired by prescription. But Paine will have none of this. To say that the right is acquired by time, is either to put time in the place of principle or make it superior to principle; whereas time has no more connection with principle than principle has with time.

> The wrong which began a thousand years ago is as much a wrong as if it began to-day, and the right which originates to-day is as much a right as if it had the sanction of a thousand years.

Political radicalism never found more complete expression than in the declaration of Paine: "Time, with respect to principles, is an eternal now."[20]

Failing to find a basis of right for hereditary government, Paine is no more successful in discovering support for the system in utility. He is blind to all elements of strength it may contain, and is able to see nothing in the hereditary system but an unnatural and absurd method of selecting governmental officials. The plan is contrary to nature and to reason; and it is, in fact, hardly conceivable how apparently sensible people ever came to adopt it. We do not attempt to secure "an hereditary mathematician," or an "hereditary wise man," or an "hereditary poet laureate"; why, then, choose our governors after this fashion? The only parallel to the doctrine of hereditary succession is found in the theological tenet of original sin.

> In Adam all sinned, and in the first electors all men obeyed; in the one all mankind were subjected to Satan, and in the other to sovereignty; our innocence was lost in the first, and our authority in the last.[21]

In the institution of monarchy Paine can discern nothing whatever that is worthy of approval, much less of imitation. Every king is to him a George III, and a George III at his worst. The whole vocabulary of epithet is exhausted in the effort to render monarchy odious and ridiculous. "Sceptred savage," "royal brute," "breathing automaton," are presented as accurate characterizations of kings. Burke's elaborate and eloquent plea for the "divinity that doth hedge about a king" was wholly unappreciated by Paine, who compared monarchy to

> something kept behind a curtain about which there is a great deal of bustle and fuss, and a wonderful air of seeming security; but when by any accident the curtain happens to open and the company see what it is, they burst into laughter.[22]

Kings are only useless and expensive figureheads—the sooner dispensed with, the better. The only function performed by the English king is that of making war and giving away places for £800,000 a year and being worshiped into the bargain.[23] Even in a representative government Paine would oppose the establishment of a single executive, because one man will always be at the head of a party and because, moreover, there is a certain debasement involved in the idea of obedience to any one individual.[24] Paine's opinion of monarchy is fairly expressed when he declares: "Of more worth is one honest man to society and in the sight of God than all the crowned ruffians that ever lived."[25] This single statement contains both his premises and his conclusions.

Aristocracy Paine disliked almost as much as monarchy; but the weight of his argument (or invective) was naturally directed against kings rather than aristocrats. George III and Louis XVI were the objective points of his attack. His principal arguments against aristocracy were: that it is kept up by family tyranny and injustice, that it establishes a body of men unaccountable to any one and therefore not to be trusted, and that it has a tendency to "degenerate" the species. "The artificial noble," he said, "shrinks into a dwarf before the noble of nature."[26] Both monarchy and aristocracy, he thought, were doomed to speedy dissolution; and he did not believe that they would "continue seven years longer in any of the enlightened countries of Europe."[27]

Rejecting all forms of "hereditary government," it appears that the only worthy form is the representative or republican. A republic, however, is with Paine more a matter of principle than of form: in fact, any government established and conducted for the public good is a republic.[28] The security that government will be so administered is found in the social contract, which guarantees the rights of all; otherwise, "despotism may be more effectually acted by many over a few than by one man over all." The essence of republican government is, therefore, that the "principle of despotism" be given up and that of contract and consent accepted. This insured, we are led up naturally to a system of "election and representation." On this question Paine parted from Rousseau and was an ardent advocate of representative government. Moreover, his idea of the extent to which the citizens should share in this representation was unusually broad. He denounced even the feeblest barrier in the form of a property qualification, and declared himself in favor of universal manhood suffrage.[29] The basis of representation, he contends, should be personal rather than property rights. Personal rights may, indeed, be regarded as a "species of property of the most sacred kind." As for wealth, as commonly understood, its possession is "no proof of moral character; nor poverty of the want of it." In regard to protection to the "landed interests," there is no reason why they should be guarded more than any other class of interests; but if there were especial cause, the surest guaranty would be found in the grant of equal rights to all. This follows, because a high property qualification excludes a majority of the population, who are likely to become hostile to the government and to endanger the security and safety of all. Furthermore, argues Paine, government is not organized on the same principle as a bank or a corporation, where property is the sole subject of discussion. In such cases it may be just to allot representation in proportion to property; but government is organized upon a different principle from such associations. It takes cognizance of every citizen, whether he has much or little or no property at all. The basis of representation should be, he urges, as broad as the subjects to which the government applies, and hence all should be entitled to the franchise: Representative government, therefore, should rest upon no narrower foundation than manhood suffrage.[30]

The tripartite division of governmental powers into executive, legislative and judicial, as marked out by Montesquieu and generally received by eighteenth-century republicans, was not acceptable to Paine. He agreed to the principle of division, but not to the form commonly adopted. Paine held that there are only two classes of governmental powers—the willing or decreeing and the executing; one corresponding to the faculties of the mind, the other to those of the body.[31] If the legislature wills and the executive fails to perform, as in a man when the mind wills and the body does not execute, a condition of imbecility results; or, if the executive acts without the predetermination of the legislature, a state of lunacy. The third and omitted power—the judiciary—is, in Paine's opinion, not a separate and distinct power at all, but is, strictly speaking, as in the modern French theory, a part of the executive. The latter he looks upon as made up of "all the official departments that execute the laws"; and of these the judiciary is the chief.[32]

For mixed or balanced governments Paine cared but little. Mixed government he derides as "an imperfect everything, cementing and soldering the discordant parts together by corruption to act as a whole."[33] In the system of checks and balances which Montesquieu found in the English constitution, Paine had little confidence. The greatest weight in any government will, he thinks, be the controlling power;[34] and, though the other powers may retard the rapidity of its motion, they are unable to prevent its ultimate success. The strongest power will finally prevail, and "what it wants in speed is supplied by time." In the English constitution the crown is the heaviest weight and, therefore, the controlling power.[35]

Paine's conception of a constitution is that of a definite body of instructions, or general rules, in accordance with which government is to be carried on.[36] The constitution is the creation, not of the government, but of the people or the society. Thus, the National Assembly of France (1791) represents the society "in its *original* character"; but, after the formation of a constitution, future Assemblies will represent the society "in its *organized* character."[37] A constitutional convention does not signify to Paine a representation of the state, but of what he calls the "society," the "people," the "nation." Paine, moreover, thinks of a constitution as something which exists, not "in name only, but in fact"; which has "not an ideal, but a real existence"; and which can, furthermore, be produced "in a visible form"—in other words, a written constitution. Burke could not produce a copy of the English constitution; therefore, "we may fairly conclude that, though it has been so much talked about, no such thing as a constitution exists."[38] Cloudy as this part of his constitutional theory may be, there are other places where Paine shows great clearness of thought. Especially is this true in regard to the amendment of constitutions. Rigidity and inflexibility he considers as highly undesirable in the organic law.[39] The constitution should contain provision for its own amendment; for, however advantageous it might be for posterity to inherit a perfect constitution, such a consummation is impossible. "We should not," he says, "allow our anxiety for their [posterity's] welfare to carry us to the pitch of doubting their capacity. They might be wiser than we are."

In his practical politics Paine favored, as we have already seen, a system of representative government, based on manhood suffrage. Further, the executive power should not be centered in the hands of one man, and should not possess a veto.[40] The legislature should consist of one house only, in which all the good and none of the bad effects of a bicameral system should be secured, by dividing the house into two sections for debate on every question, the combined vote of the two divisions being taken to determine the result.[41] In regard to the judiciary, Paine condemned tenure during good behavior, and thought that judges should be elected annually, or for the same term as other officers. Lawyers he denounces in rather severe terms—asserting, for example, that the bar "lives by encouraging the injustice it pretends to redress." He distinguishes between "lawyers' law" and "legislative law," and protests against the former, because it is "a mass of opinions and decisions, many of them contradictory to each other." Paine holds courts of arbitration in high favor and recommends resort to them, whenever possible, in preference to the ordinary tribunals.

Other points of interest and importance in Paine's politics are found in his scheme for a progressive income tax[42] and his plan for "agrarian justice."[43] The first of these suggestions is found in the **Rights of Man,** where he outlines a plan for an income tax ranging from threepence per pound, on £50 clear yearly income, to twenty shillings—or confiscation—for the twenty-third thousand of clear yearly income. In the same connection is presented an elaborate plan for state aid to the poor in the shape of pensions, donations for marriages and births, allowances for funeral expenses, employment for the causal poor in London and Westminster[44] and other like measures.

The scheme for "agrarian justice" starts with the proposition that all men have an equal right to "natural property," though not to "artificial property." The object of the plan is to make every individual secure in this right to "natural property." Estimating that the natural wealth changes hands by inheritance every thirty years, Paine proposes to tax all inheritances ten per cent and all those descending out of the direct line an additional ten per cent. From this fund every man, when he arrives at the age of twenty-one, is to be paid the sum of £15, and every person over fifty may require £10 per year. In this way every one will be secured in his original right to "natural property."

These propositions of Paine are an excellent illustration of the flexible character of "natural-right" philosophy. Government, in his theory, is at once a necessary evil, with narrowly circumscribed functions, and, on the other hand, a beneficent instrument admirably adapted to collect a confiscatory income tax or a twenty per cent inheritance tax, or to administer schemes for state assurance of employment and support. The "rights of man" are turned with equal ease to the support of either scientific anarchy or a socialistic system. Paine, it is true, was neither a socialist nor an anarchist; but there was nothing in his fundamental theory to hinder him from becoming the one or the other.

Another interesting illustration of the subjective character of the "rights of man" is furnished by Paine's answer to the remonstrance of the people of Louisiana requesting the privilege of self-government.[45] In answer to their petition for the recognition of their "natural rights," Paine asks: "Why did you not speak this when you ought to have spoken it? We fought for liberty when you stood quiet in slavery." In language strangely at variance with his **Rights of Man,** he suggests that the petitioners already enjoy a degree of liberty;

> and in proportion as you become initiated into the principles and practice of the republican system of government, of which you have yet had no experience, you will participate more and more, and finally be made partakers of the whole.

A proof of their incapacity is found in the fact that "under the name of rights you ask for powers—power to import and enslave Africans,[46] and to govern territory that *we* have *purchased.*" Inalienable rights, it would seem, may be forfeited under certain circumstances, and political liberty is not a thing to be considered apart from political capacity.

From the foregoing sketch it seems clear that Paine cannot be classed as a great political thinker. His theories of the state of nature, the rights of man, the social contract, representative government—in fact, all the great features of his system had been marked out before and better by others. Paine was not a philosopher, but an agitator. The source of his power is found in his rare faculty for popular statement of radical political ideas. Few political writers have had a more perfect mastery of the art of popular persuasion—few have played more skillfully on the popular chords than the author of **Common Sense** and the

Rights of Man. Only one voice, that of Rousseau, has proclaimed with greater effect the democratic doctrines of the natural-right school. The *Contrat Social,* however, rejected the representative system; so that Paine was, in fact, the great popular champion of radical democracy in the latter part of the eighteenth century.

The influence exerted by Paine in his advocacy of democracy, though popular rather than scientific in its nature, was by no means inconsiderable. In France he helped to combat Abbé Siéyès's plan for an hereditary monarchy and aided in the establishment of the phrases and forms, at least, of constitutional liberty, even if its life was wanting. That England was moved by his arguments in the ***Rights of Man,*** is evident from the extensive circulation of the work and the widespread controversy which it aroused. His influence is noticeable in such works as William Godwin's *Enquiry Concerning Political Justice,* published in 1793. The European influence of Paine was crippled, however, by the fact that he was imperfectly adapted to the rôle of revolutionist in either of the two states where he labored. He was too French for the English and too English for the French. No checks and balances, no monarch, no hereditary nobility, but government based upon manhood suffrage—these were ideas that ran counter to English instinct, especially in England, frightened by the scenes across the channel. On the other hand, Paine was hardly radical enough to keep even pace with the progress of the French Revolution. As he says in his reply to the Louisiana remonstrance, "You see what mischief ensued in France by the possession of power before they understood principles. They earned liberty in words, but not in fact." Paine's political ideas and political spirit were, after all, English and not French. With the French Declaration of the Rights of Man he did not disagree, but in the practical application of its ideas to political organization he was certain to differ.

In America Paine's power was weakened by the appearance of his ***Age of Reason,*** which extended his radical activity from the field of politics to that of religion. The conservatives, moreover, now that the American Revolution was accomplished, were inclined to forget the doctrines of that period and to think more of the duties than of the rights of man. So, an answer to Paine's greatest work was undertaken by J. Q. Adams, in a series of letters over the signature "Publicola." On the other hand, Jefferson and the Jeffersonian democracy accepted and approved in great part the political ideas of Paine. His hatred of England and his championship of manhood suffrage tended to make his general theory acceptable; and it is perhaps fair to say that John Adams's *Defense of the Constitutions of Government of the United States* and Paine's ***Rights of Man*** represented the political theory of the two great branches of American democracy of that day.

Notes

[1] See Moncure D. Conway, *Life of Thomas Paine* (2 vols., Putnam's Sons, 1892). Also *Writings of Thomas Paine,* edited by Conway (4 vols., Putnam's Sons, 1894-96). The references in the present article, unless otherwise stated, are to this edition of the writings.

[2] Conway says: "It is certain that the work of framing the Constitution of 1793 was mainly intrusted to Paine and Condorcet."—*Writings,* III, 128.

[3] *Writings,* III, 213 (1796). For Paine on John Adams, see III, 390.

[4] Paine was denied the right of suffrage at his home in New Rochelle in 1806.—See Life, II, 374.

[5] Conway, *Introduction to Writings of Thomas Paine.*

[6] McMaster, *History of the People of the United States,* II, 620.

[7] See *Common Sense,* I, 69; *Rights of Man,* II, 406-11.

[8] *Rights of Man,* II, 304.

[9] See Declaration of Rights in French Constitution of 1793, which contained Paine's ideas on natural rights.

[10] *Common Sense,* I, 71; also *Rights of Man,* II, 406.

[11] *Common Sense,* I, 71.

[12] *Rights of Man,* II, 407.

[13] *Ibid.,* II, 306.

[14] *Rights of Man,* II, 432.

[15] *Ibid.,* II, 384, 385.

[16] *Ibid.,* II, 308. For another classification see *Dissertations on Government,* II, 133.

[17] *Rights of Man,* II, 414; *First Principles,* III, 257.

[18] *First Principles,* III, 262.

[19] *Dissertations on Government,* II, 165. Compare Jefferson, *Works* (Ford's ed.), II, 115.

[20] *First Principles,* III, 260.—But Pennsylvania, Paine argued at another time, had no right to annual the charter of the Bank, because "the state is still the same state. The public is still the same body. . . . These are not new created every year, nor can they be displaced from their original standing, but are a perpetual

permanent body, always in being and still the same." The next generation may annual the charter, but not the present.—See *Dissertations on Government, Writings,* II, 147, 166.

[21] *Common Sense,* I, 81.

[22] *Rights of Man,* II, 426.

[23] *Common Sense,* I, 84. Paine admits that in an absolute monarchy a king may be of some service.

[24] *Letter to Washington,* III, 214.

[25] *Common Sense,* I, 84.

[26] *Rights of Man,* II, 323.

[27] *Ibid.,* II 398.

[28] *Dissertations on Government,* II, 137, 138.

[29] The Constitution of 1795, III, 280; *First Principles,* III, 265 *et seq.*

[30] *First Principles* III, 268, 269.

[31] *Answer to Four Questions,* II, 238, 239; *First Principles,* III, 275.

[32] *First Principles,* I, 276.

[33] *Rights of Man,* II, 383.

[34] *Common Sense,* I, 74.

[35] See analysis of English Constitution, I, 72-74.

[36] *Rights of Man,* II, 309.

[37] *Rights of Man,* II, 311; *Dissertations on Government,* II, 147.

[38] *Rights of Man,* II, 310.

[39] *Answer to Four Questions,* II, 249-251.

[40] See *Constitutional Reform,* IIII, Appendix G.

[41] *Four Questions,* II, 236; *Constitutional Reform,* IIII, 462. In the *Four Questions* he "is a little inclined to admit the idea of two chambers with an arbitrary and reciprocal veto." (II, 244.)

[42] *Rights of Man,* II, 497.

[43] *Agrarian Justice,* III, 322-344; see also his *Maritime Compact,* III, 421, and other propositions in the latter part of the *Rights of Man.*

[44] *Rights of Man,* II, 501, 502.

[45] For the Remonstrance, see Annals of Congress, 1804-1805, p. 1597; Paine's *Reply* (1804), in *Writings,* III, 430-436.

[46] Paine's first essay for publication was on *African Slavery in America—Writings,* I, 4.

Woodrow Wilson, twenty-eighth president of the United States, on *Common Sense*:

One such [pamphlet] took precedence of all others, whether for boldness or for power, the extraordinary pamphlet which Thomas Paine, but the other day come out of England as if upon mere adventure, gave to the world as ***Common Sense***. It came from the press in Philadelphia early in January, 1776, the year the Congress uttered its Declaration of Independence, and no writing ever more instantly swung men to its humor. It was hard to resist its quick, incisive sentences, which cut so unhesitatingly to the heart of every matter they touched; which spoke, not the arguments of the lawyer or the calculations of the statesman, but the absolute spirit of revolt, and were as direct and vivid in their appeal as any sentences of Mr. Swift himself could have been. They were cast, every one, not according to the canons of taste, but according to the canons of force, and declared, every one, without qualification, for independence.

Woodrow Wilson, in A History of the American People, *Harper and Brothers, 1902.*

Harry Hayden Clark (essay date 1933)

SOURCE: "Thomas Paine's Theories of Rhetoric," in *Transactions of the Wisconsin Academy of Sciences, Arts and Letters,* Vol. 28, 1933, pp. 307-39.

[*In the following essay, Clark presents Paine as a literary "craftsman" who abided by a set of guidelines for effective writing, including clarity, boldness, wit, and appeal to feeling. Clark also suggests that Paine's view of language originated in his views of religion and nature.*]

Thomas Paine has long been recognized as foremost among those who brought the rationalism of the eighteenth century home to the plain people and, in revolting against throne and altar, encouraged them to strive for democracy and the religion of humanity. If authorities on the history of political theory are agreed that in spite of his vast influence "Paine cannot be classed as a great political thinker" since "his theories of the state of nature, the rights of man, the social contract, representative government—in fact, all the great features of his system [—] had been marked out before and better by others," if the "source of his power is found in his rare faculty for popular statement," if "few political writers have had a more perfect mastery of the art of popular persuasion,"[1] it should be of interest to ascertain as far as possible the literary theories which helped to make the great republican the "prince of pamphleteers."[2] Of course, being neither a literary critic nor an aesthete, being concerned not with "pure" but with "applied" literature, Paine had relatively little to say regarding abstract literary theories. Nevertheless, if the criterion of the success of applied literature is its acceptance by those in whose cause it is applied, the fact that the demand for ***Common Sense*** and the ***Rights of Man*** ran to half a million copies of each[3] suggests that, the same ideas being available in other forms, their style embodied a congruency to the human mind and heart which is after all the badge of a valid literary theory and which gives what Paine does have to say of his literary theory a rather unusual claim to our attention.

Before coming directly to a consideration of this theory, however, it may be well to remind ourselves that the contemporary effectiveness of Paine's work was due in part to other factors than the intrinsic merit of its style. Applied writing depends in no small measure for its success upon the condition of the point of application, and probably at no time in history had economic distress and political inefficiency done so much to make acceptable Paine's mordant criticism of monarchy and his ardent advocacy of humanitarian reform.[4] He himself remarks in ***Common Sense,*** which is often credited with having single-handed caused a somersault in opinion as to the American Revolution, that he found "the disposition of the people such, that they might have been led by a thread and governed by a reed,"[5] a situation which does not suggest the need of any very violent power to overcome inertia. And it has been plausibly argued that Paine was not so much the creator as the voice of popular opinion,[6] moulded by an infinite variety of other factors. In England "the chief activities [of the Society for Constitutional Information] were confined to spreading the writings of Thomas Paine in cheap editions, printing 'Proclamations' and letters advocating their principles, and attempting to cooperate in these measures with various similar organizations."[7] Unfortunately, all writers cannot rely upon such an organization for distributing their work!

Furthermore, Paine's literary effectiveness may depend upon intangible factors, in part, integral with his general outlook and character. "What I write," he said, "is pure nature, and my pen and my soul have ever gone together."[8] It is probably true, as I hope to demonstrate in detail elsewhere, that Paine wrote in the light of an all-embracing central principle, essentially religious,[9] and such a principle, regardless of its intrin-

sic validity, helps to give a man's writing focus and unity and driving power, as well as the sort of effectiveness which comes from hitting the reader repeatedly on the same nerve. No doubt Paine's devotion to geometry and to scientific methods essentially deductive tended to give his work syllogistic convincingness and the air of dogmatic assurance which springs from the absence of a tedious inductive approach and a distracting regard for qualifications and exceptions. His general programme of returning to the simplicity of nature and his ostensible contempt for book-learning as opposed to the universal and sufficient light of nature[10] tended, furthermore, to free his style from pedantic literary allusions which so often clogged earlier American style, as for example that of Cotton Mather's *Magnalia*. If the rank and file of robust men are attracted by a good fight, Paine handled words as the pugilist handles his gloves; he delights in verbal knock-outs. Witness the way in which this so-called Quaker apostle of humanitarian brotherhood salutes an opponent: "Remember thou hast thrown me the glove, Cato, and either thee or I must tire. I fear not the field of fair debate, but thou hast stepped aside and made it personal. Thou hast tauntingly called on me by name; and if I cease to hunt thee from every lane and lurking hole of mischief, and bring thee not a trembling culprit before the public bar, then brand me with reproach, by naming me in the list of your confederates."[11] At the period of the birth of the nation the Fathers were outspoken, believing in free speech as a means of "conveying *heat* and *light*," (especially heat!) as Paine's friend Benjamin Rush said, "to every individual in the Federal Commonwealth."[12] After an age when opponents of monarchy and ecclesiasticism, living at their mercy, had been obliged to take refuge in sinuous methods and guarded analogies, many vigorous spirits no doubt found Paine's outspoken bluntness refreshing, if not contagious. Finally, if, as Emerson remarks, a man can excel in nothing who does not believe that what he is doing is at the moment the most important thing in the world, Paine's solemn conviction that he was a messiah sent to liberate mankind from "the tributary bondage of the ages" to throne and altar, to usher in "the birthday of a new world,"[13] steeled him with self-confidence, economic and political history having given him a sympathetic audience, which inspired his pen in its consecration to a noble cause with a fervour apostolic. His spirit was dampened by no paralyzing surrender to determinisms, economic or mechanistic, or by any misgivings as to the efficacy of his tools: he was enraptured by the magic witchery of words, confident that if mankind were to be regenerated, it would be through the mighty power of the pen. A perfectibilian dedicated to the current faith that conduct is the mere externalization of opinion, he regarded "one philosopher though a heathen" as of "more use" than "all the heathen conquerors that ever existed," the French Revolution being literally truth clad in hell-fire, "no more than the consequence of a mental revolution priorly existing in France"[14] engendered by "the writings of the French philosophers." "There is nothing which obtains so great an influence over the manners and morals of a people as the Press."[15] "Letters, the tongue of the world," represent the fighting wedge of progress, the writer commanding "a scene as vast as the world. . . . Jesus Christ and his apostles could not do this."[16]

If such general factors, integral with Paine's general outlook, help in part to explain his power, it must also be borne in mind that his mastery of his art was conditioned, in no small measure, by a knowledge of the achievements and methods of other writers and thinkers. It has been conventional to take him at his word—"I neither read books, nor studied other people's opinion"[17]—notwithstanding the fact that he contradicted this assertion repeatedly in word and act; it has been conventional to assume as axiomatic that he was distinguished by an "immense ignorance of history and literature."[18] Ignorant he no doubt was, if one uses the learning of a Coleridge or an Arnold as a standard; but such a view of Paine's knowledge of books, which has never been thoroughly investigated, would seem rather naively to neglect certain somewhat unique considerations. If, as in the case of Franklin, his formal schooling ended at an early age, he was aflame with an insatiable curiosity, and he had most unusual opportunities for satisfying it. "I seldom passed five minutes of my life however circumstanced," he confides, "in which I did not acquire some knowledge."[19] To begin with, contemporary doggerel records that as a result of his repeated triumps in debate at the "White Hart Evening Club" his fellow-townsmen at Lewes crowned "Immortal Paine . . . General of the Headstrong War," his ability being such that the excisemen of England finally appointed him to plead with Parliament on behalf of **"The Case of the Officers of the Excise,"** 1772. He had served as a school-teacher, and Franklin, who sponsored his coming to America, supposed he would continue that calling there. There, however, as editor of *The Pennsylvania Magazine,* he received and commented upon current publications in America, England, and France. It appears that before 1775 he had "received much pleasure from perusing" such English magazines as *The Gentleman's,* the *London,* the *Universal,* the *Town and Country,* the *Covent-Garden,* and the *Westminster.*[20] The Continental Congress regarded him as competent to serve as "secretary for foreign affairs almost two years,"[21] a position in which he read and wrote a vast number of important letters. These opportunities for securing information, however, are trivial compared with his immense opportunities as a result of his multitudinous contacts, in Franklin's circle in America, Godwin's circle in England, and Condorcet's circle in France.[22] What could he not have learned regarding ideas, perhaps from books whose names were unmentioned, from listening to the conversation not only of the men mentioned but

of such men as Jefferson, Barlow, Dr. Rush, John Adams, Horne Tooke, Holcroft, Burke (whose earlier work Paine admired), Brissot, Lafayette, and countless others who were Paine's frequent companions and his hosts?

The fact that Paine seldom refers to other writers may not be inconsistent with a knowledge of their ideas, especially when one takes into account the indirect conversational sources suggested above and the considerations which follow. First, as a perfectibilian condemning the past and gazing hopefully into the future, as a sworn enemy of a socially mediated tradition, Paine was generally too much of a logician to cite that tradition as support for an attack upon it. Second, as a naturalistic opponent of philosophies and religions dependent upon books which were for him rooted in traditional imposture and national and temporal idiosyncrasies, Paine advocated, through the scientific quest for universal and immutable natural law, the study not of books but of nature, which was supposed to be everywhere, to all times and peoples, a uniform and universal revelation of a wisdom and benevolence divine; consequently, he could not logically appear to depend himself upon books. Indeed, contemporary critics taunted him upon the inconsistency of himself condemning a book-religion by means of a book and offering a book as a remedy.[23] Third, it was part of the established campaign strategy of the Godwinian circle, which saw to the details of publishing the **Rights of Man** in England, to cite "no authorities."[24] Fourth, Citizen Egotism, as Paine was called, posing as an original genius, was not anxious to share the glory of having "a range in political writing beyond, perhaps, what any man ever possessed in any country,"[25] of having "arrived at an eminence in political literature the most difficult of all lines to succeed and excel in, which aristocracy with all its aids has not been able to reach or to rival,"[26] of having by his pen equalled the power of Washington's sword, his book which liberated America having "the greatest sale that any performance ever had since the use of letters."[27]

Fifth, considering that Paine was the spokesman of the unschooled and the illiterate, priding himself upon his ability to resolve imposing sophistry to its simple elements, to avoid the artificiality of an aristocratic culture, it would be unlikely that Paine would strain toward literary allusions. And finally, it was an effective part of his strategy in *The Age of Reason,* as Richard Watson scrupulously noted,[28] to disclaim all learned appeals to other books, and "to undertake to prove, from the Bible itself, that it is unworthy of credit." How Paine revels in demonstrating, as he thinks, that the Bible is "book of lies, wickedness, and blasphemy"[29] without going for proof beyond what was regarded as the sacred Word of God![30] Considering such a confessed controversial strategy, it would seem rather obvious that the paucity of other books cited could not be taken as valid evidence of the author's "immense ignorance." This, however, is but one of many instances of inadequate interpretations of Paine as a result of a failure to read individual passages in the light of both the contemporary climate of opinion and the man's central philosophical outlook. I would not imply that Paine was in any sense a prodigy of learning, but I do think that he had a decent knowledge of contemporary currents of opinion and literary methods. With the six considerations just suggested in mind, it would seem that what references Paine does make directly to other writers might be taken at somewhat more than their customary face-value, since such references conflicted with his whole philosophy and his controversial method, inviting taunts, painful to a logician and moralist, of an inability to follow his own precepts. Elsewhere[31] I hope to discuss Paine's references to more than an hundred such figures as the following, and to show his knowledge, in varying degrees, of their work; these are: Homer, Xenophon, Aesop, Herodotus, Thucydides, Plato, Aristotle, Zoroaster, Confucius, Cicero, Virgil, Pliny, Tacitus, Scaliger, Dragonetti, Augustine, Maimonides, Origen, Spinoza, Luther, Cervantes, Shakespeare, Ben Jonson, Barclay, Milton, Bunyan, Tillotson, Locke, Sydney, Henry Lord, Descartes, Newton, 'Hudibras' Butler, Grotius, Denham, Dryden, Defoe, Swift, Pope, Smollett, Thomson, Allan Ramsay, Chatterton, James Ferguson, Benjamin Martin, Conyers Middleton, Churchill, Robertson, Chesterfield, Wilkes, Blackstone, 'Junius', George Lewis Scott, Samuel Rogers, Fox, Burke, Johnson, Shelburne, Robert Merry, Blake, Sampson Perry, Godwin, Mary Wollstonecraft, Holcroft, Priestly, Cobbett, Rapin, Burgh, Price, David Levi, Ferguson, Sir William Jones, Whiston, 'Peter Pindar', Adam Smith, David Williams, Franklin, Jefferson, Barlow, John Adams, James Wilson, Samuel Adams, Christie, Edward Fitzgerald, Towers, Mackintosh, Washington, Gouverneur Morris, Monroe, Palmer, Montesquieu, Voltaire, Rousseau, Turgot, Quesnay, Raynal, Helvétius, Boulauger, Brissot, Lafayette, and Condorcet. But could the 'rebellious staymaker' read critically and digest the ideas of such authors? His diabolically acute analysis of the Holy Scriptures suggests that he could. At least he should have been able to profit by the theory and practice of these authors in formulating his own literary theories, which are for the most part in close accord with those of his age.[32]

Having now considered extra-literary factors which aided Paine and having suggested that he was not quite so ignorant of literary tradition as generally supposed, let us turn directly to a presentation of what he himself has to say regarding literary theory and the art of writing controversial prose. What were his avowed aims?

First among these aims is candour, simplicity, and clarity. He would "rid our ideas of all superfluous words, and consider them in their natural bareness and simplicity."[33] "I speak a language full and intelligible," he remarks in summing up his writing on "every subject." "I deal not in hints and intimations. I have several reasons for this: First, that I may be clearly understood. Secondly, that it may be seen I am in earnest; and, thirdly, because it is an affront to truth to treat falsehood with complaisance."[34] He describes the **Rights of Man** as "a book calmly and rationally written, . . . in a fair, open, and manly manner,"[35] and he tells us elsewhere that he forbade himself "the use of equivocal expression or mere ceremony."[36] When Americans were reluctant on account of sentimental ties to break the bond which bound them to the Fatherland, he exclaimed impatiently, "I bring reason to your ears, and in language as plain as A, B, C, hold up truth to your eyes."[37] No doubt John Adams came as near hating Paine as any man, and as a Federalist he increasingly abominated his anti-traditional[38] and equalitarian principles, yet he was honest enough to recognize that he himself "could not have written anything in so manly and striking a style [as **Common Sense**]," and that it contained "a great deal of good sense delivered in clear, simple, concise, and nervous style."[39] This first ideal of Paine's was of course in line with that of eighteenth-century prose writers from Defoe to his beloved patron Franklin, although Paine was conspicuously lacking in Franklin's inoffensive Socratic approach and his skill in winning assent without antagonizing. As Franklin wrote Hume, who had pronounced him the first man-of-letters of the New World, "certainly in writings intended for persuasion and for general information, one can not be too clear; and every expression in the least obscure is a fault . . . The introducing new words, where we are already possessed of old ones sufficiently expressive, I confess must be generally wrong."[40] Moreover, Paine's mastery of his familiar friend's ideal in this respect is attested by the fact, as Jefferson remarked,[41] that **Common Sense,** which Paine submitted to Franklin for criticism, was first attributed to Franklin.

One may designate *boldness* Paine's second ideal, one, unfortunately, as it seems to me, which not seldom carried him, as he confessed, beyond the "common track of civil language."[42] It is, he says, "curious to observe how soon this spell [of sentimental attachment to monarchy] can be dissolved. A single expression, boldly conceived and uttered, will sometimes put a whole company into their proper feelings: and whole nations are acted on in the same manner."[43] In transferring this literary method acquired in the rough-and-tumble of politics to religion, Paine was conscious of pioneering in "a style of thinking and expression different to what had been customary in England."[44] As he wrote Elihu Palmer, whose "Principles of Nature" carried on Paine's tradition in America, "The hinting and intimidating manner of writing that was formerly used on subjects of this kind, produced skepticism, but not conviction. It is necessary to be bold. Some people can be reasoned into sense, and others must be shocked into it. Say a bold thing that will stagger them, and they will begin to think.[45] And in speaking of the agitation caused by the boldness of the first part of *The Age of Reason,* he concludes, "I have but one way to be secure in my next work, which is, to go further than in my first. I see that *great rogues* escape by the excess of their crimes, and, perhaps, it may be the same in honest cases."[46] I do not choose to stain these pages by quoting examples of the scarlet and profane Billingsgate and the coarse innuendoes which Paine unworthily employed as an attack upon Christianity in his illiberal and intolerant endeavour to prove that "the only true religion is deism."[47] If Franklin was an agnostic, he was also tolerant of most religions and rich in the benign wisdom of silence. Where the master feared to tread, the disciple rushed in, with the result that whereas Franklin died the venerated Citizen of the World, beloved of mankind, Paine literally became an object of fear and pity, spending his last years in a vain endeavour to patch together the floating fragments of a wrecked renown. We cannot digress from our restricted purpose here to discuss the vast problems involved in Paine's deism. One observation might be ventured, however. Just as Paine's view that the dead have no authority over the living, that one generation can renounce its obligation to its predecessor, has been undermined by modern doctrines of the inexorable continuity of evolution, so his religious view that one must "vindicate the moral justice of God against the calumnies of the Bible,"[48] in which God is presented as cruel, by forsaking the Bible for nature, has likewise been undermined by the modern evolutionists' demonstration that nature is more cruel than the God of the Old Testament in her indifference to the struggle for existence and the survival of the fittest. Evolution has reinforced, unexpectedly, the famous nature-argument of Butler's *Analogy* (1736), against the earlier deists, who were sure that nature was all benevolence, an argument which Richard Watson tellingly used against Paine in 1796.[49]

If, as a political thinker, his chief weakness lay in his blindness to the unconscious and historical element in human association, the recognition of which constitutes "Burke's supreme claim to greatness,"[50] as a religious thinker this handicap is much more pronounced, since as a rationalist Paine sees but one path to truth, discounting insight, faith, illusion, and the religious imagination, which have guided such seers as Plato and Dante, as mere obscurantism. And this defect is furthermore aggravated by the fact that, with one or two exceptions, he was totally unfitted, by his external, mechanistic concept of God as a watchmaker and by his doctrine that worship consists only in external humanitarian service, to "be a Columbus to whole continents and worlds within," which has constituted the central objective of the American transcendental-

ists and of most distinctively religious people. Thus does the iniquity of oblivion, at the behest of time, scatter her poppy, and in rendering the boldest affirmations untenable instruct us in the wisdom of philosophic humility and the avoidance of unseemly dogmatism and violence of expression.

Of course Paine's boldness of phrase is merely the outward garment of the perfectibilian's black-and-white philosophy, according to which all rulers of the past were devils[51] while all rulers of the future will be saints. "The present state of civilization is as odious as it is unjust. It is absolutely the opposite of what it should be."[52] "The politics of Britain, so far as respects America, were originally conceived in idiotism and acted in madness."[53] He is forever the implacable enemy of "mixed governments," middle courses, and gradual methods; nothing will do but "a total reformation."[54] To this apostle of the religion of humanity his former sovereign, afflicted with mental infirmity, is his "Madjesty,"[55] otherwise a "Royal Wretch,"[56] a "Royal Criminal,"[57] or "a sceptred savage."[58] The long struggles of the English people for a "freedom slowly broadening down from precedent to precedent" are to him nothing; in the background he sees not Magna Charta but William of Normandy, to him the "son of a prostitute and the plunderer of the English nation." His universal ascription of dark motives to men of the past would better become a believer in total depravity than a believer in liberalism and natural goodness. Indeed, his brutality toward his opponents accords oddly with his professed monopoly on virtues humanitarian. If Paine's ideal of boldness must be pronounced one of the regrettable weaknesses of his literary theory, we should recall that it was a weakness he shared with his contemporaries, whose ungentle ways, it must be admitted, were not conducive to temperate expression. William Cobbett, for example, whose later affection for Paine caused him to bring his remains back to his native land, called him "a profane fool," a "blockhead," a "bloodhound," "an ass," and "red-nosed Tom, . . . the impostor, the liar, and the disturber of mankind." "Men will learn to express all that is *base, malignant, treacherous, unnatural,* and blasphemous, by the single monosyllable Paine."[59] And Paine's good friend Samuel Adams, who argued that "the natural liberty of man is to be free from any superior power on earth, and not to be under the will or legislative authority of man, but only to have the law of nature for his rule,[60] was addressed by American opponents as "the foulest, subtlest, and most venomous serpent ever issued from the egg of sedition." And in England, of course Paine's boldness was in accord with that of such writers as Junius, "the favorite model of political writers,"[61] whose "brilliant pen . . . enraptured" Paine, who said that "in the plenitude of its rage it might be said to give elegance to bitterness."[62] "No writer of the time came so near to the style of Junius," it had been said, "as Paine."[63]

Somewhat akin to Paine's ideal of boldness was his third ideal, that of *wit*. "Wit," he explained, "is naturally a volunteer, delights in action, and under proper discipline is capable of great execution. 'Tis a perfect master in the art of bush-fighting; and though it attacks with more subtility than science, has often defeated a whole regiment of heavy artillery . . . 'Tis a qualification which, like the passions, has a natural wildness, that requires governing. Left to itself, it soon overflows its banks, mixes with common filth, and brings disrepute on the fountain. We have many valuable springs of it in America, which at present run purer streams, than the generality of it in other countries."[64] He may have been thinking of the wit of Franklin, rising to the surface of his work like sparkling bubbles in wine, or the wit of Freneau, or of Barlow and the Hartford Wits. Occasionally Paine gives us a mild cerebral tickle as when, in speaking of peace terms unpopular with the democrats, he remarked, "this is what the tories call making their peace, 'a peace which passeth all understanding' indeed."[65] Often, however, as Romilly said, he is "flat where he attempts wit,"[66] as when he described the traitor Arnold boarding "the *Vulture* sloop of war lying in the North River; on which it may be truly said, that one vulture was receiving another." And often his wit is winged with a desire to pain. John Adams, who had been a target for Paine, attributed the Federalists' defeat in part to a failure to guard themselves against "that scoffing, scorning wit, and that caustic malignity of soul, which appeared so remarkably in all the writings of Thomas Paine."[67] Certainly in respect to his wit, and his deficiency in humour, Paine was a true citizen of that rationalistic century which produced such wits as Swift, Defoe, Bolingbroke, Pope, Churchill, Peter Pindar, Wilkes, and Junius, all of whom Paine read and admired.

Paine's fourth ideal—perhaps unexpected in one who was essentially a rationalist otherwise—may be described as an *appeal to feeling* and a regard for those niceties of composition, such as connotation, antithesis, balance, and cadence, which are productive of emotional or poetic pleasure. This aspect of Paine's work has been, I think, little noticed, and yet I venture to think it has stood him in good stead in his conflict with oblivion. "I had some turn," he confessed, reminiscently, "and I believe some talent for poetry; but this I rather repressed than encouraged, as leading too much into the field of imagination."[68] Nevertheless, this repressed feeling for the poetic is seldom far beneath the surface, fertilizing his art, giving it at times, as even his enemies admitted, an elevation which was not without beauty. At first, although I think it is not generally known, this hard-headed rationalist was much given to wandering in fairy lands of fancy, as one will note who reads his early papers in *The Pennsylvania Magazine* for the year 1775 on such topics as "Cupid and Hymen." Enchanted with his new-found home,

Paine wandered fancifully in "the groves of Arcadia," charmed with the "lovely appearance," the "air of pleasantness," every shepherdess being "decorated with a profusion of flowers," while amidst the "little cottages" and the "jessamine and myrtle" "the sound of labour was not heard" but only "a sweet confusion of voices mingled with instrumental music."[69] It is in this scene that Cupid rescues the beauteous Ruralinda from Gothic, Lord of the Manor, and returns her to her shepherd swain with whom she lives happily ever after. No wonder Paine, who is popularly pictured in this period as a sort of fireeater, wrote Franklin, "I thought it very hard to have the Country set on fire about my Ears almost the moment I got into it."[70] Nevertheless, he was summoned forth from this Arcadian fairyland to publish **Common Sense,** the call to arms, January 10, 1776, which presages his matured prose style embodied fifteen years later in the **Rights of Man.** As I have suggested, his style in 1775 was, for the most part, ornate, involved, artificial, rich in languorous emotional overtones which caress the sentimental fancies of an Arcadian; his style in 1791 is essentially bare, terse, swift, metallic, and epigrammatic, not without an echo, here and there, of stately eloquence. What accounts for this interesting stylistic evolution?[71] It cannot be attributed entirely to the outgrowing of youthful sentimentalism, for Paine was thirty-eight when he wrote the passages just quoted. No doubt, as in the case of Sidney Lanier later, the author's personal experience in the war had something to do with helping him to view things realistically and to give his words the ring of sincerity. For Paine was an aide to General Greene, and took part in an engagement which involved rowing "in an open boat to Fort Mifflin during the cannonade," a "*very* gallant act," as a contemporary said, "that shows what a fearless man Mr. Paine was."[72] Such an experience in the teeth of a cannonade has a way of making a man think less about Cupids and shepherdesses and fairies and Necromancers' cells. No wonder he poured out **The Crisis** in "a passion of patriotism,"[73] writing, it is said, on the head of a drum in the light of flickering campfires while the wornout army slumbered. More important, however, was the intellectual influence of associating on intimate terms, as Secretary of Foreign Affairs, fellow-author, or guest, with the leaders of Revolutionary thought such as Jefferson and Franklin, and the natural tendency to assimilate not only their thought[74] but their ideals as regards the art of writing, which were in the direction of sobriety, clarity, precision, ease, vigour and purposeful didacticism. He confessed that, while he formerly had no interest in politics,[75] "it was the American revolution that made me an author,"[76] and that as regards his later work such as the **Rights of Man** "the principles. . . . were the same as those in **Common Sense,**[77] learned in America. Henceforth, the ever-growing faith in the natural man and Utopian progress, which throbbed and pounded and exulted through his work, was in his mind given philosophic sanction by what he took to be the concrete and successful embodiment of it in the history of America. In such an interpretation, however, it is manifest that he, like other naturalists of the French Revolutionary era, failed to perceive the extent to which the American "order and decorum,"[78] which Paine expected in vain in the French Revolution, and which he attributed to natural goodness, were the inherited habitude of a Puritan liberalism, mindful of the dark impulses of the human heart, which strove not to make men masterless but self-mastered.[79] Such an entrancing vision of being instrumental in "regenerating the Old World by the principles of the New,"[80] by merely modifying the external machinery of government, in conjunction with the stylistic ideals of such intimate friends as Franklin and Jefferson,[81] made him impatient not only of fanciful writing but even of non-didactic or non-historical writing such as the drama. "Mr. Burke should recollect," he says, "that he is writing history and not *plays;* and that his readers will expect truth, and not the spouting to rant of high-toned exclamation."[82] Jefferson, in the interest of "reason and fact, plain and unadored," had condemned the undidactic novel for its "poison" of "fancy."

As I have suggested, however, Paine's early delight in the poetic did not desert him, but, being repressed, indirectly fertilized his style, giving it, at its best, colour, connotation, and cadence, enabling him to hold in thrall not only the reader's head but his heart. For the "prince of pamphleteers" knew that "the mind of a *living* public . . . feels first and reasons afterwards."[83] Everyone, of course, is familiar with his picturesque retort to Burke, who in the French Revolution pitied the rich but forgot the poor. As Paine remarked, "He is not affected by the reality of distress touching his heart, but by the showy resemblance of it striking his imagination. *He pities the plumage, but forgets the dying bird.*"[84] In metaphors of such haunting beauty Paine often succeeds in pointedly compressing his argument, rendering it strikingly memorable and quotable. "The palaces of kings are founded on the bowers of paradise." "Government, like dress, is the badge of lost innocence." "Cannons are the barristers of kings." If "there is in Paine's style none of the organ's roll which hushes Burke's listeners into a state of veneration and awe,"[85] a statement to which there are many exceptions, he is a master of epigrams, clothed often in homely phrases, which "became catchwords; household proverbs; verbal banners to flaunt before the astonished vision of a comfortable aristocracy and a contented conservatism."[86] This facility in the art of epigrams stems, no doubt, partly from the neo-classical delight in the general rather than the particular, partly from Paine's delight in logical abstraction as opposed to historic relativism, and partly from the fact that his delight in the university of natural law led to a delight in framing major premises in terms universal. I venture to think, however, that Paine's writing de-

rives no small measure of its vibrating power from his ability, as a retentive student of the English Bible, to clothe his thought in the moving diction and haunting cadences of that masterpiece of beauty which has left its authentic stamp upon most of what is great in English letters. For Paine did not condemn all the Bible, even in content. He never tires of praising the Book of Job, especially for its style. "As a composition, it is sublime, beautiful, and scientific: full of sentiment, and abounding in grand metaphorical description . . . In the last act, where the Almighty is introduced as speaking from the whirlwind, to decide the controversy between Job and his friends, it is an idea as grand as poetic imagination can conceive."[87] And it will be found, I think, that usually wherever Paine attains a dignity and impressiveness of style, an earnest and lofty eloquence, and a telling incisiveness of phrase, there are subtle echoes of the book he condemned. "The vanity and presumption of governing beyond the grave is the most ridiculous and insolent of all tyrannies. Man has no property in man; neither has any generation a property in the generations which are to follow."[68] "The farce of monarchy in all countries is following that of chivalry, and Mr. Burke is dressing for the funeral. Let it then pass gently to the tomb of all other follies and the mourners be comforted." "It is [quoting] authority against authority all the way, till we come to the divine origin of the rights of man at the creation. Here our enquiries find a resting place and our reason finds a home."[89] And in the following sentence, notice not only the biblical echoes in this attack on the Bible, but the balance and antithesis, and the stately cadence: " . . . the terrors and inquisitorial fury of the Church, like what they tell us of the flaming sword that turned every way, stood sentry over the New Testament; and time, which brings everything to light, has served to thicken the darkness that guards it from detection."[90] Paine's nice regard for rythmical units and for the music of the spoken word are obvious, and this regard must have been effectively advanced by his manner of composing, which was also, incidentally, not unlike that of Emerson. "His manner of composing, as I have heard persons who have heard him relate," writes Hogg, "was thus. He walked backwards and forwards about a room until he had completed a sentence to his satisfaction; he then wrote it down entire and perfect and never to be amended. When the weather was fair, if there was a garden, a field, a courtyard at hand, he walked about out of doors for a while, and then came in and put down the sentence which he had arranged mentally, and went out again and walked until he was ready to be delivered of another."[91] No wonder he could make his words, terrible but beautiful, march like soldiers with trumpets; no wonder he could make his words vibrate with the indignation of a Hebrew prophet foretelling the destruction of "Sodom and Gomorrah."[92] In praising his timely appeal to feeling, however, I have in mind not so much his war propaganda, a type of work with which we are all unpleasantly familiar, as that portion of his writing inspired by passion social and humanitarian. For the bitterness with which he hated the oppressors was of course merely the reverse side of the tenderness with which he pitied the oppressed. "I defend," he said, "the cause of the poor, . . . of all those on whom the real burden of the taxes fall—but above all, I defend the cause of humanity." "I speak an open and disinterested language, dictated by no passion but that of humanity . . . my country is the world, and my religion is to do good."[93] If Paine was blind to most of what the historic majesty of the past has to teach, and if his idyllic prophecies of a New Jerusalem come on earth were belied by the events of the future, if few can accept today either his religion or political doctrines, which subsume a benevolence in nature and the natural man which realistic observation and evolution has tended to disprove, it may turn out that his most important contribution was the impetus which he gave toward a wider recognition of social evils and a quest for concrete remedies. A contemporary and reader of humanitarians such as Thomson, Cowper, Blake, Mary Wollstonecraft, Franklin, Jefferson, Voltaire, Rousseau, Raynal, Brissot and Condorcet, it is no wonder that, in elaborating his many practical suggestions[94] for the relief of social suffering, whereby life's blessings were to be more equally distributed, his words throb with a contagious sympathy[95] which brought hope to the unfortunate, the poor, and the oppressed. For, much as he tempered his earlier addiction to the sentimental, he never forgot that "the mind of a living public . . . feels first, and reasons afterwards." In this respect, Paine approaches, for a moment, the view of Burke, whose essay on "The Sublime and the Beautiful" (1756) he evidently read, who held that an ideal sentence should involve first, a thought, second, an image, and, third, a sentiment.

If the rationalist Paine was not unmindful of an appeal to the reader's feelings, if he aimed "to make the reader feel, fancy, and understand justly at the same time,"[96] his practice had the support of a typically neo-classic theory of a desired balance between Memory, Judgment and Imagination, a balance which may be said to constitute his *fifth* literary ideal. It is interesting to note, incidentally, that the literary effectiveness of his defence of liberty is in no small measure dependent upon an allegiance to a principal of control. His statement of his theory is so important that I must beg leave to quote it in full, long as it is:

> "The three great faculties of the mind", he wrote, much as did Sir William Jones, whom Paine read,[97] "are *Imagination, Judgment* and *Memory*. Every action of the mind comes under one or the other of these faculties . . . [The mind being like a watch,[98]] the main spring which puts all in motion corresponds to the imagination; the pendulum which corrects and regulates that motion, corresponds to the judgment; and the hand and

dial, like the memory, record the operation. . . . if the judgment sleeps whilst the imagination keeps awake . . . the master of the school is gone out and the boys are in an uproar."[99]

". . . How very few men there are in any country," he remarks in censuring Raynal, "who can at once, and without the aid of reflection and revisal, combine warm passions with a cool temper, and the full expansion of the imagination with the natural and necessary gravity of judgment, so as to be rightly balanced within themselves, and to make a reader feel, fancy, and understand justly at the same time. To call three powers of the mind into action at once, in a manner that neither shall interrupt, and that each shall aid and invigorate the other, is a talent very rarely possessed. It often happens that the weight of an argument is lost by the wit of setting it off; or the judgment disordered by an intemperate irritation of the passions: yet a certain degree of animation must be felt by the writer, and raised in the reader, in order to interest the attention; and a sufficient scope given to the imagination, to enable it to create in the mind a sight of the persons, characters and circumstances, of the subject: for without these, the judgment will feel little or no excitement to office, and its determinations will be cold, sluggish, and imperfect. But if either or both of the two former are raised too high, or heated too much, the judgment will be jostled from its seat, and the whole matter, however, important in itself, will diminish into a pantomine of the mind, in which we create images that promote no other purpose than amusement."[100]

It is often erroneously supposed that the neo-classicists and the radical rationalists were implacably hostile to the imagination. It is true, as we have seen, that Paine repressed his interest in poetry as "leading too much into the field of imagination";[101] his hostility toward what he calls "the vapours of the imagination",[102] however, refers only to the unbalanced and undisciplined use of that faculty. For to Paine, as to many of his contemporaries, the imagination, as he described it above, is the "main-spring" of the mind. We should notice carefully, however, exactly what he means by imagination. To Paine it not so much an Aristotelian faculty, essentially moral, whereby ethical universals are envisaged on the basis of particulars purged of what is accidental or idiosyncratic, a conception held by such men as Burke, Sir Joshua Reynolds, and the mature James Russell Lowell,[103] as it was a creative arranger of images furnished by memory and controlled by judgment. If we recall how exuberant were Paine's early flights of fancy, how strongly he leaned toward the over-ornate and the Arcadian, we will understand how difficult, and necessary, in his case was self-discipline, and we will perhaps be more charitable toward his frequent and deplorable inability to bring his writing, often done under stress of emergencies which forbade revision, into complete harmony with his ideal of a fruitful and purposeful balance between the Memory, the Judgment and the Imagination. With regard to this ideal, as with others, he was in accord with the main current of his age. For, as Professor F. B. Kaye reminded us, "The neo-classicist distrusted only the undisciplined use of the faculty [imagination]; the disciplined imagination he required. The following is a typical neo-classic statement: 'In a good poem, whether it be *epic* or *dramatic;* as also in *sonnets, epigrams,* and other pieces, both judgment and fancy are required . . .'[104] This was a doctrine preached by Pope and Addison [whom Paine read, admired and quoted]. That the neo-classicists could hardly help respecting the imagination is shown by their conceptions of the creative art. The central psychological theory was that of Hobbes and Locke, according to which the judgment separates the impressions stored in the memory by the senses and the imagination joins and relates them. Imagination, therefore, was as necessary to controlled thinking as judgment, and shared its good repute."[105]

Sixth, having advocated this difficult balance of faculties necessary to the writer, Paine aimed to adjust language to thought with such exquisite precision as to create exactly the impression he wished to produce and no other. The ex-soldier knew that ammunition is not more necessary than infallible aiming. As he himself sums the matter up. "To fit the powers of thinking and the turn of language to the subject, so as to bring out a clear conclusion that shall hit the point in question and nothing else, is the true criterion of writing."[106] Conscious of his own earlier weaknesses, he is aware that the means should be always subordinated to the end, the part to the whole, that writing may fail "through an excess of graces", if as in Raynal's case, "the coloring is too high for the original", even though "the conception is lofty and the expression elegant".[107] As he boasted later, reviewing, no doubt, his own struggles for literary self-control and for artistic integrity, "All the world knows, for it cannot help knowing, that to judge *rightly,* and to write *clearly,* and that upon all sorts of subjects, to be able to command thought and as it were to play with it at pleasure, and be always master of one's temper in writing, is the faculty only of a serene mind, and the attribute of a happy and philosophical temperament."[108]

Like Milton, whose work he read,[109] Paine recognized that literary success depends upon far more than verbal carpentry and astute craftsmanship, important as these are; he recognized, like the greater and more profound radical, the organic relation between character and literary creation, the fact that the life of a poet must itself be a genuine and living poem. The deist, grossly libelled as an atheist or infidel, who spent his life ringing the changes on his master-theme that "It is only in the Creation [nature] that all our ideas and conceptions of a *word of God* can unite,"[110] was not slow to grasp the parallel idea that the literary creation of man is a revelation of its human creator, noble or ignoble in proportion as the deeper springs of his character are in fruitful harmony with what Emerson, like Paine in this respect, called "the law alive and beautiful",[111] the Oversoul. And if Paine's writing is not flawless, if he wanders far at times from the high-road he charted, it is perhaps not unrelated to the fact that he never completely achieved the "happy and philosophical" self-command he sought,[112] that he did not escape what his defender, Shelley,[113] called the "contagion of the world's slow stain". On the other hand, it should be borne in mind that this ultimate stress upon self-discipline in literary art is in the last analysis the inevitable result, in literary terms, of the contemporary outlook of religious radicals, or deists, culminating with Bolingbroke and Pope, whom Paine admired as "Free-thinkers".[114] For, as I hope to show elsewhere, the views of such religious radicals as Paine represents have been somewhat misunderstood, and important political, humanitarian, and literary results of such views largely ignored. Paine was anything but an atheist or an anarchist. If he advocated, like Pope, following nature, the concept "nature" must be interpreted in the light of the contemporary climate of opinion. He did not mean by following nature to return to the actual physical life of a savage in a wilderness. For to Paine, as to most of the deists, nature had a special meaning, confirmed by Newtonion science: as Paine expressly says, "nature is of divine origin. It is the laws by which the universe is governed";[115] nature "is no other than the laws the Creator has prescribed to matter", laws operating in "unerring order and universal harmony",[116] and perceptible through the study of science by means of "the divine gift of reason".[117] *Nature is law, eternal, immutable, universal.*[118] Now, whatever were the facts of the personal life of Paine, philosophically, far from preaching lustful license or do-as-you-please, the ultimate virtue to him, as his deist contemporaries in England, was living in harmony with this law which is nature, a conformity involving no little discipline, as has been demonstrated in the case of Shaftesbury.[119] Thus, to indicate Paine's accord with the spirit of the age, in this matter of a disciplined precision, "the true criterion of writing", we may recall that to Pope, as to Paine, "prayerbooks are the toys of age",[120] while God is revealed in nature, in "the stupendous whole" harmony of nature's laws, which are universal—"still the same". Thus, unlike the "original genius" naturalists such as Edward Young, whose cult of following nature led to a literary diversitarianism, a quest of the eccentric, of nonconformity, Pope and Paine urge us to "first follow nature, which is still the same",[121] a quest of the concentric or the universal, an ideal, in Pope's case, if less faithfully in practice in Paine's, which involved the most intense literary self-discipline as regards craftsmanship in the interest of finality of expression, of what was "ne'er so well expressed". The crowning stress, then, which Paine lays upon harmonizing a writer's powers by allegiance to a judgment which "corrects and regulates", and upon being able "to command thought and as it were to play with it at pleasure", to hit the point in question and nothing else", this crowning stress upon control in writing was but a reflection of the central philosophy of that day, wherein man found his salvation by a self-disciplined conformity to nature's law, the "unerring order and universal harmony", and it can be only inadequately, if not falsely, interpreted when divorced from that philosophic background of deism and Newtonian law.[122]

Having satisfied himself as to the perfection of the units of his composition, striving, as we have seen, for candour, simplicity, and clarity, for boldness, for wit, for an appeal not only to reason but to feeling, for a balance between judgement and imagination, and for a purposeful and precise adjustment between language and ideas with reference to a definite audience, Paine strove, finally, to arrange his units, his carefully constructed sentences, in an architectonic pattern designed to give them their maximum effectiveness. He worshipped order in everything, but especially in literary composition, and as a critic he is especially sensitive to faults in order and method. His friend Rickman testifies that "he used to speak highly of the sentimental parts of Raynal's History",[123] and he acknowledged that the Frenchman who cloaked humanitarianism under history "displays great powers of genius, and is a master of style and language".[124] Yet as an apostle of orderly method in the development of an argument, he cannot overlook the fact that "the greater part of the abbé's writings, (if he will pardon me the remark) appear to me uncentral, and burdened with variety. They represent a beautiful wilderness without paths; in which the eye is diverted by everything, without being particularly directed to anything . . ."[125] The same fault loomed large to him in the writing of "Cato", whose attack on **Common Sense** called forth Paine's Forester papers: "Cato's manner of writing has as much order in it as the motion of a squirrel. He frequently writes as if he knew not what to write next, just as the other jumps about, only because it cannot stand still".[126] And especially, in answering Burke's *Reflections,* he lamented the difficulty of imposing an orderly pattern upon the **Rights of Man,** since, as he remarked in one of his happy phrases, he had to tread "a pathless widerness of rhapsodies".[127] In common with the main figures of his era, devoted to the beauty of symmetry and the progressive unfolding of a rationalistic argument, Paine exclaims, "I love method, because I see and am convinced of its beauty and advantage. It is that which makes all business easy and understood, and without which, everything becomes embarrassed and difficult."[128] For "it is only by reducing complicated things to method and orderly connexion that they can be understood with advan-

tage, or pursued with success."[129] Paine's own practice of this theory is, as everyone knows, imperfect. He never succeeded in bringing his compositions into that faultless harmony with geometrical method illustrated so finely by the structure of Godwin's *Political Justice.* Nevertheless, as he remarks regarding one subject, he "endeavoured to give it as systematical an investigation as the short time allowed."[130] His manner of lighting the way through his compositions is simple: in general, at his best, he follows the old playwright's advice of telling us what he is going to do, of telling us he is doing it, and then telling us he has done it. Thus we find him making use, regularly, of what one may call "sign-post" sentences,[131] and "flash-backs" such as the "Recapitulation" at the end of Part I of *The Age of Reason*.[132] Such a method of securing method, added to his "damnable iteration" of his master-ideas, made it practically impossible for even the most unliterary reader to miss his meaning, so clear did he make it. Thus we are eventually come full circle, his last ideal of method serving to make possible his first ideal of clear simplicity. Just as the first is ultimately grounded on his deistic faith that "man must go back to nature for information", since "perfection consists in simplicity", so his last ideal, that of order, is also grounded on his deistic faith that the test of the revelation even of God himself is that "harmonious, magnificent order that reigns throughout the visible universe," an order which is "the standard to which everything must be brought."[133] Like his theories political, economic, humanitarian, and educational, his theories of rhetoric ultimately stem from and are fully explainable only in the light of Newtonian science and deism. *The pivot round which his thought revolved was scientific deism.* As I have suggested, in espousing orderly method in writing Paine was in full accord with his contemporaries; witness his idol, Franklin, giving typically prosaic and practical suggestions whereby his friend Benjamin Vaughan could overcome his want of "perspicuity" which Franklin traced "principally to a neglect of method".[134] If there are splendours and glooms of the human soul which the eighteenth century seldom cared to explore, if in general, as compared with the Age of Wordsworth, the Age of Pope is inferior in moral and imaginative sublimity, it is well to remember that the latter is preeminent in its regard for form and for exquisiteness of literary order. Deism, with its belief in God, man, and nature as sharply distinct, its belief in what Paine called divinely "unerring order", is parallelled in literature and art and landscape gardening by order;[135] whereas pantheism, with its belief in unity, or the fusion of God, man, and nature, is parallelled in these same fields, by comparative disorder. "Order," said Pope, "is Heav'n's first law." The apotheosis of order, and this is the point I would stress, whether or not a result of deism, was characteristic of Paine's age. Loving "unerring order" and finding it sublimely present in the "eternal harmony" of the stars, symbols of light and law, Paine said that "my belief in the perfection of the Deity will not permit me to believe that a book [the Bible] so manifestly obscure, disorderly, and contradictory can be his work",[136] but Thomas Burnet in 1759 deplored the "disorder", even of the stars, because they did not conform to the neo-classic demand for a symmetrical pattern:

> They lie carelessly scattered as if they had been sown in the heaven like seed, by handfuls, and not by a skilful hand neither. What a beautiful hemisphere they would have made if they had been placed in rank and order; if they had all been disposed into regular figures, and the little ones set with due regard to the greater, and then all finished and made up into one fair piece or great composition according to the rules of art and symmetry![137]

Could a passion for order go beyond this?

If Paine suffered many disappointments, was the object of much public and private malice, and was ultimately disillusioned with the French Revolution, and obliged to "despair of seeing the great object of European liberty accomplished,"[138] Jefferson, his great idol, the father of democracy, recognized the precious services of his pen:

> "No writer", Jefferson wrote, "has exceeded Paine in ease and familiarity of style, in perspicuity of expression, happiness in elucidation, and in simple and unassuming language. In this he may be compared with Dr. Franklin; and indeed his Common Sense was, for a while, believed to have been written by Dr. Franklin."[139]

And as he wrote Paine himself, "You must not be too much elated and set up when I tell you my belief that you are the only writer in America who can write better than your obliged and obedient servant—Thomas Jefferson."[140]

"I am in hopes," he wrote Paine in 1801, "you will find us returned generally to sentiments worthy of former times. In these it will be your glory to have steadily laboured and with as much effect as any man living."[141]

And in the attainment of this superlative "glory", Paine was guided by literary theories which, if by no means ideal, at least bore the test of practice. For he commanded the attention of half a million readers, vigorously stirring them to contemplate the political, religious, and social doctrines which helped to call into being the American and French Revolutions as well as many humanitarian movements of later days, doctrines forcefully and clearly presented in a style which served as a trusty tool and was occasionally not without elements of beauty.

Notes

[1] C. E. Merriam, "The Political Theories of Thomas Paine," *Political Science Quarterly,* XIV, 402. See also C. B. R. Kent, *English Radicals,* London, 1899, 115. As regards *The Age of Reason,* I. W. Riley concludes, "there is not an idea in it which cannot be matched in the writings of the English free-thinkers of the Georgian era." (*American Philosophy. The Early Schools,* New York, 1907, 299).

[2] *The Cambridge History of English Literature,* XI, 53.

[3] M. D. Conway, *The Life of Thomas Paine,* New York, 1892, I, 69, and *The Writings of Thomas Paine* (hereafter referred to as *Writings*), edited by Conway, New York, 1894-96, III, 382.

[4] See W. P. Hall, *British Radicalism,* 1791-97, New York, 1912, especially the earlier part.

[5] *Writings,* I, 275.

[6] R. G. Adams, *Political Ideas of the American Revolution,* Durham, North Carolina, 1922, p. 112, and Sir George O. Trevelyan, *The American Revolution,* London, 1903, I, 162. One should remember that Paine was only one of a vast number of propagandists. See P. Q. Davidson, Jr., "Revolutionary Propaganda in New England, New York, and Pennsylvania, 1763-76." *University of Chicago Abstracts of Theses,* Humanistic Series, VII, pp. 239-42.

[7] *The Life of Thomas Holcroft,* (ed. by Colby), London, 1925, II, 34. According to C. B. R. Kent (*The English Radicals,* p. 111), "In the end it [the second part of the *Rights of Man*] was adopted by the Constitutional Society as a kind of democratic Magna Charta, and sent by them to all the Corresponding Societies in England, France, and Scotland." See also Julius West, *A History of the Chartist Movement,* London, 1920, p. 22.

[8] Conway, *Life of Paine,* I, 88.

[9] This is also asserted by E. Halévy, *The Growth of Philosophic Radicalism,* London, 1928, pp. 188-89.

[10] *Writings,* IV, 339-40. "Man must go back to Nature for information" (*ibid.,* II, 402). "Perfection consists in Simplicity."

[11] *Writings,* I, 133.

[12] H. Niles, *Principles and Acts of the Revolution in America,* 235. The Continental Congress, according to its *Journal* (edition of 1904, I, 108), stood for freedom of the press "whereby oppressive officials are

shamed *or intimidated* into more honourable or just modes of conducting affairs." See T. Schroeder's "Intellectual Liberty and Literary Style," *Open Court,* XXXIV, 275 ff.

[13] *Writings,* I, 119.

[14] *Ibid.,* II, 333.

[15] *Ibid.,* I, 16.

[16] *Ibid.,* II, 102-3; IV, 287.

[17] *Writings,* II, 463.

[18] *Cambridge History of English Literature,* XI, 53.

[19] Quoted by his friend, T. C. Rickman, *The Life of Thomas Paine,* London, 1819. "As to the learning that any person gains from school education, it serves only, like a small capital, to put him in the way of beginning learning for himself afterwards. Every person of learning is finally his own teacher . . .". *Writings* IV, 64.

[20] *Writings,* I, 15.

[21] *Ibid.,* I, 413.

[22] See Conway's *Life of Paine,* I, 225; M. C. Tyler's *Literary History of the Revolution,* New York, 1897, I, 455-56; John Adams, *Works,* Boston, 1850-56, II, 507.

[23] *Writings,* IV, 83. See William Cobbett (*Observations on Paine's Age of Reason,* p. 1-2): "You offer wonders of inconsistency for our digestion. We are to believe you on your word, that we, infallible men of reason, having the Bible of Creation (as you call it) daily before our noses, are not withstanding, in imminent danger of losing sight even of morality, humanity, and theology—that a *work,* a *written book on Religion,* is not only *necessary,* but even *exceedingly* necessary for our preservation; that our Creator has not provided for such a work, but has abandoned mankind to the pernicious effects of seduction and immorality; that he is surpassed in benevolence by you; and that he has left the production of a work *exceedingly necessary, in a moral point of view,* to the care of *poor, silly* Tom Paine . . ."

[24] Witness Godwin's advice to Thelwall: "Amass as much knowledge as you please, but no authorities. To quote authorities is a vulgar business; every soul-less hypocrite can do that. To quote authorities is a cold business; it excites no responsive sentiments and produces no heart-felt conviction . . . Appeal to that eternal law which the heart of every man of common-sense recognizes immediately. Make your justification as palpable to the unlearned as the studious. Strip it of all superfluous appendages; banish from it all useless complexity." (Quoted by C. Cestre, *John Thelwell,* London, 1906, 202).

[25] *Writings,* II, 463.

[26] *Writings,* II, 462-3.

[27] *Ibid.,* IV, 431.

[28] *An Apology for the Bible, in a series of Letters Addressed to Thomas Paine . . .* Cork, 1796, p. 96.

[29] *Writings,* IV, 103.

[30] *Ibid.,* IV, 105.

[31] I have begun this task in a study of "Thomas Paine's Relation to Voltaire and Rousseau," which will be found in the *Revue Anglo-Américaine,* April and June, 1932. Two quotations from Rousseau, unnoted there, have since come to my attention; see *Writings,* III, 104, (80-81) and I, 150. F. J. C. Hearnshaw (*Development of Political Ideas,* 1927, pp. 56-57) says Paine "disseminated Rousseau's doctrines."

[32] Unfortunately, little study has been devoted to the literary theories underlying the applied literature of Americans such as Franklin, Jefferson, Adams, Barlow and Hamilton. If the birth of the nation was in no small measure rendered possible by the literary efforts of these men, it would seem that the theories underlying these efforts deserve presentation and analysis. Most critics who have approached them from the literary point of view have been content with registering their merely subjective likes and dislikes.

[33] *Writings,* II, 238.

[34] *Ibid.,* IV, 406.

[35] *Writings,* III, 54-55.

[36] *Ibid.,* III, 115. "Plain language may perhaps sound uncouthly to an ear vitiated by courtly refinements, but words were made for use." *Ibid.,* I, 182.

[37] *Writings,* I, 178. "I offer nothing more than simple facts, plain arguments, and common sense." (*Ibid.,* I, 84).

[38] See *Writings,* III, 61.

[39] *Works,* I, 205.

[40] From Franklin's letter quoted by W. C. Bruce, *Benjamin Franklin Self-Revealed,* New York, 1917, II, 439. Franklin summed up his own conception of what constitutes a good piece of writing as follows:

"To be good it ought to have a tendency to benefit the reader, by improving his virtue or his knowledge. But, not regarding the intention of the author, the method should be just; that is, it should proceed regularly from things known to things unknown, distinctly and clearly without confusion. The words used should be the most expressive that the language affords, provided that they are the most generally understood. Nothing should be expressed in two words that can be as well expressed in one; that is, no synonymes should be used, or very rarely, but the whole should be as short as possible, consistent with clearness; the words should be so placed as to be agreeable to the ear in reading; summarily it should be smooth, clear and short, for the contrary qualities are displeasing." (Quoted by W. C. Bruce, *Franklin Self-Revealed*, II, 440).

[41] *Works* (ed. Ford), New York, 1904-5, X, 183.

[42] *Writings*, I, 140.

[43] *Ibid.*, II, 481. See also the passage (*ibid.*, I, 133-134) where Paine tries to rationalize his delight in abusiveness, arguing that "personality is concerned in any political debate."

[44] *Writings*, II, 394. Thomas Seccombe (The Age of Johnson, London, 1900, p. 115-16) says that Paine's manner, as applied to Christianity, was "of a rather different kind to any that had preceded it in England."

[45] Conway, *Life of Paine*, II, 298. See also *Writings*, III, 404.

[46] *Ibid.*

[47] *Writings*, IV, 167. See also IV, 190.

[48] *Writings*, IV, 96.

[49] *Apology*, 8-9. See Joseph Butler's *The Analogy of Religion, Natural and Revealed, to the Constitution and Course of Nature*, ed. Halifax, Oxford, 1844, p. 5 and p. 11; and see W. Grisenthwaite, *A Refutation of . . . Thomas Paine, etc.*, Wells, 1822, pp. 10-11.

[50] C. P. Gooch, *Cambridge Modern History*, VIII, 756-57.

[51] "What scenes of horror, what perfection of iniquity, present themselves in contemplating the character and reviewing the history of such governments! If we would delineate human nature with a baseness of heart and hypocrisy of countenance that reflexion would shudder at and humanity disown, it is Kings, courts and cabinets that must sit for the portrait". (*Writings*, II, 413; see also, *ibid.*, IV, 256).

[52] *Writings*, III, 337.

[53] *Ibid.*, II, 122. "Everything in the English government appears to me the reverse of what it ought to be, and of what it is said to be," (*ibid*, II, 315).

[54] *Ibid.*, II, 120.

[55] Conway's *Life,* II, 31.

[56] *Writings*, I, 123.

[57] *Ibid.*, I, 161.

[58] *Ibid.*, I, 132.

[59] *Observations on Paine's Age of Reason*, pp. 1, 3, 4, 6, 7, 8.

[60] As quoted in J. T. Adam's *The Epic of America*, 83. See the correspondence between Samuel Adams and Paine, *Writings*, IV, 200-8. As examples of Samuel Adams's boldness of language see *Writings of Samuel Adams*, ed. Cushing, New York, 1904-8, II, 313-21. ("Vindex" in *Boston Gazette,* April 20, 1772) and II, 332-37. ("Valerius Poplicola" in *Boston Gazette,* Oct. 5, 1772). R. V. Harlow (*Samuel Adams,* New York, 1923, p. 183) says "There are pages upon pages of this sort of thing in Adams's extant works."

[61] J. B. Daly, *The Dawn of Radicalism*, London, 1886, 105.

[62] *Writings*, II, 198.

[63] W. H. Burr, *Paine, Was He Junius?* 1890, p. 14. The argument that Paine was Junius seems to me inconclusive; but might not the "three hundred parallels of character, conduct, opinion, style, sentiment, and language" suggest that Junius, whom Paine read, influenced him?

[64] *Writings*, 1, 16. Paine wrote elsewhere (ibid., IV, 342), anonymously, "With respect to morality, the writings of Thomas Paine are remarkable for purity and benevolence; and though he often enlivens them with wit and humour, he never loses sight of the real solemnity of his subject."

[65] *Writings*, I, 177.

[66] Sir Samuel Romilly, *Memoirs*, etc., I, 415-16. "There have been several answers to Burke since you left us, but none that have much merit except one by Paine . . . It is written in his own wild but forcible style; inaccurate in point of grammar [for an exhaustive list of such errors see F. Oldys, *Life of Paine,* London, 1792, pp. 46, 67, 88, 98 ff.] flat where he attempts wit, and often ridiculous when he indulges

himself in metaphors; but, with all that, full of spirit and energy, and likely to produce a very great effect. It has done that, indeed, already; in the course of a fortnight, it has gone through three editions; and, what I own has a good deal surprised me, has made converts of many persons who were before enemies to the [French] Revolution." See also *Tom Paine's Jests: Being an entirely new and select collection of Patriotic Bon Mots, Repartees, Anecdotes, Epigrams, Observations, &c. on Political Subjects,* By Thomas Paine and other supporters of the Rights of Man . . . London, 1794. (A copy of this rare volume, of 56 pages, sold at sixpence, will be found in the British Museum, No. 8135. a. 65).

[67] John Adams, *Works,* IX, 278. In arranging terms of a debate with the Abbe Siéyes on monarchy, Paine promised to "treat the subject seriously and sincerely," but held himself "at liberty to ridicule, as they deserve, Monarchical obsurdities, whensoever the occasion shall present itself." His so-called wit directed at the Virgin Mary and Mary Magdalene is of course especially painful. Richard Watson censured him for introducing "railing for reasoning, vulgar and illiberal sarcasm in the room of argument," (*Apology,* 14) and the anonymous author of *Christianity the Only True Theology; as an answer to Mr. Paine's Age of Reason,* (London, n. d.), censures Paine's neglect of "a serious and impartial examination of truth" for "illiberal satyr, and impertinent witticism," for "the lighter weapons of ludicrous description and impudent buffoonry". (pp. 7, 58-59).

[68] *Writings,* IV, 63. This attitude toward poetry was in accord with that of Paine's contemporaries. Witness Franklin's advice to Ralph: "I approved the amusing one's self with poetry now and then, so far as to improve one's language but no farther." *Writings,* I, 270. Madison argued that "something more substantial, more durable, more profitable [than poetry] befits our riper age." See II. H. Clark, *Poems of Freneau,* New York, 1928, especially pp. xlvii-lviii, for a consideration of Deism as related to the genesis of American poetry. On Paine's editorship in relation to early American journalism and its literary ideals see Lyon N. Richardson, *A History of Early American Magazines, 1741-1789.* New York, 1931, and A. H. Smyth. *The Philadelphia Magazines and Their Contributors 1741-1850,* Philadelphia, 1892.

[69] *Writings,* I, 36. As further examples of this sort of style, see *Writings.* I, 26-27, where he delights, in a "pleasant kind of melancholy," when even "the trees seemed to sleep," in crossing the Styx to the "Plutonian world" in quest of Alexander the Great, marvelling at a chariot "drawn by eight horses in golden harness" and all the splendour which "shined so luminously". The tendencies here suggested are found elaborated in the work of Paine's contemporary and admirer, Philip

Freneau. (See H. H. Clark, "What Made Freneau the Father of American Prose?" (*Wisconsin Academy of Sciences, Arts, and Letters.* XXV, May 1930, pp. 39-50). And see the purple patch (*Writings,* I, 22-23) which suggests that the deist's delight in nature was not so exclusively cold-blooded and scientific as might be imagined: "Tho' nature is gay, polite, and generous abroad, she is sullen, rude, and niggardly at home: Return the visit, and she admits you with all the suspicion of a miser, and all the reluctance of an antiquated beauty retired to replenish her charms. Bred up in antediluvian notions, she has not yet acquired the European taste of receiving visitants in her dressing-room: she locks and bolts up her private precesses with extraordinary care, as if not only resolved to preserve her hoards, but to conceal her age, and hide the remains of a face that was young and lovely in the days of Adam. He that would view nature in her undress and partake of her internal treasurers, must proceed with the resolution of a robber, if not of a ravisher. She gives no invitation to follow her to the cavern. The external earth makes no proclamation of the interior stores, but leaves to chance and industry, the discovery of the whole. In such gifts as nature can annually re-create, she is noble and profuse, and entertains the whole world with the interest of her fortunes; but watches over the capital with the care of a miser. Her gold and jewels lie concealed in the earth, in caves of utter darkness; and hoards of wealth, heaps upon heaps, mould in the chests, like the riches of a Necromancer's cell." One would hardly suspect that this passage constitutes a good share of a so-called "useful" essay on ways and means of mining! For evidence regarding Paine's authorship of these and other early articles, see Frank Smith, "New Light on Thomas Paine's First Year in America," *American Literature,* I, 347-371.

[70] *Writings,* I, 393.

[71] It should be borne in mind, of course, that between Paine's early work in 1775 and the *Rights of Man* in 1791 and 1792, there was a general reaction in America against stilted and grandiloquent language, which was satirized, for example, by the Hartford Wits' *Echo,* See the ridiculous examples of contemporary high-flown artificiality quoted at length by C. B. Todd, *Life and Letters of Joel Barlow,* New York, 1886, pp. 52-53.

[72] Conway, *Life of Paine,* I, 99.

[73] *Writings,* IV, 431.

[74] See M. R. Eiselen, *Franklin's Political Theories,* New York, 1928; and G. Chinard, *Thomas Jefferson,* Boston, 1929.

[75] *Writings,* IV, 63 ff.

[76] *Ibid.*, III, 402.

[77] *Ibid.*, III, 382.

[78] *Writings*, II, 463.

[79] See J. W. Thornton, *The Pulpit of the American Revolution*, Boston, 1860: and Alice M. Baldwin, *The New England Clergy and the American Revolution*, Durham, North Carolina, 1928.

[80] *Writings*, III, 98.

[81] Jefferson (*Works*, ed. Ford, VIII, 65) wrote, in 1801, regarding poetry: "In earlier life I was fond of it, and easily pleased. But as age and cares advanced, the powers of fancy have declined . . . So much has my relish for poetry deserted me that, at present, I cannot read even Virgil with pleasure . . . The very feelings to which it [poetry] is addressed are among those I have lost." Although as a young man Jefferson did not object to novels provided they were sufficiently didactic and morally "useful" (*Works*, Ford, ed. I, 396), in general he considered them fanciful, and hence objectionable: "A great obstacle to good education is the inordinate passion prevalent for novels, and the time lost in that reading which should be instructively employed. When this poison infects the mind, it destroys its tone and revolts it against wholesome reading. Reason and fact, plain and unadorned, are rejected. Nothing can engage attention unless dressed in all the figments of fancy, and nothing so bedecked comes amiss. The result is a sickly judgment, and disgust towards all the real business of life." (*Works*, ed. Ford, X, 104). It should be remembered, also, that Benjamin Martin, the Newtonian popularizer whose lectures impressed Paine at the age of twenty (Writings, IV, 63), proclaimed "As to Poetry, it is so far from being the Source of any Learning, that, on the contrary, it has, for its subject, *pure Fiction*, which is quite its Opposite: If *Wit* and *Fancy* be your *Taste*, read Poetry; if *Wisdom* and Learning, attend on [natural] Philosophy". (*A Panegyrick*, p. 54).

[82] *Writings*, II, 286-87. "I consider Mr. Burke's book in scarcely any other light than a dramatic performance; and he must, I think, have considered it in the same light himself, by the poetical liberties he has taken of omitting some facts, distorting others, and making the whole machinery bend to produce a stage effect." (*Ibid.*, II, 297).

[83] *Writings*, I, p. 395.

[84] *Ibid.*, II, 288.

[85] Seccombe, *op. cit.*, 86-87.

[86] W. P. Hall, *op. cit.*, 87.

[87] *Writings*, IV, 276. See also his appreciation of the nineteenth Psalm (*ibid.*, IV, 337).

[88] *Ibid.*, II, 278.

[89] *Writings*, II, 304.

[90] *Ibid.* IV, 405.

[91] Hogg, *Life of Shelley* ed. Dowden, 517.

[92] *Writings*, I, 208.

[93] *Writings*, II, 472.

[94] Among Paine's humanitarian interests were abolition of slavery, arbitration schemes to avoid war, land reforms, income taxes, old age pensions, more practical and universal education, remedies for yellow fever, copyright laws, and many inventions for saving time and life.

[95] See, for example, the moving passage (*Writings*, II, 493) which conclude's Paine's presentation of his fourteen concrete suggestions, in the second part of the *Rights of Man*, for alleviating suffering.

[96] *Ibid*, II, 69-70.

[97] Paine seems to have drawn some of his knowledge of Eastern religions from Sir William Jones's *Asiatic Researches* (*Writings*, IV, 330); and Jones's *Principles of Government* (1782), which ran to five edition by 1818, is strikingly paralleled by passages in Paine's later political writing. In "A Discourse on the Institution of a Society," etc., p. 8, Jones writes: "Human knowledge has been elegantly analysed according to the three great faculties of the mind, *Memory, Reason,* and *Imagination;* which we constantly find employed in arranging and retaining, comparing and distinguishing, combining and diversifying the idea, which we receive through our senses, or acquire by reflection."

[98] In 1804, after Paley's works were published, Paine wrote: "When we see a watch, we have as positive evidence of the existence of a watchmaker as if we saw him; and in the same manner the creation is evidence to our reason and our senses of the existence of a Creator." (*Writings*, IV, 317) If Paine may have borrowed this mechanical figure from Paley, Paley's political philosophy of natural rights has interesting resemblances to Paine's, elaborated in print before most of Paley's works had appeared.

[99] *Writings*, IV, 360-62.

[100] *Writings*, II, 69-70.

[101] *Ibid.*, IV, 63.

[102] *Ibid.,* I, 178. "But priests, preachers, and fanatics, put imagination in the place of faith, and it is the nature of the imagination to believe without evidence." *Ibid.,* IV, 422.

[103] See Norman Foerster, *American Criticism,* Boston, 1928, on Lowell's imagination; H. H. Clark, "Lowell's Criticism of Romantic Literature," *Publications of the Modern Language Association,* XLI, 209-228, and also "Lowell-Humanitarian. Nationalist, or Humanist?" *Studies in Philology,* XXVII, 411-441 (July, 1930). Paine, of course, had little in common with the contemporary heralds of original genius who used the imagination mainly as a means of escape, or a means of creating what was idiosyncratic or unique. In a paper on "The Romanticism of Edward Young" (*Wisconsin Academy of Sciences, Arts and Letters,* XXIV) I have discussed the neo-classical as contrasted with the classical imagination, although I should have given more stress to the idea that the neo-classicists were not hostile to the sort of imagination just described.

[104] Hobbes, *Of Man,* Pt. I, sect. 8.

[105] In the *Philological Quarterly,* VII, 178. See also, Charles Gildon. *The Complete Art of Poetry,* 1718, I, 125; "For Fancy and Judgment must join in every great Poet, as Courage and Judgment in every great General; for where either is wanting, the other is useless, or of small Value. Fancy is what we generally call *Nature,* or a *Genius, Judgment* is what we mean by Art, the union of which in one Man makes a complete Poet."

[106] *Writings,* II, 110.

[107] *Writings,* II, 110.

[108] *Ibid.,* III, 402.

[109] *Ibid.,* I, 91. John Adams, Works, II, 508, records that Paine came "to my lodgings and spent an evening with me," and in discussing the portion of *Common Sense* dealing with monarchy, he "said he had taken his ideas in that part from Milton".

[110] *Writings,* IV, 46. He was the champion, unlike Rousseau, of representative government (*Ibid.,* II, 414-429) and he was among the first to see that "the union of America is the foundation-stone of her independence; the rock on which it is built . . ." (*Ibid.,* I, 340; see all of *Crisis,* XIII).

[111] Emerson, *Complete Works* (Centenary Edition), III, 283. See H. H. Clark, "Emerson and Science", *Philological Quarterly,* X, 225-260. Where evidence is presented to show that on one side Emerson's thought had a strong kinship with that of the deists.

[112] Of course Paine has been unpardonably libelled as regards his personal character, especially by such biographers as Cheetham. His sympathetic champion, however, M. D. Conway, was obliged to accept the fact that he was dismissed from the excise for a violation of his trust, and his best friends have reluctantly Admitted that in later life he "give in to the too frequent indulgence of drinking, neglected his appearance, and retired, mortified and disgusted, from an all-judging, unkind, unjust world, into coarse obscurity, and the association of characters in inferior life." This is the testimony of Rickman, (*Life of Paine,* London, 1819, p. 11), and it is substantiated by other friends such as Barlow (C. B. Todd, *Life and Letters of Joel Barlow,* New York, 1886, see Barlow's long letter on Paine quoted pp. 236-39). See also C. Wilmont, *An Irish Peer on the Continent* (1801-3), pp. 26-27. James Monroe, who had Paine released from prison and who nursed him back to health in his own ambassadorial residence, was grieved that Paine "would commit such a breach of confidence as well as of gratitude", as that involved in publishing from his host's home pamphlets which compromised his host, the United States' ambassador, and according to B. Fay, "Paine shattered his work", (*The Revolutionary Spirit in France and America,* New York, 1927, trans. by R. Guthrie, pp. 379-380; *Writings of James Monroe,* New York, 1898-1903, II, 440-42: III, 20-21; III, 27).

[113] *The Shelley Correspondence in the Bodleian Library,* ed. R. H. Hill, Oxford, 1926, p. 21 ff., Letter XXVI, "Shelley to J. H. Hunt, 3 November, 1819, on the conviction of Richard Carlile for Publishing Paine's 'Age of Reason'." (The first and third sheets only of this letter had been printed, as in editions by Forman and Ingpen).

[114] *Writings,* IV 391-93 and 342.

[115] *Ibid.,* IV, 311.

[116] *Writings,* IV, 339.

[117] *Ibid.,* IV, 315-16, and 322.

[118] In another study, "Newtonianism and Thomas Paine", I have endeavoured to define and outline Paine's central assumptions in the light of contemporary thought, especially that of Newtonians such as James Ferguson and Benjamin Martin, who were Paine's teachers.

[119] Esther Tiffany, "Shaftesbury as Stoic", *Publications of the Modern Language Association,* XXXVIII (1923), 642-84.

[120] "Essay on Man" (1734).

[121] "Essay on Criticism". Mary Segar has recently argued, inconclusively, as it seems to me, that Pope's

deism may be reconciled with his nominal Catholicism. ("Some Notes on Pope's Religion", *Dublin Review,* No. 381, April, 1932).

[122] This vastly important subject of the relation between literary ideals and Newtonian deism awaits, so far as I am aware, thorough investigation, both in England and America. A suggestive but very brief tabulation of meanings of the term "nature" in criticism of the seventeenth and eighteenth century will be found in a paper on "'Nature' as Aesthetic Norm" by A. O. Lovejoy (*Modern Language Notes,* XLII, 1927, pp. 444-50). As regards America, Carl Becker has admirably shown how important were widespread Newtonian naturalism and deism in moulding political theory and history; he does not mention Paine, but it should be evident that if Paine imbibed Newtonianism earlier in England through indirect sources, he must have had his faith reinforced by breathing its prevailing atmosphere in America. (*The Declaration of Independence. A Study in the History of Political Ideas,* New York, 1922, Ch. II). And see B. F. Wright, Jr., "American Interpretations of Natural Law", *American Political Science Review,* XX, (1926), 524-47; and A. O. Lovejoy (*Modern Philology,* XXIX, Feb. 1932, pp. 281-299) "The Parallel of Deism and Classicism". A. Bosker, *Literary Criticism in the Age of Johnson* (The Hague, 1930), surveys his subject in the light of the stock interpretations and romantic assumptions.

[123] Rickman, *Life of Paine,* 136. See also p. 32: "Distinctness and arrangement are the peculiar characteristics of his writings: this reflection brings to mind an observation once made to him by an American girl, that his head was like an orange—it had a separate apartment for every thing it contained."

[124] *Writings,* II, 79.

[125] *Writings,* II, 110. See also *ibid.* IV, 379: "Isaiah is, upon the whole, a wild disorderly writer, preserving in general no clear chain of perception in the arrangement of his ideas, and consequently producing no definite conclusions from them."

[126] *Ibid.* I, 138.

[127] *Ibid,* II, 302.

[128] *Writings,* I.

[129] *Ibid,* I.

[130] *Ibid,* II, 24. Watson (*Apology,* p. 8) taxes *The Age of Reason,* Part II, with "much repetition, and a defect of proper arrangement," a criticism also made by T. Meek, *Sophistry Detected, or, a Refutation of T.*

Paine's Age of Reason, New-castle, *MDCCXCV,* p. 28.

[131] Such as, "Having done A, we will now turn to B," etc. See especially, for examples, *Writings* II, 520; II, 83-4; III, 331; IV, 62; I, 290; I, 329.

[132] *Ibid.,* IV, 83-84.

[133] *Writings,* IV, 339-40.

[134] "What I would therefore recommend to you is, that, before you sit down to write on any subject, you would spend some days in considering it, putting down at the same time, in short hints, every thought which occurs to you as proper to make a part of your intended piece. When you have thus obtained a collection of the thoughts, examine them carefully with this view, to find which of them is properest to be presented *first* to the mind of the reader that he, being possessed of that, may the more easily understand it, and be better disposed to receive what you intend for the second; and thus I would have you put a figure before each thought, to mark its future place in your composition. For so, every preceding proposition preparing the mind for that which is to follow, and the reader often anticipating it, he proceeds with ease, and pleasure, and approbation, as seemingly continually to meet with his own thoughts. In this mode you have a better chance for a perfect production; because the mind attending first to the sentiments alone, next to the method alone, each part is likely to be better performed, and I think too in less time." Quoted by W. C. Bruce, *Fran-klin Self-Revealed,* II, 441. It is interesting to observe that Franklin, who read "Shaftesbury and Collins", was the friend of Henry Pemberton, author of *A View of Sir Isaac Newton's Philosophy,* (London, 1729), and who confessed that he "became a thorough deist", placed high among his cardinal virtues the virtue of order.

[135] See Myra Reynolds, *The Treatment of Nature in English Poetry,* Chicago, 1919, p. 327 ff.

[136] *Writings,* IV, 222 and 216.

[137] Thomas Burnet, *The Sacred Theory of the Earth,* London, 1759. See the chapter entitled "Stars".

[138] *Writings,* III, 135.

[139] Jefferson's *Works,* ed. Ford, X, 183.

[140] Quoted in D. E. Wheller's *Life and Writings of Thomas Paine,* I, 327.

[141] Jefferson's *Works,* VIII, 19, and proudly quoted by Paine himself, *Writings,* III, 428.

Joseph Dorfman (essay date 1938)

SOURCE: "The Economic Philosophy of Thomas Paine," in *Political Science Quarterly,* Vol. LIII, No. 3, September, 1938, pp. 372-86.

[*In the following essay, Dorfman depicts Paine as an advocate of free trade and charts some of his engagements with the development of American economic thought.*]

On the eve of the Revolutionary War, Thomas Paine, a failure in England, landed in America and threw in his fortunes with the revolting colonists, fighting "for the security of their natural rights and the protection of their own property."[1] Then began a career which made him one of the most powerful pamphleteers of the eighteenth century. Not only did he play a prominent rôle in the American Revolution but also in that of France, and many English authorities feared that he might instigate one in his native land. Like any impecunious pamphleteer, he sought wealth, and like any enlightened child of the eighteenth century, he believed that success in business affairs was evidence of God's good will. But his was the luckless fate of the general run of pamphleteers. His life continued to be a precarious one, and his biographer must pass over in silence more than one instance where the necessities of livelihood required that the language of lofty idealism serve special interests.

In *Common Sense,* Paine justified independence on the ground of natural right, interest and common sense. Government must be distinguished from society. Men by natural gravitation join in society in order to assist one another to satisfy their wants; that is, society consists of the bonds created by exchange and contracts. It is produced by our wants. Government, on the other hand, is produced by men's wickedness. It is a necessary evil, a badge of man's fall or corruption. It can do no positive good; at best it restrains men's vices. Security of property is the end of government. Therefore men surrender a part of their property to furnish the means of protecting the rest.

The inequality of wealth is natural for it arises from differences in "industry, superiority of talents, dexterity of management, extreme frugality, fortunate opportunities." It is not due to oppression and avarice. Oppression may be the consequence of riches, but is seldom the cause, and avarice generally makes men too timid to be wealthy.

On the other hand, the distinction between king and subject cannot be termed natural. It is a violation of the mutual compact and is the result of oppression and conquest. People remain blind to this interference with natural right and pecuniary interest through the force of fear, superstition, prejudice and prepossession. Hereditary monarchy has the least justification, for no generation has the right to bind future generations to a definite form of government.[2]

By eliminating commercial restraints and the expense of maintaining useless royalty and aristocracy, Paine argued, independence would promote the security and increase of property. Freedom of trade is the principal source of wealth for a trading nation. England's protection is unnecessary, for America's "plan is commerce", and since it is Europe's interest to have access to American trade, America will enjoy the friendship of Europe. American independence would even benefit the important classes of the English nation, the merchants and the manufacturers, because the increased commerce will enhance their profits. At the same time, America's commercial rights must be extended, for independence without commercial prosperity is hollow.[3]

The cause of America stood on "the broad foundation of property and popularity" and the latter depended on the former. True, a country's valor is evidenced by the character of the inhabitants and the bravery of the soldiers, but confidence of success is best evidenced by the support of men of substance. In this way a war becomes really popular.

The cost of the war is nominal. The creation of a national debt would be beneficial, for it would be a national bond. Since taxes are distributed within the country, they are a spur to industry; consequently in the absence of tax levies, the country would be poverty-stricken, just as without commerce, people would be indolent. An import duty is the best type of taxation, for it keeps foreign trade in the hands of Americans, and forces foreigners to contribute to the national defense.[4]

In the midst of his efforts in behalf of the revolutionary cause, Paine illustrated his philosophy of contract by publishing a pamphlet denying Virginia's claims to Western lands. He supported the contentions of land companies, with ambiguous titles, that the land belonged to the United States which alone could decide its disposition. He advocated that Congress organize the land with a view to creating new states. Effective government, which Virginia could not possibly furnish these frontier areas, would result in a rapid appreciation of land values. He now argued that land rather than trade was the real source of riches. The riches of other countries, based on industry and trade, were fictitious. They were matters of convention, subject to risk, but lands constantly increase in value with the growth of population. The Western lands were the property of the United States and the inhabitants had no right of self-government until they reached a certain number. Even when they became states, they were to have but limited Congressional rights for seven years. Paine felt that such new states would at first require more aid from the Confederacy than they could give to it, and that the inhabitants being largely composed of immigrants would require further tutelage. After the appearance of this pamphlet the Virginia legislature voted down a proposed land grant for Paine.[5]

In 1786, in the controversy over the Bank of North America, Paine developed the doctrine that a charter granted by the legislature is an irrevocable contract. Robert Morris, while financier general, promoted the Bank of North America which possessed, among its privileges, the power to issue bank notes. He obtained a perpetual charter from Congress in 1781 and another from Pennsylvania in 1782, with powers exceeding those of its model, the Bank of England. No other bank charter could be granted. Although it was to be under private control and for private profit, its incorporators justified its establishment on the ground that it was essential to supply the war needs of the government. Most of its funds came from the government's deposits of foreign loans, and the bank did not begin operations until after the surrender of Cornwallis, when the war, in fact, was over. It paid dividends at the rate of twelve to sixteen per cent. In 1785, petitions from various localities poured in to the Pennsylvania Assembly demanding the abrogation of the bank's charter.

These petitions denounced the bank as a vicious monopoly and money power, creating the prevailing havoc, insecurity and distress in the commercial community and causing the exportation of specie. They also accused the bank of discriminating in favor of speculators, of throwing the husbandmen and mechanics into bankruptcy and paying no share of its enormous profits to the government. Further, the petitions held that the large profits would attract foreign investment in the bank and the resulting foreign influence would reduce the American people to dependency on European courts and their intrigues. Even if the ownership were confined to Americans, this accumulation of wealth in a private society claiming perpetual duration would result in destroying freedom and equality in America, and the bank directors would be able to dictate legislation. Instead of being dependent on the government, the bank would control the government. Already the bank had threatened to destroy the state's paper money, by refusing to accept it. The arguments presented in the petitions led to the formation of a legislative committee which investigated the matter, and soon the charter was repealed.

Benjamin Franklin, who like Paine was a stockholder, persuaded Paine to writer in behalf of the bank, and at the same time, Morris entered the Assembly to endeavor to reopen the case.[6] The result was a pamphlet entitled *Dissertations on Government, the Affairs of the Bank and Paper Money*. In it Paine maintained that the citizens should be aware of certain self-evident truths not because the bank is concerned, but because constitutional rights and privileges are involved. If the legislature has the power to repeal the charter or in any way interfere with the bank, then the laws of the land and the courts of justice are useless. When people form a republic, which means a government for the public good, rich and poor mutually pledge themselves to the rule of equal justice. This gives security to the rich and consolation to the poor, for it permits every man to have his own and protects him from the despotism of the majority. Since the people in this original compact renounce as unjust the tyrannical right to break contracts, the assumption of this right by their representatives, the government, destroys the sovereign principle of the republic and installs despotism. Like contracts between individuals, contracts by the legislature, as a representative of the public, with a person or persons cannot be broken or changed without the consent of both parties. A legislature is prohibited from voiding a contract not only by legal and constitutional restrictions, but also by "natural reasons, or those reasons which the plain rules of common sense point out to every man." If such prohibition did not exist, a government of established principles administered by established rules would become a government with discretionary powers during the existence of one legislature, and a new revolution would occur with the election of every new legislature. The charter of the Bank of North America, established by "the enterprising spirit of patriotic individuals", constituted a contract.

In answer to the objection to a perpetual charter, Paine admitted that no generation has a right to bind a future one; nor has it the right to break a contract into which it has originally entered. Future generations may do as they see fit in accordance with the pecuniary canons of justice. Unfortunately, however, Paine did not determine when a new generation begins, or how the contract may be broken. As for paying part of the profits to the government, Paine felt that taking tolls for charters smacked of British tyranny. The assertion that the bank should be dependent on government he regarded as "treason", since the citizens who compose the bank will not be free if they are dependent on every new legislature. This would be exercising an authority over them which the legislature does not exercise over other citizens, and thereby would destroy the equality of freedom which is the bulwark of the Constitution. Purchase of bank stock by foreigners is a good instead of an evil, for where their money is, there go their hearts, and so we obtain a stronger influence over them than they can exercise over us.

Instead of monopolizing the money of the country, the bank is merely a steward, a useful depository for its real owners—the holders of bank notes and deposits. By making available otherwise idle money, the bank quickens business and creates employment. Through the invigorated commerce, the government derives a revenue. Least of all should the agrarians complain, for the additional funds available prevent a monopoly of the market by the few wealthy merchants. Thus, for honor rather than for their own interest, the incorporators have established the bank. True, discounts have been stopped and loans have been called, but this was done either to settle accounts or to prevent exportation of specie.

Paine bitterly denounced the issuance of paper money by the state. The Pennsylvania Constitution contains nothing which gives the Assembly the power to issue paper money. Those urging paper emissions on the fictitious ground of scarcity of money are base debtors, hoping to defraud their creditors through depreciation. Specie is the emission of nature, but paper causes the exportation of specie. The value of specie is determined by the quantity nature made, and man has no share in its value whether it bears a government stamp or not. The love of specie may produce covetousness, but covetousness is not properly a vice but "frugality run to an extreme." Paper, however, costs only a trifle, and thus inevitably becomes too plentiful. Since its value depends on caprice and accident, the value varies greatly and thus becomes the object of jobbery and schemes of deceit. Every principle of justice is violated, and the bond of society is dissolved. An act to suppress the issuance of paper money is really an act to suppress vice and immorality. To make the paper legal tender is a violation of contract, destroying morality, and undermining freedom, security and property. "The punishment of a member [of the assembly] who should move for such a law ought to be *death*."

Bank notes, however, are not of this character, for they are redeemable in specie. For the restoration of credit Paine proposed an ingenious scheme whereby the bank would more effectively control the finances of the government and the wealth of the community. Instead of having the state issue paper, he suggested that the government borrow from the bank sufficient bank notes for its financial needs, and the bank and related mercantile interests would bring in money to pay the notes, since the interest on the loans would be a bounty to import specie. Such combining of authority with usefulness is the distinguishing characteristic of a republican system.

The bank obtained a new charter, but Paine temporarily lost his reputation among his old democratic friends.[7]

The French Revolution proved to be another great opportunity for Paine's talents. When he arrived in England, reform was in the air. Burke's bitter denunciations of the French Revolution were at first coolly received, and Paine replied to him with his finest work, *The Rights of Man,* which in large part recapitulated the arguments of *Common Sense.*

The origin and continuation of monarchy, aristocracy and church establishments, Paine insisted, are due to force and fraud. The beneficiaries are really beggars. Heavy taxation, needed to support them, causes riots and disturbances. If primogeniture is abolished, estates will be left equally among the heirs, and there will no longer be any need for sinecures in church and state for the younger sons of noble families.

Paine demanded removal of property qualification for voting on the ground of property rights. The disfranchised are slaves because, without the vote, they are not guaranteed the essential property right, that of freedom from restrictions in acquiring a living. Furthermore, every man over twenty-one pays taxes from his property or from his labor which is property. Above all, a property qualification renders property insecure, since men, deprived of rights through it, will rise against the cause of their oppression. However, Paine was really interested in obtaining the franchise for the business classes. In England in some places, he remarked, the lowest characters without visible means of support could vote; in other places, great merchants, manufacturers and tenant farmers with heavy capital investments could not.[8]

Paine strongly advocated less government and more society. Men are not improved by government, and "I take my stand" on the argument that his condition is to be improved by means of his interest instead of "mere theoretical reformation." The landholder, farmer, merchant and trader prosper from the aid each obtains from the others. "Common interest regulates their concerns", and the usages growing out of this intercourse are more influential than the acts of government. Society performs almost everything attributed to governments. The more civilized man is, the less need there is for government, and the natural operation of the parts satisfies men. The laws of trade and commerce are laws of nature, or the laws of society, and they are obeyed not because of government but because of interest. In the trading associations, where men act on the principle of society, the units unite naturally. Were governments suddenly to disappear, mankind would proceed in much the same fashion. Governments follow precedent and oppose enterprise, but improvements in agriculture, arts and commerce are due to the enterprise of individuals and private associations. The promoter asks only that the government leave him alone. The government functionaries are merely stewards with the duty to maintain the property and freedom of the people. The need of government is limited to the fact that every man wishes to pursue his occupation and enjoy the fruits of his property. Consequently combinations of laborers to raise wages are unlawful, and the practice of fixing maximum prices, though famine prevails, causes the greatest distress.[9]

Commerce, Paine asserted, is the great civilizing force. Nature has made commerce the means of eliminating war, for it is cheaper to obtain commodities through commerce rather than through war. Commerce is beneficial, because merchants get rich from the natural increase in value of the objects exchanged. Thus, while foreign commerce is advantageous, domestic commerce is more so, for all rather than one-half the benefits lie within the nation. Furthermore, since commerce is fostered only by the reciprocal interest of nations, attempts to control commerce by navies and conquest are a futile waste of resources and the heavy cost involved leads to domestic oppression. Therefore, Paine reasoned that the combined reduced fleets of England, Holland, France and the United States could force Spain to give South America her independence and thus open countries of immense wealth to world commerce. This area would provide a ready market for English manufacturers, whereas England at the moment was drained of specie to pay for the imports of competing manufactures from India. With good reason, Paine declared that "in all my publications, wherever the matter would admit, I have been an advocate for commerce."[10]

Paine's suggestions for financial reform were designed to relieve the business classes of heavy taxes. The support given to useless government establishments could be directed toward eliminating the poor rates. The discontent of the poor would be allayed and poor relief abolished by such measures as education, old-age pensions, and work barracks for the unemployed. Education was to consist of "reading, writing and arithmetic". Thereby the children could obtain a profitable living and cease to be a drain on the industrious. Old-age pensions were to consist of small annual payments of £6 to those between the ages of fifty and sixty, and £10 thereafter. Taxes paid by the consumer, such as the excise and customs taxes, should be retained so that trade would not be disturbed. Taxation of land and land incomes was to be arranged to encourage division of the estates, and thereby eliminate the institution of primogeniture. However, "it would be impolitic to set bounds to property acquired by industry."[11]

The English financial system, as one of credit, was based on paper rather than real money. Credit was the child of credulity and, if the holders of Bank of England notes were to demand specie, the entire system would collapse. The contradiction between his views on the Bank of North America and those on the Bank of England was somewhat resolved by his argument that to the extent that the Bank of England issued paper, based on discounted bills growing out of commercial transactions, it was engaged in legitimate business.

In fact, Paine would tamper but little with the debt. Its origins might be shady, but it was not the crime of the present holders. Furthermore, the interest should not be touched for it might affect adversely legitimate credit and commerce. As the interest was paid in Bank of England notes, it kept alive a capital useful to commerce and thereby neutralized to a considerable degree its own burden. Since the amount of specie was inadequate, it would be bad policy as well as unjust to eliminate a capital that met the defect of the circulating medium. Still, in view of the discontent over the national debt, it would be good policy for the holders to allow a slight tax on the interest.[12]

As a result of attacking monarchy in his *Rights of Man*, Paine was ordered to stand trial. At first, this did not disturb him, because reform was a common cry, and a trial would give wide publicity to his works. However, when the British government became intent on ruthlessly suppressing even nominal demands for reform, Paine left the country to take a seat in the French National Convention.

In France, Paine once more advocated his ideas. As in the case of England, he suggested reforms which would relieve the poor without disturbing trade, commerce or the unrestricted accumulation of wealth. Toward this end, he published *Agrarian Justice*. It was occasioned by the unsuccessful communist revolt led by Babeuf against the reactionary French government. Paine denounced the leaders for attempting to overthrow society instead of waiting for the customary elections or proposing useful measures. Of course, the great mass of poor are ever increasing and have become a hereditary race. In the natural state, poverty did not exist, but civilization has created both splendor and wretchedness side by side. This situation has been caused by the rise of ownership of land, whereas in the original state land was common property and every man was a joint proprietor in its products. Increasing population necessitated private cultivation, and since it is impossible to differentiate the improvement from the land itself, the latter became private property also. To obtain for the dispossessed poor their share in the common or natural property, a fund was to be raised by levying a death duty of ten per cent. Personal property should be subject to the tax because it is the effect of society, not that the individual owes society the property, but that without society an individual cannot acquire it. According to Paine's plan, the fund was to provide the rather small amount of £15 for each individual, rich or poor, on reaching the age of twenty-one, and a yearly pension of £10 after the age of fifty. The scheme would have many beneficial results. The national lands would sell at better rates. A young couple could obtain land and stock, and become profitable citizens rather than burdens on society. The wealthy classes particularly would benefit, for the unjust character of modern civilization might lead to violence against property. When display of wealth simply serves to arouse the masses to question the right of property, it is only in a system of justice that the possessors can rest secure. Such danger would be removed by the tax. The masses would see that the riches of one above another increase the national fund proportionately and that the more riches a man acquires the better it is for the poor. Paine truthfully said, "I am a friend of riches."[13]

On his return to the United States in 1802 Paine found that the prevailing sentiment was hostile. Jefferson, who was in his second presidential year, had praised *The Rights of Man*, as the orthodox doctrine of American political theory, but the Federalists regarded Paine as a regicide. In religious circles he was denounced as an atheist for his *Age of Reason* which expounded Deism. He had written that God was known through nature and the laws of science were the formulations of the laws of inscrutable, beneficent nature. Therefore, if men would be happy and moral, they should follow the ways of nature as expressed in the "wise and economical sayings" of Franklin.[14] The church members, however, only noticed his diatribes on organized religion and his characterization of the Bible as an obscene document; they failed to see his metaphysical defense of business practice and ways of conduct.

Jefferson sought Paine's advice on important questions, but made little effort to aid him. Paine wrote the President that when Napoleon had conquered England, the United States should seize Canada and the Bermudas. In another communication he expounded views which were later expressed in the Monroe Doctrine. He thought that the United States should mediate between France and rebellious Santo Domingo, and guarantee the settlement. This would give the United States great political and commercial influence in Santo Domingo.[15] Paine advised Jefferson on how Louisiana could be obtained from Napoleon. He suggested that Jefferson propose to purchase the territory, and then inform Napoleon that the inhabitants of the Western territories were growing so powerful and restive, that it was impossible to restrain them from seizing New Orleans, and that it was equally impossible for France to prevent them.[16]

Jefferson was worried over his constitutional right to make the purchase, but Paine informed him that the Constitution had nothing to do with the matter since its framers could never have foreseen the occasion. The transaction was within the president's jurisdiction. It was a sale and purchase similar to any financial transaction. The object was an increase of territory for a valuable consideration.

Concerning the government of the territory, Paine recommended a period of tutelage for the French inhabitants, since they were not acquainted with democratic institutions. At the same time he asked Jefferson about the acquisition of lands in the territory by individuals, for he had friends by principle in the British Isles who had funds to purchase unlimited amounts. He suggested that indentured servants be obtained as a labor supply, since sale of lands and settlement would be retarded until laborers were obtained. Indentured servants yield more revenue to the government than negro slaves, for their consumption of imported articles is much greater. The government, therefore, should supervise a system of indentured servitude in the newly acquired territory. On the expiration of their service, Congress, rather than their masters, should give them a few acres which would serve as an incentive to purchase more at a later date. Paine pointed to the good done by the Quaker merchants of Pennsylvania. They went extensively into the business of importing indentured servants, for it was consistent with their moral principles of bettering the condition of the poor and ending negro slavery. Free negroes might also be imported into the territory through government financial aid. Congress should supply the passage to New Orleans, and the negroes, after working for the planters for a few years, should be made share croppers.[17]

When the inhabitants of the Louisiana territory petitioned for self-government, they advanced Paine's political philosophy of the rights of self-government in accordance with "the laws of nature." The colonial arguments against England were cited. Paine replied that the Louisianans were not experienced in the representative system, that the colonies had obtained their rights by an expensive war, that it was not the duty of the United States to fight the world's battles for the world's profit, that the territory was not a contracting party to the cession but had merely been purchased. Congress was the guardian of this valuable property for all the United States, and it would be unwise to place the territory under the jurisdiction of the people whose freedom had just been purchased. Repayment of the purchase price must come from the land sales. It was better for the inhabitants that Congress govern, since its effective government would encourage increased population and thereby raise the land values. The fear of the inhabitants that governors with no interest in the welfare of the territory might be appointed was unfounded. True, despotic governments, like those of their former masters, might do so, but their references to practices of their old rulers revealed that the inhabitants did not understand the principles or interest of a republic, or the difference between governments distant and despotic and those domestic and free.[18]

During this period Paine's views regarding banks underwent a change to a more democratic philosophy. Scandals had occurred in connection with bank charters, particularly in Pennsylvania. He now claimed that neither the Pennsylvania Constitution nor that of any other state gave the government the right to grant charters or monopolies. The spirit of the times was against all such speculations. Furthermore, long term charters were a violation of the principle of annual election of the legislature. Charters for more than one year meant that one legislature could pass measures beyond the power of succeeding legislatures to correct. Paine did not suggest that incorporation should be forbidden, but rather he proposed a device which he had originally suggested to prevent the revocation of the charter of the Bank of North America. Extraordinary matters such as incorporations should be passed by two successive legislatures. If the citizens disliked a measure, they could refuse to reëlect those who had supported it.[19]

As a whole the works of Thomas Paine present a scheme of things closely resembling that of the Benthamites, which came a generation later. His views foreshadow Herbert Spencer's philosophy of a contrast between a system of status and one of free contract. Abolition of church, aristocracy and royalty would solve all social problems by leaving individuals to the natural play of free contracts. Just as *Common Sense* advocated independence through the elimination of unnecessary expense and the abolition of restrictions on commerce and property, and thus on personal rights, so on the same basis *The Rights of Man* called for the abolition of royalty and aristocracies, and *The Age of Reason,* of organized religion.

This elimination of all institutions, except those involving property and its security, would permit the expansion of business enterprise. Paine's opponents, including Hamilton, did not appreciate the drift of his writings, for his objective was theirs. Hamilton felt that wealth could be secure only with a strong government in the hands of men of great wealth, for the mass of men were ignorant and turbulent. Paine believed in the democracy of property owners, which by virtue of the beneficence of the uniting bond of property and contract would duly recognize the sanctity of all contracts including all agreements made by the legislature with individuals.

So easily did these two schools of economic thought fuse, that the major argument used by Paine to deny the right of the Pennsylvania legislature to abrogate the charter of the Bank of North America was precisely the one used by Hamilton to deny the right of Jefferson to reform the federal judiciary in 1801. Both the grant of the charter and the establishment of the judiciary were in the nature of contracts, and no legislature could interfere with the original terms except with the approval of the other contracting body.[20]

Notes

[1] *Crisis* (1782), republished in M. C. Conway, *The Writings of Thomas Paine* (New York and London, 1894-1896), vol. I, p. 334.

[2] *Common Sense* (1776), "First Principles of Government" (1795), in *Writings,* vol. I, pp. 70, 75-84, vol. III, p. 268.

[3] *Common Sense, Crisis* (III, 1777, IV, 1778), "Peace and The New Foundland Fisheries" (I, III, 1779), in *Writings,* vol. I, pp. 88, 204, 287, vol. II, pp. 3, 14.

[4] "Common Sense", "Crisis" (IX, 1780, X, 1782), in *Writings,* vol. I, pp. 102, 305, 321, 340.

[5] "Public Good" (1780), in *Writings,* vol. II, pp. 61, 63, 65-66.

[6] William Graham Sumner, *The Financier and the Finances of the American Revolution* (New York, 1891), vol. I, pp. 25-35, 183-189; William M. Gouge, *A Short History of Paper and Banking in the United States* (Philadelphia, 1833), Part II, pp. 31-38, 237-240.

[7] M. C. Conway, *The Life of Thomas Paine* (New York and London, 1892), vol. I, pp. 213, 215, 265, vol. II, p. 466; "Dissertations on Government; The Affairs of the Bank; and Paper Money" (1786), in *Writings,* vol. II, pp. 132-187; Tom Callendar, *Letters to Hamilton,* 1802, p. 36.

[8] *The Rights of Man* (1791-1792), "Address to the Addressers" (1792), in *Writings,* vol. II, pp. 312, 321, 409, 472, 499, 500, vol. III, pp. 88-89.

[9] *The Rights of Man,* pp. 406, 407-408, 409, 442-443, 456; "Letter to Danton" (1793), in *Writings,* vol. III, p. 137.

[10] *The Rights of Man,* pp. 456-457, 459-460, 511-512.

[11] *Ibid.,* pp. 471-480, 483, 484, 487, 494, 496-497.

[12] *Ibid.,* pp. 374, 376, 378, 506, 507; "Prospects on the Rubicon" (1787), "The Decline and Fall of the English System of Finance" (1796), in *Writings,* vol. II, p. 214, vol. III, pp. 286-312.

[13] *Agrarian Justice* (1797), in *Writings,* vol. III, pp. 324-344.

[14] *The Age of Reason* (1796), in *Writings,* vol. IV, p. 35.

[15] *Life,* vol. II, pp. 333, 344, 346.

[16] Letter to Jefferson, Dec. 25, 1802, in *Writings,* vol. III, pp. 379-380.

[17] *Life,* vol. II, pp. 319-320, 321-323, 332, 347-349, 350.

[18] "To the French Inhabitants of Louisiana" (1804), in *Writings,* vol. III, pp. 430-436.

[19] "Constitutions, Governments and Charters" (1805), in *Writings,* vol. IV, pp. 468-469.

[20] For a general discussion of Hamilton's economic philosophy, see Rexford Guy Tugwell and Joseph Dorfman, "Alexander Hamilton: Nation Maker", *Columbia University Quarterly,* Dec. 1937, March 1938.

Howard Penniman (essay date 1943)

SOURCE: "Thomas Paine—Democrat," in *The American Political Science Review,* Vol. XXXVII, No. 2, April, 1943, pp. 244-62.

[*In the essay that follows, Penniman parallels the moment in which he writes—during World War II— with the tumultuous time in which Paine wrote. He goes on to summarize the fundamental principles that girded the democracy that Paine ultimately espoused.*]

These may be "the times that try men's souls," as President Roosevelt recently told the nation, but they may also be the times when free and courageous men may push forward toward the better society of which Thomas Paine dreamed when he pleaded with the colonists for unity in the cause of freedom. When Paine first wrote those words 165 years ago, America had an opportunity to break away from the tyranny of Europe. But Paine was not content to win a war of independence for America alone. Like many today he talked of world revolution aimed at the tyranny of the few over the many. He, too, argued that men—all men—should have an equal opportunity to shape their own destinies and the destiny of the world in which they found themselves. In an era when men are fighting to preserve and extend a heritage of freedom, it would be well to reëxamine the ideas of Paine, whose writings inspired men of his day in America, in England, and in France to work and to die that they might be free.

The examination will be based primarily on the pamphlets and articles written after 1791; for, as Vernon L. Parrington has said, "the maturest elaboration of Paine's political philosophy is found in ***The Rights of Man,***" [1] which was written in that year. It is only in the book mentioned that Paine attempted to set down in any detail his beliefs on the general nature of the state and government. Later pamphlets and essays served to expand and elaborate the reasons for particular conclusions stated in his reply to Burke's *Reflections on the Revolution in France.* Because he was, as Charles E. Merriam suggests, primarily an "agitator" whose influence was "popular rather than scientific," [2] Paine was not as concerned with writing a complete philosophy as in securing results in specific instances. However, in his many articles on immediate issues after 1791 he remained consistent with the general position adopted in his major work.

As a democrat—and in his later years he was a democrat [3]—Paine believed that sovereignty ought to reside in the people, that decisions of the sovereign ought to be made by the numerical majority, that all members of the society ought to have equal political rights with an equal opportunity to determine the decisions of the majority, and that some means ought to be provided whereby the majority may make its decisions known. [4]

The remainder of this essay will consider the political doctrines of Paine with respect to each of these items of his democratic creed.

I. Popular sovereignty

In order to discover who ought to possess sovereignty, Paine posited a state of nature. This state of nature was never a pre-historic age when men lived apart from each other as isolated individuals. Man naturally came into society because he was a friend of man, [5] and because he could not as well satisfy his wants if he remained apart from other men. [6] A state of nature, then, was any society in which there was no regularly constituted, functioning government. Thus he referred to the members of the National Assembly of France as "delegates of the nation in its *original* character; future assemblies will be delegates of the nation in its *organized* character." [7]

All governments must either grow "*out* of the people or *over* the people." [8] Governments which "grow out of the people" are based upon "the common interest of society and the common rights of man." [9] They are set up by a compact among all the members of society, "each in his personal and sovereign right . . . and this is the only mode in which governments have a right to arise, and the only principle on which they have a right to exist." [10] Governments which are "over" the people arise through usurpation and are based upon superstition or force. They may be called governments of priestcraft or of conquerors. [11]

Because all men enter into the compact, "sovereignty, as a matter of right, appertains to the Nation only and not to any individual; and a Nation has at all times an inherent indefeasible right to abolish any form of government it finds inconvenient, and *to establish such as accords with its interest, disposition, and happiness.*"[12] The constitution or compact (Paine uses the terms synonymously) antedates government and is supreme over it. Government cannot be a partner to the compact which establishes it, and therefore cannot alter the terms of the pact.[13] Government may "control men only as individuals," but men collectively control both the terms of the compact and the powers of government.[14]

The nation may delegate power to representatives in a legislature, who hold that power as a trust as long as the people wish and no longer. "But the right of the Nation is an original right as universal as taxation. The Nation is the paymaster of everything, and everything must conform to its general will."[15] A mixed constitution, which divides authority between the representatives of the people and groups which are not responsible to the nation, is contrary to the nature of legitimate government because the irresponsible elements may control the responsible representatives.[16]

Sovereignty inheres in a people, and they cannot relinquish it either for themselves or for posterity. Paine denied Burke's contention that the people of England must continue to be ruled by a king because a Parliament in 1688 had pledged their obedience to William and Mary and their children forever.[17] The rule of the living by the dead is the worst of all tyrannies. A compact which binds posterity to a particular ruler and deprives it of political rights is similar to a will in which A bequeaths the property of B to C. It is both unjust and absurd.[18]

Representative government (i.e., democracy) based upon popular sovereignty is *"nothing more than a national association acting on the principles of society."*[19] It is concerned with the "management of the affairs of the nation,"[20] and is for the "good of the nation and not for the emolument or aggrandisement of particular individuals."[21] It is, then, a republic, established for the "good of all, as well individually as collectively."[22]

In his earlier writings, Paine took exception to the doctrine of popular sovereignty in so far as it applied to certain kinds of economic contracts. Neither the legislature nor the people had the right to revoke certain kinds of economic contracts agreed to by a preceding legislature and another party.[23] If both the government and the other party agreed to revise or discard the contract, then, and only then, could it be modified or revoked. Disputes arising out of these contracts must be submitted to a court for a decision.[24] No question could be decided by either party alone.[25] Yet, even in this essay—written before Paine

had completely worked out his political philosophy— he argued that contracts must have a limited duration. He suggested thirty years. To grant a charter "forever" can have no meaning, because "our forever" ends when the "forever" of our children begins, and we can no more bind our children to economic contracts than we can set up a government for posterity.[26]

No such limitations upon popular sovereignty were recognized in *The Rights of Man* written five years later. Paine did not consider economic contracts except in passing, but he left no doubt about his beliefs concerning political charters granted by the government. In demanding the abolition of the English "rotten boroughs," he discussed the relationship of charters to equality of rights and popular sovereignty.

> Rights are inherently in all the inhabitants; but charters, by annulling those rights, in the majority, leave the right by exclusion in the hands of the few. If charters were constructed so as to express in direct terms *"that every inhabitant, who is not a member of a corporation, shall not exercise the right of voting,"* such charters would, in the face, be charters not of rights but of exclusion. . . . They do not give rights to A, but they make a difference in favour of A by taking the right of B, and consequently are instruments of injustice.[27]

In his last political essay, written fourteen years after *The Rights of Man,* Paine denied his earlier contention in the *Dissertation on Government* that certain economic contracts could not be annulled by a legislature even if the contracts were contrary to the expressed will of the people. He admitted that if one legislature could pass an act which was beyond the power of succeeding legislatures to revise, it would be contrary to the "very intention, essence, and principle of annual elections."[28] He therefore suggested that acts which require permanency—"sales or grants of lands, acts of incorporation, public contracts with individuals or companies beyond a certain amount"—should be proposed by one legislature and adopted by a second legislature after the people had expressed their desires on the measure through an intervening election.[29] Apparently (the essay is not entirely clear on this point)[30] Paine believed that his proposal would give some degree of permanency to those kinds of economic contracts mentioned above, even though it was within the power of the people to change or annual the contracts (presumably by following the same procedure by which the contracts had been adopted originally). If this interpretation is correct, Paine had accepted in the sphere of economic contracts the position which he had argued in *The Rights of Man* in connection with political contracts. The one limitation upon popular sovereignty—that of forcing the people to wait a year before agreeing to changing a contract—is too minor to constitute any real exception to the doctrine.

It has been contended by at least one writer, however, that Paine held that rights to property are inalienable, that they constitute a limitation upon sovereignty of the people, and that government was instituted for the security and benefit of property owners.[31] But an analysis of Paine's later works (i.e., after 1791) indicates quite clearly that this is not the case, and that Paine, with the minor exception noted above, believed fully in popular sovereignty. He argued that the only inalienable rights which men possess are the natural rights that belong to them by right of their existence,[32] namely, freedom of religion,[33] freedom of discussion,[34] and the right of citizenship, with its appendage—the vote.[35] Possession of these natural rights depends only upon the willingness of a man to recognize the claim to the same right by other men. Rights and duties are reciprocal, and a statement of rights, by its nature, is also a statement of duties.[36] Even the right to vote, which has no "equivalent counterpoise," may be taken away from those who would deprive others of that right.[37]

Property is frequently spoken of as a right, but only on one occasion was it spoken of as an inalienable right, and then by implication. In *The Rights of Man,* Paine gave general approval to the first three articles of the "Declaration of the Rights of Man and Citizens,"[38] in which property was referred to as one of the "natural and imprescriptable rights of man."[39] But elsewhere in the same essay he commended the action of the French Republic in selling the lands of the church to pay the national debt,[40] and he also proposed a progressive income tax to raise money for the aid of the poor, aged, newly-married, etc. The tax was to become confiscatory for incomes above 20,000 pounds.[41] This would be difficult to reconcile with an inalienable right to property.

The relationship of property to society is stated in some detail in *Agrarian Justice*. Land was originally held in common, but with the development of cultivation this became impractical. Improvement resulting from cultivation cannot be separated from the land itself. Nevertheless, all members of society deserve some remuneration from the land, even though some do not occupy any of it. Those who live upon the land, therefore, should pay ground-rents or an inheritance tax of ten per cent into the national treasury for distribution among the members of the nation.[42] A portion of personal property also should be given "back to society from whence the whole came," because "any accumulation beyond that which a man's own hands could produce" is made possible by his living in society.[43]

Paine advised those who owned property to make it "productive of a national blessing,"[44] because only then could the owners be assured of retaining even a part of their possessions. The advice was given, if we can judge from the general tenor of his works, not out of any love for property and its "rights" as such, but because he held a functional concept of property. His proposal of high taxes on lands and personal property would, he thought, peacefully relieve misery and provide all members of society with at least the material essentials of life. Failure to give the people the necessities would mean the expropriation of property by violence, when "wealth and splendour, instead of fascinating the multitude, excite emotions of disgust . . . [and] when the ostentatious appearance it makes serves to call the right of it in question,"[45] Government, not private individuals, should put the functional concept of property into practice, because private charity cannot accomplish the job effectively.[46]

If our summary of Paine's attitude toward property is accurate, it is difficult to accept a recent interpretation of his economic ideas which argues that his concern in *Agrarian Justice* was the protection of property against the caprice of the multitude; and that he urged property-owners to give up some of their holdings because he wished them to save the rest and not because he wished to improve the material circumstances of men.[47] The more probable explanation of his urging owners to give up part of their holdings is that he acted like some present-day reformers who attempt to persuade business men that it is to their own interest to have trade unions organized within their industries. The argument, whether valid or invalid, is not made out of any desire to aid business men but to aid labor. It is no easier to accept the statement by the same author that both Paine and Hamilton were seeking the same economic objective.[48] To argue that Paine and Hamilton believed in the same sort of economic organization has no more meaning than to argue that President Roosevelt and Henry Ford both believe in capitalism. It is probably true that neither Paine nor Hamilton would have taken away all property from its owners, but at this point the similarity ceases. Paine wished property to serve all in society; Hamilton wished the state to preserve property for those who owned it, and certainly not to take it from them to help others.[49]

Parrington is right when he says that Paine believed that property rights were "limited by social needs,"[50] and that the people were to determine those needs because there can be for Paine "no law superior to this popular will expressed through the majority."[51] Although he spoke of the "rights of property," Paine emphasized that they were rights *"not of the most essential kind,"*[52] and could not be compared with, e.g., the right to vote.[53] If the rights of property are inferior to the natural rights, it seems reasonable to assume that they are not inalienable rights and that they may be regulated through the use of the natural rights.

II. Majority Rule

That the sovereignty of the people should be expressed through the decision of the majority, Paine never doubted in his later writings.[54] So convinced was he that majority-rule was the only reasonable method of making decisions in a representative society that he found it necessary to mention "majority" only briefly in *The Rights of Man*. His belief in the efficacy of majority-rule is expressed in a description of the ratification of the American constitution by the Massachusetts convention, where "the majority was not above nineteen or twenty in about three hundred members; but such is the nature of representative government that it quietly decides all matters by majority."[55] "If it prefer a bad or defective government to a reform or chuse to pay ten times more taxes than there is any occasion for, it has a right so to do; and so long as the majority do not impose conditions on a minority, different from what they impose upon themselves, though there may be much error, there is no injustice."[56] He carried the idea of decisions by majority vote into the legislature. He objected to a bicameral legislature because "it always admits of the possibility, and is often the case in practice, that a minority governs a majority, and that in some instances to a degree of great inconsistency."[57]

A more complete statement of his belief in majority-rule is to be found in *Dissertation on First Principles of Governments*, which was written in support of his arguments in *The Rights of Man:*

> In all matters of opinion, the social compact, or principle by which society is held together, requires that the majority of opinions become the rule for the whole, and that the minority yield practical obedience thereto. This is perfectly conformable to the principle of equal rights: for, in the first place, every man has a *right to give an opinion* but no man has a right that his opinion should *govern the rest*. In the second place, it is not supposed to be known beforehand on which side of any question, whether for or against, any man's opinion will fall. He may happen to be in a majority upon some questions, and in a minority upon others; and by the same rule that he expects obedience in the one case, he must yield it in the other. . . . The principle of equal rights has been repeatedly violated and that not by the majority but by the minority, and *that minority has been composed of men possessing property, as well as of men without property; property, therefore, even upon the experience already had, is no more a criterion of character than it is of rights.* It will sometimes happen that the minority are right, and the majority are wrong, but as soon as experience proves this to be the case, the minority will increase to a majority, and the error will reform itself by the tranquil operation of freedom of opinion and equality of rights. Nothing, therefore, can justify an insurrection, neither can it ever be necessary where rights are equal and opinions free.[58]

Political parties or factions around which majorities may rally at election time received little attention from Paine. He apparently accepted the fact that parties arise wherever there are representative institutions. Usually he mentioned parties only in passing, and then without comment. Once he declared that the only safeguard against parties ruling in their own interest is a constitution to which they are subject. Even here, it will be noted, he does not condemn parties as such, but only suggests that they must not be supreme. On a later occasion he expressed the belief that the "fate of every party is decided by its principles," because a majority will not long support a party with a poor or wrong program. Perhaps it was Paine's wider experience with political factions in England and France that prevented his falling into the then prevalent American notion that all parties necessarily subvert the will of the people.[59]

"The majority are, politically, the people,"[60] not only because a society of equals ought to be ruled by a majority, but also because any attempt of a minority to govern "will unite them (i.e., the majority) in a common interest against the government and against those who support it; and *as the power is always with the majority, they can overturn such a government and its supporters whenever they please*."[61] Having taken part in two revolutions which displaced kings, Paine failed to see that inertia might well prevent a disorganized majority from ruling in the face of a determined, disciplined minority. Nor did he foresee that the day would come when minorities backed by armies *can* control majorities—the mere strength of numbers meaning little in the face of modern military forces.[62]

Because governmental action needs the support of the people, minorities ought not rule even when they are certain that their decisions are correct.[63] If power is not lodged in the majority of an inclusive electorate, there is no logical stopping point short of one-man rule.[64] And it is impossible for one man to be so wise in all things that he can instruct the people and make their decisions.[65]

Unanimous agreement would be, he conceded, the preferable method of making decisions. But such is the nature of man that common consent will be consistently given only to the proposition that the majority should rule. Society will give the power to the majority because of the absolute necessity that decisions be made, and because "it is a mode of decision derived from the primary original right of every individual concerned; *that* right being first individually exercised in giving an opinion, and whether that opinion shall arrange with the minority or the majority, is a subsequent accidental thing that neither increases or diminishes the individual original right itself."[66]

III. Equality

Our discussion of Paine's belief in majority-rule has also indicated his belief in equality of political rights. As in the case of his discussion of popular sovereignty and majority-rule, he conducts his argument on two levels. He maintains that equality springs from ultimate principles or natural law, and also insists that equality should be granted for practical reasons, saying that those who have the power to bring about equality should do so for their own interest. As in all such arguments, he places greatest emphasis on the "justice" of the proposition.

The basis of equality is to be found in the origin of man. When he came from the hand of his Maker, his "high and only title" was man.[67] All accounts of the beginning of man, although differing from all others in many particulars, are agreed on one point, "*the unity of man;* by which I mean that all men are of *one degree,* and consequently that all men are born equal, and with equal natural right, in the same manner as if posterity had been continued by *creation* instead of generation . . . ; and consequently every child born into the world must be considered as deriving its existence from God. The world is as new to him as it was to the first man that existed, and his right in it is of the same kind."[68] There is "but one species of man, [and therefore] there can be but one element of human power; and that element is man himself."[69]

Upon leaving society in its "original" state to become a part of society in its "organized" state, every individual, "each in his own personal and sovereign right, *entered into a compact with each other to produce a government . . .*";[70] therefore, each "is a member of the Sovereignty"[71] with equal political rights based upon his natural rights.[72] That the rights of man in society "shall be equal is not a matter of opinion but of right, and consequently of principle."[73] Any limitation upon equality would be admitting that some men have property in others.[74]

"The right of voting for persons charged with the execution of the laws that govern society is inherent in the word Liberty, and constitutes equality of personal rights."[75] If the right to vote is "attached to inanimate matter,"[76] such as place of residence, property, or payments of direct taxes, "the dignity of the suffrage is thus lowered . . . in placing it with an inferior thing. . . . It is impossible to find an equivalent counterpoise for the right of suffrage, because *it alone* is worthy of its own basis, and cannot thrive as a graft, or an appendage. . . ."[77] A man should lose his right to vote only if he attempts to exclude another from voting. By his attempt, he automatically forfeits his claim to the right by refusing to recognize a similar claim on the part of others.[78]

On the practical side of the question, Paine argued that it was unwise to limit the suffrage to those with great property-holdings because this would, by excluding the majority, unite them, and they would seize control anyway.[79] If the suffrage were based upon a small amount of property, it would be based upon accident.[80] To associate the vote with property in any fashion would be to place the right on the most precarious of bases, because men are constantly gaining and losing property—frequently through no fault of their own. Men would, if property were a criterion, lose not only property but the right to vote when it "would be of most value."[81] To limit the vote to those who pay taxes would be meaningless, because all men pay taxes in some form.[82] If the payment of a direct tax were required, it would be dangerous because corrupt politicians could buy elections by paying the poll taxes for those who could not afford the fee.[83] If exceptions to the property qualifications are made in favor of those who have served in the army, they will fail in their purpose, because the soldier will not fight harder, realizing that his children cannot have the right which he is acquiring at the risk of his life.[84] The wisest criterion for voting is age, because "nothing but dying before that time can take it away."[85]

Nor is it wise to grant special representation to particular interests, because they will legislate for their own welfare to the detriment of the rest of society. Besides, what right have they "to a distinct and separate interest from the general interest of the nation?"[86] To discriminate against any group is to "make poverty their choice."[87] A wise man of property, Paine said, recognizes that security of his interest rests upon equal political rights for all, because the people never injure property if they are accorded equality of rights.[88] Property is not safe, however, when it is employed "criminally . . . [as] a criterion for exclusive rights."[89] Men of property should remember that "it is possible to exclude men from the right of voting, but it is impossible to exclude them from the right of rebelling against that exclusion; and when all other rights are taken away, the right of rebellion is made perfect."[90]

IV. Popular Consultation

To remove the necessity of resorting to violence to secure their ends, the people must be given some means of expressing their desires both in the changing of the fundamental law and in the selection of representatives. Paine believed that elections, frequently held,[91] prevent "inconveniences accumulating, till they discourage reformation or promote revolution."[92]

Constitutions, as we have seen, cannot be modified even by elected representatives, because the government would then be removed from the people after the first election.[93] Constitutions should state the methods by which the people may make "alterations, amendments, or additions."[94] A provision for constitutional amendment is one of the greatest steps toward the "security and progress of Constitutional liberty."[95] The wisest provision for amendment is probably one which calls for a periodic convention—perhaps every seven years[96]—because "it provides frequent opportunity of using it [the right of constitutional revision] and thus helps to keep the government within the principles of the constitution."[97] By electing special assemblies for the consideration of proposed revisions, "the general WILL, whether to reform or not, or what the reform shall be, or how far it shall extend, will be known, and it cannot be known by any other means."[98] When the convention has finished its work, the revisions should be submitted to the people for their approval.[99] Paine was clear that the calling of conventions at regular intervals must not be interpreted as barring revisions during the interim, because the powers of "forming and reforming, generating and regenerating constitutions . . . are always before a country *as a matter of right*. . . ."[100]

The people cannot meet together to pass on ordinary laws, so representatives must be kept in close touch with their constituents.[101] Legislators who are not held accountable to the people cease to represent the nation and represent only themselves.[102] They are no better than the aristocracy, who, being "accountable to nobody, ought not be trusted by anybody."[103] Free discussion,[104] aided by complete reports to the people by government officials, is essential to the maintenance of representative government. The reason for every government act must be given, because each citizen is a "proprietor of government, and considers it a necessary part of his business to understand."[105]

Paine gives more attention to the election of the members of the legislature than to the election of the members of the executive branch of government, because he assumed that the legislature in a democracy would be supreme. Nevertheless, he believed that both arms of the executive branch—the judiciary was not a separate branch of government[106]—should be kept responsible to the people through elections. Applying his beliefs to the American scene, he insisted that presidential electors should be selected by the people rather than by the legislature, as was true in some states.[107] Judges should also be made immediately responsible to the people. Terms for "good behavior" are open to objection because they have no legal or moral meaning.[108] In monarchies, judges should be independent of the king, but in democracies an irresponsible court cannot be tolerated. In a monarchy, the judges may protect the people against the tyranny of the king. In a democracy, an independent judiciary is a limitation upon the rights of the people to self-government. If presidents, governors, and legislators can be replaced by elections, why is it that judges can be removed only by "the tedious and ex-

pensive formality of impeachment?"[109] Perhaps, Paine suggested, because judges are lawyers, and lawyers always draw up the sections of constitutions dealing with the judiciary.[110]

V. Democracy and Deism

If the above analysis is correct, Paine's political ideas, at least in his later writings, satisfy all the requirements of the majority-rule democrat. There remains to discuss briefly the relationship of his belief in democracy and his belief in ultimate, immutable principles and absolute moral laws which may be objectively discovered—a notion which pervades all his writings.[111]

His "scientific" deism held that God revealed himself in nature, and that by observing nature man could find the laws which govern society, just as Newton found the laws which govern the world of physics.[112] A democratic or representative government is best fitted to follow the laws of nature because it "takes society and civilization for its basis; nature, reason, and experience for its guide."[113] Being in accord with laws of nature, the democratic society can discover other laws which govern the conduct of society.

Men are by nature both rational and good.[114] They know that to do good is to act in their own interest.[115] All that is necessary to put natural laws into practice is to have wise men inform the people of their findings about the nature of society, and the people will insist that right principles be followed.[116] "Reason, like time, will make its own way,"[117] and the errors committed at one time will be corrected by the people as soon as they recognize their mistakes.[118] The people may be trusted with power, because it is to their interest, i.e., to the interest of the majority, that right be done.[119] Superior members, who guide and inform the mass of men, spring from every section of society, but only a democratic state can take advantage of their wisdom, because only a democratic state allows all sections of the nation to take part in government.[120] Inferior members of the community may occasionally inform superior members, and therefore it would be unwise to bar them from participation.[121] When all members of society take part in its governance, all views are expressed, thus adding to the general enlightenment necessary for the passage of good acts.[122] It appears, then, that it is right that decisions should be made by the people, as expressed by the majority, because in the long run the majority will decide rightly.[123]

When the few are allowed to rule—and Paine assumed that minority-rule would be hereditary—the likelihood of government according to natural law is diminished. The interest of the few is not necessarily the interest of the entire society, and hence is not in accord with God's principles.[124] Succeeding generations of minorities become less and less qualified to rule because wisdom is not hereditary; in-breeding among the minority weakens the off-spring; and because the children are reared in an atmosphere conductive to oppression, not justice.[125]

The principles of a democratic society, stated above, have been discovered through the "science of government," although that science is still in its infancy.[126] Students of government have also found that forms of government must correspond to its principles to produce harmony and "a rational order of things."[127] Future generations will discover new laws and modify or change present forms of government to harmonize with God's revealed principles. Because of the magnificent advances during the last quarter of the eighteenth century toward an understanding of the natural laws and principles which govern society, "the present age will hereafter merit to be called the Age of Reason. . . ."[128]

Notes

[1] Vernon L. Parrington, *Main Currents in American Thought,* Vol. I, p. 334.

[2] C. E. Merriam, "Thomas Paine's Political Theories," *Political Science Quarterly,* Vol. XIV, p. 402 (Sept., 1899). See also Max Lerner, *It is Later Than You Think,* p. 109. Lerner calls Paine a "demagogue," that is, one of those Americans who were "good artists in majority politics."

[3] Some of the undemocratic features of Paine's earlier writings will be referred to briefly to indicate the historical development of his thinking.

[4] For a full discussion of the belief of a majority-rule democrat, see the excellent discussion in Willmoore Kendall, *John Locke and the Doctrine of Majority-Rule,* esp. pp. 24-38.

[5] *The Rights of Man, Writings of Thomas Paine* (M. D. Conway, ed.), Vol. II, p. 388.

[6] *Ibid.,* pp. 406-407. See also *Common Sense,* Vol. I, p. 70. Here Paine spoke of the possibility of men attempting to live as individuals, but soon joining each other when they realized that they could live better by a division of labor.

[7] *Ibid.,* p. 311. Italics are Paine's. He also referred to the United States as being in a state of nature between 1775 and the time of the adoption of the Articles of Confederation. See Vol. II, p. 407.

[8] *Ibid.,* pp. 309, 310. Italics are Paine's.

[9] *Ibid.,* p. 308.

[10] *Ibid.,* p. 309.

[11] *Ibid.,* p. 308. See also *ibid.,* pp. 277-281, 310.

[12] *Ibid.,* p. 385. Italics are mine. See also "Address to the Addressers," Vol. II, p. 68. The term "nation" as used by Paine always refers to all the citizens of a particular country.

[13] *Ibid.,* pp. 309-310. This does not mean that Paine believed in judicial review. See section on Popular Consultation.

[14] *Ibid.,* p. 436.

[15] *Ibid.,* p. 361. Italics are mine. See also p. 238, where Paine argues that an elective body no longer responsible to the people is as despotic as any king who usurped power originally. The phrase "as universal as taxation" is to be found frequently in Paine's writings. Paine himself did not believe that voting should be based upon the payment of taxes (see section on Political Equality), but was quite willing to use the term for persuasive purposes. He usually went ahead to explain that everyone pays taxes in some form, and therefore acceptance of the phrase necessitates acceptance of the notion of political equality.

[16] *Thomas Paine's Answer to Four Questions on the Legislative and Executive Powers*, Vol. II, pp. 238-239.

[17] *Rights of Man,* Vol. II, pp. 276-277, 365-366.

[18] *Ibid.,* p. 366.

[19] *Ibid.,* p. 411. Italics are Paine's. For similar definitions, see also pp. 443, 446. In the latter passages, Paine did not include the last phrase, "acting on the principles of society." It will be noted that his definition makes no distinction between the "state" and "government," or between the "state" and "society." The word "state" is never used by Paine except to describe the "thirteen American states." As we noticed earlier, a democratic state differs from society only because it is organized. In *Common Sense,* Vol. I, p. 69, Paine distinguished between the origin of society and of the state. The former arose because of the needs of man, the latter because of his wickedness. The duty of the state was to preserve law and order. Not until he identified representative government with organized society was Paine able to give the state the positive function of promoting the common good.

[20] *Ibid.,* p. 385.

[21] *Ibid.,* p. 397.

[22] *Ibid.,* pp. 421-422, 443. Republic, said Paine, came from the word *res-republica,* meaning public affairs. A republic, then, does not describe a form of govern-

ment, but the purpose of government. He added, however, that representative government is the only kind which actually deals with public affairs or the good of the nation.

[23] *Dissertation on Government; the Affairs of the Bank; and Paper Money*, Vol. II, p. 147. If the people or government break a contract, it is contrary to the terms of the original compact in which men "renounced as despotic, detestable and unjust, the right of breaking and violating their engagements, contracts and compacts with, or defrauding, imposing or tyrannizing over each other."

[24] *Ibid.*, p. 146.

[25] *Ibid.*, p. 148.

[26] *Ibid.*, pp. 164-166.

[27] *The Rights of Man*, Vol. II, pp. 465-466.

[28] "Constitutions, Governments, and Charters," Vol. IV, p. 468.

[29] *Ibid.*, pp. 468, 469.

[30] In the essay, Paine argued that certain acts, i.e., the contracts mentioned, differ from ordinary laws which may be repealed at any time. He argued that these special acts required permanency without being clear what he meant by "permanency." However, he spoke of the value of elections in insuring just contracts because "it is always to the interest of a much greater number of people in a country, to have a thing right than to have it wrong, [and therefore] the public sentiment is always worth attending to. It may sometimes err, but never intentionally, and *never long*." The last sentence indicates that the people will be allowed to correct their "errors," even at the expense of permanency. He also argued that the people of New York had "vetoed" the specific contract in question when they defeated the legislators who enacted the measure.

[31] Joseph Dorfman, "The Economic Philosophy of Thomas Paine," *Political Science Quarterly*, Vol. 53, pp. 372-386 (Sept., 1938).

On the other hand, see V. L. Parrington, *op. cit.*, Vol. I, p. 139, where it is suggested that Paine may well have believed in a socialized order, but that his desire to secure a measure of relief from intolerable conditions prevented him from bluntly stating his full position. Also see C. E. Merriam, *op. cit.*, esp. pp. 397, 400, where he remarks that Paine argues that the state should not interfere much in the affairs of business, but that he also suggests a number of instances when government ought to regulate economic conditions even more stringently than they were then regulated.

[32] *The Rights of Man, op. cit.*, Vol. II, p. 306. Paine sometimes spoke of these as "personal rights" or "rights of the mind."

[33] *Ibid.*, pp. 307, 325-326, 328. Religious freedom, he said was essential to all other rights.

[34] *Ibid.*, pp. 397, 330. Also see "Address to the Addressers," Vol. III, p. 68.

[35] *Ibid.*, pp. 328, 361. Also see *Dissertation on First Principles of Government*, Vol. III, p. 265, and *Agrarian Justice*, Vol. III, p. 325.

[36] *Ibid.*, pp. 354-355.

[37] *Dissertation on First Principles of Government*, Vol. III, p. 267.

[38] *Rights of Man*, Vol. II, p. 355.

[39] Quoted in *Rights of Man*, Vol. II, p. 351.

[40] *The Rights of Man*, Vol. II, p. 380.

[41] *Ibid.*, pp. 484-500.

[42] *Agrarian Justice*, Vol. III, pp. 330-332.

[43] *Ibid.*, p. 340.

[44] *Ibid.*, p. 341.

[45] *Ibid.*

[46] *Ibid.*, pp. 337-338.

[47] Dorfman, *op. cit.*, p. 380.

[48] *Ibid.*, p. 386.

[49] See Dixon Wecter, "Hero in Reverse," *Virginia Quarterly Review*, Vol. XVIII, 243-259 (Spring, 1942). Wecter tells of the hatred for Paine among the conservatives in his day because of his economic beliefs. If he and Hamilton agreed on economic ideas, Hamilton and his supporters were curiously unaware of the similarity. See esp. pp. 244, 245, 248.

[50] Parrington, *op. cit.*, Vol. I, p. 338.

[51] *Ibid.*, p. 333. We need not follow Parrington's speculation that Paine would have carried his arguments to a more radical conclusion, had he not confined his writing to immediately attainable objectives. See p. 339.

[52] *Dissertation on First Principles of Government*, Vol. III, p. 269. Italics are mine.

[53] *Ibid.,* p. 267.

[54] In *Common Sense,* Vol. I, p. 97, Paine suggests that Congress might pass acts by a vote of three-fifths of the members "in order that nothing might pass into a law which is not satisfactorily just." In no other pamphlet does Paine suggest rule by any number other than a simple majority.

[55] *Rights of Man,* II, p. 434.

[56] *Ibid.,* p. 509. See also "Constitutional Reform," Vol. IV, App. G., p. 465.

[57] *Ibid.,* p. 444. For a more detailed criticism of bicameralism, see "Thomas Paine's Answer to Four Questions on the Legislative and Executive Powers," Vol. II, pp. 241-244.

[58] *Dissertation on First Principles of Government,* Vol. III, pp. 273-274. Italics are Paine's.

[59] *Ibid.,* p. 277; "To Citizens of the United States" (no. 5), Vol. III, p. 405. For other comments on parties in Paine's later writings, see *Rights of Man,* Vol. II, pp. 278, 468; "The Eighteenth Fructidor," Vol. III, p. 347.

[60] See "Letter to Samuel Adams, January 1, 1803," Vol. IV, p. 207.

[61] *Dissertation on First Principles of Government,* Vol. II, p. 266. Italics are mine. See also *The Rights of Man,* Vol. II, pp. 428, 509.

[62] "Letter to the Citizens of the United States" (no. 3), Vol. III, p. 392. In this article, Paine did express some doubt of the ability of majorities to control minorities when he spoke of "the doubtful contest of civil war."

[63] See *The Rights of Man,* Vol. II, p. 514, n.

[64] *Dissertation on First Principles of Government,* Vol. III, pp. 271-272.

[65] *The Rights of Man,* Vol. II, pp. 367, 416-417. See also "Dissertation on Government; etc.," Vol. II, p. 135.

[66] "Letter Addressed to the Addressers, etc.," Vol. III, pp. 91-92. Italics are Paine's.

[67] *The Rights of Man,* Vol. II, p. 303.

[68] *Ibid.,* pp. 304-305. Italics are Paine's. He cites the Mosaic account of the creation which says that God made man in his own image, distinguishing between the sexes, "but no other distinction is implied."

[69] *Ibid.,* p. 385.

[70] *Ibid.,* p. 309. Italics are Paine's.

[71] *Ibid.,* p. 386.

[72] "Letter Addressed to the Addressers, etc.," Vol. III, pp. 91-92. See also, "Constitutional Reform," Vol. IV, App. G., p. 465.

[73] *Dissertation on First Principles of Government,* Vol. III, p. 273.

[74] *The Rights of Man,* Vol. II, p. 278.

[75] *Agrarian Justice,* Vol. III, p. 325.

[76] "Letter Addressed to the Addressers, etc.," Vol. III, p. 88.

[77] *Agrarian Justice,* Vol. III, p. 325.

[78] *Dissertation on First Principles of Government,* Vol. III, pp. 265, 267.

[79] *Ibid.,* p. 266.

[80] *Ibid.,* p. 267. Paine suggested that it might well be that a man's right to vote would depend upon such a thing as the birth of a mule. In that case, he wonders who should have the vote—the mule or the man. See Dorfman, *op. cit.,* p. 379, for a curious statement of Paine's belief in the equality of suffrage. Dorfman ignored most of the arguments stated by Paine in an effort to prove that the sole purpose for removing property qualifications for voting was the protection of property rights. Dorfman's argument is based entirely upon carefully selected sections of *The Rights of Man* and "Letter Addressed to the Addressers," ignoring completely the two pamphlets which were most explicit on the question of suffrage. (*Agrarian Justice* and *Dissertation on First Principles of Government.*)

[81] "Letter Addressed to the Addressers, etc.," Vol. III, p. 88. See also "Constitutional Reform," Vol. IV, App. G., p. 462.

[82] *Ibid.,* pp. 75, 88.

[83] *Agrarian Justice,* Vol. III, p. 326.

[84] "On the Constitution of 1795," Vol. III, pp. 283-284.

[85] "Address to the Addressers," Vol. III, p. 88

[86] *The Rights of Man,* Vol. II, p. 468.

[87] *Ibid.,* p. 399.

[88] *Dissertation on First Principles of Government,* Vol. III, p. 269.

[89] *Ibid.,* p. 268. See *The Rights of Man,* Vol. II, p. 296, where Paine suggests that the mob is the safest asylum possible, and that even a miser would cease to think only of money if he were to mix with a mob. He uses "the mob" both to threaten those of property and to idealize "the common man."

[90] *Ibid.,* pp. 267-268.

[91] "Constitutional Reform," Vol. IV, App. G., p. 460. Paine agreed with Franklin that "where annual elections end, tyranny begins."

[92] *The Rights of Man,* Vol. II, pp. 452, 517. See also "Constitutional Reform," Vol. IV, App. G., p. 457, and "Letter to the Citizens of the United States" (No. 3), Vol. III, p. 392.

[93] *Ibid.,* p. 438. Also see p. 311.

[94] *Ibid.,* p. 311.

[95] *Ibid.,* p. 452.

[96] *Ibid.,* p. 431.

[97] *Thomas Paine's Answer to Four Questions on Legislative and Executive Powers,* Vol. II, p. 250.

[98] "Letter Addressed to the Addressers, etc.," Vol. III, p. 87. See also p. 81, and "Constitutional Reform," Vol. IV, App. G., p. 457.

[99] "Constitutional Reform," Vol. IV, App. G., p. 457.

[100] *The Rights of Man,* Vol. II, pp. 397-398. See also "Letter Addressed to the Addressers, etc.," Vol. III, p. 86.

[101] *Common Sense,* Vol. I, p. 71.

[102] "Constitutional Reform," Vol. IV, App. G, p. 460.

[103] *The Rights of Man,* Vol. II, p. 323. See also "Anti-Monarchical Essay for Use of New Republicans," Vol. III, p. 108, for a curious passage illustrating the lengths to which Paine would go to assure legislative responsibility. "With representatives, frequently renewed, who neither administer nor judge, whose functions are determined by laws; with national conventions, with primary assemblies, which can be convoked at any moment; with a people knowing how to read, and how to defend itself; with good journals, guns, and pikes; a Legislature would have a good deal of trouble in enjoying many months of tyranny."

[104] "Letter to Citizens of the United States" (no. 4), Vol. III, pp. 414-417. This essay was written against the Sedition Act of 1798.

[105] *The Rights of Man,* Vol. II, pp. 427-428.

[106] *Dissertation on First Principles of Government,* Vol. III, p. 275. See also "Thomas Paine's Answer to Four Questions, etc., Vol. II, pp. 238-239.

[107] "Constitutional Reform," Vol. IV, App. G., p. 461.

[108] *Ibid.,* p. 464.

[109] *Ibid.*

[110] *Ibid.*

[111] See, for example, *Dissertation on Government, etc.,* Vol. II, p. 132. "There are such things as right and wrong in the world." And *Dissertation on First Principles of Government,* Vol. III, p. 260. ". . . time has no more connection with, or influence upon principle, than principle has upon time."

[112] See, for example, *The Age of Reason,* Vol. IV, p. 45, "*The word of God is the creation we behold:* And it is in *this word* that God speaketh universally to man." (Italics are Paine's.) See also p. 191: "The principles we discover are eternal and of divine origin. . . ." For a brief analysis of the relationship of Paine's religious beliefs to his political, economic, and social thinking, see the excellent article by H. H. Clark, "Toward a Re-interpretation of Thomas Paine," *American Literature,* Vol. V, pp. 133-145.

[113] *The Rights of Man,* Vol. II, pp. 418, 423.

[114] *Ibid.,* pp. 403, 508. See also "The Reasons for Preserving the Life of Louis Capet," Vol. III, p. 122; "Thomas Paine's Answer to Four Questions, etc.," Vol. II, p. 248.

[115] *Ibid.,* p. 435. *Thomas Paine's Answer to Four Questions, etc.,* Vol. II, p. 246; "Letter to the Citizens of the United States" (no. 4), Vol. III, p. 405; "Constitutions, Governments, and Charters," Vol. IV, App. H., pp. 468.

[116] "Letter Addressed to the Addressers, etc.," Vol. III, pp. 45-46. "Address and Declaration of the Thatched House Tavern," Vol. II, p. 256; *The Rights of Man,* Vol. II, p. 296.

[117] *The Rights of Man,* Vol. II, p. 403.

[118] *Ibid.,* p. 509.

[119] *Ibid.,* p. 435.

[120] *Ibid.,* pp. 418-420.

[121] *Thomas Paine's Answer to Four Questions, etc.,* Vol. II, p. 242.

[122] *The Rights of Man,* Vol. II, p. 386. See also "Anti-Monarchical Essay for the Use of New Republicans," Vol. III, p. 103.

[123] *Ibid.,* p. 384. "Constitutions, Governments, and Charters," Vol. IV, App. H., p. 457; see also "Letter to Citizens of the United States" (no. 4), Vol. III, p. 400, "The Right will always become the popular." Compare this position with Max Lerner, *op. cit.* p. 107, " . . . the majority in a state represents a good bet in the long pull of history." See Kendall, *op. cit.,* Ch. X, where the question is raised as to whether the belief in the "rightness" of majorities underlies all modern theories of majority rule.

[124] *Ibid.,* p. 321.

[125] *Ibid.,* pp. 322-323.

[126] *Thomas Paine's Answer to Four Questions, etc.,* Vol. II, p. 245; "Memorial Addressed to James Monroe," Vol. III, p. 176.

[127] *The Rights of Man,* Vol. II, p. 332.

[128] *Ibid.,* p. 512.

John Adams, second president of the United States, in a letter to Benjamin Waterhouse (1805):

I am willing you should call this the Age of Frivolity as you do, and would not object if you had named it the Age of Folly, Vice, Frenzy, Brutality, Daemons, Buonaparte, Tom Paine, or the Age of the Burning Brand from the Bottomless Pit, or anything but the Age of Reason. I know not whether any man in the world has had more influence on its inhabitants or affairs for the last thirty years than Tom Paine. There can be no severer satyr on the age. For such a mongrel between pig and puppy, begotten by a wild boar on a bitch wolf, never before in any age of the world was suffered by the poltroonery of mankind, to run through such a career of mischief. Call it then the Age of Paine.

John Adams, in Statesman and Friend, *1927, reprinted in* Paine, *by David Freeman Hawke, Harper and Row, 1974.*

Harry Hayden Clark (essay date 1944)

SOURCE: "Thomas Paine," in *Thomas Paine: Representative Selections, with Introduction, Bibliography, and Notes,* American Book Company, 1944, pp. xi-cxviii.

[*In the following chapter from his book, Clark examines the various religious influences on Paine's thought.*

Focusing on the significance of Paine's Quaker heritage, Clark examines it in conjunction with the rationalist, Newtonian concept of nature.]

I. Religious and Ethical Ideas

Broadly speaking, Paine's importance rests on the fact that he was an idealist, a man who envisaged a happier way of life for all men in the future, who thought in the light of first principles such as the equality and sacredness of all souls before God, and who, since he believed that in the past the life of the common people had been miserable, demanded a sharp break with the past, with tradition. During Paine's first years in America, as we shall see, while he was feeling his way along as an apprentice at propaganda, his ideas were not entirely consistent with one another and not without considerable elements of conservativism, as in **Common Sense**. After he went to France, however, and joined the cause of the ideologues, such as Condorcet, who motivated the French Revolution, he spoke consistently as an antitraditionalist who thought society could be reconstructed in the light of principles and ideals, "abstracted from time and usage."

Granting, then, his American apprenticeship, it seems best to begin our consideration of him in the light of his basic, governing religious and ethical ideas. John Adams, as we shall see, testified that Paine had doubts of religious traditionalism in 1776, and Paine himself said in 1791 that "for several years past"[1] he had intended to publish the ideas he advanced in **The Age of Reason**. Therefore it may not actually be such a violation of chronology as it might appear to consider his religious ideals first, especially since they involve at the outset the Quakerism which was his birthright.

1. The Influence of Quakerism

The development of Paine's religious and ethical ideas can be understood best, perhaps, in relation to four main religious influences: Quakerism, Newtonianism, classicism, and the exotic concepts of the Druids and ancient Persia and Egypt. The earliest and most difficult to analyze in its effect upon him was Quakerism. His best biographer, Moncure Conway, insisted that he was "explicable only by the intensity of his Quakerism . . ."[2] And there can be no serious question that many early and lasting ideas and attitudes were given him by it. Though never a member of any meeting, Paine could have been a "birthright Friend," for, as he wrote, "My father being of the Quaker profession, it was my good fortune to have an exceedingly good moral education, and a tolerable stock of useful learning."[3] One can easily see the influence of his father's religion in the experience which, intense enough at the time to be remembered decades later, must have bent or helped bend Paine's subconscious mind permanently. "I well remember," he says, "when about seven or eight years of age, hearing a sermon read by a relation of mine, who was a great devotee of the church, upon the subject of what is called *Redemption by the death of the Son of God*. After the sermon was ended, I went into the garden, and as I was going down the garden steps (for I perfectly recollect the spot) I revolted at the recollection of what I had heard, and thought to myself that it was making God Almighty act like a passionate man, that killed his son, when he could not revenge himself any other way; and as I was sure a man would be hanged that did such a thing, I could not see for what purpose they preached such sermons. This was not one of those kind of thoughts that had any thing in it of childish levity; it was to me a serious reflection, arising from the idea I had that God was too good to do such an action, and also too almighty to be under any necessity of doing it. I believe in the same manner to this moment; and I moreover believe, that any system of religion that has any thing in it that shocks the mind of a child, cannot be a true system."[4]

Throughout his religious writings he professed deep admiration for the "moral and benign part"[5] of the Quakers' thought: "I reverence their philanthropy,"[6] he proclaimed. The charity which led them to be pioneers in the abolition of slavery, prison reform, and a dozen other humanitarian enterprises found, of course, its ready response from Paine whose whole life was devoted to reforms for the good of mankind. He cited the Quakers as the sole exception to the general cruelty of Christian sects, and regarded them as "the only sect that has not persecuted . . ."[7] Indeed, it was on the grounds of the reconstruction of society according to principles of good-will and mutual profit that Paine and the Quakers found themselves in complete agreement, and there, in an absolute sense, alone. He had reinforced childhood notions of their doctrines by reading the theologian Barclay[8]; but, after all, the mystical apprehension of truth through the Inner Light and Paine's insistence that a dry and rigid rationalism alone could be depended on were mutually exclusive. He often claimed that the Quakers were deists if they but knew it. It is noteworthy, however, that he never brought them to reciprocate.

Attention must be paid statements like the following from Mr. Conway: "Paine's political principles were evolved out of his early Quakerism. He was potential in George Fox. The belief that every human soul was the child of God, and capable of direct inspiration from the Father of all, without mediator or priestly intervention, or sacramental instrumentality, was fatal to all privilege and rank. The universal Fatherhood implied universal Brotherhood, or human equality."[10] And Conway adds that it was to protect this ideal from "oppression by the majority" that Paine developed his theory of inviolable private rights. Certainly Paine's readiness to flout temporal authorities and

outworn traditions in the cause of what he felt to be the right was in the Quaker tradition. His ability to live frugally and sacrifice financially for his causes, and his not too consistent passion for simplicity, probably stemmed from Quakerism.

Of this much we can be sure. Paine did have a Quaker background. He himself affirmed that his belief in a benevolent deity whose most important attribute was loving Fatherhood came to him from it. His passionate humanitarianism; sense of brotherhood with all men, and its corollary, the sense of the equality of all men's rights; readiness to think and move independently; and his willingness to go "all out" for his beliefs could have come from Quakerism. There is every reason to believe, therefore, that he operated throughout life with Quaker attitudes and ideas in the back of his mind. Perhaps it is important to remember that usually they were in the back of his mind and did not emerge in anything like pure form.

It is hardly accurate, then, to say that Paine is "explicable only" in the light of Quakerism despite his reverence for their doctrines in general. His home was not intensely Quakeristic, since his father had "married out of meeting" and been expelled from the Society.[11] He was never actively affiliated with the Quakers, and he said in 1776, "I profess myself a member" of "the English church."[12] He attacked the Quakers' pacifism,[13] and he was so far from being considered "in his time the greatest exponent"[14] of Quakerism that they, ordinarily the most charitable of sects, refused his dying plea to be buried with their brethren. Certainly Paine's general theology and that of his contemporary, the Quaker saint John Woolman, were in many ways mutually repellent. And on the personal side the mystical Woolman and rationalistic Paine had as little in common intellectually as they did in outward action. Woolman strove for humility, gentle persuasiveness, and freedom from bondage to the flesh. Paine, though capable of generosity and high friendship, was at times outrageously egotistical, bellicose, and subject in his later life to coarseness. Finally, the typically Quaker Woolman, though interested in reforms such as the abolition of slavery, believed the essential achievement of man to be self-conquest, and inner victory over self-indulgence and sin; Paine, the deistic humanitarian, saw man's warfare to be with principalities and institutionalized powers alone in which outward service overcame outward obstacles and would usher in Utopia.[15]

2. *The Influence of Newtonianism*

One must look elsewhere for much of the motivation underlying the four major religious premises made by Paine: (*a*) that nature, in the eye of rationalistic science, is a divine revelation; (*b*) that such science reveals "a harmonious, magnificent order"[16]—that nature is law; (c) that the natural man shares the divine benevolence and that in this harmonious order his "wants, acting upon every individual, impel the whole of them into society, as naturally as gravitation acts to a center"[17]; (d) and that an attempt to re-establish in politics and religion a lost harmony with this uniform, immutable, universal, and eternal law and order, and to modify or overthrow whatever traditional institutions have obscured this order and thrown its natural harmony into discord will constitute progress, will rapidly decrease human misery, and will rapidly usher in "the birthday of a new world." Perhaps his inherited Quaker independence made it easier for him to break with the historical majesty of tradition which inhered in the Christianity of his time and place. But it seems likely that Paine derived these four major premises mainly from popularizations of Newtonian science and deism and from the climate of opinion which rationalism had helped to develop for over a century, and which is roughly denominated "The Enlightenment."[18]

Paine, with his natural bent toward science[19] and ardent self-education,[20] may have read Newton's *Principia* (1687, widely translated after 1729); if he did not read Newton himself, he could hardly have escaped learning the main outlines of his thought from the current popular diffusion of Newtonianism, which was almost literally "in the air."[21] For a man of Paine's delight in social discussion and debate, interested in science, Newtonianism and deism were accessible in scores of places, and especially in the social circles he frequented which gathered around Franklin in America, Godwin in England, and Condorcet in France. Some of the semipopular sources of his first information are known, however. In speaking of the period (1757-1759) when at the age of twenty he lived in London as a staymaker in the employ of Mr. Morris, Paine says, "As soon as I was able, I purchased a pair of globes, and attended the philosophical lectures of Martin and Ferguson, and became . . . acquainted with Dr. Bevis, of the society called the Royal Society, then living in the Temple, and an excellent astronomer."[22]

Let us now return to an exposition of what have been called Paine's four premises. The author of *The Age of Reason* "honors Reason as the choicest gift of God to man, and the faculty by which he is enabled to contemplate the power, wisdom, and goodness of the Creator displayed in the creation."[23] If he appears to be attacking the Christian religion in the light of reason, it should be borne in mind that this reason was itself associated with religion and the supernatural. Since only "the creation is the Bible of the deist,"[24] "the principles we discover there are eternal and of divine origin,"[25] "for the Creator of man is the creator of science, and it is through that medium that man can see God, as it were, face to face."[26] "That which is now called natural philosophy, embracing the whole circle of science, of which astronomy occupies the chief place, is the study of the works of God, and of the power and Wisdom of God in his works, and is the true theology."[27] To Paine "the Creator of the Universe" is "the Fountain of all Wisdom, the Origin of all Science, the Author of all Knowledge, the God of Order and of Harmony."[28] "When we see a watch, we have as positive proof of the existence of a watchmaker, as if we saw him; and in like manner the creation is evidence to our reason and our senses of the existence of a creator."[29]

At once an empiricist and a supernaturalist, Paine held that "It is comfortable to live under the belief of the existence of an infinite protecting power; and it is an addition to that comfort to know that such a belief is not a mere conceit of the imagination . . . ; nor a belief founded only on tradition or received opinion; but a belief deducible by the action of reason upon the things that compose the system of the universe; a belief rising out of visible facts: and so demonstrable . . . that matter and the properties it has will not account for the system of the universe, and that there must necessarily be a superior cause."[30] Like the Newtonians, Paine never ceased to "hope for happiness beyond this life"[31]; "the belief of a future state is a *rational belief,* founded on facts visible in the creation: for it is not more difficult to believe that we shall exist hereafter in a better state and form than at present, than that a worm should become a butterfly. . . ."[32]

In conscious revolt against the indoor, book-religion of the "gloomy Calvinists" and "the absurd and impious doctrine of predestination"[33] taught by "these fanatical hypocrites,"[34] his mind finds "a happiness in Deism, when rightly understood, that is not be found in any other system of religion."[35] "Do we not see a fair creation prepared to receive us the instant we are born—a world furnished to our hands, that cost us nothing? . . . Whether we sleep or wake, the vast machinery of the universe still goes on."[36] "Do we want to contemplate [God's] munificence? We see it in the abundance with which he fills the earth. Do we want to contemplate his mercy? We see it in his not withholding that abundance even from the unthankful."[37] "The moral duty of man consists in imitating the moral goodness and beneficence of God manifested in the creation toward all his creatures."[38]

It should be borne in mind that Paine's revolt against the Christian tradition, itself dualistic, was motivated by the perception that the historic relativism of a book-tradition was the prey of time and change; "the continually progressive change to which the meaning of words is subject, the want of an universal language which renders translation necessary, the errors to which translations are again subject, the mistakes of copyists and printers, together with the possibility of wilful alteration, are themselves evidences that human language, whether in speech or in print, cannot be the vehicle of the Word of God," the eternity and universality of which demand "the idea, not only of unchangeableness, but of the utter impossibility of any change."[39] Hence, under the tutelage of the Newtonians, he turned from books to nature, a testimony to all times and nationalities, which, approached reverently with "the divine gift of reason" and the method of science, reveals to him an immaterial Creator whose eternal and universal benevolence are manifest in "invariable principles and unchangeable order."[40]

Now it is of sovereign importance, if we would adequately interpret and judge Paine, that we should interpret his appeal not only to reason but to nature in the light of the contemporary meaning these two focal concepts had in the minds of the teachers who molded his mind in its plastic age. For the Newtonians and Paine mean, when they appeal to nature, vastly more than the original chaos of the pathless wilderness or a supine surrender to the capricious dictates of a savage appetite. *Usually, nature meant to them harmony, law, and order;* and hence an appeal to nature can scarcely be interpreted as an appeal to anarchy. Paine is careful to define what he means by nature: "Man could not invent and make a universe—he could not invent nature, for *nature is of divine origin. It is the laws by which the universe is governed.* When, therefore, we look through nature up to nature's God, we are in the right road of happiness . . ."[41] "As to that which is called *nature, it is no other than the laws* by which motion and action of every kind, with respect to unintelligible matter, is regulated."[42] "When we survey the works of Creation, the revolutions of the planetary system, and the whole economy of what is called *nature, which is no other than the laws* the Creator has prescribed to matter, we see unerring order and universal harmony reigning throughout the whole. . . . Here is *the standard to which everything must be* brought that pretends to be the work . . . of God."[43] Having interpreted Paine's mind in the light of contemporary philosophic definitions and their relative emphasis given by men whom Paine acknowledged as his teachers, we have now arrived at the very core of his thought, "the standard to which everything must be brought," which is a divinely revealed and sanctioned law and order, in harmonious conformity to which society finds its happiness. Thus Newtonian deism, as interpreted by Paine, involved discipline and order just as did Calvinistic Federalism in America, or Anglican Toryism, in England, although the difference in background and terminology has prevented many critics from recognizing it, at least in the case of Paine. Although Paine wrote *The Rights of Man* as a refutation of Burke's *Reflections on the French Revolution,* the ultimate and underlying assumptions of the former are no more an intentional defense of anarchy than those of the latter. For Paine's "standard" was a divinely ordained "harmonious magnificent order."[44]

Since Newtonianism had supplied mathematical proof of a universal, all-embracing, divinely-ordered harmony, a universe throbbing with the rhythm of benevolence, and since the Creator and the creation cannot therefore be at strife, it follows that man, the crown of creation, shares this divine harmony manifesting the "infinite goodness" of the Creator. Newtonianism, by positing a cosmic harmony, furnished, in place of Puritan convictions of man's total depravity, what seemed a mathematical foundation for a faith in the light of nature and in the pregnant theory of natural goodness. Thus Paine wrote, "man, where he is not corrupted by governments, is naturally the friend of man, . . . human nature is not of itself vicious."[45] "The great mass of people are always just,"[46] and "the safest asylum, especially in times of general convulsion when no settled form of government prevails, is *the love of the people.*"[47] Hence Paine argued that the representative government must supplant monarchy, for if "the representative system is always parallel with the order and immutable laws of nature and meets the reason of man in every part,"[48] such being "the order of nature, the order of government must . . . follow it."[49] He held that "the sovereign authority in any country is in the power of making laws," that "the government of a free country, properly speaking, is not in the persons, but in the laws,"[50] and that executives "are no other than authorities to superintend the execution of the laws,"[51] which are ultimately to be safe-guarded by a constitution sanctioning not only the control of lawless individuals but also of aggressive parties.[52] The popular notion that Paine's naturalism led him to plead for lawlessness would therefore appear to be based upon ludicrous misunderstandings. For the nature he wished to follow was the law and order of the harmonious Newtonian universe which promised a harmony among men whereby they could establish a parallel civil law and order.

This brings us to the last of what I have tried to define as Paine's major premises. Paine's contemporaries noted that in *Common Sense* (1776), *The Crisis,* and other early work, including *The Rights of Man* (1791-1792), if he had occasion to speak of the Christian religion, he did so in decent, if not respectful language; and the intolerant view that "the only religion that has not been invented . . . is pure and simple Deism,"[53] coupled with his astonishing violence in denouncing the Bible and Christianity, appears only in *The Age of Reason* (1793-1795).

It seems probable that he honestly, if illogically, tried for a time to reverence both astronomy and a broad, rational Christianity,[54] especially since in England and America, on account of the elasticity of Protestantism, most deists regarded themselves as still Christians. His liberally religious friends such as Franklin, Jefferson, Barlow, Martin, and Ferguson, and deistic predecessors such as Bolingbroke, Middleton, Pope, and others, maintained a loosely tolerant relationship with the church, setting a precedent the breaking of which required considerable provocation, even in the case of a man such as Paine.

It appears, then, that his *private* religious views became increasingly radical from his twentieth year, and increasingly conditioned other phases of his thought, although he gave *public* expression to his radicalism only as a result, perhaps, of such factors as (*a*) the danger in France of losing "sight of morality, of humanity, and of the theology that is true" following "the total abolition" of the priesthood[55]; (*b*) Burke's constant argument that a secular hierarchy is ultimately grounded upon an ecclesiastical and spiritual hierarchy, his defense therefore of the union of church and state, and his agency in defeating the repeal of the Corporation and Test Acts by charging that the Dissenters championed the French Revolution[56]; (*c*) an economic crisis in England and in the France of 1789 described by Arthur Young, during which the melioration of social suffering was discouraged, as Paine thought, by the royalists' argument that poverty was the divine will[57]; and (*d*) by contact with brilliant minds such as those of Voltaire,[58] Raynal, Boulanger, and Condorcet, whose social plans demanded the destruction of faith in the Church as the last refuge of obscurantism, persecution, and the divine right of kings. For it was such minds as these in conjunction with the current historical situation which helped to turn Paine's earlier and genially tolerant Newtonianism into channels destructive.

Science, as we have seen, aided by "the divine gift of reason," revealed to Paine a harmonious and universal order, progressive conformity to which constitutes progress. Such was the faith, in conjunction with the concrete example of America,[59] which enabled him to march in the vanguard of that dauntless band who dedicated themselves to the fair dream of perfectibility.[60] If "the world has walked in darkness for eighteen hundred years, both as to religion and government,"[61] if men are naturally creatures of society, since their benevolent interests "impel the whole of them into society, as naturally as gravitation acts to a center,"[62] if "a great portion of mankind, in what are called civilized countries, are in a state of poverty and wretchedness far below the condition of an Indian, . . . the cause . . . lies not in any natural defect in the principles of civilization, but in preventing those principles having a universal operation."[63]

Even if a modern skeptic should regard religion as the vainest of theorizing about the unknowable, he cannot ignore religion in the case of Paine, for it was the fountainhead of his concrete work; and without understanding his religion one can scarcely understand and interpret correctly practical programs which, as Franklin said, had a "prodigious" effect in the actual,

physical world. For Paine was in his mental habits essentially after 1787 an ideologue, especially devoted to methods deductive and *a priori*. He tells us again and again that his concern is with "principles, and not persons," "the principles of universal society,"[64] and his opponent Burke's alarm derived from the fundamentalism of the "religious war" against "an armed doctrine."[65] Once the polar star of Newtonian deism had risen above Paine's mental horizon, he found his way, and henceforth he had but to walk toward the light. For Newtonian science, with its doctrine of the universality of law, had liberated him, as he thought, from the stifling bondage to historic relativism, from nationalism and a concern with local circumstances and temporal peculiarities, under which he thought Burke still labored.

This was the vantage ground from which Paine dauntlessly approached the temporal tribulations of a world where a progressive departure from the "harmonious, magnificent order" of nature and dependence upon the natural benevolence of the people, wherein lies social happiness, had been embalmed by blind "custom and usage."

3. The Influence of Classical Antiquity

We come now to the third main influence on Paine's religious thought—that of Classical Antiquity. In common with other deists, when pressed by Churchmen with the assertion that men could not lead serene and moral lives without the aid of Christian revelation, Paine naturally retorted with the example of the classical sages, who lived exalted lives before Christ. "Aristotle, Socrates, Plato . . . were truly great or noble." They arrived "at fame by merit and universal consent."[66] He hopes that "what Athens was in miniature (the wonder of the ancient world), America will be in magnitude."[67] However, probably being guided by "the immortal Montesquieu" who praised the ancient republics,[68] Paine says that "Aristides, Epaminondas, Pericles, Scipio, Camillus, and a thousand other Grecian and Roman heroes would never have astonished the world with their names, had they lived under royal governments."[69] They needed republicanism, but they did not need Christianity to be noble. In the second place, he regards Christianity as a debased "steal" from classicism—"the Christian Church, sprung out of the tail of heathen mythology." Following Conyers Middleton's *Letter from Rome* (Paine praised him as having courage, honesty, and "a strong original mind"),[70] he argued that "the trinity of gods . . . was no other than a reduction of the former plurality, which was about twenty or thirty thousand. The statue of Mary succeeded the statue of Diana of Ephesus. The deification of heroes changed into the canonization of saints," and so on. "The Christian theory is little else than the idolatry of the ancient mythologists, accommodated to the purposes of power and revenue."[71] And finally,

Paine used the classicism of ancients such as Cicero to reinforce his Newtonian concept of immutable and universal natural law, deriving his knowledge through Middleton who wrote a life of Cicero. "In Cicero," Paine says, "we see that vast superiority of mind, that sublimity of right reasoning and justness of ideas, which man acquires, not by studying bibles and testaments, and the theology of schools built thereon, but by studying the creator in the immensity and unchangeable order of his creation, and the immutability of his law. 'There cannot,' says Cicero, 'be one law now, and another hereafter; but the same eternal immutable law comprehends all nations, at all times, under one common master and governor of all—God.'" Because of the disparity of the "laws" in the Old and the New Testaments, Paine concludes that they are "impositions, fables, and forgeries," since contradictions cannot derive from a God whose wisdom is "unchangeable."[72]

4. The Influence of the Early Eastern Religions and Freemasonry

In addition to Quakerism, Newtonianism and classicism, a fourth general influence bearing on Paine's religious writings is that derived from a sketchy acquaintance with the religions of ancient Egypt, the Druids, and the Persians, especially as they related to Freemasonry. As expressed particularly in his **Origin of Masonry** and **Answer to the Bishop of Llandaff,** these ideas were gathered from second-hand and third-hand sources which intrigued Paine's speculative but unscholarly mind.[73] This rather crude study in comparative religions merely reinforced ideas Paine had adopted much earlier from many other sources. He envisioned a world-wide, pre-Christian natural religion or rough deism, essentially the same in Persians, Druids, and Egyptians, and far superior in truth and purity to the jumbled corruptions of their ideas borrowed by the ancient Hebrews to form the Bible. The origin of Masonry he saw in an underground effort of these original deists to preserve the truth from the persecutions of a dominant Christianity. The purpose of this tenuous learning, however, was to attack the system developed by the church fathers into modern Christianity as a mere literal-minded corruption of Eastern allegories and myths combined with a shrewd plan for exploiting the people. The result of an interest which came late in life and was never thoroughly developed, Paine's knowledge of these esoteric religions was employed as a controversial weapon and cannot be ranked with Quakerism or Newtonianism as a truly formative factor in his personal idealism.

It was easy for Paine as a Newtonian to sympathize with the ancient sun worshippers. He worshipped God in the eternal and immutable laws which bound the universe to harmony and order. If they, born in a less enlightened age, mistook for the Creator of Order its

central fact, the Sun, their error could be understood. The old religions Paine felt to be essentially one: "The religion of the Druids . . . was the same as the religion of the ancient Egyptians. The priests of Egypt were the professors and teachers of science, and were styled priests of Heliopolis, that is, the *City of the Sun*. The Druids in Europe . . . were the same order of men . . . The word Druid signifies a *wise man*. In Persia they were called Magi, which signifies the same thing."[74] This "ancient religion of the Gentiles," moreover, was a deism "which consisted in the adoration of a first cause of the works of the creation, in which the sun was the great visible agent. It appears to have been a religion of gratitude and adoration, and not of prayer and discontented solicitation." Druidism, he insists, "that wise, elegant, philosophical religion, was the faith opposite to the faith of the gloomy Christian church."[75] And the "scientific purity and religious morality" of its rites proved the members "a wise, learned, and moral class of men."[76]

To counteract the reverence felt for the ancient Hebrews as authors of the Bible, Paine made a particular point of comparing them unfavorably with his natural religionists; calling them unscientific and "most ignorant of all the illiterate world,"[77] and sure to corrupt "a religion founded upon astronomy."[78]

The essay on Masonry is a fragment of an intended continuation of **The Age of Reason.** Paine was undoubtedly trying to enlist the support of this very powerful social movement of his day[79] by showing that its doctrines and his had always been fundamentally the same. He made extensive and ingenious extracts from what sources[80] he could find on the ideas of Masonry to prove that "*Masonry* . . . is derived from the remains of the ancient Druids; who, like the Magi of Persia and the Priests of Heliopolis in Egypt, were Priests of the Sun. They paid worship to this great luminary, as the great visible agent of a great invisible first cause, whom they stiled 'Time without Limits.'"[81] The reason for Masonic secrecy, he maintained, was that Christianity, as soon as it became dominant, had begun systematic persecutions which made it necessary for Christians who "remained attached to their original religion to meet in secret, and under the strongest injunctions of secrecy. Their safety depended upon it . . . From the remains of the religion of the Druids, thus preserved, arose the institution which, to avoid the name of Druid, took that of Mason, and practiced under this new name the rites and ceremonies of Druids."[82] His immediate use of the theory was to say: "The Christian religion and Masonry have one and the same common origin: both are derived from the worship of the Sun. The difference between their origin is, that the Christian religion is a parody on the worship of the Sun, in which they put a man whom they call Christ, in the place of the Sun, and pay him the same adoration . . ."[83]

Thus, in popularizing the exotic researches of pioneer scholars like Sir William Jones and others, Paine was himself something of a pioneer popularizer of the historical study of comparative religions and of the idea (which is perhaps the essence of deism) of the wisdom of transcending narrow sectarianisms by reducing religion to those broad elemental principles which all nations and creeds have held in common. Such principles, having won the *consensus gentium* in all ages and lands, must represent, Paine thought, the pure gold of religious thought. As he wrote his old friend Samuel Adams, who, political liberal as he was, shrank back from Paine's religious liberalism, "the World has been overrun with fable and creeds of human invention, with sectaries of whole Nations against all other Nations, and sectaries of those sectaries in each of them against each other. Every sectary, except the Quakers, has been a persecutor. Those who fled from persecution persecuted in their turn, and it is this confusion of creeds that has filled the World with persecution and deluged it with blood. Even the depredation on your commerce by the barbary powers sprang from the Crusades of the church against those powers. It was a war of creed against creed, each boasting of God for its author, and reviling each other with the name of Infidel."[84] He felt it high time to return to the universal and loving principles he believed would derive from a religion in accordance with natural law such as he thought the ancient religions had been.

If Paine did in the heat of conflict appear to attack Christianity as a whole, we should remember that at that time in France he identified it with Catholicism (which was used as a sinister political weapon of oppression and torture). In the light of the new science and the Higher Criticism, he thought he was obliged to attack the Church's obscurantist hostility to the free play of thought. He was also driven to his position by the way in which so-called Christians like Bishop Watson were distorting Christianity to preach resignation to remediable evils and to discourage charity to the poor and oppressed. The exalted and charitable morality he preached, inculcating man's imitation of God's benevolence, was surely based on Christianity, as his best-intentioned opponents agreed. And at the risk of endangering the logic of his position, he is always reverent toward the Founder of Christianity. "The morality that he preached and practiced was of the most benevolent kind," and "it has not been exceeded by any."[85] He is steadfast in his praise of Quakerism, which surely embodies many of the doctrines most respected by modern Christians. And in the light of Unitarianism and modern liberal theology, it appears that Paine was far more of a Christian than he himself believed. In so far as modern Christianity has agreed with St. Paul that the greatest of the triune Christian virtues is charity, has agreed with Christ himself in his saying that inasmuch as you have done it unto the least of one of these you have done it unto me, it would have found support from Paine as a pioneer in what he called "the religion of humanity.". . .

Notes

[1] *The Writings of Thomas Paine,* edited by Moncure D. Conway, IV, 21, preface to *The Age of Reason.* (This is the standard edition of Paine. 4 vols. New York, 1894-1896. Hereafter referred to as *Writings.*)

[2] M. D. Conway, *Life of Paine* (New York, 1892), II, 201.

[3] *Writings,* IV, 62.

[4] *Writings,* IV, 64-65; see also p. 308, where he says that if all the people of the time of the Crucifixion had been Quakers, all would "have been damned because they were too good to commit murder."

[5] *Ibid.,* IV, 65.

[6] *Ibid.,* IV, 66.

[7] *Ibid.,* IV, 185.

[8] *Ibid.,* I, 123.

[9] *Ibid.,* IV, 65, 185, *et passim.*

[10] *Writings,* II, 262.

[11] T. C. Rickman, *Life of Thomas Paine* (London, 1814), p. 33.

[12] *Writings,* I, 156.

[13] *Ibid.,* I, 121 ff., and 206 ff.

[14] Mary A. Best, *Thomas Paine, Prophet and Martyr of Democracy* (New York, 1927), p. 406.

[15] For further evidence refuting the thesis that Quakerism is the key to Paine, see R. B. Falk's excellent article, "Thomas Paine: Deist or Quaker?" *Pennsylvania Magazine of History and Biography,* January, 1938.

[16] *Writings,* IV, 340.

[17] *Ibid.,* II, 406.

[18] For full orientation consult Preserved Smith, *A History of Modern Culture* (New York, 1934), II, with an elaborate bibliography. Smith places primary emphasis on science and rationalism, and the way they affected attitudes in philosophy, politics, economics, humanitarianism, literature, and religion. See also Carl Becker, *The Declaration of Independence* (New York, 1922)

and *The Heavenly City of the Eighteenth-Century Philosophers* (New Haven, 1932); Kingsley Martin, *French Liberal Thought in the Eighteenth Century* (Boston, 1929); G. A. Koch, *Republican Religion; the American Revolution and the Cult of Reason* (New York, 1933); and H. M. Morais, *Deism in Eighteenth-Century America* (New York, 1934).

[19] *Writings*, IV, 63.

[20] *Ibid.*, IV, 64.

[21] See Herbert Drennon, "James Thomson and Newtonism," *University of Chicago Abstracts of Theses* (Humanistic Series, 1930), VIII, 524. Paine's American friend, David Rittenhouse, the astronomer, was an ardent Newtonian. In a paper to be published shortly in the *Transactions of the Wisconsin Academy*, I have dealt at considerable length with "The Influence of Science on American Literature, 1775-1809." Voltaire had of course popularized Newtonianism in France. In summing up the work of the French Encyclopedists, John Morley (*Diderot*, London, 1880, p. 4) says, "Broadly stated, the great central moral of it all was this: that human nature is good, that the world is capable of being made a desirable abiding place, and that the evil of the world is the fruit of bad education and bad institutions."

[22] *Writings*, IV, 63, and see Conway's *Life*, I, 15-17. Conway says Paine "continued his studies in Thetford," and speaks of his "scientific books" which he unfortunately does not name. The parallels between Paine's ideas and those in the published lectures by Martin and Ferguson are cited in H. H. Clark's "An Historical Interpretation of Thomas Paine's Religion," *University of California Chronicle*, XXXV, 56-87 (January, 1933).

[23] *Writings*, IV, 322. See also IV, 192; 315-16; 334-35.

[24] *Ibid.*, IV, 189.

[25] *Ibid.*, IV, 191.

[26] *Ibid.*, IV, 191.

[27] *Ibid.*, IV, 50.

[28] *Ibid.*, IV, 216.

[29] *Ibid.*, IV, 317.

[30] *Ibid.*, IV, 244. In view of the widespread belief that Paine was a "filthy little atheist" (popularized even by so intelligent a man as Theodore Roosevelt in his *Gouverneur Morris*, Boston, 1893, p. 289), it is interesting to notice that Paine insists that materialism alone cannot explain the universe because that does not account for the *motion* imparted to the planets: a God, a "Creator of motion," is necessary (*Writings*, IV, 240-241). As Conway points out (*ibid.*, IV, 238), Paine's discourse on "The Existence of God" is a "digest of Newton's Letters to Bentley, in which he postulates a divine power as necessary to explain planetary motion. . . ."

[31] *Ibid.*, IV, 21.

[32] *Ibid.*, IV, 179. On immortality, see also *ibid.*, IV, 188; 285; 420.

[33] *Ibid.*, IV, 427, also 324 f., 334 ff., 355, 424 ff.

[34] *Ibid.*, IV, 324.

[35] *Ibid.*, IV, 316.

[36] *Ibid.*, IV, 31.

[37] *Ibid.*, IV, 46.

[38] *Ibid.*, IV, 83.

[39] *Writings*, IV, 38.

[40] *Ibid.*, IV, 412.

[41] *Ibid.*, IV, 311. Paine remarks of his own discovery of a ratio in financial laws, "I have not made the ratio any more than Newton made the ratio of gravitation," which was of divine origin (*ibid.*, III, 292).

[42] *Ibid.*, IV, 242 ff. It should be noted that in the light of changeless and inexorable law Paine attacked the idea of prayer as not only futile but "an attempt to make the Almighty change his mind, and act otherwise than he does" (*ibid.*, IV, 44). See also his letter to Samuel Adams, *ibid.*, IV, 202 ff.

[43] *Ibid.*, IV, 339. (Italics mine.) The thought here expressed is reiterated, *ibid.*, IV, 46; 340; 366.

[44] *Writings*, IV, 340.

[45] *Ibid.*, II, 453.

[46] Quoted in Conway's *Life*, II, 4.

[47] *Writings*, I, 159. Of course Paine's faith that an altruistic social life is natural may have been conditioned by earlier thinkers than Martin and Ferguson. We have noted his later familiarity with Grotius, who supported the above assumption by summarizing (*De jure belli et pacis*, "Prolegomena") relevant views of ancient and Christian writers. And later references and quotations (*Writings*, IV, 325) suggest his familiarity

with Tillotson, who had refuted Hobbes long before Shaftesbury or the followers of Newton, arguing that *"men are naturally a-kin and Friends" (Works of Dr. John Tillotson* [London, 1728], I, 305, March 8, 1688/ 9), and that "the frame of our Nature disposeth us to it [charitable altruism], and our inclination to society, in which there can be no pleasure, no advantage, without mutual Love and Kindness" (*ibid.,* I, 171, December 3, 1678). Anthony Collins, one of the militant deists, praised Tillotson as one "whom all *English Free Thinkers own as* their Head" (*A Discourse of Free Thinking* [London, 1713], p. 171); and he proceeds to quote Tillotson on the light of nature and the naturalness of altruism. And there can be little question, I think, that Paine's faith in this sort of natural goodness was reinforced by heralds of the French Revolution such as Rousseau (see *Writings,* I, 150; II, 334; III, 80-81 and 104), and by American democrats such as Jefferson.

48 *Ibid.,* II, 426.

49 *Ibid.,* II, 416-419.

50 *Ibid.,* II, 428.

51 *Ibid.,* III, 276.

52 *Ibid.,* III, 277.

53 *Ibid.,* IV, 190. Since it has now been shown that the vigorous deistic book entitled *Reason the Only Oracle of Man* (Bennington, 1784) was mainly the work not of Ethan Allen but of Dr. Thomas Young of Philadelphia, it is probable that Paine was familiar with its general viewpoint, because Young and Paine were close associates while trying to formulate the constitution of 1776. (See G. P. Anderson, "Who Wrote Ethan Allen's 'Bible'?" *New England Quarterly,* X, 685-696, December, 1937.)

54 For Paine's favorable earlier references to Christianity see *Writings,* I, 56-57; 75-79; 92-99; 100; 171; 184; 188; 208; 212; 247; 250; 266. Most of these references are vague and incidental, although certainly tolerant. He speaks of himself, for example, in 1776, as one "who never dishonors religion either by ridiculing or cavilling at any denomination whatsoever" (*ibid.,* I, 121), and in *The Rights of Man,* Part Two, he argued that "the great Father of all is pleased with variety of devotion" and he urged better pay for "the inferior clergy" (*ibid.,* II, 503-504), although it is there, in 1792, that he shows his hostility to "the connection which Mr. Burke recommends, . . . the *Church Established by Law,"* the adulterous union of Church and State. J. Auchincloss (*Paine's Confession of the Divinity of the Holy Scriptures: or the Sophistry of the second part of The Age of Reason* [Stockport, 1796, 2nd ed.], pp. 7 ff.) presents a list of quotations from

Common Sense and *The Age of Reason* which contradict each other regarding the divinity of the scriptures.

55 *Writings,* IV, 21.

56 On the details regarding this controversy in Parliament and out of it, see W. T. Laprade, "England and the French Revolution, 1789-1797," *Johns Hopkins University Studies in History and Political Science,* Nos. VIII-XII, pp. 22-23 (August-December, 1909).

57 See W. P. Hall, *British Radicalism, 1791-1797* (New York, 1912), especially the early part on economic distress; and see the attitude toward the poor not only expressed by Burke but by such supporters as Hannah More (*Village Politics*) and Bishop Richard Watson ("The Wisdom and Goodness of God in having made both Rich and Poor").

58 See H. H. Clark, "Thomas Paine's Relation to Voltaire and Rousseau," in the *Revue Anglo-américaine,* avril et juin, 1932. That Paine's destructive violence may have owed something to the similar spirit of the *Examen critique de la vie . . . de Saint Paul* (1770) by N. A. Boulanger, is suggested by Paine's extensive quotations from this work in *The Age of Reason* (*Writings,* IV, 173). For orientation see F. A. Aulard's *Christianity and the French Revolution,* London, 1927.

59 *Writings,* I, 15.

60 See J. Delvaille, *L'histoire de l'idée de progrès* (Paris, 1910), p. 52.

61 *Writings,* IV, 380.

62 *Ibid.,* II, 406.

63 *Ibid.,* II, 454.

64 *Ibid.,* II, 121.

65 Edmund Burke, *Works,* VIII, 179.

66 *Writings,* III, 269.

67 *Ibid.,* II, 424. For discussion see L. M. Levin, *The Political Doctrine of Montesquieu's "Esprit des Lois": Its Classical Background* (New York, 1936), especially pp. 16-296.

68 *Writings,* I, 164 f.

69 *Ibid.,* I, 166.

70 *Writings,* IV, 407. Paine shows his knowledge of Middleton's *Letter from Rome* in saying that Middleton "made a journey to Rome, from whence he wrote letters to show that the forms and ceremonies of the

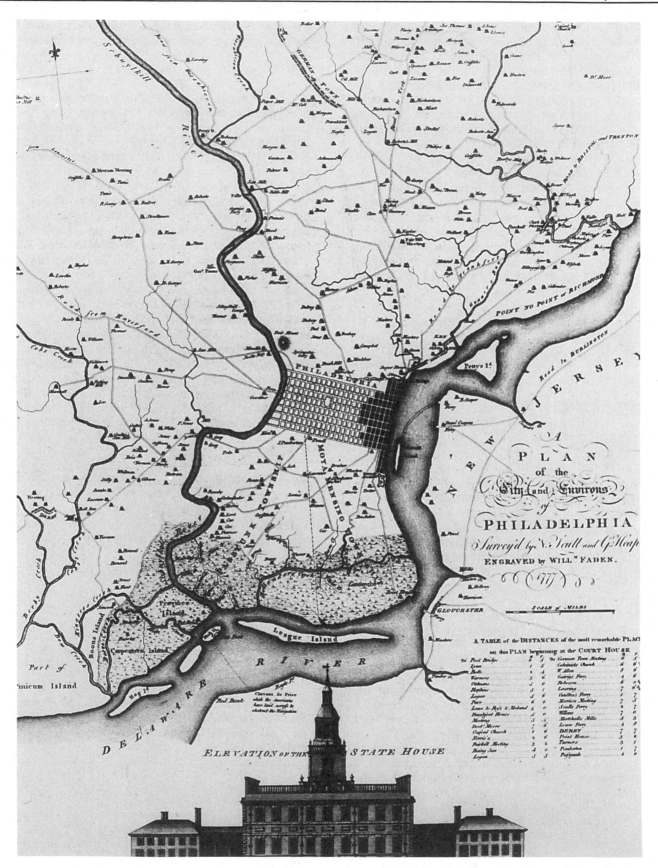

Map of Philadelphia in 1777, engraved by William Faden.

Romish Christian church were taken from the degenerate state of the heathen mythology, as it stood in the latter times of the Greeks and Romans."

[71] *Ibid.,* IV, 25.

[72] *Ibid.,* IV, 411.

[73] For the exotic religions Paine used: Sir William Jones, *On the Gods of Greece, Italy, and India* (n.p., n.d.) and *Supplemental Volumes to the Works of Sir William Jones containing the Whole of the Asiatick Researches hitherto Unpublished* (London, 1801), bound with Samuel Davis, *On the Astronomical Computations of the Hindus;* and Henry Lord, *Religion of the Persees* (London,1630).

[74] *Writings,* IV, 301.

[75] *Ibid.,* IV, 296.

[76] *Ibid.,* IV, 298.

[77] *Ibid.,* IV, 278-9. Needless to say, Paine, the champion of tolerance, was not anti-Semitic toward contemporaries.

[78] *Ibid.,* IV, 299.

[79] See Bernard Faÿ, *Revolution and Freemasonry, 1680-1800* (Boston, 1935).

[80] Aside from his many Masonic friends, Paine's sources were George Smith, *The Use and Abuse of Masonry,* and an address by Mr. Dodd in dedicating the Freemason's Hall in London.

[81] *Writings,* IV, 293.

[82] *Ibid.,* IV, 303.

[83] *Ibid.,* IV, 293.

[84] *Writings,* IV, 204.

[85] *Ibid.,* IV, 26. . . .

A. Owen Aldridge (essay date 1955)

SOURCE: "The Poetry of Thomas Paine," in *The Pennsylvania Magazine of History and Biography,* Vol. LXXIX, No. 1, January, 1955, pp. 81-99.

[*Addressing the much-neglected body of Paine's poetical writings, the essay that follows summarizes and assesses some of Paine's most read and more notable poems.*]

Even the most fanatic devotees of Thomas Paine have had very little to say concerning his verse. Some of his admirers maintain that his prose has merit enough to secure him a respected place in American literature without the need of poetry. Others say that since he proved his talents in verse to be worthy of his prose, it is regrettable that he failed to encourage his poetic vein. Actually, Paine devoted more attention to poetry than most people realize. In *The Age of Reason* he discussed the differences between poetry and prose and illustrated the manner in which the books of Isaiah and Jeremiah could be transposed into English couplets.[1] More important, he was the author of two poems of unusual merit, as well as a number of bagatelles in verse.

His early literary reputation rested in some measure on the first of these poems, an elegy on General Wolfe, published first in March, 1775, in the *Pennsylvania Magazine,* which Paine was editing. The second poem, a scathing denunciation of George III which appeared in the *Pennsylvania Packet* shortly after the appearance of *Common Sense,* had a greater vogue than any of his other verse, but after the original printing it appeared under a variety of titles, which have completely obscured the full meaning of the poem for subsequent readers. The purpose of the poem may be seen only in the original text with the original title, not in the versions printed in any of the standard editions of Paine's works. Contrary to the suggestion in the most recent edition, moreover, this poem was not the only verse Paine wrote during the War for Independence.[2] He wrote another of similar scope for the same newspaper on the subject of Governor Johnstone's attempts to bribe members of the American Congress. Fired by indignant wrath, he castigated the British as a people less honorable than the devils in hell. Although not the equal of the poem against King George, this verse has a certain epigrammatic wit, as well as satirical vigor.

The poem on the death of General Wolfe has not received the critical attention it deserves. Better than any of Paine's other verse it illustrates his notion that poetry leads "too much into the field of imagination." This Paine asserted in the 1790's in *The Age of Reason,* adding that distrust of imagination had led him to repress rather than encourage his poetic talent.[3] After his death, William Cobbett, repeating the testimony of Mme. Bonneville, asserted that Paine "rather delighted in ridiculing poetry. He did not like it: he said it was not a serious thing, but a sport of the mind, which often had not common sense."[4] Near the end of his life, however, Paine had a good opinion of his verse. In a letter to Jefferson, January 25, 1805, in which he mentioned the possibility of collecting his works, he proposed to include "some pieces of poetry which I believe have some claim to originality."[5] Paine's song on Wolfe reveals that at the time of its composition he had deliberately sought to penetrate farther into the realm of imagination than he felt contemporary poets were venturing. In his remarks introducing the poem to the *Pennsylvania Magazine,* Paine asserts that he has not "pursued the worn out tract of modern song," but has "thrown it into fable." This means that instead of eulogizing the fallen hero by means of simple statement, he had elevated his theme by the device of personification. His method derives from the method of Collins, who, in his well-known odes "Occasion'd by the Death of Mr. Thompson" and "Written in the Beginning of the Year 1746," expressed grief by means of pictorial—not abstract—symbols. To the personification of Collins, Paine added a fable based on classical mythology.

In the poem, Britannia is portrayed mourning in a "mouldering cave" for her fallen son, Wolfe. Jupiter sends Mercury to comfort her. Mercury reveals that Wolfe had been called to heaven to participate in a battle there between the gods and "the proud giants of old," who had broken out from their subterranean abodes. In a note Paine explains that "The heathen mythology after describing the defeat of the giants by Jupiter, says, that he confined them under mountains." When Mercury announced to Wolfe on the plains of Quebec that he was needed in heaven, the hero begged merely to stay where he was until victory was won. The god, however, sealing his eyes, bore him away in an urn,

> Lest the fondness he bore to his own native shore,
> Should induce him again to return.

This final turn accords well with the ingenious conceit upon which the entire song is constructed.

Paine probably wrote this song in England when he was a member of a social, intellectual club at Lewes. According to legend, he recited it at one of the meetings of this society at an inn called the White Hart. This song has been more generally praised than any of Paine's other verse. Benjamin Rush wrote to Paine's enemy James Cheetham that this song, together with Paine's prose reflections on the death of Lord Clive, gave the *Pennsylvania Magazine* "a sudden currency which few works of that kind have since had in our country."[6] Even Cheetham considered it a "beautiful song." Perhaps Paine also considered it to be his best work, and it may have been this ode which he recited to Horne Tooke, who afterwards sneered at all of Paine's work, prose and poetry. According to Tooke's biographer, Tooke once repeated from Paine "a distich, replete with the *bathos, . . .* as it had been recited to him by the author, who deemed it his masterpiece."[7] A contributor to the *Port Folio* felt that the poem on Wolfe had more faults than virtues and that it did not deserve its "high and general popularity."[8]

> If any thing had been wanting to complete the climax of absurdity which marks this ballad, it is amply supplied in the four last lines. Where, we

will not say in elegiac, but even in mock heroic poetry, can we find a more forced conceit, or a more ludicrous representation, than that of Mercury deliberately blindfolding the ghost of general Wolfe, cramming it into an urn, and, when thus disposed of, carrying it off under his arm, for the purpose of having it appointed generalissimo of the celestial armies. . . . Let those who deem it so denominate this a fine thought—a lofty conception; we cannot view it as other than an overstrained, distorted, and most ludicrous conceit—a caricature attempt at the sentimental sublime.

This opinion was echoed a number of years later in the *North American Review.*[9] Here the song is described as "a paltry conceit, of Jupiter snatching General Wolfe from earth to fight his battles against some celestial rebels, . . . rendered in tripping Bacchanalian metre. . . . Dr. Rush must have been a better judge of pills than poetry, if he sincerely praised such stuff as this."

Paine also printed in the *Pennsylvania Magazine,* July, 1775, his **"Liberty Tree,"** another song widely reprinted by his contemporaries.[10] Although the subtitle "A Song, Written Early in the American Revolution" was added subsequently, readers of the song on its first appearance were still not aware that a revolution had begun. The first two of its four stanzas describe the transplanting of the Liberty Tree from the celestial regions to America. The third and fourth stanzas, printed below, describe the unrewarded efforts of the American colonists to support British maritime power, and complain of the tyrannical measures of "Kings, Commons, and Lords."

> Beneath this fair tree, like the patriarchs of old,
>   Their bread in contentment they ate,
> Unvexed with the troubles of silver or gold,
>   The cares of the grand and the great.
> With timber and tar they Old England
>   supplied,
>   And supported her power on the sea:
> Her battles they fought, without getting a groat,
>   For the honor of Liberty Tree.
>
> But hear, O ye swains ('tis a tale most
>   profane),
>   How all the tyrannical powers,
> Kings, Commons, and Lords, are uniting amain
>   To cut down this guardian of ours.
> From the East to the West blow the trumpet
>   to arms,
>   Thro' the land let the sound of it flee:
> Let the far and the near all unite with a cheer,
>   In defense of our Liberty Tree.

Some time after the Revolution, Paine revised the song to make it fit all popular revolts against autocratic government. The revised version, a manuscript in

Paine's handwriting found among the papers of his friend Colonel John Fellows, has been previously printed only once—in a very obscure deistical periodical, *The Beacon,* edited by Paine's first sympathetic American biographer, Gilbert Vale.[11] In revising the song, Paine eliminated entirely the original third stanza, and caused the fourth (which became the third in the new version) to condemn Kingcraft and Priestcraft instead of merely "Kings Commons, and Lords."

> But hear, O ye swains! 'tis a tale most
>   profane,
>   How all the tyrannical powers
> Of Kingcraft and Priestcraft are joining amain
>   To cut down this guardian of ours.
> Fell Discord, dire torment of gods and of men,
>   Attacks the celestial decree,
> With snake-twisted locks she creeps out
>   from her den,
>   To strike at our Liberty Tree.

A new, highly optimistic concluding stanza forecasts the universal triumph of freedom and good will.

> Ye gods who preside o'er the empire of man,
>   Dispers'd o'er the face of the globe,
> Look cheerfully down and survey thine own plan,
>   And spare not, if wanted, the probe.
> Bid Concord descend from thy charming
>   abodes,
>   Bid Discord and Jealousy flee,
> And then in a bumper of nectar, ye gods,
>   Drink health to our Liberty Tree.

There is another poem in the *Pennsylvania Magazine* almost certainly by Paine which does not appear in the latest edition of his works. This is **"The Tale of the Monk and the Jew Versified,"** which appeared in March, 1775, and bears Paine's most common pseudonym in the magazine, Atlanticus.[12] It was printed as a Paine piece in an early, but undated, English collection made by William Dugdale of *The Theological Works of Thomas Paine.* The theme was apparently not original with Paine, for he introduced it with the following comment: "The tale of the Monk and Jew (versified) having appeared in some of the English magazines, but as I am no admirer of that sort of wit which is dashed with profaneness, I herewith send you a versification of the same tale, by a gentleman on this side of the water." The importance of this poem, a satire, is that it reveals an early vein of anticlerical thought. One of the problems of Paine's biography is to explain why Paine seemed to have turned abruptly from political to theological subjects during the French Revolution. It may be that his interest in religion was not at all a new development.

Paine's next two poems, written when the American Revolution had reached its height, served as propaganda pieces, almost identical in purpose with the *Crisis* papers which were appearing concurrently.

In June, 1778, Governor George Johnstone, one of a British commission to restore peace, attempted to bribe a number of members of Congress to desert the American cause, and also inspired a number of publications designed to turn the people against Congress.[13] His activities were immediately exposed and denounced. Among the denunciations hurled at Johnstone, none were more scathing than a hitherto undiscovered poem by Paine in the Philadelphia press. For the first time in his career Paine adopted the satirical style of Pope. He succeeded in capturing the sharp precision of Pope's couplets, but in a sense reduced the rigor of his scorn by the cumbersome length of his title—nonetheless typical of Pope—**"To Governor Johnstone, one of the British Commissioners, on his late letters and offers to bribe certain eminent characters in America, and threatening afterwards to appeal to the public."**

The poem appeared in the *Pennsylvania Packet,* July 28, 1778, bearing Paine's signature Common Sense. There can be no doubt that all contributions in this newspaper at this time with the signature Common Sense were written by Paine. The newspaper began publication in July, 1778. During the next twelve months two numbers of Paine's *Crisis,* as well as his two poems, appeared with the signature Common Sense, which was recognized as Paine's property. On February 4, 1779, Paine, over his initials T. P., condemned a writer in the rival *Pennsylvania Journal* for stealing his nom de plume. Since the poem on Johnstone has never before been reprinted, it is given here in full.

> WHEN Satan first from Heaven's bright
>   region fell,
> And fix'd the gloomy monarch of hell,
> Sin then was honest; Pride led on the tribe;
> No Devil receiv'd—no Devil propos'd a bribe:
> But each infernal, while he fought, abhorr'd
> The meaner mongrel arts of sap and fraud;
> Brave in his guilt, he rais'd his daring arm,
> And scorn'd the heavens, unless obtain'd by storm.
>
> But Britain—Oh! how painful 'tis to tell!
> Commits a sin that makes a blush in hell;
> Low in the ruins of demolish'd pride
> She basely skulks to conquer with a bribe,
> And when detected in the rank offence,
> Throws out a threat—to turn King's
>   evidence.
>
> Yet while we scorn the lure, despise the plan,
> We feel an angry sorrow at the man;
> Was there no wretch, whose cold unkindl'd mind
> Ne'er knew one gen'rous passion for
>   mankind,

Whose hackney'd soul, the purchase of a
   pound,
No guilt could blacken and no shame
   confound?
No slave to act the dirty work—and spare,
From men of sentiment, the painful tear?

   Must Johnstone be the man? Must he,
     whose tongue
Such able peals of elocution rung,
Whose tow'ring genius seem'd at times to rise,
And mix a kindred fervor with the skies,
Whose pointed judgment, and connected
   sense,
Gave weight to wit, and worth to eloquence;
Must he, Oh shame to genius! be the first
To practise acts himself so loudly curst?
Must he exhibit to a laughing mob,
A turn coat patriot conquer'd by a jobb;
And prove from under his adult'rous pen
How few are just of all the sons of men?

   When the sad echo of St. Pulchre's bell
Tolls to the carted wretch, a last farewell,
Or when the tyrant sees the lifted steel,
They feel those pains which Johnstone
   ought to feel.
Man may a while in infamy survive,
And by deception think himself alive,
But time will prove to his eternal shame
He dies in earnest who outlives his fame.
    Of PITT *and* YOU *this contrast may be said,*
    The dead is living; and the living dead.

Paine realized that unrestrained invective is seldom effective in satire. He condemned Johnstone indirectly therefore—but nevertheless forcefully—by complimenting the devils of hell for their political behavior, which seemed honest in comparison to Johnstone's. Mingling praise of Johnstone's intellectual qualities with condemnation of his moral corruption, Paine lamented instead of cursed his lapse from gentlemanly conduct. The somewhat theatrical final stanza concludes with an epigram disparaging Johnstone by contrasting him with the recently deceased Pitt. But lest he be accused of praising British statesmen, Paine retracts his compliment to Pitt in a footnote: "Late accounts from Europe mention the death of this honest, though haughty and ambitious statesman; and though his principles respecting America cannot be justified either by sound policy or universal benevolence, yet, even his enemies must allow that he had a soul too noble for bribery and corruption." Some years later in his *Letter to the Abbé Raynal* (1782), Paine even further reduced his estimate of Pitt. "Death," he wrote, "has preserved to the memory of this statesman, *that fame,* which he, by living, would have lost."[14]

The archvillain of the Revolution, however, Paine considered to be George III. It is true that in *Common Sense* he attacked the political institution of monarchy without personal reference to the British King, but as time passed he grew more and more bold and sardonic in referring to "His Madjesty," a later phrase of his own coinage for the insane George. The poem which appears in Paine's works under the title **"An Address to Lord Howe"** was originally called **"To the King of England"** when it appeared in the *Pennsylvania Packet,* November 14, 1778. There is nothing whatsoever in the poem to link it to Lord Howe; in fact, the line "From George the murderer down to murderous Cain" ("From CAIN to GEORGE, and back from GEORGE to CAIN" in the original version) clearly shows to whom it is addressed. Neither Lord Richard Howe, crown commissioner, nor his brother General William Howe, commander in chief of the American armies, was despised by the colonists; in fact, they were regarded as personally decent and honorable. Franklin, for example, in addressing Lord Howe on his mission to effect reconciliation spoke of the "well-founded Esteem, and . . . Affection" which he would always have for Howe as an individual.[15] Even Paine in *Crisis* No. II treated the joint commissioners in a jocular rather than a bitter tone. His harshest words refer ironically to their announced policy of hanging all armed citizens found without an officer accompanying them. "This is the humane Lord Howe and his brother, whom the Tories and their three-quarter kindred, the Quakers, or some of them at least, have been holding up for patterns of justice and mercy!"[16] This has little in common with the tone of hatred and contempt in **"To the King of England,"** which accuses George III of inhuman sentiments and prays for his death.

When Paine's friend Thomas Clio Rickman published the poem in *Letters From Thomas Paine to the Citizens of America* (London, 1804), the first British publication of the poem that I know of, it bore the title **"Verses to a Friend After a Long Conversation on War."** Richard Carlile gave it the shorter title **"Verses on War"** in his London edition of Paine's *Miscellaneous Poems* (1819), and further shortened it to **"On War"** in his deistical periodical, *The Republican.*[17] In other English editions the poem appeared completely without a title. I have seen in European libraries outside England, as well as in the British Museum, an undated pamphlet, *Address and Declaration of Universal Peace and Liberty, Held at the Thatched House Tavern, St. James's Street. August 20th 1791. By Thomas Paine. . . . Together with some Verses by the same Author, which were printed in a Pennsylvania Newspaper.* The verses, printed without title, are those on King George. None of Paine's other poems seem to have been used as propaganda pieces in this way. English publishers of the poem were obliged to drop the title referring to the King or they would have been prosecuted for treason. This does not explain, however, why the title **"An Address to Lord Howe"** was substituted in America.

Since this work seems to have circulated more widely than any of Paine's other poetry—both because of its sentiments and because of its inherent aesthetic value—and since the original version from the *Pennsylvania Packet* has never been reprinted verbatim, the entire text is printed here.

THE rain pours down—the city looks
    forlorn—
And *gloomy* subjects suit the howling morn.
Close by my fire; with doors and windows fast,
And sweetly shelter'd from the driving blast,
To gayer thoughts, I bid a day's adieu,
To spend a scene of solitude with you.

So of't has black revenge engross'd the care
Of all the leisure hours man finds to spare;
So oft has guilt in all its thousand dens
Call'd forth the vengeance of chastising pens;
That when I fain would ease my heart on you,
No thought is left untold—no passion new.
From flight to flight the mental path appears
Worn with the steps of near six thousand years,
And fill'd throughout with ev'ry scene of pain,
From CAIN to GEORGE, and back from
    GEORGE to CAIN.

Alike in cruelty, alike in hate,
In guilt alike, and more alike in fate;
Both curs'd supremely (for the blood they drew)
Each from the rising world while each was new.

Go second Cain, true likeness of the first,
And strew thy blasted head with homely dust—
In ashes sit—in wretched sackcloth weep—
And with unpitied sorrows cease to sleep.
Go, haunt the tombs, and single out the place
Where earth itself shall suffer a disgrace.
Go, spell the letters on some mould'ring urn,
And ask if he who sleeps there can return.
Go, count the numbers that in silence lie,
And learn by study what it is to die.

For sure that heart—if any heart you own—
Conceits that man expires without a groan;
That he who lives, receives from you a grace,
Or death is nothing but a change of place;
That peace is dull; that joy from sorrow
    springs,
And war the royal raree-show of things.

Else why these scenes that wound the
    feeling mind,
This sport of death—this cockpit of
    mankind.
Why sobs the widow in perpetual pain;
Why cries the orphan—*"Oh my father's slain."*
Why hangs the sire his paralytic head,
And nods with manly grief,—*"My son is dead."*

[Why shrieks the maiden, (robb'd of ease
    and sense,)
*"He's gone—He's kill'd—Oh! Heavens take
    me hence."*]
Why drops the tear from off the sister's
    cheek,
And sweetly tells the sorrows she would
    speak.
[*Why lisps* the infant on its mother's lap,
And looking round the parlour—*"Where is
    pap."*
Why weeps the mother when the question's
    ask'd,
And kiss an answer as the easiest task;]
Or why with lonely steps does pensive John
To all the neighbour's [*sic*] tell—*"Poor
    master's gone."*

Oh! could I paint the passions I can feel,
Or point a horror that would wound like
    steel,
To thy unfeeling, unrelenting mind,
I'd send a torture and relieve mankind.

Thou, that art husband, father, brother, all
The tender names that kindred learn to call,
Yet like an image, carv'd in massy stone,
Thou bear'st the shape, but sentiment has
    none;
Allied by dust and figure, not by mind,
Thou only herd'st but lives not with
    mankind,
[And prone to love like some outrageous ape
Thou know'st each class of beings by their
    shape.]

Since then no hopes to civilize remain,
And all petitions have gone forth in vain,
One prayer is left, which dreads no proud
    reply,
That HE *who made you breathe,* WOULD BID
    YOU DIE.

In this early version—written and published in haste—some lines are painfully flat and prose-like. One could read thousands of contemporary couplets without finding a line to match the ludicrousness of

. . . looking round the parlour—*"Where is pap."*

In later versions, however, Paine eliminated his amateurish phrases. The lines in brackets above he simply dropped. The above text should not, therefore, supplant the revised version printed in standard editions, but the original title should be restored. In its improved form this poem deserves the wide circulation it seems to have enjoyed. It successfully creates a somber mood and then rises to a high degree of emotional intensity over the evils of war. This is a rather difficult achievement, since Paine deals with war considered in the abstract, not with a specific campaign or particular fallen hero. Without its title, this poem has nothing even to connect it to the American Revolution.

Although not modeled on any single precursor, the first stanza resembles eighteenth-century poetry of the melancholy tradition. The next three stanzas anticipate the concern of later romanticists with malevolent influences. To be sure the later romantic hero ordinarily portrayed himself as the embodiment of diabolic forces, whereas Paine associates the British monarch with Satan. Nevertheless, the essential theatrical properties are the same: Cain, mental guilt, cruelty, hate, and unreasoned bloodshed. It is precisely because these sensational qualities are attributed to a historical personage rather than to the author himself that the work is saved from affectation and artificiality.

In addition to the final line, hoping for the death of George III, the poem has another very neat conceit. In comparing the British monarch to Cain, the author cleverly refers to the recent nativity of the American nation.

> Both curs'd supremely (for the blood they drew)
> Each from the rising world while each was new.

"To the King of England" is a notable work, and certainly Paine's best poem.

The most recent editor of Paine's works has included as a Paine piece an "Epitaph on General Charles Lee" found in manuscript in a volume in the John Carter Brown Library entitled *Anecdotes of the Late Charles Lee, Esq.* (London, 1797). This epitaph is almost certainly not by Paine. It appeared in the Philadelphia *Freeman's Journal,* July 23, 1783, where it was ascribed to the London *St. James's Chronicle.*[18] Had Paine been the author, he probably would not have sent it to the London press for its first publication. The title of the epitaph in the newspaper, which differs from that in the manuscript, shows, moreover, that it was written by an Englishman, not an American or sympathizer with the American cause: "To the MEMORY of General LEE, who died in America, having served more Nations than Britain." The text itself also shows that the author is an Englishman, who condemns Lee for defection. The newspaper text has a few verbal differences from the manuscript text, giving further proof that Paine was not the author. A line in the manuscript version

> At best a true republican at heart

appears in the newspaper version

> At best a sad republican at heart.

Paine could hardly have written the latter. Paine also would not have described Lee as "Above all kings, and yet of gold the slave." A very close friendship existed between Lee and Paine. It was Lee who invented the famous expression concerning Paine—"he burst forth upon the world like Jove in thunder."[19] Paine was always on the best of terms with the controversial general, and after Paine fell out with Washington he suggested that Lee had been Washington's superior in strategy.[20] Paine cannot be held responsible for the half-hearted elegy, admirable as it may be as a poetic composition.

Paine continued his poetic activity during his sojourn in France. A crude version of the song published in collections of his works under the title **"Hail Great Republic"** was printed in *Tom Paine's Jests* (Philadelphia, 1796). The first two stanzas of this text are almost identical with later printed versions, but the subsequent stanzas, printed below, later went through great modifications.

> From thee may rudest nations learn,
>   To prize the cause thy sons began;
> From thee may future, may future tyrants
>   know,
>   That sacred are the Rights of Man.
>   *Chorus.*
>
> From thee may hated discord fly,
>   With all her dark, her gloomy train;
> And o'er thy fertile, thy fertile wide domain,
>   May everlasting friendship reign.
>   *Chorus.*
>
> Of thee may lisping infancy,
>   The pleasing wond'rous story tell;
> And patriot sages in venerable mood,
>   Instruct the world to govern well.
>   *Chorus.*
>
> Ye guardian Angels watch around,
>   From harms protect the new born State;
> And all ye friendly, ye friendly nations join,
>   And thus salute the Child of Fate.
>   *Chorus.*

The New-York Historical Society has a manuscript text of this song in Paine's handwriting, signed T. P. It is endorsed on the recto in another hand "presented by the author to Mr. R. L. Livingston Paris July 1802." This text is closer to the final form of the poem, but there are still a number of divergences.

In Paris Paine also wrote four occasional pieces on subjects of love and gallantry: **"From the Castle in the Air to the Little Corner of the World," "The New Covenant," "Contentment; or, If You Please, Confession,"** and **"To Sir Robert Smyth: What Is Love."**

The first of these, the only one with any claim to literary merit, was printed by Joseph Dennie in his *Farmer's Weekly Museum,* June 12, 1797. In the critical essay in the *Port Folio* which we have already discussed, "Remarks on the Pretensions of Thomas Paine . . . To the Character of a Poet," the author repudiates the song on Wolfe as evidence of Paine's poetic reputation, but adds that

> while the **"Castle in the Air"** remains to testify in its favour, its case is not desperate. In that sprightly and fine effusion of fancy we perceive much to praise and very little to blame. Although wild and irregular, the imagery is highly picturesque and beautiful; and in no instance does it offend either the judgment or the taste. The conceptions, too, are lofty and spirited, the sentiments unexceptionable, and the language, for the most part, appropriate and chaste.[21]

There are miscellaneous comments to be made on other poems. **"Lines Extempore, by Thomas Paine, July, 1803"** appeared for the first time in the *Philadelphia General Advertiser (Aurora),* August 6, 1803. Cheetham in his highly derogatory life of Paine maintains that Paine wrote his description of three peddlers traveling to a fair (**"Star in the East"**) at the house of a mutual friend, William Carver, while Paine was drunk. Carver later accused Cheetham of deliberate misrepresentation, asserting that the poem had been written in France. Cheetham knew that his statement was false, Carver alleged, since Cheetham had heard Paine repeat the poem long before Paine took up residence with Carver.[22] Paine's well-known epigram on Washington, which Foner prints from Barlow's notebook, Cheetham says was written at the same time as the famous letter to Washington and was given to Cheetham soon after Paine's arrival in New York.[23]

A piece of doggerel satire in the *Pennsylvania Packet* of December 29, 1778, is probably Paine's. Entitled **"By the Goddess of Plain Truth, A Manifesto and Proclamation,"** the verse pretends to be a repudiation by the goddess of Truth of the writings which had been appearing against Paine under the pseudonym Plain Truth. Another brief poem in the Philadelphia press may also be Paine's. In the *Federal Gazette,* May 18, 1789, appears a short poem written at a tea table. When the author was asked what kind of woman he would prefer, he replied:

> Give me kind Heav'n—if this wide world has one—
> The girl that loves me for myself alone. . . .

The poem is signed Common Sense. It is possible that some other writer had adopted the name after Paine's return to England, but the title previously had been reserved to Paine in Pennsylvania, and he had used it in the *Pennsylvania Gazette* as late as March, 1787.

There are three other of Paine's poems which do not appear in the latest edition of his works. Rickman in *Letters from Thomas Paine* (1804), published an **"Epigram on a Long-Nosed Friend,"** written in Paris in 1800. This appears also in Carlile's edition of *Miscellaneous Poems* (1819), and in an undated collection of *The Theological Works of Thomas Paine* printed by William Dugdale. The chief interest in this epigram is that it concerns an actual historical personage, Count Zenobio, whom Paine knew in Paris.

> Going along the other day,
>   Upon a certain plan
> I met a nose upon the way,
>   Behind it was a man.
> I called up to the nose to stop.
>   And when it had done so,—
> The man behind it—he came up,
>   They made ZENOBIO.

Carlile and Dugdale also printed **"The Strange Story of Korah, Dathan, and Abiram, Numbers, Chap. XVI, Accounted For,"** a doggerel ballad too long for quotation here, and **"On the British Constitution,"** a doggerel epigram. Dugdale alone printed the following **"Epigram."**[24]

> Some, for the sake of titles grand
> Oft stoop to kiss a sovereign's hand;
> Others, at Rome, will stoop so low,
> They'll kiss the holy father's toe;
> But I exceed them all in bliss
> When Flora's ruby lips I kiss.

It is interesting to note in connection with Paine's verse that many years after his death an effort was made to father upon him a long poem with pretensions to epic grandeur. The attribution to Paine was apparently a puffing scheme on the part of some unknown to attract attention to his merits. Although it excited nobody, the work deserves some attention as one of the curiosities of American literature.

The author used the names of both Paine and Thomas Jefferson to promote his work. In August, 1826, an Albany weekly reported on the authority of the *Boston Courier* that "Thomas Paine, near the close of his life, committed to the care of Mr. Jefferson . . . a manuscript work entitled 'The Religion of the Sun.'"[25] The *Port Folio,* reporting the same story, joined with "the editor of one of our Philadelphia papers in condemning anything of that description, from such a source, to the hands of the common hangman."[26] The moment for launching the story had been well chosen. Since Jefferson had just died, he could not be called upon to deny or confirm this report. The *Escritor* had to be content with inquiring "whether such a manuscript was left by Mr. Jefferson among his papers? and if so, what disposition is to be made of it?" Needless to say, such a manuscript has never appeared among Jefferson's papers. Two months later, however, on October 7, 1826, the *Escritor* reported the discovery of the manuscript and quoted an ecstatic report from the *Philadelphia Album:*

> The poetical world will doubtless be thrown into a ferment at the discovery of a celebrated poem, entitled *The Religion of the Sun,* which, for dignity of diction, sublimity of metaphor, elegance and perspicuity of period, sprightliness of fancy, and sally of genius, I understand from accurate judges who have had an opportunity of examining this recently discovered manuscript, will not find a parallel in the calendars of Parnassus. These excellencies, combined with the irresistible talent of the author, will render it the Iliad of America.

The poem itself, which appeared in Philadelphia as a pamphlet of twenty-eight pages in November, 1826, contains a confused preface signed S.Y.A. (Samuel Yorke Atlee?), asserting that he had found the manuscript signed by Paine in a secondhand bookshop. The highly Latinized blank verse imitates Milton, but the structure of the poem has more in common with Blake's prophetic books. The device of a war taking place on the sun has some resemblance to the battle between the good and the bad angels in *Paradise Lost,* but the philosophical concepts of the piece belong to the deistical tradition. To the commonplace notion of a plurality of inhabited worlds, the author adds the more original concept of a hierarchy among the planets. He indicates that a being which seems to be a man in one world is only an ape in another.

The following descriptive passage illustrates the style of the whole.

> The mighty God, eternal, infinite,
> Omnipotent, omnivident, omniscient,
> Whose grandeur is announc'd, from the
>   nerv'd wing
> Of viewless insect, to the mighty mass
> Of worlds—his hand pancratic knit the
>   tendons
> That wheel, with instant revolution, round
> The insect's eye; and arm'd the vivid storm.

It is perhaps unfair to introduce *The Religion of the Sun* in a discussion of Paine's poetry since it has nothing in common with the verse Paine actually wrote, which is ineffably superior. Even though Paine was not the greatest poet of the American Revolution, he was a poet. Unlike other masters of political prose, like Bolingbroke, Burke, and Jefferson, who seldom or never followed the lyric impulse, Paine amused himself with a variety of verse forms. Despite a conscious effort to discourage his own poetic vein, he continued to write verse during every period of his life. In France he wrote one or two pleasant songs, and on his return to America he continued to cultivate

the Muse. It is of some significance that the first work from his pen to achieve more than local fame was in verse, his ode on the death of Wolfe. Although his address to King George, his most forceful poem, seems to have enjoyed its celebrity primarily as a propaganda piece, it has intrinsic merits to justify our attention to it as a work of art.

Notes

[1] Philip S. Foner, ed., *The Complete Writings of Thomas Paine* (New York, 1945), I, 475.

[2] Paine wrote four poems which can be considered "patriotic." Only the two which appeared in the *Pennsylvania Packet* were written during the Revolution. "Liberty Tree" was published in July, 1775, and "Hail Great Republic" was probably not written until 1795.

[3] Foner, I, 496.

[4] Moncure D. Conway, *Life of Thomas Paine* (New York, 1892), II, 459.

[5] Foner, II, 1460.

[6] Rush to Cheetham, July 17, 1809, in James Cheetham, *Life of Thomas Paine* (London, 1817), 21.

[7] Alexander Stephens, *Memoirs of John Horne Tooke* (London, 1813), II, 323. Stephens is responsible for preserving an amusing Paine item. Among the "Stephensia" in the *Monthly Magazine,* December, 1822, appears the following anecdote: Paine "wrote the following epigrams on the heir to the Onslow estates, who then signalised himself as *a four-in-hand,* by driving a team of little cropped horses, compared to tom-tits or tit-mice, and which begot him the nickname of 'Tommy Titmouse.'

> Pray what can Tommy Titmouse do?
> Why drive a phaeton and two.
> Can Tommy Tit do nothing more?
> Yes,—drive a phaeton and four!"

[8] "Remarks on the Pretensions of Thomas Paine, Author of 'Common Sense,' To the Character of a Poet," *Port Folio* (Philadelphia, 1815), 488-497.

[9] *North American Review* (April, 1843), 9-51, a review article by William B. Reed of "An Oration delivered at the Celebration . . . of the Birthday of Thomas Paine by John Alberger." This is the most denigratory account of Paine ever to be published. Unlike Paine's other detractors, this reviewer condemns even *Common Sense,* which he calls "trashy jargon."

[10] We can be sure that three other poems in the *Pennsylvania Magazine* are Paine's: "Farmer Short's Dog

Porter," "The Snowdrop and the Critic," and "An Account of the Burning of Bachelors' Hall." These were attributed to Paine by Mathew Carey in *Works of Thomas Paine* (Philadelphia, 1797) and by Richard Carlile, *Miscellaneous Poems* (London, 1819).

[11] Feb. 3, 1844. Vale also prints in the same issue "From Mr. Paine to Mr. Jefferson" (Foner, II, 1101-1102). Conway printed these lines (*Collected Writings of Thomas Paine* [New York, 1894-1896], IV, 493) from a manuscript among the papers of William Cobbett. They had also been printed in R. D. Owen's *Free Enquirer,* Feb. 20, 1830, where they had been forwarded by Fanny Wright.

[12] Conway includes it in his *Writings of Thomas Paine,* IV, 482-483.

[13] See Benjamin Franklin's letter to Hartley, Oct. 26, 1778, in A. H. Smyth, ed., *Writings of Benjamin Franklin* (New York, 1905-1907), VII, 197. See also the Declaration of Congress, *Pennsylvania Evening Post,* Aug. 13, 1778.

[14] Foner, II, 255.

[15] Smyth, VI, 461.

[16] Jan. 13, 1777, Foner, I, 65.

[17] *The Republican,* II, 390-391.

[18] Later it appeared also in the *American Museum,* IV (1788), 189.

[19] This expression appears in the preface to *Memoirs of the Life of the Late Charles Lee* (London, 1792). Richard Carlile, by printing this preface in Paine's *Miscellaneous Letters and Essays on Various Subjects* (London, 1819), suggests that Paine was the author, but this is unlikely since the editor of the *Memoirs* remarks that Lee's papers had been delivered to him in London in 1786, and Paine did not return to England until 1787. The complimentary sentiments of the preface, nevertheless, accorded well with Paine's opinion of Lee.

[20] Foner, II, 922.

[21] Foner remarks (II, 1096), "The original manuscript of this poem, in Paine's handwriting, is in the New York Historical Society. . . . There is another copy in Paine's handwriting in the manuscript division of the New York Public Library." Actually neither manuscript is in Paine's handwriting and neither has any authority whatsoever as a text. The best is still that of Carlile's *Miscellaneous Poems* (London, 1819).

[22] *Beacon,* Mar. 14, 1840. The text in the Foner edition (II, 1103-1106) is said to be based on "the origi-

nal, undated manuscript . . . in the New York Historical Society." Actually the manuscript in the New-York Historical Society is not in Paine's handwriting, and this text has no authority whatsoever.

[23] Foner, II, 690; Cheetham, 109.

[24] The lines on Zenobio and "The Strange Story of Korah" appear in the Conway edition, but the epigram printed by Dugdale does not. So far as I know, "The Strange Story of Korah" was first printed in Cheetham's *Life of Thomas Paine* (New York, 1809), 272-278. It was dropped from the London edition.

[25] *The Escritor: or Masonic & Miscellaneous Album,* I, 239.

[26] *Port Folio,* XXI (September, 1826), 261. After the publication of the poem a Boston paper echoed the view that it should be burned by the hangman. The *New York Correspondent,* Apr. 7, 1827, replied with a defense of Paine, toleration, and free speech.

James T. Boulton (essay date 1962)

SOURCE: "Literature and Politics I: Tom Paine and the Vulgar Style," in *Essays in Criticism,* Vol. XII, No. 1, January, 1962, pp. 18-33.

[*In the following essay, Boulton seeks to re-evaluate the "vulgarity" of Paine's style in light of its efficacy and purpose; although it may not have suited the aesthetic standards of the era, Boulton argues, it did suit itself to Paine's intended audience and sense of urgency.*]

Prose—especially political prose—written for a largely uneducated audience seems to present the literary critic with a difficult problem of evaluation. Writers—such as those examined by John Holloway in *The Victorian Sage*—who cater for an audience alert to subtleties of allusion, tone, rhythm, imagery and so forth, and who in consequence are able to manipulate a large range of literary techniques, confident of their readers' response—such writers lend themselves readily to conventional literary analysis. But because our critical tools are not normally sharpened on his kind of writing an author like Tom Paine tends to be ignored. He receives a nod from compilers of 'social settings' and 'literary scenes', as if what he had to say and the manner of saying it can safely be disregarded, but no serious critical attention.

It is noticeable that no attempt has been made by literary critics to account for the remarkable impact of one of the best known of political pamphlets, the first part of Paine's ***Rights of Man*** (1791). There is no need to insist on the reality of Paine's influence in his own day, it is too well known (though the reminder may be timely in view of the complete absence of his name from the 'Penguin Guide' covering the Revolutionary period). And it is not adequate to leave it to the political historian to explain this influence, or merely to claim, with some eighteenth-century critics, that Paine's was an appeal to the political have-nots against the ruling class. When it is remembered that upwards of fifty books and pamphlets were written in reply to Burke's *Reflections,* many of them addressed to the same audience as Paine's, this explanation obviously does not account for the distinctive success of the **Rights of Man** or for the sale (according to Paine) of 'between four and five hundred thousand' within ten years of publication.

One principal reason for Paine's success was the apparent simplicity of his revolutionary doctrine and the lucid directness with which he expressed it. For example, he enters the great eighteenth-century debate on social contract; he rejects the notion that government is a compact between 'those who govern and those who are governed' as 'putting the effect before the cause', and asserts that initially.

> the *individuals themselves,* each in his own personal and sovereign right, *entered into a compact with each other* to produce a Government: and this is the only mode in which Governments have a right to arise, and the only principle on which they have a right to exist.
>
> (Everyman's edn., p. 47.)

Any government that, like the British, was the result of conquest and was founded on the power of a ruling caste and not on the free choice of the people, was *ipso facto* no true government. Paine will have no truck with Burkean arguments which start from the idea that man is the product of countless ages of human and political development; as in the above quotation he insists on beginning *ab initio,* 'when man came from the hand of his Maker. What was he then? Man. Man was his high and only title, and a higher cannot be given him' (p. 41). The argument is naïve but its persuasive force lies in its simplicity; only by its consequences does the reader recognise how deceptive and how rigorous is the apparent simplicity— man's essential equality is established, privileges claimed as a result of so-called noble descent or hereditary succession vanish, and it is an easy step to the assertion that sovereignty resides in the collective will of a nation (expressed by its freely elected representatives) and not in a single man who has come by chance to the position of king. From the same source springs the belief that 'Man is not the enemy of Man but through the medium of a false system of Government' (p. 137), or, as he expresses it in Part II of the **Rights of Man** (published 1792), 'man, were he not corrupted by Governments, is naturally the friend of man,

and human nature is not of itself vicious' (p. 210). From this premise, expressed with such disarming directness, there follows a conclusion of vast importance for an age of dynastic conflicts: wars are the means by which non-representative governments maintain their power and wealth. (There is little wonder that Horace Walpole was perturbed when 'vast numbers of Paine's pamphlet were distributed both to regiments and ships' on the second anniversary of the fall of the Bastille.) (*Letters,* ed. Lewis, XI, 314.)

Time and again Paine makes statements which appear commonplace in a context of political theory; they prove to be revolutionary in their implications.

> The duty of man . . . is plain and simple, and consists but of two points. His duty to God, which every man must feel; and with respect to his neighbour, to do as he would be done by (p. 44).

The assertion seems innocuous enought but, as in Swift's writings, only when the reader has swallowed the bait does he realise how firmly he is hooked. The duty to one's neighbour should be recognised by all men, by rulers as well as the ruled; Paine's reader then discovers that the moral injunction has become a means by which rulers are to be assessed and that those who act well according to this principle will be respected, those who do not will be despised; and finally, the last jerk on the hook, 'with regard to those to whom no power is delegated, but who assume it, the rational world can know nothing of them'. The logic by which this last position is reached is not unimpeachable but there is sufficient appearance of logic to obtain general acceptance of the conclusion from a quite impeccable premise.

There is no need to labour the point or to outline Paine's political philosophy in full detail; based on the French 'Declaration of the Rights of Man and of Citizens' (which Paine includes in translation), his own doctrine has the same clarity that marks the deceptive simplicity of that document. Furthermore it is reinforced by Paine's buoyant confidence: the 'system of principles as universal as truth and the existence of man' which had been operative in the revolutions of America and France would inevitably operate throughout Europe. It would, therefore, 'be an act of wisdom to anticipate their approach, and produce Revolutions by reason and accommodation, rather than commit them to the issue of convulsions'. This conclusion to Part I is matched by the equally confident finish to Part II with its allegory of the budding of trees in February:

> . . . though the vegetable sleep will continue longer on some trees and plants than on others, and though some of them may not *blossom* for

two or three years, all will be in leaf in the summer, except those which are *rotten*. What pace the political summer may keep with the natural, no human foresight can determine. It is, however, not difficult to perceive that the spring is begun.

The allegory is as simple as biblical parable, its message is clear and the experience it draws on is universal; moreover the writer has succeeded in detaching himself from his own powerful feelings and has embodied them in a vivid and concrete image which precisely conveys the desired sense of inevitability. Paine is indeed a conscious artist.

This conclusion so far lacks convincing evidence to support it but it is necessary to introduce it at an early stage. Paine was aware that he was doing something new in the art of political pamphleteering; the first part of the **Rights of Man** was intended to test 'the manner in which a work, written in a style of thinking and expression different to what had been customary in England, would be received' (p.143). Immediate reactions to the literary quality of the pamphlet were, of course, coloured by political prejudice, but they remain important for our purpose. For Horace Walpole Paine's style 'is so coarse, that you would think he meant to degrade the language as much as the government' (*Letters,* XI, 239); the Whig pamphleteer, Sir Brooke Boothby, considered Paine had 'the eloquence of a night-cellar' and found his book 'written in a kind of specious jargon, well enough calculated to impose upon the vulgar' (*Observations . . . on Mr. Paine's Rights of Man,* 1792, pp. 106n., 273-4); and *The Monthly Review,* to some extent sympathetic to Paine's politics (it found his principles 'just and right on the whole'), felt obliged to remark that his style

> is desultory, uncouth, and inelegant. His wit is coarse, and sometimes disgraced by wretched puns, and his language, though energetic, is awkward, ungrammatical, and often debased by vulgar phraseology. (May, 1791, p. 81.)

On the other hand, Fox is reported as saying of the **Rights of Man** that 'it seems as clear and simple as the first rule in arithmetic' (*Atlantic Monthly* (1859), IV, 694).

Both extremes are to some extent right. The book is 'clear' but it is also inelegant and occasionally ungrammatical; Paine can certainly be said to use 'vulgar phraseology'. Yet it was an effective piece of pamphleteering, it 'worked': T. J. Mathias, writing in 1797, observed that 'our peasantry now read the **Rights of Man** on mountains, and moors, and by the wayside' (*The Pursuits of Literature,* IV, ii); it handled serious and fundamental issues; and it provided a healthy counterblast to Burke. Moreover, it remains readable. The modern critic, then, finds himself in the position of having to accept that, given the urgency of the situation and the needs of the audience, Paine's effectiveness depended in part at least on his 'vulgarity'. Now 'vulgarity' in normal critical terminology is pejorative; it is the term used by a Boothby or an eighteenth century reviewer accustomed to aristocratic standards of accepted literary excellence; it is the term associated with the word 'mob' as Ian Watt has shown it to have been used in Augustan prose (Paper at the Third Clark Library Seminar, University of California, 1956); and it is, of course, still current. But when the term is applied to Paine and his style the pejorative is completely out of place; 'vulgar' is necessary as a critical word but it should be descriptive, meaning, not boorish or debased, but plain, of the people, *vulgus*. Reluctance to accept this view leads to an unnecessarily restrictive limitation on the scope of literary criticism; criticism then is in danger of forgetting the principle of the suitability of means to ends and of becoming confined for its standards to those works only which are considered fit for aesthetic 'contemplation'.

Admitting, therefore, that Paine's achievement in the **Rights of Man** has little to offer to the 'contemplative', what can the critic say about the vulgar style? Take for example a passage ironically described by Walpole as one of Paine's 'delicate paragraphs':

> It is easy to conceive, that a band of interested men, such as placemen, pensioners, lords of the bed-chamber, lords of the kitchen, lords of the necessary-house, and the Lord knows what else besides, can find as many reasons for Monarchy as their salaries, paid at the expense of the country, amount to (p. 113).

The humour is crude, decorum is absent, the alliteration is of the kind that occurs in agitated conversation, and the logic is questionable (for others besides sycophants can justify monarchy)—but what are the advantages of such a style? In the first place there is—here and throughout the book—a philosophical claim inherent in the language used: Paine is suggesting by his choice of idiom, tone, and rhythm, that the issues he is treating can and ought to be discussed in the language of common speech; that these issues have a direct bearing on man's ordinary existence—monarchy involves the citizen in heavy taxation for its support; and that they ought not to be reserved (as Burke's language implies they should) for language whose aura of biblical sanctity suggests that such issues are above the head of the common man. Paine's language, his 'vulgarity', is indeed part of his critical method; to use a colloquial idiom about issues which Burke treats with great solemnity and linguistic complexity at once goes some way towards establishing the points just mentioned. Secondly, of course, Paine's style gains in intelligibility and immediacy, and, as one result, his readers were provided with quotable phrases which would become part of their verbal armoury for use against the *status quo*. And, thirdly, there is a rombustious energy (such as Burke lacked) about this writing; it marks out the writer as a man of vigorous and healthy common sense. Paine, in fact, is creating an image of himself as one of the vulgar, using the language of the masses with just sufficient subtlety to induce their acceptance of his views. (His understanding of the importance of a persona is further illustrated and confirmed in the second part of the pamphlet where, for example, his sympathy with the economic circumstances of his poorer readers prompts him to remind them: 'my parents were not able to give me a shilling beyond what they gave me in education; and to do this they distressed themselves' (p. 234).) If one may accept Paine's own phraseology as describing his intended audience—'the farmer, the manufacturer, the merchant, the tradesman, and down through all the occupations of life to the common labourer' (p. 113)— then his is the kind of idiom to make a direct impact.

It is, moreover, all of a piece with Paine's criticism of Burke's language. More attention will be given to this matter later, but it might be observed here how frequently Paine selects a passage from the *Reflections* in order to point out the obscurity of Burke's meaning.

> As the wondering audience, whom Mr. Burke supposes himself talking to, may not understand all this learned jargon, I will undertake to be its interpreter (p.103).

Not only does this kind of remark cement the link between Paine and his unlearned reader, and give him an opportunity to score a witty point through the interpretation that follows, it also implies that the supporters of the *status quo* wrap up their sophistries in elevated obscurity. By translating Burke's language into the idiom of everyday Paine diminishes his opponent's stature and suggests that his seeming authority resides in the bombastic quality of his diction rather than in the validity of his argument. Paine, on the other hand, is seen to make his points in words that are readily understood; he does not have recourse (so he would have us believe) to any jargon, learned or unlearned, but uses vulgar speech, the language of common sense and common experience.

As his diction is of everyday, so Paine's imagery and allusions are drawn from the common stock. He claims, for instance, that by requiring wisdom as an attribute of kingship Burke has, 'to use a sailor's phrase . . . swabbed the deck' (p. 102); Court popularity, he says, 'sprang up like a mushroom in a night' (p. 116); a State-Church is 'a sort of mule-animal, capable only of destroying, and not of breeding up' (p. 67); or his famous comment that Burke 'pities the plumage, but forgets the dying bird' (p. 24). Immediately intelligible

as they are, such phrases also suggest (as do similar ones in Bunyan) the writer's nearness to and feeling for the life lived by his readers; he is using their phrases and thus implies his oneness with their political position. He is, furthermore, adding to the status of vulgar speech (as Wordsworth did in the first *Lyrical Ballads*) by showing its capacity for dealing with important issues at a fundamental level; Burke's language, on the other hand, suggests that these issues are the exclusive concern of men using a refined and aristocratic medium.

Similar remarks are prompted by Paine's limited use of literary allusion. Burke's adulation of chivalry is ridiculed by a reference to Quixote and the windmills (p. 22); the interrelation (for the French) between the fall of the Bastille and the fall of despotism is described as 'a compounded image . . . as figuratively united as Bunyan's Doubting Castle and Giant Despair' (p. 25); Burke's researches into antiquity are not rigorously pursued, Paine asserts, in case 'some robber or some Robin Hood should rise' and claim to be the origin of monarchy (p. 104); or again he enquires whether the 'metaphor' of the Crown operates 'like Fortunatus' wishing-cap, or Harlequin's wooden sword' (p. 112). Where Paine refers beyond what might be called folk literature (and *Don Quixote* had assumed this character in England), he requires little in the way of literary training: a reference to the 'Comedy of Errors' for example, is valuable only for what is invoked by the title itself; it does not depend for its effectiveness, as do some of Burke's Shakespearean allusions, on a knowledge of the play. The only literary knowledge on which Paine counts to any extent is a knowledge of the Bible and the Book of Common Prayer. He is confident that an allusion to the Israelites' struggle for freedom, through the mention of 'bondmen and bondwomen' (p. 72), will suggest an analogy with contemporary affairs; he clearly expects the language and rhythm of, 'our inquiries find a resting place, and our reason finds a home' (p. 41), to be evocative, and the Litany to be recalled by, 'From such principles, and such ignorance, Good Lord deliver the world' (p. 111). It is noticeable, too, that the only occasion on which irony depends on a literary allusion, a biblical reference is used. Having asserted that a love of aristocratic titles is childish, Paine goes on: 'A certain writer, of some antiquity, says: *"When I was a child, I thought as a child . . ."* ' (p. 59). The irony is, of course, directed at Burke's love of antiquity and precedents, but the interesting point is that Paine is attributing to the ordinary man the literary alertness to appreciate the irony. But, for the most part, Paine relies on the force of his facts and the arguments based on them, and thereafter only on his audience's response to the metaphorical use of language which demanded a minimum of literary awareness. The metaphors involved in the description of the Bastille as 'the high altar and castle of despotism' (p.

30) rely for their effect on political and religious prejudice; the claim that France had 'outgrown the baby-cloaths of *Count* and *Duke,* and breeched itself in manhood' (p. 59) requires none but normal experience to achieve its persuasive effect.

As in this last Paine frequently relies on metaphors which are rooted in popular experience. The experiments in aeronautics in the nine years preceding the publication of the **Rights of Man**—culminating in the Channel flight of Blanchard and Jeffries in 1785—probably account for the charge that Burke has 'mounted in the air like a balloon, to draw the eyes of the multitude from the ground they stand upon' (p. 53). This charge is reiterated elsewhere but here Paine gives it imaginative embodiment in a way that would have popular appeal. Again, Paine draws heavily on what Mr. Christopher Hill has called the 'Norman Yoke' tradition in English political literature, the theory that before 1066 the Anglo-Saxons were blessed with liberty and representative government, whereas the coming of the Normans meant the end of both and the establishment of oppressive monarchy and oligarchy.[1] The theory had been current since at least the sixteenth century, it gained new vitality in the writings of the Civil War period, it reappeared in Defoe and then, most vociferously, in Paine. When, therefore, Paine refers to 'the vassalage class of manners' (p. 72) that leads subjects to humble themselves in the presence of kings, or describes William the Conqueror as 'the son of a prostitute and the plunderer of the English Nation' (p. 104), he is writing within a popular tradition which would excite even the most unsophisticated among his readers. Their tendency to look back to a golden age before the advent of tyrannic government would be powerfully stimulated by allusions to this unhistorical but very emotive and widely-held theory. But the kind of popular experience most often exploited by Paine is the dramatic and theatrical. The century abounded with farces, ballad-operas, 'entertainments', pantomime, and such-like theatrical performances; he clearly felt able to rely on experience of them. As Gay had satirised the Walpole 'gang' on the stage, so Paine uses stage-terms in his prose effectively to convey his contempt for the court and aristocracy. The unnatural degradation of the masses results, he says, in bringing forward 'with greater glare, the puppet-show of State and Aristocracy' (p. 33); courtiers may despise the monarchy but 'they are in the condition of men who get their living by a show, and to whom the folly of that show is so familiar that they ridicule it' (p. 72); and the enigma of the identity of a monarch in 'a mixed government', when king, cabinet, and dominant parliamentary group are barely distinguishable, is described as 'this pantomimical contrivance' in which 'the parts help each other out in matters which neither of them singly would assume to act' (p. 132). Furthermore, we hear of 'the Pantomime of Hush', of Fortunatus and Harlequin (favourite characters of pan-

tomime), of the magic lanthorn, and so on. The achievement of this frame of reference is important. It obviously shows Paine drawing on experiences shared with his readers, and this is a significant factor in persuasion. It also allows him to ridicule the constitution Burke defends and generally to identify it as a mode of comic entertainment (since Paine's theatrical allusions are invariably used for the purpose of attack). Consequently the common reader is induced to regard the constitution in the same light and with the same insouciance as he viewed his kind of dramatic entertainment. Some humorous as well as some serious purpose is involved. And it is noteworthy that while Burke himself frequently refers to the drama in the *Reflections* his is a different purpose: it is more obviously to arouse the emotional fervour normally associated with serious drama and to suggest that the proper state of mind for observers of the French Revolution is that appropriate to watching a tragedy.

To recognise that Paine also conducts a great deal of his literary criticism of the *Reflections* in terms of dramatic criticism is to see that the concept of drama is more than simply a persuasive technique: it embodies something central in Paine's own thesis. In his 'Conclusion' he lays it down as an axiom that 'Reason and Ignorance, the opposite to each other, influence the great bulk of mankind' and that the government in any country is determined by whichever of these principles is dominant. Reason leads to government by election and representation, Ignorance to government by hereditary succession. Leaving aside the logic of this assertion it becomes plain that the axiom is organic with Paine's choice of literary methods and the nature of his attack on Burke. It may have been no more than fortuitous that what he felt to be a popular interest—theatrical entertainment—provided him with a key metaphor to focus his analysis of Burke's arguments and literary techniques; what is certain is that the essential business of drama—the imaginative interpretation of reality in terms of figures created to embody the dramatist's attitudes and values—perfectly focuses Paine's charges against Burke. (In this sense, for example, Burke 'created' the Marie Antoinette who appears in the *Reflections;* he did not present the woman from the world of fact.) Used as a metaphor, the drama draws attention to the dichotomy between reason and ignorance, or reality and appearance, life and art, fact and fiction—between, indeed, the position claimed by Paine and the one he attributed to Burke. This is the conflict with which, in some shape or another, Paine constantly faces his readers; his choice of metaphor by which to conduct the argument suggests insight of no ordinary kind.

Once this is grasped, the references to drama fall into place. Burke, says Paine, is 'not affected by the reality of distress touching his heart, but by the showy resemblance of it striking his imagination'; he 'degenerates into a composition of art'; and he chooses to present a hero or a heroine, 'a tragedy-victim expiring in show', rather than 'the real prisoner of misery' dying in jail (p. 24). Again, Burke makes 'a tragic scene' out of the executions following the fall of the Bastille; unlike Paine he does not relate the factual circumstances which gave rise to the event.

> As to the tragic paintings by which Mr. Burke has outraged his own imagination, and seeks to work upon that of his readers, they are very well calculated for theatrical representation, where facts are manufactured for the sake of show, and accommodated to produce, through the weakness of sympathy, a weeping effect. But Mr. Burke should recollect that he is writing History, and not *plays,* and that his readers will expect truth, and not the spouting rant of high-toned exclamation (p. 22).

> I cannot consider Mr. Burke's book in scarcely any other light than a dramatic performance; and he must, I think, have considered it in the same light himself, by the poetical liberties he has taken of omitting some facts, distorting others, and making the whole machinery bend to produce a stage effect. Of this kind is his account of the expedition to Versailles (p. 34).

These are statements at length of Paine's literary-political criticism of Burke; in them the clash between truth and fiction, reality and art, reason and imagination, concentrated by the metaphor of the drama, is evident enough. Proof of what is essentially the same approach occurs frequently elsewhere. Seen in this light Paine's frequent use of factual information takes on an extra significance. He charges Burke with focusing attention solely on the deleterious effects of the Revolution and of ignoring the facts which made it necessary and inevitable.

> It suits his purpose to exhibit the consequences without their causes. It is one of the arts of the drama to do so. If the crimes of men were exhibited with their sufferings, stage effect would sometimes be lost, and the audience would be inclined to approve where it was intended they should commiserate (p. 34).

Consequently when Paine provides factual details he is not only giving information to justify and propagate his own political attitudes; his intention is to confront 'art' with 'life' and to shatter what he considers is an imaginative façade; he is also attempting to dispel the ignorance which Burke fosters by his 'dramatic method' (as defined above) and which encourages the continued existence of despotic government. It is not necessary to labour any claim for Paine's accuracy as literary critic although it seems to me that his line of approach is sound. Burke merits comparison with a

dramatist; he concentrates attention on single human figures who embody attitudes and values he regards as important (or despicable); his narrative of events is essentially conducted by 'scenes'; he stresses human actions to convey the character of a political movement; he does, in a sense, make a tragic heroine out of Marie Antoinette, and so forth. Paine, on his side, is justified in trying to break down the splendid, tragic isolation with which Burke invests the Queen; he is equally shrewd in trying to shift the emphasis that Burke places on Louis as the personal object of revolutionary assault, on to an issue of principle. There is, then, substance in Paine's literary-critical approach; he shows perhaps more insight in this respect than many later critics of Burke; but what is chiefly important here is the way in which his literary criticism coheres with his larger political theory.

The corrolary to his critical onslaught on Burke is that Paine should show himself guided by reason, that his style—by its simplicity and lucidity—should mirror his emphasis on fact and common sense. He should, in other words, write the plain vulgar style in contrast to (what he would describe as) the refined and lofty obscurity of his opponent. If Burke 'confounds everything' (p. 47) by failing to make distinctions and refusing to define his terms, Paine should work by definition and clarity; if Burke's book is 'a pathless wilderness of rhapsodies' (p. 40), then Paine's should be well-ordered and comprehensible. If Paine's writing is found to possess these desired characteristics one's conclusion will not necessarily be that he is superior to Burke as a writer: one would conclude that his style and literary methods embody his political and moral values as effectively as Burke's quite different style and methods are an embodiment of his.

In part the shape of the ***Rights of Man*** is dictated by Paine's task: to refute the *Reflections*. He was compelled to take up separate claims advanced by his antagonist; where he felt it necessary he had to provide evidence omitted by Burke, as in his account of the Versailles incident or his review of the influences leading to the outbreak of the Revolution; and he had to argue his own political theory. The nature of his task led, then, to some disjointedness; he was determined to reason 'from minutiae to magnitude' (p. 53). Again, the presence of a 'Miscellaneous Chapter' may be urged as proof of disorderliness. There is, in fact, some truth in *The Monthly Review*'s charge of desultoriness in presentation. Yet there is a sense in which this had to be. Some roughness of style, the absence of refinement and decorum, an energy that mirrored a scarcely-controllable anger on behalf of the poor and unenfranchised—these things were signs of political good faith and honesty of purpose. From the nature of the theory argued in Paine's book, he had to eschew the literary methods associated with an aristocratic culture linked, in its turn, with the politics of the establishment. There is, then, a significant truth in Sir Brooke Boothby's sneering comment that Paine 'writes in defiance of grammar, as if syntax were an aristocratical invention' (*Observations,* p. 106n.).

Whatever one's final judgment on the mode of presentation, there is no doubt that Paine's writing is simple and lucid.

> There never did, there never will, and there never can exist a Parliament, or any description of men, or any generation of men, in any country, possessed of the right or the power of binding and controlling posterity to the *'end of time'* . . . (p 12).

> When we survey the wretched condition of Man under the monarchical and hereditary systems of Government, dragged from his home by one power, or driven by another, and impoverished by taxes more than by enemies, it becomes evident that those systems are bad, and that a general Revolution in the principle and construction of Governments is necessary (p. 134).

Writing such as this—and the examples are innumerable—has the merits of clarity, directness, energy, and the powerful conviction carried by the speaking voice. There is a balance about the phrasing which is not 'literary' but vulgar in the nonpejorative sense; it results from a determination to ensure the reader's agreement by insistent affirmation, the accumulation of facts, and the colloquial phrasing of an accomplished popular orator. Where Paine attempts the kind of 'literary' style that is Burke's province he fails utterly:

> In the declaratory exordium which prefaces the Declaration of Rights, we see the solemn and majestic spectacle of a Nation opening its commission, under the auspices of its Creator, to establish a Government; a scene so new, and so transcendently unequalled by anything in the European world, that the name of a Revolution is diminutive of its character, and it rises into a REGENERATION OF MAN (p. 99).

This is rhetoric of the worst kind; it is vague and rhapsodic, pretentious and inflated—it is, indeed, guilty of the faults with which Paine charges Burke. But it is not normal: the two examples previously quoted are more representative of Paine's general style. He is invariably concerned to place his views 'in a clearer light' (p. 46); to enable us 'to possess ourselves of a clear idea of what Government is, or ought to be' (p. 47); and to avoid any word 'which describes nothing' and consequently 'means nothing' (p. 60).

Paine obviously felt that an argument visibly divided into sections was necessary for his audience; his readers presumably required the kind of signposting denoted by phrases such as, 'I will here cease the comparison . . . and conclude this part of the subject', or,

'it is time to proceed to a new subject'. Occasionally he contrives to turn what is avowedly a transition into an opening for humour:

> Hitherto we have considered Aristocracy chiefly in one point of view. We have now to consider it in another. But whether we view it before or behind, or sideways, or any way else, domestically or publicly, it is still a monster (p. 62).

The use of clearly-defined stages is a pointer to Paine's understanding of the capacity of his readers. They required guidance and reassurance; they were not to lose themselves in 'a pathless wilderness'. Nor could Paine count on a willingness in his audience to follow a lengthy discussion of abstract theory—hence his use of anecdote, of plain narrative carefully punctuated with information about the passing of time ('He arrived at Versailles between ten and eleven at night', 'It was now about one in the morning', pp. 37-8), of snatches of conversation with an ordinary soldier or a plain-speaking American, of humorous interjections, and the like. Paine was, indeed, well aware of the necessity 'of relieving the fatigue of argument' (p. 57). And the constant use of facts, the frequent recourse to definition, the impress of personal authority and experience ('I wrote to [Burke] last winter from Paris, and gave him an account how prosperously matters were going on', p. 73), the enumeration of points established—in fact the general concreteness of reference recalling Defoe or the Swift of the *Drapier's Letters* is based on a thorough understanding of the needs of his audience.

When men are sore with the sense of oppressions, and menaced with the prospect of new ones, is the calmness of philosophy, or the palsy of insensibility to be looked for?' (p. 31). Paine's rhetorical question brings sharply into focus the difficulty posed by his kind of writing for the literary critic. By normal standards his writing must be rated low, and yet what has been said here should confirm his mastery of techniques appropriate to the occasion: if effective adaptation of means to ends be a test of literary merit, the ***Rights of Man*** passes the test. The urgency of the times, the seriousness of the issues, and the needs both literary and political of his readers all underline the value of the vulgar style such as he provided.

Notes

[1] See Christopher Hill, *Puritanism and Revolution* (1958), chapter 3, especially pp. 99-100.

R. R. Fennessy (essay date 1963)

SOURCE: "Paine Replies to Burke: *Rights of Man,*" in *Burke, Paine and the Rights of Man: A Difference of*

Political Opinion, Martinus Nijhoff, 1963, pp. 160-80.

[*In the following chapter from his book, Fennessy investigates the connection of Paine's* Rights of Man *to Edmund Burke's famous indictment of the French Revolution,* Reflections on the Revolution in France. *Overall, Fennessy describes Paine as, first, failing to understand Burke's work and, second, making many logical errors in his own.*]

Paine plans to write on the revolution

After writing his letter to Burke,[1] Paine stayed on in Paris, watching with approval the progress of the revolution. He now planned to take an active part in it himself, by some publication which, he hoped, would have an influence comparable to that of **Common Sense** in the American revolution. He was in close contact with Lafayette, who seems to have supplied him with materials for an account of the events of 1789. In January 1790 Lafayette wrote to Washington: "Common Sense is writing for you a brochure in which you will see a portion of my adventures. The result will be, I hope, happy for my country and for humanity."[2] This brochure was never published, but there can be little doubt that the material for it was incorporated in **Rights of Man,** Part I, which was, in fact, dedicated to George Washington.

Further evidence of Paine's desire to take part in revolutionary events is to be found in his letter to William Short in which he mentions a paper on French affairs which he had written and which he wished to have translated into French, and published in Paris as the work of a Frenchman.[3] Paine evidently wished to have a personal influence on the course of the revolution. In later years he did, indeed, regard himself as one of those responsible for it: "Of all those who began that Revolution," he wrote in 1802, "I am almost the only survivor."[4] The claim was unfounded; Paine had nothing to do with the beginning of the revolution, apart from his acquaintance with such men as Lafayette, Condorcet and Chastellux.[5] Certainly he did his best to improve that acquaintance: for example, by his repeated letters to Lafayette during the summer of 1790. Lafayette however did not reply.[6]

Either because of the coolness of his Paris friends or for some other reason, the paper on French affairs, like the brochure dedicated to Washington, was never published. Perhaps Paine was waiting for a suitable opportunity. He needed some occasion or pretext which would give him a starting-point, and also act as a stimulus. Burke's book would admirably fulfil these functions. Paine was still in Paris when, some 'weeks after writing to Burke, he heard of the latter's speech against the revolution, and of his intention to publish a public letter explaining and justifying his opinions.[7]

Paine let it be known to his friends, and to Burke himself, that he would reply to such a publication.[8]

Paine returned to London in April 1790, and the morning after his arrival hastened to the publisher and bookseller Debrett, for the news of Burke's expected publication.[9] He was told that Burke was still at work on it, revising and correcting so much that there were rumours he would never publish at all. In fact, *Reflections* did not appear until November. In the meantime Paine met Burke a number of times, apparently on friendly terms. There was, however, an explicit understanding between them that they should not discuss French affairs. "This agreement is very fair," wrote Paine, "because he knows that I intend to reply to his Book."[10]

Paine fails to understand Burke

At last the Book appeared, and Paine immediately set to work. He was now addressing the English public for the first time since the failure of his **Prospects of the Rubicon** in 1787; and the fact that he could now publish his opinions in the form of a reply to Burke certainly gained for them more publicity than they would otherwise have enjoyed. In his "Preface to the English Edition" Paine took care to stress his acquaintance with Burke, and thus contrived to place himself on the same level, and gain the attention of the public who were discussing Burke's book.

Paine was so eager to reply to Burke, and so full of confidence in his own ability to do so, that he did not bother to read *Reflections* carefully before beginning. He himself makes it clear that he had not read all of it when he started his answer—if indeed he ever did.[11] There is some excuse for this negligence: Paine must have found the book difficult going. If Burke's extempore rhetoric was frequently too recondite for the house of commons,[12] it is not to be wondered at that the carefully-constructed prose and subtle argument of *Reflections* was too much for Tom Paine. His puzzlement is obvious when he says "Mr Burke's language . . . continually recedes and presents itself at a distance before you . . . It is therefore difficult to reply to him."[13] He complains of "the disorderly cast of his genius," "pathless wilderness of rhapsodies," "mob of ideas tumbling over and destroying one another."[14] At best, Burke's ideas seem to Paine "paradoxical," by which he means that Burke undertakes to defend something that is obviously wrong or out of date, such as aristocracy, chivalry, or the union of church and state. The whole book is a "wild unsystematical display of paradoxical rhapsodies," a "general enigma."[15]

A particular example of Paine's inability to understand Burke may be found in one place where he undertakes to quote from *Reflections* and comment on the text:

"Ten years ago," says he, "I could have felicitated France on her having a Government, without inquiring what the nature of that Government was, or how it was administered." Is this the language of a rational man?[16]

It is certainly not the language of Burke, who had asked a rhetorical question "Ten years ago, *could I have felicitated France . . . ?*"[17] The misquotation is significant because it shows that Paine had missed the whole point of Burke's argument: this was to the effect that a country cannot be congratulated on its "liberty" until we know what kind of liberty it is, just as it cannot be congratulated on its "government," until we know what kind of government it is. Paine simply failed to see the point. And this is by no means the only instance where he failed to grasp Burke's meaning. As often as not, what he "refutes" is a mere travesty of Burke's position:

> He tells them, and he tells the world to come, that a certain body of men who existed a hundred years ago, made a law, and that there does not now exist in the Nation, nor ever will, nor ever can, a power to alter it.[18]

> The method that Mr Burke takes to prove that the people of England have no such rights . . . is of the same marvellous and monstrous kind . . . ; for his arguments are that the persons, or the generation of persons, in whom they did exist, are dead, and with them the right is dead also.[19]

Paine does not appear to be conscious of, and is certainly not deterred by, his own inability to understand his opponent. Indeed, when he comes to a passage that he thinks to be particularly obscure, he offers to interpret it for the reader. After quoting (again inaccurately) Burke's passage "The rights of men in governments are their advantages etc."[20] he continues:

> As the wondering audience, whom Mr Burke supposes himself talking to, may not understand all this learned jargon, I will undertake to be its interpreter. The meaning, then, good people, of all this is, That Government is governed by no principle whatever; that it can make evil good, or good evil, just as it pleases. In short, that Government is *arbitrary power*.[21]

Paine likes to attribute to himself the role of "Common Sense," exposing the pretentious and fallacious arguments of the high and mighty Burke for the benefit of the man in the street—of the "good people." And it seems to be part of his purpose to discredit Burke personally with that part of the public who might still consider him a "friend to mankind"[22] and an enemy of tyranny and oppression:

> He writes neither in the character of a Frenchmen nor an Englishman, but in the fawning character of that creature . . . a Courtier.[23]

> It is power, and not principles, that Mr Burke venerates.[24]

The issue, for Paine, is quite clear: Burke has taken sides with hereditary government, and therefore with "arbitrary power," and oppression, with wars and high taxes, and against the cause of rational government, representative assemblies, cheap and honest public administration, enlightenment and peace.

Why should a man like Burke, whose public career had hitherto been devoted to the cause of liberty, have thus gone over to the enemy? Paine does not scruple to repeat a particularly damaging rumour which had already been put into circulation by Burke's enemies:

> Mr Burke is labouring in vain to stop the progress of knowledge; and it comes with the worse grace from him, as there is a certain transaction known in the city which renders him suspected of being a pensioner in a fictitious name.[15]

Paine, then, does not think he needs to be particular about the means he uses to refute and discredit a man whom he believes to be insincere, a renegade, a paid government agent. Similarly he does not think Burke's arguments need to be taken seriously or carefully studied—Burke himself probably does not believe in them; there is no need to unravel the lengthy periods: they are constructed to mislead, not to enlighten. Furthermore, Burke is fighting a losing battle: the revolution which he attacks is already successful in France, and cannot be overthrown; and it is to be expected that the tide of enlightenment will continue to flow, and will reach England. The real purpose of *Rights of Man* is not to reply to Burke, but to enlighten the British public as *Common Sense* had enlightened the American public. Paine wanted to "get the ear of John Bull."[26] As he later explained to Jefferson, Burke's book "served me as a background to bring forward other subjects upon."[27]

These subjects were: Paine's interpretation of the French revolution, in terms of his own political theory, and especially the theory of rights; his rejection of the hereditary principle in government; his detestation of the British system of government, and of the British royal house; his belief in the inevitability of revolutionary change in England. Such are the themes that recur in the pages of *Rights of Man,* spiced with occasional derisive or contemptuous references to Burke.

Paine's interpretation of the French revolution

For Paine the revolution is above all a matter of *principle:* it is, quite simply, the substitution of a system of government based on right principles for a system based on wrong principles. His point of view is typically abstract and theoretical. Despite the fact that he lived in Paris during the last months of 1789 and the beginning of 1790, he makes no attempt to justify or explain the revolution in terms of the actual social and economic situation. Nowhere does he mention the industrial crisis, the poor harvests, the scarcity of bread; he has nothing to say about the *cahiers,* and their demand for far-reaching reforms; nothing about the effect of seigniorial rights and feudal obligations; nothing about the incidence of taxation. Paine was not concerned with such petty details: it was the system itself that was wrong: government based on heredity and aristocracy was bound to produce such evils. His scathing comment on Burke's romantic portrait of Marie Antoinette is well known: "He pities the plumage, but forgets the dying bird."[28] But the "dying bird" that Paine refers to is not the ordinary French worker, or peasant, or tradesman, but the prisoner in the Bastille, the victim of "arbitrary power."

Again, the revolution had to be a *complete* and *universal* change of the system of government. No partial reform would have been sufficient, because despotism had spread throughout the whole administration:

> The original hereditary despotism resident in the person of the king, divides and subdivides itself into a thousand shapes and forms . . . and against this species of despotism, proceeding on through an endless labyrinth of office . . . there is no mode of redress.[29]

The sweeping changes in France that had so astonished and alarmed Burke are thus simply and dogmatically explained. Burke's failure to understand merely goes to show that he is one of those men who

> are not qualified to judge of this Revolution. It takes in a field too vast for their views to explore, and proceeds with a mightiness of reason they cannot keep pace with.[30]

This insistence on "principle" enables Paine to get round a rather awkward point. **Rights of Man** was meant to be read in France as well as in England; and France was still a monarchy, and presumably loyal to its king. Paine's anti-monarchism therefore placed him in rather a delicate situation. Besides, he had no wish to criticize Louis XVI, who had given aid and comfort to the American revolution. He therefore insists that the revolution was not against Louis XVI personally, but against "the principle" of despotism. In his account of the events of July and August 1789, he tries to show that Louis was on the side of "the Nation," though he may have been deceived at times by his intriguing advisers:

> The King (who has since declared himself deceived . . . [31]
> The King, who, very different from the general class called by that name, is a man of good heart. . .[32]

> The King, who was not in the secret of this business . . . [33]

The necessity of being kind to Louis XVI must have been an embarrassment to Paine, who was much more at his ease when showing that all kings are fools and rogues. But he was quite sincere in his benevolent attitude to the French king: this he afterwards proved in the Convention, at considerable danger to himself.[34] However, he did not think, even in 1791, that the French monarchy was destined to last:

> In America it (i.e. Monarchy) is considered as an absurdity; and in France it has so far declined, that the goodness of the man, and the respect for his personal character, are the only things that preserve the appearance of its existence[35]

According to Paine's political theory, there is, of course, no place for a king in France or in any other country. The national assembly appears as the true representative of the nation, competent, and alone competent, to govern, and to fix the terms of the constitution. Strictly speaking, says Paine, the national assembly is "the *personal social compact.*"[36] By this he means that its members represent the nation considered in its original constitution-making character. It is as though all Frenchmen, feeling the need for a government, were met for the first time under "some convenient tree" to form one. It equivalently abolishes all history and all precedent, and gives the nation a fresh start.

The national assembly not only represents and embodies the French nation in its original character, it also represents the spirit of reason and enlightenment. It is prepared to ignore all existing institutions, all the accretions of time, all accumulated superstitions and privileges, in order to place government on a purely rational basis. Paine is apparently unconscious of any incongruity when he claims that he had done his best to explain all this to Burke, before the latter had committed himself against the revolution:

> I referred to the happy situation the National Assembly were placed in . . . Their station requires no artifice to support it, and can only be maintained by enlightening mankind . . . The National Assembly must throw open a magazine of light . . . In contemplating the French Constitution, we see in it a rational order of things.[37]

It followed that all those who opposed the national assembly were the enemies of a light and reason. Whereas for Burke, Paine and his friends were nothing but a small band of conspirators trying to gain control of the assembly so as to force their own ideas on it (a belief which must have been strengthened by Paine's letter), for Paine the only "conspiracy" was on the other side. It was the courtiers and their friends who were desperately conspiring and intriguing to prevent the triumph of light and reason. When the last of the nobility and higher clergy joined the assembly, this, says Paine,

> was only a cover to the machinations that were secretly going on . . . But in a few days time from this the plot unravelled itself.[38]

One of Paine's complaints against Burke is that he

> never speaks of plots *against* the Revolution; and it is from those plots that all the mischiefs have arisen.[39]

Paine possessed that characteristic attribute of the born revolutionary—the absolute and unwavering conviction of the rightness and legitimacy of his revolution from the first moment of its existence, and the absolute wrongness of all who oppose it, no matter what their position or public authority may be. Again and again he states the issue in terms of black and white: "The event was to be freedom or slavery";[40] "Accustomed to slavery themselves, they had no idea that Liberty was capable of such inspiration."[41] "They had a cause at stake, on which depended their freedom or their slavery."[42] In similar fashion Paine deals with the writers who had prepared French opinion for the revolution: they were those, like Montesquieu, Voltaire and Rousseau, in whose writings "the spirit of Liberty" appeared, even though they lived "under a despotic Government."[43] The French officers and soldiers who went to help the Americans in their war of independence were "placed in the school of Freedom, and learned the practice as well as the principles of it by heart."[44] It is precisely this assumption of virtue, and this use of abstract concepts like Liberty and reason to produce simplified statements of complex political problems, that Burke protested against in *Reflections*. But Paine is quite unaware even of the nature and import of the protest. As far as he is concerned, all Burke's book means is that Burke has gone over to the side of oppression, despotism, and slavery.

It would, however, be wrong to think that Paine repeated such words without having any idea of what he meant by them. His meaning was indeed a simplified one: but he thoroughly understood it, and kept it constantly in mind. Freedom meant living under a properly-constructed government, and enjoying the rights of man. Slavery was living under the wrong kind of government, that is, any government not purely representative. On these points the voice of nature and reason was as loud and clear to Paine as it was in the days when he wrote *Common Sense;* and, apart from some elaboration of the idea of rights, the message was the same.

Man and his rights

To establish man's rights, Paine has recourse to the "method of origins." Burke, he complains, has tried to limit the rights of the English nation by appealing to historical documents—"musty records and mouldy parchments."[45] But why does he not go back further? Why does he stop at a particular point, instead of going back to the very origin of man?

> If we proceed on, we shall at last come out right; we shall come to the time when man came from the hand of his Maker. What was he then? Man. Man was his high and only title . . . We are now got at the origin of man, and at the origin of his rights.[46]

In *Common Sense,* Paine had attributed the necessity of government to a lack of moral virtue, and had thereby implied that its purpose is merely to preserve order among men, and prevent the stronger from imposing on or exploiting the weaker. However, since his return to Europe, Paine had been thinking over the subject of rights, and discussing it with Jefferson and Lafayette, and this had led him to form a more positive view of the function of government.

He bases his reasoning on a distinction between natural and civil rights which he first explained in a letter to Jefferson written early in 1788:

> Suppose twenty persons, strangers to each other, to meet in a country not before inhabited. Each would be a Sovereign in his own natural right. His will would be his law, but his power, in many cases, inadequate to his rights; and the consequence would be that each might be exposed, not only to each other, but to the other nineteen . . .

It is worth noting that here "natural right" implies, in the first place, individual *will*. The individual is originally sovereign: he disposes of himself according to his own will, without any reference to others. In *Rights of Man* Paine modifies this slightly:

> Natural rights are those which appertain to man in right of his existence. Of this kind are all the intellectual rights, or rights of the mind, and also all those rights of acting as an individual for his own comfort and happiness, *which are not injurious to the natural rights of others.*[47]

No doubt remembering his own doctrine that men live in society before they live under civil government, Paine here introduces a moral limitation of individual rights: they must be exercised with due regard for the corresponding rights of others. But this appears to be a moral obligation governing the *use* of the right; the right itself is the power of self-determination by free will.

It is because the free self-determination of each individual (which he possesses "in right of his existence") may be in fact hindered by the presence and activity of other men, that he enters into a state of civil government with them; and this is the origin of civil rights: "Civil rights are those which appertain to man in right of his being a member of society."[48]

Paine's theory appears to be this: whatever the human individual can do for himself he has a natural right to do. For example, a man can walk, eat, think, clothe and protect himself. He has these powers from his Maker, and not from other men; or as Paine awkwardly puts it, he has them "in right of his existence." Therefore he can exercise them by his own authority, without permission from anybody else: they are in this sense his "right"—that is, his personal prerogative and privilege. The only limitation of these natural rights that Paine seems to admit is the moral one that each individual ought to respect the rights of others.

However, Paine notes that there are some things an individual may want to do

> in which, though the right is perfect in the individual, the power to execute them is a defective . . . A man, by natural right, has a right to judge in his own cause; and so far as the right of the mind is concerned, he never surrenders it. But what availeth it him to judge, if he has not power to redress?[49]

Though he does not say so, Paine is evidently here thinking of a limitation of individual power, arising from the presence or activity of other men. A man may judge that a certain thing is his property. His power to think so is perfect, and cannot be taken from him. But he may not be able to enforce his claim against other men. This then is the occasion for the formation of civil society, and the submission of men to a common rule. It is not very different from the "defect of moral virtue" mentioned in *Common Sense*.[50] The explanation in *Rights of Man* proceeds:

> He therefore deposits this right in the common stock of society, and takes the arm of society, or which he is a part, in preference and in addition to his own. Society *grants* him nothing. Every man is a proprietor on society, and draws on the capital as a matter of right.[51]

Paine does not see that he is using the word "right" in several different senses, or rather that he fails to give it any precise sense; and that his distinction between natural and civil rights is, in fact, based on a thorough muddle. His original "natural rights" in each individual are nothing more than the individual's *power of acting*

for his own benefit, which is conceived to be his "right," because he holds it independently of other men. But such a concept is, strictly speaking, inapplicable to the relationships between men in civil society, that is, living under a common rule. The common rule is necessarily a limitation of individual action, not an extension or enlargement of it: it cannot be based on, or derived from, the original individual "right" which it excludes or limits. Hence it is ridiculous to say that

> Every civil right grows out of a natural right; or, in other words, is a natural right exchanged.[52]

It is precisely this method of reasoning about rights that Burke criticized when he wrote:

> . . . how can any man claim under the conventions of civil society, rights which do not so much as suppose its existence? rights which are absolutely repugnant to it?[53]

But here as elsewhere Paine does not grasp the import of the criticism to which he is supposed to be replying.

Paine's theory of rights, however muddled it may be, nevertheless serves him as a basis for the explanation of the origin and purpose of government. The only legitimate form of government is that which arises when men, already living together in society, agree among themselves to set up a government, and to live under common rules in order to gain certain advantages; the most notable advantage being the exchange of their "defective" natural rights for effective civil rights.[54] In typical fashion, Paine finds that a firm grasp of this one clear idea makes it easy for him to interpret the contemporary political scene:

> In casting our eyes over the world, it is extremely easy to distinguish the Governments which have arisen out of society, or out of the social com-pact, from those which have not; but to place this in a clearer light than what a single glance may afford, it will be proper to take a review of the several sources from which Governments have arisen and on which they have been foun-ded.

> They may be all comprehended under three heads.

> First, *Superstition.*

> Secondly, *Power.*

> Thirdly, *The common interest of society and the common rights of man.*

> The first was a Government of Priestcraft, the second of Conquerors, and the third of Reason.[55]

Government by Superstition and by Power are dismissed in a few words:

> I become irritated at the attempt to govern mankind by force and fraud, as if they were all knaves and fools, and can scarcely avoid disgust at those who are thus imposed upon.[56]

The only form of government which does not arouse Paine's irritation and disgust is that which arises "out of society," that is, which arises when individuals come together "each in his own personal and sovereign right," and enter into a compact to form a government. "This is the only mode in which Governments have a right to arise."[57]

From a consideration of how governments *ought* to be formed Paine passes, perhaps unconsciously, to a statement of the nature of civil power, and propounds an extremely mechanistic theory:

> *Civil power properly considered as such is made up of the aggregate of that class of the natural rights of man, which becomes defective in the individual in point of power, and answers not his purpose, but when collected to a focus becomes competent to the purpose of every one.*[58]

Here again, Paine does not appear to be aware of any difficulty. He conceives natural rights as individual powers of self-determination, and yet he imagines that by being put together in "a focus," they are somehow transformed into a principle of government, which is the opposite of self-determination. He does not see anything gratuitous in his assertion that

> Society *grants* him nothing. Every man is a proprietor in society, and draws, on the capital as a matter of right.[59]

As though society were a joint banking account. He does not suspect that he may be involved in a contradiction when he says that each individual "takes the arm of society . . . *in preference,* and *in addition* to his own."[60]

A further function of Paine's theory of rights is to provide him with a principle by which he may limit and define the competence of legitimate government over its citizens:

> *The power produced from the aggregate of natural rights, imperfect in power in the individual, cannot be applied to invade the natural rights which are retained in the individual, and in which the power to execute is as perfect as the right itself.*[61]

Paine has thus secured an area of freedom for the individual living under government—an area of self-determination into which the civil authority may not legitimately enter. His theory thus fulfils the two purposes which were the aim of most eighteenth-century natural-right doctrines: to show that a government is not to be considered legitimate unless it arises from the consent, direct or indirect, of its citizens; and to establish a principle of limitation of the competence of rulers, especially in the domains of opinion, discussion, and religion.

There is another aspect of Paine's theory of rights, which was to become more prominent in the second part of **Rights of Man**. He has pictured society as somehow forming a "common stock." a capital on which the individual citizen is entitled to draw. He has said that government exists for "the common interest of society" as well as for the "common rights of Man." This suggests that the citizens may look to government for certain benefits, and in the second part of **Rights of Man,** Paine draws up a plan of such benefits, in which some commentators have seen an anticipation of the Welfare State. Here again, Paine is apparently unaware that this conception may be quite incompatible with his other idea that society consists of separate, self-sufficient individuals, each looking after himself, enjoying his individual rights, and merely looking to society for protection from the "defect of moral virtue" in others. However, this anomaly does not concern us here, since it has little to do with Paine's reply to Burke. This he continues with an attack on the British constitution, and in particular on the hereditary principle in government.

Paine's attack on the constitution of England

Legitimate governments can easily be recognized, from the fact that they are set up by a conscious act of their citizens, and therefore have a positive, indeed a written, constitution. Paine had no time for any implicit contract between ruler and ruled. The pooling of defective rights by which citizens set up government was a specific historical transaction, which would naturally be recorded in a document. A constitution is not an act of government, but an act of the citizens whereby they set up a government, and determine its organs, functions, and powers:

> It is the body of elements, to which you can refer, and quote article by article.[62]

The English constitution, therefore, of which Burke is so proud, is not a constitution at all. Where is it? Burke cannot produce it. He has promised to compare it with the French constitution, but has notably failed to do so. The English constitution, concludes Paine triumphantly, does not exist:

> Can, then, Mr Burke produce the English Constitution? If he cannot, we may fairly conclude

that though it has been so much talked about, no such thing as a Constitution exists, or ever did exist, and consequently that the people have yet a Constitution to form.[63]

America and France, on the contrary, can show their written constitutions, made by the people in their "original capacity," and "personal social compact," and therefore evidence that these governments have arisen in the proper way "out of society." By contrast, Paine criticizes the "ill construction of all old Governments in Europe, England included with the rest."[64]

The radical defect of the English system of government is that it did not arise "out of society," or from the people, but was imposed on them from above:

> The English Government is one of those which arose out of a conquest, and not out of society, and consequently it arose over the people; and though it has been much modified from the opportunity of circumstances since the time of William the Conqueror, the country has never yet regenerated itself, and is therefore without a Constitution.[65]

Rejection of the hereditary principle in government

The hereditary principle is the means by which governments based on conquest or superstitition are perpetuated. To show how wrong it is, Paine develops an argument which he had already outlined in ***Common Sense***. Since government can arise legitimately only from the coming together of citizens to set it up, and since this is their natural right, it follows that succeeding generations of men have the same right; in other words, they are not bound by the decisions of their predecessors unless they choose to assent to them. But the hereditary principle means that the form of government and the persons of the rulers are designated by a given generation of citizens, and imposed on their posterity. Posterity is thus deprived of its natural right to choose its own rulers and settle its form of government. Hereditary government is thus always indefensible in principle: it is fundamentally unjust.[66]

Secondly, hereditary government is inefficient. "Civil government," says Paine bluntly, "is republican government."[67] Monarchy and aristocracy are not part of the process of public administration, which can be carried on perfectly well without them. They merely mean superfluous pomp, courts, titles, undignified subservience, and above all, unnecessary public expense:

> It is easy to conceive that a band of interested men, such as placemen, pensioners, lords of the bed-chamber, lords of the kitchen, lords of the

necessary-house, and the Lord knows what besides, can find as many reasons for Monarchy as their salaries, paid at the expence of the country, amount to; but if I ask the farmer, the manufacturer, the merchant, the tradesman, and down through all the occupations of life to the common labourer, what service Monarchy is to him? he can give me no answer.[68]

Paine's opinion of kings is no higher than it was in 1776, nor, despite his respect for Louis XVI, is his language more flattering:

> If there existed a man so trancendently wise above all others, that his wisdom was necessary to instruct a Nation, some reason might be offered for Monarchy; but when we cast our eyes about a country, and observe how every part understands its own affairs; and when we look around the world, and see that of all men in it, the race of Kings are the most insignificant in capacity, our reason cannot fail to ask us—What are those men kept for?[69]

Together with monarchy, Paine rejects aristocracy. He ridicules titles of nobility as mere "nicknames"[70] because they do not correspond to any useful social function, and because they actually detract from human dignity, instead of adding to it, as they are erroneously supposed to do. The abolition of titles by the national assembly shows "the elevated mind" of France:

> France has not levelled, it has exalted. It has put down the dwarf, to set up the man. The punyism of a senseless word like *Duke* or *Earl* has ceased to please.[71]

Paine particularly criticizes the principle of primogeniture as unjust to younger children, an offence against Nature, and a cause of unnecessary public expense. "Establish family justice and Aristocracy falls."[72]

Aristocracy cannot be a good system of government, because, like monarchy, it presupposes that wisdom is inherited. "The idea of hereditary legislators is as inconsistent as that of hereditary judges . . . as absurd as an hereditary mathematician."[73] Aristocracy is fundamentally wrong because it is founded in conquest "and the base idea of man having property in man."[74] Finally, aristocracy tends to "degenerate the human species"[75] by constant inter-marriage between a small number of families. Paine's criticism is rounded off with an appeal to history and nature combined:

> Mr Burke talks of nobility; let him show what it is. The greatest characters the world have known have risen on the democratic floor. Aristocracy has not been able to keep a proportionate pace with Democracy. The artificial NOBLE shrinks into a dwarf before the NOBLE of Nature.[76]

Rejection of state religion

Besides defending the hereditary principle in government, Burke had been at pains to justify one other important feature of the English constitution: church establishment. Paine objects to the union of church and state on two grounds. First, it is a violation of the individual right of conscience. Religion is something between each man and his Maker:

> It is man bringing to his Maker the fruits of his *heart;* and though those fruits may differ from each other like the fruits of the earth, the grateful tribute of every one is accepted.[77]

Since the Creator is content with whatever worship the individual sees fit to offer, it is presumptuous of an earthly ruler to impose any particular form of worship:

> Who then are thou, vain dust and ashes! by whatever name thou art called, whether a King, a Bishop, a Church, or a State, a Parliament or anything else, that obtrudest thine insignificance between the soul of man and its maker? Mind thine own concerns.[78]

The second objection to church establishment is that it deforms religion itself. Religion is by its nature "kind and benign," but when it unites itself with the civil power it becomes "vicious, cruel, persecuting or immoral":

> Persecution is not an original feature in *any* religion; but it is always the strongly-marked feature of all law-religions, or religions established by law.[79]

The error is fortunately easy to correct: "Take away the law-establishment and every religion reassumes its original benignity." This has been done in America, with the happy result that there

> a Catholic priest is a good citizen, a good character, and a good neighbour; and Episcopalian minister is of the same description; and this proceeds, independently of the men, from there being no law establishment in America.[80]

The same desirable effect is to be expected in France, where the national assembly has followed the example of America and established "UNIVERSAL RIGHT OF CONSCIENCE."[81]

Criticism of the English financial system

Here again Paine endeavours to show that the French position is superior to the English. Before the revolution, the French government was insolvent, but the nation was not.[82] The present French government has restored public finances by reducing expenditure, and by selling, on behalf of the nation, the monastic and ecclesiastical landed estates which "the priesthood" had wrongly kept "for themselves."[83] As a result of the revolution, Paine confidently predicts, "the annual interest of the debt of France will be reduced at least six millions sterling."[84] By contrast Paine considers English finance to be thoroughly unsound. His criticism is based on two clear and simple ideas: first, that money is made of gold and silver, not of paper; second, that to be rich means to have a lot of money. With the aid of these propositions Paine shows that England is not only poorer than France, but is much poorer than she ought to be, given the extent of her commerce:

> Either, therefore, the commerce of England is unproductive of profit, or the gold and silver which it brings in leak continually away by unseen means . . . and it absence is supplied by paper.[85]

This account of the relative financial situation of France and England in 1791 is an extreme example of Paine's blindness to facts which did not fit in with his theories. English finance had in fact been placed on a sound basis by six years of careful administration and progressive reform by Pitt;[86] while French finance was still bedevilled by the chaos of the revenue and the inflationary effect of the issue of *assignats*.[87] Paine's economic ideas, however firmly held and confidently stated, have not been found entirely clear and consistent by subsequent commentators.[88] The discussion does not concern us here; it is in any case clear that the primary purpose of Paine's incursion into economics in ***Rights of Man*** is to show the excellence of the new system of government in France in contrast to the absurdities and abuses of the English system.

It may be remarked that Paine's attitude to the old regime in France is free from passion or resentment. To the French monarchy he is as polite as he can manage. He objects to the principle of aristocracy, but he shows none of that hatred of the nobles as a class which already animated such revolutionary leaders as Mirabeau and Robespierre, and even his friends Condorcet and Brissot;[89] nor does he share their dread of a counter-revolution, since he is quite confident that the revolution cannot be undone. Similarly, he shows no anticlericalism: no dislike or contempt for priests, prelates, or monks. Now that the property they wrongly held has been restored to the nation, and the pernicious principle of union of church and state abandoned, Paine believes that clerics will be useful, kind, and benign citizens.

It is only when he turns to his native country that Paine shows active personal dislike; and its object is the English crown and parliamentary system of government.

Attack on the English crown and parliamentary system of government

The English system of government, which Burke has tried to defend, is in Paine's eyes nothing more than a fraud, a gigantic imposition, which, however, is destined soon to be exposed, and rejected by the English nation.

The boasted English constitution is a fraud: it does not really exist at all:

> One member says this is constitution, and another says that is constitution—to-day it is one thing, tomorrow it is something else—while the maintaining the debate proves there is none.[90]

The English parliament is a fraud, because it does not truly represent the nation. The house of commons is elected by only a "small part of the Nation," while the house of lords is

> an hereditary Aristocracy, assuming and asserting indefeasible, irrevocable rights and authority, wholly independent of the Nation.[91]

The so-called "Mixed Government" of king, lords, and commons is a fraud, because in reality it is the Cabinet that governs, by means of corruption:

> What is supposed to be the King in a Mixed Government is the Cabinet; and as the Cabinet is always a part of the Parliament, and the members justifying in one character what they advise and act in another, a Mixed Government becomes a continual enigma; entailing upon a country, by the quantity of corruption necessary to solder the parts, the expence of supporting all the forms of Government at once.[92]

Above all, the crown itself is a fraud: it is a "*metaphor* shown at the Tower for sixpence."[93] The English monarchy, in Paine's view, serves no useful purpose whatever:

> After all, what is the metaphor called a Crown, or rather what is Monarchy? Is it a thing, or is it a name, or is it a fraud? Is it a "contrivance of human wisdom," or of human craft to obtain money from a Nation under specious pretences?[94]

The English monarchy is particularly contemptible because it was founded by "William of Normandy . . . the son of a prostitute and the plunderer of the English Nation,"[95] and because of the present royal family's connection with German despotism:

> A German Elector is in his electorate a despot; how then could it be expected that he should be

attached to principles of liberty in one country while his interest in another was to be supported by despotism? . . . The Dutchy of Mecklenburg, where the present Queen's family governs, is under the same wretched state of arbitrary power, and the people in slavish vassalage.[96]

Such passages leave little room for doubt about Paine's intention: it is to undermine the faith of the English people in their political institutions, so as to prepare the way for a radical change in the English system of government. He makes no secret of this belief that such a change must come about. The English nation, he says "runs in the line of being conquered, and it ought to rescue itself from this reproach."[97] The English people are not responsible for the present defects of their government,

> but, that sooner or later, it must come into their hands to undergo a constitutional reformation, is as certain as that the same thing has happened in France.[98]

Paine does not mean to incite his fellow-countrymen to rebellion: his aim is to enlighten them: to show them that they are living under a false and despotic system of government, and thus to create a body of public opinion in favour of the change which he believes to be inevitable, though he does not say how it is to be brought about. The final paragraphs of *Rights of Man* are a statement of this confidence, and a warning to "old governments" and their supporters not to stand in the way of progress:

> As it is not difficult to perceive, from the enlightened state of mankind, that hereditary Governments are verging to their decline, and that Revolutions on the broad basis of national sovereignty and Government by representation, are making their way in Europe, it would be an act of wisdom to anticipate their approach, and produce Revolutions by reason and accomodation, rather than commit them to the issue of convulsions.[99]

Conclusion

Our conclusions concerning the first part of *Rights of Man* may be summed up as follows:

First, so far as the French revolution is concerned, Paine's purpose is not so much to reply to Burke as to establish himself with the public as a revolutionary author. His account of the events of the summer and autumn of 1789, derived from Lafayette, was almost certainly written, or prepared, before Burke's book appeared. His interpretation of the revolution is in terms of his own political notions, scarcely changed since 1776. He shows little knowledge of the actual social and economic situation in France, or of the various interests and currents of opinion that influenced the course of events in 1789 and 1790.

Second, Paine does not understand Burke's arguments and ideas, much less refute them. He simply treats Burke as a political renegade, a man who has gone over to the opposition, for reasons which are probably discreditable.

Third, Paine intended **Rights of Man** to be an important political manifesto which would achieve in England what he believed **Common Sense** had achieved in America, that is, which would prepare public opinion for a revolutionary change of government.

Thus Paine, like Burke, addressed the English people on the issue of radical constitutional change. It remains for us to see what was the effect of their appeals on English opinion.

Notes

[1] Paine to Burke, 17 January 1790, Boulton, "An Unpublished Letter from Paine to Burke," 51-53.

[2] Lafayette to Washington, 12 January 1790; quoted Aldridge, *Man of Reason*, 126-127.

[3] *Ibid.*, 133. Short was the American *chargé d'affaires* in Paris.

[4] *To the Citizens of the United States, Letter I* (1802), Foner, *Complete Writings*, II, 909.

[5] For an account of Paine's friends and activities in Paris, see Aldridge, "Condorcet et Paine, leurs rapports intellectuels."

[6] Aldridge, *Man of Reason*, 132. . . .

[7] Aldridge, *Man of Reason*, 130.

[8] *Ibid.*, 130, 132; *Rights of Man* (Ev.), 143; *The Writings*, II, 394.

[9] Paine to [Unknown], 16 April 1790, Foner, *Complete Writings*, II, 1300.

[10] Aldridge, *Man of Reason*, 132.

[11] *Rights of Man* (Ev.), 23, note; *The Writings* II, 288, note.

[12] Hazlitt, *Complete Works*, XII, 266.

[13] *Rights of Man* (Ev.), 22; *The Writings*, II, 286.

[14] *Ibid.* (Ev.), 53, 40, 101; *The Writings*, II, 314, 302, 357.

[15] *Ibid.* (Ev.), 52, 128; *The Writings*, II, 313, 381.

[16] *Ibid.* (Ev.), 21; *The Writings*, II, 286.

[17] *Reflections* (Ev.), 6; *Works*, II, 282.

[18] *Rights of Man* (Ev.), 14; *The Writings*, II, 279.

[19] *Ibid.* (Ev.), 10-11; *The Writings*, II, 276.

[20] *Reflections* (Ev.), 59; *Works*, II, 335.

[21] *Rights of Man* (Ev.), 103; *The Writings*, II, 358-359.

[22] *Ibid.* (Ev.), 4; *The Writings*, II, 269.

[23] *Ibid.* (Ev.), 128; *The Writings*, II, 381.

[24] *Ibid.* (Ev.), 21; *The Writings*, II, 286.

[25] *Ibid.* (Ev.), 104-105; *The Writings*, II, 360. The accusation that Burke was a pensioner had already been made in Wollstonecraft, *A Vindication of the Rights of Men* (1790). . . .

[26] Paine to Hall, 25 November 1791, Foner, *Complete Writings*, II, 1322.

[27] Paine to Jefferson, 1 October 1800, Foner, *Complete Writings*, II, 1412.

[28] *Rights of Man* (Ev.), 24; *The Writings*, II, 288.

[29] *Ibid.* (Ev.), 20; *The Writings*, II, 285.

[30] *Ibid.* (Ev.), 20; *The Writings*, II, 284.

[31] *Ibid.* (Ev.), 90; *The Writings*, II, 347.

[32] *Ibid.* (Ev.), 89; *The Writings*, II, 346.

[33] *Ibid.* (Ev.), 92; *The Writings*, II, 349.

[34] See Aldridge, *Man of Reason*, 190-192.

[35] *Rights of Man* (Ev.), 112; *The Writings*, II, 366.

[36] *Ibid.* (Ev.), 49; *The Writings*, II, 311. . . .

[37] *Rights of Man* (Ev.), 73; *The Writings*, II, 332.

[38] *Ibid.* (Ev.), 92; *The Writings*, II, 349.

[39] *Ibid.* (Ev.), 34; *The Writings*, II, 297.

[40] *Ibid.* (Ev.), 27; *The Writings*, II, 291.

[41] *Ibid.* (Ev.), 28; *The Writings*, II, 292.

[42] *Ibid.* (Ev.), 29; *The Writings*, II, 293.

[43] *Ibid.* (Ev.), 75; *The Writings*, II, 333-334.

[44] *Ibid.* (Ev.), 76; *The Writings*, II, 335.

[45] *Ibid.* (Ev.), 17; *The Writings*, II, 282.

[46] *Ibid.* (Ev.), 41; *The Writings* II, 303. . . .

[47] *Rights of Man* (Ev.), 44; *The Writings*, II, 306. (Italics mine).

[48] *Ibid.*

[49] *Rights of Man* (Ev.), 45; *The Writings*, II, 307.

[50] *The Writings*, I, 70.

[51] *Rights of Man* (Ev.), 45; *The Writings*, II, 307.

[52] *Ibid.*

[53] *Reflections* (Ev.), 57; *Works*, II, 332. See above. . . .

[54] *Rights of Man* (Ev.), 46; *The Writings*, II, 308.

[55] *Ibid.* (Ev.), 46; *The Writings*, II, 308.

[56] *Ibid.* (Ev.), 47; *The Writings*, II, 308.

[57] *Ibid.* (Ev.), 47; *The Writings*, II, 309.

[58] *Ibid.* (Ev.), 45; *The Writings*, II, 307.

[59] *Ibid.*

[60] *Ibid.* (Italics mine).

[61] *Ibid.*

[62] *Ibid.* (Ev.), 48; *The Writings*, II, 310.

[63] *Ibid.* (Ev.), 48-49; *The Writings*, II, 310.

[64] *Ibid.* (Ev.), 33; *The Writings*, II, 296.

[65] *Ibid.* (Ev.), 49; *The Writings*, II, 310. . . .

[66] *Rights of Man* (Ev.), 109-111; *The Writings*, II, 364-366.

[67] *Ibid.* (Ev.), 113; *The Writings*, II, 367.

[68] *Ibid.* (Ev.), 113; *The Writings*, II, 368.

[69] *Ibid.* (Ev.), 112; *The Writings*, II, 367.

[70] *Ibid.* (Ev.), 59; *The Writings*, II, 319.

[71] *Ibid.* (Ev.), 59; *The Writings*, II, 320.

[72] *Ibid.* (Ev.), 61; *The Writings*, II, 321.

[73] *Ibid.* (Ev.), 62; *The Writings*, II, 322-323.

[74] *Ibid.* (Ev.), 63; *The Writings*, II, 323.

[75] *Ibid.* (Ev.), 63; *The Writings*, II, 323.

[76] *Ibid.*

[77] *Ibid.* (Ev.), 66; *The Writings*, II, 326.

[78] *Ibid.*

[79] *Ibid.* (Ev.), 68; *The Writings*, II, 327.

[80] *Ibid.* (Ev.), 68; *The Writings*, II, 327.

[81] *Ibid.* (Ev.), 68; *The Writings*, II, 328.

[82] *Ibid.* (Ev.), 126; *The Writings*, II, 379.

[83] *Ibid.* (Ev.), 127; *The Writings*, II, 380.

[84] *Ibid.*

[85] *Ibid.* (Ev.), 124; *The Writings*, II, 377-378.

[86] Watson, *The Reign of George III*, 283 *seq.*

[87] Thompson, *The French Revolution*, 176 *seq.*

[88] Dorfman, "The Economic Philosophy of Thomas Paine"; Penniman, "Thomas Paine—Democrat."

[89] Palmer, *The Age of the Democratic Revolution*, 470 *seq.*

[90] *Rights of Man* (Ev.), 119; *The Writings*, II, 373.

[91] *Ibid.* (Ev.), 118; *The Writings*, 11, 372.

[92] *Ibid.* (Ev.), 132; *The Writings*, II, 383-384.

[93] *Ibid.* (Ev.), 55; *The Writings*, II, 316.

[94] *Ibid.* (Ev.), 111; *The Writings*, II, 366.

[95] *Ibid.* (Ev.), 104; *The Writings*, II, 359.

[96] *Ibid.* (Ev.), 114-115; *The Writings*, II, 369.

[97] *Ibid.* (Ev.), 57; *The Writings*, II, 317.

[98] *Ibid.* (Ev.), 120; *The Writings*, II, 373-374.

[99] *Ibid.* (Ev.), 138; *The Writings*, II, 389.

Works Cited

Aldridge, A. O. "Condorcet et Paine, leurs rapports intellectuels." in: *Revue de littérature comparée*, (jan.-mars 1958), 47-65.

————. *Man of Reason. The Life of Thomas Paine*. London: Cresset Press, 1960. Short title: Aldridge, *Man of Reason*.

Burke, E. *Reflections on the French Revolution*. (Everyman's Library, 460) London: J. M. Dent & Sons, 1910. Short title: *Reflections* (Ev.).

Conway, M. D. (ed.) *The Writings of Thomas Paine*. Edited by Moncure Daniel Conway. 4 vols. New York: Putnam's Sons, 1894-1896. Short title: *The Writings*.

Dorfman, H. "The Economic Philosophy of Thomas Paine." in: *Political Science Quarterly*, LIII (Sept. 1938), 372-386.

Foner, P. S. (ed.) *The Complete Writings of Thomas Paine*. Edited by Philip S. Foner. 2 vols. New York: Citadel Press, 1945. Short title: Foner, *Complete Writings*.

Hazlitt, W. *The Complete Works of William Hazlitt*. Edited by P. P. Howe. London: J. M. Dent & Sons, 1931.

Paine, T. *The Rights of Man*. Introduction by G. J. Holyoake. (Everyman's Library, 718). London: J. M. Dent & Sons, 1906. Short title: *Rights of Man* (Ev.).

Palmer, R. R. *The Age of the Democratic Revolution. A Political History of Europe and America 1760-1800. The Challenge*. Princeton N. J.,: Princeton University Press, 1959.

Thompson, J. M. *The French Revolution*. Oxford: Basil Blackwell, 1955.

Watson, J. S. *The Reign of George III 1760-1815*. Oxford: Clarendon Press, 1960.

Wollstonecraft, M. *A Vindication of the Rights of Men, in a Letter to the Rt. Hon. Edmund Burke . . .* London: J. Johnson, 1790.

Evelyn J. Hinz (essay date 1972)

SOURCE: "The 'Reasonable' Style of Tom Paine," in *Queen's Quarterly*, Vol. 79, No. 2, Summer, 1972, pp. 231-41.

[*In the essay that follows, Hinz argues against the assumption that, because Paine declared his faith in reason alone, his works sought to convince via the laws of reason; Hinz contends quite the converse—that Paine employed many alogical strategies in his efforts to persuade readers.*]

"In the following pages I offer nothing more than simple facts, plain arguments, and common sense . . ." wrote Thomas Paine in the first of the trio of works—***Common Sense, The Rights of Man*** and ***The Age of Reason***—which has established his fame as the great American spokesman for democratic principles in thought, politics, and religion.[1] Political historians inform us that actually Paine's importance lay less in his ideas, which were common to the times, than in his role as a popularizer, in his "mastery of the art of popular persuasion".[2] What is curious is that in consequently assessing Paine's style literary critics have tended to accept his own explanation of his effectiveness. In his Introduction to *Thomas Paine*, Harry Hayden Clark, for example, organizes his discussion of Paine's practice by quoting his avowed stylistic principles, and then goes on to conclude: "Such were the literary theories which guided him in his literary practice, which enabled him to command the attention of more than half a million readers, vigorously stirring them to accept the political, religious, economic, and social doctrines that helped to call into being the American Republic and the French Republic, as well as many humanitarian movements of later days."[3] Without suggesting that such evaluations are inaccurate, I believe it is important to recognize that a good portion of Paine's writing will not bear the scrutiny of common sense, that much of his persuasiveness, consequently, must be explained as demagogic strategy rather than as the presentation of simple facts and the development of plain arguments. I have no desire to appear iconoclastic, but specifically in view of what has been called "The Resurgence of Thomas Paine",[4] and generally in view of recent romantic trends in revolution on the one hand, and of the populist structuring of so many contemporary political appeals on the other hand, an inquiry into the methods of a master propagandist may be timely.

Though each of Paine's three major works has a specific angle, their common subject—Paine's controlling thesis—may be summarized as follows: all men are born equal and with two kinds of natural rights, intellectual (the right to *reason* on all subjects) and civil (the right to act to promote one's physical happiness and well-being). Man's intellectual rights can never be given or taken away; his civil rights the individual may voluntarily surrender in terms of the social compact. The origin of government, therefore, and the continual source of its power comes from the people. But monarchy and its cultural affiliations, according to Paine, have usurped both of man's natural rights; tradition and superstition have put man's reason in bondage; monarchical political systems have taken away man's civil rights by convincing him—by way of divine right theory and hereditary kingship—that the power of government lies in the rulers rather than in the ruled. Whether his point is positive or negative, then, Paine's password is "reason", and it is therefore logical that he should announce "simple facts, plain arguments, and common sense" as his stylistic touchstones.

In practice, however, Paine's characteristic method is repeatedly to *invoke* common sense and repeatedly to *assert* that he is using plain reason. "It is repugnant to reason, to the universal order of things, to all examples from former ages, to suppose that this continent can long remain subject to any external power", he writes on the eve of the American Revolution (*CS,* 25); "The plain truth is, that the antiquity of English monarchy will not bear looking into" (*CS,* 16). "Mankind, as it appears to me, are always ripe enough to understand their true interest, provided it be presented clearly to their understanding, and that in a manner not to create suspicion by anything like self-design, nor to offend by assuming too much", he writes in the Dedication to *The Rights of Man* (166), employing at the same time as he subtly implies his rhetorical strategy. Similarly, in the Dedication to *The Age of Reason,* which title in itself is self-advertisement, he announces, "The most formidable weapon against errors of every kind is reason. I have never used any other, and I trust I never shall" (234). It is not that the passages preceding and following such declarations are necessarily illogical, but, generally, that assertion is not demonstration, and, specifically, that such protestations have the effect of making his appeal appear more rational than it really is. Commenting upon the secret of his success, a modern demagogue, Hitler, is supposed to have said that if you tell a big enough lie often enough the masses will believe you; according to Paine, "A single expression, boldly conceived and uttered, will sometimes put a whole company into their proper feelings, and a whole nation are acted upon in the same manner" (*RM,* 231).

The converse of Paine's emphasis upon the rationality of his approach is his habit of branding the theories of his opponents as irrational and illogical. If reason to him is the positive *ne plus ultra,* absurdity or an equivalent is the negative. The English constitution is "A mere absurdity!" for example: "There is something exceedingly ridiculous in the composition of monarchy; it first excludes a man from the means of information, yet impowers him to act in cases where the highest judgement is required. The state of a king shuts him off from the world, yet the business of a king requires him to know it thoroughly; wherefore the different parts, by unnaturally opposing and destroying each other, prove the whole character to be absurd and useless" (*CS,* 7-8). Edmund Burke's theory of hereditary rights can simply be labelled "nonsense,

for it deserves no better name" (*RM,* 136), while with respect to established Christianity, "It is an inconsistency scarcely possible to be credited that anything should exist, under the name of *religion,* that held it to be *irreligious* to study and contemplate the structure of the universe that God had made. But the fact is too well established to be denied" (*AR,* 272). As these examples demonstrate, Paine's technique is to present his opponents in a ridiculous light by drastically oversimplifying and restyling their principles and then rightly to conclude that the picture is absurd, and further the implication that he is a man of eminent common sense for having exposed it. "In England a king hath little more to do than to make war and give away places; which in plain terms is to impoverish the nation and set it together by the ears. A pretty business indeed for a man to be allowed eight hundred thousand sterling a year for, and worshipped in the bargain!" (*CS,* 18). Only the moral indignation and appeal to rationality make this description of royalty different from the discussions of monarchy and government in *The Adventures of Huckleberry Finn!*

"It is from our enemies that we often gain excellent maxims, and are frequently surprised into reason by their mistakes", observes Paine in *Common Sense* (42). It is therefore only poetically just that other of Paine's strategies can be formulated in terms of his attacks upon the discursive methods of his opponents. In *The Rights of Man,* for example, he writes that "it is difficult to answer [Burke's] book without apparently meeting him on the same ground" because "circumstances are put for arguments" (141). One of Paine's favourite techniques is to make analogy bear the burden of argument. As one would expect, considering that Paine is an eighteenth-century figure, most of his similes can be grouped under three headings—those drawn from human nature, those from natural science, and those from mechanical technology—and by the same token his use of such similes can in part be attributed to the enlightened belief that one Order manifested itself in all aspects of creation. Still, the nature of his arguments in this mode suggests enough demagogical craft to characterize the writer as a clever propagandist as much as straightforward Deist.

The design of the analogies drawn from human nature has the effect of making the reader feel personally involved in the political issue and morally obliged to credit Paine's interpretation. For example, by way of concluding the first section of *Common Sense,* and introducing the second, Paine writes: "An inquiry into the *constitutional errors* in the English form of government is at this time highly necessary; for as we are never in a proper position of doing justice to others while we continue under the influence of some leading partiality, so neither are we capable of doing it to ourselves while we remain fettered by any obstinate prejudice. And as a man who is attached to a prostitute is unfitted to choose or judge of a wife, so any prepossession in favour of a rotten constitution of government will disable us from discerning a good one" (*CS*, 9). Had the argument ended without analogy, the reader could have dismissed Paine's implications as biased politics; by ending with a recourse to morals, Paine blackmails the reader into hearing him out.

More insidious, because reliant upon sentimentality as well as morality, is his second use of a similar analogy in *Common Sense*. His argument now is no longer for consideration of the *errors* of the British system of government but for separation: "Ye that tell us of harmony and reconciliation, can ye restore to us the time that is past? Can ye give to prostitution its former innocence? Neither can ye reconcile Britain and America" (*CS*, 34). By virtue of such a presentation, the reader who believes in the possibility of reconciliation is cornered into defending his position by accepting an impossible and irrelevant moral challenge.

One of the favourite passages of those who admire Paine's literary flair is his analogy in *The Rights of Man* between the inevitability of political revolution and seasonal rebirth. According to James Boulton, "The Allegory is as simple as biblical parable, its message is clear and the experience it draws on is universal."[5] Granting this, one may still ask whether the analogy operates by providing additional evidence or by distracting the reader into the acceptance of a *non sequitur*:

> It is now towards the middle of February. Were I to take a turn into the country, the trees would present a leafless, wintery appearance. As people are apt to pluck twigs as they go along, I perhaps might do the same, and by chance might observe that a *single bud* on that twig had begun to swell. I should reason very unnaturally, or rather not reason at all, to suppose *this* was the *only* bud in England which had this appearance. Instead of deciding thus, I should instantly conclude that the same appearance was beginning or about to begin everywhere; and though the vegetable sleep will continue longer on some trees and plants than on others, and though some of them may not *blossom* for two or three years, all will be in leaf in the summer, except those which are *rotten*. What pace the political summer may keep with the natural, no human foresight can determine. It is, however, not difficult to perceive that spring is begun. (*RM*, 233)

It is, of course, the reader who substitutes revolution for spring in the conclusion, but he has been manipulated into doing so as a result of Paine's metaphorical identification in the penultimate line. "Political summer" is the agent by which the logic of the seasonal argument is brought to bear on a totally different subject.

In a similar way, Paine's argument for separation between America and England depends upon a false analogy and then upon the transference of the logic of the vehicle to that of the tenor. "Small islands not capable of protecting themselves are the proper objects for government to take under their care; but there is something absurd in supposing a continent to be perpetually governed by an island. In no instance hath nature made the satellite larger than its primary planet; and as England and America, with respect to each other, reverse the common order of nature, it is evident that they belong to different systems. England to Europe: America to itself" (*CS*, 26). To put the argument into syllogistic form is all one needs to do to highlight the rhetoric: In nature, the smaller does not rule the larger; England is smaller than America; therefore, it is unnatural for England to rule America. As in the former example, and in all of Paine's natural analogies, the effectiveness of the technique depends upon the reader attending to the logic of the isolated terms and discounting the appropriateness or logic of the analogy itself. Is the relationship between England and America simply one of physical magnitude? And what about relative populations?

Since Paine's technological analogies proceed according to similar rhetorical strategies, one example of the type should be sufficient. The best occurs in his attempt to prove that while in theory the English constitution grants parliament the power to check the king, in fact the monarch is all-powerful: "for as the greater weight will always carry up the less, and as all the wheels of a machine are put in motion by one, it only remains to know which power in the constitution has the most weight, for that will govern; and though the others, or a part of them, may clog, or check the rapidity of its motion, yet so long as they cannot stop it, their endeavours will be ineffectual; the first moving power will at last have its way, and what it wants in speed is supplied by time" (*CS*, 8). This certainly is a common-sensical description of mechanical principles, but it is hardly evidence that the king is a tyrant, although that is the conclusion it is designed to prove: "That the crown is this overbearing part in the English constitution needs not be mentioned, and that it derives its whole consequence merely from being the giver of places and pensions is self-evident; wherefore, though we have been wise enough to shut and lock a door against absolute monarchy, we at the same time have been foolish enough to put the crown in possession of the key" (*CS*, 8-9). In literature and poetry, analogy has the effect of awakening the reader to the possibilities of new realities; in politics and propaganda it may have the effect of blinding the reader to the actualities, first, by turning the reader's attention away from the issue at hand, and second, by creating the impression that real evidence has been offered.

A corollary to Paine's reliance upon analogy as argument is his use of what might be called the implied premise. On the subject of English-American relations, for example, he asks, "To bring the matter to one point, Is the power who is jealous of our prosperity, a proper power to govern us?" (*CS,* 28). Reason demands, even of a royalist, that a negative answer be given to the question thus phrased; as stated, that is, the question is one of general principles. But as Paine's answer indicates, the abstract question is a means to a very specific end: "Whoever says *No* to this question is an independent, for independency means no more than this, whether we shall make our own laws, or whether the king, the greatest enemy this continent hath, or can have, shall tell us, *There shall be no laws but such as I like*" (28). In saying *No,* in short, the reader is trapped into saying that the king is the enemy, because the seemingly abstract question is implicitly preceded by the proposition that England is jealous of American prosperity. Structured according to the same principle, but made doubly forceful by the explicit appeal to reason is the statement, "Common sense will tell us that the power which hath endeavoured to subdue us, is, of all others, the most improper to defend us" (*CS,* 37). What common sense, and Thomas Paine, have not told us, however, is that England has, in terms of Paine's definition, attempted to *subdue* America. It is ironical that in arguing against reconciliation in another instance, Paine should quote from John Milton, for the best precedent for his use of the implied premise is to be found in Satan's attempts to convince Eve of the jealousy of God in *Paradise Lost.*

The use of adjectival qualifications suggests a similar method of cornering the reader into an acceptance of his theories. In ***Common Sense,*** for example, Paine writes that "the good people of this country are grievously oppressed" by the power politics of England (3). By making "good" and "people" and "grievously" and "oppressed" mutually identical terms, Paine leaves the dissenter with no other choice but to announce himself as morally reprobate and unchristian, at the same time that he makes the assenter feel morally righteous and humanitarian because of his anti-aristocratic biases. Similarly, when Paine argues that "in a well-conditioned republic" (*RM,* 161) political chicanery is impossible because representation by definition makes for coordination rather than competition, one should consider how the qualification anticipates any logical objections the reader may have to the idea in general. It is like saying, "a good man cannot be bad" when what is demanded is proof that "men are good".

And if the use of one qualification silences objection, the use of two forces the reader into acceptance: "Of more worth is one honest man to society, and in the sight of God, than all the crowned ruffians that ever lived" (*CS,* 18). The statement appears as the conclusion to Paine's discussion of monarchy and heredity, and its purpose therefore is to assert that kings are, by nature, no better than ordinary men. But as it is presented, the implicitly neutral terms have been so qualified that it is no longer king and commoner but two very different things that are being contrasted: honest and crowned, man and ruffians, with the consequent implication that all common men are honest and all kings are ruffians, while the balancing of the "one" against "all" is designed to suggest both the oppression of the single man by the royal multitudes and the Tennysonian purity which enables him to have "the strength of ten".

"Before anything can be reasoned upon to a conclusion, certain facts, principles, or data, to reason from, must be established, admitted, or denied", writes Paine by way of introducing an attack upon Burke for his "contemptible opinion of mankind" (*RM,* 85 and 187); "He investigates nothing to its source, and therefore he confounds everything" (91). A better case of self-exposure would be hard to find. To explain, according to Paine man is not naturally depraved but on the contrary naturally altruistic. The cause of evil lies not in man Paine repeats and repeats: "man, were he not corrupted by governments, is naturally the friend of man . . . human nature is not of itself vicious" (*RM,* 222); "If we would delineate human nature with baseness of heart and hypocrisy of countenance that reflection would shudder at and humanity disown, it is kings, courts, and cabinets, that must sit for the portrait. Man, as he is naturally, with all his faults about him is not up to the character" (*RM,* 182). And this natural goodness, it is well to add, pertains, according to Paine, not—as the traditional explanation of the origin of evil would have it—merely to prelapsarian man but to all men, because in all respects all men are created equal (*CS,* 9, 13; *RM,* 86-87; *AR,* 251, 256). But whence then, one asks, does evil arise? A Deist, Paine will not even consider the Hesiodic suggestion that man's plight originates with the gods; and enlightened thinker, he rejects the reality of Satan; instead his answer is that evil comes from governments: "man, were he not corrupted by governments, is naturally the friend of man" (*RM,* 222). But where, one logically asks, does government come from? why do naturally good men suddenly become unnaturally evil? To answer this question, Paine resorts to what must be the funniest expedient on political record: "It could have been no difficult thing in the early and solitary ages of the world, while the chief employment of men was that of attending flocks and herds, for a banditti of ruffians to overrun a country, and lay it under contribution. Their power being thus established, the chief of the band contrived to lose the name of robber in that of monarch; and hence the origin of monarchy and kings" (*RM,* 181). After such a *tour de force,* it almost seems unkind to ask where the convenient banditti came from, and how honest men came to be ruffians in the first place.

It is less unkind, however, to point out Paine's willingness to contradict himself should the occasion demand it. We have been observing, for example, Paine's thesis that monarchical government and evil are alien to man and his natural goodness: "We must not confuse the peoples with their governments" (*RM,* 55). Yet when the issue is the origin of government and the consequent source of its power, the identity of man and government is presented as a *donnée* that only an imbecile would challenge: "If governments, as Mr. Burke asserts, are not founded on the rights of *man,* and are founded on *any rights* at all, they consequently must be founded on the rights of *something* that is not *man.* What, then, is that something?" (*RM,* 208). Before presenting Paine's answer to this carefully structured dilemma, it is profitable to mention that but a few pages earlier Paine had written with respect to an either-or statement by a contemporary, "Such a mode of reasoning on such a subject is inadmissible, because it finally amounts to an accusation of providence, as if she had left to man no other choice with respect to government than between two evils . . ." (*RM,* 186). Either, therefore, Paine is naturally absent-minded or masterfully politic when in answer to his restructuring of Burke's theories he writes, "Generally speaking, we know of no other creatures that inhabit the earth than man and beast; and in all cases where only two things offer themselves and one must be admitted, a negation proved on one amounts to an affirmative on the other, and therefore, Mr. Burke, by proving against the rights of *man,* proves in behalf of the *beast* . . ." (*RM,* 208). Here, by ridiculing Burke, in short, Paine argues that government does come from man. It is not, however, merely that in doing so he contradicts his earlier argument that people must not be confused with their governments, but that immediately following this attack on his opponent, Paine writes, "For want of a constitution in England to restrain and regulate the wild impulse of power, many of the laws are irrational and tyrannical, and the administration of them vague and problematical" (208). Such a statement, it should be obvious, would suggest that Burke's "contemptible opinion of mankind" is indeed nearer the truth than Paine's romantic one, for whence comes the "wild impulse"? On this note, it is also appropriate to point out that while Paine repeatedly argues that it is rights that must make for government, when the need arises he is quite willing to argue that might makes right: "for if they cannot conquer us they cannot govern us" (*CS,* 26), he says of England's right to rule America—an argument, incidentally, which is essentially comparable to Gulliver's comment upon his opponents: "As they were able to offer no resistance, so they could expect no mercy." And as in the case of his calling upon Milton, it is ironic that Paine has elsewhere enlisted Swift in his cause (*RM,* 216).

In *The Age of Reason,* Paine attacks the Christian theory of redemption as a commercial idea structured upon a quibble concerning the meaning of "to die", (251-57) and throughout *The Rights of Man* his characteristic method of condemning Burke's principles is to decry his style of writing as purposely deceptive. A final aspect of Paine's rhetoric is his own facility in this respect. Significantly, one of the best examples is his continual play on the multiple meanings of that key word in his platform, the word "right", and one of the best instances is in the Introduction to *Common Sense.* "Perhaps the sentiments contained in the following pages are not *yet* sufficiently fashionable to procure them general favour; a long habit of not thinking a thing *wrong* gives it a superficial appearance of being *right,* and raises at first a formidable outcry in defense of custom" (3). Here, clearly he is employing the term to imply both historical or factual accuracy and moral correctness or propriety. As he continues, right comes to mean in addition political power and also *propria persona:* "As a long and violent abuse of power is generally the means of calling the right of it in question . . . and as the king of England hath undertaken in his *own right* to support the parliament in what he calls *theirs,* and as the good people of this country are grievously oppressed by the combination, they have an undoubted privilege [right] to inquire into the pretensions of both, and equally to reject the usurpation of *either.*" The purpose of such word-play is obviously to establish the political issue as a moral, historical, and personal one so that on the one hand whosoever denies his theory of natural rights becomes a moral reprobate and a misguided political thinker, and so that the reader is disposed to be subjective in his reaction to the discussion, on the other. This being the case, one expects to hear, in *The Rights of Man,* that "the bill of rights is more properly a bill of wrongs and insults" (206).

The Introduction to *Common Sense* also introduces a second key word upon which Paine plays expedient variations: "The cause of America is, in a great measure, the cause of all mankind. Many circumstances have, and will arise, which are not local, but universal, and through which the principles of all lovers of mankind are affected, and in the event of which their affections are interested" (3). The appeal here is clearly to the altruism which throughout his writings Paine announces as a characterizing attribute of man. "Interested", therefore means simply involved, and, by reason of the context, emotionally concerned with the moral well-being of others. Yet, but a few pages later, we meet with a very different definition of interest: "We have boasted the protection of Great Britain without considering that her motive was *interest* not *attachment;* and that she did not protect us from *our enemies* on *our account,* but from her enemies on her own account, from those who had no quarrel with us on any *other account,* and who will always be our enemies on the *same account*" (*CS,* 20). Suddenly, interest has come to mean the opposite of altruism, has come to mean political advantage and commercial profit. Americans are called upon to despise such interestedness through an appeal to that very quality.

According to Vernon Parrington, "The amazing influence of **Common Sense** on a public opinion long befogged by legal quibble flowed from its direct and skillful appeal to material interests."[6] Better than many, Parrington has seized upon the basis of Paine's appeal, but not upon his method, which is to disguise personal and commercial motives as altruism and humanitarianism: "our duty to mankind at large, as well as to ourselves, instruct [sic] us to renounce the alliance: because any submission to, or dependence on, Great Britain, tends directly to involve this continent in European wars and quarrels, and set us at variance with nations who would otherwise seek our friendship, and against whom we have neither anger nor complaint. . . . 'Tis the true interest of America to steer clear of European connections, which she can never do while by her dependence she is made the makeweight in the scale of British politics" (*CS*, 22-23). Thus it is that once again Paine's tactic boomerangs, for what better description of his practice here is there than the following exposé of the art of his opponents: "and though the expressions be pleasantly arranged, yet when examined they appear idle and ambiguous; and it will always happen that the nicest construction that words are capable of, when applied to the description of something which either cannot exist or is too incomprehensible to be within the compass of description, will be words of sound only, and though they may amuse the ear, they cannot inform the mind" (*CS*, 8).

The purpose of this essay has been to suggest that Paine's style is better labelled demagogic than democratic, that his tactic is to invoke reason rather than to persuade through reason. To this end I have attempted to indicate his reliance upon assertion to create the impression of common sense, his propensity to dismiss his opponents as absurd, his tendency to substitute analogy for argument and to imply premises, his circular argument concerning the origin of evil and his expedient willingness to contradict himself, his habit of directing response through the use of qualifications, and finally his ambiguous and multi-levelled diction. Whether or not these techniques, in turn, account for the popular success of Paine's work, it can be safely said that in his drama of the Irish Rebellion, *Juno and the Paycock,* Sean O'Casey perfectly characterizes the best audience for Paine's work in his portrayal of the romantic Captain Boyle and his fairweather friend, Joxer Daly. Boyle has just announced to his buddy that he will no longer be imposed upon by his wife, Juno, to which Joxer replies:

> *Joxer.* Them sentiments does you credit, Captain; I don't like to say anything as between man an' wife, but I say as a butty, as a butty, Captain, that you've stuck it too long, an' that it's about time you showed a little spunk.

> "How can a man die betther than facin' fearful odds,
> "For th' ashes of his fathers an' the temples of his gods?"

> *Boyle.* She has her rights—ther's no one denyin' it, but haven't I me rights too?

> *Joxer.* Of course you have—the sacred rights o' man!

> *Boyle.* To-day, Joxer, there's goin' to be issued a proclamation be me, establishin' an independent Republic, an' Juno'll have to take an oath of allegiance.

If these domestic rebels have taken Paine too literally and subjectively, it is perhaps because it is in the nature of his style to make readers do so.

Notes

[1] Paine, *Common Sense,* in *Thomas Paine: Representative Selections.* With Introduction, Bibliography, and Notes by Harry Hayden Clark, Revised Edition (New York: Hill and Wang, 1961), p. 18. Henceforth all quotations from Paine will be from this readily accessible American Century Series Edition, and will be identified by page number in parenthesis, with the following abbreviations: *Common Sense* (*CS*); *The Rights of Man* (*RM*); *The Age of Reason* (*AR*). I am indebted to Frank H. Ellis for encouraging me to undertake this study; to John J. Teunissen for alerting me to the methods of demagogues; and finally to the Canada Council for providing the financial assistance that enabled me to research this subject and bring it to completion.

[2] C. E. Merriam, "The Political Theories of Thomas Paine," *Political Science Quarterly,* 14 (September 1899), 389-404.

[3] See also Clark's more detailed discussion, "Thomas Paine's Theories of Rhetoric," *Transaction of the Wisconsin Academy of Sciences, Arts, and Letters,* 28 (1933), 307-39.

[4] Richard Gimbel, "The Resurgence of Thomas Paine," *Proceedings of the American Antiquarian Society,* 69 (October 1959), 97-111.

[5] James T. Boulton, "Literature and Politics I. Tom Paine and the Vulgar Style," *EC,* 12 (January 1962), 21.

[6] Vernon Louis Parrington, *Main Currents in American Thought.* Vol. I: *1620-1800, The Colonial Mind* (New York: Harcourt, Brace and Company, 1954), p. 335.

Olivia Smith (essay date 1984)

SOURCE: "*Rights of Man* and Its Aftermath," in *The Politics of Language, 1791-1819*, Clarendon Press, 1984, pp. 35-67.

[*In this chapter from her landmark book* The Politics of Language, 1791-1819, *Smith uses a close reading of Paine's word choice and grammar in order to establish the significance of his impact on language and political thought.*]

> John Simple, speaking of his wife's stay-maker to Mr Worthy: 'He is one of the prettiest-spoken men in the world'.[1]

The publication of **Rights of Man** demonstrated that a language could be neither vulgar nor refined, neither primitive nor civilized. Such dichotomies of theory did not account for the possibility of an intellectual vernacular speaker, nor did literary values account for the possibility of an intellectual vernacular prose. Even a writer as bold and as experienced as Thomas Paine was somewhat constrained by conventions of language. Describing the reason for the interval between the two parts of his book, he states: 'I wished to know the manner in which a work, written in a style of thinking and expression different to what had been customary in England, would be received before I proceeded further.'[2] Other factors besides Paine's talent contributed to the possibility of his writing such a uniquely audacious book. Paine was not denounced as a vulgar author until he had written **Rights of Man**. The respect of such people as Edmund Burke and the Duke of Portland might well have increased his ability to disregard conventional standards. Also, Paine began writing in revolutionary America, a time and place where English concepts of language lacked a strong ideological hold. That he hesitated at all indicates the tenacity of concepts of language and suggests the greater difficulty of writers who remained in England.

Thomas Paine was hindered by literary convention but not by living within social relations which imposed limits to his abilities and interests, as were his English counterparts. Francis Place, for instance, described the financial necessity of disguising his inappropriate tendency to read. He carefully kept his library hidden because he lost valuable customers when they discovered he was 'bookish': 'Had these persons been told that I never read a book, that I was ignorant of every thing except my business, that I sotted in a public house, they would not have made the least objection to me.'[3] The most devastating aspect of eighteenth-century assessment of language was its philosophic justification of this notion of vulgarity. While criticizing the stultification resulting from a rigid class society, Paine simultaneously demonstrated that the limits it imposed were fictitious. He stressed the intellectual and moral capability of his audience and wrote in a language that was alleged not to exist, an intellectual vernacular prose.

Thomas Paine wrote the **Rights of Man** in reply to Edmund Burke's *Reflections on the Revolution in France,* and the two books stand in a curious relation. Generally, the *Reflections* was received with gratitude by the radical movement for bringing greater definitiveness to political ideas. John Thelwall (principal orator of the London Corresponding Society) claimed that he did not consciously hold a political position until he read the *Reflections*. Only then did he realize that he had previously believed in the frequently reiterated phrase 'the glorious and happy constitution' and that he believed in it no longer. Others, he reports, responded similarly to the book. Burke

> wrote the most raving and fantastical, sublime, and scurrilous, paltry and magnificent, and in every way most astonishing book ever sent into the world. A book, I will venture to say, which has made more democrats, among the thinking part of mankind, than all the works ever written in answer to it.[4]

Radical democratic clubs, such as the Norwich Society, praised Burke for initiating the great debate 'by which he has opened unto us the dawn of a glorious day'.[5] Fully describing a conservative viewpoint, Burke established a background which enabled others to recognize their own thought. Ideas which had previously been unformulated were now held consciously or disowned.

By writing about politics in an unusual manner, Burke made the radical position more capable of being articulated. Making political thought more conscious, in itself, makes it more expressible. This is the usual benefit of good discussion and both Thelwall and the Norwich Society were grateful for it. Also, Burke disregarded various literary conventions in the *Reflections* which hindered the development of an intellectual vernacular. He wrote in a manner that was recognized as both refined and vulgar. Philip Francis, who read the *Reflections* before publication, advised Burke not to publish it. It was too emotive, the language was too wide-ranging, it would serve the radical cause, and it would initiate a pamphlet war.[6] Reviews of the book concur with Francis's initial assessment. The *Monthly Review,* which has also been cited in the first chapter, was both awed and offended by the book. Burke's writing drew on an unfamiliarly wide range of metaphors, 'sublime and grovelling, gross and refined'.[7] Its vehemence, its disorder, and its disregard of elegance were the characteristics of his prose that did not accord with prevalent appraisals of the refined language. While reading the published and expanded version of the book, Francis sent further criticism to Burke:

Once for all, I wish you would let me teach you to write English. To me, who am to read every thing you write, it would be a great comfort, and to you no sort of disparagement. Why will you not allow Yourself to be persuaded, that polish is material to preservation?

(*The Correspondence,* p. 151)

Francis's confident tone derives from an authority that was fully supported by an intact and well-known literary code.

Burke held various ideas which disagreed with the basic tenets of language theory. He did not believe that the rationalism of Greek and Roman civilization constituted the most valuable strain of European culture. The inclusion of feeling in feudal modes of behaviour and government makes it superior to Greek and Roman forms:

> It is this ['the mixed system of sentiment and opinion'] which has given its character to modern Europe. It is this which has distinguished it under all its forms of government, and distinguished it to its advantage, from the states of Asia, and possibly from those states which flourished in the most brilliant periods of the antique world.[8]

Burke's idiosyncratic admiration of chivalry included a criticism of the late eighteenth-century's assessment of reason. By arguing against the Dissenters, Burke argued against an ideology which had a radical form, and which also held pervasive sway. The political stance of the *Reflections,* as Conor Cruise O'Brien explains it, was of a peculiar kind: 'These writings—which appear at first sight to be an integral defence of the established order—constitute in one of their aspects . . . a heavy blow against the established order in the country of Burke's birth, and against the dominant system of ideas in England itself' (Introduction to the *Reflections,* pp. 34-5). Burke's style is one means by which he both attacks and defends the established order. The frequency of such phrases as 'influenced by the inborn feelings of my nature' (p. 168), indicate the extent of Burke's disagreement with theorists who had isolated reason as an autonomous faculty. Burke's willingness to rely on experience, his assumption that emotions are not transitory and irrational but a valid component of thought, and his unwillingness to detach himself from the ordinary world by his diction are the eccentric characteristics of his prose. Burke attacked the Dissenters with a charge that, in fact, does not belong specifically to them but to anyone who concurred with the dominant theory of language: 'They despise experience as the wisdom of unlettered men' (p. 148).

Paradoxically, Burke disregarded literary conventions in order to maintain the status quo. Vulgar language appears in his book with full consciousness of its vulgarity, usually portraying the minimal sensibility that would prevail if the radicals were successful: 'The state ought not to be considered as nothing better than a partnership agreement in a trade of pepper and coffee, callico or tobacco, or some other such low concern' (p. 194). Such uses of language are effective because their recognizably vulgar vocabulary condemns the minds and morals of those who think in such terms. The alignment of intellectual and spiritual values with class affected by theorists of language allows Burke to insult the radicals by his choice of diction. What is unusual here, however, is Burke's distinctive notion of vulgarity. He employs vulgar terms to portray sensibility that relies only on reason—what was usually considered to be the greatest achievement of the refined languages. Burke's use of vulgar terms does not portray a plebeian and irrational mind, but the brutality of a mind that performs with only one faculty. Elsewhere Burke uses vulgar terms without the pointedness of his comment here. Whereas Philip Francis sarcastically apologizes for the 'elegant' phrase 'I *vow to God*' in his letter to Burke (*The Correspondence,* p. 87), Burke adopts the language of workers to convey his meaning more precisely. To do this without apology is extremely unusual: 'A politician, to do great things, looks for a *power,* what our workmen call a *purchase*' (p. 267). With a style that was recognizably deviant, Burke brought vulgar terms, arguments based on experience, and impassioned speech into political discourse. For Paine to break the same conventions for the purpose of disrupting traditional class alignments might have been more difficult to achieve without the unsettling of literary conventions performed by the *Reflections.*

Other contributing factors should be considered before we return to Burke. Paine's reading of French authors and his experience of revolutionary America provided him with a range of conventions that was foreign to English literature and English concepts of language. This externality was essential to his becoming an author and to his becoming the type of author he became. Although he was admired as a debater and had written an unpublished pamphlet while in England, his arrival in the United States brought aimless talents sharply into focus: 'It was the cause of America that made me an author'.[9] By the time of writing **Rights of Man,** Thomas Paine had already contributed to the development of an intellectual vernacular in the United States. Eric Foner points out that Paine's achievement with **Common Sense** is analogous to his achievement in England with the **Rights of Man**. With that pamphlet also he was the first pamphleteer to address a broadly-based audience with colloquial language and to articulate political ideas that had remained unexpressed.[10]

Paine's experience of a culture which was considering the political implications of a range of questions, including language, undoubtedly gave him a greater freedom from the restrictions on language use than was possible in England. The revolutionary movement was quick to recognize the importance of language. By 1789, Noah Webster had developed a critique of the class bias of English theories and practice of language. He argued that language had been distorted in the grammar texts in order to make it more closely resemble Latin and Greek, that the model of grammar should be the spoken tongue, and that English usage had been artificially constructed to maintain and perpetuate class distinctions. According to Webster, the cumulative effect of the works of Johnson, Lowth, Sheridan, and others was to hinder the process of speaking and writing:

> The general practice of a nation is not easily changed, and the only effect that an attempt to reform it can produce, is, to make *many* people doubtful, cautious, and consequently uneasy; to render a *few* ridiculous and pedantic by following nice criticism in the face of customary propriety; and to introduce a distinction between the learned and unlearned, which serves only to create difficulties for both.[11]

Although English ideas and concepts of language were present in America (Lindley Murray was American), they did not have the monolithic status which they had in England. There is no need to establish that Paine had read Webster's theory of language. His own writings had helped to create an intellectual vernacular, and his associates in the United States, Franklin and Jefferson for example, were skilled writers of vernacular prose. The literary training of William Cobbett and Joel Barlow in the States, as well as Thomas Paine, is not coincidental. One of the achievements of the radical movement in England, the extension of literature to an increasingly large portion of the population, was greatly furthered by the more flexible literary and linguistic traditions of the United States.

Paine recognized, however, that *Rights of Man* was a different type of project from *Common Sense* or *The Crisis*. These earlier works were shorter pieces written to argue specific positions. *Rights of Man* portrays a class structure and analyses its contribution to the survival of the English form of government. Paine's task in writing his book was to portray his full sense of that class structure, while also equalling the skills of Edmund Burke, who had an extensive education and was a respected member of the literati. The stylistic combat is an exciting component of the *Rights of Man* because Paine's ability represents the possible achievements of any member of his audience. In any situation, one of the pleasures of reading exceptionally good prose lies in discovering that the language can achieve more than one had imagined. To the early readers of Paine's book, this pleasure must have been especially strong due to the alleged incapacity of the language in which he wrote. Other replies to Burke, such as James Mackintosh's, refuted Burke's ideas, but they did not challenge the scope of the debate or alter the extent of possibilities. Thomas Paine, with more political acumen, understood that the problem presented by the *Reflections* lay equally in Burke's style and his definition of the audience. Thus, Paine had not only to write a political vernacular prose, as he had already done, but to write in a manner that would refute the political implications of the literary skills represented by Edmund Burke.

There is more fulness to Paine's writing in *Rights of Man* than that of *Common Sense* or *The Crisis,* and that may have been encouraged by the *Reflections*. A greater use of metaphor, a more vividly present narrator, and a keener awareness of his audience are the characteristics of Paine's prose that match Burke's use of himself as a narrative device, his broad range of images, and the frequent attention he pays to his readers. Paine seems to have augmented his own skills in the combined gesture of learning and retaliation. Although Burke's style is allusive and literary, and although he distrusted the vulgar populace intensely, he does not write in a language that scorns the vernacular. The *Reflections* was adapted for the emerging audience simply by the process of omitting certain passages.[12] Such writings as Mackintosh's *Vindiciae Gallicae* or Godwin's *Enquiry concerning Political Justice* could not be adapted without being extensively rewritten. If the book had been written by an author with a more conventional sense of the gentlemanly language, Paine could not have augmented his own skills in the process of rebuttal while also developing an intellectual vernacular. By disregarding restrictions on prose style, Burke enabled Paine both to meet Burke on his own ground and to write in a manner that was, in spite of the glimmering precedent, revolutionary.

Burke and Paine employ a personal narrator in distinct ways, but both of them convey to their readers a full sense of their personalities and rely on their skill in conveying themselves as the fundamental proof of their argument. Burke had accused the French and English radicals of being unfeeling, and he relied on portraying his sensitivity to support his argument. This accusation pervades Burke's writing sufficiently to require an answer. The balance Paine achieves between a response that is called for by the content of the *Reflections* and one that is called for by his democratic politics reveals how fully Paine had appraised his opponent and how consciously he employs his own style. To answer the charge of insensibility, Paine chooses to portray himself as a sensitive writer whose reasoning and emotions are unexceptional. By diminishing himself, Paine eventually builds up a clear and powerful portrayal of ordinary men. The Preface and the opening pages of the book contain the most explicit contrast between Paine and Burke. Paine's experience of the French Revolution and of having known Edmund Burke accord Paine some status, but he does not make so much of them that his political thought is portrayed as a result of his unusual life. Paine recognized the necessity of contrasting himself with Burke while concurrently not calling much attention to himself, for such a ploy would undermine the basic assumption of the prose style, that everyone's thought is adequate for political participation. Paine's narrative stance manages both to define himself clearly and to pay an unusual amount of attention to his readers. As a narrator, Paine is both intensely present and unusually self-abnegating. One of the means which enables Paine to manage such a paradoxical position, is to define himself not by direct portrayal, but by leaving readers to recognize the contrast between his characterization of Burke and the image Paine creates of himself by the style of his prose.

In *The Language of Politics,* J. T. Boulton describes the contrapuntal relationship of the two: 'If Burke "confounds everything" by failing to make distinctions and refusing to define his terms, Paine should work by definition and clarity; if Burke's book is a "pathless wilderness of rhapsodies" then Paine's should be well ordered and comprehensible.' (p. 146.) The difference exists in the formulation of Paine's sentences, as well as in the book's overall organization. The spaciousness and clarity of Paine's writing depend on the syntactical emphasis on the nouns and verbs. There are few adjectives and adverbs in Paine's prose. This conveys the sense that Paine's efforts are concentrated on fundamental issues. Setting a paragraph of the *Reflections* against the **Rights of Man** will clarify several of these points.

> Always acting as if in the presence of canonized forefathers, the spirit of freedom, leading in itself to misrule and excess, is tempered with an awful gravity. This idea of a liberal descent inspires us with a sense of habitual native dignity, which prevents that upstart insolence almost inevitably adhering to and disgracing those who are the first acquirers of any distinction. By this means our liberty becomes a noble freedom. It carries an imposing and majestic aspect. It has a pedigree and illustrating ancestors. It has its bearings and its ensigns armorial. (p. 121)

Burke's tendency to couple nouns and adjectives presents the impression that there is one way in which we are compelled to respond to things. It emphasizes appearance because our response is determined by publicly manifested attributes which are uncontestable. Verbs are hardly noticeable in this passage. They serve to augment the power of objects while they do not acknowledge the possibility of choice or action. In Paine's prose, nouns and verbs are rarely modified. In the passage below, Paine employs an unusual number of adjectives and adverbs while he describes Burke's concept of the crown. He presents his own view with a simpler sentence organization. Such a style places great emphasis on the nature of things and the consequences that follow.

> Mr Burke talks about what he calls an hereditary crown, as if it were some production of Nature; or as if, like Time, it had a power to operate, not only independently, but in spite of man; or as if it were a thing or a subject universally consented to. Alas! it has none of those properties, but is the reverse of them all. It is a thing in imagination, the propriety of which is more than doubted, and the legality of which in a few years will be denied. (ii. 363)

Such phrases as 'what he calls the hereditary crown' remind readers that the power of certain terms depends on the credence given to them and not on qualities inherent in the object itself. Paine treats monarchy, titles, aristocracy, mixed government, and the church and state as the products of social organization. Terms are defined, not according to an immutable identity, but according to how they came to exist and the bearing they have on 'the sphere of man's felicity' (ii. 320).

During Paine's trial for writing Part Two, the Attorney-General objected to Paine's discussion of the constitution, not only because Paine scorned the thing itself, but also because he thought of the word with too much historical specificity. While Paine discussed the constitution as an identifiable object which had been shaped by the historical process and the needs of various social groups, the Attorney-General presented it as an autonomous idea. The sense he conveyed of it, as changing according to its own life rather than human interference, was common to conservative pamphlets of the time. It 'has been growing,—not as Mr Paine would have you believe, from the Norman Conquest—but from time almost eternal,—impossible to trace' (*ST* [*State Trials: A Complete Collection of State Trials,* Compiled by William Cobbett and later by T. B. Howells, 34 vols.], xxii. 384). Behind their contrary interpretations lies an alteration in the word which had resulted from the American Revolution. In John Adams's *Answer to Pain's Rights of Man* (the Attorney-General relies on this work later in the trial), Adams also considers Paine's use of the word. To Paine's argument that England had no constitution, he replies:

> Of course there never was a people that had a constitution, previous to the year 1776. But the word with an idea affixed to it, had been in use, and commonly understood, for centuries before that period, and therefore Mr Pain must, to suit his purpose, alter its acceptations, and in the warmth of his zeal for revolutions, endeavour to bring about a revolution in language also.[13]

As well as reflecting a change in the word due to the American Revolution, the disagreement between Paine and the Attorney-General also pertains to their differing concepts of signification. Adams's sense that Paine's use of 'constitution' indicates a 'revolution in language also' was borne out by a recently published work on language. John Horne Tooke, an associate of Paine's and a fellow member of the London Constitutional Society, wrote the *Diversions of Purley,* a work which would refute conventional notions of abstract vocabulary. . . . . To consider 'constitution' as the Attorney-General does here, is to consider it within the framework of the late eighteenth century's concept of abstract ideas. 'Monarchy' and 'constitution' within such a scheme, had an eternal existence whose value was confirmed by their status as ideas 'COMMON TO MANY INDIVIDUALS; not only to Individuals which exist now, but which existed in ages past, and will exist in ages future' (Harris, p. 341). Paine had a sense of such terms as magical because their power as words disguised their historical identities. To give them credence is to be 'immured in the Bastille of a word' (ii. 320). By treating them as concrete nouns, Paine transforms them from permanently fixed ideas to objects which could be produced, altered or removed:

> A constitution is not a thing in name only, but in fact. It has not an ideal, but a real existence; and wherever it cannot be produced in a visible form, there is none. (ii. 309)

> By engendering the church with the state, a sort of mule-animal, capable only of destroying, and not of breeding up, is produced, called *the Church established by Law.* (ii. 327)

The shift in perspective that Paine performs in the **Rights of Man** made a tremendous difference. Words which had protected political institutions by the manner in which those words were considered were made vulnerable to 'a style of thinking and expression different to what had been customary'. More than any other discrete facet of his work, this one 'destroyed with one book century-old taboos'.[14]

Whereas Burke's diction and metaphors define his class allegiance and his aesthetic sensibility (in the passage cited, for example, Burke transforms the 'spirit of liberty' into 'bearings and ensigns armorial'), Paine's is non-individuating. His literary allusions refer to works that were generally read, such as *Pilgrim's Progress,* the Bible and *Don Quixote* (Boulton, *Language of Politics,* p. 141), and his vocabulary does not contain unusual words or words used idiosyncratically. Although Paine considers such words as 'monarchy' in an unusual way, he considers them with a strictly ordinary vocabulary. This gives readers the impression that his words derive from his ideas and not from an eccentric sensibility. Paradoxically, it confirms their faith in the independence of his thought, while confirming also that he is not very distinct from themselves.

Because Paine does not choose to discuss himself directly, his style of writing is the primary ground for substantiating the author's identity. To refute Burke's charge that radicals are unfeeling, Paine describes Burke as a man without compassion who is struck by his own aesthetic vision and not the actual event of human suffering. The portrayal of Burke's reasoning as 'strange and marvellous' (ii. 276) culminates in several pages wherein Paine attacks him with a metaphorical onslaught. The culmination of Paine's portrait of Burke is resounding—one of the moments in the text when Paine's words strike readers with the energy of a sudden and new idea of their own:

> It is painful to behold a man employing his talents to corrupt himself. Nature has been kinder to Mr Burke than he is to her. He is not affected by the reality of distress touching his heart, but by the showy resemblance of it striking his imagination. He pities the plumage, but forgets the dying bird. (ii. 288)

Here, Paine's portrayal of himself implied in his criticism of another and the confirmation of this portrayal in his language, are well co-ordinated. Paine presents his response to Burke as if everyone would have the discernment and the kindness to respond in the same way. His reaction is grounded in general truth, and his compassion, by the parallel construction of the first two sentences, shares in the qualities and scope of nature's kindness.

The structured appearance of these sentences is a general feature of Paine's prose. Two sentences of equal length are followed by a sentence twice as long divided into two equal parts. The three sentences are summarized by a short sentence divided into two unusually short phrases. The symmetry is pleasing in itself, and, at its best, the expanding and contracting syntax provides for a changing rhythm that marks the pace of Paine's thought. In this instance, the general statement and the specific case are of the same length. A sentence twice as long establishes the contrast between them, and the short phrases of the third appear with a quickness that is designed to imitate the imagination. In another instance, previously cited, a short phrase presents a fact, while the two following phrases, of approximately similar length, describe two results occurring at different times: 'It [the crown] is a thing in imagination, the propriety of which is more than doubted, and the legality of which in a few years will be denied.' The syntax implies that every thought is in its correct place, receiving due weight and completed to the end of its course. Paine's presentation of untraditional and disruptive ideas was muted by their appearance in a grammatical background of order and symmetry. The writer appears more as someone who is fulfilling the form of his sentences than as someone expressing extremely unusual opinions.

Further, the structured syntax heightens the vernacular rhythm of the prose. Paine, in an unusual manner, brings formality and colloquialism together to serve each other's purpose. The syntax conveys the informality of speech rhythm and the traditional eighteenth-century values of balance, order and logic:

> The circumstances of the world are continually changing, and the opinions of men change also; and as Government is for the living, and not for the dead, it is the living only that has any right to it. That which may be thought right and found convenient in one age may be thought wrong and found inconvenient in another. In such cases, Who is to decide, the living or the dead? (ii. 281)

The interplay of the vernacular diction and the formal syntax is more reminiscent of Augustan poetry ('Absalom and Achitophel' or *The Dunciad,* for example) than of late eighteenth-century prose, as are other characteristics of Paine's style; the brevity and self-containment of his sentences, a tendency to present ideas in two parts of similar length, and the accentuated rhythm. At times Paine comes strikingly close to the couplet form by concluding two parallel phrases with words, which although they do not rhyme are closely related to each other by their meaning: 'He pities the plumage, but forgets the dying bird'; 'Our enquiries find a resting place, and our reason finds a home' (ii. 304). To bring formal syntax and vernacular diction together as successfully as Paine does implies that the attributes of syntactical order are inherently compatible with the spoken language, when formal syntax was widely held to distinguish vulgar from refined usage.

To return to the 'dying bird' passage, the concluding image is all the more effective because it is contained within an extremely balanced framework. Syntactical expertise was an eighteenth-century skill. In the Preface to his *Dictionary,* the fullness of Johnson's emotions struggles against the confines of his syntax, and the tension between the two is moving. Here the order of the syntactical arrangement does not prepare the readers for the sudden extension of meaning. The tension lies between the intellectual excitement experienced by the readers and the denial of it by the syntax. Paine's ability to perceive beyond appearances is portrayed in an image that simultaneously confirms Burke's cruelty to nature. So much meaning in a four-word phrase provokes an experience of totality when the readers expect the addition of another part.

Paine's criticism of Burke for being a spectator of his own prose contrasts with the casualness of Paine's relation to his own images. As in the 'dying bird' passage, Paine usually disregards his own images while the readers are surprised by them. This is another facet of his self-abnegation as an author for it implies that such skills are unexceptional. It also confirms Paine's refusal to be distracted and his continuing with a steady pace to concentrate on fundamental issues. In one instance, however, Paine pulls back and responds to his own writing. After describing how the 'wondering cheated multitude' was duped by the fusion of the church and state he reacts to the phrase:

> When I contemplate the natural dignity of man, when I feel (for Nature had not been kind enough to me to blunt my feelings) for the honour and happiness of its character, I become irritated at the attempt to govern mankind by force and fraud, as if they were all knaves and fools, and can scarcely avoid disgust at those who are thus imposed upon. (ii. 308)

Paine does not appear as a first-person narrator without special occasion. He usually does so to convey information that his readers would not share, such as his first-hand knowledge of events in France, or, as here, to portray his own reaction. The parenthetical phrase is one of the many instances when Paine can strike off repercussive ideas in the readers with a short and seemingly inadvertent phrase. In contrast to the imaginative basis of Burke's hysteria, Paine grounds his emotions in nature and contemplation. His feelings are shown to be a part of his thought, some of which he trusts and others of which he disciplines.

Paine makes the difference between his and Burke's style important by using them as a means of contrasting two political systems. Burke's style embodies methods of the state, for both he and tyrannical governments reduce the population to passive spectators of a theatrical show. Paine's theatre images are effective because they flexibly combine various components of his argument. His incorporation of a public audience points out that Burke ignored an essential factor of his own imagery—the audience, which is the body politic. Again, the extent of Burke's vision is shown to be near-sighted. By referring to less élitist forms of theatre, Paine's imagery is applicable to the experience of a larger reading audience (Boulton, *Language of Politics,* 143). Finally, Paine adapts an aesthetic image into a political one. Burke's theatre portrayed his response to events in France, especially as he compared the downfall of the Queen to viewing a Greek tragedy. Paine employs the same image to define the political relation between suppressive governments and the oppressed population: 'A vast mass of mankind are degradedly thrown into the back-ground of the human picture, to bring forward, with greater glare, the puppet-show of state and aristocracy' (ii. 296). Paine deflates the grandeur of Burke's scenario by altering Burke's image. By combining many aspects of his argument into an image—one which always contrasts with nature—their interrelation in the exposition also has an imaginative life. The theatre imagery provides a basis for Paine to manoeuvre, with great agility, around his portrait of the state.

Paine equates Burke's style and methods of the state both imaginatively and by discussing political variations in the customs of language use. Paine admires La Fayette's prose for directing attention to the living and for provoking thought with 'clear, concise, and soul-animating sentiments' (ii. 282). Elsewhere, he expresses admiration for Rousseau and Abbé Raynal for a 'loveliness of sentiment in favor of liberty, that excites respect, and elevates the human faculties' (ii. 334). The elected representatives of the National Assembly speak in a style that reflects the dignity of their status as representatives:

> They have not to hold out a language which they do not themselves believe, for the fraudulent purpose of making others believe it. Their station requires no artifice to support it, and can only be maintained by enlightening mankind. It is not their interest to cherish ignorance, but to dispel it. They are not in the case of a ministerial or an opposition party in England, who, though they are opposed, are still united to keep up the common mystery. (ii. 332)

The language of Parliament is corrupted both by its origins and by the manner of elections. Members of the House of Commons must ask the King's permission to speak, and the King refers to both Houses as 'my parliament' (ii. 330). Such a practice reflects the origin of the Houses in a grant from the crown. Paine maintains that English political language is a remnant of the Norman Conquest, for it reminds the speakers of their subjection.

> That this vassalage idea and style of speaking was not got rid of even at the Revolution of 1688, is evident from the declaration of Parliament to William and Mary in these words: 'We do most humbly and faithfully *submit* ourselves, our heirs and posterities, for ever.' Submission is wholly a vassalage term, repugnant to the dignity of freedom, and an echo of the language used at the Conquest. (ii. 331)

Generally too much an internationalist to stress the belief that English liberty was based on the more democratic forms of Anglo-Saxon government, Paine apparently believed a linguistic version of the Norman yoke myth. A specific language was brought to England during the Conquest which supported alien and authoritative forms. Language usage is creative in Paine's view in the sense that it defines and perpetuates political relations. Changing the style of language is a means of political and moral reformation. The aim of Paine's writing is similar to his description of the task of the National Assembly: 'The National Assembly must throw open a magazine of light. It must show man the proper character of man; and the nearer it can bring him to that standard, the stronger the National Assembly becomes.' (ii. 332.)

Paine's narrative stance performs an analogous gesture: while disregarding his own position as the author, Paine focuses an intense degree of attention on to his readers. His own thought—the actuality of having conceived and expressed his own ideas—is frequently denied. His thoughts appear in terms of speaking the obvious and the commonplace or recognizing the impossible and the absurd:

> There never did, there never will, and there never can, exist a Parliament, or any description of men, or any generation of men, in any country, possessed of the right or the power of binding and controuling posterity to the *'end of time'*. (ii. 277)

> A greater absurdity cannot present itself to the understanding of man than what Mr Burke offers to his readers. (ii. 279)

> The weaker any cord is, the less it will bear to be stretched, and the worse is the policy to stretch it. (ii. 280)

Such presentations rapidly build up the readers' sense that there exists a public understanding that is intellectually adroit and competent to deal with political questions. The style of Paine's prose foregoes the necessity of having to establish this point by replacing a contentious idea with a self-evident assumption maintained by the manner of introducing other ideas. Surprisingly, Paine never explicitly states in the ***Rights of Man*** that people are generally intelligent enough to merit participating in government. A pamphlet of 1782, written by Sir William Jones, reveals the difficulty of politely convincing the populace that they are intelligent without inadvertently stressing the distance between social classes:

> *Peasant:* Why should humble men, like me, sign or set marks to petitions of this nature? It is better for us peasants to mind our husbandry, and leave what we cannot comprehend to the King and Parliament.

> *Scholar:* You can comprehend more than you imagine; and, as *a free member of a free state,* have higher things to mind than you may conceive.[15]

(Sir William Jones, later to become the famous linguist, was a member of the London Constitutional Society, as were Thomas Paine and John Horne Tooke.) Paine's style is more gracious. He compels his readers to be aware that they are thinkers and that their ability to think is powerful:

> We have now, in a few words, traced man from a natural individual to a member of society. (ii. 307)

> In casting our eyes over the world, it is extremely easy to distinguish . . . (ii. 308)

By frequent use of rhetorical questions and frequent reference to an understanding shared between himself and the readers, Paine brings his readers into the book. 'I' and 'we' become two identities which share a relation and various activities. The signposts (as J. T. Boulton describes such statements as those cited above, p. 119) that indicate the progress of the argument serve more than the function of ordering Paine's ideas. They show Paine to be a skilled and conscious craftsman who knows what needs to be done at which point: 'To possess ourselves of a clear idea of what government is, or ought to be, we must trace its origin' (ii. 309). He reveals explicitly the progress of his argument in order to show how it is done and to remind readers of what has been accomplished. Tasks are designated and achieved with skilful ease. The signposts elucidate the process of thought and make thinking a conscious process by commenting upon the process as the readers are engaged in it. They give to the readers a keen, and at times exhilarating, sense of the 'mightiness of reason' (ii. 284).

The signposts convey a sense of progress and intimacy by disrupting the distinction between writers and readers. By using the present tense and the pronoun 'we', Paine presents the illusion that he and the readers share the activity of constructing an argument. At times, Paine dramatically breaks out of the standard relationship of an author and his audience: 'The instant we ask ourselves this question, reflection feels an answer' (ii. 296). This is an intense moment, when readers self-consciously share the thoughts and feelings of someone else. Elsewhere, Paine discusses his book as if it were a dialogue, and such discussions awaken the rhythm of the prose and the colloquialism of the language. Generally there is a sense that the writer and the readers are engaging in conversation at its best—free-ranging, intellectual, and vivid. This general tone becomes explicit and suddenly lively when Paine starts talking to his readers: 'What will Mr. Burke place against this? I will whisper his answer.' (ii. 315.)

Paine's images are also congenial. The following metaphor is a shared one, not only because it describes an ordinary event, but because Paine describes it in such a way as to make his past and the readers' present as synonymous as they can be:

> I know a place in America called Point-no-Point, because as you proceed along the shore, gay and flowery as Mr Burke's language, it continually recedes and presents itself at a distance before you; but when you have got as far as you can go, there is no point at all. Just thus it is with Mr Burke's three hundred and sixty-six pages. (ii. 286)

Paine's presentation of an event in his own memory as a present experience of the readers eliminates the separation between the two. The metaphor performs the same trick again. Readers are told at the end of the sentence that there is 'no point at all'. Paine's comparison of the landscape to Burke's writing is irrefutable because readers are sensing the emptiness which Paine says describes the process of reading the *Reflections*. Again, the readers and the writer align. The credibility of the metaphor is enhanced also by Paine's use of Burke's language to describe the landscape. The passage concludes with an inversion of the tenor and vehicle. The landscape described by Burke's language turns into a description of the three hundred pages. The metaphor seems remarkably complete and has the thoroughness of a sound argument. The ability of the tenor and vehicle to change positions clenches the analogous nature of the two.

A similar process occurs on a larger scale throughout the book. Shared experience, the inversions of tenor and vehicle, and a convincing use of surprise distinguish Paine's use of metaphor. Paine skilfully controls the reader's experience by turning previous material into imaginative and descriptive language. Analogies between Burke and the state are not overtly stated, but are made by describing the two in similar terms. Readers are familiar with the various elements of the following passage, but reading it has a strong impact because the elements appear in a new configuration:

> It is not from his prejudices only, but from the disorderly cast of his genius, that he is unfitted for the subject he writes upon. Even his genius is without a constitution. It is a genius at random, and not a genius constituted. But he must say something. He has therefore mounted in the air like a balloon, to draw the eyes of the multitude from the ground they stand upon. (ii. 314)

The metaphors here condense an argument by recombining earlier descriptions of authoritative power. The image of Burke turning himself into a balloon carries with it previous descriptions of authoritative governments, false elevation, and inventions. Conquering governments had combined the church and state while 'the wondering cheated multitude worshipped the invention' (ii. 308). The English government had been criticized for being one which arose '*over* the people' (ii. 310). And the mob exists because 'it is by distortedly exalting some men, that others are distortedly debased, 'till the whole is out of nature' (ii. 296). The passage alludes to previously disparate moments in the book while it combines them into a single imaginative description. To the Attorney-General of Paine's trial, this interrelation of the text compounded its wickedness:

> to see the whole malignity of it, it is necessary to have a recollection of several preceding passages . . . extracts of it can be made to contain the whole marrow; and at the same time that each passage, taken by itself, will do mischief enough, any man reading them together, will see that mischief come out much clearer. (*ST,* xxii. 387)

Such words as 'constitution' and 'machine' stimulate a response that is not called for or acknowledged by the passage. Paine can forego the necessity of making an argument by relying on the ability of his diction to portray the analogy between Burke and authoritative governments.

While Paine's prose determines the impact of the images, it simultaneously, and, despite the contradiction, leaves the reader free to respond to the material with an independent imagination. In the *Pennsylvania Packet* Paine discusses briefly the inability of Gouverneur Morris to lead readers to an idea without explaining it to them in a dull fashion. (Morris later became the American ambassador to France. Against the wishes of the American government, he made little attempt to shorten Paine's imprisonment under Robespierre or to lessen the threat of his execution.) Although Paine is talking specifically about humour here, the passage is pertinent to Paine's ability to depend on readers to complete his thought:

> He has yet to learn that affectation of language is incompatible with humour. Wit may be elegantly spoken, but humour requires a peculiar quaintness of expression, just sufficient to give birth to the conception, and leaving, at the same time, room enough for the fancy of a reader to work upon.[16]

Paine apparently believed that refined language was unsuitable to a prose style that granted the readers some independence of mind. Elegance emphasizes the position of the writer to the extent of excluding participation by the readers. In *Rights of Man* Paine leaves 'room enough' by relying on the ability of his diction to stimulate his readers' imagination, an imagination which the previous material has already shaped and guided. While Paine's skill lays the groundwork for such passages, readers suddenly perceive more impli-

cations to an argument, and the perception appears to be their own. Paine's type of imagery makes the readers aware of what their minds can do by urging them half-way to an idea and then leaving them to complete it. As he does by his narrative stance, Paine abnegates his own position to emphasize the intellectual activity of his readers.

One means Paine has of surprising his readers is to transform previous topics of discussion into images: 'Even his genius is without a constitution' (ii. 314); 'He has stormed it [the French Revolution] with a mob of ideas tumbling over and destroying one another' (ii. 357). Objects of analysis suddenly become part of the imaginative life. By turning what had previously been discussed into a means of description, the scope of an idea enlarges with a discernible sense of expansion. In *A Letter Addressed to the Abbé Raynal* Paine discusses the ability of an author to strike several faculties at once as one of the achievements of good prose. Writers must

> combine warm passions with a cool temper, and the full expansion of the imagination with the natural and necessary gravity of judgement, so as to feel rightly balanced within themselves, and to make a reader feel, fancy, and understand justly at the same time. To call three powers of the mind into action at once, in a manner that neither shall interrupt, and that each shall aid and invigorate the other, is a talent very rarely possessed.[17]

Paine's prose can achieve this. Readers, at times, feel themselves reflecting a 'rightly balanced' author. Judgement, understanding, and the imagination can be simultaneously active. By using previous ideas as a source of imagery, Paine transforms ideas from an object the readers perceive into a means of perception. This is the inversion of tenor and vehicle on a large and repercussive scale. The transformation is exciting because the difference between the argument and the image is the difference between a discrete idea and consciousness.

To say that Thomas Paine animated his audience would be something of an understatement. His desire to enliven his readers, in the full sense that he used the term, was clearly fulfilled. New readers were brought into the reading public when the *Rights of Man* initiated a new type of reading material. By November 1792, it was claimed that *Rights of Man* 'is now made as much a standard book in this country as Robinson Crusoe and the *Pilgrim's Progress*'.[18] Accounts of the sale and distribution of it vary, but not to a great extent. Part One, at the price of three shillings, sold fifty thousand copies in 1791 (for the sake of contrast, Burke's *Reflections* sold thirty thousand copies in two years, and he believed the sales to be unprecedented). Part One was reprinted when Part

Two was published in April 1792, both selling at the price of six pence. E. P. Thompson accepts the figure of two hundred thousand for Parts One and Two between 1791 and 1793, including the number of abridged versions distributed by the democratic clubs and the extensive circulation of the book in Ireland (p. 108). Richard Altick finds this less credible but accepts the figure of fifty thousand for the sale of Part One (and Part Two sold more, as he and others point out) 'in a few weeks'.[19] In 1802 Paine estimated the sale of both parts at four or five hundred thousand, and in 1809, at 1,500,000, a figure which includes foreign translations. Of this figure, everyone is doubtful, and accounts of the circulation of the *Rights of Man* conclude with suspecting the figure and then claiming a less huge, yet still vast extent of circulation.

The intriguing question behind such figures is the unknown numbers of those who began to read or write specifically because of the *Rights of Man* or because of the continuing political debate. There is sufficient evidence to demonstrate that such a phenomenon occurred. John Butler's *Brief Reflections on the Liberty of the British Subject,* was one of the many pamphlets which responded to Edmund Burke. Butler apologizes for his style by exerting his talents to portray the 'several disadvantages peculiar to men in servile stations':

> I assure you, sir, that there is but little besides the present production to constitute me an author. Honours, titles, places or preferments, I have none. No study to cultivate reflection but a cold chamber, no hours of leisure but the hours destined to the refreshing slumber of soft repose; no assistance but the light of Reason, which lays grovelling under the disadvantages of a barren and uncultivated education.[20]

Similarly, *A Letter to William Paley from a Poor Labourer* (1793) replied to the misrepresentation of poverty in Paley's *Reasons for Contentment.* Although the *Reflections* and other works stimulated people who had not written before to write, contemporaries most frequently associated the extension of literacy with the *Rights of Man:* 'We no longer look for learned authors in the usual places, in the retreats of academic erudition, and in the seats of religion. Our peasantry now read the *Rights of Man* on mountains, and on moors, and by the wayside.'[21] The excitement of reading ideas presented as powerfully as Paine presents them, in a style that suddenly brought one's own language into the realm of the literary, must have been immense. Richard Carlile, a radical important in the early nineteenth century, describes the impact of the book on himself in terms that would have warmed Paine's heart. He felt the dissolution of an unnamed confusion and the intellectual awakening which Paine

portrayed as the greatest value of political consciousness. Characterizing himself before he read Paine's works, he wrote 'I was a weed left to pursue its own course'.[22] William Cobbett, writing in 1805, described the impact of reading the *Rights of Man* in vivid terms, even though he was at that moment a conservative defending himself against the charge of former radicalism:

> I explicitly stated, that, previous to my *seeing* what republicanism was, I had not only imbibed its principles, I had not only been a republican, but an admirer of the writings of PAINE. The fault, therefore, if there was any, was in the head, and not in the heart; and, I do not think, that even the head will be much blamed by those who duly reflect, that I was, when I took up PAINE's book, a novice in politics, that I was boiling with indignation at the abuses I had witnessed, and that, as to the power of the book itself, it required first a proclamation, then a law, and next the suspension of the *habeas-corpus* act, to counteract them. (*PR* [*Political Register,* ed. William Cobbett, 1802-36, 89 vols.], viii. 523)

For both Carlile and Cobbett, reading *Rights of Man* initiated politically active and literary careers. Cobbett wrote his first political pamphlet, *The Soldier's Friend* (1792) in the mood he describes here, buffeted by his experience of corruption in the army and encouraged by the exposition of corruption in the *Rights of Man.*[23] Richard Carlile did not read the book until the nineteenth century when the economic hardship of 1816 led him to consider political questions. Then he began his long, stubborn and eventually successful attack on the legal limitations of freedom of speech by republishing Paine's works. The influence of the *Rights of Man* extended also to those who had less spectacular political careers.

Its history among the democratic societies further reveals the book's intellectual impact. Among the new political clubs the book was distributed, read out aloud, and debated. Francis Place describes the self-respect which resulted from discussions of such books:

> The moral effects of the London Corresponding Society were considerable. It induced men to read books, instead of wasting their time in public houses, it taught them to respect themselves, and to desire to educate their children. It elevated them in their own opinions. (p. 198)

The Constitutional Information Society in Sheffield (founded in the late months of 1791) was the first political club to be founded by mechanics. In that year, it sent Thomas Paine a request for permission to publish two thousand copies of Part One 'for themselves'. Other localities similarly sent Paine requests to print a cheaper edition: ' . . . from Rotherham, from

Leicester, from Chester, from several towns in Scotland; and Sir James Mackintosh . . . brought me a request from Warwickshire, for leave to print ten thousand copies in that county. I had already sent a cheap edition to Scotland.'[24] The publication of the book led to increased activities and the founding of new societies. Paine provided them with both a political ideology and an heroic figure: 'All the leading members of the London Corresponding Society were republicans . . . This they were taught by the writings of Thomas Paine.'[25] During 1791, the London Constitutional Society, a more gentlemanly organization that had existed since the 1780s, was primarily concerned with distributing Part One. When Part Two appeared, various members left due to disagreements over Paine's discussion of the economy. The Society then stepped up its activities. Members, especially Horne Tooke, assisted the new London Corresponding Society, communicated with groups outside London, began to liaise with the new French government, and distributed other radical pamphlets (E. P. Thompson, *The Making,* p. 111). The political activity of the 1790s (and this is equally true of the repression) was entangled until at least 1795 with the publication of the **Rights of Man**. Expressions of gratitude for the book from societies in Manchester, Norwich, and Sheffield (these are the societies mentioned in Thomas Hardy's trial for high treason: there were others as well), indicated the energy and hope which the book brought: 'To Mr. Thomas Paine our thanks are especially due for the First and Second parts of the **Rights of Man,** and we sincerely wish that he may live to see his labours crowned with success in the general diffusion of liberty and happiness among mankind.'[26] The book was instrumental to the democratic movement of the 1790s which 'marked the emergence of "lower and middling classes of society" into organised radical politics' (E. Foner, p. 220).

Thomas Paine taught members of the London Corresponding Society to accomplish the unfamiliar task of writing their ideas (E. Foner, p. 225). There is a metaphorical truth to the anecdote that is only rarely discernible. The extent to which Paine facilitated expression by writing in a vernacular language is the invisible extent of his influence. The accounts of Cobbett and Carlile suggest that in their cases, reading the *Rights of Man* was virtually a precondition to their writing. Conservative pamphlets frequently portray workers questioning squires or master workmen about the ideas in Paine's book or picking up the pen for the first time to join in the political debate (these will be discussed in the third chapter). Even those who did not want literacy to increase, regretfully gave accounts of the new and active literacy and associated it especially with the **Rights of Man**. A study which attempted to appraise its influence on the writers who did not have an accustomed position among the reading public would be worth doing. Richard Altick's assessment that the major impact of the book, in spite of the broadening of the literary territory, was in the repression and retaliation that followed, must be appraised with an awareness that discussions in Parliament, accounts in provincial newspapers, King's proclamations, and the activities of Hannah More or the Association for preserving Liberty and Property are more ready to hand than accounts of the stimulation that would lead people to read or write (Altick, p. 72). The repression was widespread and thoroughgoing. Although the literary audience may well have shrunk back to its previous size when repression prohibited the publication of radical tracts in 1795, it reappeared with greater strength in the second decade of the nineteenth century. Thomas Paine's work was instrumental both to the repression of the 1790s and to the movement which countered that repression later in the nineteenth century.

The intellectual excitement released by the book was paralleled by a great deal of terror. Particularly at the end of 1792 and the first few months of 1793, Thomas Paine became a mythical figure, provoking a complex response of fear, vehemence, and glee. He was frequently burned in effigy, in one instance 'with a large Cabbage under one arm and an old pair of Stays under the other'.[27] In Littleton 'a wooden image of Paine was pounded to bits with a sledge hammer with such vigour that the executioner's hands ran with blood' (E. P. Thompson, *The Making,* p. 112). In January and February, the *Nottingham Journal* reported several events in which Paine was ritualistically killed. At a dinner and dance, ladies stoned Paine's effigy: 'It appeared an entertainment of sweet things, for there were no less than nineteen dozen of China oranges eat, and many of the young ladies fired thirty rounds each at Citizen Tom whose effigy was hung on the eastern arch of the old abbey.' (xlix (9 Feb. 1793), 3.) A week later the journal reported another adaptation of Thomas Paine into a form of entertainment. The following account of his arrest and execution occurs in a column of otherwise factual events.

> He was sentenced to be Hanged on the arm of a large tree, near the above Village, which was accordingly done, amidst a great concourse of people; he was left hanging on the tree a considerable time, after which the company retired to the Coffee-House for refreshment . . . Paineites had laid a plan to convey the remains of their Champion away from the Tree, which the LOYALISTS being aware of, fell on, routed, and put to flight; the whole GANG of them. (xlix, (16 Feb. 1793), 3)

By 1793 Paine was perceived half as a ghoulish figure and half as a more realistic danger because of his book's stimulus to new forms of political organization. These two ways of perceiving him were not entirely distinct. Even the King's Proclamation against Seditious Writings (May 1792), conjured a new character of Thomas Paine to suit the purpose of persecution. When members of the House objected that there was no need to hunt out secretive authors when authors were not disguising their identities, the Attorney General and Secretary Dundas replied that 'Paine' was a common name and might easily be a pseudonym for one author or a group of authors (*PD* [Hansard's *Parliamentary Debates*. Initially edited by William Cobbett and continuing to the present], xxix. 1504, 1513). The information Paine supplies about himself, as well as his fame, must have made such an answer appear hollow.

Between 1792 and 1795, the circulation of Paine's work was one of the main reasons given for the passage of repressive legislation and one of the main reasons given for the arrests of those charged with high treason. From the King's Proclamation of 1792, to Paine's trial in December, to the Report of the Committee of Secrecy, to the Suspension of the Habeas Corpus Act, to the treason trials of 1794, and to the passage of the Treasonable Practices Act, Parliament debated and attempted to contain the political and intellectual energy released by Paine's writings. Throughout these procedures the *Rights of Man* and its circulation by the democratic societies were major topics of discussion. The combination of factors which the government recognized as threatening was accurate: the distribution of an inexpensive edition, the correspondence of societies from different parts of the United Kingdom, and the class composition of the societies. Speaking in 1794 in favour of the Habeas Corpus Suspension Bill, Lord Grenville described May 1792, when the London Constitutional Society began to distribute Part One, as initiating an ever-increasing fervour of treasonable activity:

> Precisely at this period it was, that these societies came forward. . .; they began their operations by endeavouring to corrupt the minds of the lower classes of the public, by disseminating pamphlets, containing the whole of their system: they passed a resolution of the 18th of May, 1792, to distribute a cheap edition of a book intituled 'Rights of Man'. Here was the foundation of that system which had since ripened into treasonable practices by subsequent proceedings, which were followed up with incredible activity. (*PD*, xxxi. 576)

Until 1795 the government often asserted that the distribution of the *Rights of Man* initiated a profound and dangerous change.

During Paine's trial in December 1792, the prosecuting attorney stressed the alarming availability of Part Two: 'all industry was used . . . to obtrude and force this upon that part of the public whose minds cannot be supposed to be conversant with subjects of this sort' (*ST*, xxii. 381). Part One had not been prosecuted because the price of the book prevented those who could not argue against it from reading it: 'and when confined to the judicious reader, it appeared to me that such a man would refute it as he went along' (*ST*, xxii. 381). Price and style were the two means by which the government determined whether or not a work should be prosecuted. Until 1798, works confined to a small audience, such as Godwin's *Enquiry concerning Political Justice*, remained unhindered by prosecution. In a simplistic manner, the trials for sedition or libel estimated intellectual understanding by a financial scale. An inexpensive price was evidence of the author's malicious intent because it established that the books were addressed 'to the ignorant, to the credulous, to the desperate' (*ST*, xxii. 383). Also, Paine's style confirmed that the *Rights of Man* was not a work of reason. During his trial, the language of gentlemen was contrasted to Paine's 'phrase and manner' (*ST*, xxii. 383). As theories of language had established one type of reasoning, and identified it with a particular class, such comments did not require much argument. The style, the author, and the audience confirmed the identity of each other.

Conservatives seemed to have no means of identifying a non-upper-class movement except in terms of conspiracy and treason. If the political activity was not the spontaneous outburst of a section of society that was by definition undisciplined, inarticulate and emotive, then it was necessarily disciplined by an externally imposed conspiratorial design. Discussing the Report of the Committee of Secrecy (1794), Pitt described these two possible alternatives:

> Such language as this, coming from people apparently so contemptible in talents, so mean in their description, and so circumscribed in their power, would, abstractedly considered, be supposed to deserve compassion, as the wildest workings of insanity; but the researches of the committee would tend to prove, that it had been the result of deep design, matured, moulded into shape, and fit for mischievous effect when opportunity should offer. (*PD*, xxxi. 502)

Treason and conspiracy were more admissible concepts than that of a politically aware vulgar population. Accordingly, Horne Tooke was tried for high treason in 1794 for being the detached conspiratorial genius of the democratic societies. As leader of the Constitutional Society who was a friend of Thomas Paine and who aided the London Corresponding Society, he provided a focal point for an alleged systematic network. The Attorney-General describes the societies as Horne Tooke's unsuspecting private army:

> It was by the strength of the Corresponding Society, consisting of some thousands—by the

strength of all these societies, in different parts of the kingdom, that were to be affiliated and associated with this [Tooke's] society, that the objects of this society were to be carried into execution, without much of personal hazard to those who were the real authors of the plan that was in agitation, and was well nigh ripening. (*ST,* xxv. 538-9)

Such arguments denied the possibility that the movement for political reform was an intellectual choice performed by numerous members of the population. The charge of treason and the belief in a deep malevolent design classified the movement as evil and precluded the necessity of giving it serious attention. The trials of Thomas Hardy, John Thelwall, and John Horne Tooke were in effect, a trial of the democratic societies generally. The inclusion of resolutions passed by other societies, the stress placed on the distribution of Paine's book, and the inclusion of the publications of various societies as evidence indicates that the trial was not of an individual but of a political movement.

The Attorney-General, in his opening argument, stakes the credibility of his case on proving that the principles of the democratic societies were those of Thomas Paine and were therefore necessarily treasonable:

> I claim no credit for the veracity with which I assert, that this conspiracy has existed, unless I show you by subsequent acts of this society, that at this moment they meant what Mr. Paine says, in principle and practice, is the only rational thing—a *representative government*; the direct contrary of the government which is established here. (*ST,* xxiv. 294).

As the government also intended to prove the existence of acts that were more obviously treasonable—that the democratic societies were manufacturing arms and that the convention in Scotland was an extra-parliamentary legislative body—a surprising amount of weight and attention was given to **Rights of Man**. The Attorney-General proceeded on the basis of an extravagant equation between the ideas of Paine's book and the alleged intentions of the society. Examining a cutler from Sheffield, he asked him:

> How do you understand the passage I have read to you, that 'monarchy would not have existed so many ages in the world, had it not been for the abuses it protects'? Did you understand that to be a recommendation, to the people of England, to protect and cultivate the monarchical principle, or to destroy it as soon as they could? (*ST,* xxiv. 1045)

This is an unconvincing assessment of the process of reading; if Thomas Paine says that monarchy is cor-

rupt, his readers will directly proceed to violence. Because high treason was legally defined as the 'compassing of the death of the King', the Attorney-General emphasized the emotive and violent character of the book's readers in order to justify the charge.

The danger which originally justified the suspension of habeas corpus was disproved during these trials. Of the twelve who were arrested, Tooke, Hardy, and Thelwall were tried and acquitted, the remaining charges were dropped. Arguments to continue the suspension included further discussion of **Rights of Man** (*PD,* xxxi. 1159), and the suspension was reactivated yearly until 1801. The discrepancy of attempting to convict on the basis of physical danger to the throne when the danger lay in changing patterns of thought became obvious with the outcome of the trials: 'It was ridiculous in the extreme to have it high treason to kill the king, and not high treason to destroy the monarchy itself' (*PD,* xxxii. 247). Legislation passed in 1795 and 1798 established laws which were designed to curtail the possibility of certain intellectual exchanges. It reasserted the boundaries that had previously been maintained by the hegemonic status of literature and language.

Notes

[1] Unsigned, *A Dialogue between Mr. Worthy and John Simple,* 1792, p. 4.

[2] 'The Rights of Man', *The Writings of Thomas Paine,* ed. Maurice D. Conway, 1894-6, 4 vols., ii. 394. Conway's edition differs considerably from P. S. Foner's.

[3] *Autobiography of Francis Place,* ed. Mary Thrale, Cambridge, 1972, p. 223.

[4] John Thelwall, *The Tribune,* 1795-6, 3 vols., ii. 220.

[5] 'Resolutions of the United Constitutional Societies of Norwich', cited during the trial of Thomas Hardy, in *A Complete Collection of State Trials,* initially compiled by William Cobbett and later by T. B. Howells, 34 vols., xxiv. 292. The *State Trials* will be abbreviated as *ST.*

[6] *The Correspondence of Edmund Burke;* vol. vi, ed. Alfred Cobban and Robert A. Smith, Cambridge, 1967, pp. 85-7.

[7] *Monthly Review,* 2nd series, iii (1791), 314.

[8] *Reflections on the Revolution in France,* ed. Conor Cruise O'Brien, 1969, p. 170.

[9] Thomas Paine, 'The Crisis', no. 14, *The Writings of Thomas Paine,* i. 375.

[10] Eric Foner, *Tom Paine in Revolutionary America,* 1976, p. 79.

[11] *Dissertations on the English Language,* 1789, EL no. 54, p. 205.

[12] James T. Boulton, *The Language of Politics in the Age of Wilkes and Burke,* Westport, Connecticut, 1975, p. 261. The chapter is generally indebted to this book.

[13] 1793, p. 10. Misspelling Paine's name was a frequent device of authors who disagreed with his politics. The American edition which the Attorney-General refers to appeared earlier than the London edition.

[14] E. P. Thompson, *The Making of the English Working Class,* New York, 1966, p. 92.

[15] *Principles of Government in a Dialogue between a Scholar and a Peasant,* 1782, p. 1.

[16] *Pennsylvania Packet; or, the General Advertiser* (16 March 1779), p. 1.

[17] *Writings,* ii. 69-70.

[18] Benjamin Vaughan, 30 Nov. 1792, Home Office papers, 42.22, cited by E. P. Thompson, *The Making,* p. 108.

[19] *The English Common Reader: A Social History of the Mass Reading Public, 1800-1900,* Chicago, 1957, p. 70.

[20] Canterbury, undated, pp. 9-10.

[21] T. J. Mathias, *Pursuits of Literature,* 2nd edn., 1797, p. 238.

[22] Guy A. Aldred, *Richard Carlile, Agitator; His Life and Times,* Glasgow, 1941, p. 20.

[23] My attributing the pamphlet to Cobbett will be discussed in the next chapter.

[24] 'Letter Addressed to the Addressers on the Late Proclamations', *Writings,* iii. 65.

[25] Cited from BL Add. MS 27812 fo. 64 by E. Foner, p. 234.

[26] Cited from the 'Resolutions of the United Constitutional Societies of Norwich', *ST,* xxiv. 292.

[27] *The Nottingham Journal,* xiviii (12 Jan. 1793), 3.

A. Owen Aldridge (essay date 1984)

SOURCE: "The *Crisis,*" in *Thomas Paine's American Ideology,* University of Delaware Press, 1984, pp. 240-53.

[*In the essay that follows, Aldridge reviews the series of pamphlets collectively titled the* Crisis, *which Paine published during the course of the Revolutionary War and which, consequently, reflect the array of issues and ideas that then permeated American thought.*]

Much less has been written about Paine's *Crisis* than his **Common Sense,** probably because it concerns itself primarily with events and circumstances in the military and diplomatic struggle and devotes relatively little attention to ideology.

Its title, like that of Paine's first publication, had previously been used in England. An anti-administration periodical entitled simply *The Crisis* flourished in London throughout 1775 and 1776. A total of ninety-one numbers were published, as well as one *Crisis Extraordinary,* a title which Paine also later adopted.[1] The London *Crisis* vigorously supported the colonies in their struggle for liberty and after July 1776 for independence, and it was widely circulated in the colonies. As a matter of fact, many more separate reprintings of this work throughout America in the one year 1775 are known than of all of Paine's more famous *Crisis* throughout the eight years of the Revolution. Even the London *Crisis Extraordinary* had an American reprinting. If one were to judge by these individual issues alone, one would be forced to conclude that the London *Crisis* had a much greater vogue in the thirteen former colonies than had Paine's **The American Crisis.** This conclusion would be faulty, however, since it would fail to take into consideration newspaper printings. Nearly every number of Paine's *Crisis,* including the first, was reprinted in at least one newspaper, and most of them were reprinted in newspapers all over the continent.

Paine added the adjective *American* to the title of his first five numbers to distnguish them from the London work. These were printed originally as pamphlets or broadsides; later numbers were newspaper articles, some labeled simply **The Crisis** and others having no uniform title.

Although Paine gave the number 13 to his last **Crisis,** symbolizing the number of states in the union, several more than thirteen essays had been published, including some described as "Supernumerary" or "Extraordinary." Paine himself did not assign the numbers 10 or 12 to any of his articles, and to this day one cannot be absolutely sure of what pieces he felt should be included in the complete text of **The Crisis.**

Paine recalled that he wrote *Crisis* No. 1 in "a passion of patriotism,"[2] and like the rest of the series it reflects fervor and propaganda much more than argument and ideas. It opens with one of the most inspiring sentences in American literature, "These are the times that try men's souls," and concludes with one of the worst jokes, the grim prediction that if the colonists do not resist British troops and German mercenaries, they will see their homes "turned into barracks and bawdy-houses for Hessians, and a future race to provide for, whose father we shall doubt of." Paine, nevertheless, portrays the military situation from an optimistic perspective. He scornfully rejects "the summer soldier and the sunshine patriot" and exhorts his loyal fellow citizens to patriotic dedication, hard work, and sacrifice.

Subsequent numbers of the *Crisis* maintain this tone of cheerful gloom, portraying actual and potential hardships, disadvantages, and defeats as near disasters, but assuring his readers that American right and reason will triumph in the end. As a group, the *Crisis* papers have more in common with exhortatory sermons than with political essays, but they nevertheless embody some segments important in themselves or relevant to Paine's other writings.

Paine embroiders the theme introduced in *Common Sense* of the uniqueness of America and its favored status in the divine dispensation. The theme remains somewhat subdued in *Common Sense* by virtue of the title-page statement on the second and subsequent editions, "Written by An Englishman," and by Paine's insistence that he is writing for all mankind. In the *Crisis,* however, Paine writes as a full-fledged American and addresses himself to particular problems and policies of his country and his countrymen.

He is deliberately ambivalent concerning the extent to which divine providence is entering the military campaign, aware as he is that deciding between the role of the Almighty and that of human enterprise had been a constant dilemma in colonial America. He solemnly affirms that God will not allow a peaceful people to be destroyed and adds even more dramatically, "Neither have I so much of the infidel in me, as to suppose that HE has relinquished the government of the world, and given us up to the care of devils."[3] At the same time he calls upon all America not to throw "the burden of the day upon Providence." He exhorts his readers in proverbial language to "lay your shoulders to the wheel" (Burton, *Anatomy of Melancholy,* part 2, sec. 1, memb. 2). And in biblical style, he urges them to "show your faith by your works."[4]

In *Crisis* No. 8, Paine introduces the theory that the physical size of America exercises a kind of metaphysical influence upon the inhabitants of the country by endowing them with sublime thoughts and superior abilities, a theme which he later developed in *Rights of Man* and which became celebrated in the bombastic phrases of his admirer, Walt Whitman. Paine suggests that "there is something in the extent of countries, which among the generality of people, insensibly communicates extension of the mind. The soul of an is-

lander, in its native state, seems bounded by the foggy confines of the water's edge, and all beyond affords to him matters only for profit or curiosity, not for friendship. His island is to him his world, and fixed to that, his every thing centers in it; while those who are inhabitants of a continent, by casting their eye over a longer field, take in likewise a larger intellectual circuit, and thus approaching nearer to an acquaintance with the universe, their atmosphere of thought is extended, and their liberality fills a wider space."[5] In 1789, Paine wrote in similar vein to Sir Joseph Banks: "Great scenes inspire great Ideas. The natural Mightiness of America expands the Mind and it partakes of the greatness it contemplates."[6] In almost identical terms, he maintains in *Rights of Man* that the scene which America "presents to the eye of a spectator, has something in it which generates and encourages great ideas. . . . The mighty objects he beholds, act upon his mind by enlarging it, and he partakes of the greatness he contemplates."[7]

The notion of the strong effect of sublime natural scenery on the emotions is a commonplace in European aesthetics of the eighteenth and nineteenth centuries, but Paine was the first to give the notion a political connotation, that is, to associate the influence of the landscape with the destiny of a particular nation. It is significant that neither he nor the many Americans after him who exulted in the uplifting effect of the topography of the New World gave any thought to the landscape in South America, the Caribbean, or Canada on the Spanish and French populations in these areas or, perhaps an even greater omission, on the indigenous ones, the Indians. Paine in later works continued to stress the salubrious environment of America with such insistence that one of his critics remarked caustically that he tries to make his readers believe "that every thing began the other day in America, and that nothing really had ever existed before."[8]

In *Crisis* No. 10, Paine affirms that the advantages of America are as much material as spiritual; he initiates, in other words, the myth that the American standard of living is the highest in the world. In his words, "There are not three millions of people in any [other] part of the universe, who live so well, or have such a fund of ability."[9] We have seen that in *Common Sense,* Paine launched another myth associated with America—that of its eternal youth. In *Crisis* No. 5, he interprets the youth or newness of America as aggravating the heinousness of Britain's crime in attacking her. "America was young, and compared with other countries, was virtuous. None but a Herod of uncommon malice would have made war upon infancy."

Paine's obsession with newness and modernity presents a paradox when compared with his rhapsodic portrayal in *Crisis* No. 3 of the pleasures and advantages in the contemplation of history, which he defines as looking back "even to the first periods of infancy," and tracing "the turns and windings through which we have passed." The historical retrospect in America leads to the conclusion that the business of an age has been crowded into a few months. "Never did men grow old in so short a time!"[10] Too little attention to the past, according to Paine, interferes with our judgment, and the act of comparing the present with the past frequently imparts wisdom. In very modern terms, Paine explains that "it is a kind of countermarch," by which we get into the rear of time, and mark the movements and meanings of things as we make our return." He suggests that a pattern exists in human events; at least explanations are always available if events are properly studied. In reference to "sentimental differences," by which he presumably means the syndrome of romantic love, however, Paine admits that logic is not always effective. Frequently "some striking circumstance, or some forcible reason quickly conceived, will affect in an instant what neither argument nor example could produce in an age."

We have already noticed Paine's early statement concerning the superiority of the moderns over the ancients in the *Pennsylvania Magazine.* He recurs to the theme in *Crisis* No. 5, where he seems to be attempting to overthrow the entire European tradition of historical writing, which uniformly portrays classical antiquity as a kind of golden age. Montesquieu in France and Bolingbroke in England are good examples of this historical classicism, in which, in Paine's words, "the wisdom, civil governments, and sense of honor of the States of Greece and Rome, are frequently help up as objects of excellence and imitation." Paine observes that "mankind have lived for little purpose" if it is necessary continually to go back two or three thousand years for lessons and examples. In his opinion, "could the mist of antiquity be taken away and men and things viewed as they then really were, it is more than probable that they would admire us, rather than we them."[11] The short period of American settlement, Paine maintains, has furnished the world "with more useful knowledge and sounder maxims of civil government than were ever produced in any age before." For this reason Paine refuses to yield "the palm of the United States to any Grecians or Romans that were ever born." He particularly seeks to take away from the ancients the universal acclaim which had been generally accorded to them for cherishing freedom. According to Paine, "the Grecians and Romans were strongly possessed of the *Spirit* of liberty, but *not* the principle, for at the time they were determined not to be slaves themselves, they employed their power to enslave the rest of mankind." This concept was soon versified by David Humphreys, in a brief poem "On the Love of Country."

Perish the Roman pride a world that braves,
To make for one free state all nations
    slaves;
Their boasted patriotism at once exprest,
Love for themselves and hate for all the
    rest.[12]

Paine not only denies liberty to the ancients, but actually maintains that "had it not been for America there had been no such thing as freedom left throughout the whole universe." Here we see a further stage of his survey of the progress of freedom. In his poem **"Liberty Tree"** he had hailed the appearance of the Goddess of Liberty "In a chariot of light, from the regions of day." In *Common Sense,* he had described Freedom as being "hunted round the globe," and had called upon America to "receive the fugitive, and prepare in time an asylum for mankind."[13] Now, in the *Crisis,* he proudly affirms that the present era in America, in contrast to the ancient world, "is blotted by no one misanthropical vice" and the revolution in progress may be styled "the most virtuous and illustrious . . . that ever graced the history of mankind."[14]

Paine echoes his ethical indictment of the ancients in a letter to Henry Laurens in the next year, affirming that "all the histories of ancient wars . . . promote no moral reflection, but like the *Beggar's Opera* renders the villain pleasing in the hero."[15] In similar vein, he charges in *Crisis* No. 13 that "Rome, once the proud mistress of the universe, was originally a band of ruffians" and that her wealth came from plunder and rapine and her greatness from the "oppression of millions." By contrast, everything in America bears the mark of honor, including her birth and the stages by which she has risen to empire. While not discounting the inspirational value of "the remembrance . . . of what is past," Paine calls upon America to look to the future in order to add to "the fair fame she began with," to let the world witness "that she can bear prosperity: and that her honest virtue in time of peace, is equal to the bravest virtue in time of war."[16]

In *Crisis* No. 10, Paine repeats from *Common Sense* the argument that the geographical location of America is a major justification for its independence, suggesting that the eventual military triumph of America over any attempt by an island to conquer her "was as naturally marked in the constitution of things, as the future ability of a giant over a dwarf is delineated in his features while an infant."[17] As British visions of totally subjugating America had been dissipated by military-topographical reality, Paine in *Crisis* No. 12 ridicules the inconsistencies of parliamentary speeches which on one hand boast of the superiority of the British forces and on the other declare that without the economic riches of America the empire is nothing. "Was America, then, the giant of the empire," he taunts, "and England only her dwarf in waiting! Is the case so strangely altered, but those who once thought we could not live without them, are now brought to declare that they cannot exist without us?"[18]

In *Crisis* No. 6 Paine refutes another geopolitical concept, the notion that geographical location in itself inevitably makes certain nations mutually antagonistic. The idea was generally attributed in the eighteenth century to the French writer Mably, who asserted in 1757 that "neighboring states are naturally enemies one to the other."[19] The notion had been introduced into the American context in 1778 by British peace commissioners who attempted to insert a wedge between the Americans and their French allies by issuing a proclamation to the American people describing France as "the late mutual and natural enemy" of both Britain and America. Going back to the concept of the state of nature, Paine vehemently denies that there exists such a principle as natural animosity. "The expression is an unmeaning barbarism, and wholly unphilosophical, when applied to beings of the same species, let their station in the creation be what it may."[20] Paine justifies this assertion on primarily theological grounds, appealing to doctrines which have more in common with Christianity than with deism. Indeed, if his principles in this place can be considered as anything other than Christian, they are pure Manichaeism. "We have," according to Paine, "a perfect idea of a natural enemy when we think of the devil, because the enmity is perpetual, unalterable, and unabateable." But men "become friends or enemies as the change of temper, or the cast of interest inclines them. The Creator of man did not constitute them the natural enemy of each other." Expanding his doctrine to include animals in the chain of being, Paine closes with the statement, "even wolves may quarrel, still they herd together." Here he comes close to repeating an argument which Shaftesbury had used against Hobbes: "Wolves are to wolves very kind and loving creatures."[21]

Readdressing himself to all of the commissioners, Paine condemns England as a barbarous nation the conduct of which is unworthy of comparison to the civilized behavior of France. He closes with a customary barb at the American Tories, whom he dismisses as "a set of wretched mortals, who having deceived themselves, are cringing, with the duplicity of a spaniel."

In the introduction to *Common Sense,* Paine had declared the cause of America to be in great measure the cause of all mankind. In keeping with this pronouncement, he suggests in the opening lines of *Crisis* No. 2 that his remarks there are meant for the world at large even though his subject matter is mainly local. "Universal empire is the prerogative of a writer. His concerns are with all mankind, and though he cannot command their obedience, he can assign them their duty."[22] Several years previously Gibbon had prescribed

that "he who writes for all mankind should draw his imagery only from sources common to all, from the human heart and the spectacle of literature."[23] Paine's ability to probe universal experience explains the success and enduring popularity of his writing. As he sees it, "what I write is pure nature, and my pen and my soul have ever gone together."[24] He therefore expresses confidence that this *Crisis,* like *Common Sense,* will make its way to England and inform its people of the design of the Americans to help them.[25]

He affirms that it would be easier for the Americans to bring about a revolution in England than for the British to conquer America, for military expeditions sent to England "with the declared design of deposing the present king, bringing his ministers to trial, and setting up the Duke of Gloucester in his stead, would assuredly carry their point." Paine came back to this notion of an invasion of England many times throughout his career, particularly during and after the French Revolution. It is significant that in the *Crisis* he does not suggest erecting a republican government for the English people, but merely effecting a change in rulers. In other words, he was at this time committed to republicanism in America, but not in Great Britain. His universalism, in other words, did not embrace republicanism. In *Crisis* No. 2 he also touches upon two of his other recurrent themes, British cruelties in India, the Caribbean, and Africa, and the imminent bankruptcy of the British government.

Paine says little in the *Crisis* about the operation of the human intellect except for echoing from *Common Sense* his belief that reason strikes the mind with automatic conviction. He tells his readers in *Crisis* No. 2 that "what I write is pure nature," and in No. 5 he observes that "what we now have to do is as clear as light, and the way to do it is as strait as a line."[26] Paine is almost Cartesian in the metaphors he uses to describe the operation of reason and the beauties of method. According to Paine, the intellectual realm reacts upon reason as the world of objects reacts upon the eye. Reason seems to have visual force as knowledge is imparted with clarity, directness, and distinctness. In *Crisis* No. 10, Paine, with his customary cheerfulness, affirms that "misfortune and experience have now taught us system and method; and the arrangements for carrying on the war are reduced to rule and order."[27] Shortly after this he adds, "I love method, because I see and am convinced of its beauty and advantage. It is that which makes all business easy and understood, and without which everything becomes embarrassed and difficult."[28] In a newspaper article supporting *Crisis* No. 10, Paine repeats his prescription of "order, system and method." "Method," he says, "is to natural power, what weight is to human strength, without which a giant would lose his labour and a country waste its force."[29] These passages share the rapture concerning order of a more famous one in *The Age of Reason* on the attributes of God. "Do we want to contemplate His power? We see it in the immensity of the creation. Do we want to contemplate His wisdom? We see it in the unchangeable order by which the incomprehensible whole is governed."[30] It is not surprising that one of Paine's pseudonyms should be "A Lover of Order."

Paine's political theory, although expressed only fragmentarily in the *Crisis,* is by and large identical with that in *Common Sense.* In *Crisis* No. 3, he suggests that his "creed of politics" is purely pragmatic, embodying a divorce between government and politics. In his words, "if an English merchant receives an order, and is paid for it, it signifies nothing to him who governs the country."[31] This is not quite the same as the dichotomy between government and society, but rather one between government and economic activity. In a newspaper letter following upon *Crisis* No. 10, he makes the assertion, which we have discussed in chapter 4, that "Government and the people do not in America constitute distinct bodies."[32] By this he means merely that the members of Congress and the state governments are drawn from the people and do not lose their identity as citizens by becoming lawmakers. In *Crisis* No. 10, moreover, he describes the war of America against Britain as "the country's war, the public's war, or the war of the people in their own behalf, for the security of their natural rights, and the protection of their own property. It is not the war of Congress, the war of the assemblies, or the war of government in any line whatever."[33] This is certainly a reaffirmation of the principle that government and society are separate.

In his letter following upon *Crisis* No. 10, Paine introduces a concept equivalent to Rousseau's theory that sovereignty in a nation is the expression of the general will. Referring to members of the Congress and the Assembly, Paine explains that they are "the representatives of majesty, but not majesty itself," and that the latter power exists in the "universal multitude." Paine uses the term *majesty* instead of Rousseau's *sovereignty*; otherwise the the theories are the same. In his later *Dissertations on Government,* 1786, Paine adopts the word *sovereignty* in essentially the same context and explains it in some detail.[34] In 1782, however, when Paine was intent mainly upon persuading his readers that increased taxation was the vital need for the survival of the nation, he did not develop the abstract significance of his theory of sovereignty but used it merely to establish a sentiment of national identification or homogeneity.

In *Crisis* No. 7, Paine expands his theories of national honor, perhaps in response to the various references to honor in the polemics over *Common Sense.* He associates personal and national honor by means of his maxim: "That which is the best character for an individual is the best character for a nation."[35] Yet on an international level, according to Paine, mankind seems not to have developed from its primitive origins but to have retained "as nations all the original rudeness of nature." Here, it will be noted, primitive times are not portrayed as being quite so salutary as they seem in *Common Sense.* The British as individuals, Paine maintains, judge other people on the basis of their national origins, their religion, and their wealth. Collectively, they seem to consider honor as consisting in "national insult" and in threatening with the rudeness of a bear and devouring with the ferocity of a lion. Paine completely demolishes the concept of a mother country in reference to Britain's relations with America. Instead of conforming to the natural direction suggested by this image, consisting of "everything that is fond, tender and forbearing," Britain, he says, has intruded its false notions of national honor revealing "the violence of resentment, the inflexibility of temper, or the vengeance of execution." All this is, of course, a repetition of the argument from *Common Sense* that Britain cannot be appropriately termed the parent country since even "brutes do not devour their young, nor savages make war upon their families."[36] In further expanding the connotations of the political term "mother country," Paine observes in the *Crisis* that the metaphor should have taught the necessity of independence, for all children eventually grow into adults and set up for themselves. "Nothing hurts the affections both of parents and children so much, as living too closely connected, and keeping up the distinction too long."[37] Paine states that the natural and the most beneficial policy of Britain would have been to maintain good relations with America and in this way to have preserved her reputation of military strength, which was rapidly being eroded by her impotence in the American campaign. Paine refers to "this method of studying the progress of the passions in order to ascertain the probable conduct of mankind" as a philosophy of politics which the British ministry have no conception of.[3]

Turning to the question of finance, Paine argues that England is so ridden by obligations that the interest on the national debt is almost equal to annual income. In seeking to demonstrate that British financiers count their debt as part of their national wealth but that it is actually a drain on the country which will bring the whole financial system to eventual collapse, Paine anticipates the argument of one of his later pamphlets, *The Decline and Fall of the English System of Finance* (1796). America, unlike England, could easily pay the expenses of the war, Paine maintains, since it has no debt of any kind other than its non-interest bearing paper currency.[39]

In reference to the internal political structure of the British nation, Paine draws attention to a conflict of interest between Parliament and the Crown which would have come to a head had Britain won the war.

The fundamental question concerned which political segment could be considered responsible for such a victory and which should reap the benefit. As Paine explains the situation, Parliament claimed a legislative right over America, but the army presumably belonged to the Crown; in the event of subduing the colonies, it would not be clear whether Parliament or the Crown would then be in control. This situation, hypothetical as it is, leads Paine to ask among a series of questions whether thc people are not the source of the power and honor of any country, whether there is any such thing as the English constitution, and "whether a congress constituted like that of America, is not the most happy and consistent form of government in the world."[40] Answers to these queries had already been suggested in *Common Sense,* and they were to be further developed in the pages of *Rights of Man*.

Paine addresses the last part of *Crisis* No. 7 to the "mercantile and manufacturing part" of the English nation, for whose benefit he had already observed that it is never worth while to go to war for profit's sake. Attempting to win over this segment of his readers by describing them as the "bulwark of the nation," he embroiders the theme introduced in *Common Sense* that trade is more profitable with an independent nation than with a subjugated one. Since a treaty of alliance had already been concluded with France, Painc warns the English merchants against allowing their government to provoke France into a declaration of war. Having already pointed to a conflict of interest between the Crown and Parliament, Paine now maintains that both forces are inimical to the welfare of the business community. "Your present king and ministry will be the ruin of you; and you had better risk a revolution and call a congress, than be thus led on from madness to despair, and from despair to ruin."[41] In addressing as a final note the ministry and the merchants collectively, Paine characteristically reduces politics to a "simple thought" and describes his own prescription of applying "the domestic politics of a family" to the national scene as an "easy and natural line."

We have already pointed out that Paine in 1776 in his *Four Letters* expressed the doctrine of the supremacy of the union over local governments; the concept is suggested also in *Common Sense* by his warning that "the continental belt is too loosely buckled"[42] and his axiom, "'tis not in numbers but in unity that our great strength lies."[43] Paine further insisted on the supremacy of the union in his newspaper essay related to *Crisis* No. 10 (*Pennsylvania Gazette,* 3 April 1782) in order to persuade his readers that the central government must maintain its autonomy in financial matters, in other words, that "the expenses of the United States for carrying on the war, and the expenses of each state for its own domestic government" must be kept separate and distinct. In Paine's realistic terms, taxes levied for national defense are "properly our insurance money." To establish the principle, Paine declares that "the union of America is the foundationstone of her independence, the rock on which it is built, and is something so sacred in her constitution, that we ought to watch every word we speak, and every thought we think, that we injure it not, even by mistake." This warning was needed to avert conflicts between loyalty to state and loyalty to the union, psychological divisions made particularly acute because some states were still bearing the brunt of British attack while others were remote from it. Paine solemnly affirms, therefore, that "with respect to those things which immediately concern the union, and for which the union was purposely established, and is intended to secure, each state is to the United States what each individual is to the state he lives in. And it is on this grand point, this movement upon one centre, that our existence as a nation, our happiness as a people, and our safety as individuals, depend."

Throughout *The Crisis* Paine expounds the primary theme of *Common Sense,* the moral justification of the war of independence. In *Crisis* No. 3, he summarizes the principal arguments in support of independence and concludes that it is "the *moral advantages*" which weigh most with all men of serious reflection."[44] In this section, however, he concerns himself with only one moral issue, that it is wrong for America through its colonial status to be involved in British wars. In *Common Sense,* he had framed the argument in political terms, affirming the principle of isolation from the political affairs of Europe.[45] In *Crisis* No. 3, he stresses ethical considerations: in Paine's words, "America neither could nor can be under the government of Britain without becoming a sharer of her guilt, and a partner in all the dismal commerce of death."[46] According to this train of thought, Britain has a dishonorable record of international belligerence going back for centuries, and the lot of America were she not set free would be to abet in every quarrel. "It is a shocking situation to live in, that one country must be brought into all the wars of another, whether the measure be right or wrong, or whether she will or not."

In *Crisis* No. 11, Paine defends the alliance between America and France on ethical grounds, specifically arguing that "the United States have as much honor as bravery" and that their conduct is based upon firm principle, not hazard or circumstance.[47] At least two years previously, Paine had suspected that the British were considering the notion of abandoning prosecution of the war in favor of seducing America to abandon her alliance with France, and he had written a paragraph denouncing this tactic as revealing "such a disposition to perfidiousness, and such disregard of honor and morals, as would add the finishing vice to national corruption." But Paine held back the paragraph because of the arrival of news indicating British determination to continue with military operations. He later inserted the paragraph in the eleventh *Crisis,* however, because of hints in the New York Tory press that the scheme of dividing America from her allies was reviving in British strategy. He thereupon provides evidence of peace gestures which had been made by the British to the courts of France and warns America to be on guard against the same insidious arts should they be used with her. The mere suggestion of coming to a separate arrangement, he denounces as an insult to America. In a realistic metaphor, he observes that no man attempts to seduce a truly honest woman; the very thought of it is a defamation of her good name.

In a passage highly revealing of his own moralistic mode of thinking, Paine affirms that he will not use the argument of selfish interest to defend the alliance but "go a step higher, and defend it on the ground of honor and principle."[48] Paine argues that since the French have treated America with the same respect which they would have shown to an old, established country, America cannot do less than fulfill her obligations. "Character is to us, in our present circumstances, of more importance than interest." Paine somewhat weakens the nobility of this sentiment by adding that since America is a young nation the rest of the world is observing its behavior to see whether it is worthy of trust. Also he uses a phrase which he had earlier ridiculed as stale and hackneyed, "the eye of the world is upon us."[49] He returns to high morals and vigorous style, however, by affirming that Britain and the world must be shown "that we are neither to be bought nor sold; that our mind is great and fixed; our prospect clear; and that we will support our character as firmly as our independence."

Paine summarizes the moral argument in his *Crisis Extraordinary* of 1782, joining it with the theme of youthfulness. "America is a new character in the universe," he maintains. "She started with a cause divinely right, and struck at an object vast and valuable. Her reputation for political integrity, perseverance, fortitude, and all the manly excellencies, stands high in the world; and it would be a thousand pities that, with those introductions into life, she suffered the least spot or blow to fall upon her *moral* fame."[50]

The thirteenth *Crisis,* symbolic of the number of states in the American union, is dated 19 April 1783, eighth anniversary of the battles of Lexington and Concord. Last of the series which Paine himself considered to constitute the *Crisis,* it begins with the triumphant declaration "'The times that tried men's souls,' are over—and the greatest and completest revolution the world ever knew, gloriously and happily accomplished." This is the first time Paine uses the word *revolution* to describe the events which had been taking place,

although he is equally hyperbolical in *Common Sense* in his reference to beginning the world over again. At the end of the war, he says, America has earned the honor and "power to make a world happy, to teach mankind the art of being so," and "to exhibit on the theatre of the universe, a character hitherto unknown."[51] Echoing the language of the Scriptures, he describes the pastoral scenes now opening for America, comprising not the "cypress shade of disappointment," but "the sweet of her labors, and the reward of her toil" in "her own land, and under her own vine" (Apocrypha 1 Maccabees 14: 12) In this situation, Paine declares, acquiring "a fair national reputation, is of as much importance as independence." A few paragraphs later he observes, "Character is much easier kept than recovered, and that man, if any such there be, who, from any sinister views, or littleness of soul, lends unseen his hand to injure it, contrives a wound it will never be in his power to heal."

Liberal thinkers throughout Europe, particularly in France and England, had supported the cause of the American colonists, but their adherence had been in the main emotional and humanitarian rather than ideological, comparable to the rhapsodic sponsorship which Boswell and Rousseau had accorded to Paoli in the latter's efforts to bring about a new regime in Corsica. There had been little said on ideological grounds about the ramifications of American independence, and one of the most daring depositories of advanced ideas, the abbé Raynal's *Histoire philosophique des deux Indes,* even reflected some doubts concerning the principles which were motivating the American "insurgens." Paine published in 1782, as we shall see later, a reply to Raynal consisting of a detailed vindication of the moral integrity of the American independence movement. The thirteenth *Crisis* offered Paine an additional opportunity of reasserting its ideological significance. He roundly affirms, therefore, that the revolution must be "an honor to the age that accomplished it" to "the end of time" and that it has "contributed more to enlighten the world, and diffuse a spirit of freedom and liberality among mankind, than any human event (if this may be called one) that ever preceded it."[52] Noteworthy in this proclamation is the suggestion of divine guidance or supervision, a religious attitude which conforms to both *Common Sense* and *Age of Reason*.

In a kind of balance sheet for America at the close of the war, Paine finds only one item on the debit side and two on the credit. The single liability consists in the national debt, which he considers as hardly worth mentioning in comparison with the compensating advantages. The two great assets consist of gaining complete freedom in the economic realm and of acquiring an ally, obviously France, "whose exemplary greatness, and universal liberality," according to Paine, "have extorted a confession even from her enemies." In a footnote supporting a principle originally presented in **Common Sense,** that the struggle "never could have happened at a better time," Paine affirms that "the great hinge on which the whole machine turned is the UNION OF THE STATES." Observing that no single state or combination of single states can equal in strength "the whole of the present United States," he stresses the advantages and necessity of "strengthening that happy union which has been our salvation, and without which we should have been a ruined people." Finally, in this footnote, Paine quotes from **Common Sense** the passages concerning the appropriateness of the timing of the struggle for independence—"THE TIME HATH FOUND US"—and the indispensable nature of the glorious union—"It is not in numbers, but in a union, that our great strength lies."[53]

All this is introductory to a forceful argument on the continued necessity of union after America had become a nation and achieved sovereignty, an argument foreshadowing the influential *Federalist* papers to be published a few years later in favor of the new constitution. Paine's major principle is based upon the relationship of the United States to the other nations in the world. The individual states lack the wealth and resources to function by themselves; only as the United States, conceived as a wisely regulated and cemented union, can they obtain the respect of other nations, make treaties, protect their commerce in foreign ports, and provide their security at home. Some measure of local autonomy must in the process be sacrificed. Echoing his **Four Letters,** Paine observes, "It is with confederated states as with individuals in society; something must be yielded up to make the whole secure." Citizenship of a particular state is merely a local distinction, but "citizenship in the United States is our national character. . . . Our great title is, AMERICANS— our inferior one varies with the place."

In the remainder of his remarks, Paine makes a number of personal revelations. In characterizing and vindicating his individual conduct throughout the war, he once more foreshadows a political attitude which became of great consequence in the early years of the republic—the view that political parties are harmful in a nation by fomenting irrational divisions and should, therefore, be avoided if at all possible. This opinion, prevalent in the speeches of George Washington, with whom it is generally associated, is clearly portrayed in Paine's summary of his own political career. "So far as my endeavours could go, they have all been directed to conciliate the affections, unite the interests and draw and keep the mind of the country together; and the better to assist in this foundation work of the revolution, I have avoided all places of profit or office, either in the state I live in, or in the United States; kept myself at a distance from all parties and party connections, and even disregarded all private and inferior concerns: and when we take into view the great work we have gone through, and feel, as we ought to feel,

the just importance of it, we shall then see, that the little wranglings and indecent contentions of personal party, are as dishonorable to our characters, as they are injurious to our repose."[54] This statement, apart from its ideological reflection on party divisions, must be considered in the nature of a political appeal and as such interpreted in a very broad sense. In actuality, Paine had served as secretary to the committee on foreign relations of the Congress and as clerk of the Pennsylvania Assembly, and he had several times before the writing of **Crisis** No. 13 appealed to various national leaders to be reimbursed for his services.

Paine reveals his pride of authorship by adding that if he has served the cause of America in the course of more than seven years by opposing "an unnatural reconciliation" with Britain, he has "likewise added something to the reputation of literature, by freely and distinterestedly employing it in the great cause of mankind, and shewing there may be genius without prostitution." He formally takes his leave of the subject—and in a sense of America—speculating upon "whatever country I may hereafter be in"—affirming that "I shall always feel an honest pride at the part I have taken and acted, and a gratitude to Nature and Providence for putting it in my power to be of some use to mankind."

Notes

[1] Paul Leicester Ford, "The Crisis," *Bibliographer* 1 (1902): 139-52.

[2] *Writings* [*of Thomas Paine,* ed. by Moncure D. Conway (New York: Putnam, 1894-96), 4 vols.],

[3] *Writings,* 1:51.

[4] *Writings,* 1:55.

[5] *Writings,* 1:164.

[6] A. O. Aldridge, *Man of Reason: The Life of Thomas Paine* (Philadelphia: J.B. Lippincott, 1959), p. 109.

[7] *Writings,* 1:354.

[8] William Lewelyn, *An Appeal to Men against Paine's Rights of Man* (London, 1793), p. 43.

[9] *Writings,* 1:203.

[10] *Writings,* 1:74.

[11] *Writings,* 1:123.

[12] *Miscellaneous Works* (New York, 1804), p. 132.

[13] *Writings,* 1:30-31.

[14] *Writings*, 1:123.

[15] *Writings*, 2:1179.

[16] *Writings*, 1:231.

[17] *Writings*, 1:193.

[18] *Writings*, 1:224.

[19] *Des Principes des négociations* in *Collection complète des oeuvres* (Paris 1794-95), 5:93.

[20] *Writings*, 1:136.

[21] *Characteristics of Men, Manners, Opinions, Times* (London, 1711), 2:320.

[22] *Writings*, 1:58.

[23] "The Study of Literature," in J. W. Spadden, ed., *Miscellaneous Works* (New York, 1907), p. 10.

[24] *Writings*, 1:72.

[25] *Writings*, 1:71. As a matter of fact, the first four numbers of the *Crisis* appeared in Almon's *Remembrances . . . For the Year 1778*, and later issues of this periodical published the rest of the *Crisis* with the exception of Nos. 10, 11, and 12.

[26] *Writings*, 1:125.

[27] *Writings*, 1:195.

[28] *Writings*, 1:205.

[29] *Pennsylvania Gazette*, 3 April 1782.

[30] *Writings*, 1:483.

[31] *Writings*, 1:72.

[32] *Pennsylvania Gazette*, 3 April 1782.

[33] *Writings*, 1:198.

[34] *Writings*, 2:369. . . .

[35] *Writings*, 1:147.

[36] *Writings*, 1:19.

[37] *Writings*, 1:154.

[38] *Writings*, 1:148.

[39] *Writings*, 1:149.

[40] *Writings*, 1:152.

[41] *Writings*, 1:155.

[42] *Writings*, 1:44.

[43] *Writings*, 1:31.

[44] *Writings*, 1:81.

[45] *Writings*, 1:20.

[46] *Writings*, 1:81.

[47] *Writings*, 1:209.

[48] *Writings*, 1:214.

[49] *Writings*, 2:65; 1:215.

[50] *Pennsylvania Gazette*, 6 April 1782. This paper, which was intended as a continuation of *Crisis* No. 10, has never been republished. See A. O. Aldridge, *Man of Reason*, pp. 92-93.

[51] *Writings*, 1:231.

[52] *Writings*, 1:232.

[53] *Writings*, 1:232-33.

[54] *Writings*, 1:234-35.

Jack Fruchtman, Jr. (essay date 1993)

SOURCE: "Nature and Man's Democratic Calling," in *Thomas Paine and the Religion of Nature*, Johns Hopkins University Press, 1993, pp. 38-56.

[*In the following chapter from his book, Fruchtman demonstrates that Paine's rationalist view of nature as product of God and reason at once shaped his belief that democracy was the only political form consistent with human nature and rights.*]

Human nature was one dimension of nature in Paine's ministry. Another was the physical world: the landscape and the heavens as God had created them. In the act of creation, God gave his people the trees, the sea, and the sky as well as human freedom and the rights of man. Human beings possessed freedom and rights as naturally as trees produced leaves or the ocean swelled into waves. The idea that human nature was directly joined to freedom and rights provided Paine with still another powerful argument to attack the government of kings, lords, and their supporters. By showing that this form of government conflicted with human nature, hence with God's physical creation, Paine also showed that it was necessarily evil and satanic.

In turning to the natural world, one mode of discourse Paine drew on, consciously or not, was the pastoral, which from the Greek poet Theocritus and the Roman Virgil to Paine's own time focused on the bucolic ideal of peace and serenity. No evidence shows definitively whether Paine used this tradition merely to embellish his style or whether he truly believed the physical world was godly. Elements of the bucolic clearly appear in his writings, especially in *The Age of Reason*. Throughout this and other works, he demonstrated his fascination with nature, which he made into a veritable religion. Through a series of secular sermons, he was certain he could convince Americans and Europeans that the moment for political transformation had arrived.

According to one literary historian, "the bucolic ideal stands at the opposite pole from the Christian one, even if it believes with the latter that the lowly will be exalted and that only bad shepherds are shepherds of men."[1] Paine's ideas mirrored this description. He denounced Christianity as a religion which institutionalized myth and fable. More significantly, the lowly, those enslaved by royalty and aristocracy, would someday conquer their masters. Although he never saw himself as a literary shepherd who left the corrupt cities for quiet musings in the countryside, he shared with pastoral writers the belief in the importance of the world of sight and sound, where lies and superstitions had no place.

The pastoral tradition focused on the plight of the dispossessed as a critical social problem in ways that the gospels could never effectively do. Paine worried about the condition of the poor and outlined social programs for them in *Rights of Man* and *Agrarian Justice*. In these works, he expressed his desire that poverty be ended and commercial prosperity achieved. He preached that all people had a duty to aid the lowly.

Two problems immediately arise here: who were the lowly and who were the "people" he expected to help them? Paine never defined the "lowly" only as disadvantaged people at the lowest rung of society. The lowly also included all those below what he called the "exalted" status of king, lord, or priest. As for the people to whom Paine preached this message, in the second part of *Rights of Man* especially, we can see that he was appealing to the same kind of people whom hc wanted to read *Common Sense:* an audience who understood his direct language, sometimes saturated with phrases they themselves might use. Thus, his appeal was to the lower orders, the artisans and tradesmen, and the middle classes, the merchants and financiers. He asserted that Burke's language was so sophisticated and learned that it was incomprehensible,

and he offered to translate it. "As the wondering audience, whom Mr. Burke supposes himself talking to, may not understand all this learned jargon, I will undertake to be its interpreter." Burke's logic was as silly as his language: "What a stroke Mr. Burke has now made! To use a sailor's phrase, he has swabbed the deck" (*RM* 117).

At any rate, the trappings of royalty or nobility did not complicate the physical landscape, which was simple and ordered, pure and virtuous. It was, in short, in the tradition of the bucolic. To engage in invention we must look to "a principle in nature, which no art can overturn, viz. that the more simple anything is, the less liable it is to be disordered" (*CS* 68).[2]

Richard Price, friend of Paine's and a leading Dissenter and minister of Newington Green, once advised the same thing: that men would be better off if they lived according to nature. "Let us then value more the simplicity and innocence of life agreeable to nature; and learn to consider nothing as savageness but malevolence, ignorance, and wickedness. The order of nature is wise and kind. In a conformity to it consists health and long life; grace, honour, virtue, and joy. But nature turned out of its way will always punish."[3] In a passage in *Rights of Man* that echoed these themes, Paine urged his readers to observe the good things that nature in America, the New World, had to offer:

> The scene which that country presents to the eye of a spectator, has something in it which generates and encourages great ideas. Nature appears to him in magnitude. The mighty objects he beholds, act upon his mind by enlarging it, and he partakes of the greatness he contemplates.—Its first settlers were emigrants from different European nations, and of diversified professions of religion, retiring from the governmental persecutions of the old world, and meeting in the new, not as enemies, but as brothers. The wants which necessarily accompany the cultivation of a wilderness produced among them a state of society, which countries, long harassed by the quarrels and intrigues of governments, had neglected to cherish. In such a situation man becomes what he ought. He sees his species, not with the inhuman idea of a natural enemy, but as kindred; and the example shows to the artificial world, that man must go back to Nature for information. (*RM* 159-60)[4]

This passage suggests Paine's desire that those in the "artificial world" return to nature but not to an original state of mankind. The possibility that America presented to the world of invention was that of a natural environment where all people might learn (he said seek "information") from the example that nature offered.

This passage contains an explicit statement about the relationship among nature, humanity's needs, and political organization. From ancient times to the present, human beings had made great material progress in the world. But moral failure accompanied this material progress. Duping and tricking into kingship was immoral. For a few men to control the lives of many was immoral. Common sense, the very attribute that made man different from the lower animals, had failed when this happened. It was obviously a fallible faculty. Man could no longer enjoy the rights, freedom, and equality that God had given him. Paine seemed certain that his explanations would enable the common people who read his work to understand his message, whereas they could not comprehend the rich phrases of an Edmund Burke.

Paine was thus often preoccupied with natural phenomena and the physical landscape in his French revolutionary writings. This was due, in part, to his new environment, which he found particularly striking. He wrote Franklin his impressions in the summer of 1787. "The country from Havre to Rouen is the richest I ever saw. The crops are abundant, and the cultivation is nice and beautiful order. Everything appeared to be in fulness; the people are very stout, the women excessively fair, and the horses of a vast size and very fat" (*CW* 2:1262).

His preoccupation with the physical environment in the 1790s was also due, in part, to two Parisian encounters. First, there was his association with the Theophilanthropists and their worship of the sun as both a symbol and a reflection of God's illumination in man's mind and soul. Second, and perhaps more tellingly, there was his close relationship with Nicholas de Bonneville, whom he met in 1791, and *le Cercle Social,* whose principles included a curious combination of continental Illuminism and French Masonry.[5] Moreover, he knew Rousseau's work, often used it in his own writings, and was inspired by the Swiss author's emphasis on and use of nature.[6]

These two influences aroused in Paine the desire to preach that average men, his lower- and middle-class readers, could now reawaken their common sense, and in effect, as he said in **Rights of Man,** "go back to Nature for information." Had American independence alone come about, this reawakening could not have taken place. But independence was "accompanied by a revolution in the principles and practices of government" on a continental scale (*RM* 159). This revolution provided an environment to which people could revive common sense and return to nature. Then they could determine their true needs and legitimate desires in a genuinely democratic society. On this basis, they would then fashion a political order that they themselves legitimized.

If the Old World was to experience the same revolution America had, it would need to look to nature. This evocation of the natural world as a symbol of a

person's return to his senses, so to speak, was Paine's way of longing for a new Age of God, a new Arcadian world of perfect justice. At times, he focused on this vision, especially in his rhetorical flourishes, which sang of the common people's power to begin the world over again.

But though Paine often used utopian language . . . he never espoused a thoroughly utopian vision. He was too much the realist for that. A return to nature never entailed departing from urban areas for the primitive or rural reaches of the countryside, where he would go unclothed without modern facilities and pursue a natural condition of life. Neither Locke nor Rousseau advocated such a return either, though Rousseau did believe that man was best when he was fresh out of the state of nature and society had not yet corrupted him.

Paine never went that far. Nature for him exemplified simplicity, innocence, and order. The natural environment taught lessons in moral dignity. Nature told people what to do. Paine often personified her and gave her a distinctive personality. "Nature justifies," said Paine, or, "Nature cannot figure." Or "he who takes nature for his guide" or "the simple voice of nature says." Physical nature's moral grandeur included those rights which a person possessed as a part of his physical existence. The outdoors and democracy were united in such a way that, like Rousseau, Paine "turned the pastoral vision into a vehicle for the democratic idea."[7] If people were to progress, they must learn God's purposes from nature.[8]

The Prize of Nature

Paine, like Rousseau and other eighteenth-century writers concerned with nature, had no desire to go beyond the frontier, to return, in effect, to the state of nature.[9] He was essentially the product of an urban environment, although he had his early experience of the outdoors in small English Midlands towns. He spent the first nineteen years of his life in the small country town of Thetford. According to Conway, Paine's first serious biographer, the town "conveys the pleasant impression of a fairly composite picture of its eras and generations. There is a continuity between the old Grammar School, occupying the site of the ancient cathedral, and the new Guildhall, with its Mechanics' Institute. The old churches summon their flocks from eccentric streets suggestive of literal sheep-paths."[10] A more recent assessment noted that the area "was rich in wildlife and flowers, river and grassland. The young Paine could have plucked the tall-stalked, blue-flowered Viper's Bugloss, the musk thistle and wild mignonette, and watched the flight of innumerable birds, including the Great Bustard who long ago left our shores." These sights and experiences undoubtedly impressed the young Thomas Paine. During the Seven

Years' War, his experiences at sea on the *King of Prussia* must also have had a profound effect. Audrey Williamson notes that he could, "on starry nights, have dreamed his dreams by the ship's sail, and had a vision of those inhabited worlds in space which so prophetically intrude into his book of deistic dissent, *The Age of Reason*."[11] The boundlessness of space and an apparently infinite sea surely impressed the young sailor. After the war, he pursued his interest in the outdoors purchasing globes and a telescope in England from the famous astronomer Dr. John Bevis of the Royal Society. "The natural bent of my mind was to science," he reported in *The Age of Reason* (*CW* 1:496).

His adventures at sea might account for his myriad uses of nautical metaphor and his particular interest in navies and gunboats.[12] Moreover, his interest in astronomy might directly relate to his theory that "the probability . . . is that each of those fixed stars is also a sun, round which another set of worlds or planets, though too remote for us to discover, performs its revolutions, as our system of worlds does round our central sun" (*Age of Reason, CW* 1:502). His projection of "a plurality of worlds" and "a multiple creation" might have resulted from stargazing in Thetford and at sea. Even his excise work provided "a healthy, open air life and Paine probably enjoyed it."[13] There can be no doubt that early experiences provided him with the grist for his religion of nature.

While Paine was a wanderer, he was no pioneer, like some rude and gruff fellow. He was satisfied with the scientific and cultural atmosphere of modern, urbane Philadelphia, London, and Paris. As he wrote to the Abbé Raynal in 1782, civilized man was no longer a "barbarian. . . . Man finds a thousand things to do now which before he did not. Instead of placing his ideas of greatness in the rude achievements of the savage, he studies arts, sciences, agriculture and commerce, the refinements of the gentleman, the principles of society, and the knowledge of the philosopher" (*CW* 2:241). These activities were all good, and Paine busied himself with many of them. One, of course, was writing. He had a natural facility for writing, and he used it powerfully.[14]

Although he was awed "by the immensity of space," the study of nature included all of God's works, including the microscopic world beyond perception. "Every tree, every plant, every leaf serves not only as a habitation but as a world to some numerous race, till animal existence becomes so exceedingly refined that the effluvia of a blade of grass would be food for thousands" (*Age of Reason, CW* 1:499-500).[15] From the vastness of the heavens to the secret, quiet world beyond man's sight, nature was a great reflection of God's creative genius.

And yet nature, in its primitive and wilderness form, was not a habitable place for Paine though he thought it possessed a part of God's divinity. God was the foundation of all life in the universe. A Quaker by upbringing, Paine noted that, while he agreed with the morality of the Friends, "if the taste of a Quaker could have been consulted at the Creation what a silent and drab-colored Creation it would have been! Not a flower would have blossomed its gayeties, nor a bird been permitted to sing" (*Age of Reason, CW* 1:498). The loss to him of these natural wonders, which he loved so much, would have been immeasurable.

Nature, Invention, and the Bastille

Like many eighteenth-century writers, Paine distinguished nature from invention—those things which had come into being through natural (or divine) causes from those things which exist because of man's creativity. This distinction focused first on things natural, which a person's common sense identified as good. Opposed to these were human inventions which, depending on the purposes for which they were used, might either be good or bad.[16]

To Paine, man's most evil institutions were monarchy, aristocracy, and the priesthood (and, later, political factions such as the Federalists). All of these worked against the dictates of common sense. The people could create good government only if they went "back to Nature for information." This hearkening back to nature was a constant knell sounded in his French revolutionary writings. He used it to argue that the revolution possessed a historical dimension so profound that it had a cosmic meaning. The very future of the world was at stake. In using images from nature during the 1790s, Paine expresses his desire about the future.

His intention was to show that the alternative to monarchy and aristocracy was what nature herself justified. What was a "natural" political association for mankind? The democratic republic was comparable to an organic, hence natural, being. "Like the nation itself, it possesses a perpetual stamina, as well of body as of mind, and presents itself on the open theatre of the world in a fair and manly manner" (*RM* 182). Indeed, "the representative system is always parallel with the order and immutable laws of nature" (*RM* 183). Monarchy, on the contrary, was "a mode of government that counteracts nature" (*RM* 182).

If all men were makers, Paine found it unthinkable that some men were barred from political decision making. He failed to understand, much less be convinced by, Burke's argument that the propertied class born to wealth should govern society. For Burke, any other class's claim to govern was foolish and wrongheaded and against nature.

As ability is a vigorous and active principle, and as property is sluggish, inert, and timid, it never can be safe from the invasions of ability, unless it be, out of all proportion, predominant in the representation. It must be represented too in great masses of accumulation, or it is not rightly protected. The characteristic essence of property, formed out of the combined principles of its acquisition and conservation, is to be *unequal*. The great masses therefore which excite envy, and tempt rapacity, must be put out of the possibility of danger.[17]

Paine's response was that anything that compromised "things natural" (such as Burke's myth of the gentry) was unnatural or, in the case of Christianity, supernatural. People like Burke compromised nature to obtain political control for their own insidious purposes. Indeed, they misused language to convince their audiences of what (to Paine, at least) was wrong, misleading, and confusing.

Paine desired a return not to nature herself but to nature's calling. He argued that through common sense man knew what was natural. By studying God's creation, people could learn to use common sense wisely. There was a direct connection between the power of one's mind and heart and the natural physical world. Through individualization and self-realization, the self develops to its greatest potential. But first it is necessary to learn from nature. Two of Paine's best-known passages, both from his French revolutionary writings, reflect his use of physical nature to draw lessons from. The first occurs at the end of the second part of **Rights of Man** and focuses on the arrival of spring, the budding revolutionary era that had started in America and was now flowing into France in 1789 and from there throughout the world. The renewal of the earth symbolically represents the coming regeneration of continental government. This kind of symbolism is also part of Paine's homiletic style.

It is now towards the middle of February. Were I to take a turn into the country, the trees would present a leafless winterly appearance. As people are apt to pluck twigs as they walk along, I perhaps might do the same, and by chance observe, that a single bud on that twig had begun to swell. I should reason very unnaturally, or rather not reason at all, to suppose this was the only bud in England which had this appearance. Instead of deciding thus, I should instantly conclude, that the same appearance was beginning, or about to begin, everywhere; and though the vegetable sleep will continue longer on some trees and plants than on others, and though some of them may not blossom for two or three years, all will be in leaf in the summer, except those which are rotten. What pace the political summer may keep with the natural, no human foresight can determine. It is, however, not difficult to perceive that the spring is begun.[18] (**RM** 272-73)

In this famous passage, Paine drew together several elements of his political ideology with natural imagery to make a powerful argument.[19] First, of course, was nature herself. Walking in the country in midwinter the observer might be tempted to conclude that all was yet dormant. But common sense told him this was not the case. The natural transformation that the change of seasons brings has already begun to happen, as has the transvaluation of human political principles. The springtime of political renewal was just beginning. This springtime was different from all other springs. It was to last forever, and the people would never return to "the present winter," something the Americans also had experienced before their revolution (**CS** 89).

The new spring was inevitable, just as it was the fate of the worm to become a butterfly, an image he used in **The Age of Reason**. The worm in this image is different from the worms he used to represent kings. Like the spring, the transformation of the worm parallels the transvaluation of politics.

The most beautiful parts of the creation to our eye are the winged insects, and they are not so originally. They acquire that form and that inimitable brillancy by progressive changes. The slow and sleeping caterpillar-worm of today passes in a few days to a torpid figure and a state resembling death; and in the next change comes forth in all the miniature magnificence of life, a splendid butterfly. (**CW** 1:592)

The lowliest of creatures, the worm, once emblematic of the king, has now been transformed into a new being. A transvaluation of kingship to democracy has taken place with the transformation of worm to butterfly. First, the worm appeared to enter a deathlike state, but not death itself. It was rather "a state resembling death." From this state, the new creature emerged. Like the passage from winter to spring, this change was quite natural. And as the new springtime was permanent, worms would never again be like kings. Now only butterflies and springtime abound. From cold, dark slavery and tyranny, man entered into a new era of light, freedom, and democracy.

In this connection, the storming and subsequent destruction of the Bastille in 1789 became a powerful metaphor for revolutionary action.[20] Its fall, like the transformation of the king-worm into the butterfly, eliminated an unnatural creation. Here Paine's homiletics reached a heightened sense of immediacy: his tone was full of anxiety and fear. As we will soon see, for Paine, it was a battle in extremis. The Bastille, a physical extension of monarchy, had to be destroyed. On its site, Parisians erected nature herself: a statue of great fertility, where on 10 August 1793, a celebration took place, a celebration that the great revolutionary artist, Jacques-Louis David himself, arranged:[21]

The gathering will take place on the site of the Bastile [*sic*]. In the midst of its ruins will be erected the fountain of Regeneration representing nature. From her fertile breasts (which she will press with her hands) will spurt an abundance of pure and healthful water of which shall drink, each in his turn, eighty-six commissioners, sent by the primary assemblies—one, namely from each department, seniority being given the preference.

A single cup shall serve for all. After the president of the National Convention shall have watered the soil of liberty by a sort of libation, he shall be the first to drink; he shall then pass the cup in succession to the commissioners of the primary assemblies. They shall be summoned alphabetically to the sound of the drum, a salvo of artillery shall announce the consummation of this act of fraternity.[22]

Paine pronounced the Bastille "the high altar and castle of despotism" (*RM* 56). Even the conservative Horace Walpole called it "a curious sample of ancient castellar dungeons, which the good fools the founders took for palaces—yet I always hated to drive by it, knowing the miseries it contained."[23]

David described what would happen as the great August procession continued through the streets of Paris:

At [Liberty's] feet will be an enormous pyre, reached by steps from on all sides: there in profoundest silence shall be offered in expiatory sacrifice the impostured attributes of royalty. There, in the presence of the beloved goddess of the French, eighty-six commissioners, each with a torch in his hand, shall vie with each other in applying the flame; there the memory of the tyrant shall be devoted to public execration and then immediately thousands of birds restored to liberty and bearing on their necks light bands on which shall be written some articles of the declaration of the rights of man, shall take their rapid flight through the air and carry to heaven the testimony of liberty restored to earth.[24]

David here combined the elements that Paine, too, believed were united into a single whole: nature in all her glory, the new light that emanated from Liberty, the rights of man, and eternal freedom. David's report of this celebration, this *fête révolutionnaire,* was very Rousseauistic. Rousseau had presaged just such a *fête* in *Emile* (474) when he wrote of the festivals that Emile and Sophie might bring to countryside. For the French after 1789, their newly won freedom became a cause for celebration in a natural setting. Indeed, as early as 1758, Rousseau noted, in his *Letter to d'Alembert,* that "we already have many of these public festivals; let us have even more. . . . It is in the open air, under the sky, that you ought to gather and give yourselves

to the sweet sentiment of your happiness. . . . Plant a stake crowned with flowers in the middle of a square; gather the people together there, and you will have a festival."[25] The French celebrated such open-air festivals in Paris in just the way David described the transformation of the Bastille into "a ball-room beneath the trees" and the symbolic transformation of the Champ de Mars from a field of military assembly to "a natural earthen arena" to commemorate the first anniversary of the revolution.[26] Thereafter, the revolution was dedicated to nature, especially the sun, the symbol of the great illumination that had taken place in 1789. It was "pure fire, eternal eye, soul and source of all the world," one historian has remarked.[27] Fire was present in the spectacular burning of the remnants of royalty, from clothes and crown to sword and shield, as David noted. As for Rousseau, the idea of open spaces and an illuminated sky was paramount. This meant that "the national festivals can have no other boundary than the vault of heaven, since the sovereign, that is to say, the people, can never be enclosed in a circumscribed and covered space and because it is alone its own object and greatest ornament."[28]

Such *fêtes* took place throughout the early 1790s. No Paine biographer mentions whether he ever personally participated in or witnessed them (nor did he ever mention them), but he surely must have known of them. The same images that Rousseau had used and the idea of the celebrations themselves run throughout his major works. The Bastille stood prominently in Paine's constellation of evils at the opposite pole of nature. His description of the revolutionaries' assault on the fortress was filled with symbolic darkness and dread. "The Bastille was to be either the prize or the prison of the assailants" (*RM* 52). It was all or nothing, salvation or doom, said Paine, who was in part responsible for turning the fall of the Bastille into historical myth. "The event was to be freedom or slavery," which to him meant that forces of absolute good were pitted against forces of absolute evil. "On one side, an army of nearly thirty thousand men; on the other, an unarmed body of citizens: for the citizens of Paris, on whom the National Assembly must then immediately depend, were as unarmed and as undisciplined as the citizens of London are now" (*RM* 54).

The image of a free people, anomic at first, but then drawn together for a cause greater than anything they had achieved before, was articulated in livid language designed to instill a similar response in the reader. The people, though unarmed, possessed "desperate resolution" to destroy the shackles that bound them to feudal institutions. Paine applauded the heroism of those who struck out at the hated symbol of evil. He hoped that a similar downfall of the British government would soon follow.

The Bastille fell with hardly a fight. Nature was victorious because the people had triumphed, inspired by "the highest animation of liberty" (*RM* 56).[29] Taken and then crushed, the Bastille crumbled, and the earth returned to its natural condition. The revolution had just begun.

The Great Oak

With the transformation of the Bastille into "a ballroom" under the trees, other natural images served Paine's linguistic and ideological purposes. One of these was the great oak, an often used emblem in eighteenth-century poetry and literature, and one that Paine emphasized in America in the 1770s and in France in the 1790s.[30] The oak had both pagan and patriotic overtones.[31] The American Sons of Liberty prayed at a "liberty tree," usually an oak because of its great strength, for God's blessing on the righteousness of their cause.

The oak suggested a set of sentiments with which both Americans and Europeans could identify: it was a creation of God through which a person might return to nature and to his own true, natural self. Joining together, taking a solemn oath of solidarity beneath its full boughs, true patriots pledged their lives, fortunes, and sacred honor to the cause of freedom and its blessings. Its sacred image served Paine's homiletics perfectly as he argued that its height and power reflected virtuous strength and security.

The great oak served opposite purposes as well. Burke, for example, used the tree to pinpoint the power of monarchy and aristocracy in the English historical tradition. In 1782, he wrote to the Duke of Richmond that

> you people of great families and hereditary trusts and fortunes are not like such as I am, who whatever we may be by the rapidity of our growth and of the fruit we bear, flatter ourselves that while we creep on the ground we belly into melons that are exquisite for size and flavour, yet still we are but annual plants that perish with our season and leave no sort of traces behind us. You if you are what you ought to be are the great oaks that shade a country and perpetuate your benefits from generation to generation. In my eye—the immediate power of a Duke of Richmond or a Marquis of Rm is not so much of moment but if their conduct and example hand down their principles to their successors; then their houses become the publick repositories and offices of record for the constitution, not like the Tower or Rolls Chappel where it is searched for and sometimes in vain in rotten parchments under dripping and perishing walls; but in full vigour and acting with vital energy and power in the characters of the leading men and natural interests of the country.[32]

The attempt to "root out" this organic link of time, family, and nature was the cause of all social and political ills. Such "hacking" and "rooting out" Burke thought were the activities of the mean-spirited, misguided few who would destroy what history had wrought, including the brilliant settlement of 1688. "We [English people] are taught to look with horror on those children of their country who are prompt rashly to hack that aged parent in pieces, and put him into the kettle of magicians, in hopes that by their poisonous weeds, and wild incantations, they may regenerate the paternal constitution, and renovate their father's life."

Burke rejected the claim of British noisemakers, rabble like Richard Price, that they themselves represented a majority in English society. "No such thing," he thundered, "I assure you."

> Because a half a dozen grasshoppers under a fern make the field ring with their importunate chink, whilst thousands of great cattle, reposed beneath the shadow of the British oak, chew the cud and are silent, pray do not imagine, that those who make the noise are the only inhabitants of the field, that of course, they are many in number; or that, after all, they are other than the little shrivelled, meagre, hopping, though loud and troublesome insects of the hour."[33]

The "shadow of the British oak" extended far. It stultified the annoying bugs that made all the commotion beneath its great branches.

Paine would have none of it. The British oak must come down, or it would rot. So must the French oak. For Paine, the tree directly contrasted with the castle prison of the Bastille. In 1791, speaking at the Thatched House Tavern in London, Paine congratulated the French people "for having laid the axe to the root of tyranny, and for erecting government on the sacred *hereditary rights of man.*"[34] In its place, in the place of the aristocratic oak of Edmund Burke, free men could now plant a liberty tree.

Rousseau used this same natural imagery when he described "bands of peasants . . . regulating their affairs of state under an oak tree, and always acting wisely."[35] Echoing this, Paine early on had cited the precedent that men long ago had gathered to form their first government "at some convenient tree" to "afford them a State House, under the branches of which, the whole colony may assemble to deliberate on public matters" (*CS* 67).[36] This tree, Paine's version of the oak, was emblematic not only of their association, but of men's free choice to join together. In the shade of this tree, they found comfort and solace, which was quite different from what the English found under "the shadow of the British oak." Here, they found that they could naturally use their innate capabilities without outside interference. It was not by accident that they chose a tree to do it under. Like the earth, the tree united the community to nature.

They gathered there to deliberate the great issues of the day. The tree was not left to those sleepy-eyed, cud-chewing cows in the pasture lying in a somnolent state under its rotten branches. For Paine, the grasshoppers (in Burke's imagery) now abounded. They were not merely noisemakers, that is, they were different from the ungainly mobs of the Gordon riots, "who committed the burnings and devastations in London" (*RM* 58). Those engaged in revolution were, for the most part, now behaving naturally. "The Almighty hath implanted in us these unextinguishable feelings for good and wise purposes. They are the guardians of his image in our hearts" (*CS* 99-100). This was true of all people. No matter what anyone, including Burke, said, this could not be changed. After all, said Paine, "whatever appertains to the nature of man, cannot be annihilated by man" (*RM* 44). Man in his person reflected the justice of God. No person could ever destroy this phenomenon.

Addressed to the Americans in 1775, Paine's poem, **"Liberty Tree,"** allowed the poet to sing of the arrival of "the Goddess Liberty" in "a chariot of light." She brought with her a gift: a plant, which was "a pledge of her love." She called the plant "Liberty Tree."

> The celestial exotic stuck deep in the
> ground,
>   Like a native it flourished and bore;
> The fame of its fruit drew the nations
> around,
>   To seek out this peaceable shore.
> Unmindful of names or distinctions they
> came,
>   For freemen like brothers agree;
> With one spirit endued, they one friendship
> pursued,
>   And their temple was Liberty Tree.

These "freemen" thrived beneath its boughs. But England, which he mentioned by name, showed

> How all the tyrannical powers,
> Kings, Commons, and Lords, are uniting
> amain
>   To cut down this guardian of ours.

For the poet, the tree would survive this assault and grow to full fruition for all people everywhere, because they would "unite with a cheer, / In defense of our Liberty Tree."[37]

No barriers, then, separated the American people from nature, or from God. Nor, in fact, did they separate any people anywhere from God. "Before any institution of government was known in the world, there existed, if I may so express it, a compact between God and Man, from the beginning of time; and that as the relation and condition which man in his *individual person* stands in towards his Maker, cannot be changed" (*RM* 113).

Burke would have wanted intermediaries (kings, lords, and priests) to stand between the people and God, on the one hand, and between the people and nature, on the other. Not so Paine: For the first time, a person could become truly conscious of his status in the natural world. He could learn what nature meant him to be and what nature had imparted to him. It was a powerful argument, expressed clearly and homiletically, and especially frightening for the British establishment, which feared the spread of revolutionary ideas and actions to their island nation. Paine's case was so forcefully made that **Rights of Man** (like *The Age of Reason* within a few years) was banned in England, and Paine outlawed.

God, Nature, and Light

In considering this permanent bond among the people, God, and nature, we should wonder how far Paine was willing to take it. In a 1797 pamphlet, written as a letter to Thomas Erskine, in which Paine defended **The Age of Reason,** he contended that he had a right to deny the truth of the Bible. He then set out to argue why it was "a duty which every man owes himself, and reverentially to his Maker, to ascertain by every possible inquiry whether there be a sufficient evidence to believe [the scriptures] or not." In the course of his analysis, Paine suddenly broke off, as he was wont to do, and wondered why it was necessary for anyone to have to explain contradictory and miraculous stories. Having concluded that such contradictions should cause any reasonably intelligent person "to suspect that it is not the word of God," he continued:

> What! does not the Creator of the universe, the Fountain of all wisdom, the Origin of all science, the Author of all knowledge, the God of order and harmony, know how to write? When we contemplate the vast economy of the creation, when we behold the unerring regularity of the visible solar system, the perfection with which all its several parts revolve, and by corresponding assemblage form a whole;—when we launch our eye into the boundless ocean of space, and see ourselves surrounded by innumerable words, not one of which varies from its appointed place—when we trace the power of a creator, from a mite to an elephant, from an atom to a universe—can we suppose that the mind that could conceive such a design and the power that executed it with incomparable perfection, cannot write without inconsistence, or that a book so written can be the work of such a power?[38]

On the simplest level, this passage reflected Paine's deism. He presented God, nature's God, as a creator, a first cause, who brought order and harmony to the universe and who was the author of human reason. And yet, something deeper, more mystical, was going on here. The bond that he saw between the people, God, and nature placed him in the company of those whom Margaret C. Jacob has termed members of "the Radical Enlightenment:" the freemasons and pantheists who, like Paine, were mystical, democratic thinkers at the end of the eighteenth century.

There are indications that Paine's version of the bond among God, the people, and nature tended to mimic in language the radical Enlightenment, which included pantheistic elements, a curious notion for a deist. Even so, the essentials of this tendency included the idea that God was more than the creator, more than the force that ordered the universe. He resided in that very order itself. He was "the Grand Architect," whose spirit dwelled within every living creature in the natural world.[39] This spirit empowered people to rule themselves without the intervention of kings, lords, and priests. Nature and man were linked in a way that had mystical, almost magical, connotations. It was the convergence of these three elements—God, the people, and nature—which gave substance to Paine's religion of nature, the way in which he expressed his worship of God's manifest creation in his own peculiar way (largely through his writings).

Paine's evocation of an orderly and well-regulated universe in his letter to Erskine went beyond a Newtonian vocabulary. God was more than a watchmaker. He was a divine immanence in the world. His power was traceable throughout all creation: from the lowliest, tiny mite to the gigantic elephant; from the atom, the smallest known element, to the entire universe itself. God not only created but continued to create the universe. His spirit and power were eternally present in time and space as a continual creation. Paine said in *The Age of Reason* that "the Creation speaks a universal language. . . . It is an *ever-existing* original, which every person can read" (*CS* 1:483). Do we want to know what God is? We will find God only in what we are, what we see, what we feel. God was in our very being. A person reflected God's nature, and a person's common sense, through its combination of reason and sensibility, reflected God's wisdom. Follow the dictates of your heart and mind, and your "moral life will follow," said Paine, adding an "of course" to the end of this sentence (*CS* 1:485). Through the medium of the natural world, through nature herself, "God speaketh universally to man." Study nature, Paine advised, and you will not only find "the works of God" but will soon discover that the power of God dwells in all living things (*CW* 1:487).

Shortly before writing to Erskine, Paine helped form an association in Paris whose purpose was to underscore the bond of the people, God, and nature. This association was the Society of the Theophilanthropists, the "adorers of God and friends of man."[40] While it remains debatable that Paine was ever a member of a Freemasonry lodge, he was definitely an early member of the society. Its records show that he addressed its membership at its gatherings, and he probably had a hand in drafting its bylaws.[41] Attached to the Erskine letter was a history of the Theophilanthropists, which Paine himself wrote.

The term *theophilanthropist* embodied the spiritual linkage that Paine thought existed among God, the people, and nature. Paine's history of the society made clear that worship of God was a matter of individual faith and belief. Not only were interventions by priests and appeals to superstition unnecessary; they were beyond the bounds of belief. God-in-his-natural-creation was the only subject of the theophilanthropists' adoration. The ethical traditions recounted in their "festivals," as Paine called their worship (echoing perhaps the celebrations and *fêtes révolutionnaires* in the 1790s), were not foreign to Paine. After all, "the wise precepts that have been transmitted by writers of all countries and in all ages" provided the foundation for these ethical traditions. Theirs was a universal understanding of God-in-nature, and their ideas were the same ones he incorporated into *The Age of Reason.*[42]

Paine's linkage of the people, God, and nature was even more pronounced in his discussion of Freemasonry. He often used the contrast between dark and light to emphasize the transvaluation of life in the new revolutionary age. While darkness might be as much a part of nature as light, blackness embodied evil and slavery. In *Rights of Man,* he preached that "what we have to do is clear as light" and that the rights of man emanated as "illuminating and divine principles." A person could know this immediately and automatically, for "the sun needs no inscription to distinguish him from darkness" (*RM* 159). Paine's understanding of Freemasonry and its origins fitted into this scheme. It originated with the ancient druids, whose primary focus was sun worship. Their beliefs, pure and virtuous, were grounded in a simple, innocent piety that served as a model for those who claimed to be in the community of the faithful.

The druids' sun worship greatly inspired Paine. In the course of his discussion, independent even of his history of Freemasonry, he remarked that the sun was "this great luminary." In "Origins of Freemasonry" he called it "the great visible agent" of God.[43] He evidently admired the centrality of nature in the druids' lives. They possessed "that wise, elegant, philosophical religion," which he took for the exact "opposite to the faith of the gloomy Christian Church" (*CS* 2:835).

Those who founded their practices and who formulated their beliefs were obviously "a wise, learned, and moral class of men," everything that Paine hoped he could be (*CW* 2:837). Through them, all people could learn true moral duty and acquire a love of nature that worked its way directly and inevitably to the divine itself.

Paine worshiped the sun as a reflection of the luminescence of God's creation. It is difficult to pinpoint exactly how Paine arrived at a religion of nature. His experiences in Thetford and the English countryside in early life were important influences on his love of and appreciation for the physical landscape. They may explain the place of nature in his work of the 1770s and 1780s. But his later writings led in an alternative direction toward his French experiences, in particular to his long association with one of the most interesting and curious journalists of the time, the romantic Nicholas de Bonneville.

Paine met Bonneville perhaps as early as 1791 and visited him often from 1797 until his return to America in 1802.[44] Bonneville's wife, Marguerite, with her three sons (one of whom was Paine's godson and namesake, Thomas Paine Bonneville), followed Paine to America the next year and at various times lived on his farms in Bordentown and New Rochelle. Paine provided for them in his will to ensure their financial stability. In the meantime, he took it upon himself to look after two of her sons (the eldest in 1804 returned to his father) and saw to their education.[45] Paine and Nicholas de Bonneville, twenty-three years his junior, were intimate friends. After 1802, in correspondence, Paine continually urged Bonneville to come to America, but it appears that he was unable to emigrate under the Napoleonic regime. He finally arrived after Paine's death.[46]

Bonneville was the founder of a revolutionary organization called *"le Cercle Social,"* of which Paine was probably a member.[47] As a journalist, he edited several newspapers, some of which printed Paine's writings. For James H. Billington, the Social Circle "combined the Masonic ideal of a purified inner *circle* with the Rousseauist ideal of a *social,* and not merely a political contract."[48] Bonneville was an early follower of Illuminism (which, because he spoke German, he helped bring to France from Germany). Illuminism paralleled existing French Masonic ideas of peace and brotherhood, light and brilliance. These were things that Paine was interested in as well. From the Social Circle, Bonneville declared, there would "emanate a *circle of light* which will uncover for us that which is hidden in the symbolic chaos of masonic innovations."[49]

The Social Circle was a small, secret, Masonic-like organization whose members adopted assumed names and carried secret identity cards. To support it, Bonneville organized a larger mass association, "the Universal Confederation of the Friends of Truth," the "servant of the Social Circle" and "of all the circles 'of free brothers affiliated with it.'"[50] Bonneville envisioned it producing yet another new society for the new breed of men: the new Illuminati, the men of vision. "The Circle of Free People [will] pour forth with a sure hand thy luminous rays into the dark climates."[51] The French newspaper *Mercure* reported that Bonneville addressed these remarks to the sun with the words, "Eclairé, le monde sera éclairé!"[52]

It is difficult, if not impossible, to know with certainty whether long association with Bonneville and his Illuminist ideals directly or indirectly stimulated Paine's religion of nature. His ideas were certainly suggestive. Because fire destroyed much of Paine's work after his death, the difficulty is compounded. And yet, the pattern that Paine established in his writing does, however circumstantially, point to Bonneville and his followers.

The brilliant spirit and power of God penetrated the natural world. The people reflected this spirit and power through their inventive capabilities, particularly their power to transform the world, if they wished. The Freemasons, the Theophilanthropists, the Illuminati all focused on nature's link to God and the people. In so doing, they provided a means, indeed an entire language, for Paine to attack those who, in his opinion, denied the people what was theirs by nature, and hence by God. By using common sense, people could know that the natural world, from the landscape to the rights of man, was authentic, virtuous, and ultimately sacred.

Natural rights were inherent qualities of all mankind to a greater extent than anyone before had suspected. A person had a natural right, in effect, to these rights because they were part of nature with its indwelling presence of God and his power. More important, the people possessed a divine right to them, because God from the beginning of time itself, from eternity, had ordained it. This was the lesson Paine preached in the 1790s to his audience of common people, principally in America and England, but also in France. He hoped this message would soon spread to Britain and eventually throughout the continent to induce all Europeans to restore the rights of man.

Notes

[1] Renato Poggioli, *The Oaten Flute: Essays on Pastoral Poetry and the Pastoral Ideal* (Cambridge: Cambridge University Press, 1975), 1.

[2] See McWilliams, *Fraternity in America,* 178-80; "The environment, after all, had been the basis for the messianic hopes that European visionaries held for

America. Ours was the environment of nature, where man could begin again" (178). . . .

[3] Richard Price, *Observations on Reversionary Payments,* second ed. (London, 1772), 276.

[4] See A. Owen Aldridge, "The Apex of American Literary Nationalism," in *Early American Literature: A Comparative Approach* (Princeton: Princeton University Press, 1982), 186-208, esp. 296, and Robert Hole, *Pulpits, Politics and Public Order in England, 1760-1832.* (Cambridge: Cambridge University Press, 1989), 115-18.

[5] These are discussed later in this chapter.

[6] Robbins, "Lifelong Education of Paine," 138, admonishes that we ought not exaggerate Paine's debt to Rousseau. Certainly the emphasis on nature in both suggests a greater debt than Robbins concedes.

[7] Poggioli, *Oaten Flute,* 216, 214. For Paine's relation to William Blake in regard to things natural, see Robert N. Essick, "William Blake, Thomas Paine, and Biblical Revelation," *Studies in Romanticism* 30 (Summer 1991): 189-212.

[8] While Paine's bucolic vision was rooted mostly in the French landscape, his feelings about America indicate an earlier preoccupation with the physical landscape. Thus, he offered a grand vista ranging from the far reaches of the western lands to the newly cultivated frontier to the rural countryside near and around the towns of America. See Thomas Paine, *Public Good* (1780), *CW* 2:303-33, esp. 332. For the power of the physical landscape in the late eighteenth and early nineteenth centuries, see Peter S. Onuf, *The Origins of the Federal Republic: Jurisdictional Controversies in the United States, 1775-1787* (Philadelphia: University of Pennsylvania Press, 1983); R.W.B. Lewis, *The American Adam: Innocence, Tragedy, and Tradition in the Nineteenth Century* (Chicago: University of Chicago Press, 1955); Charles L. Sanford, *The Quest for Paradise: Europe and the American Moral Imagination* (Urbana: University of Illinois Press, 1961); Leo Marx, *The Machine in the Garden: Technology and the Pastoral Ideal in America* (New York: Oxford University Press, 1964); Henry Nash Smith, *Virgin Land: The American West as Symbol and Myth* (Cambridge: Harvard University Press, 1950).

[9] Paine thought the wilderness, which he once called a "savage uncivilized life," was a kind of state of nature (*RM* 211). Intriguing comparisons could be made with Rousseau, especially the "Idyll of the Cherries" in the *Confessions.* See James Miller, *Rousseau: Dreamer of Democracy* (New Haven: Yale University Press, 1984); Christopher Frayling and Robert Wokler, "From the Orang-Utan to the Vampire: Towards an Anthro-pology of Rousseau," in *Rousseau after Two Hundred Years: Proceedings of the Cambridge Bicentennial Colloquium,* edited by R. A. Leigh (Cambridge: Cambridge University Press, 1982), 109-29. Parallels can also be found in Crèvecoeur, though there is no evidence Paine even heard of this rural Tory writer in New York State. See J. Hector St. John de Crèvecoeur, *Letters from an American Farmer and Sketches of Eighteenth-Century America,* edited by Albert E. Stone (Harmondsworth: Penguin, 1981), 7, 55-56, 61, 67, 69, 70-71; Myra Jehlen, "J. Hector St. John de Crèvecoeur: A Monarcho-Anarchist in America," *American Quarterly* 31 (Summer 1979): 204-22; and Marx, *Machine in the Garden,* 107-16.

[10] Conway, *Life of Paine,* 1:6.

[11] Audrey Williamson, *Thomas Paine,* 21, 27. See Alyce Barry, "Thomas Paine, Privateersman," *Pennsylvania Magazine of History and Biography* 101 (October 1977): 451-61.

[12] Barry, "Privateersman," 460-61.

[13] Williamson, *Thomas Paine,* 29, 43.

[14] One of his early pieces in the *Pennsylvania Magazine* (Feb. 1775) was "Useful and Entertaining Hints," an essay which was in part an admiring ode to nature. There, he remarked that

> in such gifts as nature can annually re-create, she is noble and profuse, and entertains the whole world with the interest of her fortunes; but watches over the capital with the care of a miser. Her gold and jewels lie concealed in the earth, in caves of utter darkness; and hoards of wealth, heap upon heaps, mould in the chests, like the riches of a necromancer's cell. It must be very pleasant to an adventurous speculist to make excursions into these Gothic regions; and in his travels he may possibly come to a cabinet locked up in some rocky vault, whose treasure shall reward his toil, and enable him to shine on his return, as splendidly as nature herself. (*CW* 2:1023)

[15] Even Paine's idea of his bridge came from the natural world. "I took the idea of constructing it from a spider's web, of which it resembles a section, and I naturally supposed that when nature enabled that insect to make a web she taught it the best method of putting it together." Letter to Sir George Staunton, Bart., Spring 1789, *CW* 2:1044-45. See also *RM* 181-82 and letter to Joseph Banks, 25 May 1789, cited in Aldridge, *Man of Reason* 109.

[16] Paine seems to approach a rudimentary theory of utility here, but he never explicitly says that he believed that all natural phenomena, like natural disasters, were good.

[17] Edmund Burke, *Reflections on the Revolution in France,* edited by Conor Cruise O'Brien (Harmondsworth: Penguin, 1969), All references are to this edition.

[18] Boulton, *Language of Politics,* 137, calls this passage an "allegory . . . as simple as biblical parable[;] its message is clear and the experience it draws on is universal." See also Smith, *Politics of Language,* 35-67. For comparison with other revolutions, see Ronald Paulson, "Revolution and the Visual Arts," in Roy Porter and Mikulas Teich, eds., *Revolution in History* (Cambridge: Cambridge University Press, 1986), 240-60, esp. 254.

[19] See Paulson, *Representations of Revolution,* 73-74.

[20] Ibid., 41-47, 75-76.

[21] This festival actually took place. See Mona Ozouf, *Festivals and the French Revolution,* translated by Alan Sheridan (Cambridge: Harvard University Press, 1988), 83-84, 172-74.

[22] Ernest F. Henderson, *Symbol and Satire in the French Revolution* (New York: G. P. Putnam's, 1912), 357-58. See also Bronislaw Backo, *Lumières de l'utopie* (Paris: Payot, 1978), 263-71.

[23] Horace Walpole to Hannah More, 10 Sept. 1789, in *Horace Walpole's Correspondence,* edited by W.S. Lewis Vol. 31 (New Haven: Yale University Press, 1961), 323.

[24] Henderson, *Symbol and Satire,* 361-62.

[25] Jean-Jacques Rousseau, "Letter to M. d'Alembert on the Theatre," in *Politics and the Arts,* edited by Allan Bloom (Ithaca: Cornell University Press, 1968), 125-26.

[26] James H. Billington, *Fire in the Minds of Men: Origins of the Revolutionary Faith* (New York: Basic Books, 1980), 48. The transformation of the Bastille into "a ballroom beneath the trees" (a public park) is from Ozouf, *Festivals,* 149.

[27] J. Tiersot, *Les Fêtes et les chants de la révolution française* (Paris: Hachette, 1908), 40.

[28] Quoted by Ozouf, *Festivals,* 129.

[29] For a quite different set of arguments for his American audience, see Paine's view of an urban institution, the bank, in chapter 6 and chapter 8 for his cosmic use of this nature imagery.

[30] Arthur Schlessinger, "Liberty Tree: A Genealogy," *New England Quarterly,* 25 (Dec. 1952): 435-48.

[31] Jordan, "Familial Politics," 294-308. See also Ozouf, *Festivals,* 217-61.

[32] Edmund Burke to the Duke of Richmond, 15 Nov. 1772, in *The Correspondence of Edmund Burke,* edited by Thomas W. Copeland (Cambridge: Cambridge University Press, 1960), 2:377.

[33] Burke, *Reflections,* 194; 181.

[34] "Address and Declaration" (London, 1791), *CW* 2:534. See also *RM* 58, where Paine makes his famous statement, "Lay then axe to the root, and teach governments humanity."

[35] Jean-Jacques Rousseau, *On the Social Contract,* edited by Donald A. Cress (Indianapolis: Hackett, 1983), 79.

[36] For a different view, see Aldridge, *Paine's American Ideology,* 104 and 304, n. 33.

[37] "Liberty Tree," *Philadelphia Evening Post* (16 Sept. 1775), *CW* 2:1091-92. See A. Owen Aldridge, "Poetry of Thomas Paine."

[38] *Prosecution of "The Age of Reason"* (1797), *CW* 2:729, 732.

[39] Margaret C. Jacob, *The Radical Enlightenment: Pantheists, Freemasons and Republicans* (London: George Allen & Unwin, 1981), 110.

[40] *Prosecution of "The Age of Reason", CW* 2:745. See McWilliams, *Idea of Fraternity,* 182, 203-9.

[41] Foner, *Paine and Revolutionary America,* 252-53; Hawke, *Paine,* 326; Jacob, *Radical Enlightenment,* 154; Williamson, *Thomas Paine,* 237. Jacob says that Paine was a Freemason. Williamson says there is no proof he was. Aldridge and Hawke say nothing. The conclusion now is that we do not have enough evidence to make a final judgment.

[42] *Prosecution of "The Age of Reason," CW* 2:747. See also "The Existence of God" (Paris, 1797), *CW* 2:248-56.

[43] "Origins of Freemasonry" (unpublished, 1805), *CW* 2:833.

[44] Aldridge, *Man of Reason,* 255-56; Hawke, *Paine,* 332; Williamson, *Thomas Paine,* 249-50, 253; Billington, *Fire in the Minds of Men,* 42 (on Paine's introduction to Bonneville in 1791).

[45] Aldridge, *Man of Reason,* 271-72, 186-87; Williamson, *Thomas Paine,* 274; Hawke, *Paine,* 394. The youngest son, Benjamin, became an important

military officer in the United States and the subject of a biography by Washington Irving.

[46] Thanks largely to the nefarious biography by Paine's enemy, James Cheetham, a great deal has been made over whether Marguerite de Bonneville was Paine's paramour, whether Paine really fathered her two youngest sons, and ironically, whether Paine was impotent during most of his life. Paine's biographers discount all of this. On Bonneville's detention in France, see Conway, *Life of Paine,* 2:432-33.

[47] Aldridge, *Man of Reason,* 146, claims he was. For the history of this extraordinary group, see Gary Kates, *The Cercle Social, the Girondins and the French Revolution* (Princeton: Princeton University Press, 1985).

[48] Billington, *Fire in the Minds of Men,* 39, 66.

[49] Nicholas de Bonneville, *The Jesuits Driven from Free Masonry* (Paris, 1788), 1:26, quoted in Billington, *Fire in the Minds of Men,* 97.

[50] C. Delacroix, "Récherches sur le Cercle Social (1790-1791)," Doctoral thesis, University of the Sorbonne, 1975, 33-34, quoted by Billington, *Fire in the Minds of Men,* 39.

[51] Nicholas de Bonneville, *On the Spirit of Religions* (Paris, 1792), quoted in Billington, *Fire in the Minds of Men,* 41.

[52] Billington, *Fire in the Minds of Men,* 522, n. 124.

Works Cited

Aldridge, Alfred Owen. *Man of Reason: The Life of Thomas Paine.* Philadelphia: Lippincott, 1959.

―――. "The Poetry of Thomas Paine." *Pennsylvania Magazine of History and Biography* 79 (Jan. 1951): 89-93.

―――. *Thomas Paine's American Ideology.* Newark: University of Delaware Press, 1985.

Billington, James H. *Fire in the Minds of Men: Origins of the Revolutionary Faith.* New York: Basic Books, 1980.

Boulton, James T. *The Language of Politics in the Age of Wilkes and Burke.* Westport, Conn.: Greenwood Press, 1975.

[Burke, Edmund]. *Reflections on the Revolution in France,* edited by Conor Cruise O'Brien. Harmondsworth: Penguin, 1969.

Conway, Moncure D. *The Life of Thomas Paine.* 2 vols. New York: Putnam, 1892.

Foner, Eric. *Tom Paine and Revolutionary America.* New York: Oxford University Press, 1976.

Hawke, David Freeman. *Paine.* New York: Harper & Row, 1974.

Henderson, Ernest F. *Symbol and Satire in the French Revolution.* New York: G. P. Putnam's, 1912.

Jacob, Margaret C. *The Radical Enlightenment: Pantheists, Freemasons and Republicans.* London: George Allen & Unwin, 1981.

Jordan, Winthrop D. "Familial Politics: Thomas Paine and the Killing of the King." *Journal of American History* 60 (Sept. 1973): 294-308.

Marx, Leo. *The Machine in the Garden: Technology and the Pastoral Ideal in America.* New York: Oxford University Press, 1964.

McWilliams, Wilson Carey. *The Idea of Fraternity in America.* Berkeley: University of California Press, 1973.

Ozouf, Mona. *Festivals and the French Revolution,* translated by Alan Sheridan. Cambridge: Harvard University Press, 1988.

[Paine, Thomas.] *The Complete Writings of Thomas Paine,* edited by Philip S. Foner. 2 vols. New York: Citadel, 1945.

―――. *Rights of Man,* edited by Henry Collins, with an introduction by Eric Foner. Harmondsworth: Penguin, 1984.

Paulson, Ronald. *Representations of Revolution 1789-1820.* New Haven: Yale University Press, 1983.

Poggioli, Renato. *The Oaten Flute: Essays on Pastoral Poetry and the Pastoral Ideal.* Cambridge: Cambridge University Press, 1975.

Robbins, Caroline. "The Lifelong Education of Thomas Paine 1737-1809: Some Reflections upon His Acquaintance among Books." *Proceedings of the American Philosophical Society* 127 (June 1983): 135-42.

Rousseau, Jean-Jacques. *The Confessions,* edited by J. M. Cohen. Harmondsworth: Penguin, 1979.

Smith, Olivia. *The Politics of Language, 1791-1819.* Oxford: Clarendon Press, 1984.

Williamson, Audrey. *Thomas Paine: His Life, Work and Times.* London: George Allen & Unwin, 1973.

Edward H. Davidson and William J. Scheick (essay date 1994)

SOURCE: "Paine Reads the Bible," in *Paine, Scripture,
and Authority:* The Age of Reason *as Religious and
Political Idea,* Lehigh University Press, 1994, pp. 70-
87.

[*Focusing on* The Age of Reason, *the following chapter from Davidson and Scheick's book analyzes Paine's
effort to undermine the authority of the Bible and his
effort to create a sense of authority for himself.*]

Paine intended *The Age of Reason* to present what he
called "the theology that is true" (1:464). His own
faith, he professed, contained two articles: "I believe
in one God, and no more; . . . and I believe that
religious duties consist in doing justice, loving mercy,
and endeavoring to make our fellow creatures happy"
(1:464). For Paine, the Deity is worthy of belief and
worship, not as He is described in the Bible, but as He
is made known, represented, in the ever-widening
knowledge of science.

The Age of Reason, as Paine affirmed, was designed
to counter the atheism coming as an effect of the
French Revolution and to clarify a belief in God based
on "true" religion, free from cant and superstition, and
based on the uniform laws of nature and human
thought. The "Almighty lecturer" speaks "universally
to man" in "all nations" on "all worlds" through the
"universal language" of his creation (1:482-83).

Paine conceded (1:485), however, that occasionally
the Bible conveyed something of this divine revelation,
particularly in the book of Job and in the Nineteenth

Psalm (as paraphrased in Joseph Addison's well-
known hymn). Paine also affirmed his belief in the person of
Jesus as a good man who lived and died at a certain
time in history. Paine accepted the Bible as a history
of a people over a long span of time, a history of the
great effects of certain patriarchs on the lives of their
people. Paine recognized elements of truth in Scripture
that were, he thought, acceptable to persons of reason.

Nevertheless, to appreciate these features of the Bible,
Paine maintained, it is necessary to penetrate through
the pretensions, flaws, discrepancies, and errors in its
narrative. Only then could the Word have any place or
pertinence in the human future that Paine prophesied.
It was to this end, as a requirement for his underlying
political agenda, that Paine set out in *The Age of
Reason* to reveal the true nature of Scripture.

Tradition and Authority in Biblical Interpretation

As we observed in the last chapter, for centuries old
questions about Scripture had been raised by scholars,
exegetes, and commentators: How had the Bible come
to be? Who wrote it? Can it be rightly called "the Book
of God," or was it the work of human hands? Paine
had his own answers to these long-considered questions. Although, . . . he had been exposed to something of this legacy, he indicated that he had no need
for it, that he would inquire into these and other matters
on his own, authorized only by the universal human
attribute of "reason and philosophy" (1:467).

One truism of this long-established and generally unquestioned heritage (at least from Luther onward in
Protestant thought) held that "scripture doth best interpret itself." Holy Writ contains everything necessary for its understanding. All that is needed to read
and perceive its truth is a humble inquirer, enlightened
(some would say "saved") by the very Word itself and
the spirit of God acting in and through the Word. As
authorities and lay readers averred, Scripture requires
no exegesis or commentary to be efficacious.[1]

This long Protestant tradition, that the Word explains
itself, prevailed side by side with a different idea, the
Pauline notion that Scripture can be difficult and obscure. The Bible could reveal itself only because it
was divine in origin; but this divine origin necessarily
meant that the truth scripturally revealed to postlapsarian
humanity must finally be an ultimate truth far beyond
the limits of human language (the means) and human
understanding (the end). Thus, according to this second tradition, even if the Word accommodates the
language and ways of human thinking, there always
must be a significant distance between its divine origin
and purpose, on the one hand, and its human reception
and understanding, on the other. This sense of the
Bible as a deep and complex mystery, as Paine himself

perceived it, persisted together with the tradition affirming that Scripture readily interprets itself to human readers.

Also, tradition taught that Holy Writ offers its divine teaching in human verses, that is, in small compact pieces. Whether single verses, chapters, or books, these pieces are, nonetheless, parts of a uniform whole. Believing in such an association, interpreters followed a course through these small segments, units of thoughts, and little increments to disclose this whole. Therefore, tradition held, people should read Scripture—telling what the Book opens to them and what they are privileged to know—by following in order the compact segments and then by speaking in their own voice. Their voice is empowered, not by itself, but by the form and power of the Bible, with its every unit in place leading to the complete text as designed and executed when the Word itself was revealed.

But how had every word of Scripture been given at that revelation, and how had every word been put in place just as it is printed in the Bible? And how can the verses in their divine order be made clearly understandable as revelation if human comprehension depends on a translation of this revelation into the inadequate terms of everyday speech? Such awareness of the need for an extreme translation to bring revelation of the divine Word to human words included, as well, an awareness of the need for an arduous retranslation of these human words to render the revelation of the divine Word. Obviously, Holy Writ, for all its surface simplicity and ordinariness, is not plainness all through, as is suggested by the notion that Scripture best interprets itself.

Paine made use of both points of view. First, in a disingenuous gesture, he seemed to accept the tradition that Scripture best interprets itself. He affirmed at one point, "The evidence I shall produce is contained in the book itself; I will not go out of the Bible for proof against the supposed authenticity of the Bible" (1:531). But, second, when he added in the next sentence that "false testimony is always good against itself," he suggested the other biblical tradition concerning Scripture as a deep and complex mystery that is not plainness all through.

The latter tradition prevails in *The Age of Reason,* with the primary difference that Paine emphasized, with a vengeance, the distance between divine revelation and human expression. For him, finally, the Bible should be approached solely in the light of what such a distance implies: not only that the divinity of Scripture should be doubted, but also that its commentary should be empirically assessed primarily in terms of contemporary thought and human behavior. Paine read Holy Writ the same way he read a historical narrative, a moral argument, or a social or political treatise of his

own time—each of which, in fact, he assumed Scripture to be. It could, then, like any narrative, argument, or treatise, be answered and countered.

Such an approach naturally led to Paine's reconsideration of those centuries-old questions: Who wrote the Bible? Are the names attributed to its individual books accurate designators of their authors? If Holy Writ is both divine revelation and human expression, how did it come to be in the form it now has? When did it receive this form?

From the outset Paine alleges that the Bible has no claim to divine authorship or authority. He concedes that while some of its parts seem to have divine sanction, equal importance cannot be given to most of the scriptural narratives. Some of these narratives, he is sure, are authentic historical records, and many of the prophecies, poems, and wise sayings express the age in which they were composed.

The Bible is, for Paine, a collection of various kinds of writings that resemble similar assemblages by other people of ancient times. Fragments of history in some written form, documents, poems, declarations, speeches, and various certificates of governmental action comprised the original records that the Jews kept throughout times of war and settlement. There was as well, in Paine's view, something of a long-surviving original narrative—including stories, poems, and sayings—that had been orally transmitted from one generation to another and perhaps crudely recorded in the Bible.

Because Paine sees a glaring discrepancy between this original simple narrative and what (to him) quite obviously was editorially manipulated and distorted later, he assumes a two-stage composition of the scriptural documents. The book of Ruth, for example, strikes Paine as essentially a simple folktale concerning a young woman who worked in the fields of a wealthy man, was taken to his bed, and eventually became his wife; but at some later stage this story was made to account for the beginning of a generation of Israelite kings who represent the founding of David's royal line. Paine concludes that, in this instance as throughout the Old Testament, the later "compilers were ignorant" of the identity of "the first narrators" and "confounded the writings of different authors with each other" (1:552-53). These later editors elaborated on early folktales to give them an allegorical and sacral significance. Through this endeavor these editors sought to inspire the Jewish people with a sense of their religious and national destiny; but they also connived for personal advantage in their management of the scriptural texts. That such corrupting *political* intentions inform much of Scripture is a critical feature of Paine's argument in *The Age of Reason.*

Paine accordingly assumes that he can read the Old Testament both for what "the first narrators" had seen or known, and for what they could not have seen or known but what was credited to them afterward. Despite Paine's hostility toward these original narrators, toward Moses and other famous Old Testament patriarchal figures, he, in some sense, imaginatively identifies with them, as if he too were a first recorder. Like them, he sets out to tell the truth. In another sense, he imaginatively identifies with the later "compilers," with the important difference that (in his opinion) he demystifies, rather than mystifies, the texts. Like these later priests or scribes, Paine discloses the form and character of the scriptural records.

Primarily he discloses how the "contradictions in time, place, and circumstances that abound in the books" were the handiwork of three different but related designers: the "Bible-makers," the "chronologists," and the "compilers" (1:531, 551). The Bible-makers put together the separate books as they were given an early and perhaps tentative form. The chronologists put the books in their order according to a design of history that the Bible seemed to reveal to them. And, as we saw, the compilers edited the text in its present form. In Paine's opinion, each group was unaware of what the other was doing, although the Bible-makers had not completed their undertaking when the chronologists set about their task, and although while these two groups were still making their final decisions and additions, the compilers entered the process. Besides numerous contradictions and discrepancies, this confusion of hands strikes Paine also as evidence of fraud. The books of the Bible, Paine concludes, were made to promise far more than was ever intended at first and were made to perpetuate false beliefs for the purpose of controlling human minds and maintaining a tyrannical state.

The Historical Books of the Old Testament

In demystifying the Old Testament, Paine conducts two inquiries. The first concerns the accuracy of dating; the second concerns the attribution of authorship.

Paine reasons that the Old Testament chronology should successfully withstand the test of mathematical judgment. Besides the fact that the fourth book is titled Numbers, the Scriptures evidence throughout a scrupulous concern with such matters as the populations of neighbors, the size of triumphant or slain armies, and the number of sheaves of grain. Aided by Ussher's chronology (which . . . seemed to many to be a part of Holy Writ itself),[2] Paine tests the accuracy of the Bible by what he assumes is Scripture's own testimony.

Paine establishes two dates central to the biblical record: the death of Moses in 1,451 B.C. and the fall of Jerusalem and the Babylonian Captivity in 588 B.C. These dates, Paine contends, are reliable because of evidence from ancillary pagan commentaries; hence, these dates can serve as an accurate measure for a biblical chronology. Subtracting the date of Moses' death from earlier dates, Paine deduces that the historical placement of the Israelite patriarchs is in all respects correct.

While assessing the accuracy of these dates, Paine makes two particularly noteworthy mistakes. He places the death of Joshua 331 years after the death of Moses, resulting in an improbable statistic for the duration of Joshua's life that conflicts with the scriptural report that Joshua died twenty years after Moses' passing. Likewise, after reviewing the chronology of Judges, Paine sets the difference between chapters 16 and 17-21 as twenty-eight years, whereas the scriptural dating amounts to 286 years.

Concerning his other primary inquiry, the attribution of authorship, Paine especially focuses on the Pentateuch. From the outset Paine assumes that Moses could not have written its books:

> They were not written in the time of Moses, nor till several hundred years afterward; . . . they are no other than an attempted history of the life of Moses, and of the times in which he is said to have lived, . . . written by some very ignorant and stupid pretenders to authorship several hundred years after the death of Moses, as men now write histories of things that happened, or are supposed to have happened, several hundred or several thousand years ago. (1:521)

The Pentateuch, particularly the account of Creation, Paine reports, owed much to its being based on "a tradition which the Israelites had among them before they came out of Egypt; and after their departure from that country they put it [the story of the Creation] at the head of their history" (1:473). One reason why an Egyptian legend appears at the beginning of an Israelite history, and was assigned to Moses, Paine deduces, was that this patriarch "was not an Israelite," but had "been educated among the Egyptians, who were a people as well skilled in science, and particularly in astronomy, as any people of their day" (1:474).[3]

Paine also adduces that the style of the Pentateuch represents a "person speaking of Moses" in the third person. "Any man might speak of himself in that manner," Paine reasons, but it cannot be supposed "that it is Moses who speaks" concerning his own meekness (Numb. 12:3) or his own death and burial in the land of Moab (Deut. 34:5-6) "without rendering Moses truly ridiculous and absurd." On the basis of these details and other "fallibilities," Paine concludes that the Pentateuch was written by "some Jewish priest, who lived . . . at least three hundred and fifty years after the time of Moses" (1:521-24).[4]

After enumerating other "fallibilities"—including references to Dan and to Israelite kings that make Mosaic authorship impossible—Paine turns from the Pentateuch to the subsequent historical books of the Old Testament. He claims that Job is the oldest book in the Bible, that it contains astronomical allusions foreign to the Israelites, and that, as we noted in chapter 3, it was originally a Gentile work "translated from another language into Hebrew" (1:547). The historical books from Samuel, through Kings and Chronicles, Paine indicates, betray in every chapter the haphazard joint work of their editors.[5] The Psalms, too, Paine affirms in correspondence with contemporary scholarship, were not all written by King David, but "by different song-writers, who lived at different times" from the Israelites' occupation of the Holy Land to the Babylonian Captivity (1:549). Nor were the Canticles or Proverbs, with matter clearly dating after the death of Solomon, entirely composed by that "worn-out debauchee" with "seven hundred wives and three hundred concubines" (1:550).

The Prophetic Books of the Old Testament

Paine's consideration of these historical books is surpassed by his interest in the prophetic books of the Old Testament, "the writings of the Jewish poets" that "deserve a better fate than that of being bound up . . . with the trash that accompanies them, under the absurd name of the Word of God" (1:477).[6] He constructs a chronological table and assigns to each prophet his time and place according to that determining date, 588 B.C. when Jerusalem was destroyed. By subtracting this date from the number assigned to each prophet, Paine arranged all the prophets from Isaiah to Malachi, from the year 760 to 397 B.C. He erred in assigning the dates of Hosea by one hundred years, of Amos by two years, Obadiah by ten years, Habbakuk by four years and Haggai by eighteen years.

Paine registers a special interest in the books of Isaiah and Jeremiah, which were the prophecies most highly regarded by Jews and Christians throughout the centuries. Both, Paine argues, have been made to appear as prophecies inspired by God, but both reveal that they are only self-betraying and disordered assemblages— like "a bundle of newspapers" (1:556)—of anecdotes and scraps of historical accounts surviving by word-of-mouth or in priestly records. As a result, what might have been intended as prophecies in the original statements may have been clear to their composers (whoever they may have been), but the transcriptions of these prophecies with interpolated interpretations several centuries later were based on a language obscured during the Babylonian Captivity and on a confusion and mystery of meanings that were lost.

Paine's discussion of these two books is very detailed. Typical of his argument is his consideration of the prophecy of the virgin and child in Isaiah, which book also foretells that King Ahaz of Judah would defeat in battle two kings who challenged him. This prophecy, Paine is quick to point out, was wrong, and significantly wrong: "Ahaz was defeated and destroyed, a hundred and twenty thousand of his people were slaughtered, Jerusalem was plundered, and two hundred thousand women, and sons and daughters, carried into captivity" (1:555).[7]

The book of Jeremiah, Paine contends, is similarly plagued by "contradictory accounts" emerging from its origin in a "medley of detached, unauthenticated anecdotes" assembled later by some unknown and "stupid book-maker" (1:559): the prophet is imprisoned for being a spy in one verse, but for being a false prophet in another verse; the prophet predicts Nebuchadnezzar's slaughter of the inhabitants of Jerusalem, but they were spared and taken into captivity;[8] and the prophet reassures Zedekiah of his safety, but this king of Judah is mutilated and imprisoned until he dies.

Furthermore, Paine observes, if the prophecies in the Old Testament had indeed forecast the events of the New Testament, surely the writers of the Gospels would have made the connection. Yet no such clear association occurs, only vague implications. Paine suspects that the books of the prophets are not, after all, about prophecy.

When Paine considers who were the original personages whose sayings have been assembled, edited, interpreted, and distorted, he indicates that they were not in their time considered to be soothsayers. They were like the entertainers in medieval courts who told stories celebrating "the event of battle . . . or of a journey, or of [an] enterprise" (1:561), either in the past or in the future. They were seers not only in expressing hopeful expectations, but especially in composing verses; for the term *seer,* Paine asserts, meant poet as well as fortune-teller. Transmitted to later generations, these seers' elemental stories—"fictitious, and often extravagant, and not admissible in any other kind of writing than poetry" (1:475n)—acquired great importance as the various assemblers of the Bible embellished these simple, primitive narratives with profound religious and cultural implications.

In a very important move in his book, Paine argues that the composers of these original narratives were members of parties, akin to political alignments and factions in contemporary politics: "They prophesied for or against, according to the party they were with, as the poetical and political writers of the present day write in defense of the party they associate with against the other" (1:562). This alignment of the poet-prophets to parties became crucial after the death of Solomon, when the kingdom splintered into Israel and Judah.

"Each party had its prophets, who abused and accused each other of being false prophets, lying prophets, impostors," Paine concludes; "the prophets of the party of Judah prophesied against the prophets of the party of Israel; and those of the party of Israel against those of Judah" (1:562).

This political dimension emerges somewhat differently in the books of Daniel and Ezekiel, which Paine allows were indeed written by the individuals named in their headings but which he disallows as prophecies.[9] Paine reads these two books as an effort by their captive authors to relate to their compatriots back in Jerusalem certain "political projects and opinions." They did so, however, "in obscure and metaphysical terms," and masqueraded their views and intentions as "dreams and visions" to evade detection by their captors. However "wild as . . . dreams and visions," Paine notes, these remarkable documents concealed the political hopes of a captured people for their restoration (1:564-65). Paine's reading of these books, like his reading of the Pentateuch as bearing *political* implications, is an important component in his agenda underlying the biblical commentary in *The Age of Reason*.

The New Testament

Paine also questions the authenticity of the New Testament. Whereas he allows that Jesus was indeed a "virtuous reformer and revolutionist" (1:469), he disallows everything else in the New Testament as a fiction perpetrated as divine inspiration by Jesus' followers long after his death. Finding discrepancies in the gospel account of Jesus' genealogy, Paine concludes that this genealogy is as much a fabrication as is the attribution of the Gospels to the names appearing at their headings. Since the Gospels are fictional, as the "impositions" of the Crucifixion, Resurrection, and Ascension particularly suggest, the Pauline epistles, dependent on these Gospels, are similarly suspect. Paine claims thereby to have shown that the Gospels were "forgeries" on the basis of evidence "extracted from the books themselves" (1:594).[10]

One of Paine's most outspoken, and perverse, conclusions is that none of the Four Gospels could have been composed before three hundred years after the death of Jesus (1:585-86). Instead of offering any evidence, he let this assertion stand as the well-supported conclusion of other authorities. Perhaps in reaching this conclusion he had in mind the First Council of the early church (Laodicea), which fixed the canon of Scripture in 363.[11] By dating the Gospels this late, Paine challenged their accuracy and their inspiration as divine expression. From the fourth century to the present, Paine believed, Christianity has been an imposition on credulous and trusting people.

The followers of Jesus at first were unaffected by priesthood, Paine speculates, but they had the example of Judaism, from which they had separated. Within a century or so, these Christians organized themselves much on the model of their religious predecessors, Jewish as well as pagan, in order to achieve a coherence and authority, both important to the survival of the new faith. Accordingly, Paine reports, they made Jesus, who was originally a simple man-founder of their faith, into a figure quite out of proportion to what he had been in real life, a figure now empowered with the ability to work miracles. This process of mystification included the attribution to Jesus of all manner of wonderful perquisites typical of a god: mysterious comings and goings, strange Orphic sayings, obscure hints, cryptic messages, magical workings, and divine descent. Now he had become the Messiah prophesied centuries before his time.

Thus, for Paine, the books of the New Testament are as replete with fable and superstition as are the books of the Old Testament. Although the first Christians lived in a time when certain rays of the light of reason illuminated the Greek and Roman world, they (like the people of classical antiquity) were still the victims of priests in league with rulers, both of whom enforced the worship of idols and gods as a way of sustaining their own very human power. Recalling similar observations about the scribal work in the Pentateuch and the role of the poetic seers in the prophetic books, this conclusion about the New Testament similarly touches on Paine's underlying political agenda in *The Age of Reason*.

The Question of Miracles and Political Power

Church authorities argued that the accounts of the miracles attributed to Jesus in the New Testament are trustworthy because they were either witnessed by persons who were present on the occasion or were recorded by intelligent persons not long afterward. One official version held that the evidence for miracles is identical to that for natural facts and events as experienced by people: both involve signs, actions, and results verifiable at the time of their occurrence by reliable witnesses close enough to the events to testify to their truth. Although miracles, by their nature, are in other ways separate from natural facts, nevertheless, authorities claimed, there is sufficient reason to trust those reported in the New Testament because of the sufficient number and the unbiased nature of the witnesses. In short, church spokesmen imputed a dual character to these divine and true gospel episodes: the events were extraordinary, but the persons reporting these events were not unusual, even if inspired.

What could be accepted as evidence for miracles in their own time, and what could be construed as evidence for miracles that could be sustained and believed in later times? Was that evidence the same or different? Orthodox authorities argued that the reasons for belief in miracles remained the same throughout time. Miracles were necessary, they indicated, not to excite wonder, but to herald and characterize the divine nature of the revelation contained in Christ's precepts and teachings. Consequently, the first baptism in the River Jordan required the appearance of a dove and the hearing of a voice; the celebration of the Last Supper required the transmutation of bread and wine; and the promise of eternal life required the death and resurrection of Jesus.

Nearly all the defenses of miracles and revealed religion depend on this principle: that the most enlightened moral system the world has ever known, Christianity, could have come into the world only in the way the biblical accounts provide. To deny the evidence for and the reliability of the New Testament accounts of miracles is to deny the claims for the Christic divine revelation they herald. Without this evidence, the Christian faith and its moral system disintegrate.

Of course, Paine denies the authenticity of this evidence. He advances arguments and language similar to those articulated by Conyers Middleton and the circle of Paul Henry Thiry, Baron d'Holbach. . . . Like Middleton, Paine asserts the function of mere human credulity in the biblical accounts of miracles, accounts composed by weak-minded narrators. Moreover, Paine repeats several of the related conclusions of the *coterie holbachique,* especially concerning Paul's invention of miraculous events to create a mystique about himself and his narratives. Paine and the clique of d'Holbach agree, too, that in the period when Christianity was gaining recognition in the Roman Empire and when it set about legitimatizing its power, self-aggrandizing church fathers altered and further corrupted the scriptural texts—mystified them with a sense of the miraculous—during councils of ecclesiastical legislation. "It was upon the vote of such men as Athanasius," Paine declared, "that the Testament was decreed to be the Word of God; and nothing can present to us a more strange idea than that of decreeing the word of God by vote" (1:594).

This last point is the final link in what is a chain of associations for Paine in *The Age of Reason.* In this scheme, the church fathers had exerted on the New Testament a corrupting priestly manipulation just as, before them, had the disciples of Jesus who themselves had followed the example of the scribes and prophets of the Old Testament. From the Pentateuch, through the books of the prophets, to the Gospels and epistles of the New Testament, and to the later interpretations of them by the church fathers, Paine contends, there has been one long and continuous history of priestly conspiracy to maintain a superstitious mystique in support of their own authority.

This authority has always meant worldly power over people, and so Paine is not surprised to find that these priests throughout time aligned themselves to parties, to the political forces of civil magistracy. In regard to the Judeo-Christian tradition, this alignment dated back to "the wretch" Moses, who "carried on wars . . . on the pretense of religion" (1:528), and to the prophets, who "prophesied for or against, according to the party they were with, as the poetical and political writers of the present day write in defense of the party they associate with against the other" (1:562). Jesus' followers inevitably followed this Judaic example, and this same pattern was continued by the early Christians and the church fathers, who (Paine believes) became allied with the civil power of the Roman Empire, under the emperor Constantine, when the first Council of Nicea was held in 325. From that time onward, the oppressive tyranny of church and state increasingly encroached on the natural liberties of the people of the West.

Through the invention of sacred texts, stories, and legends, as well as of holy places, rites, rituals, and ceremonies, priests and magistrates mystified their own power in an effort to command unquestioned reverence and obedience from a credulous multitude "enslaved" by this claim to divine right by both their religious and civil guardians. Paine's claim here about biblical mystification recalls a political point in *Rights of Man,* which specifically addresses how the ruling class has always taken "care to represent government as a thing made up of mysteries, which only [they] themselves understood," and has always aimed to convince their property-like inherited subordinates to "believe that government is some wonderful mysterious thing" (1:361, 375). Thomas Hobbes (1588-1679) had made a similar observation in *Leviathan* (1651), which reports that the Bible derives its power from the decree of Christian rulers, who demand that the Sacred Book be regarded as divine law. Revealing this connection between church and state throughout time is the real design behind Paine's religious commentary in *The Age of Reason.* In this work he assails scriptural authority because this authority seemed to him to be the dubious foundation of both religion and state in the Western world.

Pertinent hints of this central concern typically emerge in Paine's language when he fashions such expressions as "the amphibious fraud" and "the adulterous connection of church and state" to expose how the political "sword," used to acquire "power and revenue," is the main instrument of "this impious thing called revealed religion" (1:465, 467, 586, 596). The most telling moments, however, significantly frame Paine's book. In "The Author's Profession of Faith" he says that his work is "exceedingly necessary" because "of the false systems of government and false theology," because the "institutions of churches" are "human inventions" designed to "monopolize power and profit" (1:464). And in his "Conclusion" Paine recalls this very point—the underlying point of his book—by bluntly writing, "It has been the scheme of the Christian Church, and of all the other invented systems of religion, to hold man in ignorance of the Creator, as it is of Governments to hold man in ignorance of his rights. The systems of the one are as false as those of the other, *and are calculated for mutual support*" (1:601; emphasis added). What could be clearer than this revelation of Paine's intent, of the rationale behind his subversion of the authority of Scripture, on whose imputed authenticity the Western church and state were and are founded?

The Authority of a Dismembered Hand

The issue of authority, as we have seen, is an abiding concern in Paine's major works. In *Common Sense* and the *Crisis* papers he deposes the sovereignty of monarchies; in *Rights of Man* he deposes the legitimacy of aristocratic monarchical minions such as Edmund Burke; in *The Age of Reason* he deposes the supremacy of priests, from Moses to clerics and theologians at the end of the eighteenth century. Now and then, as we have seen, the earlier works anticipate the later book; and in fact from *Common Sense* to *The Age of Reason* Paine progresses from dealing with "appearances[, which] are so capable of deceiving" (1:508), to scrutinizing origins, which are buried in the past. In attacking the authenticity of Scripture, Paine tries to uproot, expose, and destroy these hidden origins of the power attributed to church and state, that "amphibious fraud."

But from where did Paine derive his own empowerment to pontificate on Scripture? We noted . . . his exposure to the ideas of several previous French and English commentators and to prevalent notions circulating within the international intellectual milieu of his time. But such an encounter was hardly sufficient, and Paine claimed (albeit disingenuously) it was utterly unnecessary (although in infrequent lapses he mentions scriptural authorities sympathetic to his position). In resorting to the dual, contrary biblical traditions holding that Holy Writ is its own best interpreter and that the Word could be difficult and obscure, Paine proclaimed (as we remarked) his autonomy in reading Scripture: "The evidence I shall produce is contained in the book itself; I will not go out of the Bible for proof against the supposed authenticity of the Bible" (1:531). As we have also seen in *Common Sense* and *Rights of Man,* however, such claims to self-fathering are fraught with paradox, and this paradox reaches a fascinating epitome in Paine's strategies for self-authorization in *The Age of Reason*.

Some of Paine's maneuvers in this book recall those in his earlier writings. There is, first, his enablement through opposition, the instating of himself by virtue of the substantiality of his priestly opponents, without whom his voice would have no cause to perform, indeed no *raison d'être*. There is, second, his use of the mechanism of transference or displacement when he insists on and repeats his claim to write by the light (the Inner Light, as it were) of "reason and philosophy," even if this formulation, as a mere abstract assertion, lacks any evidence of the empiricality imputed to it in Paine's invocations. In a related maneuver, reminiscent of a strategy in *Rights of Man,* Paine consigns the authorization of his book of "consolation" to the historical moment—"the times and the subject demand it be done" (1:472)—and to the example of others who have met peoples' need for "consolation" at this moment:

> As several of my colleagues and others of my fellow-citizens of France, have given me the example of making their voluntary and individual profession of faith, I also will make mine; and I do this with all that sincerity and frankness with which the mind of man communicates with itself. (1:464)

As these strategies, and his ever-so-subtle sympathetic identification with the "the reformer[s] and revolutionist[s]" Jesus and Luther (1:469, 495) suggest, Paine's claim of independent self-communication, his reiteration of sole reliance on pure reason, does not, in fact, prevail. Nor does he successfully demonstrate his claim to be his own patriarch or priest in his "own mind," as his "own church," where "almost all the knowledge" that he has acquired has derived from the revelation (from whence?) of "thoughts . . . that bolt into [his] mind of their own accord" (1:464, 497). Such an effort to appropriate extreme independence falters because, as our Introduction indicated, the assertion of self-authorization is a performance always caught between dependency and autonomy; it is an act always conflicted by rage against the established priestly patriarchy and by fear of the self-inflicted, potentially suicidal wound of becoming (as Paine himself pejoratively uses the expression) "altogether fatherless" (1:534)—that is, without authenticity.

In *The Age of Reason* Paine attempts another mode of the mechanism of transference, one that he had briefly suggested in *Rights of Man* and one that pretends a sort of hermetic closure with himself, as if an otherwise elusive sense of autonomy has indeed been attained. In this gambit, Paine grounds his authority on his previous performance, in effect telling his audience, "All of you already know who I am, what I stand for." And that this audience did know mattered, of course; but Paine's recourse to this manner is nonetheless a rhetorical tactic for self-authorization.

"You will do me the justice to remember, that I have always strenuously supported the right of every man to his own opinion" (1:463), contains phrasing not only looking backward ("remember") but also forward to what is to come: Paine's controversial opinion. This comment at once asserts dependence on the past and assertion of independence from it, a gesture recalling the same dilemma in Paine's earlier writings, which overtly, at least, declare the need for a complete emancipation from the past but always fail to achieve it. That the authority invoked from the past is Paine's own authority does not dismiss the conflicted implications of the stratagem itself.

This curious backward-and-forward looping is even more evident when Paine evokes, for the purpose of authorizing his present controversial discourse, the reader's memory of his role in the American Revolution (the past) and especially of *Common Sense*, falsely said to be "the first work [he] ever did publish," as the foreground of *The Age of Reason:* "I believe I should never have been known in the world as an author on any subject whatsoever had it not been for the affairs of America" (1:496-97). Covertly he instates himself as already "known"; and this worldly reputation, dependently grounded not only on his own past performance, but also on the substantial past success of a whole nation, authenticates Paine's present authorship/authority in *The Age of Reason*.

If such reflexivity seems on first encounter to signify a sort of hermeneutic of self suggesting an autonomous authority, on second thought it reveals a dependency on a past as witnessed by others, who must remember Paine, that alleged autonomous self, in a double regression to critical precedent events: the publication of his book, itself founded on the evident substantiality of the new American republic. This contestatory engagement of dependency on the past and freedom in the present in Paine's authorship of *The Age of Reason* registers in another form as well, the paradox that has been evident in his previous writings.

This paradox inheres in all of the tactics for authorization to which Paine resorts. First, his enablement through opposition: if Paine successfully deposes all priestcraft, there would then be an erasure of the substantial cause of the performance of his voice, which in any event is defined (and thereby curiously identified with) priestly fraud. Second, the resort to the abstract assertion of reason and rights amounts to a nonevidentiary empiricality, an absence, which in effect opens a void behind Paine's speech. Third, the reference to the late eighteenth century for authorization results, in effect, in a vacancy because all times are transient and, worse still, become the very pernicious past that Paine seeks to drive out of existence, even out of human memory. Fourth, references to the

example of others' work and others' lives disable claims to autonomy, not only by yoking Paine's present performance to the always corrupt past to be buried, but also by eradicating any sense of the individuality, uniqueness, even substantiality of Paine's voice. Fifth, and most fascinating, the invocation of *Common Sense* raises a number of instances of this paradox of erasure.

Paine published *Common Sense* anonymously, perhaps a clue to a hesitation at that time to take responsibility for the authority literally asserted in his book. An anonymous author is, in effect, an absent author; yet in *The Age of Reason* this "authorless" *Common Sense* is invoked as authorizing. This maneuver is all the more puzzling because in *The Age of Reason* Paine specifically disparages anonymity, as if he forgets that he used it previously himself in *Common Sense,* the very book he now calls on to authenticate his biblical commentary. "The book of Genesis is anonymous and without authority," he states, repeating this point later when he speaks of the two works attributed to Samuel as "anonymous and without authority" like "all [the] former books" of the Bible (1:526, 535). This attribution of the absence of authority subverts Paine's strategy of predicating his new book on his old anonymous book.

This predication evinces another dilemma. In deriving authenticity from *Common Sense* Paine implies something positive about the durability of language. Although he does suggest in one place that writing is as close to immortality as one can come (1:591), he contrarily notes that languages die (1:491), that print is corruptible (1:585n), and that words are always an unreliable vehicle for expressing reality and truth. For Paine, it is not just that "the Word of God cannot exist in any written or human language" because of, among other reasons, "the continually progressive change to which the meaning of words is subject"; for Paine, "human language is [always] local and changeable, and is therefore incapable of being used as the means of unchangeable and universal information" (1:477, 482; cf. 483). Oddly, Paine has appropriated Burke's sense of his opponents' language as Babel-like, which we observed in chapter 2. Paine's notion of the inability of language to convey "universal information" annihilates his claim that *The Age of Reason* is based on and expresses "reason and philosophy"; and it does violence to its other prop of displaced authorization, the invocation of *Common Sense*.

The stratagem of recalling *Common Sense* as an enabling agent for Paine's proclamations in *The Age of Reason* is vexed by more than Paine's attack, in the latter book, on the efficacy of language in relation to reality and truth. . . . [In] *Common Sense* Paine confiscated regal scriptural authority to support his assertions. A paradox occurs when Paine resorts to a book credited by its arrogation of scriptural authority to authenticate his performance in a book explicitly deposing "Bible authority" (1:517). Paine's effort to close hermetically with him-self, by privileging his authority on the basis of previous authorship in this instance, enters a logical void.

All of these conflicted strategies, at once enabling and disabling the claims for authority in *The Age of Reason,* dramatize the stagelike middle ground between independence and dependence on which Paine is necessarily situated. And it is at this site of spectacle that the paradox of mimicry also occurs, as it did in *Common Sense* and *Rights of Man,* Paine faults the patriarch Moses, the poet-prophets, the Old Testament scribes, the followers of Jesus, and the church fathers for "performances by sleight-of-hand" (1:508) when they religiously mystified natural and human matters, particularly in Scripture, in order to empower themselves politically as tyrants over others. But a close consideration of Paine's many tactics for dramatizing his own priestly authority in *The Age of Reason,* which he hopes might become (scripturally?) immortal as self-evident revelation (1:591), may also be seen as a bare performance similar to his opponents' sleight of hand. If their authority is vacant, as he asserts, then so is his own, which mimics their manner of mystifying origins whenever he uses his *religious* argument *politically* to authorize his own millennial vision of what humanity might ideally become.

While debunking miracles Paine fashions an image that we find to be remarkably reflective of this dilemma concerning authority and, as well, of Paine's self-doubt, here masked as skepticism toward others' claims to authority:

> Suppose I were to say that when I sat down to write this book a hand presented itself in the air, took up the pen and wrote every word that is herein written; would anybody believe me? Certainly they would not. Would they believe me a whit more if the thing had been a fact? Certainly they would not. (1:508)

In this passage Paine imaginatively reduces himself to a metonymic image, a mere hand. There is no body, no substantive identity behind this hand; yet it writes, and it specifically writes *this book,* the very book in the reader's hands. The author may this time have a name—Thomas Paine—but his identity is anonymous, erased in the void behind the hand. Dismembered from something empirically substantial, the identityless hand is necessarily insubstantial and unsubstantiated; yet, as if by a kind of miracle, it writes, it represents and thereby authenticates the author, who is reified and known only through the performance, the very spectacle of authorship.

What analogy could be more apt in summarizing the many conflicts informing Paine's struggle for authority in *The Age of Reason?* At the very core of this analogy lies the dilemma that Paine's literary acts of self-fathering authorship inherently incur the dismembering wound of father-lessness; and, as Paine defined the term, to be fatherless is to be without authority. In short, self-authorization is merely an act of self-authoring, a "fictitious, and often extravagant" performance, as Paine observed of the biblical prophets. That he himself should have fashioned this image of the authoring/authorizing hand may well be a testament to his belief that "our own existence is a mystery" (1:505).

Notes

[1] A detailed inquiry into biblical commentary in the eighteenth century is provided by Thomas P. Preston, "Biblical Criticism Literature, and the Eighteenth-Century Reader," in *Books and Their Readers in Eighteenth-Century England,* ed. Isabel Rivers (New York:St. Martin's Press, 1982), pp. 97-126. See also Robert M. Grant and David Tracy, *A Short History of the Interpretation of the Bible* (Philadelphia: Fortress Press, 1963); and Robert Morgan and John Barton, *Biblical Interpretation* (Oxford: Oxford University Press, 1988).

[2] Whether Paine knew the "Bible Chronology" he used was the creation of Bishop Ussher remains uncertain. In the years of the publication of *The Age of Reason* and the attendant controversy, three large and imposing chronologies appeared: Robert Walker's *Analysis of Researches into the Origin and Progress of Historical Time* (London, 1796), Philip Howard's *The Scripture History of the Earth and Mankind* (London, 1797), and Thomas Falconer's *Chronological Tables* (London, 1796). They reviewed all the dates provided by scriptural and pagan history and confirmed the chronological scheme of Ussher. The reviews of these works signify the wide acceptance of this system of dating, one review even concluding that "divine truth shall gain a full ascendancy by its native energy" (*Critical Review* 23 [1797]: 180). There is no hint of the existence of any forces aimed at undercutting and destroying such systems of chronology. See, for example, *Critical Review* 23 (1798): 169-80; and *Gentleman's Magazine* 66 (1796): 762-65.

[3] Traditional arguments for the Mosaic authorship of the Pentateuch rested on the principle that Ezra could not have been the composer because he himself ascribed the books of the law to Moses (Ezra 3:2), that every subsequent book of the Old Testament implies and relies on the existence of the Pentateuch (Josh. 1:7, 8; 8:31; 23;6; 1 Kings 2:3; 2Kings 14:6; 2 Chron. 17:9; 24:6); that Hebrew ceased to be a living language among the Israelites before or about the time of the

Babylonian Captivity; and that the law of Moses was deposited in the Temple and read to the people every seventh year from the time of its bestowal to the setting down of the record (Deut. 31:10, 24).

4 Curiously, Paine makes no mention of the two disinct accounts of the Creation in the first two chapers of Genesis, a problem well known in intellectual circles of Paine's time and supportive of his case against the literal accuracy of the Pentateuch. However, in defending himself in his "Letter to Mr. Erskine" (1797), addressed to the barrister who prosecuted the publisher of *The Age of Reason,* Paine clearly distinguishes between the two accounts in Genesis. "Here are," he concludes, "two different stories contradicting each other" (2:731), a point he repeated in his "Reply to the Bishop of Llandaff" (2:764-65).

5 Even with a copy of the Bible at hand, Paine nearly himself invents a passage of Scripture when he describes David's taking of Jerusalem (1 Chron. 5:4ff.; 14:4ff.) as evidencing a bloodthirstiness not supported by the biblical account: "It is not said . . . that they *utterly destroyed men, women, and children; that they left not a soul to breathe,* as is said of their other conquests" (1:535). Paine may have made up this seeming quotation out of Josh. 11:11-14 and 1 Sam. 27:9, where the vengefulness is nearly as strong as expressed in Paine's invented verse.

6 The argument for prophecy had been set forth with great vigor in Samuel Clarke's Boyle lectures of 1705; as he wrote in the ninth edition of *A Discourse Concerning the Being and Attributes of God, the Obligations of Natural Religion, and the Truth and Certainty of the Christian Revelation* (London: James and John Knapton, 1738), p. 371, Christian prophecy *"is positively and directly proved, to be actually and immediately sent to us from God, by the many infallible Signs and Miracles which the Author of it worked publickly as the evidence of his Divine Commission."* For the savants and biblical scholars of the eighteenth century, the controversy concerning prophecy began in 1724, when the mathematician William Whiston published a tract that provided Anthony Collins with an opportunity to attack the argument from prophecy in his *Discouse of the Grounds and Reasons of the Christian Religion* (1724). The major treatment of prophecy, especially in respect to Paine's handling of the subject, was Nathaniel Lardner's *Credibility of the Gospel History* (1730), which disclosed that the Old Testament prophecies were fulfilled in the New Testament and were, in turn, confirmed by passages of ancient authors who were contemporary with Jesus and the apostles or who lived not long afterward. Lardner offered testimony from the earliest church fathers down through the saints and martyrs to the time of Constantine the Great and the Councils, including Josephus and opponents, to the year 1325, all showing that the prophetic scheme of Scripture was infallible and confirmed by every testimony.

7 This tragic outcome was not relevant to Isaiah 7 nor to the prophecy of the virgin and the child. By the verses concerning the defeat of Ahaz, Paine saw in his Bible a small-print, italicized reference to 2 Chron. 28, to which he apparently turned and there found what had happened to Ahaz. Matthew, who is surely the first to do so, takes the word *virgin* in the prophecy to mean specifically the Virgin Mary and thus introduced a miraculous element into what was meant by the prophet to be simply a way of measuring time between the virgin's conceiving and of the land's coming into production and fruition. Paine, however, reverses the process and speaks of the "lying prophet" who devised such a "barefaced perversion of this story, that the book of Matthew, and the impudence and the . . . sordid interests of priests in later times, have founded a theory which they call the Gospel . . . 700 years after this foolish story was told" (1:555).

8 Paine apparently discovered this discrepancy by following the marginal reference in his Bible that linked Jer. 37:11-13 with Jer. 21:1-8 and 38:1-17. So the prophet, in Paine's view, stood condemned of falsehood by his own words, or in the words given to him by others long afterward.

9 He also rules against the book of Jonah, which he reads as a simple tale of how a Jew was treated by Gentiles and as a critique of prophecy itself: "As a moral, it preaches against the malevolent spirit of prediction; for as certainly as a man predicts ill, he becomes inclined to wish it" (1:569). And of the minor prophets, Paine claims they were only "itinerant preachers who mixed poetry, anecdote, and devotion together" (1:477).

10 The "Harmonists" were a number of leading expositors and defenders of Scripture who responded to the attacks of the Deists. Their chief works included Philip Doddridge's six-volume *The Family Expositer* (1739-56), Thomas Townson's *Discourse on the Evangelical History* (1793), and James Mcknight's *Harmony of the Gospels* (1778). Joseph Priestley criticized the last volume in *A Harmony of the Evangelists* (1780), and for a time he engaged in a series of *Letters* with Newcome, archbishop of Armagh.

11 For an authoritative account, in Paine's time, of the fixing of the canon of the New Testament and the recognition of Christianity as the official religion of the Roman Empire, see William Paley, *A View of the Evidences of Christianity* (London: R. Faulder, 1794), 2:199-203.

FURTHER READING

Bibliography

Gimbel, Richard. *A Bibliographical Check List of* Common Sense *with an Account of Its Publication.* New Haven: Yale University Press, 1956, 124 p.

> Comprehensive bibliography of the publication history of *Common Sense* and subsequent responses.

Lasser, Michael L. "In Response to *The Age of Reason,* 1794-1799." *Bulletin of Bibliography and Magazine Notes* 25, No. 2 (January-April 1967): 41-43.

> Brief essay and extensive bibliography documenting the contemporary replies to Paine's religious work, *The Age of Reason.*

Pendleton, Gayle Trusdel. "Towards a Bibliography of the *Reflections* and *Rights of Man* Controversy." *Bulletin of Research in the Humanities* 85, No. 1 (Spring 1982): 65-103.

> Bibliography of the cited works, plus an essay suggesting the issues integral to a full-scale study of the debate between Paine and Burke.

Wilson, Jerome D. "Thomas Paine in America: An Annotated Bibliography 1900-1973." *Bulletin of Bibliography and Magazine Notes* 31, No. 4 (October/December 1974): 133-56.

> Comprehensive list of works that the compiler hopes will "serve as the basis of a complete twentieth-century Paine bibliography."

Biography

Aldridge, Alfred Owen. *Man of Reason: The Life of Thomas Paine.* Philadelphia and New York: J. B. Lippincott Company, 1959, 348 p.

> Study by a major scholar of Paine's works. Presents its subject as "a symbol of the rationalistic spirit of his age."

Anonymous. "The English Voltaire: Tom Paine: Citizen of the World." *The Times Literary Supplement,* No. 1826 (January 30, 1937): 65-66.

> A relatively favorable review of Paine's life; nonetheless, finds his work "not very stirring" and "far less important than Paine believed."

Berthold, S. M. *Thomas Paine: America's First Liberal.* Boston: Meador Publishing Company, 1938, 264 p.

> Seeks to advance Paine's emergence from obscurity with the view that he "served . . . in causes of enlightenment and freedom."

Bradford, Gamaliel. "Thomas Paine." In his *Damaged Souls,* pp. 53-83. Boston and New York: Houghton Mifflin, 1931.

> Characterizes Paine both as a "commonplace rebel, entirely practical, a trifle sordid" and as a man "inspired by the love of humanity."

Cheetham, James. *The Life of Thomas Paine.* 1809. Reprint, Scholars' Facsimiles & Reprints, 1989, 347 p.

> Landmark biography of Paine that depicted him as a drunken blasphemer—an image that held in public perception for another century. Introduction by Lawrence M. Lasher places Cheetham's work in historical context.

Conway, Moncure Daniel. *The Life of Thomas Paine.* 1892. Reprint, Watts & Co., 1909, and Benjamin Blom, Inc., 1969. Edited by Hypatia Bradlaugh Bonner. 352 p.

> Landmark biography and revaluation of Paine. Helped instigate the resurgence of Paine's reputation in the twentieth century.

Dyck, Ian, ed. *Citizen of the World: Essays on Thomas Paine.* London: Christopher Helm, 1987, 152 p.

> Offers a series of essays on Paine's biography and several significant aspects of his career; most essays are by scholar George Spater.

Foner, Eric. *Tom Paine and Revolutionary America.* New York: Oxford University Press, 1976, 326 p.

> Focuses on crucial points in Paine's life in order to "trace . . . the relationships between a particular individual and his times and between a particular brand of radical ideology and the social and political history of revolutionary America."

Gimbel, Richard. "The Resurgence of Thomas Paine." *Proceedings of the American Antiquarian Society* 69 (October 21, 1959): 97-111.

> Brief biographical essay precedes a discussion of the changes in Paine's image in the years and decades after his death.

Ingersoll, Robert G. "Thomas Paine." *The North American Review* CLV, No. 429 (August 1892): 181-95.

> A review of Moncure D. Conway's biography. Briefly recounts Paine's life and offers a positive image of the revolutionary.

Keane, John. *Tom Paine: A Political Life.* London: Bloomsbury, 1995, 644 p.

> Attempts to fill certain gaps in Paine's biographies to date, especially his early life in England and his career in France.

Palmer, R. R. "Tom Paine: Victim of the Rights of Man." *The Pennsylvania Magazine of History and Biography* LXVI, No. 2 (April 1942): 161-75.

> Portrays Paine both as emblematic of eighteenth-century rationalism and as a "man of simple and immovable faith."

Powell, David. *Tom Paine: The Greatest Exile.* London: Croom Helm, 1985, 303 p.

> Evokes Paine's life and environment through a combination of documentation and imaginative reconstruction.

Washburne, E. B. "Thomas Paine and the French Revolution." *Scribner's Monthly* XX, No. 5 (September 1880): 771-86.

> Hailing Paine for his "ability, zeal and usefulness," recounts his initial involvement with the revolution and his imprisonment during the Terror.

Wilson, Jerome D., and William F. Ricketson. *Thomas Paine.* Boston: Twayne, 1989, 156 p.

> Develops a largely positive biography of Paine from a study of his written work.

Criticism

Adler, Felix. "Thomas Paine." *Standard* 22, No. 5 (February 1936): 123-28.

> Reassesses *The Age of Reason,* lauding Paine's humanity and sincerity, but finding his "criticism of religion . . . false."

Aldridge, Alfred Owen. "Thomas Paine in Latin America." *Early American Literature* 3, No. 3 (Winter 1968-69): 139-46.

> Charts the influence of Paine's work in Latin America through translations and distributions of his writings—one as early as 1811—as well as echoes in the works of Latin American writers.

Bailyn, Bernard. "Thomas Paine: A Reappraisal of *Common Sense,* the Most Extraordinary Pamphlet of the American Revolution." *The UNESCO Courier* 29 (July 1976): 20-22, 27-28.

> Declaration, by a leading scholar of revolutionary America, that *Common Sense* was a "work of genius." Also includes a brief narrative of its role in the Revolution.

Christian, William. "The Moral Economics of Tom Paine." *Journal of the History of Ideas* XXXIV, No. 3 (July-September 1973): 367-80.

> Contends that Paine's "major innovation in English thought was his attempt to outline the role government would play in a society which subordinated economics to morality."

Clark, Harry H. "Introduction: Thomas Paine the Conservative." In *Six New Letters of Thomas Paine,* pp. vii-xxxii. Madison: University of Wisconsin Press, 1939.

> Offers a corrective view of Paine's earlier career, arguing that previous to the French Revolution he "had considerably more in common with those who were later regarded as conservatives."

Falk, Robert P. "Thomas Paine: Deist or Quaker?" *The Pennsylvania Magazine of History and Biography* LXII, No. 1 (January 1938): 52-63.

> Argues that Paine's Quaker heritage may have played a greater role in his political views than he acknowledged.

Foner, Philip S. "Introduction." In *The Complete Writings of Thomas Paine,* edited by Philip S. Foner, pp. ix-lix. New York: Citadel Press, 1945.

> Seminal scholarly review of Paine's life and work, providing comprehensive summaries of his major writings and the historical context in which they were written.

Furniss, Tom. "Burke, Paine, and the Language of Assignats." In *The Yearbook of English Studies* 19 (1989): 54-70.

> Conducts close readings of Burke's *Reflections on the Revolution in France* and Paine's *Rights of Man* in order to determine the relationship in each between language and economics.

Ginsberg, Elaine K. "Style and Identification in *Common Sense.*" *Philological Papers* 23 (January 1977): 26-36.

> Undertakes one of the first close studies of the rhetoric and persuasive strategies Paine employed in his first important pamphlet.

Gummere, Richard M. "Thomas Paine: Was He Really Anticlassical?" *Proceedings of the American Antiquarian Society* 75 (October 20, 1965): 253-69.

> Reviews Paine's biography and writings in light of his familiarity with and possible use of classical sources.

Jordon, Winthrop D. "Familial Politics: Thomas Paine and the Killing of the King, 1776." *The Journal of American History* LX, No. 2 (September 1973): 294-308.

> Employs a psychological framework to argue that *Common Sense* was instrumental in the metaphorical regicide/patricide achieved by the American Revolution.

Kates, Gary. "From Liberalism to Radicalism: Tom Paine's *Rights of Man.*" *Journal of the History of Ideas* L, No. 4 (October-December 1989): 569-87.

> Asserts that Paine's involvement in the French Revolution "transformed" his political ideology.

Kramnick, Isaac. An Introduction to *Common Sense,* by Thomas Paine, pp. 7-59. London: Penguin, 1976.

> Provides extensive context for the novice reader, including the general history of the age and Paine's biography.

Leffman, Henry. "The Real Thomas Paine, Patriot and Publicist. A Philosopher Misunderstood." *The Pennsylvania Magazine of History and Biography* XLVI, No. 2 (1922): 81-99.

> Attempts to salvage Paine's reputation from the dismissal of the nineteenth century, particularly in terms of his contribution to the revolutions in France and America.

Nursey-Bray, P. F. "Thomas Paine and the Concept of Alienation." *Political Studies* XVI, No. 2 (1968): 223-42.

> Examines the impact of Paine's concept of alienation, or individual self-estrangement, on both his success

as a pamphleteer and his weakness as a political philosopher.

Paine, Thomas. *Political Writings*. Edited by Bruce Kuklick. Cam-bridge and New York: Cambridge University Press, 1989, 260 p.

Presents Paine's major works from *Common Sense* to Part I of *The Age of Reason,* as well as an editor's introduction and a biographical chronology.

Parrington, Vernon Louis. "Political Thinkers: The French Group." In *Main Currents of American Thought*, Vol. I: *1620-1800, The Colonial Mind*, pp. 333-62. SanDiego, Calif.: Harcourt Brace Jovanovich, 1927.

Portrays Paine as a great revolutionary and advocate of human rights whose works presented, in distilled and powerful form, the most progressive philosophies of the age.

Roth, Martin. "Tom Paine and American Loneliness." *Early American Literature* 22, No. 2 (Fall 1987): 175-82.

Reads Paine's early works for their imagery, contending that he "gives us a melodrama of isolation in an embryo" that will become characteristic of American literature and American identity.

Thompson, Tommy R. "The Resurrection of Thomas Paine in American Popular Magazines." *The Midwest Quarterly* XXXIII, No. 1 (Autumn 1991): 75-92.

Documents Paine's image in the American press, particularly during the nineteenth and early twentieth centuries; includes a bibliography.

Wector, Dixon. "Thomas Paine and the Franklins." *American Literature* 12, No. 3 (November 1940): 306-17.

Narrative and comparative study that reproduces many of the letters exchanged between the two men.

Woodcock, Bruce, and John Coates. "Writing the Revolution—Aspects of Thomas Paine and his Prose." In their *Combative Souls: Romantic Writing and Ideology: Two Contrasting Interpretations,* pp. 79-98. Hull, England: University of Hull Press, 1988.

Analyzes Paine's prose as the product of his belief that writing constituted a vital political action and could alter the forms of power.

Woolf, Leonard. "The World of Books: 'A Filthy Little Atheist.'" *The Nation and Athenaeum* 41, No. 19 (August 13, 1927), p. 638.

Briefly refutes the prevailing view of Paine and calls for a more in-depth examination of his work. Woolf, the husband of novelist Virginia Woolf, was a significant political progressive in England in his own era.

Zacharias, Donald W. "Tom Paine: Eloquent Defender of Louis XVI." *The Central States Speech Journal* XIII, No. 3 (Spring 1962): 183-88.

Focuses on Paine's French career and, in particular, the details of his effort to save the deposed king from execution.

Additional coverage of Paine's life and career is contained in the following source published by Gale Research: *Dictionary of Literary Biography,* Vols. 31, 43, and 73.

Nineteenth-Century Literature Criticism

Cumulative Indexes
Volumes 1-62

How to Use This Index

The main references

> Calvino, Italo
> 1923-1985.....CLC 5, 8, 11, 22, 33, 39,
> 73; SSC 3

list all author entries in the following Gale Literary Criticism series:

BLC = *Black Literature Criticism*
CLC = *Contemporary Literary Criticism*
CLR = *Children's Literature Review*
CMLC = *Classical and Medieval Literature Criticism*
DA = *DISCovering Authors*
DAB = *DISCovering Authors: British*
DAC = *DISCovering Authors: Canadian*
DAM = *DISCovering Authors Modules*
  DRAM: Dramatists module
  MST: Most-studied authors module
  MULT: Multicultural authors module
  NOV: Novelists module
  POET: Poets module
  POP: Popular/genre writers module

DC = *Drama Criticism*
HLC = *Hispanic Literature Criticism*
LC = *Literature Criticism from 1400 to 1800*
NCLC = *Nineteenth-Century Literature Criticism*
PC = *Poetry Criticism*
SSC = *Short Story Criticism*
TCLC = *Twentieth-Century Literary Criticism*
WLC = *World Literature Criticism, 1500 to the Present*

The cross-references

> See also CANR 23; CA 85-88;
> obituary CA 116

list all author entries in the following Gale biographical and literary sources:

AAYA = *Authors & Artists for Young Adults*
AITN = *Authors in the News*
BEST = *Bestsellers*
BW = *Black Writers*
CA = *Contemporary Authors*
CAAS = *Contemporary Authors Autobiography Series*
CABS = *Contemporary Authors Bibliographical Series*
CANR = *Contemporary Authors New Revision Series*
CAP = *Contemporary Authors Permanent Series*
CDALB = *Concise Dictionary of American Literary Biography*
CDBLB = *Concise Dictionary of British Literary Biography*

DLB = *Dictionary of Literary Biography*
DLBD = *Dictionary of Literary Biography Documentary Series*
DLBY = *Dictionary of Literary Biography Yearbook*
HW = *Hispanic Writers*
JRDA = *Junior DISCovering Authors*
MAICYA = *Major Authors and Illustrators for Children and Young Adults*
MTCW = *Major 20th-Century Writers*
NNAL = *Native North American Literature*
SAAS = *Something about the Author Autobiography Series*
SATA = *Something about the Author*
YABC = *Yesterday's Authors of Books for Children*

Literary Criticism Series
Cumulative Author Index

Abasiyanik, Sait Faik 1906-1954
See Sait Faik
See also CA 123

Abbey, Edward 1927-1989...... CLC 36, 59
See also CA 45-48; 128; CANR 2, 41

Abbott, Lee K(ittredge) 1947-...... CLC 48
See also CA 124; CANR 51; DLB 130

Abe, Kobo
1924-1993.......... CLC 8, 22, 53, 81;
DAM NOV
See also CA 65-68; 140; CANR 24; MTCW

Abelard, Peter c. 1079-c. 1142 ... CMLC 11
See also DLB 115

Abell, Kjeld 1901-1961............ CLC 15
See also CA 111

Abish, Walter 1931-.............. CLC 22
See also CA 101; CANR 37; DLB 130

Abrahams, Peter (Henry) 1919- ..... CLC 4
See also BW 1; CA 57-60; CANR 26;
DLB 117; MTCW

Abrams, M(eyer) H(oward) 1912-... CLC 24
See also CA 57-60; CANR 13, 33; DLB 67

Abse, Dannie
1923- ... CLC 7, 29; DAB; DAM POET
See also CA 53-56; CAAS 1; CANR 4, 46;
DLB 27

Achebe, (Albert) Chinua(lumogu)
1930- ..... CLC 1, 3, 5, 7, 11, 26, 51, 75;
BLC; DA; DAB; DAC; DAM MST,
MULT, NOV; WLC
See also AAYA 15; BW 2; CA 1-4R;
CANR 6, 26, 47; CLR 20; DLB 117;
MAICYA; MTCW; SATA 40;
SATA-Brief 38

Acker, Kathy 1948- .... CLC 45
See also CA 117; 122; CANR 55

Ackroyd, Peter 1949-.......... CLC 34, 52
See also CA 123; 127; CANR 51; DLB 155;
INT 127

Acorn, Milton 1923-........ CLC 15; DAC
See also CA 103; DLB 53; INT 103

Adamov, Arthur
1908-1970 .... CLC 4, 25; DAM DRAM
See also CA 17-18; 25-28R; CAP 2; MTCW

Adams, Alice (Boyd)
1926-.......... CLC 6, 13, 46; SSC 24
See also CA 81-84; CANR 26, 53;
DLBY 86; INT CANR-26; MTCW

Adams, Andy 1859-1935......... TCLC 56
See also 1

Adams, Douglas (Noel)
1952-......... CLC 27, 60; DAM POP
See also AAYA 4; BEST 89:3; CA 106;
CANR 34; DLBY 83; JRDA

Adams, Francis 1862-1893....... NCLC 33

Adams, Henry (Brooks)
1838-1918 ...... TCLC 4, 52; DA; DAB;
DAC; DAM MST
See also CA 104; 133; DLB 12, 47

Adams, Richard (George)
1920-....... CLC 4, 5, 18; DAM NOV
See also AAYA 16; AITN 1, 2; CA 49-52;
CANR 3, 35; CLR 20; JRDA; MAICYA;
MTCW; SATA 7, 69

Adamson, Joy(-Friederike Victoria)
1910-1980 .... CLC 17
See also CA 69-72; 93-96; CANR 22;
MTCW; SATA 11; SATA-Obit 22

Adcock, Fleur 1934-.............. CLC 41
See also CA 25-28R; CAAS 23; CANR 11,
34; DLB 40

Addams, Charles (Samuel)
1912-1988 .... CLC 30
See also CA 61-64; 126; CANR 12

Addison, Joseph 1672-1719 .... LC 18
See also CDBLB 1660-1789; DLB 101

Adler, Alfred (F.) 1870-1937 ...... TCLC 61
See also CA 119

Adler, C(arole) S(chwerdtfeger)
1932-..................... CLC 35
See also AAYA 4; CA 89-92; CANR 19,
40; JRDA; MAICYA; SAAS 15;
SATA 26, 63

Adler, Renata 1938-............. CLC 8, 31
See also CA 49-52; CANR 5, 22, 52;
MTCW

Ady, Endre 1877-1919 .... TCLC 11
See also CA 107

Aeschylus
525B.C.-456B.C........ CMLC 11; DA;
DAB; DAC; DAM DRAM, MST
See also DLB 176; YABC

Afton, Effie
See Harper, Frances Ellen Watkins

Agapida, Fray Antonio
See Irving, Washington

Agee, James (Rufus)
1909-1955 .... TCLC 1, 19; DAM NOV
See also AITN 1; CA 108; 148;
CDALB 1941-1968; DLB 2, 26, 152

Aghill, Gordon
See Silverberg, Robert

Agnon, S(hmuel) Y(osef Halevi)
1888-1970 .... CLC 4, 8, 14
See also CA 17-18; 25-28R; CAP 2; MTCW

Agrippa von Nettesheim, Henry Cornelius
1486-1535 .... LC 27

Aherne, Owen
See Cassill, R(onald) V(erlin)

Ai 1947-.................... CLC 4, 14, 69
See also CA 85-88; CAAS 13; DLB 120

Aickman, Robert (Fordyce)
1914-1981 .... CLC 57
See also CA 5-8R; CANR 3

Aiken, Conrad (Potter)
1889-1973 .... CLC 1, 3, 5, 10, 52;
DAM NOV, POET; SSC 9
See also CA 5-8R; 45-48; CANR 4;
CDALB 1929-1941; DLB 9, 45, 102;
MTCW; SATA 3, 30

Aiken, Joan (Delano) 1924-........ CLC 35
See also AAYA 1; CA 9-12R; CANR 4, 23,
34; CLR 1, 19; DLB 161; JRDA;
MAICYA; MTCW; SAAS 1; SATA 2,
30, 73

Ainsworth, William Harrison
1805-1882 .... NCLC 13
See also DLB 21; SATA 24

Aitmatov, Chingiz (Torekulovich)
1928-...................... CLC 71
See also CA 103; CANR 38; MTCW;
SATA 56

Akers, Floyd
See Baum, L(yman) Frank

Akhmadulina, Bella Akhatovna
1937-........... CLC 53; DAM POET
See also CA 65-68

Akhmatova, Anna
1888-1966 .... CLC 11, 25, 64;
DAM POET; PC 2
See also CA 19-20; 25-28R; CANR 35;
CAP 1; MTCW

Aksakov, Sergei Timofeyvich
1791-1859 .... NCLC 2

Aksenov, Vassily
See Aksyonov, Vassily (Pavlovich)

Aksyonov, Vassily (Pavlovich)
1932-................ CLC 22, 37, 101
See also CA 53-56; CANR 12, 48

Akutagawa, Ryunosuke
1892-1927 .... TCLC 16
See also CA 117; 154

Alain 1868-1951 .... TCLC 41

Alain-Fournier.................... TCLC 6
See also Fournier, Henri Alban
See also DLB 65

Alarcon, Pedro Antonio de
1833-1891 .... NCLC 1

Alas (y Urena), Leopoldo (Enrique Garcia)
1852-1901 .... TCLC 29
See also CA 113; 131; HW

Albee, Edward (Franklin III)
1928-...... CLC 1, 2, 3, 5, 9, 11, 13, 25,
53, 86; DA; DAB; DAC; DAM DRAM,
MST; WLC
See also AITN 1; CA 5-8R; CABS 3;
CANR 8, 54; CDALB 1941-1968; DLB 7;
INT CANR-8; MTCW

Alberti, Rafael 1902- . . . . **CLC 7**
See also CA 85-88; DLB 108

Albert the Great 1200(?)-1280. . . . **CMLC 16**
See also DLB 115

Alcala-Galiano, Juan Valera y
See Valera y Alcala-Galiano, Juan

Alcott, Amos Bronson 1799-1888 . . **NCLC 1**
See also DLB 1

Alcott, Louisa May
1832-1888 . . . . . **NCLC 6, 58; DA; DAB;**
DAC; DAM MST, NOV; WLC
See also AAYA 20; CDALB 1865-1917;
CLR 1, 38; DLB 1, 42, 79; DLBD 14;
JRDA; MAICYA; 1

Aldanov, M. A.
See Aldanov, Mark (Alexandrovich)

Aldanov, Mark (Alexandrovich)
1886(?)-1957 . . . . **TCLC 23**
See also CA 118

Aldington, Richard 1892-1962 . . . . . . **CLC 49**
See also CA 85-88; CANR 45; DLB 20, 36,
100, 149

Aldiss, Brian W(ilson)
1925- . . . . **CLC 5, 14, 40; DAM NOV**
See also CA 5-8R; CAAS 2; CANR 5, 28;
DLB 14; MTCW; SATA 34

Alegria, Claribel
1924- . . . . **CLC 75; DAM MULT**
See also CA 131; CAAS 15; DLB 145; HW

Alegria, Fernando 1918- . . . . **CLC 57**
See also CA 9-12R; CANR 5, 32; HW

Aleichem, Sholom . . . . **TCLC 1, 35**
See also Rabinovitch, Sholem

Aleixandre, Vicente
1898-1984 . . . . **CLC 9, 36; DAM POET;**
PC 15
See also CA 85-88; 114; CANR 26;
DLB 108; HW; MTCW

Alepoudelis, Odysseus
See Elytis, Odysseus

Aleshkovsky, Joseph 1929-
See Aleshkovsky, Yuz
See also CA 121; 128

Aleshkovsky, Yuz . . . . **CLC 44**
See also Aleshkovsky, Joseph

Alexander, Lloyd (Chudley) 1924- . . **CLC 35**
See also AAYA 1; CA 1-4R; CANR 1, 24,
38, 55; CLR 1, 5; DLB 52; JRDA;
MAICYA; MTCW; SAAS 19; SATA 3,
49, 81

Alexie, Sherman (Joseph, Jr.)
1966- . . . . **CLC 96; DAM MULT**
See also CA 138; DLB 175; NNAL

Alfau, Felipe 1902- . . . . **CLC 66**
See also CA 137

Alger, Horatio, Jr. 1832-1899 . . . . . **NCLC 8**
See also DLB 42; SATA 16

Algren, Nelson 1909-1981 . . . . **CLC 4, 10, 33**
See also CA 13-16R; 103; CANR 20;
CDALB 1941-1968; DLB 9; DLBY 81,
82; MTCW

Ali, Ahmed 1910- . . . . **CLC 69**
See also CA 25-28R; CANR 15, 34

Alighieri, Dante 1265-1321 . . . . **CMLC 3, 18**
See also YABC

Allan, John B.
See Westlake, Donald E(dwin)

Allen, Edward 1948- . . . . **CLC 59**

Allen, Paula Gunn
1939- . . . . **CLC 84; DAM MULT**
See also CA 112; 143; DLB 175; NNAL

Allen, Roland
See Ayckbourn, Alan

Allen, Sarah A.
See Hopkins, Pauline Elizabeth

Allen, Woody
1935- . . . . **CLC 16, 52; DAM POP**
See also AAYA 10; CA 33-36R; CANR 27,
38; DLB 44; MTCW

Allende, Isabel
1942- . . . . **CLC 39, 57, 97; DAM MULT,**
NOV; HLC
See also AAYA 18; CA 125; 130;
CANR 51; DLB 145; HW; INT 130;
MTCW; YABC

Alleyn, Ellen
See Rossetti, Christina (Georgina)

Allingham, Margery (Louise)
1904-1966 . . . . **CLC 19**
See also CA 5-8R; 25-28R; CANR 4, 58;
DLB 77; MTCW

Allingham, William 1824-1889 . . . **NCLC 25**
See also DLB 35

Allison, Dorothy E. 1949- . . . . **CLC 78**
See also CA 140

Allston, Washington 1779-1843 . . . . **NCLC 2**
See also DLB 1

Almedingen, E. M. . . . . **CLC 12**
See also Almedingen, Martha Edith von
See also SATA 3

Almedingen, Martha Edith von 1898-1971
See Almedingen, E. M.
See also CA 1-4R; CANR 1

Almqvist, Carl Jonas Love
1793-1866 . . . . **NCLC 42**

Alonso, Damaso 1898-1990 . . . . **CLC 14**
See also CA 110; 131; 130; DLB 108; HW

Alov
See Gogol, Nikolai (Vasilyevich)

Alta 1942- . . . . **CLC 19**
See also CA 57-60

Alter, Robert B(ernard) 1935- . . . . . . **CLC 34**
See also CA 49-52; CANR 1, 47

Alther, Lisa 1944- . . . . **CLC 7, 41**
See also CA 65-68; CANR 12, 30, 51;
MTCW

Altman, Robert 1925- . . . . **CLC 16**
See also CA 73-76; CANR 43

Alvarez, A(lfred) 1929- . . . . **CLC 5, 13**
See also CA 1-4R; CANR 3, 33; DLB 14,
40

Alvarez, Alejandro Rodriguez 1903-1965
See Casona, Alejandro
See also CA 131; 93-96; HW

Alvarez, Julia 1950- . . . . **CLC 93**
See also CA 147

Alvaro, Corrado 1896-1956 . . . . **TCLC 60**

Amado, Jorge
1912- . . . . **CLC 13, 40; DAM MULT,**
NOV; HLC
See also CA 77-80; CANR 35; DLB 113;
MTCW

Ambler, Eric 1909- . . . . **CLC 4, 6, 9**
See also CA 9-12R; CANR 7, 38; DLB 77;
MTCW

Amichai, Yehuda 1924- . . . . . . **CLC 9, 22, 57**
See also CA 85-88; CANR 46; MTCW

Amiel, Henri Frederic 1821-1881 . . **NCLC 4**

Amis, Kingsley (William)
1922-1995 . . . . . **CLC 1, 2, 3, 5, 8, 13, 40,**
44; DA; DAB; DAC; DAM MST, NOV
See also AITN 2; CA 9-12R; 150; CANR 8,
28, 54; CDBLB 1945-1960; DLB 15, 27,
100, 139; DLBY 96; INT CANR-8;
MTCW

Amis, Martin (Louis)
1949- . . . . **CLC 4, 9, 38, 62, 101**
See also BEST 90:3; CA 65-68; CANR 8,
27, 54; DLB 14; INT CANR-27

Ammons, A(rchie) R(andolph)
1926- . . . . **CLC 2, 3, 5, 8, 9, 25, 57;**
DAM POET; PC 16
See also AITN 1; CA 9-12R; CANR 6, 36,
51; DLB 5, 165; MTCW

Amo, Tauraatua i
See Adams, Henry (Brooks)

Anand, Mulk Raj
1905- . . . . **CLC 23, 93; DAM NOV**
See also CA 65-68; CANR 32; MTCW

Anatol
See Schnitzler, Arthur

Anaximander
c. 610B.C.-c. 546B.C. . . . . **CMLC 22**

Anaya, Rudolfo A(lfonso)
1937- . . . . **CLC 23; DAM MULT, NOV;**
HLC
See also AAYA 20; CA 45-48; CAAS 4;
CANR 1, 32, 51; DLB 82; HW 1; MTCW

Andersen, Hans Christian
1805-1875 . . . . **NCLC 7; DA; DAB;**
DAC; DAM MST, POP; SSC 6; WLC
See also CLR 6; MAICYA; 1

Anderson, C. Farley
See Mencken, H(enry) L(ouis); Nathan,
George Jean

Anderson, Jessica (Margaret) Queale
. . . . **CLC 37**
See also CA 9-12R; CANR 4

Anderson, Jon (Victor)
1940- . . . . **CLC 9; DAM POET**
See also CA 25-28R; CANR 20

Anderson, Lindsay (Gordon)
1923-1994 . . . . **CLC 20**
See also CA 125; 128; 146

Anderson, Maxwell
1888-1959 . . . . . . **TCLC 2; DAM DRAM**
See also CA 105; 152; DLB 7

Anderson, Poul (William) 1926- . . . . **CLC 15**
See also AAYA 5; CA 1-4R; CAAS 2;
CANR 2, 15, 34; DLB 8; INT CANR-15;
MTCW; SATA 90; SATA-Brief 39

Anderson, Robert (Woodruff)
1917- .... **CLC 23; DAM DRAM**
See also AITN 1; CA 21-24R; CANR 32;
DLB 7

Anderson, Sherwood
1876-1941 .... **TCLC 1, 10, 24; DA;**
DAB; DAC; DAM MST, NOV; SSC 1;
WLC
See also CA 104; 121; CDALB 1917-1929;
DLB 4, 9, 86; DLBD 1; MTCW

Andier, Pierre
See Desnos, Robert

Andouard
See Giraudoux, (Hippolyte) Jean

Andrade, Carlos Drummond de ...... **CLC 18**
See also Drummond de Andrade, Carlos

Andrade, Mario de 1893-1945..... **TCLC 43**

Andreae, Johann V(alentin)
1586-1654 .... **LC 32**
See also DLB 164

Andreas-Salome, Lou 1861-1937... **TCLC 56**
See also DLB 66

Andrewes, Lancelot 1555-1626 .... **LC 5**
See also DLB 151, 172

Andrews, Cicily Fairfield
See West, Rebecca

Andrews, Elton V.
See Pohl, Frederik

Andreyev, Leonid (Nikolaevich)
1871-1919 .... **TCLC 3**
See also CA 104

Andric, Ivo 1892-1975 .... **CLC 8**
See also CA 81-84; 57-60; CANR 43;
DLB 147; MTCW

Angelique, Pierre
See Bataille, Georges

Angell, Roger 1920- .... **CLC 26**
See also CA 57-60; CANR 13, 44; DLB 171

Angelou, Maya
1928- .... **CLC 12, 35, 64, 77; BLC; DA;**
DAB; DAC; DAM MST, MULT, POET,
POP
See also AAYA 7, 20; BW 2; CA 65-68;
CANR 19, 42; DLB 38; MTCW;
SATA 49; YABC

Annensky, Innokenty (Fyodorovich)
1856-1909 .... **TCLC 14**
See also CA 110; 155

Annunzio, Gabriele d'
See D'Annunzio, Gabriele

Anon, Charles Robert
See Pessoa, Fernando (Antonio Nogueira)

Anouilh, Jean (Marie Lucien Pierre)
1910-1987 ...... **CLC 1, 3, 8, 13, 40, 50;**
DAM DRAM
See also CA 17-20R; 123; CANR 32;
MTCW

Anthony, Florence
See Ai

Anthony, John
See Ciardi, John (Anthony)

Anthony, Peter
See Shaffer, Anthony (Joshua); Shaffer,
Peter (Levin)

Anthony, Piers 1934- .. **CLC 35; DAM POP**
See also AAYA 11; CA 21-24R; CANR 28,
56; DLB 8; MTCW; SAAS 22; SATA 84

Antoine, Marc
See Proust, (Valentin-Louis-George-Eugene-)
Marcel

Antoninus, Brother
See Everson, William (Oliver)

Antonioni, Michelangelo 1912- ..... **CLC 20**
See also CA 73-76; CANR 45

Antschel, Paul 1920-1970
See Celan, Paul
See also CA 85-88; CANR 33; MTCW

Anwar, Chairil 1922-1949 .... **TCLC 22**
See also CA 121

Apollinaire, Guillaume
1880-1918 .... **TCLC 3, 8, 51;**
DAM POET; PC 7
See also Kostrowitzki, Wilhelm Apollinaris
de
See also CA 152

Appelfeld, Aharon 1932- .... **CLC 23, 47**
See also CA 112; 133

Apple, Max (Isaac) 1941-........ **CLC 9, 33**
See also CA 81-84; CANR 19, 54; DLB 130

Appleman, Philip (Dean) 1926-..... **CLC 51**
See also CA 13-16R; CAAS 18; CANR 6,
29, 56

Appleton, Lawrence
See Lovecraft, H(oward) P(hillips)

Apteryx
See Eliot, T(homas) S(tearns)

Apuleius, (Lucius Madaurensis)
125(?)-175(?) .... **CMLC 1**

Aquin, Hubert 1929-1977......... **CLC 15**
See also CA 105; DLB 53

Aragon, Louis
1897-1982 ..... **CLC 3, 22; DAM NOV,**
POET
See also CA 69-72; 108; CANR 28;
DLB 72; MTCW

Arany, Janos 1817-1882........ **NCLC 34**

Arbuthnot, John 1667-1735.......... **LC 1**
See also DLB 101

Archer, Herbert Winslow
See Mencken, H(enry) L(ouis)

Archer, Jeffrey (Howard)
1940- .... **CLC 28; DAM POP**
See also AAYA 16; BEST 89:3; CA 77-80;
CANR 22, 52; INT CANR-22

Archer, Jules 1915- .... **CLC 12**
See also CA 9-12R; CANR 6; SAAS 5;
SATA 4, 85

Archer, Lee
See Ellison, Harlan (Jay)

Arden, John
1930- ..... **CLC 6, 13, 15; DAM DRAM**
See also CA 13-16R; CAAS 4; CANR 31;
DLB 13; MTCW

Arenas, Reinaldo
1943-1990 ...... **CLC 41; DAM MULT;**
HLC
See also CA 124; 128; 133; DLB 145; HW

Arendt, Hannah 1906-1975 ..... **CLC 66, 98**
See also CA 17-20R; 61-64; CANR 26;
MTCW

Aretino, Pietro 1492-1556 .... **LC 12**

Arghezi, Tudor.................... **CLC 80**
See also Theodorescu, Ion N.

Arguedas, Jose Maria
1911-1969 .... **CLC 10, 18**
See also CA 89-92; DLB 113; HW

Argueta, Manlio 1936-............ **CLC 31**
See also CA 131; DLB 145; HW

Ariosto, Ludovico 1474-1533........ **LC 6**

Aristides
See Epstein, Joseph

Aristophanes
450B.C.-385B.C......... **CMLC 4; DA;**
DAB; DAC; DAM DRAM, MST; DC 2
See also DLB 176; YABC

Arlt, Roberto (Godofredo Christophersen)
1900-1942 ..... **TCLC 29; DAM MULT;**
HLC
See also CA 123; 131; HW

Armah, Ayi Kwei
1939- .... **CLC 5, 33; BLC;**
DAM MULT, POET
See also BW 1; CA 61-64; CANR 21;
DLB 117; MTCW

Armatrading, Joan 1950-.......... **CLC 17**
See also CA 114

Arnette, Robert
See Silverberg, Robert

Arnim, Achim von (Ludwig Joachim von
Arnim) 1781-1831....... **NCLC 5**
See also DLB 90

Arnim, Bettina von 1785-1859.... **NCLC 38**
See also DLB 90

Arnold, Matthew
1822-1888 ..... **NCLC 6, 29; DA; DAB;**
DAC; DAM MST, POET; PC 5; WLC
See also CDBLB 1832-1890; DLB 32, 57

Arnold, Thomas 1795-1842 ...... **NCLC 18**
See also DLB 55

Arnow, Harriette (Louisa) Simpson
1908-1986 .... **CLC 2, 7, 18**
See also CA 9-12R; 118; CANR 14; DLB 6;
MTCW; SATA 42; SATA-Obit 47

Arp, Hans
See Arp, Jean

Arp, Jean 1887-1966............... **CLC 5**
See also CA 81-84; 25-28R; CANR 42

Arrabal
See Arrabal, Fernando

Arrabal, Fernando 1932- ... **CLC 2, 9, 18, 58**
See also CA 9-12R; CANR 15

Arrick, Fran.................... **CLC 30**
See also Gaberman, Judie Angell

Artaud, Antonin (Marie Joseph)
1896-1948 ... **TCLC 3, 36; DAM DRAM**
See also CA 104; 149

Arthur, Ruth M(abel) 1905-1979.... **CLC 12**
See also CA 9-12R; 85-88; CANR 4;
SATA 7, 26

Artsybashev, Mikhail (Petrovich)
1878-1927 .... **TCLC 31**

Arundel, Honor (Morfydd)
1919-1973 . . . . CLC 17
See also CA 21-22; 41-44R; CAP 2;
CLR 35; SATA 4; SATA-Obit 24

Arzner, Dorothy 1897-1979 . . . . CLC 98

Asch, Sholem 1880-1957 . . . . TCLC 3
See also CA 105

Ash, Shalom
See Asch, Sholem

Ashbery, John (Lawrence)
1927- . . . . . . CLC 2, 3, 4, 6, 9, 13, 15, 25,
41, 77; DAM POET
See also CA 5-8R; CANR 9, 37; DLB 5,
165; DLBY 81; INT CANR-9; MTCW

Ashdown, Clifford
See Freeman, R(ichard) Austin

Ashe, Gordon
See Creasey, John

Ashton-Warner, Sylvia (Constance)
1908-1984 . . . . CLC 19
See also CA 69-72; 112; CANR 29; MTCW

Asimov, Isaac
1920-1992 . . . . . . CLC 1, 3, 9, 19, 26, 76,
92; DAM POP
See also AAYA 13; BEST 90:2; CA 1-4R;
137; CANR 2, 19, 36; CLR 12; DLB 8;
DLBY 92; INT CANR-19; JRDA;
MAICYA; MTCW; SATA 1, 26, 74

Assis, Joaquim Maria Machado de
See Machado de Assis, Joaquim Maria

Astley, Thea (Beatrice May)
1925- . . . . CLC 41
See also CA 65-68; CANR 11, 43

Aston, James
See White, T(erence) H(anbury)

Asturias, Miguel Angel
1899-1974 . . . . CLC 3, 8, 13;
DAM MULT, NOV; HLC
See also CA 25-28; 49-52; CANR 32;
CAP 2; DLB 113; HW; MTCW

Atares, Carlos Saura
See Saura (Atares), Carlos

Atheling, William
See Pound, Ezra (Weston Loomis)

Atheling, William, Jr.
See Blish, James (Benjamin)

Atherton, Gertrude (Franklin Horn)
1857-1948 . . . . TCLC 2
See also CA 104; 155; DLB 9, 78

Atherton, Lucius
See Masters, Edgar Lee

Atkins, Jack
See Harris, Mark

Atkinson, Kate . . . . CLC 99

Attaway, William (Alexander)
1911-1986 . . . . CLC 92; BLC;
DAM MULT
See also BW 2; CA 143; DLB 76

Atticus
See Fleming, Ian (Lancaster)

Atwood, Margaret (Eleanor)
1939- . . . . . CLC 2, 3, 4, 8, 13, 15, 25, 44,
84; DA; DAB; DAC; DAM MST, NOV,
POET; PC 8; SSC 2; WLC
See also AAYA 12; BEST 89:2; CA 49-52;
CANR 3, 24, 33; DLB 53;
INT CANR-24; MTCW; SATA 50

Aubigny, Pierre d'
See Mencken, H(enry) L(ouis)

Aubin, Penelope 1685-1731(?) . . . . LC 9
See also DLB 39

Auchincloss, Louis (Stanton)
1917- . . . . CLC 4, 6, 9, 18, 45;
DAM NOV; SSC 22
See also CA 1-4R; CANR 6, 29, 55; DLB 2;
DLBY 80; INT CANR-29; MTCW

Auden, W(ystan) H(ugh)
1907-1973 . . . . . CLC 1, 2, 3, 4, 6, 9, 11,
14, 43; DA; DAB; DAC; DAM DRAM,
MST, POET; PC 1; WLC
See also AAYA 18; CA 9-12R; 45-48;
CANR 5; CDBLB 1914-1945; DLB 10,
20; MTCW

Audiberti, Jacques
1900-1965 . . . . . . CLC 38; DAM DRAM
See also CA 25-28R

Audubon, John James
1785-1851 . . . . NCLC 47

Auel, Jean M(arie)
1936- . . . . CLC 31; DAM POP
See also AAYA 7; BEST 90:4; CA 103;
CANR 21; INT CANR-21; SATA 91

Auerbach, Erich 1892-1957 . . . . TCLC 43
See also CA 118; 155

Augier, Emile 1820-1889 . . . . NCLC 31

August, John
See De Voto, Bernard (Augustine)

Augustine, St. 354-430 . . . . . . CMLC 6; DAB

Aurelius
See Bourne, Randolph S(illiman)

Aurobindo, Sri 1872-1950 . . . . TCLC 63

Austen, Jane
1775-1817 . . . . . NCLC 1, 13, 19, 33, 51;
DA; DAB; DAC; DAM MST, NOV;
WLC
See also AAYA 19; CDBLB 1789-1832;
DLB 116

Auster, Paul 1947- . . . . CLC 47
See also CA 69-72; CANR 23, 52

Austin, Frank
See Faust, Frederick (Schiller)

Austin, Mary (Hunter)
1868-1934 . . . . TCLC 25
See also CA 109; DLB 9, 78

Autran Dourado, Waldomiro
See Dourado, (Waldomiro Freitas) Autran

Averroes 1126-1198 . . . . CMLC 7
See also DLB 115

Avicenna 980-1037 . . . . CMLC 16
See also DLB 115

Avison, Margaret
1918- . . . . CLC 2, 4, 97; DAC;
DAM POET
See also CA 17-20R; DLB 53; MTCW

Axton, David
See Koontz, Dean R(ay)

Ayckbourn, Alan
1939- . . . . . . CLC 5, 8, 18, 33, 74; DAB;
DAM DRAM
See also CA 21-24R; CANR 31; DLB 13;
MTCW

Aydy, Catherine
See Tennant, Emma (Christina)

Ayme, Marcel (Andre) 1902-1967 . . . CLC 11
See also CA 89-92; CLR 25; DLB 72;
SATA 91

Ayrton, Michael 1921-1975 . . . . CLC 7
See also CA 5-8R; 61-64; CANR 9, 21

Azorin . . . . CLC 11
See also Martinez Ruiz, Jose

Azuela, Mariano
1873-1952 . . . . . TCLC 3; DAM MULT;
HLC
See also CA 104; 131; HW; MTCW

Baastad, Babbis Friis
See Friis-Baastad, Babbis Ellinor

Bab
See Gilbert, W(illiam) S(chwenck)

Babbis, Eleanor
See Friis-Baastad, Babbis Ellinor

Babel, Isaac
See Babel, Isaak (Emmanuilovich)

Babel, Isaak (Emmanuilovich)
1894-1941(?) . . . . . . TCLC 2, 13; SSC 16
See also CA 104; 155

Babits, Mihaly 1883-1941 . . . . TCLC 14
See also CA 114

Babur 1483-1530 . . . . LC 18

Bacchelli, Riccardo 1891-1985 . . . . . CLC 19
See also CA 29-32R; 117

Bach, Richard (David)
1936- . . . . . . CLC 14; DAM NOV, POP
See also AITN 1; BEST 89:2; CA 9-12R;
CANR 18; MTCW; SATA 13

Bachman, Richard
See King, Stephen (Edwin)

Bachmann, Ingeborg 1926-1973 . . . . . CLC 69
See also CA 93-96; 45-48; DLB 85

Bacon, Francis 1561-1626 . . . . LC 18, 32
See also CDBLB Before 1660; DLB 151

Bacon, Roger 1214(?)-1292 . . . . . . CMLC 14
See also DLB 115

Bacovia, George . . . . TCLC 24
See also Vasiliu, Gheorghe

Badanes, Jerome 1937- . . . . CLC 59

Bagehot, Walter 1826-1877 . . . . . . NCLC 10
See also DLB 55

Bagnold, Enid
1889-1981 . . . . . . CLC 25; DAM DRAM
See also CA 5-8R; 103; CANR 5, 40;
DLB 13, 160; MAICYA; SATA 1, 25

Bagritsky, Eduard 1895-1934 . . . . . TCLC 60

Bagrjana, Elisaveta
See Belcheva, Elisaveta

Bagryana, Elisaveta . . . . CLC 10
See also Belcheva, Elisaveta
See also DLB 147

Belloc, (Joseph) Hilaire (Pierre Sebastien
    Rene Swanton)
    1870-1953 ... **TCLC 7, 18; DAM POET**
    See also CA 106; 152; DLB 19, 100, 141,
    174; 1

Belloc, Joseph Peter Rene Hilaire
    See Belloc, (Joseph) Hilaire (Pierre Sebastien
    Rene Swanton)

Belloc, Joseph Pierre Hilaire
    See Belloc, (Joseph) Hilaire (Pierre Sebastien
    Rene Swanton)

Belloc, M. A.
    See Lowndes, Marie Adelaide (Belloc)

Bellow, Saul
    1915- ...... **CLC 1, 2, 3, 6, 8, 10, 13, 15,
        25, 33, 34, 63, 79; DA; DAB; DAC;
        DAM MST, NOV, POP; SSC 14; WLC**
    See also AITN 2; BEST 89:3; CA 5-8R;
    CABS 1; CANR 29, 53;
    CDALB 1941-1968; DLB 2, 28; DLBD 3;
    DLBY 82; MTCW

Belser, Reimond Karel Maria de   1929-
    See Ruyslinck, Ward
    See also CA 152

Bely, Andrey .... **TCLC 7; PC 11**
    See also Bugayev, Boris Nikolayevich

Benary, Margot
    See Benary-Isbert, Margot

Benary-Isbert, Margot   1889-1979... **CLC 12**
    See also CA 5-8R; 89-92; CANR 4;
    CLR 12; MAICYA; SATA 2;
    SATA-Obit 21

Benavente (y Martinez), Jacinto
    1866-1954 ..... **TCLC 3; DAM DRAM,
                                          MULT**
    See also CA 106; 131; HW; MTCW

Benchley, Peter (Bradford)
    1940- ..... **CLC 4, 8; DAM NOV, POP**
    See also AAYA 14; AITN 2; CA 17-20R;
    CANR 12, 35; MTCW; SATA 3, 89

Benchley, Robert (Charles)
    1889-1945 .... **TCLC 1, 55**
    See also CA 105; 153; DLB 11

Benda, Julien   1867-1956 .... **TCLC 60**
    See also CA 120; 154

Benedict, Ruth (Fulton)
    1887-1948 .... **TCLC 60**
    See also CA 158

Benedikt, Michael   1935- .... **CLC 4, 14**
    See also CA 13-16R; CANR 7; DLB 5

Benet, Juan   1927-................ **CLC 28**
    See also CA 143

Benet, Stephen Vincent
    1898-1943 ...... **TCLC 7; DAM POET;
                                          SSC 10**
    See also CA 104; 152; DLB 4, 48, 102; 1

Benet, William Rose
    1886-1950 ...... **TCLC 28; DAM POET**
    See also CA 118; 152; DLB 45

Benford, Gregory (Albert)   1941-.... **CLC 52**
    See also CA 69-72; CAAS 27; CANR 12,
    24, 49; DLBY 82

Bengtsson, Frans (Gunnar)
    1894-1954 .... **TCLC 48**

Benjamin, David
    See Slavitt, David R(ytman)

Benjamin, Lois
    See Gould, Lois

Benjamin, Walter   1892-1940 ..... **TCLC 39**

Benn, Gottfried   1886-1956........ **TCLC 3**
    See also CA 106; 153; DLB 56

Bennett, Alan
    1934- ... **CLC 45, 77; DAB; DAM MST**
    See also CA 103; CANR 35, 55; MTCW

Bennett, (Enoch) Arnold
    1867-1931 .... **TCLC 5, 20**
    See also CA 106; 155; CDBLB 1890-1914;
    DLB 10, 34, 98, 135

Bennett, Elizabeth
    See Mitchell, Margaret (Munnerlyn)

Bennett, George Harold   1930-
    See Bennett, Hal
    See also BW 1; CA 97-100

Bennett, Hal .... **CLC 5**
    See also Bennett, George Harold
    See also DLB 33

Bennett, Jay   1912-.............. **CLC 35**
    See also AAYA 10; CA 69-72; CANR 11,
    42; JRDA; SAAS 4; SATA 41, 87;
    SATA-Brief 27

Bennett, Louise (Simone)
    1919- ..... **CLC 28; BLC; DAM MULT**
    See also BW 2; CA 151; DLB 117

Benson, E(dward) F(rederic)
    1867-1940 .... **TCLC 27**
    See also CA 114; 157; DLB 135, 153

Benson, Jackson J.   1930-.......... **CLC 34**
    See also CA 25-28R; DLB 111

Benson, Sally   1900-1972 .... **CLC 17**
    See also CA 19-20; 37-40R; CAP 1;
    SATA 1, 35; SATA-Obit 27

Benson, Stella   1892-1933........ **TCLC 17**
    See also CA 117; 155; DLB 36, 162

Bentham, Jeremy   1748-1832 ..... **NCLC 38**
    See also DLB 107, 158

Bentley, E(dmund) C(lerihew)
    1875-1956 .... **TCLC 12**
    See also CA 108; DLB 70

Bentley, Eric (Russell)   1916-...... **CLC 24**
    See also CA 5-8R; CANR 6; INT CANR-6

Beranger, Pierre Jean de
    1780-1857 .... **NCLC 34**

Berdyaev, Nicolas
    See Berdyaev, Nikolai (Aleksandrovich)

Berdyaev, Nikolai (Aleksandrovich)
    1874-1948 .... **TCLC 67**
    See also CA 120; 157

Berdyayev, Nikolai (Aleksandrovich)
    See Berdyaev, Nikolai (Aleksandrovich)

Berendt, John (Lawrence)   1939-.... **CLC 86**
    See also CA 146

Berger, Colonel
    See Malraux, (Georges-)Andre

Berger, John (Peter)   1926- ...... **CLC 2, 19**
    See also CA 81-84; CANR 51; DLB 14

Berger, Melvin H.   1927- .... **CLC 12**
    See also CA 5-8R; CANR 4; CLR 32;
    SAAS 2; SATA 5, 88

Berger, Thomas (Louis)
    1924- .... **CLC 3, 5, 8, 11, 18, 38;
                                          DAM NOV**
    See also CA 1-4R; CANR 5, 28, 51; DLB 2;
    DLBY 80; INT CANR-28; MTCW

Bergman, (Ernst) Ingmar
    1918- .... **CLC 16, 72**
    See also CA 81-84; CANR 33

Bergson, Henri   1859-1941 .... **TCLC 32**

Bergstein, Eleanor   1938-........... **CLC 4**
    See also CA 53-56; CANR 5

Berkoff, Steven   1937-............. **CLC 56**
    See also CA 104

Bermant, Chaim (Icyk)   1929- ...... **CLC 40**
    See also CA 57-60; CANR 6, 31, 57

Bern, Victoria
    See Fisher, M(ary) F(rances) K(ennedy)

Bernanos, (Paul Louis) Georges
    1888-1948 .... **TCLC 3**
    See also CA 104; 130; DLB 72

Bernard, April   1956- .... **CLC 59**
    See also CA 131

Berne, Victoria
    See Fisher, M(ary) F(rances) K(ennedy)

Bernhard, Thomas
    1931-1989 .... **CLC 3, 32, 61**
    See also CA 85-88; 127; CANR 32, 57;
    DLB 85, 124; MTCW

Berriault, Gina   1926-............. **CLC 54**
    See also CA 116; 129; DLB 130

Berrigan, Daniel   1921-............ **CLC 4**
    See also CA 33-36R; CAAS 1; CANR 11,
    43; DLB 5

Berrigan, Edmund Joseph Michael, Jr.
    1934-1983
    See Berrigan, Ted
    See also CA 61-64; 110; CANR 14

Berrigan, Ted..................... **CLC 37**
    See also Berrigan, Edmund Joseph Michael,
    Jr.
    See also DLB 5, 169

Berry, Charles Edward Anderson   1931-
    See Berry, Chuck
    See also CA 115

Berry, Chuck..................... **CLC 17**
    See also Berry, Charles Edward Anderson

Berry, Jonas
    See Ashbery, John (Lawrence)

Berry, Wendell (Erdman)
    1934- .... **CLC 4, 6, 8, 27, 46;
                                          DAM POET**
    See also AITN 1; CA 73-76; CANR 50;
    DLB 5, 6

Berryman, John
    1914-1972 ...... **CLC 1, 2, 3, 4, 6, 8, 10,
        13, 25, 62; DAM POET**
    See also CA 13-16; 33-36R; CABS 2;
    CANR 35; CAP 1; CDALB 1941-1968;
    DLB 48; MTCW

Bertolucci, Bernardo   1940- .... **CLC 16**
    See also CA 106

Bertrand, Aloysius   1807-1841 .... **NCLC 31**

Bertran de Born   c. 1140-1215 ..... **CMLC 5**

Besant, Annie (Wood)   1847-1933 ... **TCLC 9**
    See also CA 105

Bodker, Cecil 1927- .... **CLC 21**
See also CA 73-76; CANR 13, 44; CLR 23;
MAICYA; SATA 14

Boell, Heinrich (Theodor)
1917-1985 .... **CLC 2, 3, 6, 9, 11, 15, 27,
32, 72; DA; DAB; DAC; DAM MST,
NOV; SSC 23; WLC**
See also CA 21-24R; 116; CANR 24;
DLB 69; DLBY 85; MTCW

Boerne, Alfred
See Doeblin, Alfred

Boethius 480(?)-524(?) .... **CMLC 15**
See also DLB 115

Bogan, Louise
1897-1970 .... **CLC 4, 39, 46, 93;
DAM POET; PC 12**
See also CA 73-76; 25-28R; CANR 33;
DLB 45, 169; MTCW

Bogarde, Dirk .... **CLC 19**
See also Van Den Bogarde, Derek Jules
Gaspard Ulric Niven
See also DLB 14

Bogosian, Eric 1953- .... **CLC 45**
See also CA 138

Bograd, Larry 1953- .... **CLC 35**
See also CA 93-96; CANR 57; SAAS 21;
SATA 33, 89

Boiardo, Matteo Maria 1441-1494 .... **LC 6**

Boileau-Despreaux, Nicolas
1636-1711 .... **LC 3**

Bojer, Johan 1872-1959 .... **TCLC 64**

Boland, Eavan (Aisling)
1944- .... **CLC 40, 67; DAM POET**
See also CA 143; DLB 40

Bolt, Lee
See Faust, Frederick (Schiller)

Bolt, Robert (Oxton)
1924-1995 ...... **CLC 14; DAM DRAM**
See also CA 17-20R; 147; CANR 35;
DLB 13; MTCW

Bombet, Louis-Alexandre-Cesar
See Stendhal

Bomkauf
See Kaufman, Bob (Garnell)

Bonaventura .... **NCLC 35**
See also DLB 90

Bond, Edward
1934- ... **CLC 4, 6, 13, 23; DAM DRAM**
See also CA 25-28R; CANR 38; DLB 13;
MTCW

Bonham, Frank 1914-1989 .... **CLC 12**
See also AAYA 1; CA 9-12R; CANR 4, 36;
JRDA; MAICYA; SAAS 3; SATA 1, 49;
SATA-Obit 62

Bonnefoy, Yves
1923- ...... **CLC 9, 15, 58; DAM MST,
POET**
See also CA 85-88; CANR 33; MTCW

Bontemps, Arna(ud Wendell)
1902-1973 .... **CLC 1, 18; BLC;
DAM MULT, NOV, POET**
See also BW 1; CA 1-4R; 41-44R; CANR 4,
35; CLR 6; DLB 48, 51; JRDA;
MAICYA; MTCW; SATA 2, 44;
SATA-Obit 24

Booth, Martin 1944- .... **CLC 13**
See also CA 93-96; CAAS 2

Booth, Philip 1925- .... **CLC 23**
See also CA 5-8R; CANR 5; DLBY 82

Booth, Wayne C(layson) 1921- ..... **CLC 24**
See also CA 1-4R; CAAS 5; CANR 3, 43;
DLB 67

Borchert, Wolfgang 1921-1947 ..... **TCLC 5**
See also CA 104; DLB 69, 124

Borel, Petrus 1809-1859........ **NCLC 41**

Borges, Jorge Luis
1899-1986 ... **CLC 1, 2, 3, 4, 6, 8, 9, 10,
13, 19, 44, 48, 83; DA; DAB; DAC;
DAM MST, MULT; HLC; SSC 4; WLC**
See also AAYA 19; CA 21-24R; CANR 19,
33; DLB 113; DLBY 86; HW; MTCW

Borowski, Tadeusz 1922-1951 ...... **TCLC 9**
See also CA 106; 154

Borrow, George (Henry)
1803-1881 .... **NCLC 9**
See also DLB 21, 55, 166

Bosman, Herman Charles
1905-1951 .... **TCLC 49**

Bosschere, Jean de 1878(?)-1953... **TCLC 19**
See also CA 115

Boswell, James
1740-1795 ...... **LC 4; DA; DAB; DAC;
DAM MST; WLC**
See also CDBLB 1660-1789; DLB 104, 142

Bottoms, David 1949-............. **CLC 53**
See also CA 105; CANR 22; DLB 120;
DLBY 83

Boucicault, Dion 1820-1890...... **NCLC 41**

Boucolon, Maryse 1937(?)-
See Conde, Maryse
See also CA 110; CANR 30, 53

Bourget, Paul (Charles Joseph)
1852-1935 .... **TCLC 12**
See also CA 107; DLB 123

Bourjaily, Vance (Nye) 1922- .... **CLC 8, 62**
See also CA 1-4R; CAAS 1; CANR 2;
DLB 2, 143

Bourne, Randolph S(illiman)
1886-1918 .... **TCLC 16**
See also CA 117; 155; DLB 63

Bova, Ben(jamin William) 1932-.... **CLC 45**
See also AAYA 16; CA 5-8R; CAAS 18;
CANR 11, 56; CLR 3; DLBY 81;
INT CANR-11; MAICYA; MTCW;
SATA 6, 68

Bowen, Elizabeth (Dorothea Cole)
1899-1973 ...... **CLC 1, 3, 6, 11, 15, 22;
DAM NOV; SSC 3**
See also CA 17-18; 41-44R; CANR 35;
CAP 2; CDBLB 1945-1960; DLB 15, 162;
MTCW

Bowering, George 1935-........ **CLC 15, 47**
See also CA 21-24R; CAAS 16; CANR 10;
DLB 53

Bowering, Marilyn R(uthe) 1949-... **CLC 32**
See also CA 101; CANR 49

Bowers, Edgar 1924- .... **CLC 9**
See also CA 5-8R; CANR 24; DLB 5

Bowie, David .... **CLC 17**
See also Jones, David Robert

Bowles, Jane (Sydney)
1917-1973 .... **CLC 3, 68**
See also CA 19-20; 41-44R; CAP 2

Bowles, Paul (Frederick)
1910- .... **CLC 1, 2, 19, 53; SSC 3**
See also CA 1-4R; CAAS 1; CANR 1, 19,
50; DLB 5, 6; MTCW

Box, Edgar
See Vidal, Gore

Boyd, Nancy
See Millay, Edna St. Vincent

Boyd, William 1952-........ **CLC 28, 53, 70**
See also CA 114; 120; CANR 51

Boyle, Kay
1902-1992 ..... **CLC 1, 5, 19, 58; SSC 5**
See also CA 13-16R; 140; CAAS 1;
CANR 29; DLB 4, 9, 48, 86; DLBY 93;
MTCW

Boyle, Mark
See Kienzle, William X(avier)

Boyle, Patrick 1905-1982.......... **CLC 19**
See also CA 127

Boyle, T. C. 1948-
See Boyle, T(homas) Coraghessan

Boyle, T(homas) Coraghessan
1948- ..... **CLC 36, 55, 90; DAM POP;
SSC 16**
See also BEST 90:4; CA 120; CANR 44;
DLBY 86

Boz
See Dickens, Charles (John Huffam)

Brackenridge, Hugh Henry
1748-1816 .... **NCLC 7**
See also DLB 11, 37

Bradbury, Edward P.
See Moorcock, Michael (John)

Bradbury, Malcolm (Stanley)
1932- .... **CLC 32, 61; DAM NOV**
See also CA 1-4R; CANR 1, 33; DLB 14;
MTCW

Bradbury, Ray (Douglas)
1920- ..... **CLC 1, 3, 10, 15, 42, 98; DA;
DAB; DAC; DAM MST, NOV, POP;
WLC**
See also AAYA 15; AITN 1, 2; CA 1-4R;
CANR 2, 30; CDALB 1968-1988; DLB 2,
8; INT CANR-30; MTCW; SATA 11, 64

Bradford, Gamaliel 1863-1932..... **TCLC 36**
See also DLB 17

Bradley, David (Henry, Jr.)
1950- ..... **CLC 23; BLC; DAM MULT**
See also BW 1; CA 104; CANR 26; DLB 33

Bradley, John Ed(mund, Jr.)
1958- .... **CLC 55**
See also CA 139

Bradley, Marion Zimmer
1930- .... **CLC 30; DAM POP**
See also AAYA 9; CA 57-60; CAAS 10;
CANR 7, 31, 51; DLB 8; MTCW;
SATA 90

Bradstreet, Anne
1612(?)-1672 ...... **LC 4, 30; DA; DAC;
DAM MST, POET; PC 10**
See also CDALB 1640-1865; DLB 24

Brady, Joan 1939- .... **CLC 86**
See also CA 141

Bragg, Melvyn 1939- . . . . CLC 10
See also BEST 89:3; CA 57-60; CANR 10,
48; DLB 14

Braine, John (Gerard)
1922-1986 . . . . CLC 1, 3, 41
See also CA 1-4R; 120; CANR 1, 33;
CDBLB 1945-1960; DLB 15; DLBY 86;
MTCW

Bramah, Ernest 1868-1942. . . . . . . TCLC 72
See also CA 156; DLB 70

Brammer, William 1930(?)-1978 . . . . CLC 31
See also CA 77-80

Brancati, Vitaliano 1907-1954. . . . . TCLC 12
See also CA 109

Brancato, Robin F(idler) 1936- . . . . . CLC 35
See also AAYA 9; CA 69-72; CANR 11,
45; CLR 32; JRDA; SAAS 9; SATA 23

Brand, Max
See Faust, Frederick (Schiller)

Brand, Millen 1906-1980. . . . . CLC 7
See also CA 21-24R; 97-100

Branden, Barbara . . . . CLC 44
See also CA 148

Brandes, Georg (Morris Cohen)
1842-1927 . . . . TCLC 10
See also CA 105

Brandys, Kazimierz 1916- . . . . CLC 62

Branley, Franklyn M(ansfield)
1915- . . . . CLC 21
See also CA 33-36R; CANR 14, 39;
CLR 13; MAICYA; SAAS 16; SATA 4,
68

Brathwaite, Edward Kamau
1930- . . . . CLC 11; DAM POET
See also BW 2; CA 25-28R; CANR 11, 26,
47; DLB 125

Brautigan, Richard (Gary)
1935-1984 . . . . CLC 1, 3, 5, 9, 12, 34, 42;
DAM NOV
See also CA 53-56; 113; CANR 34; DLB 2,
5; DLBY 80, 84; MTCW; SATA 56

Brave Bird, Mary 1953-
See Crow Dog, Mary (Ellen)
See also NNAL

Braverman, Kate 1950- . . . . CLC 67
See also CA 89-92

Brecht, Bertolt
1898-1956 . . . . . . TCLC 1, 6, 13, 35; DA;
DAB; DAC; DAM DRAM, MST; DC 3;
WLC
See also CA 104; 133; DLB 56, 124; MTCW

Brecht, Eugen Berthold Friedrich
See Brecht, Bertolt

Bremer, Fredrika 1801-1865 . . . . . NCLC 11

Brennan, Christopher John
1870-1932 . . . . TCLC 17
See also CA 117

Brennan, Maeve 1917- . . . . CLC 5
See also CA 81-84

Brentano, Clemens (Maria)
1778-1842 . . . . NCLC 1
See also DLB 90

Brent of Bin Bin
See Franklin, (Stella Maraia Sarah) Miles

Brenton, Howard 1942- . . . . CLC 31
See also CA 69-72; CANR 33; DLB 13;
MTCW

Breslin, James 1930-
See Breslin, Jimmy
See also CA 73-76; CANR 31; DAM NOV;
MTCW

Breslin, Jimmy . . . . CLC 4, 43
See also Breslin, James
See also AITN 1

Bresson, Robert 1901- . . . . CLC 16
See also CA 110; CANR 49

Breton, Andre
1896-1966 . . . . . CLC 2, 9, 15, 54; PC 15
See also CA 19-20; 25-28R; CANR 40;
CAP 2; DLB 65; MTCW

Breytenbach, Breyten
1939(?)- . . . . . . CLC 23, 37; DAM POET
See also CA 113; 129

Bridgers, Sue Ellen 1942- . . . . CLC 26
See also AAYA 8; CA 65-68; CANR 11,
36; CLR 18; DLB 52; JRDA; MAICYA;
SAAS 1; SATA 22, 90

Bridges, Robert (Seymour)
1844-1930 . . . . TCLC 1; DAM POET
See also CA 104; 152; CDBLB 1890-1914;
DLB 19, 98

Bridie, James. . . . . TCLC 3
See also Mavor, Osborne Henry
See also DLB 10

Brin, David 1950- . . . . CLC 34
See also AAYA 21; CA 102; CANR 24;
INT CANR-24; SATA 65

Brink, Andre (Philippus)
1935- . . . . CLC 18, 36
See also CA 104; CANR 39; INT 103;
MTCW

Brinsmead, H(esba) F(ay) 1922- . . . . CLC 21
See also CA 21-24R; CANR 10; MAICYA;
SAAS 5; SATA 18, 78

Brittain, Vera (Mary)
1893(?)-1970 . . . . CLC 23
See also CA 13-16; 25-28R; CANR 58;
CAP 1; MTCW

Broch, Hermann 1886-1951. . . . . . . TCLC 20
See also CA 117; DLB 85, 124

Brock, Rose
See Hansen, Joseph

Brodkey, Harold (Roy) 1930-1996 . . CLC 56
See also CA 111; 151; DLB 130

Brodsky, Iosif Alexandrovich 1940-1996
See Brodsky, Joseph
See also AITN 1; CA 41-44R; 151;
CANR 37; DAM POET; MTCW

Brodsky, Joseph
1940-1996 . . CLC 4, 6, 13, 36, 100; PC 9
See also Brodsky, Iosif Alexandrovich

Brodsky, Michael (Mark) 1948- . . . . CLC 19
See also CA 102; CANR 18, 41, 58

Bromell, Henry 1947-. . . . . CLC 5
See also CA 53-56; CANR 9

Bromfield, Louis (Brucker)
1896-1956 . . . . TCLC 11
See also CA 107; 155; DLB 4, 9, 86

Broner, E(sther) M(asserman)
1930- . . . . CLC 19
See also CA 17-20R; CANR 8, 25; DLB 28

Bronk, William 1918-. . . . . CLC 10
See also CA 89-92; CANR 23; DLB 165

Bronstein, Lev Davidovich
See Trotsky, Leon

Bronte, Anne 1820-1849. . . . . NCLC 4
See also DLB 21

Bronte, Charlotte
1816-1855 . . . . . NCLC 3, 8, 33, 58; DA;
DAB; DAC; DAM MST, NOV; WLC
See also AAYA 17; CDBLB 1832-1890;
DLB 21, 159

Bronte, Emily (Jane)
1818-1848 . . . . NCLC 16, 35; DA; DAB;
DAC; DAM MST, NOV, POET; PC 8;
WLC
See also AAYA 17; CDBLB 1832-1890;
DLB 21, 32

Brooke, Frances 1724-1789 . . . . LC 6
See also DLB 39, 99

Brooke, Henry 1703(?)-1783 . . . . LC 1
See also DLB 39

Brooke, Rupert (Chawner)
1887-1915 . . . . TCLC 2, 7; DA; DAB;
DAC; DAM MST, POET; WLC
See also CA 104; 132; CDBLB 1914-1945;
DLB 19; MTCW

Brooke-Haven, P.
See Wodehouse, P(elham) G(renville)

Brooke-Rose, Christine 1926(?)- . . . . CLC 40
See also CA 13-16R; CANR 58; DLB 14

Brookner, Anita
1928- . . . . CLC 32, 34, 51; DAB;
DAM POP
See also CA 114; 120; CANR 37, 56;
DLBY 87; MTCW

Brooks, Cleanth 1906-1994 . . . . . CLC 24, 86
See also CA 17-20R; 145; CANR 33, 35;
DLB 63; DLBY 94; INT CANR-35;
MTCW

Brooks, George
See Baum, L(yman) Frank

Brooks, Gwendolyn
1917- . . . . . . CLC 1, 2, 4, 5, 15, 49; BLC;
DA; DAC; DAM MST, MULT, POET;
PC 7; WLC
See also AAYA 20; AITN 1; BW 2;
CA 1-4R; CANR 1, 27, 52;
CDALB 1941-1968; CLR 27; DLB 5, 76,
165; MTCW; SATA 6

Brooks, Mel. CLC 12
See also Kaminsky, Melvin
See also AAYA 13; DLB 26

Brooks, Peter 1938-. . . . . CLC 34
See also CA 45-48; CANR 1

Brooks, Van Wyck 1886-1963. . . . . . CLC 29
See also CA 1-4R; CANR 6; DLB 45, 63,
103

Brophy, Brigid (Antonia)
1929-1995 . . . . CLC 6, 11, 29
See also CA 5-8R; 149; CAAS 4; CANR 25,
53; DLB 14; MTCW

Brosman, Catharine Savage 1934-. . . . CLC 9
See also CA 61-64; CANR 21, 46

Brother Antoninus
See Everson, William (Oliver)

Broughton, T(homas) Alan 1936- ... **CLC 19**
See also CA 45-48; CANR 2, 23, 48

Broumas, Olga 1949- .... **CLC 10, 73**
See also CA 85-88; CANR 20

Brown, Alan 1951- .... **CLC 99**

Brown, Charles Brockden
1771-1810 .... **NCLC 22**
See also CDALB 1640-1865; DLB 37, 59, 73

Brown, Christy 1932-1981 .... **CLC 63**
See also CA 105; 104; DLB 14

Brown, Claude
1937- ..... **CLC 30; BLC; DAM MULT**
See also AAYA 7; BW 1; CA 73-76

Brown, Dee (Alexander)
1908- .... **CLC 18, 47; DAM POP**
See also CA 13-16R; CAAS 6; CANR 11, 45; DLBY 80; MTCW; SATA 5

Brown, George
See Wertmueller, Lina

Brown, George Douglas
1869-1902 .... **TCLC 28**

Brown, George Mackay
1921-1996 .... **CLC 5, 48, 100**
See also CA 21-24R; 151; CAAS 6; CANR 12, 37; DLB 14, 27, 139; MTCW; SATA 35

Brown, (William) Larry 1951- ...... **CLC 73**
See also CA 130; 134; INT 133

Brown, Moses
See Barrett, William (Christopher)

Brown, Rita Mae
1944- ..... **CLC 18, 43, 79; DAM NOV, POP**
See also CA 45-48; CANR 2, 11, 35; INT CANR-11; MTCW

Brown, Roderick (Langmere) Haig-
See Haig-Brown, Roderick (Langmere)

Brown, Rosellen 1939- .... **CLC 32**
See also CA 77-80; CAAS 10; CANR 14, 44

Brown, Sterling Allen
1901-1989 .... **CLC 1, 23, 59; BLC; DAM MULT, POET**
See also BW 1; CA 85-88; 127; CANR 26; DLB 48, 51, 63; MTCW

Brown, Will
See Ainsworth, William Harrison

Brown, William Wells
1813-1884 .... **NCLC 2; BLC; DAM MULT; DC 1**
See also DLB 3, 50

Browne, (Clyde) Jackson 1948(?)- ... **CLC 21**
See also CA 120

Browning, Elizabeth Barrett
1806-1861 .... **NCLC 1, 16, 61; DA; DAB; DAC; DAM MST, POET; PC 6; WLC**
See also CDBLB 1832-1890; DLB 32

Browning, Robert
1812-1889 .... **NCLC 19; DA; DAB; DAC; DAM MST, POET; PC 2**
See also CDBLB 1832-1890; DLB 32, 163; YABC; 1

Browning, Tod 1882-1962 .... **CLC 16**
See also CA 141; 117

Brownson, Orestes (Augustus)
1803-1876 .... **NCLC 50**

Bruccoli, Matthew J(oseph) 1931- .. **CLC 34**
See also CA 9-12R; CANR 7; DLB 103

Bruce, Lenny .... **CLC 21**
See also Schneider, Leonard Alfred

Bruin, John
See Brutus, Dennis

Brulard, Henri
See Stendhal

Brulls, Christian
See Simenon, Georges (Jacques Christian)

Brunner, John (Kilian Houston)
1934-1995 ...... **CLC 8, 10; DAM POP**
See also CA 1-4R; 149; CAAS 8; CANR 2, 37; MTCW

Bruno, Giordano 1548-1600 .... **LC 27**

Brutus, Dennis
1924- ..... **CLC 43; BLC; DAM MULT, POET**
See also BW 2; CA 49-52; CAAS 14; CANR 2, 27, 42; DLB 117

Bryan, C(ourtlandt) D(ixon) B(arnes)
1936- .... **CLC 29**
See also CA 73-76; CANR 13; INT CANR-13

Bryan, Michael
See Moore, Brian

Bryant, William Cullen
1794-1878 ..... **NCLC 6, 46; DA; DAB; DAC; DAM MST, POET**
See also CDALB 1640-1865; DLB 3, 43, 59

Bryusov, Valery Yakovlevich
1873-1924 .... **TCLC 10**
See also CA 107; 155

Buchan, John
1875-1940 .... **TCLC 41; DAB; DAM POP**
See also CA 108; 145; DLB 34, 70, 156; 2

Buchanan, George 1506-1582 .... **LC 4**

Buchheim, Lothar-Guenther 1918- ... **CLC 6**
See also CA 85-88

Buchner, (Karl) Georg
1813-1837 .... **NCLC 26**

Buchwald, Art(hur) 1925- .... **CLC 33**
See also AITN 1; CA 5-8R; CANR 21; MTCW; SATA 10

Buck, Pearl S(ydenstricker)
1892-1973 .... **CLC 7, 11, 18; DA; DAB; DAC; DAM MST, NOV**
See also AITN 1; CA 1-4R; 41-44R; CANR 1, 34; DLB 9, 102; MTCW; SATA 1, 25

Buckler, Ernest
1908-1984 .. **CLC 13; DAC; DAM MST**
See also CA 11-12; 114; CAP 1; DLB 68; SATA 47

Buckley, Vincent (Thomas)
1925-1988 .... **CLC 57**
See also CA 101

Buckley, William F(rank), Jr.
1925- .... **CLC 7, 18, 37; DAM POP**
See also AITN 1; CA 1-4R; CANR 1, 24, 53; DLB 137; DLBY 80; INT CANR-24; MTCW

Buechner, (Carl) Frederick
1926- ...... **CLC 2, 4, 6, 9; DAM NOV**
See also CA 13-16R; CANR 11, 39; DLBY 80; INT CANR-11; MTCW

Buell, John (Edward) 1927- .... **CLC 10**
See also CA 1-4R; DLB 53

Buero Vallejo, Antonio 1916- ... **CLC 15, 46**
See also CA 106; CANR 24, 49; HW; MTCW

Bufalino, Gesualdo 1920(?)- .... **CLC 74**

Bugayev, Boris Nikolayevich 1880-1934
See Bely, Andrey
See also CA 104

Bukowski, Charles
1920-1994 .... **CLC 2, 5, 9, 41, 82; DAM NOV, POET; PC 18**
See also CA 17-20R; 144; CANR 40; DLB 5, 130, 169; MTCW

Bulgakov, Mikhail (Afanas'evich)
1891-1940 .... **TCLC 2, 16; DAM DRAM, NOV; SSC 18**
See also CA 105; 152

Bulgya, Alexander Alexandrovich
1901-1956 .... **TCLC 53**
See also Fadeyev, Alexander
See also CA 117

Bullins, Ed
1935- .... **CLC 1, 5, 7; BLC; DAM DRAM, MULT; DC 6**
See also BW 2; CA 49-52; CAAS 16; CANR 24, 46; DLB 7, 38; MTCW

Bulwer-Lytton, Edward (George Earle Lytton)
1803-1873 .... **NCLC 1, 45**
See also DLB 21

Bunin, Ivan Alexeyevich
1870-1953 .... **TCLC 6; SSC 5**
See also CA 104

Bunting, Basil
1900-1985 .... **CLC 10, 39, 47; DAM POET**
See also CA 53-56; 115; CANR 7; DLB 20

Bunuel, Luis
1900-1983 .... **CLC 16, 80; DAM MULT; HLC**
See also CA 101; 110; CANR 32; HW

Bunyan, John
1628-1688 ...... **LC 4; DA; DAB; DAC; DAM MST; WLC**
See also CDBLB 1660-1789; DLB 39

Burckhardt, Jacob (Christoph)
1818-1897 .... **NCLC 49**

Burford, Eleanor
See Hibbert, Eleanor Alice Burford

Burgess, Anthony
. **CLC 1, 2, 4, 5, 8, 10, 13, 15, 22, 40, 62, 81, 94; DAB**
See also Wilson, John (Anthony) Burgess
See also AITN 1; CDBLB 1960 to Present; DLB 14

Chernyshevsky, Nikolay Gavrilovich
  1828-1889 . . . . NCLC 1

Cherry, Carolyn Janice   1942-
  See Cherryh, C. J.
  See also CA 65-68; CANR 10

Cherryh, C. J. . . . . CLC 35
  See also Cherry, Carolyn Janice
  See also DLBY 80; SATA 93

Chesnutt, Charles W(addell)
  1858-1932 . . . . TCLC 5, 39; BLC;
                            DAM MULT; SSC 7
  See also BW 1; CA 106; 125; DLB 12, 50,
    78; MTCW

Chester, Alfred   1929(?)-1971. . . . . . . CLC 49
  See also CA 33-36R; DLB 130

Chesterton, G(ilbert) K(eith)
  1874-1936 . . . . TCLC 1, 6, 64;
                            DAM NOV, POET; SSC 1
  See also CA 104; 132; CDBLB 1914-1945;
    DLB 10, 19, 34, 70, 98, 149, 178; MTCW;
    SATA 27

Chiang Pin-chin   1904-1986
  See Ding Ling
  See also CA 118

Ch'ien Chung-shu   1910- . . . . CLC 22
  See also CA 130; MTCW

Child, L. Maria
  See Child, Lydia Maria

Child, Lydia Maria   1802-1880 . . . . NCLC 6
  See also DLB 1, 74; SATA 67

Child, Mrs.
  See Child, Lydia Maria

Child, Philip   1898-1978 . . . . CLC 19, 68
  See also CA 13-14; CAP 1; SATA 47

Childers, (Robert) Erskine
  1870-1922 . . . . TCLC 65
  See also CA 113; 153; DLB 70

Childress, Alice
  1920-1994 . . . . CLC 12, 15, 86, 96; BLC;
                    DAM DRAM, MULT, NOV; DC 4
  See also AAYA 8; BW 2; CA 45-48; 146;
    CANR 3, 27, 50; CLR 14; DLB 7, 38;
    JRDA; MAICYA; MTCW; SATA 7, 48,
    81

Chin, Frank (Chew, Jr.)   1940- . . . . DC 7
  See also CA 33-36R; DAM MULT

Chislett, (Margaret) Anne   1943- . . . . CLC 34
  See also CA 151

Chitty, Thomas Willes   1926- . . . . CLC 11
  See also Hinde, Thomas
  See also CA 5-8R

Chivers, Thomas Holley
  1809-1858 . . . . NCLC 49
  See also DLB 3

Chomette, Rene Lucien   1898-1981
  See Clair, Rene
  See also CA 103

Chopin, Kate
  . . . . TCLC 5, 14; DA; DAB; SSC 8
  See also Chopin, Katherine
  See also CDALB 1865-1917; DLB 12, 78;
    YABC

Chopin, Katherine   1851-1904
  See Chopin, Kate
  See also CA 104; 122; DAC; DAM MST,
    NOV

Chretien de Troyes
  c. 12th cent. - . . . . CMLC 10

Christie
  See Ichikawa, Kon

Christie, Agatha (Mary Clarissa)
  1890-1976 . . . . . . CLC 1, 6, 8, 12, 39, 48;
                            DAB; DAC; DAM NOV
  See also AAYA 9; AITN 1, 2; CA 17-20R;
    61-64; CANR 10, 37; CDBLB 1914-1945;
    DLB 13, 77; MTCW; SATA 36

Christie, (Ann) Philippa
  See Pearce, Philippa
  See also CA 5-8R; CANR 4

Christine de Pizan   1365(?)-1431(?) . . . . LC 9

Chubb, Elmer
  See Masters, Edgar Lee

Chulkov, Mikhail Dmitrievich
  1743-1792 . . . . LC 2
  See also DLB 150

Churchill, Caryl   1938- . . . CLC 31, 55; DC 5
  See also CA 102; CANR 22, 46; DLB 13;
    MTCW

Churchill, Charles   1731-1764. . . . . LC 3
  See also DLB 109

Chute, Carolyn   1947- . . . . CLC 39
  See also CA 123

Ciardi, John (Anthony)
  1916-1986 . . . . CLC 10, 40, 44;
                                        DAM POET
  See also CA 5-8R; 118; CAAS 2; CANR 5,
    33; CLR 19; DLB 5; DLBY 86;
    INT CANR-5; MAICYA; MTCW;
    SATA 1, 65; SATA-Obit 46

Cicero, Marcus Tullius
  106B.C.-43B.C. . . . . CMLC 3

Cimino, Michael   1943- . . . . CLC 16
  See also CA 105

Cioran, E(mil) M.   1911-1995. . . . . . . CLC 64
  See also CA 25-28R; 149

Cisneros, Sandra
  1954- . . . . . CLC 69; DAM MULT; HLC
  See also AAYA 9; CA 131; DLB 122, 152;
    HW

Cixous, Helene   1937- . . . . CLC 92
  See also CA 126; CANR 55; DLB 83;
    MTCW

Clair, Rene. . . . . CLC 20
  See also Chomette, Rene Lucien

Clampitt, Amy   1920-1994 . . . CLC 32; PC 19
  See also CA 110; 146; CANR 29; DLB 105

Clancy, Thomas L., Jr.   1947-
  See Clancy, Tom
  See also CA 125; 131; INT 131; MTCW

Clancy, Tom. . . . . CLC 45; DAM NOV, POP
  See also Clancy, Thomas L., Jr.
  See also AAYA 9; BEST 89:1, 90:1

Clare, John
  1793-1864 . . . . NCLC 9; DAB;
                                        DAM POET
  See also DLB 55, 96

Clarin
  See Alas (y Urena), Leopoldo (Enrique
    Garcia)

Clark, Al C.
  See Goines, Donald

Clark, (Robert) Brian   1932-. . . . . . . CLC 29
  See also CA 41-44R

Clark, Curt
  See Westlake, Donald E(dwin)

Clark, Eleanor   1913-1996 . . . . CLC 5, 19
  See also CA 9-12R; 151; CANR 41; DLB 6

Clark, J. P.
  See Clark, John Pepper
  See also DLB 117

Clark, John Pepper
  1935- . . . . CLC 38; BLC; DAM DRAM,
                            MULT; DC 5
  See also Clark, J. P.
  See also BW 1; CA 65-68; CANR 16

Clark, M. R.
  See Clark, Mavis Thorpe

Clark, Mavis Thorpe   1909- . . . . CLC 12
  See also CA 57-60; CANR 8, 37; CLR 30;
    MAICYA; SAAS 5; SATA 8, 74

Clark, Walter Van Tilburg
  1909-1971 . . . . CLC 28
  See also CA 9-12R; 33-36R; DLB 9;
    SATA 8

Clarke, Arthur C(harles)
  1917- . . . . CLC 1, 4, 13, 18, 35;
                            DAM POP; SSC 3
  See also AAYA 4; CA 1-4R; CANR 2, 28,
    55; JRDA; MAICYA; MTCW; SATA 13,
    70

Clarke, Austin
  1896-1974 . . . . . . CLC 6, 9; DAM POET
  See also CA 29-32; 49-52; CAP 2; DLB 10,
    20

Clarke, Austin C(hesterfield)
  1934- . . . . CLC 8, 53; BLC; DAC;
                            DAM MULT
  See also BW 1; CA 25-28R; CAAS 16;
    CANR 14, 32; DLB 53, 125

Clarke, Gillian   1937- . . . . CLC 61
  See also CA 106; DLB 40

Clarke, Marcus (Andrew Hislop)
  1846-1881 . . . . NCLC 19

Clarke, Shirley   1925-. . . . . CLC 16

Clash, The
  See Headon, (Nicky) Topper; Jones, Mick;
    Simonon, Paul; Strummer, Joe

Claudel, Paul (Louis Charles Marie)
  1868-1955 . . . . TCLC 2, 10
  See also CA 104

Clavell, James (duMaresq)
  1925-1994 . . . . CLC 6, 25, 87;
                            DAM NOV, POP
  See also CA 25-28R; 146; CANR 26, 48;
    MTCW

Cleaver, (Leroy) Eldridge
  1935- . . . . . . CLC 30; BLC; DAM MULT
  See also BW 1; CA 21-24R; CANR 16

Cleese, John (Marwood)   1939- . . . . . CLC 21
  See also Monty Python
  See also CA 112; 116; CANR 35; MTCW

Cleishbotham, Jebediah
  See Scott, Walter

Cleland, John   1710-1789 . . . . LC 2
  See also DLB 39

Clemens, Samuel Langhorne 1835-1910
See Twain, Mark
See also CA 104; 135; CDALB 1865-1917;
DA; DAB; DAC; DAM MST, NOV;
DLB 11, 12, 23, 64, 74; JRDA;
MAICYA; 2

Cleophil
See Congreve, William

Clerihew, E.
See Bentley, E(dmund) C(lerihew)

Clerk, N. W.
See Lewis, C(live) S(taples)

Cliff, Jimmy .... **CLC 21**
See also Chambers, James

Clifton, (Thelma) Lucille
1936- .... **CLC 19, 66; BLC;**
DAM MULT, POET; PC 17
See also BW 2; CA 49-52; CANR 2, 24, 42;
CLR 5; DLB 5, 41; MAICYA; MTCW;
SATA 20, 69

Clinton, Dirk
See Silverberg, Robert

Clough, Arthur Hugh 1819-1861.. **NCLC 27**
See also DLB 32

Clutha, Janet Paterson Frame 1924-
See Frame, Janet
See also CA 1-4R; CANR 2, 36; MTCW

Clyne, Terence
See Blatty, William Peter

Cobalt, Martin
See Mayne, William (James Carter)

Cobbett, William 1763-1835 ..... **NCLC 49**
See also DLB 43, 107, 158

Coburn, D(onald) L(ee) 1938- ...... **CLC 10**
See also CA 89-92

Cocteau, Jean (Maurice Eugene Clement)
1889-1963 .... **CLC 1, 8, 15, 16, 43; DA;**
DAB; DAC; DAM DRAM, MST, NOV;
WLC
See also CA 25-28; CANR 40; CAP 2;
DLB 65; MTCW

Codrescu, Andrei
1946- .... **CLC 46; DAM POET**
See also CA 33-36R; CAAS 19; CANR 13,
34, 53

Coe, Max
See Bourne, Randolph S(illiman)

Coe, Tucker
See Westlake, Donald E(dwin)

Coetzee, J(ohn) M(ichael)
1940- ...... **CLC 23, 33, 66; DAM NOV**
See also CA 77-80; CANR 41, 54; MTCW

Coffey, Brian
See Koontz, Dean R(ay)

Cohan, George M. 1878-1942 ..... **TCLC 60**
See also CA 157

Cohen, Arthur A(llen)
1928-1986 .... **CLC 7, 31**
See also CA 1-4R; 120; CANR 1, 17, 42;
DLB 28

Cohen, Leonard (Norman)
1934- .... **CLC 3, 38; DAC; DAM MST**
See also CA 21-24R; CANR 14; DLB 53;
MTCW

Cohen, Matt 1942-.......... **CLC 19; DAC**
See also CA 61-64; CAAS 18; CANR 40;
DLB 53

Cohen-Solal, Annie 19(?)- .... **CLC 50**

Colegate, Isabel 1931- .... **CLC 36**
See also CA 17-20R; CANR 8, 22; DLB 14;
INT CANR-22; MTCW

Coleman, Emmett
See Reed, Ishmael

Coleridge, Samuel Taylor
1772-1834 ..... **NCLC 9, 54; DA; DAB;**
DAC; DAM MST, POET; PC 11; WLC
See also CDBLB 1789-1832; DLB 93, 107

Coleridge, Sara 1802-1852 ...... **NCLC 31**

Coles, Don 1928- .... **CLC 46**
See also CA 115; CANR 38

Colette, (Sidonie-Gabrielle)
1873-1954 .... **TCLC 1, 5, 16;**
DAM NOV; SSC 10
See also CA 104; 131; DLB 65; MTCW

Collett, (Jacobine) Camilla (Wergeland)
1813-1895 .... **NCLC 22**

Collier, Christopher 1930-......... **CLC 30**
See also AAYA 13; CA 33-36R; CANR 13,
33; JRDA; MAICYA; SATA 16, 70

Collier, James L(incoln)
1928- .... **CLC 30; DAM POP**
See also AAYA 13; CA 9-12R; CANR 4,
33; CLR 3; JRDA; MAICYA; SAAS 21;
SATA 8, 70

Collier, Jeremy 1650-1726.......... **LC 6**

Collier, John 1901-1980........... **SSC 19**
See also CA 65-68; 97-100; CANR 10;
DLB 77

Collingwood, R(obin) G(eorge)
1889(?)-1943 .... **TCLC 67**
See also CA 117; 155

Collins, Hunt
See Hunter, Evan

Collins, Linda 1931-.............. **CLC 44**
See also CA 125

Collins, (William) Wilkie
1824-1889 .... **NCLC 1, 18**
See also CDBLB 1832-1890; DLB 18, 70,
159

Collins, William
1721-1759 .... **LC 4; DAM POET**
See also DLB 109

Collodi, Carlo 1826-1890........ **NCLC 54**
See also Lorenzini, Carlo
See also CLR 5

Colman, George
See Glassco, John

Colt, Winchester Remington
See Hubbard, L(afayette) Ron(ald)

Colter, Cyrus 1910- .... **CLC 58**
See also BW 1; CA 65-68; CANR 10;
DLB 33

Colton, James
See Hansen, Joseph

Colum, Padraic 1881-1972........ **CLC 28**
See also CA 73-76; 33-36R; CANR 35;
CLR 36; MAICYA; MTCW; SATA 15

Colvin, James
See Moorcock, Michael (John)

Colwin, Laurie (E.)
1944-1992 .... **CLC 5, 13, 23, 84**
See also CA 89-92; 139; CANR 20, 46;
DLBY 80; MTCW

Comfort, Alex(ander)
1920- .... **CLC 7; DAM POP**
See also CA 1-4R; CANR 1, 45

Comfort, Montgomery
See Campbell, (John) Ramsey

Compton-Burnett, I(vy)
1884(?)-1969 ...... **CLC 1, 3, 10, 15, 34;**
DAM NOV
See also CA 1-4R; 25-28R; CANR 4;
DLB 36; MTCW

Comstock, Anthony 1844-1915 .... **TCLC 13**
See also CA 110

Comte, Auguste 1798-1857....... **NCLC 54**

Conan Doyle, Arthur
See Doyle, Arthur Conan

Conde, Maryse
1937-....... **CLC 52, 92; DAM MULT**
See also Boucolon, Maryse
See also BW 2

Condillac, Etienne Bonnot de
1714-1780 .... **LC 26**

Condon, Richard (Thomas)
1915-1996 ..... **CLC 4, 6, 8, 10, 45, 100;**
DAM NOV
See also BEST 90:3; CA 1-4R; 151;
CAAS 1; CANR 2, 23; INT CANR-23;
MTCW

Confucius
551B.C.-479B.C........ **CMLC 19; DA;**
DAB; DAC; DAM MST
See also YABC

Congreve, William
1670-1729 .... **LC 5, 21; DA; DAB;**
DAC; DAM DRAM, MST, POET;
DC 2; WLC
See also CDBLB 1660-1789; DLB 39, 84

Connell, Evan S(helby), Jr.
1924-....... **CLC 4, 6, 45; DAM NOV**
See also AAYA 7; CA 1-4R; CAAS 2;
CANR 2, 39; DLB 2; DLBY 81; MTCW

Connelly, Marc(us Cook)
1890-1980 .... **CLC 7**
See also CA 85-88; 102; CANR 30; DLB 7;
DLBY 80; SATA-Obit 25

Connor, Ralph .... **TCLC 31**
See also Gordon, Charles William
See also DLB 92

Conrad, Joseph
1857-1924 .... **TCLC 1, 6, 13, 25, 43, 57;**
DA; DAB; DAC; DAM MST, NOV;
SSC 9; WLC
See also CA 104; 131; CDBLB 1890-1914;
DLB 10, 34, 98, 156; MTCW; SATA 27

Conrad, Robert Arnold
See Hart, Moss

Conroy, Donald Pat(rick)
1945- ... **CLC 30, 74; DAM NOV, POP**
See also AAYA 8; AITN 1; CA 85-88;
CANR 24, 53; DLB 6; MTCW

Darwin, Charles 1809-1882 ...... **NCLC 57**
See also DLB 57, 166

Daryush, Elizabeth 1887-1977.... **CLC 6, 19**
See also CA 49-52; CANR 3; DLB 20

Dashwood, Edmee Elizabeth Monica de la Pasture 1890-1943
See Delafield, E. M.
See also CA 119; 154

Daudet, (Louis Marie) Alphonse
1840-1897 .... **NCLC 1**
See also DLB 123

Daumal, Rene 1908-1944 .... **TCLC 14**
See also CA 114

Davenport, Guy (Mattison, Jr.)
1927- .... **CLC 6, 14, 38; SSC 16**
See also CA 33-36R; CANR 23; DLB 130

Davidson, Avram 1923-
See Queen, Ellery
See also CA 101; CANR 26; DLB 8

Davidson, Donald (Grady)
1893-1968 .... **CLC 2, 13, 19**
See also CA 5-8R; 25-28R; CANR 4;
DLB 45

Davidson, Hugh
See Hamilton, Edmond

Davidson, John 1857-1909 .... **TCLC 24**
See also CA 118; DLB 19

Davidson, Sara 1943- .... **CLC 9**
See also CA 81-84; CANR 44

Davie, Donald (Alfred)
1922-1995 .... **CLC 5, 8, 10, 31**
See also CA 1-4R; 149; CAAS 3; CANR 1,
44; DLB 27; MTCW

Davies, Ray(mond Douglas) 1944- .. **CLC 21**
See also CA 116; 146

Davies, Rhys 1903-1978 .... **CLC 23**
See also CA 9-12R; 81-84; CANR 4;
DLB 139

Davies, (William) Robertson
1913-1995 ..... **CLC 2, 7, 13, 25, 42, 75,**
91; DA; DAB; DAC; DAM MST, NOV,
POP; WLC
See also BEST 89:2; CA 33-36R; 150;
CANR 17, 42; DLB 68; INT CANR-17;
MTCW

Davies, W(illiam) H(enry)
1871-1940 .... **TCLC 5**
See also CA 104; DLB 19, 174

Davies, Walter C.
See Kornbluth, C(yril) M.

Davis, Angela (Yvonne)
1944- .... **CLC 77; DAM MULT**
See also BW 2; CA 57-60; CANR 10

Davis, B. Lynch
See Bioy Casares, Adolfo; Borges, Jorge
Luis

Davis, Gordon
See Hunt, E(verette) Howard, (Jr.)

Davis, Harold Lenoir 1896-1960 .... **CLC 49**
See also CA 89-92; DLB 9

Davis, Rebecca (Blaine) Harding
1831-1910 .... **TCLC 6**
See also CA 104; DLB 74

Davis, Richard Harding
1864-1916 .... **TCLC 24**
See also CA 114; DLB 12, 23, 78, 79;
DLBD 13

Davison, Frank Dalby 1893-1970 ... **CLC 15**
See also CA 116

Davison, Lawrence H.
See Lawrence, D(avid) H(erbert Richards)

Davison, Peter (Hubert) 1928- ..... **CLC 28**
See also CA 9-12R; CAAS 4; CANR 3, 43;
DLB 5

Davys, Mary 1674-1732 .... **LC 1**
See also DLB 39

Dawson, Fielding 1930- .... **CLC 6**
See also CA 85-88; DLB 130

Dawson, Peter
See Faust, Frederick (Schiller)

Day, Clarence (Shepard, Jr.)
1874-1935 .... **TCLC 25**
See also CA 108; DLB 11

Day, Thomas 1748-1789 .... **LC 1**
See also DLB 39; 1

Day Lewis, C(ecil)
1904-1972 .... **CLC 1, 6, 10;**
DAM POET; PC 11
See also Blake, Nicholas
See also CA 13-16; 33-36R; CANR 34;
CAP 1; DLB 15, 20; MTCW

Dazai, Osamu .... **TCLC 11**
See also Tsushima, Shuji

de Andrade, Carlos Drummond
See Drummond de Andrade, Carlos

Deane, Norman
See Creasey, John

de Beauvoir, Simone (Lucie Ernestine Marie Bertrand)
See Beauvoir, Simone (Lucie Ernestine
Marie Bertrand) de

de Brissac, Malcolm
See Dickinson, Peter (Malcolm)

de Chardin, Pierre Teilhard
See Teilhard de Chardin, (Marie Joseph)
Pierre

Dee, John 1527-1608 .... **LC 20**

Deer, Sandra 1940- .... **CLC 45**

De Ferrari, Gabriella 1941- .... **CLC 65**
See also CA 146

Defoe, Daniel
1660(?)-1731 .... **LC 1; DA; DAB; DAC;**
DAM MST, NOV; WLC
See also CDBLB 1660-1789; DLB 39, 95,
101; JRDA; MAICYA; SATA 22

de Gourmont, Remy(-Marie-Charles)
See Gourmont, Remy (-Marie-Charles) de

de Hartog, Jan 1914- .... **CLC 19**
See also CA 1-4R; CANR 1

de Hostos, E. M.
See Hostos (y Bonilla), Eugenio Maria de

de Hostos, Eugenio M.
See Hostos (y Bonilla), Eugenio Maria de

Deighton, Len .... **CLC 4, 7, 22, 46**
See also Deighton, Leonard Cyril
See also AAYA 6; BEST 89:2;
CDBLB 1960 to Present; DLB 87

Deighton, Leonard Cyril 1929-
See Deighton, Len
See also CA 9-12R; CANR 19, 33;
DAM NOV, POP; MTCW

Dekker, Thomas
1572(?)-1632 ..... **LC 22; DAM DRAM**
See also CDBLB Before 1660; DLB 62, 172

Delafield, E. M. 1890-1943 .... **TCLC 61**
See also Dashwood, Edmee Elizabeth
Monica de la Pasture
See also DLB 34

de la Mare, Walter (John)
1873-1956 .... **TCLC 4, 53; DAB; DAC;**
DAM MST, POET; SSC 14; WLC
See also CDBLB 1914-1945; CLR 23;
DLB 162; SATA 16

Delaney, Franey
See O'Hara, John (Henry)

Delaney, Shelagh
1939- .... **CLC 29; DAM DRAM**
See also CA 17-20R; CANR 30;
CDBLB 1960 to Present; DLB 13;
MTCW

Delany, Mary (Granville Pendarves)
1700-1788 .... **LC 12**

Delany, Samuel R(ay, Jr.)
1942- .... **CLC 8, 14, 38; BLC;**
DAM MULT
See also BW 2; CA 81-84; CANR 27, 43;
DLB 8, 33; MTCW

De La Ramee, (Marie) Louise 1839-1908
See Ouida
See also SATA 20

de la Roche, Mazo 1879-1961 ...... **CLC 14**
See also CA 85-88; CANR 30; DLB 68;
SATA 64

Delbanco, Nicholas (Franklin)
1942- .... **CLC 6, 13**
See also CA 17-20R; CAAS 2; CANR 29,
55; DLB 6

del Castillo, Michel 1933- .... **CLC 38**
See also CA 109

Deledda, Grazia (Cosima)
1875(?)-1936 .... **TCLC 23**
See also CA 123

Delibes, Miguel .... **CLC 8, 18**
See also Delibes Setien, Miguel

Delibes Setien, Miguel 1920-
See Delibes, Miguel
See also CA 45-48; CANR 1, 32; HW;
MTCW

DeLillo, Don
1936- ..... **CLC 8, 10, 13, 27, 39, 54, 76;**
DAM NOV, POP
See also BEST 89:1; CA 81-84; CANR 21;
DLB 6, 173; MTCW

de Lisser, H. G.
See De Lisser, H(erbert) G(eorge)
See also DLB 117

De Lisser, H(erbert) G(eorge)
1878-1944 .... **TCLC 12**
See also de Lisser, H. G.
See also BW 2; CA 109; 152

Drummond, William Henry
1854-1907 .... **TCLC 25**
See also DLB 92

Drummond de Andrade, Carlos
1902-1987 .... **CLC 18**
See also Andrade, Carlos Drummond de
See also CA 132; 123

Drury, Allen (Stuart) 1918- .... **CLC 37**
See also CA 57-60; CANR 18, 52;
INT CANR-18

Dryden, John
1631-1700 .... **LC 3, 21; DA; DAB;**
DAC; DAM DRAM, MST, POET;
DC 3; WLC
See also CDBLB 1660-1789; DLB 80, 101,
131

Duberman, Martin 1930- .... **CLC 8**
See also CA 1-4R; CANR 2

Dubie, Norman (Evans) 1945- ...... **CLC 36**
See also CA 69-72; CANR 12; DLB 120

Du Bois, W(illiam) E(dward) B(urghardt)
1868-1963 .... **CLC 1, 2, 13, 64, 96;**
BLC; DA; DAC; DAM MST, MULT,
NOV; WLC
See also BW 1; CA 85-88; CANR 34;
CDALB 1865-1917; DLB 47, 50, 91;
MTCW; SATA 42

Dubus, Andre
1936- .... **CLC 13, 36, 97; SSC 15**
See also CA 21-24R; CANR 17; DLB 130;
INT CANR-17

Duca Minimo
See D'Annunzio, Gabriele

Ducharme, Rejean 1941- .... **CLC 74**
See also DLB 60

Duclos, Charles Pinot 1704-1772 ..... **LC 1**

Dudek, Louis 1918- .... **CLC 11, 19**
See also CA 45-48; CAAS 14; CANR 1;
DLB 88

Duerrenmatt, Friedrich
1921-1990 ...... **CLC 1, 4, 8, 11, 15, 43;**
DAM DRAM
See also CA 17-20R; CANR 33; DLB 69,
124; MTCW

Duffy, Bruce (?)- .... **CLC 50**

Duffy, Maureen 1933- .... **CLC 37**
See also CA 25-28R; CANR 33; DLB 14;
MTCW

Dugan, Alan 1923- .... **CLC 2, 6**
See also CA 81-84; DLB 5

du Gard, Roger Martin
See Martin du Gard, Roger

Duhamel, Georges 1884-1966 .... **CLC 8**
See also CA 81-84; 25-28R; CANR 35;
DLB 65; MTCW

Dujardin, Edouard (Emile Louis)
1861-1949 .... **TCLC 13**
See also CA 109; DLB 123

Dulles, John Foster 1888-1959 .... **TCLC 72**
See also CA 115; 149

Dumas, Alexandre (Davy de la Pailleterie)
1802-1870 .... **NCLC 11; DA; DAB;**
DAC; DAM MST, NOV; WLC
See also DLB 119; SATA 18

Dumas, Alexandre
1824-1895 .... **NCLC 9; DC 1**

Dumas, Claudine
See Malzberg, Barry N(athaniel)

Dumas, Henry L. 1934-1968 ..... **CLC 6, 62**
See also BW 1; CA 85-88; DLB 41

du Maurier, Daphne
1907-1989 .... **CLC 6, 11, 59; DAB;**
DAC; DAM MST, POP; SSC 18
See also CA 5-8R; 128; CANR 6, 55;
MTCW; SATA 27; SATA-Obit 60

Dunbar, Paul Laurence
1872-1906 ...... **TCLC 2, 12; BLC; DA;**
DAC; DAM MST, MULT, POET; PC 5;
SSC 8; WLC
See also BW 1; CA 104; 124;
CDALB 1865-1917; DLB 50, 54, 78;
SATA 34

Dunbar, William 1460(?)-1530(?) .... **LC 20**
See also DLB 132, 146

Duncan, Dora Angela
See Duncan, Isadora

Duncan, Isadora 1877(?)-1927 ..... **TCLC 68**
See also CA 118; 149

Duncan, Lois 1934- .... **CLC 26**
See also AAYA 4; CA 1-4R; CANR 2, 23,
36; CLR 29; JRDA; MAICYA; SAAS 2;
SATA 1, 36, 75

Duncan, Robert (Edward)
1919-1988 .... **CLC 1, 2, 4, 7, 15, 41, 55;**
DAM POET; PC 2
See also CA 9-12R; 124; CANR 28; DLB 5,
16; MTCW

Duncan, Sara Jeannette
1861-1922 .... **TCLC 60**
See also CA 157; DLB 92

Dunlap, William 1766-1839 .... **NCLC 2**
See also DLB 30, 37, 59

Dunn, Douglas (Eaglesham)
1942- .... **CLC 6, 40**
See also CA 45-48; CANR 2, 33; DLB 40;
MTCW

Dunn, Katherine (Karen) 1945- ..... **CLC 71**
See also CA 33-36R

Dunn, Stephen 1939- .... **CLC 36**
See also CA 33-36R; CANR 12, 48, 53;
DLB 105

Dunne, Finley Peter 1867-1936.... **TCLC 28**
See also CA 108; DLB 11, 23

Dunne, John Gregory 1932- .... **CLC 28**
See also CA 25-28R; CANR 14, 50;
DLBY 80

Dunsany, Edward John Moreton Drax
Plunkett 1878-1957
See Dunsany, Lord
See also CA 104; 148; DLB 10

Dunsany, Lord .... **TCLC 2, 59**
See also Dunsany, Edward John Moreton
Drax Plunkett
See also DLB 77, 153, 156

du Perry, Jean
See Simenon, Georges (Jacques Christian)

Durang, Christopher (Ferdinand)
1949- .... **CLC 27, 38**
See also CA 105; CANR 50

Duras, Marguerite
1914-1996 ..... **CLC 3, 6, 11, 20, 34, 40,**
68, 100
See also CA 25-28R; 151; CANR 50;
DLB 83; MTCW

Durban, (Rosa) Pam 1947-........ **CLC 39**
See also CA 123

Durcan, Paul
1944- .... **CLC 43, 70; DAM POET**
See also CA 134

Durkheim, Emile 1858-1917 ...... **TCLC 55**

Durrell, Lawrence (George)
1912-1990 .... **CLC 1, 4, 6, 8, 13, 27, 41;**
DAM NOV
See also CA 9-12R; 132; CANR 40;
CDBLB 1945-1960; DLB 15, 27;
DLBY 90; MTCW

Durrenmatt, Friedrich
See Duerrenmatt, Friedrich

Dutt, Toru 1856-1877........... **NCLC 29**

Dwight, Timothy 1752-1817...... **NCLC 13**
See also DLB 37

Dworkin, Andrea 1946- .... **CLC 43**
See also CA 77-80; CAAS 21; CANR 16,
39; INT CANR-16; MTCW

Dwyer, Deanna
See Koontz, Dean R(ay)

Dwyer, K. R.
See Koontz, Dean R(ay)

Dylan, Bob 1941- ...... **CLC 3, 4, 6, 12, 77**
See also CA 41-44R; DLB 16

Eagleton, Terence (Francis) 1943-
See Eagleton, Terry
See also CA 57-60; CANR 7, 23; MTCW

Eagleton, Terry .... **CLC 63**
See also Eagleton, Terence (Francis)

Early, Jack
See Scoppettone, Sandra

East, Michael
See West, Morris L(anglo)

Eastaway, Edward
See Thomas, (Philip) Edward

Eastlake, William (Derry)
1917-1997 .... **CLC 8**
See also CA 5-8R; 158; CAAS 1; CANR 5;
DLB 6; INT CANR-5

Eastman, Charles A(lexander)
1858-1939 ..... **TCLC 55; DAM MULT**
See also DLB 175; NNAL; 1

Eberhart, Richard (Ghormley)
1904- .. **CLC 3, 11, 19, 56; DAM POET**
See also CA 1-4R; CANR 2;
CDALB 1941-1968; DLB 48; MTCW

Eberstadt, Fernanda 1960-........ **CLC 39**
See also CA 136

Echegaray (y Eizaguirre), Jose (Maria Waldo)
1832-1916 .... **TCLC 4**
See also CA 104; CANR 32; HW; MTCW

Echeverria, (Jose) Esteban (Antonino)
1805-1851 .... **NCLC 18**

Echo
See Proust, (Valentin-Louis-George-Eugene-)
Marcel

Eckert, Allan W. 1931- .... **CLC 17**
See also AAYA 18; CA 13-16R; CANR 14,
45; INT CANR-14; SAAS 21; SATA 29,
91; SATA-Brief 27

Eckhart, Meister 1260(?)-1328(?) .. **CMLC 9**
See also DLB 115

Eckmar, F. R.
See de Hartog, Jan

Eco, Umberto
1932- ... **CLC 28, 60; DAM NOV, POP**
See also BEST 90:1; CA 77-80; CANR 12,
33, 55; MTCW

Eddison, E(ric) R(ucker)
1882-1945 .... **TCLC 15**
See also CA 109; 156

Eddy, Mary (Morse) Baker
1821-1910 .... **TCLC 71**
See also CA 113

Edel, (Joseph) Leon 1907- ...... **CLC 29, 34**
See also CA 1-4R; CANR 1, 22; DLB 103;
INT CANR-22

Eden, Emily 1797-1869 .... **NCLC 10**

Edgar, David
1948- .... **CLC 42; DAM DRAM**
See also CA 57-60; CANR 12; DLB 13;
MTCW

Edgerton, Clyde (Carlyle) 1944- .... **CLC 39**
See also AAYA 17; CA 118; 134; INT 134

Edgeworth, Maria 1768-1849... **NCLC 1, 51**
See also DLB 116, 159, 163; SATA 21

Edmonds, Paul
See Kuttner, Henry

Edmonds, Walter D(umaux) 1903- .. **CLC 35**
See also CA 5-8R; CANR 2; DLB 9;
MAICYA; SAAS 4; SATA 1, 27

Edmondson, Wallace
See Ellison, Harlan (Jay)

Edson, Russell .... **CLC 13**
See also CA 33-36R

Edwards, Bronwen Elizabeth
See Rose, Wendy

Edwards, G(erald) B(asil)
1899-1976 .... **CLC 25**
See also CA 110

Edwards, Gus 1939- .... **CLC 43**
See also CA 108; INT 108

Edwards, Jonathan
1703-1758 .... **LC 7; DA; DAC;**
DAM MST
See also DLB 24

Efron, Marina Ivanovna Tsvetaeva
See Tsvetaeva (Efron), Marina (Ivanovna)

Ehle, John (Marsden, Jr.) 1925- .... **CLC 27**
See also CA 9-12R

Ehrenbourg, Ilya (Grigoryevich)
See Ehrenburg, Ilya (Grigoryevich)

Ehrenburg, Ilya (Grigoryevich)
1891-1967 .... **CLC 18, 34, 62**
See also CA 102; 25-28R

Ehrenburg, Ilyo (Grigoryevich)
See Ehrenburg, Ilya (Grigoryevich)

Eich, Guenter 1907-1972 .... **CLC 15**
See also CA 111; 93-96; DLB 69, 124

Eichendorff, Joseph Freiherr von
1788-1857 .... **NCLC 8**
See also DLB 90

Eigner, Larry .... **CLC 9**
See also Eigner, Laurence (Joel)
See also CAAS 23; DLB 5

Eigner, Laurence (Joel) 1927-1996
See Eigner, Larry
See also CA 9-12R; 151; CANR 6

Einstein, Albert 1879-1955 .... **TCLC 65**
See also CA 121; 133; MTCW

Eiseley, Loren Corey 1907-1977 ..... **CLC 7**
See also AAYA 5; CA 1-4R; 73-76;
CANR 6

Eisenstadt, Jill 1963- .... **CLC 50**
See also CA 140

Eisenstein, Sergei (Mikhailovich)
1898-1948 .... **TCLC 57**
See also CA 114; 149

Eisner, Simon
See Kornbluth, C(yril) M.

Ekeloef, (Bengt) Gunnar
1907-1968 .... **CLC 27; DAM POET**
See also CA 123; 25-28R

Ekelof, (Bengt) Gunnar
See Ekeloef, (Bengt) Gunnar

Ekwensi, C. O. D.
See Ekwensi, Cyprian (Odiatu Duaka)

Ekwensi, Cyprian (Odiatu Duaka)
1921- ...... **CLC 4; BLC; DAM MULT**
See also BW 2; CA 29-32R; CANR 18, 42;
DLB 117; MTCW; SATA 66

Elaine .... **TCLC 18**
See also Leverson, Ada

El Crummo
See Crumb, R(obert)

Elia
See Lamb, Charles

Eliade, Mircea 1907-1986 .... **CLC 19**
See also CA 65-68; 119; CANR 30; MTCW

Eliot, A. D.
See Jewett, (Theodora) Sarah Orne

Eliot, Alice
See Jewett, (Theodora) Sarah Orne

Eliot, Dan
See Silverberg, Robert

Eliot, George
1819-1880 ..... **NCLC 4, 13, 23, 41, 49;**
DA; DAB; DAC; DAM MST, NOV;
WLC
See also CDBLB 1832-1890; DLB 21, 35, 55

Eliot, John 1604-1690 .... **LC 5**
See also DLB 24

Eliot, T(homas) S(tearns)
1888-1965 ..... **CLC 1, 2, 3, 6, 9, 10, 13,**
15, 24, 34, 41, 55, 57; DA; DAB; DAC;
DAM DRAM, MST, POET; PC 5;
WLC 2
See also CA 5-8R; 25-28R; CANR 41;
CDALB 1929-1941; DLB 7, 10, 45, 63;
DLBY 88; MTCW

Elizabeth 1866-1941 .... **TCLC 41**

Elkin, Stanley L(awrence)
1930-1995 ...... **CLC 4, 6, 9, 14, 27, 51,**
91; DAM NOV, POP; SSC 12
See also CA 9-12R; 148; CANR 8, 46;
DLB 2, 28; DLBY 80; INT CANR-8;
MTCW

Elledge, Scott .... **CLC 34**

Elliot, Don
See Silverberg, Robert

Elliott, Don
See Silverberg, Robert

Elliott, George P(aul) 1918-1980..... **CLC 2**
See also CA 1-4R; 97-100; CANR 2

Elliott, Janice 1931- .... **CLC 47**
See also CA 13-16R; CANR 8, 29; DLB 14

Elliott, Sumner Locke 1917-1991 ... **CLC 38**
See also CA 5-8R; 134; CANR 2, 21

Elliott, William
See Bradbury, Ray (Douglas)

Ellis, A. E. .... **CLC 7**

Ellis, Alice Thomas .... **CLC 40**
See also Haycraft, Anna

Ellis, Bret Easton
1964- .... **CLC 39, 71; DAM POP**
See also AAYA 2; CA 118; 123; CANR 51;
INT 123

Ellis, (Henry) Havelock
1859-1939 .... **TCLC 14**
See also CA 109

Ellis, Landon
See Ellison, Harlan (Jay)

Ellis, Trey 1962- .... **CLC 55**
See also CA 146

Ellison, Harlan (Jay)
1934- ...... **CLC 1, 13, 42; DAM POP;**
SSC 14
See also CA 5-8R; CANR 5, 46; DLB 8;
INT CANR-5; MTCW

Ellison, Ralph (Waldo)
1914-1994 .... **CLC 1, 3, 11, 54, 86;**
BLC; DA; DAB; DAC; DAM MST,
MULT, NOV; SSC 26; WLC
See also AAYA 19; BW 1; CA 9-12R; 145;
CANR 24, 53; CDALB 1941-1968;
DLB 2, 76; DLBY 94; MTCW

Ellmann, Lucy (Elizabeth) 1956- .... **CLC 61**
See also CA 128

Ellmann, Richard (David)
1918-1987 .... **CLC 50**
See also BEST 89:2; CA 1-4R; 122;
CANR 2, 28; DLB 103; DLBY 87;
MTCW

Elman, Richard 1934- .... **CLC 19**
See also CA 17-20R; CAAS 3; CANR 47

Elron
See Hubbard, L(afayette) Ron(ald)

Eluard, Paul .... **TCLC 7, 41**
See also Grindel, Eugene

Elyot, Sir Thomas 1490(?)-1546 ..... **LC 11**

Elytis, Odysseus
1911-1996 .... **CLC 15, 49, 100;**
DAM POET
See also CA 102; 151; MTCW

Farley, Walter (Lorimer)
1915-1989 .... **CLC 17**
See also CA 17-20R; CANR 8, 29; DLB 22;
JRDA; MAICYA; SATA 2, 43

Farmer, Philip Jose 1918- .... **CLC 1, 19**
See also CA 1-4R; CANR 4, 35; DLB 8;
MTCW; SATA 93

Farquhar, George
1677-1707 .... **LC 21; DAM DRAM**
See also DLB 84

Farrell, J(ames) G(ordon)
1935-1979 .... **CLC 6**
See also CA 73-76; 89-92; CANR 36;
DLB 14; MTCW

Farrell, James T(homas)
1904-1979 .... **CLC 1, 4, 8, 11, 66**
See also CA 5-8R; 89-92; CANR 9; DLB 4,
9, 86; DLBD 2; MTCW

Farren, Richard J.
See Betjeman, John

Farren, Richard M.
See Betjeman, John

Fassbinder, Rainer Werner
1946-1982 .... **CLC 20**
See also CA 93-96; 106; CANR 31

Fast, Howard (Melvin)
1914- .... **CLC 23; DAM NOV**
See also AAYA 16; CA 1-4R; CAAS 18;
CANR 1, 33, 54; DLB 9; INT CANR-33;
SATA 7

Faulcon, Robert
See Holdstock, Robert P.

Faulkner, William (Cuthbert)
1897-1962 ..... **CLC 1, 3, 6, 8, 9, 11, 14,
18, 28, 52, 68; DA; DAB; DAC;
DAM MST, NOV; SSC 1; WLC**
See also AAYA 7; CA 81-84; CANR 33;
CDALB 1929-1941; DLB 9, 11, 44, 102;
DLBD 2; DLBY 86; MTCW

Fauset, Jessie Redmon
1884(?)-1961 .... **CLC 19, 54; BLC;
DAM MULT**
See also BW 1; CA 109; DLB 51

Faust, Frederick (Schiller)
1892-1944(?) ..... **TCLC 49; DAM POP**
See also CA 108; 152

Faust, Irvin 1924- .... **CLC 8**
See also CA 33-36R; CANR 28; DLB 2, 28;
DLBY 80

Fawkes, Guy
See Benchley, Robert (Charles)

Fearing, Kenneth (Flexner)
1902-1961 .... **CLC 51**
See also CA 93-96; DLB 9

Fecamps, Elise
See Creasey, John

Federman, Raymond 1928- ...... **CLC 6, 47**
See also CA 17-20R; CAAS 8; CANR 10,
43; DLBY 80

Federspiel, J(uerg) F. 1931- .... **CLC 42**
See also CA 146

Feiffer, Jules (Ralph)
1929- ...... **CLC 2, 8, 64; DAM DRAM**
See also AAYA 3; CA 17-20R; CANR 30;
DLB 7, 44; INT CANR-30; MTCW;
SATA 8, 61

Feige, Hermann Albert Otto Maximilian
See Traven, B.

Feinberg, David B. 1956-1994 ..... **CLC 59**
See also CA 135; 147

Feinstein, Elaine 1930- .... **CLC 36**
See also CA 69-72; CAAS 1; CANR 31;
DLB 14, 40; MTCW

Feldman, Irving (Mordecai) 1928- .... **CLC 7**
See also CA 1-4R; CANR 1; DLB 169

Felix-Tchicaya, Gerald
See Tchicaya, Gerald Felix

Fellini, Federico 1920-1993 ..... **CLC 16, 85**
See also CA 65-68; 143; CANR 33

Felsen, Henry Gregor 1916- .... **CLC 17**
See also CA 1-4R; CANR 1; SAAS 2;
SATA 1

Fenton, James Martin 1949- .... **CLC 32**
See also CA 102; DLB 40

Ferber, Edna 1887-1968 .... **CLC 18, 93**
See also AITN 1; CA 5-8R; 25-28R; DLB 9,
28, 86; MTCW; SATA 7

Ferguson, Helen
See Kavan, Anna

Ferguson, Samuel 1810-1886 ..... **NCLC 33**
See also DLB 32

Fergusson, Robert 1750-1774 .... **LC 29**
See also DLB 109

Ferling, Lawrence
See Ferlinghetti, Lawrence (Monsanto)

Ferlinghetti, Lawrence (Monsanto)
1919(?)- .... **CLC 2, 6, 10, 27;
DAM POET; PC 1**
See also CA 5-8R; CANR 3, 41;
CDALB 1941-1968; DLB 5, 16; MTCW

Fernandez, Vicente Garcia Huidobro
See Huidobro Fernandez, Vicente Garcia

Ferrer, Gabriel (Francisco Victor) Miro
See Miro (Ferrer), Gabriel (Francisco
Victor)

Ferrier, Susan (Edmonstone)
1782-1854 .... **NCLC 8**
See also DLB 116

Ferrigno, Robert 1948(?)- .... **CLC 65**
See also CA 140

Ferron, Jacques 1921-1985 ... **CLC 94; DAC**
See also CA 117; 129; DLB 60

Feuchtwanger, Lion 1884-1958 ..... **TCLC 3**
See also CA 104; DLB 66

Feuillet, Octave 1821-1890 ...... **NCLC 45**

Feydeau, Georges (Leon Jules Marie)
1862-1921 ..... **TCLC 22; DAM DRAM**
See also CA 113; 152

Fichte, Johann Gottlieb
1762-1814 .... **NCLC 62**
See also DLB 90

Ficino, Marsilio 1433-1499 .... **LC 12**

Fiedeler, Hans
See Doeblin, Alfred

Fiedler, Leslie A(aron)
1917- .... **CLC 4, 13, 24**
See also CA 9-12R; CANR 7; DLB 28, 67;
MTCW

Field, Andrew 1938- .... **CLC 44**
See also CA 97-100; CANR 25

Field, Eugene 1850-1895 .... **NCLC 3**
See also DLB 23, 42, 140; DLBD 13;
MAICYA; SATA 16

Field, Gans T.
See Wellman, Manly Wade

Field, Michael .... **TCLC 43**

Field, Peter
See Hobson, Laura Z(ametkin)

Fielding, Henry
1707-1754 ...... **LC 1; DA; DAB; DAC;
DAM DRAM, MST, NOV; WLC**
See also CDBLB 1660-1789; DLB 39, 84,
101

Fielding, Sarah 1710-1768 .... **LC 1**
See also DLB 39

Fierstein, Harvey (Forbes)
1954- ..... **CLC 33; DAM DRAM, POP**
See also CA 123; 129

Figes, Eva 1932- .... **CLC 31**
See also CA 53-56; CANR 4, 44; DLB 14

Finch, Robert (Duer Claydon)
1900- .... **CLC 18**
See also CA 57-60; CANR 9, 24, 49;
DLB 88

Findley, Timothy
1930- ...... **CLC 27; DAC; DAM MST**
See also CA 25-28R; CANR 12, 42;
DLB 53

Fink, William
See Mencken, H(enry) L(ouis)

Firbank, Louis 1942-
See Reed, Lou
See also CA 117

Firbank, (Arthur Annesley) Ronald
1886-1926 .... **TCLC 1**
See also CA 104; DLB 36

Fisher, M(ary) F(rances) K(ennedy)
1908-1992 .... **CLC 76, 87**
See also CA 77-80; 138; CANR 44

Fisher, Roy 1930- .... **CLC 25**
See also CA 81-84; CAAS 10; CANR 16;
DLB 40

Fisher, Rudolph
1897-1934 .... **TCLC 11; BLC;
DAM MULT; SSC 25**
See also BW 1; CA 107; 124; DLB 51, 102

Fisher, Vardis (Alvero) 1895-1968.... **CLC 7**
See also CA 5-8R; 25-28R; DLB 9

Fiske, Tarleton
See Bloch, Robert (Albert)

Fitch, Clarke
See Sinclair, Upton (Beall)

Fitch, John IV
See Cormier, Robert (Edmund)

Fitzgerald, Captain Hugh
See Baum, L(yman) Frank

FitzGerald, Edward 1809-1883 .... **NCLC 9**
See also DLB 32

Fitzgerald, F(rancis) Scott (Key)
1896-1940 .... **TCLC 1, 6, 14, 28, 55;
DA; DAB; DAC; DAM MST, NOV;
SSC 6; WLC**
See also AITN 1; CA 110; 123;
CDALB 1917-1929; DLB 4, 9, 86;
DLBD 1; DLBY 81, 96; MTCW

Galsworthy, John
1867-1933 ...... **TCLC 1, 45; DA; DAB;
DAC; DAM DRAM, MST, NOV;
SSC 22; WLC 2**
See also CA 104; 141; CDBLB 1890-1914;
DLB 10, 34, 98, 162

Galt, John 1779-1839 .... **NCLC 1**
See also DLB 99, 116, 159

Galvin, James 1951- .... **CLC 38**
See also CA 108; CANR 26

Gamboa, Federico 1864-1939 ..... **TCLC 36**

Gandhi, M. K.
See Gandhi, Mohandas Karamchand

Gandhi, Mahatma
See Gandhi, Mohandas Karamchand

Gandhi, Mohandas Karamchand
1869-1948 ..... **TCLC 59; DAM MULT**
See also CA 121; 132; MTCW

Gann, Ernest Kellogg 1910-1991.... **CLC 23**
See also AITN 1; CA 1-4R; 136; CANR 1

Garcia, Cristina 1958- .... **CLC 76**
See also CA 141

Garcia Lorca, Federico
1898-1936 ... **TCLC 1, 7, 49; DA; DAB;
DAC; DAM DRAM, MST, MULT,
POET; DC 2; HLC; PC 3; WLC**
See also CA 104; 131; DLB 108; HW;
MTCW

Garcia Marquez, Gabriel (Jose)
1928- .... **CLC 2, 3, 8, 10, 15, 27, 47, 55,
68; DA; DAB; DAC; DAM MST,
MULT, NOV, POP; HLC; SSC 8; WLC**
See also AAYA 3; BEST 89:1, 90:4;
CA 33-36R; CANR 10, 28, 50; DLB 113;
HW; MTCW

Gard, Janice
See Latham, Jean Lee

Gard, Roger Martin du
See Martin du Gard, Roger

Gardam, Jane 1928- .... **CLC 43**
See also CA 49-52; CANR 2, 18, 33, 54;
CLR 12; DLB 14, 161; MAICYA;
MTCW; SAAS 9; SATA 39, 76;
SATA-Brief 28

Gardner, Herb(ert) 1934- .... **CLC 44**
See also CA 149

Gardner, John (Champlin), Jr.
1933-1982 ..... **CLC 2, 3, 5, 7, 8, 10, 18,
28, 34; DAM NOV, POP; SSC 7**
See also AITN 1; CA 65-68; 107;
CANR 33; DLB 2; DLBY 82; MTCW;
SATA 40; SATA-Obit 31

Gardner, John (Edmund)
1926- .... **CLC 30; DAM POP**
See also CA 103; CANR 15; MTCW

Gardner, Miriam
See Bradley, Marion Zimmer

Gardner, Noel
See Kuttner, Henry

Gardons, S. S.
See Snodgrass, W(illiam) D(e Witt)

Garfield, Leon 1921-1996 .... **CLC 12**
See also AAYA 8; CA 17-20R; 152;
CANR 38, 41; CLR 21; DLB 161; JRDA;
MAICYA; SATA 1, 32, 76;
SATA-Obit 90

Garland, (Hannibal) Hamlin
1860-1940 .... **TCLC 3; SSC 18**
See also CA 104; DLB 12, 71, 78

Garneau, (Hector de) Saint-Denys
1912-1943 .... **TCLC 13**
See also CA 111; DLB 88

Garner, Alan
1934- .... **CLC 17; DAB; DAM POP**
See also AAYA 18; CA 73-76; CANR 15;
CLR 20; DLB 161; MAICYA; MTCW;
SATA 18, 69

Garner, Hugh 1913-1979 .... **CLC 13**
See also CA 69-72; CANR 31; DLB 68

Garnett, David 1892-1981 .... **CLC 3**
See also CA 5-8R; 103; CANR 17; DLB 34

Garos, Stephanie
See Katz, Steve

Garrett, George (Palmer)
1929- .... **CLC 3, 11, 51**
See also CA 1-4R; CAAS 5; CANR 1, 42;
DLB 2, 5, 130, 152; DLBY 83

Garrick, David
1717-1779 .... **LC 15; DAM DRAM**
See also DLB 84

Garrigue, Jean 1914-1972 .... **CLC 2, 8**
See also CA 5-8R; 37-40R; CANR 20

Garrison, Frederick
See Sinclair, Upton (Beall)

Garth, Will
See Hamilton, Edmond; Kuttner, Henry

Garvey, Marcus (Moziah, Jr.)
1887-1940 .... **TCLC 41; BLC;
DAM MULT**
See also BW 1; CA 120; 124

Gary, Romain .... **CLC 25**
See also Kacew, Romain
See also DLB 83

Gascar, Pierre .... **CLC 11**
See also Fournier, Pierre

Gascoyne, David (Emery) 1916- .... **CLC 45**
See also CA 65-68; CANR 10, 28, 54;
DLB 20; MTCW

Gaskell, Elizabeth Cleghorn
1810-1865 .... **NCLC 5; DAB;
DAM MST; SSC 25**
See also CDBLB 1832-1890; DLB 21, 144,
159

Gass, William H(oward)
1924- ... **CLC 1, 2, 8, 11, 15, 39; SSC 12**
See also CA 17-20R; CANR 30; DLB 2;
MTCW

Gasset, Jose Ortega y
See Ortega y Gasset, Jose

Gates, Henry Louis, Jr.
1950- .... **CLC 65; DAM MULT**
See also BW 2; CA 109; CANR 25, 53;
DLB 67

Gautier, Theophile
1811-1872 .... **NCLC 1, 59;
DAM POET; PC 18; SSC 20**
See also DLB 119

Gawsworth, John
See Bates, H(erbert) E(rnest)

Gay, Oliver
See Gogarty, Oliver St. John

Gaye, Marvin (Penze) 1939-1984 ... **CLC 26**
See also CA 112

Gebler, Carlo (Ernest) 1954- .... **CLC 39**
See also CA 119; 133

Gee, Maggie (Mary) 1948- .... **CLC 57**
See also CA 130

Gee, Maurice (Gough) 1931- .... **CLC 29**
See also CA 97-100; SATA 46

Gelbart, Larry (Simon) 1923- ... **CLC 21, 61**
See also CA 73-76; CANR 45

Gelber, Jack 1932- .... **CLC 1, 6, 14, 79**
See also CA 1-4R; CANR 2; DLB 7

Gellhorn, Martha (Ellis) 1908- .. **CLC 14, 60**
See also CA 77-80; CANR 44; DLBY 82

Genet, Jean
1910-1986 ...... **CLC 1, 2, 5, 10, 14, 44,
46; DAM DRAM**
See also CA 13-16R; CANR 18; DLB 72;
DLBY 86; MTCW

Gent, Peter 1942- .... **CLC 29**
See also AITN 1; CA 89-92; DLBY 82

Gentlewoman in New England, A
See Bradstreet, Anne

Gentlewoman in Those Parts, A
See Bradstreet, Anne

George, Jean Craighead 1919- ...... **CLC 35**
See also AAYA 8; CA 5-8R; CANR 25;
CLR 1; DLB 52; JRDA; MAICYA;
SATA 2, 68

George, Stefan (Anton)
1868-1933 .... **TCLC 2, 14**
See also CA 104

Georges, Georges Martin
See Simenon, Georges (Jacques Christian)

Gerhardi, William Alexander
See Gerhardie, William Alexander

Gerhardie, William Alexander
1895-1977 .... **CLC 5**
See also CA 25-28R; 73-76; CANR 18;
DLB 36

Gerstler, Amy 1956- .... **CLC 70**
See also CA 146

Gertler, T. .... **CLC 34**
See also CA 116; 121; INT 121

gfgg .... **CLC XvXzc**

Ghalib .... **NCLC 39**
See also Ghalib, Hsadullah Khan

Ghalib, Hsadullah Khan 1797-1869
See Ghalib
See also DAM POET

Ghelderode, Michel de
1898-1962 .... **CLC 6, 11; DAM DRAM**
See also CA 85-88; CANR 40

Ghiselin, Brewster 1903- .... **CLC 23**
See also CA 13-16R; CAAS 10; CANR 13

Ghose, Zulfikar 1935- .... **CLC 42**
See also CA 65-68

Ghosh, Amitav 1956- .... **CLC 44**
See also CA 147

Giacosa, Giuseppe 1847-1906 ...... **TCLC 7**
See also CA 104

Gibb, Lee
See Waterhouse, Keith (Spencer)

Gibbon, Lewis Grassic . . . . TCLC 4
See also Mitchell, James Leslie

Gibbons, Kaye
1960- . . . . CLC 50, 88; DAM POP
See also CA 151

Gibran, Kahlil
1883-1931 . . . . TCLC 1, 9; DAM POET,
POP; PC 9
See also CA 104; 150

Gibran, Khalil
See Gibran, Kahlil

Gibson, William
1914- . . . . CLC 23; DA; DAB; DAC;
DAM DRAM, MST
See also CA 9-12R; CANR 9, 42; DLB 7;
SATA 66

Gibson, William (Ford)
1948- . . . . CLC 39, 63; DAM POP
See also AAYA 12; CA 126; 133; CANR 52

Gide, Andre (Paul Guillaume)
1869-1951 . . . . TCLC 5, 12, 36; DA;
DAB; DAC; DAM MST, NOV; SSC 13;
WLC
See also CA 104; 124; DLB 65; MTCW

Gifford, Barry (Colby) 1946- . . . . CLC 34
See also CA 65-68; CANR 9, 30, 40

Gilbert, W(illiam) S(chwenck)
1836-1911 . . . . . TCLC 3; DAM DRAM,
POET
See also CA 104; SATA 36

Gilbreth, Frank B., Jr. 1911- . . . . CLC 17
See also CA 9-12R; SATA 2

Gilchrist, Ellen
1935- . . . . CLC 34, 48; DAM POP;
SSC 14
See also CA 113; 116; CANR 41; DLB 130;
MTCW

Giles, Molly 1942- . . . . CLC 39
See also CA 126

Gill, Patrick
See Creasey, John

Gilliam, Terry (Vance) 1940- . . . . CLC 21
See also Monty Python
See also AAYA 19; CA 108; 113;
CANR 35; INT 113

Gillian, Jerry
See Gilliam, Terry (Vance)

Gilliatt, Penelope (Ann Douglass)
1932-1993 . . . . CLC 2, 10, 13, 53
See also AITN 2; CA 13-16R; 141;
CANR 49; DLB 14

Gilman, Charlotte (Anna) Perkins (Stetson)
1860-1935 . . . . TCLC 9, 37; SSC 13
See also CA 106; 150

Gilmour, David 1949- . . . . CLC 35
See also CA 138, 147

Gilpin, William 1724-1804 . . . . NCLC 30

Gilray, J. D.
See Mencken, H(enry) L(ouis)

Gilroy, Frank D(aniel) 1925- . . . . CLC 2
See also CA 81-84; CANR 32; DLB 7

Gilstrap, John 1957(?)- . . . . CLC 99

Ginsberg, Allen (Irwin)
1926-1997 . . . . . CLC 1, 2, 3, 4, 6, 13, 36,
69; DA; DAB; DAC; DAM MST, POET;
PC 4; WLC 3
See also AITN 1; CA 1-4R; 157; CANR 2,
41; CDALB 1941-1968; DLB 5, 16, 169;
MTCW

Ginzburg, Natalia
1916-1991 . . . . CLC 5, 11, 54, 70
See also CA 85-88; 135; CANR 33;
DLB 177; MTCW

Giono, Jean 1895-1970. . . . . CLC 4, 11
See also CA 45-48; 29-32R; CANR 2, 35;
DLB 72; MTCW

Giovanni, Nikki
1943- . . . . . . CLC 2, 4, 19, 64; BLC; DA;
DAB; DAC; DAM MST, MULT, POET;
PC 19
See also AITN 1; BW 2; CA 29-32R;
CAAS 6; CANR 18, 41; CLR 6; DLB 5,
41; INT CANR-18; MAICYA; MTCW;
SATA 24; YABC

Giovene, Andrea 1904- . . . . CLC 7
See also CA 85-88

Gippius, Zinaida (Nikolayevna) 1869-1945
See Hippius, Zinaida
See also CA 106

Giraudoux, (Hippolyte) Jean
1882-1944 . . . . TCLC 2, 7; DAM DRAM
See also CA 104; DLB 65

Gironella, Jose Maria 1917- . . . . CLC 11
See also CA 101

Gissing, George (Robert)
1857-1903 . . . . TCLC 3, 24, 47
See also CA 105; DLB 18, 135

Giurlani, Aldo
See Palazzeschi, Aldo

Gladkov, Fyodor (Vasilyevich)
1883-1958 . . . . TCLC 27

Glanville, Brian (Lester) 1931- . . . . . . CLC 6
See also CA 5-8R; CAAS 9; CANR 3;
DLB 15, 139; SATA 42

Glasgow, Ellen (Anderson Gholson)
1873(?)-1945 . . . . TCLC 2, 7
See also CA 104; DLB 9, 12

Glaspell, Susan 1882(?)-1948 . . . . . TCLC 55
See also CA 110; 154; DLB 7, 9, 78; 2

Glassco, John 1909-1981 . . . . CLC 9
See also CA 13-16R; 102; CANR 15;
DLB 68

Glasscock, Amnesia
See Steinbeck, John (Ernst)

Glasser, Ronald J. 1940(?)- . . . . CLC 37

Glassman, Joyce
See Johnson, Joyce

Glendinning, Victoria 1937- . . . . CLC 50
See also CA 120; 127; DLB 155

Glissant, Edouard
1928- . . . . CLC 10, 68; DAM MULT
See also CA 153

Gloag, Julian 1930- . . . . CLC 40
See also AITN 1; CA 65-68; CANR 10

Glowacki, Aleksander
See Prus, Boleslaw

Gluck, Louise (Elisabeth)
1943- . . . . CLC 7, 22, 44, 81;
DAM POET; PC 16
See also CA 33-36R; CANR 40; DLB 5

Glyn, Elinor 1864-1943 . . . . TCLC 72
See also DLB 153

Gobineau, Joseph Arthur (Comte) de
1816-1882 . . . . NCLC 17
See also DLB 123

Godard, Jean-Luc 1930-. . . . . CLC 20
See also CA 93-96

Godden, (Margaret) Rumer 1907-. . . CLC 53
See also AAYA 6; CA 5-8R; CANR 4, 27,
36, 55; CLR 20; DLB 161; MAICYA;
SAAS 12; SATA 3, 36

Godoy Alcayaga, Lucila 1889-1957
See Mistral, Gabriela
See also BW 2; CA 104; 131; DAM MULT;
HW; MTCW

Godwin, Gail (Kathleen)
1937- . . . . CLC 5, 8, 22, 31, 69;
DAM POP
See also CA 29-32R; CANR 15, 43; DLB 6;
INT CANR-15; MTCW

Godwin, William 1756-1836. . . . . . NCLC 14
See also CDBLB 1789-1832; DLB 39, 104,
142, 158, 163

Goebbels, Josef
See Goebbels, (Paul) Joseph

Goebbels, (Paul) Joseph
1897-1945 . . . . TCLC 68
See also CA 115; 148

Goebbels, Joseph Paul
See Goebbels, (Paul) Joseph

Goethe, Johann Wolfgang von
1749-1832 . . . . NCLC 4, 22, 34; DA;
DAB; DAC; DAM DRAM, MST,
POET; PC 5; WLC 3
See also DLB 94

Gogarty, Oliver St. John
1878-1957 . . . . TCLC 15
See also CA 109; 150; DLB 15, 19

Gogol, Nikolai (Vasilyevich)
1809-1852 . . . . . . NCLC 5, 15, 31; DA;
DAB; DAC; DAM DRAM, MST; DC 1;
SSC 4; WLC
See also DLB 198

Goines, Donald
1937(?)-1974 . . . . CLC 80; BLC;
DAM MULT, POP
See also AITN 1; BW 1; CA 124; 114;
DLB 33

Gold, Herbert 1924-. . . . . . . CLC 4, 7, 14, 42
See also CA 9-12R; CANR 17, 45; DLB 2;
DLBY 81

Goldbarth, Albert 1948-. . . . . CLC 5, 38
See also CA 53-56; CANR 6, 40; DLB 120

Goldberg, Anatol 1910-1982 . . . . CLC 34
See also CA 131; 117

Goldemberg, Isaac 1945- . . . . CLC 52
See also CA 69-72; CAAS 12; CANR 11,
32; HW

Golding, William (Gerald)
1911-1993 .... **CLC 1, 2, 3, 8, 10, 17, 27, 58, 81; DA; DAB; DAC; DAM MST, NOV; WLC**
See also AAYA 5; CA 5-8R; 141; CANR 13, 33, 54; CDBLB 1945-1960; DLB 15, 100; MTCW

Goldman, Emma 1869-1940 ...... **TCLC 13**
See also CA 110; 150

Goldman, Francisco 1955- .... **CLC 76**

Goldman, William (W.) 1931- .... **CLC 1, 48**
See also CA 9-12R; CANR 29; DLB 44

Goldmann, Lucien 1913-1970 ...... **CLC 24**
See also CA 25-28; CAP 2

Goldoni, Carlo
1707-1793 .... **LC 4; DAM DRAM**

Goldsberry, Steven 1949- .... **CLC 34**
See also CA 131

Goldsmith, Oliver
1728-1774 ...... **LC 2; DA; DAB; DAC; DAM DRAM, MST, NOV, POET; WLC**
See also CDBLB 1660-1789; DLB 39, 89, 104, 109, 142; SATA 26

Goldsmith, Peter
See Priestley, J(ohn) B(oynton)

Gombrowicz, Witold
1904-1969 .... **CLC 4, 7, 11, 49; DAM DRAM**
See also CA 19-20; 25-28R; CAP 2

Gomez de la Serna, Ramon
1888-1963 .... **CLC 9**
See also CA 153; 116; HW

Goncharov, Ivan Alexandrovich
1812-1891 .... **NCLC 1**

Goncourt, Edmond (Louis Antoine Huot) de
1822-1896 .... **NCLC 7**
See also DLB 123

Goncourt, Jules (Alfred Huot) de
1830-1870 .... **NCLC 7**
See also DLB 123

Gontier, Fernande 19(?)- .... **CLC 50**

Gonzalez Martinez, Enrique
1871-1952 .... **TCLC 72**
See also HW

Goodman, Paul 1911-1972 .... **CLC 1, 2, 4, 7**
See also CA 19-20; 37-40R; CANR 34; CAP 2; DLB 130; MTCW

Gordimer, Nadine
1923- .... **CLC 3, 5, 7, 10, 18, 33, 51, 70; DA; DAB; DAC; DAM MST, NOV; SSC 17**
See also CA 5-8R; CANR 3, 28, 56; INT CANR-28; MTCW; YABC

Gordon, Adam Lindsay
1833-1870 .... **NCLC 21**

Gordon, Caroline
1895-1981 ... **CLC 6, 13, 29, 83; SSC 15**
See also CA 11-12; 103; CANR 36; CAP 1; DLB 4, 9, 102; DLBY 81; MTCW

Gordon, Charles William 1860-1937
See Connor, Ralph
See also CA 109

Gordon, Mary (Catherine)
1949- .... **CLC 13, 22**
See also CA 102; CANR 44; DLB 6; DLBY 81; INT 102; MTCW

Gordon, Sol 1923- .... **CLC 26**
See also CA 53-56; CANR 4; SATA 11

Gordone, Charles
1925-1995 ..... **CLC 1, 4; DAM DRAM**
See also BW 1; CA 93-96; 150; CANR 55; DLB 7; INT 93-96; MTCW

Gorenko, Anna Andreevna
See Akhmatova, Anna

Gorky, Maxim .... **TCLC 8; DAB; WLC**
See also Peshkov, Alexei Maximovich

Goryan, Sirak
See Saroyan, William

Gosse, Edmund (William)
1849-1928 .... **TCLC 28**
See also CA 117; DLB 57, 144

Gotlieb, Phyllis Fay (Bloom)
1926- .... **CLC 18**
See also CA 13-16R; CANR 7; DLB 88

Gottesman, S. D.
See Kornbluth, C(yril) M.; Pohl, Frederik

Gottfried von Strassburg
fl. c. 1210- .... **CMLC 10**
See also DLB 138

Gould, Lois .... **CLC 4, 10**
See also CA 77-80; CANR 29; MTCW

Gourmont, Remy (-Marie-Charles) de
1858-1915 .... **TCLC 17**
See also CA 109; 150

Govier, Katherine 1948- .... **CLC 51**
See also CA 101; CANR 18, 40

Goyen, (Charles) William
1915-1983 .... **CLC 5, 8, 14, 40**
See also AITN 2; CA 5-8R; 110; CANR 6; DLB 2; DLBY 83; INT CANR-6

Goytisolo, Juan
1931- ..... **CLC 5, 10, 23; DAM MULT; HLC**
See also CA 85-88; CANR 32; HW; MTCW

Gozzano, Guido 1883-1916 .... **PC 10**
See also CA 154; DLB 114

Gozzi, (Conte) Carlo 1720-1806 .. **NCLC 23**

Grabbe, Christian Dietrich
1801-1836 .... **NCLC 2**
See also DLB 133

Grace, Patricia 1937- .... **CLC 56**

Gracian y Morales, Baltasar
1601-1658 .... **LC 15**

Gracq, Julien .... **CLC 11, 48**
See also Poirier, Louis
See also DLB 83

Grade, Chaim 1910-1982 .... **CLC 10**
See also CA 93-96; 107

Graduate of Oxford, A
See Ruskin, John

Grafton, Garth
See Duncan, Sara Jeannette

Graham, John
See Phillips, David Graham

Graham, Jorie 1951- .... **CLC 48**
See also CA 111; DLB 120

Graham, R(obert) B(ontine) Cunninghame
See Cunninghame Graham, R(obert) B(ontine)
See also DLB 98, 135, 174

Graham, Robert
See Haldeman, Joe (William)

Graham, Tom
See Lewis, (Harry) Sinclair

Graham, W(illiam) S(ydney)
1918-1986 .... **CLC 29**
See also CA 73-76; 118; DLB 20

Graham, Winston (Mawdsley)
1910- .... **CLC 23**
See also CA 49-52; CANR 2, 22, 45; DLB 77

Grahame, Kenneth
1859-1932 .... **TCLC 64; DAB**
See also CA 108; 136; CLR 5; DLB 34, 141, 178; MAICYA; 1

Grant, Skeeter
See Spiegelman, Art

Granville-Barker, Harley
1877-1946 ...... **TCLC 2; DAM DRAM**
See also Barker, Harley Granville
See also CA 104

Grass, Guenter (Wilhelm)
1927- ..... **CLC 1, 2, 4, 6, 11, 15, 22, 32, 49, 88; DA; DAB; DAC; DAM MST, NOV; WLC**
See also CA 13-16R; CANR 20; DLB 75, 124; MTCW

Gratton, Thomas
See Hulme, T(homas) E(rnest)

Grau, Shirley Ann
1929- .... **CLC 4, 9; SSC 15**
See also CA 89-92; CANR 22; DLB 2; INT CANR-22; MTCW

Gravel, Fern
See Hall, James Norman

Graver, Elizabeth 1964- .... **CLC 70**
See also CA 135

Graves, Richard Perceval 1945- .... **CLC 44**
See also CA 65-68; CANR 9, 26, 51

Graves, Robert (von Ranke)
1895-1985 ...... **CLC 1, 2, 6, 11, 39, 44, 45; DAB; DAC; DAM MST, POET; PC 6**
See also CA 5-8R; 117; CANR 5, 36; CDBLB 1914-1945; DLB 20, 100; DLBY 85; MTCW; SATA 45

Graves, Valerie
See Bradley, Marion Zimmer

Gray, Alasdair (James) 1934- ...... **CLC 41**
See also CA 126; CANR 47; INT 126; MTCW

Gray, Amlin 1946- .... **CLC 29**
See also CA 138

Gray, Francine du Plessix
1930- .... **CLC 22; DAM NOV**
See also BEST 90:3; CA 61-64; CAAS 2; CANR 11, 33; INT CANR-11; MTCW

Gray, John (Henry) 1866-1934 .... **TCLC 19**
See also CA 119

Hansberry, Lorraine (Vivian)
1930-1965 . . . . . . **CLC 17, 62; BLC; DA;**
DAB; DAC; DAM DRAM, MST,
MULT; DC 2
See also BW 1; CA 109; 25-28R; CABS 3;
CANR 58; CDALB 1941-1968; DLB 7,
38; MTCW

Hansen, Joseph 1923- . . . . **CLC 38**
See also CA 29-32R; CAAS 17; CANR 16,
44; INT CANR-16

Hansen, Martin A. 1909-1955 . . . . . **TCLC 32**

Hanson, Kenneth O(stlin) 1922- . . . . **CLC 13**
See also CA 53-56; CANR 7

Hardwick, Elizabeth
1916- . . . . **CLC 13; DAM NOV**
See also CA 5-8R; CANR 3, 32; DLB 6;
MTCW

Hardy, Thomas
1840-1928 . . . . . . **TCLC 4, 10, 18, 32, 48,**
53, 72; DA; DAB; DAC; DAM MST,
NOV, POET; PC 8; SSC 2; WLC
See also CA 104; 123; CDBLB 1890-1914;
DLB 18, 19, 135; MTCW

Hare, David 1947- . . . . **CLC 29, 58**
See also CA 97-100; CANR 39; DLB 13;
MTCW

Harford, Henry
See Hudson, W(illiam) H(enry)

Hargrave, Leonie
See Disch, Thomas M(ichael)

Harjo, Joy 1951- . . . **CLC 83; DAM MULT**
See also CA 114; CANR 35; DLB 120, 175;
NNAL

Harlan, Louis R(udolph) 1922- . . . . . **CLC 34**
See also CA 21-24R; CANR 25, 55

Harling, Robert 1951(?)- . . . . **CLC 53**
See also CA 147

Harmon, William (Ruth) 1938- . . . . . **CLC 38**
See also CA 33-36R; CANR 14, 32, 35;
SATA 65

Harper, F. E. W.
See Harper, Frances Ellen Watkins

Harper, Frances E. W.
See Harper, Frances Ellen Watkins

Harper, Frances E. Watkins
See Harper, Frances Ellen Watkins

Harper, Frances Ellen
See Harper, Frances Ellen Watkins

Harper, Frances Ellen Watkins
1825-1911 . . . . **TCLC 14; BLC;**
DAM MULT, POET
See also BW 1; CA 111; 125; DLB 50

Harper, Michael S(teven) 1938- . . **CLC 7, 22**
See also BW 1; CA 33-36R; CANR 24;
DLB 41

Harper, Mrs. F. E. W.
See Harper, Frances Ellen Watkins

Harris, Christie (Lucy) Irwin
1907- . . . . **CLC 12**
See also CA 5-8R; CANR 6; DLB 88;
JRDA; MAICYA; SAAS 10; SATA 6, 74

Harris, Frank 1856-1931 . . . . **TCLC 24**
See also CA 109; 150; DLB 156

Harris, George Washington
1814-1869 . . . . **NCLC 23**
See also DLB 3, 11

Harris, Joel Chandler
1848-1908 . . . . **TCLC 2; SSC 19**
See also CA 104; 137; DLB 11, 23, 42, 78,
91; MAICYA; 1

Harris, John (Wyndham Parkes Lucas)
Beynon 1903-1969
See Wyndham, John
See also CA 102; 89-92

Harris, MacDonald . . . . **CLC 9**
See also Heiney, Donald (William)

Harris, Mark 1922- . . . . **CLC 19**
See also CA 5-8R; CAAS 3; CANR 2, 55;
DLB 2; DLBY 80

Harris, (Theodore) Wilson 1921- . . . . **CLC 25**
See also BW 2; CA 65-68; CAAS 16;
CANR 11, 27; DLB 117; MTCW

Harrison, Elizabeth Cavanna 1909-
See Cavanna, Betty
See also CA 9-12R; CANR 6, 27

Harrison, Harry (Max) 1925- . . . . . . **CLC 42**
See also CA 1-4R; CANR 5, 21; DLB 8;
SATA 4

Harrison, James (Thomas)
1937- . . . . **CLC 6, 14, 33, 66; SSC 19**
See also CA 13-16R; CANR 8, 51;
DLBY 82; INT CANR-8

Harrison, Jim
See Harrison, James (Thomas)

Harrison, Kathryn 1961- . . . . **CLC 70**
See also CA 144

Harrison, Tony 1937- . . . . **CLC 43**
See also CA 65-68; CANR 44; DLB 40;
MTCW

Harriss, Will(ard Irvin) 1922- . . . . . . **CLC 34**
See also CA 111

Harson, Sley
See Ellison, Harlan (Jay)

Hart, Ellis
See Ellison, Harlan (Jay)

Hart, Josephine
1942(?)- . . . . **CLC 70; DAM POP**
See also CA 138

Hart, Moss
1904-1961 . . . . . . **CLC 66; DAM DRAM**
See also CA 109; 89-92; DLB 7

Harte, (Francis) Bret(t)
1836(?)-1902 . . . . **TCLC 1, 25; DA; DAC;**
DAM MST; SSC 8; WLC
See also CA 104; 140; CDALB 1865-1917;
DLB 12, 64, 74, 79; SATA 26

Hartley, L(eslie) P(oles)
1895-1972 . . . . **CLC 2, 22**
See also CA 45-48; 37-40R; CANR 33;
DLB 15, 139; MTCW

Hartman, Geoffrey H. 1929- . . . . **CLC 27**
See also CA 117; 125; DLB 67

Hartmann von Aue
c. 1160-c. 1205 . . . . **CMLC 15**
See also DLB 138

Hartmann von Aue 1170-1210 . . . . **CMLC 15**

Haruf, Kent 1943- . . . . **CLC 34**
See also CA 149

Harwood, Ronald
1934- . . . . **CLC 32; DAM DRAM, MST**
See also CA 1-4R; CANR 4, 55; DLB 13

Hasek, Jaroslav (Matej Frantisek)
1883-1923 . . . . **TCLC 4**
See also CA 104; 129; MTCW

Hass, Robert
1941- . . . . **CLC 18, 39, 99; PC 16**
See also CA 111; CANR 30, 50; DLB 105;
SATA 94

Hastings, Hudson
See Kuttner, Henry

Hastings, Selina . . . . **CLC 44**

Hathorne, John 1641-1717 . . . . **LC 38**

Hatteras, Amelia
See Mencken, H(enry) L(ouis)

Hatteras, Owen . . . . **TCLC 18**
See also Mencken, H(enry) L(ouis); Nathan,
George Jean

Hauptmann, Gerhart (Johann Robert)
1862-1946 . . . . . . **TCLC 4; DAM DRAM**
See also CA 104; 153; DLB 66, 118

Havel, Vaclav
1936- . . . . **CLC 25, 58, 65;**
DAM DRAM; DC 6
See also CA 104; CANR 36; MTCW

Haviaras, Stratis . . . . **CLC 33**
See also Chaviaras, Strates

Hawes, Stephen 1475(?)-1523(?) . . . . . **LC 17**

Hawkes, John (Clendennin Burne, Jr.)
1925- . . . . . . **CLC 1, 2, 3, 4, 7, 9, 14, 15,**
27, 49
See also CA 1-4R; CANR 2, 47; DLB 2, 7;
DLBY 80; MTCW

Hawking, S. W.
See Hawking, Stephen W(illiam)

Hawking, Stephen W(illiam)
1942- . . . . **CLC 63**
See also AAYA 13; BEST 89:1; CA 126;
129; CANR 48

Hawthorne, Julian 1846-1934 . . . . . **TCLC 25**

Hawthorne, Nathaniel
1804-1864 . . . . **NCLC 39; DA; DAB;**
DAC; DAM MST, NOV; SSC 3; WLC
See also AAYA 18; CDALB 1640-1865;
DLB 1, 74; 2

Haxton, Josephine Ayres 1921-
See Douglas, Ellen
See also CA 115; CANR 41

Hayaseca y Eizaguirre, Jorge
See Echegaray (y Eizaguirre), Jose (Maria
Waldo)

Hayashi Fumiko 1904-1951 . . . . **TCLC 27**
See also DLB 180

Haycraft, Anna
See Ellis, Alice Thomas
See also CA 122

Hayden, Robert E(arl)
1913-1980 . . . . . . **CLC 5, 9, 14, 37; BLC;**
DA; DAC; DAM MST, MULT, POET;
PC 6
See also BW 1; CA 69-72; 97-100; CABS 2;
CANR 24; CDALB 1941-1968; DLB 5,
76; MTCW; SATA 19; SATA-Obit 26

Hayford, J(oseph) E(phraim) Casely
See Casely-Hayford, J(oseph) E(phraim)

Hayman, Ronald 1932-........... **CLC 44**
See also CA 25-28R; CANR 18, 50;
DLB 155

Haywood, Eliza (Fowler)
1693(?)-1756 .... **LC 1**

Hazlitt, William 1778-1830 ...... **NCLC 29**
See also DLB 110, 158

Hazzard, Shirley 1931- .... **CLC 18**
See also CA 9-12R; CANR 4; DLBY 82;
MTCW

Head, Bessie
1937-1986 .... **CLC 25, 67; BLC;**
DAM MULT
See also BW 2; CA 29-32R; 119; CANR 25;
DLB 117; MTCW

Headon, (Nicky) Topper 1956(?)- ... **CLC 30**

Heaney, Seamus (Justin)
1939- ...... **CLC 5, 7, 14, 25, 37, 74, 91;**
DAB; DAM POET; PC 18
See also CA 85-88; CANR 25, 48;
CDBLB 1960 to Present; DLB 40;
DLBY 95; MTCW; YABC

Hearn, (Patricio) Lafcadio (Tessima Carlos)
1850-1904 .... **TCLC 9**
See also CA 105; DLB 12, 78

Hearne, Vicki 1946-.............. **CLC 56**
See also CA 139

Hearon, Shelby 1931-............. **CLC 63**
See also AITN 2; CA 25-28R; CANR 18,
48

Heat-Moon, William Least......... **CLC 29**
See also Trogdon, William (Lewis)
See also AAYA 9

Hebbel, Friedrich
1813-1863 .... **NCLC 43; DAM DRAM**
See also DLB 129

Hebert, Anne
1916- .... **CLC 4, 13, 29; DAC;**
DAM MST, POET
See also CA 85-88; DLB 68; MTCW

Hecht, Anthony (Evan)
1923- ...... **CLC 8, 13, 19; DAM POET**
See also CA 9-12R; CANR 6; DLB 5, 169

Hecht, Ben 1894-1964 .... **CLC 8**
See also CA 85-88; DLB 7, 9, 25, 26, 28, 86

Hedayat, Sadeq 1903-1951........ **TCLC 21**
See also CA 120

Hegel, Georg Wilhelm Friedrich
1770-1831 .... **NCLC 46**
See also DLB 90

Heidegger, Martin 1889-1976 ...... **CLC 24**
See also CA 81-84; 65-68; CANR 34;
MTCW

Heidenstam, (Carl Gustaf) Verner von
1859-1940 .... **TCLC 5**
See also CA 104

Heifner, Jack 1946- .... **CLC 11**
See also CA 105; CANR 47

Heijermans, Herman 1864-1924 ... **TCLC 24**
See also CA 123

Heilbrun, Carolyn G(old) 1926-..... **CLC 25**
See also CA 45-48; CANR 1, 28, 58

Heine, Heinrich 1797-1856 .... **NCLC 4, 54**
See also DLB 90

Heinemann, Larry (Curtiss) 1944- .. **CLC 50**
See also CA 110; CAAS 21; CANR 31;
DLBD 9; INT CANR-31

Heiney, Donald (William) 1921-1993
See Harris, MacDonald
See also CA 1-4R; 142; CANR 3, 58

Heinlein, Robert A(nson)
1907-1988 ...... **CLC 1, 3, 8, 14, 26, 55;**
DAM POP
See also AAYA 17; CA 1-4R; 125;
CANR 1, 20, 53; DLB 8; JRDA;
MAICYA; MTCW; SATA 9, 69;
SATA-Obit 56

Helforth, John
See Doolittle, Hilda

Hellenhofferu, Vojtech Kapristian z
See Hasek, Jaroslav (Matej Frantisek)

Heller, Joseph
1923- .... **CLC 1, 3, 5, 8, 11, 36, 63; DA;**
DAB; DAC; DAM MST, NOV, POP;
WLC
See also AITN 1; CA 5-8R; CABS 1;
CANR 8, 42; DLB 2, 28; DLBY 80;
INT CANR-8; MTCW

Hellman, Lillian (Florence)
1906-1984 ...... **CLC 2, 4, 8, 14, 18, 34,**
44, 52; DAM DRAM; DC 1
See also AITN 1, 2; CA 13-16R; 112;
CANR 33; DLB 7; DLBY 84; MTCW

Helprin, Mark
1947- .... **CLC 7, 10, 22, 32;**
DAM NOV, POP
See also CA 81-84; CANR 47; DLBY 85;
MTCW

Helvetius, Claude-Adrien
1715-1771 .... **LC 26**

Helyar, Jane Penelope Josephine 1933-
See Poole, Josephine
See also CA 21-24R; CANR 10, 26;
SATA 82

Hemans, Felicia 1793-1835 ...... **NCLC 29**
See also DLB 96

Hemingway, Ernest (Miller)
1899-1961 .... **CLC 1, 3, 6, 8, 10, 13, 19,**
30, 34, 39, 41, 44, 50, 61, 80; DA; DAB;
DAC; DAM MST, NOV; SSC 25; WLC
See also AAYA 19; CA 77-80; CANR 34;
CDALB 1917-1929; DLB 4, 9, 102;
DLBD 1; DLBY 81, 87, 96; MTCW

Hempel, Amy 1951- .... **CLC 39**
See also CA 118; 137

Henderson, F. C.
See Mencken, H(enry) L(ouis)

Henderson, Sylvia
See Ashton-Warner, Sylvia (Constance)

Henley, Beth .... **CLC 23; DC 6**
See also Henley, Elizabeth Becker
See also CABS 3; DLBY 86

Henley, Elizabeth Becker 1952-
See Henley, Beth
See also CA 107; CANR 32; DAM DRAM,
MST; MTCW

Henley, William Ernest
1849-1903 .... **TCLC 8**
See also CA 105; DLB 19

Hennissart, Martha
See Lathen, Emma
See also CA 85-88

Henry, O........ **TCLC 1, 19; SSC 5; WLC**
See also Porter, William Sydney

Henry, Patrick 1736-1799 .... **LC 25**

Henryson, Robert 1430(?)-1506(?).... **LC 20**
See also DLB 146

Henry VIII 1491-1547............. **LC 10**

Henschke, Alfred
See Klabund

Hentoff, Nat(han Irving) 1925-..... **CLC 26**
See also AAYA 4; CA 1-4R; CAAS 6;
CANR 5, 25; CLR 1; INT CANR-25;
JRDA; MAICYA; SATA 42, 69;
SATA-Brief 27

Heppenstall, (John) Rayner
1911-1981 .... **CLC 10**
See also CA 1-4R; 103; CANR 29

Heraclitus
c. 540B.C.-c. 450B.C......... **CMLC 22**
See also DLB 176

Herbert, Frank (Patrick)
1920-1986 ...... **CLC 12, 23, 35, 44, 85;**
DAM POP
See also AAYA 21; CA 53-56; 118;
CANR 5, 43; DLB 8; INT CANR-5;
MTCW; SATA 9, 37; SATA-Obit 47

Herbert, George
1593-1633 .... **LC 24; DAB;**
DAM POET; PC 4
See also CDBLB Before 1660; DLB 126

Herbert, Zbigniew
1924- .... **CLC 9, 43; DAM POET**
See also CA 89-92; CANR 36; MTCW

Herbst, Josephine (Frey)
1897-1969 .... **CLC 34**
See also CA 5-8R; 25-28R; DLB 9

Hergesheimer, Joseph
1880-1954 .... **TCLC 11**
See also CA 109; DLB 102, 9

Herlihy, James Leo 1927-1993 ...... **CLC 6**
See also CA 1-4R; 143; CANR 2

Hermogenes fl. c. 175- .... **CMLC 6**

Hernandez, Jose 1834-1886...... **NCLC 17**

Herodotus c. 484B.C.-429B.C..... **CMLC 17**
See also DLB 176

Herrick, Robert
1591-1674 ..... **LC 13; DA; DAB; DAC;**
DAM MST, POP; PC 9
See also DLB 126

Herring, Guilles
See Somerville, Edith

Herriot, James
1916-1995 .... **CLC 12; DAM POP**
See also Wight, James Alfred
See also AAYA 1; CA 148; CANR 40;
SATA 86

Herrmann, Dorothy 1941-........ **CLC 44**
See also CA 107

Herrmann, Taffy
See Herrmann, Dorothy

Hersey, John (Richard)
1914-1993 .... **CLC 1, 2, 7, 9, 40, 81, 97;**
DAM POP
See also CA 17-20R; 140; CANR 33;
DLB 6; MTCW; SATA 25;
SATA-Obit 76

Herzen, Aleksandr Ivanovich
1812-1870 .... **NCLC 10, 61**

Herzl, Theodor 1860-1904 .... **TCLC 36**

Herzog, Werner 1942- .... **CLC 16**
See also CA 89-92

Hesiod c. 8th cent. B.C.- .... **CMLC 5**
See also DLB 176

Hesse, Hermann
1877-1962 .... **CLC 1, 2, 3, 6, 11, 17, 25,**
69; DA; DAB; DAC; DAM MST, NOV;
SSC 9; WLC
See also CA 17-18; CAP 2; DLB 66;
MTCW; SATA 50

Hewes, Cady
See De Voto, Bernard (Augustine)

Heyen, William 1940- .... **CLC 13, 18**
See also CA 33-36R; CAAS 9; DLB 5

Heyerdahl, Thor 1914- .... **CLC 26**
See also CA 5-8R; CANR 5, 22; MTCW;
SATA 2, 52

Heym, Georg (Theodor Franz Arthur)
1887-1912 .... **TCLC 9**
See also CA 106

Heym, Stefan 1913- .... **CLC 41**
See also CA 9-12R; CANR 4; DLB 69

Heyse, Paul (Johann Ludwig von)
1830-1914 .... **TCLC 8**
See also CA 104; DLB 129

Heyward, (Edwin) DuBose
1885-1940 .... **TCLC 59**
See also CA 108; 157; DLB 7, 9, 45;
SATA 21

Hibbert, Eleanor Alice Burford
1906-1993 .... **CLC 7; DAM POP**
See also BEST 90:4; CA 17-20R; 140;
CANR 9, 28; SATA 2; SATA-Obit 74

Hichens, Robert S. 1864-1950 ..... **TCLC 64**
See also DLB 153

Higgins, George V(incent)
1939- .... **CLC 4, 7, 10, 18**
See also CA 77-80; CAAS 5; CANR 17, 51;
DLB 2; DLBY 81; INT CANR-17;
MTCW

Higginson, Thomas Wentworth
1823-1911 .... **TCLC 36**
See also DLB 1, 64

Highet, Helen
See MacInnes, Helen (Clark)

Highsmith, (Mary) Patricia
1921-1995 .... **CLC 2, 4, 14, 42;**
DAM NOV, POP
See also CA 1-4R; 147; CANR 1, 20, 48;
MTCW

Highwater, Jamake (Mamake)
1942(?)- .... **CLC 12**
See also AAYA 7; CA 65-68; CAAS 7;
CANR 10, 34; CLR 17; DLB 52;
DLBY 85; JRDA; MAICYA; SATA 32,
69; SATA-Brief 30

Highway, Tomson
1951- ..... **CLC 92; DAC; DAM MULT**
See also CA 151; NNAL

Higuchi, Ichiyo 1872-1896 ...... **NCLC 49**

Hijuelos, Oscar
1951- .... **CLC 65; DAM MULT, POP;**
HLC
See also BEST 90:1; CA 123; CANR 50;
DLB 145; HW

Hikmet, Nazim 1902(?)-1963 ...... **CLC 40**
See also CA 141; 93-96

Hildegard von Bingen
1098-1179 .... **CMLC 20**
See also DLB 148

Hildesheimer, Wolfgang
1916-1991 .... **CLC 49**
See also CA 101; 135; DLB 69, 124

Hill, Geoffrey (William)
1932- .... **CLC 5, 8, 18, 45; DAM POET**
See also CA 81-84; CANR 21;
CDBLB 1960 to Present; DLB 40;
MTCW

Hill, George Roy 1921- .... **CLC 26**
See also CA 110; 122

Hill, John
See Koontz, Dean R(ay)

Hill, Susan (Elizabeth)
1942- .. **CLC 4; DAB; DAM MST, NOV**
See also CA 33-36R; CANR 29; DLB 14,
139; MTCW

Hillerman, Tony
1925- .... **CLC 62; DAM POP**
See also AAYA 6; BEST 89:1; CA 29-32R;
CANR 21, 42; SATA 6

Hillesum, Etty 1914-1943 .... **TCLC 49**
See also CA 137

Hilliard, Noel (Harvey) 1929- ...... **CLC 15**
See also CA 9-12R; CANR 7

Hillis, Rick 1956- .... **CLC 66**
See also CA 134

Hilton, James 1900-1954 .... **TCLC 21**
See also CA 108; DLB 34, 77; SATA 34

Himes, Chester (Bomar)
1909-1984 .... **CLC 2, 4, 7, 18, 58; BLC;**
DAM MULT
See also BW 2; CA 25-28R; 114; CANR 22;
DLB 2, 76, 143; MTCW

Hinde, Thomas .... **CLC 6, 11**
See also Chitty, Thomas Willes

Hindin, Nathan
See Bloch, Robert (Albert)

Hine, (William) Daryl 1936- .... **CLC 15**
See also CA 1-4R; CAAS 15; CANR 1, 20;
DLB 60

Hinkson, Katharine Tynan
See Tynan, Katharine

Hinton, S(usan) E(loise)
1950- .... **CLC 30; DA; DAB; DAC;**
DAM MST, NOV
See also AAYA 2; CA 81-84; CANR 32;
CLR 3, 23; JRDA; MAICYA; MTCW;
SATA 19, 58

Hippius, Zinaida .... **TCLC 9**
See also Gippius, Zinaida (Nikolayevna)

Hiraoka, Kimitake 1925-1970
See Mishima, Yukio
See also CA 97-100; 29-32R; DAM DRAM;
MTCW

Hirsch, E(ric) D(onald), Jr. 1928- ... **CLC 79**
See also CA 25-28R; CANR 27, 51;
DLB 67; INT CANR-27; MTCW

Hirsch, Edward 1950- .... **CLC 31, 50**
See also CA 104; CANR 20, 42; DLB 120

Hitchcock, Alfred (Joseph)
1899-1980 .... **CLC 16**
See also CA 97-100; SATA 27;
SATA-Obit 24

Hitler, Adolf 1889-1945 .... **TCLC 53**
See also CA 117; 147

Hoagland, Edward 1932- .... **CLC 28**
See also CA 1-4R; CANR 2, 31, 57; DLB 6;
SATA 51

Hoban, Russell (Conwell)
1925- .... **CLC 7, 25; DAM NOV**
See also CA 5-8R; CANR 23, 37; CLR 3;
DLB 52; MAICYA; MTCW; SATA 1,
40, 78

Hobbes, Thomas 1588-1679 .... **LC 36**
See also DLB 151

Hobbs, Perry
See Blackmur, R(ichard) P(almer)

Hobson, Laura Z(ametkin)
1900-1986 .... **CLC 7, 25**
See also CA 17-20R; 118; CANR 55;
DLB 28; SATA 52

Hochhuth, Rolf
1931- ..... **CLC 4, 11, 18; DAM DRAM**
See also CA 5-8R; CANR 33; DLB 124;
MTCW

Hochman, Sandra 1936- .... **CLC 3, 8**
See also CA 5-8R; DLB 5

Hochwaelder, Fritz
1911-1986 ...... **CLC 36; DAM DRAM**
See also CA 29-32R; 120; CANR 42;
MTCW

Hochwalder, Fritz
See Hochwaelder, Fritz

Hocking, Mary (Eunice) 1921- ..... **CLC 13**
See also CA 101; CANR 18, 40

Hodgins, Jack 1938- .... **CLC 23**
See also CA 93-96; DLB 60

Hodgson, William Hope
1877(?)-1918 .... **TCLC 13**
See also CA 111; DLB 70, 153, 156, 178

Hoeg, Peter 1957- .... **CLC 95**
See also CA 151

Hoffman, Alice
1952- .... **CLC 51; DAM NOV**
See also CA 77-80; CANR 34; MTCW

Hoffman, Daniel (Gerard)
1923- .... **CLC 6, 13, 23**
See also CA 1-4R; CANR 4; DLB 5

Hoffman, Stanley 1944- .... **CLC 5**
See also CA 77-80

Hoffman, William M(oses) 1939- ... **CLC 40**
See also CA 57-60; CANR 11

Hoffmann, E(rnst) T(heodor) A(madeus)
1776-1822 .... **NCLC 2; SSC 13**
See also DLB 90; SATA 27

Hrabal, Bohumil 1914-1997..... **CLC 13, 67**
See also CA 106; 156; CAAS 12; CANR 57

Hsun, Lu
See Lu Hsun

Hubbard, L(afayette) Ron(ald)
1911-1986 .... **CLC 43; DAM POP**
See also CA 77-80; 118; CANR 52

Huch, Ricarda (Octavia)
1864-1947 .... **TCLC 13**
See also CA 111; DLB 66

Huddle, David 1942- .... **CLC 49**
See also CA 57-60; CAAS 20; DLB 130

Hudson, Jeffrey
See Crichton, (John) Michael

Hudson, W(illiam) H(enry)
1841-1922 .... **TCLC 29**
See also CA 115; DLB 98, 153, 174;
SATA 35

Hueffer, Ford Madox
See Ford, Ford Madox

Hughart, Barry 1934-............. **CLC 39**
See also CA 137

Hughes, Colin
See Creasey, John

Hughes, David (John) 1930- .... **CLC 48**
See also CA 116; 129; DLB 14

Hughes, Edward James
See Hughes, Ted
See also DAM MST, POET

Hughes, (James) Langston
1902-1967 ..... **CLC 1, 5, 10, 15, 35, 44;**
BLC; DA; DAB; DAC; DAM DRAM,
MST, MULT, POET; DC 3; PC 1;
SSC 6; WLC
See also AAYA 12; BW 1; CA 1-4R;
25-28R; CANR 1, 34; CDALB 1929-1941;
CLR 17; DLB 4, 7, 48, 51, 86; JRDA;
MAICYA; MTCW; SATA 4, 33

Hughes, Richard (Arthur Warren)
1900-1976 ..... **CLC 1, 11; DAM NOV**
See also CA 5-8R; 65-68; CANR 4;
DLB 15, 161; MTCW; SATA 8;
SATA-Obit 25

Hughes, Ted
1930- .... **CLC 2, 4, 9, 14, 37; DAB;**
DAC; PC 7
See also Hughes, Edward James
See also CA 1-4R; CANR 1, 33; CLR 3;
DLB 40, 161; MAICYA; MTCW;
SATA 49; SATA-Brief 27

Hugo, Richard F(ranklin)
1923-1982 .... **CLC 6, 18, 32;**
DAM POET
See also CA 49-52; 108; CANR 3; DLB 5

Hugo, Victor (Marie)
1802-1885 .... **NCLC 3, 10, 21; DA;**
DAB; DAC; DAM DRAM, MST, NOV,
POET; PC 17; WLC
See also DLB 119; SATA 47

Huidobro, Vicente
See Huidobro Fernandez, Vicente Garcia

Huidobro Fernandez, Vicente Garcia
1893-1948 .... **TCLC 31**
See also CA 131; HW

Hulme, Keri 1947- .... **CLC 39**
See also CA 125; INT 125

Hulme, T(homas) E(rnest)
1883-1917 .... **TCLC 21**
See also CA 117; DLB 19

Hume, David 1711-1776............. **LC 7**
See also DLB 104

Humphrey, William 1924-........ **CLC 45**
See also CA 77-80; DLB 6

Humphreys, Emyr Owen 1919-..... **CLC 47**
See also CA 5-8R; CANR 3, 24; DLB 15

Humphreys, Josephine 1945-.... **CLC 34, 57**
See also CA 121; 127; INT 127

Huneker, James Gibbons
1857-1921 .... **TCLC 65**
See also DLB 71

Hungerford, Pixie
See Brinsmead, H(esba) F(ay)

Hunt, E(verette) Howard, (Jr.)
1918- .... **CLC 3**
See also AITN 1; CA 45-48; CANR 2, 47

Hunt, Kyle
See Creasey, John

Hunt, (James Henry) Leigh
1784-1859 ...... **NCLC 1; DAM POET**

Hunt, Marsha 1946-.............. **CLC 70**
See also BW 2; CA 143

Hunt, Violet 1866-1942 .... **TCLC 53**
See also DLB 162

Hunter, E. Waldo
See Sturgeon, Theodore (Hamilton)

Hunter, Evan
1926- .... **CLC 11, 31; DAM POP**
See also CA 5-8R; CANR 5, 38; DLBY 82;
INT CANR-5; MTCW; SATA 25

Hunter, Kristin (Eggleston) 1931-... **CLC 35**
See also AITN 1; BW 1; CA 13-16R;
CANR 13; CLR 3; DLB 33;
INT CANR-13; MAICYA; SAAS 10;
SATA 12

Hunter, Mollie 1922-............. **CLC 21**
See also McIlwraith, Maureen Mollie
Hunter
See also AAYA 13; CANR 37; CLR 25;
DLB 161; JRDA; MAICYA; SAAS 7;
SATA 54

Hunter, Robert (?)-1734............. **LC 7**

Hurston, Zora Neale
1903-1960 .... **CLC 7, 30, 61; BLC; DA;**
DAC; DAM MST, MULT, NOV; SSC 4
See also AAYA 15; BW 1; CA 85-88;
DLB 51, 86; MTCW; YABC

Huston, John (Marcellus)
1906-1987 .... **CLC 20**
See also CA 73-76; 123; CANR 34; DLB 26

Hustvedt, Siri 1955-............... **CLC 76**
See also CA 137

Hutten, Ulrich von 1488-1523....... **LC 16**
See also DLB 179

Huxley, Aldous (Leonard)
1894-1963 ..... **CLC 1, 3, 4, 5, 8, 11, 18,**
35, 79; DA; DAB; DAC; DAM MST,
NOV; WLC
See also AAYA 11; CA 85-88; CANR 44;
CDBLB 1914-1945; DLB 36, 100, 162;
MTCW; SATA 63

Huysmans, Charles Marie Georges
1848-1907
See Huysmans, Joris-Karl
See also CA 104

Huysmans, Joris-Karl........... TCLC 7, 69
See also Huysmans, Charles Marie Georges
See also DLB 123

Hwang, David Henry
1957- .... **CLC 55; DAM DRAM; DC 4**
See also CA 127; 132; INT 132

Hyde, Anthony 1946-.............. **CLC 42**
See also CA 136

Hyde, Margaret O(ldroyd) 1917- ... **CLC 21**
See also CA 1-4R; CANR 1, 36; CLR 23;
JRDA; MAICYA; SAAS 8; SATA 1, 42,
76

Hynes, James 1956(?)-............ **CLC 65**

Ian, Janis 1951- .... **CLC 21**
See also CA 105

Ibanez, Vicente Blasco
See Blasco Ibanez, Vicente

Ibarguengoitia, Jorge 1928-1983.... **CLC 37**
See also CA 124; 113; HW

Ibsen, Henrik (Johan)
1828-1906 .... **TCLC 2, 8, 16, 37, 52;**
DA; DAB; DAC; DAM DRAM, MST;
DC 2; WLC
See also CA 104; 141

Ibuse Masuji 1898-1993.......... **CLC 22**
See also CA 127; 141; DLB 180

Ichikawa, Kon 1915-.............. **CLC 20**
See also CA 121

Idle, Eric 1943-.................. **CLC 21**
See also Monty Python
See also CA 116; CANR 35

Ignatow, David 1914-...... **CLC 4, 7, 14, 40**
See also CA 9-12R; CAAS 3; CANR 31, 57;
DLB 5

Ihimaera, Witi 1944- .... **CLC 46**
See also CA 77-80

Ilf, Ilya........................ TCLC 21
See also Fainzilberg, Ilya Arnoldovich

Illyes, Gyula 1902-1983............ **PC 16**
See also CA 114; 109

Immermann, Karl (Lebrecht)
1796-1840 .... **NCLC 4, 49**
See also DLB 133

Inchbald, Elizabeth 1753-1821 ... **NCLC 62**
See also DLB 39, 89

Inclan, Ramon (Maria) del Valle
See Valle-Inclan, Ramon (Maria) del

Infante, G(uillermo) Cabrera
See Cabrera Infante, G(uillermo)

Ingalls, Rachel (Holmes) 1940-..... **CLC 42**
See also CA 123; 127

Ingamells, Rex 1913-1955 .... **TCLC 35**

Inge, William (Motter)
1913-1973 .. **CLC 1, 8, 19; DAM DRAM**
See also CA 9-12R; CDALB 1941-1968;
DLB 7; MTCW

Ingelow, Jean 1820-1897 .... **NCLC 39**
See also DLB 35, 163; SATA 33

Ingram, Willis J.
See Harris, Mark

Jensen, Johannes V. 1873-1950.... **TCLC 41**

Jensen, Laura (Linnea) 1948- ...... **CLC 37**
See also CA 103

Jerome, Jerome K(lapka)
1859-1927 .... **TCLC 23**
See also CA 119; DLB 10, 34, 135

Jerrold, Douglas William
1803-1857 .... **NCLC 2**
See also DLB 158, 159

Jewett, (Theodora) Sarah Orne
1849-1909 .... **TCLC 1, 22; SSC 6**
See also CA 108; 127; DLB 12, 74;
SATA 15

Jewsbury, Geraldine (Endsor)
1812-1880 .... **NCLC 22**
See also DLB 21

Jhabvala, Ruth Prawer
1927- .... **CLC 4, 8, 29, 94; DAB;**
DAM NOV
See also CA 1-4R; CANR 2, 29, 51;
DLB 139; INT CANR-29; MTCW

Jibran, Kahlil
See Gibran, Kahlil

Jibran, Khalil
See Gibran, Kahlil

Jiles, Paulette 1943- .... **CLC 13, 58**
See also CA 101

Jimenez (Mantecon), Juan Ramon
1881-1958 ..... **TCLC 4; DAM MULT,**
POET; HLC; PC 7
See also CA 104; 131; DLB 134; HW;
MTCW

Jimenez, Ramon
See Jimenez (Mantecon), Juan Ramon

Jimenez Mantecon, Juan
See Jimenez (Mantecon), Juan Ramon

Joel, Billy .... **CLC 26**
See also Joel, William Martin

Joel, William Martin 1949-
See Joel, Billy
See also CA 108

John of the Cross, St. 1542-1591 .... **LC 18**

Johnson, B(ryan) S(tanley William)
1933-1973 .... **CLC 6, 9**
See also CA 9-12R; 53-56; CANR 9;
DLB 14, 40

Johnson, Benj. F. of Boo
See Riley, James Whitcomb

Johnson, Benjamin F. of Boo
See Riley, James Whitcomb

Johnson, Charles (Richard)
1948- .... **CLC 7, 51, 65; BLC;**
DAM MULT
See also BW 2; CA 116; CAAS 18;
CANR 42; DLB 33

Johnson, Denis 1949- .... **CLC 52**
See also CA 117; 121; DLB 120

Johnson, Diane 1934- .... **CLC 5, 13, 48**
See also CA 41-44R; CANR 17, 40;
DLBY 80; INT CANR-17; MTCW

Johnson, Eyvind (Olof Verner)
1900-1976 .... **CLC 14**
See also CA 73-76; 69-72; CANR 34

Johnson, J. R.
See James, C(yril) L(ionel) R(obert)

Johnson, James Weldon
1871-1938 .... **TCLC 3, 19; BLC;**
DAM MULT, POET
See also BW 1; CA 104; 125;
CDALB 1917-1929; CLR 32; DLB 51;
MTCW; SATA 31

Johnson, Joyce 1935-............. **CLC 58**
See also CA 125; 129

Johnson, Lionel (Pigot)
1867-1902 .... **TCLC 19**
See also CA 117; DLB 19

Johnson, Mel
See Malzberg, Barry N(athaniel)

Johnson, Pamela Hansford
1912-1981 .... **CLC 1, 7, 27**
See also CA 1-4R; 104; CANR 2, 28;
DLB 15; MTCW

Johnson, Robert 1911(?)-1938..... **TCLC 69**

Johnson, Samuel
1709-1784 ..... **LC 15; DA; DAB; DAC;**
DAM MST; WLC
See also CDBLB 1660-1789; DLB 39, 95,
104, 142

Johnson, Uwe
1934-1984 .... **CLC 5, 10, 15, 40**
See also CA 1-4R; 112; CANR 1, 39;
DLB 75; MTCW

Johnston, George (Benson) 1913- ... **CLC 51**
See also CA 1-4R; CANR 5, 20; DLB 88

Johnston, Jennifer 1930- .... **CLC 7**
See also CA 85-88; DLB 14

Jolley, (Monica) Elizabeth
1923- .... **CLC 46; SSC 19**
See also CA 127; CAAS 13

Jones, Arthur Llewellyn 1863-1947
See Machen, Arthur
See also CA 104

Jones, D(ouglas) G(ordon) 1929-.... **CLC 10**
See also CA 29-32R; CANR 13; DLB 53

Jones, David (Michael)
1895-1974 .... **CLC 2, 4, 7, 13, 42**
See also CA 9-12R; 53-56; CANR 28;
CDBLB 1945-1960; DLB 20, 100; MTCW

Jones, David Robert 1947-
See Bowie, David
See also CA 103

Jones, Diana Wynne 1934- .... **CLC 26**
See also AAYA 12; CA 49-52; CANR 4,
26, 56; CLR 23; DLB 161; JRDA;
MAICYA; SAAS 7; SATA 9, 70

Jones, Edward P. 1950-........... **CLC 76**
See also BW 2; CA 142

Jones, Gayl
1949- .... **CLC 6, 9; BLC; DAM MULT**
See also BW 2; CA 77-80; CANR 27;
DLB 33; MTCW

Jones, James 1921-1977.... **CLC 1, 3, 10, 39**
See also AITN 1, 2; CA 1-4R; 69-72;
CANR 6; DLB 2, 143; MTCW

Jones, John J.
See Lovecraft, H(oward) P(hillips)

Jones, LeRoi .... **CLC 1, 2, 3, 5, 10, 14**
See also Baraka, Amiri

Jones, Louis B. .... **CLC 65**
See also CA 141

Jones, Madison (Percy, Jr.) 1925- ... **CLC 4**
See also CA 13-16R; CAAS 11; CANR 7,
54; DLB 152

Jones, Mervyn 1922- .... **CLC 10, 52**
See also CA 45-48; CAAS 5; CANR 1;
MTCW

Jones, Mick 1956(?)- .... **CLC 30**

Jones, Nettie (Pearl) 1941- .... **CLC 34**
See also BW 2; CA 137; CAAS 20

Jones, Preston 1936-1979 .... **CLC 10**
See also CA 73-76; 89-92; DLB 7

Jones, Robert F(rancis) 1934-....... **CLC 7**
See also CA 49-52; CANR 2

Jones, Rod 1953- .... **CLC 50**
See also CA 128

Jones, Terence Graham Parry
1942- .... **CLC 21**
See also Jones, Terry; Monty Python
See also CA 112; 116; CANR 35; INT 116

Jones, Terry
See Jones, Terence Graham Parry
See also SATA 67; SATA-Brief 51

Jones, Thom 1945(?)- .... **CLC 81**
See also CA 157

Jong, Erica
1942- .... **CLC 4, 6, 8, 18, 83;**
DAM NOV, POP
See also AITN 1; BEST 90:2; CA 73-76;
CANR 26, 52; DLB 2, 5, 28, 152;
INT CANR-26; MTCW

Jonson, Ben(jamin)
1572(?)-1637 ...... **LC 6, 33; DA; DAB;**
DAC; DAM DRAM, MST, POET;
DC 4; PC 17; WLC
See also CDBLB Before 1660; DLB 62, 121

Jordan, June
1936- ..... **CLC 5, 11, 23; DAM MULT,**
POET
See also AAYA 2; BW 2; CA 33-36R;
CANR 25; CLR 10; DLB 38; MAICYA;
MTCW; SATA 4

Jordan, Pat(rick M.) 1941- .... **CLC 37**
See also CA 33-36R

Jorgensen, Ivar
See Ellison, Harlan (Jay)

Jorgenson, Ivar
See Silverberg, Robert

Josephus, Flavius c. 37-100 ...... **CMLC 13**

Josipovici, Gabriel 1940- .... **CLC 6, 43**
See also CA 37-40R; CAAS 8; CANR 47;
DLB 14

Joubert, Joseph 1754-1824 .... **NCLC 9**

Jouve, Pierre Jean 1887-1976...... **CLC 47**
See also CA 65-68

Joyce, James (Augustine Aloysius)
1882-1941 .... **TCLC 3, 8, 16, 35, 52;**
DA; DAB; DAC; DAM MST, NOV,
POET; SSC 26; WLC
See also CA 104; 126; CDBLB 1914-1945;
DLB 10, 19, 36, 162; MTCW

Jozsef, Attila 1905-1937.......... **TCLC 22**
See also CA 116

Juana Ines de la Cruz 1651(?)-1695 ... **LC 5**

Judd, Cyril
See Kornbluth, C(yril) M.; Pohl, Frederik

Kennedy, Adrienne (Lita)
1931- . . . . . **CLC 66; BLC; DAM MULT;**
DC 5
See also BW 2; CA 103; CAAS 20; CABS 3;
CANR 26, 53; DLB 38

Kennedy, John Pendleton
1795-1870 . . . . **NCLC 2**
See also DLB 3

Kennedy, Joseph Charles   1929-
See Kennedy, X. J.
See also CA 1-4R; CANR 4, 30, 40;
SATA 14, 86

Kennedy, William
1928- . . . **CLC 6, 28, 34, 53; DAM NOV**
See also AAYA 1; CA 85-88; CANR 14,
31; DLB 143; DLBY 85; INT CANR-31;
MTCW; SATA 57

Kennedy, X. J. . . . . **CLC 8, 42**
See also Kennedy, Joseph Charles
See also CAAS 9; CLR 27; DLB 5;
SAAS 22

Kenny, Maurice (Francis)
1929- . . . . **CLC 87; DAM MULT**
See also CA 144; CAAS 22; DLB 175;
NNAL

Kent, Kelvin
See Kuttner, Henry

Kenton, Maxwell
See Southern, Terry

Kenyon, Robert O.
See Kuttner, Henry

Kerouac, Jack . . . . . **CLC 1, 2, 3, 5, 14, 29, 61**
See also Kerouac, Jean-Louis Lebris de
See also CDALB 1941-1968; DLB 2, 16;
DLBD 3; DLBY 95

Kerouac, Jean-Louis Lebris de   1922-1969
See Kerouac, Jack
See also AITN 1; CA 5-8R; 25-28R;
CANR 26, 54; DA; DAB; DAC;
DAM MST, NOV, POET, POP; MTCW;
WLC

Kerr, Jean   1923- . . . . **CLC 22**
See also CA 5-8R; CANR 7; INT CANR-7

Kerr, M. E. . . . . **CLC 12, 35**
See also Meaker, Marijane (Agnes)
See also AAYA 2; CLR 29; SAAS 1

Kerr, Robert . . . . **CLC 55**

Kerrigan, (Thomas) Anthony
1918- . . . . **CLC 4, 6**
See also CA 49-52; CAAS 11; CANR 4

Kerry, Lois
See Duncan, Lois

Kesey, Ken (Elton)
1935- . . . . . . **CLC 1, 3, 6, 11, 46, 64; DA;**
DAB; DAC; DAM MST, NOV, POP;
WLC
See also CA 1-4R; CANR 22, 38;
CDALB 1968-1988; DLB 2, 16; MTCW;
SATA 66

Kesselring, Joseph (Otto)
1902-1967 . . . . . **CLC 45; DAM DRAM,**
MST
See also CA 150

Kessler, Jascha (Frederick)   1929- . . . . **CLC 4**
See also CA 17-20R; CANR 8, 48

Kettelkamp, Larry (Dale)   1933- . . . . **CLC 12**
See also CA 29-32R; CANR 16; SAAS 3;
SATA 2

Key, Ellen   1849-1926 . . . . **TCLC 65**

Keyber, Conny
See Fielding, Henry

Keyes, Daniel
1927- . . . . **CLC 80; DA; DAC;**
DAM MST, NOV
See also CA 17-20R; CANR 10, 26, 54;
SATA 37

Keynes, John Maynard
1883-1946 . . . . **TCLC 64**
See also CA 114; DLBD 10

Khanshendel, Chiron
See Rose, Wendy

Khayyam, Omar
1048-1131 . . . . **CMLC 11; DAM POET;**
PC 8

Kherdian, David   1931- . . . . **CLC 6, 9**
See also CA 21-24R; CAAS 2; CANR 39;
CLR 24; JRDA; MAICYA; SATA 16, 74

Khlebnikov, Velimir . . . . **TCLC 20**
See also Khlebnikov, Viktor Vladimirovich

Khlebnikov, Viktor Vladimirovich   1885-1922
See Khlebnikov, Velimir
See also CA 117

Khodasevich, Vladislav (Felitsianovich)
1886-1939 . . . . **TCLC 15**
See also CA 115

Kielland, Alexander Lange
1849-1906 . . . . **TCLC 5**
See also CA 104

Kiely, Benedict   1919- . . . . **CLC 23, 43**
See also CA 1-4R; CANR 2; DLB 15

Kienzle, William X(avier)
1928- . . . . **CLC 25; DAM POP**
See also CA 93-96; CAAS 1; CANR 9, 31;
INT CANR-31; MTCW

Kierkegaard, Soren   1813-1855 . . . . **NCLC 34**

Killens, John Oliver   1916-1987 . . . . . **CLC 10**
See also BW 2; CA 77-80; 123; CAAS 2;
CANR 26; DLB 33

Killigrew, Anne   1660-1685 . . . . **LC 4**
See also DLB 131

Kim
See Simenon, Georges (Jacques Christian)

Kincaid, Jamaica
1949- . . . . **CLC 43, 68; BLC;**
DAM MULT, NOV
See also AAYA 13; BW 2; CA 125;
CANR 47; DLB 157

King, Francis (Henry)
1923- . . . . **CLC 8, 53; DAM NOV**
See also CA 1-4R; CANR 1, 33; DLB 15,
139; MTCW

King, Martin Luther, Jr.
1929-1968 . . . . **CLC 83; BLC; DA; DAB;**
DAC; DAM MST, MULT
See also BW 2; CA 25-28; CANR 27, 44;
CAP 2; MTCW; SATA 14; YABC

King, Stephen (Edwin)
1947- . . . . **CLC 12, 26, 37, 61;**
DAM NOV, POP; SSC 17
See also AAYA 1, 17; BEST 90:1;
CA 61-64; CANR 1, 30, 52; DLB 143;
DLBY 80; JRDA; MTCW; SATA 9, 55

King, Steve
See King, Stephen (Edwin)

King, Thomas
1943- . . . . . **CLC 89; DAC; DAM MULT**
See also CA 144; DLB 175; NNAL

Kingman, Lee . . . . **CLC 17**
See also Natti, (Mary) Lee
See also SAAS 3; SATA 1, 67

Kingsley, Charles   1819-1875 . . . . . **NCLC 35**
See also DLB 21, 32, 163; 2

Kingsley, Sidney   1906-1995 . . . . **CLC 44**
See also CA 85-88; 147; DLB 7

Kingsolver, Barbara
1955- . . . . **CLC 55, 81; DAM POP**
See also AAYA 15; CA 129; 134; INT 134

Kingston, Maxine (Ting Ting) Hong
1940- . . . . **CLC 12, 19, 58; DAM MULT,**
NOV
See also AAYA 8; CA 69-72; CANR 13,
38; DLB 173; DLBY 80; INT CANR-13;
MTCW; SATA 53; YABC

Kinnell, Galway
1927- . . . . **CLC 1, 2, 3, 5, 13, 29**
See also CA 9-12R; CANR 10, 34; DLB 5;
DLBY 87; INT CANR-34; MTCW

Kinsella, Thomas   1928- . . . . **CLC 4, 19**
See also CA 17-20R; CANR 15; DLB 27;
MTCW

Kinsella, W(illiam) P(atrick)
1935- . . . . **CLC 27, 43; DAC;**
DAM NOV, POP
See also AAYA 7; CA 97-100; CAAS 7;
CANR 21, 35; INT CANR-21; MTCW

Kipling, (Joseph) Rudyard
1865-1936 . . . . . . **TCLC 8, 17; DA; DAB;**
DAC; DAM MST, POET; PC 3; SSC 5;
WLC
See also CA 105; 120; CANR 33;
CDBLB 1890-1914; CLR 39; DLB 19, 34,
141, 156; MAICYA; MTCW; 2

Kirkup, James   1918- . . . . **CLC 1**
See also CA 1-4R; CAAS 4; CANR 2;
DLB 27; SATA 12

Kirkwood, James   1930(?)-1989 . . . . . . **CLC 9**
See also AITN 2; CA 1-4R; 128; CANR 6,
40

Kirshner, Sidney
See Kingsley, Sidney

Kis, Danilo   1935-1989 . . . . **CLC 57**
See also CA 109; 118; 129; MTCW

Kivi, Aleksis   1834-1872 . . . . **NCLC 30**

Kizer, Carolyn (Ashley)
1925- . . . . . **CLC 15, 39, 80; DAM POET**
See also CA 65-68; CAAS 5; CANR 24;
DLB 5, 169

Klabund   1890-1928 . . . . **TCLC 44**
See also DLB 66

Klappert, Peter   1942- . . . . **CLC 57**
See also CA 33-36R; DLB 5

Klein, A(braham) M(oses)
1909-1972 . . . . **CLC 19; DAB; DAC;**
DAM MST
See also CA 101; 37-40R; DLB 68

Klein, Norma 1938-1989 . . . . **CLC 30**
See also AAYA 2; CA 41-44R; 128;
CANR 15, 37; CLR 2, 19;
INT CANR-15; JRDA; MAICYA;
SAAS 1; SATA 7, 57

Klein, T(heodore) E(ibon) D(onald)
1947- . . . . **CLC 34**
See also CA 119; CANR 44

Kleist, Heinrich von
1777-1811 . . . . **NCLC 2, 37;**
DAM DRAM; SSC 22
See also DLB 90

Klima, Ivan 1931- . . . . . **CLC 56; DAM NOV**
See also CA 25-28R; CANR 17, 50

Klimentov, Andrei Platonovich 1899-1951
See Platonov, Andrei
See also CA 108

Klinger, Friedrich Maximilian von
1752-1831 . . . . **NCLC 1**
See also DLB 94

Klopstock, Friedrich Gottlieb
1724-1803 . . . . **NCLC 11**
See also DLB 97

Knapp, Caroline 1959- . . . . **CLC 99**
See also CA 154

Knebel, Fletcher 1911-1993 . . . . **CLC 14**
See also AITN 1; CA 1-4R; 140; CAAS 3;
CANR 1, 36; SATA 36; SATA-Obit 75

Knickerbocker, Diedrich
See Irving, Washington

Knight, Etheridge
1931-1991 . . . . **CLC 40; BLC;**
DAM POET; PC 14
See also BW 1; CA 21-24R; 133; CANR 23;
DLB 41

Knight, Sarah Kemble 1666-1727 . . . . . **LC 7**
See also DLB 24

Knister, Raymond 1899-1932 . . . . . . **TCLC 56**
See also DLB 68

Knowles, John
1926- . . . . . . **CLC 1, 4, 10, 26; DA; DAC;**
DAM MST, NOV
See also AAYA 10; CA 17-20R; CANR 40;
CDALB 1968-1988; DLB 6; MTCW;
SATA 8, 89

Knox, Calvin M.
See Silverberg, Robert

Knox, John c. 1505-1572 . . . . **LC 37**
See also DLB 132

Knye, Cassandra
See Disch, Thomas M(ichael)

Koch, C(hristopher) J(ohn) 1932- . . . **CLC 42**
See also CA 127

Koch, Christopher
See Koch, C(hristopher) J(ohn)

Koch, Kenneth
1925- . . . . **CLC 5, 8, 44; DAM POET**
See also CA 1-4R; CANR 6, 36, 57; DLB 5;
INT CANR-36; SATA 65

Kochanowski, Jan 1530-1584 . . . . **LC 10**

Kock, Charles Paul de
1794-1871 . . . . **NCLC 16**

Koda Shigeyuki 1867-1947
See Rohan, Koda
See also CA 121

Koestler, Arthur
1905-1983 . . . . **CLC 1, 3, 6, 8, 15, 33**
See also CA 1-4R; 109; CANR 1, 33;
CDBLB 1945-1960; DLBY 83; MTCW

Kogawa, Joy Nozomi
1935- . . . . . . **CLC 78; DAC; DAM MST,**
MULT
See also CA 101; CANR 19

Kohout, Pavel 1928- . . . . **CLC 13**
See also CA 45-48; CANR 3

Koizumi, Yakumo
See Hearn, (Patricio) Lafcadio (Tessima
Carlos)

Kolmar, Gertrud 1894-1943 . . . . . . **TCLC 40**

Komunyakaa, Yusef 1947- . . . . . . **CLC 86, 94**
See also CA 147; DLB 120

Konrad, George
See Konrad, Gyoergy

Konrad, Gyoergy 1933- . . . . . . **CLC 4, 10, 73**
See also CA 85-88

Konwicki, Tadeusz 1926- . . . . . **CLC 8, 28, 54**
See also CA 101; CAAS 9; CANR 39;
MTCW

Koontz, Dean R(ay)
1945- . . . . . . **CLC 78; DAM NOV, POP**
See also AAYA 9; BEST 89:3, 90:2;
CA 108; CANR 19, 36, 52; MTCW;
SATA 92

Kopit, Arthur (Lee)
1937- . . . . . **CLC 1, 18, 33; DAM DRAM**
See also AITN 1; CA 81-84; CABS 3;
DLB 7; MTCW

Kops, Bernard 1926- . . . . **CLC 4**
See also CA 5-8R; DLB 13

Kornbluth, C(yril) M. 1923-1958 . . . . **TCLC 8**
See also CA 105; DLB 8

Korolenko, V. G.
See Korolenko, Vladimir Galaktionovich

Korolenko, Vladimir
See Korolenko, Vladimir Galaktionovich

Korolenko, Vladimir G.
See Korolenko, Vladimir Galaktionovich

Korolenko, Vladimir Galaktionovich
1853-1921 . . . . **TCLC 22**
See also CA 121

Korzybski, Alfred (Habdank Skarbek)
1879-1950 . . . . **TCLC 61**
See also CA 123

Kosinski, Jerzy (Nikodem)
1933-1991 . . . . **CLC 1, 2, 3, 6, 10, 15, 53,**
70; DAM NOV
See also CA 17-20R; 134; CANR 9, 46;
DLB 2; DLBY 82; MTCW

Kostelanetz, Richard (Cory) 1940- . . **CLC 28**
See also CA 13-16R; CAAS 8; CANR 38

Kostrowitzki, Wilhelm Apollinaris de
1880-1918
See Apollinaire, Guillaume
See also CA 104

Kotlowitz, Robert 1924- . . . . **CLC 4**
See also CA 33-36R; CANR 36

Kotzebue, August (Friedrich Ferdinand) von
1761-1819 . . . . **NCLC 25**
See also DLB 94

Kotzwinkle, William 1938- . . . **CLC 5, 14, 35**
See also CA 45-48; CANR 3, 44; CLR 6;
DLB 173; MAICYA; SATA 24, 70

Kowna, Stancy
See Szymborska, Wislawa

Kozol, Jonathan 1936- . . . . **CLC 17**
See also CA 61-64; CANR 16, 45

Kozoll, Michael 1940(?)- . . . . **CLC 35**

Kramer, Kathryn 19(?)- . . . . **CLC 34**

Kramer, Larry 1935- . . **CLC 42; DAM POP**
See also CA 124; 126

Krasicki, Ignacy 1735-1801 . . . . **NCLC 8**

Krasinski, Zygmunt 1812-1859 . . . . **NCLC 4**

Kraus, Karl 1874-1936 . . . . **TCLC 5**
See also CA 104; DLB 118

Kreve (Mickevicius), Vincas
1882-1954 . . . . **TCLC 27**

Kristeva, Julia 1941- . . . . **CLC 77**
See also CA 154

Kristofferson, Kris 1936- . . . . **CLC 26**
See also CA 104

Krizanc, John 1956- . . . . **CLC 57**

Krleza, Miroslav 1893-1981 . . . . **CLC 8**
See also CA 97-100; 105; CANR 50;
DLB 147

Kroetsch, Robert
1927- . . . . **CLC 5, 23, 57; DAC;**
DAM POET
See also CA 17-20R; CANR 8, 38; DLB 53;
MTCW

Kroetz, Franz
See Kroetz, Franz Xaver

Kroetz, Franz Xaver 1946- . . . . **CLC 41**
See also CA 130

Kroker, Arthur 1945- . . . . **CLC 77**

Kropotkin, Peter (Aleksieevich)
1842-1921 . . . . **TCLC 36**
See also CA 119

Krotkov, Yuri 1917- . . . . **CLC 19**
See also CA 102

Krumb
See Crumb, R(obert)

Krumgold, Joseph (Quincy)
1908-1980 . . . . **CLC 12**
See also CA 9-12R; 101; CANR 7;
MAICYA; SATA 1, 48; SATA-Obit 23

Krumwitz
See Crumb, R(obert)

Krutch, Joseph Wood 1893-1970 . . . . **CLC 24**
See also CA 1-4R; 25-28R; CANR 4;
DLB 63

Krutzch, Gus
See Eliot, T(homas) S(tearns)

Krylov, Ivan Andreevich
1768(?)-1844 . . . . **NCLC 1**
See also DLB 150

Kubin, Alfred (Leopold Isidor)
    1877-1959 . . . . **TCLC 23**
    See also CA 112; 149; DLB 81

Kubrick, Stanley 1928- . . . . **CLC 16**
    See also CA 81-84; CANR 33; DLB 26

Kumin, Maxine (Winokur)
    1925- . . . . . **CLC 5, 13, 28; DAM POET;**
                       PC 15
    See also AITN 2; CA 1-4R; CAAS 8;
      CANR 1, 21; DLB 5; MTCW; SATA 12

Kundera, Milan
    1929- . . . . **CLC 4, 9, 19, 32, 68;**
                 DAM NOV; SSC 24
    See also AAYA 2; CA 85-88; CANR 19,
      52; MTCW

Kunene, Mazisi (Raymond) 1930- . . . **CLC 85**
    See also BW 1; CA 125; DLB 117

Kunitz, Stanley (Jasspon)
    1905- . . . . **CLC 6, 11, 14; PC 19**
    See also CA 41-44R; CANR 26, 57;
      DLB 48; INT CANR-26; MTCW

Kunze, Reiner 1933- . . . . **CLC 10**
    See also CA 93-96; DLB 75

Kuprin, Aleksandr Ivanovich
    1870-1938 . . . . **TCLC 5**
    See also CA 104

Kureishi, Hanif 1954(?)- . . . . **CLC 64**
    See also CA 139

Kurosawa, Akira
    1910- . . . . **CLC 16; DAM MULT**
    See also AAYA 11; CA 101; CANR 46

Kushner, Tony
    1957(?)- . . . . **CLC 81; DAM DRAM**
    See also CA 144

Kuttner, Henry 1915-1958 . . . . **TCLC 10**
    See also Vance, Jack
    See also CA 107; 157; DLB 8

Kuzma, Greg 1944- . . . . **CLC 7**
    See also CA 33-36R

Kuzmin, Mikhail 1872(?)-1936 . . . . **TCLC 40**

Kyd, Thomas
    1558-1594 . . . . **LC 22; DAM DRAM;**
                            DC 3
    See also DLB 62

Kyprianos, Iossif
    See Samarakis, Antonis

La Bruyere, Jean de 1645-1696 . . . . . . **LC 17**

Lacan, Jacques (Marie Emile)
    1901-1981 . . . . **CLC 75**
    See also CA 121; 104

**Laclos, Pierre Ambroise Francois Choderlos
    de** 1741-1803 . . . . **NCLC 4**

Lacolere, Francois
    See Aragon, Louis

La Colere, Francois
    See Aragon, Louis

La Deshabilleuse
    See Simenon, Georges (Jacques Christian)

Lady Gregory
    See Gregory, Isabella Augusta (Persse)

Lady of Quality, A
    See Bagnold, Enid

**La Fayette, Marie (Madelaine Pioche de la
    Vergne Comtes** 1634-1693 . . . . **LC 2**

Lafayette, Rene
    See Hubbard, L(afayette) Ron(ald)

Laforgue, Jules
    1860-1887 . . . . **NCLC 5, 53; PC 14;**
                          SSC 20

Lagerkvist, Paer (Fabian)
    1891-1974 . . . . **CLC 7, 10, 13, 54;**
                  DAM DRAM, NOV
    See also Lagerkvist, Par
    See also CA 85-88; 49-52; MTCW

Lagerkvist, Par . . . . **SSC 12**
    See also Lagerkvist, Paer (Fabian)

Lagerloef, Selma (Ottiliana Lovisa)
    1858-1940 . . . . **TCLC 4, 36**
    See also Lagerlof, Selma (Ottiliana Lovisa)
    See also CA 108; SATA 15

Lagerlof, Selma (Ottiliana Lovisa)
    See Lagerloef, Selma (Ottiliana Lovisa)
    See also CLR 7; SATA 15

La Guma, (Justin) Alex(ander)
    1925-1985 . . . . **CLC 19; DAM NOV**
    See also BW 1; CA 49-52; 118; CANR 25;
      DLB 117; MTCW

Laidlaw, A. K.
    See Grieve, C(hristopher) M(urray)

Lainez, Manuel Mujica
    See Mujica Lainez, Manuel
    See also HW

Laing, R(onald) D(avid)
    1927-1989 . . . . **CLC 95**
    See also CA 107; 129; CANR 34; MTCW

Lamartine, Alphonse (Marie Louis Prat) de
    1790-1869 . . . . . **NCLC 11; DAM POET;**
                         PC 16

Lamb, Charles
    1775-1834 . . . . . . **NCLC 10; DA; DAB;**
               DAC; DAM MST; WLC
    See also CDBLB 1789-1832; DLB 93, 107,
      163; SATA 17

Lamb, Lady Caroline 1785-1828 . . **NCLC 38**
    See also DLB 116

Lamming, George (William)
    1927- . . . . **CLC 2, 4, 66; BLC;**
                    DAM MULT
    See also BW 2; CA 85-88; CANR 26;
      DLB 125; MTCW

L'Amour, Louis (Dearborn)
    1908-1988 . . . . **CLC 25, 55; DAM NOV,**
                       POP
    See also AAYA 16; AITN 2; BEST 89:2;
      CA 1-4R; 125; CANR 3, 25, 40;
      DLBY 80; MTCW

Lampedusa, Giuseppe (Tomasi) di
    1896-1957 . . . . **TCLC 13**
    See also Tomasi di Lampedusa, Giuseppe
    See also DLB 177

Lampman, Archibald 1861-1899 . . **NCLC 25**
    See also DLB 92

Lancaster, Bruce 1896-1963 . . . . **CLC 36**
    See also CA 9-10; CAP 1; SATA 9

Lanchester, John . . . . **CLC 99**

Landau, Mark Alexandrovich
    See Aldanov, Mark (Alexandrovich)

Landau-Aldanov, Mark Alexandrovich
    See Aldanov, Mark (Alexandrovich)

Landis, Jerry
    See Simon, Paul (Frederick)

Landis, John 1950- . . . . **CLC 26**
    See also CA 112; 122

Landolfi, Tommaso 1908-1979 . . . **CLC 11, 49**
    See also CA 127; 117; DLB 177

Landon, Letitia Elizabeth
    1802-1838 . . . . **NCLC 15**
    See also DLB 96

Landor, Walter Savage
    1775-1864 . . . . **NCLC 14**
    See also DLB 93, 107

Landwirth, Heinz 1927-
    See Lind, Jakov
    See also CA 9-12R; CANR 7

Lane, Patrick
    1939- . . . . **CLC 25; DAM POET**
    See also CA 97-100; CANR 54; DLB 53;
      INT 97-100

Lang, Andrew 1844-1912 . . . . **TCLC 16**
    See also CA 114; 137; DLB 98, 141;
      MAICYA; SATA 16

Lang, Fritz 1890-1976 . . . . **CLC 20**
    See also CA 77-80; 69-72; CANR 30

Lange, John
    See Crichton, (John) Michael

Langer, Elinor 1939- . . . . **CLC 34**
    See also CA 121

Langland, William
    1330(?)-1400(?) . . . . . . **LC 19; DA; DAB;**
                DAC; DAM MST, POET
    See also DLB 146

Langstaff, Launcelot
    See Irving, Washington

Lanier, Sidney
    1842-1881 . . . . . . **NCLC 6; DAM POET**
    See also DLB 64; DLBD 13; MAICYA;
      SATA 18

Lanyer, Aemilia 1569-1645 . . . . . . **LC 10, 30**
    See also DLB 121

Lao Tzu . . . . **CMLC 7**

Lapine, James (Elliot) 1949- . . . . **CLC 39**
    See also CA 123; 130; CANR 54; INT 130

Larbaud, Valery (Nicolas)
    1881-1957 . . . . **TCLC 9**
    See also CA 106; 152

Lardner, Ring
    See Lardner, Ring(gold) W(ilmer)

Lardner, Ring W., Jr.
    See Lardner, Ring(gold) W(ilmer)

Lardner, Ring(gold) W(ilmer)
    1885-1933 . . . . **TCLC 2, 14**
    See also CA 104; 131; CDALB 1917-1929;
      DLB 11, 25, 86; MTCW

Laredo, Betty
    See Codrescu, Andrei

Larkin, Maia
    See Wojciechowska, Maia (Teresa)

Larkin, Philip (Arthur)
    1922-1985 . . . . **CLC 3, 5, 8, 9, 13, 18, 33,**
              39, 64; DAB; DAM MST, POET
    See also CA 5-8R; 117; CANR 24;
      CDBLB 1960 to Present; DLB 27;
      MTCW

Leger, (Marie-Rene Auguste) Alexis
Saint-Leger
1887-1975 . . . . . . CLC 11; DAM POET
See also Perse, St.-John
See also CA 13-16R; 61-64; CANR 43;
MTCW

Leger, Saintleger
See Leger, (Marie-Rene Auguste) Alexis
Saint-Leger

Le Guin, Ursula K(roeber)
1929- . . . . . . CLC 8, 13, 22, 45, 71; DAB;
DAC; DAM MST, POP; SSC 12
See also AAYA 9; AITN 1; CA 21-24R;
CANR 9, 32, 52; CDALB 1968-1988;
CLR 3, 28; DLB 8, 52; INT CANR-32;
JRDA; MAICYA; MTCW; SATA 4, 52

Lehmann, Rosamond (Nina)
1901-1990 . . . . CLC 5
See also CA 77-80; 131; CANR 8; DLB 15

Leiber, Fritz (Reuter, Jr.)
1910-1992 . . . . CLC 25
See also CA 45-48; 139; CANR 2, 40;
DLB 8; MTCW; SATA 45;
SATA-Obit 73

Leibniz, Gottfried Wilhelm von
1646-1716 . . . . LC 35
See also DLB 168

Leimbach, Martha 1963-
See Leimbach, Marti
See also CA 130

Leimbach, Marti . . . . CLC 65
See also Leimbach, Martha

Leino, Eino . . . . TCLC 24
See also Loennbohm, Armas Eino Leopold

Leiris, Michel (Julien) 1901-1990 . . . CLC 61
See also CA 119; 128; 132

Leithauser, Brad 1953- . . . . CLC 27
See also CA 107; CANR 27; DLB 120

Lelchuk, Alan 1938- . . . . CLC 5
See also CA 45-48; CAAS 20; CANR 1

Lem, Stanislaw 1921- . . . . CLC 8, 15, 40
See also CA 105; CAAS 1; CANR 32;
MTCW

Lemann, Nancy 1956- . . . . CLC 39
See also CA 118; 136

Lemonnier, (Antoine Louis) Camille
1844-1913 . . . . TCLC 22
See also CA 121

Lenau, Nikolaus 1802-1850 . . . . . . NCLC 16

L'Engle, Madeleine (Camp Franklin)
1918- . . . . CLC 12; DAM POP
See also AAYA 1; AITN 2; CA 1-4R;
CANR 3, 21, 39; CLR 1, 14; DLB 52;
JRDA; MAICYA; MTCW; SAAS 15;
SATA 1, 27, 75

Lengyel, Jozsef 1896-1975 . . . . CLC 7
See also CA 85-88; 57-60

Lenin 1870-1924
See Lenin, V. I.
See also CA 121

Lenin, V. I. TCLC 67
See also Lenin

Lennon, John (Ono)
1940-1980 . . . . CLC 12, 35
See also CA 102

Lennox, Charlotte Ramsay
1729(?)-1804 . . . . NCLC 23
See also DLB 39

Lentricchia, Frank (Jr.) 1940- . . . . . . CLC 34
See also CA 25-28R; CANR 19

Lenz, Siegfried 1926- . . . . CLC 27
See also CA 89-92; DLB 75

Leonard, Elmore (John, Jr.)
1925- . . . . . . CLC 28, 34, 71; DAM POP
See also AITN 1; BEST 89:1, 90:4;
CA 81-84; CANR 12, 28, 53; DLB 173;
INT CANR-28; MTCW

Leonard, Hugh . . . . CLC 19
See also Byrne, John Keyes
See also DLB 13

Leonov, Leonid (Maximovich)
1899-1994 . . . . CLC 92; DAM NOV
See also CA 129; MTCW

Leopardi, (Conte) Giacomo
1798-1837 . . . . NCLC 22

Le Reveler
See Artaud, Antonin (Marie Joseph)

Lerman, Eleanor 1952- . . . . CLC 9
See also CA 85-88

Lerman, Rhoda 1936- . . . . CLC 56
See also CA 49-52

Lermontov, Mikhail Yuryevich
1814-1841 . . . . NCLC 47; PC 18

Leroux, Gaston 1868-1927 . . . . TCLC 25
See also CA 108; 136; SATA 65

Lesage, Alain-Rene 1668-1747 . . . . . . LC 28

Leskov, Nikolai (Semyonovich)
1831-1895 . . . . NCLC 25

Lessing, Doris (May)
1919- . . . . . CLC 1, 2, 3, 6, 10, 15, 22, 40,
94; DA; DAB; DAC; DAM MST, NOV;
SSC 6
See also CA 9-12R; CAAS 14; CANR 33,
54; CDBLB 1960 to Present; DLB 15,
139; DLBY 85; MTCW; YABC

Lessing, Gotthold Ephraim
1729-1781 . . . . LC 8
See also DLB 97

Lester, Richard 1932- . . . . CLC 20

Lever, Charles (James)
1806-1872 . . . . NCLC 23
See also DLB 21

Leverson, Ada 1865(?)-1936(?) . . . . TCLC 18
See also Elaine
See also CA 117; DLB 153

Levertov, Denise
1923- . . . . . . CLC 1, 2, 3, 5, 8, 15, 28, 66;
DAM POET; PC 11
See also CA 1-4R; CAAS 19; CANR 3, 29,
50; DLB 5, 165; INT CANR-29; MTCW

Levi, Jonathan . . . . CLC 76

Levi, Peter (Chad Tigar) 1931- . . . . . CLC 41
See also CA 5-8R; CANR 34; DLB 40

Levi, Primo
1919-1987 . . . . CLC 37, 50; SSC 12
See also CA 13-16R; 122; CANR 12, 33;
DLB 177; MTCW

Levin, Ira 1929- . . . . . CLC 3, 6; DAM POP
See also CA 21-24R; CANR 17, 44;
MTCW; SATA 66

Levin, Meyer
1905-1981 . . . . CLC 7; DAM POP
See also AITN 1; CA 9-12R; 104;
CANR 15; DLB 9, 28; DLBY 81;
SATA 21; SATA-Obit 27

Levine, Norman 1924- . . . . CLC 54
See also CA 73-76; CAAS 23; CANR 14;
DLB 88

Levine, Philip
1928- . . . . CLC 2, 4, 5, 9, 14, 33;
DAM POET
See also CA 9-12R; CANR 9, 37, 52;
DLB 5

Levinson, Deirdre 1931- . . . . CLC 49
See also CA 73-76

Levi-Strauss, Claude 1908- . . . . CLC 38
See also CA 1-4R; CANR 6, 32, 57; MTCW

Levitin, Sonia (Wolff) 1934- . . . . CLC 17
See also AAYA 13; CA 29-32R; CANR 14,
32; JRDA; MAICYA; SAAS 2; SATA 4,
68

Levon, O. U.
See Kesey, Ken (Elton)

Levy, Amy 1861-1889 . . . . NCLC 59
See also DLB 156

Lewes, George Henry
1817-1878 . . . . NCLC 25
See also DLB 55, 144

Lewis, Alun 1915-1944 . . . . TCLC 3
See also CA 104; DLB 20, 162

Lewis, C. Day
See Day Lewis, C(ecil)

Lewis, C(live) S(taples)
1898-1963 . . . . . CLC 1, 3, 6, 14, 27; DA;
DAB; DAC; DAM MST, NOV, POP;
WLC
See also AAYA 3; CA 81-84; CANR 33;
CDBLB 1945-1960; CLR 3, 27; DLB 15,
100, 160; JRDA; MAICYA; MTCW;
SATA 13

Lewis, Janet 1899- . . . . CLC 41
See also Winters, Janet Lewis
See also CA 9-12R; CANR 29; CAP 1;
DLBY 87

Lewis, Matthew Gregory
1775-1818 . . . . NCLC 11, 62
See also DLB 39, 158, 178

Lewis, (Harry) Sinclair
1885-1951 . . . . . TCLC 4, 13, 23, 39; DA;
DAB; DAC; DAM MST, NOV; WLC
See also CA 104; 133; CDALB 1917-1929;
DLB 9, 102; DLBD 1; MTCW

Lewis, (Percy) Wyndham
1882(?)-1957 . . . . TCLC 2, 9
See also CA 104; 157; DLB 15

Lewisohn, Ludwig 1883-1955 . . . . . . TCLC 19
See also CA 107; DLB 4, 9, 28, 102

Leyner, Mark 1956- . . . . CLC 92
See also CA 110; CANR 28, 53

Lezama Lima, Jose
1910-1976 . . . . CLC 4, 10, 101;
DAM MULT
See also CA 77-80; DLB 113; HW

L'Heureux, John (Clarke) 1934- . . . . CLC 52
See also CA 13-16R; CANR 23, 45

Lord Houghton
See Milnes, Richard Monckton

Lord Jeffrey
See Jeffrey, Francis

Lorenzini, Carlo 1826-1890
See Collodi, Carlo
See also MAICYA; SATA 29

Lorenzo, Heberto Padilla
See Padilla (Lorenzo), Heberto

Loris
See Hofmannsthal, Hugo von

Loti, Pierre . . . . **TCLC 11**
See also Viaud, (Louis Marie) Julien
See also DLB 123

Louie, David Wong 1954- . . . . **CLC 70**
See also CA 139

Louis, Father M.
See Merton, Thomas

Lovecraft, H(oward) P(hillips)
1890-1937 . . . . **TCLC 4, 22; DAM POP;**
SSC 3
See also AAYA 14; CA 104; 133; MTCW

Lovelace, Earl 1935- . . . . **CLC 51**
See also BW 2; CA 77-80; CANR 41;
DLB 125; MTCW

Lovelace, Richard 1618-1657 . . . . **LC 24**
See also DLB 131

Lowell, Amy
1874-1925 . . . . **TCLC 1, 8; DAM POET;**
PC 13
See also CA 104; 151; DLB 54, 140

Lowell, James Russell 1819-1891 . . **NCLC 2**
See also CDALB 1640-1865; DLB 1, 11, 64,
79

Lowell, Robert (Traill Spence, Jr.)
1917-1977 . . . **CLC 1, 2, 3, 4, 5, 8, 9, 11,**
15, 37; DA; DAB; DAC; DAM MST,
NOV; PC 3; WLC
See also CA 9-12R; 73-76; CABS 2;
CANR 26; DLB 5, 169; MTCW

Lowndes, Marie Adelaide (Belloc)
1868-1947 . . . . **TCLC 12**
See also CA 107; DLB 70

Lowry, (Clarence) Malcolm
1909-1957 . . . . **TCLC 6, 40**
See also CA 105; 131; CDBLB 1945-1960;
DLB 15; MTCW

Lowry, Mina Gertrude 1882-1966
See Loy, Mina
See also CA 113

Loxsmith, John
See Brunner, John (Kilian Houston)

Loy, Mina . . . . **CLC 28; DAM POET; PC 16**
See also Lowry, Mina Gertrude
See also DLB 4, 54

Loyson-Bridet
See Schwob, (Maycr Andre) Marcel

Lucas, Craig 1951- . . . . **CLC 64**
See also CA 137

Lucas, George 1944- . . . . **CLC 16**
See also AAYA 1; CA 77-80; CANR 30;
SATA 56

Lucas, Hans
See Godard, Jean-Luc

Lucas, Victoria
See Plath, Sylvia

Ludlam, Charles 1943-1987 . . . . . **CLC 46, 50**
See also CA 85-88; 122

Ludlum, Robert
1927- . . . **CLC 22, 43; DAM NOV, POP**
See also AAYA 10; BEST 89:1, 90:3;
CA 33-36R; CANR 25, 41; DLBY 82;
MTCW

Ludwig, Ken . . . . **CLC 60**

Ludwig, Otto 1813-1865 . . . . **NCLC 4**
See also DLB 129

Lugones, Leopoldo 1874-1938 . . . . . **TCLC 15**
See also CA 116; 131; HW

Lu Hsun 1881-1936 . . . . . . **TCLC 3; SSC 20**
See also Shu-Jen, Chou

Lukacs, George . . . . **CLC 24**
See also Lukacs, Gyorgy (Szegeny von)

Lukacs, Gyorgy (Szegeny von) 1885-1971
See Lukacs, George
See also CA 101; 29-32R

Luke, Peter (Ambrose Cyprian)
1919-1995 . . . . **CLC 38**
See also CA 81-84; 147; DLB 13

Lunar, Dennis
See Mungo, Raymond

Lurie, Alison 1926- . . . . **CLC 4, 5, 18, 39**
See also CA 1-4R; CANR 2, 17, 50; DLB 2;
MTCW; SATA 46

Lustig, Arnost 1926- . . . . **CLC 56**
See also AAYA 3; CA 69-72; CANR 47;
SATA 56

Luther, Martin 1483-1546 . . . . **LC 9, 37**
See also DLB 179

Luxemburg, Rosa 1870(?)-1919 . . . . **TCLC 63**
See also CA 118

Luzi, Mario 1914- . . . . **CLC 13**
See also CA 61-64; CANR 9; DLB 128

Lyly, John 1554(?)-1606 . . . . **DC 7**
See also DAM DRAM; DLB 62, 167

L'Ymagier
See Gourmont, Remy (-Marie-Charles) de

Lynch, B. Suarez
See Bioy Casares, Adolfo; Borges, Jorge
Luis

Lynch, David (K.) 1946- . . . . **CLC 66**
See also CA 124; 129

Lynch, James
See Andreyev, Leonid (Nikolaevich)

Lynch Davis, B.
See Bioy Casares, Adolfo; Borges, Jorge
Luis

Lyndsay, Sir David 1490-1555 . . . . . . **LC 20**

Lynn, Kenneth S(chuyler) 1923- . . . . **CLC 50**
See also CA 1-4R; CANR 3, 27

Lynx
See West, Rebecca

Lyons, Marcus
See Blish, James (Benjamin)

Lyre, Pinchbeck
See Sassoon, Siegfried (Lorraine)

Lytle, Andrew (Nelson) 1902-1995 . . **CLC 22**
See also CA 9-12R; 150; DLB 6; DLBY 95

Lyttelton, George 1709-1773 . . . . **LC 10**

Maas, Peter 1929- . . . . **CLC 29**
See also CA 93-96; INT 93-96

Macaulay, Rose 1881-1958 . . . . . **TCLC 7, 44**
See also CA 104; DLB 36

Macaulay, Thomas Babington
1800-1859 . . . . **NCLC 42**
See also CDBLB 1832-1890; DLB 32, 55

MacBeth, George (Mann)
1932-1992 . . . . **CLC 2, 5, 9**
See also CA 25-28R; 136; DLB 40; MTCW;
SATA 4; SATA-Obit 70

MacCaig, Norman (Alexander)
1910- . . . . . **CLC 36; DAB; DAM POET**
See also CA 9-12R; CANR 3, 34; DLB 27

MacCarthy, (Sir Charles Otto) Desmond
1877-1952 . . . . **TCLC 36**

MacDiarmid, Hugh
. . . . **CLC 2, 4, 11, 19, 63; PC 9**
See also Grieve, C(hristopher) M(urray)
See also CDBLB 1945-1960; DLB 20

MacDonald, Anson
See Heinlein, Robert A(nson)

Macdonald, Cynthia 1928- . . . . **CLC 13, 19**
See also CA 49-52; CANR 4, 44; DLB 105

MacDonald, George 1824-1905 . . . . . **TCLC 9**
See also CA 106; 137; DLB 18, 163, 178;
MAICYA; SATA 33

Macdonald, John
See Millar, Kenneth

MacDonald, John D(ann)
1916-1986 . . . . **CLC 3, 27, 44;**
DAM NOV, POP
See also CA 1-4R; 121; CANR 1, 19;
DLB 8; DLBY 86; MTCW

Macdonald, John Ross
See Millar, Kenneth

Macdonald, Ross . . . . . **CLC 1, 2, 3, 14, 34, 41**
See also Millar, Kenneth
See also DLBD 6

MacDougal, John
See Blish, James (Benjamin)

MacEwen, Gwendolyn (Margaret)
1941-1987 . . . . **CLC 13, 55**
See also CA 9-12R; 124; CANR 7, 22;
DLB 53; SATA 50; SATA-Obit 55

Macha, Karel Hynek 1810-1846 . . **NCLC 46**

Machado (y Ruiz), Antonio
1875-1939 . . . . **TCLC 3**
See also CA 104; DLB 108

Machado de Assis, Joaquim Maria
1839-1908 . . . . . **TCLC 10; BLC; SSC 24**
See also CA 107; 153

Machen, Arthur . . . . **TCLC 4; SSC 20**
See also Jones, Arthur Llewellyn
See also DLB 36, 156, 178

Machiavelli, Niccolo
1469-1527 . . . . **LC 8, 36; DA; DAB;**
DAC; DAM MST
See also YABC

MacInnes, Colin 1914-1976 . . . . . . **CLC 4, 23**
See also CA 69-72; 65-68; CANR 21;
DLB 14; MTCW

McDermott, Alice 1953- ········· **CLC 90**
See also CA 109; CANR 40

McElroy, Joseph 1930- ········ **CLC 5, 47**
See also CA 17-20R

McEwan, Ian (Russell)
1948- ········ **CLC 13, 66; DAM NOV**
See also BEST 90:4; CA 61-64; CANR 14,
41; DLB 14; MTCW

McFadden, David 1940- ··········· **CLC 48**
See also CA 104; DLB 60; INT 104

McFarland, Dennis 1950- ········ **CLC 65**

McGahern, John
1934- ··········· **CLC 5, 9, 48; SSC 17**
See also CA 17-20R; CANR 29; DLB 14;
MTCW

McGinley, Patrick (Anthony)
1937- ························· **CLC 41**
See also CA 120; 127; CANR 56; INT 127

McGinley, Phyllis 1905-1978 ······ **CLC 14**
See also CA 9-12R; 77-80; CANR 19;
DLB 11, 48; SATA 2, 44; SATA-Obit 24

McGinniss, Joe 1942- ············· **CLC 32**
See also AITN 2; BEST 89:2; CA 25-28R;
CANR 26; INT CANR-26

McGivern, Maureen Daly
See Daly, Maureen

McGrath, Patrick 1950- ··········· **CLC 55**
See also CA 136

McGrath, Thomas (Matthew)
1916-1990 ···· **CLC 28, 59; DAM POET**
See also CA 9-12R; 132; CANR 6, 33;
MTCW; SATA 41; SATA-Obit 66

McGuane, Thomas (Francis III)
1939- ··············· **CLC 3, 7, 18, 45**
See also AITN 2; CA 49-52; CANR 5, 24,
49; DLB 2; DLBY 80; INT CANR-24;
MTCW

McGuckian, Medbh
1950- ··········· **CLC 48; DAM POET**
See also CA 143; DLB 40

McHale, Tom 1942(?)-1982 ······· **CLC 3, 5**
See also AITN 1; CA 77-80; 106

McIlvanney, William 1936- ········ **CLC 42**
See also CA 25-28R; DLB 14

McIlwraith, Maureen Mollie Hunter
See Hunter, Mollie
See also SATA 2

McInerney, Jay
1955- ············· **CLC 34; DAM POP**
See also AAYA 18; CA 116; 123;
CANR 45; INT 123

McIntyre, Vonda N(eel) 1948- ····· **CLC 18**
See also CA 81-84; CANR 17, 34; MTCW

McKay, Claude
········TCLC 7, 41; BLC; DAB; PC 2
See also McKay, Festus Claudius
See also DLB 4, 45, 51, 117

McKay, Festus Claudius 1889-1948
See McKay, Claude
See also BW 1; CA 104; 124; DA; DAC;
DAM MST, MULT, NOV, POET;
MTCW; WLC

McKuen, Rod 1933- ············· **CLC 1, 3**
See also AITN 1; CA 41-44R; CANR 40

McLoughlin, R. B.
See Mencken, H(enry) L(ouis)

McLuhan, (Herbert) Marshall
1911-1980 ················ **CLC 37, 83**
See also CA 9-12R; 102; CANR 12, 34;
DLB 88; INT CANR-12; MTCW

McMillan, Terry (L.)
1951- ······· **CLC 50, 61; DAM MULT,
NOV, POP**
See also AAYA 21; BW 2; CA 140

McMurtry, Larry (Jeff)
1936- ·········· **CLC 2, 3, 7, 11, 27, 44;
DAM NOV, POP**
See also AAYA 15; AITN 2; BEST 89:2;
CA 5-8R; CANR 19, 43;
CDALB 1968-1988; DLB 2, 143;
DLBY 80, 87; MTCW

McNally, T. M. 1961- ············ **CLC 82**

McNally, Terrence
1939- ··· **CLC 4, 7, 41, 91; DAM DRAM**
See also CA 45-48; CANR 2, 56; DLB 7

McNamer, Deirdre 1950- ········· **CLC 70**

McNeile, Herman Cyril 1888-1937
See Sapper
See also DLB 77

McNickle, (William) D'Arcy
1904-1977 ······ **CLC 89; DAM MULT**
See also CA 9-12R; 85-88; CANR 5, 45;
DLB 175; NNAL; SATA-Obit 22

McPhee, John (Angus) 1931- ······ **CLC 36**
See also BEST 90:1; CA 65-68; CANR 20,
46; MTCW

McPherson, James Alan
1943- ··················· **CLC 19, 77**
See also BW 1; CA 25-28R; CAAS 17;
CANR 24; DLB 38; MTCW

McPherson, William (Alexander)
1933- ······················· **CLC 34**
See also CA 69-72; CANR 28;
INT CANR-28

Mead, Margaret 1901-1978 ········ **CLC 37**
See also AITN 1; CA 1-4R; 81-84;
CANR 4; MTCW; SATA-Obit 20

Meaker, Marijane (Agnes) 1927-
See Kerr, M. E.
See also CA 107; CANR 37; INT 107;
JRDA; MAICYA; MTCW; SATA 20, 61

Medoff, Mark (Howard)
1940- ········ **CLC 6, 23; DAM DRAM**
See also AITN 1; CA 53-56; CANR 5;
DLB 7; INT CANR-5

Medvedev, P. N.
See Bakhtin, Mikhail Mikhailovich

Meged, Aharon
See Megged, Aharon

Meged, Aron
See Megged, Aharon

Megged, Aharon 1920- ············· **CLC 9**
See also CA 49-52; CAAS 13; CANR 1

Mehta, Ved (Parkash) 1934- ······· **CLC 37**
See also CA 1-4R; CANR 2, 23; MTCW

Melanter
See Blackmore, R(ichard) D(oddridge)

Melikow, Loris
See Hofmannsthal, Hugo von

Melmoth, Sebastian
See Wilde, Oscar (Fingal O'Flahertie Wills)

Meltzer, Milton 1915- ············ **CLC 26**
See also AAYA 8; CA 13-16R; CANR 38;
CLR 13; DLB 61; JRDA; MAICYA;
SAAS 1; SATA 1, 50, 80

Melville, Herman
1819-1891 ····· **NCLC 3, 12, 29, 45, 49;
DA; DAB; DAC; DAM MST, NOV;
SSC 1, 17; WLC**
See also CDALB 1640-1865; DLB 3, 74;
SATA 59

Menander
c. 342B.C.-c. 292B.C. ········ **CMLC 9;
DAM DRAM; DC 3**
See also DLB 176

Mencken, H(enry) L(ouis)
1880-1956 ················· **TCLC 13**
See also CA 105; 125; CDALB 1917-1929;
DLB 11, 29, 63, 137; MTCW

Mendelsohn, Jane 1965(?)- ········ **CLC 99**
See also CA 154

Mercer, David
1928-1980 ······· **CLC 5; DAM DRAM**
See also CA 9-12R; 102; CANR 23;
DLB 13; MTCW

Merchant, Paul
See Ellison, Harlan (Jay)

Meredith, George
1828-1909 ·· **TCLC 17, 43; DAM POET**
See also CA 117; 153; CDBLB 1832-1890;
DLB 18, 35, 57, 159

Meredith, William (Morris)
1919- ·· **CLC 4, 13, 22, 55; DAM POET**
See also CA 9-12R; CAAS 14; CANR 6, 40;
DLB 5

Merezhkovsky, Dmitry Sergeyevich
1865-1941 ················· **TCLC 29**

Merimee, Prosper
1803-1870 ············ **NCLC 6; SSC 7**
See also DLB 119

Merkin, Daphne 1954- ············ **CLC 44**
See also CA 123

Merlin, Arthur
See Blish, James (Benjamin)

Merrill, James (Ingram)
1926-1995 ···· **CLC 2, 3, 6, 8, 13, 18, 34,
91; DAM POET**
See also CA 13-16R; 147; CANR 10, 49;
DLB 5, 165; DLBY 85; INT CANR-10;
MTCW

Merriman, Alex
See Silverberg, Robert

Merritt, E. B.
See Waddington, Miriam

Merton, Thomas
1915-1968 ·· **CLC 1, 3, 11, 34, 83; PC 10**
See also CA 5-8R; 25-28R; CANR 22, 53;
DLB 48; DLBY 81; MTCW

Merwin, W(illiam) S(tanley)
1927- ······ **CLC 1, 2, 3, 5, 8, 13, 18, 45,
88; DAM POET**
See also CA 13-16R; CANR 15, 51; DLB 5,
169; INT CANR-15; MTCW

Metcalf, John 1938- ·············· **CLC 37**
See also CA 113; DLB 60

Metcalf, Suzanne
See Baum, L(yman) Frank

Mew, Charlotte (Mary)
1870-1928 .... TCLC 8
See also CA 105; DLB 19, 135

Mewshaw, Michael 1943- .... CLC 9
See also CA 53-56; CANR 7, 47; DLBY 80

Meyer, June
See Jordan, June

Meyer, Lynn
See Slavitt, David R(ytman)

Meyer-Meyrink, Gustav 1868-1932
See Meyrink, Gustav
See also CA 117

Meyers, Jeffrey 1939- .... CLC 39
See also CA 73-76; CANR 54; DLB 111

Meynell, Alice (Christina Gertrude Thompson)
1847-1922 .... TCLC 6
See also CA 104; DLB 19, 98

Meyrink, Gustav .... TCLC 21
See also Meyer-Meyrink, Gustav
See also DLB 81

Michaels, Leonard
1933- .... CLC 6, 25; SSC 16
See also CA 61-64; CANR 21; DLB 130;
MTCW

Michaux, Henri 1899-1984 ..... CLC 8, 19
See also CA 85-88; 114

Michelangelo 1475-1564 .... LC 12

Michelet, Jules 1798-1874 ...... NCLC 31

Michener, James A(lbert)
1907(?)- .... CLC 1, 5, 11, 29, 60;
DAM NOV, POP
See also AITN 1; BEST 90:1; CA 5-8R;
CANR 21, 45; DLB 6; MTCW

Mickiewicz, Adam 1798-1855 ..... NCLC 3

Middleton, Christopher 1926- ...... CLC 13
See also CA 13-16R; CANR 29, 54;
DLB 40

Middleton, Richard (Barham)
1882-1911 .... TCLC 56
See also DLB 156

Middleton, Stanley 1919- .... CLC 7, 38
See also CA 25-28R; CAAS 23; CANR 21,
46; DLB 14

Middleton, Thomas
1580-1627 .... LC 33; DAM DRAM,
MST; DC 5
See also DLB 58

Migueis, Jose Rodrigues 1901- ..... CLC 10

Mikszath, Kalman 1847-1910 ..... TCLC 31

Miles, Jack .... CLC 100

Miles, Josephine (Louise)
1911-1985 .... CLC 1, 2, 14, 34, 39;
DAM POET
See also CA 1-4R; 116; CANR 2, 55;
DLB 48

Militant
See Sandburg, Carl (August)

Mill, John Stuart 1806-1873 .. NCLC 11, 58
See also CDBLB 1832-1890; DLB 55

Millar, Kenneth
1915-1983 .... CLC 14; DAM POP
See also Macdonald, Ross
See also CA 9-12R; 110; CANR 16; DLB 2;
DLBD 6; DLBY 83; MTCW

Millay, E. Vincent
See Millay, Edna St. Vincent

Millay, Edna St. Vincent
1892-1950 ...... TCLC 4, 49; DA; DAB;
DAC; DAM MST, POET; PC 6
See also CA 104; 130; CDALB 1917-1929;
DLB 45; MTCW; YABC

Miller, Arthur
1915- .... CLC 1, 2, 6, 10, 15, 26, 47, 78;
DA; DAB; DAC; DAM DRAM, MST;
DC 1; WLC
See also AAYA 15; AITN 1; CA 1-4R;
CABS 3; CANR 2, 30, 54;
CDALB 1941-1968; DLB 7; MTCW

Miller, Henry (Valentine)
1891-1980 .... CLC 1, 2, 4, 9, 14, 43, 84;
DA; DAB; DAC; DAM MST, NOV;
WLC
See also CA 9-12R; 97-100; CANR 33;
CDALB 1929-1941; DLB 4, 9; DLBY 80;
MTCW

Miller, Jason 1939(?)- .... CLC 2
See also AITN 1; CA 73-76; DLB 7

Miller, Sue 1943- ..... CLC 44; DAM POP
See also BEST 90:3; CA 139; DLB 143

Miller, Walter M(ichael, Jr.)
1923- .... CLC 4, 30
See also CA 85-88; DLB 8

Millett, Kate 1934- .... CLC 67
See also AITN 1; CA 73-76; CANR 32, 53;
MTCW

Millhauser, Steven 1943- ...... CLC 21, 54
See also CA 110; 111; DLB 2; INT 111

Millin, Sarah Gertrude 1889-1968 .. CLC 49
See also CA 102; 93-96

Milne, A(lan) A(lexander)
1882-1956 .... TCLC 6; DAB; DAC;
DAM MST
See also CA 104; 133; CLR 1, 26; DLB 10,
77, 100, 160; MAICYA; MTCW; 1

Milner, Ron(ald)
1938- ..... CLC 56; BLC; DAM MULT
See also AITN 1; BW 1; CA 73-76;
CANR 24; DLB 38; MTCW

Milnes, Richard Monckton
1809-1885 .... NCLC 61
See also DLB 32

Milosz, Czeslaw
1911- .... CLC 5, 11, 22, 31, 56, 82;
DAM MST, POET; PC 8
See also CA 81-84; CANR 23, 51; MTCW;
YABC

Milton, John
1608-1674 ...... LC 9; DA; DAB; DAC;
DAM MST, POET; PC 19; WLC
See also CDBLB 1660-1789; DLB 131, 151

Min, Anchee 1957- .... CLC 86
See also CA 146

Minehaha, Cornelius
See Wedekind, (Benjamin) Frank(lin)

Miner, Valerie 1947- .... CLC 40
See also CA 97-100

Minimo, Duca
See D'Annunzio, Gabriele

Minot, Susan 1956- .... CLC 44
See also CA 134

Minus, Ed 1938- .... CLC 39

Miranda, Javier
See Bioy Casares, Adolfo

Mirbeau, Octave 1848-1917 ...... TCLC 55
See also DLB 123

Miro (Ferrer), Gabriel (Francisco Victor)
1879-1930 .... TCLC 5
See also CA 104

Mishima, Yukio
.... CLC 2, 4, 6, 9, 27; DC 1; SSC 4
See also Hiraoka, Kimitake

Mistral, Frederic 1830-1914 ...... TCLC 51
See also CA 122

Mistral, Gabriela .... TCLC 2; HLC
See also Godoy Alcayaga, Lucila

Mistry, Rohinton 1952- ...... CLC 71; DAC
See also CA 141

Mitchell, Clyde
See Ellison, Harlan (Jay); Silverberg, Robert

Mitchell, James Leslie 1901-1935
See Gibbon, Lewis Grassic
See also CA 104; DLB 15

Mitchell, Joni 1943- .... CLC 12
See also CA 112

Mitchell, Joseph (Quincy)
1908-1996 .... CLC 98
See also CA 77-80; 152; DLBY 96

Mitchell, Margaret (Munnerlyn)
1900-1949 ...... TCLC 11; DAM NOV,
POP
See also CA 109; 125; CANR 55; DLB 9;
MTCW

Mitchell, Peggy
See Mitchell, Margaret (Munnerlyn)

Mitchell, S(ilas) Weir 1829-1914 .. TCLC 36

Mitchell, W(illiam) O(rmond)
1914- ...... CLC 25; DAC; DAM MST
See also CA 77-80; CANR 15, 43; DLB 88

Mitford, Mary Russell 1787-1855 .. NCLC 4
See also DLB 110, 116

Mitford, Nancy 1904-1973 .... CLC 44
See also CA 9-12R

Miyamoto, Yuriko 1899-1951 ..... TCLC 37
See also DLB 180

Mizoguchi, Kenji 1898-1956 ...... TCLC 72

Mo, Timothy (Peter) 1950(?)- ...... CLC 46
See also CA 117; MTCW

Modarressi, Taghi (M.) 1931- ...... CLC 44
See also CA 121; 134; INT 134

Modiano, Patrick (Jean) 1945- ..... CLC 18
See also CA 85-88; CANR 17, 40; DLB 83

Moerck, Paal
See Roelvaag, O(le) E(dvart)

Mofolo, Thomas (Mokopu)
1875(?)-1948 .... TCLC 22; BLC;
DAM MULT
See also CA 121; 153

Mohr, Nicholasa
1935- ..... **CLC 12; DAM MULT; HLC**
See also AAYA 8; CA 49-52; CANR 1, 32;
CLR 22; DLB 145; HW; JRDA; SAAS 8;
SATA 8

Mojtabai, A(nn) G(race)
1938- .... **CLC 5, 9, 15, 29**
See also CA 85-88

Moliere
1622-1673 ..... **LC 28; DA; DAB; DAC;**
DAM DRAM, MST; WLC

Molin, Charles
See Mayne, William (James Carter)

Molnar, Ferenc
1878-1952 ..... **TCLC 20; DAM DRAM**
See also CA 109; 153

Momaday, N(avarre) Scott
1934- ..... **CLC 2, 19, 85, 95; DA; DAB;**
DAC; DAM MST, MULT, NOV, POP
See also AAYA 11; CA 25-28R; CANR 14,
34; DLB 143, 175; INT CANR-14;
MTCW; NNAL; SATA 48;
SATA-Brief 30; YABC

Monette, Paul 1945-1995 .... **CLC 82**
See also CA 139; 147

Monroe, Harriet 1860-1936 .... **TCLC 12**
See also CA 109; DLB 54, 91

Monroe, Lyle
See Heinlein, Robert A(nson)

Montagu, Elizabeth 1917- .... **NCLC 7**
See also CA 9-12R

Montagu, Mary (Pierrepont) Wortley
1689-1762 .... **LC 9; PC 16**
See also DLB 95, 101

Montagu, W. H.
See Coleridge, Samuel Taylor

Montague, John (Patrick)
1929- .... **CLC 13, 46**
See also CA 9-12R; CANR 9; DLB 40;
MTCW

Montaigne, Michel (Eyquem) de
1533-1592 ..... **LC 8; DA; DAB; DAC;**
DAM MST; WLC

Montale, Eugenio
1896-1981 .... **CLC 7, 9, 18; PC 13**
See also CA 17-20R; 104; CANR 30;
DLB 114; MTCW

Montesquieu, Charles-Louis de Secondat
1689-1755 .... **LC 7**

Montgomery, (Robert) Bruce 1921-1978
See Crispin, Edmund
See also CA 104

Montgomery, L(ucy) M(aud)
1874-1942 .... **TCLC 51; DAC;**
DAM MST
See also AAYA 12; CA 108; 137; CLR 8;
DLB 92; DLBD 14; JRDA; MAICYA; 1

Montgomery, Marion H., Jr. 1925- .. **CLC 7**
See also AITN 1; CA 1-4R; CANR 3, 48;
DLB 6

Montgomery, Max
See Davenport, Guy (Mattison, Jr.)

Montherlant, Henry (Milon) de
1896-1972 .... **CLC 8, 19; DAM DRAM**
See also CA 85-88; 37-40R; DLB 72;
MTCW

Monty Python
See Chapman, Graham; Cleese, John
(Marwood); Gilliam, Terry (Vance); Idle,
Eric; Jones, Terence Graham Parry; Palin,
Michael (Edward)
See also AAYA 7

Moodie, Susanna (Strickland)
1803-1885 .... **NCLC 14**
See also DLB 99

Mooney, Edward 1951-
See Mooney, Ted
See also CA 130

Mooney, Ted .... **CLC 25**
See also Mooney, Edward

Moorcock, Michael (John)
1939- .... **CLC 5, 27, 58**
See also CA 45-48; CAAS 5; CANR 2, 17,
38; DLB 14; MTCW; SATA 93

Moore, Brian
1921- ...... **CLC 1, 3, 5, 7, 8, 19, 32, 90;**
DAB; DAC; DAM MST
See also CA 1-4R; CANR 1, 25, 42; MTCW

Moore, Edward
See Muir, Edwin

Moore, George Augustus
1852-1933 .... **TCLC 7; SSC 19**
See also CA 104; DLB 10, 18, 57, 135

Moore, Lorrie .... **CLC 39, 45, 68**
See also Moore, Marie Lorena

Moore, Marianne (Craig)
1887-1972 .... **CLC 1, 2, 4, 8, 10, 13, 19,**
47; DA; DAB; DAC; DAM MST, POET;
PC 4
See also CA 1-4R; 33-36R; CANR 3;
CDALB 1929-1941; DLB 45; DLBD 7;
MTCW; SATA 20; YABC

Moore, Marie Lorena 1957-
See Moore, Lorrie
See also CA 116; CANR 39

Moore, Thomas 1779-1852 .... **NCLC 6**
See also DLB 96, 144

Morand, Paul 1888-1976 .. **CLC 41; SSC 22**
See also CA 69-72; DLB 65

Morante, Elsa 1918-1985 .... **CLC 8, 47**
See also CA 85-88; 117; CANR 35;
DLB 177; MTCW

Moravia, Alberto
1907-1990 .... **CLC 2, 7, 11, 27, 46;**
SSC 26
See also Pincherle, Alberto
See also DLB 177

More, Hannah 1745-1833 .... **NCLC 27**
See also DLB 107, 109, 116, 158

More, Henry 1614-1687 .... **LC 9**
See also DLB 126

More, Sir Thomas 1478-1535 .... **LC 10, 32**

Moreas, Jean .... **TCLC 18**
See also Papadiamantopoulos, Johannes

Morgan, Berry 1919- .... **CLC 6**
See also CA 49-52; DLB 6

Morgan, Claire
See Highsmith, (Mary) Patricia

Morgan, Edwin (George) 1920- ..... **CLC 31**
See also CA 5-8R; CANR 3, 43; DLB 27

Morgan, (George) Frederick
1922- .... **CLC 23**
See also CA 17-20R; CANR 21

Morgan, Harriet
See Mencken, H(enry) L(ouis)

Morgan, Jane
See Cooper, James Fenimore

Morgan, Janet 1945- .... **CLC 39**
See also CA 65-68

Morgan, Lady 1776(?)-1859 ...... **NCLC 29**
See also DLB 116, 158

Morgan, Robin 1941- .... **CLC 2**
See also CA 69-72; CANR 29; MTCW;
SATA 80

Morgan, Scott
See Kuttner, Henry

Morgan, Seth 1949(?)-1990 .... **CLC 65**
See also CA 132

Morgenstern, Christian
1871-1914 .... **TCLC 8**
See also CA 105

Morgenstern, S.
See Goldman, William (W.)

Moricz, Zsigmond 1879-1942 ..... **TCLC 33**

Morike, Eduard (Friedrich)
1804-1875 .... **NCLC 10**
See also DLB 133

Mori Ogai .... **TCLC 14**
See also Mori Rintaro

Mori Rintaro 1862-1922
See Mori Ogai
See also CA 110

Moritz, Karl Philipp 1756-1793 ...... **LC 2**
See also DLB 94

Morland, Peter Henry
See Faust, Frederick (Schiller)

Morren, Theophil
See Hofmannsthal, Hugo von

Morris, Bill 1952- .... **CLC 76**

Morris, Julian
See West, Morris L(anglo)

Morris, Steveland Judkins 1950(?)-
See Wonder, Stevie
See also CA 111

Morris, William 1834-1896 .... **NCLC 4**
See also CDBLB 1832-1890; DLB 18, 35,
57, 156, 178

Morris, Wright 1910- ... **CLC 1, 3, 7, 18, 37**
See also CA 9-12R; CANR 21; DLB 2;
DLBY 81; MTCW

Morrison, Arthur 1863-1945 ...... **TCLC 72**
See also CA 120; 157; DLB 70, 135

Morrison, Chloe Anthony Wofford
See Morrison, Toni

Morrison, James Douglas 1943-1971
See Morrison, Jim
See also CA 73-76; CANR 40

Morrison, Jim .... **CLC 17**
See also Morrison, James Douglas

Nakos, Lilika 1899(?)- .... **CLC 29**

Narayan, R(asipuram) K(rishnaswami)
1906- ...... **CLC 7, 28, 47; DAM NOV;**
SSC 25
See also CA 81-84; CANR 33; MTCW;
SATA 62

Nash, (Frediric) Ogden
1902-1971 .... **CLC 23; DAM POET**
See also CA 13-14; 29-32R; CANR 34;
CAP 1; DLB 11; MAICYA; MTCW;
SATA 2, 46

Nathan, Daniel
See Dannay, Frederic

Nathan, George Jean 1882-1958 ... **TCLC 18**
See also Hatteras, Owen
See also CA 114; DLB 137

Natsume, Kinnosuke 1867-1916
See Natsume, Soseki
See also CA 104

Natsume, Soseki 1867-1916 ..... **TCLC 2, 10**
See also Natsume, Kinnosuke
See also DLB 180

Natti, (Mary) Lee 1919-
See Kingman, Lee
See also CA 5-8R; CANR 2

Naylor, Gloria
1950- ..... **CLC 28, 52; BLC; DA; DAC;**
DAM MST, MULT, NOV, POP
See also AAYA 6; BW 2; CA 107;
CANR 27, 51; DLB 173; MTCW; YABC

Neihardt, John Gneisenau
1881-1973 .... **CLC 32**
See also CA 13-14; CAP 1; DLB 9, 54

Nekrasov, Nikolai Alekseevich
1821-1878 .... **NCLC 11**

Nelligan, Emile 1879-1941 .... **TCLC 14**
See also CA 114; DLB 92

Nelson, Willie 1933- .... **CLC 17**
See also CA 107

Nemerov, Howard (Stanley)
1920-1991 .... **CLC 2, 6, 9, 36;**
DAM POET
See also CA 1-4R; 134; CABS 2; CANR 1,
27, 53; DLB 5, 6; DLBY 83;
INT CANR-27; MTCW

Neruda, Pablo
1904-1973 ..... **CLC 1, 2, 5, 7, 9, 28, 62;**
DA; DAB; DAC; DAM MST, MULT,
POET; HLC; PC 4; WLC
See also CA 19-20; 45-48; CAP 2; HW;
MTCW

Nerval, Gerard de
1808-1855 ..... **NCLC 1; PC 13; SSC 18**

Nervo, (Jose) Amado (Ruiz de)
1870-1919 .... **TCLC 11**
See also CA 109; 131; HW

Nessi, Pio Baroja y
See Baroja (y Nessi), Pio

Nestroy, Johann 1801-1862 ...... **NCLC 42**
See also DLB 133

Netterville, Luke
See O'Grady, Standish (James)

Neufeld, John (Arthur) 1938- ...... **CLC 17**
See also AAYA 11; CA 25-28R; CANR 11,
37, 56; MAICYA; SAAS 3; SATA 6, 81

Neville, Emily Cheney 1919- .... **CLC 12**
See also CA 5-8R; CANR 3, 37; JRDA;
MAICYA; SAAS 2; SATA 1

Newbound, Bernard Slade 1930-
See Slade, Bernard
See also CA 81-84; CANR 49;
DAM DRAM

Newby, P(ercy) H(oward)
1918- .... **CLC 2, 13; DAM NOV**
See also CA 5-8R; CANR 32; DLB 15;
MTCW

Newlove, Donald 1928- .... **CLC 6**
See also CA 29-32R; CANR 25

Newlove, John (Herbert) 1938- ..... **CLC 14**
See also CA 21-24R; CANR 9, 25

Newman, Charles 1938- .... **CLC 2, 8**
See also CA 21-24R

Newman, Edwin (Harold) 1919- .... **CLC 14**
See also AITN 1; CA 69-72; CANR 5

Newman, John Henry
1801-1890 .... **NCLC 38**
See also DLB 18, 32, 55

Newton, Suzanne 1936- .... **CLC 35**
See also CA 41-44R; CANR 14; JRDA;
SATA 5, 77

Nexo, Martin Andersen
1869-1954 .... **TCLC 43**

Nezval, Vitezslav 1900-1958 ...... **TCLC 44**
See also CA 123

Ng, Fae Myenne 1957(?)- .... **CLC 81**
See also CA 146

Ngema, Mbongeni 1955- .... **CLC 57**
See also BW 2; CA 143

Ngugi, James T(hiong'o) .... **CLC 3, 7, 13**
See also Ngugi wa Thiong'o

Ngugi wa Thiong'o
1938- ..... **CLC 36; BLC; DAM MULT,**
NOV
See also Ngugi, James T(hiong'o)
See also BW 2; CA 81-84; CANR 27, 58;
DLB 125; MTCW

Nichol, B(arrie) P(hillip)
1944-1988 .... **CLC 18**
See also CA 53-56; DLB 53; SATA 66

Nichols, John (Treadwell) 1940- .... **CLC 38**
See also CA 9-12R; CAAS 2; CANR 6;
DLBY 82

Nichols, Leigh
See Koontz, Dean R(ay)

Nichols, Peter (Richard)
1927- .... **CLC 5, 36, 65**
See also CA 104; CANR 33; DLB 13;
MTCW

Nicolas, F. R. E.
See Freeling, Nicolas

Niedecker, Lorine
1903-1970 .... **CLC 10, 42; DAM POET**
See also CA 25-28; CAP 2; DLB 48

Nietzsche, Friedrich (Wilhelm)
1844-1900 .... **TCLC 10, 18, 55**
See also CA 107; 121; DLB 129

Nievo, Ippolito 1831-1861 .... **NCLC 22**

Nightingale, Anne Redmon 1943-
See Redmon, Anne
See also CA 103

Nik. T. O.
See Annensky, Innokenty (Fyodorovich)

Nin, Anais
1903-1977 ...... **CLC 1, 4, 8, 11, 14, 60;**
DAM NOV, POP; SSC 10
See also AITN 2; CA 13-16R; 69-72;
CANR 22, 53; DLB 2, 4, 152; MTCW

Nishiwaki, Junzaburo 1894-1982 .... **PC 15**
See also CA 107

Nissenson, Hugh 1933- .... **CLC 4, 9**
See also CA 17-20R; CANR 27; DLB 28

Niven, Larry .... **CLC 8**
See also Niven, Laurence Van Cott
See also DLB 8

Niven, Laurence Van Cott 1938-
See Niven, Larry
See also CA 21-24R; CAAS 12; CANR 14,
44; DAM POP; MTCW

Nixon, Agnes Eckhardt 1927- ...... **CLC 21**
See also CA 110

Nizan, Paul 1905-1940 .... **TCLC 40**
See also DLB 72

Nkosi, Lewis
1936- ..... **CLC 45; BLC; DAM MULT**
See also BW 1; CA 65-68; CANR 27;
DLB 157

Nodier, (Jean) Charles (Emmanuel)
1780-1844 .... **NCLC 19**
See also DLB 119

Nolan, Christopher 1965- .... **CLC 58**
See also CA 111

Noon, Jeff 1957- .... **CLC 91**
See also CA 148

Norden, Charles
See Durrell, Lawrence (George)

Nordhoff, Charles (Bernard)
1887-1947 .... **TCLC 23**
See also CA 108; DLB 9; SATA 23

Norfolk, Lawrence 1963- .... **CLC 76**
See also CA 144

Norman, Marsha
1947- .... **CLC 28; DAM DRAM**
See also CA 105; CABS 3; CANR 41;
DLBY 84

Norris, Benjamin Franklin, Jr.
1870-1902 .... **TCLC 24**
See also Norris, Frank
See also CA 110

Norris, Frank
See Norris, Benjamin Franklin, Jr.
See also CDALB 1865-1917; DLB 12, 71

Norris, Leslie 1921- .... **CLC 14**
See also CA 11-12; CANR 14; CAP 1;
DLB 27

North, Andrew
See Norton, Andre

North, Anthony
See Koontz, Dean R(ay)

North, Captain George
See Stevenson, Robert Louis (Balfour)

North, Milou
See Erdrich, Louise

Northrup, B. A.
See Hubbard, L(afayette) Ron(ald)

Oneal, Elizabeth   1934-
See Oneal, Zibby
See also CA 106; CANR 28; MAICYA;
SATA 30, 82

Oneal, Zibby . . . . CLC 30
See also Oneal, Elizabeth
See also AAYA 5; CLR 13; JRDA

O'Neill, Eugene (Gladstone)
1888-1953 . . . . . . TCLC 1, 6, 27, 49; DA;
DAB; DAC; DAM DRAM, MST; WLC
See also AITN 1; CA 110; 132;
CDALB 1929-1941; DLB 7; MTCW

Onetti, Juan Carlos
1909-1994 . . . . CLC 7, 10; DAM MULT,
NOV; SSC 23
See also CA 85-88; 145; CANR 32;
DLB 113; HW; MTCW

O Nuallain, Brian   1911-1966
See O'Brien, Flann
See also CA 21-22; 25-28R; CAP 2

Oppen, George   1908-1984 . . . . CLC 7, 13, 34
See also CA 13-16R; 113; CANR 8; DLB 5,
165

Oppenheim, E(dward) Phillips
1866-1946 . . . . TCLC 45
See also CA 111; DLB 70

Origen   c. 185-c. 254 . . . . CMLC 19

Orlovitz, Gil   1918-1973 . . . . CLC 22
See also CA 77-80; 45-48; DLB 2, 5

Orris
See Ingelow, Jean

Ortega y Gasset, Jose
1883-1955 . . . . . TCLC 9; DAM MULT;
HLC
See also CA 106; 130; HW; MTCW

Ortese, Anna Maria   1914- . . . . CLC 89
See also DLB 177

Ortiz, Simon J(oseph)
1941- . . . . CLC 45; DAM MULT,
POET; PC 17
See also CA 134; DLB 120, 175; NNAL

Orton, Joe . . . . CLC 4, 13, 43; DC 3
See also Orton, John Kingsley
See also CDBLB 1960 to Present; DLB 13

Orton, John Kingsley   1933-1967
See Orton, Joe
See also CA 85-88; CANR 35;
DAM DRAM; MTCW

Orwell, George
. . . . . TCLC 2, 6, 15, 31, 51; DAB; WLC
See also Blair, Eric (Arthur)
See also CDBLB 1945-1960; DLB 15, 98

Osborne, David
See Silverberg, Robert

Osborne, George
See Silverberg, Robert

Osborne, John (James)
1929-1994 . . . . . CLC 1, 2, 5, 11, 45; DA;
DAB; DAC; DAM DRAM, MST; WLC
See also CA 13-16R; 147; CANR 21, 56;
CDBLB 1945-1960; DLB 13; MTCW

Osborne, Lawrence   1958- . . . . CLC 50

Oshima, Nagisa   1932- . . . . CLC 20
See also CA 116; 121

Oskison, John Milton
1874-1947 . . . . . TCLC 35; DAM MULT
See also CA 144; DLB 175; NNAL

Ossoli, Sarah Margaret (Fuller marchesa d')
1810-1850
See Fuller, Margaret
See also SATA 25

Ostrovsky, Alexander
1823-1886 . . . . NCLC 30, 57

Otero, Blas de   1916-1979. . . . . CLC 11
See also CA 89-92; DLB 134

Otto, Whitney   1955-. . . . . CLC 70
See also CA 140

Ouida . . . . TCLC 43
See also De La Ramee, (Marie) Louise
See also DLB 18, 156

Ousmane, Sembene   1923- . . . . CLC 66; BLC
See also BW 1; CA 117; 125; MTCW

Ovid
43B.C.-18(?) . . . CMLC 7; DAM POET;
PC 2

Owen, Hugh
See Faust, Frederick (Schiller)

Owen, Wilfred (Edward Salter)
1893-1918 . . . . . . TCLC 5, 27; DA; DAB;
DAC; DAM MST, POET; PC 19; WLC
See also CA 104; 141; CDBLB 1914-1945;
DLB 20

Owens, Rochelle   1936-. . . . . CLC 8
See also CA 17-20R; CAAS 2; CANR 39

Oz, Amos
1939- . . . . CLC 5, 8, 11, 27, 33, 54;
DAM NOV
See also CA 53-56; CANR 27, 47; MTCW

Ozick, Cynthia
1928- . . . . CLC 3, 7, 28, 62; DAM NOV,
POP; SSC 15
See also BEST 90:1; CA 17-20R; CANR 23,
58; DLB 28, 152; DLBY 82;
INT CANR-23; MTCW

Ozu, Yasujiro   1903-1963 . . . . CLC 16
See also CA 112

Pacheco, C.
See Pessoa, Fernando (Antonio Nogueira)

Pa Chin . . . . CLC 18
See also Li Fei-kan

Pack, Robert   1929-. . . . . CLC 13
See also CA 1-4R; CANR 3, 44; DLB 5

Padgett, Lewis
See Kuttner, Henry

Padilla (Lorenzo), Heberto   1932- . . . CLC 38
See also AITN 1; CA 123; 131; HW

Page, Jimmy   1944-. . . . . CLC 12

Page, Louise   1955-. . . . . CLC 40
See also CA 140

Page, P(atricia) K(athleen)
1916- . . . . CLC 7, 18; DAC; DAM MST;
PC 12
See also CA 53-56; CANR 4, 22; DLB 68;
MTCW

Page, Thomas Nelson   1853-1922. . . . SSC 23
See also CA 118; DLB 12, 78; DLBD 13

Paget, Violet   1856-1935
See Lee, Vernon
See also CA 104

Paget-Lowe, Henry
See Lovecraft, H(oward) P(hillips)

Paglia, Camille (Anna)   1947-. . . . . . CLC 68
See also CA 140

Paige, Richard
See Koontz, Dean R(ay)

Paine, Thomas   1737-1809 . . . . NCLC 62
See also CDALB 1640-1865; DLB 31, 43,
73, 158

Pakenham, Antonia
See Fraser, (Lady) Antonia (Pakenham)

Palamas, Kostes   1859-1943 . . . . TCLC 5
See also CA 105

Palazzeschi, Aldo   1885-1974 . . . . . . CLC 11
See also CA 89-92; 53-56; DLB 114

Paley, Grace
1922- . . . . CLC 4, 6, 37; DAM POP;
SSC 8
See also CA 25-28R; CANR 13, 46;
DLB 28; INT CANR-13; MTCW

Palin, Michael (Edward)   1943- . . . . . CLC 21
See also Monty Python
See also CA 107; CANR 35; SATA 67

Palliser, Charles   1947-. . . . . CLC 65
See also CA 136

Palma, Ricardo   1833-1919. . . . . TCLC 29

Pancake, Breece Dexter   1952-1979
See Pancake, Breece D'J
See also CA 123; 109

Pancake, Breece D'J. . . . . CLC 29
See also Pancake, Breece Dexter
See also DLB 130

Panko, Rudy
See Gogol, Nikolai (Vasilyevich)

Papadiamantis, Alexandros
1851-1911 . . . . TCLC 29

Papadiamantopoulos, Johannes   1856-1910
See Moreas, Jean
See also CA 117

Papini, Giovanni   1881-1956. . . . . . . TCLC 22
See also CA 121

Paracelsus   1493-1541. . . . . LC 14
See also DLB 179

Parasol, Peter
See Stevens, Wallace

Pareto, Vilfredo   1848-1923 . . . . TCLC 69

Parfenie, Maria
See Codrescu, Andrei

Parini, Jay (Lee)   1948- . . . . CLC 54
See also CA 97-100; CAAS 16; CANR 32

Park, Jordan
See Kornbluth, C(yril) M.; Pohl, Frederik

Parker, Bert
See Ellison, Harlan (Jay)

Parker, Dorothy (Rothschild)
1893-1967 . . . . CLC 15, 68;
DAM POET; SSC 2
See also CA 19-20; 25-28R; CAP 2;
DLB 11, 45, 86; MTCW

Parker, Robert B(rown)
1932- . . . . . . CLC 27; DAM NOV, POP
See also BEST 89:4; CA 49-52; CANR 1,
26, 52; INT CANR-26; MTCW

Peshkov, Alexei Maximovich 1868-1936
  See Gorky, Maxim
  See also CA 105; 141; DA; DAC;
    DAM DRAM, MST, NOV

Pessoa, Fernando (Antonio Nogueira)
  1888-1935 . . . . **TCLC 27; HLC**
  See also CA 125

Peterkin, Julia Mood 1880-1961 . . . . **CLC 31**
  See also CA 102; DLB 9

Peters, Joan K(aren) 1945- . . . . **CLC 39**
  See also CA 158

Peters, Robert L(ouis) 1924- . . . . **CLC 7**
  See also CA 13-16R; CAAS 8; DLB 105

Petofi, Sandor 1823-1849 . . . . **NCLC 21**

Petrakis, Harry Mark 1923- . . . . **CLC 3**
  See also CA 9-12R; CANR 4, 30

Petrarch
  1304-1374 . . . . **CMLC 20; DAM POET;**
                                              PC 8

Petrov, Evgeny . . . . **TCLC 21**
  See also Kataev, Evgeny Petrovich

Petry, Ann (Lane) 1908-1997 . . . **CLC 1, 7, 18**
  See also BW 1; CA 5-8R; 157; CAAS 6;
    CANR 4, 46; CLR 12; DLB 76; JRDA;
    MAICYA; MTCW; SATA 5;
    SATA-Obit 94

Petursson, Halligrimur 1614-1674 . . . . **LC 8**

Philips, Katherine 1632-1664 . . . . **LC 30**
  See also DLB 131

Philipson, Morris H. 1926- . . . . **CLC 53**
  See also CA 1-4R; CANR 4

Phillips, Caryl
  1958- . . . . **CLC 96; DAM MULT**
  See also BW 2; CA 141; DLB 157

Phillips, David Graham
  1867-1911 . . . . **TCLC 44**
  See also CA 108; DLB 9, 12

Phillips, Jack
  See Sandburg, Carl (August)

Phillips, Jayne Anne
  1952- . . . . **CLC 15, 33; SSC 16**
  See also CA 101; CANR 24, 50; DLBY 80;
    INT CANR-24; MTCW

Phillips, Richard
  See Dick, Philip K(indred)

Phillips, Robert (Schaeffer) 1938- . . . **CLC 28**
  See also CA 17-20R; CAAS 13; CANR 8;
    DLB 105

Phillips, Ward
  See Lovecraft, H(oward) P(hillips)

Piccolo, Lucio 1901-1969 . . . . **CLC 13**
  See also CA 97-100; DLB 114

Pickthall, Marjorie L(owry) C(hristie)
  1883-1922 . . . . **TCLC 21**
  See also CA 107; DLB 92

Pico della Mirandola, Giovanni
  1463-1494 . . . . **LC 15**

Piercy, Marge
  1936- . . . . **CLC 3, 6, 14, 18, 27, 62**
  See also CA 21-24R; CAAS 1; CANR 13,
    43; DLB 120; MTCW

Piers, Robert
  See Anthony, Piers

Pieyre de Mandiargues, Andre 1909-1991
  See Mandiargues, Andre Pieyre de
  See also CA 103; 136; CANR 22

Pilnyak, Boris . . . . **TCLC 23**
  See also Vogau, Boris Andreyevich

Pincherle, Alberto
  1907-1990 . . . . . **CLC 11, 18; DAM NOV**
  See also Moravia, Alberto
  See also CA 25-28R; 132; CANR 33;
    MTCW

Pinckney, Darryl 1953- . . . . **CLC 76**
  See also BW 2; CA 143

Pindar 518B.C.-446B.C. . . . . **CMLC 12; PC 19**
  See also DLB 176

Pineda, Cecile 1942- . . . . **CLC 39**
  See also CA 118

Pinero, Arthur Wing
  1855-1934 . . . . . **TCLC 32; DAM DRAM**
  See also CA 110; 153; DLB 10

Pinero, Miguel (Antonio Gomez)
  1946-1988 . . . . **CLC 4, 55**
  See also CA 61-64; 125; CANR 29; HW

Pinget, Robert 1919- . . . . **CLC 7, 13, 37**
  See also CA 85-88; DLB 83

Pink Floyd
  See Barrett, (Roger) Syd; Gilmour, David;
    Mason, Nick; Waters, Roger; Wright,
    Rick

Pinkney, Edward 1802-1828 . . . . . **NCLC 31**

Pinkwater, Daniel Manus 1941- . . . . **CLC 35**
  See also Pinkwater, Manus
  See also AAYA 1; CA 29-32R; CANR 12,
    38; CLR 4; JRDA; MAICYA; SAAS 3;
    SATA 46, 76

Pinkwater, Manus
  See Pinkwater, Daniel Manus
  See also SATA 8

Pinsky, Robert
  1940- . . **CLC 9, 19, 38, 94; DAM POET**
  See also CA 29-32R; CAAS 4; CANR 58;
    DLBY 82

Pinta, Harold
  See Pinter, Harold

Pinter, Harold
  1930- . . . . . **CLC 1, 3, 6, 9, 11, 15, 27, 58,**
                      73; DA; DAB; DAC; DAM DRAM,
                                              MST; WLC
  See also CA 5-8R; CANR 33; CDBLB 1960
    to Present; DLB 13; MTCW

Piozzi, Hester Lynch (Thrale)
  1741-1821 . . . . **NCLC 57**
  See also DLB 104, 142

Pirandello, Luigi
  1867-1936 . . . . . **TCLC 4, 29; DA; DAB;**
                      DAC; DAM DRAM, MST; DC 5;
                                              SSC 22; WLC
  See also CA 104; 153

Pirsig, Robert M(aynard)
  1928- . . . . **CLC 4, 6, 73; DAM POP**
  See also CA 53-56; CANR 42; MTCW;
    SATA 39

Pisarev, Dmitry Ivanovich
  1840-1868 . . . . **NCLC 25**

Pix, Mary (Griffith) 1666-1709 . . . . . . **LC 8**
  See also DLB 80

Pixerecourt, Guilbert de
  1773-1844 . . . . **NCLC 39**

Plaatje, Sol(omon) T(shekisho)
  1876-1932 . . . . **TCLC 71**
  See also BW 2; CA 141

Plaidy, Jean
  See Hibbert, Eleanor Alice Burford

Planche, James Robinson
  1796-1880 . . . . **NCLC 42**

Plant, Robert 1948- . . . . **CLC 12**

Plante, David (Robert)
  1940- . . . . **CLC 7, 23, 38; DAM NOV**
  See also CA 37-40R; CANR 12, 36, 58;
    DLBY 83; INT CANR-12; MTCW

Plath, Sylvia
  1932-1963 . . . . . **CLC 1, 2, 3, 5, 9, 11, 14,**
                      17, 50, 51, 62; DA; DAB; DAC;
                      DAM MST, POET; PC 1; WLC
  See also AAYA 13; CA 19-20; CANR 34;
    CAP 2; CDALB 1941-1968; DLB 5, 6,
    152; MTCW

Plato
  428(?)B.C.-348(?)B.C. . . . . . **CMLC 8; DA;**
                      DAB; DAC; DAM MST
  See also DLB 176; YABC

Platonov, Andrei . . . . **TCLC 14**
  See also Klimentov, Andrei Platonovich

Platt, Kin 1911- . . . . **CLC 26**
  See also AAYA 11; CA 17-20R; CANR 11;
    JRDA; SAAS 17; SATA 21, 86

Plautus c. 251B.C.-184B.C. . . . . **DC 6**

Plick et Plock
  See Simenon, Georges (Jacques Christian)

Plimpton, George (Ames) 1927- . . . . . **CLC 36**
  See also AITN 1; CA 21-24R; CANR 32;
    MTCW; SATA 10

Plomer, William Charles Franklin
  1903-1973 . . . . **CLC 4, 8**
  See also CA 21-22; CANR 34; CAP 2;
    DLB 20, 162; MTCW; SATA 24

Plowman, Piers
  See Kavanagh, Patrick (Joseph)

Plum, J.
  See Wodehouse, P(elham) G(renville)

Plumly, Stanley (Ross) 1939- . . . . . . **CLC 33**
  See also CA 108; 110; DLB 5; INT 110

Plumpe, Friedrich Wilhelm
  1888-1931 . . . . **TCLC 53**
  See also CA 112

Poe, Edgar Allan
  1809-1849 . . . . **NCLC 1, 16, 55; DA;**
                      DAB; DAC; DAM MST, POET; PC 1;
                                              SSC 1, 22; WLC
  See also AAYA 14; CDALB 1640-1865;
    DLB 3, 59, 73, 74; SATA 23

Poet of Titchfield Street, The
  See Pound, Ezra (Weston Loomis)

Pohl, Frederik 1919- . . . . . **CLC 18; SSC 25**
  See also CA 61-64; CAAS 1; CANR 11, 37;
    DLB 8; INT CANR-11; MTCW;
    SATA 24

Poirier, Louis 1910-
  See Gracq, Julien
  See also CA 122; 126

Pteleon
See Grieve, C(hristopher) M(urray)
See also DAM POET

Puckett, Lute
See Masters, Edgar Lee

Puig, Manuel
1932-1990 .... **CLC 3, 5, 10, 28, 65;**
DAM MULT; HLC
See also CA 45-48; CANR 2, 32; DLB 113;
HW; MTCW

Purdy, Al(fred Wellington)
1918- .... **CLC 3, 6, 14, 50; DAC;**
DAM MST, POET
See also CA 81-84; CAAS 17; CANR 42;
DLB 88

Purdy, James (Amos)
1923- .... **CLC 2, 4, 10, 28, 52**
See also CA 33-36R; CAAS 1; CANR 19,
51; DLB 2; INT CANR-19; MTCW

Pure, Simon
See Swinnerton, Frank Arthur

Pushkin, Alexander (Sergeyevich)
1799-1837 ..... **NCLC 3, 27; DA; DAB;**
DAC; DAM DRAM, MST, POET;
PC 10; WLC
See also SATA 61

P'u Sung-ling 1640-1715 .... **LC 3**

Putnam, Arthur Lee
See Alger, Horatio, Jr.

Puzo, Mario
1920- ..... **CLC 1, 2, 6, 36; DAM NOV,**
POP
See also CA 65-68; CANR 4, 42; DLB 6;
MTCW

Pygge, Edward
See Barnes, Julian (Patrick)

Pym, Barbara (Mary Crampton)
1913-1980 .... **CLC 13, 19, 37**
See also CA 13-14; 97-100; CANR 13, 34;
CAP 1; DLB 14; DLBY 87; MTCW

Pynchon, Thomas (Ruggles, Jr.)
1937- ..... **CLC 2, 3, 6, 9, 11, 18, 33, 62,**
72; DA; DAB; DAC; DAM MST, NOV,
POP; SSC 14; WLC
See also BEST 90:2; CA 17-20R; CANR 22,
46; DLB 2, 173; MTCW

Pythagoras
c. 570B.C.-c. 500B.C. .... **CMLC 22**
See also DLB 176

Qian Zhongshu
See Ch'ien Chung-shu

Qroll
See Dagerman, Stig (Halvard)

Quarrington, Paul (Lewis) 1953-.... **CLC 65**
See also CA 129

Quasimodo, Salvatore 1901-1968 ... **CLC 10**
See also CA 13-16; 25-28R; CAP 1;
DLB 114; MTCW

Quay, Stephen 1947- .... **CLC 95**

Quay, The Brothers
See Quay, Stephen; Quay, Timothy

Quay, Timothy 1947-............. **CLC 95**

Queen, Ellery.................. **CLC 3, 11**
See also Dannay, Frederic; Davidson,
Avram; Lee, Manfred B(ennington);
Marlowe, Stephen; Sturgeon, Theodore
(Hamilton); Vance, John Holbrook

Queen, Ellery, Jr.
See Dannay, Frederic; Lee, Manfred
B(ennington)

Queneau, Raymond
1903-1976 .... **CLC 2, 5, 10, 42**
See also CA 77-80; 69-72; CANR 32;
DLB 72; MTCW

Quevedo, Francisco de 1580-1645.... **LC 23**

Quiller-Couch, Arthur Thomas
1863-1944 .... **TCLC 53**
See also CA 118; DLB 135, 153

Quin, Ann (Marie) 1936-1973...... **CLC 6**
See also CA 9-12R; 45-48; DLB 14

Quinn, Martin
See Smith, Martin Cruz

Quinn, Peter 1947-............... **CLC 91**

Quinn, Simon
See Smith, Martin Cruz

Quiroga, Horacio (Sylvestre)
1878-1937 ..... **TCLC 20; DAM MULT;**
HLC
See also CA 117; 131; HW; MTCW

Quoirez, Francoise 1935-........... **CLC 9**
See also Sagan, Francoise
See also CA 49-52; CANR 6, 39; MTCW

Raabe, Wilhelm 1831-1910 .... **TCLC 45**
See also DLB 129

Rabe, David (William)
1940- ...... **CLC 4, 8, 33; DAM DRAM**
See also CA 85-88; CABS 3; DLB 7

Rabelais, Francois
1483-1553 ...... **LC 5; DA; DAB; DAC;**
DAM MST; WLC

Rabinovitch, Sholem 1859-1916
See Aleichem, Sholom
See also CA 104

Rachilde 1860-1953 .... **TCLC 67**
See also DLB 123

Racine, Jean
1639-1699 .... **LC 28; DAB; DAM MST**

Radcliffe, Ann (Ward)
1764-1823 .... **NCLC 6, 55**
See also DLB 39, 178

Radiguet, Raymond 1903-1923 .... **TCLC 29**
See also DLB 65

Radnoti, Miklos 1909-1944 ...... **TCLC 16**
See also CA 118

Rado, James 1939-............... **CLC 17**
See also CA 105

Radvanyi, Netty 1900-1983
See Seghers, Anna
See also CA 85-88; 110

Rae, Ben
See Griffiths, Trevor

Raeburn, John (Hay) 1941-........ **CLC 34**
See also CA 57-60

Ragni, Gerome 1942-1991 .... **CLC 17**
See also CA 105; 134

Rahv, Philip 1908-1973 .... **CLC 24**
See also Greenberg, Ivan
See also DLB 137

Raine, Craig 1944-............... **CLC 32**
See also CA 108; CANR 29, 51; DLB 40

Raine, Kathleen (Jessie) 1908- ... **CLC 7, 45**
See also CA 85-88; CANR 46; DLB 20;
MTCW

Rainis, Janis 1865-1929 .... **TCLC 29**

Rakosi, Carl..................... **CLC 47**
See also Rawley, Callman
See also CAAS 5

Raleigh, Richard
See Lovecraft, H(oward) P(hillips)

Raleigh, Sir Walter
1554(?)-1618 .... **LC 31, 39**
See also CDBLB Before 1660; DLB 172

Rallentando, H. P.
See Sayers, Dorothy L(eigh)

Ramal, Walter
See de la Mare, Walter (John)

Ramon, Juan
See Jimenez (Mantecon), Juan Ramon

Ramos, Graciliano 1892-1953 ..... **TCLC 32**

Rampersad, Arnold 1941-......... **CLC 44**
See also BW 2; CA 127; 133; DLB 111;
INT 133

Rampling, Anne
See Rice, Anne

Ramsay, Allan 1684(?)-1758 .... **LC 29**
See also DLB 95

Ramuz, Charles-Ferdinand
1878-1947 .... **TCLC 33**

Rand, Ayn
1905-1982 ...... **CLC 3, 30, 44, 79; DA;**
DAC; DAM MST, NOV, POP; WLC
See also AAYA 10; CA 13-16R; 105;
CANR 27; MTCW

Randall, Dudley (Felker)
1914- ...... **CLC 1; BLC; DAM MULT**
See also BW 1; CA 25-28R; CANR 23;
DLB 41

Randall, Robert
See Silverberg, Robert

Ranger, Ken
See Creasey, John

Ransom, John Crowe
1888-1974 .... **CLC 2, 4, 5, 11, 24;**
DAM POET
See also CA 5-8R; 49-52; CANR 6, 34;
DLB 45, 63; MTCW

Rao, Raja 1909- ... **CLC 25, 56; DAM NOV**
See also CA 73-76; CANR 51; MTCW

Raphael, Frederic (Michael)
1931-.................... **CLC 2, 14**
See also CA 1-4R; CANR 1; DLB 14

Ratcliffe, James P.
See Mencken, H(enry) L(ouis)

Rathbone, Julian 1935- .... **CLC 41**
See also CA 101; CANR 34

Rattigan, Terence (Mervyn)
1911-1977 .... **CLC 7; DAM DRAM**
See also CA 85-88; 73-76;
CDBLB 1945-1960; DLB 13; MTCW

Richardson, John
1796-1852 . . . . **NCLC 55; DAC**
See also DLB 99

Richardson, Samuel
1689-1761 . . . . . . **LC 1; DA; DAB; DAC;**
DAM MST, NOV; WLC
See also CDBLB 1660-1789; DLB 39

Richler, Mordecai
1931- . . . . **CLC 3, 5, 9, 13, 18, 46, 70;**
DAC; DAM MST, NOV
See also AITN 1; CA 65-68; CANR 31;
CLR 17; DLB 53; MAICYA; MTCW;
SATA 44; SATA-Brief 27

Richter, Conrad (Michael)
1890-1968 . . . . **CLC 30**
See also AAYA 21; CA 5-8R; 25-28R;
CANR 23; DLB 9; MTCW; SATA 3

Ricostranza, Tom
See Ellis, Trey

Riddell, J. H. 1832-1906 . . . . **TCLC 40**

Riding, Laura . . . . **CLC 3, 7**
See also Jackson, Laura (Riding)

Riefenstahl, Berta Helene Amalia 1902-
See Riefenstahl, Leni
See also CA 108

Riefenstahl, Leni . . . . **CLC 16**
See also Riefenstahl, Berta Helene Amalia

Riffe, Ernest
See Bergman, (Ernst) Ingmar

Riggs, (Rolla) Lynn
1899-1954 . . . . . **TCLC 56; DAM MULT**
See also CA 144; DLB 175; NNAL

Riley, James Whitcomb
1849-1916 . . . . . . **TCLC 51; DAM POET**
See also CA 118; 137; MAICYA; SATA 17

Riley, Tex
See Creasey, John

Rilke, Rainer Maria
1875-1926 . . . . **TCLC 1, 6, 19;**
DAM POET; PC 2
See also CA 104; 132; DLB 81; MTCW

Rimbaud, (Jean Nicolas) Arthur
1854-1891 . . . . . **NCLC 4, 35; DA; DAB;**
DAC; DAM MST, POET; PC 3; WLC

Rinehart, Mary Roberts
1876-1958 . . . . **TCLC 52**
See also CA 108

Ringmaster, The
See Mencken, H(enry) L(ouis)

Ringwood, Gwen(dolyn Margaret) Pharis
1910-1984 . . . . **CLC 48**
See also CA 148; 112; DLB 88

Rio, Michel 19(?)- . . . . **CLC 43**

Ritsos, Giannes
See Ritsos, Yannis

Ritsos, Yannis 1909-1990 . . . . . **CLC 6, 13, 31**
See also CA 77-80; 133; CANR 39; MTCW

Ritter, Erika 1948(?)- . . . . **CLC 52**

Rivera, Jose Eustasio 1889-1928 . . . **TCLC 35**
See also HW

Rivers, Conrad Kent 1933-1968 . . . . . . **CLC 1**
See also BW 1; CA 85-88; DLB 41

Rivers, Elfrida
See Bradley, Marion Zimmer

Riverside, John
See Heinlein, Robert A(nson)

Rizal, Jose 1861-1896 . . . . **NCLC 27**

Roa Bastos, Augusto (Antonio)
1917- . . . . . **CLC 45; DAM MULT; HLC**
See also CA 131; DLB 113; HW

Robbe-Grillet, Alain
1922- . . . . . . **CLC 1, 2, 4, 6, 8, 10, 14, 43**
See also CA 9-12R; CANR 33; DLB 83;
MTCW

Robbins, Harold
1916- . . . . **CLC 5; DAM NOV**
See also CA 73-76; CANR 26, 54; MTCW

Robbins, Thomas Eugene 1936-
See Robbins, Tom
See also CA 81-84; CANR 29; DAM NOV,
POP; MTCW

Robbins, Tom . . . . **CLC 9, 32, 64**
See also Robbins, Thomas Eugene
See also BEST 90:3; DLBY 80

Robbins, Trina 1938- . . . . **CLC 21**
See also CA 128

Roberts, Charles G(eorge) D(ouglas)
1860-1943 . . . . **TCLC 8**
See also CA 105; CLR 33; DLB 92;
SATA 88; SATA-Brief 29

Roberts, Elizabeth Madox
1886-1941 . . . . **TCLC 68**
See also CA 111; DLB 9, 54, 102;
SATA 33; SATA-Brief 27

Roberts, Kate 1891-1985 . . . . **CLC 15**
See also CA 107; 116

Roberts, Keith (John Kingston)
1935- . . . . **CLC 14**
See also CA 25-28R; CANR 46

Roberts, Kenneth (Lewis)
1885-1957 . . . . **TCLC 23**
See also CA 109; DLB 9

Roberts, Michele (B.) 1949- . . . . **CLC 48**
See also CA 115; CANR 58

Robertson, Ellis
See Ellison, Harlan (Jay); Silverberg, Robert

Robertson, Thomas William
1829-1871 . . . . **NCLC 35; DAM DRAM**

Robeson, Kenneth
See Dent, Lester

Robinson, Edwin Arlington
1869-1935 . . . . **TCLC 5; DA; DAC;**
DAM MST, POET; PC 1
See also CA 104; 133; CDALB 1865-1917;
DLB 54; MTCW

Robinson, Henry Crabb
1775-1867 . . . . **NCLC 15**
See also DLB 107

Robinson, Jill 1936- . . . . **CLC 10**
See also CA 102; INT 102

Robinson, Kim Stanley 1952- . . . . . . **CLC 34**
See also CA 126

Robinson, Lloyd
See Silverberg, Robert

Robinson, Marilynne 1944- . . . . **CLC 25**
See also CA 116

Robinson, Smokey . . . . **CLC 21**
See also Robinson, William, Jr.

Robinson, William, Jr. 1940-
See Robinson, Smokey
See also CA 116

Robison, Mary 1949- . . . . **CLC 42, 98**
See also CA 113; 116; DLB 130; INT 116

Rod, Edouard 1857-1910 . . . . **TCLC 52**

Roddenberry, Eugene Wesley 1921-1991
See Roddenberry, Gene
See also CA 110; 135; CANR 37; SATA 45;
SATA-Obit 69

Roddenberry, Gene . . . . **CLC 17**
See also Roddenberry, Eugene Wesley
See also AAYA 5; SATA-Obit 69

Rodgers, Mary 1931- . . . . **CLC 12**
See also CA 49-52; CANR 8, 55; CLR 20;
INT CANR-8; JRDA; MAICYA;
SATA 8

Rodgers, W(illiam) R(obert)
1909-1969 . . . . **CLC 7**
See also CA 85-88; DLB 20

Rodman, Eric
See Silverberg, Robert

Rodman, Howard 1920(?)-1985 . . . . . **CLC 65**
See also CA 118

Rodman, Maia
See Wojciechowska, Maia (Teresa)

Rodriguez, Claudio 1934- . . . . **CLC 10**
See also DLB 134

Roelvaag, O(le) E(dvart)
1876-1931 . . . . **TCLC 17**
See also CA 117; DLB 9

Roethke, Theodore (Huebner)
1908-1963 . . . . . . **CLC 1, 3, 8, 11, 19, 46,**
101; DAM POET; PC 15
See also CA 81-84; CABS 2;
CDALB 1941-1968; DLB 5; MTCW

Rogers, Thomas Hunton 1927- . . . . . **CLC 57**
See also CA 89-92; INT 89-92

Rogers, Will(iam Penn Adair)
1879-1935 . . . **TCLC 8, 71; DAM MULT**
See also CA 105; 144; DLB 11; NNAL

Rogin, Gilbert 1929- . . . . **CLC 18**
See also CA 65-68; CANR 15

Rohan, Koda . . . . **TCLC 22**
See also Koda Shigeyuki

Rohmer, Eric . . . . **CLC 16**
See also Scherer, Jean-Marie Maurice

Rohmer, Sax . . . . **TCLC 28**
See also Ward, Arthur Henry Sarsfield
See also DLB 70

Roiphe, Anne (Richardson)
1935- . . . . **CLC 3, 9**
See also CA 89-92; CANR 45; DLBY 80;
INT 89-92

Rojas, Fernando de 1465-1541 . . . . . . **LC 23**

Rolfe, Frederick (William Serafino Austin
Lewis Mary) 1860-1913 . . . . . . **TCLC 12**
See also CA 107; DLB 34, 156

Rolland, Romain 1866-1944 . . . . **TCLC 23**
See also CA 118; DLB 65

Rolle, Richard c. 1300-c. 1349 . . . **CMLC 21**
See also DLB 146

Rolvaag, O(le) E(dvart)
See Roelvaag, O(le) E(dvart)

Romain Arnaud, Saint
See Aragon, Louis

Romains, Jules 1885-1972 . . . . CLC 7
See also CA 85-88; CANR 34; DLB 65;
MTCW

Romero, Jose Ruben 1890-1952 . . . TCLC 14
See also CA 114; 131; HW

Ronsard, Pierre de
1524-1585 . . . . LC 6; PC 11

Rooke, Leon
1934- . . . . CLC 25, 34; DAM POP
See also CA 25-28R; CANR 23, 53

Roosevelt, Theodore 1858-1919 . . . . TCLC 69
See also CA 115; DLB 47

Roper, William 1498-1578 . . . . LC 10

Roquelaure, A. N.
See Rice, Anne

Rosa, Joao Guimaraes 1908-1967 . . . CLC 23
See also CA 89-92; DLB 113

Rose, Wendy
1948- . . . . CLC 85; DAM MULT; PC 13
See also CA 53-56; CANR 5, 51; DLB 175;
NNAL; SATA 12

Rosen, Richard (Dean) 1949- . . . . CLC 39
See also CA 77-80; INT CANR-30

Rosenberg, Isaac 1890-1918 . . . . . . TCLC 12
See also CA 107; DLB 20

Rosenblatt, Joe . . . . CLC 15
See also Rosenblatt, Joseph

Rosenblatt, Joseph 1933-
See Rosenblatt, Joe
See also CA 89-92; INT 89-92

Rosenfeld, Samuel 1896-1963
See Tzara, Tristan
See also CA 89-92

Rosenstock, Sami
See Tzara, Tristan

Rosenstock, Samuel
See Tzara, Tristan

Rosenthal, M(acha) L(ouis)
1917-1996 . . . . CLC 28
See also CA 1-4R; 152; CAAS 6; CANR 4,
51; DLB 5; SATA 59

Ross, Barnaby
See Dannay, Frederic

Ross, Bernard L.
See Follett, Ken(neth Martin)

Ross, J. H.
See Lawrence, T(homas) E(dward)

Ross, Martin
See Martin, Violet Florence
See also DLB 135

Ross, (James) Sinclair
1908- . . . . . . CLC 13; DAC; DAM MST;
SSC 24
See also CA 73-76; DLB 88

Rossetti, Christina (Georgina)
1830-1894 . . . . . NCLC 2, 50; DA; DAB;
DAC; DAM MST, POET; PC 7; WLC
See also DLB 35, 163; MAICYA; SATA 20

Rossetti, Dante Gabriel
1828-1882 . . . . NCLC 4; DA; DAB;
DAC; DAM MST, POET; WLC
See also CDBLB 1832-1890; DLB 35

Rossner, Judith (Perelman)
1935- . . . . CLC 6, 9, 29
See also AITN 2; BEST 90:3; CA 17-20R;
CANR 18, 51; DLB 6; INT CANR-18;
MTCW

Rostand, Edmond (Eugene Alexis)
1868-1918 . . . . . . TCLC 6, 37; DA; DAB;
DAC; DAM DRAM, MST
See also CA 104; 126; MTCW

Roth, Henry 1906-1995 . . . . . . CLC 2, 6, 11
See also CA 11-12; 149; CANR 38; CAP 1;
DLB 28; MTCW

Roth, Joseph 1894-1939 . . . . TCLC 33
See also DLB 85

Roth, Philip (Milton)
1933- . . . . . . CLC 1, 2, 3, 4, 6, 9, 15, 22,
31, 47, 66, 86; DA; DAB; DAC;
DAM MST, NOV, POP; SSC 26; WLC
See also BEST 90:3; CA 1-4R; CANR 1, 22,
36, 55; CDALB 1968-1988; DLB 2, 28,
173; DLBY 82; MTCW

Rothenberg, Jerome 1931- . . . . CLC 6, 57
See also CA 45-48; CANR 1; DLB 5

Roumain, Jacques (Jean Baptiste)
1907-1944 . . . . TCLC 19; BLC;
DAM MULT
See also BW 1; CA 117; 125

Rourke, Constance (Mayfield)
1885-1941 . . . . TCLC 12
See also CA 107; 1

Rousseau, Jean-Baptiste 1671-1741 . . . LC 9

Rousseau, Jean-Jacques
1712-1778 . . . . LC 14, 36; DA; DAB;
DAC; DAM MST; WLC

Roussel, Raymond 1877-1933 . . . . . TCLC 20
See also CA 117

Rovit, Earl (Herbert) 1927- . . . . CLC 7
See also CA 5-8R; CANR 12

Rowe, Nicholas 1674-1718 . . . . LC 8
See also DLB 84

Rowley, Ames Dorrance
See Lovecraft, H(oward) P(hillips)

Rowson, Susanna Haswell
1762(?)-1824 . . . . NCLC 5
See also DLB 37

Roy, Gabrielle
1909-1983 . . . . CLC 10, 14; DAB; DAC;
DAM MST
See also CA 53-56; 110; CANR 5; DLB 68;
MTCW

Rozewicz, Tadeusz
1921- . . . . CLC 9, 23; DAM POET
See also CA 108; CANR 36; MTCW

Ruark, Gibbons 1941- . . . . CLC 3
See also CA 33-36R; CAAS 23; CANR 14,
31, 57; DLB 120

Rubens, Bernice (Ruth) 1923- . . . CLC 19, 31
See also CA 25-28R; CANR 33; DLB 14;
MTCW

Rubin, Harold
See Robbins, Harold

Rudkin, (James) David 1936- . . . . . . CLC 14
See also CA 89-92; DLB 13

Rudnik, Raphael 1933- . . . . CLC 7
See also CA 29-32R

Ruffian, M.
See Hasek, Jaroslav (Matej Frantisek)

Ruiz, Jose Martinez . . . . CLC 11
See also Martinez Ruiz, Jose

Rukeyser, Muriel
1913-1980 . . . . CLC 6, 10, 15, 27;
DAM POET; PC 12
See also CA 5-8R; 93-96; CANR 26;
DLB 48; MTCW; SATA-Obit 22

Rule, Jane (Vance) 1931- . . . . CLC 27
See also CA 25-28R; CAAS 18; CANR 12;
DLB 60

Rulfo, Juan
1918-1986 . . . . CLC 8, 80; DAM MULT;
HLC; SSC 25
See also CA 85-88; 118; CANR 26;
DLB 113; HW; MTCW

Rumi, Jalal al-Din 1297-1373 . . . . CMLC 20

Runeberg, Johan 1804-1877 . . . . . . NCLC 41

Runyon, (Alfred) Damon
1884(?)-1946 . . . . TCLC 10
See also CA 107; DLB 11, 86, 171

Rush, Norman 1933- . . . . CLC 44
See also CA 121; 126; INT 126

Rushdie, (Ahmed) Salman
1947- . . . . . . CLC 23, 31, 55, 100; DAB;
DAC; DAM MST, NOV, POP
See also BEST 89:3; CA 108; 111;
CANR 33, 56; INT 111; MTCW; YABC

Rushforth, Peter (Scott) 1945- . . . . . CLC 19
See also CA 101

Ruskin, John 1819-1900 . . . . TCLC 63
See also CA 114; 129; CDBLB 1832-1890;
DLB 55, 163; SATA 24

Russ, Joanna 1937- . . . . CLC 15
See also CA 25-28R; CANR 11, 31; DLB 8;
MTCW

Russell, George William 1867-1935
See Baker, Jean H.
See also CA 104; 153; CDBLB 1890-1914;
DAM POET

Russell, (Henry) Ken(neth Alfred)
1927- . . . . CLC 16
See also CA 105

Russell, Willy 1947- . . . . CLC 60

Rutherford, Mark . . . . TCLC 25
See also White, William Hale
See also DLB 18

Ruyslinck, Ward 1929- . . . . CLC 14
See also Belser, Reimond Karel Maria de

Ryan, Cornelius (John) 1920-1974 . . . CLC 7
See also CA 69-72; 53-56; CANR 38

Ryan, Michael 1946- . . . . CLC 65
See also CA 49-52; DLBY 82

Ryan, Tim
See Dent, Lester

Rybakov, Anatoli (Naumovich)
1911- . . . . CLC 23, 53
See also CA 126; 135; SATA 79

Ryder, Jonathan
See Ludlum, Robert

Ryga, George
1932-1987 . . CLC 14; DAC; DAM MST
See also CA 101; 124; CANR 43; DLB 60

Search, Alexander
See Pessoa, Fernando (Antonio Nogueira)

Sebastian, Lee
See Silverberg, Robert

Sebastian Owl
See Thompson, Hunter S(tockton)

Sebestyen, Ouida 1924- . . . . **CLC 30**
See also AAYA 8; CA 107; CANR 40;
CLR 17; JRDA; MAICYA; SAAS 10;
SATA 39

Secundus, H. Scriblerus
See Fielding, Henry

Sedges, John
See Buck, Pearl S(ydenstricker)

Sedgwick, Catharine Maria
1789-1867 . . . . **NCLC 19**
See also DLB 1, 74

Seelye, John 1931- . . . . **CLC 7**

Seferiades, Giorgos Stylianou 1900-1971
See Seferis, George
See also CA 5-8R; 33-36R; CANR 5, 36;
MTCW

Seferis, George . . . . **CLC 5, 11**
See also Seferiades, Giorgos Stylianou

Segal, Erich (Wolf)
1937- . . . . **CLC 3, 10; DAM POP**
See also BEST 89:1; CA 25-28R; CANR 20,
36; DLBY 86; INT CANR-20; MTCW

Seger, Bob 1945- . . . . **CLC 35**

Seghers, Anna . . . . **CLC 7**
See also Radvanyi, Netty
See also DLB 69

Seidel, Frederick (Lewis) 1936- . . . . . **CLC 18**
See also CA 13-16R; CANR 8; DLBY 84

Seifert, Jaroslav
1901-1986 . . . . **CLC 34, 44, 93**
See also CA 127; MTCW

Sei Shonagon c. 966-1017(?) . . . . . . **CMLC 6**

Selby, Hubert, Jr.
1928- . . . . **CLC 1, 2, 4, 8; SSC 20**
See also CA 13-16R; CANR 33; DLB 2

Selzer, Richard 1928- . . . . **CLC 74**
See also CA 65-68; CANR 14

Sembene, Ousmane
See Ousmane, Sembene

Senancour, Etienne Pivert de
1770-1846 . . . . **NCLC 16**
See also DLB 119

Sender, Ramon (Jose)
1902-1982 . . **CLC 8; DAM MULT; HLC**
See also CA 5-8R; 105; CANR 8; HW;
MTCW

Seneca, Lucius Annaeus
4B.C.-65 . . . . . . **CMLC 6; DAM DRAM;
DC 5**

Senghor, Leopold Sedar
1906- . . . . . **CLC 54; BLC; DAM MULT,
POET**
See also BW 2; CA 116; 125; CANR 47;
MTCW

Serling, (Edward) Rod(man)
1924-1975 . . . . **CLC 30**
See also AAYA 14; AITN 1; CA 65-68;
57-60; DLB 26

Serna, Ramon Gomez de la
See Gomez de la Serna, Ramon

Serpieres
See Guillevic, (Eugene)

Service, Robert
See Service, Robert W(illiam)
See also DAB; DLB 92

Service, Robert W(illiam)
1874(?)-1958 . . . . . . **TCLC 15; DA; DAC;
DAM MST, POET; WLC**
See also Service, Robert
See also CA 115; 140; SATA 20

Seth, Vikram
1952- . . . . **CLC 43, 90; DAM MULT**
See also CA 121; 127; CANR 50; DLB 120;
INT 127

Seton, Cynthia Propper
1926-1982 . . . . **CLC 27**
See also CA 5-8R; 108; CANR 7

Seton, Ernest (Evan) Thompson
1860-1946 . . . . **TCLC 31**
See also CA 109; DLB 92; DLBD 13;
JRDA; SATA 18

Seton-Thompson, Ernest
See Seton, Ernest (Evan) Thompson

Settle, Mary Lee 1918- . . . . **CLC 19, 61**
See also CA 89-92; CAAS 1; CANR 44;
DLB 6; INT 89-92

Seuphor, Michel
See Arp, Jean

**Sevigne, Marie (de Rabutin-Chantal) Marquise
de** 1626-1696 . . . . **LC 11**

Sewall, Samuel 1652-1730 . . . . **LC 38**
See also DLB 24

Sexton, Anne (Harvey)
1928-1974 . . . . **CLC 2, 4, 6, 8, 10, 15, 53;
DA; DAB; DAC; DAM MST, POET;
PC 2; WLC**
See also CA 1-4R; 53-56; CABS 2;
CANR 3, 36; CDALB 1941-1968; DLB 5,
169; MTCW; SATA 10

Shaara, Michael (Joseph, Jr.)
1929-1988 . . . . **CLC 15; DAM POP**
See also AITN 1; CA 102; 125; CANR 52;
DLBY 83

Shackleton, C. C.
See Aldiss, Brian W(ilson)

Shacochis, Bob . . . . **CLC 39**
See also Shacochis, Robert G.

Shacochis, Robert G. 1951-
See Shacochis, Bob
See also CA 119; 124; INT 124

Shaffer, Anthony (Joshua)
1926- . . . . **CLC 19; DAM DRAM**
See also CA 110; 116; DLB 13

Shaffer, Peter (Levin)
1926- . . . . . . **CLC 5, 14, 18, 37, 60; DAB;
DAM DRAM, MST; DC 7**
See also CA 25-28R; CANR 25, 47;
CDBLB 1960 to Present; DLB 13;
MTCW

Shakey, Bernard
See Young, Neil

Shalamov, Varlam (Tikhonovich)
1907(?)-1982 . . . . **CLC 18**
See also CA 129; 105

Shamlu, Ahmad 1925- . . . . **CLC 10**

Shammas, Anton 1951- . . . . **CLC 55**

Shange, Ntozake
1948- . . . . **CLC 8, 25, 38, 74; BLC;
DAM DRAM, MULT; DC 3**
See also AAYA 9; BW 2; CA 85-88;
CABS 3; CANR 27, 48; DLB 38; MTCW

Shanley, John Patrick 1950- . . . . **CLC 75**
See also CA 128; 133

Shapcott, Thomas W(illiam) 1935- . . **CLC 38**
See also CA 69-72; CANR 49

Shapiro, Jane . . . . **CLC 76**

Shapiro, Karl (Jay) 1913- . . **CLC 4, 8, 15, 53**
See also CA 1-4R; CAAS 6; CANR 1, 36;
DLB 48; MTCW

Sharp, William 1855-1905 . . . . **TCLC 39**
See also DLB 156

Sharpe, Thomas Ridley 1928-
See Sharpe, Tom
See also CA 114; 122; INT 122

Sharpe, Tom . . . . **CLC 36**
See also Sharpe, Thomas Ridley
See also DLB 14

Shaw, Bernard . . . . **TCLC 45**
See also Shaw, George Bernard
See also BW 1

Shaw, G. Bernard
See Shaw, George Bernard

Shaw, George Bernard
1856-1950 . . . **TCLC 3, 9, 21; DA; DAB;
DAC; DAM DRAM, MST; WLC**
See also Shaw, Bernard
See also CA 104; 128; CDBLB 1914-1945;
DLB 10, 57; MTCW

Shaw, Henry Wheeler
1818-1885 . . . . **NCLC 15**
See also DLB 11

Shaw, Irwin
1913-1984 . . . . **CLC 7, 23, 34;
DAM DRAM, POP**
See also AITN 1; CA 13-16R; 112;
CANR 21; CDALB 1941-1968; DLB 6,
102; DLBY 84; MTCW

Shaw, Robert 1927-1978 . . . . **CLC 5**
See also AITN 1; CA 1-4R; 81-84;
CANR 4; DLB 13, 14

Shaw, T. E.
See Lawrence, T(homas) E(dward)

Shawn, Wallace 1943- . . . . **CLC 41**
See also CA 112

Shea, Lisa 1953- . . . . **CLC 86**
See also CA 147

Sheed, Wilfrid (John Joseph)
1930- . . . . **CLC 2, 4, 10, 53**
See also CA 65-68; CANR 30; DLB 6;
MTCW

Sheldon, Alice Hastings Bradley
1915(?)-1987
See Tiptree, James, Jr.
See also CA 108; 122; CANR 34; INT 108;
MTCW

Sheldon, John
See Bloch, Robert (Albert)

Simpson, N(orman) F(rederick)
1919- . . . . **CLC 29**
See also CA 13-16R; DLB 13

Sinclair, Andrew (Annandale)
1935- . . . . **CLC 2, 14**
See also CA 9-12R; CAAS 5; CANR 14, 38;
DLB 14; MTCW

Sinclair, Emil
See Hesse, Hermann

Sinclair, Iain 1943- . . . . **CLC 76**
See also CA 132

Sinclair, Iain MacGregor
See Sinclair, Iain

Sinclair, Irene
See Griffith, D(avid Lewelyn) W(ark)

Sinclair, Mary Amelia St. Clair 1865(?)-1946
See Sinclair, May
See also CA 104

Sinclair, May . . . . **TCLC 3, 11**
See also Sinclair, Mary Amelia St. Clair
See also DLB 36, 135

Sinclair, Roy
See Griffith, D(avid Lewelyn) W(ark)

Sinclair, Upton (Beall)
1878-1968 . . . . . . **CLC 1, 11, 15, 63; DA;**
DAB; DAC; DAM MST, NOV; WLC
See also CA 5-8R; 25-28R; CANR 7;
CDALB 1929-1941; DLB 9;
INT CANR-7; MTCW; SATA 9

Singer, Isaac
See Singer, Isaac Bashevis

Singer, Isaac Bashevis
1904-1991 . . . . **CLC 1, 3, 6, 9, 11, 15, 23,**
38, 69; DA; DAB; DAC; DAM MST,
NOV; SSC 3; WLC
See also AITN 1, 2; CA 1-4R; 134;
CANR 1, 39; CDALB 1941-1968; CLR 1;
DLB 6, 28, 52; DLBY 91; JRDA;
MAICYA; MTCW; SATA 3, 27;
SATA-Obit 68

Singer, Israel Joshua 1893-1944 . . . **TCLC 33**

Singh, Khushwant 1915- . . . . **CLC 11**
See also CA 9-12R; CAAS 9; CANR 6

Sinjohn, John
See Galsworthy, John

Sinyavsky, Andrei (Donatevich)
1925- . . . . **CLC 8**
See also CA 85-88

Sirin, V.
See Nabokov, Vladimir (Vladimirovich)

Sissman, L(ouis) E(dward)
1928-1976 . . . . **CLC 9, 18**
See also CA 21-24R; 65-68; CANR 13;
DLB 5

Sisson, C(harles) H(ubert) 1914- . . . . . **CLC 8**
See also CA 1-4R; CAAS 3; CANR 3, 48;
DLB 27

Sitwell, Dame Edith
1887-1964 . . . . **CLC 2, 9, 67;**
DAM POET; PC 3
See also CA 9-12R; CANR 35;
CDBLB 1945-1960; DLB 20; MTCW

Sjoewall, Maj 1935- . . . . **CLC 7**
See also CA 65-68

Sjowall, Maj
See Sjoewall, Maj

Skelton, Robin 1925- . . . . **CLC 13**
See also AITN 2; CA 5-8R; CAAS 5;
CANR 28; DLB 27, 53

Skolimowski, Jerzy 1938- . . . . **CLC 20**
See also CA 128

Skram, Amalie (Bertha)
1847-1905 . . . . **TCLC 25**

Skvorecky, Josef (Vaclav)
1924- . . . . **CLC 15, 39, 69; DAC;**
DAM NOV
See also CA 61-64; CAAS 1; CANR 10, 34;
MTCW

Slade, Bernard . . . . **CLC 11, 46**
See also Newbound, Bernard Slade
See also CAAS 9; DLB 53

Slaughter, Carolyn 1946- . . . . **CLC 56**
See also CA 85-88

Slaughter, Frank G(ill) 1908- . . . . . . **CLC 29**
See also AITN 2; CA 5-8R; CANR 5;
INT CANR-5

Slavitt, David R(ytman) 1935- . . . . **CLC 5, 14**
See also CA 21-24R; CAAS 3; CANR 41;
DLB 5, 6

Slesinger, Tess 1905-1945 . . . . **TCLC 10**
See also CA 107; DLB 102

Slessor, Kenneth 1901-1971 . . . . **CLC 14**
See also CA 102; 89-92

Slowacki, Juliusz 1809-1849 . . . . . **NCLC 15**

Smart, Christopher
1722-1771 . . . **LC 3; DAM POET; PC 13**
See also DLB 109

Smart, Elizabeth 1913-1986 . . . . **CLC 54**
See also CA 81-84; 118; DLB 88

Smiley, Jane (Graves)
1949- . . . . **CLC 53, 76; DAM POP**
See also CA 104; CANR 30, 50;
INT CANR-30

Smith, A(rthur) J(ames) M(arshall)
1902-1980 . . . . **CLC 15; DAC**
See also CA 1-4R; 102; CANR 4; DLB 88

Smith, Adam 1723-1790 . . . . **LC 36**
See also DLB 104

Smith, Alexander 1829-1867 . . . . . **NCLC 59**
See also DLB 32, 55

Smith, Anna Deavere 1950- . . . . **CLC 86**
See also CA 133

Smith, Betty (Wehner) 1896-1972 . . . **CLC 19**
See also CA 5-8R; 33-36R; DLBY 82;
SATA 6

Smith, Charlotte (Turner)
1749-1806 . . . . **NCLC 23**
See also DLB 39, 109

Smith, Clark Ashton 1893-1961 . . . . **CLC 43**
See also CA 143

Smith, Dave . . . . **CLC 22, 42**
See also Smith, David (Jeddie)
See also CAAS 7; DLB 5

Smith, David (Jeddie) 1942-
See Smith, Dave
See also CA 49-52; CANR 1; DAM POET

Smith, Florence Margaret 1902-1971
See Smith, Stevie
See also CA 17-18; 29-32R; CANR 35;
CAP 2; DAM POET; MTCW

Smith, Iain Crichton 1928- . . . . **CLC 64**
See also CA 21-24R; DLB 40, 139

Smith, John 1580(?)-1631 . . . . **LC 9**

Smith, Johnston
See Crane, Stephen (Townley)

Smith, Joseph, Jr. 1805-1844 . . . . **NCLC 53**

Smith, Lee 1944- . . . . **CLC 25, 73**
See also CA 114; 119; CANR 46; DLB 143;
DLBY 83; INT 119

Smith, Martin
See Smith, Martin Cruz

Smith, Martin Cruz
1942- . . . . . **CLC 25; DAM MULT, POP**
See also BEST 89:4; CA 85-88; CANR 6,
23, 43; INT CANR-23; NNAL

Smith, Mary-Ann Tirone 1944- . . . . . **CLC 39**
See also CA 118; 136

Smith, Patti 1946- . . . . **CLC 12**
See also CA 93-96

Smith, Pauline (Urmson)
1882-1959 . . . . **TCLC 25**

Smith, Rosamond
See Oates, Joyce Carol

Smith, Sheila Kaye
See Kaye-Smith, Sheila

Smith, Stevie . . . . **CLC 3, 8, 25, 44; PC 12**
See also Smith, Florence Margaret
See also DLB 20

Smith, Wilbur (Addison) 1933- . . . . . **CLC 33**
See also CA 13-16R; CANR 7, 46; MTCW

Smith, William Jay 1918- . . . . **CLC 6**
See also CA 5-8R; CANR 44; DLB 5;
MAICYA; SAAS 22; SATA 2, 68

Smith, Woodrow Wilson
See Kuttner, Henry

Smolenskin, Peretz 1842-1885 . . . . **NCLC 30**

Smollett, Tobias (George) 1721-1771 . . **LC 2**
See also CDBLB 1660-1789; DLB 39, 104

Snodgrass, W(illiam) D(e Witt)
1926- . . . . **CLC 2, 6, 10, 18, 68;**
DAM POET
See also CA 1-4R; CANR 6, 36; DLB 5;
MTCW

Snow, C(harles) P(ercy)
1905-1980 . . . . **CLC 1, 4, 6, 9, 13, 19;**
DAM NOV
See also CA 5-8R; 101; CANR 28;
CDBLB 1945-1960; DLB 15, 77; MTCW

Snow, Frances Compton
See Adams, Henry (Brooks)

Snyder, Gary (Sherman)
1930- . . **CLC 1, 2, 5, 9, 32; DAM POET**
See also CA 17-20R; CANR 30; DLB 5, 16,
165

Snyder, Zilpha Keatley 1927- . . . . . . **CLC 17**
See also AAYA 15; CA 9-12R; CANR 38;
CLR 31; JRDA; MAICYA; SAAS 2;
SATA 1, 28, 75

Soares, Bernardo
See Pessoa, Fernando (Antonio Nogueira)

Stapledon, (William) Olaf
1886-1950 .... **TCLC 22**
See also CA 111; DLB 15

Starbuck, George (Edwin)
1931-1996 .... **CLC 53; DAM POET**
See also CA 21-24R; 153; CANR 23

Stark, Richard
See Westlake, Donald E(dwin)

Staunton, Schuyler
See Baum, L(yman) Frank

Stead, Christina (Ellen)
1902-1983 .... **CLC 2, 5, 8, 32, 80**
See also CA 13-16R; 109; CANR 33, 40;
MTCW

Stead, William Thomas
1849-1912 .... **TCLC 48**

Steele, Richard 1672-1729 .... **LC 18**
See also CDBLB 1660-1789; DLB 84, 101

Steele, Timothy (Reid) 1948- .... **CLC 45**
See also CA 93-96; CANR 16, 50; DLB 120

Steffens, (Joseph) Lincoln
1866-1936 .... **TCLC 20**
See also CA 117

Stegner, Wallace (Earle)
1909-1993 ... **CLC 9, 49, 81; DAM NOV**
See also AITN 1; BEST 90:3; CA 1-4R;
141; CAAS 9; CANR 1, 21, 46; DLB 9;
DLBY 93; MTCW

Stein, Gertrude
1874-1946 ...... **TCLC 1, 6, 28, 48; DA;**
DAB; DAC; DAM MST, NOV, POET;
PC 18; WLC
See also CA 104; 132; CDALB 1917-1929;
DLB 4, 54, 86; MTCW

Steinbeck, John (Ernst)
1902-1968 ...... **CLC 1, 5, 9, 13, 21, 34,**
45, 75; DA; DAB; DAC; DAM DRAM,
MST, NOV; SSC 11; WLC
See also AAYA 12; CA 1-4R; 25-28R;
CANR 1, 35; CDALB 1929-1941; DLB 7,
9; DLBD 2; MTCW; SATA 9

Steinem, Gloria 1934- .... **CLC 63**
See also CA 53-56; CANR 28, 51; MTCW

Steiner, George
1929- .... **CLC 24; DAM NOV**
See also CA 73-76; CANR 31; DLB 67;
MTCW; SATA 62

Steiner, K. Leslie
See Delany, Samuel R(ay, Jr.)

Steiner, Rudolf 1861-1925 .... **TCLC 13**
See also CA 107

Stendhal
1783-1842 .... **NCLC 23, 46; DA; DAB;**
DAC; DAM MST, NOV; WLC
See also DLB 119

Stephen, Leslie 1832-1904 .... **TCLC 23**
See also CA 123; DLB 57, 144

Stephen, Sir Leslie
See Stephen, Leslie

Stephen, Virginia
See Woolf, (Adeline) Virginia

Stephens, James 1882(?)-1950 ...... **TCLC 4**
See also CA 104; DLB 19, 153, 162

Stephens, Reed
See Donaldson, Stephen R.

Steptoe, Lydia
See Barnes, Djuna

Sterchi, Beat 1949- .... **CLC 65**

Sterling, Brett
See Bradbury, Ray (Douglas); Hamilton,
Edmond

Sterling, Bruce 1954- .... **CLC 72**
See also CA 119; CANR 44

Sterling, George 1869-1926 .... **TCLC 20**
See also CA 117; DLB 54

Stern, Gerald 1925- .... **CLC 40, 100**
See also CA 81-84; CANR 28; DLB 105

Stern, Richard (Gustave) 1928-... **CLC 4, 39**
See also CA 1-4R; CANR 1, 25, 52;
DLBY 87; INT CANR-25

Sternberg, Josef von 1894-1969 ..... **CLC 20**
See also CA 81-84

Sterne, Laurence
1713-1768 ...... **LC 2; DA; DAB; DAC;**
DAM MST, NOV; WLC
See also CDBLB 1660-1789; DLB 39

Sternheim, (William Adolf) Carl
1878-1942 .... **TCLC 8**
See also CA 105; DLB 56, 118

Stevens, Mark 1951- .... **CLC 34**
See also CA 122

Stevens, Wallace
1879-1955 .... **TCLC 3, 12, 45; DA;**
DAB; DAC; DAM MST, POET; PC 6;
WLC
See also CA 104; 124; CDALB 1929-1941;
DLB 54; MTCW

Stevenson, Anne (Katharine)
1933- .... **CLC 7, 33**
See also CA 17-20R; CAAS 9; CANR 9, 33;
DLB 40; MTCW

Stevenson, Robert Louis (Balfour)
1850-1894 ..... **NCLC 5, 14; DA; DAB;**
DAC; DAM MST, NOV; SSC 11; WLC
See also CDBLB 1890-1914; CLR 10, 11;
DLB 18, 57, 141, 156, 174; DLBD 13;
JRDA; MAICYA; 2

Stewart, J(ohn) I(nnes) M(ackintosh)
1906-1994 .... **CLC 7, 14, 32**
See also CA 85-88; 147; CAAS 3;
CANR 47; MTCW

Stewart, Mary (Florence Elinor)
1916- .... **CLC 7, 35; DAB**
See also CA 1-4R; CANR 1; SATA 12

Stewart, Mary Rainbow
See Stewart, Mary (Florence Elinor)

Stifle, June
See Campbell, Maria

Stifter, Adalbert 1805-1868 ...... **NCLC 41**
See also DLB 133

Still, James 1906- .... **CLC 49**
See also CA 65-68; CAAS 17; CANR 10,
26; DLB 9; SATA 29

Sting
See Sumner, Gordon Matthew

Stirling, Arthur
See Sinclair, Upton (Beall)

Stitt, Milan 1941- .... **CLC 29**
See also CA 69-72

Stockton, Francis Richard 1834-1902
See Stockton, Frank R.
See also CA 108; 137; MAICYA; SATA 44

Stockton, Frank R. .... **TCLC 47**
See also Stockton, Francis Richard
See also DLB 42, 74; DLBD 13;
SATA-Brief 32

Stoddard, Charles
See Kuttner, Henry

Stoker, Abraham 1847-1912
See Stoker, Bram
See also CA 105; DA; DAC; DAM MST,
NOV; SATA 29

Stoker, Bram
1847-1912 .... **TCLC 8; DAB; WLC**
See also Stoker, Abraham
See also CA 150; CDBLB 1890-1914;
DLB 36, 70, 178

Stolz, Mary (Slattery) 1920- .... **CLC 12**
See also AAYA 8; AITN 1; CA 5-8R;
CANR 13, 41; JRDA; MAICYA;
SAAS 3; SATA 10, 71

Stone, Irving
1903-1989 .... **CLC 7; DAM POP**
See also AITN 1; CA 1-4R; 129; CAAS 3;
CANR 1, 23; INT CANR-23; MTCW;
SATA 3; SATA-Obit 64

Stone, Oliver (William) 1946- ...... **CLC 73**
See also AAYA 15; CA 110; CANR 55

Stone, Robert (Anthony)
1937- .... **CLC 5, 23, 42**
See also CA 85-88; CANR 23; DLB 152;
INT CANR-23; MTCW

Stone, Zachary
See Follett, Ken(neth Martin)

Stoppard, Tom
1937- ...... **CLC 1, 3, 4, 5, 8, 15, 29, 34,**
63, 91; DA; DAB; DAC; DAM DRAM,
MST; DC 6; WLC
See also CA 81-84; CANR 39;
CDBLB 1960 to Present; DLB 13;
DLBY 85; MTCW

Storey, David (Malcolm)
1933- ..... **CLC 2, 4, 5, 8; DAM DRAM**
See also CA 81-84; CANR 36; DLB 13, 14;
MTCW

Storm, Hyemeyohsts
1935- .... **CLC 3; DAM MULT**
See also CA 81-84; CANR 45; NNAL

Storm, (Hans) Theodor (Woldsen)
1817-1888 .... **NCLC 1**

Storni, Alfonsina
1892-1938 ..... **TCLC 5; DAM MULT;**
HLC
See also CA 104; 131; HW

Stoughton, William 1631-1701 ...... **LC 38**
See also DLB 24

Stout, Rex (Todhunter) 1886-1975 ... **CLC 3**
See also AITN 2; CA 61-64

Stow, (Julian) Randolph 1935- .. **CLC 23, 48**
See also CA 13-16R; CANR 33; MTCW

Stowe, Harriet (Elizabeth) Beecher
1811-1896 ..... **NCLC 3, 50; DA; DAB;**
DAC; DAM MST, NOV; WLC
See also CDALB 1865-1917; DLB 1, 12, 42,
74; JRDA; MAICYA; 1

Tallent, Elizabeth (Ann) 1954- ..... **CLC 45**
See also CA 117; DLB 130

Tally, Ted 1952- .... **CLC 42**
See also CA 120; 124; INT 124

Tamayo y Baus, Manuel
1829-1898 .... **NCLC 1**

Tammsaare, A(nton) H(ansen)
1878-1940 .... **TCLC 27**

Tam'si, Tchicaya U
See Tchicaya, Gerald Felix

Tan, Amy (Ruth)
1952- .... **CLC 59; DAM MULT, NOV,**
POP
See also AAYA 9; BEST 89:3; CA 136;
CANR 54; DLB 173; SATA 75

Tandem, Felix
See Spitteler, Carl (Friedrich Georg)

Tanizaki, Jun'ichiro
1886-1965 ...... **CLC 8, 14, 28; SSC 21**
See also CA 93-96; 25-28R; DLB 180

Tanner, William
See Amis, Kingsley (William)

Tao Lao
See Storni, Alfonsina

Tarassoff, Lev
See Troyat, Henri

Tarbell, Ida M(inerva)
1857-1944 .... **TCLC 40**
See also CA 122; DLB 47

Tarkington, (Newton) Booth
1869-1946 .... **TCLC 9**
See also CA 110; 143; DLB 9, 102;
SATA 17

Tarkovsky, Andrei (Arsenyevich)
1932-1986 .... **CLC 75**
See also CA 127

Tartt, Donna 1964(?)- .... **CLC 76**
See also CA 142

Tasso, Torquato 1544-1595 .... **LC 5**

Tate, (John Orley) Allen
1899-1979 .... **CLC 2, 4, 6, 9, 11, 14, 24**
See also CA 5-8R; 85-88; CANR 32;
DLB 4, 45, 63; MTCW

Tate, Ellalice
See Hibbert, Eleanor Alice Burford

Tate, James (Vincent) 1943- ... **CLC 2, 6, 25**
See also CA 21-24R; CANR 29, 57; DLB 5,
169

Tavel, Ronald 1940- .... **CLC 6**
See also CA 21-24R; CANR 33

Taylor, C(ecil) P(hilip) 1929-1981... **CLC 27**
See also CA 25-28R; 105; CANR 47

Taylor, Edward
1642(?)-1729 .... **LC 11; DA; DAB;**
DAC; DAM MST, POET
See also DLB 24

Taylor, Eleanor Ross 1920- .... **CLC 5**
See also CA 81-84

Taylor, Elizabeth 1912-1975 ... **CLC 2, 4, 29**
See also CA 13-16R; CANR 9; DLB 139;
MTCW; SATA 13

Taylor, Henry (Splawn) 1942- ...... **CLC 44**
See also CA 33-36R; CAAS 7; CANR 31;
DLB 5

Taylor, Kamala (Purnaiya) 1924-
See Markandaya, Kamala
See also CA 77-80

Taylor, Mildred D. .... **CLC 21**
See also AAYA 10; BW 1; CA 85-88;
CANR 25; CLR 9; DLB 52; JRDA;
MAICYA; SAAS 5; SATA 15, 70

Taylor, Peter (Hillsman)
1917-1994 ..... **CLC 1, 4, 18, 37, 44, 50,**
71; SSC 10
See also CA 13-16R; 147; CANR 9, 50;
DLBY 81, 94; INT CANR-9; MTCW

Taylor, Robert Lewis 1912- .... **CLC 14**
See also CA 1-4R; CANR 3; SATA 10

Tchekhov, Anton
See Chekhov, Anton (Pavlovich)

Tchicaya, Gerald Felix
1931-1988 .... **CLC 101**
See also CA 129; 125

Tchicaya U Tam'si
See Tchicaya, Gerald Felix

Teasdale, Sara 1884-1933......... **TCLC 4**
See also CA 104; DLB 45; SATA 32

Tegner, Esaias 1782-1846........ **NCLC 2**

Teilhard de Chardin, (Marie Joseph) Pierre
1881-1955 .... **TCLC 9**
See also CA 105

Temple, Ann
See Mortimer, Penelope (Ruth)

Tennant, Emma (Christina)
1937- .... **CLC 13, 52**
See also CA 65-68; CAAS 9; CANR 10, 38;
DLB 14

Tenneshaw, S. M.
See Silverberg, Robert

Tennyson, Alfred
1809-1892 .... **NCLC 30; DA; DAB;**
DAC; DAM MST, POET; PC 6; WLC
See also CDBLB 1832-1890; DLB 32

Teran, Lisa St. Aubin de .... **CLC 36**
See also St. Aubin de Teran, Lisa

Terence
195(?)B.C.-159B.C..... **CMLC 14; DC 7**

Teresa de Jesus, St. 1515-1582...... **LC 18**

Terkel, Louis 1912-
See Terkel, Studs
See also CA 57-60; CANR 18, 45; MTCW

Terkel, Studs .... **CLC 38**
See also Terkel, Louis
See also AITN 1

Terry, C. V.
See Slaughter, Frank G(ill)

Terry, Megan 1932- .... **CLC 19**
See also CA 77-80; CABS 3; CANR 43;
DLB 7

Tertz, Abram
See Sinyavsky, Andrei (Donatevich)

Tesich, Steve 1943(?)-1996...... **CLC 40, 69**
See also CA 105; 152; DLBY 83

Teternikov, Fyodor Kuzmich 1863-1927
See Sologub, Fyodor
See also CA 104

Tevis, Walter 1928-1984 .... **CLC 42**
See also CA 113

Tey, Josephine .... **TCLC 14**
See also Mackintosh, Elizabeth
See also DLB 77

Thackeray, William Makepeace
1811-1863 ..... **NCLC 5, 14, 22, 43; DA;**
DAB; DAC; DAM MST, NOV; WLC
See also CDBLB 1832-1890; DLB 21, 55,
159, 163; SATA 23

Thakura, Ravindranatha
See Tagore, Rabindranath

Tharoor, Shashi 1956- .... **CLC 70**
See also CA 141

Thelwell, Michael Miles 1939- ..... **CLC 22**
See also BW 2; CA 101

Theobald, Lewis, Jr.
See Lovecraft, H(oward) P(hillips)

Theodorescu, Ion N. 1880-1967
See Arghezi, Tudor
See also CA 116

Theriault, Yves
1915-1983 .. **CLC 79; DAC; DAM MST**
See also CA 102; DLB 88

Theroux, Alexander (Louis)
1939- .... **CLC 2, 25**
See also CA 85-88; CANR 20

Theroux, Paul (Edward)
1941- .... **CLC 5, 8, 11, 15, 28, 46;**
DAM POP
See also BEST 89:4; CA 33-36R; CANR 20,
45; DLB 2; MTCW; SATA 44

Thesen, Sharon 1946-............. **CLC 56**

Thevenin, Denis
See Duhamel, Georges

Thibault, Jacques Anatole Francois
1844-1924
See France, Anatole
See also CA 106; 127; DAM NOV; MTCW

Thiele, Colin (Milton) 1920- .... **CLC 17**
See also CA 29-32R; CANR 12, 28, 53;
CLR 27; MAICYA; SAAS 2; SATA 14,
72

Thomas, Audrey (Callahan)
1935- .... **CLC 7, 13, 37; SSC 20**
See also AITN 2; CA 21-24R; CAAS 19;
CANR 36, 58; DLB 60; MTCW

Thomas, D(onald) M(ichael)
1935- .... **CLC 13, 22, 31**
See also CA 61-64; CAAS 11; CANR 17,
45; CDBLB 1960 to Present; DLB 40;
INT CANR-17; MTCW

Thomas, Dylan (Marlais)
1914-1953 ... **TCLC 1, 8, 45; DA; DAB;**
DAC; DAM DRAM, MST, POET;
PC 2; SSC 3; WLC
See also CA 104; 120; CDBLB 1945-1960;
DLB 13, 20, 139; MTCW; SATA 60

Thomas, (Philip) Edward
1878-1917 ......**TCLC 10; DAM POET**
See also CA 106; 153; DLB 19

Thomas, Joyce Carol 1938-........ **CLC 35**
See also AAYA 12; BW 2; CA 113; 116;
CANR 48; CLR 19; DLB 33; INT 116;
JRDA; MAICYA; MTCW; SAAS 7;
SATA 40, 78

Thomas, Lewis 1913-1993 .... **CLC 35**
See also CA 85-88; 143; CANR 38; MTCW

Thomas, Paul
See Mann, (Paul) Thomas

Thomas, Piri 1928-............... CLC 17
See also CA 73-76; HW

Thomas, R(onald) S(tuart)
1913- .... CLC 6, 13, 48; DAB;
DAM POET
See also CA 89-92; CAAS 4; CANR 30;
CDBLB 1960 to Present; DLB 27;
MTCW

Thomas, Ross (Elmore) 1926-1995 .. CLC 39
See also CA 33-36R; 150; CANR 22

Thompson, Francis Clegg
See Mencken, H(enry) L(ouis)

Thompson, Francis Joseph
1859-1907 .... TCLC 4
See also CA 104; CDBLB 1890-1914;
DLB 19

Thompson, Hunter S(tockton)
1939- .... CLC 9, 17, 40; DAM POP
See also BEST 89:1; CA 17-20R; CANR 23,
46; MTCW

Thompson, James Myers
See Thompson, Jim (Myers)

Thompson, Jim (Myers)
1906-1977(?) .... CLC 69
See also CA 140

Thompson, Judith .... CLC 39

Thomson, James
1700-1748 ..... LC 16, 29; DAM POET
See also DLB 95

Thomson, James
1834-1882 ..... NCLC 18; DAM POET
See also DLB 35

Thoreau, Henry David
1817-1862 .... NCLC 7, 21, 61; DA;
DAB; DAC; DAM MST; WLC
See also CDALB 1640-1865; DLB 1

Thornton, Hall
See Silverberg, Robert

Thucydides c. 455B.C.-399B.C. .... CMLC 17
See also DLB 176

Thurber, James (Grover)
1894-1961 .... CLC 5, 11, 25; DA; DAB;
DAC; DAM DRAM, MST, NOV; SSC 1
See also CA 73-76; CANR 17, 39;
CDALB 1929-1941; DLB 4, 11, 22, 102;
MAICYA; MTCW; SATA 13

Thurman, Wallace (Henry)
1902-1934 .... TCLC 6; BLC;
DAM MULT
See also BW 1; CA 104; 124; DLB 51

Ticheburn, Cheviot
See Ainsworth, William Harrison

Tieck, (Johann) Ludwig
1773-1853 .... NCLC 5, 46
See also DLB 90

Tiger, Derry
See Ellison, Harlan (Jay)

Tilghman, Christopher 1948(?)-..... CLC 65

Tillinghast, Richard (Williford)
1940- .... CLC 29
See also CA 29-32R; CAAS 23; CANR 26,
51

Timrod, Henry 1828-1867 .... NCLC 25
See also DLB 3

Tindall, Gillian 1938-............... CLC 7
See also CA 21-24R; CANR 11

Tiptree, James, Jr. .... CLC 48, 50
See also Sheldon, Alice Hastings Bradley
See also DLB 8

Titmarsh, Michael Angelo
See Thackeray, William Makepeace

**Tocqueville, Alexis (Charles Henri Maurice
Clerel Comte)** 1805-1859..... NCLC 7

Tolkien, J(ohn) R(onald) R(euel)
1892-1973 .... CLC 1, 2, 3, 8, 12, 38;
DA; DAB; DAC; DAM MST, NOV,
POP; WLC
See also AAYA 10; AITN 1; CA 17-18;
45-48; CANR 36; CAP 2;
CDBLB 1914-1945; DLB 15, 160; JRDA;
MAICYA; MTCW; SATA 2, 32;
SATA-Obit 24

Toller, Ernst 1893-1939.......... TCLC 10
See also CA 107; DLB 124

Tolson, M. B.
See Tolson, Melvin B(eaunorus)

Tolson, Melvin B(eaunorus)
1898(?)-1966 .... CLC 36; BLC;
DAM MULT, POET
See also BW 1; CA 124; 89-92; DLB 48, 76

Tolstoi, Aleksei Nikolaevich
See Tolstoy, Alexey Nikolaevich

Tolstoy, Alexey Nikolaevich
1882-1945 .... TCLC 18
See also CA 107; 158

Tolstoy, Count Leo
See Tolstoy, Leo (Nikolaevich)

Tolstoy, Leo (Nikolaevich)
1828-1910 ...... TCLC 4, 11, 17, 28, 44;
DA; DAB; DAC; DAM MST, NOV;
SSC 9; WLC
See also CA 104; 123; SATA 26

Tomasi di Lampedusa, Giuseppe 1896-1957
See Lampedusa, Giuseppe (Tomasi) di
See also CA 111

Tomlin, Lily...................... CLC 17
See also Tomlin, Mary Jean

Tomlin, Mary Jean 1939(?)-
See Tomlin, Lily
See also CA 117

Tomlinson, (Alfred) Charles
1927- .... CLC 2, 4, 6, 13, 45;
DAM POET; PC 17
See also CA 5-8R; CANR 33; DLB 40

Tomlinson, H(enry) M(ajor)
1873-1958 .... TCLC 71
See also CA 118; DLB 36, 100

Tonson, Jacob
See Bennett, (Enoch) Arnold

Toole, John Kennedy
1937-1969 .... CLC 19, 64
See also CA 104; DLBY 81

Toomer, Jean
1894-1967 ...... CLC 1, 4, 13, 22; BLC;
DAM MULT; PC 7; SSC 1
See also BW 1; CA 85-88;
CDALB 1917-1929; DLB 45, 51; MTCW;
YABC

Torley, Luke
See Blish, James (Benjamin)

Tornimparte, Alessandra
See Ginzburg, Natalia

Torre, Raoul della
See Mencken, H(enry) L(ouis)

Torrey, E(dwin) Fuller 1937-....... CLC 34
See also CA 119

Torsvan, Ben Traven
See Traven, B.

Torsvan, Benno Traven
See Traven, B.

Torsvan, Berick Traven
See Traven, B.

Torsvan, Berwick Traven
See Traven, B.

Torsvan, Bruno Traven
See Traven, B.

Torsvan, Traven
See Traven, B.

Tournier, Michel (Edouard)
1924- .... CLC 6, 23, 36, 95
See also CA 49-52; CANR 3, 36; DLB 83;
MTCW; SATA 23

Tournimparte, Alessandra
See Ginzburg, Natalia

Towers, Ivar
See Kornbluth, C(yril) M.

Towne, Robert (Burton) 1936(?)-.... CLC 87
See also CA 108; DLB 44

Townsend, Sue 1946- .. CLC 61; DAB; DAC
See also CA 119; 127; INT 127; MTCW;
SATA 55, 93; SATA-Brief 48

Townshend, Peter (Dennis Blandford)
1945- .... CLC 17, 42
See also CA 107

Tozzi, Federigo 1883-1920........ TCLC 31

Traill, Catharine Parr
1802-1899 .... NCLC 31
See also DLB 99

Trakl, Georg 1887-1914........... TCLC 5
See also CA 104

Transtroemer, Tomas (Goesta)
1931- .... CLC 52, 65; DAM POET
See also CA 117; 129; CAAS 17

Transtromer, Tomas Gosta
See Transtroemer, Tomas (Goesta)

Traven, B. (?)-1969............. CLC 8, 11
See also CA 19-20; 25-28R; CAP 2; DLB 9,
56; MTCW

Treitel, Jonathan 1959-........... CLC 70

Tremain, Rose 1943-.............. CLC 42
See also CA 97-100; CANR 44; DLB 14

Tremblay, Michel
1942- ...... CLC 29; DAC; DAM MST
See also CA 116; 128; DLB 60; MTCW

Trevanian........................ CLC 29
See also Whitaker, Rod(ney)

Trevor, Glen
See Hilton, James

Trevor, William
1928-..... **CLC 7, 9, 14, 25, 71; SSC 21**
See also Cox, William Trevor
See also DLB 14, 139

Trifonov, Yuri (Valentinovich)
1925-1981 .... **CLC 45**
See also CA 126; 103; MTCW

Trilling, Lionel 1905-1975 .... **CLC 9, 11, 24**
See also CA 9-12R; 61-64; CANR 10;
DLB 28, 63; INT CANR-10; MTCW

Trimball, W. H.
See Mencken, H(enry) L(ouis)

Tristan
See Gomez de la Serna, Ramon

Tristram
See Housman, A(lfred) E(dward)

Trogdon, William (Lewis) 1939-
See Heat-Moon, William Least
See also CA 115; 119; CANR 47; INT 119

Trollope, Anthony
1815-1882 ..... **NCLC 6, 33; DA; DAB;**
DAC; DAM MST, NOV; WLC
See also CDBLB 1832-1890; DLB 21, 57,
159; SATA 22

Trollope, Frances 1779-1863 ..... **NCLC 30**
See also DLB 21, 166

Trotsky, Leon 1879-1940 .... **TCLC 22**
See also CA 118

Trotter (Cockburn), Catharine
1679-1749 .... **LC 8**
See also DLB 84

Trout, Kilgore
See Farmer, Philip Jose

Trow, George W. S. 1943- .... **CLC 52**
See also CA 126

Troyat, Henri 1911- .... **CLC 23**
See also CA 45-48; CANR 2, 33; MTCW

Trudeau, G(arretson) B(eekman) 1948-
See Trudeau, Garry B.
See also CA 81-84; CANR 31; SATA 35

Trudeau, Garry B. .... **CLC 12**
See also Trudeau, G(arretson) B(eekman)
See also AAYA 10; AITN 2

Truffaut, Francois 1932-1984... **CLC 20, 101**
See also CA 81-84; 113; CANR 34

Trumbo, Dalton 1905-1976 .... **CLC 19**
See also CA 21-24R; 69-72; CANR 10;
DLB 26

Trumbull, John 1750-1831 .... **NCLC 30**
See also DLB 31

Trundlett, Helen B.
See Eliot, T(homas) S(tearns)

Tryon, Thomas
1926-1991 ...... **CLC 3, 11; DAM POP**
See also AITN 1; CA 29-32R; 135;
CANR 32; MTCW

Tryon, Tom
See Tryon, Thomas

Ts'ao Hsueh-ch'in 1715(?)-1763 ...... **LC 1**

Tsushima, Shuji 1909-1948
See Dazai, Osamu
See also CA 107

Tsvetaeva (Efron), Marina (Ivanovna)
1892-1941 .... **TCLC 7, 35; PC 14**
See also CA 104; 128; MTCW

Tuck, Lily 1938- .... **CLC 70**
See also CA 139

Tu Fu 712-770..................... **PC 9**
See also DAM MULT

Tunis, John R(oberts) 1889-1975 ... **CLC 12**
See also CA 61-64; DLB 22, 171; JRDA;
MAICYA; SATA 37; SATA-Brief 30

Tuohy, Frank..................... **CLC 37**
See also Tuohy, John Francis
See also DLB 14, 139

Tuohy, John Francis 1925-
See Tuohy, Frank
See also CA 5-8R; CANR 3, 47

Turco, Lewis (Putnam) 1934- ... **CLC 11, 63**
See also CA 13-16R; CAAS 22; CANR 24,
51; DLBY 84

Turgenev, Ivan
1818-1883 .... **NCLC 21; DA; DAB;**
DAC; DAM MST, NOV; DC 7; SSC 7;
WLC

Turgot, Anne-Robert-Jacques
1727-1781 .... **LC 26**

Turner, Frederick 1943-.......... **CLC 48**
See also CA 73-76; CAAS 10; CANR 12,
30, 56; DLB 40

Tutu, Desmond M(pilo)
1931- ..... **CLC 80; BLC; DAM MULT**
See also BW 1; CA 125

Tutuola, Amos
1920- .... **CLC 5, 14, 29; BLC;**
DAM MULT
See also BW 2; CA 9-12R; CANR 27;
DLB 125; MTCW

Twain, Mark
.... **TCLC 6, 12, 19, 36, 48, 59; SSC 26;**
WLC
See also Clemens, Samuel Langhorne
See also AAYA 20; DLB 11, 12, 23, 64, 74

Tyler, Anne
1941- .... **CLC 7, 11, 18, 28, 44, 59;**
DAM NOV, POP
See also AAYA 18; BEST 89:1; CA 9-12R;
CANR 11, 33, 53; DLB 6, 143; DLBY 82;
MTCW; SATA 7, 90

Tyler, Royall 1757-1826.......... **NCLC 3**
See also DLB 37

Tynan, Katharine 1861-1931 .... **TCLC 3**
See also CA 104; DLB 153

Tyutchev, Fyodor 1803-1873 ..... **NCLC 34**

Tzara, Tristan
1896-1963 .... **CLC 47; DAM POET**
See also Rosenfeld, Samuel; Rosenstock,
Sami; Rosenstock, Samuel
See also CA 153

Uhry, Alfred
1936- ..... **CLC 55; DAM DRAM, POP**
See also CA 127; 133; INT 133

Ulf, Haerved
See Strindberg, (Johan) August

Ulf, Harved
See Strindberg, (Johan) August

Ulibarri, Sabine R(eyes)
1919- .... **CLC 83; DAM MULT**
See also CA 131; DLB 82; HW

Unamuno (y Jugo), Miguel de
1864-1936 ... **TCLC 2, 9; DAM MULT,**
NOV; HLC; SSC 11
See also CA 104; 131; DLB 108; HW;
MTCW

Undercliffe, Errol
See Campbell, (John) Ramsey

Underwood, Miles
See Glassco, John

Undset, Sigrid
1882-1949 .... **TCLC 3; DA; DAB;**
DAC; DAM MST, NOV; WLC
See also CA 104; 129; MTCW

Ungaretti, Giuseppe
1888-1970 .... **CLC 7, 11, 15**
See also CA 19-20; 25-28R; CAP 2;
DLB 114

Unger, Douglas 1952-............ **CLC 34**
See also CA 130

Unsworth, Barry (Forster) 1930-.... **CLC 76**
See also CA 25-28R; CANR 30, 54

Updike, John (Hoyer)
1932- ...... **CLC 1, 2, 3, 5, 7, 9, 13, 15,**
23, 34, 43, 70; DA; DAB; DAC;
DAM MST, NOV, POET, POP;
SSC 13; WLC
See also CA 1-4R; CABS 1; CANR 4, 33,
51; CDALB 1968-1988; DLB 2, 5, 143;
DLBD 3; DLBY 80, 82; MTCW

Upshaw, Margaret Mitchell
See Mitchell, Margaret (Munnerlyn)

Upton, Mark
See Sanders, Lawrence

Urdang, Constance (Henriette)
1922- .... **CLC 47**
See also CA 21-24R; CANR 9, 24

Uriel, Henry
See Faust, Frederick (Schiller)

Uris, Leon (Marcus)
1924- .... **CLC 7, 32; DAM NOV, POP**
See also AITN 1, 2; BEST 89:2; CA 1-4R;
CANR 1, 40; MTCW; SATA 49

Urmuz
See Codrescu, Andrei

Urquhart, Jane 1949-........ **CLC 90; DAC**
See also CA 113; CANR 32

Ustinov, Peter (Alexander) 1921- .... **CLC 1**
See also AITN 1; CA 13-16R; CANR 25,
51; DLB 13

U Tam'si, Gerald Felix Tchicaya
See Tchicaya, Gerald Felix

U Tam'si, Tchicaya
See Tchicaya, Gerald Felix

Vaculik, Ludvik 1926- .... **CLC 7**
See also CA 53-56

Vaihinger, Hans 1852-1933 .... **TCLC 71**
See also CA 116

Valdez, Luis (Miguel)
1940- ..... **CLC 84; DAM MULT; HLC**
See also CA 101; CANR 32; DLB 122; HW

Voinovich, Vladimir (Nikolaevich)
1932- . . . . **CLC 10, 49**
See also CA 81-84; CAAS 12; CANR 33;
MTCW

Vollmann, William T.
1959- . . . . . . **CLC 89; DAM NOV, POP**
See also CA 134

Voloshinov, V. N.
See Bakhtin, Mikhail Mikhailovich

Voltaire
1694-1778 . . . . . **LC 14; DA; DAB; DAC;
DAM DRAM, MST; SSC 12; WLC**

von Daeniken, Erich 1935- . . . . **CLC 30**
See also AITN 1; CA 37-40R; CANR 17,
44

von Daniken, Erich
See von Daeniken, Erich

von Heidenstam, (Carl Gustaf) Verner
See Heidenstam, (Carl Gustaf) Verner von

von Heyse, Paul (Johann Ludwig)
See Heyse, Paul (Johann Ludwig von)

von Hofmannsthal, Hugo
See Hofmannsthal, Hugo von

von Horvath, Odon
See Horvath, Oedoen von

von Horvath, Oedoen
See Horvath, Oedoen von

von Liliencron, (Friedrich Adolf Axel) Detlev
See Liliencron, (Friedrich Adolf Axel)
Detlev von

Vonnegut, Kurt, Jr.
1922- . . . . . . **CLC 1, 2, 3, 4, 5, 8, 12, 22,
40, 60; DA; DAB; DAC; DAM MST,
NOV, POP; SSC 8; WLC**
See also AAYA 6; AITN 1; BEST 90:4;
CA 1-4R; CANR 1, 25, 49;
CDALB 1968-1988; DLB 2, 8, 152;
DLBD 3; DLBY 80; MTCW

Von Rachen, Kurt
See Hubbard, L(afayette) Ron(ald)

von Rezzori (d'Arczzo), Gregor
See Rezzori (d'Arezzo), Gregor von

von Sternberg, Josef
See Sternberg, Josef von

Vorster, Gordon 1924- . . . . **CLC 34**
See also CA 133

Vosce, Trudie
See Ozick, Cynthia

Voznesensky, Andrei (Andreievich)
1933- . . . . . . **CLC 1, 15, 57; DAM POET**
See also CA 89-92; CANR 37; MTCW

Waddington, Miriam 1917- . . . . **CLC 28**
See also CA 21-24R; CANR 12, 30;
DLB 68

Wagman, Fredrica 1937- . . . . **CLC 7**
See also CA 97-100; INT 97-100

Wagner, Richard 1813-1883 . . . . **NCLC 9**
See also DLB 129

Wagner-Martin, Linda 1936- . . . . **CLC 50**

Wagoner, David (Russell)
1926- . . . . **CLC 3, 5, 15**
See also CA 1-4R; CAAS 3; CANR 2;
DLB 5; SATA 14

Wah, Fred(erick James) 1939- . . . . . . ⌐LC 44
See also CA 107; 141; DLB 60

Wahloo, Per 1926-1975 . . . . **CLC 7**
See also CA 61-64

Wahloo, Peter
See Wahloo, Per

Wain, John (Barrington)
1925-1994 . . . . **CLC 2, 11, 15, 46**
See also CA 5-8R; 145; CAAS 4; CANR 23,
54; CDBLB 1960 to Present; DLB 15, 27,
139, 155; MTCW

Wajda, Andrzej 1926- . . . . **CLC 16**
See also CA 102

Wakefield, Dan 1932- . . . . **CLC 7**
See also CA 21-24R; CAAS 7

Wakoski, Diane
1937- . . . . **CLC 2, 4, 7, 9, 11, 40;
DAM POET; PC 15**
See also CA 13-16R; CAAS 1; CANR 9;
DLB 5; INT CANR-9

Wakoski-Sherbell, Diane
See Wakoski, Diane

Walcott, Derek (Alton)
1930- . . . . **CLC 2, 4, 9, 14, 25, 42, 67, 76;
BLC; DAB; DAC; DAM MST, MULT,
POET; DC 7**
See also BW 2; CA 89-92; CANR 26, 47;
DLB 117; DLBY 81; MTCW

Waldman, Anne 1945- . . . . **CLC 7**
See also CA 37-40R; CAAS 17; CANR 34;
DLB 16

Waldo, E. Hunter
See Sturgeon, Theodore (Hamilton)

Waldo, Edward Hamilton
See Sturgeon, Theodore (Hamilton)

Walker, Alice (Malsenior)
1944- . . . . **CLC 5, 6, 9, 19, 27, 46, 58;
BLC; DA; DAB; DAC; DAM MST,
MULT, NOV, POET, POP; SSC 5**
See also AAYA 3; BEST 89:4; BW 2;
CA 37-40R; CANR 9, 27, 49;
CDALB 1968-1988; DLB 6, 33, 143;
INT CANR-27; MTCW; SATA 31;
YABC

Walker, David Harry 1911-1992 . . . . **CLC 14**
See also CA 1-4R; 137; CANR 1; SATA 8;
SATA-Obit 71

Walker, Edward Joseph 1934-
See Walker, Ted
See also CA 21-24R; CANR 12, 28, 53

Walker, George F.
1947- . . . . **CLC 44, 61; DAB; DAC;
DAM MST**
See also CA 103; CANR 21, 43; DLB 60

Walker, Joseph A.
1935- . . . . **CLC 19; DAM DRAM, MST**
See also BW 1; CA 89-92; CANR 26;
DLB 38

Walker, Margaret (Abigail)
1915- . . . . **CLC 1, 6; BLC; DAM MULT**
See also BW 2; CA 73-76; CANR 26, 54;
DLB 76, 152; MTCW

Walker, Ted . . . . **CLC 13**
See also Walker, Edward Joseph
See also DLB 40

Wallace, David Foster 1962- . . . . **CLC 50**
See also CA 132

Wallace, Dexter
See Masters, Edgar Lee

Wallace, (Richard Horatio) Edgar
1875-1932 . . . . **TCLC 57**
See also CA 115; DLB 70

Wallace, Irving
1916-1990 . . . . . **CLC 7, 13; DAM NOV,
POP**
See also AITN 1; CA 1-4R; 132; CAAS 1;
CANR 1, 27; INT CANR-27; MTCW

Wallant, Edward Lewis
1926-1962 . . . . **CLC 5, 10**
See also CA 1-4R; CANR 22; DLB 2, 28,
143; MTCW

Walley, Byron
See Card, Orson Scott

Walpole, Horace 1717-1797 . . . . **LC 2**
See also DLB 39, 104

Walpole, Hugh (Seymour)
1884-1941 . . . . **TCLC 5**
See also CA 104; DLB 34

Walser, Martin 1927- . . . . **CLC 27**
See also CA 57-60; CANR 8, 46; DLB 75,
124

Walser, Robert
1878-1956 . . . . **TCLC 18; SSC 20**
See also CA 118; DLB 66

Walsh, Jill Paton . . . . **CLC 35**
See also Paton Walsh, Gillian
See also AAYA 11; CLR 2; DLB 161;
SAAS 3

Walter, Villiam Christian
See Andersen, Hans Christian

Wambaugh, Joseph (Aloysius, Jr.)
1937- . . . . **CLC 3, 18; DAM NOV, POP**
See also AITN 1; BEST 89:3; CA 33-36R;
CANR 42; DLB 6; DLBY 83; MTCW

Wang Wei 699(?)-761(?) . . . . **PC 18**

Ward, Arthur Henry Sarsfield 1883-1959
See Rohmer, Sax
See also CA 108

Ward, Douglas Turner 1930- . . . . **CLC 19**
See also BW 1; CA 81-84; CANR 27;
DLB 7, 38

Ward, Mary Augusta
See Ward, Mrs. Humphry

Ward, Mrs. Humphry
1851-1920 . . . . **TCLC 55**
See also DLB 18

Ward, Peter
See Faust, Frederick (Schiller)

Warhol, Andy 1928(?)-1987 . . . . **CLC 20**
See also AAYA 12; BEST 89:4; CA 89-92;
121; CANR 34

Warner, Francis (Robert le Plastrier)
1937- . . . . **CLC 14**
See also CA 53-56; CANR 11

Warner, Marina 1946- . . . . **CLC 59**
See also CA 65-68; CANR 21, 55

Warner, Rex (Ernest) 1905-1986 . . . . **CLC 45**
See also CA 89-92; 119; DLB 15

Warner, Susan (Bogert)
1819-1885 .... **NCLC 31**
See also DLB 3, 42

Warner, Sylvia (Constance) Ashton
See Ashton-Warner, Sylvia (Constance)

Warner, Sylvia Townsend
1893-1978 .... **CLC 7, 19; SSC 23**
See also CA 61-64; 77-80; CANR 16;
DLB 34, 139; MTCW

Warren, Mercy Otis 1728-1814... **NCLC 13**
See also DLB 31

Warren, Robert Penn
1905-1989 .... **CLC 1, 4, 6, 8, 10, 13, 18,
39, 53, 59; DA; DAB; DAC; DAM MST,
NOV, POET; SSC 4; WLC**
See also AITN 1; CA 13-16R; 129;
CANR 10, 47; CDALB 1968-1988;
DLB 2, 48, 152; DLBY 80, 89;
INT CANR-10; MTCW; SATA 46;
SATA-Obit 63

Warshofsky, Isaac
See Singer, Isaac Bashevis

Warton, Thomas
1728-1790 .... **LC 15; DAM POET**
See also DLB 104, 109

Waruk, Kona
See Harris, (Theodore) Wilson

Warung, Price 1855-1911........ **TCLC 45**

Warwick, Jarvis
See Garner, Hugh

Washington, Alex
See Harris, Mark

Washington, Booker T(aliaferro)
1856-1915 .... **TCLC 10; BLC;
DAM MULT**
See also BW 1; CA 114; 125; SATA 28

Washington, George 1732-1799 ...... **LC 25**
See also DLB 31

Wassermann, (Karl) Jakob
1873-1934 .... **TCLC 6**
See also CA 104; DLB 66

Wasserstein, Wendy
1950- .... **CLC 32, 59, 90;
DAM DRAM; DC 4**
See also CA 121; 129; CABS 3; CANR 53;
INT 129; SATA 94

Waterhouse, Keith (Spencer)
1929- .... **CLC 47**
See also CA 5-8R; CANR 38; DLB 13, 15;
MTCW

Waters, Frank (Joseph)
1902-1995 .... **CLC 88**
See also CA 5-8R; 149; CAAS 13; CANR 3,
18; DLBY 86

Waters, Roger 1944-.............. **CLC 35**

Watkins, Frances Ellen
See Harper, Frances Ellen Watkins

Watkins, Gerrold
See Malzberg, Barry N(athaniel)

Watkins, Gloria 1955(?)-
See hooks, bell
See also BW 2; CA 143

Watkins, Paul 1964-.............. **CLC 55**
See also CA 132

Watkins, Vernon Phillips
1906-1967 .... **CLC 43**
See also CA 9-10; 25-28R; CAP 1; DLB 20

Watson, Irving S.
See Mencken, H(enry) L(ouis)

Watson, John H.
See Farmer, Philip Jose

Watson, Richard F.
See Silverberg, Robert

Waugh, Auberon (Alexander) 1939-.. **CLC 7**
See also CA 45-48; CANR 6, 22; DLB 14

Waugh, Evelyn (Arthur St. John)
1903-1966 ...... **CLC 1, 3, 8, 13, 19, 27,
44; DA; DAB; DAC; DAM MST, NOV,
POP; WLC**
See also CA 85-88; 25-28R; CANR 22;
CDBLB 1914-1945; DLB 15, 162; MTCW

Waugh, Harriet 1944- .... **CLC 6**
See also CA 85-88; CANR 22

Ways, C. R.
See Blount, Roy (Alton), Jr.

Waystaff, Simon
See Swift, Jonathan

Webb, (Martha) Beatrice (Potter)
1858-1943 .... **TCLC 22**
See also Potter, Beatrice
See also CA 117

Webb, Charles (Richard) 1939-...... **CLC 7**
See also CA 25-28R

Webb, James H(enry), Jr. 1946-.... **CLC 22**
See also CA 81-84

Webb, Mary (Gladys Meredith)
1881-1927 .... **TCLC 24**
See also CA 123; DLB 34

Webb, Mrs. Sidney
See Webb, (Martha) Beatrice (Potter)

Webb, Phyllis 1927-.............. **CLC 18**
See also CA 104; CANR 23; DLB 53

Webb, Sidney (James)
1859-1947 .... **TCLC 22**
See also CA 117

Webber, Andrew Lloyd............. **CLC 21**
See also Lloyd Webber, Andrew

Weber, Lenora Mattingly
1895-1971 .... **CLC 12**
See also CA 19-20; 29-32R; CAP 1;
SATA 2; SATA-Obit 26

Weber, Max 1864-1920 .... **TCLC 69**
See also CA 109

Webster, John
1579(?)-1634(?) ...... **LC 33; DA; DAB;
DAC; DAM DRAM, MST; DC 2; WLC**
See also CDBLB Before 1660; DLB 58

Webster, Noah 1758-1843 .... **NCLC 30**

Wedekind, (Benjamin) Frank(lin)
1864-1918 ...... **TCLC 7; DAM DRAM**
See also CA 104; 153; DLB 118

Weidman, Jerome 1913-............ **CLC 7**
See also AITN 2; CA 1-4R; CANR 1;
DLB 28

Weil, Simone (Adolphine)
1909-1943 .... **TCLC 23**
See also CA 117

Weinstein, Nathan
See West, Nathanael

Weinstein, Nathan von Wallenstein
See West, Nathanael

Weir, Peter (Lindsay) 1944-....... **CLC 20**
See also CA 113; 123

Weiss, Peter (Ulrich)
1916-1982 .... **CLC 3, 15, 51;
DAM DRAM**
See also CA 45-48; 106; CANR 3; DLB 69,
124

Weiss, Theodore (Russell)
1916- .... **CLC 3, 8, 14**
See also CA 9-12R; CAAS 2; CANR 46;
DLB 5

Welch, (Maurice) Denton
1915-1948 .... **TCLC 22**
See also CA 121; 148

Welch, James
1940- ..... **CLC 6, 14, 52; DAM MULT,
POP**
See also CA 85-88; CANR 42; DLB 175;
NNAL

Weldon, Fay
1933- .... **CLC 6, 9, 11, 19, 36, 59;
DAM POP**
See also CA 21-24R; CANR 16, 46;
CDBLB 1960 to Present; DLB 14;
INT CANR-16; MTCW

Wellek, Rene 1903-1995........... **CLC 28**
See also CA 5-8R; 150; CAAS 7; CANR 8;
DLB 63; INT CANR-8

Weller, Michael 1942- .... **CLC 10, 53**
See also CA 85-88

Weller, Paul 1958-............... **CLC 26**

Wellershoff, Dieter 1925-.......... **CLC 46**
See also CA 89-92; CANR 16, 37

Welles, (George) Orson
1915-1985 .... **CLC 20, 80**
See also CA 93-96; 117

Wellman, Mac 1945- .... **CLC 65**

Wellman, Manly Wade 1903-1986 .. **CLC 49**
See also CA 1-4R; 118; CANR 6, 16, 44;
SATA 6; SATA-Obit 47

Wells, Carolyn 1869(?)-1942 ...... **TCLC 35**
See also CA 113; DLB 11

Wells, H(erbert) G(eorge)
1866-1946 .... **TCLC 6, 12, 19; DA;
DAB; DAC; DAM MST, NOV; SSC 6;
WLC**
See also AAYA 18; CA 110; 121;
CDBLB 1914-1945; DLB 34, 70, 156, 178;
MTCW; SATA 20

Wells, Rosemary 1943-............ **CLC 12**
See also AAYA 13; CA 85-88; CANR 48;
CLR 16; MAICYA; SAAS 1; SATA 18,
69

Welty, Eudora
1909- ...... **CLC 1, 2, 5, 14, 22, 33; DA;
DAB; DAC; DAM MST, NOV; SSC 1;
WLC**
See also CA 9-12R; CABS 1; CANR 32;
CDALB 1941-1968; DLB 2, 102, 143;
DLBD 12; DLBY 87; MTCW

Wen I-to 1899-1946 .... **TCLC 28**

Wentworth, Robert
See Hamilton, Edmond

Werfel, Franz (V.) 1890-1945 . . . . . . **TCLC 8**
See also CA 104; DLB 81, 124

Wergeland, Henrik Arnold
1808-1845 . . . . **NCLC 5**

Wersba, Barbara 1932-. . . . . **CLC 30**
See also AAYA 2; CA 29-32R; CANR 16,
38; CLR 3; DLB 52; JRDA; MAICYA;
SAAS 2; SATA 1, 58

Wertmueller, Lina 1928- . . . . **CLC 16**
See also CA 97-100; CANR 39

Wescott, Glenway 1901-1987. . . . . . . **CLC 13**
See also CA 13-16R; 121; CANR 23;
DLB 4, 9, 102

Wesker, Arnold
1932- . . . . **CLC 3, 5, 42; DAB;**
DAM DRAM
See also CA 1-4R; CAAS 7; CANR 1, 33;
CDBLB 1960 to Present; DLB 13;
MTCW

Wesley, Richard (Errol) 1945-. . . . . . **CLC 7**
See also BW 1; CA 57-60; CANR 27;
DLB 38

Wessel, Johan Herman 1742-1785 . . . . **LC 7**

West, Anthony (Panther)
1914-1987 . . . . **CLC 50**
See also CA 45-48; 124; CANR 3, 19;
DLB 15

West, C. P.
See Wodehouse, P(elham) G(renville)

West, (Mary) Jessamyn
1902-1984 . . . . **CLC 7, 17**
See also CA 9-12R; 112; CANR 27; DLB 6;
DLBY 84; MTCW; SATA-Obit 37

West, Morris L(anglo) 1916-. . . . . **CLC 6, 33**
See also CA 5-8R; CANR 24, 49; MTCW

West, Nathanael
1903-1940 . . . . . **TCLC 1, 14, 44; SSC 16**
See also CA 104; 125; CDALB 1929-1941;
DLB 4, 9, 28; MTCW

West, Owen
See Koontz, Dean R(ay)

West, Paul 1930- . . . . **CLC 7, 14, 96**
See also CA 13-16R; CAAS 7; CANR 22,
53; DLB 14; INT CANR-22

West, Rebecca 1892-1983 . . **CLC 7, 9, 31, 50**
See also CA 5-8R; 109; CANR 19; DLB 36;
DLBY 83; MTCW

Westall, Robert (Atkinson)
1929-1993 . . . . **CLC 17**
See also AAYA 12; CA 69-72; 141;
CANR 18; CLR 13; JRDA; MAICYA;
SAAS 2; SATA 23, 69; SATA-Obit 75

Westlake, Donald E(dwin)
1933- . . . . **CLC 7, 33; DAM POP**
See also CA 17-20R; CAAS 13; CANR 16,
44; INT CANR-16

Westmacott, Mary
See Christie, Agatha (Mary Clarissa)

Weston, Allen
See Norton, Andre

Wetcheek, J. L.
See Feuchtwanger, Lion

Wetering, Janwillem van de
See van de Wetering, Janwillem

Wetherell, Elizabeth
See Warner, Susan (Bogert)

Whale, James 1889-1957 . . . . **TCLC 63**

Whalen, Philip 1923- . . . . **CLC 6, 29**
See also CA 9-12R; CANR 5, 39; DLB 16

Wharton, Edith (Newbold Jones)
1862-1937 . . . . . . **TCLC 3, 9, 27, 53; DA;**
DAB; DAC; DAM MST, NOV; SSC 6;
WLC
See also CA 104; 132; CDALB 1865-1917;
DLB 4, 9, 12, 78; DLBD 13; MTCW

Wharton, James
See Mencken, H(enry) L(ouis)

Wharton, William (a pseudonym)
. . . . **CLC 18, 37**
See also CA 93-96; DLBY 80; INT 93-96

Wheatley (Peters), Phillis
1754(?)-1784 . . . . **LC 3; BLC; DA; DAC;**
DAM MST, MULT, POET; PC 3; WLC
See also CDALB 1640-1865; DLB 31, 50

Wheelock, John Hall 1886-1978 . . . . **CLC 14**
See also CA 13-16R; 77-80; CANR 14;
DLB 45

White, E(lwyn) B(rooks)
1899-1985 . . **CLC 10, 34, 39; DAM POP**
See also AITN 2; CA 13-16R; 116;
CANR 16, 37; CLR 1, 21; DLB 11, 22;
MAICYA; MTCW; SATA 2, 29;
SATA-Obit 44

White, Edmund (Valentine III)
1940- . . . . **CLC 27; DAM POP**
See also AAYA 7; CA 45-48; CANR 3, 19,
36; MTCW

White, Patrick (Victor Martindale)
1912-1990 . . **CLC 3, 4, 5, 7, 9, 18, 65, 69**
See also CA 81-84; 132; CANR 43; MTCW

White, Phyllis Dorothy James 1920-
See James, P. D.
See also CA 21-24R; CANR 17, 43;
DAM POP; MTCW

White, T(erence) H(anbury)
1906-1964 . . . . **CLC 30**
See also CA 73-76; CANR 37; DLB 160;
JRDA; MAICYA; SATA 12

White, Terence de Vere
1912-1994 . . . . **CLC 49**
See also CA 49-52; 145; CANR 3

White, Walter F(rancis)
1893-1955 . . . . **TCLC 15**
See also White, Walter
See also BW 1; CA 115; 124; DLB 51

White, William Hale 1831-1913
See Rutherford, Mark
See also CA 121

Whitehead, E(dward) A(nthony)
1933- . . . . **CLC 5**
See also CA 65-68; CANR 58

Whitemore, Hugh (John) 1936-. . . . . **CLC 37**
See also CA 132; INT 132

Whitman, Sarah Helen (Power)
1803-1878 . . . . **NCLC 19**
See also DLB 1

Whitman, Walt(er)
1819-1892 . . . . . **NCLC 4, 31; DA; DAB;**
DAC; DAM MST, POET; PC 3; WLC
See also CDALB 1640-1865; DLB 3, 64;
SATA 20

Whitney, Phyllis A(yame)
1903- . . . . **CLC 42; DAM POP**
See also AITN 2; BEST 90:3; CA 1-4R;
CANR 3, 25, 38; JRDA; MAICYA;
SATA 1, 30

Whittemore, (Edward) Reed (Jr.)
1919- . . . . **CLC 4**
See also CA 9-12R; CAAS 8; CANR 4;
DLB 5

Whittier, John Greenleaf
1807-1892 . . . . **NCLC 8, 59**
See also DLB 1

Whittlebot, Hernia
See Coward, Noel (Peirce)

Wicker, Thomas Grey 1926-
See Wicker, Tom
See also CA 65-68; CANR 21, 46

Wicker, Tom . . . . **CLC 7**
See also Wicker, Thomas Grey

Wideman, John Edgar
1941- . . . . **CLC 5, 34, 36, 67; BLC;**
DAM MULT
See also BW 2; CA 85-88; CANR 14, 42;
DLB 33, 143

Wiebe, Rudy (Henry)
1934- . . . . **CLC 6, 11, 14; DAC;**
DAM MST
See also CA 37-40R; CANR 42; DLB 60

Wieland, Christoph Martin
1733-1813 . . . . **NCLC 17**
See also DLB 97

Wiene, Robert 1881-1938. . . . . **TCLC 56**

Wieners, John 1934-. . . . . **CLC 7**
See also CA 13-16R; DLB 16

Wiesel, Elie(zer)
1928- . . . . . . **CLC 3, 5, 11, 37; DA; DAB;**
DAC; DAM MST, NOV
See also AAYA 7; AITN 1; CA 5-8R;
CAAS 4; CANR 8, 40; DLB 83;
DLBY 87; INT CANR-8; MTCW;
SATA 56; YABC

Wiggins, Marianne 1947-. . . . . **CLC 57**
See also BEST 89:3; CA 130

Wight, James Alfred 1916-
See Herriot, James
See also CA 77-80; SATA 55;
SATA-Brief 44

Wilbur, Richard (Purdy)
1921- . . . **CLC 3, 6, 9, 14, 53; DA; DAB;**
DAC; DAM MST, POET
See also CA 1-4R; CABS 2; CANR 2, 29;
DLB 5, 169; INT CANR-29; MTCW;
SATA 9

Wild, Peter 1940-. . . . . **CLC 14**
See also CA 37-40R; DLB 5

Wilde, Oscar (Fingal O'Flahertie Wills)
1854(?)-1900 . . . . **TCLC 1, 8, 23, 41; DA;**
DAB; DAC; DAM DRAM, MST, NOV;
SSC 11; WLC
See also CA 104; 119; CDBLB 1890-1914;
DLB 10, 19, 34, 57, 141, 156; SATA 24

Woiwode, L.
See Woiwode, Larry (Alfred)

Woiwode, Larry (Alfred) 1941-... **CLC 6, 10**
See also CA 73-76; CANR 16; DLB 6;
INT CANR-16

Wojciechowska, Maia (Teresa)
1927-..................... **CLC 26**
See also AAYA 8; CA 9-12R; CANR 4, 41;
CLR 1; JRDA; MAICYA; SAAS 1;
SATA 1, 28, 83

Wolf, Christa 1929-........ **CLC 14, 29, 58**
See also CA 85-88; CANR 45; DLB 75;
MTCW

Wolfe, Gene (Rodman)
1931-................... **CLC 25; DAM POP**
See also CA 57-60; CAAS 9; CANR 6, 32;
DLB 8

Wolfe, George C. 1954-.......... **CLC 49**
See also CA 149

Wolfe, Thomas (Clayton)
1900-1938 ..... **TCLC 4, 13, 29, 61; DA;
DAB; DAC; DAM MST, NOV; WLC**
See also CA 104; 132; CDALB 1929-1941;
DLB 9, 102; DLBD 2; DLBY 85; MTCW

Wolfe, Thomas Kennerly, Jr. 1931-
See Wolfe, Tom
See also CA 13-16R; CANR 9, 33;
DAM POP; INT CANR-9; MTCW

Wolfe, Tom .... **CLC 1, 2, 9, 15, 35, 51**
See also Wolfe, Thomas Kennerly, Jr.
See also AAYA 8; AITN 2; BEST 89:1;
DLB 152

Wolff, Geoffrey (Ansell) 1937- ..... **CLC 41**
See also CA 29-32R; CANR 29, 43

Wolff, Sonia
See Levitin, Sonia (Wolff)

Wolff, Tobias (Jonathan Ansell)
1945-..................... **CLC 39, 64**
See also AAYA 16; BEST 90:2; CA 114;
117; CAAS 22; CANR 54; DLB 130;
INT 117

Wolfram von Eschenbach
c. 1170-c. 1220 .... **CMLC 5**
See also DLB 138

Wolitzer, Hilma 1930-............ **CLC 17**
See also CA 65-68; CANR 18, 40;
INT CANR-18; SATA 31

Wollstonecraft, Mary 1759-1797...... **LC 5**
See also CDBLB 1789-1832; DLB 39, 104,
158

Wonder, Stevie .... **CLC 12**
See also Morris, Steveland Judkins

Wong, Jade Snow 1922-.......... **CLC 17**
See also CA 109

Woodcott, Keith
See Brunner, John (Kilian Houston)

Woodruff, Robert W.
See Mencken, H(enry) L(ouis)

Woolf, (Adeline) Virginia
1882-1941 .... **TCLC 1, 5, 20, 43, 56;
DA; DAB; DAC; DAM MST, NOV;
SSC 7; WLC**
See also CA 104; 130; CDBLB 1914-1945;
DLB 36, 100, 162; DLBD 10; MTCW

Woollcott, Alexander (Humphreys)
1887-1943 .... **TCLC 5**
See also CA 105; DLB 29

Woolrich, Cornell 1903-1968....... **CLC 77**
See also Hopley-Woolrich, Cornell George

Wordsworth, Dorothy
1771-1855 .... **NCLC 25**
See also DLB 107

Wordsworth, William
1770-1850 .... **NCLC 12, 38; DA; DAB;
DAC; DAM MST, POET; PC 4; WLC**
See also CDBLB 1789-1832; DLB 93, 107

Wouk, Herman
1915- .. **CLC 1, 9, 38; DAM NOV, POP**
See also CA 5-8R; CANR 6, 33; DLBY 82;
INT CANR-6; MTCW

Wright, Charles (Penzel, Jr.)
1935-.................. **CLC 6, 13, 28**
See also CA 29-32R; CAAS 7; CANR 23,
36; DLB 165; DLBY 82; MTCW

Wright, Charles Stevenson
1932-............... **CLC 49; BLC 3;
DAM MULT, POET**
See also BW 1; CA 9-12R; CANR 26;
DLB 33

Wright, Jack R.
See Harris, Mark

Wright, James (Arlington)
1927-1980 .... **CLC 3, 5, 10, 28;
DAM POET**
See also AITN 2; CA 49-52; 97-100;
CANR 4, 34; DLB 5, 169; MTCW

Wright, Judith (Arandell)
1915- .... **CLC 11, 53; PC 14**
See also CA 13-16R; CANR 31; MTCW;
SATA 14

Wright, L(auralı) R. 1939-........ **CLC 44**
See also CA 138

Wright, Richard (Nathaniel)
1908-1960 .... **CLC 1, 3, 4, 9, 14, 21, 48,
74; BLC; DA; DAB; DAC; DAM MST,
MULT, NOV; SSC 2; WLC**
See also AAYA 5; BW 1; CA 108;
CDALB 1929-1941; DLB 76, 102;
DLBD 2; MTCW

Wright, Richard B(ruce) 1937-...... **CLC 6**
See also CA 85-88; DLB 53

Wright, Rick 1945-............... **CLC 35**

Wright, Rowland
See Wells, Carolyn

Wright, Stephen Caldwell 1946- .... **CLC 33**
See also BW 2

Wright, Willard Huntington 1888-1939
See Van Dine, S. S.
See also CA 115

Wright, William 1930-............ **CLC 44**
See also CA 53-56; CANR 7, 23

Wroth, LadyMary 1587-1653(?) ..... **LC 30**
See also DLB 121

Wu Ch'eng-en 1500(?)-1582(?)........ **LC 7**

Wu Ching-tzu 1701-1754 .... **LC 2**

Wurlitzer, Rudolph 1938(?)- ... **CLC 2, 4, 15**
See also CA 85-88; DLB 173

Wycherley, William
1641-1715 ..... **LC 8, 21; DAM DRAM**
See also CDBLB 1660-1789; DLB 80

Wylie, Elinor (Morton Hoyt)
1885-1928 .... **TCLC 8**
See also CA 105; DLB 9, 45

Wylie, Philip (Gordon) 1902-1971... **CLC 43**
See also CA 21-22; 33-36R; CAP 2; DLB 9

Wyndham, John.................. CLC 19
See also Harris, John (Wyndham Parkes
Lucas) Beynon

Wyss, Johann David Von
1743-1818 .... **NCLC 10**
See also JRDA; MAICYA; SATA 29;
SATA-Brief 27

Xenophon
c. 430B.C.-c. 354B.C........ **CMLC 17**
See also DLB 176

Yakumo Koizumi
See Hearn, (Patricio) Lafcadio (Tessima
Carlos)

Yanez, Jose Donoso
See Donoso (Yanez), Jose

Yanovsky, Basile S.
See Yanovsky, V(assily) S(emenovich)

Yanovsky, V(assily) S(emenovich)
1906-1989 .... **CLC 2, 18**
See also CA 97-100; 129

Yates, Richard 1926-1992 ..... **CLC 7, 8, 23**
See also CA 5-8R; 139; CANR 10, 43;
DLB 2; DLBY 81, 92; INT CANR-10

Yeats, W. B.
See Yeats, William Butler

Yeats, William Butler
1865-1939 ..... **TCLC 1, 11, 18, 31; DA;
DAB; DAC; DAM DRAM, MST,
POET; WLC**
See also CA 104; 127; CANR 45;
CDBLB 1890-1914; DLB 10, 19, 98, 156;
MTCW

Yehoshua, A(braham) B.
1936-..................... **CLC 13, 31**
See also CA 33-36R; CANR 43

Yep, Laurence Michael 1948-...... **CLC 35**
See also AAYA 5; CA 49-52; CANR 1, 46;
CLR 3, 17; DLB 52; JRDA; MAICYA;
SATA 7, 69

Yerby, Frank G(arvin)
1916-1991 .... **CLC 1, 7, 22; BLC;
DAM MULT**
See also BW 1; CA 9-12R; 136; CANR 16,
52; DLB 76; INT CANR-16; MTCW

Yesenin, Sergei Alexandrovich
See Esenin, Sergei (Alexandrovich)

Yevtushenko, Yevgeny (Alexandrovich)
1933-............ **CLC 1, 3, 13, 26, 51;
DAM POET**
See also CA 81-84; CANR 33, 54; MTCW

Yezierska, Anzia 1885(?)-1970 ..... **CLC 46**
See also CA 126; 89-92; DLB 28; MTCW

Yglesias, Helen 1915-........... **CLC 7, 22**
See also CA 37-40R; CAAS 20; CANR 15;
INT CANR-15; MTCW

Yokomitsu Riichi 1898-1947 ...... **TCLC 47**

Literary Criticism Series
Cumulative Topic Index

This index lists all topic entries in Gale's *Classical and Medieval Literature Criticism, Contemporary Literary Criticism, Literature Criticism from 1400 to 1800, Nineteenth-Century Literature Criticism,* and *Twentieth-Century Literary Criticism.*

Topic Index

Topic Index

NCLC Cumulative Nationality Index

Nationality Index

NCLC 62 Title Index

ISBN 0-7876-1243-X

90000